THE REVOLUTION IN CORPORATE FINANCE

In memory of Merton Miller

The Revolution in Corporate Finance

FOURTH EDITION

EDITED BY

Joel M. Stern AND *Donald H. Chew, Jr.*

BLACKWELL PUBLISHING
350 Main Street, Malden, MA 02148-5020, USA
9600 Garsington Road, Oxford OX4 2DQ, UK
550 Swanston Street, Carlton, Victoria 3053, Australia

First edition published 1982
Second edition published 1992
Third edition published 1998
Fourth edition published 2003 by Blackwell Publishing Ltd

4   2007

Library of Congress Cataloging-in-Publication Data
The revolution in corporate finance / edited by Joel M. Stern and Donald H. Chew, Jr. —
4th ed.
　　p. cm.
　　Includes bibliographical references and index.
　　ISBN 978-1-4051-0781-5 (pbk: alk. paper)
　　1. Corporations–Finance. I. Stern, Joel M. II. Chew, Donald H.

　HG4026.5 .R48 2003
　658.15 — dc21   2002038488

ISBN: 978-1-4051-0781-5 (pbk: alk. paper)

A catalogue record for this title is available from the British Library.

Set in 9½ / 11½ pt Baskerville
by Newgen Imaging Systems (P) Ltd, Chennai, India
Printed and bound in Singapore
by C.O.S. Printers Pte Ltd

For further information on
Blackwell Publishing, visit our website:
www.blackwellpublishing.com

Contents

Preface to the Fourth Edition

This edition of *The Revolution in Corporate Finance* begins and ends with the late Merton Miller, winner of the 1990 Nobel Prize in Economics and widely regarded as the "father of modern finance." When Miller started on his path-breaking work with Franco Modigliani in the late 1950s, the study of finance was little more than a glorified apprenticeship system transmitting the conventional wisdom – typically packaged in the form of case studies – from one generation of corporate managers to the next. Since then, thanks to Miller and his many followers, finance has become one of the most innovative and productive of all the social sciences. As Miller writes in "The History of Finance: An Eyewitness Account" (with which this book opens), the field of finance, despite its late start, "has come to surpass many, perhaps even most, of the more traditional fields of economics in terms of the number of students enrolled in finance courses, the number of faculty teaching finance courses, and, above all, in the quantity and quality of their combined scholarly output." To this list of accomplishments must be added the profound effects of the modern theory of finance on corporate practice. Today's corporate financial decision-making – everything from valuation and the setting of corporate goals and compensation plans to risk management and securities design – bears the imprint of research that has been extended or encouraged, if not actually initiated, by Miller himself.

Miller played several important roles in transforming finance into the more systematic and scientific discipline it has become. First, of course, were his pioneering contributions to finance scholarship. The "M&M" irrelevance propositions represent the first attempt to apply rigorous economic logic to corporate *financial* decision-making. And the conclusions came as a surprise to many finance scholars as well as to most practicing corporate executives. The basic message of the M&M propositions is that there is no "magic" in leverage or dividends. M&M showed that, if we make some simplifying assumptions – if we ignore taxes and bankruptcy costs, and assume that managers make the same investment and operating decisions whether the firm is levered with 10% or 90% debt – then there is no good reason to expect changes in corporate leverage and dividend payout ratios to affect the value of the firm. Such financing decisions are simply different ways of repackaging a company's operating cash flows for investors; and provided those decisions don't affect the firm's "earnings power," they should not affect its total market value.

Although empirical testing of the M&M propositions has proven to be difficult if not impossible, there was one rather interesting, admittedly informal, test of the logic of M&M that is worth recalling. In late 1994, a profitable utility called Florida Power & Light, with some prodding from my colleagues at

Stern Stewart, announced that it was cutting its dividend by 33%. No profitable utility had ever done such a thing – and the conventional wisdom among investment bankers was that utility investors *want* dividends – and the more the better. After FPL announced the cut, the stock price fell immediately from $34 to $27, a drop of about 20%, pretty much as its investment banker predicted. The banker also said that the discount might last for as long as two years. But, in fact, the discount disappeared almost entirely in the following six weeks. What's more, as a result of the company's new dividend policy (backed up by management's announcement that it would soon begin returning the firm's excess cash through a policy of regular stock repurchases), FPL's stock suddenly became a "buy" at a number of major brokerage houses, and there was a major shift in the "clientele" holding the stock. Over the next few years, FPL was one of the top performers in the S&P Utility Index.

As this example suggests, one of the important messages of the M&M propositions is that changes in capital structure and dividends should not matter, *provided* managers find other ways of assuring investors that the company's earnings power and return on capital remain unaffected. And, of course, effective corporate communication of the new policy plays an important role in ensuring this outcome.

But perhaps the more important message of M&M to corporate practitioners is what it says about why financing decisions *might* matter. As Miller himself wrote in a 1988 article called "The Modigliani-Miller Propositions After Thirty Years" (also in this book),

The view that capital structure is literally irrelevant or that "nothing matters" in corporate finance, though still sometimes attributed to us . . . is far from what we ever actually said about the real-world applications of our theoretical propositions. Looking back now, perhaps we should have put more emphasis on the other, upbeat side of the "nothing matters" coin: showing what doesn't matter can also show, by implication, what does . . .

The M&M propositions say, in effect, that *if* corporate financing and dividend decisions matter – that is, if they can increase corporate values – they are likely to do so only for the following reasons: (1) they reduce the taxes paid by the corporation or its investors; (2) they reduce the probability of a costly bankruptcy or financial distress (which in turn could lead to value-reducing underinvestment); (3) they send a positive signal to investors about management's view of the firm's prospects; or (4) they provide managers with stronger incentives to operate efficiently and to invest only in value-adding projects. It is in this sense that M&M can be seen as laying the groundwork for the modern theory of corporate finance – they showed future scholars where to look for the *real* effects of financial decisions.

But it is not for his scholarship alone that Miller will be remembered as the father of finance. Throughout much of his career, but especially following the award of the Nobel Prize in 1990, Miller was a tireless, and very persuasive, spokesman for the financial markets he had spent his life studying. As Fischer Black put it, Miller was both a "great economist" and a "fine warrior." And as René Stulz writes in the closing article of this book, "the cause for which Miller fought until the end of his life was the social efficacy of financial markets – the idea that financial markets, when allowed to function with minimal interference from regulators and governments, are extraordinarily effective in allocating resources in ways that create social wealth."

Starting in the late '80s, and continuing throughout the '90s, Miller traveled widely and gave a remarkable series of lectures aimed directly at influencing public policy toward financial markets. Notable among these lectures were his *ten* annual Keynote Addresses, delivered in Southeast Asian cities between 1989 and 1999, to an association of finance academics and professionals called the Pacific-Basin Capital Markets (PACAP) group. In 1989, the year PACAP was formed, Miller devoted his inaugural address to a defense of stock index futures trading, which was then being blamed for the stock market crash of 1987. In December of 1990, Miller used the occasion of his Nobel Prize to deliver a speech called "Leverage." His message was that the leveraged restructuring movement of the 1980s, far from being the cause of the recession then underway, had brought major benefits to the U.S. economy by streamlining bloated and poorly run companies – and that the heavy debt financing that accompanied and facilitated this process did not present a threat to the economy.

When the corporate derivatives fiascos struck in the early '90s, Miller wrote and delivered a talk called "Financial Innovation: Achievements and Prospects" (reprinted in this book) in which he likened the proliferation of futures, options, and other "new instruments" to a "gigantic insurance company" – one that promised to achieve "more efficient risk-sharing" throughout the economy by allowing companies and investors to shift unwanted risks to others more able or willing to bear them. And when the Asian crisis was breaking out in 1998, Miller contradicted the popular wisdom by arguing (in a speech called "Financial Markets and Growth," also in this book) that the fundamental cause of the problem was not "too much reliance on financial markets" by the Asian countries, but "too little." The real culprit, in Miller's view, was the extent of the Asian economies' reliance on banks; and the main solution was developing capital market alternatives, and the conditions necessary to sustain them. (In support of Miller's analysis, the recent rise to prosperity of South Korea, which since 1998 has embraced many aspects of free markets and U.S.-style corporate governance, offers a striking contrast to the continuing problems of neighboring Japan.)

Because of his gift for conveying important – and often counterintuitive – economic insights with wit and an ample use of homespun metaphors, Miller's audiences were large and appreciative. In Tokyo in 1993, I was fortunate enough to see him explain to some 500 Japanese business leaders and regulators why the "shortsightedness" of the U.S. stock market was not a serious problem. As Miller put it,

Myopia is not the only disease of vision afflicting business managers. They may suffer from astigmatism (distorted vision) or even from hyperopia or excessive farsightedness. Looking back over the last 20 years, one may well find cases in which American firms facing strong stockholder pressures to pay out funds invested too little in some kinds of capital-intensive technology. But many Japanese firms, facing no such pressure, have clearly *over*-invested during that same period in highly capital-intensive plants that will never come close to recovering their initial investment, let alone earning a positive rate of return. And I won't even mention the trillions of yen poured into land and office buildings both at home and abroad.

Pointing to the core of the Japanese problem, Miller described the Japanese stock market as "a *Bunraku* theater, with the bureaucrats from MOF [the Japanese Ministry of Finance] backstage manipulating the puppets." And then he went to offer a classic defense of the "shareholder value principle" at the core of the U.S. corporate governance system.

Despite (or perhaps because of) his critical assessment of the Japanese Ministry, Miller was often surrounded during his visit by admiring Japanese businessmen. But none were more admiring than his hosts at the sumo tournament where, hours after his speech, this Nobel laureate could be seen and heard shouting the wrestlers' names (with a remarkably good Japanese accent) and carrying on like the Chicago Bears fan that he was.

As Eugene Fama, Miller's colleague and friend of almost 40 years, said nearly two years ago at a memorial service in Chicago:

Mert epitomized what makes a university, a department, or, indeed, a whole profession great – the willingness of talented people to contribute to the work of others simply because they love the game . . . In his death, the world of finance has lost one of its defining beacons. Many of us have lost a lifelong mentor, colleague, and friend. He cannot be replaced.

It is not only Miller's contribution to finance scholarship, then, but also his efforts to communicate the social value of financial markets to a broader audience that this book is meant to honor. Most of the book's seven sections accordingly begin with articles by Miller. And in addition to the topics of capital budgeting ("The Corporate Investment Decision"), capital structure ("The Financing Decision"), and risk management that were covered in previous editions, this edition has two new sections – one on international financing and one on international corporate governance. Both were frequent subjects of Miller's later writings, and both have received increasing attention from the entire finance profession. In both cases, moreover, these sections begin with Miller's articles, the "defining beacons" for the articles that follow.

Don Chew
New York City
August 2, 2002

Preface to the First Edition

Over the past 25 years or so, a quiet revolution in the theory of corporate finance has been taking place at select graduate business schools in the U.S. and abroad. Beginning principally with the work of Merton Miller and Francisco Modigliani in the late 1950s, the study of finance has been gradually molded through rigorous application of economic logic into the shape of a positive science. (In fact, with the recent award of the Nobel Prize to Modigliani, finance scholarship appears finally to have assumed its rightful standing as a "serious" branch of economic studies.) Now firmly grounded in principles of microeconomic theory, and aided by sophisticated statistical methods and powerful computers drawing on massive data bases, the theory of "modern finance" has made steady progress toward achieving the two major aims of a hard science: internal consistency and predictive power.

Aside from this appropriation of the scientific method, what is "revolutionary" about the modern theory of finance? The revolution in finance is at bottom a change in the theory of valuation, a displacement of older, conventional notions of how the stock market prices securities (even though, of course, many of these discarded theories continue to be propounded daily by Wall Street "authorities"). Financial academics, supported by an extensive body of empirical research, have been challenging much of the accounting-oriented intuition that continues to pass for the collective wisdom of the business community.

The rise of modern finance has brought about a confrontation, in short, between two very different views of the process by which capital markets establish the values of corporate securities. The traditional view holds that stock prices are determined primarily by reported earnings. At its most simplistic, it maintains that investors respond uncritically to financial statements, mechanically capitalizing published EPS figures at standard, industry-wide multiples. We call this the "accounting model of the firm." The rival view, the "economic model," holds that the market value of corporate stock – like the value of a bond or any other investment – is the present value of a company's future expected after-tax *cash flows*, discounted at rates which reflect investors' required returns on securities of comparable risk. According to this view, reported earnings may offer a reasonably good measure of corporate performance, but only insofar as they reflect real cash profitability. When earnings seriously misrepresent operating cash flows, accounting statements distort performance and provide an unreliable guide to value. (And dividends, we might add, are probably largely irrelevant – aside from possible tax and "information" effects – to the process of valuation.)

This fundamental difference in theory of value has in turn given rise to two distinct philosophies of corporate management. Corporate executives subscribing to the accounting model view the goal of financial management as the maximization of reported earnings per share. Those who subscribe to the "economic model" argue that public firms should be run largely as if they were private; that is, the public corporation best serves its stockholders by maximizing neither reported earnings nor earnings growth, but after-tax "free cash flow." The sophisticated investors that dominate the market pricing process are accustomed to distinguishing between accounting illusion and economic reality in setting stock prices; and they can be counted on to reward such "value-maximizing" behavior by management.

The crucial assumption underlying the "economic model" is, of course, the sophistication of market investors. And this assumption, which has been formulated and tested by academics as the "efficient markets hypothesis" (EMH), is the central tenet of modern finance. EMH is essentially an extension to capital markets of the "zero profits theorem" which economists have long applied to competitive goods markets. Briefly stated, the principle of market efficiency holds that competition among investors for information about public companies' intrinsic values ensures that the current prices of widely-traded financial assets are "unbiased predictors" of the future value of those securities. This means that a company's future stock price (adjusted for a gradually upward "drift" in which all stocks are expected to participate over time) is equally likely to be higher or lower than today's price. It also implies that new investors can expect a "normal" rate of return on their investment at any given time – no more, no less. (The failure of the vast majority of professional fund managers consistently to outperform the market is forceful testimony to the truth of the efficient markets proposition.)

For corporate management, EMH has three important implications: (1) the market is not likely to be fooled by accounting manipulations; (2) today's stock price reflects the collective wisdom of the marketplace about the future performance of the company (over the long run as well as the short); and unless management has significant inside information, the current price should be viewed as a reliable estimate of the value of the company; and (3) the market's reaction to corporate announcements, such

as announcements of acquisitions, divestitures, new securities offerings, or capital expenditure programs, should be viewed as conveying the market's best estimate of the consequences of that transaction on the (long-term) value of the company.

There exists today in the academic finance community a remarkable consensus about the validity of EMH (at least in its so-called "semi-strong" form) – a consensus which is backed by the greater body of academic research in finance conducted over the last two decades. To say this, of course, is not to minimize important remaining disagreements among financial economists about aspects of the theory. The Capital Asset Pricing Model, for example, has not done as good a job in explaining actual corporate returns as its formulators had hoped; and a challenger, known as "arbitrage pricing theory," although far from assuming a usable form, is on the rise. As another example, the widely-accepted DCF valuation framework, which has been under attack in the past few years, is now being supplemented by the use of option pricing theory to evaluate strategic business options. But such disagreements notwithstanding, the relentless testing of the proposition of market efficiency from the late 60s onward has made it – as Michael Jensen has commented – "without doubt the best-documented hypothesis in the social sciences."

But however thoroughly the principles of "modern finance" appear to have prevailed over all rivals in the business schools, they have not captured a strong following in the practicing business community. Nor, we suspect, have its many implications for corporate investment and financing been well understood. The general skepticism is based, in part, on the inevitable unwillingness of experienced practitioners to surrender their intuitive sense of a capricious market to the overly general conclusions of studies whose complex "methodologies" they cannot – or, more likely, will not take the time to – fathom. But another, perhaps more important reason for this resistance lies in the failure of the academy to state its case in a comprehensible and convincing manner.

To date, the publication of financial studies has been confined largely to academic journals. Unless readers bring to the subject a strong background in economics and quantitative methods, they will find these studies very tough going. And density of presentation aside, such journals do not encourage their contributors to lay significant stress on the practical applications of theoretical developments. As anyone who has gone through a reputable M.B.A. program can tell you, theoretical training in finance, at least as currently structured, is not designed to prepare students for the extensions and modifications of the theory that actual corporate decision-making requires.

Before the lessons of modern finance can be applied to corporate decision-making, the best current research must be identified, rid of its technical obscurities, and presented with a firm eye toward applications. The purpose of this book is to further develop the channel of communication between the academic and business communities, to help close the rift between theory and much corporate practice that now exists, by translating current academic research into practical recommendations for corporate management. Accordingly, the articles printed here reflect an attempt to achieve an ideal balance between theoretical rigor and applicability, analytical precision and compact clarity of expression.

THE SOURCEBOOKS

The *Revolution in Corporate Finance* represents a gathering up of many of the articles that have been published to date in both the *Chase Financial Quarterly* and the *Midland Corporate Finance Journal*. Before I describe the contents of this book, let me provide a brief history of these publications.

In the fall of 1981, under the aegis of the Chase Manhattan Bank, Joel Stern and I (with the help of Joe Willett) founded a publication called the *Chase Financial Quarterly* in order to supplement our corporate finance advisory work for the Bank. Its purpose, more broadly, was to help bridge what we saw as a "gulf" between modern finance theory and much corporate practice by culling from current research useful prescriptions for corporate policy.

Four issues later, in November of 1982, we and other members of our Chase Financial Policy division left the Bank to form Stern Stewart & Co., a private corporate finance advisory firm. We also renewed our publishing efforts by founding, with the sponsorship of the Midland Bank plc, the *Midland Corporate Finance Journal (MCFJ)*. The purpose of the *MCFJ*, like that of its predecessor, was

to bring to the attention of senior management the practical import of theoretical developments in finance for a wide range of corporate decisions: capital budgeting, dividend policy, capital structure planning, international performance measurement, acquisition and divestiture pricing, corporate risk management, and executive compensation.

Now beginning its fourth year of publication, the *MCFJ* has achieved a distinction we think unique among financial publications: while making a strong appeal to practicing corporate executives, it has also established a reputation among financial academics as the most creditable corporate finance publication written for the layman. For this reason, besides attracting a growing corporate following, the *MCFJ* is beginning to be used extensively in graduate business schools, especially in Executive Development Programs. The articles are now being assigned in the classrooms at such prestigious institutions as the University of Chicago (where Merton Miller, incidentally, has been using an entire issue of the *MCFJ* as the main text of a course he teaches in corporate policy), MIT's Sloan School, Wharton, Dartmouth's Tuck School, Stanford, Berkeley, UCLA, the University of Virginia, the University of Rochester, and the Harvard Business School.

IN CLOSING

What, then, does the revolution in finance theory have to say to practicing corporate executives? It is important to recognize that to the extent management views its function as the maximization of stockholder value, all financial decisions are based on some theory of capital market pricing. How management decides to use the corporate assets at its disposal, and what it chooses to tell investors, depend fundamentally on its understanding of how the stock market works.

Effective financial management, therefore, is in no small part a matter of achieving a better understanding of how capital markets work. In fact, we believe that an executive who adopts the perspective of financial markets and views himself as the steward of stockholders' savings has already taken a major step toward achieving the goal of corporate management: the most efficient use of the scarce stockholder capital at its disposal. And, when properly understood and applied, the theory of modern finance can provide corporate decision-makers with a more sensible basis for a number of corporate finance functions: setting corporate goals, evaluating the performance of divisions and subsidiaries, choosing among investment opportunities and financing vehicles, pricing acquisitions and divestitures, structuring incentive compensation schemes, finding the ideal capital structure, and communicating with the investment community.

I would like to close by expressing both Joel's and my gratitude to all the academics who have served on our Advisory Board over the past four years, as well as to our many other contributors who have made the *Chase Financial Quarterly*, the *Midland Corporate Finance Journal*, and thus this book possible.

Donald H. Chew, Jr.
New York City
February 4, 1986

PART I

Financial Markets

The book begins with Merton Miller's "History of Finance." As Miller starts by observing, the field of finance, since its relatively late start in the 1950s, "has come to surpass many, perhaps even most, of the more traditional fields of economics in terms of the number of students enrolled in finance courses, the number of faculty teaching finance courses, and, above all, in the quantity and quality of their combined scholarly output." The article then goes on to describe all of the major developments of the past 50 years using the series of Nobel Prizes in finance as the "organizing principle." Starting with Harry Markowitz's mean-variance framework, which underlies modern portfolio theory (and for which Markowitz received the Nobel Prize in 1990), the focus shifts to the Capital Asset Pricing Model (for which William Sharpe was also recognized in the same year), efficient market theory, and the M&M irrelevance propositions. In describing each of these advances, Miller emphasizes the "tension" between what he identifies as the two main streams in finance scholarship: (1) the Business School (or "micro normative') approach, which aims to help investors maximize returns and corporate managers to maximize shareholder value, while taking the prices of securities in the market as given; and (2) the Economics Department (or "macro normative') approach, which starts by assuming that investors and managers are value

maximizers and then attempts to explain the behavior of the prices themselves.

These two streams converge in the final episode of Miller's history – the breakthrough in option pricing accomplished by Fischer Black, Myron Scholes, and Robert Merton in the early 1970s (for which Merton and Scholes were awarded the Nobel Prize in 1998, "with the late Fischer Black everywhere acknowledged as the third pivotal figure'). According to Miller, the Black-Scholes option pricing model and its successors "mean that, for the first time in its close to 50-year history, the field of finance can be built, or . . . rebuilt, on the basis of 'observable' magnitudes." For finance practitioners, the ability to calculate option values using (almost entirely) observable variables made possible the spectacular growth in "financial engineering" in the '90s, the highly lucrative activity where the practice of finance has come closest to attaining the precision of a hard science. At the same time, option pricing has given rise to a relatively new field called "real options" that promises to revolutionize corporate strategy and capital budgeting (and becomes the main focus in the second chapter of this book).

As Miller's "History" also notes, it was not until the late 1960s that the stock market began to be taken seriously by economists as a proper subject for scholarly research. But since Eugene Fama introduced the notion of an "efficient" stock market to the finance literature in 1965, the growth of academic research on stock market behavior has been prodigious. In "The Theory of Stock Market Efficiency: Accomplishments and Limitations," the University of Rochester's Ray Ball provides a first-hand account of how stock market research has evolved over the past 30 years. The account is "first-hand" because Professor Ball was one of the pioneers in efficient markets research. While working at the University of Chicago in the mid-'60s, Ball and colleague Philip Brown produced what is now regarded as the first scientific study of the market's reaction to the release of financial statements.

For all its accomplishments, however, efficient markets theory has had its setbacks. As described in Ball's article, a large body of empirical studies in the 1970s provided "remarkably consistent evidence of the stock market's ability to process information in a rational, in some cases ingenious, fashion." But after a 15-year period in which one triumph of modern financial theory succeeded another – including, again, the M&M irrelevance propositions, the Sharpe-Lintner CAPM, and the Black-Scholes option pricing model – evidence began to surface of "anomalies" that appeared to contradict the theory of efficient markets. For example, the prices of both individual firms and the market as a whole were reported to "overreact" in certain circumstances; and variables such as low market-to-book ratios and low P/E ratios, as well as a pronounced "small firm effect," appeared to provide opportunities for investors to earn higher rates of return than those predicted by the CAPM.

But, as Ball argues in the second half of his article, such anomalies may stem less from flaws in stock market pricing than from the limitations of the *model* of market efficiency itself and from defects in the design of researchers' tests (particularly their mechanical application of the CAPM) of the model. "Whether," as Ball concludes, "the existence of such anomalous findings indicates a fatal flaw in the theory – or, more likely, the value of incorporating greater realism – only time and more research will tell.'

In "Market Myths," Bennett Stewart summarizes a good deal of academic evidence attesting to the rationality and sophistication of financial markets. Much of the behavior of corporate America, Stewart argues, is dictated by unthinking adherence to what he calls the "Accounting Model of Value" – at its most simplistic, the idea that the market establishes a company's value by capitalizing its current earnings at a "standard" industry-wide multiple. In place of the Accounting Model, Stewart proposes adoption of the "Economic Model of Value" as the basis for corporate decision-making. The Economic Model estimates a company's worth as the sum of all future expected operating cash flows, net of required new investment and discounted at a cost of capital that reflects risk and investors' alternative investment opportunities. It is essentially this model, Stewart claims, that the most sophisticated, influential investors (the "lead steers") use in pricing corporate securities. After a long exposition of the follies of accounting-based as opposed to value-based management, Stewart goes on to challenge a number of other popular beliefs about the market – namely, that dividends are an important fundamental variable in the pricing of stocks, and that the market responds mechanically to accounting earnings while ignoring changes in operating cash flow.

One final piece of testimony to market efficiency is furnished by "An Analysis of Trading Profits: How Trading Rooms Really Make Money." In this article, Albéric Braas and Charles Bralver of Oliver, Wyman & Co. (a bank strategy consulting group) attempt to correct some popular misconceptions about the profitability of bank trading operations. Based on their work with more than 40 large trading operations, the authors conclude that, for most trading rooms, speculative "positioning" is not a reliable source of profits. The primary source of profit is dealings with customers. Stable profits can also be expected from interdealer trade, but only from traders who work for large institutions with heavy order flows and who adopt a "jobber" style of trading.

CHAPTER 1

The History of Finance: An Eyewitness Account

*Merton H. Miller (University of Chicago)**

I am honored indeed to be Keynote Speaker at the Fifth Anniversary of the German Finance Association. Five years, of course, is not very old as professional societies go, but then neither is the field of finance itself. That field in its modern form really dates from the 1950s. In the 40 years since then, the field has come to surpass many, perhaps even most, of the more traditional fields of economics in terms of the number of students enrolled in finance courses, the number of faculty teaching finance courses and, above all, in the quantity and quality of their combined scholarly output.

The huge body of scholarly research in finance over the last 40 years falls naturally into two main streams. And no, I don't mean "asset pricing" and "corporate finance," but a deeper division that cuts across both those conventional subdivisions of the field. The division I have in mind is the more fundamental one between what I will call the Business School approach to finance and the Economics Department approach. Let me say immediately, however, that my distinction is purely "notional" not physical – a distinction over what the field is really all about, not where the offices happen to be located.

* A Keynote Address presented at the Fifth Annual Meeting of the German Finance Association in Hamburg, Germany, September 25, 1998. It was first published in the Summer 1999 issue of the *Journal of Portfolio Management*, a publication of Institutional Investor.

In the USA, as I am sure you are aware, the vast majority of academics in finance are, and always have been, teaching in Business Schools, not Economics Departments. I should add immediately, however, that in the elite schools at least, a substantial fraction of the finance faculties have been trained in – that is, have received their Ph.D.s from – Economics Departments. Habits of thought acquired in graduate school have a tendency to stay with you.

The characteristic Business School approach tends to be what we would call in our jargon "micro normative." That is, a decision-maker, be it an individual investor or a corporate manager, is seen as maximizing some objective function, be it utility, expected return or shareholder value, taking the prices of securities in the market as given. In a Business School, after all, that's what you're supposed to be doing: teaching your charges how to make better decisions. To someone trained in the classical traditions of economics, however, the famous dictum of the great Alfred Marshall stands out: "It is not the business of the economist to tell the brewer how to make beer." The characteristic Economics Department approach thus is not micro, but *macro* normative. Their models assume a world of micro optimizers, and deduce from that how the market prices, which the micro optimizers take as given, actually evolve.

Note that I am differentiating the stream of research in finance along macro versus micro lines and not along the more familiar normative versus positive line. Both streams of research in finance are thoroughly positivist in outlook in that they try to be, or at least claim to be, concerned with testable hypotheses. The normal article in finance journals over the last 40 years has two main sections: one where the model is presented, and the second an empirical section showing that real-world data are consistent with the model (which is hardly surprising because had that not been so, the author would never have submitted the paper in the first place and the editors would never have accepted it for publication).

The interaction of these two streams, the Business School stream and the Economics Department stream – the micro normative and the macro normative – has largely governed the history of the field of finance to date. I propose to review some of the highpoints of that history, taking full advantage of a handy organizing principle nature has given us – to wit, the Nobel prizes in finance. Let me emphasize again that I will not be offering a comprehensive survey of the field – the record is far too large for that – but rather a selective view of what I see as the highlights, an eyewitness account, as it were, and always with special emphasis on the tensions between the Business School and the Economics Department streams. After that overview I will offer some very personal views on where I think the field is heading, or at least where I would be heading were I just entering the field today.

MARKOWITZ AND THE THEORY OF PORTFOLIO SELECTION

The tension between the micro and macro approaches was visible from the very beginning of modern finance – from our big bang, as it were – which I think we can all agree today dates to the year 1952 with the publication in the *Journal of Finance* of Harry Markowitz's article "Portfolio Selection." Markowitz in that remarkable paper gave, for the first time, a precise definition of what had hitherto been just vague buzzwords, "risk" and "return." Specifically, Markowitz identified the yield or return on an investment with the expected value or probability-weighted mean value of its possible outcomes; and its risk with the variance or squared deviations of those outcomes around the

mean. This identification of return and risk with Mean and Variance, so instinctive to finance professionals these days, was far from obvious then. The common perception of risk even today focuses on the likelihood of losses – on what the public thinks of as the "downside" risk – not just on the *variability* of returns. Yet Markowitz's choice of the Variance as his measure of risk, counterintuitive as it may have appeared to many at the time, turned out to be inspired. It not only subsumed the more intuitive view of risk – because in the normal (or at least the symmetric) distributions we use in practice the downside risk is essentially the mirror image of the upside – but it had a property even more important for the development of the field. By identifying return and risk with Mean and Variance, Markowitz made the powerful algebra of mathematical statistics available for the study of portfolio selection.

The immediate contribution of that algebra was the famous formula for the variance of a *sum* of random variables: the weighted sum of the variance *plus* twice the weighted sum of the covariances. We in finance have been living off that formula, literally, for more than 40 years now. That formula shows, among other things, that for the individual investor, the relevant unit of analysis must always be the whole portfolio, not the individual share. The risk of an individual share cannot be defined apart from its relation to the whole portfolio and, in particular, its covariances with the other components. Covariances, and not mere numbers of securities held, govern the risk-reducing benefits of diversification.

The Markowitz Mean-Variance model is the perfect example of what I have called the Business School or micro normative stream in finance. And that is somewhat ironic in that the Markowitz paper was originally a thesis in the University of Chicago's Economics Department. Markowitz even notes that Milton Friedman, in fact, voted against the thesis initially on the grounds that it wasn't really economics. And indeed, the Mean-Variance model, as visualized by Markowitz, really *wasn't* economics. Markowitz saw investors as actually applying the model to pick their portfolios using a combination of past data and personal judgment to select the needed Means, Variances, and Covariances.

For the Variances and Covariances, at least, past data probably *could* provide at least a reasonable starting point. The precision of such estimates can always be increased by cutting the time interval into smaller and smaller intervals. But what of the Means? Simply averaging the returns of the last few years, along the lines of the examples in the Markowitz paper (and later book) won't yield reliable estimates of the return *expected* in the future. And running those unreliable estimates of the Means through the computational algorithm can lead to weird, corner portfolios that hardly seem to offer the presumed benefits of diversification, as any finance instructor who has assigned the portfolio selection model as a classroom exercise can testify.

But if the Markowitz Mean-Variance algorithm is useless for selecting optimal portfolios, why have I taken its publication as the starting point of modern finance? Because that essentially Business School model of Markowitz was transformed by William Sharpe, John Lintner, and Jan Mossin into an Economics Department model of enormous reach and power.

WILLIAM SHARPE AND THE CAPITAL ASSET PRICING MODEL

That William Sharpe was so instrumental in transforming the Markowitz Business School model into an Economics Department model continues the irony noted earlier. Markowitz, it will be recalled, submitted his thesis to an Economics Department, but Sharpe was always a business school faculty member and much of his earlier work had been in the management science/operations research area. Sharpe also maintains an active consulting practice advising pension funds on their portfolio selection problems. Yet his Capital Asset Pricing Model is almost as perfect an example as you can find of an economists' macro-normative model of the kind I described.

Sharpe starts by imagining a world in which every investor is a Markowitz Mean-Variance portfolio selector. And he supposes further that these investors all share the same expectation as to returns, variances, and covariances. But if the inputs to the portfolio selection are the same, then every investor will hold exactly the same portfolio of risky assets. And because all risky assets must be held by somebody, an immediate implication is

that every investor holds the "market portfolio," that is an aliquot share of every risky security in the proportions in which they are outstanding.

At first sight, of course, the proposition that everyone holds the same portfolio seems too unrealistic to be worth pursuing. Keep in mind first, however, that the proposition applies only to the holdings of risky assets. It does not assume that every investor has the same degree of risk aversion. Investors can always reduce the degree of risk they bear by holding riskless bonds along with the risky stocks in the market portfolio; and they can increase their risk by holding negative amounts of the riskless asset, that is by borrowing and leveraging their holdings of the market portfolio.

Second, the idea of investing in the market portfolio is no longer strange. Nature has imitated art, as it were. Shortly after Sharpe's work appeared, the market created mutual funds that sought to hold all the shares in the market in their outstanding proportions. Such index funds, or "passive" investment strategies, as they are often called, are now followed by a large and increasing number of investors, particularly, but by no means only, those of U.S. pension funds.

The realism or lack of realism of the assumptions underlying the Sharpe CAPM was never a subject of serious debate within the profession, unlike the case of the M&M propositions to be considered later. The profession, from the outset, wholeheartedly adopted the Friedman positivist view that what counts is not the literal accuracy of the assumptions, but the *predictions* of the model. And in the case of Sharpe's model, those predictions were striking indeed. The CAPM implies that the distribution of expected rates of return across all risky assets is a *linear* function of a single variable – namely each asset's sensitivity to or covariance with the market portfolio, the famous β, which becomes the natural measure of a security's risk. The aim of science is to explain a lot with a little and few models in finance or economics do so more dramatically than the CAPM.

The CAPM not only offered new and powerful theoretical insights into the nature of risk, but also lent itself admirably to the kind of in-depth empirical investigation so necessary for the development of a new field like finance. Nor have the benefits been confined narrowly to the field of finance. The great volume of empirical research testing the CAPM has led to major innovations in both theoretical and applied econometrics.

Although the single-β CAPM managed to withstand more than 30 years of intense econometric investigation, the current consensus within the profession is that a single risk factor, though it takes us an enormous length of the way, is not quite enough for describing the cross-section of expected returns. In addition to the market factor, two other pervasive risk factors have by now been identified for common stocks. One is a size effect: small firms seem to earn higher returns than large firms, on average, even after controlling for β or market sensitivity. The other is a factor, still not fully understood, but which seems reasonably well captured by the ratio of a firm's accounting book value to its market value. Firms with high book-to-market ratios appear to earn higher returns on average over long horizons than those with low book-to-market ratios, after controlling for size and for the market factor. That a three-factor model has now been shown to describe the data somewhat better than the single factor CAPM should detract in no way, of course, from our appreciating the enormous influence on the theory of asset pricing exerted by the original CAPM.

THE EFFICIENT MARKETS HYPOTHESIS

The Mean-Variance model of Markowitz and the CAPM of Sharpe et al. were contributions whose great scientific value were recognized by the Nobel Committee in 1990. A third major contribution to finance was recognized at the same time. But before describing it, let me mention a fourth major contribution that has done much to shape the development of the field of finance in the last 25 years, but which has so far not received the attention from the Nobel Committee I believe it deserves. I refer, of course, to the Efficient Markets Hypothesis, which says, in effect, that no simple rule based on already published and available information can generate above-normal rates of return. On this score of whether mechanical profit opportunities exist, the conflict between the Business School tradition in finance and the Economics Department tradition has been and still remains intense.

The hope that studying finance might open the way to successful stock market speculation served to keep up interest in the field even before the modern scientific foundations were laid in the 1950s. The first systematic collection of stock market prices, in fact, was compiled under the auspices of the Alfred Cowles Foundation in the 1930s. Cowles himself had a lifelong enthusiasm for the stock market, dimmed only slightly by the catastrophic crash of 1929. Cowles is perhaps better known by academic economists these days as the sponsor of the Cowles Foundation, currently an adjunct of the Yale Economics Department and the source of much fundamental research on econometrics in the 1940s and '50s. Cowles' indexes of stock prices have long since been superseded by much more detailed and computerized databases, such as those of the Center for Research in Security Prices at the University of Chicago. And to those computer databases, in turn, goes much of the credit for stimulating the empirical research in finance that has given the field its distinctive flavor.

Even before these new computerized indexes came into widespread use in the early 1960s, however, the mechanical approach to above-normal investment returns was already being seriously challenged. That challenge was being delivered, curiously enough, not by economists, but by statisticians like M.G. Kendall and my colleague Harry Roberts – who argued that stock prices were essentially random walks. That implied, among other things, that the record of past stock prices, however rich in "patterns" it might appear, had no predictive power for future stock prices and returns.

By the late 1960s, however, the evidence was clear that stock prices were not random walks by the strictest definition of that term. Some elements of predictability *could* be detected particularly in long-run returns. The issue of whether publicly available information could be used for successful stock market speculation had to be rephrased – a task in which my colleague Eugene Fama played the leading role – as whether the observed departures from randomness in the time series of returns on common stocks represented true profit opportunities after transaction costs and after appropriate compensation for changes in risk over time. With that shift in focus from returns to cost- and risk-adjusted returns, the Efficient Markets debate was no longer a matter of statistics, but one of economics.

This tieback to economics helps explain why the Efficient Market Hypothesis of finance remains as strong as ever despite the steady drumbeat of empirical studies directed against it. Suppose you find some mechanical rule that seems to earn above normal returns – and with thousands of researchers spinning through the mountains of tapes of past data, anomalies, like the currently fashionable "momentum effects," are bound to keep turning up. Then imitators will enter and compete away those above-normal returns exactly as in any other setting in economics. Above-normal profits, wherever they are found, inevitably carry with them the seeds of their own decay.

THE MODIGLIANI–MILLER PROPOSITIONS

Still other pillars on which the field of finance rests are the Modigliani-Miller Propositions on capital structure. Here, the tensions between the micro normative and the macro normative approaches were evident from the outset, as is clear from the very title of the first M&M paper, "The Cost of Capital, Corporation Finance and the Theory of Investment." The theme of that paper, and indeed of the whole field of corporate finance at the time, was capital budgeting. The micro normative wing was concerned with the "cost of capital," in the sense of the optimal "cut off" rate for investment when the firm can finance the project either with debt or equity or some combination of both. The macro normative or economics wing sought to express the aggregate demand for investment by corporations as a function of the cost of capital that firms were actually using as their optimal cutoffs, rather than just the rate of interest on long-term government bonds. The M&M analysis provided answers that left both wings of the profession dissatisfied. At the macro normative level, the M&M measure of the cost of capital for aggregate investment functions never really caught on, and, indeed, the very notion of estimating aggregate demand functions for investment has long since been abandoned by macro economists. At the micro level, the M&M proportions implied that the choice of financing instrument was irrelevant for the optimal cutoff. That cutoff depended solely on the risk (or "risk-class") of the investment regardless of how it was financed, hardly a happy position for professors of finance to explain to their students being trained

presumably in the art of selecting optimal capital structures.

Faced with the unpleasant action-consequences of the M&M model at the micro level, the tendency of many at first was to dismiss the assumptions underlying M&M's then-novel arbitrage proof as unrealistic. The assumptions underlying the CAPM, of course, are equally or even more implausible, as noted earlier, but the profession seemed far more willing to accept Friedman's "the assumptions don't matter" position for the CAPM than for the M&M Propositions. The likely reason is that the second blade of the Friedman positivism slogan – what *does* count is the descriptive power of the model itself – was not followed up. Tests by the hundreds of the CAPM filled the literature. But direct calibration tests of the M&M Propositions and their implications did not exist.

One fundamental difficulty of testing the M&M Propositions showed up in the initial M&M paper itself. The capital structure proposition says that if you could find two firms whose underlying earnings were identical, then so would be their market values, regardless of how much of the capital structure took the form of equity as opposed to debt. But how do you find two companies whose earnings are identical? M&M tried using industry as a way of holding earnings constant, but that sort of filter was far too crude to be decisive. Attempts to exploit the power of the CAPM were no more successful. How do you compute a β for the underlying real assets?

One way to avoid the difficulty of not having two identical firms, of course, is to see what happens when the *same* firm changes its capital structure. If a firm borrows and uses the proceeds to pay its shareholders a huge dividend or to buy back shares, does the value of the firm increase? Many studies have suggested that they do. But the interpretation of those results faces a hopeless identification problem. The firm, after all, never issues a press release saying we are just conducting a purely scientific investigation of the M&M Propositions. The market, which is forward looking, has every reason to believe that these capital structure decisions are conveying management's views about changes in the firm's prospects for the future. These confounding "information effects," present in every dividend and capital structure decision, render indecisive all tests based on specific corporate actions.

Nor can we hope to refute the M&M Propositions indirectly by calling attention to the multitude of new securities and of variations on old securities that are introduced year after year. The M&M Propositions say only that no gains could be earned from such innovations if the market were in fact "complete." But the new securities in question may well be serving to complete the market, earning a firstmover's profit to the particular innovation. Only those in Wall Street know how hard it is these days to come by those innovator's profits.

If all this seems reminiscent of the Efficient Markets Hypothesis, that is no accident. The M&M Propositions are also ways of saying that there are no free lunches. Firms cannot hope to gain by issuing what looks like low-cost debt rather than high-cost equity. They just make the higher cost equity even higher. And if any substantial number of firms, at the same time, sought to replace what they think is their high-cost equity with low-cost debt (even tax-advantaged debt), then the interest costs of debt would rise and the required yields on equity would fall until the perceived incentives to change capital structures (or dividend policies for that matter) were eliminated. The M&M Propositions, in short, like the Efficient Markets Hypothesis, are about *equilibrium* in the capital markets – what equilibrium looks like and what forces are set in motion once it is disturbed. And that is why neither the Efficient Markets Hypothesis nor the Modigliani-Miller propositions have ever set well with those in the profession who see finance as essentially a branch of management science.

Fortunately, however, recent developments in finance, also recognized by the Nobel Committee, suggest that the conflict between the two traditions in finance, the Business School stream and the Economics Department stream, may be on the way to reconciliation.

OPTIONS

That new development, of course, is the field of options, whose pioneers, recently honored by the Nobel Committee, were Robert Merton and Myron Scholes (with the late Fischer Black everywhere acknowledged as the third pivotal figure). Because the intellectual achievement of their work has been memorialized over and over this past year – and rightly so – I will not seek to review it here. Instead, in keeping with my theme today, I want to focus on what options mean for the history of finance.

Options mean, among other things, that for the first time in its close to 50-year history, the field of finance can be built, or as I will argue be rebuilt on the basis of "observable" magnitudes. I still remember the teasing we financial economists, Harry Markowitz, William Sharpe, and I, had to put up with from the physicists and chemists in Stockholm when we conceded that the basic unit of our research, the expected rate of return, was not actually observable. I tried to tease back by reminding them of their neutrino – a particle with no mass whose presence was inferred only as a missing residual from the interactions of other particles. But that was eight years ago. In the meantime, the neutrino has been detected.

To say that option prices are based on observables is not strictly true, of course. The option price in the Black-Scholes-Merton formula depends on the current market value of the underlying share, the striking price, the time to maturity of the contract, and the risk-free rate of interest, all of which are observable either exactly or very closely. But the option price depends also, and very critically, on the *variance* of the distribution of returns on the underlying share, which is not directly observable; it must be estimated. Still, as Fischer Black always reminded us, estimating variances is orders of magnitude easier than estimating the means or expected returns that are central to the models of Markowitz, Sharpe, or Modigliani–Miller. The precision of an estimate of the variance can be increased, as noted earlier, by cutting time into smaller and smaller units – from weeks to days to hours to minutes. For means, however, the precision of estimate can be increased only by lengthening the sample period, giving rise to the well-known dilemma that by the time a high degree of precision in estimating the mean from past data has been achieved, the mean itself has almost surely shifted.

Having a base in observable quantities – or virtually observable quantities – on which to value securities might seem at first sight to have benefited primarily the management science stream in finance. And, indeed, recent years have seen the birth of a new and rapidly growing specialty area within the profession, that of financial engineering (with the recent establishment of a journal with that name a clear sign that the field is here to stay). The financial engineers have already reduced the original Black-Scholes-Merton formula to model-T status. Nor has the micro normative field of *corporate* finance been left out. When it comes to capital budgeting, long a major focus of that field, the decision impact of what have come to be called "real" options – even simple ones like the right to close down a mine when the output price falls and reopen it when it rises – is substantially greater than that of variations in the cost of capital.

The options revolution, if I may call it that, is also transforming the macro normative or economics stream in finance. The hint of things to come in that regard was prefigured in the title of the original Black-Scholes paper itself, "The Pricing of Options and Corporate Liabilities." The latter phrase was added to the title precisely to convince the editors of the *Journal of Political Economy* – about as economicsy a journal as you can get – that the original (rejected) version of their paper was not just a technical *tour de force* in mathematical statistics, but an advance with wide applicability for the study of market prices.

And indeed, the Black-Scholes analysis showed, among other things, how options serve to "complete the market" for securities by eliminating or at least substantially weakening the constraints on high leverage obtainable with ordinary securities. The Black-Scholes demonstration that the shares in highly leveraged corporations are really call options also serves in effect to complete the M&M model of the pricing of corporate equities subject to the prior claims of the debt holders. But we can go even further. *Every* security can be thought of as a package of component Arrow-Debreu state-price options, just as every physical object is a package of component atoms and molecules.

But I propose to speculate no further about these and other exciting prospects for the future. Let me close rather with the question I raised in the beginning: what would I advise a young member of the German Finance Association to specialize in? What would *I* specialize in if I were starting over and entering the field today?

Well, I certainly wouldn't go into asset pricing or corporate finance. Research in those subfields has already reached the phase of rapidly diminishing returns. Agency theory, I would argue, is best left to the legal profession and behavioral finance is best left to the psychologists. So at the risk of sounding a bit like the character in the movie "The Graduate," I reduce my advice to a single word: options. When it comes to research potential, options have much to offer both the management-science business-school wing within the profession *and* the economics wing. In fact, so vast are the research opportunities for both wings that the field is surely due for a total reconstruction as profound as that following the original breakthrough by Harry Markowitz in 1953.

The shift towards options in the center of gravity of finance that I foresee should be particularly welcomed by the members of the German Finance Association. I can remember when research in finance in Germany was just beginning and tended to consist of copies of American studies using German data. But when it comes to a relatively new area like options, we all stand roughly equal at the starting line. And it's an area in which the rigorous and mathematical German academic training may even offer a comparative advantage.

It is no accident, I believe, that the Deutsche Termin Borse (or Eurex, as it has now become after merging with the Swiss exchange) has taken the high-tech road to a leading position among the world's future exchanges only eight years after a great conference in Frankfurt where Hartmut Schmidt, Fischer Black, and I sought to persuade the German financial establishment that allowing futures and options trading would not threaten the German economy. Hardware and electronic trading were the key to DTB's success; but I see no reason why the German scholarly community can't duplicate that success on the more abstract side of research in finance as well.

Whether they can should be clear by the time of your 25th Annual Meeting. I'm only sorry I won't be able to see that happy occasion.

CHAPTER 2

The Theory of Stock Market Efficiency: Accomplishments and Limitations

Ray Ball (University of Rochester)*

Thirty years have passed since Eugene Fama introduced the idea of an "efficient" stock market to the financial economics literature, and it continues to stimulate both insight and controversy. Put simply, the idea is that investors compete so fiercely in using public information that they bid away its value for earning additional returns. In so doing, they quickly incorporate all publicly available information into prices.

Harvard economist Benjamin Friedman has dismissed the idea as a "credo" – a statement of faith, not scientific research.[1] Warren Buffett, whose legendary investment performance and philosophy have caused some soul-searching among efficient markets theorists, has described the stock market as "a slough of fear and greed untethered to corporate realities."[2] In my view, the concept of efficient stock markets is one of the most important ideas in economics.

In the theory of stock market efficiency, public information that has not been fully reflected in stock prices is like gold lying in the streets; reports of either are treated with equal skepticism. Take the case of a company reporting a \$3 increase in annual EPS when the consensus forecast at the beginning of that year was a \$2 increase. How should such information, which is essentially "free" for investors to acquire the moment it is placed in the public domain, affect the company's stock price?

In an efficient market, the expected part of the earnings increase (\$2 of the \$3, in this case) should already be reflected in the price, and investors should trade on the new information (the extra \$1, or the earnings "surprise") until all the gains from so doing are competed away. The stock price adjustment to the information should be rapid (if not "instantaneous"), and the new price should make the stock a "fair game" – one which promises new investors a normal rate of return.

In the mid-1960s, while working together at the University of Chicago, Phil Brown and I set out to test these propositions by exploring how the stock market actually responds to announcements of annual earnings. We examined some 2300 annual earnings reports by about 300 New York Stock Exchange companies over the nine-year period 1956–1964. After classifying each of the 2300 reports as containing either "good news" or "bad news" based on past earnings, we calculated the stock returns to an investor holding each of the two groups of companies from one year before to six months after the announcement.

* This article draws heavily on my earlier article, "On the Development, Accomplishments and Limitations of the Theory of Stock Market Efficiency," *Managerial Finance* 20 (1994, issue no. 2/3), pp. 3–48. Permission from the editor and publisher is gratefully acknowledged.

1   Cited in R. Thaler, ed., *Advances in Behavioral Finance* (New York: Russell Sage Foundation, 1993), p. 213.
2   *The New York Times* February 18 (1995), p. 35.

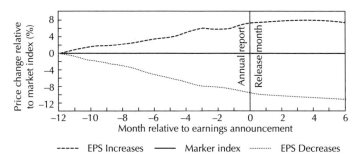

Figure 2.1   Stock Price Changes in Relation to Annual Earnings Announcements*
*Stock prices rise during the year before firms announce EPS increases as information flows into the market. Prices also fall in advance of EPS decreases. There is some price reaction at the time of the announcement. The graph shows price movements for the average firm. Firms with larger EPS changes tend to experience larger price movements. Source: Ball and Brown (1968).

What we found provided stronger support for the theory than practitioners in finance and accounting – not to mention most of our academic colleagues – had expected. The results of our study,[3] which are summarized graphically in Figure 2.1, suggested that the market had already anticipated roughly 80% of the "surprise" component in annual earnings by the time the earnings were announced. There was some further upward "drift" following the announcements of earnings increases and small downward movements following decreases. But, over the entire six-month period after the announcements, investor returns from holding each of the two groups of firms (those with unexpected EPS increases and those with decreases) would have been close to zero. Thus, prices had incorporated the information released in annual earnings reports in a way that virtually eliminated future opportunities to profit from that news. (And, since publication of our study in 1968, these results have been replicated by many other studies of different time periods in 15 different countries.)

The impact of the simple idea of market efficiency has been extensive and enduring. Stimulated in large part by a new research design known as the "event study" (introduced in a 1969 study by Fama,

Fisher, Jensen, and Roll that I discuss later), a large body of empirical research in the 1970s provided consistent evidence of the stock market's ability to process information in a rational, in some cases ingenious, fashion. This research so transformed our view of stock markets that contemporary observers cannot begin to appreciate the general suspicion of and ignorance about stock markets that prevailed 30 years ago.

At the same time it was expanding our knowledge of how the stock market processes information, the early work on market efficiency helped to establish a receptive climate for three other major developments in financial theory: the Miller-Modigliani theories of corporate financial policy; the Sharpe-Lintner Capital Asset Pricing Model (CAPM); and the Black-Scholes option pricing model. Each of these theoretical developments has in turn affected financial practice in important ways. The CAPM, for example, is widely used today both by institutional investors (in establishing their asset allocation and performance measurement criteria) and industrial corporations (in setting their investment rate-of-return targets). The Black-Scholes model is one of the most popular, if not the dominant, procedure for valuing stock options, as well as many other derivatives and so-called "contingent claims." And widespread practices such as indexing, performance measurement, and asset securitization are all unthinkable without the idea of well-functioning security markets.

---

3   R. Ball and P. Brown, "An Empirical Evaluation of Accounting Income Numbers," *Journal of Accounting Research* 6 (1968), 159–178.

Our current understanding of how information is incorporated into stock prices has also influenced corporate disclosure policy. For example, it is now common for corporations to release between two and six different earnings numbers (for example, those including and excluding earnings from businesses that were sold during the period, both before and after the effects of accounting method changes). Whereas the pre-efficiency mentality of accountants (and the SEC) was to distrust investors' judgment and thus to choose *the* earnings number for them, the dominant corporate practice today, with the blessing of the SEC, is to present and then leave it to users to digest the full range of information.

In short, the theoretical developments of the '60s and '70s have helped transform the practice of finance. And, in addition to these theoretical and practical achievements, the early empirical testing of market efficiency coincided with the more general emergence of interest in and respect for free markets that began in the 1970s, first among economists and then later among politicians. Indeed, the market efficiency literature has helped pave the way for what has proved to be a worldwide "liberalization" of financial and other markets.

Despite its insights and accomplishments, however, the theory of efficient markets has obvious limitations. For example, it treats information as a commodity that means the same thing to all investors. It also assumes – with potentially serious consequences, in my view – that information is *costlessly* incorporated into prices. In reality, of course, investors interpret events differently; they face considerable uncertainty about why others are trading; and, especially in the case of smaller firms, they face high costs (as a percentage of firm value) in acquiring and processing information. Given these limitations, it is not surprising that researchers soon began to accumulate evidence that appeared to contradict the theory. Whether the existence of such "anomalous" findings indicates a fatal flaw in the theory – or, more likely, the value of incorporating greater realism – only time and more research will tell.

My aim in this article is to provide an admittedly somewhat personal perspective on the accomplishments and limitations of the theory, and to offer a few suggestions about how the theory might be modified to explain some of the contradictory evidence. Briefly put, my view is this: the theory of efficient markets was an audacious and welcome change

from the comparative ignorance about stock market behavior that preceded it; and despite its now-obvious theoretical and empirical flaws, it has profoundly influenced both the theory and practice of finance.

THE IDEA THAT MARKETS ARE "EFFICIENT"

When Phil Brown and I started the research for our 1968 paper, academics in finance and economics conducted little or no research on stock prices, and we were strongly discouraged by highly skeptical colleagues. The prevailing view among academic economists, even at the University of Chicago, was that the stock market was not a proper subject of serious study. While part of the skepticism about our research stemmed from economists' reservations about the way accountants calculate earnings, much more could be traced to a deep suspicion of stock markets. Indeed, the notion of modelling the stock market *in rational economic terms* was academic heresy at the time.

What little research had been conducted on stock prices up to this point had been performed for the most part by statisticians. The scant empirical literature that preceded the efficient market hypothesis modelled price behavior in statistical, not economic, terms. Successive daily stock price changes seemed for the most part "independent"; that is, they displayed no discernible trends or patterns that could be exploited by investors. Prices on any given day appeared likely to go up or down with roughly equal probability. Lacking an economic explanation for this result, researchers described it in statistical language as the "random walk hypothesis."

Moreover, it was a statistician at the University of Chicago, Harry Roberts, who first saw the potential import for economics of the "random walk" literature. In an important paper published in 1959, Roberts mused, "Perhaps the traditional academic suspicion about the stock market as an object of scholarly research will be overcome." And, as he went on to say,

. . . there is a plausible rationale [for the random walk model]. If the stock market behaved like a mechanically imperfect roulette wheel, people would notice the imperfections and, by acting on them, remove them. This rationale is appealing, if for no other reason than its value as counterweight to the popular view of stock market "irrationality," but it is obviously incomplete.[4]

Among financial economists and other students of the stock market, statistical dependence in returns came to be viewed as valuable information just sitting there in the public domain, that is, as so much gold in the streets. Any predictable trends in prices over time would mean that knowledge of past returns (which is essentially costless to acquire) could be used to predict future returns. In short, dependence across time was viewed as inconsistent with rational behavior in competitive markets and thus as evidence of what later became known as "market inefficiency."[5]

The first use of the term "efficient market" appeared in a 1965 paper by Eugene Fama, who defined it as:

a market where there are large numbers of rational, profit-maximizers actively competing, with each trying to predict future market values of individual securities, and where important current information is almost freely available to all participants . . .

"In an efficient market," Fama argued,

on the average, competition will cause the full effects of new information on intrinsic values to be reflected "instantaneously" in actual prices.[6]

The economics underlying this model are very simple. Publicly-available information by definition is accessible to all investors at zero cost. While earnings reports, for example, are costly for firms to produce, once made public they are nearly costless to obtain (though not necessarily costless to interpret, as I discuss later). And since revenue and cost are equated in competitive equilibrium, the implication of stock market efficiency is that if the cost of reproducing public information is zero, then so are the expected gains. Security prices should therefore adjust to information as soon as

(if not before) it becomes publicly available. Ideas don't come much simpler in economics.

ACCOMPLISHMENTS OF THE THEORY OF STOCK MARKET EFFICIENCY

It is difficult to trace the influence of ideas because their effects range from the direct and concrete (such as the effects on financial practice I noted earlier) to the more subtle and abstract (for example, their influence on how we think about issues, and on the concepts and language we use).

To gain some appreciation of how thoroughly the research on market efficiency has changed our thinking about stock markets, imagine the mindset of an observer of stock markets prior to the research that began in the late '60s. Ordinarily we view the market's reaction to information through the lens of chronological time. Reading the daily financial press, for example, we observe the market's response at a single point in time to what is often a bewildering variety of events and circumstances affecting companies' values. There are announcements of earnings and dividend, new promotional campaigns, labor disputes, staff retrenchments, new debt and equity issues, management changes, proxy contests, asset write-offs, bond rating changes, and changes in interest rates, money supply figures, and GDP data. Thus, what we see with the unaided eye are price reactions to many events at once, without seeing the underlying pattern for any one of them.

In 1969, however, a study of the stock market reaction to stock splits by Eugena Fama, Lawrence Fisher, Michael Jensen, and Richard Roll (hereafter "FFJR") introduced the concept of "event time," which may well have been the single most important break-through in our understanding of how stock prices respond to new information.[7] In attempting to isolate the market's reaction to stock splits (by eliminating the surrounding "noise" of other events), FFJR took many instances of the same event occurring in many different companies at different times, and "standardized" them all in terms of a single "event" date (designated in the

4 H.V. Roberts, "Stock Market 'Patterns' and Financial Analysis: Methodological Suggestions," *Journal of Finance* 14 (1959), 7.
5 For a review of the random walk literature and precedents, see E.F. Fama, "Efficient Capital Markets: A Review of Theory and Empirical Work," *Journal of Finance* 25 (1970), 383–417.
6 E.F. Fama, "Random Walks in Stock Market Prices," *Financial Analysts Journal*, September–October (1965), 4.

7 E.F. Fama, L. Fisher, M.C. Jensen and R. Roll, "The Adjustment of Stock Prices to New Information," *International Economic Review* 10 (1969), 1–21.

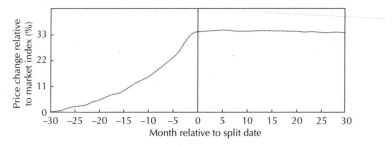

Figure 2.2 Stock Price Changes in Relation to Stock Splits*
*Stock prices rise during the 30 months before stocksplits. Because all the information in the split is public knowledge by the time it occurs, the stock price reaction to the split is complete by "month 0." The graph shows movements for the average firm. Firms with larger splits tend to experience larger price movements. Source: FFJR (1969).

literature as "$t = 0$"). In so doing, they were able to provide an "event-time" view of the market's reaction of the kind presented in Figure 2.2.

What does Figure 2.2 tell us? Conventional wisdom held then, as it does today, that stock splits are good news for investors (and, although why stock splits should be good news has long been something of a puzzle to economists, FFJR reported a plausible reason in their 1969 study: namely, 72% of the splitting firms in their research sample announced dividend increases above the NYSE average in the year *after* the split). What the conventional wisdom may not have predicted, however, but what emerges in Figure 2.2, is the speed with which investors restore the market to its equilibrium or "fair game" condition after the announcement (as revealed by the immediate flattening of the line after $t = 0$).

Thus, where we had previously seen only the chaos of daily stock price movements, FFJR's research design enabled us to see order. And the large empirical literature on market efficiency that came after FFJR both refined their "event study" technique and accumulated impressive evidence – unimaginable before the late '60s – that stock prices respond in apparently ingenious ways to information.[8] One surprising and illuminating example: announcements of new public stock offerings are associated with an immediate 3%

average stock price reduction. The prevailing explanation of this negative market response is as follows: Investors recognize that managers, as representatives of existing shareholders, are more likely to issue new stock (rather than debt) when they think the company is overvalued; hence announcements of new stock offerings are interpreted, at least in the average case, as conveying managers' private assessment of the firm's prospects relative to its current valuation.[9] Another example worth noting (in part for its touch of the bizarre): unexpected CEO deaths are associated with price *decreases* in the case of professional managers, as we might expect in an economy where most companies are well run. But, in the case of those CEOs who are also the founders, death notices are accompanied by price *increases*, with the implication that many founders tend to hang on to their companies too long.[10]

There was one other notable factor contributing to the remarkable successes of efficient markets theory in the late 1960s and early 1970s. At that time, the stock market was one of the few areas in which a large amount of data could be used to test a simple competitive economic theory. And the

---

8 For surveys with detailed analysis of individual studies and their findings, see Fama (1970), cited earlier; E.F. Fama, "Efficient Capital Markets: II," *Journal of Finance* 46 (1991), 1575–1617; and S.F. LeRoy, "Efficient Capital Markets and Martingales," *Journal of Economic Literature* 27 (1989), 1583–1621.

9 For a nice summary of how the market responds to new securities issues, see C.W. Smith, "Raising Capital: Theory and Evidence," *Midland Corporate Finance Journal*, Vol. 4 No. 1 (Spring 1986), 6–22. This article was based in turn on "Investment Banking and the Capital Acquisition Process," *Journal of Financial Economics* 15 (1986), pp. 3–29.

10 W.B. Johnson, R.P. Magee, N.J. Nagarajan and H.A. Newman, "An Analysis of the Stock Price Reaction to Sudden Executive Deaths," *Journal of Accounting and Economics* 7 (1985), 151–174.

data were unusually plentiful. The University of Chicago's Center for Research in Securities Prices (CRSP), which was established (with exceptional foresight) by James H. Lorie in 1960, provided comprehensive data on the universe of all NYSE stocks going back to 1926. Such a rich source of data – which, rare for the time, came in machine-readable form and were essentially error-free – was a luxury almost unheard-of among economists.

Influencing the climate for other financial economic theories

Together, then, the new theory and evidence on market efficiency demonstrated to economists for the first time that share price behavior could be viewed as a rational economic phenomenon. And this development in turn helped set the stage for other breakthroughs.

Two other broad areas of financial-economic enquiry were launched around the same time as efficient market theory. First were the "dividend" and "capital structure" irrelevance propositions formulated by Merton Miller and Franco Modigliani (first at Carnegie Mellon, later at the University of Chicago) and presented in papers published in 1958 and 1961.[11] Soon after came the capital asset pricing model (CAPM), which was developed separately by William Sharpe (at Stanford in a 1964 paper) and John Lintner (at Harvard in 1965).[12] The consistent evidence of market efficiency offered strong support for these concepts that shared similar assumptions about the working of financial markets. Indeed, without the impressive body of empirical research on efficiency as background, it is not clear that the equilibrium-based reasoning of the Sharpe-Lintner CAPM (and later the Black-Scholes option pricing model, introduced in 1973) would have been so well and so

quickly received.[13] Development of the CAPM (as I discuss later) was particularly important for subsequent research on market efficiency because it provided researchers with a method of estimating investors' "expected" returns – the returns passive investors would otherwise have earned in the absence of the information being tested.

A considerable body of knowledge on corporate capital structure has also been built on the work of Miller and Modigliani. The arbitrage-based arguments M&M used to buttress their "irrelevance propositions" were a novelty in corporate finance. They were developed over approximately the same period that Roberts and Fama were formulating their ideas on efficiency, and they relied in part on the same basic reasoning of competitive economic theory underlying market efficiency. Among other practical contributions, M&M's then revolutionary thinking on capital structure appears to have supplied an important part of the logic for the leveraged restructurings of the 1980s.[14] As in the case of the CAPM, finance scholars were more receptive to the M&M propositions in large part because of their consistency with the closely-related area of efficient markets.

Summing up

Encouraged, then, by its initial accomplishments and reinforced by other theoretical developments like the CAPM, research on market efficiency spread rapidly across the globe, with results that provided remarkably consistent support for the theory. This research had an enduring impact on our view of stock markets, of financial markets generally, and perhaps of markets of all kinds. Because this evidence tended to contradict prior assumptions, which were based on prejudice and casual observation rather than on systematic research, academic attention was quickly drawn to

11 F. Modigliani and M.H. Miller, "The Cost of Capital, Corporation Finance, and The Theory of Investment," *American Economic Review* 48 (1958), 261–297; and M.H. Miller and F. Modigliani, "Dividend Policy, Growth and the Valuation of Shares," *Journal of Business* 34 (1961), 411–433.
12 W.F. Sharpe, "Capital Asset Prices: A Theory of Market Equilibrium under Conditions of Risk," *Journal of Finance* 19 (1964), 425–442; and J. Lintner, "The Valuation of Risk Assets and the Selection of Risky Investments in Stock Portfolios and Capital Budgets," *Review of Economics and Statistics* 47 (1965), 13–37.

13 Teachers and researchers made frequent reference to the Sharpe-Lintner model well before it was formally tested (by Black, Jensen, and Scholes in 1972 and Fama and MacBeth in 1973), relying in part on the strong evidence of market efficiency and on the perceived overlapping of the two ideas.
14 See M.H. Miller, "The Modigliani–Miller Propositions Thirty Years After," *Journal of Applied Corporate Finance* 2(1) (Spring 1989).

it. In a surprisingly short time, academic attitudes toward stock markets had shifted from one extreme to the other, from suspicion to almost reverence.

LIMITATIONS IN THE THEORY OF EFFICIENT MARKETS

It was not long, however, before researchers began to report evidence that appeared to contradict the theory. But, as I argue below, finance scholars should not have been completely surprised by such evidence. The theory of efficient markets has not influenced theory and practice because it is free of defects. Its influence has been due to the insights it provides, not those it fails to provide. The cup remains half full, even though it is half empty.

I now discuss a number of limitations of the theory that I have divided into three overlapping categories: (1) the theory's failure to explain certain aspects of share price behavior, referred to in the literature as "anomalies"; (2) defects in efficiency as a model of markets; and (3) problems in testing the efficiency model.

Empirical anomalies: problems in fitting the theory to the data

No theory can explain all the data with which it is confronted, especially when the data are as abundant as stock prices. There is now a large body of anomalous evidence that at least appears to contradict market efficiency. The list of such "anomalies" includes:

- **Price Overreactions**. There is evidence that the prices of individual stocks overreact to information and then undergo "corrections." The resulting negative correlations in prices appear to create profit opportunities for "contrarian" trading strategies.[15]
- **Excess Volatility**. Robert Shiller, among others, has argued that the stock market in general

overreacts to events because of investors' pursuit of fads and other herd-like behavior. In support of his argument, he presents evidence suggesting that the volatility of stock prices is much too large to be explained by the volatility of dividends.[16]

- **Price Underreactions to Earnings**. In seeming contradiction of the the tendency of prices to overreact to information in general, research indicates that prices *underreact* to quarterly earnings reports, thus lending support for "earnings momentum" strategies.[17]
- **The Failure of CAPM to Explain Returns**. The Capital Asset Pricing Model, as mentioned, has provided the primary means for measuring investors' expected returns; indeed, it was the workhorse for calculating discount rates for an entire generation of practitioners as well as researchers. But evidence that high-beta stocks do not earn higher returns than low-beta stocks has led some to pronounce the horse dead.[18] (But recent research suggests that announcements of the death of beta may be premature.)[19]
- **The Explanatory Power of Non-CAPM Factors**. Stocks with (1) small capitalization, (2) low market-to-book ratios, (3) high-dividend yields, and (4) low P/E ratios tend to outperform their expected returns (as estimated by the CAPM), thus providing justification for yield-tilted, small-cap, and other popular investment strategies.
- **Seasonal Patterns**. Researchers have provided evidence of seasonal patterns of hourly, daily, monthly, and quarterly duration. Particularly puzzling is the "weekend effect": the tendency of stock returns to be negative over the period from Friday's close to Monday's opening. Such seasonals could lend support to technical analysts' claims to outperform market averages.

---

15 W.F.M. De Bondt, and R.H. Thaler, "Does the Stock Market Overreact" *Journal of Finance*, (1985), 793–805; and W.F.M. De Bondt and R.H. Thaler, "Further Evidence on Investor Overreaction and Stock Market Seasonality," *Journal of Finance* 42 (1987), 557–581.

16 R.J. Shiller, "Do Stock Prices Move Too Much to Be Justified by Subsequent Changes in Dividends?," *American Economic Review* 71, (1981a), 421–436.

17 V.L. Bernard and J. Thomas, "Evidence That Stock Prices Do Not Fully Reflect the Implications of Current Earnings for Future Earnings," *Journal of Accounting and Economics* 13 (1990), 305–340.

18 For a survey, see M. Reinganum, "The Collapse of the Efficient Market Hypothesis: A Look at the Empirical Anomalies of the 1980s," *Selected Reading in Investment Management* (Institutional Investor, 1988).

19 For a defense of beta, see S.P. Kothari and J. Shanken in this issue.

As I argue below, however, it is difficult to tell whether such anomalies should be attributed to defects in markets themselves, to flaws in "market efficiency" as a way of thinking about competitive markets, or to problems with the research itself.

Defects in "efficiency" as a model of stock markets

Failure to Incorporate Information Acquisition and Processing Costs. One of the most important explanations of these anomalies is likely to be the neglected role of information costs. Information costs are neither new to economists nor inconsistent with competitive markets. Nevertheless, the costs of acquiring and processing information have received scant attention in the theory and empirical research on stock market efficiency.

The first "event studies" such as the FFJR study of stock splits and the Ball-Brown study of annual earnings reports investigated relatively simple cases in which information is widely disseminated in the financial press and on the wire services to analysts and other investors. The cost to individual investors of acquiring such public information (as opposed to the cost of producing that same information prior to disclosure) was assumed to be negligible. The information was also assumed to be simple to use, with negligible processing (or interpretation) costs.

But what about those academic research designs that simulate trading strategies that in fact have substantial information acquisition and processing costs? In such cases, the abnormal returns reported by the research could be significantly overstated. Consider the following:

1. If 1000 professors of finance worldwide annually incur costs of $50,000 each (including salary, computer costs, and overhead) in searching for anomalies, the expected return from their discovery of pricing errors in the market could be as much as 5% per year (or $50 million) on a $1 billion portfolio. And, if they have been searching for 20 years, the expected return from producing such *private* information could be many times larger.
2. But, if the expected returns from such strategies are this large, why have some researchers published their anomalous evidence? Why have they not instead used that information for private gain?
3. More generally, what are the expected gains from producing and trading on private information?
4. What is the meaning of gains from a trading rule that is simulated using *historical* data together with *modern* computing and statistical techniques? (Does this differ from, say, the simulated gains from owning a helicopter gunship during the Middle Ages?)
5. If an analyst forecasts the earnings of 25 stocks each quarter at an annual cost of $200,000 (including salary and overhead), then the average cost of a forecast is $2000. This is one ten-thousandth of 1% of the market value of a $2 billion firm. It is one tenth of 1% of the market value of $2 million of stock in the firm held by clients. If we further assume that the gains from forecasting are approximately equal to the costs, can we reliably detect such a low number in stock rates of return?

We have no well-developed answers to such questions. To date, and for obvious reasons, researchers have tended to ignore information costs and have relied on cases of publicly-disclosed information (whose cost we somewhat arbitrarily define as zero) in testing market efficiency.

The direction of the bias from ignoring information costs is consistent with the anomalies evidence. For example, information costs are a likely candidate for explaining the small-firm effect, the tendency of small-cap stocks to produce higher returns. Such firms tend to have small analyst followings, presumably because the cost of acquiring and processing information is large relative to the amounts invested in them. Investors may rationally require higher returns (than those predicted by the CAPM) to compensate for their higher information costs (as a percentage of value).

But little more can be said without knowing more about the size of such information processing and acquisition costs, and how such costs are likely to affect actual (pre-cost) expected returns. Moreover, there can be significant differences *among* investors in the information they possess, in the extent of their efforts to seek information, and in their ability to process it. Although the CAPM is silent on this issue, it would be logical to expect more sophisticated, better-informed, and more active investors to earn higher returns. The question, however, is: How much higher? For example, what is the predicted rate of return in a competitive market for an investor like Warren Buffett who sits on the corporate board, is a close friend of the CEO, and has a voice in major corporate decisions? Much of Buffett's success may be attributed to his ability to reduce the information (and "agency") costs that confront ordinary passive investors. Lower information costs could in turn be viewed as reducing Buffett's perceived risks and required rates of return, thus making stocks more valuable to him than to ordinary investors.

Heterogeneous Information and Beliefs. This brings us to another, closely related deficiency of efficient markets theory – one which stems from its "mechanical" characterization of investors as homogeneous, wholly objective, information-processing machines. Investor sentiment and confidence play no role, and publicly available information is assumed to have the same implications for all. In reality, of course, individual investors can differ greatly in their beliefs, and a single piece of information – say, IBM's latest earnings report – may be interpreted quite differently by different investors.

The assumption of homogeneous investors was understandable at the time the theory was developed. For one thing, it allowed researchers to demonstrate to highly skeptical readers that stock prices do respond to information, and in rational ways. But there were other grounds for using such a clearly unrealistic assumption. As the great Austrian economist F.A. Hayek argued in his 1945 classic, "The Use of Knowledge in Society,"[20] market prices incorporate information that is not – and perhaps cannot – be fully known by any individual. For this reason, markets are likely to be more rational in viewing information than the individual investors who comprise them. Indeed, that is the beauty of markets.

But this does not mean markets are infallible. (To paraphrase Churchill on democracy, it's not that markets are perfect in allocating resources; it's just that all other systems are so much worse.) For all their virtues, markets cannot fully overcome the inevitable limits of individual knowledge – limits that, under certain circumstances, can have pronounced effects on market behavior.

To see how such limits might affect markets, consider that the trading decisions of individual investors are based not only on the individual's information about a given stock or commodity, but also on that individual's beliefs about the information on which *other investors* base their trading. And because an investor possessing a piece of information or holding a belief about the future cannot know with certainty the extent to which that information or belief is shared by others, he does not know the extent to which the information is already reflected in prices.

One plausible way of interpreting episodes of high turnover and rapid price changes, such as the stock market crash of 1987, is that investors' costs of becoming quickly informed about the motives for others' trades can become extraordinarily high. Under such conditions of extreme uncertainty, the "mechanistic" model of efficiency, with its assumptions of zero information costs and homogeneous investors, clearly breaks down. In such cases, investors' required rates of return can be seen as rising sharply in response to the sudden surge in price volatility, and the general uncertainty is resolved only gradually over time (in part through the commentary of market analysts and others whose economic role efficient markets theory has largely ignored).

A central question for finance theory, then, is whether events such as the crash of '87 are unambiguous evidence of market irrationality. Are we forced to conclude, along with Keynes (and the new "behaviorialist" school of thought in finance), that the market is a game of musical chairs in which "animal spirits" regularly prevail over reason? Or can such episodes plausibly be described by Hayekian models in which *rational* individuals with different information confront extreme uncertainty?

Expanding efficient markets theory to accommodate information costs and differences among investors may help us decide this issue. For, in addition to the basic uncertainty that attends all business activity, differences among investors' information and beliefs are an added source of uncertainty and hence information costs; and, in cases where such costs are high, investors may expect to earn significantly higher returns.

20 *American Economic Review* 35 (1945), 519–530.

A Brief Digression on the Role of Security Analysts. As mentioned above, efficient markets theory has virtually nothing to say about the economic role of security analysts and public commentary. The theory's silence on security analysts has even led many academics to view them as redundant.

What do stock analysts do? Besides talking to management on a regular basis, they pay close attention to economic events affecting the companies they follow, and to the accompanying market reactions. They also talk to large investors about their reasons for buying or selling and so attempt to gauge "investor sentiment." In so doing, analysts can be viewed as reducing investor uncertainty about the information and trading motives of *other* investors.

For example, analysts' earnings forecasts function as estimates of the information about near-term profitability that has already been built into current prices. The existence of such forecasts enables investors to compare their own private forecasts against what amounts to a public consensus. And by reducing one source of investors' uncertainty – namely, about why others are trading – securities analysts reduce information costs and raise the market value of publicly traded companies. Media commentary on markets can be viewed as playing a similar role.

Failure to Consider Transactions Costs. Besides assuming zero information costs and homogeneous investors, early versions of efficient markets theory also assumed that the markets themselves are costless to operate. But if stock markets are large-scale, high-turnover institutions whose primary purpose is to minimize the transactions costs associated with helping firms raise capital, they have not succeeded in *eliminating* such costs.

Having said this, it is not clear what role transactions costs play in setting stock prices. In a paper published in 1978, Michael Jensen argued that an efficient market can only be expected to adjust prices within limits defined by the cost of trading.[21] According to this view, for example, if transactions costs are 1%, an abnormal return to a trading strategy of up to 1% would be considered within

the bounds of efficiency. It could not be exploited for profit *net of costs*.

This view makes sense to traders, but it has several shortcomings from a broader economic perspective. First, there must exist some level of transactions costs at which we are unwilling to call a market "efficient." If transactions costs were extremely large, there would be few opportunities to profit from price errors, net of costs. Nevertheless, it makes little sense to describe a market with extremely large costs of trading and thus extremely large price errors as "efficient."

Second, although transactions costs of x% may be consistent with price *errors* of ±x%, they are not consistent with price *biases* of that size. Since most "event studies" and related efficiency tests study average returns, the pricing errors due to transactions costs should net to zero over a broad sample of trades; and thus transactions costs are not obviously relevant to interpreting the results of the studies.

Third, because transactions costs vary across investors, defining efficiency in terms of transactions costs can produce as many definitions as there are investors. Whose transactions costs are to be used in judging *the market* to be efficient? A possible solution might be to define efficiency in terms of the lowest-cost trader. But, because some specialists and institutional investors face transactions costs as low as one tenth of one percent, this approach can degenerate into ignoring transactions costs entirely. Thus, the role of transactions costs in the theory of market efficiency remains largely unresolved.

Market Microstructure Effects. A closely-related issue is the effect of the actual market mechanism on transacted prices, known in the literature as market "microstructure" effects. Researchers typically assume that trades could be executed at the closing prices recorded in data files such as CRSP's. These price estimates, however, have a margin of error that is as large as their quoted spreads, which run about 3% for the average NYSE-AMEX stock (and average close to 6% for NYSE-AMEX stocks with prices less than $5). To compound the problem, investors cannot always execute at quoted spreads because of illiquidity.

Such market microstructure effects can be quite large relative to the size of the short-term abnormal returns reported by many event studies. Consider the "turn of the year" or "January" effect – the

---

21 M.C. Jensen, "Some Anomalous Evidence Regarding Market Efficiency," *Journal of Financial Economics* 6 (1978), 96.

widely-recognized tendency of stocks (particularly low-price stocks) to produce large returns in the first trading days of the calendar year. A 1989 study by Donald Keim demonstrates that this effect can be explained largely by a pronounced (if unexplained) tendency of stocks to trade near the bid at the end of the year and then move toward the ask at the beginning.[22]

Similar microstructure effects may well also be exaggerating the size of the short-term price reversals, the seasonal patterns in daily or weekly returns, and even the abnormal longer-term returns reported in the anomalies literature. Such effects are especially likely to influence the findings of research on low-price stocks. In 1985, for example, Werner DeBondt and Richard Thaler published a study reporting very large gains from a contrarian strategy of buying stocks immediately after large percentage declines and holding them for five years.[23] In a study published this past year, however, two of my Rochester colleagues and I discovered that DeBondt and Thaler's results were distorted by some very large percentage gains on some very low-priced stocks. One stock earned 3500% after trading at $1/16 (which is half of $1/8, the minimum increment in which NYSE stocks are typically quoted). We also found that adjustments of $1/8 in the prices of their "loser" stocks would have reduced the five-year returns of this contrarian strategy by 2500 basis points.[24]

Like transactions costs, microstructure or trading-mechanism effects present the researcher with a dilemma. Trading mechanisms certainly are not costless to operate, and thus the prices at which trades are transacted are likely to be affected in systematic ways by institutional arrangements. This seems particularly likely for small-capitalization and low-price stocks, and for stocks and stock exchanges with low turnover. But, unlike transactions costs, it

seems unreasonable to interpret price behavior caused by the trading mechanism as evidence of market inefficiency, because recorded prices are not those at which the simulated trading strategies could have been executed at the close of trading.

Yet taking this view to its limit leads here, as in the case of transactions costs, to the perverse outcome that the probability of a market's being judged efficient increases with the size of bid/ask spreads. Thus, as with transactions costs, the precise role of market microstructure effects in the *theory* of market efficiency is not apparent.

Problems in testing "efficiency" as a model of stock markets

As noted earlier, investors' ability to exploit public information for gain can be tested only by comparing the returns earned when trading on public information against the returns otherwise expected from passive investing. In many empirical tests of market efficiency, the Capital Asset Pricing Model has been used to estimate such expected returns. But, as also mentioned, the CAPM has come under attack from empirical studies showing at best weak correlations between actual stock market returns and those predicted by the CAPM. And because tests of market efficiency are thus "joint tests" of *both* the CAPM's success in measuring expectations and the market's ability to incorporate new information in prices, flaws in the CAPM raise doubts about the reliability of the existing empirical research – both the work that appears to contradict market efficiency as well as that which supports it.

Changes in Riskless Rates and Risk Premiums. The CAPM states that a stock's expected return is equal to the riskless rate (in practice, the interest rates on Treasury notes or bonds) plus a risk premium obtained by multiplying the stock's beta times the market equity risk premium (the amount a stock of average risk is expected to earn above the riskless rate). Expressed as an equation:

$$E(R) = Rf + B (Rm - Rf).$$

Unfortunately, the model is completely silent on a number of important issues of practical as well

22 D.B. Keim, "Trading Patterns, Bid-ask Spreads and Estimated Security Returns: The Case of Common Stocks at Calendar Turning Points," *Journal of Financial Economics* 25 (1989), 75–98.

23 DeBondt and Thaler (1985), cited earlier.

24 As a more general indication of skewed returns, we found that although the median returns of "winner" and "loser" stocks differed by only 5%, the average returns differed by 57%. See R. Ball, S.P. Kothari and J. Shanken, "Problems in Measuring Portfolio Performance: An Application to Contrarian Investment Strategies," *Journal of Financial Economics* 38 (1995), 79–107.

as theoretical import. For example, what riskless rates, market risk premiums, and individual betas would be consistent with an efficient market? And how are such measures expected to change over time, if at all? (Most empirical tests of market efficiency simply assume that riskless rates, market risk premiums, or betas are constant.)

The second question is potentially troubling because the more we allow both interest rates and the market risk premium to vary over time, the less ability we have to answer a question such as: Are stock prices in general too volatile? In 1981, for example, Robert Shiller published a study concluding that the historical variance of stock prices over the 108-year period from 1871 to 1979 was much too large to be justified by the variance of corporate dividends.[25] Using the CAPM, however, it's impossible to say whether Shiller is right. Because of its assumption of constant riskless rates and market risk premiums, the CAPM provides no means of judging the "correct" amount of variance in the market index. Shiller's test, for example, assumes in the tradition of the CAPM that the market-wide expected return is constant in *nominal* terms over the entire sample period 1871–1979 in order to place bounds on the price variance allowable in an efficient market. Under this assumption, the probability of rejecting market efficiency seems almost 100%![26]

But consider what happens when we relax this assumption. Consider the S&P 500 as the value of a claim on a perpetuity of expected earnings produced by the 500 companies comprising the index. If the real riskless rate is assumed to be zero (close to its historical average), then an increase in the risk premium from 6% to 8% will reduce the value of the S&P 500 by 25%. Do we see too few or too many such percentage declines in the S&P 500? It seems quite plausible that market risk premiums could change dramatically in response to sudden changes in investors' perceptions of political risk and economic uncertainty. But the answer to this question depends on how frequently the risk premium can be expected to change by as much as 2%. (And, although the CAPM is silent on this

issue, researchers are now attempting to find ways to address it.)

Trends in Real Rates and Market Risk Premiums. Moreover, there is nothing in the CAPM that would rule out serial correlation in changes in either the riskless rate or the market risk premium.[27] In fact, the investment opportunity set facing companies and investors seems likely to exhibit positive serial correlation – that is, a tendency for increases to be followed by further increases – due to bursts of invention, among other factors. A gradual aging of the population seems likely to induce positive dependence in interest rates (as a growing number of retirees seeks to live off income from investment and a shrinking workforce operates those investments).

In contrast, the market risk premium seems particularly likely to have elements of *negative* dependence. Consider, for example, how risk premiums would change if the level of general economic uncertainty perceived by investors varies over time, but tends eventually to return to "normal" levels. Increases in perceived risk will cause the index to fall (even given the same *level* of expected corporate profits) in order to give investors a temporarily higher expected return over the period of increased uncertainty. And, if the uncertainties that trigger sharp price declines are resolved over time, the index then tends to rise.[28]

Working along with such cycles in economic uncertainty and investor confidence, changes in the *supply* of risky assets (due to the creation of new assets and the obsolescence of old) by corporations would reinforce this pattern of negative serial correlation in investors' required returns and market risk premiums. For example, suppose expectations of increased political and economic stability are associated with rising stock prices and P/E ratios

---

25 Shiller (1981), cited earlier.
26 This is a case of using an excessive and misplaced faith in the CAPM to undermine what appears, in my view at least, to be a more reasonable belief in the rationality of market pricing.

27 For some informal evidence of a sharp decline in market risk premiums over the past 20 years, see J.R. Woolridge, "Do Stock Prices Reflect Fundamental Values?," (in this issue).
28 This point has been made by E.F. Fama, *Foundations of Finance* (Basic Books, New York), p. 149; K.C. Chan, "On the Contrarian Investment Strategy," *Journal of Business* 61 (1988), 147–163; E.F. Fama and K.R. French, "Permanent and Temporary Components of Stock Prices," *Journal of Political Economy* 96 (1988), 246–273; and R. Ball and S.P. Kothari, "Nonstationary Expected Returns: Implications for Serial Correlation in Returns, Apparent Price Reversals and Tests of Market Efficiency," *Journal of Financial Economics* 25 (1989), 51–74.

(as has happened since the recent U.S. House and Senate elections) in response to declines in both interest rates and the general market risk premium. For U.S. corporations, this means a reduction in their cost of capital; and, in response to the lower cost of capital, they can be expected to expand the supply of new risky investments over the next few years. As the aggregate supply of risky assets increases, investors' required rates of return will tend to rise back toward normal levels over time, causing prices and P/E ratios to fall.

Given the above assumptions, then (all of which seem fairly plausible), an efficient market would be expected to exhibit serial dependence in both real interest rates and market risk premiums. The point of these conjectures is to illustrate that the cyclical patterns (or "mean reversion") in stock returns are not necessarily evidence of the market irrationality asserted by Shiller and the so-called behavioralists. Such negative dependence is equally consistent with rational responses by (1) investors to changes in general political and economic conditions and (2) corporations to the resulting changes in investor demand (as reflected in interest rates and risk premiums) for stocks.[29]

Changes in Betas. Finally, consider the relation between beta and market efficiency. Finance theory says nothing about how betas vary both among companies and over time. It thus offers no guidance as to what betas and what patterns of changes in observed betas are consistent with efficiency.

The current theory fails to account, for example, for the fact that betas can be expected to change in fairly predictable ways in response to changes in stock price levels. To illustrate, if we assume that a company has a given level of overall risk (a fixed "asset beta"), the beta of the company's stock (its equity beta) will rise along with increases in its degree of financial leverage (or debt-to-equity ratio). When expressed in market value terms, moreover, a company's debt-to-equity ratio will increase not only when it issues more debt, but also when its stock price falls. Loosely speaking, this means that *when a company's stock price drops sharply, investors' perception of the stock's risk and hence its required return actually increases*. Conversely, *when the stock price rises significantly, its perceived risk and required return fall*.

Such systematic changes in betas in response to large stock price changes could account for a number of the "anomalies" noted earlier. For example, the longer-term "mean reversion" of stock returns – the tendency of high stock returns to be followed by low ones, and vice versa – discovered by Gene Fama and Ken French could be explained largely by systematic shifts in beta after price changes, as could the ability of low P/E and low market-to-book stocks to outperform market averages.[30]

Seasonal Patterns in Betas. To take another example, betas could well exhibit seasonals. There is no reason in principle why securities' relative risks, or even aggregate risk, cannot vary with, say, the day-of-the-week. Consider a firm that routinely makes its major announcements – earnings, dividends, investments, acquisitions – on Thursdays, perhaps because it schedules board meetings on that day. Thursday returns then will exhibit higher variance and, possibly, covariance. To the extent this is so, what appear to be seasonal patterns of superior returns may turn out to be normal ones when adjusted for the associated temporary increases in risk.

IS "BEHAVIORAL" FINANCE THE ANSWER?

Given such limitations in the concept of market efficiency and the existing empirical tests of the

---

29 The *supply* of risky investment assets produced by corporate investment decisions is typically assumed by the CAPM to be fixed and thus unaffected by changes in prices and other financial variables. But, without any "supply-side" theory about how corporations respond to changes in real rates and risk premiums, it is difficult to see how we could be surprised by *any* observed sequence of market returns or use the sequence to judge any market to be efficient or inefficient. This is a deficiency not only of the CAPM, but of all major models in modern finance theory including the DCF present value model, the option pricing model, and efficient market theory itself. Each of these financial models is concerned exclusively with investor demand for (and hence the price of) a certain asset in relation to other assets with given prices. Indeed, I would argue that *the failure to consider the supply of investments is perhaps the greatest deficiency in modern financial economic theory*.

30 Ball and Kothari (1989) provide evidence that endogenous risk variation explains much of the serial correlation observed in Fama and French (1988). A related issue is the evidence of apparent price reversals in De Bondt and Thaler (1985, 1987). Both Chan (1988) and Ball and Kothari (1989) report that the equity betas of the most extreme "losing" stocks can be expected to increase because of the extreme increase in their market debt-equity ratios. Conversely, the extreme "winning" stocks are likely to have equity beta decreases due to extreme leverage reductions.

theory, a group of finance scholars known as behavioralists has suggested that it is time to abandon the premise of collectively rational investors on which the theory rests. Behavioralists argue that stock price "corrections" and cycles reflect systematic biases in how investors use information. Investors are said to place too much weight on current information, focusing myopically on short-term earnings, for example, while ignoring companies' long-run propects. And stock prices accordingly are viewed as highly unreliable guides to corporate resource allocation and other important decisions. But, is behavioral finance the answer to the limitations of efficient markets theory?

I don't think so. First of all, the profit opportunities created by such alleged investor myopia seem grossly inconsistent with competitive markets. They are much too large to be credible, thus casting doubt on the research methods. Moreover, the failure of the vast majority of professional money managers (including contrarians as well as earnings momentum types) to outperform market averages with any degree of consistency should reinforce our skepticism about such claims.

Second, behavioral finance has anomalies of its own. The extensive evidence of post-earnings-announcement drift cited earlier means that investors place *too little weight*, not too much, on recent earnings information. Showing that a theory has anomalies is one thing; replacing it with an anomaly-free theory is another.

Finally, behavioralists have also criticized the objectivity and openness of the research process over the 1960s and '70s, arguing that the process was slow to accept dissenting views. Benjamin Friedman, for example, comments:

It is no coincidence that the research [in support of efficient markets theory] . . . has emerged almost entirely from the nation's business schools. From the perspective of the private-interest orientation of these institutions, this identification is both understandable and appropriate.[31]

While Friedman is correct that the idea of efficiency arose in business schools, his further implication that the schools' "private-interest orientation" influenced the research findings represents not just a distortion, but in fact a complete inversion of the

incentives of both researchers and teachers. In my experience, businessmen and MBA students have been more receptive to the message that there is gold in the streets than to the lesson that fiercely competitive financial markets eliminate the easy opportunities for gain.

Many critics of the literature on market efficiency have suggested that it took too long to recognize anomalies. Consider this recent statement by Richard Thaler in his introduction to a collection of behavioralist studies in finance:

The financial world as described in Eugene Fama's 1970 efficient markets survey was one that had no urgent need for people. Markets were efficient, prices were unpredictable, and financial economists did not know how to spell the word "anomaly."[32]

This statement, perhaps precisely because it is made from the secure vantage of hindsight, is strongly at odds with my own view of how the research evolved. In our 1968 paper cited at the beginning, Phil Brown and I mentioned anomalous evidence of post-earnings-announcement "drift" in prices. Since this was the second "event study" ever conducted (in the first, FFJR found no signs of anomalies) and was published just three years after the first time the words "efficient market" appeared in print, it seems that the efficient markets literature was not slow in introducing anomalous evidence.

Moreover, the word "anomaly" was introduced to the financial economics literature in a paper I published in 1978 that surveyed a number of puzzling findings related to earnings and dividends.[33] While that survey encountered some resistance and took two years to get published, other anomalies were uncovered in the meantime. Recognizing the pattern, Michael Jensen quickly put together an issue of the *Journal of Financial*

---

31 In Thaler (1993, p. 213).

32 Thaler (1993).
33 R. Ball, "Anomalies in Relationships Between Securities' Yields and Yield-Surrogates," *Journal of Financial Economics* 6, (1978), 103–126. I borrowed the word "anomaly" from Thomas Kuhn's famous book, *The Structure of Scientific Revolutions* (University of Chicago Press, 1970), which introduced the term to the philosophy of science and scientific method. Kuhn's book, I might note, was published in the same year as Fama's review of the EMH literature, and only eight years before the word appeared in the financial economics literature.

Economics devoted entirely to studies of anomalies that was published in the same year.

Overall, then, critics of the literature's responsiveness to anomalous results seem to have overstated their case. In retrospect, I am surprised by how *quickly* the literature embraced the idea of anomalies in the late '70s. We had much more difficulty convincing people that markets were efficient a decade earlier.

CONCLUDING OBSERVATIONS

Are stock markets efficient? Yes and no. On the one hand, the research provides insights into stock price behavior that were previously unimaginable. On the other hand, as research has come to show, the theory of efficient markets is, like all theories, an imperfect and limited way of viewing stock markets. The issue will be impossible to solve conclusively while there are so many binding limitations to the asset pricing models that underlie empirical tests of market efficiency.

Our models of asset pricing began with the CAPM and thus have an accumulated history of only 30 years. With such a limited tradition in asset pricing, we could hardly expect to have a strong basis for concluding that security prices do (or do not) immediately restore equilibrium in response to new information, particularly in the presence of extreme uncertainty. Bearing such constraints in mind, I believe that much of the evidence on stock price behavior does not and cannot reliably address the *factual* issue of "efficiency" at this point in time. Our models of price equilibrium and our data are not yet up to the task.

This is not to say that empirical research cannot be informative under these circumstances. We have learned a great deal from the "anomaly chasing" of the last decade, and there are enough puzzles and clues to work on for some time. Nevertheless, I do not believe that we can reliably learn much about whether (or to what extent) markets are efficient from these results.

Do we have a better theory? I think not. But, as researchers comb through the evidence and seek more realistic ways of modelling stock price behavior, we are bound to improve the theory over time.

Have we learned much from the theory of stock market efficiency? I think so. And I think this is a better question. The economic theory of competitive markets now seems unlikely to be dislodged from its central role in stock market research, for several reasons. First, stock markets must rank highly among markets on *a priori* likelihood of being competitive: there are no entry barriers; there are many buyers and sellers, who by and large appear to be greedy and enterprising people; and transaction costs are relatively low. Second, as outlined above, the inevitability of binding limitations in both our models of efficiency and in the available data provides a credible alternative explanation for the range of anomalies that have been documented over the last decade. Third, I personally went through the transformation from the pre-EMH view of securities markets, and I am still impressed by how well prices respond to information, *relative to what we expected thirty years ago*.

CHAPTER 3

Market Myths

*G. Bennett Stewart, III (Stern Stewart & Co.)**

It is easy to forget why senior management's most important job is to create value. Of course, a higher value increases the wealth of the company's shareholders who, after all, are the owners of the enterprise. But, of greater import, society at large benefits. The quest for value drives scarce resources to their most productive uses and their most efficient users. The more effectively resources are deployed, the more robust will be economic growth and the rate of improvement in our standard of living. Adam Smith's invisible hand is at work when investors' private gain is a public virtue. And, although there are exceptions to this rule, most of the time there is a happy harmony between creating market value and enhancing the quality of life.

The pursuit of value often is made more difficult by a failure to understand how share prices are really set in the stock market. I regularly encounter senior executives and board members who believe stock prices are determined by some vague combination of earnings, growth, return, book value, cash flow, dividends, and the demand for their shares. (In one particularly memorable meeting, I was harangued for several hours by an elderly gentleman who claimed that mysterious forces – the so-called "gnomes" of Wall Street – controlled

the market. His "voodoo valuation" framework will not be formally rebutted in this book.)

Confusion over what it is that investors really want can make it difficult for management to reach sensible decisions regarding business strategy, acquisitions and divestitures, accounting methods, financial structure, dividend policy, investor relations, and, most important of all (let's be honest), bonus plans. With the competition for capital growing ever more hostile and global, the cost of ignorance is escalating. It is high time management learns the answer to the question: What is the engine that drives share prices?

IN SEARCH OF VALUE: THE ACCOUNTING MODEL VERSUS THE ECONOMIC MODEL

Right away there are two competing answers. The traditional "accounting model" of valuation contends that Wall Street sets share prices by capitalizing a company's earnings-per-share (EPS) at an appropriate price/earnings multiple (P/E). If, for example, a company typically sells at ten times earnings, and EPS is now $1.00, the accounting model would predict a $10 share price. But, should earnings fall to $0.80 per share, then – however temporary the downturn – the company's shares are expected to fall to $8.

The appeal of this accounting model is its simplicity and apparent precision. Its shortcoming is an utter lack of realism; the accounting model

---

* This article is a slightly abbreviated version of Chapter 2 of the author's book, *The Quest for Value: A Guide for Senior Management* (Harper & Row, 1990).

assumes, in effect, that P/E multiples never change. But P/E multiples change all the time – in the wake of acquisitions and divestitures, changes in financial structure and accounting policies, and new investment opportunities. P/E multiples, in short, adjust to changes in the "quality" of a company's earnings. And this makes EPS a very unreliable measure of value.

A competing explanation – the "economic model" of value to which I subscribe – holds that share prices are determined by smart investors who care about just two things: the cash to be generated over the life of a business, and the risk of the cash receipts. More precisely, the economic model states that a company's intrinsic market value is determined by discounting its expected future "Free Cash Flow" (FCF) back to a present value at a rate that reflects its "cost of capital."

The cost of capital is the rate of return required to compensate investors for bearing risk. It is a rate determined in practice by adding a premium for risk to the yield prevailing on relatively risk-free government bonds.

FCF is the cash flow generated by a company's operations that is free, or net, of the new capital invested for growth. To compute it, imagine that all of a company's cash operating receipts are deposited in a cigar-box, and that all of its cash operating outlays are taken out, regardless of whether the outlays are recorded by the accountants as expenses on the income statement or as expenditures on the balance sheet. What's left over in the cigar box is FCF.

Which is the more desirable, then, positive or negative FCF? While you may be tempted to say a positive FCF will maximize a company's value, the correct answer actually is: It depends. It depends on the expected rate of return on the new investments a company is making. A profitable company investing lots of capital to expand (such as Federal Express) has a negative FCF, while an unprofitable company shrinking its assets to pay creditors (like Western Union) generates positive FCF. Which company is worth more? In this case (and many others like it), the company with the negative FCF creates greater value.

People say to me, "Bennett, you are a great believer in cash flow. Why is it that your incentive compensation plans do not reward management for generating more Free Cash Flow, if that is what determines value?"

"Ah," I say, "because it is Free Cash Flow *over the entire life of the business* that matters. FCF in any one year is a nearly meaningless measure of performance and value. A positive or negative FCF cannot be judged to be good or bad without examining the quality of FCF – that is, the rate of return earned on the investments."

But now I am getting ahead of myself. There will be plenty of time later to expound on the finer points of the economic model. For now, let's return to the fundamental debate: Is it earnings or cash flow that truly drives stock prices?

Because most companies' earnings and cash flow move together most of the time, it can be difficult to say for sure whether stock prices truly result from capitalizing earnings or discounting cash flow. To sort out this potentially misleading correlation, academic researchers have studied how share prices react to events that cause a company's earnings and its cash flow to depart from one another.

The accounting model versus the economic model – some evidence

The accounting model relies upon two distinct financial statements – an income statement and balance sheet – whereas the economic model uses only one: sources and uses of cash. Because earnings are emphasized in the accounting model, whether a cash outlay is expensed on the income statement or is capitalized on the balance sheet makes a great deal of difference. In the economic model, where cash outlays are recorded makes no difference at all – unless it affects taxes. This conflict is highlighted when a company is permitted to choose between alternative accounting methods.

LIFO vs. FIFO. Switching from FIFO (First In, First Out) to LIFO (Last In, First Out) inventory costing in times of rising prices decreases a company's reported earnings because the most recently acquired and, hence, most costly inventory is expensed first. But, in so doing, it saves taxes, leaving more cash to accumulate in the cigar box.

Now we have an important question: Does the market focus on the decline in earnings or the increase in cash? Following the empirical tradition of the "Chicago School," let's find out what investors actually do to stock prices instead of asking them what they might do.

Professor Shyam Sunder demonstrated that companies switching to LIFO experienced on average a 5 percent increase in share price on the date the intended change was first announced. An analysis performed by a second group of researchers revealed that the share price gain was in direct proportion to the present value of the taxes to be saved by making the switch. Taken together, these studies provide powerful evidence that share prices are dictated by cash generation, not book earnings.

These findings also prove that a company adopting LIFO will sell for a higher multiple of its earnings than if it used FIFO. The higher multiple is consistent with the higher quality of LIFO earnings; inventory holding gains are purged from income, and there are the tax savings besides.

And if, as this research suggests, a company's share price depends upon the "quality" as well as the quantity of its earnings, then the accounting model of value collapses. It collapses because a company's P/E multiple is not a primary *cause* of its stock price, as the model seems to suggest, but a consequence of it. The accounting model cannot answer the question: What determines a company's stock price in the first place?

In the LIFO–FIFO example, earnings go down while cash goes up. Let us now examine a second accounting choice, one where earnings go down but there is no change in cash.

The Amortization of Goodwill. When the purchase method is used to account for an acquisition, any premium paid over the estimated fair value of the seller's assets is assigned to goodwill and amortized against earnings over a period not to exceed forty years. Because it is a non-cash, non-tax-deductible expense, the amortization of goodwill per se is of no consequence in the economic model of valuation. In the accounting framework, by contrast, it matters because it reduces reported earnings.

With pooling-of-interests accounting, by contrast, buyers merely add the book value of the sellers' assets to their own book value. No goodwill is recorded or amortized, and this usually makes the acquiror's subsequent reported earnings and return on equity look much better than if purchase accounting had been employed.

Now, if the amortization of goodwill were the only difference between pooling and purchase,

I might consider a preference for pooling accounting to be harmless. But, many times sellers will take only cash, or buyers are unwilling to issue equity, thereby ruling out pooling transactions. Avoiding a sensible transaction merely because it must be recorded under purchase rules is the height of folly.

Sad to say, it was apparently just this foolish thinking that prevented the disposition of some of Beatrice's last remaining properties. The press has reported on more than one occasion that interested suitors balked at purchasing Beatrice units because of a concern over how the market would react to the enormous goodwill they would be forced to record. H. J. Heinz, for one, canned a bid in part over just such a concern with goodwill.

Now, if Don Kelly, Beatrice's CEO at that time, was asking too high a price – one that the potential buyers could not justify by the likely future generation of cash – then that would have been a good reason for them to step back. But if, as the press suggested, the potential buyers walked away from value-adding acquisitions merely because it would have required the recognition and amortization of goodwill, then they let the accounting tail wag their business dog (and I can only shake my head in wonder).

As these cases suggest, it is important to know whether investors are fooled by the cosmetic differences between purchase and pooling, or if instead they penetrate accounting fictions to focus on real economic value. To find out which answer is correct, let us once again trust our eyes and not our ears. Let's look over the shoulders of researchers who have carefully studied the shares prices of acquiring companies.

Hai Hong, Gershon Mandelker and Robert Kaplan, while associated with Carnegie-Mellon's business school, examined the share prices of a large sample of American companies making acquisitions during the 1960s. They divided all the acquirors into two camps: those electing purchase and those using pooling. Over the interval covered by their study, it was much easier to qualify an acquisition for pooling than it is now. Most acquisitions could be recorded using either purchase or pooling, with the choice largely up to management. Thus, if it were true that investors were concerned with the recognition and amortization of goodwill, the stock prices of purchase acquirors should have underperformed the pooling acquirors. And yet, no significant difference in stock returns could be detected.

This evidence supports the view that accounting entries that do not affect cash do not affect value. It also proves that what matters in an acquisition is only how much cash (and cash-equivalent value) is paid out to consummate the transaction relative to how much cash is likely to flow in afterwards, and not how the transaction is recorded by accountants.

The studies I have cited (along with many other tests of share price behavior too numerous to review here) offer persuasive evidence that share prices are determined by expected cash generation and not by reported earnings. A company's earnings explain its share price only to the extent that earnings reflect cash. Otherwise, earnings are misleading and should be abandoned as the basis for making decisions (and, as I shall argue later, for determining bonuses).

Just say no

Just how damaging an addiction to earnings can be is illustrated by the case of RJR, the tobacco giant. As reported in a recent *Wall Street Journal article*, RJR puffed up its sales and earnings for several years prior to its LBO by "loading" cigarette inventories on its distributors. Dealers were encouraged to purchase billions of surplus cigarettes just before semi-annual price increases were put into effect. (Company officials estimated that there were a staggering 18 billion excess cigarettes on dealers' shelves as of January 1, 1989.) As a result, RJR was able to report higher sales and earnings. But, in so doing, management forfeited future sales at higher prices, accelerated the payment of excise taxes and turned off smokers with cigarettes that had turned stale.

Within months of the LBO, RJR announced it would discontinue this harmful practice cold turkey, slashing cigarette shipments 29 percent in the third quarter and 17 percent in the fourth quarter of 1989 compared to year earlier levels. "Though the accounting symptoms look bad (reported profits will be reduced by about $170 million in each quarter), the vital signs of corporate health are restored right away."

"This is a very positive development for the company as far as cash flow is concerned," noted Kurt von der Hayden, RJR's CFO. "I view it as a very positive contribution to our debt service."

Because RJR offered extended payment terms to induce its dealers to load inventories, cash flow would not be hurt by the shipment drop. But excise taxes will be postponed, production and distribution can become more efficient and fresher cigarettes may help to stem a further loss of market share to Phillip Morris.

A former senior RJR officer said that management had been aware of the problem, but couldn't withdraw from the practice because they feared the impact on earnings would have outraged Wall Street, James W. Johnston, the head of the RJR Tobacco Company, stated, "Here is probably the clearest, most positive statement of what we can accomplish by being private for a while."

For shame! What about the evidence that the stock market really responds to the generation of cash and not to illusory accounting profits? As my colleague Joel Stern puts it, "Run your public company as if it were privately-held, and you will be making the right decision for your public stockholders." And maybe you won't be vulnerable to its being taken private at twice the current stock price (RJR traded for $55 a share before being taken private for $110 a share.)

Kick the earnings habit. Join the Cash Flow generation.

MORE TROUBLES WITH EARNINGS

Is R&D an expenditure or expense?

Another problem with earnings as a measure of value is the improper accounting for research and development. Accountants are required to expense R&D outlays as if their potential contribution to value is always exhausted in the period incurred. But common sense says otherwise.

Why would Merck, the spectacularly successful pharmaceutical company, spend more than 10 percent of its sales each year on R&D if it did not expect a substantial return to follow? In fact Merck is looking for a long-term payoff from such spending, and so are its investors. The company's shares sell for a multiple of over 20 times reported earnings and nearly 10 times accounting book value. Merck's earnings and book value apparently understate the company's value by a wide margin. Expensing R&D is one of the reasons why.

While the payoff from any one of its projects is unpredictable, Merck's overall R&D spending is almost certain to bear fruit. Like any capital expenditure that is expected to create an enduring value, Merck's R&D should be capitalized onto the balance sheet and then amortized against earnings over the period of projected payoff from its successful R&D efforts. Such accounting would lead Merck to report both a higher book value and higher current earnings, thereby making the company's actual P/E and price-to-book multiples more understandable.

The accountants' cavalier dismissal of R&D is what accounts in part for the sky-high share price multiples enjoyed by the many small, rapidly growing high-tech Silicon Valley and Route 128 firms. As in Merck's case, their stock prices capitalize an expected future payoff from their R&D while their earnings are charged with an immediate expense. It is especially ironic to note that, following the acquisitions of R&D-intensive companies, the accountants will agree to record as goodwill for the buyer the R&D they had previously expensed for the seller. Thus, according to the accountants, R&D can be an asset if acquired but not if it is homegrown. (Again, I shake my head in wonder.)

What possible justification could there be for writing off R&D as an immediate expense when it is so obviously capitalized in stock market values? My answer is that the accountants are in bed with the bankers.

Accountants take downers, too

To protect their loans, bankers prefer to lend against assets that retain value even if the borrower must be liquidated. Such "tangible" assets include receivables, inventories, and property, plant and equipment – assets that have a use to others. But because an insolvent company is unlikely to recover much value from its prior R&D investments (if it did, why is it going bankrupt?), lenders are reluctant to lend against it. Their accounting

pals accommodate their desire for concreteness by expensing "intangibles" like R&D.

Accountants, to be sure, do not accept my contention that they are the unwitting slaves of the bankers. They explain their overzealous pen strokes as an adherence to the "principle of conservatism," a slogan that in practice means, "when in doubt, debit." You may have more appreciation for the poor accountants' cynical bent if I told you they are much more likely to be sued for overstating earnings than for understating them. So perhaps their conservatism is more pragmatic than principled.

The key question remains: Are the investors who set share prices knee-jerk conservatives or hardheaded realists when it comes to R&D? Do they consider R&D a cost to be expensed or an expenditure to be capitalized?

Stock prices provide the answer that economic realism prevails (the academic evidence to support this is reviewed later in this article). R&D outlays should be capitalized and amortized over their projected lives – not because they always do create value, but because they are expected to.

Full cost vs. successful efforts

One objection that might be raised to capitalizing R&D is that it may leave assets on a company's books that no longer have any value. What if the R&D fails to pay off? Should not at least the unsuccessful R&D outlays be expensed? I say no. Full-cost accounting is the only proper way to assess a company's rate of return.

The issue of successful efforts versus full cost accounting is best illustrated by oil companies. With successful efforts accounting, an oil company capitalizes only the costs associated with actually finding oil; all drilling expenditures that fail to discover economic quantities of oil are immediately expensed against earnings. While such a policy reduces earnings early on, it causes a permanent reduction in assets that eventually leads to the overstatement of future rates of return.

With full-cost accounting, by contrast, an oil company capitalizes all drilling outlays onto its balance sheet and then amortizes them over the lives of the successful wells. If you believe (as I do) that part of the cost associated with finding oil is that unsuccessful wells have to be drilled (if not, why are they drilled in the first place?), then full-cost accounting must be employed to properly measure an oil company's capital investment and thus its true rate of return.

The misuse of successful efforts accounting is not limited just to oil companies, though. Any company that writes off an unsuccessful investment will subsequently overstate the rate of return its investors have realized. Such an overstatement may tempt management to overinvest in businesses that really are not as profitable as they seem to be on paper.

Citibank illustrates the point. In 1987, Citibank took a $3 billion charge to earnings to establish a reserve for the eventual charge-off of LDC loans. Now Citibank sleeps better, for in the years after the charge-off, loan losses are charged against the reserve, never to touch earnings. And, with $3 billion of equity erased with an accounting stroke of the pen, Citibank's accounting return on equity has rebounded quite smartly. Management may wonder why, though, with such an improved return, the bank still sells for such a lowly multiple. One reason is that while Citibank has employed successful efforts accounting, the market uses full cost to judge rates of return.

To overcome such distortions, the economic model of accounting for value would reverse unusual write-offs by taking the charges off the income statement and adding them back to the balance sheet. This way a company's rate of return will rise only if there is a genuine improvement in the generation of cash from operations after the write-off.

Abraham Briloff, an accounting professor at NYU, is one who has fallen into the trap of advocating successful efforts accounting. For example, in a book entitled "Unaccountable Accounting," he chastised United Technologies for not writing down the goodwill associated with its acquisition of Mostek, a semiconductor company. He argued that, in light of the severe operating problems that materialized at Mostek in the years after the acquisition, the goodwill on UT's books clearly overstated Mostek's value to UT's stockholders, and should be written off just as if it were an unsuccessful drilling expenditure.

I am afraid that Briloff labors under the mistaken belief that a company's balance sheet somehow attempts to represent its market value. He and, it seems, the entire accounting profession apparently have forgotten one of the first principles of economics: sunk costs are irrelevant.

Burn the books

As any first year economics student knows, the cash already invested in a project is an irrecoverable sunk cost that is irrelevant to computing value. Market values are determined not by the cash that has gone into the acquisition of assets, but by the cash flow that can subsequently be gotten out of them. Therefore, a company's book value simply cannot be a measure of its market value (as Briloff seems to assume).

Rather, a company's balance sheet can at best be a measure of "capital" – that is, the amount of cash deposited by (debt as well as equity) investors in the company. Whether such "capital" translates into "value" depends upon management's success in earning a high enough discounted cash flow rate of return on that capital. This is the question that, although critical to the economic model of value, no balance sheet can answer. This judgment is best left to the stock market.

The deferred tax chameleon

The inadequacy of conventional accounting statements is further exposed by the question: Is the deferred tax reserve appearing on a company's balance sheet debt or equity? Clearly the accountants cannot decide; that's why they stick it in the no man's land between debt and equity. My answer to the question is uncomfortably close to the accountants' hedged position. I too say, "It depends."

Pity the pessimistic lenders, for they must consider the deferred tax reserve to be a debt-like liability. Bankers realize that if a company's condition deteriorates, it probably will not be able to replace the assets that give rise to the deferral of taxes. Moreover, should the assets be sold to secure debt repayment, the company may be obligated to pay a recapture of the past deferred tax benefit. In either event, the deferred tax reserve is quite rightly considered by creditors to be a quasi-liability that uses up a company's capacity to borrow money.

But if you divorce yourself from the downright depressing company of lenders and take up with the more genial society of shareholders, you will discover that the entire character of the deferred tax reserve changes right before your eyes. For as long as a company remains a viable going concern – an assumption taken for granted in the stock market valuation of most companies — the assets that give rise to the deferral of taxes will continue to be replenished. Because the shareholders in a going concern do not expect the company's deferred tax reserve ever to be repaid, it is properly considered to be the equivalent of common equity and thus a meaningless accounting segregation from net worth.

Furthermore, if the deferred tax reserve is properly considered to be a part of shareholders' equity, then to be consistent the year-to-year change in the reserve ought to be added back to reported profits. That way taxes are taken as an expense only when paid, not when provided for by the accountants.

An analogy can be drawn to the Individual Retirement Accounts (IRAs) many people opened some years back. If you are accounting for yours properly, you must consider only part of the funds in your account to be true equity. An accountant would insist that you set aside a deferred tax reserve because eventually you will have to pay taxes when you withdraw the funds from the account. Do you expect to earn a return from that part of your account that is the deferred tax reserve, or do you consider that to be a free loan from the government?

Of course, you expect to earn a return on the entire balance in your account. Nonetheless, I have heard otherwise level-headed corporate executives suggest that their corporate deferred tax reserve ought to be considered a free advance from the government. But, just as you do, corporations should expect to earn a return on all cash invested, no matter what the accountants may call it.

Steal this book

Permit me one final accounting irony. No doubt the cash you parted with to buy this book has been expensed by your company's accountants. I wish they had had the charity (if not the wisdom) to capitalize it. They insult me by assuming that, when you put this book down for the last time, you will forget everything you've read.

Where they ought to be

The accountants, then, are stuck between a rock and a hard place. They can prepare financial statements either for creditors or for stockholders – that is, either for judging a company's debt capacity or its stock market value. But they simply cannot do both at once. It should be clear by now that the lenders won this debate: The accountants take the position that a company is more dead than alive.

Managers must stop making business decisions with financial statements that assume their company is one day away from bankruptcy. To make realistic judgements of performance and value, accounting statements must be recast from the liquidating perspective of a lender to the going concern perspective of shareholders. The balance sheet must be reinterpreted as the cash invested in a "capital" account, and not as the value of "assets". To do this, all of the investments a company makes in R&D along with bookkeeping provisions that squirrel away cash from operations (for deferred tax reserve, warranty reserve, bad debt reserve, inventory obsolescence reserve, deferred income reserve, etc.) must be taken out of earnings and put back into equity capital (a topic discussed in numbing detail in a later chapter).

EARNINGS PER SHARE DO NOT COUNT

Although EPS suffers from the same shortcomings as earnings, it is such a popular measure of corporate performance that it warrants further attention.

Consider an acquisition in which a company selling for a high P/E multiple buys a firm selling for a low P/E ratio by exchanging shares. Because fewer of the high P/E shares are needed to retire all the outstanding low P/E shares, the buyer's EPS will always increase. Many think that is good news for the buyer's shareholders. And, yet, it will happen even if the combination produces no synergies.

To see how really silly is a preoccupation with EPS, reverse the transaction so that now the low

P/E firm buys the high-multiple company through a share exchange. This time the buyer's EPS must always decrease; a greater number of low-multiple shares will have to be issued to retire all the high-multiple ones. Many think such EPS dilution signals bad news for the buying company's shareholders, and advise that it be avoided at all cost.

But regardless of which company buys or which sells, the merged company will be the same, with the same assets, prospects, risks, earnings and value. Can the transaction really be desirable if consummated in one direction but not in the other? Of course not. Yet, that is what accounting EPS suggests.

Let's take an example. Assuming that two companies each currently earn $1.00 a share and have 1000 shares outstanding, and that one firm sells for 20 times earnings while the other sells at 10 times its earnings, the facts are as shown in Exhibit 3.1.

To make it simple, assume that there are no synergies and that the buyers pay precisely market price for the seller's shares. With fair value paid for value acquired, these transactions have all the excitement of kissing your sister. A proponent of the economic model would expect the acquiror's stock price to sit still.

Yet, when Hi buys Lo, EPS increases to $1.33 and when Lo buys Hi, EPS falls to $0.66. Preoccupied with EPS, accounting enthusiasts may see a good deal and a bad deal when in fact the two transactions are both the same: Lo-Hi is just Hi-Lo with a two-for-one stock split.

EPS does not matter because, in the wake of an acquisition, a company's P/E multiple will change to reflect a deterioration or improvement in the overall quality of its earnings. In our example,

Exhibit 3.1

	Hi	Lo	Hi buys Lo	Lo buys Hi
No. Shares	1,000	1,000	1,500*	3,000**
Total Earnings	$1,000	$1,000	$2,000	$2,000
Total Value	$20,000	$10,000	$30,000	$30,000
Price p/Share	$20.00	$10.00	$20.00	$10.00
EPS	$1.00	$1.00	$1.33	$0.66
P-E Ratio	20	10	15	15

*Hi must issue 500 shares at $20 to retire all 1000 of Lo's $10 shares.
**Lo must issue 2000 shares at $10 to retire all 1000 of Hi's $20 shares.

observe that no matter which firm buys and which sells, the combined company will have a P/E multiple of 15 (the consolidated value of $30,000 divided by the consolidated earnings of $2,000). Hi's 20 P/E must fall, and Lo's 10 P/E must rise.

Hi must give up part of its P/E multiple to acquire relatively more current earnings from Lo, and Lo must surrender part of its current earnings to purchase Hi's more promising future growth prospects and a higher multiple. P/E counters EPS, rendering it a meaningless measure of an acquisition's merits.

In the economic model, what does matter is the exchange of value, and not the exchange of earnings so popular with accounting enthusiasts. If a buyer receives from a seller a value greater than it gives, this difference (which I call *Net Value Added*) will accrue to the benefit of the buyer's shareholders (in many cases the benefit will show up as an increase in the value of the buyer's shares immediately after the deal is announced).

Now if this seems a simple and sensible way to judge an acquisition's merits, please note that it has nothing to do with EPS. If a prospective acquisition promises to generate a positive Net Value Added for the buyer, but the accountants inform us that EPS will be diluted, then I conclude that the acquiror will sell for a higher P/E multiple, that's all. Once again, a company's P/E multiple is not the cause of its stock price, but a consequence of it. Let's take an example.

I once advised a large telecommunications company on an acquisition in which EPS dilution was a potential stumbling block. Our client was thinking about buying a company engaged in a rapidly growing and potentially highly-profitable business – one that appeared to have an excellent strategic fit with its own capabilities and business plan. I was enthusiastic about the transaction because I saw a prospect for the value created through the combination to be shared by both the buyer and the seller (the candidate was a unit of another company).

The chairman, too, was enthusiastic until he saw how much the deal would dilute EPS. He pointed out that the P/E multiple they would have to pay was much higher than their own, so that the acquisition would lead to a substantial dilution in EPS.

I remarked that the target had far brighter growth prospects than they did so that, when the new business was added to their more mature operations, he could expect his company to command a higher P/E multiple. He said: "You mean it's like adding high-octane gas to low-octane gas; our octane rating will increase."

"Right," I said. "The candidate has supercharged earnings, and when you add them to your under-powered earnings, your pro forma earnings power will take off. Your multiple will climb, and that will counter the dilution in EPS."

"Then we are in big trouble," he said. "My compensation plan is tied to EPS. We are rewarding just the quantity of earnings. But you're telling me that the quality of our earnings matters, too. So what should we do?"

"Well, you could change your incentive compensation plan," I said, "and then make the acquisition."

Which is what they did. And on the date of the announcement of the transaction, the seller's stock price increased, our client's price increased, and a key competitor's stock price plunged. Now that is what I call a successful acquisition. The seller wins. The buyer wins. And the competition gets clobbered.

I warn you, however, that my definition of a successful acquisition is different from that of many investment bankers. For them, successful acquisitions are all those that happen.

That's no reason to spin off

A spin-off is a pro rata distribution of the shares of a subsidiary unit to the shareholders of the parent. It is simply the reverse of a stock-for-stock acquisition, and is subject to the same accounting quirks. This time, though, instead of acquiring a lower-multiple company to boost EPS, the accounting enthusiast will recommend spinning one off to boost the parent company's P/E multiple.

Referring again to the example presented above, suppose Hi did acquire Lo to form Hi-Lo, a company that sells for a P/E multiple of 15, an even blend of Hi's 20 multiple and Lo's 10 multiple. Now why not spin off Lo to leave behind a company that sells for Hi's P/E of 20? Is this really advisable? I don't think so, but for a definitive answer you will have to ask an investment banker whose finger is on the pulse of the market.

Seriously, though, the increase in P/E cannot by itself benefit Hi-Lo's shareholders. They are still stuck with their pro rata share of the low-multiple business after it is spun off. The spin-off merely takes Lo's earnings from Hi-Lo into a separate company where they are capitalized at Lo's multiple of 10. Thus, the increase in multiple that attaches to Hi's earnings is offset by the diminished multiple the market places on Lo's share of the consolidated profits. No matter how the accounting pie is sliced, it's still the same pie.

Just such a spin-off was used to "undo" R.J. Reynolds' acquisition of Sea Land, a containerized shipping operation whose P/E multiple was even lower than that of Reynolds. Several years after acquiring it, Reynolds' management decided to spin off Sea Land to its shareholders and was quite pleased to note that as a result Reynolds' P/E multiple jumped from 7.5 to 9.5. But that increase in multiple just reversed the decline suffered when Reynolds first acquired Sea Land, no doubt to increase EPS.

So what we have described here is an investment banker's fantasy – an infinite deal generator: Have Hi multiple acquire Lo multiple in an exchange of shares to improve Hi's EPS (never mind, please, the collapse in P/E), and then, after a respectable period lapses, spin off shares in Lo to improve the multiple (never mind what happens to EPS); and then have Hi reacquire Lo to improve Hi's EPS . . . and, well, you get the idea (and the investment bankers get the fees).

Now please don't get the idea that I oppose spin-offs. As a matter of fact, I believe that spin-offs have been one of the most neglected tools of corporate finance. But the merits of a spin-off and other financial restructurings simply cannot be judged by the accounting model of value.

THE PROBLEM WITH EARNINGS GROWTH

Earnings growth also is a misleading indicator of performance. While it is true that companies that sell for the highest stock price multiples are rapidly growing, rapid growth is no guarantee of a high multiple.

To see why, consider a situation in which two companies, X and Y, have the same earnings, and are expected to grow at the same rate. At this point, we would be forced to conclude that both companies would sell for the same share price and P/E multiple because, as far as we can tell, they are identical.

Suppose now that X must invest more capital than Y to sustain its growth. In this case Y will command a higher share price and P/E multiple because it earns a higher rate of return on the new capital it invests. X merely spends its way to the growth that Y achieves through a more efficient use of capital.

This example illustrates that earnings growth for any company is determined by multiplying a measure of the *quality* of its investments – the rate of return – by a measure of the *quantity* of investment – the investment rate:

Growth = Rate of Return × Investment Rate

The rate of return is measured in relevant cash flow terms before financing costs. The investment rate equals new capital investment (both for working capital and for fixed assets) divided by earnings. The investment rate is the ratio of a company's uses-of-funds for operations to its sources-of-funds from operations – one which indicates the fraction or multiple of current earnings that are plowed back into the business.

To make the example more concrete, suppose X and Y are growing earnings at 10 percent, but X must invest all of its earnings to grow at that rate whereas Y needs to invest only 80 percent of its earnings to keep pace. Y would warrant a higher value because it earns a 12.5 percent rate of return on capital, while X returns just 10 percent.

From this information, you may be tempted to conclude that X is worth less than Y simply because it would not be able to pay a dividend while Y could. However, even though X reinvests all of its earnings it still could pay a dividend simply by raising new debt or equity. In fact, X could grow at the same rate as Y, pay the same dividends as Y, and even have the same capital structure as Y (if it periodically raises equity), but still be worth significantly less.

Financial cosmetics are widely available to gloss over a company's true performance. Rate of return is the only measure that allows Y to be reliably distinguished from X.

Growth gone haywire: the case of W.T. Grant

I had an opportunity, while completing the Chase Manhattan Bank's credit training program in 1976, to analyze W.T. Grant's financial performance over the period leading up to the eventual liquidation of the company in 1975. Grant's management decided in the late 1960s to embark on an aggressive growth strategy to shift their stores from depressed inner-city locations to more attractive suburban ones. Besides the brick and mortar investment, this strategy also entailed a large initial outlay for the new stores' inventory. To build volume, store managers were compensated to generate more sales.

Not surprisingly, credit approval became quite lax. This plan led to impressive sales and reported earnings gains for a time; but, with the pile-up of receivables and inventories, it also resulted in a cash flow problem. In fact, with poor and declining rates of return on capital, Grant's Free Cash Flow was negative for each year from 1968 to 1975. And, despite this need for new capital, dividends were maintained at 30 percent of earnings and not a penny of new equity was raised. Growth was financed with new debt, commercial paper, and leases. By 1974 the grim reaper was at the company's door.

W.T. Grant's management apparently forgot one important principle: growth without a commitment to careful capital management – earning an acceptable rate of return – is a sure formula for disaster. Their bankers forgot something, too. Risky expansions should be financed with equity, not with debt.

In sum, rapid growth can be a misleading indicator of added value because it can be generated simply by pouring capital into a business. Earning an acceptable rate of return is essential to creating value. Growth adds to value only when it is accompanied by an adequate rate of return. If returns are low, growth actually reduces value. (Just ask Saatchi and Saatchi.)

THE ROLE OF LEAD STEERS

How can it be true, as I claim, that the cash generated over the life of a business (adjusted for risk) is what determines share prices when most investors seem to be preoccupied with such traditional accounting measures as earnings, EPS, and earnings growth? The answer is that prices in the stock market, like all other prices, are set "at the margin" by the smartest money in the game, leaving the majority of investors as mere price-takers. The concept of marginal pricing – one of the most difficult in all economics to grasp – can be illustrated by the metaphor of the "Lead Steers" made popular by Joel Stern. He says, "If you want to know where a herd of cattle is heading, you need not interview every steer in the herd, just the lead steer."

The stock market works in very much the same way. While millions of people invest in the stock market, a relative handful of prominent investors account for the great majority of trades. For example, about 55 percent of the volume on the NYSE consists of block trades of 10,000 shares or more, and over two-thirds of all volume is attributable to trades of 5,000 shares or more. The importance of small, unsophisticated investors has been exaggerated in the press and, I am afraid, in the minds of many senior executives.

The price of oil is set in just this way, too. When I pull my car into a gas station, I may feel in some way responsible for determining the price of oil. But, no, I am just a price-taker. Be it cash or credit, the price is posted, and I can take or leave it. I realize now that the price of oil is set by professional oil traders who compete with each other to get the price right before the other traders do.

But even this characterization is not really accurate. For the astute traders I just tipped my hat to must in turn bow to the economic forces of supply and demand. They cannot make oil depart from the price that will clear the market – the one that will leave no excess supply or unsatisfied demand. You see, even the lead steers do not really lead. They too must follow the will of economic forces.

My point is this: Let's not confuse the process by which prices are set in the market with the economic forces that truly set market prices.

A lead steer up close

Getting a "lead steer" to reveal his true investment strategy is about as easy as getting a magician to disclose the secret to his tricks. Both prefer that you enjoy their performance without figuring out how it is done. As one particularly astute investor (who wishes to remain anonymous) put it to me: "Why should I popularize my approach – that's my edge."

But there are some who will draw the curtain back for a tantalizing peek at their magic. What they reveal goes far beyond a myopic preoccupation with next quarter's EPS. Consider, as but one example, O. Mason Hawkins, president of Southeastern Asset Management, Inc. (SAM), an investment management firm located in Memphis, Tennessee. Since hanging out a shingle in 1975, Hawkins has never had a down year, and only once has he underperformed the S&P 500 – and this with a billion dollars under active management. According to CDA Investment Technologies (a firm which evaluates portfolio management), SAM was the fifth best money manager for the five years ending June 30, 1988, with an annualized return of 19.7 percent versus 14.4 percent for the market.

Here is some straight bull from Mr. Hawkins:

Our investment philosophy is based on the approach of trying to buy stocks at a significant discount from what we appraise their private market value to be. There are several ways to do that.

The first method is to determine what the free cash flow is and can be in the coming business cycle under normalized conditions. Then we buy the company at a very reasonable multiple of that free cash flow.

Another way is liquidating value; we simply add up all the assets on the balance sheet, subtracting all the liabilities, and adjust for things like understated inventories or real estate, overfunded or underfunded pensions, overdepreciated plant and equipment, and trademarks, franchises and brandnames. We come up with a net value for what the company could be liquidated for on the courthouse steps, if it came to that, and buy the company at a significant discount.

We also take sales in the marketplace, arm's length transactions between competent businessmen, and compare what they will pay for businesses versus the market value of the company we are looking at.

We talk with management, we talk with suppliers, we talk with competitors. However, we reach most of our conclusions by looking at the numbers and analyzing them.

Next comes the qualitative things, because we don't want to own stocks just because they are cheap . . . We are interested in companies whose insiders, management members and board members, have a vested interest in the company and who are adding to that

*position. We are looking for a partner rather than an adversary in
the executive office.*
— The Daily News, *April 29, 1986*

*We're trying to avoid a situation like Phillips Petroleum, where
management was virtually willing to destroy the company in order
to maintain their positions.*
— Pensions and Investment Age, *February 17, 1986*

*We'd rather get with a guy who pays himself $100,000 a year and
can make millions on his stock than someone . . . who's making a
million dollars a year and has a couple hundred shares of his stock.*
— Investor's Daily, *November 1, 1985*

Mason practices what he preaches. He sold sixty
percent of his firm to employees and then invested
the proceeds in a mutual fund that they manage.
Hawkins admits, though, that having his own
mother-in-law's money in the fund is his greatest
motivation to perform well.

Mason Hawkins' record and philosophy is typical of the "lead steer" investors who truly set stock
prices: they think like businessmen, not like
accountants. Perhaps surprisingly, many of the lead
steers have no formal association or identity with
Wall Street, preferring the anonymity and perspective that is gained by distancing themselves from
"the Street." You can't find them. They find you.

DIVIDENDS DO NOT MATTER

At this point I will make a bold statement. Not
only do earnings and earnings growth not matter;
dividends do not matter either.

In the economic model, paying dividends is an
admission of failure – management's failure – to
find enough attractive investment opportunities
to use all available cash. Companies are valued
for what they do, not for what they do not do. By
paying dividends, management has less money
available to fund growth. The value of profitable
investment opportunities forgone is subtracted
from share price.

If management chooses to raise debt or equity
to replace the dividend, then current shareholders'
interests are diluted by introducing new claims on
future cash flow. Such a policy makes a company
incur transactions costs for unnecessary financings,
and forces investors to pay taxes on dividends
that might otherwise be deferred as capital gains.
So why pay dividends?

What if a company has exhausted its investment
opportunities? Then it certainly would be better to
pay dividends rather than to make unrewarding
investments. In most cases, however, it would be
even better to use the funds to buy back stock.
Then only the investors who choose to sell will be
taxed; and they will be taxed only on the gain realized after the basis in their shares is applied against
the proceeds from the sale. Although the tax rate
on capital gains is now the same as it is for dividends, so long as the tax basis in the shares is not
zero investors will pay a lower tax on a capital gain.
The Tax Reform Act of 1986 did not make dividends attractive, only less unattractive than before.

Moreover, if paying any dividends at all is
thought to be advisable, then borrowing to pay
them all at once is probably even better. One benefit is the corporate income taxes saved when debt
replaces equity, and yet no additional tax burden is
placed on investors. Shareholders will just pay in
advance the discounted present value of the taxes
they otherwise would have paid over time.
Moreover, it will probably reassure investors to
know that the tendency of cash-rich companies
to overinvest in their undeserving basic businesses
and to make overpriced acquisitions will be reined
in by the obligation to service debt first. And, it
may also bring about the transfer of a more significant equity stake into the hands of key managers
and employees, thereby heightening their incentives to add value.

But I am getting ahead of the story at hand.
I will discuss the benefits of such financial restructurings in greater detail later on in this book. For
now, let me summarize the discussion thus far by
saying that, depending upon where a company's
cash flow is in relation to its investment needs, it
makes sense either to pay no dividends at all or to
pay them all at once. The middle of the road is the
most reckless place to drive a company's dividend
policy.

But the corporate perspective certainly is not
all that matters on this question. What about
investors? Do they want dividends?

Granted some may need cash for consumption,
and thus may require a dividend. But they can create their own dividend by selling or borrowing
against some of their shares or, better yet, by
adding income-yielding bonds and preferred
stocks to a non-dividend paying common stock

portfolio. Investors who need cash do not need to get it from every component of their portfolio.

Even so, the payment of dividends actually taking place is out of all proportion to the consumption needs of investors. Most get reinvested back into the market, but only after the brokers' turnstile has been ticked. Besides, if a cash yield is so desirable, why have deep-discount bonds, which pay no cash return at all, become so popular? Much like a non-dividend paying common stock, the return on such bonds is entirely in the form of expected price appreciation.

Does paying a dividend make a stock less risky to own? Some argue that a bird in the hand (a dividend) is worth two in the bush (capital gains). But the retort is not that dividends not paid will show up as capital gains for sure, but that dividends that are paid are capital gains lost for sure. Stock prices fall by the amount of any dividends paid, never to be recouped. Paying certain dividends out of uncertain earnings cannot make earnings, or common shares, any less risky. It only makes the residual capital gain that much riskier.

It is true that some investors will not buy the shares of companies that do not pay at least a nominal dividend. Will the share prices of companies that pay no dividends be penalized by not appealing to this group? Absolutely not. Once again, share prices are not set by a polling technique in which all investors have a vote on value. Prices in the stock market are set at the margin. So long as there are a sufficient number of investors with sufficient wealth who are not seeking dividends, companies that pay few or no dividends have no cause for concern. They will sell for their fair value.

How can the view that I am articulating for investors – namely, that "dividends do not matter" – be reconciled with the fact that dividend announcements often have a pronounced effect on stock prices? Managements and boards of directors apparently have conditioned investors to associate dividend increases with a healthy outlook and dividend cuts with impending catastrophe. For example, in 1983, Bethlehem Steel halved the dividend and the stock price collapsed. At the same time, management disclosed their intention to close basic steelmaking at the Lackawanna mill, a decision that would trigger the payment of one billion dollars in unfunded vested pension benefits.

Bethlehem's stock price would have collapsed no matter what had happened to the dividend. But, in light of the company's need for cash, cutting the dividend made sense. And thus, there is just a correlation, but not a true causal relationship, between dividend announcements and share prices. Radical changes in dividend policy simply tend to coincide with the release of other important news to the market.

The evidence on dividends

Finally, and most decisively, let us once again turn to definitive academic research to answer the question.

The most important empirical study on dividends appeared in the prestigious *Journal of Financial Economics* in 1974. Although it has been updated and retested on several occasions, the fundamental findings have withstood the test of time. The study, performed by Professors Fischer Black and Myron Scholes, tested whether the total returns achieved during the period 1936 to 1966 from 25 carefully-constructed portfolios depended upon the dividend yield or dividend payout ratios of the underlying stocks. Their analysis revealed that the return to investors was explained by the level of risk, and was not at all affected by how the return was divided between dividends and capital gains. They found that within a given risk category, some stocks paid no dividends, some paid modest dividends, and some paid a lot of dividends, but all experienced the same overall rate of return over time.

Black and Scholes concluded that investors will do best by assuming that dividends do not matter and by ignoring both payout and yield in choosing their stocks (that is, they should worry about risk, diversification, taxes and value, but not dividends per se). Their advice to corporate managers is no less important than it is to investors: Do not formulate dividend policy in an attempt to influence shareholders' returns. Instead, set dividend policy in the context of the company's own investment needs and financing options, and then carefully explain it to investors.

THE MYTH OF MARKET MYOPIA

It is easy to imagine that the pressure put on money managers to perform each quarter will force them to ignore the long-term payoffs from farsighted business decisions and instead focus only on near-term results. Here is the popular view of a myopic stock market, as articulated by Donald N. Frey, the former CEO of Bell & Howell:

When the typical institutional portfolio in the U.S. has an annual turnover rate of 50% and some smaller ones have turnover rates of more than 200%, it is no surprise that American business is hobbled compared with foreign rivals ... Playing the market the way our money managers do ignores two critical factors: the time required to bring a product from development to market and the time required to redirect resources from a maturing business to a new one ... The pressure for short-term results puts unnecessary hurdles in the way of sound management. Investors' expectations for simultaneously high dividends on stocks, high interest rates on bonds, and rapid growth in the price of securities force managers to forgo many of their most promising ventures. Ultimately, these pressures rob consumers of future products, workers of future jobs, and investors of future profits.

Frey is joined in this view by Andrew C. Sigler, chairman and CEO of Champion International Corporation, a large paper products company:

The only pressure I have on me is short-term pressure. I announce that we're going to spend half a billion dollars at Courtland, Alabama, with a hell of a payout from redoing a mill and my stock goes down two points. So I finally caved in and announced I'm going to buy back some stock, which makes no sense. If the economy is supposedly run by corporations and corporations are supposed to invest and be competitive, buying back your own stock, if you have alternatives, makes no sense. But you can't fight it. The share price today is refined constantly by that proverbial young man looking at a CRT screen. There's an assigned P-E ratio based on what I did last quarter and what I'll do next quarter.

Now, in one sense, Frey and Sigler are right. Because rates of interest have been quite high this past decade, especially in real terms, distant payoffs are more heavily discounted by investors. Projects must pay off more quickly and handsomely in order to pass muster. That is just a fact of life with which all projects must contend.

After all, the amount of capital available for companies to invest is limited. It is constrained in the aggregate to an amount equal to just what individuals throughout the world choose to save. High real interest rates are the result of too many promising projects chasing too little savings. A high rate of interest is the market's way of attracting more savings with the one hand and discouraging less rewarding capital projects with the other in order to strike a balance between the available supply of and demand for capital.

For management to ignore this obvious market signal is to misallocate capital, to destroy wealth and welfare, and to attract raiders like bees to honey. Frey and Sigler seem not to understand that capital budgeting is the process of deciding which projects ought not to be funded so that other, even more promising ones can be.

But their allegations go farther still. They claim our economic system is fundamentally flawed because of the tendency of investors – mainly professional money managers – to be unduly short-sighted. If it were true that stock prices failed to reflect the true value of insightful investment decisions, then regulations preventing hostile corporate takeovers (a fate, I might add, that eventually befell Bell & Howell) might be in order.

Unfortunately – at least for those who believe in greater market regulation – their claims are refuted by both logic and observations of share prices. Economic logic says that a company's stock price should depend upon the cash expected to be generated over the entire life of the business – otherwise there are large profit opportunities for long-term investors. The simple fact that stocks trade at multiples of current earnings is *prima facie* evidence of the stock market's extended time horizon. For, with a stock selling at a multiple of, say, just 10 times earnings, it would have to be held for ten years for the earnings to recoup just the principal paid, and held indefinitely for an appropriate return on investment to be earned.

Moreover, differences in P/E ratios indicate that the market responds to the relative prospects for profitable growth. If all the market cared about was near-term earnings, wouldn't all companies sell for the same P/E ratio? But it is precisely those companies whose prospects for long-run growth and profitability are brightest that sell for the highest P/E multiples; and this is a strong sign of market sophistication.

The CEOs also go astray when they accuse institutional investors of impatience. The long-term nature of pension and life insurance liabilities suggests that most of the large institutional investors accused of a short-term mentality actually would be better off investing in risky stocks that promise a higher long-term payoff than more conservative investments are apt to provide.

And, apparently, the institutions do just that. A study undertaken by the SEC's economics staff shows that institutional investors own a far larger percentage of the shares of R&D-intensive companies than of more mature, blue-chip stocks. Far from indicating shortsightedness, this ownership pattern reveals patience and, indeed, a positive appetite for long-run payoffs.

But even if it is true that money managers are evaluated each quarter – and no doubt many are – it still does not logically follow that share price movements each quarter are dictated by that quarter's results. In fact, because share prices are forward looking, share price movements quarter-to-quarter must be determined by the change in outlook extending beyond that quarter into the indefinite future. For, if share price movements did respond myopically to quarterly results, a simple trading rule would exist: just buy "depressed" stocks (those where the most recent earnings understate the long-term outlook) and sell short overpriced ones (where current earnings overstate long-term value), and you will outperform the market over time. But such a simple investment rule does not work.

Most fundamentally, does the frenetic trading activity that Frey in particular disparages arise from a short-term horizon on the part of American investors? And does trading activity motivated by a quick payoff depress the value of companies investing for the long term? Not at all.

For every buyer there must be a seller, and for every seller a buyer. If both buyers and sellers are equally shortsighted, trading per se would have no effect on value. For if the seller is selling because of an unwarranted concern over a near-term earnings problem, is the buyer buying because of an unjustified enthusiasm about near-term earnings prospects? Trading volume simply does not affect the level of stock prices (a theme to which I will return shortly).

The real reason why the market rises or falls is simply that the lead steers decide that intrinsic value has changed. When this happens, trading volume may surge as investors adjust their portfolios to accommodate a new market value. It may seem as if the trading volume is what causes a change in value when, in fact, it is the trading volume that results from a change in value. Beware of correlation masquerading as a cause.

I believe that the increase in trading volume this past decade is best explained as a consequence of the deregulation of brokerage commissions in May 1976 and the automation of the brokerage industry, both of which have made the U.S. the low-cost producer of trades worldwide. Lower trading costs mean more trades, and more trades mean that even more information is being digested by market participants and actively impounded into stock market values. In my view, the growing demands placed on management to invest capital wisely actually are the result of an increasingly efficient and sophisticated capital market. They are not, as the CEOs assert, some new-found institutional focus on the short term at the expense of the long term. But, again, do not take my word for it. Nor the words of Frey or Sigler, for that matter. Let's consult the academic experts who have no axe to grind.

The evidence on market myopia

Definitive evidence proving the market's far-sightedness comes from research performed by John McConnell of Purdue University and Chris Muscarella of Southern Methodist University. They examined share price reactions to announcements of capital spending plans (like Mr. Sigler's Courtland new machines), including research and development outlays. Because of the lag between making an investment and realizing its payoff, the immediate effect of an increase in a company's capital spending would be to reduce both its earnings and cash flow – a result Mr. Sigler is convinced leads inevitably to a markdown in a company's stock price.

Indeed, if the market were dominated by the callow, computer-driven automatons familiar to Mr. Sigler, then share prices would be expected to decline with almost any planned capital spending increase, no matter how significant might be the long-term payoff. If, however, the projects to be undertaken are generally sound – ones in which discounted cash flows over the lives of the investments offer promising returns – and if the market is dominated by astute, forward-looking lead steers, then share prices should rise despite any negative near-term accounting consequences. The converse would be true for an announced decrease in capital spending.

McConnell and Muscarella's evaluation of 547 capital spending announcements made by 285 different companies over the period 1975 to 1981 reveals a statistically significant share price appreciation for companies announcing an increase in capital spending, and a decrease in share price for firms announcing reductions.

Their findings do not imply that every single capital spending increase was greeted favorably (Sigler's Courtland project, for example, was not), only that most were. When in early 1984 Federal Express announced Zapmail, a service designed to preempt fax machines, the company's stock fell in price nearly $10 a share, from the mid-$40s to the mid-$30s. Several years later, the project was called off in the wake of a widespread proliferation of fax machines, and Federal's stock price rose by nearly $8 a share. Investors heaved a sigh of relief to learn that no more money would be poured into a black hole. The point, though, is that Federal Express's share price fell initially not because the market was unable to visualize the long-run payoff from the Zapmail project, but because it saw the consequences so clearly.

Will Sigler's Courtland project suffer a similar fate? Only time will tell. For now, he is free to rail against the stock market and to protest that spending half a billion dollars to redo a paper mill is the world's best use for that scarce capital (despite the fact that his stock price fell when the project was first announced and rose when, by repurchasing shares, he freed up funds for other companies to invest). Essentially, then, we have one man's opinion arrayed against the collective wisdom of market investors who, in moving stock prices, are putting their money where their mouth is.

The R & D Issue. Returning to the research of McConnell and Muscarella, let me mention that they also discovered that share prices reacted no differently to announcements of stepped-up research and development that was to be immediately expensed against earnings than they did in cases of new capital expenditures to be added to the balance sheet. Here is the proof that R&D is a capital expenditure, not an expense, and should be capitalized onto a company's books just like any other capital expenditure that is intended to create an enduring value.

They also found that 111 capital spending announcements made by 72 public utilities over the same time period had, as expected, no discernible impact on share price. The explanation here is that regulators constrain public utilities to charging prices intended to provide only a zero net present value for new capital projects.

The McConnell/Muscarella study provides impressive evidence that, far from being myopic, the market:

♦ factors into stock prices a realistic estimate of the long-run payoff from management's current investment decisions;
♦ is able to distinguish value-adding from value-neutral opportunities; and
♦ does not care whether the accountants expense or capitalize value-building outlays.

The burden of proof lies on those who think otherwise.

SUPPLY AND DEMAND

Mr. Frey's aforementioned concern about excessive trading volume is particularly confusing to me because I have met with many CEOs who are concerned that their stock price is depressed because of insufficient trading activity, a view to which I also cannot subscribe.

Both misconceptions hinge on the belief that share prices are set by a relationship between supply and demand, and that management accordingly can (and should) market its common stock in much the same fashion as any other consumer product. After all, if the number of common shares outstanding is fixed, would not advertising in concert with frequent analysts' presentations spark demand for the shares and thereby raise their price through a surge in volume?

Don Carter, Chairman and Chief Executive Officer of The Carter Organization, the world's largest proxy solicitation and corporate governance firm, is (quite predictably) a proponent of the supply/demand model of stock price behavior. "Every company," he asserts,

has a shareholder family and that family consists of many components: mom and pop shareholders, institutional shareholders, management holdings, and speculative holdings. We identify those holders and generate two-way communication by mail or visit, to learn why they own their stock. Their answer will help us in our search for new investors with similar motives. Our job is to make sure that those who are in the stock stay in it, and those who are not – come in and join the party. When you have more buyers than sellers, the stock price will rise – period. It's still supply and demand that determines stock price.

Bell South has in the past adopted this "Madison Avenue" approach to Wall Street. For some time, hardly a week would pass without a full-page advertisement appearing in the *Wall Street Journal* touting the company's investment appeal. After the reader was informed of a little-known fact – namely, that rapid growth in population in the southeastern part of the United States is expected to continue – Bell South would let us know that they were preeminently positioned to benefit from this trend. We were then advised to call our broker and purchase their shares.

To repeat our opening question: Will such a campaign increase share price? It will not, because it simply is not true that the supply of a company's shares is fixed. Instead, supply is perfectly flexible by virtue of options and short-selling. The lead steers can combine call options on Bell South stock with less risky T-bills to create a position equivalent to owning Bell South stock, but without owning Bell South stock directly. Or, they could sell Bell South shares short – that is, sell shares they do not own. When this happens, the total number of shares owned by all investors will exceed the number of shares that have been issued by the company, with the difference being accounted for by the short sales. Would you be surprised to learn that Bell South has one of the largest short positions of any stock on the Big Board?

Another, though admittedly less precise, approach to recreating the unique investment opportunity that Bell South claims it represents would be for investors to purchase certain proportions of the shares of other regional telephone companies, such as Bell Atlantic, along with, say, Walmart, or Food Lion – retailers who, like Bell South, are benefiting from the burgeoning growth of the Southeast.

Through these and other actions, sophisticated investors can create an artificial supply of a company's shares or close proxies for those shares in order to offset any surge in demand a PR campaign might generate. And the evidence on this issue reveals that efforts to promote a company's appeal to investors lead to an increase in trading volume, but not in stock price, thereby benefiting brokers (and maybe Don Carter), but not shareholders.

An elegant indictment of trading volume comes from Warren Buffet, the highly-regarded Chairman of Berkshire Hathaway:

One of the ironies of the stock market is the emphasis on activity. Brokers, using terms such as "marketability" and "liquidity," sing the praises of companies with high share turnover . . . But investors should understand that what is good for the croupier is not good for the customer. A hyperactive market is the pickpocket of enterprise.

Flexibility in the demand for a company's shares also makes trading volume an unimportant determinant of value. Investors for the most part are not interested in buying shares of stock in only a single company. To diversify risk, investors hold a portfolio of stocks. The attributes that an investor wants a portfolio to exhibit – in terms of income, risk, potential for capital appreciation, exposure to the business cycle, etc. – can be obtained by selecting shares from among a wide variety of easily substitutable companies. When shares are purchased to play a role in a portfolio, the shares of stocks in individual companies will be priced much like undifferentiated commodities; advertising will serve to raise only volume, not price.

The evidence on supply and demand

Fortunately, this important issue has also been the subject of expert academic research. A test conducted by Professor Myron Scholes as part of his doctoral dissertation at the University of Chicago provides strong evidence that share prices are determined by intrinsic values and not by an interaction between supply and demand.

His ingenious study examined secondary offerings where already-issued shares of a company's common stock are sold by investors who own them. Because no new shares are sold, a secondary offering by itself should not affect the intrinsic cash-flow value of a company. And yet, a supply-demand enthusiast would predict that, given a downward sloping demand schedule, additional shares could be sold only at a discount from market price. The greater the number of shares unleashed on the market, presumably the greater would be the discount required to induce investors to take up the shares. Another implication of the supply-demand view is that the price decline would likely be temporary. After the surplus supply of shares is absorbed into the market, a more normal share value should return.

Secondary offerings thus provide a very clear test of whether intrinsic value or supply and demand best explains how individual company's share prices are set.

Professor Scholes did find that secondary offerings reduced share price (an average of two percent measured against the market), but the price decline was unrelated to the size of the offering. It is reasonable to assume that secondary issues are timed by sellers to occur when they believe the shares are overvalued. Scholes concluded, therefore, that the price decline was caused by the adverse connotation associated with the decision to sell, and not the temporary "overhang" of supply.

He obtained further support for this interpretation by dividing the sellers into various groups. The largest price decline was associated with sales by management (as when Charles Schwab sold large blocks of Bank of America stock shortly before a more devastating decline in share price), the next largest by venture capitalists and by others close to the company, and little, if any, price decline was detected following large block sales by third-party institutions. Scholes' study showed that the quality of information rather than the quantity of shares traded is what determines the depth of the price discount.

Scholes traced the price decline several months after the offering and found that it persisted, though not in every case, as some shares recovered in value and others fell further. But, as a statistical statement, the price decline apparently was in response to some likely fundamental decline in the company's prospective economic performance.

Scholes' research offers convincing and reassuring evidence that stock prices are set by the lead steers' appraisal of intrinsic values (that is, the prospect for cash generation and risk), not supply and demand.

Lest the case be overstated, I add that that supply and demand do play a role in determining share values, but only in the aggregate. The intersection of the aggregate demand for capital relative to its worldwide supply determines the underlying level of real interest rates and hence, indirectly, the value of all stock markets. But it is only in setting the value of the market as a whole, and not for any single company, that supply and demand operate.

There are two important implications of Scholes' research. First, the objective of investor relations should be to revise expectations, rather than to stimulate demand. To increase share price, management must convince the right investors – the "lead steers" – to pay more, not simply convince more investors in the herd to buy. It is unfortunate that most of what passes for investor relations is "retail" as opposed to "wholesale" in orientation, aims to inform the herd and not the lead steers, and stimulates volume instead of price.

Second, the price decline associated with raising new equity capital can be mitigated through a clear program of financial communication and by raising equity through a pre-announced sequence of small issues (ideally a 415 shelf registration). Investment bankers' protestations about the "market overhang" from a shelf registration should be discounted as an obvious attempt to use the discredited supply-demand argument to their own benefit.

IN CONCLUSION

Earnings, earnings per share, and earnings growth are misleading measures of corporate performance. Earnings are diminished by bookkeeping entries having nothing to do with recurring cash flow, and are charged with such value-building capital outlays as research and development, all in an attempt to placate lenders' desire to assess liquidation value. EPS at best measures only the quantity of earnings, but the quality of earnings reflected in the P/E multiple matters, too. Rapid earnings growth can be manufactured by pouring capital into substandard projects; earning an adequate rate of return is far more important than growing rapidly.

While many investors are fooled by accounting shenanigans, the investors who matter are not.

Stock prices are not set through a polling technique where all investors have an equal vote. They are set rather by a select group of "lead steers" who look through misleading accounting results to arrive at true values. The rest of the herd, though blissfully ignorant of why the price is right, is well protected by the informed judgments of the "lead steers."

While it is fashionable to think so, the market is not myopic. The investors who set stock prices take into account the likely payoff from a capital project, no matter how distant, but discount it for the additional investment, risk, and time involved in getting there. On those occasions when a company's stock price responds unfavorably to a new capital project, it probably is not because the market is unable to visualize the eventual payoff. The real reason is that the market predicts that the long-run return will be inadequate; and its judgment will prove to be right more often than not. The record shows conclusively that betting against the market is simply not rewarding.

The best research on the subject shows that paying dividends does not enhance the total return received by investors over time. But paying dividends may deprive worthwhile projects of capital, or may force the company and investors to incur unnecessary transactions costs. And because boards of directors usually are loathe to cut the dividend except in the most dire circumstances, dividends become an additional and unnecessary fixed cost of running the business. Returning excess cash through periodic share repurchases, or a large, one-time, special dividend (with future dividends suspended to support the repayment of debt) is likely to be more rewarding than paying out a stream of dividends over time.

Stimulating investors' demand for shares will increase share volume, but not share price, benefiting brokers, but not shareholders. Lead steers head off a stampeding herd of investors by selling shares short or buying puts, providing an artificial supply of shares to siphon off any temporary surge in demand. To increase share price through more effective financial communication, management needs to convince the right investors that the company is worth more, not just persuade more investors to buy the stock.

The sophisticated investors, or "lead steers," who set stock prices, care about the generation of cash and the risks taken over the entire life of the business. This is the economic model of corporate value creation.

Despite the impressive evidence assembled in the academic community in support of an economic model of value, many companies still forsake truly economic decisions in deference to an earnings totem. How many senior managers of publicly-traded companies, for example, relish the thought of switching to LIFO to save taxes, gladly ignore goodwill amortization when an acquisition is contemplated, and care not a whit about the hit to earnings suffered when capital spending is increased? Not many, I suspect. They have been hypnotized by the cant of the popular press, sell-side security analysts, and many investment bankers and accountants into believing the myth that the market wants earnings, and wants it now. To make matters much worse, their incentive compensation often is tied to near-term earnings and earnings-related measures, so that they cannot afford to let their common sense be their guide.

What is the answer? Senior managers and boards of directors must be educated about how the stock market really works, and their compensation schemes must change accordingly.

CHAPTER 4

An Analysis of Trading Profits: How Most Trading Rooms Really Make Money

Albéric Braas and Charles N. Bralver
(Oliver, Wyman & Company)

Our observation of more than 40 large trading operations has led us to conclude that most trading rooms should be managed to generate stable profits by taking little positioning risk. This prescription is founded on three basic observations, each of which is developed in one of the three main parts of this article:

1. *The Myth of Speculative Positioning as the Best Source of Profit*. In this section we argue that, for most trading rooms, positioning is not a reliable source of revenues and profits.
2. *The Value of the Turn*. Here we take the view that more money is made trading interdealer volume than is customarily believed – but that it only happens if traders adopt a "jobber" style of trading.
3. *The Power of Customer Business*. Here we show the value of trading with customers and conclude that, for most trading rooms, it should be viewed as the primary source of revenue and profit.

THE MYTH OF SPECULATIVE POSITIONING AS BEST SOURCE OF PROFIT

Traders are naturally inclined to believe that the primary source of earnings in trading fixed income securities, equities, or foreign exchange is

positioning. The underlying premise is that quality traders are able to predict the movements of interest rates, foreign exchange rates, and stock prices with sufficient accuracy to "beat the market" – if not consistently, then at least more often than not.

Having analyzed trading rooms around the world, for smaller operations in regional centers as well as major players, our experience suggests the above premise is ill-founded. For most trading rooms and traders, the financial markets are in fact very efficient, and betting on price movements is not a sound business proposition. Just as economists cannot consistently predict interest rates and mutual fund managers do not outperform the market year after year, traders cannot be expected to "outguess" movements in the value of trading instruments with any degree of reliability.

It is instructive to track the pattern of traders' positions relative to subsequent market movements. Exhibit 4.1, which reflects our analysis of a large foreign exchange trading desk in New York, shows the relationship (or the conspicuous absence thereof) between one group of successful traders' positions in Swiss francs and Deutsche marks and subsequent changes in the spot market prices of those currencies. If these traders were consistently making money by taking positions, long positions would be strongly correlated with up movements and short positions with down movements; the dots would lie along an upward-sloping diagonal

Exhibit 4.1   Price Change Vs. Position Size

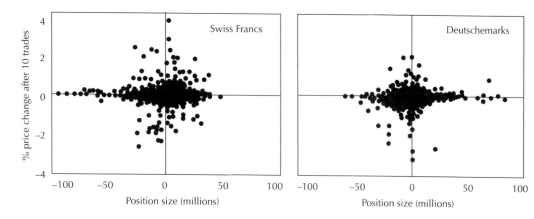

running from lower left to upper right. In this case, they do not – and it is our experience as an adviser that they seldom do.

There are, however, a few significant exceptions. We know of three situations in which traders can make money by positioning. First, position-taking tends to be profitable when the market experiences a lift or slide of significant duration. One example is the decline of the dollar in 1987, when most foreign exchange traders went short and made money. The slide may not have been foreseeable; but once it was underway, it seemed easy to call. Unfortunately, such situations are rare, and hence cannot be relied upon to generate sustained profits over time. Second, traders can make money by positioning when they have some proprietary source of information. And, third, consistent profits from positioning can also be expected if the firm has sufficient market power to influence prices. Most markets have a handful of dealers large enough to be "trend-setters" – dealers whose quotations get everybody's attention. Besides being able to influence price by their actions, these influential players also benefit from a kind of proprietary information. Because they trade in larger volume with the largest institutional investors (some of which are large enough to move the market themselves), they may be better able to anticipate market movements as they see the order flow from such dominant customers. Being a lead dealer to those customers and receiving those orders before the rest of the market constitutes a significant advantage.

Furthermore, in some cases, the use of increasingly sophisticated computer models to track and analyze data appears to have become another source of proprietary information and competitive advantage. For example, some investment banks seem to owe their success in the mortgage-backed securities market to their computer-driven fixed-income research and to the sheer volume of their trading – both of which allow them to structure, hedge, and price the instruments with more confidence and accuracy than their competitors.

In sum, position-taking is not for everybody. Only market leaders can leverage the competitive advantage acquired in the interdealer markets or in working with their customer base into their house positions; others are best advised to minimize speculative positions most of the time. This prescription also applies to institutions that hire successful traders from other trading houses; such traders often "lose their touch" when they find themselves in a disadvantaged environment. All too often, we find trading rooms that have no competitive advantage taking positions as if they did. Almost invariably, revenues and profits are disappointing and unreliable. Even in cases where there are initial or periodic bursts of profit and enthusiasm, such profits are typically dissipated in subsequent years or quarters. In these cases, the present value of the revenue stream is not likely to justify investment in state-of-the-art infrastructure and multi-desk trading floors. Our experience, in short, is that few trading rooms earn an acceptable return on the capital put at risk through positioning; and many even fail to cover expenses.

Exhibit 4.2   Market Share Vs. Interdealer Strength

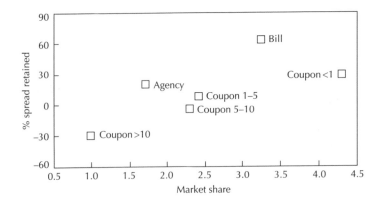

This is not to say, however, that trading must be a losing game for those institutions that do not have the competitive leverage to position effectively against market movements. There are other, more reliable, sources of profits from a trading room.

THE VALUE IN THE TURN (OR, WHO KEEPS THE BID-OFFER SPREAD?)

Any trading market, at any point in time, consists of all the parties prepared to buy or sell at specified prices. Where the buying and selling pressure meets is within the "bid-ask" (or "bid-offer") spread – the spread in the interdealer market between the best posted bid and the best posted offer at a point in time. The bid-ask spread is relatively high on illiquid securities like municipal bonds and junk bonds but very thin on liquid assets like foreign exchange.

Some traders argue that there is no such thing as a bid-offer spread in a transaction, that each trade is a bargain struck, and that the range between the bid and the offered prices is simply a negotiating framework within (or outside of) which the bargain is concluded. Our view, however, is that the price at which an interdealer bargain is struck is a function of the relative power of the two parties in the instrument traded. One party's offered price often becomes the counterparty's bid price. In repeated transactions between these two parties, this counterparty will consistently find itself on the wrong side of the market bid-offer in the bargain.

The advantaged parties in such situations generally turn out to be those players with stronger market-making capacity; and the other dealers with whom they trade are essentially forced to trade at the prices quoted by those market-makers. The possession of such an advantage in turn seems to be a function of market share. This phenomenon is especially clear in our analysis of thousands of trades for a primary dealer in U.S. Government securities. As illustrated in Exhibit 4.2, the percentage of the spread retained interdealer in each of six different trading instruments appears to be a direct function of the dealer's share of the interdealer volume in a given instrument.

Our experience has convinced us, then, that a bid-ask spread materializes when dealers with larger market share transact with smaller dealers. And, as our analysis has consistently demonstrated, a given trader's average, long-run tendency to retain that spread is a function of the "market power" of his or her institution. Market power translates into control of "bargains," which in turn translate into revenues.

A head fixed-income trader for a New York powerhouse put it best when he told us, "Any trader I put in the 5- to 7-year note chair makes a lot of money for us. Each of them thinks he is making the money with his smart calls. But it's really the chair that makes the money." Although there is some exaggeration in this statement, the message here is that the predictability and sustainability of trading profits is the result of the market-maker's ability to retain a disproportionate share of the bid-offer spread in a large volume of trades. Like the "golden crumbs" in Tom Wolfe's *Bonfire of the Vanities*, 70% spread retention on billions of dollars of daily volume represents a sizeable and consistent stream of revenue.

There are two keys to spread retention. First, the firm must have considerable financial muscle and trade flows. Second, traders must adopt a "jobbing" attitude, striving continuously to buy at or close to the bid side and to resell quickly at the offer side. This implies a lot of volume, but relatively small positions of short duration (and hence low risk).

THE POWER OF CUSTOMER BUSINESS

A good predictor of long-term success in a trading room is the status of salespeople relative to traders. The most successful Wall Street firms have long recognized that distributing and selling securities (or other financial instruments) to smaller dealers and to institutional customers not only keeps them better-informed than their competitors, but also is a stable source of earnings. Too often salespeople are viewed as second-class citizens in trading rooms – because, once again, the myth of position-taking as the best source of profit overshadows the added value in the customer side of the business. One typical result of this misconception is an undervalued, undermotivated salesforce that is required to sell an irregular flow of products based on traders' house positions and "views." The ultimate effect is a dissatisfied customer base and highly volatile earnings.

It is often argued that the interdealer business and the customer business are so closely inter-related that it is not possible to separate the revenue and the profits generated by each. We believe, however, that by marking large numbers of trans-actions to market (that is, determining where the actual price of each stood relative to the market prices at the time of sale), senior management can set transfer prices between trading and sales that provide a reasonably reliable split of revenues between the two.

Our examinations of over forty trading desks around the world have shown that, contrary to popular belief, customer business represents a sig-nificant portion of trading revenues – generally between 60 percent and 150 percent (in which case positioning loses money) of total revenues.

One of our clients, for example, reported about $10 million of pre-tax profit for a given time period in trading U.S. government securities. During the period, the client had conducted almost $400 billion of customer business and over $500 billion of inter-dealer business.

Upon closer examination, by marking indi-vidual trades to market, we decomposed the firm's "gross trading profit" of $30 million into the following categories:

Customer Revenue	$26 million
Spread Retention (Interdealer)	8 million
Trading Profit (Positioning)	(4) million
◆ Gross Trading Profit	$30 million
Expenses	(20) million
◆ Net Profit (pre-tax)	$10 million

In this case, which is far more representative than one might think, customer revenues were actually covering up positioning *losses* – losses that amounted to 40 percent of net profit.

Not all dealings with customers are profitable, however. As shown in Exhibit 4.3, many (particu-larly small) trades are in fact priced below cost. This tends to happen either because too few trading rooms really understand their fully loaded costs or because their business has become too competitive.

In general, though, a large portion of customer business yields mark-ups relative to true interdealer prices; and the value of the mark-ups is often greater than the cost of a well-organized salesforce. Dealing with customers allows you to price sales not only at the offer but often above it, while pur-chasing at or below the bid. Even when customers are powerful enough to avoid any mark-up relative to dealers' prices, they typically buy at or close to the major dealers' offer prices and sell at or close to the bid prices. For those dealers who can source most of their trades at the market bid prices and resell at the market offer, customer business gener-ates a consistently profitable revenue stream.

As shown in Exhibit 4.4, one of our clients (also a primary government securities dealer) was able to retain a consistently large percentage of the bid-offer spread in dealing with its larger cus-tomers. As in the case illustrated in Exhibit 4.2, the percentage retained in each instrument was shown to vary directly with the institution's relative posi-tion in that instrument.

Of course, the largest institutional customers sometimes hold market power comparable to that of the major dealers. Those customers, while pro-viding essential information flows, often "play the

Exhibit 4.3   Cost, Revenue per Customer Vs. Deal Size

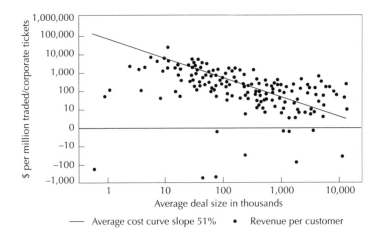

Exhibit 4.4   Percentage of Bid-Offer Spread Retained

Products	Customer trades over $1 MM	Products	Customer trades over $1 MM
Bills		**Off-the-run coupons**	
On the run	94	Less than 1 year	59
Off the run	100	1–5 years	73
		Over 5 years	100
Active coupons		**Agencies**	
2, 3, 4 years	56	Less than 5 years	91
5, 7, 10 years	92	Over 5 years	88
20, 30 years	94		

markets" themselves and know how to take advantage of the dealers' willingness to provide market liquidity. With such customers, dealers can rarely price to gain full compensation for that service.

The key to a profitable customer business, then, is to concentrate on those customer segments in which one holds (or can build) some type of comparative advantage. For this reason, the appropriate market focus will differ for every salesforce. The largest dealers typically do well with the large institutional investors who use them selectively as first-tier suppliers of securities, and whose main concerns are product depth and a knowledgeable salesforce. Regional dealers or banks generally have a competitive advantage with smaller institutional investors in their region – and that business, we have observed, can be very profitable.

It is also often argued that by making markets (by standing ready to quote prices continuously to customers), dealers often end up with unwanted positions that must be unwound at a net loss over time. The resulting losses, it is further argued, tend to offset much if not all of the other revenue from customer business.

By tracking traders' positions, however, we have demonstrated over and over again that, except in rare periods of large price movements, this argument is fundamentally groundless. Inventories, to be sure, must often be maintained in illiquid markets to allow efficient sale of securities to customers. And although such inventories are subject to the ups and downs of the markets, the resulting exposure from taking such long positions should be viewed as simply one of the costs of functioning as

Exhibit 4.5   Forex Trading Profits Large US and European FX Banks 1988

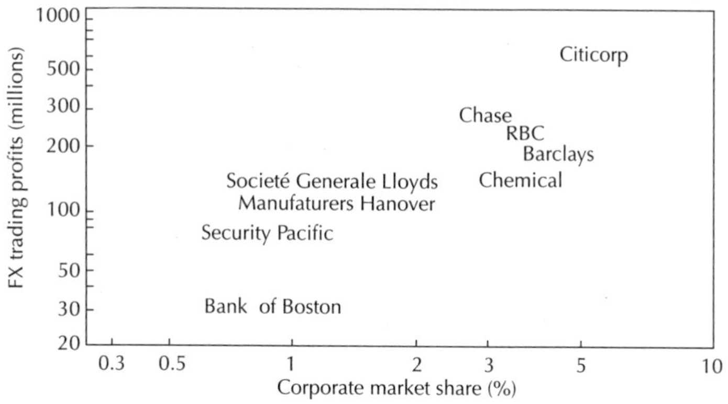

Chart: y-axis "FX trading profits (millions)" with values 20, 30, 50, 100, 200, 300, 500, 1000; x-axis "Corporate market share (%)" with values 0.3, 0.5, 1, 2, 3, 5, 10. Labels: Citicorp; Chase; RBC; Barclays; Chemical; Societé Generale Lloyds; Manufaturers Hanover; Security Pacific; Bank of Boston.

Source: Annual Reports, Bernstein Research, Euromoney, OWC Analysis

a market-maker – a cost that when properly managed, as our own work repeatedly bears out, is far outweighed by the value of a strong customer franchise.

Even in liquid markets, moreover, it is clear that customer flows determine the ability to generate consistent trading profits. The more continuous the flow of customer orders, the less positioning risk any given trader is forced to bear, thus allowing him or her to function strictly as a broker. For example, in an analysis of a client that deals in the UK equity market, we found that its trading in stocks with high customer-volume ratios produced consistently higher profits than stocks with smaller customer order flows. Further supporting evidence comes from our observation (illustrated in Exhibit 4.5) that the overall foreign exchange trading profits of some of the major banks around the world are strongly correlated with the degree of their penetration of the *customer* side of their markets.

For most trading rooms, then, sales is and will remain the principal source of consistent and stable revenue and profits. For many operations, "trading" and "trading and sales" are misnomers. The business should really be called "sales and trading," because much of what are called "trading" profits are really the result of a good customer base and the resulting flow of orders and information.

With advances in technology and increasing customer sophistication, margins in the business have narrowed; and today there are more salespeople

than the industry can profitably employ. But, in our view, the current problem of oversupply (and hence excess costs) will not reduce the value of sales in the trading environment. Customer business will simply have to be executed in a cheaper and more efficient fashion in the future.

CONCLUSION

The above insights have major implications for managing the vast majority of trading desks, including those who erroneously believe they can trade head to head with the Salomons of this world.

First, sales (and not speculative trading) is the only reliable source of stable revenues for most trading rooms. The "trading" strategy should be subordinated to the "sales" strategy and speculative positioning should be kept to the strict minimum necessary to be credible and to operate. This, of course, implies a low-risk profile that should suit many senior managements.

Second, sales and trading is much more than an opportunistic business driven by individual traders' skills at outguessing the market. It is a business in which profits are largely driven by fundamental competitive advantage. The business lends itself to strategic management by:

♦ Understanding and monitoring the real sources of revenue – in essence opening the "black box" and creating a meaningful MIS for senior management;

◆ Recognizing one's existing limitations and not letting them become weaknesses;

◆ Identifying one's existing or potential strengths (particularly with specific customer segments) and focusing one's energy on them.

The third major implication is that positioning (and market arbitrage) should be pursued as a goal in itself only by the very few competitors that, through market power or sophisticated, proprietary computer systems, can price, evaluate risk, or set trends in a manner that most others cannot.

PART II

The Corporate Investment Decision

One of the major tasks of corporate financial management is to evaluate investment opportunities. In many companies, this investment function is separated from the financing decisions typically performed by the corporate treasury, and is instead entrusted to a corporate "planning" or "strategy" group. Perhaps partly as a result of this separation of the investment and financing functions within the corporation, corporate strategy has developed for the most part independently of the discipline of financial economics.

One source of contention between financial analysts and strategists is the heavy reliance of the former on quantitative methods in evaluating possible investments. In the early 1980s, the *Harvard Business Review* ran a series of articles assailing the shortsightedness of American corporate investment practices. The blame for this alleged myopia was placed, in large part, on the widespread use of the analytical technique known as discounted cash flow analysis, or "DCF." And because DCF has long been advocated by financial economists as the most reliable method for assessing economic value, the whole of finance theory seems to have been implicated.

In "Finance Theory and Financial Strategy," MIT professor Stewart Myers sheds welcome light on this controversy by separating what may be valid in such claims from what is not. As Myers points out, much of the criticism of DCF involves a misreading of the underlying theory, and is indeed aimed not at "finance theory, but at habits of financial analysts that financial economists are attempting to reform" – and the article offers a list of the most prominent abuses of the DCF method. Nevertheless, as Myers acknowledges, part of the "gap" that has long divided the disciplines of finance and corporate strategy can be attributed to the real (as opposed to imagined) limitations of the DCF method. When properly applied, DCF remains the best available technique for evaluating certain kinds of investments: namely, those companies or investments producing fairly predictable cash flow streams. Where the DCF method falls down are in those kinds of investments that offer significant operating or strategic options – that is, for example, the right, but not the obligation, to build on a vacant property, develop an oil reserve, or expand or contract a mining operation. It is impossible to capture the value of such "real options" using the simple DCF technique; and options pricing theory, as Myers suggests, seems to hold out the best solution to this problem.

Following this attempt to integrate capital budgeting and strategy, we present two articles on the corporate cost of capital – one that defends the Capital Asset Pricing Model (CAPM) and one that attempts to supplement the CAPM with a second important variable. In addition to providing one of the central theoretical constructs of modern finance theory, the CAPM offers a practical method for estimating the risks and minimum required rates of returns (or "hurdle" rates) for corporate investments, which of course is a critical part of the capital budgeting process. But, along with the theory of market efficiency, the CAPM and its central variable beta have come under attack in the past decade – so much so that a number of academics have proclaimed the "death of beta." In their "Defense of Beta," S.P. Kothari and Jay Shanken provide an alternative interpretation of recent evidence against beta. They also report, based on the findings of their own recent study, that when betas are calculated using annual instead of monthly returns, there is a strong correlation between actual historic stock returns and the returns predicted by the CAPM.

In "The Liquidity Route to a Lower Cost of Capital," Yakov Amihud and Haim Mendelson discuss the managerial implications of their own research finding that liquidity is a major determinant (as important in fact as systematic risk or "beta") of the level of expected stock returns. Less liquid stocks earn proportionately higher rates of return (before transaction costs) over long periods of time, thus representing a higher cost of capital for corporate management. The authors also explore a number of possible corporate responses designed to reduce the cost of capital by increasing the liquidity of stocks and bonds.

The remaining two articles in this section expand on Stewart Myers's suggestion of the potential for "real options" in corporate strategy. In "The Promise of Real Options," Aswath Damodaran offers an introduction to the use of option pricing models to value real options. As illustrated in series of cases, real options are valuable sources of flexibility that are often built into corporate real (as opposed to financial) assets or activities. Some examples are the right of a mining company to expand or contract (or shut down) a mining operation, of a biotech firm (with a patent) to develop and market a drug, and of an Internet company to apply its technology to a variety of (possibly as yet unknown) products or markets. The real options *approach* is the use of option pricing models to quantify the value of such flexibility when evaluating corporate investments or strategies – a value that is not reflected in conventional discounted cash flow (DCF) analysis. Once having made

strategic decisions to invest, managers can also use the new valuation method to help decide *when* to "exercise" the options built into their investments (i.e., when to develop the reserves, take the minerals out of the ground, or make the company's big push into China or e-commerce).

In "Real Options: State of the Practice," Alex Triantis and Adam Borison use their own recent interviews with 39 representatives from 34 companies as a basis for addressing a number of questions about the current state of corporate real options practice: In the case of companies that are using real options, how and why was it initially adopted? How is it now being used – and how is it likely to be used in the future? What are the best ways to ensure that the implementation is successful?

The main impetus for corporate adoptions appears to be the rise in the number and kind of corporate investments for which DCF is not well suited – again, because of its inability to take account of the value of flexibility or strategic options. Perhaps the clearest sign of this dissatisfaction with DCF is the survey's finding that, in the majority of cases, a company's initial interest in real options came not from the finance or treasury group, but rather from people in nonfinancial disciplines such as strategy, operations, and marketing. In fact, real options has proven especially congenial to corporate strategists, who have long been forced to argue the case for flexibility (often against the treasury) without any means of assigning quantitative values to their intuitive assessments of potential investments.

The survey results also lead the authors to identify three main corporate uses of real options – as (1) a strategic way of thinking, (2) an analytical valuation tool, and (3) an organization-wide process for evaluating and then managing major capital investment projects. In illustrating the first use, the authors cite the case of corporate investments in IT and e-business initiatives, which are best viewed as "platforms for future growth" and where real options tends to function primarily as "a philosophy and process." As the authors note, "Even if it is difficult to arrive at precise valuations for these investments . . . the platforms can be designed more carefully by thinking about future uncertainty and the creation of options to mitigate the effect of downside risks as well as quickly take advantage of upside opportunities."

The second major application of real options, as a formal valuation method, is illustrated with an account of Intel's 1996 decision to invest in the "shells" of manufacturing facilities that can be quickly fitted with equipment to meet surges in demand. Although the investment would have been rejected based on conventional DCF analysis, the benefits of the flexibility (valued using both the Black-Scholes and the "binomial" approaches) provided by excess production capacity were shown to outweigh the costs.

In many companies, the evaluation of investment opportunities – and strategic planning in general – are largely divorced from ongoing corporate performance measurement. After the initial decision to invest, little effort is made to track results against plan. The third main application of real options, illustrated by the approach of Texaco, is to view major corporate investments as a portfolio of options whose value is monitored and managed over time.

In the final section of their article, the authors report on the lessons learned from attempts to *implement* real options at the surveyed companies. Perhaps not surprising, their conclusion is that such implementations should be planned and managed as a "carefully staged process of the kind that typifies real options thinking." The key steps are (1) conducting pilot projects; (2) gaining commitment from senior management; (3) "codifying" real options thinking and practice with an expert working group; and (4) "institutionalizing and integrating" real options throughout the organization. As for the future of real options, the authors see a steady increase in the rate of corporate adoptions, especially as more companies complete these first three stages and move toward firm-wide integration.

CHAPTER 5

Finance Theory and Financial Strategy*

Stewart C. Myers (Massachusetts Institute of Technology)

Strategic planning is many things, but it surely includes the process of deciding how to commit the firm's resources across lines of business. The financial side of strategic planning allocates a particular resource, capital.

Finance theory has made major advances in understanding how capital markets work and how risky real and financial assets are valued. Tools derived from finance theory, particularly discounted cash flow analysis, are widely used. Yet finance theory has had scant impact on strategic planning.

I attempt here to explain the gap between finance theory and strategic planning. Three explanations are offered:

1. Finance theory and traditional approaches to strategic planning may be kept apart by differences in language and "culture."
2. Discounted cash flow analysis may have been misused, and consequently not accepted, in strategic applications.
3. Discounted cash flow analysis may fail in strategic applications even if it is properly applied.

Each of these explanations is partly true. I do not claim that the three, taken together, add up to the whole truth. Nevertheless, I will describe both the problems encountered in applying finance theory to strategic planning, and the potential payoffs if the theory can be extended and properly applied.

The first task is to explain what is meant by "finance theory" and the gap between it and strategic planning.

THE RELEVANT THEORY

The financial concepts most relevant to strategic planning are those dealing with firms' capital investment decisions, and they are sketched here at the minimum level of detail necessary to define "finance theory."

Think of each investment project as a "minifirm," all-equity financed. Suppose its stock could be actively traded. If we know what the minifirm's stock would sell for, we know its present value. We calculate net present value (NPV) by subtracting the required investment.

In other words, we calculate each project's present value to investors who have free access to capital markets. We should therefore use the valuation model which best explains the prices of similar securities. However, the theory is usually boiled

---

* This article was first published in *Interfaces* 14: 1 January–February 1984 (pp. 126–137). It is reprinted with permission of The Institute of Management Science.

down to a single model, discounted cash flow (DCF):

$$PV = \sum_{t=1}^{T} \frac{C_t}{(1 + r)^t},$$

where PV = present (market) value;

C_t = forecasted incremental cash flow after corporate taxes – strictly speaking the mean of the distribution of possible $\tilde{C}_t$'s;

T = project life (C_T includes any salvage value);

r = the opportunity cost of capital, defined as the equilibrium expected rate of return on securities equivalent in risk to the project being valued.

NPV equals PV less the cash outlay required at t = 0.

Since present values add, the value of the firm should equal the sum of the values of all its minifirms. If the DCF formula works for each project separately, it should work for any collection of projects, a line of business, or the firm as a whole. A firm or line of business consists of intangible as well as tangible assets, and growth opportunities as well as assets-in-place. Intangible assets and growth opportunities are clearly reflected in stock prices, and in principle can also be valued in capital budgeting. Projects bringing intangible assets or growth opportunities to the firm have correspondingly higher NPVs. I will discuss whether DCF formulas can capture this extra value later.

The opportunity cost of capital varies from project to project, depending on risk. In principle, each project has its own cost of capital. In practice, firms simplify by grouping similar projects in risk classes, and use the same cost of capital for all projects in a class.

The opportunity cost of capital for a line of business, or for the firm, is a value-weighted average of the opportunity costs of capital for the projects it comprises.

The opportunity cost of capital depends on the use of funds, not on the source. In most cases, financing has a second-order impact on value: you can make much more money through smart investment decisions than smart financing decisions. The advantage, if any, of departing from all-equity financing is typically adjusted for through a somewhat lowered discount rate.

Finance theory stresses cash flow and the expected return on competing assets. The firm's investment opportunities compete with securities stockholders can buy. Investors willingly invest or reinvest cash in the firm only if it can do better, risk considered, than the investors can do on their own.

Finance theory thus stresses fundamentals. It should not be deflected by accounting allocations, except as they affect cash taxes. For example, suppose a positive-NPV project sharply reduces book earnings in its early stages. Finance theory would recommend forging ahead, trusting investors to see through the accounting bias to the project's true value. Empirical evidence indicates that investors do see through accounting biases; they do not just look naively at last quarter's or last year's EPS. (If they did, all stocks would sell at the same price-earnings ratio.)

All these concepts are generally accepted by financial economists. The concepts are broadly consistent with an up-to-date understanding of how capital markets work. Moreover, they seem to be accepted by firms, at least in part: any time a firm sets a hurdle rate based on capital market evidence and uses a DCF formula, it must implicitly rely on the logic I have sketched. So the issue here is not whether managers accept finance theory for capital budgeting (and for other financial purposes). It is why they do not use the theory in strategic planning.

THE GAP BETWEEN FINANCE THEORY AND STRATEGIC PLANNING

I have resisted referring to strategic planning as "capital budgeting on a grand scale" because capital budgeting in practice is a bottom-up process. The aim is to find and undertake specific assets or projects that are worth more than they cost.

Picking valuable pieces does not ensure maximum value for the whole. Piecemeal, bottom-up capital budgeting is not strategic planning.

Capital budgeting techniques, however, ought to work for the whole as well as the parts. A strategic commitment of capital to a line of business is an investment project. If management does invest, they must believe the value of the firm increases by more than the amount of capital committed – otherwise they are throwing money away. In other words, there is an implicit estimate of net present value.

This would seem to invite application of finance theory, which explains how real and financial assets are valued. The theory should have direct application not only to capital budgeting, but also to the financial side of strategic planning.

Of course it has been applied to some extent. Moreover, strategic planning seems to be becoming more financially sophisticated. Financial concepts are stressed in several recent books on corporate strategy.[1] Consulting firms have developed the concepts' strategic implications.[2]

Nevertheless, I believe it is fair to say that most strategic planners are not guided by the tools of modern finance. Strategic and financial analyses are not reconciled, even when the analyses are of the same major project. When low net present value projects are nurtured "for strategic reasons," the strategic analysis overrides measures of financial value. Conversely, projects with apparently high net present values are passed by if they don't fit in with the firm's strategic objectives. When financial and strategic analyses give conflicting answers, the conflict is treated as a fact of life, not as an anomaly demanding reconciliation.

In many firms, strategic analysis is partly or largely directed to variables finance theory says are irrelevant. This is another symptom of the gap, for example:

- Many managers worry about a strategic decision's impact on book rate of return or earnings per share. If they are convinced the plan adds to the firm's value, its impact on accounting figures should be irrelevant.
- Some managers pursue diversification to reduce risk – risk as they see it. Investors see a firm's risk differently. In capital markets, diversification is cheap and easy. Investors who want to diversify do so on their own. Corporate diversification is redundant; the market will not pay extra for it.

If the market were willing to pay extra for diversification, closed-end funds would sell at premiums over net asset value, and conglomerate firms would be worth more to investors than their components separately traded. Closed-end funds actually sell at discounts, not premiums. Conglomerates appear to sell at discounts, too, although it is hard to prove it since the firm's components are not traded separately.

Much of the literature of strategic planning seems extremely naive from a financial point of view. Sometimes capital markets are ignored. Sometimes firms are essentially viewed as having a stock of capital, so that "cash cows" are needed to finance investment in rapidly growing lines of business. (The firms that pioneered in strategic planning actually had easy access to capital markets, as do almost all public companies.) Firms may not like the price they pay for capital, but that price is the opportunity cost of capital, the proper standard for new investment by the firm.

The practical conflicts between finance and strategy are part of what lies behind the recent criticism of U.S. firms for allegedly concentrating on quick payoffs at the expense of value. U.S. executives, especially MBAs, are said to rely too much on purely financial analysis, and too little on building technology, products, markets, and production efficiency. The financial world is not the real world, the argument goes; managers succumb to the glamour of high finance. They give time and talent to mergers, spinoffs, unusual securities, and complex financing packages when they should be out on the factory floor. They pump up current earnings per share at the expense of long-run values.

Much of this criticism is not directed against finance theory, but at habits of financial analysis that financial economists are attempting to reform. Finance theory of course concentrates on the financial world – that is, capital markets. However, it fundamentally disagrees with the implicit assumption of the critics who say that the financial world is not the real world and that financial analysis diverts attention from, and sometimes actively undermines, real long-run values. The professors and textbooks actually say that financial values rest on real values and that most value is created on the left-hand side of the balance sheet, not on the right.

Finance theory, however, is under attack, too. Some feel that any quantitative approach is

1 See, for example, W.E. Fruhan, Jr., *Financial Strategy: Studies in the Creation, Transfer and Destruction of Shareholder Value*, (Homewood, Illinois: Richard D. Irwin, Inc., 1979); M. S. Salter and W.A. Weinhold, *Diversification Through Acquisition* (New York: The Free Press, 1979); and H. Bierman, *Strategic Financial Planning*, (New York: The Free Press, 1980).

2 See Alberts, W.A. and McTaggart, James M. 1984, "Value-based Strategic Investment Planning," *Interfaces*, Vol. 14, No. 1 (January–February), pp. 138–151.

inevitably short-sighted. Hayes and Garvin, for example, have blamed discounted cash flow for a significant part of this country's industrial difficulties. Much of their criticism seems directed to misapplications of discounted cash flow, some of which I discuss later. But they also believe the underlying theory is wanting; they say that "beyond all else, capital investment represents an act of faith."[3] This statement offends most card-carrying financial economists.

I do not know whether "gap" fully describes all of the problems noted, or hinted at, in the discussion so far. In some quarters, finance theory is effectively ignored in strategic planning. In others, it is seen as being in conflict, or working at cross-purposes, with other forms of strategic analysis. The problem is to explain why.

TWO CULTURES AND ONE PROBLEM

Finance theory and strategic planning could be viewed as two cultures looking at the same problem. Perhaps only differences in language and approach make the two appear incompatible. If so, the gap between them might be bridged by better communication and a determined effort to reconcile them.

Think of what can go wrong with standard discounted cash flow analyses of a series of major projects:

♦ Even careful analyses are subject to random error. There is a 50 percent probability of a positive NPV for a truly border line project. Firms have to guard against these errors dominating project choice.
♦ Smart managers apply the following check. They know that all projects have zero NPV in long-run competitive equilibrium. Therefore, a positive NPV must be explained by a short-run deviation from equilibrium or by some permanent competitive advantage. If neither explanation applies, the positive NPV is suspect. Conversely, a negative NPV is suspect if a competitive advantage or short-run deviation from equilibrium favors the project.

3 R.H. Hayes and D.A. Garvin, "Managing as If Tomorrow Mattered," *Harvard Business Review*, Vol. 60, No. 3 (May–June), 1982, pp. 70–79.

In other words, smart managers do not accept positive (or negative) NPVs unless they can explain them.

Strategic planning may serve to implement this check. Strategic analyses look for market opportunities – that is, deviations from equilibrium – and try to identify the firm's competitive advantages.

Turn the logic of the example around. We can regard strategic analysis which does not explicitly compute NPVs as showing absolute faith in Adam Smith's invisible hand. If a firm, looking at a line of business, finds a favorable deviation from long-run equilibrium, or if it identifies a competitive advantage, then (efficient) investment in that line must offer profits exceeding the opportunity cost of capital. No need to calculate the investment's NPV: the manager knows in advance that NPV is positive.

The trouble is that strategic analyses are also subject to random error. Mistakes are also made in identifying areas of competitive advantage or out-of-equilibrium markets. We would expect strategic analysts to calculate NPVs explicitly, at least as a check; strategic analysis and financial analysis ought to be explicitly reconciled. Few firms attempt this. This suggests the gap between strategic planning and finance theory is more than just "two cultures and one problem."

The next step is to ask why reconciliation is so difficult.

MISUSE OF FINANCE THEORY

The gap between strategic and financial analysis may reflect misapplication of finance theory. Some firms do not try to use theory to analyze strategic investments. Some firms try but make mistakes.

I have already noted that in many firms capital investment analysis is partly or largely directed to variables finance theory says are irrelevant. Managers worry about projects' book rates of return or impacts on book earnings per share. They worry about payback, even for projects that clearly have positive NPVs. They try to reduce risk through diversification.

Departing from theoretically correct valuation procedures often sacrifices the long-run health of the firm for the short, and makes capital investment choices arbitrary or unpredictable. Over time, these sacrifices appear as disappointing growth, eroding market share, loss of technological leadership, and so forth.

The non-financial approach taken in many strategic analyses may be an attempt to overcome the short horizons and arbitrariness of financial analysis as it is often misapplied. It may be an attempt to get back to fundamentals. Remember, however: finance theory never left the fundamentals. Discounted cash flow should not in principle bias the firm against longlived projects, or be swayed by arbitrary allocations.

However, the typical mistakes made in applying DCF do create a bias against long-lived projects. I will note a few common mistakes.

Ranking on internal rate of return

Competing projects are often ranked on internal rate of return rather than NPV. It is easier to earn a high rate of return if project life is short and investment is small. Long-lived, capital-intensive projects tend to be put down the list even if their net present value is substantial.

The internal rate of return does measure bang per buck on a DCF basis. Firms may favor it because they think they have only a limited number of bucks. However, most firms big enough to do formal strategic planning have free access to capital markets. They may not like the price, but they can get the money. The limits on capital expenditures are more often set inside the firm, in order to control an organization too eager to spend money. Even when a firm does have a strictly limited pool of capital, it should not use the internal rate of return to rank projects. It should use NPV per dollar invested, or linear programming techniques when capital is rationed in more than one period.[4]

Inconsistent treatment of inflation

A surprising number of firms treat inflation inconsistently in DCF calculations. High nominal discount rates are used but cash flows are not fully adjusted for future inflation. Thus accelerating inflation makes projects – especially long-lived ones – look less attractive even if their real value is unaffected.

Unrealistically high rates

Some firms use unrealistically high discount rates, even after proper adjustment for inflation. This may reflect ignorance of what normal returns in capital markets really are. In addition:

◆ Premiums are tacked on for risks that can easily be diversified away in stockholders' portfolios.
◆ Rates are raised to offset the optimistic biases of managers sponsoring projects. This adjustment works only if the bias increases geometrically with the forecast period. If it does not, long-lived projects are penalized.
◆ Some projects are unusually risky at inception, but only of normal risk once the start-up is successfully passed. It is easy to classify this type of project as "high-risk," and to add a start-up risk premium to the discount rate for all future cash flows. The risk premium should be applied to the start-up period only. If it is applied after the start-up period, safe, short-lived projects are artificially favored.

Discounted cash flow analysis is also subject to a difficult organizational problem. Capital budgeting is usually a bottom-up process. Proposals originate in the organization's midriff, and have to survive the trip to the top, getting approval at every stage. In the process political alliances form, and cash flow forecasts are bent to meet known standards. Answers – not necessarily the right ones – are worked out for anticipated challenges. Most projects that get to the top seem to meet profitability standards set by management.

According to Brealey and Myers's Second Law, "The proportion of proposed projects having positive NPV is independent of top management's estimate of the opportunity cost of capital."[5]

Suppose the errors and biases of the capital budgeting process make it extremely difficult for

---

4 See R. A. Brealey and S. C. Myers, *Principles of Corporate Finance* (New York: McGraw-Hill Book Company, 1981), pp. 101–107.

5 Brealey and Myers, *Principles of Corporate Finance*, cited in note 4, p. 238.

top management to verify the true cash flows, risks, and present value of capital investment proposals. That would explain why firms do not try to reconcile the results of capital budgeting and strategic analyses. However, it does not explain why strategic planners do not calculate their own NPVs.

We must ask whether those in top management – the managers who make strategic decisions – understand finance theory well enough to use DCF analysis effectively. Although they certainly understand the arithmetic of the calculation, they may not understand the logic of the method deeply enough to trust it or to use it without mistakes.

They may also not be familiar enough with how capital markets work to use capital market data effectively. The widespread use of unrealistically high discount rates is probably a symptom of this.

Finally, many managers distrust the stock market. Its volatility makes them nervous, despite the fact that the volatility is the natural result of a rational market. It may be easier to underestimate the sophistication of the stock market than to accept its verdict on how well the firm is doing.

FINANCE THEORY MAY HAVE MISSED THE BOAT

Now consider the firm that understands finance theory, applies DCF analysis correctly, and has overcome the human and organizational problems that bias cash flows and discount rates. Carefully estimated net present values for strategic investments should help significantly. However, would they fully grasp and describe the firm's strategic choices? Perhaps not.

There are gaps in finance theory as it is usually applied. These gaps are not necessarily intrinsic to finance theory generally. They may be filled by new approaches to valuation. However, if they are the firm will have to use something more than a straight-forward discounted cash flow method.

An intelligent application of discounted cash flow will encounter four chief problems:

◆ Estimating the discount rate,
◆ Estimating the project's future cash flows,
◆ Estimating the project's impact on the firm's other assets' cash flows – that is, through the cross . . . sectional links between projects, and

◆ Estimating the project's impact on the firm's future investment opportunities. These are the time-series links between projects.

The first three problems, difficult as they are, are not as serious for financial strategy as the fourth. However, I will review all four.

Estimating the opportunity cost of capital

The opportunity cost of capital will always be difficult to measure, since it is an expected rate of return. We cannot commission the Gallup Poll to extract probability distributions from the minds of investors. However, we have extensive evidence on past average rates of return in capital markets and the corporate sector.[6] No long-run trends in "normal" rates of return are evident. Reasonable, ballpark cost of capital estimates can be obtained if obvious traps (for example, improper adjustments for risk or inflation) are avoided. In my opinion, estimating cash flows properly is more important than fine-tuning the discount rate.

Forecasting cash flow

It's impossible to forecast most projects' actual cash flows accurately. DCF calculations do not call for accurate forecasts, however, but for accurate assessments of the mean of possible outcomes.

Operating managers can often make reasonable subjective forecasts of the operating variables they are responsible for – operating costs, market growth, market share, and so forth – at least for the future that they are actually worrying about. It is difficult for them to translate this knowledge into a cash flow forecast for, say, year seven. There are several reasons for this difficulty. First, the operating

---

6   For estimates of capital market returns over the period 1926 to the present, see R.G. Ibbotson and R.A. Sinquefield, *Stocks, Bonds, Bills and Inflation: The Past and the Future*, Financial Analysts Research Foundation, Charlottesville, Virginia, 1982. For estimates of historical returns on capital from a corporate perspective, see D.M. Holland and S.C. Myers, "Trends in Corporate Profitability and Capital Costs," in R. Lindsay, ed., *The Nation's Capital Needs: Three Studies*, Committee on Economic Development, Washington, DC, 1979.

manager is asked to look into a far future he is not used to thinking about. Second, he is asked to express his forecast in accounting rather than operating variables. Third, incorporating forecasts of macroeconomic variables is difficult. As a result, long-run forecasts often end up as mechanical extrapolations of short-run trends. It is easy to overlook the long-run pressures of competition, inflation, and technical change.

It should be possible to provide a better framework for forecasting operating variables and translating them into cash flows and present value – a framework that makes it easier for the operating manager to apply his practical knowledge and that explicitly incorporates information about macroeconomic trends. There is, however, no way around it: forecasting is intrinsically difficult, especially when your boss is watching you do it.

Estimating cross-sectional relationships between cash flows

Tracing "cross-sectional" relationships between project cash flows is also intrinsically difficult. The problem may be made more difficult by inappropriate project definitions or boundaries for lines of businesses. Defining business units properly is one of the tricks of successful strategic planning.

However, these inescapable problems in estimating profitability standards, future cash returns, and cross-sectional interactions are faced by strategic planners even if they use no financial theory. They do not reveal a flaw in existing theory. Any theory or approach encounters them. Therefore, they do not explain the gap between finance theory and strategic planning.

The links between today's investments and tomorrow's opportunities

The fourth problem – the link between today's investments and tomorrow's opportunities – is much more difficult.

Suppose a firm invests in a negative-NPV project in order to establish a foothold in an attractive market. Thus a valuable second-stage investment is used to justify the immediate project. The second stage must depend on the first: if the firm could take the second project without having taken the first, then the future opportunity should have no impact on the immediate decision. However, if tomorrow's opportunities depend on today's decisions, there is a time-series link between projects.

At first glance, this may appear to be just another forecasting problem. Why not estimate cash flows for both stages, and use discounted cash flow to calculate the NPV for the two stages taken together?

You would not get the right answer. The second stage is an option, and conventional discounted cash flow does not value options properly. The second stage is an option because the firm is not committed to undertake it. It will go ahead if the first stage works and the market is still attractive. If the first stage fails, or if the market sours, the firm can stop after Stage 1 and cut its losses. Investing in Stage 1 purchases an intangible asset: a call option on Stage 2. If the option's present value offsets the first stage's negative NPV, the first stage is justified.

THE LIMITS OF DISCOUNTED CASH FLOW

The limits of DCF need further explanation. Think first of its application to four types of securities:

1. DCF is standard for valuing bonds, preferred stocks and other fixed-income securities.
2. DCF is sensible, and widely used, for valuing relatively safe stocks paying regular dividends.
3. DCF is not as helpful in valuing companies with significant growth opportunities. The DCF model can be stretched to say that Apple Computer's stock price equals the present value of the dividends the firm may eventually pay. It is more helpful to think of Apple's price, P_0 as:

$$P_0 = \frac{EPS}{r} + PVGO, \quad \text{where}$$

EPS = normalized current earnings
r = the opportunity cost of capital
PVGO = the net present value of future growth opportunities.

Note that PVGO is the present value of a portfolio of options – the firm's options to invest in second-stage, third-stage, or even later projects.

4. DCF is never used for traded calls or puts. Finance theory supplies option valuation formulas that work, but the option formulas look nothing like DCF.

Think of the corporate analogues to these securities:

♦ There are few problems in using DCF to value safe flows, for example, flows from financial leases.
♦ DCF is readily applied to "cash cows" – relatively safe businesses held for the cash they generate rather than for strategic value. It also works for "engineering investments," such as machine replacements, where the main benefit is reduced cost in a clearly-defined activity.
♦ DCF is less helpful in valuing businesses with substantial growth opportunities or intangible assets. In other words, it is not the whole answer when options account for a large fraction of a business's value.
♦ DCF is no help at all for pure research and development. The value of R&D is almost all option value. Intangible assets' value is usually option value.

The theory of option valuation has been worked out in detail for securities – not only puts and calls, but warrants, convertibles, bond call options, and so forth. The solution techniques should be applicable to the real options held by firms. Several preliminary applications have already been worked out, for example:

♦ Calculations of the value of a Federal lease for offshore exploration for oil or gas. Here the option value comes from the lessee's right to delay the decisions to drill and develop, and to make these decisions after observing the extent of reserves and the future level of oil prices.[7]
♦ Calculating an asset's abandonment or salvage value: an active second-hand market increases an asset's value, other things equal. The second-hand market gives the asset owner a put option which increases the value of the option to bail out of a poorly performing project.[8]

The option "contract" in each of these cases is fairly clear: a series of calls in the first case and a put in the second. However, these real options last longer and are more complex than traded calls and puts. The terms of real options have to be extracted from the economics of the problem at hand. Realistic descriptions usually lead to a complex implied "contract," requiring numerical methods of valuation.

Nevertheless, option pricing methods hold great promise for strategic analysis. The time-series links between projects are the most important part of financial strategy. A mixture of DCF and option valuation models can, in principle, describe these links and give a better understanding of how they work. It may also be possible to estimate the value of particular strategic options, thus eliminating one reason for the gap between finance theory and strategic planning.

LESSONS FOR CORPORATE STRATEGY

The task of strategic analysis is more than laying out a plan or plans. When time-series links between projects are important, it's better to think of strategy as managing the firm's portfolio of real options.[9] The process of financial planning may be thought of as:

♦ Acquiring options, either by investing directly in R&D, product design, cost or quality improvements, and so forth, or as a by-product of direct capital investment (for example, investing in a Stage 1 project with negative NPV in order to open the door for Stage 2).
♦ Abandoning options that are too far "out of the money" to pay to keep.

---

7 See the article in this issue by James Paddock, Daniel Siegel, and James Smith, which deals with the use of option pricing models in valuing offshore petroleum leases.

8 See S.C. Myers and S. Majd, "Applying Option Pricing Theory to the Abandonment Value Problem," Sloan School of Management, MIT, Working Paper, 1983.

9 See W.C. Kester, "Today's Options for Tomorrow's Growth," *Harvard Business Review* (March–April 1984).

◆ Exercising valuable options at the right time – that is, buying the cash-producing assets that ultimately produce positive net present value.

There is also a lesson for current applications of finance theory to strategic issues. Several new approaches to financial strategy use a simple, traditional DCF model of the firm.[10] These approaches are likely to be more useful for cash cows than for growth businesses with substantial risk and intangible assets.

The option value of growth and intangibles is not ignored by good managers even when conventional financial techniques miss them. These values may be brought in as "strategic factors," dressed in non-financial clothes. Dealing with the time-series links between capital investments, and with the option value these links create, is often left to strategic planners. But new developments in finance theory promise to help.

BRIDGING THE GAP

We can summarize by asking how the present gap between finance theory and strategic planning might be bridged.

Strategic planning needs finance. Present value calculations are needed as a check on strategic analysis and vice versa. However, the standard discounted cash flow techniques will tend to understate the option value attached to growing, profitable lines of business. Corporate finance theory requires extension to deal with real options. Therefore, to bridge the gap we on the financial side need to:

◆ Apply existing finance theory correctly.
◆ Extend the theory. I believe the most promising line of research is to try to use option pricing theory to model the time-series interactions between investments.

Both sides could make a conscious effort to reconcile financial and strategic analysis. Although complete reconciliation will rarely be possible, the attempt should uncover hidden assumptions and bring a generally deeper understanding of strategic choices. The gap may remain, but with better analysis on either side of it.

10   See, for example, Chapter 2 of W.E. Fruhan, Jr., *Financial Strategy: Studies in the Creation, Transfer and Destruction of Shareholder Value*, (Homewood, Illinois: Richard D. Irwin, Inc., 1979).

CHAPTER 6

In Defense of Beta

S. P. Kothari and Jay Shanken (University of Rochester)

An important implication of modern finance theory is that the higher the non-diversifiable risk of a portfolio, the higher its expected return. For more than 20 years, financial academics and practitioners have used beta – the central variable in the capital asset pricing model, or CAPM – as their primary measure of non-diversifiable risk.[1]

Stated in brief, beta is a regression coefficient designed to measure the extent to which a given asset's return moves together with the broad market's. Loosely speaking, if the S&P 500 increases by 10% in a given period, a stock that also tends to rise by 10% has a beta of 1.0; and a stock that rises by 20% has a beta of 2.0. According to the CAPM, moreover, a stock with a beta of 2.0 should earn a risk "premium" (that is, a return in excess of the T-bill rate) that over long periods of time is twice the premium on a stock with a beta of 1.0.

In recent years, however, the use of beta and the underlying CAPM risk-return theory have come under severe attack from a number of empirical studies. Although several articles announcing the "death" of beta have appeared in recent years, the most serious challenge to the CAPM has come from a widely-cited article by Eugene Fama and Kenneth French published at the end of 1992.[2] There Fama and French reported that beta does a poor job of explaining "cross-sectional" variation in the average returns of stocks over the period 1963–90. They also reported that two other easily measured variables – the book-to-market ratio and the market capitalization of equity (a common measure of firm size) – together explain a significant fraction of the variation in average returns over the same period. Over the longer period 1941–90, beta fares only a bit better.

The financial press, along with the investment and academic communities, have shown keen interest in Fama and French's work. Such interest arises for at least two reasons. First, if betas are at best weakly correlated with average returns, professional investors must reevaluate their investment strategies. For, if Fama and French are right, it would make sense to shift out of high-beta stocks and into low-beta stocks. Such a strategy would reduce risk while having a minimal impact on expected return.

---

1 The CAPM derives primarily from the work of three finance scholars working largely independently of each other. For the seminal papers, see William F. Sharpe, "Capital Asset Prices: A Theory of Market Equilibrium under Conditions of Risk," *Journal of Finance*, 19 (1964), 425–442; John Lintner, "The Valuation of Risk Assets and the Selection of Risky Investments in Stock Portfolios and Capital Budgets," *Review of Economics and Statistics*, 47 (1965), 13–37; and Ian Mossin, "Equilibrium in a Capital Asset Market," *Econometrica*, 34 (1966), 768–783.

2 Eugene F. Fama and Kenneth French, "The Cross-section of Expected Returns," *Journal of Finance*, 47 (1992), 427–465.

Of course, if enough investors resort to this strategy, there will be downward pressure on the prices of high-beta stocks and upward pressure on the prices of low-beta stocks. And, because such price pressures would in turn cause high-beta stocks to earn higher returns and low-beta stocks to earn lower returns than before, the relation between beta and expected return would actually be strengthened rather than diminished. In this sense, the strategy contains the seeds of its own destruction, a familiar theme in efficient financial markets.

The second source of the interest in Fama and French's study is the prospect of using the book-to-market ratio and firm size to make more efficient portfolio investment decisions, especially if the relevance of the CAPM is in serious doubt. Since there is no conclusive theoretical explanation for how and why these two variables should affect expected returns, interpretations of the Fama-French results have varied widely (and wildly). Consistent with an efficient markets framework, Fama and French view book-to-market and firm size as proxies for other (non-beta) risk factors for which the market compensates investors with higher returns.[3] But those inclined to believe in investor irrationality have seized on the surprising explanatory power of these variables as evidence of market *in*efficiency. In this "behavioralist" view of financial markets, investor excesses (of the kind Keynes attributed to "animal spirits") provide opportunities for other investors to earn higher average returns without bearing commensurately higher risk.

We recently completed a study in which we too attempted to determine whether there really is a positively sloped relation between beta and average returns.[4] But before describing our own findings, we will provide a different perspective on the Fama-French results – one that, in our view, has been conspicuously absent from the beta debate.

To begin with, it's important to keep in mind that the CAPM risk-return relation is a statement about *expected* returns, not actual returns. Over very long periods of time, average actual returns should turn out to be roughly equivalent to expected returns; this is an important part of the definition of efficient markets. But, given the very high variability of the surprise component in actual returns, average returns over a given sample period – even one as long as 30 years – can deviate significantly from investors' expectations.

Actual investment decision-making, of course, must be based on our best-informed expectations, since this is all we have at the time a decision is made. Therefore, in assessing the empirical evidence on the risk-return relation, the relevant question is this: In light of the evidence now available, what is our best forecast (expectation) of what the compensation for bearing beta risk will be in the *future*?

Looking at the Fama-French evidence from this perspective, one notices something quite interesting. Their estimate of expected return compensation based on data for the 1941–90 period is 0.24% per month, or about 3% per year (that is, for every 1.0 increase in beta, the average annual return was roughly 3% higher). However, the standard error of this estimate is nearly the same (.23% per month); and because the conventional *t-statistic* is thus only about 1.0, we cannot reject the hypothesis that the expected risk premium is zero. It is this aspect of the evidence that has received nearly all of the media attention.

What has been neglected, however, is the simple observation that, *given the same Fama-French evidence*, a substantial annual risk premium of 6% per year (one standard error above the mean) is about as likely as no risk premium. In other words, the data permit a wide range of conclusions about the true slope of the risk-return relation. And, in the absence of more definitive evidence, our "priors" or perceptions based on considerations other than the evidence must necessarily play a major role in how we interpret the research findings and make investment decisions.

In our recent study, we began by reexamining some of the issues surrounding empirical tests of the risk-return relation. We found that, in designing tests to determine whether there is a positive reward for bearing beta risk, the measurement of betas plays a critically important role. For example, the betas of individual companies vary systematically (though not in a linear fashion) with the length of the return-measurement interval used in

---

3 The true magnitude of the book-to-market effect may be much lower than that estimated by Fama and French, however, because of certain selection biases in the data. See S.P. Kothari, Jay Shanken, and Richard G. Sloan, "Another Look at the Cross-section of Expected Returns," *Journal of Finance*, 50 (1995).

4 S.P. Kothari, Jay Shanken, and Richard G. Sloan, "Another Look at the Cross-section of Expected Returns," *Journal of Finance*, 50 (1995).

estimating betas.[5] Common practice, both in the investment and academic worlds, is to calculate betas based on *monthly* returns; that is, an individual company's beta is typically measured by regressing its monthly stock returns against the corresponding monthly returns of the S&P 500 over the past five years. But, since theory provides little guidance as to the appropriate horizon, we explored the use of annual betas as an alternative to the usual monthly horizon in academic research.

Our conclusion was that the use of annual instead of monthly returns to estimate betas, though possibly reducing precision, help avoids other measurement problems caused by trading frictions (such as transactions costs and taxes), non-synchronous trading, and seasonal patterns in returns. Each of these factors can create biases in estimating beta. For example, the betas of small-cap stocks that trade in thin markets are systematically understated by "monthly" betas. Over a period as long as a year, however, measured returns should be close to the market's assessment of changes in value, yielding less biased beta estimates.[6]

Even more noteworthy, when using annual returns to estimate betas, we found an economically and statistically significant positive relation between beta and average returns. The results of our study, discussed in more detail below, are broadly as follows: A portfolio with a beta risk of 1.5 (loosely speaking, a portfolio that is one-and-a-half times as volatile as the market index) can be expected to return 6% to 12% more per year than a portfolio with a beta of 0.5. In short, we found evidence of substantial compensation for bearing beta risk.

---

5   See David Levhari and Haim Levy, "The Capital Asset Pricing Model and the Investment Horizon," *Review of Economics and Statistics*, 59 (1977), 92–104; Puneet Handa, S.P. Kothari, and Charles E. Wasley, "The Relation between the Return Interval and Betas: Implications for the Size Effect," *Journal of Financial Economics*, 23 (1989), 79–100.
6   See Scholes, Myron S. and John Williams, 1977, "Estimating Betas from Nonsynchronous Data," *Journal of Financial Economics*, 14, 327–348; Kalman J. Cohen, Gabriel A. Hawawini, Steven F. Maier, Robert A. Schwartz, and David K. Whitcomb, "Friction in the Trading Process and the Estimation of Systematic Risk," *Journal of Financial Economics*, 12 (1983), 263–278; and Andrew W. Lo and A. Craig MacKinlay, "Data-snooping Biases in Tests of Financial asset pricing models, *Review of Financial Studies*, 3 (1990), 431–467.

SOME BACKGROUND ON BETA RESEARCH METHODS

The basics of the current method for estimating the relation between expected stock returns and beta risk, including the method used in our own study, were first provided by Gene Fama and James MacBeth in a paper published in 1973.[7] There are two main insights from this pioneering study that have continued to influence empirical tests of the risk-return relation over the past 20 years.

First, while the reward for bearing beta risk may not be positive over periods as short as a year or two, in an efficient market the reward should be positive over sufficiently long time periods. Fama and MacBeth accordingly used more than three decades of stock returns in testing whether the *average* or expected compensation for beta risk is positive.

Second, the validity of the results of a test of the risk-return relation depends critically on the accuracy with which a researcher has measured the betas of the portfolios whose returns and risks are being correlated. The less precise the estimated betas as measures of the underlying or "true" risk of the portfolios, the greater the likelihood that the researcher will err in concluding that the risk-return trade-off is too flat.

The method introduced by Fama and MacBeth is a two-step procedure. First, since the estimate of the beta of an individual stock is generally not very precise, risk-return analysis is performed by grouping stocks into *portfolios* according to their estimated betas. More specifically, they calculate an estimate of beta for each stock using the last five years of monthly stock returns and then use those estimates to classify each stock into one of 20 different portfolios arranged from lowest to highest risk. Thus, portfolio 1 consists of the 5% lowest-beta stocks and portfolio 20 consists of the 5% highest-beta stocks.

For each year in the sample, moreover, new beta estimates are calculated incorporating the past year's

---

7   For studies making contributions to these empirical procedures, see Fischer Black, Michael C. Jensen, and Myron Scholes, "The Capital Asset Pricing Model: Some Empirical Tests," in Michael C. Jensen, ed., *Studies in the Theory of Capital Markets* (Praeger, New York, NY, 1972); and Marshall E. Blume and Irwin Friend, "A New Look at the Capital Asset Pricing Model," *Journal of Finance*, 28 (1973), 19–33.

Table 6.1 Pre-ranking and Post-ranking Betas, Firm Size, and Average Returns on
20 Beta-ranked Portfolios (1927–1990)

Portfolio	Ranking-period Beta	Post-ranking Beta	Ln(Size)	Post-ranking Return
1	0.20	0.44	5.45	12.4
2	0.38	0.59	5.75	13.4
3	0.48	0.75	5.72	15.0
4	0.56	0.68	5.69	15.3
5	0.63	0.72	5.59	15.3
6	0.70	0.75	5.31	16.1
7	0.76	0.80	5.26	17.1
8	0.81	1.05	5.15	18.3
9	0.87	0.82	5.10	16.9
10	0.93	0.91	4.92	18.0
11	0.99	0.97	4.82	18.1
12	1.04	1.14	4.72	19.0
13	1.10	1.19	4.49	20.9
14	1.17	1.10	4.47	18.4
15	1.24	1.39	4.30	21.6
16	1.32	1.28	4.12	20.4
17	1.42	1.41	3.93	21.9
18	1.54	1.30	3.80	20.4
19	1.71	1.51	3.55	20.7
20	2.17	1.19	3.27	18.1

returns. The new estimates in turn could change the old rankings, thus causing the composition of the 20 portfolios to vary somewhat from year to year. This method of annually reforming the portfolios yields "biased" betas, however – that is, the betas of the lowest-beta portfolios tend to be too low and the betas of the highest-beta portfolio tend to be too high. To eliminate this bias, the portfolio betas are estimated a second time using a later set of stock returns (producing "post-ranking" betas). (For an illustration of this bias in so-called "ranking-period" betas, and how "post-ranking" betas overcome it, compare the first two columns in Table 6.1.)

In the second step of the Fama-MacBeth procedure, returns earned on the portfolios in a given month (call it "t") are regressed on the portfolio betas using the following regression model:[8]

$$R_{pt} = g_0 + g_1 b_p = u_{pt} \qquad (1)$$

where

- R_{pt} is the return on portfolio p in month t;
- b_p is the beta estimate for portfolio p;
- g_0 and g_1 are regression coefficients; and
- u_{pt} is the regression disturbance term or unexpected return.

The regression model is estimated in each month using data on the 20 beta-sorted portfolios. The "output" of such regressions are the coefficient estimates g_{0t} and g_{1t}. The size of the beta coefficient, g_{1t}, can be interpreted as the compensation for risk in month t. It will sometimes be higher, and at other times lower, than the expected compensation, depending on the actual market return that month. But if the *average* value of these coefficients is positive and statistically significant, the interpretation is that the expected reward for bearing beta risk is positive, a central prediction of the CAPM.

SOME NEW EVIDENCE

Our study used stock return data for New York and American Stock Exchange firms (available from the University of Chicago's Center for Research in

8   In some versions of the methodology the beta estimates are updated over time. In the more recent applications, a single beta is usually estimated for each portfolio over the entire period.

Security Prices (CRSP)) that go as far back as 1926. For each year from 1927 to 1990, we grouped all NYSE and ASE stocks into 20 equal-weighted portfolios according to their ranking-period betas ("ranking-period," once again, means the betas were estimated from stock returns prior to the given year). Next, to overcome the beta "bias" described earlier, we calculated post-ranking betas for each of the same 20 portfolios by examining the stock returns on the portfolios during the 12 months *after* the ranking-period beta estimation.[9] For each of the portfolios, moreover, we also calculated the average size (measured as the natural log of market equity capitalization) of the companies in the portfolio.

In Table 6.1, we report the post-ranking betas along with the 64-year averages for ranking-period betas, firm size, and returns for each of the 20 "beta-ranked" portfolios. As shown in the table, the post-ranking (or unbiased) betas ranged from a low of 0.44 for portfolio 1 to a high of 1.51 for portfolio 19 (portfolio 20 need not have the highest beta because the portfolios, as mentioned, were formed on the basis of their ranking-period betas). As the table also makes clear, firm size is inversely related to beta; that is, smaller capitalization stocks tend to have higher systematic risks than larger cap stocks.

Also apparent from Table 6.1 is that the post-ranking period returns on the 20 portfolios generally rise with the post-ranking betas, which is consistent with the CAPM's prediction that higher systematic risk is rewarded by higher average returns. The lowest average return, 12.4%, is earned by portfolio 1. The highest average annual return, 21.9%, is earned by portfolio 17, which has the second highest post-ranking beta, 1.41.

Thus, the spread in average returns across the 20 portfolios is about 9%, while the spread in betas is a little over 1.0. One could interpret this result as follows: If there are two portfolios whose betas differ by 1.0, then the higher beta portfolio would be expected to earn approximately 9% more.

Regression Results. To provide a formal test of this proposition, we next performed cross-sectional regressions of the kind pioneered by Fama and MacBeth (and described earlier). In performing these regressions, however, we used two additional procedures for grouping stocks into portfolios. Besides the 20 "beta-ranked" portfolios described above, we also grouped all stocks into 20 different portfolios according to company size (with the 5% smallest firms in portfolio 1 and the 5% largest in portfolio 20, hereafter called "size-ranked" portfolios). Because beta and size are inversely related, ranking firms according to size is an indirect way of ranking according to beta. (In fact, the size portfolios produced a greater range (highest-lowest) of post-ranking betas – 1.35, as opposed to 1.07 for the beta-ranked portfolios in Table 6.1.)

Finally, in an effort to identify the relative contributions of the "beta effect" and the "size effect," we also formed 100 portfolios that were sorted as follows: all stocks were sorted first into 10 deciles based on size; and then each of these 10 size-ranked groups were broken down into 10 more portfolios according to ranking-period beta. (We refer to the resulting 100-portfolio groupings as "first size-then-beta.")

Table 6.2 reports our regression results for each of the three portfolio-sorting procedures for each month from July 1927 to June 1991 (a total of 768 months). Both the average beta coefficients (g_1) and size coefficients (g_2) reported in Table 6.2 are statistically significant at conventional levels using all three sets of portfolios. We found a monthly risk premium of 1.02% for the "size-ranked" portfolios, a risk premium of 0.54% for the "beta-ranked" portfolios, and an intermediate 0.71% for the "first size-then-beta-ranked" portfolios. Based on these findings, one would conclude that the *ex post* compensation for beta risk over the 64-year period since 1926 was somewhere between 6.5% and 12.2% per year. (Viewed together with the magnitude of the coefficients, moreover, the relatively large t-statistics should give us considerable confidence in the reliability of the positive correlation between expected return and beta.)[10]

---

9 Such post-ranking betas were calculated using the time-series regression: $R_{pt} = a_p + b_p R_{mt} + e_{pt}$, where a_p and b_p are the intercept and slope (beta) parameters for portfolio p; R_{mt} is the annual return on the market portfolio, defined as the equal-weighted annual return on the stocks available that year on the CRSP tape; and e_{pt} is the regression disturbance term, which captures the portion of p's return that is unrelated to the market index.

---

10 We also find (but do not report in table 6.2) that the results are robust to several alternative ways of forming portfolios. Similar statistical significance is found over the shorter and less volatile 1941–90 period, although the estimated risk premia are lower.

Table 6.2 Cross-sectional Regressions of Monthly Returns on Beta and Firm Size: Equal-weighted Market Index*

Portfolios	g₀ (t-stat)	g₁ (t-stat)	g₂ (t-stat)	Adj R²
20, beta ranked	0.76 (3.25)	0.54 (1.94)		0.32
	1.76 (2.48)		−0.16 (−2.03)	0.27
	1.68 (3.82)	0.09 (0.41)	−0.14 (−2.57)	0.35
20, size ranked	0.30 (−0.18)	1.02 (3.91)		0.32
	1.73 (3.70)		−0.18 (−3.50)	0.33
	−0.05 (−0.85)	1.15 (4.61)	0.03 (0.76)	0.40
100, first size,	0.58 (1.54)	0.71 (3.39)		0.12
then beta ranked	1.72 (3.66)		−0.18 (−3.43)	0.12
	1.14 (3.78)	0.43 (2.58)	−1.10 (−2.87)	0.16

*Time-series averages of estimated coefficients from the following monthly cross-sectional regressions from 1927 to 1990, associated t-statistics in parentheses, and adjusted R²s are reported (with and without size being included in the regressions):

$$R_{pt} = g_0 + g_1 b_p + g_2 \, \text{Size}_{pt-1} + \mu_{pt}$$

Table 6.2 also contains evidence of a now well-documented negative "size effect" on expected returns.[11] (In particular, when beta and size are both included as independent variables in the regressions, the coefficient on size (g_2) is consistently two or three standard errors below zero.) This tendency of small firms to earn higher rates of return than their betas would suggest indicates that beta alone does not fully account for expected returns. One should also keep in mind, however, that the regression method we employ relies on *estimates* of beta, not the underlying or "true" betas. Since size is likely to be strongly (negatively) correlated with true beta as well as many other measures of firm risk and liquidity, it is difficult to know exactly what the coefficient on size is reflecting.[12]

One last point on the beta and size issue; using the estimates of g_0 and g_1 from Table 6.2, and plugging the beta for a particular portfolio into equation (1), we computed an estimate of expected return for that portfolio. Similarly, using the regression equation that includes size as well as beta, we computed what our evidence suggests is an even better estimate of portfolio expected return. When following this procedure, we found that the differences between the expected returns obtained using size and beta, and those derived using beta alone, averaged less than 1.0% per year across all of our portfolios and never exceeded 3.0% in any given year. By comparison, the average returns on these portfolios ranged from 8.1% to 38.2%. This finding suggests that, although beta and size are both needed to account for differences in expected return, the additional information provided by size, given that beta is already in the model, is modest.

CONCLUSIONS

In contrast to the popular interpretation of the Fama and French results as implying no compensation for beta risk, we have observed that their evidence is equally consistent with a value-weighted market risk premium of 6% per year. In addition, when betas are estimated using annual rather than monthly data, the results are highly statistically significant, with estimates of the equal-weighted market risk premium ranging from 6% to 12% per year.

11 See Rolf Banz (1981) and Marc Reinganum (1981)

12 See K.C. Chan, Nai-Fu Chen, and David A. Hsieh, "An exploratory, investigation of the firm size effect, *Journal of Financial Economics*, 14 (1985), 451–471; and Yakov Amihud and Haim Mendelson, "Asset Pricing and the Bid-ask Spread," *Journal of Financial Economics*, 17 (1986), 223–249. This difficulty is compounded by the fact that, as Richard Roll noted in 1977, our tests necessarily use a stock index as an empirical proxy for the theoretically-preferred true market portfolio.

Firm size is also statistically significant in explaining cross-sectional differences in expected returns. Although the *incremental* contribution of size beyond beta is modest, including size improves the assessment of expected return. This could be due in part to the fact that size is related to the *true* beta of a stock. Thus, while the CAPM may not provide a perfect description of expected returns, the latest pronouncements that beta is dead appear, once again, to have been premature.

CHAPTER 7

The Liquidity Route to a Lower Cost of Capital

Yakov Amihud (New York University) and Haim Mendelson (Stanford University)

Corporate finance theory says that the value of a company is the present value of the cash flows that investors expect it to generate in the future, discounted at the firm's cost of capital. The cost of capital has traditionally been assumed to be an increasing function of the level of (risk-free) interest rates and the risk of the company's stock. The cost of capital is said to contain a *risk premium* over and above the risk free interest rate because investors demand to be compensated for bearing additional risk.[1]

In a 1986 paper published in the *Journal of Financial Economics*,[2] we proposed that there is another important determinant of the corporate cost of capital: the liquidity of the company's securities or claims. We hypothesized that, in setting stock prices, investors demand not only a risk premium, but also a *liquidity premium* to compensate them for the costs they bear when buying and selling the firm's claims, whether it be stocks, bonds, or other securities. Thus, the greater the liquidity of a security (or the lower the associated liquidity costs), the lower the expected return required by investors for any given level of risk. And the

lower a company's required return, all other things equal, the higher is its stock price for a given level of earnings or operating cash flows – or in the language of market analysts, the higher its P/E ratio.

One major implication of our theory is that reductions in liquidity costs should lead to higher stock prices, even without any improvement in corporate "fundamentals" such as expected earnings. And, as we discuss in this article, there have been a number of liquidity-enhancing developments in recent years that have likely contributed to the current level of stock prices. Perhaps most dramatic, the rise of Internet trading has substantially reduced the cost of trading in a number of ways: it has reduced brokerage commissions, enabled investors to execute their own trades, and provided direct, low-cost access to information about companies. In addition to these Internet-based developments, there have also been a number of important institutional innovations. Most notable is the major reform of the Nasdaq, instituted in 1997, that allows limit orders by investors to compete directly with quotes by market makers. Such competition has reduced bid-ask spreads and, in the process, provided greater market depth. Another

---

1 The theory of finance discusses what is the risk that is relevant to investors, given their ability to diversify. There are a number of models on how to measure risk, and numerous empirical studies on whether risk is priced in the market.

2 Yakov Amihud and Haim Mendelson, "Asset Pricing and the Bid-Ask Spread," *Journal of Financial Economics* Vol. 17, (1986), 223–249.

important change is the reduction, in June 1997, of the minimum "tick" from $\$\frac{1}{8}$ to $\$\frac{1}{16}$, which has also contributed to lower bid-ask spreads and increased liquidity.

Our theory also provides a plausible explanation for an older market "anomaly" that is well-known in academic circles as the "small firm effect." As a considerable body of studies has shown, over a long period of time smaller companies produced higher (risk-adjusted) returns than large firms. And because the stocks of smaller firms are significantly less liquid (as indicated by wider bid-ask spreads and other measures) than those of large companies, the excess returns on small firm stocks can be understood as the compensation provided investors for the higher associated liquidity costs.[3]

In recent years, however, the small firm effect has disappeared – and, indeed, large companies have produced higher returns than small firms. According to our theory, the recent underperformance of small firms might be attributable to differences in the effects of these liquidity changes on the values of large and small firms. For example, the rise of Internet trading, while reducing liquidity costs in general, may have done less to stimulate trading volume for smaller firms (apart from small high tech and Internet firms) than for large ones (a possibility that has not yet been tested). To the extent that the reduction of liquidity costs for small stocks has failed to match that of large stocks, the lower realized returns experienced by small firms in recent years could be partly attributed to their becoming *relatively* less liquid than they were before. (And even if liquidity costs fall by the same amount for large and small firms, reductions in trading costs will cause bigger increases in the values of large firms because of their shareholders' greater sensitivity to trading costs.)

Finally, our theory has a major implication for corporate executives: *a company can reduce its cost of capital and raise its stock price by applying policies designed to increase the liquidity of its securities.*[4] In this paper,

after discussing the major factors that determine a firm's liquidity and reviewing the evidence of academic studies on how liquidity affects the cost of capital, we offer a number of suggestions for managements intent on increasing the liquidity of their stock. Specifically, we propose that managers (1) consider measures, such as stock splits, designed to increase their investor base by attracting small investors; (2) seek trading venues for their securities that promise to increase liquidity; and (3) provide more and better information to investors. Moreover, for smaller companies with virtually no analyst following, we suggest that they *pay analysts to cover their stock*, much as companies pay Moody's or Standard & Poors to rate their bonds.

WHAT IS LIQUIDITY?

The liquidity of a stock is a measure of the ease with which cash can be converted to an investment in the stock or vice versa. Illiquidity is driven by the explicit and implicit costs of buying or selling the stock. It is convenient to represent the costs of liquidity as the sum of three components: adverse selection costs, opportunity costs, and direct costs (commissions and fees). We now discuss each of these costs in turn.

Adverse selection costs

A major component of the costs of liquidity is *adverse selection costs*. Such costs are typically divided into two components: the bid-ask spread and market impact costs. The bid and ask prices quoted for a stock are the prices at which investors can trade a small order instantaneously; a small sell order can be instantaneously executed at the market bid price, and a small buy order can be executed instantaneously at the ask price. The difference between the highest bid (buying) price and the lowest ask (selling) price – the bid-ask spread – thus represents a liquidity cost. A liquid stock has a narrow bid-ask spread, which implies a lower cost for an instantaneous "round-trip" transaction.

In the NASDAQ stock market, the bid and ask prices are posted by designated market makers on computer screens. In auction markets like the

---

3 For evidence showing that liquidity costs are higher for small firms, see Hans R. Stoll and Robert E. Whaley, "Transaction Costs and the Small Firm Effect," *Journal of Financial Economics*, 12 (1983), 57–79.

4 For an early version of this argument, see Yakov Amihud and Haim Mendelson, "Liquidity and Asset Prices: Financial Management Implications," *Financial Management* 17, (Spring 1988), 5–15.

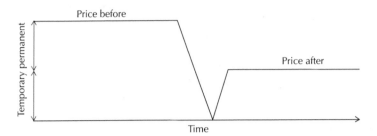

Figure 7.1   Price Effects of a Large Block Sale

New York Stock Exchange (NYSE) and the American Stock Exchange (AMEX), bid and ask prices are quoted by market participants on the floor of the exchange or on a limit order book, where the bid and ask prices represent the best price available to buy and sell, respectively.[5] Recently, there has been an increase in the number of private Electronic Communication Networks (ECNs) that manage limit order books of public orders.

The bid and ask quotes are good for limited quantities only. If a trader wants to sell a larger quantity, the transaction itself may "move" the market in a direction that hurts the trader. For example, the sale of a large quantity of stock has a negative impact on the sale price and, on average, the negative impact is an increasing function of the amount sold. Thus, the sale of a large quantity of stock typically causes a price decline, part of which is temporary but part of which remains.

Figure 7.1 shows schematically the effects of a large block sale on stock price. The sale depresses the price, but some of the price decline is subsequently reversed. In Figure 7.1, the "temporary" component of the price decline – the part that accompanies a large transaction but does not reflect an actual change in the stock's value – is the market impact cost of the transaction. The "permanent" decline measures the change in the stock's value.

In a 1996 study, Keim and Madhavan estimated the temporary market impact costs of block sales to be 1.86% for NYSE and AMEX transactions, and 3.28% for National Market System ("NMS") stocks on the NASDAQ Stock Market.[6] They also found that the market impact for institutional investors who execute large packages of stocks over time averaged almost 1% for buy packages and −0.3% for sell packages.[7]

These liquidity costs – the bid-ask spread and market impact costs – are in large part *adverse selection* costs that result from the fact that transactions may be triggered by new information that is not yet reflected in the market price of the stock. Market microstructure studies[8] distinguish

---

5   Auction markets often have a designated specialist who serves as a "lead market maker," as is the case on the NYSE and the AMEX. However, the specialist also incorporates in the bid and ask quotes the best prices available in the limit order book. In this case, the "market makers" are the traders who placed the limit orders, the specialist, and the floor traders who participate in the auction taking place on the exchange floor.

6   These numbers pertain to large blocks executed in the "upstairs" market. See Donald B. Keim and Ananth Madhavan, "The Upstairs Market for Large-Block Transactions: Analysis and Measurement of Price Effects," *Review of Financial Studies* 9, 1996, 1–36.

7   See Louis K.C. Chan and Joseph Lakonishok, "The Behavior of Stock Prices Around Institutional Trades," *Journal of Finance* 50, 1995, 1147–1174. The +1% for purchases and −0.3% for sales represent the total market impact from the opening price on the package's first day to the closing price on the package's last day.

8   See, e.g., Lawrence R. Glosten and Paul R. Milgrom, "Bid, Ask and Transaction Prices in a Specialist Market with Heterogeneously Informed Traders," *Journal of Financial Economics* 14, (1985), 71–100; Albert P. Kyle, "Continuous Auctions and Insider Trading," *Econometrica* 53, (1985), 1315–1336. For an empirical examination of the adverse selection component of the bid-ask spread, see Lawrence Glosten and Lawrence Harris, "Estimating the Components of the Bid-Ask Spread," *Journal of Financial Economics* 21, (1985), 123–142; Roger D. Huang and Hans R. Stoll, "The Components of the Bid-Ask Spread: A General Approach," *Review of Financial Studies* 10, 4 (1997), 995–1034.

between *informed* traders, who possess superior information about the stock's value, and *uninformed* traders, who trade for liquidity reasons, while having no particular information about the stock. (For example, an uninformed trader may sell the stock when he or she needs the money invested in it, or will buy the stock when he or she has excess cash.) Market makers are naturally reluctant to trade against informed traders, but the two types of traders are typically mixed.

Adverse selection means that informed traders will sell the stock when they know its price is too high and buy when they know the price is too low. For example, suppose an informed trader wants to sell a stock to a market maker at the quoted bid price. This suggests that the informed trader knows that the current market price is too high. The market maker usually buys the stock at the bid price, hoping to sell it later at the ask price and earn the difference – the bid-ask spread. However, when trading against an informed trader, the market maker is exposed to the risk that he is overpaying for the stock. The more likely it is that the seller is "informed," the lower the bid price the market maker is willing to pay. Conversely, if the market maker suspects that the buyer is informed, the ask (offer) price will be higher. For the same reason, if the market maker knows that a large sale has been initiated by an informed trader, it is likely to depress the stock price more than in the case where it was initiated by an uninformed trader. Moreover, in cases where the identity of the seller is not disclosed, the market maker will assume that a large sale is coming from an informed trader.[9]

The result is that in a market where transactions are more likely to be initiated by informed traders, the bid-ask spread is wider, market impact costs are larger, and liquidity is lower. In contrast, trading by uninformed investors does not expose market makers to adverse selection. In fact, the greater the likelihood of uninformed trading, the narrower the bid-ask spread and the smaller the market impact costs.

Consistent with the idea that uninformed trades tend to come from smaller shareholders, studies have documented that increasing the number of investors that hold a stock leads to a smaller bid-ask spread. In a 1974 study, Benston and Hagerman[10] found a negative relationship between the number of stockholders and the stocks' bid-ask spreads. This means that for a company with a given trading volume and risk, increasing the small-investor base can be expected to enhance the liquidity of the company's stock. Evidence also shows that specialists on the NYSE are more willing to provide price improvement for small orders than they do for large orders.[11] That is, the effective bid-ask spread on small orders on the NYSE is significantly smaller than the effective bid-ask spread on large orders. This finding also suggests that stock liquidity is enhanced by small orders.

Opportunity costs

The buyer or seller of a block of securities faces a tradeoff between market impact costs and execution delays. In the equity markets, traders of large blocks often search "upstairs" for better prices and approach intermediaries (typically block positioners) to solicit orders on the other side of the market. However, the delay associated with this search process can be costly because an unfavorable price change can take place between the time the trader made her initial trading decision and the execution of the trade. For example, suppose the trader decides to short a stock whose price is expected to decline. By delaying the execution, the trader is exposed to the risk that the price will decline while the search for a better price is still under way. Worse yet, the search process itself may alert the rest of the market to the impending sale of a large block, moving the market down – the very outcome the trader wanted to avoid. In that case, the delay in execution forces the trader to incur a loss.

A trader who wants to avoid paying the bid-ask cost may enter her order as a limit order.

9 See David Easley and Mureen O'Hara, "Price, Trade Size and Information in Securities Markets," *Journal of Financial Economics* 19 (1987), 69–90.

10 George J. Benston and Robert L. Hagerman, "Determinants of Bid-Asked Spreads in the Over-the-Counter Market," *Journal of Financial Economics* 1, 1974, 353–364.
11 See Lawrence Harris and Joel Hasbrouck, "Market vs. Limit Orders: The SuperDOT Evidence on Order Submission Strategy," *Journal of Financial and Quantitative Analysis* 31, 1996, 213–231.

But, again, such a strategy may create a delay in execution that imposes opportunity costs on the trader. For example, a trader wishing to buy a stock because of expectations of a price rise may choose, instead of paying the ask price, to enter a limit buy order at a lower price. However, the stock price may indeed rise, as the trader has expected, and the limit order to buy will not be executed. The delay in execution has thus imposed a cost on the trader.

While delay costs are difficult to measure, they can be substantial, especially in fast-moving markets. In a study of execution costs for equity trades by pension funds in the second and third quarters of 1997, Wagner[12] found that delay costs accounted for about half of the total cost of order execution.[13]

Securities markets can reduce these delay costs by enabling speedy executions. This can be achieved in manual or electronic auction markets with a multitude of participants who stand ready to absorb incoming orders. As a result, the search cost of contacting potential traders on the other side (for example, buyers when the order is to sell) is low and the delay is minimized. For example, on the New York Stock Exchange, where more than 50% of trading volume is in large blocks,[14] block trades take place partly "upstairs" and partly on the Exchange floor. A recent study by Madhavan and Cheng found that, for the Dow stocks, about 80% of block dollar volume is traded downstairs and, for the NYSE overall, about 73% of block volume is accounted for by "downstairs" trading.[15]

Brokerage commissions and fees

Another component of the cost of liquidity is the direct costs of trading, which include brokerage commissions, exchange fees, and taxes. Because traders are interested in their *total* cost of buying or their *net* proceeds from selling, high commissions and fees do not necessarily imply that the trader is worse off paying them, since there may be a trade-off between these direct costs and other liquidity costs. In particular, a block trader may prefer a market with higher commissions and fees if trading there results in lower market impact costs. A 1995 study by Chan and Lakonishok[16] found that, for institutional investors' sales of large equity blocks, market impact costs were negatively related to the commission expense: the higher the commission, the lower the market impact cost. Institutional investors were therefore willing to pay higher commissions in return for lower market impact costs. However, for individual investors whose market impact cost is negligible, commissions and fees can represent a significant percentage of total trading costs.

Historically, institutional brokerage commissions have declined whereas those paid by individuals have not. However, the emergence and growth of online brokerage have recently driven down retail commissions. Since the online brokerage industry has targeted primarily the discount brokers' base of customers interested in fast and cheap executions, price-cutting has been commonplace. For example, E*Trade reduced its prices seven times between 1993 to 1996, before settling down at $14.95 for most trades. The average retail commission charged by the top online trading firms has decreased by more than two thirds since the beginning of 1996. The decline in retail commissions has since continued, and they now appear to have stabilized at a level of about $17 per trade. Figure 7.2 shows the trend in weighted-average retail commissions charged by online brokerage firms over 1996–1999. Since the end of 1999, Ameritrade, Datek, and Suretrade have begun charging commissions that are less than $10 per trade.

With the increase in online trading, these trends are predicted to prevail industrywide, as shown in Figure 7.3. Thus, the commission component of the cost of illiquidity, which has historically

---

12   Wayne Wagner, Plexus Group, March 1998.
13   Specifically, the delay cost was 72 basis points compared to a total of 147 basis points (72/147) for Small-Cap Growth funds, 63/123 for Small Cap Value funds, 61/96 for Index funds, 32/63 for Large-Cap Growth funds and 13/36 for Large-Cap Value funds.
14   Defined as transactions of 10,000 shares or more or stock having a market value of $200,000 or more (whichever is less). Block trades constituted 52.3 percent of reported trading volume on the NYSE over the ten years 1989–1998. See NYSE Fact Book, 1999.
15   Madhavan and Cheng, *Op. Cit.* at 185.

16   L.K.C. Chan and J. Lakonishok, "The Behavior of Stock Prices Around Institutional Trades," *Journal of Finance* 50, 1995, 1147–1174.

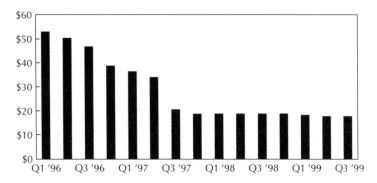

Figure 7.2   Weighted Average of Commissions per Trade Charged by Online Trading Firms, 1996–1999

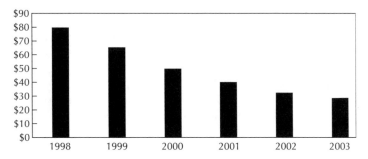

Figure 7.3   Average Industry wide Retail Commission per Trade
Source: Morgan Stanley Dean Witter estimates.

affected mainly retail investors, is declining dramatically.

But all this begs the question: How are the resulting increases in liquidity likely to affect stock prices? As suggested in our introduction, there is a growing body of evidence that suggests a direct link between increased liquidity and higher stock prices, and we now briefly review this evidence.

THE EFFECT OF LIQUIDITY ON STOCK PRICES

The effect of liquidity on asset prices follows directly from the above discussion: the more liquid the stock, the lower the company's cost of capital and, for any given level of expected cash flows generated by the company, the higher the stock price. In other words, increasing the liquidity of the stock will increases its price without changing anything in the company's "fundamentals," such as the level and risk of future earnings.

The theory of the effect of liquidity on a company's cost of capital was introduced by our 1986 JFE paper cited earlier.[17] In that paper, we argued that investors should require higher returns on less liquid stocks in order to compensate them for the liquidity costs they bear. Moreover, our study provided empirical evidence that, across a broad spectrum of securities, the less liquid the stock, the higher the return that it generates (on average), after adjusting for risk. Although the liquidity cost per transaction is usually small relative to the security's price, we showed that the cumulative effect of liquidity costs on the security's value is considerable because liquidity costs are incurred *repeatedly* – whenever the security is traded. Thus, liquidity costs represent a recurring cost stream throughout the lifetime of the stock. The value impact of this cost stream is the present value of the recurring costs, which can be substantial.

---

17   Yakov Amihud and Haim Mendelson, 1986, *op. cit.*

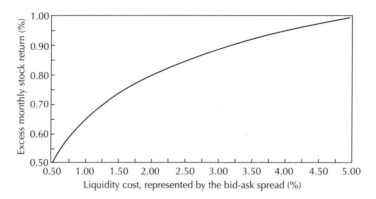

Figure 7.4 Average Excess Monthly Compensation for Illiquidity (NYSE Stocks)

To illustrate, consider a stock that is traded once every two years, with trading costs of two cents per transaction. Assume the value of a share of the stock, if it could be traded without any illiquidity costs, would be $1. The *present value* of the trading costs, discounted, say, at 8%, is $0.14. That is, illiquidity cuts the stock price from $1 to $0.86. Now, if the liquidity cost declines by 1/2 cent to 1.5 cents per transaction, the present value of the costs of trading will decline to 10.5 cents, and the stock price will rise to $0.895, an increase of about 4%. Thus, as this example suggests, a seemingly small improvement in liquidity – a small reduction in liquidity costs – can generate a substantial increase in stock prices.

The empirical evidence strongly supports this theory. Our 1986 study found that the average returns on NYSE stocks over the 20-year period 1961–1980 were significantly higher for stocks with higher bid-ask spreads, after controlling for risk. Figure 7.4 plots the excess monthly return due to illiquidity as a function of the bid-ask spread for NYSE-listed stocks. The plot shows that the greater the liquidity cost, the higher the expected return required by investors for investing in the stock.

The average stock return over a long period is assumed to reflect the rate of return required by investors. The results thus suggest that if a company is able to increase the liquidity of its stock – i.e., reduce liquidity costs (measured in our study by the bid-ask spread) – then its required return will decline and its value will rise for a given level of operating cash flow. That is, *increasing the liquidity of a stock lowers the company's equity cost of capital.*

Our study was followed by a number of studies that support the hypothesis that expected return is higher for stocks with higher liquidity costs. For example, a 1997 study by Eleswarapu[18] obtained a significant positive return-spread relationship for NASDAQ stocks for the period 1974–1990. A 1998 study by Chalmers and Kadlec[19] of NYSE/AMEX stocks over the period 1983–1992 found a significant positive relation between return and the effective bid-ask spread amortized over its holding period (following the model in our 1986 study).[20]

A comprehensive study of the effect of the cost of liquidity on stock returns was published in 1996 by Michael Brennan (a coauthor of the article immediately following) and Avanidhar Subrahmanyam.[21] For each stock in their sample, Brennan and

18 Venkat R. Eleswarapu, "Cost of Transacting and Expected Returns in the NASDAQ Market." *Journal of Finance* 52, 1997, 2113–2127.

19 Jogn M.R. Chalmers, and Gregory B. Kadlec, "An Empirical Examination of the Amortized Spread," *Journal of Financial Economics* 48, 2, 1998, 159–188.

20 Chalmers and Kadlec (1998) use amortized effective spreads, the spread divided by the stock's holding period, obtained from the turnover rate on the stock. The effective bid-ask spread is measured as the (absolute) difference between the mid-point of the quoted bid-ask spread and the transaction price that follows. The amortization over the holding period of the stock is obtained by dividing the effective bid-ask spread by the average holding period of the stock, obtained as the reciprocal of its turnover.

21 Michael J. Brennan and Avanidhar Subrahmanyam, "Market Microstructure and Asset Pricing: On the Compensation for Illiquidity in Stock Returns," *Journal of Financial Economics* 41, 1996, 441–464.

Subrahmanyam measured the adverse selection cost by estimating the transaction-by-transaction price response to the size of the (signed) order flow. The coefficient of the price change on the order size is a measure of the market impact, or adverse selection cost. In a cross-sectional analysis of stock return as a function of liquidity costs, the study found that stock returns were a significantly increasing function of liquidity costs.

In an even more recent study, Easley, Hvidkjaer, and O'Hara[22] estimated the adverse selection cost via the probability of informed trading in the stock. This probability is estimated from transaction data and a classification of trades into buy or sell based on the relationship between trade and quote data. The theory suggests that other things equal, the expected return on a stock should be an increasing function of the probability of informed trading, because of the associated adverse selection cost. As expected, the study found that informed trading is associated with a significant return premium.

Other studies have examined the return-liquidity relationship by using trading volume as a measure of liquidity.[23] For example, a 1998 study by Brennan, Chordia, and Subrahmanyam[24] found that higher stock trading volume is correlated with lower expected stock returns. Another 1998 study – by Datar, Naik and Radcliffe[25] – used stock turnover as a measure of liquidity, given that the stock holding period (the reciprocal of stock turnover) is a decreasing function of liquidity costs. That study found that stock returns fall with increases in stock turnover, consistent with the hypothesis on the negative return-liquidity relationship.

In sum, the evidence shows that expected stock returns fall with increases in a variety of measures of liquidity.

Changes in liquidity and stock prices

The next question is whether *changes* in stock liquidity bring about changes in stock prices. This question is important for policy purpose, since we propose below that firms can increase their stock values by enhancing their liquidity.

Of course, it is hard to detect a pure improvement in a stock's liquidity that can be isolated from other changes in the company. But, in a study published in 1997, we (and our colleague Beni Lauterbach)[26] examined this issue in a situation where the increase in stock liquidity was "exogenous" – that is, imposed from the outside and completely beyond the firm's control – and hence not "contaminated" with specific information about the stock. The data for our study came from the Tel Aviv Stock Exchange (TASE). Prior to 1987, stocks on the TASE were traded once a day in a call auction method. At the end of 1987, the TASE implemented a new trading system that enables (almost) continuous trading in stocks through the daily trading period. Naturally, the new continuous trading method provided stocks with greater liquidity than the former once-a-day call auction. The most important consideration, for purposes of our experiment, was that the TASE was the entity that decided which stocks would be transferred to the new trading system, and that the transfer was done periodically in small batches (an average of seven stocks per transfer). Thus, the transfer to the more liquid system did not reflect new information about the firm, which was not a party to the decision.[27]

---

22   David Easley, Soeren Hvidkjaer and Maureen O'Hara, "Is Information Risk a Determinant of Asset Returns?" Working Paper, Cornell University, November 1999.

23   In accordance with the Amihud-Mendelson model, trading turnover is expected to be higher in equilibrium for stocks with lower liquidity costs. This hypothesized relationship is tested and supported by Allen B. Atkins and Edward A. Dyl, "Transactions Costs and Holding Periods for Common Stocks," *Journal of Finance* 52, 1997, 309–325.

24   Michael J. Brennan, Tarum Cordia and Avanidhar Subrahmanyam, "Alternative Factor Specifications, Security Characteristics, and the Cross-Section of Expected Stock Returns," *Journal of Financial Economics* 49, 1998, 345–373.

25   Vinay T. Datar, Narayan Y. Naik and Robert Radcliffe, "Liquidity and Stock Returns: An Alternative Test," *Journal of Financial Markets* 1, 1998, 205–219.

26   Yakov Amihud, Haim Mendelson and Beni Lauterbach, "Market Microstructure and Securities Values: Evidence from the Tel Aviv Stock Exchange," *Journal of Financial Economics* 45, (1997), 365–390.

27   This is a major distinction between this study and other studies that examined the consequences of firms listing their stock on an exchange.

During the study period, 1987–1994, there were 17 transfers of stocks from the call to the continuous trading method, amounting to 120 stocks in all. Once the identity of stocks to be transferred was announced, the transfer was completed within a few days (three in most cases) and the stock started trading in the more liquid market. Our study examined the effect of these transfers on the following attributes: (1) liquidity; (2) market efficiency; and (3) stock price.

First of all, we found that stocks that were transferred to the continuous trading method enjoyed a sizable and significant increase in liquidity; their average trading volume as a percentage of total market volume increased from 0.266% to 0.475%, an increase of nearly 80 percent. Using a second measure that we called the "liquidity ratio," we also found that the ratio of daily (monetary) trading volume to the daily absolute stock return fell significantly after the transfers, implying that it took a considerably larger change in trading volume to "move" the stock.

The efficiency of the market in processing information about the individual stocks also improved after the transfer to the more liquid trading system, with stock prices incorporating new information more rapidly. Whereas under the old trading system, stock returns on any given day were typically still incorporating market information from the previous day, the effect of such "lagged" market returns disappeared after the transfer. In addition, the variance of the residual returns from the market model – a measure of volatility often used as proxy for lingering investor uncertainty – declined significantly after the transfer, indicating less pricing "errors."

The key question, however, is whether these improvements in liquidity and efficiency were beneficial to the firm. That is, did they increase the stock price? Our study showed a very strong and significant rise in stock prices. Stock values (as measured by the cumulative abnormal return (*CAR*) rose by at least 5.5 percent during the period from five days before the announcement to 30 days after the actual transfer. Moreover, the actual increases in value attributable to the trading change were almost certainly larger than this, since some stocks that were expected to be transferred experienced significant price increases prior to the announcement.

In short, our study provides remarkably strong evidence that improved liquidity can lead to a significant increase in stock prices.

TAKING THE LIQUIDITY ROUTE TO A HIGHER STOCK PRICE

As we have seen, then, both finance theory and a substantial body of evidence now suggests that less liquid stocks have higher expected returns in order to compensate investors for their higher liquidity costs. As a result, companies can lower the required returns and increase their stock prices by increasing the liquidity of their stocks – and without any change in the market's expectations about their future operating cash flows.

Not all of the factors that affect stock liquidity are under the control of the issuing company. Indeed, most of the different costs of liquidity are driven largely if not wholly by "outsiders" – investors, brokers, dealers, exchanges, and regulators – rather than by the company itself. To be sure, companies do think about the liquidity of their stock when they go public and select an underwriter, and when they decide to list on an exchange. Thereafter, however, management typically does not concern itself very much about the liquidity of its securities, effectively letting the decisions of market intermediaries and regulators drive its cost of capital. This may work for some companies that already enjoy high liquidity, such as highly visible companies with active trading. But, for most companies, this may be the wrong policy. As we have shown above, liquidity is capable of having a large impact on a company's market value; and, as we argue below, one of the key roles of financial management is to build and maintain the liquidity of the firm's securities.

Why aren't companies taking a more proactive role in increasing the liquidity of their shares and other financial claims? Part of the reason undoubtedly is that managements feel powerless to affect what goes on in markets. A widespread attitude among CEOs and CFOs is that maintaining liquidity is the concern of the securities exchanges and the Securities and Exchange Commission. However, the costs of liquidity are ultimately borne by the issuing company because, as we have seen, investors demand compensation for bearing these costs.

Just as the firm wants to have a say in distribution channel decisions that affect its profitability in its product market, it should seek ways to improve the liquidity of its stock so as to reduce its cost of capital. A firm that leaves all decisions that affect the liquidity of its stock in the hands of intermediaries and regulators risks is likely to pay an inflated cost of capital.[28]

The current regulatory regime limits a company's ability to determine the way its claims are traded (and we have argued elsewhere that empowering issuers to have more say would benefit issuers and their investors).[29] However, part of the blame lies with the companies themselves, which have not taken advantage of the opportunities that are now available to them. This is particularly the case for smaller firms, which may not be aware of the ways liquidity can be used to reduce their cost of capital. As we argue below, there are a number of policies they can employ to enhance their stock's liquidity. Furthermore, a corporate focus on policies that aim to improve liquidity is also likely to increase the responsiveness of the investment community in general and so end up contributing to greater liquidity.

In what follows, we discuss a number of ways in which a company can increase its value by increasing the liquidity of its stock. We show how a company can affect drivers of liquidity to its advantage.

Effect of the size and composition of the investor base on liquidity and stock price

When a company goes public, it usually seeks to increase the dispersion of its stockholding among investors, but after the IPO little attention is typically paid to managing the size of the company's investor base. As our research shows, the size and composition of the company's investor base can significantly affect its liquidity and its stock price.

As mentioned earlier, studies have found that having a larger number of shareholders is associated with lower bid-ask spreads.[30] And this raises the possibility that a company can increase its liquidity and stock price simply by increasing the number of its stockholders. In a 1999 study with Jun Uno,[31] we tested this proposition in the Japanese stock market. We chose that market because Japanese stocks were subject to minimum trading units (MTUs) – minimum numbers of shares that can be traded on an exchange (i.e., odd lot trading was prohibited) that can be determined by the issuing company. We hypothesized that Japanese companies could expand the investor base of their stocks by reducing their MTU or lot size. Small investors, we reasoned, are likely to be deterred from buying or trading Japanese stocks by large MTUs – particularly in the case of higher-priced stocks where purchasing the MTU requires a large amount of money.

Not surprisingly, the vast majority of decisions to reduce the MTU were made by companies with high-priced stocks. The average stock price in our sample of companies that reduced their MTU was 3,782 yen, well above the average price of 970 yen on the Tokyo stock exchange at that time. For the large majority of stocks, the reduction in MTU was from a trading unit of 1,000 shares to a trading unit of 100 shares (although some firms reduced the number only to 500).

As we also predicted, the reduction in MTU both expanded the investor base and increased stock liquidity. As reported in Table 7.1, the mean increase in the number of shareholders over the event year was 135 percent, and the median increase was 52 percent. Further, the increase in the number of shareholders was due almost entirely to the increase in the number of small individual investors. In fact, the number of institutional investors hardly changed – and this is not at all surprising, since such investors were not constrained by the high stock price in the first place.

28 For a discussion of why securities markets and regulators are unlikely to optimize the firm's liquidity and a proposal for a regulatory regime that addresses this problem, see Y. Amihud and H. Mendelson, "A New Approach to the Regulation of Trading Across Securities Markets," *New York University Law Review* 71 (1996), pp. 1411–1466.
29 *Ibid.*

30 See *supra* note 10.
31 Yakov Amihud, Haim Mendelson and Jun Uno, "Number of Shareholders and Stock Prices: Evidence from Japan," *Journal of Finance* 54 (1999), 1169–1184.

Table 7.1   Effect of Reduction in MTU on Investor Base and Average Holdings*

Statistic	Change in number of all shareholders	Change in number of individual shareholders	Radio of individual/all shareholders		Average number of shares held by individual shareholders[a]	
			Before[b]	After[b]	Before[b]	After[b]
Mean	+135%	+234%	0.643	0.867	4,868	2,197
Median	+52%	+139%	0.656	0.882	3,487	1,787

*Sources of data: Tokyo Stock Exchange data: the *Nihon Keizai Shimbun* NEEDS database.
[a]This ratio is obtained by dividing for each company the number of shares held by individual shareholders by the number of individual shareholders.
[b]"Before" means the end of the year before the reduction in MTU. "After" means the end of the year when the reduction took place.

As Table 7.1 also reports, the average number of shares held by an individual investor was approximately halved following the reduction in MTU. By contrast, for a control sample of stocks with comparable prices and volumes that did not reduce their MTU, the average shareholding per individual investor did not change. Moreover, as expected, we also found that the stocks with reduced MTU enjoyed a significant increase in trading volume (and hence presumably liquidity).[32]

Effect of the Increase in Investor Base on Stock Prices. We next examined whether it was worth-while for the company to increase the investor base. The results in Table 7.1 suggest that, before the reduction in MTU, many individual investors were unable to hold the stock because the monetary outlay was too large. A second interpretation – though not a mutually exclusive one – that is also consistent with our findings is that some individual investors may have been forced by the MTU to hold more shares of the stock than they considered desirable, and that after the reduction in the MTU they chose to reduce their holdings to achieve a more diversified portfolio. In either case, small investors were better off having the option to hold a smaller number of shares, which increased their willingness to pay for the stock.

We analyzed the stock-price effect of the reduction in MTU as follows. For each company reducing its MTU[33], we identified two dates: the *announcement date* (A_i), the day on which the company's board of directors decided to reduce the stock's MTU (the news appeared on the following day in *Nihon Keizai Shimbun*), and the *change date* C_i, when the reduction in MTU actually took place. The average number of trading days between the announcement and change was 75.8, with a median of 66.5 days.

Next, for each company, we calculated the cumulative abnormal return (*CAR*), the price change (net of market), and the appropriate size portfolio returns over the period from day $A_i - 5$ (i.e., 5 days prior to the announcement) through $C_i + 1$ (i.e., the day following the implementation of the smaller MTU). The average of CAR_i across all stocks (calculated as a simple or weighted average[34]) results in the (simple or weighted) average *CAR*, the average cumulative abnormal return for the event. The *CAR* measures the average price effect of reducing the MTU.

We found that the average price change over the entire period – the (simple) average *CAR* – was +4.43 percent (t = 1.81), the median *CAR* was +4.79 percent, and the weighted average *CAR* was +5.90 percent (t = 2.65, highly significant at better than 1%). Consistent with our theory, these findings suggest that the increase in investor base

---

32   Denote by Vi/Vci the ratio of the trading volume of stock i to the trading volume of the matching control stock for stock i, and denote by DVi the (logarithm of the) relative change in Vi/Vci in the year of the reduction in MTU compared to that in the year before the reduction. The evidence shows the DVi had a mean of 0.42 (t=2.71).

33   Each MTU reduction for a stock is an event.
34   In the calculation of the weighted averages, the weight of stock i was $1/\text{Var}(\varepsilon_{it})°$, where ε_{it} were obtained from model (1).

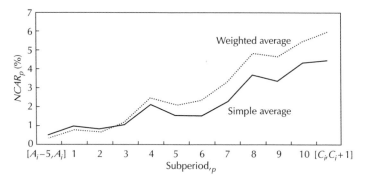

Figure 7.5 Normalized CARs Over Twelve Subperiods*

*The subperiods are $[A_i - 5, A_i]$, the deciles of (A_i, C_i) and $[C_i, C_i + 1]$. Shown are the simple and weighted averages of $NCAR_p$. Weights are the inverses of the residual variances from the market model regression (4.1). The first subperiod is $A_i - 5$ to A_i (A_i is the announcement day for company i), and the last subperiod is from day C_i to day $C_i + 1$ (C_i is the day of the reduction in the MTU). The interim period is divided into 10 equal subperiods. CAR_i is calculated for each stock i over the 12 subperiods and averaged across stocks to provide $NCAR_p$, the normalized average CAR for period p, $p = 1, 2, \ldots 12$. The weighted $NCAR$ uses as weights the inverses of the residual variances from the market model regression (1).

resulting from the reduction in MTU led to a significant price increase.

Figure 7.5 shows the behavior of the stock price appreciation (net of market) over the event interval $[A_i - 5, C_i + 1]$, which in turn was divided, for each stock, into 10 equal subintervals in order to obtain $NCAR$, the normalized average CAR.[35] There are two additional intervals, one at the beginning of a five-day pre-announcement interval (including the announcement day); and a two-day interval at the end that includes the change day and the clay after. Figure 7.5 shows the behavior of the average normalized price appreciation, $NCAR$, over the twelve subperiods, both for simple $NCAR_p$

and for weighted $NCAR_p$. As can be seen in the figure, the effect of the MTU reduction on stock prices was gradual, peaking at the last interval, $[C_i, C_i + 1]$. This is not surprising, since the benefits of enhanced liquidity could not be completely realized until the actual improvement in liquidity took place.

Also important, our results show that the stock price appreciation was greater for those stocks with larger increases in their investor base following the reduction in MTU. This was tested by the model:

$$CAR_i = \gamma_0 + \gamma_1 \times \Delta SH_i + v_i$$

where the dependent variable is the cumulative (net-of-market) price appreciation, and ΔSH_i is the logarithm of the relative change in the number of shareholders. As predicted, we found that $\gamma_1 > 0$. Stocks that had a greater increase in their investor base enjoyed a significantly greater price appreciation. These results significantly support the proposition that the increase in the firm's investor base increases its value. Moreover, the same results hold when we consider the increase in the proportion of individual shareholders to total shareholders. This finding was also consistent with our theory, since individual investors are expected to provide more uninformed or "liquidity-motivated" trading.

---

35 To account for the fact that the event intervals differ across stocks, we normalize them by dividing for each stock the period (A_i, C_i) between the announcement day and the actual MTU-reduction day into ten equal-sized intervals numbered 1, 2, 3, . . ., 10. The cumulative abnormal returns are then calculated for each stock i over twelve subperiods: the first corresponds to the pre-announcement interval $[A_i - 5, A_i]$ (including the announcement day A_i), then ten subperiods corresponding to the deciles of the period (A_i, C_i) between the announcement and the actual MTU-reduction day, and the last subperiod $[C_i, C_i + 1]$ includes the MTU-reduction day and the following trade day. In this way, the different periods between the announcement and actual reduction day are normalized across events, and we obtain $NCAR_p$, the normalized CAR, over the twelve subperiods $p = 1, 2, \ldots 12$.

Such trading, as we saw earlier, enhances liquidity because it imposes no adverse selection costs on market makers.

Having made the case for an expanded shareholder base, we should also point out that maximizing the number of shareholders is not necessarily the optimal corporate strategy. There are a number of costs associated with having a larger number of smaller shareholders. Most obvious is the fixed cost associated with servicing each shareholder. But also potentially important, as we pointed out in a 1988 study,[36] is the tendency for agency costs – reductions in value stemming from conflicts of interests between stockholders and managers – to increase as ownership becomes more dispersed among outside shareholders. Thus, companies should aim to increase their investor base only to the point where the marginal benefit of having more shareholders still exceeds the marginal cost.

Increasing the Investor Base. By setting the number of shares outstanding (and hence the offer price) at an Initial Public Offering and then splitting its stock, a company can affect the facility with which investors can invest in its stock. This decision indirectly determines the general level of the company's stock price and hence the minimum dollar amount needed to trade a round lot (100 shares). A round lot costs $2,000 when the stock is priced at $20 per share, as compared to $10,000 for a $100 share price. Providing support for the efficacy of stock splits, a 1997 study by Mukherji, Kim, and Walker[37] shows that stock splits both increase the number of investors holding the stock and at the same time increase the firm's stock price. Furthermore, the price increase at the split announcement is positively correlated with the increase in the number of shareholders.

But, again, stock splits are not costless – they may well increase the bid-ask spread as a percentage of price. The minimum bid-ask spread is one tick ($\frac{1}{16}$ for most U.S. stocks), implying that the minimal spread is 0.31% on a stock priced at $20, as compared to 0.06% for a stock priced at $100. This imposes liquidity costs on trading the

stock. On the other hand, a study by James Angel has provided evidence that a minimal spread based on tick size – at least for smaller and less followed companies – increases liquidity by providing incentives for market makers to trade the stock.[38]

In addition, stock splits increase brokerage commissions, which are typically a function of the number of shares traded. Hence, the commission as a percentage of price is lower when the price is higher. For example, online retail brokerage commissions are often 3 cents per share, amounting to 0.15% for a stock price of $20, or 0.03% for a stock price of $100. However, just as Angel has proposed that there is an optimal tick size, Brennan and Hughes[39] have argued that the higher commissions induce brokerage firms to encourage trading by providing information services through stock analysts that cover the stock, thus providing a benefit to the firm.

Companies can also increase their investor base by facilitating small investors' purchase of stock through the Internet. Direct selling of stock online through Direct Stock Purchase Plans and Dividend Reinvestment Programs enables small investors to buy the stock at low transaction costs. And when these plans are administered over the Internet using Web sites like Stockpower.com, money-paper.com and Netstockdirect.com, the process is fast and efficient for both the company and the investor.

Finally, companies can increase their investor base by increasing the familiarity of potential investors with the company. As discussed below, this can be accomplished by disclosing more and better information about the company to potential stockholders and so facilitating their purchase of stock.

---

36   Amihud and Mendelson, *Financial Management* 1988, *Op. Cit.*

37   Mukherji, Sandip, Yong H. Kim and Michael C. Walker, "The Effect of Stock Splits on the Ownership Structure of Firms," *Journal of Corporate Finance* 3, (1997), 167–188.

38   James Angel, "Tick Size, Share Prices, and Stock Splits," *Journal of Finance* 52, 2 (June 1997) Moreover, Brennan and Copeland have proposed that this increase in trading costs may serve as a credible signal about the future value of the firm. See Michael J. Brennan and Thomas E. Copeland, "Stock Splits, Stock Prices and Transaction Costs," *Journal of Financial Economics* 22, (1988), 83–101.

39   Brennan, Michael J. and Patricia J. Hughes, "Stock Prices and the Supply of Information," *Journal of Finance* 46, (1991), 1665–1691.

Disclosure of information

Making more information available about the firm can increase the liquidity of its stock by reducing the potential asymmetry of information about its value. As discussed earlier, adverse selection costs – a major component of liquidity costs – are incurred when trading takes place between investors who have access to undisclosed information and investors who do not. Thus, the firm can increase its value by disclosing information about itself to the public, or by making it easier to find out and disseminate information about the firm.

As we proposed in a 1988 study,[40] a commitment by the a firm to disclose more information than is necessary by law or regulation increases its liquidity and consequently reduces its cost of capital. Studies have shown that the provision of more informative statements in SEC filings increased the liquidity of companies that did so, as measured by a reduction in the bid-ask spread. This occurred both when firms in the petroleum industry disclosed reserve-based present value variables[41] and when companies implemented the 1970 SEC recommendation for more finely partitioned data in the form of segment disclosures.[42]

Management forecasts are another way that firms can voluntarily provide information to reduce information asymmetry about the value of their stock. A 1997 study by Coller and Yohn[43] showed that companies that released management forecasts of earnings had the following bid-ask spread patterns: *Prior* to releasing the forecast, these firms had higher bid-ask spreads than the firms in a matched control sample; *following* the management forecast, the bid-ask spreads significantly declined, close to the level of the control sample. Thus, earnings forecasts were released by the managers of firms for which asymmetric information appeared to be a problem – and the release corrected the problem, resulting in lower adverse selection costs. The evidence thus suggests that the provision of more and finer information about the firm increases stock liquidity, leading to a reduction in the firm's cost of capital.

Another example of the beneficial effects of information disclosure on liquidity was provided by a 1996 study by Bartov and Bodnar[44] in the context of foreign currency accounting. In December 1981, the FASB released SFAS No. 52 requiring companies to designate a functional currency (either the U.S. dollar or a foreign currency) for their foreign operations. Its objective was to provide "information that is generally compatible with the expected effects of exchange rate change on an enterprise cash flow and equity." Firms that chose a foreign currency as a functional currency switched to a new method of reporting accounting information about the firm (the current-rate method), whereas firms choosing the U.S. dollar as a functional currency continued to report according to the prevailing method. The new reporting method was expected by the FASB to "result in reports of financial conditions and results of operations that . . . will most closely reflect economic effects." Given that firms could voluntarily elect to switch to a foreign functional currency and thus implement the new, more informative reporting method, the effect of greater disclosure of information could be examined.

Bartov and Bodnar found that firms that chose a foreign currency as a functional currency – and thus applied the enhanced reporting method – realized an average increase of 25.6% in their annual trading volume subsequent to the switch (statistically significant). Firms that continued to use the dollar as a functional currency realized an average decline of 9.1% in their trading volume (although this last finding was statistically insignificant, the difference in the change in trading

40 Amihud and Mendelson, *Financial Management* 1988, *Op. Cit.* This proposition was formally modeled by Douglas Diamind and Robert Verecchia in "Disclosure, Liquidity and the Cost of Capital."

41 K. Raman and N. Tripathy, "The Effect of Supplemental Reserve-Based Accounting Data on the Market Microstructure." *Journal of Accounting and Public Policy* 12 (Summer 1993), pp. 113–133.

42 M. Greenstein and H. Sami, "The Impact of the SEC's Segment Disclosure Requirement on Bid-Ask Spreads," *The Accounting Review* 69, (January 1994), 179–199.

43 M. Coller and T. Yohn, "Management Forecasts and Information Asymmetry: An Examination of Bid-Ask Spreads." *Journal of Accounting Research* (Fall 1997).

44 Eli Bartov and Gordon Bodnar, "Alternative Accounting Methods, Information Asymmetry and Liquidity: Theory and Evidence," *Accounting Review* 71, 3, (July 1996).

volume between the two groups was highly statistically significant).

The choice of a more informative reporting method seems to have been motivated by a desire of firms to improve the liquidity of their stock. The study showed that the probability of a firm switching to the new reporting method was significantly higher if the firm's trading turnover[45] was lower before the switch. The results of the Bartov-Bodnar study again demonstrate that firms suffering from low stock liquidity can enhance liquidity – and increase stock price – by voluntarily providing information about their operations and finances.

Another illustration of the beneficial effect of information disclosure by firms on their stock liquidity was provided in a 1998 study of oil companies by Boone.[46] In 1978, the Securities and Exchange Commission mandated the disclosure of the discounted present value of oil and gas reserves.[47] Firms that implemented this form of disclosure realized a significant decline in their stock's bid-ask spread that was apparently permanent, persisting at least a year after the initial reserve disclosure. Given the positive relationship between the bid-ask spread and required return, it follows that the greater disclosure of information about the value of the oil companies resulted in a decline in their cost of capital.

But, of course, greater disclosure has costs as well as benefits, and we briefly mention these costs below:

♦ Disclosure provides information that can be profitably used by competitors, sometimes to the detriment of the disclosing firm. This cost (measured in absolute dollars) typically increases with the firm's scale of operations. However, small firms may be more vulnerable if the disclosure of new inside developments to bigger and better-financed competitors threatens their existence. For example, information about product development or a new successful strategy by a firm that is quickly adopted by its larger, more powerful competitor may increase the competitive pressure on the smaller firm.

♦ The provision of more detailed information may expose the disclosing firms and its managers to lawsuits in the event of errors (which are unavoidable) or to frivolous lawsuits by disenchanted stockholders. The latter are particularly likely when the information is not entirely certain and includes some conjectures and expectations, such as predictions of future earnings or the success or failure of a certain product. This creates a disincentive to disclose forthcoming but uncertain developments in the firm.

♦ The production of information is costly in terms of setting information systems to collect and process data in the firm, retaining accountants and auditors, etc. This cost increases with firm size, since larger firms tend to produce more information. However, there is a large element of fixed cost in the production of information, and thus this cost may be proportionally greater for smaller firms compared to large firms.

Naturally, a company's decision about the amount of information to be disclosed depends on balancing the cost against the benefits of disclosure. For some companies, both the costs and the benefits may be higher. For example, all three cost components of information are larger for firms with more complex and uncertain operations, but such firms are also subject to greater information asymmetry, which reduces the liquidity of their stock. In the end, the firm decides on how much information to disclose by performing a usual cost-benefit analysis.

However, companies that are unaware of the value of releasing information and the resulting beneficial effect on stock prices are likely to release less than the optimal amount and quality of information. The immediate costs of disclosure are often more directly visible and measurable than the ensuing benefits in terms of increased liquidity and lower cost of capital. Thus, firms should undertake a rigorous analysis of the benefits of liquidity enhancement, balancing them against the costs.

---

45 Turnover is defined as the annual share volume divided by shares outstanding. Bartov and Bodnar adjust this measure for unusual trading volume that results from information surprises.
46 Jeffery Boone, "Oil and Gas Reserve Value Disclosures and Bid-Ask Spreads," *Journal of Accounting and Public Policy* 17, 1, (March 1998).
47 Accounting Series Release No. 263.

THE IMPORT OF NEW TECHNOLOGY FOR CORPORATE DISCLOSURE POLICY

Until fairly recently, most companies focused their information disclosure on investment analysts and institutions. This made sense because the cost of direct disclosures to a large number of small investors was prohibitive. Disseminating information to a limited number of small, but active or influential, players economized on information dissemination costs while maintaining an informationally efficient market. Smaller investors could achieve their financial goals by resorting to asset managers or mutual funds that had access to the relevant information.

However, the Internet is changing this cost structure, enabling low-cost dissemination of more extensive and timely information to a large number of investors. This is sometimes called the "democratization of information." Today, firms can reduce informational asymmetries and improve the liquidity of their stock by releasing information either directly or indirectly (through analysts). We now discuss both of these techniques in turn.

Direct information dissemination: Communicating with the investor base

In 1999, there were more than 78 million shareowners in the U.S., of which 11% traded primarily over the Internet.[48] Forrester research expects the number of households with Internet accounts to double from 1999 to 2001, and to quadruple by 2003. Table 7.2 compares some of the characteristics of online and off-line traders.

Online shareowners tend to be more affluent, hold more individual stocks, and trade more frequently. They seek not only the low cost of online trading, but also the ability to use online information and transact quickly and efficiently. These investors expect companies to provide them information directly and conveniently over the Internet.

Table 7.2 Characteristics of Online Vs. Off-Line Shareowners*

	Online shareowner	Off-line shareowner
Age	41	48
Household financial assets	$229,000	$127,000
Household equity assets	$127,600	$70,000
Number of stocks owned	13	7
Annual stock transactions	10	1
Annual mutual fund transactions	2	1

*Numbers shown are the medians. Source: SIA survey, November 1999.

The Internet provides a new means to distribute and disseminate information about companies at low cost to both online and off-line investors.[49] The most elementary way is for a company to establish a web site that provides investor relations information to the public – something that most large companies now already do. The content of the site should be unbiased and informative, rather than serving as an advertising platform. That is, it should include independent analysts' reports about the company and analysis of its financials even if they are not flattering to the company. The important thing in this context is to convey the firm's commitment to make available all timely and relevant information, which will make the information provided on the site credible and usable.

Online traders expect more than a static Web site. They want company information to be integrated with their trading process. Standard information about the company is provided by third parties, who aggregate information and provide it to Internet portals like Yahoo! Finance, Quicken, or online brokerage web sites. This means that it is in the company's best interest to provide rich and timely information to both analysts and intermediaries, who interpret and organize it and make it available to a large investor base.

In summary, firms can use the Internet to release information directly to investors at low cost.

---

48 Source: SIA survey, November 1999. About 18% of investors surveyed have made *some* trades over the Internet.

49 "Off-line" investors prefer to trade with a broker but often use the Internet to collect company information.

This both reduces informational asymmetries and attracts active small investors, increasing the investor base. Both outcomes improve liquidity and reduce the firm's cost of capital.

Indirect information dissemination: communicating with investment analysts

We have shown that the greater availability of information about the firm enhances its liquidity and thus contributes to an increase in stock price. A major source of information about public firms is analyst reports about the firm. Analysts often perform extensive research on companies – far more extensive than would be possible for small single shareholders. The analysts disseminate the information to the public in a way that reaches a broad audience, thus reducing the difference in the amount of information about the firm held by different groups of investors. The recent move to use the Internet to disseminate analysts information further reduces the informational asymmetry between those who have in-depth information about the firm and those who do not.

The importance of analysts in providing liquidity is clearly demonstrated in a study (presented in the article immediately following) by Michael Brennan and Claudia Tamarowski.[50] The study uses two measures of liquidity: trading volume and market impact cost. The market impact cost is the percentage change in stock price as a function of the transaction size,[51] which is calculated from transaction-by-transaction data for each stock. The results of their study for each of the two measures can be summarized in the following two regressions:

(1) log (market impact cost)
   $= -0.169$ log $(1 + \#$ analysts$)$
   $+$ other variables
(2) log (average trading volume)
   $= 0.897$ log $(1 + \#$ analysts$)$
   $+$ other variables

where the other variables control for firm size (trading volume or market value), stock return variance

and stock price. The first equation indicates that market impact costs fall, and the second that trading volume increases, as the number of analysts following the firm increases. (The t statistic for the coefficients in the two equations are, respectively, 3.13 and 13.31, both highly significant.) Thus, both models show that liquidity increases with the number of analysts covering the stock.

In general, brokerage firms retain analysts as part of their overall service, with their cost being covered indirectly through brokerage commissions or through investment banking operations.[52] Analyst reports are not a profit center,[53] and the decision on what firms to cover and how much resources to allocate to such coverage are divorced from the liquidity impact of the analysis.

Securities and Exchange Commission Chairman Arthur Levitt complained of a "web of dysfunctional relationships" between analysts and the firms they cover, in which analyst coverage is driven by the brokerage firm's existing and contemplated investment banking relationships.[54] This creates a bias towards covering sectors and firms that are most likely to become investment banking customers, and making these sectors more liquid – at the expense of other firms and sectors that are less likely to result in such side business. In particular, the high-tech and Internet sectors are likely to receive more analyst attention than more traditional sectors of the economy because these are areas with a larger investment banking potential (as well as publicity).[55]

50 Michael J. Brennan and Claudia Tamarowski, "Investor Relations, Liquidity and Stock Prices," *Journal of Applied Corporate Finance*, this issue.

51 As calculated in Brennan and Subrahmanyam, *Op. cit.*

52 Some discount brokers such as Schwab provide analyst reports as an unbundled but fixed-fee service. This is an unbundled version of the "full-service" brokerage model; the unbundling rarely extends to a report-by-report fee structure. Further, the fees are waived for a period of time or for qualified customers (typically based on level of assets or number of trades).

53 While there has recently been an increase in "pay per view" analyst reports, often distributed over the Internet, the associated fee revenue is low.

54 Based on remarks by SEC Chairman Arthur Levitt to The Economic Club of New York, New York City, October 18, 1999. The SEC is proposing "Regulation FD" to combat unequal disclosure problems.

55 As one industry participant described a recent report by a PaineWebber analyst who predicted a target price of $1,000 for Qualcomm, about twice its market price prior to the report, "brokerage films have more than one agenda, and they need publicity to develop their business . . . One can never be sure what audience an analyst is preaching to."

Smaller firms in the less-glamorous sectors of the economy are likely to suffer from insufficient investment analysis, resulting in lower liquidity. Because the gathering and analysis of information about a company has a large component of fixed cost, it becomes unprofitable for a brokerage firm to invest resources to analyze small companies, unless they have a strong reason to do so. In the article just cited, Brennan and Tamarowski[56] also report finding that the number of analysts covering a stock is a (significantly) increasing function of the stock's market value. When this result is viewed together with their finding of the positive effect of the number of analysts on stock liquidity, it is clear that large stocks enjoy greater liquidity-enhancing opportunities than small stocks.

Brennan and Hughes[57] have suggested that companies effectively pay brokerage firms to increase the number of analysts covering them by increasing the level of brokerage commissions through stock splits and the resulting adjustments of their stock prices. Because brokerage commissions increase with the number of shares traded, stock splits increase brokers' revenues for a given dollar amount traded and thus encourage information gathering by investment analysts in brokerage firms about companies that split their stock.

However, stock splits are an inefficient way to pay for analysts' services. While stock splits help increase the firm's investor base and liquidity, they also increase the minimum percentage bid-ask spread (because of the existence of a minimum tick), which causes an additional cost of trading – and because the cost of the bid-ask spread does not necessarily accrue to the brokers who provide the analysts services, it constitutes a dead weight loss. Furthermore, the brokers who provide analyst services capture only a fraction of the brokerage commissions generated through the lower price, because investors who trade through other brokers free-ride on the information provided by the analysts of another brokerage firm. And, even if each broker could fully capture the commissions generated by trading on the information produced by its analysts, there would still be too little production of information because the broker cannot capture the *full* benefits from the increased liquidity that accrue to the firm whose stock is analyzed and about which information is provided.

These benefits ultimately accrue to the issuer. As discussed earlier, the loss in firm value due to liquidity costs is given by the present value of these costs over the recurring trades in the security. Given that additional analyst coverage reduces liquidity costs and increases the market value of the firm, a value-maximizing firm should be willing to *pay directly* for analyst coverage. This should be especially true of smaller firms in the less-glamorous sectors of the economy, where brokerage firms have no side incentives to increase coverage.

We therefore propose that *a smaller firm can enhance its liquidity and its market value by paying directly for analysts*. We believe that a direct, fully-disclosed payment by the firm for analyst coverage is less vulnerable to distortions than the current practice, where the payment is indirect and hidden, and it should lead to better alignment between the costs of analyst coverage and the benefits. In fact, this is exactly what is currently done with bond ratings: In order to increase the liquidity of their public bonds, firms pay the rating agencies for their rating services while having no effect on the rating results (that is, paying for ratings does not make the rating more favorable (see Amihud and Mendelson (1988)). Another current institution with a similar economic function is the auditing service that the firm retains and pays for, while the auditor provides an independent evaluation of the accuracy of the information in the firm's financial reports. We believe that the same could be done for analyst services. A small firm wanting to increase its analysts following could simply pay the analysts to cover the firm and provide the public with more information about it.

This method of payment for analyst services is more efficient than any of the arrangements that are currently employed because it is targeted to fully compensate the provider of information services. This largely solves the free-riding problem: the current firm's shareholders are the ultimate beneficiary of the enhanced liquidity of the firm's stock that is provided by the greater analyst coverage, and thus they should be willing to pay for it. Since the liquidity enhancement crucially depends on the credibility and quality of the analysis, both the firm and the analyst have an incentive to

---

56   *Op. cit.*
57   *Op. cit.*

provide unbiased information.[58] And because the firm determines the number and identity of the analysts, it has an incentive to choose them in a way that maximizes its market value; that is, it should increase the number of analysts to the point where the marginal value of additional liquidity (driven by more analysts) is equal to the marginal cost. As pointed out above, the smaller the firm, the more valuable this arrangement because large firms are already covered by a large number of analysts.

CONCLUSION

In this paper we propose that a company can raise its stock price by enhancing the liquidity of its stock. The greater the stock's liquidity, the lower the expected return that investors require, translating into a lower corporate cost of capital and a higher valuation for any given cash flows that the company generates.

We suggest a number of means that companies can use to increase the liquidity of their stock, including increasing the company's investor base and improving the dissemination of information about the stock. We show that increasing the investor base by adding small individual investors increases liquidity and raises the stock price. Volunteering to provide more information about the company reduces the asymmetry of information about its value and thus increases stock liquidity – and its price. A company should attempt to make its financial reporting as transparent as possible (without disclosing trade secrets), make prompt announcements of new information, and perhaps even pay for services that provide information to the public, such as those of analysts. This could be particularly valuable for small companies about which less information is generated and disseminated, a fact that may explain small stocks' higher expected returns and lower prices. Of course, given the cost associated with the provision of information, the final decision must weigh such costs against the benefits of increased liquidity.

---

58   Of course, this arrangement does not solve the shareholder-manager agency problem, but neither does it create a new one.

CHAPTER 8

The Promise of Real Options

Aswath Damodaran (New York University)

In corporate finance, the discounted cash flow model operates as the basic framework for most analysis. In investment analysis, for instance, the conventional view is that the net present value (NPV) of a project is the measure of the value it is expected to add to the firm. Thus, investing in a positive-NPV value project is expected to increase the value of a company and taking on a negative-NPV project to reduce it. The value of the company itself can also be estimated using conventional DCF analysis. The market value of a firm is equal to the present value of all the firm's expected after-tax (but pre-interest) cash flows discounted at the weighted average cost of capital.

In recent years, the DCF framework has come under some fire for failing to consider the options that are embedded in many corporate projects. For instance, the NPV of a project typically does not capture the value of management's ability to expand the size or scope of the project should things work out particularly well; nor does it reflect the value of delaying the start of a project until conditions become more favorable. When comparing different investment opportunities, the traditional approach of picking the model with the highest NPV is likely to shortchange investments that offer management more flexibility in making operating changes and add-on investments. In valuing acquisitions, the strategic options that might be opened up for the acquiring firm as a result of the transaction

are often not considered in DCF analysis. And a DCF valuation model is likely to ignore other options that might be owned by the firm, including patents, licenses, and rights to natural reserves.

In light of these options that seem to be everywhere, some theorists (and many corporate practitioners) believe that we should consider these options when analyzing corporate decisions. But there is no clear unanimity among this group as to what they would like to see done. Some top managers and consultants prefer to use real options simply as a rhetorical tool that can be used to justify investment and acquisition decisions for which there may be little quantitative support. The basis for this feeling is often that, while there are embedded options in most decisions, such options cannot be valued with precision. Others argue that we should use real options to attempt to quantify the value of these options, and build them into the decision process.

In this paper, I explore the existence of options in business decisions and lay out the conditions that need to be fulfilled for a real option to have significant value. I also examine how best to obtain the inputs needed to value these options and incorporate them into decision making. The paper begins with a short introduction to options, the determinants of option value, and the basics of option pricing. Without spending much time on the technicalities of option pricing, this section

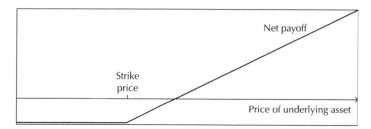

Figure 8.1 Payoff on Call Option

briefly mentions some of the special difficulties that come up when valuing real options. The rest of the paper discusses three kinds of options that are often built into investments or projects: (1) the option to delay a project until a change in prices or other circumstances makes the investment more valuable; (2) the option to expand a project if the initial investment turns out more promising than expected or reveals new opportunities; and (3) the option to abandon a project should things not work out as planned. As the paper attempts to show, the presence of any or all of these real options can make an investment worth more than its conventional DCF value.

BASICS OF OPTION PRICING

An option provides the holder with the right to buy or sell a specified quantity of an *underlying asset* at a fixed price (called a *strike price* or an *exercise price*) at or before the expiration date of the option. Since it is a right and not an obligation, the holder can choose not to exercise the right and allow the option to expire. There are two types of options: *call options* and *put options*.

A call option gives the buyer of the option the right to buy the underlying asset at a fixed price, called the strike or the exercise price, at any time prior to the expiration date of the option: the buyer pays a price for this right. If at expiration the value of the asset is less than the strike price, the option is not exercised and expires worthless. But if the value of the asset is greater than the strike price, the option is exercised; the buyer of the option buys the stock at the exercise price and the difference between the asset value and the exercise price is the gross profit on the investment. The net profit (see Figure 8.1) on the investment is the difference

between the gross profit and the price paid for the call initially.

A put option gives the buyer of the option the right to sell the underlying asset at a fixed price, again called the strike or exercise price, at any time prior to the expiration date of the option. If the price of the underlying asset is greater than the strike price, the option will not be exercised and will expire worthless. If the price of the underlying asset is less than the strike price, the owner of the put option will exercise the option and sell the stock at the strike price, claiming the difference between the strike price and the market value of the asset as the gross profit. Again, netting out the initial cost paid for the put yields the net profit from the transaction.

Determinants of option value

The value of an option is determined by a number of variables relating to the underlying asset and financial markets.

1. *Current Value of the Underlying Asset.* Options are assets that derive value from an underlying asset. Consequently, changes in the value of the underlying asset affect the value of the options on that asset. Since calls provide the right to buy the underlying asset at a fixed price, an increase in the value of the asset will increase the value of the calls. Puts, on the other hand, become less valuable as the value of the asset increase.
2. *Variance in Value of the Underlying Asset.* The buyer of an option acquires the right to buy or sell the underlying asset at a fixed price. The higher the variance in the value of the underlying asset, the greater the value of the option. This is true for both calls and puts. While it may

seem counterintuitive that an increase in a risk measure (variance) should increase value, options are different from other securities since buyers of options can never lose more than the price they pay for them; in fact, they have the potential to earn significant returns from large price movements.

3. *Strike Price of Option.* A key characteristic used to describe an option is the strike price. In the case of calls, where the holder acquires the right to buy at a fixed price, the value of the call will decline as the strike price increases. In the case of puts, where the holder has the right to sell at a fixed price, the value will increase as the strike price increases.

4. *Time to Expiration on Option.* Both calls and puts become more valuable as the time to expiration increases. This is because the longer time to expiration provides more time for the value of the underlying asset to move, increasing the value of both types of options. Additionally, in the case of a call, where the buyer has to pay a fixed price at expiration, the present value of this fixed price decreases as the life of the option increases, increasing the value of the call.

5. *Riskless Interest Rate Corresponding to Life of Option.* The riskless interest rate affects the valuation of options mainly by affecting the present value of the exercise price. Since the exercise price des not have to be paid (received) until expiration on calls (puts), increases in the interest rate will increase the value of calls and reduce the value of puts.

6. *Dividends Paid on the Underlying Asset.* The value of the underlying asset can be expected to decrease if dividend payments are made on the asset during the life of the option. Consequently, the value of a call on the asset is a *decreasing* function of the size of expected dividend payments, and the value of a put is an *increasing* function of expected dividend payments. A more intuitive way of thinking about the effect of dividend payments on call options is as costs of delaying exercise on in-the-money options. To see why, consider a call option on a traded stock. Once it is in the money, exercising the call option will provide the holder with the stock, and entitle him or her to the dividends on the stock in subsequent periods. Failing to exercise the option will mean that these dividends are forgone.

Table 8.1 Summary of Variables Affecting Call and Put Prices

Factor	Effect on call value	Put value
Increase in underlying asset's value	Increases	Decreases
Increase in Strike Price	Decreases	Increases
Increase in variance of underlying asset	Increases	Increases
Increase in time to expiration	Increases	Increases
Increase in interest rates	Increases	Decreases
Increase in dividends paid	Decreases	Increases

For a summary of the six key variables and their predicted effects on call and put prices, see Table 8.1.

The pricing model

With the exception of dividends, each of these five variables appears in the option pricing model developed by Fischer Black and Myron Scholes (with invaluable help from Robert Merton) in 1973. Although the Black-Scholes model was designed to value "dividend-protected" European options (which can be exercised only at maturity), the model can be applied, with some adjustments discussed below, to American options on dividend-paying stocks. In constructing their model, Black and Scholes used a "replicating portfolio" – a portfolio composed of the underlying asset and the risk-free asset that had the same cash flows as the option being valued – to come up with the following formula for the value of a option call:

$$V = SN(d_1) - Ke^{-rt}N(d_2) \qquad \text{eq. (1)},$$

where

- S = Current value of the underlying asset
- K = Strike price of the option
- t = Life to expiration of the option
- r = Riskless interest rate corresponding to the life of the option
- σ^2 = Variance in the ln(value) of the underlying asset.

The last of the five variables, the variance measure, shows up in the terms $N(d_1)$ and $N(d_2)$, where

$$d_1 = [\ln(S/K)+(r+\sigma^2/2)t]/\sigma\sqrt{t}$$
$$d_2 = d_1-\sigma\sqrt{t}$$

$N(d_1)$ and $N(d_2)$ are probability functions that play an important use in the analysis in that they represent, in approximate terms, the range of probability that the option will be in the money at expiration.

The process of valuing options with the Black-Scholes model involves the following steps:

Step 1 Use the inputs for the five variables listed above to estimate d_1 and d_2.

Step 2 Use d_1 and d_2 to estimate the cumulative normal distribution (or probability) functions, $N(d_1)$ and $N(d_2)$.

Step 3 Estimate the present value of the exercise price (using the continuous time version of the present value formulation) as follows: $PV = K\,e^{-rt}$.

Step 4 Estimate the value of the call with the Black-Scholes formula.

In the remainder of the paper, we use this model to value a number of corporate real options. The version of the Black-Scholes model presented above does not take into account the possibility of early exercise or the payment of dividends, both of which affect the value of options. In the Appendix, I discuss a number of possible adjustments that, while not perfect, provide partial corrections to value.

THE OPTION TO DELAY

As stated earlier, the most important limitation of the conventional DCF method for capital budgeting is its failure to reflect the value of strategic options that are often embedded in corporate real investments. The first of the three kinds of real options I consider in this paper is the option to delay a project.

Projects are typically analyzed based upon the cash flows expected and the discount rates that prevail when the analysis is being done. The NPV computed on that basis is thus a measure of its

value and acceptability *at that point in time*. Expected cash flows and discount rates change over time, however, and so does the NPV. Thus, a project that has a negative NPV now may have a positive NPV in the future. In a competitive environment in which individual firms have no special advantages over their competitors in taking projects, this may not seem significant. But, in an environment in which a project can be taken by only one firm (because of legal restrictions or other barriers to entry to competitors), the changes in the project's value over time give it the characteristics of a call option.

In the abstract, assume that a project requires an initial upfront investment of X, and that the present value of expected cash inflows computed right now is V. The net present value of this project is the difference between the two:

$$NPV = V-X$$

Now assume that the firm has exclusive rights to this project for the next n years, and that the present value of the cash inflows may change over that time because of changes in either the cash flows or the discount rate. Thus, although the project may have a negative NPV right now, it may still be a good project if the firm waits. Defining V again as the present value of the cash flows, the firm's decision rule on this project can be summarized as follows:

If $V > X$ Take the project: Project has positive NPV.

If $V < X$ Do not take the project: Project has negative NPV.

If the firm does not take the project, it incurs no additional cash outflows (though it will lose what it originally invested in the project).

This expected payoff in this case is shown in Figure 8.2, which assumes that the firm holds off committing itself until the end of the period for which it has exclusive rights to the project. Note that this payoff diagram is that of a call option. The underlying asset is the project itself, the strike price of the option is the investment needed to take the project, and the life of the option is the period for which the firm has rights to the project. The present value of the cash flows on this project and the expected variance in this present value represent the value and variance of the underlying asset.

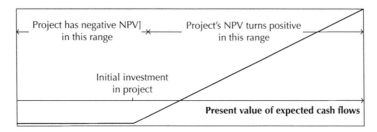

Figure 8.2 The Option to Delay a Project

The inputs needed to apply option pricing theory in valuing the option to delay are the same as those needed for any option. We need the value of the underlying asset, the variance in that value, the time to expiration on the option, the strike price, the riskless rate, and the equivalent of the dividend yield (which, again, represents the cost of delay).

Value of the Underlying Asset. In the case of product options, the underlying asset is the project itself. The current value of this asset is the present value of expected cash flows from initiating the project now, not including the upfront investment, which can be obtained by doing a standard capital budgeting analysis. Of course, there is bound to be a good deal of "noise" in the cash flow estimates. But, rather than being viewed as a problem, this uncertainty should be viewed as the main reason the project delay option has value. If the expected cash flows on the project were known with certainty and were not expected to change, there would be no need to use an option pricing framework since the option would have no value.

Variance in the Value of the Asset. As suggested, at the time of the initial investment there is likely to be considerable uncertainty associated with the cash flow estimates and the NPV measure of the value of the asset, partly because the potential market size for the product may be unknown and partly because technological shifts can change the cost structure and profitability of the product. The value of the option derives largely from the variance in cash flows – the higher the variance, the higher the value of the project delay option. Thus, the value of an option to invest in a project in a stable business will be less than the value of one in an environment where technology, competition, and markets are all changing rapidly.

The variance in the present value of the cash flows from projects can be estimated in one of three ways:

1. If similar projects have been introduced in the past, the variance in the cash flows from those projects can be used as an estimate. A consumer product company like Gillette might use this method to estimate the variance associated with introducing a new blade for its razors.
2. Probabilities can be assigned to various market scenarios, cash flows estimated under each scenario, and the variance estimated across present values. Alternatively, the probability distributions can be estimated for each of the inputs into the project analysis – the size of the market, the market share, and the profit margin, for instance – and simulations used to estimate the variance in the present values that emerge. This approach tends to work best when there are only one or two sources[1] of significant uncertainty about future cash flows.
3. The variance in the market value of companies involved in the same business (as the project being considered) can be used as an estimate of the variance. Thus, the average variance in firm value of companies involved in the software business can be used as the variance in present value of a software project.[2]

---

1 In practical terms, the probability distributions for inputs like market size and market share can often be obtained from market testing.

2 This might understate the variance in the project since firms have portfolios of projects, and the variance of this project portfolio will generally be lower than the variance of an individual project.

Exercise Price on Option. A project delay option is exercised when the firm owning the rights to the project decides to invest in it. The cost of making this investment is the exercise price of the option. The underlying assumption is that this cost remains constant (in present value dollars) and that any uncertainty associated with the product is reflected in the present value of cash flows on the product.

Expiration of the Option and the Riskless Rate. The project delay option expires when the rights to the project lapse. Investments made after the project rights expire are assumed to deliver an NPV of zero as competition drives returns down to the required rate. The riskless rate to use in pricing the option should be the rate that corresponds to the expiration of the option. While this input can be estimated easily when firms have the explicit right to a project (through a license or a patent, for instance), it becomes far more difficult to obtain when firms only have a competitive advantage to take a project. Since competitive advantages fade over time, the number of years for which the firm can be expected to have these advantages is the life of the option.

Cost of Delay (Dividend Yield). There is a cost to delaying taking a project, once the net present value turns positive. Since the project rights expire after a fixed period, and excess profits (which are the source of positive present value) are assumed to disappear after that time as new competitors emerge, each year of delay translates into one less year of value-creating cash flows.[3] If the cash flows are evenly distributed over time, and the life of the patent is n years, the annual cost of delay can be estimated as 1 divided by n. Thus, if the project rights are for 20 years, the annual cost of delay works out to 5% a year. Note, though, that this cost of delay rises each year – to $1/19$ in year 2, $1/18$ in year 3 and so on, making the cost of delaying exercise larger over time.

Valuing the option to delay a project: an illustration

Assume that you are interested in acquiring the exclusive rights to market a new product that will make it easier for people to access their e-mail on the road. If you do acquire the rights to the product, you estimate that it will cost you $500 million upfront to set up the infrastructure needed to provide the service. Based upon your current projections, you believe that the service will generate $100 million in after-tax cash flows each year. In addition, you expect to operate without serious competition for the next five years.

From a purely "static" standpoint – that is, assuming the project has no real options with material value – the NPV of this project can be computed by taking the present value of the expected cash flows over the next five years. Assuming a discount rate of 15% (based on the riskiness of this project), we obtain the following net present value for the project: $-$500 million $+$ $100 million (PV of annuity, 15%, 5 years) $=-$500 million $+$ $335 million $=-$165 million. Thus the project has a static NPV of $-$165 million.

The biggest source of uncertainty about this project is the number of people who will be interested in this product. While the current market tests indicate that you will capture a relatively small number of business travelers as your customers, the test also indicates a possibility that the potential market could get much larger over time. In fact, a simulation of the project's cash flows yields a standard deviation of 42% in the present value of the cash flows, with an expected value of $335 million.

To value the exclusive rights to this project, we first define the inputs to the option pricing model:

♦ Value of the Underlying Asset (S)=PV of Cash Flows from Project if introduced now = $335 million
♦ Strike Price (K) = Initial Investment needed to introduce the product = $500 million
♦ Variance in Underlying Asset's Value = 0.42^2 = 0.1764
♦ Time to expiration = Period of exclusive rights to product = 5 years
♦ Dividend Yield = 1/Life of the patent = $1/5$ = 0.20
♦ (Five-year) Riskless rate = 5%.

---

3 A value-creating cashflow is one that adds to the net present value because it is in excess of the required return for investments of equivalent risk.

By plugging the above variables into the Black-Scholes model presented earlier, the value of the option can then be estimated as follows: $335mm. $\exp^{(-0.2)(5)}(0.2250) - 500$mm. $(\exp^{(-0.05)(5)}(0.0451) =$ $10.18 million. This suggests that the rights to this product, which has a negative NPV if introduced now, are nevertheless worth about $10 million today.

Practical considerations

While it is quite clear that the option to delay is embedded in many projects, there are several problems associated with the use of option pricing models to value these options. First, the underlying asset in this option, which is the project, is not traded, making it difficult to estimate its value and variance. We would argue that the value can be estimated from the expected cash flows and the discount rate for the project, albeit with error. The variance is more difficult to estimate, however, since we are attempting to estimate a variance in project value over time.

Second, the behavior of prices over time may not conform to the continuous price path assumed by many (including the Black-Scholes) option pricing models. In particular, the model's assumptions that value follows a continuous "diffusion" process, and that the variance in value remains unchanged over time, may be difficult to justify in the context of a project. For instance, a sudden technological change may dramatically change the value of a project, either positively or negatively.

Third, there may be no specific period for which the firm has rights to the project. Unlike the example above, in which the firm had exclusive rights to the project for 20 years, the firm's rights may be less clearly defined, both in terms of exclusivity and time. For instance, a firm may have significant advantages over its competitors, which may in turn provide it with the virtually exclusive rights to a project for a period of time. The rights are not legal restrictions, however, and could erode faster than expected. In such cases, the expected life of the project itself is uncertain. In our valuation of the rights to the product, we used a life for the option of five years, but competitors could in fact enter sooner than we anticipated. Alternatively, the barriers to entry may turn out to be greater than

expected, and allow the firm to earn excess returns for longer than five years.

Implications of viewing the right to delay a project as an option

Several interesting implications emerge from the analysis of the option to delay a project as an option. First, a project may have a negative NPV based upon currently expected cash flows, but it may still be a "valuable" project because of the option characteristics. Thus, while a negative NPV should encourage a firm to reject a project, it should not lead it to conclude that the rights to this project are worthless.

Second, a project may now have a positive NPV but still not be accepted right away because the firm may gain by waiting and accepting the project in a future period, for the same reasons that investors do not always exercise an option just because it is in the money. This is more likely to happen if the firm has the rights to the project for a long time, and the variance of project inflows is high. To illustrate, assume that a firm has the patent rights to produce a new type of disk drive for computer systems and that building a new plant will yield a positive NPV right now. If the technology for manufacturing the disk drive is in flux, the firm may delay taking the project in the hope that the improved technology will increase the expected cash flows and the value of the pro-ject. But it also must weigh these possible benefits against the cash flows that will be forgone by not taking the project.

Third, factors that can make a project less attractive in a static analysis can actually make the rights to the project more valuable. As an example, consider the effect of uncertainty about how long the firm will be able to operate without competition and earn excess returns. In a static analysis, increasing this uncertainty increases the risk of the project and may make it less attractive. But when the project is viewed as an option, an increase in the uncertainty may actually make the option more valuable.

Valuing natural resource options

Natural resources is one of most likely candidates for the application of real options in capital budgeting. In a natural resource investment, the underlying asset is the natural resource and the value of the asset is based in large part upon just two variables: (1) the price of the resource and (2) the estimated quantity. Thus, in the case of a gold mine, for example, the underlying asset is the value of the estimated gold reserves in the mine based upon the current price of gold. In most such investments, there is an initial cost associated with developing the resource, and the difference between the value of the asset extracted and the cost of the development is the profit to the owner of the resource.

Defining the cost of development as X, and the estimated value of the resource as V, the potential payoffs on a natural resource option can be written as follows: $V - X$ if $V > X$, or 0 if $V = X$. Thus, the investment in a natural resource option has a payoff function similar to a call option.

To value a natural resource investment as an option, we need to make assumptions about a number of variables:

1. *Available reserves of the resource.* Since this is not known with certainty at the outset, it has to be estimated. In an oil tract, for instance, geologists can provide reasonably accurate estimates of the quantity of oil available in the tract.
2. *Estimated cost of developing the resource.* The estimated development cost is the exercise price of the option. Again, a combination of knowledge about past costs and the specifics of the investment have to be used to come up with a reasonable measure of development cost.
3. *Time to expiration of the option.* The life of a natural resource option can be defined in one of two ways. First, if the ownership of the investment has to be relinquished at the end of a fixed period of time, that will be the life of the option. In many offshore oil leases, for instance, the oil tracts are leased to the oil company for several years. The second approach is based upon the inventory of the resource and the capacity output rate, as well as estimates of the number of years it would take to exhaust the inventory. Thus, a gold mine with a mine inventory of three million ounces and a capacity output rate of 150,000 ounces a year will be exhausted in 20 years, which is defined as the life of the natural resource option.

4. *Variance in value of the underlying asset.* The variance in the value of the underlying asset is determined by two factors: (1) variability in the price of the resource and (2) variability in the estimate of available reserves. In the special case where the quantity of the reserve is known with certainty, the variance in the underlying asset's value will depend entirely upon the variance in the price of the natural resource; in this case, the option can be valued like any other simple option. In the more realistic case where the quantity of the reserve and the oil price can change over time, the option becomes more difficult to value; here the firm may have to invest in stages to exploit the reserves.
5. *Cost of delay.* The net production revenue as a percentage of the market value of the reserve is the equivalent of the dividend yield and is treated the same way in calculating option values. An alternative way of thinking about this cost is in terms of a cost of delay. Once a natural resource option is in-the-money (the value of the reserves is greater than the cost of developing these reserves), the firm by not exercising the option is forgoing the production revenue it could have generated by developing the reserve.

An important issue in using option pricing models to value natural resource options is the effect of development lags on the value of these options. Since the resources cannot be extracted instantaneously, a time lag has to be allowed between the decision to extract the resources and the actual extraction. A simple adjustment for this lag is to adjust the value of the developed reserve for the loss of cash flows during the development period. Thus, if there is a one-year lag in development, the current value of the developed reserve will be discounted back one year at the net production revenue/asset value ratio[4] (which we also called the dividend yield above).

---

4 Intuitively, it may seem like the discounting should occur at the risk-free rate. The simplest way of explaining why we discount at the dividend yield is to consider the analogy with a listed option on a stock. Assume that on exercising a listed option on a stock, you had to wait six months for the stock to be delivered to you. What you lose is the dividends you would have received over the six month period by holding the stock. Hence, the discounting is at the dividend yield.

Illustration: valuing a gold mine[5]

Consider a gold mine with an estimated inventory of one million ounces and a capacity output rate of 50,000 ounces per year. The price of gold is expected to grow 3% a year. The firm owns the rights to this mine for the next 20 years. The cost of opening the mine is $100 million, and the average production cost is $250 per ounce; once initiated, the production cost is expected to grow 5% a year. The standard deviation in gold prices is 20%, and the current price of gold is $375 per ounce. The riskless rate is 6%. The inputs to the model are as follows:

- Value of the underlying asset = Present Value of expected gold sales (@ 50,000 ounces a year) = (50,000*375)*[1−(1.03²⁰/(.09−.03)−(50,000*250)*[1−(1.05²⁰/1.09²⁰)]/(.09−.05) = $211.79 million − $164.55 million = $47.24 million
- Exercise price = Cost of opening mine = $100 million
- Variance in ln(gold price) = 0.04
- Time to expiration on the option = 20 years
- Riskless interest rate = 6%
- Dividend Yield = Loss in production for each year of delay = 1/20 = 5%

Based upon these inputs, the Black-Scholes model provides the following value for the call:

$d_1 = -0.1676 \quad N(d_1) = 0.4334$
$d_2 = -1.0621 \quad N(d_2) = 0.1441$
Call value $= \$47.24 \, \exp^{(-0.05)(20)} (0.4334)$
$\qquad -100 * (\exp^{(0.09)(20)} (0.1441)$
$\qquad = \$3.19 \text{ million}$

The value of the mine when viewed as an option on the price of gold is thus a positive $3.19 million. By contrast, the static capital budgeting analysis would have yielded a net present value of −$52.76 million ($47.24 million − $100 million). The additional value accrues directly from the mine's option characteristics.

Valuing an oil reserve[6]

Consider an offshore oil property with an estimated oil reserve of 50 million barrels of oil; the cost of developing the reserve is expected to be $600 million, and the development lag is two years. The firm has the rights to exploit this reserve for the next 20 years, and the marginal value per barrel of oil is currently $12[7] (price per barrel − marginal cost per barrel). Once developed, the net production revenue each year will be 5% of the value of the reserves. In this example, we assume that the only uncertainty is in the price of oil, and the variance therefore becomes the variance in ln(oil prices), which is assumed to be 0.03. If development is started today, the oil will not be available for sale until two years from now.

Given this information, the inputs to the Black-Scholes can be estimated as follows:

- Current Value of the asset = S = Value of the developed reserve discounted back the length of the (two-year) development lag at the dividend yield = $12 * 50 /(1.05)² = $544.22
- Exercise Price = Cost of developing reserve = $600 million (assumed to be fixed over time)
- Time to expiration on the option = 20 years
- Variance in the value of the underlying asset = 0.03
- Riskless rate = 8%
- Dividend Yield = Net production revenue/ Value of reserve = 5%

Based upon these inputs, the model provides the following values:

$d_1 = 1.0359 \quad N(d_1) = 0.8498$
$d_2 = 0.2613 \quad N(d_2) = 0.6030$
Call value $= \$544.22 \, \exp^{(-0.05)(20)} (0.8498)$
$\qquad -600 * (\exp^{(0.09)(20)} (0.6030)$
$\qquad = \$97.08 \text{ million}$

---

6 The following is a simplified version of the illustration provided by Siegel, Smith and Paddock to value an offshore oil property.

7 For simplicity, we will assume that while this marginal value per barrel of oil will grow over time, the present value of the marginal value will remain unchanged at $12 per barrel. If we do not make this assumption, we will have to estimate the present value of the oil that will be extracted over the extraction period.

---

5 The following is a simpler version of the example presented in Brennan and Schwartz, applying option pricing theory to value a gold mine.

Although not viable at current prices, this oil reserve is still a valuable property because of its potential to create value if oil prices go up.

Valuing a patent: the case of Avonex[8]

Biogen is a biotechnology firm with a patent on a drug called Avonex, which has passed FDA approval to treat multiple sclerosis. A product patent provides a firm with the exclusive right to develop and market a product for a fixed period of time. Since the firm will do so only if the present value of the expected cash flows from the product sales exceed the cost of development, the firm can shelve the patent and not incur any further costs. Thus, a product patent can be viewed as a call option in which the product itself is the underlying asset.

Assume that you are trying to value the patent on Avonex and that you arrive at the following estimates for use in the option pricing model:

- An internal analysis of the drug today, based upon the potential market and the price that the firm can expect to charge, yields a present value of cash flows of $3.422 billion prior to considering the initial development cost.
- The initial cost of developing the drug for commercial use is estimated to be $2.875 billion if the drug is introduced today.
- The firm has the patent on the drug for the next 17 years, and the current long-term treasury bond rate is 6.7%.
- While it is difficult to do reasonable simulations of the cash flows and present values, the average variance in firm value for publicly traded biotechnology firms is 0.224.

It is further assumed that the potential for excess returns exists only during the patent life, and that competition will wipe out excess returns beyond that period. Thus, any delay in introducing the drug, once it becomes viable, will cost the firm one year of patent-protected excess returns.

(For the initial analysis, the cost of delay will be 1/17, next year it will be 1/16, the year after 1/15 and so on.)

Based on these assumptions, we obtain the following inputs to the option pricing model:

- Present Value of Cash Flows from Introducing the Drug Now = S = $3.422 billion
- Initial Cost of Developing Drug for Commercial Use (today) = K = $2.875 billion
- Patent Life = t = 17 years
- Riskless Rate = r = 6.7% (17-year T.Bond rate)
- Variance in Expected Present Values = $\sigma^2 = 0.224$
- Expected Cost of Delay = y = 1/17 = 5.89%

These yield the following estimates for d and N(d):

$$d_1 = 1.1362 \qquad N(d_1) = 0.8720$$
$$d_2 = -0.8512 \qquad N(d_2) = 0.2076$$

Plugging these estimates back into the option pricing model, we get: Value of the patent = $3.422exp^{(-0.0589)(17)}(0.8720) - $2.875 exp^{(-0.067)(17)}(0.2076) = $907 million. In comparison, the static NPV of this project is only $547 million ($3.422 billion − $2.875 billion). Moreover, the time premium on this option suggests that the firm will be better off waiting rather than developing the drug immediately, notwithstanding the cost of delay. However, the cost of delay will increase over time, thus making exercise (development) more likely.

In the above example, we also assumed that the excess returns are restricted to the patent life, and that they disappear the instant the patent expires. In the pharmaceutical sector, the expiration of a patent does not necessarily mean the loss of excess returns. In fact, many firms continue to be able to charge a premium price for their products and earn excess returns after the patent expires, largely as a consequence of the brand name image that they built up over the project life. A simple way of adjusting for this reality is to increase the present value of the cash flows on the project (S) and decrease the cost of delay (y). The net effect is a greater likelihood that firms will delay commercial development, while they wait to collect more information and assess market demand.

---

8   This analysis was done at the time of Avonex's approval by the FDA. The product is now commercially developed.

THE OPTION TO EXPAND

Companies choose to invest in some projects because doing so allows them either to take on other projects or to enter other markets in the future. In such cases, it can be argued that the initial projects are options that allow the firm to take other projects, and the firm should therefore be willing to pay a price for such options. A firm may accept a negative NPV on the initial project because of the possibility of high positive NPVs on future projects.

To examine this option using the framework developed earlier, assume that the present value of the expected cash flows from entering the new market or investing in the new project is V, and the total investment needed to enter this market or take this project is X. Further, assume that the firm has a fixed time horizon, at the end of which it has to make the final decision on whether or not to take advantage of this opportunity. Finally, assume that the firm cannot move forward on this opportunity if it does not take the initial project. At the expiration of the fixed time horizon, the firm will enter the new market or invest in the new project if the present value of the expected cash flows at that point in time exceeds the cost of entering the market.

Valuing an option to expand: the case of The Home Depot

Assume that The Home Depot is considering opening a small store in France. The store will cost 100 million FF to build, and the present value of the expected cash flows from the store is 120 million FF. Thus, considered as a stand-alone investment, the store has a positive NPV of 20 million FF.

Assume, however, that by opening this store, the Home Depot acquires the option to expand into a much larger store any time over the next five years. The cost of expansion will be 200 million FF, and it will be undertaken only if the present value of the expected cash flows exceeds 200 million FF. At the moment, the present value of the expected cash flows from the expansion is believed to be only 150 million FF (if it were greater than 200 million FF, the company would have opened

the larger store right away). The Home Depot still does not know much about the market for home improvement products in France, and there is considerable uncertainty about this estimate. The standard deviation of the estimate is 28.3%.

The value of the option to expand can be estimated by defining the inputs to the option pricing model as follows:

- Value of the Underlying Asset (S) = PV of Cash Flows from Expansion, if done now = 150 million FF
- Strike Price (K) = Cost of Expansion = 200 million FF
- Variance in Underlying Asset's Value = $0.283^2 = 0.08$
- Time to expiration = Period for which expansion option applies = 5 years
- The five-year riskless rate = 6%.

The value of the option can be estimated as follows:

$$\text{Call value} = 150 \text{ million FF } (0.6314)$$
$$- 200 \, (\exp^{(-0.06)\,(5)}) \, (0.3833)$$
$$= 37.91 \text{ million FF}$$

When this value is added to the negative NPV of the original project under consideration (–20 million FF), the project including the option to expand has a positive NPV of 17.91 million FF. Based on this analysis, The Home Depot would decide to open the smaller store despite its negative NPV because it thereby acquires an option of much greater value.

Practical considerations

The practical considerations associated with estimating the value of the option to expand are similar to those associated with valuing the option to delay. In most cases, companies with options to expand have no specific time horizon by which they have to make an expansion decision, making these open-ended options or, more precisely, options with indefinite lives. Even in those cases where a life can be estimated for the option, neither the size nor the potential market for the product may be known, and estimating either can be problematic. To illustrate, consider the Home

Depot example discussed above. While we adopted a period of five years, at the end of which The Home Depot has to decide one way or another on its future expansion in France, it is entirely possible that this time frame is not specified at the time the store is opened. Furthermore, we have assumed that both the cost and the present value of expansion are known initially. In reality, the firm may not have good estimates for either before opening the first store, since it does not have much information on the underlying market.

Implications

The option to expand is implicitly used by many companies to rationalize taking projects that may have negative NPV, but provide significant opportunities to tap into new markets or sell new products. While the option pricing approach adds rigor to this argument by estimating the value of this option, it also provides insight into those occasions when it is most valuable. In general, the option to expand is clearly more valuable for more volatile businesses with higher returns on projects (such as biotechnology or computer software), than in stable businesses with lower returns (such as housing, utilities, or automobile production).

Strategic Considerations/Options. In many acquisitions or investments, the acquiring firm believes that the transaction will give it competitive advantages in the future. Among such competitive advantages are:

- *Access to a Growing or Large Market.* An investment or acquisition may allow the firm to enter a large or potentially large market much sooner than it otherwise would have been able to do so. A good example of this would be the acquisition of a Mexican retail firm by a U.S. firm, with the intent of expanding into the Mexican market.
- *Technological Expertise.* In some cases, the acquisition is motivated by the desire to acquire a proprietary technology that will allow the acquirer to expand either its existing market or into a new market.
- *Brand Name.* Firms sometime pay large premiums over market value to acquire firms with valuable brand names because they believe that these brand names can be used for expansion into new markets in the future.

While all of these potential advantages may be used to justify initial investments that do not meet financial benchmarks, not all of them create valuable options. As we will see later in the paper, the value of the option derives from the degree to which these competitive advantages, assuming that they do exist, translate into sustainable excess returns.

Research, Development, and Test Market Expenses. Companies that spend considerable amounts of money on R&D and test marketing are often stymied when they try to evaluate these expenses, since the payoffs are often in terms of future projects. At the same time, there is the very real possibility that after the money has been spent, the products or projects may turn out not to be viable; consequently, the expenditure is treated as a sunk cost. In fact, it can be argued that R&D has the characteristics of a call option – the amount spent on the R&D is the cost of the call option, and the projects or products that might emerge from the research provide the payoffs on the options. If these products are viable (i.e., the present value of the cash inflows exceeds the needed investment), the payoff is the difference between the two; if not, the project will not be accepted, and the payoff is zero.

Several logical implications emerge from this view of R&D. First, research expenditures should provide much higher value for firms that are in volatile technologies or businesses, since the variance in product or project cash flows is positively correlated with the value of the call option. Thus, an office product or consumer goods company should receive less value for its research than a biotechnology firm. Second, the value of research and the optimal amount to be spent on research will change over time as businesses mature. The best example is the pharmaceutical industry. In the 1980s, pharmaceutical companies invested substantial amounts in research and earned high returns on new products. In the 1990s, however, as health care costs started leveling off and the business matured, many of these companies found that they were not getting the same payoffs on research and started cutting back. Some companies moved research dollars from conventional drugs to biotechnology products, where the uncertainty about future cash flows remains high.

Multi-Stage Investments. When entering new businesses or taking new investments, companies sometimes have the option to enter the business in stages. While doing so may reduce potential upside, it also protects the firm against downside risk by allowing it, at each stage, to gauge demand and decide whether to go on to the next stage. In other words, a standard project can be recast as a series of options to expand, with each option being dependent on the previous one. There are two propositions that follow:

+ Some projects that do not look good on a full-investment basis may be value creating if the firm can invest in stages.
+ Some projects that look attractive on a full-investment basis may become even more attractive if taken in stages.

The gain in value from the options created by multi-stage investments has to be weighed against the cost. Taking investments in stages may allow competitors who decide to enter the market on a full scale to capture the market. It may also lead to higher costs at each stage, since the firm is not taking full advantage of economies of scale.

There are several implications that emerge from viewing this choice between multi-stage and one-time investments in an option framework. The projects where the gains will be largest from making the investment in multiple stages include:

+ *Projects where there are significant barriers to entry from competitors entering the market and taking advantage of delays in full-scale production.* Thus, a firm with a patent on a product or other legal protection against competition pays a much smaller price for starting small and expanding as it learns more about the product
+ *Projects where there is significant uncertainty about the size of the market and the eventual success of the project.* Here, starting small and expanding allows the firm to reduce its losses if the product does not sell as well as anticipated, and to learn more about the market at each stage. This information can then be useful in subsequent stages in both product design and marketing.
+ *Projects where there is a substantial investment needed in infrastructure (large fixed costs) and high operating leverage.* Since the savings from doing a project in multiple stages

can be traced to investments needed at each stage, they are likely to be greater in firms where those costs are large. Capital-intensive projects as well as projects that require large initial marketing expenses (a new brand name product for a consumer product company) will gain more from the options created by taking the project in multiple stages.

When are real options valuable? Some key tests

While the argument that some or many investments have valuable strategic or expansion options embedded in them has great allure, there is a danger that this argument will be used to justify poor investments. In fact, acquirers have long justified huge premiums on acquisitions on synergistic and strategic grounds. To prevent real options from falling into the same black hole, we need to be more rigorous in our measurement of the value of real options.

Quantitative Estimation. When real options are used to justify a decision, the justification has to be put in quantitative as well as qualitative terms. In other words, managers who argue for taking a project with poor returns or paying a premium on an acquisition on the basis of real options should be required to value these real options and show that the economic benefits exceed the costs. There will be two arguments made against this requirement. The first is that real options cannot be easily valued, since the inputs are difficult to obtain and often noisy. The second is that the inputs to option pricing models can be easily manipulated to back up the desired result. While both arguments have some basis, a noisy estimate is better than no estimate at all, and the process of quantitatively trying to estimate the value of a real option is in fact the first step to understanding what drives it value.

Key Tests. Not all investments have options embedded in them, and not all options, even if they do exist, have value. To assess whether an investment creates valuable options that need to be analyzed and valued, three key questions need to be answered affirmatively:

1. *Is the first investment really a prerequisite for the later investment/expansion? If not, how*

important is the first investment for the later one? Consider our earlier analysis of the value of a patent or the value of an undeveloped oil reserve as options. A firm cannot generate patents without investing in research or paying another firm for the patents, and it cannot get rights to an undeveloped oil reserve without bidding on it at a government auction or buying it from another oil company. Clearly, the initial investment here (spending on R&D, bidding at the auction) is required for the firm to have the second option. Now consider the Home Depot investment in a French store and the option to expand into the French market later. The initial store investment provides the Home Depot with information about market potential, without which it would presumably be unwilling to expand into the larger market. Thus, although the initial investment is not really a prerequisite for the second, management might view it as such. The argument becomes less defensible, however, when we look at one firm acquiring another to have the option to be able to enter a large market. Acquiring an e-tailer to get a foothold in the Internet retailing market, or buying a Brazilian brewery to preserve the option to enter the Brazilian beer market would be examples of such transactions.

2. *Does the firm have an exclusive right to the later investment/expansion? If not, does the initial investment provide the firm with significant competitive advantages on subsequent investments?* The value of the option ultimately derives not from the cash flows generated by the second and subsequent investments, but from the excess returns generated by these cash flows. The greater the potential for excess returns on the second investment, the greater the value of the option in the first investment. The potential for excess returns is closely tied to how much of a competitive advantage the first investment provides the firm when it takes subsequent investments. At one extreme, consider again the case of investing in R&D to acquire a patent. The patent gives the firm that owns it the exclusive rights to produce that product, and if the market potential is large, the right to the excess returns from the project. At the other extreme, the firm might get no competitive advantages on subsequent investments, in which case it is questionable as to whether there can be any excess returns on

these investments. In reality, most investments will fall somewhere between these two extremes, with greater competitive advantages being associated with higher excess returns and larger option values.

3. *How sustainable are the competitive advantages?* In a competitive marketplace, excess returns attract competitors, and competition drives out excess returns. The more sustainable the competitive advantages possessed by a firm, the greater will be the value of the options embedded in the initial investment. The sustainability of competitive advantages is a function of two forces. The first is the nature of the competition; other things remaining equal, competitive advantages fade much more quickly in sectors where there are aggressive competitors. The second is the nature of the competitive advantage. If the resource controlled by the firm is finite and scarce (as is the case with natural resource reserves and vacant land), the competitive advantage is likely to be sustainable for longer periods. But, if the competitive advantage comes from being the first mover in a market or technological expertise, it will come under assault far sooner. The most direct way of reflecting this in the value of the option is in its life; the life of the option can be set to the period of competitive advantage and only the excess returns earned over this period count towards the value of the option.

THE OPTION TO ABANDON

The last of the three kinds of real options considered in this paper is the option to abandon a project when its cash flows do not measure up to expectations. One way to reflect this value is through decision trees. This approach has limited applicability in most real world investment analyses; it typically works only for multi-stage projects, and it requires inputs on probabilities at each stage of the project. The option pricing approach provides a more general way of estimating and building in the value of abandonment into the value of an option.

To illustrate, assume that V is the remaining value on a project if it continues to the end of its life, and L is the liquidation or abandonment value for the same project at the same point in time. If the project has a life of n years, the value of

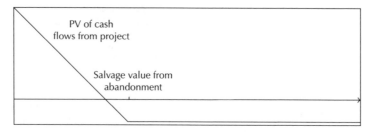

Figure 8.3 The Option to Abandon a Project

continuing the project can be compared to the liquidation (abandonment) value. If the value from continuing is higher, the project should be continued; if the value of abandonment is higher, the holder of the abandonment option could consider abandoning the project.

The payoff from owning an abandonment option is either L−V (if V = L) or 0 (if V > L). These payoffs are graphed in Figure 8.3 as a function of the expected stock price. Unlike the prior two cases, the option to abandon takes on the characteristics of a put option.

Valuing an option to abandon: an illustration

Assume that a firm is considering taking a 10-year project that requires an initial investment of $100 million in a real estate partnership, where the present value of expected cash flows is $110 million. While the net present value of $10 million is small, assume that the firm has the option to abandon this project any time in the next 10 years by selling its share of the ownership to the other partners for $50 million. The standard deviation in the present value of the cash flows from the partnership is 24.5%.

The value of the abandonment option can be estimated by determining the characteristics of the put option:

- Value of the Underlying Asset (S) = PV of Cash Flows from Project = $110 million
- Strike Price (K) = Salvage Value from Abandonment = $50 million
- Variance in Underlying Asset's Value = $0.245^2 = 0.06$

- Time to expiration = Period for which the firm has abandonment option = 10 years
- Riskless rate (ten-year maturity) is 6%.

If we further assume the property is not expected to lose value over the next 10 years, the value of the put option can be estimated as follows:[9]

Value of abandonment
$$= 50 \exp^{(-.06)\,(10)} (1 - 0.8387)$$
$$- 110^* (\exp^{(-0.04)\,(10)} (1 - 0.9737)$$
$$= \$1.53 \text{ million}$$

The value of this abandonment option has to be added to the project's static NPV of $10 million, which yields a total NPV with the abandonment option of $11.53 million. Note, moreover, that abandonment becomes a more and more valuable option as the remaining project life decreases, since the present value of the remaining cash flows will decrease.

Practical considerations

In the above analysis we assumed, rather unrealistically, that the abandonment value was clearly specified upfront and that it did not change during the life of the project. This may be true in some very specific cases, in which an abandonment option is built into the contract. More typical, however, for firms with options to abandon is that the salvage values can only be estimated with noise upfront. Further, the abandonment value may change over the life of the project, making it difficult to apply traditional option pricing techniques.

---

9 We use put-call parity to derive the value of a put as follows:
$P = Ke^{-rt} (1 - N(d_2)) - Se^{-yt}(1 - N(d_1))$.

Finally, it is entirely possible that abandoning a project may not bring in a liquidation value, but may create costs instead. A manufacturing firm may have to pay severance to its workers, for instance. In such cases, it would not make sense to abandon unless the cash flows on the project are even more negative.

We also assumed that the real estate investment was not expected to lose value over time. In a real project, there may be a loss in value as the project ages. This expected loss in value, on an annual basis, can be built in as a dividend yield and used to value the abandonment option. This has the effect of making the option more valuable.

Strategic implications

The fact that the option to abandon has value provides a rationale for firms to build in the operating flexibility to scale back or terminate projects if they do not measure up to expectations. The first, and most direct, way is to create operating flexibility contractually with those parties that are involved in the project. Thus, contracts with suppliers may be written on an annual basis rather than long term, and employees may be hired on a temporary basis rather than permanently. The physical plant used for a project may be leased on a short term basis rather than bought, and the financial investment may be made in stages rather than as an initial lump sum. While there is a cost to building in this flexibility, the gains may be much larger, especially in volatile businesses.

On the other side of the transaction, offering abandonment options to customers and partners in joint ventures can have a negative impact on value. As an example, assume that a firm that sells its products on multi-year contracts offers customers the option to cancel the contract at any time. While this may sweeten the deal and increase sales, there is likely to be a substantial cost. In the event of a recession, firms that are unable to meet their obligations are likely to cancel their contracts. When there is sufficient volatility in income, any benefits gained by the initial sale (obtained by offering the inducement of cancellation by the buyer) may be offset by the cost of the option provided to customers.

CONCLUSION

In recent years, both practitioners and academics have made the argument that traditional discounted cash flow models do a poor job of capturing the value of the options embedded in many corporate actions. This paper shows how option pricing models used in valuing financial assets could be used to value three kinds of real options that are often built into corporate projects: the option to delay, the option to expand, and the option to abandon. As a number of examples in this paper suggest, corporate investments that would be rejected using conventional DCF analysis can sometimes be justified by the value of the strategic options they provide. As the illustrations also show, however, the pricing of real options is considerably more difficult than the pricing of financial options and adjustments must often be made to capture the complexity of real investments.

Appendix: Limitations of the Black-Scholes Model and Possible Adjustments

The version of the Black-Scholes model presented earlier does not take into account the possibility of early exercise or the payment of dividends, both of which affect the value of options. Below we discuss possible adjustments that provide partial corrections to value.

1. Dividends

The payment of dividends reduces the stock price. Consequently, call options will become less valuable and put options more valuable as dividend payments increase. One approach to dealing with dividends is to estimate the present value of expected dividends paid by the underlying asset during the option life and subtract it from the current value of the asset to use as "S" in the model. Since this becomes impractical as the option life becomes longer, we would suggest an alternate approach. If the dividend yield (y = dividends/ current value of the asset) of the underlying asset is expected to remain unchanged during the life of the option, the Black-Scholes model can be modified to take dividends into account as follows.

$$C = Se^{-yt} N(d_1) - Ke^{-rt} N(d_2)$$

where

$$d_1 = [\ln(S/K) + (r - y + \sigma^2/2)t] 1/\sigma\sqrt{t}$$
$$d_2 = d_1 - \sigma t^{.5}$$

From an intuitive standpoint, the adjustments have two effects. First, the value of the asset is discounted back to the present at the divident yield to take into account the expected drop in value from dividend payments. Second, the interest rate is offset by the divident yield to reflect the lower carrying cost from holding the stock (in the replicating portfolio). The net effect wll be a reduction in the value of calls, with the adjustment, and an increase in the value of puts.

2. Early Exercise

The Black-Scholes model is designed to value European options, i.e. options that cannot be exercised until the expiration day. Most options that we consider are American options, which can be exercised any time before expiration. Without working through the mechanics of valuation models, an American option should always be worth at least as much as, and generally more than, a European option because of the early exercise option. There are two basic approaches for dealing with the possibility of early exercise. The first is to continue to use the unadjusted Black-Scholes and regard the resulting value as a floor or conservative estimate of the true value. The second approach is to value the option at each potential exercise date. With options on stocks, this basically requires that we value options to each ex-dividend day and choose the greatest of the estimated call values.

CHAPTER 9

Real Options: State of the Practice

Alex Triantis (University of Maryland) and Adam Borison
(Applied Decision Analysis/PricewaterhouseCoopers)*

In an economic environment characterized by rapid change, great uncertainty, and the need for flexibility, it has become increasingly important for corporate managers to use investment evaluation tools and processes that properly account for both uncertainty and the company's ability to react to new information. Real options has emerged as an approach that addresses this challenge more successfully than traditional capital budgeting techniques. What makes real options analysis so effective in the current business climate is its explicit recognition that future decisions designed to maximize value will depend on new information – such as changes in financial prices or market conditions – that is acquired over the course of time or through some exploratory investment. It is in this sense that real options resemble financial options: just as the value of a stock option (and the investor's decision to exercise it) depends on the future stock price, the exercise decision of a real

option is based on the future value of an underlying real asset – that is, the future value of the investment project. The real options approach thus builds on the theory and insights developed for pricing financial options, while also making use of techniques from the discipline of decision analysis.

In the mid-1980s, academics began building option-based models to value investments in real assets, laying the foundation for an extensive academic literature in this area.[1] The 1990s saw numerous conferences, several books, and many articles aimed at corporate practitioners, who began to experiment with these techniques.[2] Now, as we approach the end of 2001, real options has established a solid, albeit limited, foothold in the

* We appreciate the input of all the survey participants, particularly Rupert D'Souza, Head of Financial Planning and Strategic Analysis at Genentech, Soussan Faiz, Manager of Global Valuation Services at Texaco, and Brice Hill, Server Components Comptroller at Intel, who helped to prepare the inserts for this article. We also wish to acknowledge the useful contributions of Gardner Walkup, Partner and Leader of the Energy Practice at Applied Decision Analysis, helpful comments from UCLA professor Eduardo Schwartz, and the detailed feedback of Don Chew, the editor of this journal.

1 Four papers published in 1985 and 1986 are widely cited in the real options literature: Michael Brennan and Eduardo Schwartz, "Evaluating Natural Resource Investments," *Journal of Business*, 1985; Robert McDonald and Daniel Siegel, "Investment and the Valuation of Firms When There is an Option to Shut Down," *International Economic Review*, 1985; Robert McDonald and Daniel Siegel, "The Value of Waiting to Invest," *Quarterly Journal of Economics* and Sheridan Titman, "Urban Land Prices Under Uncertainty," *American Economic Review*, 1985.

2 A searchable database of over 500 practitioner and academic articles on real options can be found at www.rhsmith. umd.edu/finance/atriantis. The Summer 2000 issue of the *Journal of Applied Corporate Finance* contains a number of practitioner-oriented articles on real options.

Exhibit 9.1 Companies and Industries Represented in Interview Sample

Industry	Companies
Consumer & Industrial Products	DuPont, LLBean, Procter & Gamble
Financial Services	Credit Suisse, First Boston, Morgan Stanley
High Tech & Infocom	Hewlett Packard, Intel, Rockwell, Sprint, Ultratech
Life Sciences	Amgen, Genentech, Genzyme
Energy	Anadarko, Chevron, Cinergy, ConEdison, Conoco, Constellation Energy Group, Dynegy, El Paso, Enron, Lakeland Electric, Ontario Power Generation, Texaco, Wisconsin Public Service Corporation, Xcel Energy
Real Estate/Homebuilding	Beazer Homes
Transportation	Airbus, Boeing, British Airways, Canadian Pacific, General Motors

corporate world. Given this evolution, it is fair to ask, "How is real options being practiced and what impact is it having in the corporate setting?"

In this article, we address this question by synthesizing the experiences of 39 individuals from 34 companies in seven different industries. The companies that agreed to be mentioned in this article (one firm chose to remain anonymous) are listed in Exhibit 9.1. We selected individuals who were familiar with real options. In some cases, they had simply attended a conference on the topic. In other cases, they were leading efforts to implement real options on an enterprise-wide basis. The responses that we received reflect the mindset of individuals who have not only an intellectual interest in the new methods but also, in some cases, a corporate mandate to better understand and possibly apply real options to the investment decision-making process.

Most of the individuals who were interviewed held middle or senior management positions in their firms. Representative titles were Chief Financial Officer, Chief Risk Officer, and Chief Investment Strategist, as well as Director, Manager, or Vice President of areas such as Business Development, Investment Planning, Strategic Planning, Marketing, Corporate Development, Global Valuation Services, Corporate Financial Planning, Business Strategy, and Research. As these titles suggest, the individuals came from a variety of different functional areas, including strategy, marketing, business development, and finance.

In our discussions, we set out to answer three basic questions:

1. What was the impetus for using real options?
2. How and where is real options being applied?
3. What are the primary success factors in using real options?

We also asked our interviewees for their assessments of the future of real options, both in their own firms and elsewhere. The detailed questions we asked are provided in an Appendix.

While certain questions drew similar responses from most of the corporate practitioners we interviewed, it was also apparent that there is a wide range of applications and approaches, which we describe below in detail. Based on these responses, we synthesized a set of "best practices" – that is, factors and processes that appear to be necessary for a firm to take full advantage of real options. We conclude the article with some observations about the expected pace of diffusion of real options in practice and what is likely to speed it up or slow it down.

WHAT WAS THE IMPETUS FOR USING REAL OPTIONS?

For many companies, real options is perceived as a dramatic departure from the past that has the potential to alleviate important concerns, manage critical business risks, or reveal exciting growth opportunities. For example, a concern about their managers' tendency to undervalue the firm's assets during divestitures, to overpay for other firms' assets during acquisitions, or to overinvest in projects with uncertain strategic benefits has driven some firms to investigate the use of real options. Other firms have been motivated by the desire to capture fleeting new-economy growth opportunities or to solidify positions of industry leadership. Often a specific event serves as a catalyst under these conditions. Such events might include a competitive auction for an important asset, such as an oil field or spectrum rights, or a step change in the business environment, such as entry of new types of competitors.

For the great majority of firms, however, real options is not viewed as a revolutionary solution to new business conditions. Instead, it is seen as part of an evolutionary process to improve the valuation of investments and the allocation of capital, thereby increasing shareholder value. While there may be no pressing need for real options, the adoption of these techniques is viewed as providing a long-term competitive advantage through better decision-making.

The companies that have shown broad interest in real options have some common characteristics. Generally, they operate in industries where large investments with uncertain returns are commonplace, such as oil and gas or life sciences. In many cases, they are in industries that have undergone major structural change that makes more traditional valuation techniques less helpful, such as the electric power industry. Finally, they tend to be in engineering-driven industries, where use of sophisticated analytical tools has long been the rule. Surprisingly, there appears to be relatively little interest to date within the financial industry, including banking and insurance.

For most of the companies we interviewed, interest in real options has started quite recently, usually in the last three to five years. In the most common cases, someone in middle management became aware of real options by reading an article, attending a presentation at a conference, or learning about it in school. The middle manager then typically had the ear of a senior executive with the budget and inclination to proceed. In a few cases, interest was driven by a senior executive who "pushed" interest in real options down the ranks. Interestingly, in the majority of cases, it was not someone in finance who encouraged experimentation with real option tools, but rather managers directly involved in business development, strategic planning, operations, or marketing.

Different firms are attracted by different features of real options; and, as we discuss later, these features seem to drive the approaches they are using. In some cases, it is the concept of dealing with, and even profiting from, uncertainty that drives the interest. In other cases, it is the idea of rigorously quantifying the value of investments that seem to resist formal quantification. In still other cases, it is the idea of linking management decisions to capital markets that is most appealing.

HOW AND WHERE ARE REAL OPTIONS BEING APPLIED?

While virtually all the managers we spoke with indicated that they "use real options," it was readily apparent that the approach taken varies from firm to firm. We loosely categorize the techniques or processes that were described to us into the three following classes:

- *Real options as a way of thinking.* In such cases, real options is used primarily as a language that frames and communicates decision problems qualitatively.
- *Real options as an analytical tool.* Real options, and option pricing models in particular, are used primarily to value projects with known, well-specified option characteristics.
- *Real options as an organizational process.* Real options is used, as part of a broader process, as a management tool to identify and exploit strategic options.

Although some companies using the first or second approaches characterize themselves as "beginners," "lacking detailed real options expertise," or "being 50% of the way there," these three classes of approaches do not necessarily represent a progression. Instead, they are more reflective of the types of applications that firms have found most valuable.

For example, in some companies, real options is used as an input into an M&A process where formal numerical analysis plays only a small role. In such cases, real options contributes as a qualitative way of thinking, with little formality either in terms of analytical rigor or organizational procedure. In other firms, real options is used in a commodity trading environment where options in contracts are clearly specified and simply need to be valued. In this case, real options functions as an analytical tool, though generally only in specialized areas of the firm and not on an organization-wide basis. In still other firms, real options is used in a technology R&D context where the firm's success is driven by identifying and managing potential sources of flexibility. In this case, real options contributes as an organizational process with both an analytical and a conceptual core. While it is difficult to quantify exactly how many firms fall into each of these three categories, it appears that the companies we interviewed are split fairly evenly among them.

Real options as a way of thinking

Sophisticated managers have long recognized that the projects they oversee often have considerable flexibility associated with them, and that this flexibility adds significant value. A production plant may be expanded or switched over to a better use. An R&D project can be abandoned or accelerated. An alliance can be renegotiated, turned into a joint venture, or terminated. Given that these sources of flexibility have long been recognized, does it make a difference that they are now referred to as "options," such as the option to expand, the option to switch, the option to abandon, or the option to accelerate?

In fact, our discussions revealed that the development and use of a shorthand language to characterize strategic elements of a project does seem to be valuable.[3] But if the new language itself

is important for improved communication, it is the heightened awareness that options exist within a project – and that options can be created or extinguished as a result of specific actions – that is likely to represent the biggest change. This mindset also involves thinking about uncertainty in a positive light, as something that can be exploited for gain rather than something to be avoided. Similarly, it involves a better appreciation of the importance of learning, and thus the value of acquiring costly information.

In some cases, this common language is extended and formalized, and the firm explicitly works to frame decision problems as "options."[4] In fact, the process of going through a framing exercise to map out future scenarios and identify decisions that could be made at different stages of the project's life was often cited – particularly by those involved principally with strategic planning – as the key benefit of using a real options process.

The transition to the new economy has created many difficult decisions for corporations, and many have responded by adopting a real options mindset to provide some structure in making these decisions. For instance, infrastructure investments such as IT and e-business initiatives are best viewed as "platforms" whose value comes largely from the options they provide for future growth. Some of these options are exclusive, while others must effectively be shared with competitors.[5] Even if it is difficult to arrive at precise valuations for these investments using real options techniques, the platforms can be designed more carefully by thinking about future uncertainty and the creation of options to mitigate the effect of downside risks as well as quickly take advantage of upside opportunities. The issue of "scaleability," for example, can often be captured and refined when placed under a real options lens.

Among other recent changes in the business environment is the proliferation of contractual arrangements among firms, ranging from an increased prevalence of purchase and supply

3 Real options can facilitate not only internal communication, but also external communication with boards of directors, shareholders, and Wall Street analysts. The motivation is to better convey the rationale and value behind management strategy. As discussed later in the article, interest in real options among Wall Street analysts is expected to grow, which will lead to increased use of real options as an external communication device.

4 See Martha Amram and Nalin Kulatilaka (1999), *Real Options: Managing Strategic Investment in an Uncertain World*, Harvard Business School Press, and Robert Clemen (1996), *Making Hard Decisions*, 2nd Edition, Duxbury Press.
5 For an elaboration of this argument and a supporting case study in this issue, see Han Smit, "Acquisition Strategies and Option Games."

contracts along the value chain to new governance structures involving joint ventures or alliances. In companies that have adopted the real options mindset, these contracts are viewed as bundles of options, and the transactions are discussed and even negotiated using options language. Firms focus on getting options that are worth more to them than to the party they are contracting with, and on granting options if the value to the other party exceeds the expected cost to the firm. Similarly, M&A activity at many firms is being discussed from an options perspective.[6]

The process of mapping out scenarios in a tree that includes uncertainty and decision nodes is a standard procedure involved in decision analysis (or "decision and risk analysis," as it is sometimes called), and it has been around for many years. When used primarily as a qualitative way of thinking, what has real options brought to this part of the decision-making process? This question evoked two types of responses, depending upon whether or not we were talking to someone who was experienced in using decision analysis techniques before experimenting with real options techniques.

For those who had not previously used decision analysis or related techniques, real options clearly adds an entirely new dimension to strategic thinking. Discounted cash flow (DCF) analyses require point estimates or expected forecasts, and thus little thought had been given to specifying ranges of outcomes or the flexibility to respond to different scenarios when making future decisions. Real options appears to be readily accepted by some of these firms even when decision analysis is not. There are likely two reasons for this. First, unlike decision analysis, real options is seen as a natural progression from financial evaluation tools like DCF analysis. Second, the language of real options may be more appealing in certain contexts. Real options is more closely associated with valuation and investments, whereas decision analysis may be perceived to be about strategy and decisions. In some parts of an organization, there may be great interest in and openness to improved approaches to evaluating investments, while there is little interest in changing strategic decision-making processes.

What about those managers who had already been using decision analysis techniques before they became aware of real options? Interestingly, these managers feel that the real options paradigm has in fact influenced the way in which they frame decision problems. Many indicated that the real options mindset makes them think more about downstream decisions, about breaking down and measuring uncertainty, and about splitting up decisions into several stages. In decision analysis, the primary focus is often on the current decision and downstream decisions can have a "second class" status. However, in real options applications, these downstream decisions are given equal if not greater weight. Furthermore, given its financial heritage, real options helps managers focus on the metric of shareholder value – something of great significance to more and more firms.

Consequently, whether companies had a legacy of "decision-making under uncertainty" or not, real options appears to make a significant contribution to the understanding and communication of flexibility on a qualitative basis.

Real options as an analytical tool

Many managers are faced with the task of evaluating a particular project with a well-specified type of flexibility, such as a contract with exit or renewal provisions, or a plant with expansion capability. In these cases, real options is often the "tool of choice." Before discussing the real options techniques that are most actively used by firms in this context, we provide a very brief summary of the available valuation techniques, as well as a sense of why the conventional DCF technique is inappropriate for evaluating projects that involve real options.

A standard application of DCF techniques involves two key steps: (1) coming up with the best estimate of the cash flow at each point in time over a horizon, and (2) discounting these expected cash flows back to the present at a risk-adjusted discount rate (or rates).[7] The discount rate should

---

6 Ibid., and Ken Smith and Alex Triantis, "Untapped Options for Creating Value in Acquisitions," *Mergers and Acquisitions*, November–December 1994.

7 Since expected cash flows are projected over a finite horizon (often five or ten years), a terminal value calculation using multiples or simple perpetuity formulas are often used as well, based on assumptions of constant growth in cash flows and a constant risk-adjusted discount rate.

DRUG DEVELOPMENT AT GENENTECH

Drug development at Genentech and similar firms is inherently a "stage gate" process in which each successive phase depends on the success of the previous phase. Each stage is similar to purchasing a call option and the entire process can be viewed as a series of call options. The real options approach can be applied in this context at various levels of sophistication depending on the availability of data and the complexity of the problem. Real options can be as much a philosophy and process as it is a formal valuation methodology. As a philosophy and process, it involves understanding the sources and evolution of uncertainty, identifying the options, valuing them, and later exercising them appropriately. It can also involve identifying securities in the financial markets that can serve as proxies for the real assets and hence provide discipline in the valuation. If those proxies are unavailable, internal systems need to be designed to provide checks and balances on all assumptions.

At Genentech, real options has been used in this manner in the analysis of all drug development projects since 1995. One of the most important features of the real options approach is

its recognition that investment values vary over time and that management has the ability to terminate investments whose future value has fallen below zero. Traditional discounted cash flow methods generally do not account for this contingent decision-making or active management and, as a result, will undervalue flexible investments. The drug development process can be improved simply by incorporating this understanding into project valuation. Applied in this manner, real options provides a consistent language and method to evaluate and compare all projects more effectively across the company.

More recently, Genentech has begun to expand its use of real options through development of a new enterprise-wide investment planning system. In this system, Monte Carlo simulation is used to develop the appropriate distributions for relevant costs and revenues, and the risk-neutral approach is being adopted to take advantage of financial data that already exist within the company. This more sophisticated approach will extend the gains that Genentech has already made in this area.

---

take into account the systematic risk of the cash flows – that is, the extent to which the cash flows are correlated with the market as a whole.

Unfortunately, this simple technique cannot be easily used to value options. In order to come up with an expected cash flow in the future, one needs to know how the option exercise decision(s) will affect the distribution of the option payoff. This may be quite difficult when dealing with complex options, such as compound options that arise when there is a series of future decisions associated with a particular investment opportunity. Even more challenging is the task of estimating discount rates. The appropriate discount rates for options vary widely, depending on the time to maturity of the option, the volatility of the underlying asset, and the difference between the stock price and the exercise price (i.e., whether and to what extent the option is in- or out-of-the money).

The breakthroughs in option pricing theory in the 1970s resulted in valuation techniques that

circumvented the need to estimate risk-adjusted discount rates for options. The main insight behind these techniques is that once the value of the underlying asset (for example, the stock price in the case of stock options) is known, the numerator (the cash flows) can be more readily risk-adjusted than the denominator (the discount rate) when dealing with options. Essentially, risk-adjusted probabilities that are consistent with the valuation of the underlying asset can be backed out for each of the different possible values of the underlying asset at the maturity of the option.[8] These probabilities are then multiplied by the payoffs of the option for each possible underlying asset value, and the resulting risk-adjusted

---

8 If none of the uncertainties cause the risk of the project to systematically vary with the market (e.g., if it is all product related because it is linked to R&D, operations, and market penetration, rather than to general economic conditions), then the risk-adjusted and actual probabilities would be identical.

expected payoff of the option is then discounted at the risk-free rate.[9]

This basic pricing approach is embedded into a variety of different techniques that are used to value real options, including the Black-Scholes model, the binomial or other "lattice" option pricing models, Monte Carlo simulation, and risk-adjusted decision trees. These techniques, and the settings in which each of them is most appropriately applied, are briefly described below.[10]

The well-known Black-Scholes formula can be used to provide a quick estimate of the value of a real option, but will be accurate only under very restrictive conditions. The formula can be applied if there is a single decision to be made regarding an investment at a particular point in time in the future, analogous to the decision of whether to exercise a stock option at its maturity date. The value of the underlying opportunity that could be obtained upon exercise must be lognormally distributed – which is at best a very rough approximation in many cases.

The binomial option pricing model allows for much greater flexibility than the Black-Scholes model in allowing for optimal timing of the exercise decision as well as for more general specifications of the distribution of the underlying asset's value at different points in time. The term "binomial" refers to the fact that during each short "sub-period" in the model, the value of the underlying asset can take on only one of two possible values. For each node in the tree, the value of the option is calculated assuming that either (i) the option is exercised at that time or (ii) the firm continues to hold onto the option for another period. In order to calculate the latter value, the real option value must be solved in an iterative fashion, beginning at the last possible date for option exercise and working back to the current time. While binomial models are certainly more general

than the Black-Scholes formula and can be extended, they do have limitations in dealing with problems involving multiple uncertainties, "path-dependent" uncertainties or payoffs (discussed below), and complex options.

Monte Carlo simulation is a powerful technique that allows for considerable flexibility in the number and specification of the uncertainties in the decision problem. Based on assumed probability distributions for each uncertainty, a large number of possible scenarios are generated for the underlying project cash flows or value. The real option value is then calculated for each of these scenarios, and the average of these values is discounted back to the present.[11] The Monte Carlo valuation approach is useful when the cash flows from a project are "path-dependent" – that is, when they depend on prior decisions taken by the firm. While it has traditionally been difficult to use this approach to value American options, new techniques are being developed to address this shortcoming.[12]

The "risk-adjusted decision tree" is a more general, if more involved, approach. These trees allow for multiple decisions and uncertainties over time. The basic principle of such trees is that risk-adjusted (risk-neutral) probabilities are specified for the systematic, or market, uncertainties, and "actual" probabilities (generally termed "objective" probabilities by finance practitioners and "subjective" probabilities by decision analysis practitioners) are used for the private or diversifiable risks.[13]

All of the techniques described above are being used in practice to evaluate investments. The dominant methods seem to be binomial (or trinomial) lattices, Monte Carlo simulation, and risk-adjusted decision trees. The particular technique used, and

---

9 See John Hull (2000), *Options, Futures, and Other Derivatives*, 4th Edition, Prentice Hall, for a more detailed description of the "risk-neutral" valuation approach, as it is often referred to, and the option valuation techniques that build on this approach.

10 See Timothy Luehrman (1998), "Investment Opportunities as Real Options: Getting Started with the Numbers," *Harvard Business Review*, or Aswath Damodaran (2000), "The Promise of Real Options," *Journal of Applied Corporate Finance*, for illustrations of the use of the Black-Scholes model to value real options.

11 The probabilities of the scenarios can be risk-adjusted, or the cash flows can be risk-adjusted in other ways, but in either case, a risk-free rate is used for discounting. Note that the Monte Carlo procedure described here is different than Monte-Carlo simulations used by firms outside of a real options context to obtain risk profiles of a project or to examine the sensitivity of values to simultaneous changes in several input parameters.

12 See Francis Longstaff and Eduardo Schwartz (2001), "Valuing American Options by Simulation: A Simple Least-Squares Approach," *Review of Financial Studies*.

13 See James Smith and Robert Nau (1995), "Valuing Risky Projects: Option Pricing Theory and Decision Analysis" *Management Science*. This is also referred to sometimes as a "no-arbitrage" decision tree.

the way in which it is implemented, depends on the sophistication of the user, the amount of time available to conduct the analysis, and the type of project being studied.

The Black-Scholes formula was used sparingly by the firms in our sample. The following limitations of this approach were mentioned several times: corporate investments are much more complex than the simple European options the Black-Scholes formula is designed to value; the assumption of lognormally distributed project values is generally not appropriate; the formula is a "black box" and thus it is not easy to intuitively understand or explain where the value comes from; and the "volatility" input is difficult to estimate in practice.

Where the Black-Scholes formula is used, it is usually seen as a quick and easy way to arrive at a rough value for simple investment opportunities, such as an option to expand a manufacturing facility that can be exercised only at a specific date, or a growth option to launch a new product, where follow-on products are ignored. Since the Black-Scholes formula is well known even to those who are less familiar with option pricing, in some cases the formula is also used to validate the value produced by tree-based models. While this validation may be misleading, or may not be possible in many instances, for simple problems this use of Black-Scholes might provide some reassurance to senior management that the tree-based models are indeed correctly specified.

Although binomial trees and decision trees have many common characteristics (discrete time periods, two or three possible values for each uncertainty in each period, risk-adjusted probabilities), the choice of tree structure and terminology used by those we interviewed typically reflected the background of the managers as well as the complexity of the project being evaluated. Binomial models are predominantly used by those with finance training who are looking at relatively straightforward investment problems.

A typical application of the binomial model involves a single decision, such as launching a new online venture, expanding generating capacity, exercising a contractual option to purchase an aircraft, or exiting a market. It also usually involves a single underlying uncertain variable – usually the present value of the underlying project – that aggregates several uncertainties such as market size, market share, production yield, and price.

Such problems present a close analogy to standard call or put options on financial securities, where the present value of the underlying project is analogous to the price of the underlying financial asset. However, since the underlying asset value is not given, but must instead be calculated, the accuracy of this technique rests on the ability to properly estimate the underlying project value using a risk-adjusted discount rate that is based on financial market information. Specifically, this requires the existence of other investments with the same blend of underlying uncertainties, and requires faith in a model that relates rates of return to risk (such as the Capital Asset Pricing Model (CAPM)).

Many projects call for much more detailed modeling than can be captured in traditional binomial trees. For instance, an R&D investment at a pharmaceutical or biotech firm requires investment at different stages, and uncertainty about discovery must be modeled separately from other variables, such as market share and market size, since it influences the investment decisions at each stage. Similarly, for an oil and gas firm, uncertainty about the size of reserves or the technical feasibility of developing an oil field affects early exploration and development decisions, whereas the price of oil may have a more significant impact on downstream drilling decisions.

By decoupling project-specific uncertainties (such as those related to discovery and development) from market-wide uncertainties (e.g., price or consumer demand), probabilities in the decision tree can be more carefully estimated. Probability estimates for project-specific uncertainties are typically obtained from subject matter experts, and do not need to be risk-adjusted since they represent risks that can be diversified by shareholders. By contrast, risk-adjusted probabilities for market risks, such as the price of commodities or the level of interest rates, can be estimated using market price information from bond, equity, futures, and options markets.

Some firms are indeed using decision trees (or binomial trees) correctly by carefully calculating risk-adjusted cash flows and then using risk-free discount rates.[14] This ensures that decisions are

14 For an explanation of this discounting method and two alternatives to it, see the article in this issue by James Hodder and Antonio Mello, "Valuing Real Options: Can Risk-Adjusted Discounting Be Made to Work?".

consistent with the preferences of shareholders, as reflected in the risk-return relationships observed in financial markets. However, decision trees often appear to be used to generate actual (not risk-adjusted) contingent cash flows, and these cash flows are then discounted at the firm's cost of capital. This procedure implicitly assumes that the risk of the project is similar to the risk of the firm's overall portfolio of assets-in-place and future opportunities. While this is not an appropriate assumption in many cases – especially for growth options such as R&D investments that have very high risk – it still likely represents a significant improvement over using standard DCF techniques based on point estimates of cash flows.

Some firms are using Monte Carlo simulation to directly value investments with option-like features. For instance, several power companies use Monte Carlo simulation to value generating assets by viewing the assets as giving the firm a series of independent European options to generate and sell electricity over time. Since electricity prices tend to spike periodically and then return to "normal" levels (i.e., they are "mean-reverting"), Monte Carlo simulation is much better suited to value European options on electricity than the Black-Scholes formula, which relies on the lognormality assumption. As with the tree approaches, the evolution of electricity prices must be appropriately risk-adjusted in the simulation in order to value the generating assets accurately.

Other firms are using Monte Carlo simulation indirectly to support valuation by other means, or to provide distributions of project values for risk management purposes. For instance, some firms use Monte Carlo simulation to generate a distribution for the value of an underlying "developed" project using distributions of variables such as price, market share, and market size that determine the project's cash flows and value. This volatility is then used to generate a binomial tree for the evolution of the project's value over time, and the value of an American option to invest in the project is calculated using the binomial option pricing model.

When applied in this analytic mode, real options is used primarily in the operations functions of companies whose managers have strong quantitative skills and training in finance. For example, perhaps the most common application in this context is transaction evaluation and risk management

in the trading operations of energy firms. These are highly competitive businesses driven by transactions, where there is constant pressure both to construct more profitable deals and to find better ways of analyzing them. Other common applications involve capacity planning and supply chain management in manufacturing firms.

Real options has thus clearly found considerable acceptance in an analytical role in sophisticated companies with flexible investments. Companies seem to have moved away from simple closed-form approaches with limited applicability, such as Black-Scholes, and toward reliance on one of three related methods: binomial lattices, Monte Carlo simulation, and risk-adjusted decision trees.

Real options as an organizational process

Most firms have a variety of processes for evaluating and managing capital investments, both for individual projects as well as for the firm's portfolio of projects. These processes are referred to as the "portfolio process," the "capital budgeting process," or "the business case process." Such processes should be, and generally are, linked to other management processes, such as risk management and internal performance evaluation. In some firms these processes are focused on specific applications such as R&D, exploration and production, or e-business, whereas in other firms they are enterprise-wide.

These processes typically have strong, formal organizational and analytical components. Organizationally, the process is usually run by a working group of specialists from both the corporate level and the business units. The corporate-level specialists tend to refine and oversee the process, and they report to senior management in strategy or finance. The business unit specialists are more responsible for executing the process itself, specifically the investment evaluation. The working group is guided by both business unit and corporate management, and draws upon experts within and outside the firm as necessary.

Analytically, these processes are generally divided into three phases. In an initial, largely qualitative phase, the capital investment issue is structured or framed. What is the value metric?

ADOPTION OF REAL OPTIONS AT INTEL

Is it worth investing capital today to develop the shell of a manufacturing facility that can be quickly fitted with equipment and started up if demand surges for a company's products? This was a strategic decision faced by Intel back in 1996. Using best estimates of future production volumes, a traditional analysis would likely have shown that the expected benefit of excess production capacity was lower than the opportunity cost of tying up valuable capital in idle physical assets. However, key analysts at Intel recognized that this traditional analysis would miss the key feature of this investment – management flexibility.

These analysts recognized that this investment was analogous to buying a call option. Based on this understanding, the analysts valued the investment using a binomial lattice model, with demand as the key underlying uncertainty. The lattice used risk-adjusted probabilities to reflect the fact that demand had a risk component that was systematically tied to the overall state of the economy. This approach properly captured the value to Intel's shareholders of management's ability to add capacity quickly should future demand increase significantly. It clearly indicated that the investment had significant positive value.

Once the analysis was complete, it was presented to senior management. The presentation was designed to address three key issues. First, in intuitive language, what is driving the value creation, and what are you picking up that would be missed by standard valuation techniques? Second, can the details of the analysis be laid out carefully, including a clear explanation for how risk is being accounted for? Third, can the analysis be validated in any way?

Addressing the first question was simple – in fact, senior management appreciated the value of

talking about addressing future capacity needs using the language of options. Laying out the analysis, however, required a more carefully executed presentation. But it too was well received, perhaps due to the analytic capabilities of senior management in a technically driven company. As for validation, two approaches were used. First, the more widely known Black-Scholes formula was used to demonstrate that, given particular assumptions and inputs, the binomial model indeed produces a very similar value. Second, sensitivity analysis was conducted on some of the key variables in the valuation analysis to give management a sense that the changes in valuation in response to different input values were in line with their intuition. Moreover, it confirmed that the value of the investment was not overly sensitive to estimation error for the inputs.

Based on the success of this initial application and the resulting management buy-in, momentum has developed behind more widespread application of these techniques for similar applications across the firm. Presentations have been made to the company's CFO and division comptrollers, and over 300 other employees have been exposed to real options over the last three years through introductory seminars. With greater recognition of the potential benefits of real options analysis, expectations are that the implementation of these techniques will continue to spread throughout the organization. This will likely require more intensive training of employees performing the valuations, the creation of a centralized group that can advise on and review the valuations, and more streamlined methods for quick application of real options for smaller projects.

What are the alternative investment levels? How do different projects in a portfolio interact? In a second, largely quantitative phase, analytical tools are used to quantify the value of individual projects or portfolios of projects, and to prioritize projects based on their value and resource requirements. Finally, in another largely qualitative phase, the results of the analysis are summarized for review and approval by the appropriate senior management.

In many companies, real options is seen as an important evolution in techniques for valuing investments. As a result, these firms are relying on an investment evaluation process built around real options or, more commonly, are overlaying real options onto an existing process. The success of this overlay strategy is likely to depend on the nature of the existing process and the types of real options tools that are added to that process. Companies that have a legacy of formal investment evaluation under uncertainty generally have experienced success when adopting a real options approach. On the other hand, firms that have approached investment evaluation rather informally, perhaps by using point forecasts and high hurdle rates, typically have difficulty incorporating real options. In these firms, real options is often seen as competing with, rather than enhancing, the existing approach.

Typically, the addition of real options changes the process in some important ways. First, it reinforces a multi-disciplinary view in which the team proceeds through stages of framing, information gathering and analysis, and presentation of results. Second, it increases the emphasis on shareholder value, as opposed to other "intermediate" metrics related to production, revenue, or market share. Third, it puts a great deal of emphasis on dynamics and learning. Fourth, it changes the analytical tools underlying the process. Because of the more complex and non-standardized nature of options in this context, there tends to be a greater reliance on Monte Carlo simulation and risk-adjusted decision trees in particular, rather than Black-Scholes and binomial lattices.

One feature of real options in this context that deserves separate mention is the importance of follow-up. In many cases, interviewees made the point that the value calculated using real options is realized only if the firm actually executes the plan. Furthermore, they made the point that a major contribution of the real options approach is that it enforces the concept of ongoing project management. Without a real options approach, there is a tendency to conduct an evaluation simply to decide whether or not to make an investment. The management of the investment is not tied to the original analysis. In contrast, with real options, one of the key results is a roadmap of future actions. Successful firms use this roadmap to revisit an accepted project on a regular basis to ensure that appropriate decisions are being made over time (i.e., that all the embedded options are being optimally exercised). Such a project management process is particularly important in cases when there are no formal incentives for executing these options, a point we will return to shortly.

So far, the major use of real options in this project and portfolio management organizational mode is in specific areas of capital investment.

Key areas include exploration and production investments in oil and gas firms, generation plant investments in power firms, R&D portfolios in pharmaceutical and biotech firms, and technology investment portfolios in high-tech firms. In some of these firms, real options has been integrated with the broad capital investment process and the firm has adopted real options enterprise-wide.

By mapping out both uncertainties and decisions over time, real options provides an appropriate way to track not only value creation but also the risk profile of a project or portfolio of projects. Indeed, several firms reported that they have enterprise risk management processes that use the value and risk profile emerging from a real options analysis rather than a DCF analysis. For example, leading commodity-driven firms manage portfolios of derivative contracts and physical assets in this manner. Option tools are used to value both types of assets, as well as to calculate risk exposures that are then integrated across these two classes of assets and then appropriately managed.

There has been considerable discussion about designing internal performance appraisal and incentive compensation systems to reward the creation and optimal exercise of real options within the corporation. Many managers agree that current systems often provide incentives that conflict with the optimal management of the firm's portfolio of real options. For example, how many managers are rewarded for exercising a put option to contract or shut down their own business area? Or, as an example of a more subtle conflict between conventional performance measures and value maximization, how many oil and gas managers are rewarded for delaying production (and forgoing current earnings) until oil prices move well "into-the-money?"

In sum, while some firms have succeeded at integrating real options deep into their capital investment, project portfolio, and/or risk management processes, real options has yet to be formally integrated into performance evaluation and compensation.[15] But when one considers that most

---

15 Similarly, while the financing decisions of the firm should carefully reflect the risk-return profile of its portfolio of assets-in-place as well as its growth options, there do not appear to be formal systems developed to precisely tailor financial instruments or contingent financing plans based on formal real options analyses such as decision trees.

EVALUATING AND MANAGING STRATEGIC INVESTMENTS AT TEXACO

Texaco is one of a handful of major global energy companies. A great part of the success of Texaco and similar firms is their ability to identify the right major capital investments, both internal and external, and manage them appropriately. During the 1980s and early 1990s, this effort was taking place in an increasingly challenging environment. Oil and gas prices were going through major swings, including record low levels, that made intelligent investment and operational planning difficult. In addition, a new breed of "super-major" energy firms was emerging that put Texaco in direct competition with companies with substantially greater resources.

In the mid-1990s, Texaco began to recognize the critical importance of top-notch investment valuation and management. Texaco had strong analytical skills, using a variety of techniques such as DCF, Monte Carlo simulation, and decision analysis, and was doing quite well. However, experiences applying these techniques to competitive bidding for assets and in analyzing ventures in new technology were sometimes disappointing. Seeking improvements, Texaco began to explore the concept of real options, recognizing its superiority over conventional approaches. This led to an interest in piloting the application of real options on an appropriate investment opportunity.

Around the same time, real options had undergone a transformation from an academic specialty to a business-oriented practice with strong analytical and organizational foundations. Texaco found that this superior version of real options had several appealing features. First, it began with a robust and broader strategic framing of the opportunity in question, something very important to Texaco management. Second, it drew heavily on familiar tools such as DCF, decision analysis, and finance theory. Third, it

could be applied as a scaleable process that dovetailed with other management processes.

Given this background, Texaco decided to test, and potentially adopt, a real options approach. With the help of outside consultants, Texaco conducted a major pilot project on a challenging exploration and production opportunity. This project was successful at achieving buy-in among both executives and the rank-and-file. Specialists were trained in key business areas, and Texaco began wider application of the approach in other exploration and production activities as well as new technology businesses, new ventures like e-business, and an international downstream portfolio. Real options has become a key enabler to the way Texaco evaluates and manages major strategic investments.

With a great deal of accumulated experience in individual real options applications over the past few years, the issue for Texaco is how to take the next step. For the real options approach to contribute fully to Texaco's success, it needs to be better integrated with other management processes, rather than being viewed as separate and different. Two key management processes are dynamic project management to execute the investment plan, and performance appraisal. The latter is a key to providing incentives for optimal exercise of real options and value-based project management. Texaco also aspires to combine the real options approach with corporate risk management. Finally, Texaco aims, where practical, to incorporate real options into the portfolio planning process in order to provide the best overall mix of investments and strategic positioning at the corporate level. For maximum benefit, Texaco believes in a more holistic and orchestrated deployment of real options. While this is a substantial challenge, Texaco continues to move forward in this endeavor.

firms have been using real options for fewer than five years, this is not at all surprising.

WHAT ARE THE PRIMARY SUCCESS FACTORS IN USING REAL OPTIONS?

The approaches to implementing real options taken by the many different corporate managers we spoke with are quite varied. Nevertheless, whether by choice or by default, it is clear that there is a common path to the successful adoption of real options – in fact, it is a carefully staged process of the kind that typifies real options thinking. Much like the development and launch of an innovative new product, the adoption of real options involves phases analogous to R&D, prototype design, marketing, and full-scale "production"; and important gates must be passed early on to sustain momentum in the adoption process. The key steps in this process are:

♦ conducting one or more pilot projects that are explicitly experimental;
♦ getting buy-in from senior-level and rank-and-file managers based on the pilot projects;
♦ codifying real options through an expert working group, specialist training, and customization; and
♦ institutionalizing and integrating real options firm-wide.

At the completion of each stage, companies choose whether or not to continue. Nevertheless, for the vast majority of the managers interviewed, the expectation is that the firm will proceed through all these stages, though at a pace that may differ considerably among companies. In general, companies seem to be pleased with their initial work with real options, and are eager to move on to further stages, perhaps held back temporarily by lack of senior level buy-in, as we discuss below. Firms at the later stages are breaking new ground – they have the momentum to move on, but are dealing with both analytic and organizational challenges, and have relatively few role models.

Pilot projects

Very few companies want to, or should, proceed with the adoption of real options in one leap. Instead, most firms begin by experimenting with one or more pilot projects.[16] These pilot projects need to be carefully designed not only to maximize what is learned about applying real options techniques, but also to facilitate moving forward with adoption of these techniques based on a successful first implementation. Given these twin, but sometimes conflicting, goals, substantial effort must be spent on putting together the right team, choosing the most appropriate project(s) to experiment with, and benchmarking the analysis.

In most firms, the impetus to explore the use of real option techniques has been coming more from individuals involved in business development, strategic planning, operations, or marketing and much less so from those in treasury or other divisional finance groups. Real options models have immediate appeal to strategic planners since the dynamic modeling of uncertainty and decisions is broadly consistent with, and tends to reinforce, their intuition. In contrast, financial analysts are more apt to follow conventional methods employed by investment bankers and other analysts on Wall Street. Few investment bankers have to date embraced real options analysis, in large part because of the difficulty in applying real options to value a whole company rather than a single project.

One of the strongest arguments that can be made for real options is that it provides a framework that bridges the longstanding gap between strategy and finance. In fact, companies that have been quick to embrace real options models have appreciated that it presents not only a valuation tool but a framework to incorporate knowledge from various parts of the organization into the investment decision-making process. As a result, in exploring the use of real options in the organization, cross-disciplinary teams should be formed to leverage and combine all this knowledge.

Employees from operations, for instance, are often the first to recognize option features that are built into a project, such as options to expand and contract production. They also have expertise

---

16 Getting approval for a limited budget to perform a pilot project experiment has not seemed to pose a major problem in most firms, particularly if there is an advocate who has credibility with senior management.

in understanding the technical risks faced by the company that are often at the heart of the analysis. The marketing group has experience in understanding demand volatility and developing strategies to learn about market conditions before fully ramping up a project. Scientists and engineers are the appropriate experts to estimate success probabilities for different stages of R&D and resources required at each stage. Finance professionals can best appreciate the interaction between a project's risk profile and the impact on a firm's cost of capital and financing strategy. All of these aspects of a project must be integrated into a successful real options analysis.

To the extent that there are people in the organization who have had experience using decision analysis or option pricing techniques, these individuals should clearly be included in the pilot team. Frequently, outside consultants with experience in implementing real options models and processes are brought in to facilitate and participate in the pilot project analysis.

The selection of an appropriate pilot project is important as it will provide a showcase for the application of real options. In most firms, one can readily identify projects for which the use of real options is likely to provide noticeably different results from those obtained through traditional techniques. Projects that involve high volatility, large irreversible investments, and significant flexibility are good candidates.[17] While projects that have staged investments over long horizons (a series of growth options) would also highlight the importance of real options, these projects may take a long time to "prove" their value and thus provide empirical demonstration of the benefit of using real options analysis. In companies with projects (e.g., new business development) or contracts (e.g., for commodity trading) where real option ideas provide a natural fit, support for the adoption of real options analysis seems to come much more easily and quickly.

Firms that have benchmarked a real options analysis of a pilot project against a more traditional analysis that the firm would have typically followed (e.g., a DCF analysis) have found that it becomes easier to make a case for adopting real options techniques. This benchmarking exercise can serve to highlight, with the help of a concrete illustration, what is the same as and what is different from traditional approaches. The valuations generated by the alternative techniques will likely be different; but in addition, the real options approach may produce new insights about how to time or scale the investment, and about how to create flexibility in the future.

Many of the managers interviewed emphasized that great care must be taken in choosing pilot projects. In firms where there is resistance or reluctance to adopt real options, a single well-publicized failure (whether legitimate or not) can mean the end of the process. Consequently, firms that have successfully moved beyond the pilot stage typically are either careful, lucky, or both.

Senior level and rank-and-file buy-in

Assuming that the pilot projects demonstrate the feasibility and desirability of a real options approach, the next critical step is senior-level buy-in. One or more successful pilots can go a long way toward demonstrating the value of real options. However, most firms have difficulty changing processes without management support for such changes. It was quite evident from our discussions that the single most important catalyst for widespread implementation of real options in the firm's decision-making process is the buy-in of key senior-level executives. At many firms, the "pull" by senior management is lacking, and the process of selling real options internally comes more from the "push" of one or a few intellectually curious and entrepreneurial individuals who appreciate the potential of the real options framework.

There are several reasons why getting senior level buy-in has been, or continues to be, difficult at many firms. First, and perhaps most obvious, senior executives are often too busy handling issues requiring immediate attention to be willing to spend time to learn about real options. Second,

---

17 Most firms are equally able to identify projects for which traditional DCF analysis provides relatively accurate valuations. These include projects where there would be little to no value for the embedded options – either because most of the investment needs to be made immediately (there are few or insignificant downstream decisions), or because the level of uncertainty is relatively low.

there is often considerable skepticism about new techniques, particularly if the "push" is coming from external consultants rather than from an internal champion. This skepticism may be increased by the perceived complexity of the "Nobel-Prize-winning valuation tools" involved, and perhaps even by their association with well-publicized fiascos involving derivatives and their pricing techniques, such as the failure of Long-Term Capital Management.

Third, there occasionally is a perception that real options may simply be another way for strategic planners to increase the value of pet projects. This perception may have become more prevalent in the wake of the recent new-economy hysteria, when real options was sometimes promoted as a magic bullet to justify the high valuations of dot-coms and other high-tech companies. While it is true that real options will likely deliver a higher value than would a conventional DCF analysis that ignores options embedded in the project, this should not necessarily be a red flag. Such projects were often accepted based on overly optimistic, qualitative assessments of strategic value (such as the creation of future growth options, or flexibility). Real options provides a way to inject discipline into this decision process by quantifying these benefits, providing a tougher standard.

Given these challenges, how then is senior-level buy-in achieved? Our interviews suggest a few lessons. First, rather than beginning with the technical superiority of the analytic approach, the arguments in favor of real options must be couched in simple, compelling terms. For the senior managements of most firms, these terms typically involve an appeal to shareholder value and competitive advantage. Second, to the extent possible, direct evidence of the benefits of the approach should be provided in the form of the pilot projects or examples from outside the firm. Third, an approach must be suggested that recognizes the unique context of the firm, particularly the available resources. Some firms have employed outside consultants to help communicate such a story to senior management, but the case for using real options ultimately needs to come from within the organization.

While buy-in at the senior level is a necessary condition for the widespread acceptance of real options, it is not a sufficient condition. As with

senior management, rank-and-file employees are invariably busy with their existing roles and obligations, particularly in today's flatter and leaner organizations. Middle- and lower-level employees may look at real options as one more burden, especially if senior management has not made an appropriate commitment to incremental resources. Furthermore, these employees may have witnessed a variety of management fads ("flavors of the month"), and may be legitimately skeptical about the longevity of interest in real options. Again, senior management can play a role in alleviating this concern.

These issues can be compounded by inertia – the tendency to rely on known techniques – and by a lack of knowledge about real options that in turn will exaggerate its complexity. Several firms have successfully addressed resistance to real options through a concerted marketing effort directed at key personnel in the rank-and-file, involving presentations by participants in the pilot stage, circulation of other internal white papers, and even intranet sites dealing specifically with real options. Companies with many engineers and scientists tend to experience very quick acceptance of these techniques, presumably because of the ability of these individuals to understand probability distributions and their penchant for logic-based processes. One particularly effective technique is to combine a pilot project success story with a senior management endorsement.

Codifying real options

The combination of successful pilot projects and widespread buy-in sets the stage for broader use and refinement of the real options approach. Once the interest is well-established, it is critical to lower the barrier to entry by reducing the time and effort required to use real options. We refer to this as "codifying" real options. The key elements of such a plan include:

- developing a "scaleable" real option process that integrates appropriately with existing processes;
- creating a working group of experts to coordinate the real options process; and
- training specialists in key business areas.

Given the pressures of today's economy, most companies are reluctant to adopt processes that consume large amounts of calendar or people time. It is thus important to design the real options process to work with, and not against, existing processes. At the same time, the process should also be scaleable. A billion-dollar investment in a new manufacturing facility can and should be analyzed in a very systematic and detailed manner, not only to decide whether or not to proceed with the investment, but also how best to design the facility for future flexibility needs. In many firms, this is the primary application of real options. In such cases, a scaled-down analysis is not necessary but compatibility with existing processes is likely to be a major concern.

In contrast, an in-house venture capital group that has five employees and is evaluating 20 potential deals each quarter has to be able to conduct a real options analysis in an accelerated time frame. For large firms that are constantly evaluating a large number of projects, the ability to adjust the scale of the decision-making process in relation to the size of the investment is critical. As real options begins to be adopted by different groups in an organization, templates and guidelines should be developed for different types of problems (e.g., a capacity planning decision, an R&D investment, an equity investment, or a licensing agreement). These templates and guidelines should be coordinated as much as possible with other management processes.

A successful real options process typically requires oversight and coordination by a true "working" (as opposed to "managing") group. This working group, consisting of several experts, tends to be housed in the treasury department or in an in-house consulting group. As analysts throughout the organization begin to apply real options techniques, this group of experts can oversee the necessary quality control. Even if real options techniques are "hardwired" through the use of a set of internally developed standard templates, or of some externally developed software package, users may not fully understand what the inputs represent, or how to properly estimate them. Specifically, since inputs such as volatility, mean reversion, jumps, convenience yields, and correlations do not appear in standard DCF applications, there is justifiable cause for concern that lack of

experience could lead to misspecification of these inputs.[18]

This group of experts should also be involved in the training of a broad cross-section of employees. It is important for key finance and strategy personnel to be well trained in real options, and to be able to recognize when an evaluation calls for real options and when it does not.[19] It is equally important, however, for individuals from operations, marketing, and strategy to understand the benefits of the real options framework, and to develop a mindset that aims to create and preserve real options when designing projects or contracts. A handful of companies we spoke with had already exposed hundreds of their employees to the real options methodology, and had provided more detailed training to dozens of key personnel who would be conducting the analyses.

Institutionalizing real options

Once real options has been codified, the firm has reached the stage where real options can be institutionalized across the firm and integrated fully with other processes and systems. A few companies have begun to explore this stage in the adoption of real options, and they are arriving there in

---

18 Volatility estimates, or the probabilities of the stochastic variables reaching particular values over time, need to be obtained from available market or internal data, or from subject matter experts. For prices of an input or output commodity, it is also crucial to understand characteristics such as mean reversion and spikes, rather than using standard assumptions of log-normality. The "convenience yield," which is analogous to a dividend yield for a stock, is often difficult to specify; it captures the loss in project value from waiting (either due to forgone profits or the effect of competition), and may reflect differences between forward and spot prices on commodities. The degree of correlation between uncertain variables is another important variable that must be carefully estimated. For instance, while revenues and expenses associated with a new product may both be highly uncertain, if they are closely correlated, the margin on selling the product may be much less uncertain. Finally, in some applications such as R&D, the timing of each stage (analogous to the maturity date of an option) can be highly variable, adding more complexity into the analysis.

19 For instance, some options are so deep-in-the-money, i.e. will obviously be exercised in the future, that the incremental value that comes from "the right, but not the obligation" to make the future investment is minimal, and option pricing techniques are not required to properly value the opportunity.

somewhat different ways. Some firms were already using decision analysis and related techniques in the 1980s, and transformed these processes into real options analysis techniques in the 1990s. These firms have largely progressed through the first three stages and are now actively interested in the "institutionalization" stage. Other firms were using option valuation techniques to price contractual options, and the evaluation of physical assets to incorporate their option features became a natural extension. Integrating the risk management of the physical and contractual sides of their business followed naturally as well. To our knowledge, only one or two firms have made major external pronouncements to key stakeholders (e.g., Wall Street analysts) regarding their use of real options. Most of the firms in our survey have passed quickly through the early gates of the staged adoption process. But, given that the overwhelming majority have only recently become interested in real options, it is not surprising that full-scale institutionalization has not yet occurred. According to many of our interviewees, however, this appears to be only a matter of time, the inevitable result of the diffusion of real option techniques throughout the organization.

WHAT DOES THE FUTURE HOLD FOR REAL OPTIONS?

Some observers may feel that real options remains primarily an academic pursuit. Others feel that its fortunes are tied to the condition of the new economy, and that its prospects have dimmed with the plunge in Nasdaq prices. Our discussions with corporate practitioners paint a different picture. It appears that a quiet, modest evolution is occurring in important parts of many companies. These firms have built on the academic foundations, drawn upon research and consulting resources, and are actively adopting the real options approach.

Where, then, is real options going? Will this process accelerate or stall, and how will the practice of real options change over time?

Based on our interviews, the evidence seems quite clear. First, real options will serve not simply as an analytical tool, but as a general way of thinking and, in a more rigorous and intensive way,

as an organizational process. Second, and related, there will likely be increasing convergence among the various real options approaches, particularly the "decision analytic" and "option pricing" approaches.

In the long run, the continued acceptance of real options will likely depend on the answer to one very important question: Does real options help managers make better investment decisions – decisions that end up creating more wealth for the firm's shareholders? Based on our interviews, there is an overwhelming – in fact, seemingly unanimous – feeling that the answer to this question is yes. Unfortunately, it is impossible to obtain definitive proof that this process indeed leads to the right decision in an individual case, since one can observe only whether the outcome is good or bad, and the outcome is tied as much to the uncertain world as to the decision. However, over long periods of time, companies that make better decisions should prosper relative to those whose decision processes are deficient. Furthermore, if firms are able to create options and then monetize their value by divesting assets or businesses – or by selling equity positions in specific businesses in their portfolio – the gains from creating options at a discount to their value will be more quickly recognized.[20]

While the benefits of real options will determine its long-term acceptance, other factors can affect the rate of adoption dramatically. Two phenomena indicate that this rate will increase. The first is a network effect; as more companies speak the language and use similar valuation techniques for evaluating projects internally, other companies will follow their example. Such an effect is already detectable in the energy and life sciences industries. The second is a "push" from Wall Street. While real options is a difficult tool to apply accurately in valuing an entire company, it is likely that these techniques will gradually take hold on Wall Street. In so doing, they will provide a common framework and language by which value will be measured and communicated in the future.

---

20 Companies that issued stock on an internally generated dot-com were able to quickly realize the value of their Internet growth options. It may well be that they created value for the parent company not by creating options at a cost below the "true value" of the option, but rather by taking advantage of overvaluation of these options in the market.

Appendix: Survey Questions

I. *Exposure*

Where/How Did You Learn About Real Options?

1. What does "real options" mean to your firm?
2. How and when did your firm learn about it?
3. What was it about real options that interested your firm?
4. How was interest in real options communicated within your firm?
5. Who in your firm has expressed the most interest in real options? The least interest?
6. Have your stakeholders (e.g., Board, equity analysts) expressed interest in real options?

II. *Applications*

Where Have You Applied Real Options?

1. When and where did your firm first apply real options?
2. Where have you applied real options? In particular, what organizations, what issues?
3. How widely is real options used? In particular, individual projects, portfolios?

III. *Methods*

How Have You Applied Real Options?

1. How has it been applied organizationally? In particular, a center of excellence, consultants?
2. What background do real options practitioners have in your firm, and what training do they get?
3. How has it been applied analytically? In particular, trees, binomial lattices, Monte Carlo, Black-Scholes?
4. How have the applications changed as you gain more experience?
5. What kind of follow-up process do you have after a real options project to monitor progress?
6. How does real options interact with other management systems, such as compensation?

IV. *Results*

How Is Real Options Regarded?

1. How has your firm reacted to real options? In particular, is your firm satisfied? Why?
2. What has been your biggest success, failure? Why?
3. What are the major challenges you now see in applying real options? Why?
4. What do you now find most valuable, least valuable about real options? Why?
5. Which executives in your firm are now most supportive of real options? Why?

V. *The Future*

Where Is Real Options Going?

1. Do you expect the use of real options to grow in your firm? Why?
2. Do you expect the use of real options to grow generally? Why?
3. What changes must be made to the practice of real options to increase its acceptance? Why?

PART III

The Financing Decision I: Capital Structure

Does capital structure matter? And, if so, how and why does it matter? Although corporate finance scholars have debated these questions for at least 40 years, definitive answers still seem as elusive as they did in 1958 when Miller and Modigliani published the first of their two famous "irrelevance" propositions.

Following the M&M propositions, academic researchers in the 1960s and '70s turned their attention to market "imperfections" that might make firm value depend on capital structure. The main suspects were (1) a tax code that encourages debt by making interest payments but not dividends tax-deductible and (2) expected costs of financial distress that rise with increasing amounts of debt. Toward the end of the '70s, there was also discussion of "signaling" effects, such as the tendency for stock prices to fall significantly on the announcement of new equity issues and to rise on the news of stock buybacks. These effects seemed to confirm the existence of large "information costs" that could influence financing choices in predictable ways.

Such information costs took center stage in the ongoing debate when, in 1984, Stewart Myers devoted his President's address to the American Finance Association to what he called "The Capital Structure Puzzle." The puzzle was this: Most academic discussions of capital structure began with the assumption that companies making

financing decisions are guided by a *target capital structure* – a proportion of debt to equity that management aims to achieve, if not at all times, then at least as a long-run average. But the empirical evidence suggested otherwise. Rather than adhering to leverage targets, Myers observed, most large U.S. public companies appeared to follow a financing "pecking order." They used retained earnings rather than external financing when possible; and if outside capital was necessary, they issued debt first and equity only as a last resort. Based on the Darwinian principle that efficient practices prevail, Myers suggested that the pecking order maximized firm value by minimizing expected information costs – mainly, it seems, by reducing to near zero the probability that the firm would *ever* have to issue equity.

The vulnerable point in the pecking order is its seeming blanket endorsement of financial "slack"; that is, because internal funds are always preferred to outside financing, the model appears to imply that managers should hoard capital and so reduce their dependence on capital markets. Then, in 1986, Harvard's Michael Jensen entered the capital structure debate with a very different message. Pointing to the success of LBOs and leveraged acquisitions, Jensen argued that, in the case of mature companies, heavy debt financing could add value by *eliminating* financial slack and thus curbing a managerial tendency to overinvest in industries with excess capacity. And, as if to confirm that

Jensen was on the right track, the capital markets continued to supply large numbers of LBOs and other leveraged deals through the rest of the '80s – and, except for a brief halt in the early '90s, for much of that decade as well.

This section starts with Merton Miller's reassessment of the "The Modigliani–Miller Propositions After Thirty Years." It may seem odd to begin with an article by Miller, since the M&M propositions seem to say that capital structure does not affect corporate value. But, as Miller writes in the article,

the view that capital structure is literally irrelevant or that "nothing matters" in corporate finance, though still sometimes attributed to us . . . is far what we ever actually said about the real-world applications of our theoretical propositions.

The M&M propositions were intended to hold only under a deliberately restrictive set of conditions, the most important of which are as follows: (1) there are no significant differences in the tax treatment accorded different securities; (2) reliable information about the firm's earnings prospects is freely available to investors (and, by implication, what management knows about the future is not significantly different from what investors know); and (3) corporate investment decisions, as mentioned above, are not influenced by financing (or dividend) choices.

The empirical import of the M&M propositions – and thus their central message to corporate practitioners – can be seen by turning the propositions "on their heads." That is, if changes in corporate capital structure or dividends do increase stock values, they are likely to do so only for the following reasons: (1) they reduce taxes or transaction costs; (2) they provide a reliable "signal" to investors of management's confidence in the firm's earnings prospects; or (3) they increase the probability that management will undertake only profitable investments.

In this article, after recounting the thinking behind the propositions, Miller goes on to consider the contribution of each of these three factors to an explanation of the leveraged restructuring movement of the '80s. Part of the discussion focuses on the beneficial effect of debt finance on managerial efficiency and corporate reinvestment decisions, especially in companies in mature industries with too much "free cash flow." But the greatest stress

falls on the tax advantage of debt over equity, an argument put forth by Miller and Modigliani in 1963. In brief, the "tax-adjusted" M&M proposition says that the benefits of substituting tax-deductible interest payments for non-deductible (and thus twice-taxed) dividend payments could push the optimal capital structure *toward 100% debt* (provided, of course, the offsetting costs of high leverage are not too great).

In "Still Searching for Optimal Capital Structure," Stewart Myers argues that arriving at a company's optimal capital structure comes down largely to balancing the tax benefits of debt against financial distress costs, including the loss in value resulting from corporate underinvestment. Myers's special insight into the problem is his analysis of the "underinvestment problem" that is likely to arise when companies with valuable growth options use too much debt. And for corporate managers, his principal recommendation is that, while companies with substantial cash flow from tangible assets should rely heavily on debt financing to reduce taxes, companies whose current value derives mainly from strategic options to invest in future growth should be funded largely (if not entirely) with equity.

In "The Capital Structure Puzzle: Another Look at the Evidence," Michael Barclay and Clifford Smith summarize the empirical research on capital structure and then go on to argue that management incentives, taxes, financial distress costs, and information costs *all* appear to play important roles in corporate financing decisions. The key to reconciling the two main theories of capital structure – and thus to solving the capital structure puzzle mentioned above – lies in achieving a better understanding of the relation between corporate financing *stocks* (leverage ratios) and *flows* (specific choices between debt and equity). According to the authors, the bulk of the evidence on leverage ratios is consistent with the idea that companies have target leverage ratios, and that such targets depend primarily on one key variable: the company's investment opportunities. As a general rule – and consistent with Myers's analysis of the underinvestment problem – the larger the percentage of a firm's value that consists of intangible "growth options," the lower the leverage ratio.

But if the evidence on leverage ratios is largely consistent with the idea that companies set leverage targets, other research suggests that firms often deviate widely from their targets, particularly firms experiencing changes in profitability. Although such findings are generally viewed as evidence that corporate managers do not set target leverage ratios – or do not try very hard to achieve them – Barclay and Smith suggest another interpretation: Precisely because the information (and other) costs of issuing riskier securities can be very large, "[e]ven if companies have target leverage ratios, there will be an *optimal deviation* from those targets – one that depends on the costs associated with adjusting back to the target relative to the costs of deviating from the target." As the authors note in closing, "The next major step forward in solving the capital structure puzzle is almost certain to involve a more formal weighing of these two sets of costs."

In "What Do We Know About Stock Repurchases?," David Ikenberry and Gustavo Grullon provide a remarkably comprehensive review of a large and growing body of academic studies. In 1998 – and for the first time ever – the total dollar amount of stock repurchased by U.S. corporations exceeded their cash dividend payments. Why are companies buying back so much stock? As the authors note, repurchases play a critical economic role both in preventing mature companies from "overinvesting" and in allowing investors to move their capital from mature sectors with too much capital into high-growth industries with too little. But dividends, of course, accomplish the same function; so why are repurchases growing much more rapidly? Although the capital gains treatment of repurchases is part of the explanation, perhaps even more important is the greater "flexibility" provided by open market repurchase programs – flexibility to make small adjustments in capital structure, to exploit (or correct) perceived undervaluation of the firm's shares, and possibly even to increase the liquidity of the stock, particularly in bear markets.

"The Dividend Cut 'Heard 'Round the World'" is a joint product of the academic and business worlds, a collaboration between Professor Eugene Brigham and two practitioners, Paul Evanson, President of Florida Power and Light, and Dennis Soter, a partner of Stern Stewart & Co. More important, the article describes a successful innovation in corporate practice that lends support to one of the major theoretical insights of "modern" finance theory – the "dividend irrelevance" proposition formulated by Nobel laureates Merton Miller and Franco Modigliani almost 40 years ago.

The story the article describes is this: In May 1994, the FPL Group, the parent company of Florida Power & Light, announced a 32 percent reduction in its dividend, thereby becoming the first profitable utility to take this step. Although the initial market reaction was negative, FPL's stock has outperformed the S&P Electric Utility index by a significant margin in the two years following the announcement. Within six weeks of the dividend cut (but after a series of "roadshows" explaining FPL's decision to the investment community), at least 15 major brokerage houses had added the stock to their "buy" lists. And by the end of 1995, FPL's institutional ownership had increased from about 33 percent to 47 percent.

At the same time it announced the dividend cut, FPL also announced its intent to repurchase up to 10 million shares of its common stock. Besides providing a more tax-efficient means of distributing excess capital, FPL's partial substitution of stock repurchases for dividends was justified as a way of increasing the company's financial flexibility in advance of further deregulation and heightened competition among utilities. And, although few utilities have followed FPL's example to date, a remarkable number of U.S. companies now appear to be choosing stock repurchases in place of larger dividend increases – an appropriate response, as the authors suggest, to an increasingly competitive business environment.

The section ends with a "Roundtable" in which a small group of finance academics and practitioners discuss first the theory and then the practice of corporate capital structure and stock repurchase decisions. The case study of PepsiCo that follows Cliff Smith's initial overview of the theory suggests that putting the theory into practice can be far from straightforward. Consistent with the theory, Pepsi does have a target leverage ratio – and, as described by Assistant Treasurer Rick Thevenet, the company attempts to adhere to that target mainly by paying out much of its substantial free cash flow in the form of dividends and stock buybacks. But if the company's decision-making process appears broadly consistent with the theoretical framework, it also relies on conventional rating-agency criteria to an extent that surprises some of the panelists. After an unsuccessful attempt in the early '90s to persuade the agencies that a leverage target of 25 percent debt to (market) total capital was consistent with the company's desired single-A rating, Pepsi's management ended up adopting a policy of operating with "zero excess cash" while using the maximum leverage allowable under the agencies' guidelines for single-A companies.

Pepsi's policy of maintaining a single-A credit rating sets off a debate about the value of preserving access to capital markets "under all conditions." For example, Stern Stewart's Dennis Soter challenges the popular argument that a single-A is necessary to enable companies to fund large growth opportunities. In making his case, he cites the example of SPX Corporation, a double-B-rated company that, just 15 months after a large, leveraged Dutch-auction repurchase, acquired a company twice its size in a stand-alone, leveraged transaction. But the last word on this matter is provided by Tim Opler, a former academic who now advises corporate clients for Credit Suisse First Boston. As Opler suggests, Pepsi and SPX have very different business models; and when those differences are taken into account, both the "intelligent use of financial engineering" in the SPX case and the relative financial conservatism of Pepsi are likely to be value-adding strategies.

In the second part of the discussion, Rice University's David Ikenberry begins by offering four main corporate motives for stock repurchases: (1) to increase (or at least maintain) the target corporate leverage ratio; (2) to distribute excess capital and so prevent managers from destroying value by reinvesting in low-return projects (the free cash flow problem mentioned above); (3) to provide a more flexible and tax-efficient substitute for dividends; and (4) to "signal" and, possibly, to profit from undervaluation of the firm's shares. As in the first part of the discussion, the case of Pepsi largely supports the theory. Thevenet notes that, in the year 2000, the company generated free cash flow of $3 billion, of which $800 million was paid out in dividends and another $1.4 billion in stock buybacks. And each of the four motives cited above appears to have been at work in the design or execution of Pepsi's buyback policy.

There is also some discussion of a fifth motive for buybacks: the desire to boost earnings per share. Although this motive is perhaps the most widely cited by corporate managers, the idea that EPS considerations should be driving corporate buyback programs is shown to rest on flawed reasoning. First of all, as Pepsi's Thevenet points out, if one considers the return on the cash that companies would have otherwise earned had they not used it to buy back shares (something sellside analysts routinely fail to do), stock repurchases are "accretive" in the first year or so only for companies with P/Es lower than 20 (which is well below the S&P 500's average P/E of 27). And even in cases where buybacks do end up increasing EPS, the real source of the gains, as Ikenberry points out, is the previously low return on the assets used to fund the buyback. That is to say, the source of the gain is not some magical EPS effect, but rather the simple fact that corporate assets have been reallocated from low-return to higher-return uses. Or, to put the same thought in different words, holding excess cash on the corporate balance sheet tends to be a value-reducing investment.

The roundtable also raises questions about the most popular form of stock buybacks – namely, open market programs – and the lack of disclosure that surrounds such programs in the U.S. (though Pepsi's disclosure policy is an exception – one that is held up as a model of best practice). The lack of transparency surrounding buybacks is linked to what appears to be one of the tacit goals of many open market programs: to buy back as many shares at the lowest price possible. A number of panelists suggest that this kind of corporate "opportunism," while increasing EPS, could also end up discouraging trading and reducing liquidity. And in his closing comments, Soter goes so far as to argue that corporate buyback policy should be designed not to transfer wealth from selling to remaining shareholders, but to "share the gains from value-creating transactions." The basic premise behind Soter's argument is that, by providing more and better disclosure of their financing and governance policies, companies are likely to establish greater credibility with investors, thereby increasing the liquidity and long run value of their shares.

CHAPTER 10

The Modigliani–Miller Propositions After Thirty Years

Merton H. Miller (University of Chicago)*

It has now been 30 years since the Modigliani–Miller Propositions were first presented in "The Cost of Capital, Corporation Finance and the Theory of Investment," which appeared in the *American Economic Review* in June 1958. I have been invited, if not to celebrate, at least to mark, the event with a retrospective look at what we set out to do on that occasion and an appraisal of where the Propositions stand today after three decades of intense scrutiny and often bitter controversy.

Some of these controversies can by now be regarded as settled. Our Proposition I, which holds the value of a firm to be independent of its capital structure (its debt/equity ratio), is accepted as an implication of equilibrium in perfect capital markets. The validity of our then novel arbitrage proof of that proposition is also no longer disputed, and essentially similar arbitrage proofs are now common throughout finance.[1] Propositions analogous to, and

often even called, M and M propositions have spread beyond corporation finance to the fields of money and banking, fiscal policy, and international finance.[2]

Clearly Proposition I, and its proof, have been accepted into economic theory. Less clear, however, is the empirical significance of the MM value-invariance Proposition I in its original sphere of corporation finance.

Skepticism about the practical force of our invariance proposition was understandable given the almost daily reports in the financial press, then as now, of spectacular increases in the values of firms after changes in capital structure. But the view that capital structure is literally irrelevant or

---

* This article is a shortened version of an article that appeared in the *Journal of Economic Perspectives* (Fall 1988) and is reprinted here with permission of the American Economic Association, the journal's publisher. The author would like to acknowledge helpful comments on an earlier draft made by George Constantinides, Melvin Reder, Lester Telser, Hal Varian, Robert Vishny, and by the editors of the *Journal of Economic Perspectives*, Carl Shapiro, Joseph Stiglitz, and Timothy Taylor.

1 Examples include Cornell and French (1983) on the pricing of stock index futures, Black and Scholes (1973) on the

pricing of options, and Ross (1976) on the structure of capital asset prices generally. For other, and in some respects, more general proofs of our capital structure proposition, see among others, Stiglitz (1974) for a general equilibrium proof showing that individual wealth and consumption opportunities are unaffected by capital structures; Hirshleifer (1965) and (1966) for a state preference, complete-markets proof; Duffie and Shafer (1986) for extensions to some cases of incomplete markets; and Merton (forthcoming) for a spanning proof.

Full citations for all articles mentioned are listed in the References section at the end of this article.

2 See, for example, Wallace (1981) on domestic open-market operations; Sargent and Smith (1986) on central bank foreign-exchange interventions: Chamley and Polemarchakis (1984) on government tax and borrowing policies; and Fama (1980), (1983) on money, banking, and the quantity theory.

that "nothing matters" in corporate finance, though still sometimes attributed to us (and tracing perhaps to the very provocative way we made our point), is far from what we ever actually said about the real-world applications of our theoretical propositions. Looking back now, perhaps we should have put more emphasis on the other, upbeat side of the "nothing matters" coin: showing what *doesn't* matter can also show, by implication, what *does*.

This more constructive approach to our invariance proposition and its central assumption of perfect capital markets has now become the standard one in teaching corporate finance. We could not have taken that approach in 1958, however, because the analysis departed too greatly from the then accepted way of thinking about capital structure choices. We first had to convince people (including ourselves!) that there could be *any* conditions, even in a "frictionless" world, where a firm would be indifferent between issuing securities as different in legal status, investor risk, and apparent cost as debt and equity. Remember that interest rates on corporate debts were then in the 3 to 5 percent range, with equity earnings/price ratios – then the conventional measure of the "cost" of equity capital – running from 15 to 20 percent.

The paradox of indifference in the face of such huge spreads in the apparent cost of financing was resolved by our Proposition II, which showed that when Proposition I held, the cost of equity capital was a linear increasing function of the debt/equity ratio. Any gains from using more of what might seem to be cheaper debt capital would thus be offset by the correspondingly higher cost of the now riskier equity capital. Our propositions implied that the *weighted average* of these costs of capital to a firm would remain the same no matter what combination of financing sources the firm actually chose.

Though departing substantially from the then conventional views about capital structure, our propositions were certainly not without links to what had gone before. Our distinction between the real value of the firm and its financial packaging raised many issues long familiar to economists in discussions of "money illusion" and money neutrality . . .

In the field of corporate finance, however, the only prior treatment similar in spirit to our own was by David Durand in 1952 (who, as it turned out, also became our first formal critic).[3] Durand

had proposed, as one of what he saw as two polar approaches to valuing shares, that investors might ignore the firm's then-existing capital structure and first price the whole firm by capitalizing its operating earnings *before* interest and taxes. The value of the shares would then be found by subtracting out the value of the bonds. But he rejected this possibility in favor of his other extreme, which he believed closer to the ordinary real-world way of valuing corporate shares. According to this conventional view, investors capitalized the firm's net income *after* interest and taxes with only a loose, qualitative adjustment for the degree of leverage in the capital structure.

That we too did not dismiss the seemingly unrealistic approach of looking through the momentary capital structure to the underlying real flows may well trace to the macroeconomic perspective from which we had approached the problem of capital structure in the first instance. Our main concern, initially, was with the determinants of *aggregate* economic investment by the business sector. The resources for capital formation by firms came ultimately from the savings of the household sector, a connection that economists had long found convenient to illustrate with schematic national income and wealth T-accounts, including, of course, simplified sectoral balance sheets such as:

BUSINESS FIRMS		HOUSEHOLDS	
Assets	**Liabilities**	**Assets**	**Liabilities**
Productive Capital	Debts owed to households	Debts of firms	Household net worth
	Equity in firms owned by households	Equity in firms	

Consolidating the accounts of the two sectors leads to the familiar national balance sheet in which the debt and equity securities no longer appear:

Assets	Liabilities
Productive Capital	Household Net worth

3 Durand (1959).

The value of the business sector to its ultimate owners in the household sector is thus seen clearly to lie in the value of the underlying capital. And by the same token, the debt and equity securities owned by households can be seen not as final, but only as intermediate, assets serving to partition the earnings (and their attendant risks) among the many separate individual households within the sector.

Our value-invariance Proposition I was in a sense only the application of this macroeconomic intuition to the microeconomics of corporate finance; and the arbitrage proof we gave for our Proposition I was just the counterpart, at the individual investor level, of the consolidation of accounts and the washing out of the debt/equity ratios at the sectoral level. In fact, one blade of our arbitrage proof had the arbitrager doing exactly that washing out. If levered firms were undervalued relative to unlevered firms, our arbitrager was called on to "undo the leverage" by buying an appropriate portion of both the levered firm's debt and its shares. On a consolidated basis, the interest paid by the firm cancels against the interest received and the arbitrager thus owned a pure equity stream. Unlevered corporate equity streams could in turn be relevered by borrowing on individual account if unlevered streams ever sold at a discount relative to levered corporate equity. That possibility of "homemade leverage" by individual investors provided the second and completing blade of our arbitrage proof of value invariance.

Our arbitrage proof drew little flak from those who saw it essentially as a metaphor – an expository device for highlighting hidden implications of the "law of one price" in perfect capital markets. But whether the operations we called arbitrage could *in fact* substitute for consolidation when dealing with real-world corporations was disputed. Could investors, acting on their own, really replicate and, where required, wash out corporate capital structures – if not completely, as in the formal proof, then by enough, and quickly enough, to make the invariance proposition useful as a description of the central tendency in the real-world capital market? These long-standing and still not completely resolved issues of the empirical relevance of the MM propositions will be the primary focus of what follows here.

Three separate reasons (over and above the standard complaint that we attributed too much rationality to the stock market) were quickly offered by our critics for believing that individual investors could not enforce the corporate valuations implied by Propositions I and II. These lines of objection, relating to dividends, debt defaults, and taxes, each emphasized a different, distinctive feature of the corporate form of business organization. And each in turn will be reexamined here, taking full advantage this time, however, of the hindsight of thirty years of subsequent research and events . . .

ARBITRAGE, DIVIDENDS, AND THE CORPORATE VEIL

The law of one price is easily visualized in commodity settings where market institutions deliberately provide the necessary standardization and interchangeability of units. But to which of the many features of an entity as complex as an operating business firm would our financial equilibration extend?

We opted for a Fisherian rather than the standard Marshallian representation of the firm. Irving Fisher's view of the firm – now the standard one in finance, but then just becoming known – impounds the details of technology, production, and sales in a black box and focuses on the underlying net cash flow. The firm for Fisher was just an abstract engine transforming current consumable resources, obtained by issuing securities, into future consumable resources payable to the owners of the securities. Even so, what did it mean to speak of firms or cash flow streams being different, but still "similar" enough to allow for arbitrage or anything close to it?

Some of the answers would be provided, we hoped, by our concept of a "risk class," which was offered with several objectives in mind. At the level of the theory, it defined what today would be called a "spanning" set; the uncertain underlying future cash flow streams of the individual firms within each class could be assumed perfectly correlated, and hence perfect substitutes. But the characteristics of those correlated streams could be allowed to differ from class to class. Hence, at the more practical level, the risk class could be identified with Marshallian industries – groupings around which so much academic and Wall Street research had always been organized.[4] We hoped that the earnings of firms in some large industries such as oil or electricity generation might vary together closely enough not just for real-world arbitragers to carry on their work of equilibration efficiently, but also to offer us as outside observers a chance of judging how well they were succeeding. Indeed, we devoted more than a third of the original paper (plus a couple of follow-up studies) to empirical estimates of how closely real-world market values approached those predicted by our model. Our hopes of settling the empirical issues by that route, however, have largely been disappointed.[5]

INVESTOR ARBITRAGE WHEN DIVIDENDS DIFFER: THE DIVIDEND-INVARIANCE PROPOSITION

Although the risk class, with its perfect correlation of the underlying real cash streams may have provided a basis for the arbitrage in our formal proof, there remained the sticking point of how real-world market equilibrators could gain access to a firm's operating cash flows, let alone to two or more correlated ones. As a matter of law, what the individual equity investor actually gets on buying a share is not a right to the firm's underlying cash flow but only to such cash dividends as the corporation's directors choose to declare. Must these man-made payout policies also be assumed perfectly correlated along with the underlying cash flows to make the equilibration effective? If so, the likely empirical range of the value-invariance proposition would seem to be narrow indeed.

A second MM-invariance proposition – that the value of the firm was independent of its dividend policy – was developed in part precisely to meet this class of objections. The essential content of the dividend-"irrelevance" argument was already in hand at the time of the original leverage paper and led us there to dismiss the whole dividend question as a "mere detail" (not the last time, alas, that we may have overworked that innocent word "mere"). We stated the dividend-invariance proposition explicitly, and noted its relation to the leverage proof in the very first round of replies to our critics.[6] But because dividend decisions were controversial in their own right, and because considering them raised so many side issues of valuation theory and of practical policy, both private and public, we put off the fuller treatment of dividends to a separate paper that appeared three years after the first one.[7]

That the close connection in origin of the two invariance propositions has not been more widely appreciated traces not only to their separation in time, but probably also to our making no reference to arbitrage (or even to debt or equity) in the proof of the dividend-invariance proposition. Why bring in arbitrage, we felt, when an even simpler line of proof would serve? The dividend invariance proposition stated only that, *given* the firm's investment decision, its dividend decision would have no effect on the value of the shares. The added cash to fund the higher dividend payout must come from somewhere, after all; and with investment fixed, that somewhere could only be from selling off part of the firm. As long as the securities sold off could be presumed sold at their market-determined values, then, whether the analysis was carried out under conditions of certainty or uncertainty, the whole operation of paying dividends, again holding investment constant, could be seen as just a wash – a swap of equal values not much different in principle from withdrawing money from a pass-book savings account.

The informational content of dividends

Managerial decisions on dividends thus might affect the cash component of an investor's return; but they would not affect the *total* return of cash

---

4   Remember, in this connection, that the capital asset pricing models of Sharpe (1964) and Lintner (1965) and their later extensions that now dominate empirical research in finance had yet to come on the scene. For some glimpses of how more recent asset pricing frameworks can accommodate the MM propositions without reference to MM risk classes or MM arbitrage, see Ross (1988).

5   Direct statistical calibration of the goodness of fit of the MM value-invariance propositions has not so far been achieved by us or others for a variety of reasons, some of which will be noted further in due course below.

6   See Modigliani and Miller (1959), especially pages 662–668.

7   See Miller and Modigliani (1961).

plus appreciation, and the total is what mattered. In practice, of course, even changing the cash-dividend component often seemed to matter a great deal, at least to judge by the conspicuous price jumps typically accompanying announcements of major boosts or cuts in dividends. These highly visible price reactions to dividend announcements were among the first (and are still the most frequently mentioned) of the supposed empirical refutations of the MM value-invariance principle. By invoking the dividend-invariance proposition to support the leverage-invariance proposition, we seemed to have succeeded only in substituting one set of objections for another.

But, as we suggested in our 1961 dividend paper, these price reactions to dividend announce-ments were not really refutations. They were better seen as failures of one of the key assumptions of both the leverage and dividend models, *viz.* that all capital market participants, inside managers and outside investors alike, have the same information about the firm's cash flows. Over long enough time horizons, this all-cards-on-the-table assumption might, we noted, be an entirely acceptable approx-imation, particularly in a market subject to S.E.C. disclosure rules. But new information is always coming in; and over shorter runs, the firm's inside managers were likely to have information about the firm's prospects not yet known to or fully appreciated by the investing public at large. Management-initiated actions on dividends or other financial transactions might then serve, by implication, to convey to the outside market information not yet incorporated in the price of the firm's securities.

Although our concern in the 1961 dividend paper was with the observed announcement effects of dividend decisions, informational asymmetry also raised the possibility of strategic behavior on the part of the existing stockholders and/or their management agents. Might not much of the price response to dividend (and/or other capital struc-ture) announcements simply be attempts by the insiders to mislead the outsiders; and if so, what point was there to our notion of a capital market equilibrium rooted solely in the fundamentals? Our instincts as economists led us to discount the possibility that firms could hope to fool the invest-ing public systematically. But, at the time, we could offer little more support than a declaration of faith

in Lincoln's Law – that you can't fool all of the people all of the time.

By the 1970s, however, the concept of an information equilibrium had entered economics, and came soon after to the field of corporate finance as well.[8] In 1977, for example, Stephen Ross showed how debt/equity ratios might serve to signal, in the technical sense, managements' special information about the firm's future prospects.[9] But the extent to which these and subsequent asymmetric information models can account for observed departures from the "invariance" propositions has not so far been convincingly established.[10]

The interaction of investment policy and dividend policy

The dividend-invariance proposition, as we initially stated it, highlights still another way in which the corporate form of organization, and especially the separation it permits between own-ership and management, can have effects that at first sight at least seem to contradict the MM value-invariance predictions. Recall that the dividend-invariance proposition takes the firm's investment decision as given – which is just a strong way of saying that the level of investment, whatever it might be, is set by management *independently* of the dividend. Without imposing such an "other-things-equal" condition, there would, of course, be no way of separating the market's reac-tion to real investment events from reactions to the dividend and any associated, purely financial events.

In the real world, of course, the financial press reports single-company stories, not cross-sectional partial regression coefficients. In these single-company tales, the investment decision and the dividend/financing decisions are typically thor-oughly intertwined. But if the tale is actually one of cutting back unprofitable investments and paying

---

8 Bhattacharya (1979) noted the formal similarity between Spence's (1973) job-market signalling model and the MM divi-dend model with asymmetric information.

9 Ross (1977).

10 For a recent survey of results on dividend signalling, see Miller (1987). For a more general survey of asymmetric information models in finance, see Stiglitz (1982).

out the proceeds as dividends, followed by a big run-up in price, then the MM invariance proposition may seem to be failing, but is really not being put to the test. Nor is this scenario only hypothetical. Something very much like it appears in a number of the most notorious of recent takeover battles, particularly in the oil industry where some target firms had conspicuously failed to cut back their long-standing polices of investment in exploration despite the drastic fall in petroleum prices.

In a sense, as noted earlier, these gains to shareholders from ending a management-caused undervaluation of the firm's true earning power can also be viewed as a form of capital-market arbitrage, but not one that atomistic MM investors or arbitragers can supply on their own. Once again, the special properties of the corporate form intrude, this time the voting rights that attach to corporate shares and the majority-like rules (and sometimes supermajority rules) in the corporate charters that determine the control over the firm's decisions. Much of the early skepticism, still not entirely dispelled, about the real empirical force of inter-firm arbitrage (MM-arbitrage included) traces to these properties of corporate shares beyond their purely cash-flow consequences. A particular example of the obstacle they offered to effective capital market equilibrium was that of closed-end investment funds. In 1958, as still today, closed-end funds often sold at a substantial discount to net asset value – a discount that could be recaptured only by the shareholders merely (that word again) by getting enough of them to vote to convert to open-end fund status . . .

[Omitted here from the original is a section entitled "MM Invariance with Limited Liability and Risky Debt."]

THE MM PROPOSITIONS IN A WORLD WITH TAXES

We have no shortage of potential candidates for forces that might well lead the market to depart systematically and persistently from the predictions of the original MM value-invariance propositions. One such likely candidate, the third of the original lines of objection, has loomed so large in fact as to

have dominated academic discussions of the MM propositions, at least until the recent wave of corporate takeovers and restructurings became the new focus of attention. That candidate is the corporate income tax, the one respect in which everyone agreed that the corporate form really did matter.

The U.S. Internal Revenue Code has long been the classic, and by now is virtually the world's only, completely unintegrated tax system imposing "double taxation" of corporate net income. A separate income tax is first levied directly on the corporation; and, except for certain small and closely held corporations, who may elect to be taxed as partnerships under Subchapter S of the Code, a second tax is then levied at the personal level on any income flows such as dividends or interest generated at the corporate level. Double taxation of the interest payments is avoided because interest on indebtedness is considered a cost of doing business and hence may be deducted from corporate gross income in computing net taxable corporate earnings. But no such allowance has been made for any costs of equity capital.[11]

If the separate corporate income tax were merely a modest franchise tax for the privilege of doing business in corporate form, as was essentially the case when it was introduced in the early years of this century, the extra burden on equity capital might be treated as just one more on the long list of second-order differences in the costs of alternative sources of capital for the firm. But, at the time of our 1958 article, the marginal tax rate under the corporate income tax had been close to and sometimes over 50 percent for nearly 20 years, and it remained there for almost another 30 years until dropped to 34 percent by the recent Tax Reform Act of 1986. The cost differentials of this size were just too big to be set aside in any normative or empirical treatments of real-world capital structure choices.

Strictly speaking, of course, there is one sense, albeit a somewhat strained one, in which the basic value-invariance does go through even with corporate taxes. The Internal Revenue Service can be

---

11 Two exceptions should be noted for the record. An undistributed profits tax from which dividends were deductible was in force for two years in the late 1930s. The excess-profits tax during World War II also allowed a deduction not for dividends, but for the "normal profits" of the firm.

considered as just another security holder, whose claim is essentially an equity one in the normal course of events (but which can also take on some of the characteristics of secured debt when things go badly and back taxes are owed). Securities, after all, are just ways of partitioning the firm's earnings: the MM propositions assert only that the sum of the values of all the claims is independent of the number and the shapes of the separate partitions.

However satisfying this government-as-a-shareholder view may be as a generalization of the original model, the fact remains that the government, though it sometimes gives negative taxes or subsidies for some kinds of investment, does not normally buy its share with an initial input of funds that can serve to compensate the other stockholders for the claims on income they transfer to the Treasury. Nor are we talking here of taxation-according-to-the-benefits or of the rights of eminent domain, or even of whether the corporate tax might ultimately be better for the shareholders, or for the general public, than alternative ways of raising the same revenue. For the nongovernment equity claimholders, the government's claim to the firm's earnings is a net subtraction from their own.

THE MM TAX-ADJUSTED LEVERAGE PROPOSITION

Allowing for that subtraction can lead to a very different kind of MM Proposition, though one, as we showed in our Tax Correction article (1963), that can still be derived from an arbitrage proof along lines very similar to the original.[12] This time, however, the value of the firm (in the sense of the sum of the values of the private, nongovernmental claims) is *not* independent of the debt/equity division in the capital structure. In general, thanks to the deductibility of interest, the purely private claims will increase in value as the debt ratio increases. In fact, under conditions which can by no means be dismissed out of hand as implausible, we showed that the value of the private claims might well have no well-defined interior maximum. The optimal capital structure might be all debt!

In many ways this tax-adjusted MM proposition provoked even more controversy than the original invariance one – which could be, and often was, shrugged off as merely another inconsequential paradox from some economists' frictionless dream-world. But this one carried direct and not very flattering implications for the top managements of companies with low levels of debt. It suggested that the high bond ratings of such companies, in which the management took so much pride, may actually have been a sign of their incompetence; that the managers were leaving too much of their stockholders' money on the table in the form of unnecessary corporate income tax payments – payments which in the aggregate over the sector of large, publicly-held corporations clearly came to many billions of dollars.

We must admit that we too were somewhat taken aback when we first saw this conclusion emerging from our analysis. The earlier modeling of the tax effect in our 1958 paper, which the 1963 paper corrected, had also suggested tax advantages in debt financing, but of a smaller and more credible size. By 1963, however, with corporate debt ratios in the late 50s not much higher than in the low tax 1920s,[13] we seemed to face an unhappy dilemma: either corporate managers did not know (or perhaps care) that they were paying too much in taxes; or something major was being left out of the model. Either they were wrong or we were.

The offsetting costs of debt finance

Much of the research effort in finance over the next 25 years has been spent, in effect, in settling which it was. Since economists, ourselves included, were somewhat leerier then than some might be now in offering mass ineptitude by U.S. corporate management as an explanation for any important and long-persisting anomalies, attention was naturally directed first to the possibly offsetting costs of leveraging out from under the corporate income tax. Clearly, leveraging increased the riskiness of the shares, as we ourselves had stressed in our original Proposition II and its tax-adjusted

---

12 Modigliani and Miller (1963).

13 See Miller (1963).

counterpart. A sequence of bad years, moreover, might wipe out the firm's taxable income and, given the very ungenerous treatment of losses in our tax law, that could reduce, possibly quite substantially, any benefits from the interest tax shields. A run of very bad years might actually find a highly-levered firm unable (or, as the option theorists might prefer, unwilling) to meet its debt-service requirements, precipitating thereby any of the several processes of recontracting that go under the general name of bankruptcy. These renegotiations can be costly indeed to the debtor's estate, particularly when many separate classes of creditors are involved.[14]

The terminal events of bankruptcy are not the only hazards in a high-debt strategy. Because the interests of the creditors and the stockholders in the way the assets are managed need not always be congruent, the creditors may seek the additional protection of restrictive covenants in their loan agreement. These covenants may not only be costly to monitor but may foreclose, if only by the time delay in renegotiating the original terms, the implementation of valuable initiatives that might have been seized by a firm less constrained. Nor should the transaction and flotation costs of outside equity financing be neglected, particularly in the face of information asymmetries. Prudence alone might thus have seemed to dictate the maintenance of a substantial reserve of untapped, quick borrowing power, especially in an era when those managing U.S. corporations (and the financial institutions buying their debt securities) still had personal memories of the debt refinancing problems in the 1930s.

We dutifully acknowledged these well-known costs of debt finance, but we were hard put at the time to see how they could overweigh the tax savings of up to 50 cents per dollar of debt that our model implied. Not only did there seem to be potentially large amounts of corporate taxes to be saved by converting equity capital to tax-deductible interest debt capital, but there appeared

to be ways of doing so that avoided, or at least drastically reduced, the secondary costs of high-debt capital structures. The bankruptcy risk exposure of junior debt could have been blunted with existing hybrid securities such as income bonds, to take just one example, under which deductible interest payments could be made in the good years, but passed or deferred in the bad years without precipitating a technical default.

For reducing the moral hazards and agency costs in the bondholder-stockholder relation, the undoing-of-leverage blade in the original MM proof offered a clue: let the capital suppliers hold some of each – equity as well as debt – either directly or through convertible or exchangeable securities of any of a number of kinds. In sum, many finance specialists, myself included, remained unconvinced that the high-leverage route to corporate tax savings was either technically unfeasible or prohibitively expensive in terms of expected bankruptcy or agency costs.

JUNK BONDS, LEVERAGED BUYOUTS AND THE FEASIBILITY OF HIGH-LEVERAGE STRATEGIES

A number of recent developments in finance can be seen as confirming the suspicions of many of us academics in the early 1960s that high-leverage strategies to reduce taxes were indeed entirely feasible. Among these, of course, is the now large outstanding volume of what are popularly known as "junk bonds." The very term is a relic of an earlier era in which the distinguishing characteristic of bonds as investments was supposedly their presence at the low-risk end of the spectrum. High-risk, high-yield bonds did exist, of course, but were typically bonds issued initially with high ratings by companies that had subsequently fallen on hard times. The significant innovation in recent years – and it is still a puzzle as to why it took so long – has been in the showing that, contrary to the conventional wisdom, junk bonds could in fact be issued and marketed successfully by design, and not just as "fallen angels."

The designs utilizing new risky-debt securities have often taken the very conspicuous form of "leveraged buyouts" of the outside shareholders by a control group typically led by the existing top

---

14 The perceived complexity of the present bankruptcy code (and perhaps even the very reason for having such a code) reflect mainly the need for resolving conflicts within and between the various classes of creditors. The difficulties parallel those encountered elsewhere in "common pool" problems (see Jackson 1987).

management. The device itself is an old one, but had been confined mainly to small firms seeking both to assure their continuity after the death or retirement of the dominant owner-founder, and to provide more liquidity for the entrepreneur's estate. The new development of recent years has been the ability, thanks in part to the market for junk bonds, to apply the technique to a much wider range of publicly-held, big businesses with capitalizations now routinely in the billions, and with new size records being set almost every year.

The debt/equity ratios in some recent LBOs have reached as high as 9 to 1 or 10 to 1 or even more – far beyond anything we had ever dared use in our numerical illustrations of how leverage could be used to reduce taxes. The debtor/creditor incentive and agency problems that might be expected under such high leverage ratios have been kept manageable partly by immediate asset sales, but over the longer term by "strip financing" – trendy investment banker argot for the old device of giving the control and most of the ownership of the equity (except for the management incentive shares) to those providing the risky debt (or to the investment bankers they have designated as monitors). The same hold-both-securities approach, as in our arbitrage proof, has long been the standard one in Japan where corporate debt ratios are, or are at least widely believed to be, substantially higher than for their U.S. counterparts.

Some possible non-tax gains from leveraging

The recent surge of leveraged buyouts not only shows the feasibility of high-leverage capital structures for reducing corporate income taxes, but also suggests at least two other possible sources for the gains to the shareholder that may accompany a major recapitalization with newly-issued debt. The firm may, for example, already have had some long-term debt outstanding when the additional debt needed to accomplish the buyout was arranged. Even in a world without taxes, the no-gain-from-leverage implication of the original MM invariance proposition might fail if the new debt was not made junior in status to the old, if the old bond covenant was "open ended," as many still are, and if the new bonds were issued under it. Assuming no

change in the underlying earning power from the recapitalization, the original creditors would then find the value of their claim diluted. The benefits of this dilution of the old bondholders accrue, of course, to the stockholders, which is why it has often been labeled "theft," particularly by the adversely affected bondholders. (Finance specialists prefer the less emotionally charged term "uncompensated wealth transfer.")

The high debt ratios in LBOs also redirect attention to the assumption, shown earlier to be crucial to the MM dividend-invariance proposition, that the firm's financial decisions can be taken as independent of its real operating and investment decisions. That assumption never sits well and certainly the notion that heavy debt burdens might indeed lead to overcautious business behavior has long been part of the folk wisdom on the dangers of debt. The new wrinkle to the interdependence argument brought in recently by the defenders of LBOs has been to stress the positive *virtues* of having managers face large debt obligations. Managements in such firms must work hard and diligently indeed to achieve any earnings above interest to enhance the value of the residual equity they hold in the firm. By accepting such heavy debt-service burdens, moreover, the managers are making a binding commitment to themselves and to the other residual equity holders against yielding to the temptations, noted earlier, to pour the firm's good money down investment ratholes.[15]

Voluntary recapitalizations and the MM dividend proposition

High debt ratios have been installed in some U.S. firms in recent years, not just by outside-initiated LBOs but through voluntary recapitalizations – sometimes, it is true, merely for fending off an imminent hostile takeover, but sometimes also with the tax benefits very clearly emphasized. Even apart from the tax angles, nothing in the practice of finance these days could be more quintessentially MM than these often highly visible "self takeovers," as some

---

15 This view of debt service as a device for reining in managerial discretion is a major strand in what has come to be called the "free cash flow" theory of corporate finance. For an account of that theory, see Jensen (1988).

wag has dubbed them. Leverage-increasing recap-italizations of this kind do indeed raise the firm's debt/equity ratio, but because the proceeds of the new bonds floated are turned over to the share-holders, the self takeovers also reunite in a single operation the two Siamese-twin MM propositions, the leverage proposition and the dividend proposi-tion (joined together originally at birth, but soon parted and living separate lives thereafter).

The dividend proposition, as noted earlier, was put forward initially to overcome a line of objection to the leverage proof. But how dividends might actually affect real-world prices raises other issues which in turn have led to as much controversy, and to an even larger number of discordant empirical findings, than for the leverage propositions. Once again, moreover, major tax differentials intruded, this time the gap between rates on dividends and capital gains under the personal income tax, with again what seemed in the late 50s and early 60s to be strikingly unorthodox policy implications. Some high-income stockholders clearly would have been better off if the firm paid no dividends and simply reinvested its earnings or bought shares in other corporations. That much every real-world con-glomerator and every public finance specialist surely knew.

But the value-for-value presumption of the MM dividend proposition carried within it some further advice. There were better ways to avoid taxes on dividends than pouring the firm's money down ratholes: use the money to buy back the firm's shares! For the taxable shareholders, buybacks at market-determined prices could transform heavily-taxed dividends into less-heavily taxed capital gains and, better yet, into unrealized capital gains for shareholders who choose not to sell or trade their shares. Unlike a declared regular dividend, more-over, an announced share repurchase, whether by tender or by open market purchases, carried no implied commitments about future payouts.

Personal-Corporate Tax Interactions and Capital Market Equilibrium

These tax-advantaged dividend-substitution prop-erties of share repurchase may also offer a clue as to why the leveraging of corporate America out

from under the corporate income tax may have been so long delayed. The point is not so much that share repurchase by itself has been a major vehicle deliberately invoked by corporations to reduce the personal income taxes of their shareholders, though its potential for that purpose certainly has not been lost on corporate treasurers and direc-tors.[16] But the very presence of such a possibility at the corporate level serves as a reminder that the U.S. tax system has not one but two distinct taxes that bear on capital structure choices. Any model of capital market equilibrium must allow for both, and for their interactions.

In particular, under reasonable assumptions, the joint corporate-personal tax gains from corporate leverage, G_L, can be expressed in the following relatively transparent formula:

$$G_L = \left[1 - \frac{(1-t_c)(1-t_{PS})}{(1-t_{PB})}\right] B_L$$

where B_L is the value of the levered firm's interest-deductible debts, t_c is the marginal corporate tax rate, and t_{PS} and t_{PB} are the marginal investor's personal marginal tax rates on, respectively, income from corporate shares and income from interest-bearing corporate debts.[17] In the special case in which the personal income tax makes no distinction between income from debt or from equity (i.e., $t_{PS} = t_{PB}$), the gain from leverage reduces to $t_c B_L$, which is precisely the expression in the MM tax model.[18] But in the contrasting extreme special case in which (a) the capital gains provisions or other special reliefs have effectively eliminated the personal tax on equity income, (b) full loss offsets are available at the corporate level, and (c) the marginal personal tax rate on

---

16 Most economists, upon first hearing about share repurchase as an alternative to dividend payments, assume that the Internal Revenue Service must surely have some kind of magic bullet for deterring so obvious a method of tax avoidance. It doesn't, or at least not one that will work in the presence of even minimally-competent tax lawyers.

17 See Miller (1977).

18 That special case assumes, among other things, that debt, once in place, is maintained or rolled over indefinitely. For valuing the tax savings when debts are not perpetuities, see the comment on this paper by Franco Modigliani that appears in the same issue of *Journal of Economic Perspectives* (Fall 1988) as this article originally appeared in.

interest income just equals the marginal corporate rate ($t_{PB} = t_c$), the purely tax gains from corporate leverage would vanish entirely. The gains from interest deductibility at the corporate level would be exactly offset by the added burden of interest includability under the personal tax – an added burden that, in equilibrium, would be approximated by risk-adjusted interest rate premiums on corporate and Treasury bonds over those on tax-exempt municipal securities.

This somewhat surprising special case of zero net gain from corporate leverage has inevitably received the most attention, but it remains, of course, only one of the many potentially interesting configurations for market equilibrium. Stable intermediate cases are entirely possible in which some gains to corporate leverage still remain, but thanks to the capital gains or other special provisions driving t_{PS} below t_{PB}, or to limitations on loss offsets, those gains at the corporate level are substantially below those in the original MM tax model. The tax gains from leverage might, in fact, even be small enough, when joined with reasonable presumed costs of leverage, to resolve the seeming MM anomaly of gross under-leveraging by U.S. corporations.[19]

THE MM PROPOSITIONS AND THE RECENT TAX REFORM ACT

Any such "Debt and Taxes" equilibrium, however, that the corporate sector might have reached in the early 1980s by balancing costs of debt finance against MM tax gains from leverage must surely have been shattered by the Tax Reform Act of 1986. That act sought, among other things, to reverse the long steady slide, accelerating in the early 1980s, in the contribution of corporate income taxes to total federal tax revenues. But, in attempting to increase the load on corporations, Congress seemed to have overlooked some of the interactions between corporations and individual investors that lie at the heart of the MM propositions and their later derivatives. For shareholders taxable at high marginal rates

on interest or dividends under the personal income tax, for example, maintaining assets in corporate solution and suffering the corporate tax hit might make sense, provided enough of the after-corporate tax earnings could be transmuted into long-deferred, low-taxed capital gains by profitable reinvestment in real assets. In fact, over much of the life of the income tax, when shares were held largely by wealthy individuals and hardly at all by pension funds or other tax-exempt holders, the corporate form of organization for businesses with great growth potential may well have been the single most important tax shelter of all.

But the pattern of tax advantages that encouraged the accumulation of wealth in corporate form appears to have been altered fundamentally by the Tax Reform Act of 1986. The Investment Tax Credit and related tax subsidies to fixed investment have been phased out. The marginal rate on the highest incomes under the personal income tax has now been driven to 28 percent and, hence, below the top corporate rate of 34 percent. The long-standing personal income tax differential in favor of long-term realized capital gains has been eliminated, though income in that form still benefits from a variety of timing options and from the tax-free write-up of any accumulated gains when the property passes to heirs. The analogous tax free write-up privileges for corporate deaths or liquidations, however, formerly allowed under the so-called *General Utilities* doctrine, have now been cut back by the TRA and some of its recent predecessors, reducing still further the tax benefits of the corporate form.

To finance specialists familiar with the MM propositions, these combined changes suggest that Congressional hopes of substantially increasing the yield of the corporate income-tax – that is to say, their hopes of reinstating the double taxation of corporate profits – may well be disappointed.[20] Our capital markets and legal institutions offer too many ways for averting the double hit. Corporations can split off their cash-cow properties into any of a variety of non-corporate "flow-through" entities such as master limited partnerships or royalty trusts. And, as has been the running theme of this

---

19 For some recent empirical tests of such an intermediate equilibrium using the premium over municipals, see Buser and Hess (1986). Kim (1987) offers a wide-ranging survey of recent theoretical and empirical research on capital market equilibrium in the presence of corporate-personal income tax interactions.

---

20 For some recent signs of Congressional concerns on this score, see Brooks (1987) and Canellos (1987).

entire section, firms retaining corporate form can always gut the corporate tax with high-leverage capital structures. In fact, under not entirely implausible conditions (notably that the marginal bondholder is actually a tax-exempt pension fund rather than a taxable individual investor, implying that the t_{PB} is zero) the incentive to leverage out from under the corporate tax may now actually be as high or higher than it was back in 1963. The statutory top corporate tax rate has indeed been cut; but with the Investment Tax Credit and Accelerated Depreciation also blown away by the Tax Reform Act of 1986, many capital-intensive corporations may now, for the first time in a very long while, be facing the unpleasant prospect of actually paying substantial corporate taxes.

And perhaps that observation can serve as a fitting note of uncertainty, or at least of unfinished business, on which to close this look back at the MM propositions. The open questions about those propositions have long been the empirical ones, as noted here at many points. Are the equilibria the propositions imply really strong enough attractors to demand the attention of those active in the capital markets either as practitioners or as outside observers? In the physical or biological sciences, one can often hope to answer such questions by deliberately shocking the system and studying its response. In economics, of course, direct intervention of that kind is rarely possible, but nature, or at least Congress, can sometimes provide a substitute. The U.S. tax system is a pervasive force on business decisions of many kinds, but especially so on the class of financial decisions treated in the MM propositions. Tax considerations have for that reason always figured prominently in the field of finance. Occasionally, the profession may even see changes in the tax regime drastic enough for the path of return to a new equilibrium to stand out sharply against the background of market noise. Whether the Tax Reform Act of 1986 is indeed one of those rare super shocks that can validate a theory remains to be seen.

References

Bhattacharya, Sudipto, "Imperfect Information, Dividend Policy and the 'Bird in the Hand' Fallacy." *Bell Journal of Economics* 10.1 (Spring 1979): 259–70.

Black, Fischer, and Cox, John, "Valuing Corporate Securities: Some Effects of Bond Indenture Provisions." *Journal of Finance* 31.2 (May 1976): 351–67.

Black, Fischer, and Scholes, Myron, "The Pricing of Options and Corporate Liabilities." *Journal of Political Economy* 81.3 (May–June 1973): 637–54.

Brooks, Jennifer J. S., "A Proposal to Avert the Revenue Loss from 'Disincorporation.'" *Tax Notes* 36.4 (July 27 1987): 425–28.

Buser, Stephen A., and Hess, Patrick J., "Empirical Determinants of the Relative Yields on Taxable and Tax-exempt Securities." *Journal of Financial Economics* 17 (May 1986): 335–56.

Canellos, Peter C., "Corporate Tax Integration: By Design or by Default?" *Tax Notes* 35.8 (June 8 1987): 999–1008.

Chamley, Christopher, and Polemarchakis, Heraklis, "Assets, General Equilibrium and the Neutrality of Money." *Review of Economic Studies* 51.1 (January 1984): 129–38.

Cornell, Bradford, and French, Kenneth, "Taxes and the Pricing of Stock Index Futures." *Journal of Finance* 38.3 (June 1983): 675–94.

Duffie, Darrell, and Shafer, Wayne, "Equilibrium and the Role of the Firm in Incomplete Markets." Manuscript (August 1986).

Durand, David, "Costs of Debt and Equity Funds for Business: Trends and Problems of Measurement." In Conference on Research in Business Finance. National Bureau of Economic Research. New York. (1952): 215–47.

Durand, David, "The Cost of Capital. Corporation Finance and the Theory of Investment: Comment." *American Economic Review* 49.4 (September 1959): 639–55.

Fama, Eugene, "Banking in the Theory of Finance." *Journal of Monetary Economics* 6.1 (January 1980): 39–57.

Fama, Eugene, "Financial Intermediation and Price Level Control." *Journal of Monetary Economics* 12.1 (January 1983): 7–28.

Hirshleifer, Jack, "Investment Decision under Uncertainty: Choice Theoretic Approaches." *Quarterly Journal of Economics* 79 (November 1965): 509–36.

Hirshleifer, Jack, "Investment Decision under Uncertainty: Applications of the State Preference Approach." *Quarterly Journal of Economics* 80 (May 1966): 611–17.

Jackson, Thomas H., *The Logic and Limits of Bankruptcy Law*. Cambridge. Mass.: Harvard University Press. 1987.

Jensen, Michael C., "Takeovers: Their Causes and Consequences." *Journal of Economic Perspectives* 2 (Winter 1988): 21–48.

Kim, E. Han, "Optimal Capital Structure in Miller's Equilibrium." in *Frontiers of Financial Theory*. Edited by Sudipto Bhattacharya and George Constantinides [Totowa. N.J.: Renan and Littlefleld. 1987]. forthcoming.

Lintner, John. "The Valuation of Risk Assets and the Selection of Risky Investments in Stock Portfolios and Capital Budgets." *Review of Economics and Statistics* 47 (February 1965): 13–37.

Merton, Robert C., "Capital Market Theory and the Pricing of Financial Securities." in *Handbook of Monetary Economics* edited by Benjamin Friedman and Frank Hahn. Amsterdam: North Holland. forthcoming.

Merton, Robert C., "On the Pricing of Corporate Debt: The Risk of Interest Rates." *Journal of Finance* 29.3 (May 1974): 449–70.

Miller, Merton H., "The Corporate Income Tax and Corporate Financial Policies." In *Stabilization Policies*, The Commission on Money and Credit, Prentice-Hall. Inc., New Jersey. (1963): 381–470.

Miller, Merton H., "Debt and Taxes." *Journal of Finance* 32.2 (May 1977): 261–75.

Miller, Merton H., "The Informational Content of Dividends." In *Macroeconomics and Finance: Essays in Honor of Franco Modigliani*. Editors Rudiger Dornbusch. Stanley Fischer and John Bossons. MIT Press. Cambridge. MA. (1987): 37–58.

Miller, Merton H., and Modigliani, Franco, "Dividend Policy. Growth and the Valuation of Shares." *Journal of Business* 34.4 (October 1961): 411–33.

Miller, Merton H., and Modigliani, Franco, "Some Estimates of the Cost of Capital to the Utility Industry, 1954–7." *American Economic Review* 56.3 (June 1966): 333–91.

Miller, Merton H., and Scholes, Myron S, "Dividends and Taxes." *Journal of Financial Economics* 6.4 (December 1978): 333–64.

Modigliani, Franco, "Debt, Dividend Policy, Taxes, Inflation and Market Valuation." *Journal of Finance* 37.2 (May 1982): 255–73.

Modigliani, Franco, and Miller, Merton H., "The Cost of Capital. Corporation Finance and the Theory of Investment." *American Economic Review* 48.3 (June 1958): 261–97.

Modigliani, Franco, and Miller, Merton H., "The Cost of Capital, Corporation Finance and the Theory of Investment: Reply." *American Economic Review* 49.4 (September 1959): 655–69.

Modigliani, Franco, and Miller, Merton H., "Corporate Income Taxes and the Cost of Capital: A Correction." *American Economic Review* 53.3 (June 1963).

Ross, Stephen, "The Determination of Financial Structure: The Incentive Signalling Approach." *Bell Journal of Economics* 8.1 (Spring 1977): 23–40.

Ross, Stephen, "Return, Risk and Arbitrage." In *Risk and Return in Finance*. Editors Irwin Friend and James Bicksler. Vol. 1. Ballinger. Cambridge MA. (1976): 189–219.

Rubinstein, Mark, "Derivative Assets Analysis." *Journal of Economic Perspectives* 1 (Fall 1987): 73–93.

Sargent, Thomas J., and Smith, Bruce D., "The Irrelevance of Government Foreign Exchange Operations." Manuscript, 1986.

Sharpe, William F., "Capital Asset Prices: A Theory of Market Equilibrium under Conditions of Risk." *Journal of Finance* 19 (September 1964): 425–42.

Spence, Michael, "Job-Market Signalling." *Quarterly Journal of Economics* 87.3 (August 1973): 355–79.

Stiglitz, Joseph, "A Re-Examination of the Modigliani-Miller Theorem." *American Economic Review* 59, 5 (December 1969): 784–93.

Stiglitz, Joseph, "On the Irrelevance of Corporate Financial Policy." *American Economic Review* 64.6 (December 1974): 851–66.

Stiglitz, Joseph, "Information and Capital Markets." In *Financial Economics: Essays in Honor of Paul Cootner*. Editors William F. Sharpe and Cathryn Gootner, Prentice Hall, New Jersey (1982): 118–58.

Stoll, Hans R. "The Relationship Between Put and Call Option Prices," *Journal of Finance* 24 (December 1969): 801–24.

Wallace, Neil, "A Modigliani-Miller Theorem for Open Market Operations." *American Economic Review* 71.5 (June 1981): 267–74.

CHAPTER 11

Still Searching for Optimal Capital Structure

Stewart C. Myers (Massachusetts Institute of Technology)*

The optimal balance between debt and equity financing has been a central issue in corporate finance ever since Modigliani and Miller (MM) showed in 1958 that capital structure was irrelevant.

Thirty years later the MM analysis is textbook fare, not in itself controversial. Yet in practice it seems that financial leverage matters more than ever. I hardly need document the aggressive use of debt in the 1980s, especially in leveraged buyouts (LBOs), hostile takeovers and restructurings, and the recently renewed appreciation of the comforts of equity.

Of course none of these developments disproves MM's irrelevance theorem, which is just a "no magic in leverage" proof for a taxless, frictionless world. MM's practical message is this: *If* there is an optimal capital structure, it should reflect taxes or some specifically identified market imperfections. Thus managers are often viewed as trading off the tax savings from debt financing against costs of financial distress, specifically the agency costs generated by issuing risky debt and the deadweight costs of possible liquidation or reorganization. I call this the *static tradeoff* theory of optimal capital structure.

My purpose here is to see whether this or competing theories of optimal capital structure can explain actual behavior and recent events in financial markets. I consider the static tradeoff theory, a *pecking order* theory emphasizing problems of asymmetric information, and a preliminary *organizational* theory which drops the assumed objective of shareholder value maximization.

In the end none of these theories is completely satisfactory. However, the exercise of trying to apply them forces us to take the firm's point of view and to think critically about the factors which may govern actual decisions.[1]

THE STATIC TRADEOFF THEORY

Figure 11.1 summarizes the static tradeoff theory. The horizontal base line expresses MM's idea that

---

* An earlier version of this paper was prepared for the Federal Reserve Bank of Boston's conference on "Are Distinctions between Debt and Equity Disappearing?" in October 1989 and published in the conference proceedings: R.W. Kopke and E.S. Rosengren, *Are the Distinctions between Debt and Equity Disappearing?* (Federal Reserve Bank of Boston, 1990). This version contains expanded explanations of several points. Also a few anachronisms have been eliminated.

---

1 This is not a self-contained survey article. I have stated theories intuitively and not attempted to derive them. I have attempted to cite interesting and representative research by others but have nevertheless skipped over many useful empirical and theoretical contributions. For an extensive survey and bibliography, see Ronald Masulis, *The Debt-Equity Choice* (New York: Ballinger Publishing Co., 1988).

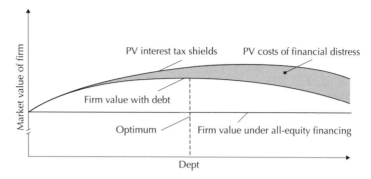

Figure 11.1 The Static–tradeoff Theory of Capital Structure

V, the market value of the firm – the aggregate market value of all its outstanding securities – should not depend on leverage when assets, earnings, and future investment opportunities are held constant. But the tax-deductibility of interest payments induces the firm to borrow to the margin where the present value of interest tax shields is just offset by the value loss due to agency costs of debt and the possibility of financial distress.

The static tradeoff theory has several things going for it. First, it avoids "corner solutions" and rationalizes moderate borrowing with a story that makes easy common sense. Most business people immediately agree that borrowing saves taxes and that too much debt can lead to costly trouble.

Second, closer analysis of costs of financial distress gives a testable prediction from the static tradeoff story; since these costs should be most serious for firms with valuable intangible assets and growth opportunities, we should observe that *mature* firms holding mostly *tangible* assets should borrow more, other things constant, than growth firms or firms which depend heavily on R&D, advertising, etc. Thus we would expect a pharmaceutical company to borrow less than a chemical manufacturer, even if the two firms' business risk (measured by asset beta, for example) are the same. This predicted inverse relationship between (proxies for) intangible assets and financial leverage has been confirmed by several studies.[2]

The static tradeoff theory may also seem to draw support from studies of the reaction of stock prices to announcements of security issues, retirements, or exchanges. Clifford Smith's 1986 summary of this research shows that almost all leverage-increasing transactions are good news, and leverage-decreasing transactions bad news.[3] Thus announcements of common stock issues drive down stock price, but repurchases push them up; exchanges of debt for equity securities drive up stock prices, but equity-for-debt exchanges depress them. These impacts are often striking and generally strong enough to bar quibbles about statistical significance; the only exception seems to be debt issue announcements, which on average have no significant effect.[4]

These "event studies" could be interpreted as proving investors' appreciation of the value of interest tax shields, thus confirming the practical importance of the static tradeoff theory's chief motive for borrowing. But on balance this evidence works *against* the theory. First, the competing pecking order theory can explain the same facts as the market's rational response to the issue or retirement of common equity, even if investors are totally

ratios are negatively related to marketing and selling expenses and R&D expenses. These expenses are obvious proxies for intangible assets, although Titman and Wessels interpret them as proxies for "uniqueness." See S. Titman and R. Wessels, "The Determinants of Capital Structure Choice," *Journal of Finance*, vol. 43, no. 1, March 1988, 1–19. See also note 23 below.

3 Clifford Smith, "Investment Banking and the Capital Acquisition Process." *Journal of Financial Economics*, vol. 15, no. 12, January–February 1986, 3–29.

4 See L. Shyam-Sunder, "The Stock Price Effect of Risky versus Safe Debt," *Journal of Financial and Quantitative Analysis*, vol. 26, no. 4, December 1991, 549–558.

2 See Michael Long and Ileen Malitz in "Investment Patterns and Financial Leverage," in B. Friedman, ed., *Corporate Capital Structure in the United States* (Chicago: University of Chicago Press, 1985). Also, Sheridan Titman and Roberto Wessels find that debt

indifferent to changes in financial leverage. This point is discussed further in the next section.

Second, the simple static tradeoff theory does not predict what the event studies find. If the theory were true, managers would be diligently seeking optimal capital structure, but find their firms bumped away from the optimum by random events. A couple years of unexpectedly good operating earnings or the unanticipated cash sale of a division might leave a firm below its optimal debt ratio, for example; another firm suffering a string of operating losses might end up too highly levered.

Thus we would expect to observe some firms issuing debt and/or retiring equity to regain the optimal debt ratio – they would move to the right, up the left-hand side of Figure 11.1. But other firms would be reducing leverage and moving to the left, up the right-hand slope of the figure. The movement should be value-increasing in both cases, and good news if it is news at all.

It's possible, of course, that the leverage-increasing transactions reflect reductions in business risk and increases in target debt ratios. If investors can't observe these changes directly, then a debt-for-equity exchange is good news; it demonstrates management's confidence in the level and safety of future earnings.

It's also possible that managers are not value-maximizers and do not attempt to lever up to the optimum. If most firms are sitting comfortably but inefficiently on the left of the upward-sloping value curve in Figure 11.1, then any increase in leverage is good news, and any decrease bad news. However, we can't just explain away the event study results without thinking more carefully about how a "managerial" firm would want to arrange its financing. Would it always prefer low debt, for example? This too is left to a later section of the paper.

The most telling evidence against the static tradeoff theory is the strong inverse correlation between profitability and financial leverage. *Within an industry*, the most profitable firms borrow less, the least profitable borrow more. In an extensive study of debt policy in U.S. and Japanese manufacturing corporations, Carl Kester finds that return on assets is the most significant explanatory variable for actual debt ratios. There is other supporting evidence as well.[5]

To repeat: high profits mean low debt. Yet the static tradeoff story would predict just the opposite relationship. Higher profits mean more dollars for debt service and more taxable income to shield. They should mean *higher* target debt ratios.

Could the negative correlation between profitability and leverage reflect delays in firms' adjustment to their optimum debt ratios? For example, a string of unexpectedly high (low) profits could push a firm's actual debt ratio below (above) the target. If transaction costs prevent quick movements back to the optimum, a negative correlation is established – a negative correlation between profitability and *deviations* from target debt ratios.

This explanation is logically O.K. but not credible without some specific theory or evidence on how firms manage capital structures over time. Expositions of the static tradeoff story rarely mention transaction costs;[6] in fact they usually start by accepting MM's Proposition I (the flat base line in Figure 11.1), which assumes that transaction costs are second order.

None of the evidence noted so far justifies discarding the static tradeoff theory. However, it's

---

5   W.C. Kester, "Capital and Ownership Structure: A Comparison of United States and Japanese Manufacturing

Corporations," *Financial Management*, vol. 15, no. 1, Spring 1986, 5–16. J. Baskin gets results similar to Kester's, and cites about a dozen other corroborating studies, in "An Empirical Investigation of the Pecking Order Hypothesis," *Financial Management*, vol. 18, no. 1, Spring 1989, 26–35. Further, Titman and Wessels (1988), cited in note 2, find a significant negative relationship between (an estimate of latent) profitability and market-value debt ratios, but no significant relationship to book ratios. Note, however, that "no significant relationship" does not support the static tradeoff theory, which predicts a positive impact of profitability on book debt ratios.

6   One exception is the target adjustment models used in empirical studies of capital structure choice. See, for example, A. Jalilvand and R.S. Harris, "Corporate Behavior in Adjusting to Capital Structure and Dividend Targets: An Econometric Study," *Journal of Finance*, vol. 39, no. 1, March 1984, 127–144. In these models, random events change actual capital structures, but transaction costs force firms to work back only gradually towards actual capital structures. Actual capital structures are mean-reverting.

These models work fairly well if one assumes the static tradeoff theory holds and that each firm has a well-defined target debt ratio. Unfortunately, the models work equally well when the firm has no target and follows a pure pecking order strategy. (See S.C. Myers and L. Shyam-Sunder, "Testing Static Tradeoff against Pecking Order Theories of Capital Structure," Working paper, MIT Sloan School of Management, February 1993.) In other words, the models offer no support for the static tradeoff theory against that competitor.

foolish not to be skeptical. The theory sounds right to financial economists, and business people will give it lip service if asked. It may be a weak guide to average behavior. It is not much help in understanding any given firm's decisions.

THE PECKING ORDER THEORY

The pecking order theory of capital structure reasons as follows:

1. Dividend policy is "sticky."
2. Firms prefer internal to external financing. However, they seek external financing if necessary to finance positive-NPV real investments.
3. If they do require external financing, they will issue the safest security first – i.e., they will choose debt before equity financing.
4. As the firm seeks more external financing, it will work down the pecking order of securities, from safe to risky debt, perhaps to convertibles and other quasi-equity instruments, and finally to equity as a last resort.[7]

In the pecking order theory, there is no well-defined target debt ratio. The attraction of interest tax shields and the threat of financial distress are assumed to be second-order. Debt ratios change when there is an imbalance of internal cash flow, net of dividends, and real investment opportunities. Highly profitable firms with limited investment opportunities work down to a low debt ratio. Firms whose investment opportunities outrun internally generated funds are driven to borrow more and more.

This theory gives an immediate explanation for the negative intra-industry correlation between profitability and leverage. Suppose firms generally invest to keep up with industry growth. Then rates of real investment will be similar within an industry. Given sticky dividend payout, the least profitable firms in the industry will have less internal funds for new investment and will end up borrowing more.

The pecking order story is not new. There are longstanding concerns about corporations who rely too much on internal financing to avoid the

"discipline of capital markets." Gordon Donaldson, for example, has observed pecking order behavior in careful case studies.[8] But, until Nicholas Majluf's and my papers published in 1984,[9] the preference for internal financing and the aversion to new equity issues was viewed as managerial behavior contrary to shareholders' interests. Our papers showed that managers who act solely in (existing) shareholders' interests will rationally prefer internal finance and will issue the least risky security if forced to seek outside funds.

The pecking order theory reflects problems created by asymmetric information – a fancy way of saying that managers know more about their firms than outside investors do. How do we know managers have superior information? Well, outside investors clearly think they do because stock prices react to firms' announcements of earnings, major capital expenditures, exchange offers, stock repurchases, etc. The market learns from managers' actions because the managers are believed to have better or earlier information.

Consider the following story:

1. Because managers know more about their firms than outside investors do, they are reluctant to issue stock when they believe their shares are undervalued. They are more likely to issue when their shares are fairly priced or overpriced.
2. Investors understand that managers know more and that they try to "time" issues.
3. Investors therefore interpret the decision to issue as bad news, and firms which issue equity can do so only at a discount.
4. Faced with this discount, firms which have worked down the pecking order and need external equity may end up passing by good investment opportunities (or accepting "excessive" leverage) because shares can't be sold at what managers consider a fair price.

7 Warrants would be even lower on the pecking order. However, warrants are usually issued in a package with debt – roughly equivalent to a convertible bond.

8 Gordon Donaldson, *Managing Corporate Wealth: The Operation of a Comprehensive Financial Goals System* (New York: Praeger, 1984).
9 See S.C. Myers and N.S. Majluf, "Corporate Financing and Investment Decisions When Firms Have Information That Investors Do Not Have," *Journal of Financial Economics*, vol. 13, no. 2, June 1984, 187–221; and S.C. Myers, "The Capital Structure Puzzle," *Journal of Finance*, vol. 39, no. 3, July 1984, 575–592.

This story has three immediate implications. First, internal equity is better than external equity. (Note that the static tradeoff theory makes no distinction between equity from retained earnings and equity from stock issues.) Because dividends are sticky and debt service predetermined, retention of any excess operating cash flow is more or less automatic and does not convey information to investors.

Second, financial slack is valuable. It relieves managers' fear of passing by a positive-NPV outlay when external equity finance is required, but shares can only be issued at a substantial discount to intrinsic value.

Financial slack means cash, marketable securities, and readily saleable real assets. It also means the capacity to issue (nearly) default-risk free debt. If a new debt issue carries no default risk, potential investors do not have to worry about whether the firm as a whole is over- or undervalued by the market.

Third, debt is better than equity if external financing is required, simply because debt is safer than equity. Asymmetric information drives the firm to issue the safest possible security. This establishes the pecking order.

Why are safer securities better? Not because the manager always wants to issue them. On the contrary, when the market overvalues the firm, the manager would like to issue the most overvalued security: not debt, but equity. (Warrants would be even better.) If the market undervalues the firm, the manager would like to issue debt in order to minimize the bargain handed to investors.

But no intelligent investor would let the manager play this game. Suppose you are a potential buyer of a new security issue, either debt or equity. You know the issuer knows more than you do about the securities' true values. You know the issuer will want to offer equity only when it is overvalued – i.e., when the issuer is more pessimistic than you are. Would you ever buy equity if debt were an alternative? If you do the issuer is guaranteed to win and you to lose. Thus you will refuse equity and only accept debt. The firm will be forced to issue debt, regardless of whether the firm is over- or undervalued.

Issuing safer securities minimizes the manager's information advantage. Any attempt to exploit this information advantage more aggressively will fail because investors cannot be forced to buy a security they infer is overvalued. An equity issue

becomes feasible in the pecking order only when leverage is already high enough to make additional debt materially expensive, e.g., because of the threat of costs of financial distress. If the manager is known to have a good reason to issue equity rather than debt and is willing to do so in some cases where the equity is actually *under*priced, then purchase of new equity can be a fair game for investors, and issue of new equity becomes feasible despite the manager's information advantage.

In practice the pecking order theory cannot be wholly right. A counterexample is generated every time a firm issues equity when it could have issued investment-grade debt. Nevertheless, the theory immediately explains otherwise puzzling facts, such as the strong negative association between profitability and leverage. It also explains why almost all corporate equity financing has come from retention rather than new issues.[10]

The pecking order model also explains why stock price falls when equity is issued. If the firm acts in the interest of its existing shareholders, the announcement of an equity issue is always bad news.[11] So is an equity-for-debt exchange offer – not because the exchange reduces financial leverage, but because it amounts to a new issue of common stock. The fact that investors pay for the issue with an unusual currency (the issuing firms' previously outstanding debt securities) is irrelevant.

Conversely, a debt-for-equity exchange is good news not because it increases outstanding debt, but because it amounts to a repurchase of equity. If investors believe managers have superior knowledge, then their decision to repurchase signals optimism and pushes stock price up.

Thus the pecking order theory neatly explains why equity issues reduce stock prices, but plain-vanilla debt issues do not. If the probability of default is low, then managers' information advantage is not a major concern to potential buyers of a debt issue. The smaller the managers' advantage, the less information is released by the decision to issue. The pecking order theory would predict a small negative impact when a debt issue is

10 See R.A. Brealey and S.C. Myers, *Principles of Corporate Finance*, 4th ed. (New York: McGraw-Hill Book Co., 1991), Table 14-3, pp. 326–327.
11 Majluf and Myers (1984), cited in note 9.

announced (all corporate debt carries some default risk), but for most public issues the effect should be very small and likely to be lost in the noise of the market.

AN ORGANIZATIONAL THEORY OF CAPITAL STRUCTURE

Both of the theories reviewed so far assume that managers act in their current stockholders' interests. This is a useful convention of modern corporate finance theory but hardly a law of nature.

Witnesses to the market for corporate control in the 1980s have to admit the existence of conflicts between managers and stockholders. Plenty of takeovers, LBOs, and restructurings were undertaken to solve "free cash flow" problems, in which firms with excess cash flow were inclined to waste it rather than paying it out to investors.

Competition tends to punish such waste. We would not expect to find it in toughly competitive industries. But if product market competition doesn't do the job, then competition in the market for corporate control may take its place. U.S. automobile companies were forced to slim down their organizations by their Japanese competitors. However, the Japanese don't pump oil, and so United States oil companies were forced to diet by (actual or threatened) takeovers.

Suppose we accept for sake of argument that there are important divergences between organizations' and investors' interests. What does that say about the role financing decisions play in the market for corporate control? What help does it give us to understand financing decisions made by corporations that are not disciplined by the threat of takeover? In other words, what would a managerial or organizational theory of capital structure look like?

Managerial theories would model capital structure choices in terms of top management's *personal* utility functions, compensation schemes, and opportunities for alternative employment. Perhaps managers' personal risk aversions lead the firm to use too little debt – at least that is a common casual hypothesis.[12] (Ideal compensation schemes could

induce value-maximizing financing decisions, eliminating the need for a managerial theory of capital structure.)

Michael Jensen and William Meckling's path-breaking paper on agency costs stresses managers' natural tendency to extract too many perquisites and analyzes the monitoring, bonding, and contracting undertaken to minimize the net costs of the managers' rational but self-interested behavior.[13,14] Obviously these costs increase as the managers' personal ownership stake in the firm decreases. This supplies an argument for debt financing and against "public" equity – that is, against equity contributed by non-management investors who can not monitor management effectively.

This agency cost approach is most dramatically expressed in Jensen's free cash flow hypothesis, which starts from the alleged tendency of managers to plow excessive amounts into mature businesses or ill-advised acquisitions. "The problem," Jensen says, "is how to motivate managers to disgorge the cash rather than investing it below the cost of capital or wasting it in organizational inefficiencies."[15]

If that's the problem, debt financing is better than equity because it bonds the firm to pay out cash. The ideal debt level would leave the firm with just enough cash in the bank to finance all

---

manager sets the mix of debt and equity to his own best advantage, thereby signaling the firm's true value to investors. See S.A. Ross, "The Determination of Financial Structure: the Incentive-Signalling Approach," *Bell Journal of Economics and Management Science*, vol. 8, no. 1, Spring 1977, 23–40.

13 M.C. Jensen and W.H. Meckling, "Theory of the Firm: Managerial Behavior, Agency Costs and Ownership Structure," *Journal of Financial Economics*, vol. 3, no. 4, October 1976, 305–360.

14 The problem is not that managers get perks but that they would rather have cash. If a manager's contribution justifies a salary of $100,000, there's no inefficiency in giving $80,000 in cash and $20,000 in perks freely chosen by the manager. The problem is that cash payments are much more easily controlled than perks extracted. Given the opportunity, a manager may take perks that he would not buy with his own money. Thus he may end up costing $80,000 in cash and $40,000 in perks but still view his cash-equivalent compensation as $100,000. The $20,000 cost, plus the costs of bonding and monitoring to prevent the manager from taking more than $40,000 in perks, is a net drain on the value of the firm.

15 M.C. Jensen, "Agency Costs of Free Cash Flow, Corporate Finance, and Takeovers," *American Economic Review*, vol. 76, no. 2, May 1986, p. 323.

---

12 Stephen Ross presents a more sophisticated incentive signaling model in which a rational (and possibly risk-neutral)

Table 11.1 Organizational Balance Sheet*

PV Existing Assets, Pre-Tax	PVA	Existing Debt	D
PV Growth Opportunities, Pre-Tax	PVGO	Employees' Surplus	S
PV Future Taxes	PVTAX	Existing Equity	E
After-Tax Value	V	After-Tax Value	V

Corporate Wealth = Employees' Surplus + Equity

W   =   S   +   E

*All entries at Market Value.

positive-NPV projects but not a penny left over.[16] Perhaps growth and size are the ultimate perks, but debt can supply the necessary discipline.

This gives a rationale for LBOs, restructurings, and debt-financed takeovers. The "good guys," who are willing to take on debt and disgorge cash, oust the "bad guys" and put their firms on a diet. The good guys stay good because the new management has a substantial equity interest and is more tightly monitored by lenders and the new equity investors.

Unfortunately these ideas are more useful in thinking about the market for corporate control than about capital structure. Suppose we look at other times or places where incumbent management is not threatened by the good guys. Are we reduced to saying that mature firms will (1) invest too much and (2) borrow too little? Why hasn't natural economic selection devised compensation arrangements which lead managers to reach value-maximizing debt levels and disgorge all excess cash?

We can clarify some of these issues by stepping away from managers' personal attributes and incentives, and thinking instead of the firm as a value-maximizing organism.

The Organizational Balance Sheet. Table 11.1 presents an organizational balance sheet. This has no necessary, direct connection with the firm's books. It is just a way of expressing the identity between the market value of assets and liabilities.

On the left is PVA, the present value of future cash flows from existing assets, plus PVGO, the present value of growth opportunities, less the present value of the government's tax claim,

PVTAX. Note that PVGO can be negative if the firm is expected to waste money on negative-NPV capital investments or to overpay for acquisitions.

On the right is D, existing debt; E, equity; plus S, the present value of *organizational surplus*. This surplus reflects the present value of the future costs of perks, overstaffing, above-market wages, etc. Note that PVA and PVGO are defined *before* this surplus is subtracted; that is, PVA and PVGO represent the potential values if management maximized total firm value.

Think of organizational surplus as a junior financial claim, a preferred share for example. It is junior because creditors can usually force the firm to go on a diet if debt service is threatened. It is not a true residual claim because many elements of surplus – overstaffing and above-market salaries, for example – tend to be "smoothed," and there are limits to the amount of surplus that can be extracted.[17]

Jack Treynor has suggested that "the financial objective of the corporation is to conserve, and when possible, to enhance the corporation's power to distribute cash," which depends on the net market value of the firm.[18] For a public corporation traded in well-developed capital markets, market value is fungible. Therefore the "power to distribute cash" is proportional to *corporate wealth*. This is the sum of equity and employee surplus, W = E + S.

---

16 This argument has been formalized and generalized by Rene Stulz in "Managerial Discretion and Optimal Financing Policies," *Journal of Financial Economics*, vol. 26, no. 1, March 1990, 3–27.

17 There is no simple junior–senior ordering between surplus and equity. In some cases surplus may be the true residual claim. Consider an incorporated consulting company or investment bank, where human capital is the most important asset and employee compensation is heavily weighted towards year-end bonuses. The bonuses may have more variance than dividends paid to shareholders.

18 J.L. Treynor, "The Financial Objective in the Widely Held Corporation," *Financial Analysts Journal*, March–April 1981, p. 70.

Gordon Donaldson concluded from his extensive case studies of mature public corporations that "the financial objective that guided the top managers of the companies studied [was] maximization of corporate wealth. Corporate wealth is *that wealth over which management has effective control* and is an assured source of funds."[19]

Of course standard corporate finance theory also assumes the firm maximizes wealth. But it is *shareholders*' wealth. Standard theory says that that dividend policy is irrelevant in perfect, frictionless markets because paying a dollar per share dividend reduces share price by exactly a dollar; shareholders' wealth is unchanged. However, *corporate* wealth declines by a dollar per share. That dollar is no longer under the effective control of management.

Treynor and Donaldson lead us to think of the firm as a coalition. Managers' personal risk aversion is not important because corporate wealth is marketable and risks can be hedged as appropriate with zero-NPV transactions. We are concerned with the behavior of the organization as a whole rather than the personal motives and decisions of a few people at the top of the corporate hierarchy. The coalition maximizes value, and we can work with PVs and NPVs just as in ordinary corporate finance theory.

This may be a powerful simplification, though it is not yet clear whether the objective should be to maximize total corporate wealth ($W = E + S$) or the net wealth of the organizational coalition (S only). For now we will take Treynor and Donaldson literally and assume the objective is to maximize W.

Investment and Financing Decisions by Firms Seeking to Maximize Corporate Wealth. Consider how several common financial decisions would be analyzed by a firm which maximizes corporate wealth. For simplicity I will assume the organization's decisionmakers have no information advantage over outside investors and also that existing debt is (close to) default-risk free, so there is no temptation to undertake transactions to undercut existing creditors.

Because corporate wealth is measured by market value, rules for ranking capital investments are

exactly the same as in standard finance theory. The firm always seeks positive NPV and prefers more NPV to less.

Suppose the firm issues debt to finance additional capital investment projects which happen to have NPV = 0.[20] Then there is no change in corporate wealth: the market value of additional real assets are offset by the new debt liability. Thus with debt financing, there is no incentive to overinvest in negative-NPV projects.

However, an issue of debt that replaces equity, holding PVA and PVGO constant, *decreases* corporate wealth. As debt increases, corporate wealth, which is the sum of equity and organizational surplus, must go down.

This could be good news for stockholders. First, PVTAX, the government's claim on the firm, could be significantly decreased by interest tax shields on the new debt. Some of the tax savings might be captured in increased surplus, but some would flow through to equity.

Second, the value of organizational surplus would decrease, transferring value to equity. Surplus is similar to a subordinated debt claim, whose market value falls when more senior debt is inserted between the junior debt and the firm's assets.[21]

Thus the organizational theory can explain why debt-for-equity changes are good news for stockholders. (Of course one has to accept that interest tax shields have significant value and that surplus is an important entry on the organizational balance sheet.) The theory also predicts that firms will not undertake debt-for-equity exchanges except under pressure, say, from threat of a takeover.

An issue of equity that replaces debt would be bad news for investors. The reasoning is just as for a debt-for-equity exchange, with signs of course reversed. But would a new equity issue, or retention of an unanticipated increase in earnings, be bad news if the money is put to a zero-NPV use on the asset side of the balance sheet?

Yes, because employees' surplus increases. Remember that this surplus resembles a junior debt, whose value increases when the firm adds

---

19 Donaldson (1984), cited in note 8, p. 22; emphasis in original.

20 The present value of interest tax shields on debt supported by the project is included in the project's NPV.
21 An issue of debt to finance zero-NPV real investment would trigger a similar, but smaller transfer to equity.

equity-financed assets. Suppose the new equity money is raised by a share issue. Then new equity investors anticipate the value transfer from equity to surplus and mark down the purchase price of the new shares accordingly. The increase in surplus must therefore be extracted from existing equity.

The equity issue may be even worse news if the proceeds are not productively invested. If $10 million is raised and invested in a project with a value of only $6 million, existing shareholders lose $4 million (and also lose whatever the employees gain from appreciation in the value of their junior claim). Other things constant, corporate wealth nevertheless *increases* by $6 million, and surplus clearly increases, too.

Thus the negative stock market reaction to equity issues is guaranteed if investors fear that marginal investments are negative-NPV. But why should the corporate-wealth-maximizing firm ever accept a negative-NPV project? Why can't it issue equity and buy marketable securities, which presumably have NPV = 0? Then a $10 million equity issue should add $10 million to corporate wealth.

This is not an easy question for the organizational theory, but there are some possible answers. First, buying marketable debt securities amounts to lending money. If there is a significant tax advantage to borrowing, there must be a corresponding disadvantage to lending. Thus investment in a Treasury bill should have NPV < 0 after tax. Second, if another company's equity securities are purchased, an additional layer of taxation is created, which should drive NPV negative. This layer of tax is eliminated if the other company is taken over, but takeovers not motivated by real economic gains are also likely to be negative-NPV once transaction costs and takeover premiums are recognized.

Limits to Corporate Wealth. Assume, then, that outlets for investment with zero or positive NPV are limited. That limit defines the maximum scale of a shareholder-value maximizing firm. What limits the scale of a firm that maximizes corporate wealth? It seems that any new equity issue inevitably increases corporate wealth *and* organizational surplus when the proceeds are used to buy real assets. (Corporate wealth and surplus also increase if earnings are retained rather than paid out as dividends.) This is so even if the assets' NPVs are negative, so long as they have any value

at all. Why doesn't the firm issue more and more equity, expanding and generating practically unlimited corporate wealth? If corporate wealth is the objective, the firm does not care about the *price* of new shares.

This, too, is not an easy question. One can appeal to the threat of takeover by other firms seeking to maximize *their* corporate wealth by preying on other firms with large employee surpluses or substantial negative-NPV investments. However, takeovers did not appear as a significant threat to large public corporations until relatively recently.[22]

Second, one can also argue that growth firms need to maintain share price to assure access to new equity as needed to finance future real investment. But this does not help explain behavior of mature firms whose internal cash flow outruns positive-NPV opportunities.

A third argument refers to PVGO, the present value of growth opportunities shown in Table 11.1. A corporation that invests heavily in negative-NPV assets today may lead investors to expect similar future investments. Investors mark PVGO down and eventually set it negative. In extreme cases, where the firm is more or less throwing money away, this year's additions to corporate wealth through PVA could be more than offset by the reduction in corporate wealth from an increasingly negative PVGO.

Corporate wealth is in the end not determined by the corporation but by investors. Only *market* value can be translated into "the power to distribute cash." That depends on what investors are willing to pay. That willingness depends on their assessment of the intelligence of the future operating and investment plans of the firm.

There is a fourth – I think deeper – argument. A large public corporation with management separate from ownership must maintain an adequate market value of equity in order to operate its business efficiently.

The inefficiencies of *not* supporting "adequate" equity value can be seen in an extreme case. Consider a firm that expands assets and corporate

22   One can also note the compensation schemes of top management, whose fortunes are tied more closely to equity earnings and stock prices than most of their employees. However, it's not clear why a wealth-maximizing organization would adopt such schemes.

wealth at the expense of shareholders so aggressively that the market value of its shares is driven to a small fraction of the firm's potential value. Organizational surplus is then very large; in effect the coalition of employees expropriates most of the potential equity value. I will suppose that this firm is somehow protected from takeover and that internal cash flow more than covers future investment outlays.

In this case organizational surplus must serve as the capital base of the business. There is no equity to support contracts or relationships with suppliers, employees, and customers, or to guarantee the firm's ability to pay its debts.

The present value of organizational surplus could serve as capital if its value were observable. But S is not a traded asset. It can only be valued from scratch, i.e. by valuing the firm's assets and liabilities, then subtracting any debt claims (and the residual market value of equity). For a large firm with many business units, international operations, significant going concern value and other intangible assets, uncertain growth opportunities, and possibly hidden liabilities, this would be a costly and notoriously inaccurate exercise. But absent the exercise it would be imprudent to enter into a contractual or business relationship with such a firm.

The costs and delays that would be imposed on the firm's operations are obvious.[23]

A firm that landed in this box would see two ways out:

1. Eliminate the separation between ownership and control, recreating inside equity investors – perhaps an LBO partnership – with the power and credible incentive to restrict employee surplus. Of course such owners would also prevent the firm from expanding into negative-NPV assets.[24]
2. Make a deal with outside equity investors which limits the size of organizational surplus

and reestablishes a significant, objective equity value for the firm. This would also limit negative-NPV expansion.

For all these reasons we see that too aggressive pursuit of corporate wealth at the expense of shareholders does not maximize organizational surplus. The employee coalition therefore seeks, or accepts, an accommodation with shareholders. That leads us to dividend policy.

Dividend policy. Why are shareholders willing to pay anything at all for a mature firm's shares, absent effective voting power or the threat of takeover? The answer is that the firm has somehow bonded itself to distribute cash to shareholders. Obviously the bond is not contractual, as it is with debt, but implicit. This is the reason why firms have fairly well-defined, sticky policies that regulate dividends per share.

A stock issue increases equity value only if this bonded or "promised" future payout increases. Consider the two extreme cases. First suppose a firm issues $10 million in new equity but does not "promise" to pay out any additional future dividends. (Aggregate dividends are maintained but dividends per share drop in proportion to the number of new shares issued.) Then existing shareholders must absorb a $10 million capital loss. In other words, the decision to issue new stock breaks the firm's "promise" to old shareholders. But having just broken that promise, it's not clear where the firm would find any rational *new* shareholders. In other words, an equity issue would probably be infeasible.

At the other extreme the firm could accept an implicit obligation to maintain dividends per share and to pay out additional future dividends with a present value of $10 million. This fully "covers" the newly issued shares, so existing shares maintain their value. Total equity value increases by $10 million.

Corporate wealth also increases by $10 million. However, not much of this goes to employees. The firm has $10 million more assets but has also promised $10 million to new shareholders. Nothing is left over for organizational surplus, except for the transfer to surplus from existing equity, which occurs because employees now hold better protected junior claims on the firm's assets.

Perhaps this tells us why firms prefer to retain earnings when profits unexpectedly increase. Suppose the firm has "promised" to pay out

---

23 This argument resembles Sheridan Titman's argument that firms with "unique" products and long-term relationships with suppliers and customers should favor conservative debt ratios. S. Titman, "The Effect of Capital Structure on a Firm's Liquidation Decision," *Journal of Financial Economics*, vol. 13, no. 1, March 1984, 137–151.

24 This may happen automatically. If E falls close to zero, then ownership and control passes to the employee coalition, in which case they should act as inside equity investors.

dividends according to some sticky rule. Then if earnings are higher than anticipated, much of the increase is free for employees to deploy; it has not been promised to shareholders. On the other hand, if there is an unanticipated shortfall, dividends are to some extent protected, and the firm reduces the flow to surplus or turns to outside financing for real investment.

This begins to look like a pecking order. The organizational theory of capital structure may be able to explain why the most profitable firms typically borrow the least. Their higher than "normal" or expected earnings are retained because their contract with shareholders does not require them to be paid out. If real investment opportunities do not increase in proportion to earnings – as is likely for mature firms – and if immediate cash flows to surplus are also sticky, then higher earnings mean greater retention, less reliance on external financing, and presumably a lower debt ratio.

The organizational theory also seems to explain stock market reactions to announcements of security issues, retirements, and exchanges. Overall it is a promising alternative to capital structure theories based on shareholder wealth maximization.

Yet caution is called for. I have not been able to develop the theory fully and formally in this paper. I have not analyzed the implicit contract between the firm and its shareholders or attempted a link-up to the literature on dividend policy. I have compared employees' surplus to a junior debt liability without giving a detailed description of the properties of this claim, and I have implicitly treated organizational surplus as a kind of tax which does not reduce the *potential* value of existing assets and growth opportunities. This is almost certainly oversimplified.

Finally, I have accepted Treynor and Donaldson's suggested objective of maximizing corporate wealth. The discussion above of equity issues and the firms' implicit contract with shareholders suggests that maximizing corporate wealth may not always be in the employees' interest, even if all employees could act as one.

CONCLUSIONS

This paper has briefly reviewed three theories – perhaps I should say two theories and one story – of capital structure. I have tried to match them to firms' actual behavior and to judge their ability to explain the two most striking facts about corporate financing.

The first fact is that investors regard almost all leverage-increasing security issues or exchanges as good news, and leverage-decreasing transactions as bad news. The only exception is plain-vanilla debt issues, which apparently are no news at all. The second fact is the strong negative correlation between profitability and financial leverage.

The widely-cited static tradeoff theory, taken literally, explains neither fact. It is at best a weak guide to average behavior.

The pecking order theory, though apparently a minority view, seems to explain both facts.

The organizational theory described in this paper is a first try at restating Jensen's free cash flow theory of the market for corporate control as a general theory of capital structure choice. It may be able to explain the two facts, though its predictions are not as clear and definite as the pecking order model's. A more thorough and formal development of the organizational theory is obviously needed.

The initial plausibility of the organizational theory derives from the financial history of the 1980s, particularly the aggressive use of leverage in LBOs, takeovers, and restructurings. Jensen properly interprets much of this activity as follows: high debt ratios were effective in forcing mature companies on a diet and preventing them from making negative-NPV capital investments or acquisitions. The debt is viewed as a contractual bond which forced overweight companies to distribute cash to investors.

The organizational theory is an extension of this argument, and therefore broadly consistent with it. The static tradeoff theory gives no help with the events of the 1980s unless it is assumed that companies are systematically underleveraged and therefore not maximizing shareholder value. But in that case the static tradeoff theory is no more than an open invitation to develop an organizational theory.

Thus there are really only two contenders in the race to explain capital structure: models such as the pecking order theory which assert asymmetric information as the chief underlying problem, and models which start from the proposition that organizations act in their own interests.

CHAPTER 12

The Capital Structure Puzzle: Another Look at the Evidence

Michael J. Barclay and Clifford W. Smith, Jr.
(University of Rochester)

A perennial debate in corporate finance concerns the question of optimal capital structure: Given a level of total capital necessary to support a company's activities, is there a way of dividing up that capital into debt and equity that maximizes current firm value? And, if so, what are the critical factors in setting the leverage ratio for a given company?

Although corporate finance has been taught in business schools for almost a century, the academic finance profession has found it remarkably difficult to provide definitive answers to these questions – answers that can guide practicing corporate executives in making their financing decisions. Part of the difficulty stems from how the discipline of finance has evolved. For much of this century, both the teaching of finance and the supporting research were dominated by the case-study method. In effect, finance education was a glorified apprenticeship system designed to convey to students the accepted wisdom – often codified in the form of rules of thumb – of successful practitioners. Such rules of thumb may have been quite effective in a given set of circumstances, but as those circumstances change over time such rules tend to degenerate into dogma. An example was Eastman Kodak's longstanding decision to shun debt financing – a policy stemming from George Eastman's brush with insolvency at the turn of the century that was not reversed until the 1980s.

But this "anecdotal" approach to the study of finance is changing. In the past few decades, financial economists have worked to transform corporate finance into a more scientific undertaking, with a body of formal theories that can be tested by empirical studies of market and corporate behavior. The ultimate basis for judging the usefulness of a theory is, of course, its consistency with the facts – and thus its ability to predict actual behavior. But this brings us to the most important obstacle to developing a definitive theory of capital structure: namely, the difficulty of designing empirical tests that are powerful enough to distinguish among the competing theories.

What makes the capital structure debate especially intriguing is that the different theories represent such different, and in some ways almost diametrically opposed, decision-making processes. For example, some finance scholars have followed Miller and Modigliani by arguing that both capital structure and dividend policy are largely "irrelevant" in the sense that they have no significant, predictable effects on corporate market values. Another school of thought holds that corporate financing choices reflect an attempt by corporate managers to balance the tax shields of greater debt against the increased probability and costs of financial distress, including those arising from corporate underinvestment. But if too much debt can destroy value by causing financial distress and underinvestment, others have argued that *too little* debt – at least in large, mature companies – can lead to *over*investment and low returns on capital.

Still others argue that corporate managers making financing decisions are concerned primarily with the "signaling" effects of such decisions – for example, the tendency of stock prices to fall significantly in response to common stock offerings (which can make such offerings very expensive for existing shareholders) and to rise in response to leverage-increasing recapitalizations. Building on this signaling argument, MIT professor Stewart Myers has suggested that corporate capital structures are simply the cumulative result of individual financing decisions in which managers follow a financial *pecking order* – one in which retained earnings are preferred to outside financing, and debt is preferred to equity when outside funding is required. According to Myers, corporate managers making financing decisions are not really thinking about an optimal capital structure – that is, a long-run targeted debt-to-equity ratio they eventually want to achieve. Instead, they simply take the "path of least resistance" and choose what then appears to be the low-cost financing vehicle – generally debt – with little thought about the future consequences of these choices.

In his 1984 speech to the American Finance Association in which he first presented the pecking order theory, Professor Myers referred to this conflict among the different theories as the "capital structure puzzle." As we already suggested, the greatest barrier to progress in solving the puzzle has been the difficulty of devising conclusive tests of the competing theories. Over 30 years ago, researchers in the *capital markets* branch of finance, with its focus on portfolio theory and asset pricing, began to develop models in the form of precise mathematical formulas that predict the values of traded financial assets as a function of a handful of (mainly) observable variables. The predictions generated by such models, after continuous testing and refinement, have turned out to be remarkably accurate and useful to practitioners. For example, the Black-Scholes option pricing model – variations of which have long been widely used on options exchanges – has enabled traders to calculate the value of traded options of all kinds as a function of just six variables (all but one of which can be directly observed).

The key to financial economists' success in capital markets is this: Armed with specific hypotheses, they have been able to develop sophisticated and powerful empirical tests. The evidence from such tests has in turn allowed theorists to increase the "realism" of their models to the point where they have been used, and in some cases further refined, by practitioners. And while no one would argue that all major asset pricing issues have been resolved, the continuing interaction between theory and testing has yielded a richer understanding of risk-return tradeoffs than anyone might have imagined decades ago.

Empirical methods in corporate finance have lagged behind those in capital markets for several reasons. First, our models of capital structure decisions are less precise than asset pricing models. The major theories focus on the ways that capital structure choices are likely to affect firm value. But rather than being reducible, like the option pricing model, to a precise mathematical formula, the existing theories of capital structure provide at best qualitative or directional predictions. They generally identify major factors like taxes or bankruptcy costs that would lead to an association between particular firm characteristics and higher or lower leverage. For example, the tax-based theory of capital structure suggests that firms with more non-interest tax shields (like investment tax credits) should have less debt in their capital structures; but the theory does not tell us how much less.

Second, most of the competing theories of optimal capital structure are not mutually exclusive. Evidence consistent with one theory – say, the tax-based explanation – generally does not allow us to conclude that another factor – the value of debt in reducing overinvestment by mature companies – is unimportant. In fact, it seems clear that taxes, bankruptcy costs (including incentives for underinvestment), and information costs all play some role in determining a firm's optimal capital structure. With our current tests, it is generally not possible to reject one theory in favor of another.

Third, many of the variables that we think affect optimal capital structure are difficult to measure. For example, signaling theory suggests that the managers' "private" information about the company's prospects plays an important role in their financing choices. But, since there is no obvious way to identify when managers have such proprietary information, it is hard to test this proposition.

For all of these reasons and others, the state of the art in corporate finance is less developed than in asset pricing. Thus it is important for the academic community to continue to develop the theory to yield more precise predictions, and to devise more powerful empirical tests as well as better proxies for the key firm characteristics that are likely to drive corporate financing decisions.

In this paper, we offer our assessment of the current state of the academic finance profession's understanding of these issues and suggest some new directions for further exploration. We also offer in closing what we feel is a promising approach to reconciling the different theories of capital structure.

THE THEORIES[1]

Current explanations of corporate financial policy can be grouped into three broad categories: (1) taxes, (2) contracting costs, and (3) information costs. Before discussing these theories, it is important to keep in mind that they are not mutually exclusive and that each is likely to help us understand at least particular facets of corporate financing. Our aim is to determine the relative importance of the different theories and to identify those aspects of financial policy that each theory is most helpful in explaining.

Taxes

The basic corporate profits tax allows the deduction of interest payments but not dividends in the calculation of taxable income. For this reason, adding debt to a company's capital structure lowers its expected tax liability and increases its after-tax cash flow. If there were only a corporate profits tax and no individual taxes on corporate securities, the value of a levered firm would equal that of an identical all-equity firm plus the present value of its interest tax shields. That present value, which represents the contribution of debt financing to the market value of the firm, could be estimated simply by multiplying the company's marginal tax rate (34% plus state and local rates) times the principal amount of outstanding debt (assuming the firm expects to maintain its current debt level).

The problem with this analysis, however, is that it overstates the tax advantage of debt by considering only the corporate profits tax. Many investors who receive interest income must pay taxes on that income. But those same investors who receive equity income in the form of capital gains are taxed at a lower rate and can defer any tax by choosing not to realize those gains. Thus, although higher leverage lowers the firm's corporate taxes, it increases the taxes paid by investors. And, because investors care about their *after-tax* returns, they require compensation for these increased taxes in the form of higher yields on corporate debt – higher than the yields on, say, comparably risky tax-exempt municipal bonds.

The higher yields on corporate debt that reflect investors' taxes effectively reduce the tax advantage of debt over equity. In this sense, the company's shareholders ultimately bear all of the tax consequences of its operations, whether the company pays those taxes directly in the form of corporate income tax or indirectly in the form of higher required rates of return on the securities its sells. For this reason alone,[2] the tax advantage of corporate debt is almost certainly not 34 cents for every dollar of debt. Nor is it likely to be zero, however, and so a consistently profitable company that volunteers to pay more taxes by having substantial unused debt capacity is likely to be leaving considerable value on the table.

Contracting costs

Conventional capital structure analysis holds that financial managers set leverage targets by balancing

---

1 This section draws on the discussion of capital structure theory in Michael J. Barclay, Clifford W. Smith, Jr. and Ross L. Watts "The Determinants of Corporate Leverage and Dividend Policies," *Journal of Applied Corporate Finance*, Vol. 7 No. 4 (Winter 1995).

2 The extent to which a company benefits from interest tax shields also depends on whether it has other tax shields. For example, holding all else equal, companies with more investment tax credits or tax loss carryforwards should have lower leverage ratios to reflect the lower value of their debt tax shields. See Harry DeAngelo and Ronald Masulis, "Optimal Capital Structure Under Corporate and Personal Taxation," *Journal of Financial Economics*, Vol. 8 No. 1 (1980), pp. 3–29.

the tax benefits of higher leverage against the greater probability, and thus higher expected costs, of financial distress. In this view, the optimal capital structure is the one in which the next dollar of debt is expected to provide an additional tax subsidy that just offsets the resulting increase in expected costs of financial distress.

Costs of Financial Distress (or the Underinvestment Problem). Although the *direct* expenses associated with the administration of the bankruptcy process appear to be quite small relative to the market values of companies,[3] the *indirect* costs can be substantial. In thinking about optimal capital structure, the most important indirect costs are likely to be the reductions in firm value that result from cutbacks in promising investment that tend to be made when companies get into financial difficulty.

When a company files for bankruptcy, the bankruptcy judge effectively assumes control of corporate investment policy – and it's not hard to imagine circumstances in which judges do not maximize firm value. But even in conditions less extreme than bankruptcy, highly leveraged companies are more likely than their low-debt counterparts to pass up valuable investment opportunities, especially when faced with the prospect of default. In such cases, corporate managers are likely not only to postpone major capital projects, but to make cutbacks in R&D, maintenance, advertising, or training that end up reducing future profits.

This tendency of companies to underinvest when facing financial difficulty is accentuated by conflicts that can arise among the firm's different claimholders. To illustrate this conflict, consider what might happen to a high-growth company that had trouble servicing its debt. Since the value of such a firm will depend heavily on its ability to carry out its long-term investment plan, what the company needs is an infusion of equity. But there is a problem. As Stewart Myers pointed out in his classic 1977 paper entitled "Determinants of Corporate Borrowing,"[4] the investors who would be asked to provide the new equity in such cases recognize that much of the value created (or preserved) by their investment would go to restoring the creditors' position. In this situation, the cost of the new equity could be so high that managers acting on their shareholders' behalf might rationally forgo both the capital and the investment opportunities.

Myers referred to this as "the underinvestment problem." And, as he went on to argue, companies whose value consists primarily of intangible investment opportunities – or "growth options," as he called them – will choose low-debt capital structures because such firms are likely to suffer the greatest loss in value from this underinvestment problem. By contrast, mature companies with few profitable investment opportunities where most of their value reflects the cash flows from tangible "assets in place" incur lower expected costs associated with financial distress. Such mature companies, all else equal, should have significantly higher leverage ratios than high-growth firms.

The Benefits of Debt in Controlling Overinvestment. If too much debt financing can create an underinvestment problem for growth companies, too little debt can lead to an *over*investment problem in the case of mature companies. As Michael Jensen has argued,[5] large, mature public companies generate substantial "free cash flow" – that is, operating cash flow that cannot be profitably reinvested inside the firm. The natural inclination of corporate managers is to use such free cash flow to sustain growth at the expense of

---

3 Perhaps the best evidence to date on the size of direct bankruptcy costs comes from Jerry Warner's study of 11 railroads that declared bankruptcy over the period 1930–1955. (Jerold B. Warner, "Bankruptcy Costs: Some Evidence," *Journal of Finance*, Vol. 32 (1977), pp. 337–347.) The study reported that out-of-pocket expenses associated with the administration of the bankruptcy process were quite small relative to the market value of the firm – less than 1% for the larger railroads in the sample. For smaller companies, it's true, direct bankruptcy costs are a considerably larger fraction of firm value (about five times larger in Warner's sample). Thus there are "scale economies" with respect to *direct* bankruptcy costs that imply that larger companies should have higher leverage ratios, all else equal, than smaller firms. But, even these higher estimates of direct bankruptcy costs, when weighted by the probability of getting into bankruptcy in the first place, produce *expected costs* that appear far too low to make them an important factor in corporate financing decisions.

4 Stewart C. Myers, "Determinants of Corporate Borrowing," *Journal of Financial Economics*, Vol. 5 (1977), pp. 147–175.

5 See Michael C. Jensen, "Agency Costs of Free Cash Flow, Corporate Finance, and Takeovers," *American Economic Review*, Vol. 76 (1986), pp. 323–329.

profitability, either by overinvesting in their core businesses or, perhaps worse, by diversifying through acquisition into unfamiliar ones.

Because both of these strategies tend to reduce value, companies that aim to maximize firm value must distribute their free cash flow to investors. Raising the dividend is one way of promising to distribute excess capital. But major substitutions of debt for equity (for example, in the form of leveraged stock repurchases) offer a more reliable solution because contractually obligated payments of interest and principal are more effective than discretionary dividend payments in squeezing out excess capital. Thus, in industries generating substantial cash flow but facing few growth opportunities, debt financing can add value simply by forcing managers to be more critical in evaluating capital spending plans.[6]

Information costs

Corporate executives often have better information about the value of their companies than outside investors. Recognition of this information disparity between managers and investors has led to two distinct, but related theories of financing decisions – one known as "signaling," the other as the "pecking order."

Signaling. With better information about the value of their companies than outside investors,

managers of undervalued firms would like to raise their share prices by communicating this information to the market. Unfortunately, this task is not as easy as it sounds; simply announcing that the companies are undervalued generally isn't enough. The challenge for managers is to find a *credible* signaling mechanism.

Economic theory suggests that information disclosed by an obviously biased source (like management, in this case) will be credible only if the costs of communicating falsely are large enough to constrain managers to reveal the truth. Increasing leverage has been suggested as one potentially effective signaling device. Debt contracts oblige the firm to make a fixed set of cash payments over the life of the loan; if these payments are missed, there are potentially serious consequences, including bankruptcy. Equity is more forgiving. Although stockholders also typically expect cash payouts, managers have more discretion over these payments and can cut or omit them in times of financial distress.

For this reason, adding more debt to the firm's capital structure can serve as a credible signal of higher future cash flows.[7] By committing the firm to make future interest payments to bondholders, managers communicate their confidence that the firm will have sufficient cash flows to meet these obligations.

Debt and equity also differ with respect to their sensitivity to changes in firm value. Since the promised payments to bondholders are fixed, and stockholders are entitled to the residual (or what's left over after the fixed payments), stock prices are much more sensitive than bond prices to any proprietary information about future prospects. If management is in possession of good news that has yet to be reflected in market prices, the release of such news will cause a larger increase in stock prices than in bond prices; and hence current stock prices (prior to release of the new information) will appear more undervalued to managers than current bond prices. For this reason, signaling theory suggests that managers of companies that believe their assets are undervalued will generally choose to issue debt – and to use equity only as a last resort.

---

6   More generally, the use of debt rather than equity reduces what economists call the agency costs of equity – loosely speaking, the reduction in firm value that arises from the separation of ownership from control in large, public companies with widely dispersed shareholders. In high-growth firms, the risk-sharing benefits of the corporate form are likely to outweight these agency costs. But, in mature industries with limited capital requirements, heavy debt financing has the added benefit of facilitating the concentration of equity ownership. To illustrate this potential role of debt, assume that the new owner of an all-equity company with $100 million of assets discovers that the assets can support $90 million of debt. Reducing the firm's equity from $100 million to $10 million greatly increases the ability of small investor groups (including management) to control large asset holdings.

The concentration of ownership made possible by leverage appears to have been a major part of the value gains achieved by the LBO movement of the '80s, and which has been resurrected in the 1990s. And, to the extent there are gains from having more concentrated ownership (and, again, these are likely to be greatest for mature industries with assets in place), companies should have higher leverage ratios.

---

7   Stephen Ross, "The Determination of Financial Structure: The Incentive Signaling Approach," *Bell Journal of Economics*, Vol. 8 (1977), pp. 23–40.

To illustrate this with a simple example, let's suppose that the market price of a stock is $25.00. Investors understand that its "real" value – that is, the value they would assign if they had access to the same information as the firm's managers – might be as high as $27.00 or as low as $23.00; but given investors' information $25.00 is a fair price. Now let's suppose that the managers want to raise external funds and they could either sell equity or debt. If the managers think the stock is really worth only $23.00, selling shares for $25.00 would be attractive – especially if their compensation is tied to stock appreciation. But if the managers think the stock is really worth $27.00, equity would be expensive at $25.00 and debt would be more attractive.

Investors understand this – and so if the company announces an equity offer, investors reassess the current price in light of this new information. Since it is more likely that the stock is worth $23.00 than $27.00, the market price declines. Such a rapid adjustment in valuation associated with the announcement thus eliminates much of any potential gain from attempting to exploit the manager's superior information.

Consistent with this example, economists have documented that the market responds in systematically negative fashion to announcements of equity offerings, marking down the share prices of issuing firms by about 3% on average. By contrast, the average market reaction to new debt offerings is not significantly different from zero.[8] The important thing to recognize is that most companies issuing new equity – those that are undervalued as well as those that are overvalued – can expect a drop in stock prices when they announce the offering. For those firms that are fairly valued or undervalued prior to the announcement of the offering, this expected drop in value represents an economic dilution of the existing shareholders' interest. Throughout the rest of this paper, we refer to this dilution as part of the "information costs" of raising outside capital.

The Pecking Order. Signaling theory, then, says that financing decisions are based, at least in part, on management's perception of the "fairness" of the market's current valuation of the stock. Stated as simply as possible, the theory suggests that, in order to minimize the information costs of issuing securities, a company is more likely to issue debt than equity if the firm appears undervalued, and to issue stock rather than debt if the firm seems overvalued.

The pecking order theory takes this argument one step farther, suggesting that the information costs associated with issuing securities are so large that they dominate all other considerations. According to this theory, companies maximize value by systematically choosing to finance new investments with the "cheapest available" source of funds. Specifically, they prefer internally generated funds (retained earnings) to external funding and, if outside funds are necessary, they prefer debt to equity because of the lower information costs associated with debt issues. Companies issue equity only as a last resort, when their debt capacity has been exhausted.[9]

The pecking order theory would thus suggest that companies with few investment opportunities and substantial free cash flow will have low debt ratios – and that high-growth firms with lower operating cash flows will have high debt ratios. In this sense, the theory not only suggests that interest tax shields and the costs of financial distress are at most a second-order concern; the logic of the pecking order actually leads to a set of predictions that are *precisely the opposite* of those offered by the tax and contracting cost arguments presented above.

THE EVIDENCE

Having discussed the different theories for observed capital structure, we now review the available empirical evidence to assess the relative "explanatory power" of each.

8 More generally, the evidence suggests that leverage-increasing transactions are associated with positive stock price reactions while leverage-reducing transactions are associated with negative reactions. In reaction to large debt-for-stock exchanges, for example, stock prices go up by 14% on average. The market also reacts in a predictably negative way to *leverage-reducing* transactions, with prices falling by 9.9% in response to common-for-debt exchanges and by 7.7% in preferred-for-debt exchanges. For a review of this evidence, see Clifford Smith, "Investment Banking and the Capital Acquisition Process," *Journal of Financial Economics*, Vol. 15 (1986), pp. 3–29.

9 See Stewart Myers, "The Capital Structure Puzzle," *Journal of Finance*, Vol. 39 (1984), pp. 575–592.

Evidence on contracting costs

Leverage Ratios. Much of the previous evidence on capital structure supports the conclusion that there is an optimal capital structure and that firms make financing decisions and adjust their capital structures to move closer to this optimum. For example, a 1967 study by Eli Schwartz and Richard Aronson showed clear differences in the average debt to (book) asset ratios of companies in different industries, as well as a tendency for companies in the same industry to cluster around these averages.[10] Moreover, such industry debt ratios seem to align with R&D spending and other proxies for corporate growth opportunities that the theory suggests are likely to be important in determining an optimal capital structure. In a 1985 study, Michael Long and Ileen Malitz showed that the five most highly leveraged industries – cement, blast furnaces and steel, paper and allied products, textiles, and petroleum refining – were all mature and asset-intensive. At the other extreme, the five industries with the lowest debt ratios – cosmetics, drugs, photographic equipment, aircraft, and radio and TV receiving – were all growth industries with high advertising and R&D.[11]

Other studies have used "cross-sectional" regression techniques to test whether the theoretical determinants of an optimal capital structure actually affect financing decisions. For example, in their 1984 study, Michael Bradley, Greg Jarrell, and Han Kim found that the debt to (book) asset ratio was negatively related to both the volatility of annual operating earnings and to advertising and R&D expenses. Both of these findings are consistent with high costs of financial distress for growth companies, which tend to have more volatile earnings as well as higher spending on R&D.[12]

Several studies have also reported finding that the debt ratios of individual companies seem to revert toward optimal targets. For example, a 1982 study by Paul Marsh estimated a company's target ratio as the average ratio observed over the prior ten years. He then found that the probability that a firm issues equity is significantly higher if the firm is above its target debt ratio, and significantly lower if below the target.[13]

As described in a 1995 article in this journal, we (together with colleague Ross Watts) attempted to add to this body of empirical work on capital structure by examining a much larger sample of companies that we tracked for over three decades.[14] For some 6,700 companies covered by Compustat, we calculated "market" leverage ratios (measured as the book value of total debt divided by the book value of debt and preferred stock plus the *market* value of equity) over the period 1963–1993. Not surprisingly, we found considerable differences in leverage ratios, both across companies in any given year and, in some cases, for the same firm over time. Although the average leverage ratio for the 6,700 companies over the 30-year period was 25%, one fourth of the cases had market leverage ratios that were higher than 37.5% and another one fourth had leverage ratios less than 10.3%.

To test the contracting cost theory described earlier in this paper, we attempted to determine the extent to which corporate leverage choices can be explained by differences in companies' investment opportunities. As suggested earlier, the contracting cost hypothesis predicts that the greater these investment opportunities (relative to the size of the company), the greater the potential underinvestment problem associated with debt financing and, hence, the lower the company's target leverage ratio. Conversely, the more limited a company's growth opportunities, the greater the potential overinvestment problem and, hence, the higher should be the company's leverage.

To test this prediction, we needed a measure of investment opportunities. Because stock prices reflect intangible assets such as growth opportunities but corporate balance sheets do not, we reasoned that the larger a company's "growth options" relative to its "assets in place," the higher on average will be its market value in relation to its

10 Eli Schwartz and J. Richard Aronson, "Some Surrogate Evidence in Support of Optimal Financial Structure," *Journal of Finance*, Vol. 22 No. 1 (1967).

11 Michael Long and Ileen Malitz, "The Investment-Financing Nexus: Some Empirical Evidence," *Midland Corporate Finance Journal*, Vol. 3 No. 3 (1985).

12 Michael Bradley, Greg Jarrell, and E. Han Kim, "The Existence of an Optimal Capital Structure: Theory and Evidence," *Journal of Finance*, Vol. 39 No. 3 (1984).

13 Paul Marsh, "The Choice Between Equity and Debt," *Journal of Finance*, Vol. 37 (1982), pp. 121–144.

14 Barclay, Smith, and Watts (1995), cited above.

book value. We accordingly used a company's market-to-book ratio as our proxy for its investment opportunity set.

The results of our regressions provide strong support for the contracting cost hypothesis. Companies with high market-to-book ratios had significantly lower leverage ratios than companies with low market-to-book ratios. (The t-statistic on the market-to-book ratio in the leverage regression was about 130.) To make these findings a little more concrete, our results suggest that, as one moves from companies at the bottom 10th percentile of market-to-book ratios (0.77) to the 90th percentile (2.59), the predicted leverage market ratio falls by 14.3 percentage points – which is a large fraction of the average ratio of 25%. (For further discussion of these results, see the box on the page 161.)

Moreover, such a negative relation between corporate leverage and market-to-book ratios appears to hold outside the U.S. as well. In a 1995 study, Raghuram Rajan and Luigi Zingales examined capital structure using data from Japan, Germany, France, Italy, the U.K. and Canada, as well as the U.S. They found that, in each of these seven countries, leverage is lower for firms with higher market-to-book ratios and higher for firms with higher ratios of fixed assets to total assets.[15]

The above evidence on leverage ratios, it should be pointed out, is also generally consistent with the tax hypothesis in the following sense: The same low-growth companies that face low financial distress costs and high free-cash-flow benefits from heavy debt financing are also likely to have greater use for interest tax shields than high-growth companies. At the same time, the above evidence is inconsistent with the predictions of the pecking order theory – which, again, suggests that low-growth firms with high free cash flow will have relatively low debt ratios.

Debt Maturity and Priority. Like this article up to this point, most academic discussions of capital structure focus just on the leverage ratio. In so doing, they effectively assume that all debt financing is the same. In practice, of course, debt differs in several important respects, including maturity, covenant restrictions, security, convertibility and call provisions, and whether the debt is privately placed or held by widely dispersed public investors. Each of these features is potentially important in determining the extent to which debt financing can cause, or exacerbate, a potential under-investment problem. For example, debt-financed companies with more investment opportunities would prefer to have debt with shorter maturities (or at least with call provisions, to ensure greater financing flexibility), more convertibility provisions (which reduce the required coupon payments), less restrictive covenants, and a smaller group of private investors rather than public bondholders (which makes it easier to reorganize in the event of trouble). By recognizing this array of financing choices, we can broaden the scope of our examination and raise the potential power of our tests, while at the same time increasing the relevance of the analysis for managers who must choose the design of their debt securities.

As described in our 1996 article in this journal,[16] we designed an empirical test of the suggestion – offered by Stewart Myers in his 1977 article – that one way for companies with lots of growth options to control the underinvestment problem is to issue debt with shorter maturities. The argument is basically this: A firm whose value consists mainly of growth opportunities could severely reduce its future financing and strategic flexibility – and in the process destroy much of its value – by issuing long-term debt. Not only would the interest rate have to be high to compensate lenders for their greater risk, but the burden of servicing the debt could cause the company to defer strategic investments if their operating cash flow turns down. By contrast, shorter-term debt, besides carrying lower interest rates in such cases, would also be less of a threat to future strategic investment because, as the firm's current investments begin to pay off, it will be able over time to raise capital on more favorable terms.[17]

---

15 See Raghuram Rajan and Luigi Zingales, "What Do We Know About Capital Structure? Some Evidence From International Data," *Journal of Finance*, Vol. 50 No. 5 (1995). These relations are statistically significant for each country for the coefficient on growth options and for every country but France and Canada for the coefficient on assets in place.

16 Michael J. Barclay and Clifford W. Smith, Jr., "On Financial Architecture: Leverage, Maturity, and Priority," *Journal of Applied Corporate Finance*, Vol. 8 No. 4 (1996).
17 If the firm's debt matures before a company's growth options must be exercised, the investment distortions created by the debt are eliminated. Since these investment distortions are most severe, and most costly, for firms with significant growth options, high-growth firms should use more short-term debt.

ROBUSTNESS OF THE EVIDENCE ON CONTRACTING COSTS

A number of empirical tests of the contracting cost hypothesis have taken the form of a regression with market leverage (measured as the ratio of the book value of debt to the total market value of the firm) as the dependent variable and the corporate market-to-book ratio together with a few "control" variables as the independent variables. Because the market value of the firm appears on both the left and right hand sides of this regression (in the denominator of the leverage ratio and in the numerator of the market-to-book ratio), some researchers have questioned whether the strong negative relation between these variables really supports the theory or is simply the "artificial" result of large variations in stock prices.

To examine the robustness of these results, our 1995 study with Ross Watts used other proxies for the firms' investment opportunities (the independent variable) that do not rely on market values. For example, when we substituted a company's R&D and advertising as a percentage of sales for its market-to-book ratio, our results were consistent with the contracting cost hypothesis. The coefficients on both of our alternative proxies for the firm's investment opportunities had the correct sign, and the t-statistics, although lower than 130, were still impressive – about 65 in the R&D regression and 18 in the advertising regression.

In a more recent series of tests, we used two different proxies for leverage (the dependent variable): (1) the ratio of total debt to the *book* value of assets; and (2) the interest coverage ratio (EBIT over interest).

On purely theoretical grounds, these regressions are expected to produce less significant results. Recall that the contracting cost hypothesis predicts that tangible "assets in place" provide good collateral for loans while intangible investment opportunities do not. If leverage is measured as the ratio of total debt to the book value of assets, we are really measuring the extent to which the firm has leveraged just its tangible (book) assets while essentially ignoring the intangible assets. For this reason, the theory predicts less variation in leverage when measured in relation to book assets than when measured in relation to total market value.

Nevertheless, when we re-estimated the leverage regression substituting book leverage as the dependent variable, the results again supported the contracting cost hypothesis. The regression coefficient on the market-to-book ratio in the book-leverage regression was smaller (with a somewhat lower t-statistic), as predicted. But the coefficient was still reliably negative, with a t-statistic greater than 45.

A similar problem arises with the coverage ratio. In this case, the benefits of intangible growth opportunities (in the form of higher expected future cash flow) are not reflected in current earnings when we use the coverage ratio as our proxy for leverage. Yet, even so, the correlation coefficient was positive; that is to say, companies with higher market-to-book values tended to have significantly higher interest coverage ratios (the t-statistic exceeded 70).

When we tested this prediction (again using market-to-book as a measure of growth options), we found that growth companies tended to have significantly less debt with a maturity greater than three years than companies with limited investment opportunities. More specifically, our regressions suggest that moving from companies at the 10th to the 90th percentile of market-to-book ratios (that is from 0.77 to 2.59) reduces the ratio of long-term debt to total debt by 18 percentage points (a significant reduction, given our sample average ratio of 46%).

Moreover, we also found in the same study that the debt issued by growth firms is significantly more concentrated among high-priority classes. Consistent with our results indicating that firms with more growth options tend to have lower leverage ratios, we find that changing the market-to-book ratio from the 10th to the 90th percentile is associated with reductions in leasing of 89%, in secured debt of 71%, in ordinary debt of 78%, and in subordinated debt of almost 250%. Our explanation for this is as follows: When firms get into financial difficulty, complicated capital structures with claims of different priorities can generate serious conflicts among creditors, thus exacerbating the underinvestment problem described earlier.

And because such conflicts and the resulting under-investment have the greatest potential to destroy value in growth firms, those growth firms that do issue fixed claims are likely to choose mainly high-priority fixed claims.

The evidence on information costs

Leverage. Signaling theory says that companies are more likely to issue debt than equity when they are undervalued because of the large information costs (in the form of dilution) associated with an equity offering. The pecking order model goes even farther, suggesting that the information costs associated with riskier securities are so large that most companies will not issue equity until they have completely exhausted their debt capacity. Neither the signaling nor the pecking order theory offers any clear prediction about what optimal capital structure would be for a given firm. The signaling theory seems to suggest that a firm's actual capital structure will be influenced by whether the company is perceived by management to be undervalued or overvalued. The pecking order model is more extreme; it implies that a company will not have a target capital structure, and that its leverage ratio will be determined by the gap between its operating cash flow and its invest-ment requirements over time. Thus, the pecking order predicts that companies with consistently high profits or modest financing requirements are likely to have low debt ratios – mainly because they don't need outside capital. Less profitable compa-nies, and those with large financing requirements, will end up with high leverage ratios because of managers' reluctance to issue equity.

A number of studies have provided support for the pecking order theory in the form of evidence of a strong negative relation between past prof-itability and leverage. That is, the lower are a company's profits and operating cash flows in a given year, the higher is its leverage ratio (measured either in terms of book or market values).[18] Moreover, in an article published in 1998, Stewart Myers and Lakshmi Shyam-Sunder added to this series of studies by showing that this relation explains more of the time-series variance of debt ratios than a simple target-adjustment model of

capital structure that is consistent with the con-tracting cost hypothesis.[19]

Such findings have generally been interpreted as confirmation that managers do not set target lever-age ratios – or at least do not work very hard to achieve them. But this is not the only interpreta-tion that fits these data. Even if companies have target leverage ratios, there will be an *optimal devia-tion* from those targets – one that will depend on the transactions costs associated with adjusting back to the target relative to the costs of deviating from the target. To the extent there are fixed costs and scale economies in issuing securities, compa-nies with capital structure targets – particularly smaller firms – will make infrequent adjustments and often will deliberately overshoot their targets. (And, as we argue in the closing section of this paper, a complete theory of capital structure must take account of these adjustment costs and how they affect expected deviations from the target.)

In our 1995 paper with Ross Watts, we attempted to devise our own test of how information costs affect corporate financing behavior. According to the signaling explanation, undervalued companies will have higher leverage than overvalued firms. One major challenge in testing this signaling argument is coming up with a reliable proxy for undervaluation that can be readily observed. In devising such a measure, we began with the assumption that corpo-rate earnings follow a random walk, and that the best predictor of a company's next year's earnings is thus its current year's earnings. We then classified firms as undervalued in any given year in which their earn-ings (excluding extraordinary items and discontinued operation and adjusted for any changes in shares outstanding) increased in the following year. We designated as overvalued all firms whose ordinary earnings decreased in the next year.

Our regressions showed a very small (but statistically significant) positive relation between a

---

18 See, for example, Carl Kester, "Capital and Ownership Structure: A Comparison of Unites States and Japanese Manufacturing Corporations," *Financial Management*, Vol. 15 (1986); Rajan and Zingales (1995); and Sheridan Titman and Roberto Wessels, "The Determinants of Capital Structure Choice," *Journal of Finance*, Vol. 43 (1988), pp. 1–19.
19 Lakshmi Shyam-Sunder and Stewart Myers, "Testing Static Tradeoff Against Pecking Order Models of Capital Structure," *Journal of Financial Economics*, Vol. 51 No. 2.

company's leverage ratio and its unexpected earnings, thus suggesting that this undervaluation variable has a trivial effect on corporate capital structure. For example, moving from the 10th percentile of abnormal earnings in our sample (those firms whose earnings decreased by 12%) to the 90th percentile (those whose earnings increased by 13%) raised the predicted leverage ratio by only 0.5 percentage points. Moreover, in our 1996 study (which also uses COMPUSTAT data, although for a somewhat different time period), we again found a small relation between leverage and unexpected earnings. In this regression, however, the relation was *negative*.

Maturity and Priority. Signaling theory implies that undervalued firms will have more short-term debt and more senior debt than overvalued firms because such instruments are less sensitive to the market's assessment of firm value and thus will be less undervalued when issued. The findings of our 1996 study are inconsistent with the predictions of the signaling hypothesis with respect to debt maturity. Companies whose earnings were about to increase the following year in fact issued less short-term debt and more long-term debt than firms whose earnings were about to decrease. And, whereas the theory predicts more senior debt for firms about to experience earnings increases, the ratio of senior debt to total debt is lower for overvalued than for undervalued firms.

In sum, the results of our tests of managers' use of financing choices to signal their superior information to the market are not robust, and the economic effect of any such signaling on corporate decision-making seems minimal.

According to the pecking order theory, the firm should issue as much of the security with the lowest information costs as it can. Only after this capacity is exhausted should it move on to issue a security with higher information costs. Thus, for example, firms should issue as much secured debt or capitalized leases as possible before issuing any unsecured debt, and they should exhaust their capacity for issuing short-term debt before issuing any long-term debt. But these predictions are clearly rejected by the data. For example, when we examined the capital structures of over 7,000 companies between 1980 and 1997 (representing almost 57,000 firm-year observations), we found that 23% of these observations had no secured debt, 54% had no capital leases, and 50% had no debt that was originally issued with less than one year to maturity.

To explain these more detailed aspects of capital structure, proponents of the pecking order theory must go outside their theory and argue that other costs and benefits determine these choices. But once you allow for these other costs and benefits to have a material impact on corporate financing choices, you are back in the more traditional domain of optimal capital structure theories.

The evidence on taxes

Theoretical models of optimal capital structure predict that firms with more taxable income and fewer non-debt tax shields should have higher leverage ratios. But the evidence on the relation between leverage ratios and tax-related variables is mixed at best. For example, studies that examine the effect of non-debt tax shields on companies' leverage ratios find that this effect is either insignificant, or that it enters with the wrong sign. That is, in contrast to the prediction of the tax hypothesis, these studies suggest that firms with more non-debt tax shields such as depreciation, net operating loss carryforwards and investment tax credits have, if anything, *more* not less debt in their capital structures.[20]

But before we conclude that taxes are unimportant in the capital structure decision, it is critical to recognize that the findings of these studies are hard to interpret because the tax variables are crude proxies for a company's effective marginal tax rate. In fact, these proxies are often correlated with other variables that influence the capital structure choice. For example, companies with investment tax credits, high levels of depreciation, and other non-debt tax shields also tend to have mainly tangible fixed assets. And, since fixed assets provide good collateral, the non-debt tax shields may in fact be a proxy not for limited tax benefits, but rather for low contracting costs associated with debt financing. The evidence from the studies just cited is generally consistent with this interpretation.

20   See, for example, Bradley, Jarrell, and Kim (1984); Titman and Wessels (1988); Barclay, Smith, Watts (1995), all of which are cited above.

Similarly, firms with net operating loss carry-forwards are often in financial distress; and, since equity values typically decline in such circumstances, financial distress itself causes leverage ratios to increase. Thus, again, it is not clear whether net operating losses proxy for low tax benefits of debt or for financial distress.

More recently, several authors have succeeded in detecting tax effects in financing decisions by focusing on incremental financing choices (that is, *changes* in the amount of debt or equity) rather than on the levels of debt and equity. For example, a 1990 study by Jeffrey Mackie-Mason examined registered security offerings by public U.S. corporations and found that firms were more likely to issue debt if they had a high marginal tax rate and to issue equity if they had a low tax rate.[21] In another attempt to avoid the difficulties with crude proxy variables, a 1996 study by John Graham used a sophisticated simulation method to provide a more accurate measure of companies' marginal tax rates.[22] Using such tax rates, Graham also found a positive association between changes in debt ratios and the firm's marginal tax rate.

On balance, then, the evidence appears to suggest that taxes play a least a modest role in corporate financing and capital structure decisions. Moreover, as mentioned earlier, the results of our tests of contracting costs reported above can also be interpreted as evidence in support of the tax explanation.

TOWARD A UNIFIED THEORY OF CORPORATE FINANCIAL POLICY

In addition to explaining the basic leverage (or debt vs. equity) decision, a useful theory of capital structure should also help explain other capital structure choices, such as debt maturity, priority, the use of callability and convertibility provisions, and the choice between public and private financing. As discussed above, the contracting-cost theory provides a unified framework for analyzing the entire range of capital structure choices while most other theories, such as the signaling and pecking order theories, are at best silent about – and more often inconsistent with – the empirical evidence on these issues.

We now take this argument one step further by suggesting that a productive capital structure theory should also help explain an even broader array of corporate financial policy choices, including dividend, compensation, hedging, and leasing policies. The empirical evidence suggests that companies choose coherent *packages* of these financial policies. For example, small high-growth firms tend to have not only low leverage ratios and simple capital structures (with predominantly short-maturity, senior bank debt), but also low dividend payouts as well as considerable stock-based incentive compensation for senior executives. By contrast, large mature companies tend to have high leverage, more long-term debt, more complicated capital structures with a broader range of debt priorities, higher dividends, and less incentive compensation (with greater reliance on earnings-based bonuses rather than stock-based compensation plans).[23] Thus, corporate financing, dividend, and compensation policies, besides being highly correlated with each other, all appear to be driven by the same fundamental firm characteristics: investment opportunities and (to a lesser extent) firm size. And this consistent pattern of corporate decision-making suggests that we now have the rudiments of a unified framework for explaining most, if not all, financial policy choices.

As mentioned earlier, proponents of the pecking order theory argue that the information costs associated with issuing new securities dominate all other costs in determining capital structure. But, as we also noted, the logic and predictions of the pecking order theory are at odds with, and thus incapable of explaining, most other financial policy choices. For example, in suggesting that firms will always use the cheapest source of funds, the model implies that companies will not simultaneously pay

21   Jeffrey Mackie-Mason, "Do Taxes Affect Corporate Financing Decisions?," *Journal of Finance*, Vol. 45 (1990), pp. 1471–1494.

22   John Graham, "Debt and the Marginal Tax Rate, *Journal of Financial Economics*, Vol. 41 (1996), pp. 41–73.

23   See Clifford W. Smith and Ross L. Watts, "The Investment Opportunity Set and Corporate Financing, Dividend and Compensation Policies," *Journal of Financial Economics*, Vol. 32 (1992), pp. 263–292.

dividends and access external capital markets. But this prediction can, of course, be rejected simply by glancing at the business section of most daily newspapers. With the exception of a few extraordinarily successful high tech companies like Microsoft and Amgen, most large, publicly traded companies pay dividends while at the same time regularly rolling over existing debt with new public issues. And, as already discussed, although the pecking order predicts that mature firms that generate lots of free cash flow should eventually become all equity financed, they are among the most highly levered firms in our sample. Conversely, the pecking order theory implies that high-tech startup firms will have high leverage ratios because they often have negative free cash flow and incur the largest information costs when issuing equity. But, in fact, such firms are financed almost entirely with equity.

Thus, as we saw in the case of debt maturity and priority, proponents of the pecking order must go outside of their theory to explain corporate behavior at both ends of the corporate growth spectrum. In so doing, they implicitly limit the size and importance of information costs; they concede that, at least for the most mature and the highest-growth sectors, information costs are less important than other considerations in corporate financing decisions.

Integration of stocks and flows

Although the pecking order theory is incapable of explaining the full array of financial policy choices, this does not mean that information costs are unimportant in corporate decision-making. On the contrary, such costs will influence corporate financing choices and, along with other costs and benefits, must be part of a unified theory of corporate financial policy.

In our view, the key to reconciling the different theories – and thus to solving the capital structure puzzle – lies in achieving a better understanding of the relation between corporate financing *stocks* and *flows*. The theories of capital structure discussed in this paper generally focus either on the stocks (that is, on the levels of debt and equity in relation to the target) or on the flows (the decision of which security to issue at a particular time). For example, the

primary focus of the contracting-cost theories has been leverage ratios, which are measures of the *stocks* of debt and equity. By contrast, information-based theories like the pecking order model generally focus on flows – for example, on the information costs associated with a new issue of debt or equity. But, since both stocks and flows are likely to play important roles in such decisions, neither of these theoretical approaches taken alone is likely to offer a reliable guide to optimal capital structure.

In developing a sensible approach to capital structure strategy, the CFO should start by thinking about the firm's target capital structure in terms of stock measures – that is, *a ratio of debt to total capital that can be expected to minimize taxes and contracting costs* (although information costs may also be given some consideration here). That target ratio should take into consideration factors such as the company's projected investment requirements; the level and stability of its operating cash flows; its tax status; the expected loss in value from being forced to defer investment because of financial distress; and the firm's ability to raise capital on short notice (without excessive dilution).

If the company is not currently at or near its optimal capital structure, the CFO should come up with a plan to achieve the target debt ratio. For example, if the firm has "too much" equity (or too much capital in general), it can increase leverage by borrowing (or using excess cash) to buy back shares – a possibility that the pecking order generally ignores. (And the fact that U.S. corporate stock repurchases have been growing at almost 30% per year for most of this decade is by itself perhaps the single most compelling piece of evidence that corporate managers *are* thinking in terms of optimal capital structure.) But, if the company needs more capital, then managers choosing between equity and various forms of debt must consider not only the benefits of moving toward the target, but also the associated adjustment costs. For example, a company with "too much" debt may choose to delay an equity offering – or issue convertibles or PERCS instead – in order to reduce the cost of issuing securities that it perceives to be undervalued.

As a more general principle, the CFO should adjust the firm's capital structure whenever the costs of adjustment – including information costs as well as out-of-pocket transactions costs – are less than the costs of deviating from the target. Based on the existing research, what can we say about such adjustment costs? The available evidence on the size and variation of such costs suggests that there is a material fixed component – one that again includes information costs as well as out-of-pocket costs.[24] And, since average adjustment costs fall with increases in transaction size, there are scale economies in issuing new securities that suggest that small firms, all else equal, are likely to deviate farther from their capital structure targets than larger companies.

Although the different kinds of external financing all exhibit scale economies, the structure of the costs varies among different types of securities. Equity issues have both the largest out-of-pocket transactions costs and the largest information costs. Long-term public debt issues, particularly for below-investment-grade companies, are less costly.[25] Short-term private debt or bank loans are the least costly. And, because CFOs are likely to weigh

these adjustment costs against the expected benefits from moving closer to their leverage target, it is not surprising that seasoned equity offerings are rare events, that long-term debt issues are more common, and that private debt offerings or bank loans occur with almost predictable regularity. Moreover, because of such adjustment costs, most companies – particularly smaller firms – are also likely to spend considerable time away from their target capital structures. Other things equal, larger adjustment costs will lead to larger deviations from the target before the firm readjusts.

In sum, to make a sensible decision about capital structure, CFOs must understand both the costs associated with deviating from the target capital structure and the costs of adjusting back toward the target. The next major step forward in solving the capital structure puzzle is almost certain to involve a more formal weighing of these two sets of costs.

---

24   See, for example, David Blackwell and David Kidwell, "An Investigation of Cost Differences Between Private Placements and Public Sales of Debt," *Journal of Financial Economics*, 22 (1988), pp. 253–278; and Clifford Smith, "Alternative Methods for Raising Capital: Rights vs. Underwritten Offerings," *Journal of Financial Economics*, Vol. 5 (1977), pp. 273–307.

---

25   See, in this issue, Sudip Datta, Mai Iskandar-Datta, and Ajay Patel, "The Pricing of Debt IPOs," *Journal of Applied Corporate Finance*, Vol. 12 No. 1 (Spring 1999).

CHAPTER 13

What Do We Know About Stock Repurchases?

Gustavo Grullon and David L. Ikenberry (Rice University)*

The modern corporation has a colorful history spanning centuries. Yet it has only been within the last two decades that public corporations have seized upon a previously little used mechanism for returning capital to their shareholders – the share repurchase. Although companies have long been permitted to buy back their stock, it was not until the early 1980s that U.S. corporations began adopting share repurchase programs in large numbers. This surge in activity was fueled by an explosion in the use of open market repurchase programs. In the 1990s, this movement went global as countries like Canada and the U.K., with repurchase laws already in place, also saw an increase in repurchase activity. In addition, a host of countries that formerly prohibited stock repurchases, such as Germany, Taiwan, Hong Kong, and Japan, adopted provisions allowing resident firms to repurchase equity in the open market for the first time.

The magnitude of this shift in corporate policy has been significant. Consider that, in the five-year period between 1995 and 1999, U.S. corporations announced intentions to repurchase roughly $750 billion worth of stock. Moreover, in 1998 – and for the first time in history – U.S. corporations distributed more cash to investors through share repurchases than through cash dividends.[1] Only time will tell whether companies will continue to repurchase stock at the same pace as witnessed recently. Yet what does seem clear is that given today's regulatory, tax, and economic climate, stock buybacks are likely to remain a dominant transaction going forward. Repurchase activity can also be expected to grow globally as more countries adopt enabling regulations.

Just as share repurchases have grown in popularity and importance, research about how and why firms buy back stock continues to evolve. In this paper, we provide a comprehensive review of this literature and, in so doing, shed light on economists' collective understanding of how and why stock repurchases affect stock prices. The rest of the paper unfolds as follows: In the second section, we provide an overview of the three dominant methods that companies use to repurchase stock: fixed-price tender offers, Dutch-auction tender offers, and open market repurchases. Because open market programs are by far the most popular choice, we focus heavily on various aspects of this mechanism. In the third section, we examine how

* We appreciate receiving helpful comments from Don Chew (the editor), Jeff Fleming, Aaron Halfacre, Jaemin Kim, Bob Marchesi, Brad McWilliams, Raghu Rau, Jeff Smisek, and Theo Vermaelen.

1 For a comprehensive review of dividends compared to repurchases, see Gustavo Grullon and Roni Michaely (2000), "Dividends, Share Repurchases, the Substitution Hypothesis," Rice University and Cornell University working paper.

share repurchase activity in the U.S. has evolved over the last 20 years. In the fourth section, we review the primary reasons offered for why companies repurchase stock and consider the extent to which such reasons are consistent with the empirical evidence on how repurchases affect shareholder wealth. In the fifth section, we discuss various aspects of open market programs, including liquidity effects, financial flexibility and completion rates, and the regulatory environment. Finally, we present a number of policy recommendations for both executives who set corporate financial policy and for regulators charged with monitoring corporate dealings with investors. (In the Appendix, we discuss execution strategies for buying back stock, including several innovative strategies involving the use of equity derivative such as puts and calls.)

TYPES OF SHARE REPURCHASES

There are essentially three ways that companies repurchase shares in the U.S.: (1) the fixed-price tender offer, (2) the Dutch-auction tender offer, and (3) the open market repurchase program. Although the use of share repurchases became widespread only after the mid-1980s, both tender-offer and open market repurchases have been available to U.S. corporations for many decades.[2] The Dutch-auction mechanism, by contrast, is a relatively recent transaction in the U.S.

As the name suggests, fixed-price tender offers involve the firm offering a single price to all shareholders for a specific number of shares. This offer is typically valid for a limited period of time and may or may not be contingent on a minimum threshold of shares being tendered. If the offer is oversubscribed, management has the option to increase the size of the repurchase. When managers do not make such extensions and the offer is oversubscribed, each shareholder receives a pro-rated amount of cash and the balance of their tender is returned in stock.[3]

The Dutch-auction repurchase is also a fixed-price deal. In this transaction, managers solicit information from shareholders that allows them to form a final price. This price is revealed toward the end of the process as opposed to being set initially by management under the traditional approach. The process starts with managers announcing a range of prices at which they will accept offers from shareholders. Shareholders choosing to participate in the offer then tell the firm the price at which they are willing to part with their shares and the number of shares they are tendering. At the close of the offer period, management collects the individual offers and sorts them by price. The precise price level at which the repurchase is completed is determined by adding the number of shares offered starting at the lowest end of management's price range. The price stops at that point at which the cumulative number of shares equals the size of the repurchase program. All shareholders who tender at or below that specified level are included in the repurchase program, and all receive the same price per share. All investors who tendered at prices above the clearing price are excluded from the deal, and their shares are returned to them.

These two approaches, fixed-price tender offers and Dutch-auctions, allow management to achieve a variety of goals. First, these programs tend to be an efficient way to retire a large block of shares in a relatively short period of time. Several studies have reported that the typical tender-offer involves about 15% of the outstanding shares. For this reason, tender offers may be an ideal mechanism for companies intent on making dramatic (and rapid) changes in capital structure. Because of their large size and relative speed, tender offers have also been suggested as an effective way for managers to convey information about future profitability or to signal to the market their belief that the firm is undervalued. This signaling motive is thought to be particularly important in the case of fixed-price tender offers, where management offers investors a significant "premium" (about 16%, on average) for their shares.[4] By contrast, in Dutch-auction programs, where managers are culling information from the market and thus revealing less about their own views, the premiums are smaller (about 12.5%) and the signal is said to be weaker. In sum, Dutch-auctions are likely to be preferred over tender offers by companies who want to buy lots of

---

2 For example, it was in 1942 that a stock repurchase executed under rather questionable circumstances lead the SEC to adopt Rule 10b-5, a rather sweeping rule governing all aspects of company disclosure.

3 In some cases, managers may deviate slightly from precise pro-rata repurchases to buy out odd-lot shareholders in order to reduce future servicing costs.

stock and distribute large amounts of capital in a short period of time, but also want to pay less of a premium.

Yet among the three approaches firms use to repurchase stock, fixed-price methods are relatively uncommon. Clearly, the preferred technique for buying back stock is the open market repurchase program. In such cases companies either directly or through intermediaries buy their own stock on the open market. In the U.S., the legal framework surrounding open market repurchase programs is relatively ambiguous, particularly when compared to the legal structure (both for the process and the disclosure) of a country like Canada. In the U.S., open market repurchases are treated as material events. They are approved by company boards and, because of their materiality, are formally announced to the public. Yet apart from this initial announcement, no formal disclosure or registration (aside from what is buried in the standard accounting documents) is required to be filed with either the government or any stock market or exchange. There is no limit on program size or duration (although several studies have found that the typical open market program is for roughly 5% of the share base).[5] Wall Street practitioners generally characterize open market programs as lasting two to three years, and this generalization has been confirmed by a recent study reporting that companies take roughly three years on average to complete their open market repurchase programs.[6]

RECENT TRENDS IN SHARE REPURCHASES

The level of repurchase activity, both in the U.S. and abroad, has changed remarkably in the past 20 years. Table 13.1 reports both the number and total dollar value for U.S. repurchase announcements for each of the three major repurchase methods over the period 1980 to 1999.[7] For convenience, we also plot in Figure 13.1 the combined dollar volume of repurchase announcements. A few points are readily apparent. First, open market programs are the dominant mechanism by which U.S. firms repurchase stock. Over the 20-year period reported here, we find that open market programs comprised roughly 91% of the total value of all repurchase announcements. In the last five years of our sample period, this market share increased further, varying from 95% in 1997 to 98% in 1995. A second trend clearly evident is the abrupt increase in repurchase activity starting in the mid-1980s, an increase due almost entirely to the sharp rise in open market programs. The surge of open market buybacks in the '80s was followed by another wave of open market programs in the mid-1990s. Since 1996, open market share repurchase announcements have remained above the $100 billion mark.[8]

In sum, share repurchase activity in the U.S. has experienced a profound transformation in the last 15 years. Before the mid-1980s, stock repurchases in the U.S. (from all three methods) were relatively uncommon. The rising importance of stock repurchases can perhaps best be summed up by looking at changes in a single ratio. As reported in a recent study (co-authored by one of the present writers), total corporate payouts in share repurchase programs during the period 1972–1983 amounted to

4 For example, a 1991 study by Robert Comment and Gregg Jarrell of repurchase tender offers in the early 1980s reported that the median premium was 16.0% measured relative to three days prior to the repurchase announcement. Robert Comment and Gregg Jarrell, "The Relative Signaling Power of Dutch-Auction and Fixed-Price Self-Tender Offers and Open-Market Share Repurchases," *Journal of Finance*, 46 (1991).

5 As an extreme example of the limitless flexibility of open market repurchases, Continental Airlines announced in late 1999 that the board authorized an indefinite open market program limited each year to half the firm's cash flows.

6 Clifford Stephens and Michael Weisbach, "Actual Share Reacquisitions in Open-Market Repurchase Programs," *Journal of Finance*, 53 (1998).

7 The data for open market programs was obtained by merging information from Securities Data Company (SDC) with the dataset of David Ikenberry, Josef Lakonishok and Theo Vermaelen, "Market Underreaction to Open Market Share Repurchases," *Journal of Financial Economics*, 39 (1995). This table does not distinguish between new programs and program extensions. Some firms announce a program and, after fulfilling most of it, announce a program extension. For clarity, we treat each announcement as a separate event. For the two fixed-price methods, we obtained all of our information from SDC. For all three methods, the sample is limited to firms trading on the NYSE, ASE or Nasdaq.

8 The dominance of open market programs in the 1980s and 1990s reported here is similar to that reported elsewhere including Murali Jagannathan, Clifford Stephens, and Michael Weisbach, "Financial Flexibility and the Choice between Dividends and Stock Repurchases," *Journal of Financial Economics*, forthcoming (2000) and Grullon and Michaely (2000), cited earlier.

Table 13.1 Number and Value of Share Repurchase Announcements*

Year	Dutch auctions		Tender Offers		Open market	
	Cases	Dollars (millions)	Cases	Dollars (millions)	Cases	Dollars (millions)
1980	—	—	1	5	86	1,429
1981	—	—	44	1,329	95	3,013
1982	—	—	40	1,164	129	3,112
1983	—	—	40	1,352	53	2,278
1984	1	9	67	10,517	236	14,910
1985	6	1,123	36	13,352	159	22,786
1986	11	2,332	20	5,492	219	28,417
1987[a]	9	1,502	42	4,764	132	34,787
1988	21	7,695	32	3,826	276	33,150
1989	22	5,044	49	1,939	499	62,873
1990	10	1,933	41	3,463	778	39,733
1991	4	739	51	4,715	282	16,139
1992	7	1,638	37	1,488	447	32,635
1993	5	1,291	51	1,094	461	35,000
1994	10	925	52	2,796	824	71,036
1995	8	969	40	542	851	81,591
1996	22	2,774	37	2,562	1,111	157,917
1997	30	5,442	35	2,552	967	163,688
1998	20	2,640	13	4,364	1,537	215,012
1999	19	3,817	21	1,790	1,212	137,015

*This table provides a breakdown by year of the number announcements and the total dollar value of the three repurchase mechanisms in the U.S. over the period 1980 to 1999. This data is obtained by merging information from Securities Data and from the dataset of Ikenberry, Lakonishok and Vermaelen (1995) and includes announcements only for firms trading on the NYSE, ASE or Nasdaq. This table does not distinguish between new programs and program extensions. Each announcement by a firm is treated as a separate event.

[a]Because of an extreme clustering of announcements after the 1987 crash, this table does not include open market program announcements made in the last quarter of 1987.

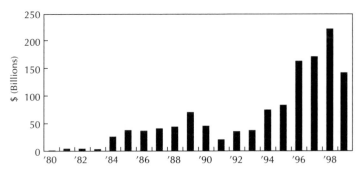

Figure 13.1 Market Value of Share Repurchase Announcements*
*This figure depicts the market value of share repurchase announcements (for tender offers, Dutch-auctions, and open market programs combined) in the U.S. over the period 1980 to 1999. This data is obtained by merging information from Securities Data and from the datasets of Ikenberry, Lakonishok and Vermaelen (1995) and only includes announcements for firms trading on the NYSE, ASE or Nasdaq. This table does not distinguish between new programs and program extensions. All announcements are treated as a separate event.

less than 4.5% of total earnings. Over the period 1984 to 1998, this same ratio exceeded 25%.[9]

To what can we attribute this surge in repurchase activity? Several factors have been at work. An important one was a major change in the regulatory environment. Prior to 1982, the regulatory environment relating to repurchase programs was ambiguous and structured only by ill-defined case law. This regulatory ambiguity and the associated litigation risk were substantially reduced in late 1982 when the SEC adopted rule 10b-18. Beyond this, two other factors affecting repurchase program activity relate to the level of market prices and the underlying condition of the economy. While research suggests that the actual dollar payouts associated with repurchase programs are not closely associated with market movements, there is evidence that program announcements are inversely related to broader moves in the market; that is, when stock prices fall, announcements of repurchases rise. For example, although evidence from the 1987 crash is excluded from the data reported in Table 13.1, several hundred firms announced repurchases in the weeks following that market break. Similar fluctuations occurred in October 1989 and later in the summer of 1998 after the market disturbance stemming from trouble in global bond markets. In 1990 and 1991, the U.S. economy entered into and pulled out of recession and then rallied into one of the most sustained periods of peace-time economic expansion. There is evidence that some portion of the corporate cash flows generated during this expansion that might have been used to increase dividends was instead channeled into share repurchases.

WHY DO COMPANIES BUY BACK THEIR STOCK?

Those who study markets tend to search for the one explanation, or the single primary factor, that describes some trend or activity. But it is clear that there is no single dominant motive for corporations to repurchase stock. In fact, in any given company, managers may find several factors encouraging them to buy back their stock. In this section, we discuss the more common explanations

and the economic factors that drive them. We start with the explanation that is most commonly provided by managers and corporate practitioners generally – namely, that stock repurchases can be used to boost earnings per share. After showing the fallacy of that argument, we turn to the corporate motives that are taken seriously by finance scholars.

The explanation most widely discussed by financial economists is that corporate managers use repurchases to "signal" their optimism about the firm's prospects to the market. Although this point is often overlooked even in academic discussions, there are two different versions of this "signaling" story. One says that repurchases are intended to convey management's expectation of future increases in the firm's earnings and cash flow – a view that is not shared by the market. The second version holds that managers are not attempting to convey new information to the market, but are instead expressing their disagreement with how the market is pricing their current performance. In either case, the firm's management views the stock as undervalued. The disagreement between the two stories is over the cause of the discrepancy between price and fair value. In the first case, it is the company's inability (without the repurchase) to communicate its prospects convincingly to the market; in the second, it is the market's failure to reflect publicly available information in the current price, a market "inefficiency" if you will.

The earnings bump

In both executive surveys and company press releases that accompany buyback programs, managers often say that they are repurchasing stock in order to increase earnings per share.[10] Investment bankers and stock analysts often cite this "EPS bump" as a major, if not the primary, benefit of stock buybacks. It is true that, as long as earnings fall by less (in percentage terms) than the percentage of shares outstanding, then EPS will indeed go up. And, if we assume that the market sets prices by

9 Grullon and Michaely (2000), cited earlier.

10 A recent press account (*Wall Street Journal*, March 6, 2000, page c. 17) for example reads "The appeal behind a share repurchases is . . . fairly straightforward. A company buys a portion of its shares outstanding which gives a boost to its earnings-per share figures."

mechanically capitalizing reported EPS at industry-wide multiples, then stock prices will also go up.

But there is a fundamental flaw – or at least a hidden assumption – in this logic. It effectively assumes that the firm has idle or unproductive assets; and that, by getting rid of such assets, as opposed to some magical EPS effect, the firm's productivity (e.g., its EVA or return on capital) increases. For example, take the case where the firm is simply using excess cash (as opposed to raising new debt) to buy back its shares. In such a case, the firm is effectively choosing to shrink its asset base.[11] Theory suggests that shrinking the size of the firm adds value only if the firm is failing to earn its cost of capital on its marginal investments (and holding excess cash is generally viewed as a negative-NPV investment). If this is the case, then the real source of the gain is not some kind of market alchemy, but (as we discuss below) a reallocation of capital to higher-valued uses. But what about the case where the repurchase is funded with new debt? Although earnings may also increase, such an increase comes at the cost of higher financial risk, thus calling into question whether the market would use a constant multiple to price the shares.

Cash flow signaling

We typically think of a firm's management as being better informed about the company's true value than outside shareholders. This informational "asymmetry" can lead to occasions where managers have good news about future profitability, yet prevailing stock prices cannot reflect this because investors have access only to public information. Consequently, the stock can be priced below its intrinsic value. Of course, managers could try to eliminate the pricing discrepancy by simply telling investors whatever good news they

have. Yet, economists argue that such simple announcements are likely to lack credibility.[12]

What can managers do to convey their private information in a credible way? There is a well-developed literature that argues that managers provide credible signals of their optimism about future earnings by engaging in actions, like stock repurchase programs, that impose constraints on managers' flexibility. For example, Merton Miller and Kevin Rock argue that managers anticipating better-than-expected earnings are more likely to distribute cash in advance to their shareholders, whether through dividends or share repurchases.[13] According to this explanation, managers are willing to commit themselves to making these cash outflows today because they expect that future capital needs can be financed with anticipated increases in future earnings. Companies that foresee a decrease in earnings are less likely to take the same action because significant distributions to stockholders could not only force them to forgo profitable investment opportunities, but might also push them into financial distress.[14]

The implications for the first version of the signaling story thus seem clear: repurchasing firms should, on average, experience increases in future earnings and cash flows. But the empirical evidence is not so clear. Early studies generally found some evidence of earnings improvement after repurchase announcements.[15] However, these studies focused

---

11 See Larry Y. Dann, 1983, "Is Your Common Stock Really Worth Buying Back?," *Directors & Boards* 7, no. 4, 23–29.

12 If the costs of producing misleading forecasts is low, all managers, not just those with good news, have an incentive to tell the market about "bright" expectations for future earnings. In such an environment, investors cannot rely on any of the announcements they hear since they cannot distinguish between under-and overvalued firms. The finance literature refers to this phenomenon as a pooling equilibrium. In such a market, news about earnings is incorporated into stock prices only when the actual results are published.

13 Merton Miller and Kevin Rock, "Dividend Policy Under Asymmetric Information," *Journal of Finance* 40 (1985).

14 Using a similar argument, Sudipto Bhattacharya shows that the cost of raising new capital to finance future investment opportunities prevents overvalued firms from repurchasing shares or paying dividends. See Sudipto Bhattacharya, "Imperfect Information, Dividend Policy, and 'the Bird in the Hand' Fallacy," *Bell Journal of Economics* 10 (1979).

15 See for example, Larry Dann, 1981, "Common Stock Repurchases: An Analysis of Returns to Bondholders and Stockholders," *Journal of Financial Economics* 9 (1981); Theo Vermaelen, "Common Stock Repurchases and Market Signaling," *Journal of Financial Economics* 9 (1981); Larry Dann, Ronald Masulis and David Mayers, "Repurchase Tender Offers and Earning Information," *Journal of Accounting and Economics* 14 (1991); Michael Hertzel and Prem Jain, "Earning and Risk Changes Around Stock Repurchase Tender Offers," *Journal of Accounting and Economics* 14 (1991); Erik Lie and John McConnell, "Earnings Signals in Fixed-Price and Dutch Auction Self-Tender Offers," *Journal of Financial Economics* 49 (1998); Tom Nohel and Vefa Tarhan, "Share Repurchases and Firm Performance: New Evidence on the Agency Costs of Free Cash Flow," *Journal of Financial Economics* 49 (1998).

mainly on fixed-price repurchases. Significant increases in operating performance and cash flow are clearly to be expected in such cases, where the stronger commitment to distribute cash and the willingness to pay a fixed premium make a more powerful statement to the market.

But these situations differ from the far more typical case where managers are quietly buying shares on the open market. Here, the evidence that such transactions anticipate increases in future profits is less supportive. Early papers found modest evidence of earnings growth.[16] However, a recent study by one of the present writers (cited hereafter as Grullon (2000)), takes a more thorough and comprehensive look at the evidence and comes to a different conclusion.[17] Looking at all open market share repurchase programs announced between 1980 and 1994, this study finds a significant *decline* in operating income as a percentage of total assets. The study also finds that investment analysts' forecasts of future earnings tend to go *down* after repurchase announcements.

In sum, the results of Grullon (2000) contradict the hypothesis that managers announcing stock repurchase programs are signaling good news about future cash flow or earnings. Instead, the evidence points to a reduction in earnings and profitability. But it's important to keep in mind that since many open market programs are funded with cash rather than new debt, they often have the effect of shrinking the firm's asset and capital base. For many companies in mature or declining industries, the decision to shrink the firm by repurchasing stock may turn out to be an important, if not a critical, value-increasing strategy for reasons we discuss later.

Market undervaluation

If there is little evidence to support the first signaling story, what about the second possibility – that managers are signaling their disagreement with how the market is pricing existing public information?

With their fundamental understanding of the firm and its industry, a firm's managers are perhaps best positioned to recognize when market prices diverge from their true value. This explanation is consistent with the statements managers often make when announcing buyback programs such as their stock is "undervalued" or "a good buy" or "prices don't reflect the underlying value of the firm."

But, as we discuss later, companies that announce open market programs don't always carry them out. And talk, of course, is cheap. Moreover, the initial market reaction to announcements of open market programs is generally only about 4% (as compared to about 15% for fixed-price offers), a result that seems small if stocks are indeed such a bargain. Either many companies announcing buybacks are not so undervalued or the market is skeptical of management's claims and thus underreacts to the initial announcement.

To examine this question of whether managers are responding to what they perceive as undervaluation, a 1995 study by Josef Lakonishok, Theo Vermaelen, and one of the present writers (henceforth ILV (1995)) investigated stock returns for a four-year period following repurchase announcements for over 1,200 open market programs announced by U.S. firms and reported in the *Wall Street Journal* between 1980 and 1990.[18] As reported in Table 13.2, ILV (1995) found excess returns of 12.14% over the four-year period for their entire sample of firms. This finding is, of course, consistent with the possibility that such firms are undervalued at the time they announced a repurchase.

But, in an attempt to focus more carefully on mispricing as opposed to other reasons, ILV (1995) also considered the book-to-market ratio of the companies when they announced their repurchase programs. Companies with high book-to-market ratios are often viewed as "value" stocks; and, in such cases, perceived undervaluation is likely to be a primary factor in the decision to repurchase. For growth stocks at the other extreme, undervaluation seems less likely to be the dominant motivating factor.

As shown in Panel B of Table 13.2, the sample of repurchasing stocks in ILV (1995) is *not* overly tilted to value stocks. In fact, the distribution is relatively even between the growth and value stocks.

---

16 Vermaelen (1981), cited earlier, and Eli Bartov, 1991, "Open-Market Stock Repurchase as Signals for Earnings and Risk Changes," *Journal of Accounting and Economics* 14 (1991), find weak evidence that there are positive unexpected earnings after the announcement of these programs.

17 Gustavo Grullon (2000), "The Information Content of Share Repurchase Programs," Rice University working paper.

18 Ikenberry, Lakonishok and Vermaelen (1995), cited earlier.

Table 13.2 Long-run Stock Returns Following Open Market Share Repurchase Announcements*

	n	Year 1	Year 2	Year 3	Year 4
PANEL A: COMPOUNDED RETURN DIFFERENCES OVERALL					
All Firms	1,208	2.04%	5.16%	12.60%	12.14%
		(.064)	(.011)	(.000)	(.012)
PANEL B: COMPOUNDED RETURN DIFFERENCES BY BOOK-TO-MARKET RATIO					
Quintile 1	201	−1.11%	0.18%	−1.98%	−4.31%
(Glamour stocks)		(.687)	(.526)	(.397)	(.358)
Quintile 2	260	2.16%	−0.81%	5.96%	0.08%
		(.206)	(.625)	(.220)	(.498)
Quintile 3	276	3.03%	4.63%	11.32%	7.54%
		(.087)	(.174)	(.058)	(.308)
Quintile 4	225	0.59%	3.66%	12.47%	16.27%
		(.374)	(.197)	(.058)	(.144)
Quintile 5	241	4.66%	16.36%	34.29%	45.29%
(Value stocks)		(.054)	(.003)	(.000)	(.000)

*This table summarizes long-horizon evidence for 1,208 U.S. open market stock repurchase programs announced between 1980 and 1990 as reported in Ikenberry, Lakonishok and Vermaelen (1995). Here, annual returns for repurchase are calculated beginning in the month following the announcement. Equal-weighted portfolios are formed in event-time and are rebalanced each year. These returns are compared to a benchmark portfolio formed on the basis of size and book-to-market. The compounded difference in returns between the repurchase sample portfolio and the benchmark portfolio is reported below for a four-year period following the repurchase announcement. Significance is determined using a randomized-bootstrap methodology. The p-values from these tests are reported in parenthesis.

Thus, to the extent a high book-to-market ratio correctly identifies undervaluation as a primary factor, the evidence would seem to suggest that companies buy back stock for reasons other than just market mispricing.

Also worth noting in Panel B of Table 13.2 is that, for those firms in the highest book-to-market quintile at the time of the buyback announcement, the compounded excess return was extremely high, on average, increasing from 4.7% in the first year to 45.3% in the fourth year. On an annualized basis, this excess performance translates into roughly 10% per year, a level roughly *double* the risk premium most would consider typical of common stocks during this time period. But, as we move toward lower book-to-market quintiles, where undervaluation seems less likely to be a driving factor, we see little evidence of undervaluation. As a group, these firms appeared to be fairly priced at the time of the announcement, a result consistent with the idea that these firms are repurchasing stock for reasons other than undervaluation.

At least in some cases, then, managers seem to be indicating that their firm is undervalued. Interestingly, the evidence also suggests that the market seems to underreact to these signals. If managers are deliberating trying to send a message, the market appears to be reacting with skepticism. This apparent contradiction with efficiency has led some to question the robustness of these findings. Two recent papers shed light on this issue. In a recent study of 1,060 Canadian stock repurchases, Ikenberry, Lakonishok, and Vermaelen (ILV (2000)) re-examine the question of undervaluation.[19] Using data from a different country and from a more recent time-period (1989 to 1997), they report similar evidence of positive long-term returns. Over a three-year window following the repurchase announcement, ILV (2000) found excess returns in Canada to be 0.587% per month, or roughly 7% per year. Like their 1995 study of the U.S. market, this study divided the Canadian firms into two parts according to whether the book-to-market ratio at the time of the announcement was above or below average for Canadian firms

19 David Ikenberry, Josef Lakonishok and Theo Vermaelen, "Stock Repurchases in Canada: Performance and Strategic Trading," *Journal of Finance*, forthcoming (2000).

overall. For the growth firms, they found excess returns of roughly 3.3% per year (t=2.13) over the three-year period following the announcement. And, remarkably similar to the U.S. value firms, Canadian value firms announcing repurchases earned excess annual returns of 9.1% (t=3.77).

In another recent study, Chan, Ikenberry and Lee (CIL (2000)) examined long-horizon returns for a sample of over 4,000 open market programs announced by U.S. firms from 1980 to 1996.[20] Like ILV (1995), but using six years of post-1990 data, CIL (2000) also reported evidence of abnormal stock returns. In addition, the study found some evidence of excess performance by growth stocks, a result similar to the evidence from the Canadian market in the 1990s. In attempting to explain the long-term returns, CIL (2000) also looked at two additional factors: (1) whether insiders were trading around the time of the repurchase announcement, and (2) whether the firms actually bought shares in the market. The results for insider trading were inconclusive; that is, there was no evidence that managers trade sympathetically with the share repurchase program. However, the authors do find evidence of higher long-run abnormal returns when companies actually buy back stock in the first year of the program, particularly for value stocks.

Agency costs of free cash flows

As agents of the shareholders, we would like to think that managers work to increase shareholder wealth by always making decisions that increase the market value of the firm. But this view ignores one of the important consequences of the separation of ownership and control in the large, modern corporation, a concern that dates from at least as early as the 1930s.[21] As shareholders lose control, managers have the ability to put their own interests ahead of their shareholders'. Of critical concern is the extent to which managers allocate capital into unprofitable activities, pursuing growth and size at the expense of profitability and value. For some managers in some

circumstances, the perks of managing a larger, more influential organization are likely to outweigh the benefits of having satisfied shareholders. The costs that arise from this conflict between growth and value maximization are known in finance theory as agency costs – or, more specifically, as the agency costs of "free cash flow."[22]

Companies at risk for overinvesting, or investing in non-productive activities, are those with large amounts of excess capital – particularly liquid capital like cash – for which the firm has no (foreseeable) positive-NPV projects. In two seminal papers, Frank Easterbrook and Michael Jensen argued that one way to at least mitigate such potential free cash flow problems is for firms to return cash back to shareholders in the form of higher dividends, particularly in cases of companies with excess or surplus capital.[23] Like dividends, stock repurchases are an effective tool for addressing this problem. The free cash flow hypothesis suggests that repurchase announcements are likely to be good news for the simple reason that they reduce management's ability to divert capital to uses that are not in the best interest of shareholders. By reducing financial slack in the firm, managers who repurchase stock have fewer opportunities to adopt value-reducing projects. In sum, any repurchase can be a good repurchase, provided it doesn't jeopardize the firm's ability to fund promising investment opportunities that might arise in the future.

Several studies have examined this issue of whether share repurchases are at least partly motivated by the agency problems of free cash flow. In their 1993 study of leveraged recaps, David and Diane Denis provided evidence of the role of heavy debt in adding value by reducing excessive capital investment.[24] Other early studies focused on whether the market reaction to announcements of fixed-price tender offers was stronger for firms

20 Konan Chan, David Ikenberry and Inmoo Lee (2000), "Do managers knowingly repurchase stock on the open market?," Rice University working paper.
21 See Adolf Berle and Gardiner Means, 1932, *The Modern Corporation and Private Property*, New York: Macmillan.
22 See Michael Jensen and William Meckling, "Theory of the Firm: Managerial Behavior, Agency Costs and Ownership Structure," *Journal of Financial Economics*, 3 (1976).
23 Frank Easterbrook, "Two Agency-Cost Explanations of Dividends," *American Economic Review*, 74 (1984); Michael Jensen, "Agency Costs of Free Cash Flow, Corporate Finance, and Takeovers," *American Economic Review*, 76 (1986).
24 David J. Denis and Diane K. Denis, 1993, "Managerial Discretion, Organizational Structure, and Corporate Finance: A Study of Leverage Recapitalizations," *Journal of Accounting and Economics* 16, 209–236.

with low Tobin's Q than for those with high Tobin's Q.[25] (Tobin's Q is the market value of the firm relative to the replacement value of the firm and, as such, can be similar to the market-to-book ratio.) The rationale for this test is that if the market is responding to concerns over agency problems, the reaction to tender offer announcements should be more positive for those companies most likely to overinvest. Conceivably, these might be cases where the market did not foresee future growth opportunities, thus implying lower Q ratios. Although the findings of one early study did not support this prediction,[26] several more recent studies report evidence consistent with the agency cost story. For example, Lie (2000) finds that firms that announce repurchase tender offers have higher levels of cash than their industry peers, and that the market reaction to such announcements is positively related to the amount of excess cash in the announcing firm.[27]

In the case of open market share repurchases, Grullon (2000) finds that the market reaction to these events is negatively correlated with the firm's operating return on investment. In other words, the market reacts favorably to buyback programs announced by companies whose investment opportunities appear to have declined. This evidence is also consistent with the next corporate motive we consider, the idea that companies use stock repurchases as a means of re-allocating capital from less productive to more productive areas in our economy.

Capital market allocation

A central function of financial markets is to allocate capital among competing investment opportunities. Ideally, all projects that add value should receive new capital in order to maximize the wealth of an economy. Sometimes, however,

this efficient allocation cannot be achieved due to market "imperfections" (other than the misalignment of incentives between managers and stockholders just discussed). One important imperfection in this context is the information "asymmetries" between managers and outside investors that we discussed earlier.

Consider an economy where all the funds available for investment projects are given to a single firm, Firm Y, at a specific point in time. Suppose that in the following year Firm Y is generating cash flows, but it has no new profitable investment opportunities. And there is a new Firm X that has positive NPV projects. Clearly, if Firm Y does not distribute the excess capital it has amassed, the welfare of this economy suffers.

A central premise of how capital is allocated in a free economy is that corporations should consider returning capital to shareholders when they have run out of value-adding investment opportunities. Shareholders are then free to reallocate this capital to other more productive uses. Although the capital market allocation hypothesis is similar in spirit to the free cash flow hypothesis, this hypothesis asserts that even without agency problems shareholders are better off with a share repurchase program. The reason for this is that shareholders can allocate funds more effectively than corporate managers, if only because they have a broader view of economy-wide opportunities.

If this capital market allocation hypothesis is correct, then firms announcing share repurchase programs should experience a reduction in their investment opportunities. What empirical evidence we have seems consistent with this explanation. In the case of repurchase tender offers, a 1998 study by Nohel and Tarhan found that, on average, companies shrink their asset bases after the transactions. In the case of open market programs, Grullon (2000) finds that firms that make such announcements also show a subsequent reduction in their capital expenditures.

In short, one important reason for share repurchases has to do with the natural birth and death process of companies in a capitalist system.[28] Although corporate managers appear to use stock repurchases simply to address their own perceived undervaluation problems, the financial markets at large effectively use repurchases as a principal means of liberating capital from a moribund

---

25   For a detailed discussion of this test, see Larry Lang and Robert Litzenberger, "Dividend Announcements: Cash Flow Signaling vs. Free Cash Flow Hypothesis," *Journal of Financial Economics*, 24 (1989).

26   Keith Howe, Jia He, and G. Wenchi Kao, "One-Time Cash Flow Announcements and Free Cash-Flow Theory: Share Repurchases and Special Dividends," *Journal of Finance*, 47 (1992).

27   Erik Lie, "Excess Funds and Agency Problems: An Empirical Study of Incremental Cash Disbursements," *Review of Financial Studies*, 13 (2000).

economic sector so that it can be channeled into more promising ones. Viewed in this light, although repurchases may have the effect of shrinking the size of an organization, they are certainly not undesirable or unhealthy, nor should they be viewed as a sign of managerial failure or lack of imagination.[29] They are essential to any dynamic economy that hopes to have voluntary reallocations of capital from the "old" to the "new" economy.

Dividend substitution

Before stock repurchases became popular in the 1980s, cash dividends were the principal means of returning excess capital to shareholders. For companies that are fairly priced, the two approaches are economic equivalents, with one important difference – the tax treatment of investors' income. In a share repurchase, investors who choose to sell to the firm incur capital gains taxes. Non-selling shareholders receive a pro-rata increase in their ownership in the firm, but pay no immediate tax bill. Although the benefit of long-term capital gains over ordinary income tax rates has varied over time, there is generally a clear preference.[30] This differential is even larger if we consider that investors typically have the option to postpone the realization of capital gains taxes.[31]

Thus, it is possible that the surge in repurchase activity in recent years may reflect, in part, a broad tax-motivated substitution of repurchases for dividends.[32] There has been some recent debate as to the extent to which such substitution is occurring. Special dividends, those occasional payments that companies typically tell their investors not to expect again, have almost vanished from the marketplace.[33] On the other hand, their decline was apparent well before the recent surge in buyback activity. It is not clear that repurchases are responsible for the absence of special dividends today, although the logic for why special dividends might no longer exist is certainly clear.

Special dividends are often thought of as distributions to investors of large, non-recurring cash inflows, as opposed to regular cash dividends, which tend to be funded with recurring earnings and so are generally expected to be paid in a stable fashion over time. But stock repurchases, because of their flexibility, might offer firms another means of distributing their "lumpy," non-recurring cash flows. In support of this possibility, a recent study by Jagannathan, Stephens, and Weisbach (2000) finds that repurchasing firms have more volatile earnings than dividend-paying firms.[34]

Although this result suggests that repurchases and dividends overlap only to a limited extent, more compelling evidence for the dividend substitution hypothesis is provided by another recent study. Grullon and Michaely (2000) report that while the dividend payout ratio of U.S. companies has been declining since the mid-1980s, the total payout ratio has remained more or less constant (at around 26–28%), suggesting that corporations have been substituting repurchases for dividends. That study shows the average dividend payout ratio fell

---

28 For an important study that discusses the economic role of leverage, dividends, stock repurchases, and takeovers, see Michael C. Jensen, "The Modern Industrial Revolution, Exit, and the Failure of Internal Control Systems," *Journal of Finance* 48, 1993, 831–880.

29 This reallocation function of share repurchases has, in the past, been held with some suspicion. Consider the headlines in The Washington Post, February 23, 1995: "A Debate Over Disinvestment: Is Buying Back Stock Such a Capital Idea For Companies?" The central thesis of this article suggested that share repurchases somehow reduce the productive capital base and thus are destructive to the economy.

30 In 1999, for example, the top marginal rate on dividend income was 39.6%, while the top marginal rate on capital gains was roughly half this amount, only 20%.

31 For example, previous research has estimated the present value of the capital gains tax liability to be about 7% of the realized gain. See Aris Protopapadakis, "Some Indirect Evidence on Effective Capital Gains Tax Rates," *Journal of Business*, 56 (1983).

32 Grullon and Michaely (2000), cited earlier, and Erik Lie and Heidi Lie, "The Role of Personal Taxes in Corporate Decisions: An Empirical Analysis of Share Repurchases and Dividends," *Journal of Financial and Quantitative Analysis*, 34 (1999) show that aggregate expenditures on share repurchases are positively correlated with the relative tax benefit of capital gains.

33 Harry DeAngelo, Linda DeAngelo, and Douglas Skinner, "Special Dividends and the Evolution of Dividend Signaling," *Journal of Financial Economics*, forthcoming (2000).

34 Jagannathan, Stephens and Weisbach (2000), cited earlier.

35 The decline in the use of dividends among U.S. firms has also been documented in a recent paper by Eugene Fama and Kenneth French, "Disappearing Dividends: Changing Firm Characteristics or Lower Propensity to Pay," The Center for Research Securities Prices working paper (2000).

from 22.3% in 1974 to 13.8% in 1998,[35] while the average repurchase payout ratio increased from 3.7% to 13.6% during the same period.

Grullon and Michaely also find that companies initiating capital distributions today prefer repurchases over dividends. The frequency of firms initiating a distribution through a repurchase (as opposed to a dividend) increased from 27% in 1973 to 81% in 1998. In addition, they find that established companies dramatically increased their repurchase activity, while their cash dividends have not increased at nearly the same rate. With the aid of regression analysis, moreover, they provide evidence that expenditures on share repurchases by established firms have been financed in large part with what would otherwise have been increases in dividends.

Grullon and Michaely also provide some evidence that the stock market recognizes, and takes a favorable view of, this shift from dividends to stock repurchases. They find that the market reaction to a dividend cut, which tends to be sharply negative for most firms, is *not* statistically different from zero if the corporation has repurchased shares in the recent past. Furthermore, the study shows that the market reaction to a repurchase announcement is stronger when the expected tax benefits for dividend substitution are higher.

Capital structure adjustments

Another reason often suggested as to why corporations repurchase their own stock is to adjust their debt-to-equity ratios. In the case of tender offers, this is clearly an important motive since corporations typically retire a large fraction of stock in such transactions, and thus their leverage ratios increase. For open market programs, however, this motive is less compelling. Open market share repurchase programs are typically smaller in scope – several studies report that the typical program is for 5% of the share base. Moreover, corporations often take several years to complete a program. Given the predominance of open market programs over other forms of corporate stock repurchase, dramatic adjustments in capital would not appear to be a primary motive.

Although open market repurchases have only a small effect on the capital structure in the short run, it is possible that corporations repurchase shares in the open market to avoid having to make larger adjustments in their leverage ratios. That is, companies may use small open market programs as a way to fine-tune their leverage over time. For example, in some press releases that accompany open market programs, managers have commented on the need to obtain shares for their ESOPs (employee stock ownership plans) or DRIPs (dividend reinvestment plans). Perhaps more important, firms will announce that they are buying shares to offset "dilution" from employee and executive stock options incentive plans. A number of recent studies (including Chan, Ikenberry, and Lee (2000), cited earlier) have shown that repurchase announcements often occur around the time of the exercise of executive stock options.

This need of companies to issue additional shares comes from a variety of sources and is more or less continuous. To the extent that companies do not repurchase stock, each of these activities has the effect of a small equity offering. The impact on capital structure of these issuance commitments can be substantial. Left unchecked, the firm is effectively decreasing its leverage over time.

With respect to executive stock options, there is an interesting side-issue to consider. When managers receive stock options, the strike price in most of these contracts is not "dividend-protected" – that is, reduced to reflect increases in the payout. Consequently, managers who hold a significant number of options have an incentive to avoid increases in dividends and instead re-channel those funds into repurchases. In fact, Christine Jolls finds that the increasing use of executive stock options is a major factor in the general increase in repurchase activity in the 1990s.[36] But, of course, managers intent on maximizing the value of their options might be tempted to eliminate dividends entirely – and we rarely see companies take such an extreme step. Nevertheless, if the corporation is compelled to pay out capital to shareholders for whatever reason, managers who are heavily compensated through options may feel more inclined to choose a share repurchase over a cash dividend.

---

36   See Christine Jolls, "The Role of Incentive Compensation in Explaining the Stock-Repurchase Puzzle," Harvard University working paper (1996).

OTHER CONSIDERATIONS IN OPEN MARKET SHARE REPURCHASES

Our focus up to this point has been on understanding why companies repurchase stock. We now discuss a number of other issues that arise in planning repurchase programs, particularly as they relate to open market programs. We begin with the possible impact of stock repurchases on liquidity. Open market programs are, by design, flexible in terms of when and how managers buy back stock. Thus we devote some discussion to this flexibility and the issue of completion rates. The last part of this section reviews some of the disclosure and other regulatory aspects of open market programs in the U.S.

Share repurchases and stock liquidity

When companies retire stock, particularly a large block, it is often assumed that liquidity must fall because of the reduction in float and in the number of investors capable of trading the stock. Yet a reduction in liquidity may not be an inevitable outcome for several reasons. For one thing, as we mentioned earlier, companies are often issuing shares on a continuous basis for a variety of reasons. Second, and more important, is the possibility that the company's trades during the buyback may actually have a beneficial impact on liquidity.

Several theoretical and empirical studies have considered the likely effect of stock repurchases on "market microstructure." Some finance theorists have argued that open market repurchase programs should be detrimental to market dynamics because the firm's presence in the market increases the fraction of "informed" traders – traders with an informational advantage over other investors. The larger presence of informed traders is in turn thought to give rise to an "adverse selection" problem. The problem is this: When a better-informed trader (such as the firm itself) enters a market, market-makers respond by widening their bid-ask spreads, thereby increasing transaction costs for all investors and so reducing liquidity. And there is some evidence to support this argument: A 1988 study by Michael Barclay and Clifford Smith found that bid-ask spreads widened after the

announcement of an open market repurchase program.[37]

But there is also a reasonable counterargument – namely, that share repurchases may actually improve liquidity by increasing depth on the sell-side of the market. Here companies can be thought of as supporting their market-makers(s) and adding downside liquidity in falling stock markets. Furthermore, the presence of a large buyer in a falling market may give confidence to market participants and reduce the number of sellers in the market. For example, many market observers have maintained that the large number of share repurchase programs announced during and after the market crash of October 1987 was partly motivated by the desire to increase liquidity.

More recent evidence supports this idea that share repurchase programs can be used to increase liquidity. Using a different sample and methodological procedure than that used by Barclay and Smith, a 1995 study by James Miller and John McConnell found no evidence of an increase in bid-ask spreads after buyback announcements.[38] And a number of other studies have produced evidence that bid-ask spreads actually decline when repurchase programs are announced.[39] Perhaps most interesting is a recent study by Jaemin Kim that examines this issue using high-frequency, intraday data.[40] Although this study does not report

37 Michael Barclay and Clifford Smith, Jr., "Corporate Payout Policy: Cash Dividends versus Open-Market Repurchases," *Journal of Financial Economics*, 22(1988).

38 James Miller and John McConnell, "Open-Market Share Repurchase Programs and Bid-Ask Spreads on the NYSE: Implications for Corporate Payout Policy," *Journal of Financial and Quantitative Analysis*, 30 (1995).

39 See, for example, James Wiggins, "Open Market Stock Repurchase Programs and Liquidity," *Journal of Financial Research*, 17 (1994); Ajai Singh, Mir Zaman and Chandrasekhar Krishnamurti, "Liquidity Changes Associated with Open Market Repurchases," *Financial Management*, 23 (1994); Diana Franz, Ramesh Rao, Niranjan Tripathy, "Informed Trading Risk and Bid-Ask Spread Changes around Open Market Stock Repurchases in the NASDAQ Market," *Journal of Financial Research*, 18 (1995); J. Chris Leach, Douglas Cook, and Laurie Krigman, "Corporate Repurchase Programs: Evidence on the Competing-Market-Maker Hypothesis," University of Colorado at Boulder working paper (1995).

40 Jaemin Kim, "Open Market Share Repurchase Announcements: Their Impact on Liquidity," University of Washington working paper (2000).

sample-wide increases in liquidity after share repurchase announcements, it does provide evidence of reduced volatility after share repurchase announcements as well as a decrease in bid-ask spreads among smaller, less illiquid stocks. This finding seems consistent with the liquidity-enhancement argument, since illiquid stocks would be most likely to benefit from the company's deep pockets.

Does the market reward companies for adding liquidity in this manner? The early evidence suggests that the answer is no – at least at the time of the announcement. Grullon (2000) examines the relation between the short-term market reaction to share repurchase announcements and the level of liquidity of the stock. Using stock turnover as a proxy for liquidity, this study finds that illiquid stocks experience essentially the same market reaction when announcing repurchase programs as do more liquid firms. This result can be interpreted in one of two ways: either shareholders do not place much value on the added liquidity or the benefits of added liquidity are priced into the stock only gradually over time as investors become aware of them.

One final important question that remains is whether companies are indeed a useful source of liquidity during market downturns. If this contention is true, then the stock returns of firms that are actively repurchasing their shares should be less sensitive to market-wide movements in a declining or bearish market. To examine this hypothesis, we perform a simple econometric analysis using the ILV (1995) dataset of all corporate repurchases announced between 1980 and 1990 in the *Wall Street Journal* as well as the open market programs recorded by SDC over the period 1991 to 1996. Our analysis involves estimating the following regression equation:

$$r_{it} = \beta_0 + \beta_1 r_{mt} + \beta_2 r_{mt} \times DUMNEG_t + \beta_3 r_{mt} \times DUMNEG_t \times DUMREPO_t + \varepsilon_{it},$$

where r_{it} is the daily return for repurchase firm i, r_{mt} is the daily value-weighted market return, DUMNEG is a dummy variable equal to 1 if the market return is negative, zero otherwise, and DUMREPO is a dummy variable equal to 1 if the observation falls in a quarter where the corporation repurchased shares, zero otherwise. Information on actual repurchases was gathered from COMPUSTAT files.

The interaction variable $r_{mt} \times DUMNEG_t \times DUMREPO_t$, β_3, captures the impact we are looking for. It measures the market sensitivity of the firm's returns on days when the market is declining and the company is also buying stock. This term can be thought of as the change in market beta for repurchasing companies when markets are bearish. If firms trade in a way that is designed to support their stocks, this coefficient should be negative – in other words, their beta risk should be decreasing. Consistent with this prediction, Table 13.3 shows that the average estimated value of β_3 for all the firms in our sample was negative (–0.042) and statistically significantly different from zero (at the 1 percent level). We also found that β_3 becomes more negative as the repurchase activity of the firm increases. The average β_3 for firms with low repurchase yields (Quintile 1) is essentially zero. At the other extreme, the average β_3 for firms with high repurchase yields (Quintile 5) is negative (–0.075) and highly significant.

Although the "economic" magnitude of this change in beta may seem fairly small, repurchases do appear to provide at least some support in a declining market. Moreover, a few things are working against us in this analysis. First, our data is "noisy" since we did not have access to daily data on company repurchase activity and so could only approximate such activity using quarterly numbers. More important, many repurchase programs are not explicitly managed to provide liquidity benefits. For example, as discussed in the Appendix, many companies implement VWAP, or volume weighted average price, contracts with their brokers. Such contracts motivate brokers to trade with volume as opposed to supporting downside liquidity. In sum, our inability to find more striking reductions in betas during open market programs is complicated by limitations of the data. Moreover, this result is likely compounded by the fact that some companies may unwittingly be forgoing liquidity benefits by the way they manage their programs.

Financial flexibility and completion rates

By design, open market repurchase programs allow managers flexibility as to when or even if they buy stock. Moreover, tracking actual repurchase trades is not always straightforward. For example, in the U.S. there are no disclosure requirements like those

Table 13.3 The Effect of Share Repurchases on Stock Returns*

	Average regression coefficient				
	β_0	β_1	β_2	β_3	N
Entire Sample	0.0009[a]	0.7196[a]	0.2116[a]	−0.0418[a]	1,913
SORTED BY REPURCHASE YIELD:					
Quintile 1 (Low)	0.0012[a]	0.7138[a]	0.2486[a]	−0.0002	386
Quintile 2	0.0010[a]	0.7103[a]	0.2834[a]	−0.0381[c]	382
Quintile 3	0.0007[a]	0.7880[a]	0.1318[a]	−0.0353	381
Quintile 4	0.0008[a]	0.6747[a]	0.2071[a]	−0.0611[a]	382
Quintile 5 (High)	0.0008[a]	0.7115[a]	0.1863[a]	−0.0749[a]	382

*This table reports the average estimated coefficients of the regression shown in the text. The regression coefficients are estimated over a period of four years surrounding the share repurchase announcement. The sample consists of firms that announced open market share repurchases over the period 1980–1990. Information on actual repurchases is gathered from the quarterly COMPUSTAT files. a, b, and c denote significantly different from zero at the 1%, 5%, and 10% level, respectively.

mandated for insider trades. Most U.S. firms do not provide details of their repurchases on a periodic basis in the same way they publicize, for example, their earnings and dividend payouts.

This dearth of disclosure has led regulators and institutional investors to express concern over completion rates and whether firms are making good-faith efforts to buy the shares they authorize for repurchase. For example, Canadian stock exchanges such as the Toronto Stock Exchange oversee the approval of share repurchase programs.[41] Canadian regulators are said to be less inclined to authorize new repurchase programs if the company has a poor track record in completing previous programs. A primary concern of both regulators and investors is that, because of the flexibility and modest disclosure requirements associated with open market repurchase programs (particularly in the U.S.), there is some potential for companies to mislead investors by announcing repurchase programs while having no intention of buying stock. While such opportunistic behavior is always a possibility, it is not clear that the lack of full completion rates can or should be construed as deliberate deception on the part of corporate

managers. Just as firms repurchase for a variety of reasons, their propensity to buy all the stock they authorize for repurchase will also vary as well.

First, what is the track record on completion rates? In the U.S., this simple question is difficult to answer because mandatory disclosure about actual repurchases is limited to a few pieces of information scattered throughout the firm's financial statements. Typically, for U.S. firms this disclosure is limited to line items in the cash flow statements published in the 10-Q and 10-K reports. Other parts of the financial statements, including the management discussion and analysis section, may provide information on the number of shares repurchased. This information is not always straightforward to follow and, of course, it is published well after the trades are executed. The difficulty in tracking actual repurchase activity in the U.S. is further complicated by the fact that the duration of open market programs is typically not defined; programs often run many years.

A 1998 study by Stephens and Weisbach has produced what is probably the most reliable estimate of completion rates for U.S. stocks. This study takes a variety of approaches that range from measuring expenditures from the cash flow statement to examining changes in shares outstanding. Experience suggests that this last approach is inadequate because of the significant "leakage" of share issuances for executive stock options, ESOP obligations or DRIPs – all of which

41 To be more precise, open market programs in Canada are referred to as normal course issuer bids. We thank Timothy Baikie, Special Counsel Market Regulation for the Toronto Stock Exchange, for sharing with us some of the practices Canadian firms follow when repurchasing stock.

can increase shares outstanding while the firm is buying back stock. In the case of Microsoft, for example, this leakage is so great that the balance of outstanding shares actually increases over time even though the firm is actively buying back stock. Focusing on cash expenditures, Stephens and Weisbach report that during the period 1981 to 1990, U.S. firms completed roughly 75% of their authorized shares during the period three years from the initial announcement.

In Canada, disclosure of actual repurchase activity is far more extensive and meaningful. There the exchanges gather and publish each month the previous month's trading activity for all authorized programs. Thus, it is easy to find the exact level of repurchase activity at any point in time, the number of shares still authorized for repurchase, and the program's termination date. In examining this data, ILV (2000) find that, for their sample of 1,060 Canadian repurchases announced between 1989 and 1997, the average completion rate after 12 months was 28.6% and rising throughout their sample period. Only one-third of the sample bought at least half of their initial authorization. Less than one in ten firms completed 90% or more of their authorization. Direct comparison of Canadian completion rates to U.S. rates is not very meaningful because Canadian law limits all programs to 12 months or less. Nevertheless, taking this into account, Canadian completion rates appear to be slightly lower than those for U.S. firms.

Besides variable completion rates, ILV (2000) also find other indications of strategic trading by management. For example, completion rates were higher, on average, for value stocks than for growth stocks. The study also finds that companies buy more shares in a declining market – consistent with both the liquidity support and signaling hypotheses we discussed earlier – and buy fewer shares when prices are rising.[42]

Is it possible that some firms in Canada are intentionally misleading the market? ILV consider this question by looking at how long-horizon stock returns vary with differences in completion rates.

---

42 This result may also be affected by trading limits like Rule 10b-18. Canada has similar rules that discourage firms from executing trades in a rising market. Because of trade limits on "up-ticks," it is easier for firms to collect shares in declining markets.

Table 13.4 Long Run Stock Returns for Canadian Firms According to Buyback Completion Rates*

	Year 1	Years 2 and 3
No shares	11.5%	0.6%
Up to 30%	9.1%	11.3%
More than 30%	2.6%	6.8%

*This table summarizes (annualized) abnormal returns reported by Ikenberry, Lakonishok and Vermaelen (2000). They examine 1,060 Canadian repurchase programs announced between 1989 and 1997. They examine performance beginning in the month following the announcement. They separate performance into two periods, the first year following the announcement and then the two subsequent years. Performance is estimated by forming calendar-time portfolios and applying the Fama-French (1993) three-factor model. Completion rates are reported by all Canadian firms and are split into cases where no shares were bought, where at least some shares but less than 30% of the initial authorization were bought, and finally cases where firms bought at least 30% of their initial authorization.

The study divides their sample into three groups: those cases where no shares were bought; those where at least some shares but less than 30% of the initial authorization were bought; and those cases where firms bought at least 30% of their initial authorization. Of particular interest here are those cases where firms did not purchase a single share during the program. If management was trying to mislead investors, one would expect to find either no evidence of excess performance or perhaps even a decline. However, as reported in Table 13.4, this is not the case. In fact, we see the opposite: the highest levels of abnormal performance in year 1 are those cases where no shares were bought. Moreover, if we look at years 2 and 3, there is no evidence of abnormal performance. As for cases where the managers bought more than 30% of the stock, Table 13.4 shows the opposite pattern: comparatively low stock returns (2.6%) in year 1 and higher returns (6.8%) in years 2 and 3. Thus, while it is always possible that managers in some cases may consider using repurchases to mislead investors, the evidence does not show this to be prevalent. A more plausible interpretation would appear to be that managers simply choose not to buy their stock when prices rise and the undervaluation problems that may have prompted the share repurchase authorization in the first place are resolved. In cases were the market is slower to react, managers appear to be more aggressive in buying back stock.

This provides at least some explanation for why completion rates, after the fact, are not always 100%. However, is it even reasonable to think that managers fully anticipate buying all the shares they authorize for repurchase? A 1996 study by Ikenberry and Vermaelen suggests not.[43] After noting that open market programs are not firm commitments and that companies frequently state that "shares may be purchased from time to time depending on market conditions," this study views the flexibility that open market programs provide managers as an *exchange option*. The basic idea is that authorization of an open market program effectively gives managers an option to repurchase stock whenever they feel their stock price falls below fair value. Consistent with their model, the study finds that the market reaction is more positive in cases where the implied option value is higher – for example, when the stock's (non-market-related) volatility is relatively high.

An interesting further ramification of this exchange option model is that one should expect open market repurchase authorizations to be quite common precisely *because* of this flexibility. Given that these programs are not too costly to establish, that companies bear little or no penalty for not buying stock, and that the option to buy stock quietly in the market at various times is valuable; one would expect to see *most* firms at least authorize a repurchase program even if they view themselves as fairly valued. To investigate this prediction, we examined the percentage of S&P 100 and 500 companies that authorized open market programs from January 1, 1995 through January 1, 2000. As shown in Table 13.5, in 1999 alone roughly one out of every four companies in both the S&P 100 and 500 announced a repurchase program. Moreover, during the period from 1997 through the end of 1999, a three-year period often considered typical for open market programs, the authorization rate was 58% for the S&P 500 and 62% for the S&P 100. Going back five years, fully 70% of S&P 500 firms and 80% S&P 100 firms have at one point or another authorized a program. Such high authorization rates are consistent with this idea that open market programs give

Table 13.5 Open Market Share Repurchase Programs Announced by Large Firms*

Within the last:	S&P 500	S&P 100
One Year	25.0%	26.0%
Two Years	46.4%	50.0%
Three Years	58.2%	62.0%
Four Years	66.8%	74.0%
Five Years	70.2%	80.0%

*This table reports the percentage of firms included in the S&P 500 and S&P 100 indices as of January 1, 2000 that had authorized an open market repurchase program within the past one to five years. This information was obtained from Securities Data Corporation and Standard & Poor's.

managers a valuable, and relatively inexpensive, option to repurchase stock. And, given the flexibility provided by such options, we should not be surprised to see completion rates well below 100%.

Regulatory issues

Although U.S. companies have been repurchasing stock on the open market for decades, the practice was limited until 1982. Before then, there was no regulatory road map to guide corporate buybacks. Because of the firm's market power, concerns over potential accusations of price manipulation undoubtedly kept many companies out of the market.[44] Then, in November 1982, after a long debate over various proposals, the SEC adopted rule 10b-18, the first and only rule that provides any legal structure and protection to the buyback process. Although this rule is not statutory law, it sufficiently reduced litigation uncertainty to allow the surge in share repurchase activity in the '80s and '90s.

The rule narrowly applies to trading activities and does not address any other associated aspects of buybacks, including the disclosure of actual trades. However, a critical point about rule 10b-18 is that it provides no limitations as to what companies can and cannot do. Instead the rule is a "safe-harbor" and provides legal protection against accusations of price manipulation as long as four

---

43 David Ikenberry and Theo Vermaelen, "The Option to Repurchase Stock," *Financial Management*, 25 no. 4 (1996).

44 For example, when rule 10b-18 was adopted, SEC chairman John Shad is quoted as saying "without the change, companies are inhibited from making big open-market buys."

trading limits are followed. Issuers and their affiliates are deemed not to violate the anti-manipulative provisions of other SEC rules (section 9a2 and rule 10b-5) if the company's transactions on any given day:

1. are made through only one broker or dealer;
2. are not executed at the opening or during the last half hour of trading;
3. are not done at a price exceeding the highest current independent bid price or the last independent sale price, whichever is higher; and
4. if the total repurchase volume does not exceed 25% of average daily trading volume (excluding block-trades) calculated over the preceding four calendar-weeks.

The framework for these four guidelines came from a widely publicized court case in the 1960s where price manipulation was indeed the central issue.[45] The rule does not apply to trades executed for an employee stock ownership plan nor does it apply to prices or volumes set for self-tenders or negotiated trades done off-market.

The four basic limits achieve different objectives. The first limit is intended to place some responsibility on the broker/dealer for following the rules and also limits the firm from appearing to hide its trades. The limit of one broker/dealer is applied on a day-to-day basis, not for the entire program. Thus firms have considerable freedom to move their brokerage business around (though it is not clear that many behave this way). The second provision, which relates to time of day limits the firm from affecting prices at either the opening or close, two times at which the firm's last traded price can be an important benchmark value for establishing exchange ratios in takeovers or determining payouts from compensation reward plans.

The last two items of the safe-harbor are intended to reduce the price impact of the firm's own trading. The third provision essentially serves as an "up-tick" limit and keeps the company from forcing its share price to trade at a higher price tick. A side effect of this provision, however, is that it also keeps the company from trading aggressively when the market is rising. Instead, this rule encourages companies to be suppliers of liquidity on the lower side of the market and to execute trades when the market is falling. At times, including the crash of 1987, the SEC has lifted various aspects of the rule, including these last two items, thus encouraging companies to trade more aggressively on extreme occasions. In fact, the SEC recently eased some of the 10b-18 restrictions during "market-wide breaks" with the aim of encouraging companies to be more aggressive in supporting their stock.

As mentioned, Rule 10b-18 is a safe-harbor rule, meaning that firms can rely on this rule for protection against litigation for price manipulation if they comply with the trading limits. Yet the rule poses no mandatory limit on the firm's ability to trade. For smaller companies whose trading volume or liquidity may be restricted, the lack of any statutory limit may be an important factor. Even for more widely traded stocks, companies are not required to, nor do they always obey, the specific limits outlined in the rule. A 1997 study by Cook, Krigman, and Leach, after carefully collecting data on 64 repurchase programs done between March 1993 and March 1994, found that less than 10% of the programs followed the absolute letter of each provision in rule 10b-18.[46] Roughly a third of the programs violated daily volume limits at one time or another. The up-tick rule is perhaps most limiting. Here, the study reported that more than 85% of the companies violated this aspect of the rule at some time during their program. In fact, about 10% of all the NYSE repurchase trades were done at prices above the safe-harbor limit. For NASDAQ stocks, *a majority* of the trades were not compliant, a result not entirely unexpected given the comparatively smaller and less liquid companies that trade in that market.

---

45 In the early- and mid-1960s, Georgia Pacific was acquiring companies through stock transactions. The exchange ratio in these acquisitions was set as a function of Georgia Pacific's stock price at certain points in time. At the same time, the company was repurchasing shares on the open market which it claimed were for employee bonuses. The SEC claimed that the repurchases were intentionally timed to affect the last traded price on the NYSE and thus lower the effective exchange ratio in its acquisitions. As a result, the court issued an injunction, the four elements of which closely resemble what is now Rule 10b-18.

46 J. Chris Leach, Laurie Krigman, and Douglas Cook, "Safe Harbor or Smoke Screen? Compliance and Disclosure under SEC Rule 10b-18," University of Colorado at Boulder working paper (1997).

Generally speaking, companies appear to be at least sensitive to the spirit of 10b-18. In the past, many companies announcing repurchase programs have stated their intent to follow rule 10b-18. And, while the rule does not apply to ERISA trades, companies still often instruct their brokers to execute these trades according to 10b-18 limitations. But despite such possible good intentions, the evidence suggests that firms either cannot or choose not to follow the rule's limits for each trade they execute.

Apart from Rule 10b-18, there is a surprising lack of regulatory structure. In Canada, for example, while its trading limits are similar to those in the U.S., there is considerably more regulatory structure governing the entire buyback process.[47] Open market repurchase programs in Canada are mandated to last no more than one year and cannot be for more than the higher of 5% of the share base or 10% of the public float. Companies wishing to purchase shares in subsequent years must have their programs renewed again by the board and must also reapply for approval from the stock exchange their shares trade on. For U.S. companies, by contrast, there are no regulatory limits other than the mandated initial disclosures to the market.

Perhaps the most troubling regulatory gap in the U.S. relates to disclosure of actual repurchase trades. Besides the minimal summary information provided in the quarterly and annual financial statements, companies have no obligation to disclose any aspect of their trades on a periodic basis or otherwise. This contrasts markedly, for example, with the disclosure required for insider trading activity. Although firms repurchasing stock are not required to disclose any of their trades, if management makes the same decision on a personal account, details about the trades must be promptly disclosed to the SEC and then made public in short order. In Canada, by contrast, the exchanges publish each month a comprehensive table showing repurchase activity (as well as the absence of such activity) for all authorized programs. Although specific trade details such as price are not reported, overall volume is clearly reported and available on a timely basis.

A final regulatory inconsistency regarding share repurchases concerns the practice of "black-out dates," rules that companies impose on their insiders limiting when they can buy or sell company stock. Typically, these self-imposed rules limit trading around the time of material events, such as earnings announcements. And such limitations are pervasive. A recent study by Carr Bettis, Jeffrey Coles, and Michael Lemmon finds that over 90% of a sample of U.S. firms restrict insider trading and nearly 80% have explicit black-out dates where managers are prohibited from trading.[48] Although there is no specific regulatory statute that applies any such limits to repurchases, some corporate legal departments nevertheless extend the same limits on insider trading to corporate repurchase activity as well.

SOME POLICY RECOMMENDATIONS FOR COMPANIES AND REGULATORS

Stock repurchases by U.S. companies, particularly those done on the open market, experienced a remarkable increase in popularity in the 1980s and '90s. In 1998, for the first time ever, the total value of all stock repurchased by U.S. companies exceeded the total amount paid in dividends. And the U.S. repurchase movement has gone global in the past few years, spreading not only to other "market-based" economies like Canada and the U.K., but also to countries like Japan and Germany, where such transactions were prohibited until recently.

Why are companies buying back their stock in such numbers? The most common reason cited by corporate executives and stock analysts is that stock repurchases boost reported earnings per share. But as we point out, this argument is nothing more than accounting sleight of hand. Although repurchases do increase EPS in many cases, it has this effect only when the assets used to buy back the shares have no productive use inside the firm. And if the assets have no productive internal use, then managers will increase the firm's overall productivity and thus add value simply by

---

47 A key distinction however is that the Canadian equivalent of rule 10b-18 was not enacted as a safe-harbor guideline, but instead as statutory limits.

48 J. Carr Bettis, Jeffrey L. Coles and Michael L. Lemmon, 2000, Corporate Policies Restricting Trading by Insiders, forthcoming *Journal of Financial Economics*.

distributing them to their shareholders. Thus, like dividend payments, repurchases are a means for companies to get rid of their excess capital, a process that has two main benefits. First, it helps prevent companies from "overinvesting" – that is, pursuing corporate size and growth at the expense of profitability and value. Second, by returning capital to investors, repurchases (and dividends) play the critically important economic function of allowing investors to channel their investment from mature or declining sectors of the economy to more promising sectors.

But if stock repurchases and dividends serve the same basic economic function, why have repurchases gained popularity in the U.S. only in the past two decades? A primary factor was the SEC's adoption of rule 10b-18 in 1982, which had the effect of reducing the regulatory ambiguity that had previously surrounded repurchases. With at least some shield against litigation risk over price manipulation, companies had the ability to take advantage of some of the important differences between repurchases and dividends. For example, because repurchases are taxed as capital gains and dividends as ordinary income, repurchases have been a more tax-efficient way of returning capital to shareholders than dividends (particularly with the widening of the gap between ordinary income and capital gains tax rates in the '90s). In addition, repurchases give managers more flexibility than dividends – flexibility to make small adjustments in capital structure, to exploit perceived undervaluation of the shares, and even perhaps to increase the liquidity of the stock (which may be particularly valuable in bear markets).

Of course, dividends and stock repurchases have both been held up as means of raising stock prices by "signaling" management's confidence in the firm's prospects to investors. But, as discussed in this paper, there are two distinct versions of the signaling story with respect to repurchases. One says that repurchases signal future unexpected increases in corporate cash flows and profitability; but the evidence is supportive only in the case of fixed-price offers, but not in open market programs, the dominant means by which companies buy back stock. The second version says that management is simply signaling its disagreement with the current market price; and, in this case, there is persuasive evidence that companies announcing

open market repurchase programs provide superior long-term returns to their stockholders. Moreover, this performance is much more evident for value stocks (those with high book-to-market ratios) than for growth stocks, suggesting that buybacks are in part a response to perceived undervaluation.

What policy issues should industry and regulators consider with respect to buybacks, particularly those on the open market? First, companies should consider the value of the flexibility that open market programs provide them in responding to changing market conditions (and, as discussed in the Appendix, they should also take into account how some repurchase execution strategies can reduce this flexibility). In some cases, it may be more important to express management's firm commitment to buy back shares by means of a tender offer or Dutch auction. But, in the vast majority of cases, preserving the flexibility of managers to buy (or not to buy) stock is likely to be an important consideration. Indeed, many companies may be using open market programs primarily to "support" their stock prices and supply liquidity during a downturn.

For U.S. regulators, the growth in stock buybacks poses a variety of interesting issues, most of which revolve around helping to define both the disclosure and the structure of the repurchase process. In the case of open market programs, companies are not required to (and rarely do) furnish their investors with details about a given program's structure, execution method, or even its duration. Interestingly, disclosure requirements for activities such as insider trading are far more comprehensive than for buybacks – which, after all, are strikingly similar transactions made on behalf of the firm where the economic threat to market credibility is seemingly far greater. The regulatory guidelines for shelf-offerings in the U.S. also differ greatly from the ill-defined structure of open market programs.

The evidence suggests that U.S. markets were well served when SEC rule 10b-18 was adopted in 1982. Yet, because this rule is narrow in scope and purpose, policy regulators and corporate leaders should consider some of the benefits provided by other systems, notably Canada's, which provide greater transparency and more guidelines for the repurchase process. In the absence of such an organized framework and disclosure environment, it is puzzling why some U.S. companies have not adopted some voluntary reporting standard, particularly given investors' enthusiasm about corporate repurchase activity. One possibility may relate to the costs of choosing to disclose in some periods, while preferring not to disclose in other periods because of a lack of activity.

Appendix: Open Market Execution Strategies

Open market programs offer managers considerable flexibility in choosing when to buy stock or even whether to buy any stock at all. Companies are not required to provide, and most managers do not volunteer, details about the timing, price, or volumes of their stock repurchases. Compared to other corporate activities, one might characterize open market repurchase programs as obscure.

An equally obscure aspect concerns the process by which firms actually acquire stock in the open market. There are essentially two basic approaches. The first might be considered a traditional "cash-based" strategy. This is the approach envisioned when the SEC crafted rule 10b-18. Here managers trade just as investors might, buying stock and delivering cash. The degree of managerial attention this approach requires varies and is at the discretion of management. In some cases, managers prefer to have close control and essentially execute the program "in-house." In other cases, management only oversees the process and delegates most of the execution details. Here managers will often provide their agent with a target amount of stock they would like executed over some period of time ranging from a day, week, month, quarter, or even longer.

While there are variations of the cash approach (one of which we will mention later), the second basic class of strategies is the "synthetic repurchase." This approach has numerous variations that involve the firm either purchasing call options and/or selling put options on their own stock. The purchase of call options allows managers to lock-in a maximum price for repurchasing a given quantity of stock. If the price settles below the strike at expiration, the option expires worthless; but this also means that market prices have not moved against the firm, thus allowing it to collect shares in the open market at what it may view as attractive prices. If the market moves up and prices close above the strike at expiration, the firm can take delivery of its shares while paying only the lower

strike price. This application of a synthetic strategy has an insurance element to it. For firms worried about their ability to repurchase sufficient quantities of stock at a given price, such an approach might be helpful. Yet insurance is never free and this approach comes, of course, with a price.

A second reason for this kind of synthetic strategy concerns the trading volume and price limits suggested in SEC rule 10b-18. Shares that are acquired through option contracts are considered negotiated trades and are not subject to open market trading limitations. In fact, by using long call options, firms can regulate to some extent just how many shares they wish to accumulate, thus bypassing 10b-18, simply by adjusting the strike price. As the strike is lowered into the money, the probability that management will take delivery also increases. A quick approach to determining this probability is simply to observe the option's "delta."

A second well-known synthetic approach is for the firm to sell put options. In this case, managers collect an up-front premium[49] and, in effect, "promise" to buy stock should market prices fall below a specific point. This approach has been characterized by some as an efficient way for firms to collect a large number of shares at "bargain prices" while again avoiding some of the SEC's trading limitations. Some companies with bullish expectations have been known to sell out-of-the-money puts as a means of collecting premiums on what they view as overvalued puts.

If one sells a put and simultaneously applies those proceeds to the purchase of a call with the same parameters, they have created a synthetic forward contract at the strike. Under this arrangement, regardless of whether prices move up or down, managers have a pre-set price and will be assured of taking delivery once the options reach maturity.[50] If managers pull the strike prices apart by setting the call's strike price higher and the put's

---

49　In the U.S., this premium is non-taxable and falls straight to the bottom line.

50　Given the costs involved, it is not entirely clear why a firm would do this. One possibility is that management might believe that such an approach would allow them to obtain a larger number of shares in a shorter period of time than would be possible in the open market. Thus this approach might be lower in cost to say a fixed-price tender offer which are much more visible and where the firm typically pays a premium.

lower, they essentially create a repurchase collar. This way the company accomplishes its goals for repurchasing stock, but has synthetically transferred all of their trading activity into the option market. Although these synthetic products are widely discussed in practice, determining the actual extent of their use is difficult because most firms disclose little about their use of such contracts to investors.[51]

Do these synthetic approaches add value? They clearly add value for investment bankers; the mark-up on such products dominates the revenue they typically receive as broker-agents in basic cash-based strategies. For companies, however, the answer is not so clear. These synthetic approaches may be cost-effective in allowing the firm to gather shares in an orderly manner that it might otherwise have problems replicating in the cash market. As mentioned earlier, these transactions fall outside the domain of rule 10b-18. But, in other cases, these plans could cause problems. For example, the short-put strategy is appealing if one is convinced that bargain prices arise only as a result of noisy markets. But low prices can also result from unexpectedly bad operating performance. A short put may amplify the effect of whatever bad news is affecting the stock price since this strategy pre-commits the firm to spending capital to purchase shares. The firm will, ex-post, be buying shares at prices above the prevailing market at times when its fundamental cash flow may be reduced. Clearly, both management and the board should appreciate this exposure. One way around this dilemma is for the firm to have other options in place that "undo" a portion of their commitment should prices drop to extreme levels, thus giving relief when doomsday-like situations arise. Other variations of this basic theme also exist.

In short, managers should be aware of the possible consequences of synthetic repurchase strategies, particularly those that *obligate* the firm to certain actions. For example, when firms sell puts on their own stock, they forgo the inherent flexibility that explicitly motivates open market programs. A similar caveat applies to a popular variation of the basic cash-based repurchase strategy, known generically as "accelerated repurchase programs."

Here investment bankers go into the market and borrow company stock from other investors. The bank then shorts these shares to the firm in one negotiated trade. The investment bank then settles their short position by buying stock in the market over some set period of time. Typically, the bank purchases a fixed number of shares each day during the repurchase window. In many accelerated programs, the company agrees to reimburse the bank the difference between the initial negotiated price and the VWAP, or volume-weighted average price. This price is determined from all trades that occurred that day. Thus, the company is assured in advance that on any given day, it pays only the average market price and is not exposed to any trading risk from the banker.

One alleged advantage of this strategy is the mythical "EPS bump" that we discussed earlier. An accelerated repurchase immediately reduces the average number of shares, thus increasing reported earnings more than would otherwise occur if the same transactions spanned a longer period of time. But, as discussed earlier, it is important to remember that this earnings gain arises only to the extent that the firm has an inefficient allocation of assets, as opposed to any accounting sorcery or hand-waving.

Yet, like synthetic repurchase strategies, accelerated repurchase programs also remove some of the financial flexibility that open market programs provide. In cases where firms feel committed to disgorge cash and are not overly price sensitive (such as in cases involving dividend substitution), entering in an accelerated repurchase may indeed be appropriate. Unfortunately, a VWAP contract does not allow the firm to take full advantage of the opportunity it has to increase downside liquidity. By design, the VWAP contract gives the banker a strict incentive to trade with volume. This is good for the firm if markets are falling on high volume. On such occasions, the investment banker's buy-oriented trades provide a source of downside liquidity. However if a stock has naturally weak volume and the same decline is experienced, the banker is exposed should he or she choose to provide liquidity in this falling market. Moreover, the same incentive contract forces the investment banker to trade and compete aggressively for buy-side liquidity when markets are increasing on heavy volume. Both of these

---

51   See for example, "More Firms Use Options to Gamble on Their Own Stock," *Wall Street Journal*, May 22, 1997.

actions are opposite from what managers might otherwise prefer.

Companies choosing to preserve some liquidity benefit from repurchasing stock might consider instituting a series of revolving downside limit orders. In bearish markets, the firm collects shares and provides downside liquidity. But, on days where markets are rising, the company can choose to save its resources and not compete against other traders in the market.

CHAPTER 14

The Dividend Cut "Heard 'Round the World": The Case of FPL

Dennis Soter (Stern Stewart & Co.) Eugene Brigham (University of Florida) and Paul Evanson (Florida Power & Light Company)

> [FPL's decision was] *"the dividend cut heard 'round the world."*
> – Morgan Stanley analyst report, June 1994

On May 9, 1994, FPL Group, the parent company of Florida Power & Light Company, announced a 32% reduction in its quarterly dividend payout, from 62 cents per share to 42 cents. This was the first-ever dividend cut by a healthy utility. A number of utilities had reduced their dividends in the past, but only after cash flow problems – often associated with nuclear plants – had given them no other choice.

In its announcement, FPL stressed that it had studied the situation carefully and that, given the prospect of increased competition in the electric utility industry, the company's high dividend payout ratio (which had averaged 90% in the past four years) was no longer in its stockholders' best interests. The new policy resulted in a dividend payout of about 60% of the prior year's earnings. Management also announced that, starting in 1995, the dividend payout would be reviewed in February instead of May to reinforce the linkage between dividends and annual earnings. In so doing, the company wanted to minimize unintended "signaling effects" from any future changes in the dividend.

At the same time it announced this change in dividend policy, FPL Group's board authorized the repurchase of up to 10 million shares of common stock over the next three years; and FPL's management indicated that 4 million shares would be repurchased over the next 12 months, depending on market conditions. (In fact, the company repurchased 4 million shares in the last eight months of 1994 and 1.9 million shares in 1995, at a total cost of $193 million.) In adopting this strategy, the company noted that changes in the U.S. tax code since 1990 had made capital gains more attractive than dividends to shareholders. Whereas dividends are taxed at ordinary income rates, gains from stock sales are taxed at lower capital gains rates. Furthermore, capital gains are taxed only when realized, thus providing each shareholder the opportunity to defer that tax.

Besides providing a more tax-efficient means of distributing excess capital to its stockholders, FPL's substitution of stock repurchases for dividends was also designed to increase the company's financial flexibility in preparation for a new era of deregulation and heightened competition among utilities. Although much of the cash savings from the dividend cut would be returned to investors in the form of stock repurchases, the rest would be used to retire debt at Florida Power & Light and so reduce the company's leverage ratio. This deleveraging and strengthening of FPL's financial condition were intended both to prepare the company for an increase in business risk and to provide the financial resources to take advantage of future growth opportunities.

The stock market's initial reaction to FPL's announcement was negative. On the day of the

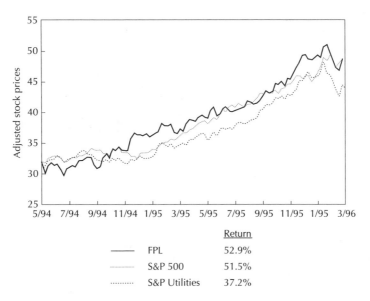

Figure 14.1   Adjusted Stock Prices for FPL, the S&P 500, and the S&P Utilities (5/6/94-3/29/96)

announcement, the company's stock price fell from $31.88 to $27.50, a drop of nearly 14%. (Given that FPL's average stock price during the prior month was about $33.75, and that the stock under-performed the S&P Utilities Index by about 4% during that month, a better estimate of the market's negative response is probably about 18–20%.) But, as analysts digested the news and considered the reasons for the reduction, they concluded that the action was not a signal of financial distress but rather a strategic decision that would improve the company's long-term financial flexibility and prospects for growth. This view spread throughout the financial community, and FPL's stock began to recover.

On May 31, less than a month after the announcement, FPL's stock closed at $32.17 (adjusted for the quarterly dividend of 42 cents), or about 30 cents higher than the pre-announcement price. By the middle of June, at least 15 major broker-age houses had placed FPL's common stock on their "buy" lists. On May 9, 1995 – exactly one year after the announcement of the cut – FPL's stock price closed at $37.75, giving stockholders a one-year post-announcement return (including dividends) of 23.8%,[1] more than double the 11.2% of the S&P 500 Index and well above the 14.2% of the S&P Utilities Index over the same

period. As this article went to press (April 1, 1996), FPL's stock was trading at $45.25 (or $48.73 adjusted for dividends), providing stockholders with a two-year post-announcement return of 52.9% – again, well above the 37.2% return of the S&P Utilities Index over the same period. (For a graphic illustration of FPL's stock return relative to the S&P Utilities Index, see Figure 14.1.)

Management's decision, however, was not an easy one. FPL had achieved the longest record of continuous annual dividend increases of any electric utility – 47 years – and the third longest of any company traded on the New York Stock Exchange. Moreover, dividend cuts are almost invariably followed by sharp reductions in stock price. Anticipating that the market's initial reaction would be negative, management undertook a major investor relations campaign to explain the company's change in dividend policy as a critical part of its overall business and financial strategy. That campaign took the form of a series of "road shows" comparable to those used in launching

---

1   Measured from the $31.88 stock price prior to the announcement. If we measure the return instead from the prior month's average of $33.75, the return would have been about 17%, still above the S&P return of 14.2%.

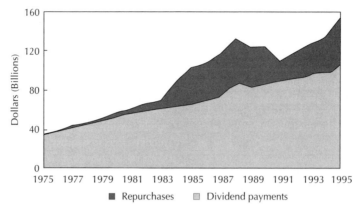

Figure 14.2 Total Dividend Payments and Repurchases*
Source: Compustat. 1995 repurchases are estimated based on first three quarters.
*This figure is taken from Jean Helwege, David Laster, and Kevin Cole, "Stock Market Valuation Indicators: Is This Time Different?," *Financial Analysts Journal* (forthcoming, 1996).

IPOs. The comparison seems apt because, in an important sense, FPL was becoming a *new* company – or at least it was a company in the process of transforming itself to confront a new competitive business environment.

FPL was not alone, however, either in reconsidering its dividend policy, or in making a partial substitution of stock repurchases for dividends. With companies in many industries facing greater competition, boards of directors are increasingly deciding that stock buybacks are a more effective means than dividends of committing management to distribute excess cash to stockholders. In the past three years, the dividend payout ratio of the S&P 500 has fallen from a 70-year historical average of about 55% to under 40%.[2] Stock market "bears" continue to point to a market dividend yield that has fallen from an historical average of about 4% to below 2.4%. What such analysis typically fails to recognize is the growing extent to which stock repurchases are being used to supplement dividends as a method of paying out excess cash. Between 1991 and 1995, total corporate dividends increased from $82.6 billion to an estimated $98.7 billion, an average annual growth rate of about 4%. Over the same period, the total amount

of stock repurchased by U.S. companies grew from $21.3 billion to $55.3 billion, an average annual growth rate of over 30%.[3] (For an illustration of the growth of stock repurchases relative to dividends since 1976, see Figure 14.2.)[4] In 1995 alone, over 800 U.S. companies announced plans to repurchase a total of $98 billion of stock – a 42% increase over the prior year.

> **THE CASE OF GE**
>
> *In the first five years of the eighties . . . GE returned to its share owners about $840 million a year in dividends. Throughout the following five years, ending in 1990 . . . we returned nearly double that – about $1.4 billion in annual dividends and repurchased $2.6 billion of stock. During the past five years, we've returned to share owners about $2.3 billion a year in dividends and repurchased an additional $5.5 billion of our stock. The pace continued to accelerate in 1995 when . . . [we paid] $2.8 billion in dividends and [repurchased] $3.1 billion [of our stock].*
>
> – Jack Welch
> 1995 Annual Report of General Electric

2 See Jean Helwege, David Laster, and Kevin Cole, "Stock Market Valuation Indicators: Is This Time Different?" *Financial Analysts Journal* (forthcoming, 1996).

3 Ibid.
4 As the figure shows, the first major spurt of growth in stock repurchases begins in 1984 and then rises to a peak in 1989. Much of these repurchases in the 1980s, however, were part of defensive recapitalizations and were thus not entirely "voluntary" decisions on the part of management. In the 1990s, by contrast, stock repurchases have been largely voluntary – that is, undertaken without pressure from a hostile bidder.

Other utilities, as well as companies in other rapidly changing industries, are wrestling with the dividend issue. Neither financial economists nor Wall Street operators have a magic formula for establishing the optimal payout policy. Indeed, many academics are still engaged in a 35-year-old debate as to whether dividend policy matters at all. The FPL case can be seen as contributing to the dividend debate in the following sense: It suggests that while there may not be a single dividend payout ratio that maximizes a company's value, the wrong policy may end up reducing value. More important, it makes clear that the right dividend policy for an individual company depends primarily on the business environment in which the firm operates – and that changes in the business environment are likely to dictate changes in financial policy. As the FPL story also shows, making the right dividend decision is not a trivial undertaking.

THE CHANGING ECONOMIC ENVIRONMENT

Dividend policy cannot be established in a vacuum. It must be viewed as part of an integrated financial strategy that includes a company's target capital structure and its expected future requirements for outside capital. The most important determinants of a company's financial strategy, as we will argue below, are its business strategy and the nature and extent of its investment opportunities. When the dynamics of the business change, as the case of FPL will illustrate, corporate strategy and financial policies – including dividends – also must change.

Under traditional rate-of-return regulation, FPL and other utilities had relatively stable earnings and paid out a high percentage of earnings as dividends. Largely because of the stability of their earnings, dividends on utility stocks tended to be quite predictable, much like the interest earned on corporate bonds. For this reason, utility stocks were typically purchased as "income" stocks and, like bonds, are highly sensitive to changes in interest rates. In fact, many utilities maintained their dividends throughout the Great Depression and, as a result, attracted income-oriented investors – the so-called "widow and orphan" clientele, who are said to place a special value on high payouts and high dividend yields.

Historically, utilities have been natural monopolies and have been granted monopoly franchises for their service areas. In return, they are required to provide customers with power on demand. They have operated subject to a "regulatory compact" under which regulators are supposed to allow them to earn a rate of return on their invested capital that is "commensurate with returns on investments in other enterprises having corresponding risks." That means, in effect, that the utility can earn its cost of capital on funds supplied by investors, but no more. Because of regulation, utilities have limited upside potential, but they have also been thought to have relatively little downside risk.

However, the regulatory compact began to be revamped during the 1970s and 1980s when many utilities were charged, with 20-20 hindsight, with having made "imprudent" investments, especially in nuclear plants. Regulatory actions during those years made it clear that a utility could no longer make investments with the assurance that revenues would be sufficient to provide a reasonable rate of return.

The most significant federal legislation affecting the electric utility industry was the Energy Policy Act of 1992. This act required utilities to open their transmission lines for wholesale transactions to any utility or independent power producer, and it allowed any company to build, own, and operate power plants. While the act specifically precluded the Federal Energy Regulatory Commission (FERC) from ordering transmission access for "retail wheeling" – that is, sales directly to retail customers – it did not prevent states from allowing retail competition.

Since the passage of this Act, there has been growing pressure at both the federal and state levels for customer choice. In Washington, Republican Congressman Dan Schaefer of Colorado, the chairman of the House Commerce Subcommittee on Energy and Power, has been strongly advocating a rapid transition to full retail competition. Bills have already been introduced in both the House and the Senate that would require states to prescribe some form of retail competition. At present, 35 states are considering regulatory or legislative proposals for retail competition.

To illustrate the significance of wheeling for the industry, on April 20, 1994 (just two weeks before the FPL dividend announcement), the California

Public Utilities Commission released its proposal to phase in retail wheeling beginning in 1996. In the week following that proposal, California's three largest utilities together lost over $1.8 billion of market value – an average loss of 8%.

This announcement was by no means the first sign that the electric utility industry was becoming a riskier place in which to operate and invest. Perhaps the most dramatic statement about the financial future of the industry came in October 1993 – six months prior to the FPL dividend action – when Standard & Poor's took the unprecedented step of revising its bond rating outlook on 22 utilities (representing about one-third of all utilities with rated debt) from "stable" to "negative." To reflect the more competitive environment, S&P also announced that it was changing its rating guidelines for the industry to take greater account of factors such as revenue dependencies and vulnerabilities, fuel diversity, and the regulatory environment.[5]

In sum, FPL and other utilities today find themselves increasingly subject to competition and so can no longer make investments with the expectation that they will earn a "fair" rate of return because of their status as a regulated monopoly. The shift in utilities' position from low-risk, regulated monopolies to riskier, competitive companies began in the late 1960s and is still going on today. Furthermore, different utilities have been affected in different ways and at different times. Still, FPL and all other utilities now face a drastically different future than under the old rules of the game, and this new situation requires new and different financial policies.

FINANCIAL IMPACTS

Panel A of Figure 14.3 shows dividend payout ratios for FPL, the utility industry, and the S&P 400 industrials over the past 30 years. The two most striking features of the figure are (1) the high payouts of utilities relative to other industries' and (2) the fact that FPL's payout, although below that of the average utility in the early years, had become substantially higher than the industry average by 1993.

As shown in Panel B, FPL's dividends grew at roughly the same rate as earnings in the years from 1965 until the beginning of the 1990s. During the second half of the 1980s, for example, earnings were trending upward, dividends were increasing at about 4% annually, and FPL's payout ratio fell within a fairly narrow range of 60–70%. Over the period 1990–1993, however, earnings fell about 10% from their late '80s levels; and, even though dividend increases were held to less than 2% per year, FPL ended up paying out an average of 90% of its earnings over this four-year period.

In short, FPL's dividends were increasing faster than its earnings. Under the old regulatory regime, the company might have chosen to maintain the dividend growth rate by resorting to new stock or bond issues.[6] (In fact, over the five-year period 1989–1993, FPL's total dividend payments were roughly equivalent to the company's proceeds from new equity

---

6 A major potential drawback to issuing stock is the fact that the announcement of a stock offering is generally taken by investors to be a negative signal about management's outlook for the future. If future prospects looked brighter to management than to investors, and hence the stock was in management's view undervalued, then the company would want to finance with debt rather than stock so as to avoid unnecessary dilution. On the other hand, if management was more pessimistic than investors, it would view the stock as overvalued; and in this situation management would tend to choose stock rather than debt financing. Because investors know that this is the way management can be expected to act, the announcement of a stock offering is construed as a negative signal, on average, and stock prices tend to decline when stock offerings are announced.

Under the old regulatory compact, however, this announcement effect probably did not apply to most utilities. The size of the market's negative response to a stock offering announcement is likely to depend on the extent of the "information asymmetry" between management and investors. That is, if investors know a great deal about a company and its operations, then the announcement (and the reasons for it) will have been anticipated, and there will be relatively little pressure on the stock price. Because of regulation, investors know more about utilities than about most other companies, so the price pressure when utilities issue stock is relatively small. Therefore, other things equal, utilities are better able to provide stockholders with cash dividends and then raise equity by issuing stock.

As we argue in this article, in the new competitive environment for utilities a new financing rule is likely to prevail – namely, "cash is king." Because the managements of utilities can no longer count on equity capital being available on favorable terms, they are likely to see a greater need to "control their own destiny" by conserving equity capital, maintaining higher cash balances, and reducing their target debt-to-capital ratios.

---

5 See Ben Esty, "Dividend Policy at FPL Group, Inc. (A)," Harvard Business School Case 9-295-059, p. 6.

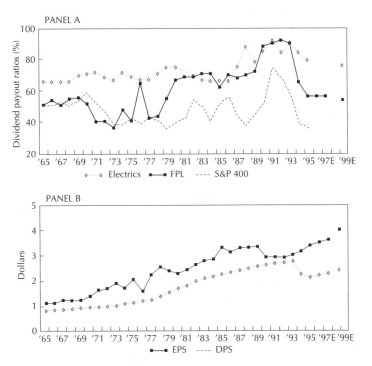

Figure 14.3   Trends in Dividend Payout Ratios: FPL, The Electric Utility Industry, and the S&P 400

issues[7] – and thus the company was effectively just recycling equity capital, paying out cash with one hand that it would soon take back with another in the form of a new stock offering.) Facing the prospect of greater competition and less predictable earnings, FPL's management wanted to increase its financial flexibility and end its past dependence on regular infusions of outside equity capital, especially since access to capital could be limited in the future.

FPL was not alone in wanting to escape from this pattern of dividends financed by new debt and equity offerings. Many utilities suspected that their payout ratios were getting too high, but they also felt compelled to maintain or even increase their dividends. Partly completed plants were in the pipeline, and capital was needed to finish these plants. Debt was being used aggressively, which in turn required additional equity. Most companies debated internally and with their investment bankers the pros and cons of getting the needed equity by cutting dividends versus issuing new stock.

The conclusion that was invariably reached – one that reflects the conventional wisdom of the utility industry and its financial advisers – can be summarized as follows: Investors in utilities *expect* annual dividend increases (that is why they buy the stocks in the first place), and so a dividend cut by a utility would immediately, drastically, and perhaps even permanently lower the stock price. The subsequent drop in stock price would in turn make it virtually impossible for the utility to issue new stock in the future – or, at best, the new stock could be sold only at a very low and dilutive price. That dilution would in turn lead to lower future earnings, which would lead to still lower stock prices in subsequent issues. In this fashion, a dividend cut would lead to a downward spiral in the market value of utilities.

The upshot of this conventional reasoning for FPL, and for most other utilities, was a series of dividend increases in the early '90s that exceeded earnings growth and, hence, high and rising payout ratios. As we have observed, the typical utility entered the 1990s with a payout ratio much higher than most industrials', even as the industry was facing rapidly increasing competition. Many utility executives were concerned about this situation.

---

7   We are indebted to Ben Esty's Harvard case study, cited earlier, for this observation.

They wanted to improve the alignment of their financial policies with the new market realities, but they were afraid of what might happen to stock prices if they cut the dividend or held the increase to less than what was expected by investors.

In 1994, FPL's management concluded that its dividend payout was too high. But determining the best course of action, and getting agreement from the Board, required further work and study, along with considerable input from Stern Stewart & Co.

THE THEORY OF DIVIDENDS

Financial economists have been producing studies of dividend policy for at least 30 years; but, as often happens, different researchers have come to different conclusions. There are three major theories that attempt to explain investors' "demand" for dividends.

The traditional justification for high dividends is that stockholders want current income. They could sell a portion of their shares each year to get that income, but in doing so they would incur transactions costs and possibly capital gains taxes. Stockholders are also commonly said to prefer dividends to retained earnings because "a dollar of dividends in the hand is better than a dollar of hoped-for capital gains in the bush." In other words, dividends are less risky and, hence, more valuable to investors than retained earnings.

A second theory maintains that investors as a group care only about total returns, not about whether they receive them in the form of dividends or price appreciation. This "dividend irrelevance" proposition, formulated by Nobel Prize winners Franco Modigliani and Merton Miller in the early '60s, is based on the argument that dividend policy is "merely a financing decision," a way of dividing up the pie of corporate earnings. In this view, the only important determinant of a company's value is its future earnings power. Thus, whether companies choose to pay low dividends and finance themselves with retained earnings, or pay high dividends and retrieve the capital with new stock or debt, is largely a matter of indifference to investors.

A third theory says that investors care about how their total returns are divided between dividends and price appreciation primarily because of the tax code. To the extent dividends are taxed at higher rates than capital gains, investors collectively will prefer a lower payout policy.

Empirical studies have been conducted to test these three theories, but statistical problems make the results inconclusive. For example, studies of announcements of dividend changes confirm, without exception, that the market responds positively to dividend increases, on average, and negatively to dividend cuts.[8] On the other hand, there are also studies that show that companies announcing dividend cuts outperform the market significantly in the year following the dividend cut.[9] None of the existing studies provides a conclusive answer to the issue confronted by FPL – namely, whether companies that choose to pay out higher proportions of their earnings as dividends end up producing higher (or lower) total returns for their stockholders.[10]

There are, however, a number of insights from academic research on dividends that managers should at least take into account when thinking about dividend policy. We review them (in order of ascending importance) below.

---

8 See, for example, among many others, Paul Asquith and David W. Mullins, "The Impact of Initiating Dividend Payments on Stockholders' Wealth," *Journal of Business*, vol. 56, January 1983, pp. 77–96; Terry E. Dielman and Henry R. Oppenheimer, "An Examination of Investor Behavior During Periods of Large Dividend Changes," *Journal of Financial and Quantitative Analysis*, vol. 19, June 1984; and Robert H. Litzenberger and Krishna Ramaswamy, "The Effects of Dividends on Common Stock Prices: Tax Effects or Information Effects," *Journal of Finance*, vol. 37, May 1982, pp. 429–443.

9 See Randall Woolridge and Chinmoy Ghosh, "Dividend Cuts? Do They Always Signal Bad News," *Midland Corporate Finance Journal* Vol. 3 No. 2 (Summer 1985).

10 The first major broad-based study of the relationship between dividends and stock prices was published in 1974 by the late Fischer Black and Myron Scholes. (See "The Effects of Dividend Yield and Dividend Policy on Common Stock Prices and Returns," *Journal of Financial Economics*, Vol. 1 No. 1 (May 1974).) For each year between 1935 and 1966, Black and Scholes grouped all NYSE stocks into one of 25 portfolios on the basis of dividend yield and risk, and then attempted to test whether stock returns varied in any systematic fashion with yields (holding risk constant). Finding no significant relationship between yield and return, the study concluded that the market is essentially "neutral" toward dividends.

Dividend policy and signaling

Perhaps the most obvious is the "signaling" effect of dividends that is said to arise from "information asymmetries" between managers and outside investors. The argument in brief is this: Managers are extremely reluctant to cut dividends, and so they generally increase the dividend only if they are confident that future earnings and cash flows will enable them to maintain the new, higher payout. Investors are aware of this behavior (indeed, they have been conditioned to respond to it by decades of experience). Because investors also know that managers are likely to have a clearer view of their companies' prospects than outsiders, a dividend increase functions as a fairly reliable signal that managers foresee a rosy future, and a dividend reduction signals a gloomy forecast.[11]

In most cases, however, providing investors with accurate signals about the company's future will not be the *primary* purpose of a change in financial policy. In the case of FPL's dividend cut, management did not of course intend to send a negative signal (companies sometimes do, for example, when they alert analysts to an expected downturn in earnings). Moreover, the company attempted to offset the negative signal from the dividend with the simultaneous announcement of a major stock repurchase, which typically communicates management's confidence about the future. However, management's principal aim in changing dividend policy was not to provide accurate signals to the market, but rather, as we discuss below, to establish the right financial structure for a more competitive environment.

Managing clientele effects

A second, related, consideration is the "clientele effect" associated with changing dividend policy. The argument here is that companies, by virtue of their past dividend payouts, attract investors whose characteristics cause them to prefer a particular company's dividend policy. Thus, utilities have traditionally attracted investors who like high dividend payouts. Such investors want regular cash income, are in relatively low tax brackets, and seek relatively safe, "defensive" investments. "Growth" companies, on the other hand, pay lower dividends, reinvest more of their earnings, and provide a greater percentage of their total returns in the form of capital gains. Investors in high tax brackets with no pressing need for cash income tend to be attracted to such companies.

Clientele theory suggests that management should attempt to maintain a stable dividend policy because change could require stockholders to switch companies, which would involve brokerage costs, and, possibly, capital gains taxes. Perhaps the best definition of a stable dividend policy would include two elements: (1) avoid if at all possible reducing the dividend, both to avoid giving investors incorrect signals and also to provide investors with a stable flow of cash income; (2) if conditions permit, increase the dividend at some reasonable rate, because the combination of inflation and earnings retention should lead to rising earnings and an increased capacity to pay dividends.

On the other hand, in well-functioning capital markets, there is no compelling reason for companies to prefer one investor clientele to another. If the stock price drops because of selling by one group of investors, the theory says that "value-based" bargain hunters should be attracted to the firm's stock.[12] The case history of FPL appears to bear out this logic.

---

11 Note that since a dividend increase requires that an optimistic forecast be backed up with cash, managers are limited in their ability to mislead investors with higher-than-sustainable dividends. For this reason, a dividend increase is regarded as a more credible signal of future good times than just, say, a management forecast of higher future earnings. On the other hand, some companies might increase dividends because of a decline in available investment opportunities, which would not generally be regarded by investors as good news. Thus, while dividend actions can be used to convey useful information, they are by no means perfect signals, and their expected role may change in the future as more companies substitute stock repurchases for dividends.

---

12 Indeed, more recent developments in corporate investor relations – in particular, the practice of targeting large, sophisticated investors – suggest that companies may increase their values by seeking out and cultivating more active and better-informed investors. See John Bird et al., "Finance Theory and the New Investor Relations," *Journal of Applied Corporate Finance*, Vol. 6 No. 2 (Summer 1993). See also the "Stern Stewart Roundtable on Relationship Investing and Shareholder Communication," in the same issue of the *JACF*.

ARE CLIENTELE EFFECTS IMPORTANT?: THE CASE OF EQUIFAX

In 1992, Stern Stewart & Co. advised Equifax on a major leveraged recapitalization involving the repurchase of 12% of the company's common stock. This case was somewhat different from FPL's in that Equifax was increasing its leverage ratio to take advantage of unused debt capacity.

What Equifax has in common with FPL is that a dramatic shift in the company's financial strategy led to a major change in the company's investor clientele. As in the case of FPL, when Equifax announced its leveraged recap, many of its traditional investors sold while a number of larger, "value-based" investors became significant buyers. As in the case of FPL, the experience of Equifax suggests that clientele effects are at most "second-order" concerns, and they should not prevent companies from taking actions that improve their long-run competitive position.

Of course, it would have been desirable to have been able to accommodate FPL's high-dividend clientele – and, yes, those investors who sold undoubtedly incurred transactions costs. However, as we argued earlier, the primary aim of FPL's management was not to avoid sending unintended signals, nor was it necessarily to preserve its existing clientele – it was to achieve the right financial structure going forward.

Nevertheless, the existence of clientele effects may have one important implication for FPL. Given that the company had decided that a 90% payout ratio no longer made sense, management should make a sufficiently large cut in the dividend that the probability of future cuts is low. In the case of FPL, as we suggest later, reducing the company's dividend payout by 32% in 1994 may well have been the only way of ensuring *future* dividend stability. In this sense, FPL's dividend action was designed to accommodate those dividend-seeking investors who chose not to sell their shares and to attract new income-seeking investors looking for consistent dividend growth from an electric utility even in the face of industry uncertainties. The dividend reduction, while significant, nevertheless kept FPL's payout and yield within the range of electrics generally. This way, traditional utility investors could continue to invest in FPL for current income, but with the expectation of greater stock appreciation.

Balancing agency costs and flotation costs

Economists have tended to dismiss the notion that dividends are more valuable than capital gains because they are more reliable and hence less risky. What this bird-in-the-hand theory fails to recognize is that dividends can ultimately be paid only out of future cash flow, and it is the riskiness of the future cash flow stream that determines the degree of certainty with which investors can view future dividends.

More recent academic thinking, however, has provided an interesting variation of this "bird-in-the-hand" argument. As Michael Jensen has observed, companies in mature industries with excess capital have a tendency to retain and then waste that capital, either by overinvesting in core businesses or diversifying through acquisitions.[13] High dividends represent one solution to this "free cash flow" problem. Other possible solutions are special dividends or open market stock repurchase programs – and, in more extreme cases of excess capital, larger tender offers for the firm's own stock financed with new borrowings.

One recent study provides strong empirical support for this argument. After examining 6,700 companies over the period 1961–1991, Michael Barclay, Clifford Smith, and Ross Watts conclude that "mature" companies – those with few promising investment opportunities (as indicated by low market-to-book ratios and high depreciation expense) – tend to have significantly higher dividend yields and leverage ratios than "growth" companies (with high market-to-book ratios and heavy R&D spending).[14] With few investment opportunities and thus limited requirements for new capital, mature companies pay high dividends in part to prevent themselves from wasting their excess cash, or from becoming a takeover target as a consequence of having too much cash.

Conversely, growth companies tend to have lower dividend payouts and debt ratios not only

13 See Michael C. Jensen, "Agency Costs of Free Cash Flow, Corporate Finance, and Takeovers," *American Economic Review* 76 (1986), 323–329.

14 Michael J. Barclay, Clifford W. Smith, Jr. and Ross L. Watts (1995) "The Determinants of Corporate Leverage and Dividend Policies," *Journal of Applied Corporate Finance* 7: 4, 4–19.

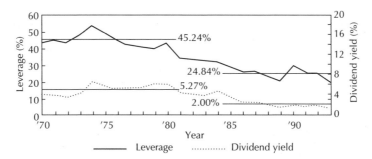

Figure 14.4 Changes in Leverage and Dividend Yield in Response to Deregulation of the Telecommunications Industry: 1970–1993

because there is no temptation to waste capital (after all, such firms by definition have many profitable investment opportunities), but because raising outside capital can be very costly. Though there are exceptions to this rule, growth companies tend to be in riskier businesses than mature companies, and higher business risk is likely to mean a greater likelihood of not having access to capital at reasonable cost across market cycles. In such cases, a policy of high dividends can lead to high flotation costs (including dilution of equity as well as investment banker fees) or, still worse, an inability to capitalize upon valuable investment opportunities. For this reason, high-risk companies tend to use equity-dominated capital structures and to conserve their equity capital by retaining rather than paying out earnings.

Barclay, Smith, and Watts also find that regulation – and, by implication, a change from regulated to unregulated status – has predictable effects on a company's dividend (and overall financing) policy. Specifically, their study shows that regulated companies have systematically higher dividend payouts and leverage ratios than unregulated firms. The study also furnishes evidence (see Figure 14.4) that the deregulation of the telecommunications industry that began in the early 1980s has led to a significant reduction in the dividend yields and leverage ratios of those companies.

Both of these findings, as we discuss below, have a direct bearing on FPL because management was anticipating a change in its fundamental business from that of a heavily regulated, low-risk enterprise to a competitive, riskier one.

BACK TO FPL

The academic thinking summarized above – buttressed by the findings of Smith, Barclay, and Watts just described – suggests that a company's target dividend payout ratio should reflect primarily the following considerations:

(1) its expected capital requirements (that is, the amount of projected capital expenditures and strategic investments over and above its expected level of operating cash flow);
(2) the riskiness of its business (as reflected in the expected *variability* of its cash flow);
(3) the company's target capital structure (also partly a function of risk); and
(4) the availability and cost of outside capital (which are both a function of and important factors in setting target capital structure).

According to its own financial projections, FPL was not expecting a sharp increase in its investment requirements in the foreseeable future. In fact, management was projecting a large and growing cash operating *surplus* (net income plus depreciation minus capital expenditures) in each of the next five years. FPL was thus not a traditional "growth" company in the sense of having profitable growth opportunities requiring outside funding.

But if greater competition would not increase FPL's investment requirements in the near term, it was expected to lead to a significant increase in business risk and, hence, in the variability of its earnings and operating cash flows. An increase in cash flow variability in turn implies reductions in both the company's optimal leverage ratio and dividend payout.

As stated earlier, FPL chose to reduce its dividend payout ratio from over 90% to about 60% of annual earnings. Management's decision-making process can be summarized as follows:

◆ FPL's operating cash flows and investment requirements were projected over each of the next five years (1994–1998). Operating cash flow (net income plus depreciation) was projected to increase at a steady rate while capital expenditures were projected to fall sharply. With this decline in capital spending, the amount of cash flow available to pay dividends was projected to turn positive in 1994, and to exceed the projected dividend in 1995.

◆ Having thus projected both the level of its operating cash flows and its funding requirements, FPL's next step was to determine its target capital structure. Here the critical consideration was the expected increase in management's uncertainty about future operating cash flows due to deregulation. In the past, FPL had operated with a capital structure composed of about 48% long-term debt, 6% preferred, and 46% common equity. The expected increase in business risk caused management to raise its targeted percentage of common equity to 50%.

◆ After having decided on a target capital structure, the final step was to determine the dividend payout ratio. The company looked at the payout ratios of other electric utilities, of companies in other industries that had recently been deregulated (telecommunications and trucking, for example), and of competitive industries generally. Management's goal was to set a dividend level that would increase in tandem with the expected growth in earnings and that the company would be able to maintain in almost any business environment, including that of full competition. At the same time, the payout was designed to preserve management's ability to invest in growth opportunities in preparation for worldwide deregulation of the electric utility industry.

STOCK REPURCHASES AS A SUBSTITUTE FOR CASH DIVIDENDS

What if management significantly underestimated FPL's future earnings power and, as a consequence

of cutting the dividend, the firm became awash in excess cash? FPL's decision to cut its dividend was announced simultaneously with an authorization to buy back up to 10 million shares over the next three years. From the company's point of view, dividends and stock repurchases represent alternative means of distributing excess capital to stockholders. There are two basic reasons why stock repurchases may be a more efficient means of returning capital to stockholders.

The first has to do with taxes. Stock repurchases substitute returns in the form of capital gains for returns in the form of dividends, and taxable investors typically pay higher rates on dividend income than on capital gains. Since 1990, the spread between the marginal tax rate on dividends and capital gains has widened from zero to 11.6% (39.6% vs. 28%). Moreover, those stockholders who choose to tender their shares pay capital gains only on the difference between the repurchase price and their tax basis in the stock. Of course, those stockholders who choose not to sell their shares can defer taxes indefinitely. For all these reasons, investors as a group are likely to pay lower taxes on corporate distributions when stock repurchases take the place of dividends.

The second motive for substituting stock repurchases for dividends – and by far the more important in FPL's case – is the financial flexibility that a policy of selective stock buybacks can be expected to provide management in the future. As we just observed, although the firm's capital requirements are projected to decline in the next five years, the increase in competition is expected to reduce the stability of FPL's operating cash flows over time. In addition, deregulation in the U.S. and around the world may present attractive investment opportunities for the company. As a result, there is greater uncertainty about how much "free cash flow" will be left over to pay dividends.

Substituting a policy of selective stock repurchases for roughly one third of FPL's past dividend payout effectively provided management an option – execute the repurchase or, if management has better uses for the capital, wait until a better time. The value of this option can be viewed as rising in tandem with increases in the expected variability of future operating cash flow and with the emergence of new investment opportunities. As stated earlier, one clear aim of FPL's new financial policy is to reduce its past dependence on new equity issues. Under the old funding regime, FPL, like other utilities, paid out ever higher dividends and then simply raised more capital as necessary through new stock and debt issues. The new competitive environment is giving rise to a new financing rule that can be summed up in the expression "cash is king." Because equity capital will not always be available on favorable terms, companies in competitive industries are likely to see a greater need to "control their own destiny" by conserving equity capital, maintaining higher cash balances, and reducing their target debt-equity ratios. Substituting a policy of discretionary stock repurchases for regular cash dividends contributes to each of these objectives.

INVESTOR REACTION

As noted earlier, the initial market reaction to the announcement of FPL's dividend cut was decidedly negative. Because of the market's strong past association of dividend cuts with reduced profitability, the announcement clearly signaled diminished earnings prospects to some of FPL's stockholders. What seems equally clear from the FPL story, however, is the willingness of other investors to accept the idea that a dividend cut *by a profitable company* can be a value-increasing financial strategy, a move to be applauded rather than condemned. It is interesting to note that FPL's institutional ownership has increased since the dividend action – from 34% at the end of 1993 to 47% at the end of 1995.

Could FPL have avoided the initial price drop, and should it have done more to prepare the market for the announcement? In fact, management did inform analysts early in 1994 that it was reviewing its dividend payout level, pointing out that FPL's payout was high relative to other utilities', and that industry payouts were high relative to historic industry standards. Moreover, the company did attempt to stabilize its price by announcing the dividend cut and stock repurchase program simultaneously. But the fact that this measure had only limited effect, at least initially, is not surprising. FPL was a pioneer in this undertaking – the first utility to cut its dividend for strategic reasons – and there are bound to be costs as well as

benefits from being ahead of the market's learning curve. Our financial markets, as sophisticated as they are, must to some extent learn "by doing." Trial and error may be a necessary prelude to valuable innovation.

The good news for other companies is that the market appears to catch on very quickly. For example, after the market closed on October 13, 1995, Texas Utilities cut its dividend by 35%. On the next morning, the company's stock price opened *higher*, and its price has since remained above its pre-announcement level. Our prediction is that when other profitable utilities follow FPL's lead, as some surely will, the market's immediate response will be positive in more cases than not.

CONCLUSION: DO THE RIGHT THING

Since the formulation of the celebrated M&M "dividend irrelevance" proposition in 1961, financial economists – and an increasing number of industry practitioners and money managers – have been arguing that dividends "do not matter." That is, whether a company pays out 10% or 100% of its earnings in the form of dividends is likely to have no material effect on its long-run market value.

In one sense, the FPL story can be viewed as confirming the validity of the M&M logic. After experiencing an initial drop of some 20% in value, FPL's shares quickly recovered their lost value and went on to outperform the S&P Utility Index by a significant margin over the two-year period following the announcement.

To say that investors collectively do not care whether they receive their returns in the form of dividends or capital appreciation is not the same as saying that the dividend policies of individual companies do not matter. In fact, dividend policy may matter greatly in certain circumstances. For mature companies with highly stable cash flows, paying out too little of operating cash flows may cause managers to overinvest – for example, through value-destroying diversifying acquisitions or misguided attempts to maintain market share at the expense of profitability. On the other hand, for companies in higher-growth or riskier businesses, paying out too much may reduce financial flexibility to the point that management is forced to pass up valuable investment opportunities.

As the case of FPL demonstrates, stock repurchases are likely to be a superior alternative to dividends for distributing excess capital to investors, especially for companies confronting a riskier business environment. Besides potential tax advantages for investors, a policy of substituting stock repurchases for dividends increases a company's financial flexibility. In the case of FPL, the improvement in financial condition was designed to provide management with the financial flexibility to respond to increased competition, and to make strategic acquisitions in an industry expecting further consolidation.

CHAPTER 15

Stern Stewart Roundtable on Capital Structure and Stock Repurchase*

Clifford Smith (University of Rochester); Tim Opler (Credit Suisse First Boston); Rick Thevenet (PepsiCo); Dennis Soter (Stern Stewart & Co.); David Ikenberry (Rice University); Erik Sirri (Babson College). Moderated by Donald Chew (Stern Stewart & Co.)

DONALD CHEW: Good morning, and welcome to Stern Stewart & Company and to this discussion of corporate capital structure. I'm Don Chew, one of the founding partners of Stern Stewart as well as editor of the *Journal of Applied Corporate Finance*, and I will be serving as moderator.

Our discussion will fall into two parts. The first will focus on questions of capital structure planning: Is there such a thing as an optimal capital structure? That is, given a level of total capital necessary to support a company's activities, is there a way of dividing up that capital into debt and equity that maximizes *current* firm value? And, if so, what are the critical factors in setting the leverage ratio for a given company? What are the most important benefits and costs of debt financing? Should a company's capital structure be designed to maintain at least an investment-grade rating, or does such a financing strategy end up leaving substantial value on the table?

The second part of the discussion will focus on what has become an increasingly popular method of returning excess capital to shareholders – stock repurchases. In 1998, for the first time ever, the total dollars spent by U.S. companies in buying back their stock exceeded their total dividend payments. We will explore the causes of this explosion of stock repurchase activity, and the extent to which distributions to buy back shares are substituting for dividend payments. I also want to raise the issue of whether many U.S. companies may be buying back their stock for what most of us around this table are likely to feel is the wrong reason – namely, to increase their near-term earnings per share. To judge from reports by the financial press and sellside analysts, boosting EPS is one of the most important corporate motives for repurchases – it's right up there with buying back undervalued stock as a corporate "investment." The focus on EPS may be largely responsible for what many observers feel is the inadequacy of current disclosure surrounding corporate repurchase activity – an issue we will take up at the end of the discussion. There we will consider the possibility that many companies, in an attempt to buy back as many shares at the lowest price possible, are actually *reducing* liquidity and share values.

To explore these issues, we have brought together a small but distinguished group of academics and

---

* February 27, 2001, New York City.

practitioners. And I will take a moment now to introduce each of them:

To my immediate left is **CLIFFORD SMITH**, who is the Louise and Henry Epstein Professor of Business Administration at the University of Rochester's Simon School of Business. In a career at the Simon School that stretches back to 1974, Cliff has done research in the fields of corporate finance, financial institutions, and derivative securities that has resulted in 14 books and over 80 articles in leading finance and economics journals. Besides being one of the most prolific researchers in corporate finance, Cliff has received a remarkable 26 Superior Teaching Awards, 10 from MBA students and 16 from students in the Simon School's Executive Development program. And I can vouch for the quality of that teaching, since it was Cliff's corporate finance course at Rochester that served as my own introduction to the subject back in the late '70s. In the last 25 years, Cliff has done as much as any academic in finance to demonstrate how and why corporate executives can add value through capital structure, risk management, and financial policies generally.

To Cliff's left is **ERIK SIRRI**, who is currently an Associate Professor of Finance at Babson College. From 1996 to 1999, Erik was the Chief Economist of the U.S. Securities and Exchange Commission, where he served as the senior advisor to the Commission and its Chairman on major economic policy issues. During his tenure at the SEC, Erik also conducted research in areas such as the role of information and disclosure in securities markets, private securities issuance and the 144a market, and the reform of the issuance process. His current research focuses on the interaction between securities law and financial economics. Before joining the SEC, Erik was an Assistant Professor of Finance at the Harvard Business School.

Next to Erik is **TIM OPLER**, who has had an interesting career as an academic theorist and teacher and, more recently, as a practitioner of corporate finance. After earning a Ph.D. from UCLA – as did Erik Sirri, by the way – Tim taught finance at SMU and Ohio State and did research in corporate finance. Then, in 1996, he left the academy and became a corporate financial adviser to the clients of Deutsche Bank. In 1999, Tim joined W.R. Hambrecht, where he advised companies on issues of capital structure, stock repurchase, and corporate finance generally. And he has recently become Director of the Financial Strategy Group at Credit Suisse First Boston. Tim has done a considerable amount of research in corporate finance, including highly regarded studies of capital structure, corporate cash holdings, and the costs associated with financial distress.

Across the table from Tim is **DAVID IKENBERRY**, who has been Associate Professor of finance at Rice University for over ten years since getting his Ph.D. at the University of Illinois. Dave has done a lot of work on stock repurchase – so much that I would describe him as the world's foremost authority on the subject. In the Spring 2000 issue of this journal, Dave and a colleague at Rice wrote an article called "What Do We Know About Stock Repurchase?" that has received an extraordinary amount of attention, including circulation by a Swedish investment bank throughout Sweden, where stock repurchase was recently legalized. In addition to four published studies on stock repurchase, Dave has published empirical studies that address an array of corporate decisions, including proxy fights, exchange listings, and stock splits.

Next to Dave is **RICHARD THEVENET**. Rick is Assistant Treasurer at PepsiCo, Inc., where he has worked for the past eight years. And, as he will tell us, Pepsi has been quite aggressive in recent years in buying back its stock and otherwise pursuing the interests of its stockholders. After earning an MBA at the University of Chicago in 1982, Rick went to work at Mobil Oil, and then for a number of years here at Stern Stewart. He has also worked in the treasury areas at International Paper and Banker's Trust.

Last but not least is **DENNIS SOTER**, my colleague and fellow partner at Stern Stewart. Dennis runs our corporate finance advisory activity and also oversees implementations of EVA (Economic Value Added) performance measurement and incentive systems in middle market companies. In the past few years, Dennis has served as a financial adviser in three highly successful leveraged recapitalizations. Each of these deals involved borrowing substantial amounts of new debt to buy back shares – and two involved major changes in dividend policy as well. Prior to joining Stern Stewart, Dennis was National Director of Ernst & Whinney's Mergers & Acquisitions practice.

PART ONE: CAPITAL STRUCTURE

So with that as general introduction, I'm going to start things off by asking Cliff Smith to give us an overview of the theory of corporate capital structure. Cliff, what is the current thinking in the academic finance profession about optimal capital structure? Does capital structure play a major role in management's efforts to maximize shareholder value? Or is financial policy, as Modigliani and Miller suggested back in 1958, largely "irrelevant"?

The theory

CLIFF SMITH: Well, I agree that Modigliani and Miller is the logical place to begin this discussion. Most people in my profession would date the beginning of "modern" corporate finance from the publication of the first M&M paper in 1958. That paper basically said that if you make three assumptions – (1) no taxes paid by the corporation or its investors, (2) no bankruptcy or other contracting costs, and (3) no effect of financing choices on managers' investment decisions – then the current market value of the firm should not be affected by how you structure the liability side of the firm's balance sheet. Given these three assumptions, M&M showed that the right-hand side of the balance sheet cannot have any material effect on the real source of corporate value – the operating cash flows generated by the business.

M&M's fundamental insight was that differences in leverage or in the kinds of securities the firm issues are nothing more than different ways of dividing up those cash flows and repackaging them for investors. And as long as these financial decisions don't affect the "real" decisions in any predictable way – for example, as long as the firm's managers make the same investment and operating decisions whether the leverage ratio is 10% or 90% – financial decisions are not going to affect the total value of the firm – that is, the sum of the value of its debt and equity.

Now, what does the M&M proposition have to say to corporate treasurers and CFOs, to all those people who get paid good money to make decisions that "don't matter"? There are really two messages – one negative and one positive. The negative

message is that, as Stewart Myers likes to put it, there is no "magic" in leverage. Investment bankers peddling different kinds of debt instruments love to show their clients the wonderful effect of increasing leverage on pro forma earnings per share. The message of M&M is that this effect is an illusion. It certainly is true that if companies issue debt, then EPS will go up so long as the return on that incremental invested capital exceeds the after-tax corporate borrowing rate – but I don't have to tell anyone in this room that this is not an acceptable standard of profitability. The problem with this strategy, as M&M showed, is that as companies take on more financial leverage, the risk of the equity goes up along with it. And as the risk of the equity increases, stockholders raise their *required* rate of return, the P/E ratio of the firm goes down, and the net effect is that total firm value remains unchanged.

The positive message of the M&M proposition, and its main message to corporate practitioners, can best be seen by standing the proposition on its head. That is, if changes in capital structure are going to affect corporate market values, they will do so only for the following three reasons: First, the firm's choice of financing policy affects its tax liabilities. Second, how you structure the liability side of the balance sheet affects the firm's information costs, contracting costs, or transactions costs – a category that includes the costs arising from bankruptcy or financial distress. And third, how you structure the liability side of the firm's balance sheet today affects management's operating and investment decisions, either now or in the future.

Much of the work in corporate finance that has taken place since the original M&M paper in '58 has been the development of theories that elaborate on one of these three possibilities. For example, in a 1963 paper, Modigliani and Miller themselves looked at the implications of the tax deductibility of interest payments. And in the so-called "tax-adjusted" M&M proposition presented there, they argued that the value of the tax shields generated by interest payments could push the optimal capital structure to 99% debt.

But, of course, corporate leverage ratios in the real world were nowhere near those levels when M&M wrote their paper – and, despite the sharp increase in at least book leverage ratios in the 1980s, they are nowhere near 90% today (though we did see some LBOs in that territory). Clearly,

Clifford Smith   Photographs by Clay Enos

something was missing from this explanation. Either the tax benefits of leverage were being overstated, or there were major offsetting costs to high leverage that were being overlooked. So, the finance profession faced a dilemma of sorts: If the tax benefits amounted to 34 cents per dollar of debt financing – and I'm using today's corporate tax rate for the sake of illustration – why were companies volunteering to pay so much in additional taxes; why were they leaving so much value on the table?

Merton Miller himself provided part of the answer to this question in his 1976 Presidential Address to the American Finance Association that he titled "Debt and Taxes." Miller pointed out that the tax savings of corporate debt financing were exaggerated by the failure to account for the taxes paid by the *holders* of corporate debt. Noting that equity is more tax-advantaged than debt *for investors*, Mert went on to show that the tax savings from turning equity into debt at the corporate level are at least partly offset by the higher pre-tax promised rate of return on debt that bondholders require as compensation for the taxes they pay on their interest income.

But if the tax benefits were overstated by the "tax-adjusted" M&M proposition, some recent research suggests that there continues to be a material tax advantage of debt. In fact, John Graham has a paper that concludes that, for a U.S. company with an average leverage ratio of about 25% debt to capital (in market value terms), the tax benefits of debt today amount to about 7–10% of total firm value.

Now, if you accept the idea that there is a material tax advantage to debt financing, then the main reason we don't see companies with 99% leverage ratios must have to do with the *costs* of debt financing. But it was not immediately clear to finance academics what those costs were. After all, the assets of bankrupt firms don't just vanish; they often get transferred to other firms without losing any of their value. And in 1976, my Rochester colleague Jerry Warner published a study suggesting that the direct bankruptcy costs for a sample of large railroads were quite low – no more than one percent of firm value. It was only when people began to examine what are now called the "indirect" costs of financial distress – a category that includes things like value-reducing managerial behavior when operating under a pile of debt – that the story began to change.

One of the most important contributions to our understanding of the costs of high leverage came from a paper by Stewart Myers called "Determinants of Corporate Borrowing," which was published by the *Journal of Financial Economics* in 1977. In that paper, Stew began by viewing the values of companies as made up of two pieces: (1) "assets in place," those more or less tangible assets that are generating the firm's current cash flows; and (2) intangible "growth options," or opportunities to make future investments that arise from the firm's current capabilities. He then proceeded to demonstrate why companies whose value mainly reflects assets in place use more leverage than firms whose value comes mainly from growth options. The principal danger in using debt to finance growth companies was referred to by Myers as the "underinvestment problem." Stew's basic argument was that debt-financed companies, when faced with a downturn in operating cash flows, are more likely than firms financed with equity to pass up valuable investment opportunities because much of the gain from the investment works to shore up the bondholders' position instead of increasing shareholder value. So, the bottom line here is that firms with a lot of intangible growth options are going to find debt more expensive – both initially when raising it, and perhaps later when attempting to service it – because the debt burden can cause managers to turn down positive-NPV projects.

Now, this was the state of thinking on corporate capital structure in the late '70s and early '80s: It was a matter of weighing moderate tax benefits from debt against some potentially significant costs, particularly for growth companies. But with the wave of LBOs and other leveraged transactions in the 1980s, the academic finance profession was forced to come up with a more satisfying explanation of the *benefits* of debt. That explanation was provided in a 1986 paper by Michael Jensen called "The Agency Costs of Free Cash Flow, Corporate Finance and Takeovers." Now, the arguments in this paper were not entirely new. As early as 1976, when he was still at Rochester, Mike Jensen and our colleague Bill Meckling had pointed to another possible benefit of debt financing in their pioneering paper on "agency costs." Jensen and Meckling showed that, in a world where managers often pursue their own interests at their shareholders' expense, raising equity from outside investors can be costly because of this conflict of interest between ownership and control that ends up reducing the value of publicly traded companies. And as Mike and Bill argued in that paper, replacing equity with debt could lead to higher firm value by reducing the agency costs associated with having outside equity holders.

It was Jensen's 1986 "free cash flow" paper that provided an important application of Jensen and Meckling's theory to the events of the 1980s. In that paper, Mike defined free cash flow as that portion of a company's operating cash flow in excess of the amount necessary to fund all its available positive-NPV projects. He argued that unless such cash flow is paid out to investors, managers have a tendency to destroy value through empire-building, costly attempts to maintain market share, or just plain failure to make hard decisions to cut back when appropriate. And if you go back to the investment opportunity spectrum described by Stew Myers, firms with lots of assets in place that generate substantial cash flow but have little in the way of profitable reinvestment opportunities have a tendency to develop this kind of free cash flow problem. For such firms, high leverage is likely to add value because it *commits* the managers to pay out free cash flow to investors. And in Jensen's view, that was a major part of what was going on in the '80s: the massive substitution of debt for equity in LBOs and other highly leveraged transactions was adding value by reducing overinvestment in mature industries that had lots of cash flow but few promising investment opportunities.

Now, the interesting thing to me is that when you set Jensen's free cash flow story alongside Myers's underinvestment argument, you get a perfectly complementary set of explanations for corporate financing behavior that revolves around a single variable: the company's investment opportunities. When you combine the two stories, you're left with the following generalization: For companies with lots of free cash flow and limited growth opportunities, it makes sense to weight the capital structure toward debt, both to shield income from taxes and to reduce managerial incentives to waste free cash flow – and the fact that such firms have limited investment opportunities means that the costs of high leverage stemming from potential *under*investment are not a big concern. At the other end of the spectrum, companies whose current value consists mainly of future growth opportunities will find that it generally makes sense to avoid debt financing. And in the case of high-tech companies with little or no current earnings or cash flow, it will make sense to have "negative leverage" – that is, cash on the balance sheet in excess of outstanding debt.

CHEW: Cliff, there's one major strand in the academic capital structure literature that you haven't discussed – the so-called signaling theories that focus on the information costs associated with raising outside capital. And although you've placed considerable emphasis on Stew Myers's concept of the corporate underinvestment problem, you haven't mentioned another of Stew's major contributions to the academic debate over capital structure – the so-called "pecking order" theory of corporate financing. Could you say a word about signaling and the pecking order?

SMITH: Don, when you were setting up this roundtable, you told me to summarize everything we know about corporate finance in *five minutes*. Subject to that constraint, I decided to limit myself to presenting what is essentially a theory of *optimal* capital structure. I've started with the assumption that most corporate managers have target capital structures – targeted percentages of debt to capital that, even if companies move away from them for long periods of time, still serve as long-term guides in their financial planning process.

Now, as you suggest, there is another potentially important cost of leverage that I haven't mentioned. It's a set of costs that stem from what academics call the "information asymmetry" problem – and let's just call them "information costs" for short. The basic idea here is that because managers are in a position to know more about the firm's prospects than outsiders, decisions by companies to raise outside capital – particularly equity capital – may cause investors to suspect that management thinks the firm is overvalued, at least based on their view of the firm's near-term prospects. In terms of "signaling" theory, the company's decision to raise new equity sends a negative signal to investors, who rationally respond by reducing the firm's share price – by about 3%, in the average case. Now, for those companies that feel they are fairly valued at the time of the announcement of the new offering (and this is not the average case, by the way; the average firm issuing equity *is* overvalued by about 3%), that negative stock price reaction represents a cost to the firm, a dilution of the value of existing stockholders' claims.

And this brings me to Stew Myers's pecking order model. Building on this signaling argument, Stew suggested that corporate capital structures are simply the cumulative result of individual financing decisions in which managers systematically prefer internal funds over outside financing, and debt over equity if outside funding is required. In fact, an equity offering is typically viewed as a very expensive last resort, something to be avoided if at all possible. The pecking order, then, is basically a strategy that aims to minimize "information costs" while essentially ignoring all the other costs and

benefits of debt I mentioned earlier. And as I interpret the model, it says that corporate managers making financing decisions are not really thinking about an optimal capital structure – a long-run target leverage ratio they eventually want to achieve. Instead they take the path of least resistance and choose what then appears to be the lowest-cost financing vehicle – generally either internal funds or debt – with little thought about the future consequences of these choices.

Now, there is some evidence – particularly in the form of lots of highly profitable firms with low leverage ratios – that at least appears to be consistent with the predictions of this pecking order theory. That evidence suggests to me that information costs and, more generally, the desire to preserve access to capital markets are very important considerations in managerial decision-making. They are considerations that, when viewed in the context of this underinvestment problem I've been harping on, act to limit the corporate use of debt. But let me also briefly throw out one last comment about the evidence in support of the pecking order. My own belief is that companies incur some major costs, including information costs, in making sudden large adjustments in capital structure. And because of those adjustment costs, many firms find it cost-effective to deviate from what they consider to be their target leverage ratios for long periods of time. But that behavior shouldn't be allowed to obscure the fact that most firms *do* have at least implicit, if not explicitly formulated and articulated, capital structure targets.

The evidence

CHEW: Cliff, you mentioned some empirical work that supports the pecking order story. Can you tell us a little about the recent studies that you and others have done in support of the idea of optimal capital structure?

SMITH: Well, let me start by saying that the entire field of empirical research in capital structure is still in its formative stages. It's primarily been within the last decade that the finance profession has attempted to test the different propositions, to bring standard statistical tools to bear on trying to sort out the relative importance of taxes, contracting and information costs, managerial investment incentives, and so forth. And as I just suggested about research on the pecking order, we're still early enough in the process that different people can look at the same studies, and yet take away somewhat different things from them.

In support of the idea of an optimal capital structure, researchers have long detected definite patterns in leverage ratios across different industries. A 1967 study by Eli Schwartz and Richard Aronson showed clear differences in the average debt to (book) asset ratios of companies in different industries, along with a tendency for companies within the same industry to cluster around these averages. And as our theory would suggest, those industry debt ratios were significantly lower for industries characterized by heavy R&D spending and other proxies for corporate growth opportunities. I also would mention a 1985 study by Mike Long and Ileen Malitz that showed that the five most highly leveraged industries at the time – cement, steel, paper products, textiles, and oil refining – were all mature and asset-intensive. At the other extreme, the five industries with the lowest debt ratios – cosmetics, drugs, cameras, aircraft, and radio and TV receiving – were all growth industries with high advertising and R&D. Yet another study – a 1984 study by Mike Bradley, Greg Jarrell, and Han Kim using "cross-sectional" regression techniques – reported that book leverage ratios were negatively related both to the volatility of operating earnings and to advertising and R&D expenses. These findings are all consistent with high costs of financial distress for growth companies, which tend to have more volatile earnings as well as higher spending on R&D.

And these findings are also consistent with what two of my Rochester colleagues – Mike Barclay and Ross Watts – and I found in our more recent work. In a series of papers published in the 1990s, we looked at the leverage ratios of all the companies covered by COMPUSTAT – some 6,700 in total – over a 30-year period from 1963–1993. Like a number of studies by others, we used a company's market-to-book ratio as a proxy for the extent to which its current value consists of intangible assets or growth opportunities. The basic idea behind this assumption is that, because stock prices reflect intangible assets such as growth opportunities but accounting balance sheets generally do not, the larger a company's growth options relative to its assets in place, the higher on average will be its market value in relation to its book value.

What we found was that companies with high market-to-book ratios had significantly lower leverage ratios than companies with low market-to-book ratios. And these statistical results appear extremely robust. To make these findings a little more concrete, let me cite some industry averages we came up with. When we looked at the average ratios for eight different industries over the period 1989–1993, we found that the two industries with the highest market-to-book values, drugs and medical equipment, had average market leverage ratios of 6.6% and 11.7%, respectively. The two industries with the lowest market-to-book values, railroad equipment and lumber, had market leverage ratios of 32.5% and 28%. The average leverage ratio for the entire sample, I might add, was 25%.

Now, some people in the profession have objected that the way we set up the test – the fact that the market value of the firm appears on both the left- and right-hand sides of this regression – ended up driving our results. In response to this objection, we experimented with a bunch of different variables on both sides of the regression. In place of market-to-book ratios, we used things like R&D and advertising budgets as proxies for growth opportunities, and we used depreciation of fixed plant and equipment as a measure of assets in place. In place of market leverage ratios, we used both book debt ratios and interest coverage ratios. And whatever way we ran these tests, the results suggest a robust and consistent relation between leverage and measures of the firm's investment opportunities.

A second relation that also seems very robust is the effect of the regulatory environment on the firm's leverage ratio. Every study that I've ever seen finds that regulated firms have materially more leverage than similar unregulated firms. Our explanation is that regulation, by limiting both the extent and scope of the firm's investment opportunities, reduces managers' discretion in responding to such opportunities, which in turn reduces the underinvestment costs of debt. And because the managers of regulated firms have less latitude in changing investment policy, potential bondholders also have much stronger assurances that the firm's strategy is not about to undergo a dramatic shift after the bonds have been issued – a problem that academics refer to as "asset substitution."

Tim Opler   Photographs by Clay Enos

More evidence

CHEW: Thanks, Cliff. Let's turn to Tim Opler, who has not only done a good deal of research on capital structure, but also now makes a living advising companies on capital structure and other financial issues. Tim, you took part in a study of corporate cash holdings that was published just last year in the *Journal of Financial Economics*. Are your results broadly consistent with Cliff's findings?

OPLER: That's a good question. I say that because corporate decisions to hold or not to hold cash should be – and in fact turn out to be – closely related to the decision to use debt. Or, to put the same thought in different words, the same company characteristics that make debt costly – notably, high risk and lots of growth opportunities – are also likely to make cash holdings advantageous. As Cliff suggested earlier when talking about high-tech companies, a company's *excess* cash – the amount over and above what it needs to handle its routine transactions – represents in effect *negative* leverage. In this sense, cash holdings are an important part of a firm's capital structure.

There are a couple of notable findings in our study. First of all, small companies in general tend to hold significantly larger cash balances as a percentage of total assets than larger companies with otherwise similar characteristics. And although Cliff didn't mention it, that finding is consistent with his own study's finding that smaller firms, all else equal, tend to have lower leverage ratios. We also find that companies with high market-to-book ratios – as well as firms with larger R&D budgets as a percent of sales – tend to hold more cash as a

percentage of total assets. Again, this is consistent with Cliff's story about the incompatibility of high leverage and growth options. What's more, we find that companies with greater business risk, as measured by the standard deviation of both their operating and stock returns, tend to hold more cash as a percentage of firm assets. By contrast, companies with investment-grade credit ratings tend to have lower cash balances – and this should come as no surprise, since such companies tend to be larger and less risky, and thus have better access to capital, than firms without investment-grade ratings.

So I would say that, yes, our results are broadly consistent with Cliff's study and with his general argument. But there are some differences worth mentioning. For one thing, we find that companies that generate large operating cash flows as a percentage of assets – firms that Cliff earlier characterized as having mainly "assets in place" – also tend to have large cash balances. Cliff's model would suggest that these firms should have relatively high leverage ratios, both to reduce taxes and control the free cash flow problem. And to be consistent with that model, such firms should also probably have fairly low cash holdings instead of the high balances that we find. Now Cliff may be right to suggest that such firms may be in the middle of a gradual adjustment process toward higher leverage and lower cash holdings – because our study does find that companies that generate a lot of cash flow also make large distributions to stockholders in the form of dividends and stock repurchases. But if we consider cash as negative leverage, this tendency of cash-generating companies to retain a significant part of their surplus cash rather than paying it out immediately provides support for the pecking order theory. It suggests that many companies, if they have any leverage target at all, aren't in a great hurry to get there.

There is also another part of our study that works somewhat against the grain of Cliff's argument. After looking for patterns in cash holdings, we then attempted to see whether cash-rich companies have a tendency to waste much of that cash by "overinvesting." Using regression analysis, we came up with a model that estimates a company's *expected* cash holdings as a function of several firm characteristics, including size, risk, market-to-book ratio, and R&D spending. And by calculating a firm's actual cash holdings against the predicted level, we estimated its *excess* cash. But when we then examined the spending behavior of firms with excess cash, we found little evidence of the free cash flow problem that Cliff described earlier. It's true that companies with excess cash made more acquisitions than their cash-poor counterparts. But capital expenditures – excluding acquisitions – as a percentage of total assets for both kinds of firms were about the same. And as I mentioned earlier, we found that cash-laden companies tend to make larger distributions to their shareholders than firms with moderate or low cash holdings – a finding that suggests that if these cash-rich firms do have a free cash flow problem, their managers are at least trying to do something about it. So, while there may be some evidence of a free cash flow problem in our study, my reading of the evidence is that most companies make fairly judicious use of their cash. They don't allow it to burn a hole in their pockets, as agency theory suggests they might.

And let me make one last comment about our study. As in Cliff's study, our results are consistent with the idea that companies attempt to balance potential agency costs associated with having too much cash against a variety of financial distress costs associated with having too little. But where Cliff's work places most of its emphasis on costs arising from the corporate underinvestment problem, we focus on other kinds of financial distress costs as well. For example, we pay a lot of attention to the negative effects of corporate overleveraging and illiquidity on the firm's customers and on its suppliers. Our general sense is that those costs are quite significant in driving corporate decisions both to hold more cash and to limit their leverage ratios.

CHEW: Tim, you've also done a study of financial distress costs that focuses on retailing, as well as a number of other specific industries. Can you briefly summarize what you found?

OPLER: In a paper I did with Sheridan Titman, we looked at a large group of companies that were in industries that subsequently experienced financial difficulty. What we found is that those companies that went into a downturn with higher leverage tended to perform substantially worse – both in terms of EBITDA and stock returns – than less levered firms in the same situation. And we were not at all surprised by that result. After all, think about how the customers of a car manufacturer would respond if the company got into financial difficulty.

CHEW: Okay, so you're saying that a major cost of leverage takes the form of a negative customer response. It's not just a matter of leveraged companies cutting back on vital investment – of, say, overleveraged retailers failing to refurbish their stores. It's also a matter of customers shying away from financially troubled companies.

OPLER: There are several factors that I think contributed to our findings. Certainly some companies facing financial stress have cut back on investments they should have made. And there's no question that customers often avoid buying goods from companies that are in financial difficulty. But another cause of problems is the response of suppliers that worry about getting paid. There are many examples in the retailing industry of suppliers refusing to extend credit to financially troubled retailers.

CHEW: Retailing is an industry that may not fit neatly into these categories that Cliff has set up. On the one hand, it seems to be an industry that generates lots of cash flow. And the fact that there were a number of LBOs and other leveraged transactions in the industry during the '80s – Campeau and Macy's, two failed deals, come to mind – suggests that there was a big free cash flow problem. That is, like so many U.S. industries during this period, retailing was suffering from huge excess capacity; there was clearly too much capital chasing too few investment opportunities – and leverage can help add value in such cases. But, Tim, your study seems to reach a different conclusion – namely, that some retailers, by *over*leveraging, made themselves more vulnerable to a downturn, whether because they were less able to respond to price competition, their financial problems scared away their customers or suppliers, or they were unable to reinvest in their stores.

So my question is, where does that put retailing? Do retailers in general have lots of profitable growth opportunities that require investment – or at least lots of investments that have to be made in order for them to remain competitive? Or are they cash cows waiting to be milked?

OPLER: Retailing in general has not been a high-growth industry, although there are exceptions, of course, like Wal-Mart. What we do know about retailers is that they tend on average to have debt-to-capital ratios that are in the middle of the pack. But there is a lot of variation. If you look at the distribution of capital structures in the retailing industry, you'll find that the newer, more risky retailers tend to be less leveraged, while the more established firms tend to operate with more debt.

DENNIS SOTER: Tim, when you look at retailers, do you factor the off-balance-sheet leases into the calculation of leverage?

OPLER: Yes, definitely.

SOTER: And you still find them to be in the middle of the pack with respect to leverage?

OPLER: In general, yes. The reason that's true is that some of the largest retailers in this country tend to be relatively unlevered in relation to their actual cash flow and ability to service debt. For example, I suspect that companies like Wal-Mart operate with low leverage because they have major expansion plans that may require significant funding in the future.

CHEW: On balance, then, is the lesson from your study that retailers have overleveraged themselves? Or are they instead using what appears to be an optimal amount of leverage, at least at the time of issuance – and the leverage then has the effect of weeding out less competitive players when over-capacity sets in? If the latter is correct, then the capital markets can almost be seen as *pushing* the companies to lever up in order to correct the industry's free cash flow and overcapacity problems.

OPLER: In general I would say that the retailers have not used too much leverage – and your point about leverage and excess capacity is well taken in the sense that most retailers would find it very difficult to raise equity on anything but punitive terms. But there are enough differences among retailers and their strategies that it makes no sense to talk about an optimal leverage ratio for the entire industry.

On the other hand, there are industries that seem clearly to me to operate with too little leverage. The oil and gas industry – the one that Jensen focused on when developing his free cash flow argument – clearly comes to mind.

SMITH: Let me go back for a moment to this issue about where retailing fits into the asset categories I set up earlier. I don't have any difficulty with saying that most retailers have more assets in place than growth opportunities. But let me also say that, although our study was set up to learn as much as we could from looking at just one variable, the capital structure problem clearly has more than just this one dimension. I agree with Tim that leverage can create problems in companies because there are other parties to the collection of contracts that make up the firm than just the stockholders and the bondholders. As Tim said, the CFO's choice of leverage could have major effects on the firm's relationship with its customers. But I would also point out that the relationship is going to be very different if the firm's product is one whose quality can be readily observed before purchase as opposed to a product whose quality cannot really be determined until after the dust settles on the whole transaction. Imagine that I'm the fellow at Eastman Kodak who buys the silver used in producing film. If somebody arrives with a truckload of silver, even if he's never done business with Kodak before, I can have the silver assayed and determine the quality of the product to any degree of certitude I'm willing to pay for, *before* the transaction takes place. But now let's take the case of air travel. If you buy a plane ticket, you can't tell the quality of that plane ticket until you've landed, gotten off the plane, and picked up your baggage.

Excess cash and the case of Chrysler

DAVID IKENBERRY: Another issue to consider in setting capital structure is the durability of the firm's products. I'm not too worried about the capital structure of my local grocer because I'm going to consume that head of lettuce by the end of the week. But if I go to Chrysler to buy a K Car, I will be fairly concerned about the longer-run viability of that company. When Lee Iacocca went to the government to get a federal guarantee of Chrysler's debt, the biggest benefit to Chrysler's shareholders was not the reduction in interest payments, but rather the resulting increase in sales – because consumers were convinced that Chrysler was now too big to fail.

SMITH: And the first thing Chrysler did after receiving that government guarantee of their debt was to increase their warranty from twelve months and 12,000 miles to five years and 50,000 miles. By changing that contract with the customer, they materially increased the demand for the product. (And in making the warranty more valuable to its customers, by the way, Chrysler enlarged the value of the government's guarantee to the company itself – all at the expense of U.S. taxpayers.) So the lesson here is that your financial structure and how you structure these details of your product may not be independent decisions.

CHEW: Tim, is that why Chrysler found it necessary to have some $10 billion in cash on its balance sheet before being acquired by Daimler? To reassure the firm's customers? And in your study of corporate cash holdings, was Chrysler's $10 billion an "outlier," or was it pretty much in the middle of the pack?

OPLER: As a percentage of total assets, Chrysler's cash holdings were actually a fairly representative case, at least when you take into account the cyclicality or high risk of the business. In 1995, Bob Eaton told the investment community that Chrysler needed $7 billion in cash to ensure its ability to get through the next recession. And if you recall, Chrysler stockholders Kerk Kerkorian and Jerry Ork responded by saying, "That's way too much; probably $3 billion would be enough." But guess what? Here we are in the year 2001, and it's now Daimler Chrysler. And not long ago, Daimler Chrysler's cash position got as high as $22 billion. At the moment, the company is losing cash at a rate of $3–4 billion per quarter. And I think we will now see just how much cash the car companies really need to weather a downturn. As Bob Eaton said at the time, "When it rains in the car industry, it's not just a regular storm; it's a monsoon." My guess is that in retrospect the arguments made at the time by Chrysler were right on the money.

CHEW: But you might also recall that when Chrysler said that it needed the $7 billion to weather the recession, Kerkorian said that, as a major holder of Chrysler's stock, it was the presence of that $7 billion cushion that troubled him the most. And in that sense, I *could* offer a completely different interpretation of the same events. The fact that Chrysler is losing so much money today might be taken to imply that having that huge cash cushion blunted the drive for efficiency inside the firm. All that cash may have insulated management from capital market pressures that would have forced the company to make the necessary improvements to become really efficient.

OPLER: I have to disagree. The auto industry has always been one that's extremely cyclical, with periods of boom followed by bust. And when there's a bust, the companies cannot and should not expect the banks or the capital markets to bail them out.

CHEW: Well, you may be right. But I would also argue that the severity of the boom-and-bust cycle is in large part a consequence of chronic overcapacity in the industry. And the overcapacity itself may in fact be a fairly predictable result of all this cash and capital sitting on the balance sheets of all these players.

SOTER: Tim, how much did Chrysler spend when it bought its stake in Mitsubishi? It's very hard to argue that Chrysler's shareholders benefited from that acquisition. And I find it hard to believe that Chrysler's willingness to do the deal had nothing to do with the fact that they had all this liquidity on their balance sheet.

OPLER: I don't know enough about the Mitsubishi deal to comment on that. But let me come back and address the broader question: Was Chrysler, before the purchase by Daimler, wasting money? Was it an inefficient company? I don't doubt that there were dollars that were disbursed from the treasury that shouldn't have been. But I think many people would agree that Chrysler was a very well-run company. It created terrific products like the Jeep Cherokee and the minivans, and it gained significant market share relative to the other car companies.

So I don't personally believe that Chrysler's management ran the company more inefficiently because they had excess cash. Of course, there were probably a few occasions when having the extra cash encouraged them to make what turned out to be negative-NPV investments. But I would be hard pressed to say that the company's behavior was driven by an inefficient, growth-at-all-costs mentality.

Capital structure in practice: the case of Pepsi

CHEW: Okay, let's now turn to Rick Thevenet. As a member of Pepsi's treasury group, Rick is the only bonafide practitioner of corporate finance in the room. In recent years, Pepsi has acquired a reputation for managing its capital very efficiently. Rick, would you tell us a little about the role of capital structure in Pepsi's overall business strategy and in its drive for efficiency?

THEVENET: One of our financial aims at Pepsi is to minimize the amount of cash on our books. More precisely, our objective is to have zero *excess* cash on the books – that is, cash in excess of our normal intra-day float and whatever is trapped offshore for tax reasons. At the same time, we try to have the maximum amount of debt that we can while still maintaining our single-A credit rating.

So, we do have a capital structure or leverage target. And we arrive at that target by determining the largest leverage ratio consistent with our desired credit rating. Once we get to that leverage target, we try to stay there. How do we stay there? Mainly by using our excess cash to buy back stock.

CHEW: Why do you operate with so little cash?

THEVENET: Well, one reason is that we have very good access to commercial paper. If we really need to raise cash, we just go out and issue commercial paper. On occasion, we've issued as much as $3 billion in commercial paper on 15 minutes' notice. So, again, our cash management objective is to have zero in the checking account at eleven o'clock in the morning. It's a very easy objective to measure and, given our access to commercial paper, it's easy to achieve.

CHEW: So the key calculation is how much money you can raise in the commercial paper market without lowering your rating?

THEVENET: Right. As I said, we aim to maintain a single-A credit rating. We want to be single-A because that gives us immediate access, under almost any conditions, to large amounts of cash at

the best rates from all the commercial paper markets in the U.S., Europe, and Japan.

Now, while our financial policies are aimed at maintaining that single-A rating, we also have an investment policy that forces us to look carefully at all of our major investments and expenditures. When viewed together, our financial and investment policies have the effect of putting constraints on the amount of cash we're willing to invest back in the business. The most important constraint is whether or not the project is expected to yield a positive net present value. Having that kind of discipline in evaluating investments is important to Pepsi, in large part because the company now generates almost $3 billion in cash more than it spends on new projects. In Cliff's terms, that's about $3 billion of free cash flow that might be wasted by a less financially disciplined management team. To avoid that problem, we pay out much of that cash to our stockholders. Last year Pepsi paid out $800 million in dividends while also spending $1.4 billion to buy back its stock.

We attempt to keep our cash to a minimum because we share the investment community's concern that if we have $3 billion in excess cash sitting on our balance sheet, management will be tempted to spend the money unwisely. And by "unwisely" I mean, for example, acquiring brands where the purchase price is at such a premium that we cannot possibly earn an adequate rate of return on our investment.

CHEW: Is there a past history of that kind of behavior in the organization?

THEVENET: In the '80s we had high hopes for growth and large returns from buying back restaurant franchises. With 20–20 hindsight, some of these individual purchases didn't pan out. On a small number of the restaurants we bought, we earned less than our cost of capital. But when we adopted our new financial and investment policies in the late '80s, we shut off the investment spigot.

At the same time, we discovered that we could create significant value simply by divesting assets that we already owned. For example, in some instances we found that we could sell restaurants for more than they were worth to Pepsi. Then, in a more dramatic step, we spun off the restaurants into a separate company called Tricon. Pepsi's stock rose nearly 15% on the announcement of the spinoff, and Tricon has appreciated more than

50% since the spin. Part of the gains in this case came from leverage; whereas Pepsi then had only 7% (market) leverage, Tricon was levered at 50%. Thus, one of the things we accomplished by getting rid of our excess cash was to force management to examine more carefully not only acquisition candidates, but existing assets too – to ensure that they would provide us with a fair return of capital. And having done that, we discovered that we suddenly had a lot more cash to buy back stock. Historically we have used stock buybacks to manage our leverage. But with the Quaker transaction being recorded as a "pooling of interests," our buyback is on hold.

So, our decision to minimize our cash levels and maintain maximum leverage – again, while still being consistent with a single-A rating – helped to reinforce our new strategy of more disciplined, value-based management. Prior to making this change in strategy, Pepsi was a more or less conventional "growth" company. Management's main concerns then were top-line growth and bottom-line growth. As a result, capital was never a concern for us. If the company wanted to make a major investment – say, a big acquisition – it had a lot of internal cash. And if the company didn't have enough cash, it could always issue debt.

As a general rule, then, if there is a lot of excess cash or unused debt capacity, companies will generally find a way to spend it. For example, if you have an M&A department whose sole function is to go out and buy other companies, and you also have lots of excess cash, then you're likely to end up buying some companies that don't add value.

But the value-based approach at Pepsi differs greatly from that of most growth companies. Today all investments have to show that they are likely to add value, to earn more than the cost of capital. And our cash and capital structure policies reinforce that message. As I said earlier, we use our excess cash to buy back stock and to keep our leverage ratio at the top of the single-A range. With less cash on the books, there is less temptation for us to overpay to acquire other corporations, or make uneconomic investments in our core businesses.

CHEW: Has your target leverage ratio increased during that time?

THEVENET: In 1991, which was a year or two before I joined the company, we had a target

leverage ratio of 25% debt in relation to the *market* value of total capital. Our rationale for using market values – and the rationale used by many academic studies of capital structure, including Cliff's – was that the stock price is a forward-looking measure of the company's ability to service debt. And to the extent the market was expecting an increase in the company's future cash profits, the company could support a higher debt ratio than was implied in the use of book values.

But if we were successful in convincing ourselves that this was the right approach, the rating agencies didn't buy it. We had an ongoing battle to get them to accept that our target was consistent with a single-A rating. As we kept telling them, by using conventional book leverage and historical coverage ratios, you're effectively looking at this year's debt in relation to last year's cash flows. But they were not persuaded. One factor that complicated the discussion was the volatility of our P/E multiple, which has increased in the past ten years from about 20 to as high as 35 in the past few months. According to the rating agencies, if we had adhered to that same 25% market leverage target with a P/E of 35, we would have almost doubled our book leverage ratio and become dramatically overleveraged.

So, we have given up our attempt to convert the rating agencies to our market-based way of thinking about leverage ratios. On the plus side, they no longer look at us on a book leverage basis. We now target cash flows and, in particular, earnings coverage ratios when looking at our ratings.

CHEW: So earnings coverage ratios are a key variable?

THEVENET: They seem to be *the* key variable for the rating agencies.

IKENBERRY: Just a quick question, Rick. Cliff started out this discussion by telling us what M&M and other academics think are the most important considerations in arriving at optimal capital structure. Then you started out by suggesting that when Pepsi went through a similar thought process guided by most of the same considerations, the company came up with an optimal leverage ratio of 25% of total market cap. But now you tell us that the determining factor in this capital structure decision is the need to maintain a single-A rating.

Now, I have to say that although I hear this story from corporate treasurers all the time, I still find it pretty extraordinary. Why, given what I think is a

Rick Thevenet   Photographs by Clay Enos

pretty compelling theory, do companies keep coming back to what appear to us to be these outmoded rating-agency criteria? Why not follow the theory if the theory would lead you down a more sensible path?

THEVENET: I guess the best way to respond to your question is to tell you what happens if you fail to maintain your credit rating. And let me illustrate my point using the commercial paper market. The CP markets for A1/P1 credits like Pepsi have about $1.2 trillion outstanding. But if you fall into the A2/P2 category – a category that is roughly equivalent to a triple-B rating on corporate bonds – the market size shrinks to about $180 billion. On top of that, whereas the largest corporate CP programs for individual A1/P1 issuers run from $60 to $80 billion, the largest programs for A2/P2 firms are only around $2 billion. So, the amount that you can have outstanding as an A2/P2 is dramatically restricted. You can't get immediate access and the rates are considerably higher. And if there's a default in A2/P2, the markets often shut down completely, and you just cannot get access to cash.

IKENBERRY: But why do you need this instant access to such large amounts of cash? Does Pepsi have incredibly perishable growth options – the kind that, if you don't exercise them by five o'clock, they're gone?

THEVENET: Our concern at Pepsi is that if we didn't have access to the A1/P1 commercial paper market, we wouldn't be able to buy brands like the Quaker Oats brand that we're now looking to buy. Now, in that case, we are using stock to make the acquisition. But let's take the case of South Beach, or SoBe. Other people were "in the hunt" for SoBe, and we ended up paying about $300 million dollars in cash. If we were in A2/P2 commercial

paper, we could not have made that acquisition because of the lead time required to lock up financing in the A2/P2 markets.

ERIK SIRRI: So, what you're saying, then, is that commercial paper is a substitute for cash. That's your critical source of financial flexibility, and that's why you want to maintain your single-A rating.

THEVENET: That's right. If we were an A2/P2 commercial paper issuer, we would have to keep loads of cash on the books to handle those periods when we wouldn't be able to access the debt market. In that case, we would have a capital structure with $4 or $5 billion in debt and as much as $1 billion of cash. Under our current structure, we have $7 billion of debt and no cash – and our feeling is that our current structure is much more efficient for us.

Another important reason for maintaining our access to cash is to respond to possible competitive threats. We face some pretty formidable competitors, and if one of them should mount a major attack in one of our key markets, a double-B credit rating could drastically limit our range of responses. But, as a single-A, we feel pretty confident in our ability to deal with our competition.

When investment grade may not be optimal: the case of SPX

CHEW: This is probably a good time to turn the floor over to my colleague, Dennis Soter, who, as I said earlier, is in charge of Stern Stewart's corporate finance advisory practice. Dennis, you have achieved a certain fame – or "notoriety" is probably a better word – for suggesting that most U.S. companies are underleveraged, and that the optimal

Dennis Soter   Photographs by Clay Enos

capital structure for most firms is below investment grade. How do you respond to Rick's argument?

SOTER: Well, I can see where the prospect of intense competition might cause you to want to maintain a single-A rating. But I do want to question the idea that such a rating is necessary for most companies to capitalize on their investment opportunities or growth options.

There is a wealth of evidence on leveraged acquirers doing deals where they take their case "to the market," so to speak, by raising capital for a specific transaction. In this kind of financing, the acquirer puts in anywhere from 10% to 25% equity and then, in effect, subjects the wisdom of the investment to the scrutiny of investors. In the 1980s, the source of financing would have been the junk bond market. In the '90s, it was more likely to be the syndicated bank market. In either event, the transactions had to stand on their own merits to get done. They did not have the benefit of a single-A bond rating.

CHEW: Dennis, would you give us an example of such a transaction?

SOTER: Well, the best example that I've been involved with was an acquisition by a company in Muskegon, Michigan called SPX Corporation. In 1997, SPX did a leveraged restructuring where it bought back 18% of its shares using a Dutch auction selftender. Just prior to the transaction, the company had one issue of rated debt outstanding, and it was rated single-B – although if you adjust for the fact that the issue was deeply subordinated, that would suggest a double-B-minus as SPX's corporate credit rating. In order to do the stock repurchase, SPX first had to do a tender offer to retire that debt issue, because the repurchase itself would otherwise have caused the company to violate a covenant.

As a result of completing both transactions – first retiring the old debt issue and then issuing new debt to finance the stock repurchase – the company's book debt-to-capital ratio went above 100%. In fact, it went to about 115%, which means that the company now had a significantly *negative* accounting net worth. But, far from being a cause of concern to the market, the transaction apparently had a favorable impact on the investment community's expectations for future profitability. The fact that management was prepared to add to the leverage of an already highly leveraged company appeared to send a very positive signal to the market. During the eight to ten weeks following the announcement of the transaction, SPX's stock price went from the mid-$40s to about $70 per share – and it stayed there.

But that's not the most interesting part of the SPX story. Under the new leadership of the company, which effectively came into place late in 1995, the company had restructured its operations to place less emphasis on the auto parts supply business and more on what it perceived to be a higher-growth segment, specialty service tools. This meant that management was willing to take on high leverage even when it saw the company as having significant investment opportunities. And the high leverage did not end up interfering with these plans. About 15 months after its leveraged stock repurchase, SPX announced that it had reached an agreement to acquire General Signal, a company that was approximately twice its size, for $2 billion.

Now, given that this was just 15 months after it had gone through a major leveraging, SPX was clearly not going to write a check or draw down a line of credit for $2 billion. To do this deal, which also involved the assumption of $400 million of General Signal's debt, SPX ended up putting together a syndicated loan package for $1.65 billion. It was difficult to do, but it got done. And that acquisition has been a major contributor to SPX's remarkable increase in value since then.

Besides illustrating the ability of our capital markets to provide funding for promising investments, the SPX case also shows what can be accomplished by an aggressive and highly motivated management team. Before these transactions took place, John Blystone and his management team were granted a significant number of well-out-of-the-money stock options. And with the help of a bonus plan tied to EVA, management has added a lot of value in a fairly short time.

CHEW: But, Dennis, the basic business strategy of SPX seems considerably different from that of a company like Pepsi. SPX has basically chosen to discard its old business model, to move away from its traditional auto supply business and become what I see as a kind of industrial counterpart of KKR. Management is effectively saying that it's getting into the business of buying underperforming businesses and fixing them. Like KKR, they don't mind using financial leverage to get control. But I would also be surprised if SPX didn't attempt, like most LBO firms, to pay down a lot of that debt fairly quickly. And, as Cliff pointed out in a roundtable that we ran over 15 years ago, I'm not sure the LBO model can serve as a reliable guide to optimal capital structure for companies that are not in the business of buying and fixing other companies.

SOTER: That may be true. But the point of my story is to question this idea – and it's one that I hear all the time – that you need a single-A rating to have access to capital markets. The business risk of SPX, in terms of the volatility and predictability of cash flows, is arguably significantly greater than the business risk of a company like Pepsi. I haven't looked at the stability of your cash flows, Rick. But we've worked with a number of successful consumer products companies, and they tend to generate very stable cash flows. For example, we worked with Quaker Oats a few years ago and found they had very high and stable free cash flow. And, in my mind, that's the perfect candidate to use a lot of leverage. In fact, it's not inconceivable that Pepsi could have borrowed

$13 or $14 billion and acquired Quaker in an all-cash deal.

CHEW: But could they have done that today, given the depressed state of the junk bond market?

SOTER: That might have been tough in the current environment. But not that long ago, borrowing $13 billion at an interest rate of, say, 10% – or, say, five percentage points over the ten-year Treasury rate – would have involved only another $130 million in annual interest payments. The interest coverage would have been tight, but I'm sure Pepsi could have done that. And with the free cash flows generated in the future, it could then have paid down the debt within some reasonable period of time. I'm not suggesting, by the way, that that would necessarily be the value-maximizing strategy for Pepsi. It's quite possible, as you said, that a competitor might respond by going after you in the product markets.

But I don't know whether a single-A rating is necessary to take advantage of the growth options that you perceive. And my general feeling is that the managers of large public companies tend to use too little debt. For every company that thinks about debt as a means of reducing taxes or controlling agency costs, we seem to run across two or three firms that just follow Stew Myers's pecking order and take the path of least resistance.

THEVENET: I would argue that Pepsi has good investment opportunities and that substantial value would be lost if we were unable to finance them. Our earnings have been growing at 15% percent a year, and we fully expect that to continue. We also estimate that our returns on incremental invested capital have averaged – and will continue to average – between 15% and 25%.

Dennis mentioned earlier that our businesses produce fairly stable cash flow. After all, how cyclical can the snack chip business be? But we do occasionally run into roll-out and timing problems in our international markets, and there are a number of other risks that show up in our business operations from time to time. And a big part of our ongoing strategy is to invest heavily in brand-building and value-creating acquisitions.

It's also important to keep in mind that our capital structure policy is part of the company's comprehensive risk management program. We have an overall risk management approach that says that because the company faces risks on the operating side, and from foreign exchange fluctuations as well, we've decided to limit the risk arising from financial leverage.

What could we accomplish by increasing our leverage? We estimate that our weighted average cost of capital right now is about 9%. If we doubled our leverage, my own estimate suggests that our cost of capital would fall by at most 50 basis points. There's not much value added from that. Now, would higher leverage stop our management from making a lot of bad investments? We don't think so. We think our value-based management approach, combined with our zero cash and stock repurchase programs, prevent that. As a firm with one of the highest P/E multiples in our industry, we think we're performing significantly better than most of our competitors. And the potential value added from levering up appears fairly insignificant when set against the potential loss in value from reduced financing and operating flexibility.

So, Pepsi today has lots of valuable growth opportunities. And when we compare ourselves to companies in other industries with similar P/E ratios, we think of ourselves as a "pseudo-pharmaceutical," a company with high potential returns and good growth prospects. Most of the current value of the company rests on our ability to make those investments, and we don't want to jeopardize that future by taking on too much financial risk.

OPLER: I think to some degree both Dennis and Rick are right. The SPX case study provides a good illustration of what the intelligent use of financial engineering and leverage can do for a company in the value-creation process. But I also think PepsiCo is probably not wrong to have the leverage policy that it has. While I agree with Dennis that Pepsi could add substantially more debt to its balance sheet and probably avoid most of the costs associated with debt that have been discussed in the academic community, I think Rick's argument about the company's potential loss of access to the CP market, and to capital markets in general, is one that has to be taken very seriously.

One of my main reasons for saying this has to do with the ongoing trend toward global consolidation in many industries. If you're a large global multinational in the food business, you have to be prepared to respond to global consolidation. There are players out there like Unilever that have very stable cash flows but are nonetheless operating with very conservative balance sheets. And although Unilever has been criticized for being too conservative, the company's goal is to continue to grow through consolidation – and, in so doing, to take advantage of the tremendous economies of scale that exist in a world that's getting bigger and more efficient all the time. For example, Unilever was recently able to buy BestFoods on a leveraged basis. They were able to go to the market in a very tough time and do a $7 billion deal.

CHEW: Tim, wouldn't that argument also apply to the telecom industry, where a number of companies seem to have wound up with more leverage than they want?

OPLER: That's right. Four or five years ago, there was a large rush of competitors into the telecom and wireless industries. Many of these new companies chose to fund themselves with junk bonds – mainly, it seems to me, because the capital was available on such favorable terms. But now there is enormous overcapacity in these businesses. And as investors have gotten wind of this overcapacity in the last year or so, the value of most of those bonds has dropped pretty sharply, the cost of borrowing has gone up, and the companies themselves are struggling to raise new capital. And so even though some of these firms might have a solid strategy for competing against the incumbent telecoms, they're now in a position where their growth potential is severely restricted.

At the same time, some of the bigger players in the industry seem to have clearly benefited from their decisions not to use leverage. For example, some of the RBOCs in the U.S. like Bell South, Verizon, and SBC are relatively unlevered compared to the rest of the industry. And they will tell you that being conservatively financed is part of their strategy because, like companies in the food industry, they are facing global consolidation. Now, I'm not at all suggesting that these conservatively leveraged companies have the *optimal* capital structure. But they have certainly managed to avoid the problems now faced by many of their would-be competitors.

CHEW: One of Mike Milken's first great successes was the MCI deal in the early 1980s, which was funded with convertible bonds. The argument in that case was that although the company had these great growth opportunities, and though they might have needed financing flexibility to take on ATT, equity was just too expensive. The story is that every time the CFO gave any indication of an intent to raise equity, the stock price would drop 10% to 20%. So they decided to issue lower-coupon convertibles with equity kickers attached. Would that financing strategy have helped some of the current telecom companies by reducing their current coupon rates?

OPLER: MCI did a brilliant job of financing themselves in markets that were not as deep as they are today. And a lot of today's telcos have been using converts. But the question that one has to ask is, "Let's suppose that you were back at MCI in 1983, but there were 20 other MCIs out there trying to do the same thing. Would you then have wanted to be as aggressive as MCI in putting leverage on the balance sheet?"

I would argue that the answer is no. Now, I agree with you that if you can't issue equity in those circumstances, then converts are better than straight debt; they help preserve financial flexibility to some degree. But when you see very heavy entry and potential overcapacity in your industry, then you want to be cautious about leverage if you're a company that really has something to add to an industry and wants to have staying power.

To me the important message here is that if you're a financial officer of a company, you need to think through these issues and not make decisions about financial strategy through inertia. It's important to go through the thought process that we're talking about today, and to evaluate and even quantify the tradeoffs between different financial strategies as carefully as you can.

PART TWO: STOCK REPURCHASE

CHEW: Let's turn now to the second major topic of this discussion, corporate stock repurchases. I earlier introduced David Ikenberry as the world's foremost authority on the subject, and I've asked Dave to start us off by providing an overview of the different methods companies have been using to buy back their stock, along with a brief discussion of their motives.

IKENBERRY: The U.S. corporate experience with share repurchases is relatively recent, at least in the grand scheme of things. While the transaction has been around for many decades, the history of buybacks as a popular transaction is confined to the

last 20 years – to the period following the enactment by the SEC of Rule 10b-18 in the early 1980s. That rule, by providing a legal safe harbor against the possibility of investor litigation, really opened the door to all the repurchase activity that we see today.

There are three basic methods a company can use to buy back its stock. Probably the most dramatic approach, the one that really grabs the headlines, is the fixed-price tender offer. In this case, the manager shouts out a price and a quantity and then waits for the market to respond. A second, in some ways equally showy, approach is the Dutch-auction process. In this case, the manager shouts a quantity and a range of possible prices, and the market responds with a demand schedule. As in the fixed-price offer, the company ends up repurchasing all shares tendered at the same price. But in the Dutch-auction process, the price is the minimum level that brings in the desired quantity – or if that quantity is not forthcoming, the price becomes the top of the range.

It is important to keep in mind, however, that these two flashy mechanisms – the fixed-price offer and Dutch auctions – together account for only about 5% of the total transaction volume. Over 90% of repurchases are accomplished using the third mechanism, the open market repurchase. Here the company trades basically like any investor in the open marketplace – although corporate activity is limited to a slight degree by some SEC "guidelines" that we can discuss later. The companies establish brokerage accounts with one or more brokers, though they generally use only one on any given day. And the brokers are given varying degrees of decision-making authority, ranging from programs where the company itself makes almost all trading decisions to cases in which the repurchases are entrusted completely to outside agents operating under general guidelines.

In addition to these three basic methods, some companies are using what I call "derivative layover" strategies. Such strategies typically involve the company buying call options on its own stock, selling put options, or some variation of these strategies. These options generally have the effect of "locking in" repurchases at certain price levels. They also fall outside the jurisdiction of Rule 10b-18.

Why do companies repurchase their shares? When we talk to CFOs and practitioners, we hear a variety of stories and motivations. But

David Ikenberry   Photographs by Clay Enos

underlying all this variety, there are clearly some common themes, and I've come up with a classification scheme that groups them into four major categories. As you will see, the four explanations are not mutually exclusive. In fact, some companies at any point in time might be buying shares for all four of these reasons.

One common explanation for stock buybacks is that they provide companies with a means of adjusting their capital structure. If a company feels it has too little debt and more equity than it needs, a stock repurchase can restore the proper debt-equity balance. And for companies looking to make very rapid and dramatic changes in leverage ratios, both fixed-price offers and Dutch auctions financed by new debt offerings are appealing choices.

But changes in capital structure can also take a more subtle form. What I have in mind here are corporate repurchases of shares for use in executive stock option programs. To me, this is really quite similar in spirit to thinking about a capital structure problem. For example, the typical U.S. firm is said to experience "equity dilution" from stock option programs of about 2–3% a year – and for many high-tech firms, this run-rate can be substantially higher. If you cumulate that 2–3% over a five-year period, you are talking about a 10–20% expansion of the share base. So, for companies that make significant stock option grants each year, it's not unreasonable to think that they are going to need repurchases, perhaps on an ongoing basis, to keep the firm's leverage ratio from falling over time.

A second major motivation that I see for repurchases is one that we've already discussed – namely, to get rid of a company's free cash flow, the excess cash that cannot be profitably reinvested in the

business and that is likely to be wasted if left on the balance sheet. You can even extend this free cash flow model a little bit further to an idea that I refer to as "abandonment." Take the case of an industry where all growth options have just completely evaporated, and the company's only value-preserving strategy is to exit the industry. In such cases, harvesting the cash flows or borrowing money to buy back shares can be an effective way of returning assets or resources back to the capital markets.

Now, you often hear analysts and other commentators criticize stock repurchases as a managerial admission of failure, a sign of management's lack of imagination. But while such criticism may be appropriate in a handful of cases, it generally completely misses the point of a repurchase. In most cases, repurchases are management's way of telling their shareholders that the company has more capital than it can profitably employ. Far from being an admission of failure, it's a statement of their responsibility to shareholders to invest only in positive-NPV projects. And when viewed as part of a broad economic cycle, repurchases provide a means of liberating capital from mature, though perhaps still quite profitable, companies and channeling that capital into growth companies. In this sense, repurchases are an important part of the natural birth, growth, and maturation cycle that all companies go through. They're a key way of moving capital from the old economy into the new economy.

Repurchases represent an act of managerial humility as opposed to managerial hubris. It's a way of managers saying to the capital markets, "Here is my excess cash, take it; you have better opportunities for it than we do." And when this happens, despite the objections of some analysts, the markets generally applaud.

A third major motive for repurchases is that they provide a more flexible and tax-advantaged substitute for dividend payments – which, of course, are the more conventional way of returning excess capital to shareholders. Finance academics have been struggling for years to try to understand why companies pay dividends in the first place, given their tax treatment. But once you accept the idea that companies are sometimes prone to wasting excess capital, repurchases provide a more tax-efficient approach to paying it out. And besides reducing investor taxes, repurchases also give management a great deal more financing flexibility than dividends. Whereas dividends are expected to be paid every quarter, buybacks can be accelerated or deferred in response to changes in the firm's profitability or investment requirements.

Consistent with this motive of dividend substitution, there are a number of academic studies that provide clear evidence that traditional cash dividends as a percentage of total corporate distributions have declined sharply while the fraction accounted for by repurchases has grown. And, as Don mentioned earlier, 1998 was the first year in U.S. history that more cash flow was returned to shareholders in the form of repurchases than through dividends.

But my sense, however, is that dividends are not going away completely. Most companies that have paid dividends in the past are not eliminating or phasing them out. What we're really seeing is a phenomenon that I would call dividend "capitation"; that is, most dividend-paying companies seem to be providing fairly modest increases, while the amounts of capital they return to investors through stock repurchase are growing at much higher rates.

The fourth common motive for stock buybacks is to "signal" – and, in many cases, to profit from – a perceived undervaluation of the firm. I like to refer to this idea as "market mispricing." When you read all these corporate press releases describing the company's stock as a "bargain," you get a sense that mispricing is a big factor in these decisions. And some research that I've been involved in – and I'm sure we'll come back to this – provides suggestive evidence of this mispricing or undervaluation.

Now such underpricing, to the extent it exists, presents a bit of a puzzle for finance scholars who are wedded to the idea of an efficient stock market. One possible interpretation is that managers have access to private or privileged information that hasn't been disclosed to the market. And according to the signaling argument that Cliff mentioned earlier, managers may be using stock repurchases to transmit a signal to the market about the firm's future, to communicate to investors their confidence in the firm's prospects. In this interpretation, although the company's stock would not be undervalued based on *publicly available* information, it is mispriced on the basis of managers' private information.

The other possible interpretation of such mispricing is what might be called temporary market "inefficiencies" – occasional deviations of a company's traded market value from its intrinsic value. As I've already mentioned, a great many corporate managers use this argument – in many cases in public press releases – to justify their repurchases. That is, after the investor relations department has failed to convince the market that the firm deserves a higher valuation through other means – analyst presentations and the like – managers then "put their money where their mouth is" and buy back what they perceive to be undervalued shares. So, in many of these cases, I see repurchases functioning as last-ditch efforts to communicate a message to the market that the stock is undervalued. In other words, the problem isn't so much how to reveal hidden value; rather it's a disagreement about how the market is evaluating information that is already publicly available.

And I think that finance scholars need to take this idea of temporary inefficiency fairly seriously. In my own work on buybacks, I continually run across statements where companies will say, "We are repurchasing shares because we view ourselves as *extremely* undervalued." In a society as litigious as ours, that's really stepping out on a limb. It certainly serves to provoke those lawyers who make a living pushing lawsuits for unhappy investors. And I think there's considerable evidence in this repurchase area – particularly in the form of the abnormally high stock returns of companies *after* buying back their stock – of undervaluation due to a simple failure of the market to process publicly available information.

Some evidence on stock buybacks

CHEW: I agree with you, Dave, that the market does occasionally appear to get out of whack – and that a stock repurchase is an effective managerial device for getting it back in line. For example, think about what happened about two years ago when so many old-economy companies were trading at less than six times earnings. They started lining up to buy back their stock. And, as you suggest, this was probably their last resort, the only way they could signal to the market that they weren't going to fall off the earth.

But are the abnormal returns that you're finding necessarily evidence of a *market* inefficiency? The more stories I read in the business press in which the market is "surprised" by corporate earnings, the more I'm convinced of the importance of this information asymmetry problem that Cliff talked about earlier. My sense is that, even in large, widely followed companies, there is a big barrier between the people on the inside and the investors on the outside trying to find out what's really going on. And for that reason, conveying the confidence of insiders to the investment community, especially in difficult economic times, is a big challenge. So, what you are labeling a market inefficiency may just be a reflection of very high "information costs."

IKENBERRY: Well, on the one hand, I find this idea of an information barrier between insiders and outsiders a very plausible one. If companies' prospects were really that transparent, money managers could make a lot of easy money just by stepping in to correct some pretty obvious discrepancies between stock prices and fair value.

But if this were the case, the undervaluation should be a fairly short-lived phenomenon, and that's not what the research seems to say. The findings of studies that I have been involved in – and this has been confirmed by other studies as well – show that by simply buying and holding a portfolio of companies repurchasing their shares, investors earn abnormal returns year after year for as long as a four-year period. As a group, these companies don't have unusually high levels of risk. They are not growth companies, but rather fairly steady cash generators. But their stock returns over a multi-year period are really quite extraordinary. And this suggests that the market has simply made a mistake in valuing these companies – and the managers have responded to the mispricing by buying back the shares.

CHEW: But when the industrial firms were all trading at six times earnings, my sense was that the market was almost waiting for *the companies* to announce that they were going to buy back stock. That is, investors were experiencing great uncertainty; and until the companies stepped forward and announced the buybacks, the investors were going to stay on the sidelines. The market was saying in effect, "Well, they're trading at only six times earnings, but management doesn't seem very confident; they're letting the price sit there without doing anything about it." So maybe there's kind of a market equilibrium at work in which stock repurchases are now *expected* to play an important role in communicating insider information.

IKENBERRY: I would agree. A classic example of that is what happened after the crash of 1987. In one day, we saw the stock prices of large-cap companies drop about 20% and smaller-cap firms lost almost 30%. That crash happened on a Monday. That evening there were several thousand corporate board meetings held telephonically. And about 750 repurchase programs were authorized and reported in the newspapers the following morning.

Now, the really fascinating thing to me was the difference between the subsequent performance of the companies that announced their intent to buy back stock and those that did not. The companies that bellied up to the bar and said, "We don't agree with this 20% rollback of our value and we're ready to commit resources to back our beliefs" – those were the companies that, by and large, recovered during the fourth quarter of 1987. But the other companies did not. What's more, a study of the '87 crash by Jeff Netter and Mark Mitchell reported that those companies that said they were willing to buy back their stock ended up not doing so. Why? Because they never had to. The market woke up and said, "Well, we may have gone a little bit too far."

So, this tells me that stock repurchases, especially in times of great investor uncertainty, can provide a credible signal of management's confidence. And the failure to announce a buyback, at least in some circumstances, can signal lack of confidence.

The EPS effect

CHEW: Dave, you've mentioned four reasons to buy back stock. But isn't there a fifth motive – namely, to increase earnings per share? That's one we tend to hear quite often both from corporate managers and sellside analysts.

IKENBERRY: As financial academics, we tend to dismiss the possibility that managers are really doing this. A lot of managers may believe that they are buying back shares mainly to increase EPS – and surveys confirm that this is a dominant motive – but as academics we try to understand the more fundamental forces that are driving this behavior. We attempt to find something real underlying the accounting cosmetics that are often used to justify corporate decisions.

Now, when you look a little more closely at what happens in these share repurchases, you often do find some real economic benefits behind this increase in EPS. If a company repurchases shares and then gets an earnings per share pop, that tells me that the company had an inefficient allocation of assets *before* it bought back the shares. For example, a company with lots of "idle" cash on its balance sheet may get a boost in EPS from buying its shares; but I would argue that the real underlying benefit is not the EPS effect per se, but the improvement in the allocation of capital and the resulting increase in return on capital. So, the EPS benefits of stock buybacks are really a matter of real-locating assets on the left-hand side of the balance sheet to higher-valued uses. Or, as I suggested earlier, it's about returning a company's excess capital to investors and so increasing the overall rate of return.

THEVENET: The size of any EPS increase depends on the algebraic relationship between the firm's E/P ratio – the inverse of its P/E – and the return on its cash. If you earn 5% after taxes on your cash, then buybacks are accretive only if your P/E is less than 20 – that is, only if your E/P is above 5%. There is no information content in the accretion, no value creation; it's just simple algebra. And since the S&P 500 has an average P/E of 27, the average S&P 500 company would actually suffer dilution from stock buybacks in the first year or two.

Now, a lot of sellside analysts talk about earnings pick-up. But when they do their analysis, they almost always fail to consider that the cash used to repurchase stock would otherwise have been used to pay down debt or to generate interest income. The conventional analysis effectively assumes that the companies found some money on the sidewalk and used it to buy back stock. But if you do the analysis properly, the majority of U.S. firms get no pick-up their first or second year. It's only the low P/E companies that get any pick-up at all in the first year. And even their pick-up is usually less than a tenth of a cent per share.

So, this great EPS effect is mainly an illusion. If you do the math right, it just doesn't exist. And in those few cases where it exists, it couldn't possibly drive the share price. After all, how much of a stock price move can you get if your EPS goes up by only one or two tenths of a cent? But having said that, there are cumulative effects by buybacks, over a five-or six-year period, that can amount to much more.

CHEW: In the case of a company like IBM, the analysts always seem to dwell on how much the stock buyback contributed to the past year's earnings. But, given that IBM's P/E is over 20, you're saying that it doesn't really contribute at all to IBM's EPS?

THEVENET: Not if you take into account IBM's alternative uses for the cash. And I think this is a real blind spot in sellside analysts. Many of them fail to do the math properly, to consider the interest income that is forgone when a company buys back stock.

OPLER: IBM is a great example of a company that has been criticized by some analysts for using share buybacks to increase its EPS. As Dave said earlier, a lot of critics view the buybacks as a sign of management failure. And I agree with Dave that that view really misses the mark. In most cases, the announcement of a stock buyback is a managerial statement about the firm's discipline in using shareholder capital.

SMITH: I'd like to make one quick comment about this EPS business. While it may be true that there is no near-term EPS benefit for many firms from buying back their stock, EPS considerations still affect a company's buyback strategy in the following sense: Any manager whose main goal is to report higher EPS – if not in the next quarter, then in the next couple of quarters down the road – is going to want to buy back shares at the lowest price possible.

What kinds of companies buy back their stock?

CHEW: Dave, you've done some work on the characteristics of companies that buy back stock. Do they tend to be mainly value companies with low P/Es? Or are there also lots of growth companies with high P/E ratios?

IKENBERRY: We have looked at repurchasing companies mainly in terms of their price-to-book ratios, which, as Cliff said earlier, are often used as a proxy for a company's growth opportunities. When I first started research in the area of stock repurchase about ten years ago, my initial thought was that undervaluation was a big driver of this activity, and that therefore we should expect to see a clear tilt towards the value side of the spectrum. But we found almost no evidence of such a tilt in the buybacks of the 1980s. We basically found a uniform distribution; that is, companies from all parts of the price-to-book and P/E continuum were buying back stock. And it was this initial finding that led me to my current view that companies are not buying back shares for just one reason. A CFO might have two or three major motivations pushing him or her down the buyback path.

But even though we saw repurchase activity by all kinds of companies, the very high stockholder returns came from the companies at the low price-to-book or value end of the spectrum. Our findings can be summed up as follows: If you had bought all the U.S. companies ranked in the bottom price-to-book quintile (relative to their market cap) that announced stock repurchases in the 1980s and then held the stocks for four years, you would have outperformed value stocks in general by about 45% during that period.

SMITH: Dave, what can you tell us about the market's initial reaction to the repurchase announcements? Was the response to announcements by high price-to-book firms any different from the response to low price-to-book firms?

IKENBERRY: What we found in our work on stock repurchases in the '80s – and we haven't checked this in the '90s – is that the typical price reaction to announcements of open market repurchases by value companies was virtually identical to the reaction to growth companies. It was a positive 3.5% for growth companies, and it was also 3.5% for value companies. At the same time, we found

substantially larger positive reactions in the case of smaller firms – about 7–8%, on average – as compared to only 1–2% for large firms like GM and Pepsi. What this finding may be suggesting is that small firms have greater information problems and hence bigger mispricing problems.

SMITH: I'm frankly a little surprised at your findings, and for the following reason: When a firm whose value comes primarily from assets in place announces that it is making a major stock repurchase, you've got a pretty clear message there. Because the firm is volunteering to increase its payout, investors' interpretation of that announcement logically should be that the firm's ability to generate cash from those assets in place has improved. But in the case of companies whose values come primarily from growth opportunities, there's the potential for a mixed message. On the one hand, it could be that their ability to generate cash has improved. On the other hand, they may also be telling investors that they don't have as many profitable reinvestment opportunities as they once had.

IKENBERRY: Let's consider the case of Internet companies about two years ago. Companies with negative cash flow and extraordinary growth opportunities are the last firms that we would expect to be volunteering to buy back shares. But when growth companies begin to make share repurchase announcements, they are likely to be signaling that they are moving from a very high to a somewhat lower growth trajectory. And I think there is a lot of evidence that is consistent with that idea, particularly in terms of the slowing of growth rates of companies after they begin to buy back stock. But we don't seem to see this showing up in the market reactions to share repurchase announcements.

CHEW: Well, there is some evidence that the market is making this kind of distinction in the case of changes in dividend policy. A study by Kose John and Larry Lang found that when low-growth or value firms increase their dividend, there is a highly significant positive reaction. But when growth companies increase their dividends, there's not much of a market reaction – which is consistent with Cliff's point about larger distributions sending mixed messages for growth companies.

And isn't it also true, Dave, that the growth companies in your own studies are much less likely than the value firms to carry out their announced repurchase programs and actually buy back the stock? If so, that makes a lot of sense because growth companies in general are much less likely to have large amounts of excess capital. It seems to me that such companies – provided they really have the growth opportunities that seem to be reflected in their stock prices – would much prefer that the buyback announcement have the effect of raising their prices so they will not actually have to use their capital to buy back their stock.

IKENBERRY: We have looked at completion rates for Canadian companies – the amount of stock actually repurchased as a percentage of the amount the firm said it planned to repurchase. The reason we chose Canada is because the disclosure of actual buybacks there is relatively transparent, and much more extensive than in the U.S. What we found is that completion rates for Canadian value firms tend to be significantly higher than for growth firms. And this finding is consistent with the idea that although value firms may be using repurchases at least in part to get rid of their free cash flow, growth firms are not.

But let me come back to this issue of how to interpret the market's reaction to these announcements. My overall feeling is that while the initial market reaction is helpful for understanding the motives for transactions, there's increasing evidence that the initial reaction is not complete. For example, in the case of share repurchases by value companies, although the initial market reaction was only 3.5%, the abnormal return for that transaction over the next four years was an additional 45%! That's a big number.

CHEW: What were the abnormal returns for the growth companies that bought back stock?

IKENBERRY: We found no evidence of abnormal returns for U.S. growth firms in the 1980s. That suggests to me that growth companies are repurchasing shares for some other reason than to signal their undervaluation.

SOTER: One possibility, as you suggested earlier, Dave, is that growth companies are buying back more shares to offset dilution from stock option programs.

IKENBERRY: We do see companies like Microsoft and Intel with extraordinary growth opportunities repurchasing large amounts of their own stock. Now, why would corporations like that be using their capital to buy back stock instead of investing in growth opportunities? Well, part of the answer is that such companies use stock options in place of salary or cash bonuses. And if companies are not repurchasing shares at the same time they grant options, they're essentially raising new equity from the capital markets as a way of supplementing salaries and funding total compensation. Viewed in this light, a policy of regular stock buybacks and stock option grants can be seen as a way of avoiding going to the capital markets to raise expensive equity capital.

SOTER: But if that's your intention, wouldn't it be simpler just to use stock appreciation rights, which are funded out of treasury? This way the companies can avoid the dilution and transaction costs of issuing new shares and use the cash to fund long-term incentive plans.

IKENBERRY: That's true, and some companies do that. But let me come back to Cliff's suggestion that managers might be conveying through stock repurchases their conviction that cash flows in the future are going to increase. When we actually looked at the growth in year-over-year earnings of companies buying back their stock, the numbers were not very impressive.

CHEW: What if I looked at just the value repurchasers? Do their announcements portend future increases in earnings?

IKENBERRY: No, not as best as we can find. What our results suggest is that the market is simply mispricing the firms on the basis of publicly available information. After all, we built our sample of value firms using just publicly available information. And, as I said, that strategy produced a 45% abnormal return.

CHEW: So, you're saying these companies outperformed the market by 45% over a four-year period without *any* increase in their earnings or cash flow?

IKENBERRY: Well, there is a modest increase in earnings, but we're not talking about blowout earnings performance.

SMITH: If you had bought other firms in the same industry, would you have gotten different results, either in terms of earnings or stock returns?

IKENBERRY: That's a good question, because our findings do not use industry controls or benchmarks. When you compare the stock returns of companies that buy back shares to other firms in the same industry that don't repurchase shares, part of the abnormal performance goes away. And although we haven't put this theory in print, this evidence provides support for an investment strategy known as "sector rotation" – the idea that you concentrate your investment in sectors where companies are buying back stock and sell short sectors in which the firms are net issuers of stock.

Sector rotation seems to work in part because of the tendency of brokerage firms and their sellside analysts to downgrade entire sectors – say, airlines or pharmaceuticals – while upgrading others. It also reflects the operation of industry-wide factors that are beyond management's control. For example, in 1992 and '93, when we had a transition from the Bush administration to the Clinton administration, the prospects for the healthcare industry suddenly became very uncertain. The stock prices of the ethical drug industry fell dramatically. And in response to those price drops, there was an explosion in repurchases across the entire industry. Essentially every single company in the industry was repurchasing shares.

CHEW: But you wouldn't classify drug companies as value stocks, would you?

IKENBERRY: No, but they represent cases where managers could say to themselves, "We have a strong pipeline of projects, and this seems to be an incredible opportunity to invest in our own stock." And while some of this apparent mispricing may be attributable to managers' better information, such an investment opportunity could also suggest a temporary market inefficiency, if you will.

SMITH: Well, I for one would be very reluctant to conclude that this was evidence of a market inefficiency. It seems to me that if Hillary Clinton's task force had worked out differently, even the strongest pipelines would have been worth a lot less than they were before. The possibility of price controls on drugs in the U.S. seems to me to be a very good reason for reducing my estimates of these firms' ability to generate cash flow in the future. So, this is just a special case of the problems we run into when trying to generalize from case studies.

IKENBERRY: That's right – we're talking about a sample size of one. On the other hand, we're also talking about a case in which the management of every firm in that industry chose to make the same repurchase decision during that period of time.

The link between payout policy and how managers are paid

OPLER: Well, let's talk about another example; let's fight an anecdote with another anecdote. We earlier mentioned IBM, and I think IBM is a very good example of a stock repurchase success story. When Lou Gerstner came on board in the early 1990s, one of the first things the company did was to cut the dividend very sharply. But, in 1996, after IBM had returned to profitability, Gerstner announced that the company was going to hold the line on dividend increases. Instead they were going to distribute excess capital by increasing their stock repurchase program. And in every year for the last five or six years, IBM has bought back about $5 billion worth of stock. The argument the company used when they initiated this program was that their own stock is one of their best investments. And their stock price has, of course, performed very well in the past five years.

SMITH: What has happened to IBM's executive compensation plan during that period?

OPLER: Well, I'm sure it's heavy on stock options, and I'm sure IBM's managers have been amply rewarded by the price increases.

SMITH: I'm not surprised to hear that. If I had to offer one single explanation for the sharp rise of repurchases relative to dividends in the last decade, I would point to a change in the U.S. tax code in the early '90s – and it's a tax change that has nothing to do with the tax treatment of repurchases or dividends themselves. The tax change I have in mind is the one that made it harder for companies to pay senior managers more than $1 million in a given year and still get a tax deduction. That tax change undoubtedly helped convince a lot of companies that stock options were a more tax-efficient way to compensate top management. And if you're a manager who owns a lot of stock options relative to shares of stock, you have an incentive to substitute stock repurchases for dividends.

In talking about capital structure policy earlier, we spent a lot of time discussing the linkage between corporate investment policy and financing policy, and between investment policy and payout policy. But I want to suggest that when thinking about these issues, it's also important to consider the role of compensation policy. As a general proposition, changes in a company's internal structure – things like how much decision-making authority line managers are given, and the details of the performance measurement and reward system – need to be coordinated with changes in its financial policies. And a company's payout policy needs to be coordinated with how it compensates its managers and employees. If there are good reasons for companies to use more incentive compensation in the form of stock options or restricted stock or stock appreciation rights, one of the ways to make those programs more effective and more valuable to the managers is to make distributions to stockholders in the form of share repurchase programs rather than quarterly checks in the mail. Because unless you combine that stock option or stock appreciation right program with dividend units, the option holder is going to get a claim only on the expected capital gain, not on the total return.

THEVENET: Pepsi makes extensive use of stock options for incentive compensation. And in making our decision to shift cash from dividends to stock buyback programs, we took care to align managers' interests with those of shareholders. For instance, if a firm has $1 billion of extra cash and a billion shares outstanding, it has two choices. It could pay out the cash in a special $1 dividend and watch the stock fall by $1 on the ex-dividend date. If it does that, the value of all the managers' options would also fall by $1. We would then be punishing the managers for taking the right action and paying out the excess cash! Alternatively, we could use the cash to buy back $1 billion of stock. And if the buyback is viewed by the market as NPV neutral or better, we have at least not punished our managers, and may in fact have rewarded them for returning excess cash to the shareholders.

SOTER: The issue of stock options and payout policy also came up in the SPX case I cited earlier. As I said, the company's aggressive use of leverage to finance growth could be attributed in large part to the use of out-of-the-money options to motivate top management. What I failed to mention was that, as part of the financial restructuring, the board also voted to discontinue the payment of cash dividends. Now, this policy change actually had two major benefits. First, as Cliff suggested, it increased the value to management and hence the effectiveness of the company's stock option program.

Second, it helped increase the company's ability to service its higher debt load. In fact, the annual savings from the elimination of dividend payments was roughly equal to the after-tax interest expense on the new debt used to fund the stock buyback – a benefit that was not reflected, by the way, in the coverage ratios used by the rating agencies.

Buybacks and corporate disclosure

SIRRI: There's a bit of evidence in the organizational behavior literature that might shed light on an issue that Dave mentioned earlier – namely, companies' failure to carry out authorized stock repurchase programs. A paper by two organizational behavior professors, James Westphall and Ed Zajac, attempted to provide an explanation for why some companies announce repurchase programs and end up never purchasing a single share, or buying back only a fraction of the specified number of shares. According to this study, there are two important explanatory variables: one is the power of the CEO in relation to the board and the second is the presence of interlocking directorates.

What does this tell us? Well, I interpret it essentially as confirmation of the free cash flow story. That is, although the company would like to get the signaling benefits from announcing a buyback – the pop in the stock price – the CEO really doesn't want to disgorge the resources; he or she wants to keep them for use internally. And the interlocking directorates in this story function as a kind of information network that lets the CEO know that other firms have done this, and therefore he can do it, too.

What I also find especially interesting about this study – what lends credence to the story – is its finding that the same companies that fail to carry out their repurchase programs also show a similar tendency to back off from announced executive compensation programs. So, what we have here is an agency cost story, evidence of a corporate governance problem. And although stock buybacks are potentially a mechanism for solving one agency problem – the tendency of managers to waste free cash flow – the ability of companies to announce buybacks without any real intention of following through suggests that the solution may be flawed or incomplete.

IKENBERRY: In Canada especially, this issue has received a good deal of attention. When doing stock repurchases, Canadian companies not only have to get their boards to authorize the repurchase, as they do in the U.S., they also have to get a stamp of approval from the Toronto Stock Exchange. And in conversations with people at the TSE, I have been told that the exchange is very concerned about the possibility that companies are using repurchase announcements to mislead investors.

In a study I co-authored with Josef Lakonishok and Theo Vermaelen last year, we checked to see how widespread this "bait and switch" tactic is and how it affects the stockholders. We looked at all the Canadian firms that announced their intent to buy back stock, and then we grouped them into three categories: (1) those cases where they bought back a lot of stock; (2) those where they bought back a modest amount; and (3) those where they bought back not a single share. What we found is that those companies that didn't buy a single share were the stocks that actually performed the best! In Canada, authorized repurchase programs are good for only 12 months and then expire. And during the one-year period their programs were in force, the abnormal performance of those companies that bought no shares at all was a full ten percentage points above the market. The one-year returns of the most aggressive buyers were lower, although still significant.

Now one way of interpreting these findings is that, in the case of the firms that bought back no shares, the market woke up in response to the announcement – and management accordingly saw no need to buy the shares. And in those cases where management did buy lots of shares, the market failed to respond. And so management either really did intend to buy back shares, perhaps to get rid of their free cash flow – or they saw this huge amount of value lying on the table and kept right on buying. Or maybe both factors were at work at the same time.

So, our study suggests that most managers came into these transactions with a conviction that their shares were undervalued and with a genuine intent to buy back the shares. But when the market raised the values, the managers changed their minds. I should also tell you that, in those same cases, the abnormal returns were limited to the first year. There was no evidence of abnormal returns in the second and third years – that is, after the programs had ceased.

SOTER: But, Dave, if you really thought your stock was undervalued, wouldn't a more persuasive signaling device be to use a tender offer as opposed to an open market program?

IKENBERRY: I agree completely. For example, if you've got private information that you want to convey to public markets, why not just shout a price and shout a quantity? This way you're slapping the market on the side of the face. And since you're openly declaring your intention, you don't have to worry about any disclosure issues that can arise in open market programs.

The big concern with tender offers, however, is the possibility of a large wealth transfer from your existing stockholders to selling stockholders. If you're buying back at $50 when your true value turns out to be $30, you've transferred $20 of wealth to shareholders who have left the firm. The possibility of such wealth transfers is greatly reduced in open market programs, where the repurchases are spread over time and made at different prices.

THEVENET: Echoing Dave's point, we have looked at stock buyback tender offers from an execution standpoint, and our analysis shows that although the stock price tends to go up in response to the announcement, in many cases it falls back after the buyback to where it started or even farther. So our feeling is that we're better off spending the same billion dollars buying back aggressively in the open market rather than going out and tendering for the shares. If you have a temporary pop in your price, the gains end up going to outsiders.

We also think open market repurchases can be used to build credibility. Once you have developed a reputation for announcing programs and then carrying them through, there's no need to do a tender offer. You've created a covenant with your shareholders that says, "When we have more cash than we can profitably invest, we're going to give it back in the form of stock repurchases." And for companies that have established this kind of credibility, a tender offer is unnecessary. You don't have to stand in front of the press and beat your chest and make promises.

CHEW: What do you tell your stockholders? Do you have an investor relations program that discusses the details of your open market programs?

THEVENET: In Canada, as Dave will tell you, companies make monthly announcements of how many shares they've bought back, and how much they've spent doing it. We release that same information in our quarterly statements. And until the recent passage of Reg FD, we would tell stock analysts in our monthly meetings how much we had bought back during the latest month and quarter.

CHEW: Do you tell the analysts what your decision criteria are when buying back the stock? For example, do you say you will buy only if the price falls below a certain level?

THEVENET: We don't get that specific. When we launched our most recent program, we said that ours would be an "opportunistic" program in which we plan to buy $4.5 billion worth of our stock over the next three years. Now, since we're currently involved in a purchase of Quaker Oats that will be accounted for as a pooling of interest, we have been forced to suspend our buyback program. But in our programs in the past, we have always delivered on what we promised to do. And in cases where we have announced two- or three-year programs, we have ended up buying back the stock from six months to a year ahead of schedule.

So we've now built up a lot of credibility. And our shareholders know that if we have cash in excess of our positive-NPV projects, we will return it in an orderly fashion to our investors. We don't wait until we have $50 or $100 million of cash on the books; we do it every day of the week.

CHEW: How does the level of your stock price affect your decision to buy back stock? Do you buy it back whenever you have excess cash, regardless of the price? Or do you instead have a trading rule that says buy if the price falls below X?

THEVENET: I give an average of six talks a year on stock repurchase, and during the coffee breaks the people from different companies compare notes. Based on these conversations, there seems to be two schools of thought on this question. One is the kind of program in which the chairman thinks he's got a hot hand, and he will say, "Today our stock's undervalued; go out and buy a $100 million." The other approach is to have a trading rule that allows the decision-making to be delegated to somebody in treasury, or to an outside broker.

Other firms tell us that when the chairman gets involved, those stock buyback programs invariably turn out to be the worst-performing ones. Why? The story I hear time and time again is that when the chairman gets involved, he gets cold feet when the stock is at bargain prices. He says, "Oh my God, the world is coming to an end," and he doesn't buy it back. Instead he buys it back when the stock's not far off its high and he's feeling reasonably comfortable. He buys high, he doesn't buy low.

At Pepsi we have a different process. We have a simple metric or trading rule that is based on our P/E multiple, and where our stock price is relative to our industry peers and to the S&P 500. Now, in each quarter that one of our repurchase programs is in effect, there is a minimum and a maximum amount of our stock that we commit ourselves to buying. And when our stock looks expensive in terms of our trading rule – what we refer to as the top quartile of relative value – then we scale back our repurchases to the minimum level. But when our stock is in the inexpensive range, or the bottom quartile, we buy like gangbusters; we buy the maximum amount.

And this procedure has worked well in the following sense: During the past five years, Pepsi has bought back over $9 billion of stock. In the year 2000, the average price of our repurchases ended up being $3 below our volume-weighted average price for the year. The worst year we ever had was 50 cents lower than the volume-weighted average.

Liquidity and stock repurchases

CHEW: Is there any obvious downside to this kind of corporate "opportunism," to having a program whose basic aim is to buy stock from public investors at prices that turn out to be below average? Cliff, you wrote a paper in the late '80s that suggested that the liquidity of a company's stock might decline in the wake of an open market stock repurchase program. Can you tell us what you were thinking about then?

SMITH: In that paper, Mike Barclay and I were struggling with a very basic question about payout policy. Given that stock repurchases have a definite tax advantage over dividends, and that open market repurchases also give companies more financing flexibility, why don't repurchases completely dominate dividends as a way of distributing cash to stockholders? And one possibility that we wanted to explore was that the very flexibility on the part of the firm's management team could operate as something of a two-edged sword. That is, if I'm an outside investor and I know that I'm going to be trading with people who ought to have substantially more information about the firm's prospects, what effect is that likely to have on the bid-ask spread and the liquidity of the stock? And we found some evidence that in fact bid-ask spreads widened.

Why is liquidity a matter of concern? We have pretty good evidence that wider bid-ask spreads tend to be associated with a higher cost of capital, and hence lower stock prices. And if I take this argument to its logical next step, corporate stock buyback plans that attempt to increase EPS by buying back stock at the lowest possible prices could actually end up reducing firm value by discouraging people from trading and so reducing liquidity.

CHEW: Dave, in your article on buybacks in this journal, you argued that stock buybacks may actually *increase* liquidity for certain kinds of firms. What's your take on this issue?

IKENBERRY: Well, there have actually been a number of papers in this area, Cliff's being the first. And as Cliff said, the big concern of these papers was that liquidity could be reduced by repurchases. The basic argument was that the presence of a "well-informed" trader might cause less-informed players – that is, most of the investing public – to avoid trading.

But, as best we can tell, more recent evidence using different measures of liquidity than the bid-ask spread suggests that repurchase activity does not reduce liquidity. And, in fact, there are certain kinds of companies where the repurchase activity may be beneficial. For firms with volatile and highly illiquid stocks, where liquidity is defined in terms of market price impact or shares traded per day, there's some evidence that when companies are buying back stock, their trading activity actually serves to dampen volatility and the price impacts associated with selling.

CHEW: This is true mainly for small and riskier firms?

IKENBERRY: Yes, that's essentially the story. There's a Ph.D. dissertation by Jaemin Kim at the University of Washington that reports that while conventional metrics of liquidity like trading volume don't improve, some of the non-conventional metrics of liquidity, such as overall volatility and price impact, do tend to improve for those companies that score lowest on these metrics. Now, based on this evidence, a company like PepsiCo is not likely to see much of a change in its liquidity. But when we look at firms where liquidity may be on the low side, stock repurchase can actually have a beneficial impact.

SOTER: We had an interesting experience along those lines three or four years ago. We were advising a company in Grand Rapids, Michigan called Knape & Vogt. It's a small Nasdaq company with very low float. It has two classes of stock, one of which is owned by the family and doesn't trade. So, it's a typical closely held company. And we were faced with the following problem: We wanted to recapitalize the company to a higher degree of leverage, and the only way to do it quickly was to do a tender offer. If we had done it in the public market subject to the safe harbor, it would have taken too long. The dilemma we faced was this: How do you tender for your shares when you have so little float?

But our concern proved to be groundless. The tender offer, rather than reducing the float, actually had the effect of increasing liquidity. What happened was that we created a "liquidity event" by virtue of the fact that we went to the marketplace and bought back nearly 20% of the shares. In so doing, we gave institutions with positions in the shares an opportunity to get out without having a significant downward impact on the stock price.

Our initial concern was that our offer would not get any takers. But the outcome was quite the opposite: We were able to buy the shares back at a very modest premium over the stock price – and the company realized a significant increase in the trading volume of its shares in the year or so after the tender offer.

And let me make one last point about this case: I'm not saying that buying back the shares at a small premium is necessarily a good or bad thing in and of itself. In fact, my advice to companies is that, provided you don't overpay, the price you pay to buy back shares doesn't matter. In our view,

Erik Sirri   Photographs by Clay Enos

managers have a fiduciary duty to selling share-holders as well as remaining shareholders; and it seems to me that the sellers are entitled to part of the gains from a value-increasing transaction.

Back to disclosure

SMITH: Well, let me turn the discussion back to the issue of corporate disclosure that we touched on earlier – because I think most people would agree that these issues are closely related in the sense that the effect of stock repurchases on liquidity is likely to be determined in part by the amount of information the company provides investors about its own trading activity. And, as a general proposition, the more information the market has about the firm's trading procedures, the more liquid the stock should be.

Now, there are some SEC-mandated disclosures for companies that plan to buy back stock. But it would also seem to me that a corporate management team intent on maximizing firm value has incentives, quite apart from complying with regulations, to convince outside investors that stock buybacks are not a game they're playing that ends up making management better off at the expense of their selling stockholders.

And since we've got the former Chief Economist of the SEC in our midst, let me ask him that question. Erik, what kinds of disclosures are, first of all, mandated by the SEC? Second, what kinds of corporate disclosures over and above those regulatory mandated minimums have you

seen and would you recommend to others? And related to this question, what are the costs associated with going the extra step and voluntarily providing some of the information that the Canadian firms provide? Is that a sensible thing to do, or is that stepping in front of a beartrap?

SIRRI: Well, let me start by focusing on what is mandated by the SEC, because I think that has a lot to do with the currently low level of disclosure surrounding stock buybacks in the U.S. My feeling is that the main reason we see so little information produced can be stated very simply: The body of securities law is aimed primarily at the companies that are issuing stock, not at those who are buying it. There are really only two provisions in U.S. securities law that apply to repurchases. The first says that if a company is going to repurchase shares, the board of directors has to approve the plan. And if the repurchase is deemed to be "material," then you've got to make a statement to the public of the number of shares the firm intends to repurchase and the time period over which it may be conducting such operations. If the repurchases are not deemed to be material, you don't even have to volunteer that information.

Now, as Dave mentioned, SEC Rule 10b-18 provides a safe harbor for repurchasing companies. It's essentially an anti-manipulation rule that says if you follow a set of four or five rules – for example, use only one broker at a given time, don't buy at the opening price, and don't buy too much in any given day – then you will qualify for the safe harbor protecting the firm against charges of stock manipulation.

In fact, there is nothing in the securities law that says that companies have to follow those safe harbor guidelines. And a recent study by Krigman and Leach reported that the trading practices of only 6 out of 24 repurchasing firms in their sample were consistent with the safe harbor.

IKENBERRY: That study also reports that the repurchase programs of the vast majority of Nasdaq firms violate one or more of the safe-harbor guidelines.

SIRRI: That's right. And the guideline that most firms tended to violate was the limit on daily volume. The main reason companies ignore this limit is pretty well captured in Dennis's story about Knape & Vogt's tender offer. That is, it just isn't efficient to repurchase in very small quantities over long periods of time. If you want to buy the stuff, you've got to buy the stuff.

But let me return to a point that Dave made earlier. He said he found it remarkable that corporate announcements of stock repurchases regularly describe the company's stock as "significantly undervalued" because such statements might provide grounds for lawsuits by disappointed investors. But, considered from just a legal point of view, corporate repurchases actually create an obligation for firms to say *something*. After all, they're taking the unusual step of going out into the market and buying their own stock. And if they don't say anything about why they're buying, and it can later be demonstrated that management had private information that suggested they were undervalued, then they can get caught for fraud. For example, if a gold mining firm has struck gold and it buys back its stock before revealing that information, it can be sued for fraud. So, if you as a manager of a repurchasing company really feel the firm is undervalued, then you have to say so.

IKENBERRY: It sounds to me like a Catch-22. Look at a case like Samsonite, where the company's management said that it was "grossly undervalued" when buying back the stock. Today the price is a fraction of where they bought back the stock, and the ambulance chasers are just out in droves. You're damned if you do and damned if you don't.

SIRRI: Well, it's a question of degree. Under normal circumstances, if a firm is not attempting to access capital markets or buy back shares and management gets news that leads it to believe the firm is undervalued, it is under no obligation to say anything. But if you're repurchasing, that triggers an obligation to disclose good news immediately; you can't wait.

Disclosure and equity derivatives

SMITH: Okay, you've told us about the *mandated* disclosures. But all that does is put a floor on things; it's not a statement about best practice. So let's take the next step: What advice would you offer managers? What is likely to be the *value-maximizing* disclosure strategy?

SIRRI: Well, there's nothing that stops you from putting objective information in your financial statements. And I like Pepsi's approach – that is, announcing your broad intent and then giving the analysts regular updates on how many shares you've repurchased and at what price.

SMITH: Dave just mentioned ambulance-chasing lawyers. What kinds of litigation possibilities arise from making statements about a company's buyback plan?

SIRRI: As long as you're reporting factual information, you're pretty much clear. But you want to stay away from saying what you intend to do. So, for instance, when companies announce repurchases, they will say things like "the board has authorized" and "the company *may* purchase up to x amount of shares." But they will almost always avoid binding themselves to do something.

IKENBERRY: Cliff raises an interesting question: That is, given that the level of U.S. disclosure surrounding buybacks is so low, why aren't we seeing companies volunteering to create higher standards of disclosure? I think there is a move by the Fortune 100 or 200 companies toward quarterly disclosures of buyback activity. But in my experience, even those disclosures are communicated in a rather indirect, informal process. You know, if you're in on the call, you get to hear the number. But if you're not in on the call, or if you're acting as a historian like me, it's almost impossible to tell how many shares were actually repurchased by a given company in a given period. For example, if you asked me to find out how many shares were actually bought back by IBM in 1997, there's no way I could get that information from publicly revealed documents. And why we

Don Chew   Photographs by Clay Enos

haven't moved to some low-cost, but uniform standard is beyond me.

SMITH: Well, let's imagine we were all sitting around the board table at the New York Stock Exchange trying to decide what the disclosure requirements should be for listing on the exchange. The NYSE has a big interest in seeing that its companies provide investors with the right amount of information, not too much and not too little. This way of thinking about the issue is a useful one given that, in the past century or so, there have been a number of cases where the NYSE has chosen to impose higher disclosure requirements on its members than the SEC.

IKENBERRY: I think an interesting model in that setting would be to turn to Canada and look at what they're doing. Every month the exchange collects data on the repurchase activities of all companies and then makes it available on one big spreadsheet.

SMITH: Well, the academic in me says that there are no obvious externalities in this disclosure process, no obvious material costs associated with providing more disclosure. And if the benefits of disclosing something exceed the costs of disclosing it, normal market forces should see to it that the information gets disclosed. But we don't see this disclosure occurring. So, my question is: What are the benefits to greater disclosure? And what are the costs that seem to be getting in the way of more disclosure?

CHEW: Let me ask what is essentially the same question in a slightly different way: What effect would greater corporate disclosure about

repurchase programs have on longer-term values? Would it increase them, reduce them, or have little effect either way? I raise this question because it seems to me that most companies buying back their shares – even those whose basic aim is to distribute excess capital in the most tax-efficient way – are *executing* their buyback programs in ways that aim to boost their EPS. As Cliff said earlier, the company that ends up buying more of its shares with fewer dollars ends up reporting higher EPS than it otherwise would. And mainly for this reason, it appears to me, many repurchasing companies want their repurchase activity to be a secretive process. They think this helps them buy more of their stock at lower prices.

So, there seems to be a lot of EPS-driven behavior in this share buyback area – and it also seems likely that at least some of this behavior is going to end up reducing the values of companies, if not at the end of the next quarter, then over the longer term. As Dave told us earlier, some companies are even writing put options on their own stock. Although put writing doesn't affect reported earnings, it appears to me to be an essentially speculative activity. It's also an activity that actually brings cash *into the firm* – and that works against the idea that repurchases are designed mainly to get rid of excess cash.

Tim, you advise companies on repurchases. Do these concerns have any basis in what you see in your work?

OPLER: I'm not sure I would go as far as you do, Don. But I agree that companies sometimes seem to want to cloak their buyback activity. Moreover, I think that one reason to have more voluntary or mandatory disclosure is that it helps to reduce the problem of companies announcing buybacks that don't follow through. And that's why I agree with Dennis's argument about the signaling power associated with tender offers. They are completely credible promises to buy back shares. And that credibility is lacking in a world where you don't have to disclose whether you bought some stock or not until the end of the quarter. So, I think the open market programs would have a more powerful signaling effect if companies either volunteered, or were obligated, to provide more disclosure.

THEVENET: Every quarter Pepsi discloses the number of shares bought back and the average price at which we bought back the stock. What I would like to see is a lot more disclosure on the corporate use of equity derivatives. There are a lot of put-writing programs going on and there is very little disclosure of the amounts and practices involved. The way these put-writing programs work is essentially as follows: As long as the company's stock price does not go down after the put is sold, proceeds from the put sale have the effect of reducing the average buyback price. What isn't disclosed is the amount of liquidity or financial risk the companies are taking on by having hundreds of millions of shares out there in puts. There are cases where companies with these programs have seen their stock take a 20% hit – and the net impact has been hundreds of millions of dollars of losses from being forced to buy back stock above the put prices. So, my feeling is that many of these programs are a time bomb waiting to explode. And, as I said, I'd like to see more disclosure on that.

SIRRI: In fact, there is some required disclosure for these transactions. The current market-based risk requirements require disclosures of the firm's commodity, equity, and fixed-income risks at the end of every quarter. So, companies are forced to disclose some information about these transactions at most three months after the fact.

SMITH: This is something that hasn't received a lot of academic attention – and I'm talking not about disclosure, but about the practice of writing puts on the company's own stock. If I sell puts as part of a buyback program, that means I've introduced a new element of volatility into the firm's market leverage ratio. As we all know, a company's market leverage ratio rises when its stock price falls, and vice versa. But once you

introduce these puts, a drop in the stock price results in a disproportionately large increase in leverage. Selling puts means that you're greasing the skids just when things start going downhill. And if you're worried about underinvestment problems from conventional forms of leverage, then these put programs really ought to scare you.

THEVENET: That's right. Using these puts means that you're likely to be creating financial losses at precisely the same time you've got operating cash flow problems – that is, when your stock price is falling. It forces you to buy back stock just when you have the least ability to finance such repurchases.

CHEW: Tim, is it your impression that the kinds of companies that use these put programs are mainly firms like Microsoft and Intel, where financial distress is not really a conceivable problem?

OPLER: There's no question that some of the major users have been high-tech companies with fairly modest amounts of leverage.

SMITH: Well, if Xerox had been doing this 12 months ago, would you have said Xerox is a firm that could wind up in financial trouble? Or take half of the Nasdaq, and look at them 18 months ago and ask yourself, "Were these firms facing any real possibility of financial distress?"

IKENBERRY: Three years ago I asked the treasurer of a large high-tech firm the same question. There had been a big *Wall Street Journal* story about the problems from selling puts. And when I asked him about this issue, his response was, "Well, we've been writing puts all the way up." So I said, "What if your stock now goes down? Are you in a position to buy them back all the way down? Aren't you going to have some long conversations with the board about this?" And his response was, "I would love to be in a position where I had to buy them back. I have a voracious appetite for shares; I couldn't fill my appetite for shares unless the puts were there."

So it's not as if the companies are unaware of these issues and have walked into these positions blindly. But I would generally agree with you, Cliff, that these things can be very dangerous.

THEVENET: We frequently get pitches for these put programs by investment bankers. And we've been to a number of conferences where corporate treasury people will talk about their strategies. In virtually every case, some guy whose stock has gone up for 18 straight months thinks that he's invincible; people like that think they're the next

Dell or Microsoft. They almost never point out that these put programs can lose substantial sums of money. And there is a tremendous amount of career risk if these companies get it wrong.

OPLER: I would make two comments on this issue of puts. One of them is that the quality of disclosure is not what it should be. Companies do have a lot of discretion when disclosing their derivatives positions, and some of them do these transactions in significant size. When you read what companies say in the footnotes about their put-writing programs, you can't tell much about things like the maturities and strike prices of the puts. So it's tough for someone on the outside to understand what the companies are doing.

The second thing I would say is that the securities analysts ought to be paying more attention to this. Many are either not aware of, or choose to ignore, the fact that companies are using these programs and the problems they can cause. It's important because, as Cliff said, it effectively increases the firm's leverage.

But I don't want to make a blanket condemnation of the practice. Put writing can be valuable in some circumstances. As Dave said earlier, they can be used to "lock in" the price at which the firm buys back its shares.

In closing

SIRRI: Let me come back to this issue Cliff posed earlier: Why don't companies disclose more about their repurchases, whether they use derivatives or not? Why is it so difficult to determine how much of a company's earnings arise from repurchase activity, or covering options positions, as opposed to normal business operations?

My answer to this question is simple: all things equal, the managers of most companies would rather not disclose things if they don't have to. They don't want you to see exactly what they're doing, to see the little bets they are taking. If things turn out well, they can choose to reveal their strategy; and if things don't work out well, they bury the losses. So obfuscation serves their interests; it gives them another degree of freedom in producing results that are acceptable to stockholders.

At least that was certainly the feeling I got while working at the SEC. We were always trying to get

better risk disclosure, but the issuers always seemed to be stonewalling. The firms were saying, "We don't want to disclose information on how we're hedging equity risk. We don't want to tell you what we're doing with derivatives for interest rate risk management."

CHEW: But I was always taught that the market assigns a discount for uncertainty, not a premium. And if this is true, what you seem to be suggesting is that most managers are really not attempting to maximize value.

SIRRI: I frankly don't think most managers buy your premise – or if they do, their main interest is in meeting short-term earnings targets. The long term is made up of a series of short terms, and anything that helps them make it through the next quarter effectively gives them an option to get to the next period where bad bets may work out. And as I said, obfuscation serves their interests in doing this.

SOTER: Well, I think the short-sighted behavior resulting from this focus on quarterly EPS can really end up hurting companies. It can destroy their credibility with investors. If a company were to make an investment or an acquisition and not disclose anything about it, management would be strongly criticized by the investment community.

And I think the same thinking ought to apply in the case of stock repurchases. When CEOs and CFOs ask me if I think stock buybacks are a good idea, my answer is always, "I don't know; it depends on the company and on the circumstances." As Cliff was saying earlier, a stock repurchase decision, whether it's in the open market or whether it's a tender offer, is just one component of the company's overall financial strategy; it's part of an entire package of financial policies. And a company's financial strategy has to be designed in the larger context of the company's investment or business strategy, taking account of both its funding needs and the risks of the business.

Now, when we help companies think through their financial strategies, if we do reach a decision to buy back shares, the last phase of the engagement always deals with communication of that decision to the investment community. And whether the company chooses to work through the open market or through a tender offer or Dutch auction, we feel it is very important that investors understand both the underlying reasons for and the goals of the repurchases. Buying out the largest number of shareholders at the lowest price is not the goal of a repurchase. For example, in the case of the SPX Dutch auction I cited earlier, we actually failed to buy back the desired amount of stock because not enough stockholders tendered their shares. The announcement of the Dutch auction drove the price above the high end of the range. And when the Dutch auction was completed, the company then launched an open market program to complete the recapitalization. Also important, when management announced the repurchases, it took great pains to show how the substitution of stock repurchases for dividends was going to increase the financing flexibility of the firm, as well as saving taxes for investors.

So I strongly recommend that companies volunteer as much information as they can about why they're buying back their stock, and how they plan to do it. I have never recommended, by the way, that a company say in a press release that it believes its stock is undervalued. I think it's much more credible to address that issue in terms of what management perceives to be the business's prospects and what the investment community should expect going forward in terms of the company's investment and financing policies. I would also argue that it even makes sense to talk about a company's compensation policies. I can tell you from experience that if management's bonuses are tied to EPS growth, it may be in their interest to take short-sighted actions and use all kinds of accounting machinations to manufacture earnings and mislead investors. We see a big difference in behavior between those leadership teams that are under EVA incentive plans versus those that are designed to increase GAAP earnings.

CHEW: Dennis, I didn't think we'd be able to get out of this meeting without at least one commercial for EVA. Now that's behind us, I think we can adjourn. Thank you all for taking part in this discussion.

PART IV

The Financing Decision II: The Financing Vehicles

The previous section of the book addressed the general question of corpoate capital structure: What is the "optimal" debt-equity mix for a given public corporation? This part focuses on the specific financing vehicles that can be used by corporate treasurers to bring about the desired capital structure. Following a general introductory review of various financing instruments, we feature a series of articles analyzing a number of more or less innovative financing vehicles: convertible bonds, hybrid debt, and project finance.

In "Raising Capital: Theory and Evidence," Clifford Smith begins with a concise review of academic research bearing on (1) the stock market's response to announcements by public companies of different kinds of securities offerings and (2) the relative efficiency of different methods of marketing corporate securities – that is, rights vs. underwritten offerings, negotiated vs. competitive bid contracts, and traditional vs. shelf registration. Somewhat surprisingly, at least to academics, the research confirms that the average market reaction to security offerings of all kinds – debt and equity, straight and convertible, and issued by utilities as well as industrials – is "consistently either negative or not significantly different from zero . . . Furthermore, the market's response to common stock issues is more strongly negative than its response to preferred stock or debt offerings. It is also more negative to announcements of convertible than non-convertible

securities, . . . and to offerings by industrials than utilities."

In the first half of the article, Smith evaluates a number of explanations that have been offered to account for these findings. For example, the expected dilutive effect of new equity and convertibles on EPS is dismissed as an "accounting illusion" that should have no effect on economic values. Skepticism is also expressed about the time-honored "price-pressure" argument that maintains that large issues of new securities must be offered at a discount from market prices, even in heavily traded markets like the New York Stock Exchange. In place of these traditional arguments, Smith suggests that the most plausible explanation of the market's systematically negative response to equity and convertibles is the "information asymmetry" hypothesis. In brief, the argument holds that because of the possibility of inside information and the incentives of management as insiders to issue overvalued securities, the mere act of announcing new equity or convertibles often releases a negative signal to the market about the firm's cash flow prospects (at least, relative to those reflected in its current stock price), thus causing stock prices to fall on average.

In the second part of the article, Smith uses this "information asymmetry" argument to explain why firm commitment underwritten offerings predominate over rights offerings, negotiated over competitive bids, and traditional registration over the new shelf registration procedure. The mere possibility of insider information creates a demand by potential investors for the issuing firm to hire reputable underwriters to "certify" the value of the new securities. The guarantee of quality, as well as the commitment to maintain an after-market, provided to investors is much stronger in the case of firm underwritten offerings, especially those which are negotiated with a single investment banker rather than auctioned through a competitive bid and registered using the traditional rather than the new shelf procedure. In cases where such certification services are unnecessary, however, shelf registration can provide significant savings in transaction costs.

In "Financing Corporate Growth," Professors Alan Shapiro and Brad Cornell provide a broad survey of financing issues faced by all public corporations – tax consequences, concerns about financial and operating flexibility, potential conflicts among bondholders and stockholders, effects on management incentives, and establishing credibility with investors. They then go on to narrow their focus to the financing problems confronting so-called "growth" companies. Growth companies, especially those whose value resides largely in intangible assets, are likely to need lots of equity and perhaps large cash balances to provide the flexibility necessary to execute their investment plans in the most timely way. Because of the uncertainty and risks they represent for investors, such companies are likely to find the use of public capital markets expensive, and the discounts on their securities steep.

For this reason, the authors argue, bank loans or other forms of "inside" debt such as private placements may provide a special financing opportunity for such companies because of the flexibility offered by the close relationship between borrower and investor. For those growth companies large enough to tap public credit markets, convertible bonds may also be especially useful because of their stock-option-like conversion feature, which helps overcome bondholders' normal reluctance to bear large and ill-defined risks.

In "Are Banks Still Special?," Chris James and David Smith present new evidence that announcements of bank loans continue to elicit a positive reaction from the stock market (in contrast to announcements of almost other kinds of capital-raising transactions, including public debt and equity as well as private placements). Although this is an old finding, the authors offer an intriguing new explanation for it – one in which bankers play an important role in financing large corporations (under certain circumstances) as well as the traditional, smaller, "story" credits.

In "Convertible Bonds: Matching Financial and Real Options," David Mayers argues that for companies whose value consists in large part of real options (and high-tech and biotech stocks come readily to mind), convertible bonds are likely to prove a cost-effective financing approach because of the ability they offer management to match capital inflows with expected investment outlays. That is, as a company's real options move into the money and its stock price rise to reflect that, the call provision in convertibles effectively gives management the option to call the bonds and force conversion into equity. Besides eliminating the cash flow drain from servicing the debt, the new infusion of equity can in turn be used to support additional debt (or convertible) financing precisely when the company needs growth capital. Of course, this kind of matching would not be of much use in "perfect" capital markets, where companies are assumed to be able to raise money at the drop of a hat simply by revealing their valuable projects to investors. But, in a world where companies face significant costs from having either too much (particularly equity) capital or too little, the matching provided by convertibles could be a value-adding financing strategy.

As evidence for this argument, Mayers cites the findings of his recent study of convertibles in the *Journal of Financial Economics*. After analyzing a sample of 289 companies that called their convertibles during the period 1971–1990, the study reports significant increases in corporate investment activity beginning in the year of the call and continuing for the next three years. The companies also showed increased financing activity following the call, mainly in the form of new long-term debt issues (many of them also convertibles) in the year of the call.

In "The Uses of Hybrid Debt in Managing Corporate Risk," Charles Smithson and Don Chew attempt to explain the popularity of hybrid debt during both the early 1980s and the early

1990s. In the early 1980s, when interest rates were much higher than they are today, hybrids like Sunshine Mining's silver-linked bond issue were used by riskier companies to help reduce their interest costs to manageable levels. But though rates are much lower in the early 1990s, credit *spreads* widened considerably for all but blue-chip borrowers. In many cases, companies used hybrid debt to lower their risk profile and thus avoid the higher funding costs now associated with being a riskier corporate borrower.

In "Using Project Finance to Fund Infrastructure Investments," Richard Brealey, Ian Cooper, and Michel Habib argue that the complex web of contractual agreements underlying most project financings can be viewed as attempts to shift a variety of project risks – operating risks, political risks, currency risks – to the parties best able to appraise and control them. In this sense, risk management also involves structuring the incentives of the various parties in ways designed to increase efficiency. The equity investment by the project's operators is seen as working together with high debt ratios and the web of contracts to reduce "agency" problems that arise in the management of large projects (and, indeed, in all organizations, public and private). The authors also explain why most project financing takes the form of limited recourse bank loans rather than, say, public bonds with full recourse to the sponsors.

CHAPTER 16

Raising Capital: Theory and Evidence*

Clifford W. Smith, Jr. (University of Rochester)

Corporations raise capital by selling a variety of different securities. The *Dealers' Digest* (1985) reports that over $350 billion of public securities sales were underwritten between 1980 and 1984. Of that total, 63 percent was straight debt, 24 percent was common stock, 6 percent was convertible debt, 5 percent was preferred stock, and the remaining 2 percent was convertible preferred stock. Besides choosing among these types of securities, corporate management must also choose among different methods of marketing the securities. In issues that accounted for 95 percent of the total dollars raised between 1980 and 1984, the contracts were negotiated between the issuing firm and its underwriter; in only 5 percent of the offers was the underwriter selected through a competitive bid. Shelf registration, a relatively new procedure for registering securities, was employed in issues accounting for 27 percent of the total dollars raised; the remaining 73 percent was raised through offerings using traditional registration procedures.

Despite the critical role that capital markets play in both financial theory and practice, financial economists have only recently begun to explore the

alternative contractual arrangements in the capital raising process and the effect of these choices on a company's cost of issuing securities. This article has two basic aims: (1) to examine the theory and evidence concerning the market's response to security offer announcements by public corporations; and (2) to evaluate the different methods of marketing corporate securities (rights versus underwritten offers, negotiated versus competitive bid contracts, traditional vs. shelf registration, etc.), with attention given to the special case of initial public equity offers.

MARKET REACTIONS TO SECURITY OFFER ANNOUNCEMENTS

A public company seeking external capital must first decide what type of claim to sell. In making that decision, it is important to understand the market's typical reaction to these announcements.

Presented in Table 16.1 is a summary of the findings of recent academic research on the market's response to announcements of public issues (grouped by industrial firms and utilities) of common stock, preferred stock, convertible preferred stock, straight debt and convertible debt. Perhaps surprisingly, the average abnormal returns (that is, the price movements adjusted for general market price changes) are consistently either negative or

* This article is based on "Investment Banking and the Capital Acquisition Process," *Journal of Financial Economics* (1986). This research was supported by the Managerial Economics Research Center, Graduate School of Management, University of Rochester.

Table 16.1 The Stock Market Response to Announcements of Security Offerings (In the columns below are the average two-day abnormal common stock returns and average sample size (in parentheses) from studies of announcements of security offerings. Returns are weighted averages by sample size of the returns reported by the respective studies listed below. (Unless noted otherwise, returns are significantly different from zero.) Most of these studies appear in the forthcoming issue of the University of Rochester's *Journal of Financial Economics* 15 (1986), but full citations for all can be found in the reference section at the end of this issue.)

| | Types of issuer | |
Type of security offering	Industrial	Utility
Common Stock	−3.14%[a]	−0.75%[b]
	(155)	(403)
Preferred Stock	−0.19%[c,*]	+0.08%[d,*]
	(28)	(249)
Convertible Preferred Stock	−1.44%[d]	−1.38%[d]
	(53)	(8)
Straight Bonds	−0.26%[e,*]	−0.13%[f,*]
	(248)	(140)
Convertible Bonds	−2.07%[e]	n.a.[g]
	(73)	

[a]*Source*: Asquith/Mullins (1986), Kolodny/Suhler (1985), Masulis/Korwar (1986), Mikkelson/Partch (1986), Schipper/Smith (1986)
[b]*Source*: Asquith/Mullins (1986), Masulis/Korwar (1986), Pettway/Radcliffe (1985)
[c]*Source*: Linn/Pinegar (1986), Mikkelson/Partch (1986)
[d]*Source*: Linn/Pinegar (1986)
[e]*Source*: Dann/Mikkelson (1984), Eckbo (1986), Mikkelson/Partch (1986)
[f]*Source*: Eckbo (1986)
[g]Not available (virtually none are issued by utilities)
*Interpreted by the authors as not statistically significantly different from zero

not significantly different from zero; in no case is there evidence of a significant positive reaction. Furthermore, the market's response to common stock issues is more strongly negative than its response to preferred stock or debt offerings. It is also more negative to announcements of convertible than non-convertible securities, and more negative to announcements of offerings by industrials than utilities.

I would first like to examine potential explanations of these findings. Let me start by briefly noting a number of arguments that have been proposed to account for at least parts of this overall pattern of market responses, and then go on to consider each in more detail.

EPS Dilution. The increase in the number of shares outstanding resulting from an equity (or convertible) offering is expected to reduce (fully diluted) reported earnings per share, at least in the near term. New equity is also expected to reduce

reported ROE. It has been suggested that such anticipated reductions in accounting measures of performance reduce stock prices.

Price Pressure. The demand curve for securities slopes downward. A new offering increases the supply of that security relative to the demand for it, thus causing its price to fall.

Optimal Capital Structure. A new security issue changes a company's capital structure, thus altering its relationship to its optimal capital structure (as perceived by the market).

Insider Information. Management may possess important information about the company that the market doesn't share. Investors recognize this information disparity and revise their estimate of a company's value in response to management's announced decisions. This effect works through two channels:

Implied Cash Flow Change: Security offers reveal inside information about operating profitability;

that is, the requirement for external funding may reflect a shortfall in recent or expected future cash flows.

Leverage Change: Increases in corporate leverage are interpreted by the market as reflecting management's confidence about the company's prospects. Conversely, decreases in leverage, such as those brought about by equity offers, reflect management's lack of confidence about future profitability.

Unanticipated Announcements. To the extent an offer is anticipated, its economic impact is already reflected in security prices. Thus, market reactions to less predictable issues should be greater, other things equal, than to more predictable issues.

Ownership Changes. Some security offerings accompany actual or expected changes in the ownership or organization of the company, which in turn can influence market reaction to the announcement.

Before considering each of these possibilities at greater length, let me emphasize that some of the above arguments have more explanatory power than others. But no single explanation accounts, to the exclusion of all others, for the complete pattern of market responses documented by the research.

EPS DILUTION

Many analysts argue that announcements of new equity issues depress stock prices because the increase in the number of shares outstanding is expected to result in a reduction, at least in the near term, of reported earnings per share. The expected fall in (near-term) EPS causes stock prices to fall.

Underlying this argument is the assumption that investors respond uncritically to financial statements, mechanically capitalizing EPS figures at standard, industry-wide P/E multiples. Such a view is, of course, completely at odds with the theory of modern finance. In an efficient market, the value of a company's equity – like the value of a bond or any other investment – should reflect the present value of all of its expected future after-tax *cash flows* (discounted at rates which reflect investors' required returns on securities of comparable risk). This view thus implies that even if near-term EPS is expected to fall as the result of a new equity

offering, the issuing company's stock price should not fall as long as the market expects management to earn an adequate rate of return on the new funds. In fact, if the equity sale is perceived by the market as providing management with the means of undertaking an exceptionally profitable capital spending program, then the announcement of an equity offering (combined perhaps with an announcement of the capital expenditure plan) should, if anything, cause a company's price to rise.

There remains a strong temptation, of course, to link the negative stock price effects of new equity announcements to the expected earnings reduction. But to accept this argument is to mistake correlation for causality. We must look to other events to assess whether it is the expected earnings dilution that *causes* the market reaction, or whether there are other, more important factors at work. I believe that studies of stock price reactions to accounting changes have provided convincing testimony to the sophistication of the market, which contradicts the claims of the EPS dilution argument.[1] Such studies provide remarkably consistent evidence that markets see through cosmetic accounting changes, and that market price reactions generally reflect changes in the expected underlying cash flows – that is, in the long-run prospects for the business. In short, there is no plausible theoretical explanation – nor is there credible supporting evidence – that suggests that the reductions in expected EPS accompanying announcements of stock offerings should systematically cause the market to lower companies' stock prices.

PRICE PRESSURE

In a somewhat related explanation, some argue that the price reduction associated with the announcement of a new equity or convertible issue is the result of an increase in the supply of a company's equity. This price pressure argument is based on the premise that the demand schedule for the shares of any given company is downward

---

1   For an excellent review of this research, see Ross Watts, "Does It Pay to Manipulate EPS?," *Chase Financial Quarterly* (Spring 1982). Reprinted in *Issues in Corporate Finance* (New York: Stern Stewart & Co., 1983).

sloping, and that new shares can thus be sold only by offering investors a discount from the market price. The greater the proportional amount of new shares, the larger the discount necessary to effect the sale.

Modern portfolio theory, however, attaches little credibility to the price pressure argument – not, at least, in the case of widely-traded securities in well-established secondary markets. The theory says that investors pricing securities are concerned primarily with risk and expected return. Because the risk and return characteristics of any given stock can be duplicated in many ways through various combinations of other stocks, there are a great many close substitutes for that stock. Given this abundance of close substitutes, economic theory says that the demand curve for corporate securities should more closely approximate a horizontal line than a sharply downward sloping one. A horizontal demand curve in turn implies that an issuing company should be able to sell large quantities of new stock without any discount from the current market price (provided the market does not interpret the stock sale itself as releasing negative insider information about the company's prospects relative to its current value).

What does the available research tell us about the price pressure hypothesis? I will simply mention a few studies bearing on this question.

The first serious study of price pressure was Myron Scholes's doctoral dissertation at the University of Chicago. Scholes examined the effect on share prices of large blocks offered through secondary offerings. According to the price pressure hypothesis, the larger the block of shares to be sold, the larger the price decline would have to be to induce increasing numbers of investors to purchase the shares. By contrast, the intrinsic value view suggests that the stock price would be unaffected by the size of the block to be sold. It says that at the right price, the market would readily absorb additional shares.

Scholes found that while stock prices do decline upon the distribution of a large block of shares, the price decline appears to be unrelated to the size of the distribution. This finding suggests that the price discount necessary to distribute the block is better interpreted as a result of the adverse information communicated by a large block sale than as a result of selling pressure. This interpretation was

reinforced by the additional finding that the largest price declines were recorded when the secondary sale was made by corporate officers in the company itself – that is, by insiders with possibly privileged information about the company's future.[2]

In another study on price pressure, Avner Kalay and Adam Shimrat recently examined bond price reactions to new equity offers. They reason that if price pressure (and not adverse information) causes the negative stock price reaction, there should be no reduction in the value of the company's outstanding bonds upon the announcement of the stock issue – if anything, the new layer of equity should provide added protection for the bonds and cause their prices to rise. The study, however, documented a significant drop in bond prices, suggesting that the market views an equity offering as bad news, reducing the value of the firm as a whole.[3]

Another recent study of price pressure was conducted by Scott Linn and Mike Pinegar. They examined the price reaction of outstanding preferred stock issues to announcements of new preferred stock issues by the same company. They found that the price of an outstanding preferred stock did not fall with the announcement of an additional new preferred issue, thus providing no support for the operation of price pressure in the market for preferred stock.[4]

In short, there is little empirical evidence in support of price pressure in the market for widely-traded stocks. The observed stock price declines, as I shall suggest later, are more plausibly attributed to negative "information" effects.

OPTIMAL CAPITAL STRUCTURE

Financial economists generally agree that firms have an optimal capital structure and a number of researchers have suggested that the price reactions

---

2   For the published version of Scholes's dissertation, see "Market for Securities: Substitution versus Price Pressure and the Effects of Information on Share Prices," *Journal of Business* 45 (1972), 179–211.

3   Avner Kalay and Adam Shimrat, "Firm Value and Seasoned Equity Issue: Price Pressure, Wealth Redistribution, or Negative Information," New York University working paper, 1986.

4   See Scott Linn and J. Michael Pinegar, "The Effect of Issuing Preferred Stock on Common Stockholder Wealth," Unpublished manuscript, University of Iowa, 1985.

documented in Table 16.1 reflect companies' attempts to move toward that optimum. This explanation might be useful if we found broad samples of firms experiencing positive market responses to their new security issues. But because the market reaction to most security offerings appears systematically negative (or at best neutral), it is clear that any attempt by firms to move toward a target capital structure is not the dominating factor in the market's response. If we were to use the market's reaction to new security offerings as the basis for any useful generalization about companies' relationship to their optimal structure, we would be put in the embarrassing position of arguing that new security offerings routinely move companies away from, not toward, such an optimum. Thus, I raise this possibility largely to dismiss it.

INFORMATION DISPARITY BETWEEN MANAGEMENT AND POTENTIAL INVESTORS

The documented reductions in firm value associated with security sales – which, after all, are voluntary management decisions – thus present financial economists with a puzzle. One possible explanation is that new security sales are optimal responses by management to changes for the worse in a company's prospects. Alternatively, a company's current market valuation may seem to management to reflect excessive confidence about the future, and it may attempt to exploit such a difference in outlook by "timing" its equity offerings. Investors habituated to stock offerings under such conditions will discount, as a matter of course, the stock prices of companies announcing security offerings. In such circumstances, even if a security sale increases the value of the firm by allowing it to fund profitable projects, it could lead potential investors to suspect that management has a dimmer view of the company's future than that reflected in its current market value.

It is now well documented that managers have better information about the firm's prospects than do outside investors.[5] There is also little doubt that

outsiders pay attention to insider trading in making their own investment decisions. Given these observations, I believe that the findings in Table 16.1 are driven in large part by this potential disparity of information between management and the market, and the incentives it offers management in timing the issue of new securities.

Furthermore, I would argue that, as a result of this potential information disparity, new security offerings affect investors' outlook about a company through two primary channels: (a) the implied change in expected net operating cash flow and (b) the leverage change.

Implied Changes in Net Operating Cash Flow. Investors, of course, are ultimately interested in a company's capacity to generate cash flow. Although a new security offering might imply that the company has discovered new investment opportunities, it might also imply a shortfall in cash caused by poor current or expected future operating performance. As accounting students learn in their first year of business school, "sources" must equal "uses" of funds. Consequently, an announcement of a new security issue must imply one of the following to investors: (1) an expected increase in new investment expenditure, (2) a reduction in some liability (such as debt retirement or share repurchase) and hence a change in capital structure, (3) an increase in future dividends, or (4) a reduction in expected net operating cash flow. If new security sales were generally used only in anticipation of profitable new investment or to move capital structure closer to an optimal target ratio, then we should expect positive stock price reactions to announcements of new offerings. But if unanticipated security issues come to be associated with reductions in future cash flows from operations, then investors would systematically interpret announcements of security sales as bad news.

This argument can be generalized to consider other announcements which do not explicitly link sources and uses of funds. Using the above line of reasoning, we would interpret announcements of stock repurchases, increases in investment expenditures, and higher dividend payments as signaling increases in expected operating cash flow and, thus, as good news for investors. Conversely, security offerings, reductions in investment expenditures, and reductions in dividend payments all would imply reductions in expected operating cash flow.

---

5 See Jeffrey Jaffe's seminal study of insider trading, "Special Information and Insider Trading," *Journal of Business* 47 (1974), 410–420.

Table 16.2 The Stock Market Response to Announcements of Changes in Financing, Dividend, and Investment Policy (In the columns below are the average two-day common stock abnormal returns and average sample size from studies of changes in financing, dividend, and investment policy grouped by implied changes in corporate cash flows. Returns are weighted averages by sample size of the returns reported by the respective studies. (Unless otherwise noted, returns are significantly different from zero.) Full citations for all studies mentioned can be found in the reference section at the end of this issue.)

Type of announcement	Average sample size	Two-day announcement period-return
Implied Increase in Corporate Cash Flow		
Common Stock Repurchases:		
Intra-firm tender offer[a]	148	16.2%
Open market repurchase[b]	182	3.6
Targeted small holding[c]	15	1.6
Calls of Non-Convertible Bonds[d]	133	−0.1*
Dividend Increases:		
Dividend initiation[e]	160	3.7
Dividend increase[f]	280	0.9
Specially designated dividend[g]	164	2.1
Investment Increases[h]	510	1.0
Implied Decrease in Corporate Cash Flow		
Security Sales:		
Common stock[i]	262	−1.6
Preferred stock[j]	102	0.1*
Convertible preferred[k]	30	−1.4
Straight debt[l]	221	−0.2*
Convertible debt[l]	80	−2.1
Dividend Decreases[f]	48	−3.6
Investment Decreases[h]	111	−1.1

[a]*Source*: Dann (1981), Masulis (1980), Vermalen (1981), Rosenfeld (1982)
[b]*Source*: Dann (1980), Vermalen (1981)
[c]*Source*: Bradley/Wakeman (1983)
[d]*Source*: Vu (1986)
[e]*Source*: Asquith/Mullins (1983)
[f]*Source*: Charest (1978), Aharony/Swary (1980)
[g]*Source*: Brickley (1983)
[h]*Source*: McConnell/Muscarella (1985)
[i]*Source*: Asquith/Mullins (1986), Masulis/Korwar (1986), Mikkelson/Partch (1986), Schipper/Smith (1986), Pettway/Radcliff (1985)
[j]*Source*: Linn/Pinegar (1986), Mikkelson/Partch (1986)
[k]*Source*: Linn/Pinegar (1986)
[l]*Source*: Dann/Mikkelson (1984), Eckbo (1986), Mikkelson/Partch (1986)
*Interpreted by the authors as not significantly different from zero.

The academic evidence on market responses to announcements of new securities sales, stock repurchases, dividend changes, and changes in capital spending (summarized in Table 16.2) is broadly consistent with this hypothesis. As shown in the upper panel of Table 16.2, announcements of security repurchases, dividend increases, and increases in capital spending are greeted systematically by increases in stock prices. The market responds negatively, as a rule, to announcements of security sales, dividend reductions, and decreases in new investment (an exception has been the oil industry in recent years, in which case the market's response to increases in capital spending has been negative, and positive to announced cutbacks in investment). On the basis of this evidence, the market appears to make inferences about changes in operating cash flow from announcements that do not explicitly associate sources with uses of funds.

I should point out, however, that although this explanation helps to explain non-positive price reactions to announcements of all security sales, it provides no insight into the questions of why investors respond more negatively to equity than debt sales, to convertible than non-convertible issues, and to sales by industrials rather than utilities.

Information Disparity and Leverage Changes. Suppose that a potential purchaser of securities has less information about the prospects of the firm than management. Assume, furthermore, that management is more likely to issue securities when the market price of the firm's traded securities is higher than management's assessment of their value. In such a case, sophisticated investors will revise their estimate of the value of the firm if and when management announces a new security issue. Furthermore, the larger the potential disparity in information between insiders and investors, the greater the revision in expectations and the larger the negative price reaction to the announcement of a new issue.

Because debt and preferred stock are more senior claims on corporate cash flows, the values of these securities are generally less sensitive to changes in a company's prospects than is the value of common stock. Thus, this problem of potential insider information that management faces whenever it issues a new security is most acute in the case of equity offerings. Similarly, the values of convertible debt and convertible preferred stock are also generally more sensitive to changes in firm value than non-convertible debt and preferred because of their equity component – but less sensitive, of course, than common stock; hence the information disparity should be more problematic for convertible than for straight securities.

The case of utility offerings is somewhat different. In the rate regulation process, managers of utilities generally petition their respective regulatory authorities for permission to proceed with a new security issue. This petitioning process should reduce the price reaction of utilities announcements relative to

industrials for three reasons: (1) it could reduce the differential information between manager and outsiders; (2) it could limit managers' discretion as to what security to sell; (3) it could reduce managers' ability to "time" security offerings to take advantage of inside information. Because of this regulatory process, utilies do not face as great a problem in persuading the market to accept its securities at current prices.

Thus, while this information disparity hypothesis does not predict whether the response to announcements of debt and preferred issues will be negative or positive, it does predict that the reaction to common stock sales will be more negative than the response to preferred or debt, more negative to convertible than non-convertible issues, and to industrial than utility offerings.[6]

This second, leverage-related channel through which the information disparity problem operates can be distinguished from the implied cash flow explanation by examining evidence from events that *explicitly* associate sources and uses of funds: namely, exchange offers, conversion-forcing calls of convertible securities, and security sales in which the proceeds are explicitly intended for debt retirement. Research on announcements of these transactions (summarized in Table 16.3) documents the following: (1) the market responds positively to leverage-increasing transactions and negatively to leverage-decreasing transactions; (2) the larger the change in leverage, the greater the price reaction. Accordingly, debt-for-common offers have larger positive stock price reactions than preferred-for-common offers, and common-for-debt offers have larger negative price reactions than common-for-preferred offers.

In Table 16.4 the analysis of the two channels is combined to provide additional insight into the information disparity explanation. The events to the upper left of the table tend to have positive

---

6   But if the evidence across classes of securities is consistent with the information asymmetry hypothesis, some data within security classes is apparently inconsistent. When Eckbo (1986) and Mikkelson/Partch (1986) disaggregate their bond data by rating class, neither study finds higher rated, less risky (and thus less sensitive to firm value) bonds to be associated with smaller abnormal returns. Eckbo also finds more negative abnormal returns to mortgage bonds than non-mortgage bonds. (References for studies are cited in full at the end of this issue.)

Table 16.3 The Stock Market Response to Announcements of Pure Financial Structure Changes: Exchange Offers, Security Sales with Designated Uses of Funds, and Calls of Convertible Securities. (Below is a summary of two-day announcement effects associated with the events listed above. Because each of these transactions explicitly associate sources with uses of funds, they represent virtually pure financial structure changes. (Unless otherwise noted, returns are significantly different from zero.) Full citations for all studies mentioned can be found in the reference section at the end of the article.)

Type of transaction	Security issued	Security retired	Average sample size	Two-day announcement period return
Leverage-Increasing Transactions				
Stock Repurchase[a]	Debt	Common	45	21.9%
Exchange Offer[b]	Debt	Common	52	14.0
Exchange Offer[b]	Preferred	Common	9	8.3
Exchange Offer[b]	Debt	Preferred	24	2.2
Exchange Offer[c]	Income Bonds	Preferred	24	2.2
Transactions with No Change in Leverage				
Exchange Offer[d]	Debt	Debt	36	0.6*
Security Sale[e]	Debt	Debt	83	0.2*
Leverage-Reducing Transactions				
Conversion-forcing Call[e]	Common	Convertible	57	−0.4*
Conversion-forcing Call[e]	Common	Preferred	113	−2.1
Security Sale[f]	Convertible Debt	Convertible Bond	15	−2.4
Exchange Offer[b]	Common	Debt	30	−2.6
Exchange Offer[b]	Preferred	Preferred	9	−7.7
Security Sale[f]	Common	Debt	12	−4.2
Exchange Offer[b]	Common	Debt	20	−9.9

[a]*Source*: Masulis (1980)
[b]*Source*: Masulis (1983) (Note: These returns include announcement days of both the original offer and, for about 40 percent of the sample, a second announcement of specific terms of the exchange.)
[c]*Source*: McConnell/Schlarbaum (1981)
[d]*Source*: Dietrich (1984)
[e]*Source*: Mikkelson (1981)
[f]*Source*: Eckbo (1986) and Mikkelson/Partch (1986)
*Not statistically different from zero.

stock price reactions, those in the lower right tend to have negative reactions while those along the diagonal tend to be insignificant. Hence, a common stock offering, which implies both a reduction in future operating cash flow and a reduction in leverage, prompts the largest negative market response of all the security offers. A stock repurchase, by contrast, suggests increases both in operating cash and leverage, and accordingly receives strong endorsement by the market. It seems to provide a credible expression to investors of management's confidence about the company's future performance (at least relative to its current value).

UNANTICIPATED ANNOUNCEMENTS

Because stock price changes reflect only the unanticipated component of announcements of corporate events, the stock price change at the announcement of a security offering will be larger, all else equal, the more unpredictable is the announcement. For example, debt repayment (either from maturing issues or sinking-fund provisions) requires the firm to issue additional debt to maintain its capital structure. Given a target capital structure and stable cash flows, debt repayment must be matched with a new

Table 16.4

		Implied Cash Flow Change	
	Negative	No Change	Positive
Negative	Common Sale	Convertible Bond Sale To Retire Debt Common/Preferred E.O. Preferred/Debt E.O Common/Debt E.O Common Sale to Retire Debt Call of Convertible Bonds Call of Convertible Preferred	Calls of Non-Convertible Bonds
Leverage Change **No Change**	Convertible Preferred Sale Convertible Debt Sale Investment Decrease Dividend Decrease	Debt/Debt E.O.	Dividend Increases Investment Increases
Positive	Preferred Sale Debt Sale	Common Repurchase Finance with Debt Debt/Common E.O. Preferred/Common E.O. Debt/Preferred E.O. Income Bond/Preferred E.O.	Common Repurchase

Significant Negative Stock Price Reaction	Insignificant Stock Price Reaction	Significant Positive Stock Price Reaction

debt issue; hence the more predictable are principal repayments, the more predictable will be new debt issues. Similarly, the predictability of earnings (and thus internally generated equity) will determine the predictability of a new equity issue. Therefore, one should expect a new debt issue to be more predictable than a new equity issue because principal repayments are more predictable than earnings.

Another reason for the greater predictability of public debt offerings is related to the cost structures of public versus private debt. Flotation costs for publicly-placed debt appear to have a larger fixed component and more pronounced economies of scale than bank debt. Thus, a firm tends to use bank lines of credit until an efficient public issue size is reached; then the firm issues public debt and retires the bank debt. If investors can observe the amount of bank borrowing and the pattern of public debt issues, then more predictable announcements of public bond issues should have smaller price reactions.

Utilities use external capital markets with far greater frequency than industrials, thus making utility issues more predictable. For this reason alone, we would expect utilities' stock prices to exhibit a smaller reaction to announcements of new security sales. In short, the relative predictability of announcements of security offerings helps explain both the observed differences in market reactions to common stock versus debt issues and to the offerings of industrials versus those of utilities.

CHANGES IN OWNERSHIP AND CONTROL

Some security sales involve potentially important changes in ownership or organizational structure. In such transactions, part of the observed price reaction may reflect important changes in the ownership and control of the firm. For example, equity carve-outs (also known as partial public offerings) are transactions in which firms sell a minority interest in the common stock of a previously wholly-owned subsidiary. In contrast to the negative returns from the sale of corporate common stock reported earlier, equity carve-outs are associated with significant *positive* returns of 1.8 percent for the five days around the announcement.

In this case, the problem of the potential information disparity which appears to plague equity offerings seems to be offset by positive signals to investors. What are these signals? As Katherine Schipper and Abbie Smith argue in the article following this one, equity carve-outs may suggest to the market that management feels the consolidated firm is not receiving full credit in its current stock price for the value of one of its subsidiaries. If such is the information management communicates by offering separate equity claims on an "undervalued" subsidiary, then carve-outs could provide a means of raising new equity capital that neutralizes the negative signal released by announcements of seasoned equity offerings. Also worth nothing, the public sale of a minority interest in a subsidiary carries potentially important control implications. For example, the sale of subsidiary stock allows management of the subsidiary to have a market-based compensation package that more accurately reflects the subsidiary's operating performance. In fact, 94 percent of the carve-outs studied adopted incentive compensation plans based on the subsidiary's stock.[7]

Academic research in general suggests that changes in ownership and organization affect stock prices (see Table 16.5). The evidence summarized in the upper panel suggests that voluntary organizational restructuring on average benefits stockholders. The research findings summarized in the lower panel suggests that announcements of transactions that increase ownership concentration raise share prices while those that reduce concentration lower share prices. For example, in equity offers where a registered secondary offering by the firm's management accompanied the primary

equity, the average stock price reaction was −4.5 percent, almost 1.5 percent more negative than the average response to industrial equity offerings. This is the case, incidentally, in which the information problem becomes most acute: not only is the firm issuing new stock, but management is using the offering to further reduce its ownership stake – the reverse of a leveraged buyout.

SUMMING UP THE MARKET'S REACTION TO SECURITIES OFFERINGS

Table 16.6 offers a pictorial summary of the various hypotheses and how each contributes to our understanding of the research findings on new security issues. Those arguments focusing on the information gap between management and investors appear to have the most explanatory power. The extent to which announcements are unanticipated helps explain differences in the market's response to debt vs. equity offerings, and to industrial vs. utility issues. And in the special cases when the offer accompanies ownership or organizational changes, there are important additional insights available. The price pressure hypothesis may have some validity, but for widely-traded securities I remain skeptical. The dilutive effects on EPS and ROE of new equity and convertible offerings are nothing more than accounting illusions; *given* that the security is fairly priced at issue, and that management expects to earn its cost of capital on the funds newly raised, there is no real economic dilution of value caused by a new equity offering. Finally, optimal capital structure theories, at this stage of development, seem to offer little insight into the general pattern of price reactions to new security sales.

ALTERNATIVE METHODS OF MARKETING SECURITY OFFERINGS

Once having decided on the terms of a security to sell, management then must choose among a number of methods to market the issue. It can offer the securities on a pro rata basis to its own stockholders through a rights offering, it can hire an underwriter to offer the securities for sale to the public, or it can place the securities privately. If

7 See the article immediately following in this journal: Katherine Schipper and Abbie Smith, "Equity Carve-outs." See also the academic piece on which the above article is based, "A Comparison of Equity Carve-outs and Seasoned Equity Offerings: Share Price Effects and Corporate Restructuring," *Journal of Financial Economics* 15 (1986), pp. 153–186.

Table 16.5   The Market Response to Announcements of Organizational and Ownership Changes (In the columns below are summaries of the cumulative average abnormal common stock returns and average sample size from studies of announcements of transactions which change corporate control or ownership stucture. Returns are weighted averages by sample size of the returns reported by the respective studies. (Unless otherwise noted, returns are significantly different from zero.) Full citations for all studies mentioned can be found in the reference section at the end of this issue.)

Type of announcement	Average sample size	Cumulative abnormal returns
Organizational Restructuring		
Merger: Target[a]	113	20.0%
Bidder[a]	119	0.7*
Spin-Off[b]	76	3.4
Sell-Off: Seller[c]	279	0.7
Buyer[d]	118	0.7
Equity Carve Out[e]	76	0.7*
Joint Venture[f]	136	0.7
Going Private[g]	81	30.0
Voluntary Liquidation[h]	75	33.4
Life Insurance Company Mutualization[i]	30	56.0
Savings & Loan Association Charter Conversion[j]	78	5.6
Proxy Fight[k]	56	1.1
Ownership Restructuring		
Tender Offer: Target[l]	183	30.0
Bidder[l]	183	0.8*
Large Block Acquisition[m]	165	2.6
Secondary Distribution: Registered[n]	146	−2.9
Non-Registered[n]	321	−0.8
Targeted Share Repurchase[o]	68	−4.8

[a]*Source*: Dann (1980), Asquith (1983), Eckbo (1983), Jensen/Ruback (1983)

[b]*Source*: Hite/Owers (1983), Miles/Rosenfeld (1983), Schipper/Smith (1983), Rosenfeld (1984)

[c]*Source*: Alexander/Benson/Kampmeyer (1984), Rosenfeld (1984), Hite/Owers (1985), Jain (1985), Klein (1985), Vetsuypens (1985)

[d]*Source*: Rosenfeld (1984), Hite/Owers (1985), Jain (1985), Klein (1985)

[e]*Source*: Schipper/Smith (1986)

[f]*Source*: McConnell/Nantell (1985)

[g]*Source*: DeAngelo/DeAngelo/Rice (1984)

[h]*Source*: Kim/Schatzberg (1985)

[i]*Source*: Mayers/Smith (1986)

[j]*Source*: Masulis (1986)

[k]*Source*: Dodd/Warner (1983)

[l]*Source*: Bradley/Desai/Kim (1985), Jensen/Ruback (1983)

[m]*Source*: Holderness/Sheehan (1985), Mikkelson/Ruback (1985)

[n]*Source*: Mikkelson/Partch (1985)

[o]*Source*: Dann/DeAngelo (1983), Bradley/Wakeman (1983)

*Interpreted by the authors as not significantly different from zero.

Table 16.6

Potential Explanations	Research Finding: Returns ≤ 0	Common ≤ Debt or Preferred	Convertibles ≤ Non-Convertibles	Industrials ≤ Utilities
Optimal Capital Structure	No	No	No	No
Implied Cash Flow Change	Yes	No	No	No
Leverage Change	No	Yes+	Yes	Yes
Unanticipated Announcements	No	Yes	No	Yes
Ownership Changes	Yes*	Yes*	Yes*	No
Price Pressure	No	No	No	No

+But only for Debt, not Preferred.
*In Special Cases.

management chooses to use an underwriter, it can negotiate the offer terms with the underwriter, or it can structure the offering internally and then put it out for competitive bid. the underwriting contract can be a firm commitment or a best efforts offering. Finally, the issue can be registered with the Securities and Exchange Commission under its traditional registration procedures; or, if the firm qualifies, it can file a shelf registration in which it registers all securities it intends to sell over the next two years.

Let's look at the major alternatives for marketing securities to provide a better understanding of why certain methods predominate.

RIGHTS VERSUS UNDERWRITTEN OFFERINGS

The two most frequently used methods by which public corporations sell new equity are firm-commitment underwritten offerings and rights offerings. In an underwritten offering, the firm in effect sells the issue to an investment bank, which resells the issue to public investors (or forms a syndicate with other investment banks to do so). The initial phases of negotiation between the issuing company and the investment banker focus on the amount of capital, the type of security, and the terms of the offering. If the firm and its chosen underwriter agree to proceed, the underwriter begins to assess the prospects, puts together an underwriting syndicate, prepares a registration statement, and performs what is known as a "due diligence" investigation into the financial condition of the company.

In a rights offering, each stockholder receives options (or, more precisely, warrants) to buy the newly issued securities. One right is issued for each share held. Rights offerings also must be registered with the SEC.

Despite evidence that the out-of-pocket expenses of an equity issue underwritten by an investment banker are from three to 30 times higher than the costs of a non-underwritten rights offering,[8] over 80 percent of equity offerings employ underwriters. Perhaps the most plausible rationale for using underwriters is that they are effective in monitoring the firm's activities and thus provide implicit guarantees to investors when they sell the securities. This monitoring function would be especially valuable in light of the information disparity between managers and outside stockholders discussed in the first part of this article.

Thus, in addition to providing distribution channels between issuing corporations and investors, the

8 See my paper, "Alternative Methods for Raising Capital: Rights versus Under-Written Offerings," *Journal of Financial Economics* 5 (1977), 273–307.

investment banker performs a monitoring function analogous to that which bond rating agencies perform for bondholders and auditing firms perform for investors and other corporate claimholders. While such activities are expensive, such monitoring of management increases the value of the firm by raising the price investors are willing to pay for the company's securities.

NEGOTIATED VERSUS COMPETITIVE BID CONTRACTS

The evidence also suggests that competitive bid offerings involve lower total flotation costs than negotiated offers.[9] In fact, it has been estimated that companies which use negotiated contracts can expect their total issue costs to be higher, on average, by 1.2 percent of the proceeds. Nevertheless, the primary users of competitive bids are regulated firms which are required to do so. Companies not facing this regulatory constraint (Rule 50 of the Public Utilities Holding Company Act) appear overwhelmingly to choose negotiated offers.

This behavior may be attributed partly to the fact that the variance of issuing costs has been found to be higher for competitive bid than for negotiated offers. Executives whose compensation is tied to accounting earnings might prefer a more stable, if somewhat lower, bottom line resulting from the use of negotiated offerings. Another potentially important problem with competitive bids is the difficulty in restricting the use of information received by investment bankers not awarded the contract. Hence, companies with valuable proprietary information are likely to find the confidentiality afforded by negotiated bids more attractive.

Probably most important, though, is that the monitoring, and thus the guarantee provided investors, is much more effective in the case of negotiated offerings than in competitive bids. With a negotiated offer, the issuing firm has less control over the terms and timing of the offer; hence, investors have fewer worries that the issue will be structured to exploit their information disadvantage.

This leads me to generalize about the kinds of companies which are likely to benefit from using competitive bids. The less the potential disparity between management's and the market's estimation of the value of the company, the greater are the likely savings to a company from using the competitive bidding process. For this reason, regulated utilities (those not already subject to Rule 50) stand to benefit more from the use of competitive bids than unregulated firms. Also, in the case of more senior claims such as debt and preferred stock, the informational asymmetry problem is less pronounced, as I have suggested, because the value of the claim is less sensitive to firm value. Thus straight debt, secured debt and non-convertible preferred stock should all be sold through competitive bids more frequently than common stock, convertible preferred stock or convertible bonds. And this is apparently the case.[10]

SHELF VERSUS TRADITIONAL REGISTRATION

Prior to any public security offering, the issue must be registered with the SEC. Using traditional registration procedures, the issuing firm, its investment banker, its auditing firm, and its law firm all typically participate in filing the required registration statements with the SEC (as well as with the appropriate state securities commissions). The offering can only proceed when the registration statement becomes effective.

In March of 1982, however, the SEC authorized Rule 415 on an experimental basis, and it was made permanent in November 1983. It permits companies with more than $150 million of stock held by investors unaffiliated with the company to specify and register the total dollar amount of securities they expect to offer publicly over the next two years. The procedure is called shelf registration because it allows companies to register their securities, "put them on the shelf," and then issue the securities whenever they choose.

---

9 See Sanjai Bhagat and Peter Frost, "Issuing Costs to Existing Shareholders in Competitive and Negotiated Underwritten Public Utility Equity Offerings," *Journal of Financial Economics* 15 (1986).

10 See the article which appears later in this issue, James R. Booth and Richard L. Smith, "The Certification Role of the Investment Banker in the Pricing of New Issues." The article is based on their study, "Capital Raising, Underwriting and the Certification Hypothesis," *Journal of Financial Economics* 15 (1986).

After the securities are registered, management can then offer and sell them for up to two years on a continuous basis. Rule 415 also allows the company to modify a debt instrument and sell it without first filing an amendment to the registration statement. Thus, shelf registration allows qualifying firms additional flexibility both in structuring debt issues and in timing all security issues.

Because of the additional flexibility afforded management by the shelf procedure, there is greater opportunity for management to exploit its inside information and issue (temporarily) overvalued securities. Thus, the information disparity problem attending new issues should be especially great in cases of shelf registration. Potential investors anticipating this problem will exact an even larger discount in the case of shelf offerings than in offerings registered through traditional procedures. Hence, stock price reactions to announcements of new offerings registered under Rule 415 could be more negative, other things equal, than those under traditional registration procedures.

It is largely for this reason, I would argue, that shelf registration has been used far more frequently with debt than with equity offerings.

A SPECIAL CASE: INITIAL PUBLIC OFFERINGS

Private firms that choose to go public typically obtain the services of an underwriter with which to negotiate an initial public equity offering (IPO). IPOs are an interesting special case of security offers. They differ from offerings previously discussed in two important ways: (1) the uncertainty about the market clearing price of the offering is significantly greater than for public corporations with claims currently trading; (2) because the firm has no traded shares, examination of stock price reactions to initial announcements is impossible. The first difference affects the way these securities are marketed; the second limits the ways researchers can study the offerings.

UNDERPRICING

The stock price behavior of IPOs from the time the initial offer price is set until the security first

trades in the aftermarket demonstrates unmistakably that the average issue is offered at a significant discount from the price expected in the aftermarket. In fact the average underpricing appears to exceed 15 percent. (For a summary of the results of studies of offer prices for initial public equity offerings as well as new issues of seasoned equity and bonds, see Table 16.7.) Once the issue has begun trading in the aftermarket, however, the returns to stockholders appear to be normal.

In an IPO, as suggested, there is a large amount of uncertainty about the market-clearing price. Furthermore, as some observers have argued, this uncertainty creates a special problem if some investors are considerably more knowledgable than others – for example, institutions relative to, say, individuals (especially since the Rules of Fair Practice of the NASD prohibit raising the price if the issue is oversubscribed). Assume, for the sake of simplicity, that we can divide all potential investors into two distinct groups: "informed" and "uninformed." Under these conditions, if the initial offer price were set at its expected market-clearing price, it is not difficult to demonstrate that uninformed investors would earn systematically below normal returns. If an issue is believed by informed investors to be underpriced, then those investors will submit bids and the issue will be rationed among informed and uninformed investors alike. If the issue is overpriced, however, informed investors are less likely to submit bids and the issue is more likely to be undersubscribed. In this process, uninformed investors systematically receive more of overpriced issues and less of underpriced issues.[11]

Recognizing their disadvantaged position in this bidding process, uninformed investors will respond by bidding for IPOs only if the offer price is systematically below their estimate of the aftermarket price in order to compensate them for their expected losses on overpriced issues. Such a bidding process would also account for the well-documented observation that underpricing is greater for issues with greater price uncertainty.

The above explanation has been tested using data from IPOs in the following way. Given that

11 For a systematic formulation of this "informed-uninformed" investor dichotomy and its effects on IPO pricing, see Kevin Rock, "Why New Issues Are Underpriced," *Journal of Financial Economics* 15 (1986).

Table 16.7 The Underpricing of New Security Issues (Presented below is a summary of estimates of the underpricing of new securities at issuance by type of offering. Underpricing is measured by the average percentage change from offer prices to aftermarket price. Full citations for all studies mentioned can be found in the reference section at the end of this issue.)

Type of offering	Study	Sample period	Sample size	Estimated underpricing
Initial Public Equity Offering	Ibottson (1974)	1960–1969	120	11.4%
Initial Public Equity Offering	Ibbotson/Jaffe (1975)	1960–1970	2650	16.8
Initial Public Equity Offering	Ritter (1984)	1960–1982	5162	18.8
		1977–1982	1028	26.5
		1980–1981	325	48.4
Initial Public Equity Offering:	Ritter (1985)	1977–1982		
Firm Commitment			664	14.8
Best Efforts			364	47.8
Initial Public Equity Offering:	Chalk/Peavy (1985)	1974–1982	440	13.8
Firm Commitment			415	10.6
Best Efforts			82	52.0
Equity Carve-Outs	Schipper/Smith (1986)	1965–1983	36	0.19
Seasoned New Equity Offering	Smith (1977)	1971–1975	328	0.6
Seasoned New Utility	Bhagat/Frost (1986)	1973–1980	552	−0.30
Equity Offering:				
Negotiated			479	−0.25
Competitive Bid			73	−0.65
Primary Debt Issue	Weinstein (1978)	1962–1974	412	0.05
	Sorensen (1982)	1974–1980	900	0.50
	Smith (1986)	1977–1982	132	1.6

there is an equilibrium amount of underpricing (i.e., one which has proved to be acceptable to issuers in order to sell the issue), we can hypothesize that an investment banker that repeatedly prices issues below this equilibrium level will lose the opportunity for further business. If the investment banker repeatedly overprices (or does not underprice by enough), however, he loses investors.

A recent study by Randy Beatty and Jay Ritter estimated an underpricing equilibrium and then examined the average deviation from that level of underpricing by 49 investment bankers who handled four or more initial public offerings during the period 1977–1981. When they compared the subsequent performance of the 24 underwriters whose average deviation from their estimated normal underpricing was greatest with that of the remaining 25 underwriters, the market share of those 24 firms fell from 46.6 to 24.5 percent during 1981–1982; and five of the 24 actually closed down. For those 25 with the smallest deviation from

the estimated underpricing equilibrium, market share goes from 27.2 to 21.0 percent, and only one of the 25 ceases operation. (The remaining 54.5 percent of the business in 1981–1982 was underwritten by firms which did fewer than four IPOs from 1977–1981.)[12]

As Table 16.7 shows, security issues by public corporations are also typically underpriced, but much less so than in the case of IPOs. Seasoned new equity issues have been found to be underpriced by 0.6 percent. There is some disagreement about the degree of underpricing of seasoned bonds, with estimates ranging from 0.05 percent to as high as 1.2 percent of the offer price. Seasoned equity issues by utilities, however, appear to be *overpriced* by 0.3 percent.

---

12 See Randolph P. Beatty and Jay R. Ritter, "Investment Banking, Reputation, and the Underpricing of Initial Public Offerings," *Journal of Financial Economics* 15 (1986).

BEST EFFORTS VERSUS FIRM COMMITMENT CONTRACTS

There are two alternative forms of underwriting contracts that are typically used in IPOs. The first is a firm commitment underwriting agreement, in which the underwriter agrees to purchase the whole issue from the firm at a specified price for resale to the public. The second is a "best efforts" agreement. In such an arrangement, the underwriter acts only as a marketing agent for the firm. The underwriter does not agree to purchase the issue at a predetermined price, but simply sells as much of the security as it can and takes a predetermined spread. The issuing company gets the net proceeds, but without any guarantee of the final amount from the investment banker. This agreement generally specifies a minimum amount that must be sold within a given period of time; if this amount is not reached, the offering is cancelled. From 1977–1982, 35 percent of all IPOs were sold with best efforts contracts. Those issues, however, raised only 13 percent of the gross proceeds from IPOs over that period, implying that larger IPOs tend to use the firm commitment method.

The choice between firm commitment and best efforts comes down, once again I think, to resolving the problems created by the information disparity between informed and uninformed investors. The preceeding argument for underpricing firm commitments can be contrasted with the incentives in a best efforts contract. Consider that in the case of a best efforts IPO, if the issue is overpriced and the issue sales fall short of the minimum specified in the underwriting contract, the offer is cancelled and the losses to uninformed investors are reduced. Structuring the contract in this manner reduces the problem faced by uninformed potential security holders, and thus reduces the discount necessary to induce them to bid.

Thus, the relative attractiveness of the two types of contracts will be determined, in part, by the amount of uncertainty associated with the price of the issue. The prohibition against raising prices for an oversubscribed issue (imposed by the NASD's Rules of Fair Practice) means that the company has effectively given a free call option to potential stockholders. Thus, relative to a best efforts contract, the expected proceeds to the issuer in a firm

commitment IPO are reduced as the amount of uncertainty about after-market prices increases. In a best efforts contract, the firm provides potential investors not only with an implicit call option (because of the rule against raising the price), but also gives them the option to put the shares back to the firm if the issue is undersubscribed. Because of these implicit options provided investors in best efforts contracts, the greater the uncertainty about the after-market price of an IPO, the more attractive are best efforts contracts to investors; hence, the more likely are issuers to choose that form over a firm commitment.

To summarize, firm commitment offerings are more likely the less the uncertainty about the market-clearing security price. Consistent with this hypothesis, one study found that the average standard deviation of the aftermarket rates of returns for 285 best efforts offerings was 7.6 percent in contrast to a 4.2 percent standard deviation for 641 firm commitment offerings.[13]

STABILIZATION ACTIVITY AND THE GREEN SHOE OPTION

Underwriters typically attempt to stabilize prices around the offer date of a security. In the case of primary equity offers by listed firms, this stabilization is accomplished by placing a limit order to purchase shares with the specialist on the exchange. I believe this activity represents a bonding mechanism by the investment banker – one that promises investors that if the issue is overpriced, they can sell their shares into the stabilizing bid, thereby cancelling the transaction.

The Green Shoe option (so named because it was originally used in an offering by the Green Shoe Company) is frequently employed in underwritten equity offers. It gives the underwriter the right to buy additional shares from the firm at the offer price. This is equivalent to granting the investment banker a warrant with an exercise price equal to the offer price in the issue. The total quantity of shares exercisable under this option

---

13   See Jay Ritter, "The 'Hot Issue' Market of 1980," *Journal of Business* 57 (1984).

typically ranges between 10 and 20 percent of the offer. Obviously, the option is more valuable if the offer price is below the market value of the shares; thus, the Green Shoe option is another potentially effective bonding mechanism by which the investment banker reassures investors that the issue will not be overpriced. That is, if a new offering prospectus contains a Green Shoe provision, potential investors (especially the less-informed) will reduce their forecast of the probability that the issue will be overpriced because the returns to the underwriter from the Green Shoe are lower if the warrant cannot be exercised.

IMPLICATIONS FOR CORPORATE POLICY

Recent research on the stock market response to new security offers consistently documents a significant negative reaction (on the order of 3 to 4 percent on average) to announcements of new equity issues by industrial companies. Convertible issues, both debt and preferred, also typically are greeted by a negative, though smaller, price change (of roughly 1 to 2 percent). By contrast, the market reaction to straight debt and preferred issues appears to be neutral.

The critical question, of course, is – Why does the market systematically lower the stock prices of companies announcing new stock and convertible offers? Such financing decisions, after all, are voluntary choices by management intended, presumably, to increase the long-run value of the firm by providing necessary funding.

After consideration of several possible explanations, I argue that the primary cause of this negative response is the potential for management to exploit its inside information by issuing overvalued equity (or convertibles, which of course have an equity component). Investors recognize their vulnerability in this process and accordingly reduce their estimate of the firm's value. The result, in the average case, is that the new equity is purchased by investors at a discount from the pre-announcement price.

This theory and evidence has a number of managerial implications. Perhaps the most important is that management should be sensitive to the way the market is likely to interpret its announcement of a new issue. For example, if the company is

contemplating a primary equity offering and an executive asks to include a registered secondary in the offer, the board of directors should recognize that this can be a very expensive perk; in such cases the market price typically falls by almost 5 percent upon the announcement. This is probably the surest means of arousing the market's suspicion that insiders have a different view of the company's future than that reflected in the current stock price.

Perhaps the best way for management to overcome this information problem is to state, as clearly as possible, the intended uses for the funds. For example, if management intends to use the proceeds for plant expansion, management should say so – emphatically. We know that the market responds positively, on average, to announcements of increases in capital spending plans (with the exception of the case of oil companies in recent years, where the reverse has been true).[14] Consequently, short of revealing proprietary information which could compromise the firm's competitive position,[15] management should benefit from the attempt to be as forthright as possible in sharing with the investment community its investment opportunities, corporate objectives, capital structure targets, and so forth.

This strategy is not meant to contradict the obvious: namely, that current stockholders benefit when management issues stock or convertibles when the market price proves to have been high; and that debt or preferred stock is better if the company proves to be undervalued (though, in the absence of significant inside information, I would suggest that this can only be determined with hindsight). The problem, however, is that this kind of managerial opportunism may prove an expensive strategy for a firm that wants to maintain its access to capital markets. If management develops a reputation for exploiting inside information, the price

---

14 A study by John McConnell and Chris Muscarella ("Corporate Capital Expenditure Decisions and the Market Value of the Firm," *Journal of Financial Economics* 14 (1985)) found that announcements of increases of corporate capital spending were accompanied by a 1 percent increase, on average, of the announcing company's stock price.

15 For example, when Texas Gulf Sulphur discovered substantial mineral deposits in Canada, immediate release of that information would have substantially increased the cost of adjacent mineral rights then under negotiation.

discount the market exacts for accepting subsequent new issues could be even larger.

In the second part of the article, I attempt to show how the use of investment bankers as underwriters also helps to solve this financing problem arising from the possibility of insider information. The fact that management may have an incentive to issue overvalued securities causes a demand for "bonding" the firm's actions – that is, investors will offer more for the securities if they are provided a credible promise that they will not be exploited.

In those cases where the information disparity between management and investors is likely to be greatest, and to have the worst potential consequences for new investors (i.e., for equity holders, and especially in the case of smaller firms in less heavily traded markets), the demand for the bonding or certification provided by the banker is also likely to be the greatest. For this reason I have argued that underwritten issues provide stronger gurantees to investors than rights offers; issues with negotiated underwriting contracts are more strongly bonded than competitive bid issues; issues registered using traditional procedures are more strongly bonded than those employing the new shelf registration procedures; and issues containing a Green Shoe option are more strongly bonded than those without. Therefore, for example, an industrial equity issue should more frequently be registered using traditional rather than shelf registration procedures, and sold under a negotiated, firm commitment rather than a competitive bid contract; it is also more likely to include a Green Shoe option. By contrast, a non-convertible debt issue by a utility is more likely to be sold under a competitive bid contract and registered using the new shelf registration procedures.

The above argument is not to deny that shelf registration procedures have significantly lowered the fixed costs of public issues for some industrial companies. In fact it should be especially cost-effective for large, well-established companies, especially in the case of public debt offers.

To take greatest advantage of the potential savings from shelf registration, I believe that management must change some of its practices with respect to debt offerings. Instead of using a line of credit at a bank until a large public issue can be made, qualifying companies could use the shelf registration process to place several smaller issues. In order to retain the additional liquidity in secondary markets associated with large issues, I expect companies to begin offering multiple issues with the same coupon rate, coupon dates, maturity dates, and covenants – instead of designing all new issues to sell at par.

CHAPTER 17

Financing Corporate Growth

Bradford Cornell (University of California, Los Angeles) and Alan C. Shapiro (University of Southern California)

Rapid growth poses special problems for financial managers. They must raise large amounts of cash to fund this growth, often for risky and relatively young firms. Nonetheless, it is misleading to speak of "financial management for growing companies" as if it were a special subject unrelated to financial management in general. The ultimate goal of financial policy, whether a company is growing or not, is to maximize the value of shareholders' equity. In addition, the set of financial instruments and policies available to a financial manager does not change just because a company is growing rapidly. It makes sense, therefore, to examine the financial tools available to all firms to boost market value before talking about the appropriate financial strategies for growing firms.

Broadly speaking, there are two basic approaches for using finance to increase the value of the firm. Both these approaches can be illustrated by thinking of the firm as producing a cash flow "pie" – that is, total operating cash flow distributable to all investors (debtholders, stockholders, and others). The first approach takes the size of the cash flow pie to be independent of financial policy, so that the principal role of finance is to divide the pie into slices by issuing varying types of securities. The object of this division is to match the securities' characteristics with the desires of investors so as to maximize the total proceeds from the sale of the securities.

The second approach focuses on ways in which financial policy can increase the size of the value pie by affecting operating and investment decisions. Underlying this approach is the view that a company is a complex web of "contracts" tying together disparate corporate stakeholders such as investors, management, employees, customers, suppliers, and distributors. This approach assumes that the firm's future operating cash flow may depend significantly upon the perceptions and incentives of the firm's noninvestor stakeholders. Financial policy can be used to increase the size of the cash flow pie by strengthening stakeholder relationships – for example, by improving management incentives or increasing the confidence of suppliers and customers.

The next two sections of the paper examine each of these approaches in greater detail. Once the basic tools of financial management have been laid out, we turn in Section 3 to the issue of what constitutes a growth company. Sections 4 and 5 address the main questions of the paper: How are growth companies unique, and given these special characteristics, what financial management techniques are best suited for such companies?

SLICING THE PIE

Even if corporate operating cash flow is unaffected by financial policy, it may be possible to sell claims to a given cash flow pie at a higher aggregate price by cleverly packaging these claims. In this sense, corporate finance is analogous to marketing. The firm needs money to finance future investment projects. Instead of selling some of its existing assets to raise the required funds, it will sell the rights to the future cash flows generated by its current and prospective projects. It can sell these rights directly and become an all-equity financed firm. But the firm may get a better price for the rights to its future cash flows by repackaging these rights before selling them to the investing public.

There are two basic situations in which such repackaging may add to firm value. First, since different securities are taxed in different ways, repackaging can potentially reduce the government's share of the pie and thereby increase the cash flow available for eventual distribution to investors. Second, total revenue from the sale of rights to the pie may be increased if securities can be devised for which specific investors are willing to pay a higher price. There are four circumstances in which investors may pay more in the aggregate for claims to the cash flow pie: (1) the securities are better designed to meet the special needs and desires of a particular class of investors; (2) the securities are more liquid; (3) the securities reduce transaction costs; or (4) the security structure reduces the "credibility gap" between management and potential investors that exists whenever companies raise capital from outside sources.

Tax factors in financing

The uneven tax treatment of various components of financial cost introduces the possibility of reducing after-tax financing costs by reducing the government's share of the cash flow pie. Most notably, many firms consider debt financing to be less expensive than equity financing because interest payments are tax deductible whereas dividends are paid out of after-tax income.

As Merton Miller has noted, however, this comparison is misleading for two reasons.[1] First, it ignores personal taxes. Second, it ignores the supply response of corporations to potential tax arbitrage. In the absence of any restrictions, the supply of corporate debt can be expected to rise as long as corporate debt is less expensive than equity. As the supply of debt rises, the yield on this debt must increase in order to attract investors in progressively higher tax brackets. This process continues until the tax rate for the marginal debtholder equals the marginal corporate tax rate. At that point, there is no longer a corporate tax incentive for issuing more debt.

This process illustrates a key insight that underlies Miller's argument: The supply of securities in the capital markets is almost infinitely elastic. As soon as there is a small advantage to issuing one type of security rather than another, alert financial managers and investment bankers quickly alter their behavior to profit from this discrepancy. They will continue to issue the cheaper security until the discrepancy disappears. For this reason, opportunities to create value through the issuance of new securities are small and unlikely to persist.

Only in rare instances will a tax advantage persist "at the margin." The example of zero coupon bonds illustrates one such case. In 1982, PepsiCo issued the first long-term, zero-coupon bond. Although they have since become a staple of corporate finance, zero-coupon bonds initially were a startling innovation. Zeros don't pay interest, but are sold at a deep discount from par. For example, the price on PepsiCo's 30-year bonds was around $60 for each $1,000 face amount of the bonds. Investors' gains come from the difference between the discounted price and the face value they receive at maturity.

These securities appeal to those investors who like to be certain of their long-term return. The locked-in return means that investors know the maturity value of their investment, an important consideration for pension funds and other buyers who have fixed future commitments to meet. Normal bonds don't provide that certainty, because the rate at which coupons can be

1 Merton H. Miller, "Debt and Taxes," *Journal of Finance*, May 1977, pp. 261–276.

reinvested is unknown at the time of issue. But despite the potential market for such bonds, they did not exist until PepsiCo's 1982 issue.

The pent-up demand for its $850 million face value offering gave PepsiCo an extraordinarily low cost of funds. The net borrowing cost to the company was under 10 percent, almost four percentage points lower than the yield at that time on U.S. Treasury securities of the same maturity. But zero-coupon bonds did not remain such a low-cost source of funds for long. Once firms saw these low yields, the supply of zero-coupon debt expanded rapidly. In addition, clever Wall Street firms discovered how to manufacture zeros from existing bonds. They bought Treasury bonds, stripped the coupons from the bonds, repackaged the coupons, and sold the coupons and the principal separately as a series of annuities and zero-coupon bonds.

The increase in the supply relative to the demand for zeros resulted in a jump in their required yields, negating their previous cost advantage. But the tax advantage – one which is associated with any original issue discount debt (OID) – remained. The tax advantage to a firm from issuing zeros rather than current coupon debt stems from the tax provision that allows companies to amortize as interest the amount of the original discount from par over the life of the bond. The firm benefits by receiving a current tax write-off for a future expense. By contrast, if it issues current coupon debt, the firm's tax write-off and expense occur simultaneously. The tax advantage from OIDs, which is maximized by issuing zero-coupon bonds, translates into a reduction in the company's cost of debt capital.

But these tax savings don't tell the whole story. Investors must pay tax on the amortized portion of the discount each year even though they receive no cash until the bond matures. Thus the tax advantage to the firm from issuing zeros has been offset by the higher pre-tax yields required by investors to provide them with the same after-tax yields they could earn on comparable-risk current coupon debt. As a result, corporations issuing zeros will only realize a tax benefit to the extent that the marginal corporate tax rate exceeds the marginal investor tax rate. At the extreme, if these marginal tax rates are equal, the tax advantage to an issuing corporation will be completely eliminated by the tax disadvantage to the investor.

The initial purchasers of zero-coupon bonds were primarily of two groups: (1) tax-exempt institutional investors such as pension plans and individual investors (for their tax-exempt IRAs) who sought to lock in higher yields; and (2) Japanese investors, for whom the discount was treated as a non-taxable capital gain if the bonds were sold prior to maturity. Selling to the tax-exempt segment of the market yielded maximum benefits to the issuers of zeros since the disparity in marginal tax rates was at its greatest.

The supply of tax-exempt institutional money, however, is limited. Furthermore, the Japanese government has ended the tax exemption for zero-coupon bond gains; Japanese investors have accordingly demanded higher yields to compensate for their tax liability. The reaction by the Japanese government illustrates another important point concerning financial strategy: If one devises a legal way to engage in unlimited tax arbitrage through the financial markets, the government will eventually change the law.

More limited tax arbitrage, however, may persist for some time. For example, companies with tax losses or excess tax credits can sell preferred stock to other corporations and thereby reduce investor taxes without a corresponding increase in their taxes. The reason is that corporate investors can exclude from taxable income 70 percent of the preferred (or common) dividends they receive. This means that a corporate investor in the 34 percent tax bracket faces an effective tax rate of only 10.2 percent ($0.3 \times 34\%$) on preferred dividends. As a result, corporate investors are willing to accept a lower yield on preferred stock than on comparable debt securities. Hence, companies in low tax brackets (who are unable to make full use of the interest tax write-off) should be able to raise funds at a lower after-tax cost with preferred stock instead of debt. Similarly, leasing (rather than buying) assets enables low tax bracket companies to raise funds at a lower cost by passing along the depreciation tax deduction to investors in higher tax brackets in return for a lower effective interest rate.

Financial innovation

To the extent that the firm can design a security that appeals to a special niche in the capital market, it can attract funds at a cost that is less than the required return on securities of comparable risk. But as we noted in the case of zeros, such a rewarding situation is likely to be temporary because the demand for a security that fits a particular niche in the market is not unlimited, and because the supply of securities designed to tap such niches is likely to increase dramatically once a niche is recognized.

As one further example of this process, major investment banks are currently trying to create value by exploiting what they perceive as profitable niches in the mortgage market. Investment banks such as First Boston, Salomon Brothers, and Goldman Sachs have been purchasing mortgages and repackaging them into complex derivative securities which offer unique risk-return combinations. To the extent that such unique securities are desirable to investors, the investment banks can sell them for more than the cost of the mortgages. Once a particular security structure proves to be profitable, however, other firms aggressively enter the business and drive profits down.

In general, the high elasticity of supply means that repackaging a security's payment stream so that it reallocates risk from one class of investors to another is unlikely to be a sustainable way of creating value. The only niche that is likely to persist as a profitable opportunity in the face of competitive pressure is a niche that involves the government. For instance, by substituting its credit for the credit of a ship buyer, the U.S. government, under the Merchant Marine Act of 1936, subsidizes the financing of U.S.-built vessels. Other subsidized loan programs include those administered by the Synfuels Corporation, Economic Development Administration, the Farmers Home Administration, the Export-Import Bank, and the ubiquitous Small Business Administration.

However, even these governmental niches are not free from competition. For instance, when the government makes subsidized loans available to "small business," it produces an incentive for firms to restructure to satisfy the criteria for being "small." Furthermore, the government severely restricts the supply of securities that can take advantage of these loan subsidy programs.

Increasing liquidity

Liquidity or marketability is an important attribute of a financial security. One measure of a security's marketability is the spread between the bid and ask prices at which dealers are willing to satisfy buyers' or sellers' demands for immediate execution of their trades. There is substantial empirical evidence that investors are willing to accept lower returns on more liquid assets.[2] Other things being equal, therefore, a firm can increase its market value by increasing the liquidity of the claims it issues.

There are a number of ways in which firms can increase the liquidity of their claims. The most important include going public, standardizing their claims (which includes the securitization of bank loans), underwriting new public issues, buying insurance for a bond issue, and listing on organized exchanges.

Because most liquidity-enhancing measures entail significant costs (for example, legal and underwriting fees and reporting costs), however, the firm must trade off the benefits of increased liquidity against the costs. This cost-benefit calculation can best be formulated by expressing the value of increased liquidity as the market value of the firm's equity multiplied by the percentage reduction in its required return.

This expression implies that the advantages of liquidity enhancement tend to be greatest for large firms (which have higher market values) and for firms whose securities are already highly liquid. The latter implication also follows from the observation that low-liquidity assets tend to be held by investors who are willing to hold assets for longer periods of time. Thus, liquidity is less valuable to them than to investors in more liquid assets.[3]

---

2 See, for example, Yakov Amihud and Haim Mendelson, "Asset Pricing and the Bid-Ask Spread," *Journal of Financial Economics*, 17, 1986, pp. 223–249.
3 Liquidity may also have disadvantages in some circumstances. In situations where management commitment is critical and uncertainty is high, such as leveraged buyouts and venture capital, management arguably should be "locked in" to the firm, at least for a while.

Reducing transaction costs

By reducing transaction costs associated with raising money, the firm can increase its net proceeds. The use of investment bankers to underwrite new security issues, shelf registration under Rule 415, and extendible notes are ways in which the costs of raising money can be reduced. Similarly, the use of secured debt and leasing can reduce enforcement costs by giving a lender or lessor clear title to the pledged or leased assets. Because the costs associated with repossessing assets are more likely to be incurred the higher the probability of bankruptcy, companies in shakier financial positions will find this particular benefit of leasing or secured borrowing more valuable than those in better financial shape.

Bridging the credibility gap

One of the key costs associated with issuing new securities arises from the financing problem caused by so-called informational "asymmetries." In plainer terms, corporate management may have inside information about the company's prospects that it can use to exploit potential investors by issuing overpriced securities.[4] Recognizing management's ability and incentives to exploit them by issuing overvalued securities, rational investors will revise downward their estimates of a company's value as soon as management announces its intent to issue new securities. For example, on February 28, 1983, AT&T announced its plan to issue about $1 billion of new common stock. Investors took the equity issue as a bad sign and responded by reducing AT&T's market value by $2 billion.[5]

For companies trying not to misrepresent the value of their assets, the credibility problem imposes a potentially large cost on the use of securities to raise funds. This cost should not be confused with the cost of capital – the return required by investors to hold the company's securities. Rather the cost of issuing securities referred to here is an added discount at which these securities must be sold because of the potential for important inside information.

The riskier the security being issued, the more important this credibility gap becomes, and the larger the discount applied by investors fearful of buying lemons. Conversely, if the firm can issue essentially riskless debt the discount will be zero because the return to the new debt does not depend on management's information advantage.

These observations imply that companies can overcome the credibility problem by raising funds in accordance with what Stewart Myers calls the financing "pecking order."[6] The most common corporate practice, as Myers observes, is to use the least risky source first – that is, retained earnings – and then use progressively riskier sources such as debt and convertibles; common stock offerings are typically used only as a last resort. Myers's explanation for this pattern of financing preferences is that it reduces the security price discount imposed by investors when companies raise new capital. By using internal funds, companies avoid the credibility problem altogether. If companies must go to the capital markets, they face smaller discounts by issuing securities in ascending order of risk: first debt, then hybrids such as convertible bonds, and finally equity.

This set of financing practices has two results: (1) it minimizes the amount of new equity that must be raised and (2) it forces companies to issue equity only when necessary. By limiting management's discretion over when to issue new equity, adherence to the financing pecking order reduces investors' suspicion that management is simply trying to "time" the market and "unload" overpriced stock.

By reducing this credibility gap, then, companies get better prices for their securities. And when they are forced to issue new equity, where the credibility problem is most acute, all but the largest companies tend to use firm commitment offerings (rather than, say, shelf registration or best efforts).

---

4. The problem of informational asymmetry is discussed in Stewart C. Myers and Nicholas Majluf, "Corporate Financing and Investment Decisions When Firms Have Information Investors Do Not," *Journal of Financial Economics*, 1984, pp. 187–221.

5 For information on the events surrounding this issue, see "American Telephone and Telegraph Company (1983)" in Butters, Fruhan, Mullins, and Piper, *Case Problems in Finance* 9th edition (Homewood, Ill.: Richard D. Irwin, 1987).

6 Stewart C. Myers, "The Capital Structure Puzzle," *Journal of Finance*, July 1984, pp. 575–592.

Besides providing distribution channels for new issues, underwriters also perform an implicit role of "certifying" to outside investors that the securities are fairly valued. They do this by putting their reputation on the line with investors when pricing new issues.[7]

USING FINANCE TO INCREASE THE CASH FLOW PIE

The modern corporation, as we said before, is an interrelated set of contracts among a variety of stakeholders: shareholders, lenders, employees, managers, suppliers, distributors, and customers. Although these stakeholders have a common interest in the firm's success, there are potentially costly conflicts of interests. To the extent that financial policy can reduce these conflicts, it can enlarge the cash flow pie and thereby increase the value of the firm.

In this respect, recent research has identified three sources of conflict related to financial policy. The first problem stems from the separation of ownership and control. Professional managers who do not own a significant fraction of equity in the firm are likely to be more directly interested in maximizing their own "utility" than the value of the firm. This creates a conflict between managers and outside shareholders.

A second area of conflict involves stockholders and bondholders. Because the value of common stock equals the market value of the firm (that is, total assets) minus the value of its liabilities, managers can increase shareholder wealth by reducing the value of the bonds. This possibility is at the root of stockholder–bondholder conflicts.

Third, under certain circumstances, firms may have incentives to act in ways that conflict with the best interests of the individuals that do business with them. For example, an airline in financial distress may choose to reduce maintenance expense in order to improve short-run cash flow.

Stockholder–manager conflicts

Managers, like all other economic agents, are ultimately concerned with maximizing their own utility, subject to the constraints they face. Although management is legally mandated to act as the agent of shareholders, the laws are sufficiently vague that management has a good deal of latitude to act in its own behalf. This problem, together with the separation of ownership and control in the modern corporation, results in potential conflicts between the two parties. The agency conflict between managers and outside shareholders derives from three principal sources.[8]

The first conflict arises from management's tendency to consume some of the firm's resources in the form of various perquisites. But the problem of overconsumption of "perks" is not limited to corporate jets, fancy offices, and chauffeur-driven limousines. It also extends, with far greater consequences for shareholders, into corporate strategic decision-making. As Michael Jensen points out, managers have an incentive to expand the size of their firms beyond the point at which shareholder wealth is maximized.[9] Growth increases managers' power and perquisites by increasing the resources at their command. Because changes in compensation are positively related to sales growth, growth also tends to increase managerial compensation.[10]

As Jensen has argued persuasively, the problem of overexpansion is particularly severe in companies that generate substantial amounts of "free cash flow" – that is, cash flow in excess of that required to undertake all economically sound investments (those with positive net present values). Maximizing shareholder wealth dictates that free cash flow be paid out to shareholders. The problem is how to get managers to return excess cash to

---

7 The certification role of investment bankers is discussed in Clifford W. Smith, Jr., "Investment Banking and the Capital Acquisition Process," *Journal of Financial Economics*, 1986 and James R. Booth and Richard Smith, "Capital Raising, Underwriting and the Certification Hypothesis," *Journal of Financial Economics*, 1986.

8 The agency conflict is discussed in Michael C. Jensen and William H. Meckling, "Theory of the Firm: Managerial Behavior, Agency Costs and Ownership Structure," *Journal of Financial Economics*, October 1976, pp. 305–360.

9 Michael C. Jensen, "Agency Costs of Free Cash Flow, Corporate Finance, and Takeovers," *American Economic Review*, May 1986, pp. 323–329.

10 Evidence on this point is supplied by Kevin J. Murphy, "Corporate Performance and Managerial Remuneration: An Empirical Analysis," *Journal of Accounting and Economics*, April 1985, pp. 11–42.

the shareholders instead of investing it in projects with negative net present values or wasting it through organizational inefficiencies.

A second conflict arises from the fact that managers have a greater incentive to shirk their responsibilities as their equity interest falls. They will trade off the costs of putting in additional effort against the marginal benefits. With a fixed salary and a small equity claim, professional managers are unlikely to devote energy to the company equivalent to that put forth by an entrepreneur.

Finally, their own risk aversion can cause managers to forgo profitable investment opportunities. Although the risk of potential loss from an investment may be diversified in the capital markets, it is more difficult for managers to diversify the risks associated with losing one's salary and reputation. Forgoing profitable, but risky, projects amounts to the purchase by management of career insurance at shareholder expense.

Stockholder–bondholder conflicts

An important feature of corporate debt is that bondholders have prior but fixed claims on a firm's assets, while stockholders have limited liability for the firm's debt and unlimited claims on its remaining assets. In other words, stockholders have the option to "put" the firm to the bondholders if things go bad, but to keep the profits if the firm is successful. This option becomes more valuable as company cash flows increase in variability because the value of equity rises, and the value of debt declines, with increases in the volatility of corporate cash flows. If there is a significant amount of risky debt outstanding, the option-like character of equity gives shareholders an incentive to engage in risk-increasing activities – for example, highly risky projects – that have the potential for big returns. (Witness the behavior of many of the troubled Texas S & Ls.) Similarly, management can also reduce the value of pre-existing bonds and transfer wealth from current bondholders to stockholders by issuing a substantial amount of new debt, thereby raising the firm's financial risk.

Alternatively, if the firm is in financial distress, shareholders may pass up projects with positive net present values that involve added equity

investment because most of the payoffs go to bondholders. The failure to invest in such projects reduces the value of bondholder claims on the firm as well as the total value of the firm.

Non-investor stakeholder conflicts

The potential conflict between a company and its non-investor stakeholders can best be understood by viewing stakeholders as buying a set of implicit claims from the company.[11] For example, the manufacturer of a car, a pump, or a refrigerator is implicitly committed to supplying parts and service as long as the article lasts. Similarly, although managers typically have no formal employment contract, they often perceive an implicit contract that guarantees lifetime jobs in exchange for competence, loyalty, and hard work. Before deciding to carry a new product line, a retailer frequently receives promises from the manufacturer about delivery schedules, advertising, and future products and enhancements. Implicit claims are also sold to other stakeholders, such as suppliers and independent firms that provide repair services and manufacture supporting products.

EXAMPLES OF IMPLICIT CLAIMS BOUGHT BY STAKEHOLDERS

CUSTOMERS:
- continuing stream of service and parts
- durability
- performance/timeliness of delivery
- availability of complementary products and services

EMPLOYEES AND MANAGERS:
- safe work environment
- fair evaluation process
- opportunity for advancement
- lifetime employment in return for competence and loyalty

SUPPLIERS AND DISTRIBUTORS:
- advertising
- future products and enhancements

---

11 This section is based on Bradford Cornell and Alan C. Shapiro, "Corporate Stakeholders and Corporate Finance," *Financial Management*, April 1987, pp. 5–14.

These examples illustrate two key characteristics of implicit claims. First, they are too nebulous and depend too heavily upon external circumstances to be reduced to written contracts at reasonable cost. Second, because implicit claims cannot be reduced to writing, they cannot be unbundled from and traded independently of the goods and services the firm buys and sells.

In general terms, the firm is promising its stakeholders that it will make a "best efforts" attempt to satisfy them whatever happens in the future. This implicit claim clearly cannot be reduced to a legal agreement, but stakeholders' assessments of what such claims are worth are likely to be a key determinant of, for example, how much customers will pay for the company's products and the effort that employees, suppliers, and other stakeholders will make on behalf of the company.

The price stakeholders will pay for implicit claims depends on their expectations of future payoffs. In forming these expectations, stakeholders understand that it may turn out to be in the company's interest to renege on such claims after the fact; that is, absent other information about a firm, they will expect the firm to promise the maximum payout *ex ante*, but only to deliver the amount that maximizes the value of the firm *ex post*.[12] Firms can engage in this type of behavior because implicit claims have little legal standing. Typically, the firm can default on its implicit claims without going bankrupt. This means that corporate stakeholders such as customers, suppliers, and employees must look to the firm, not the courts, for assurance that their implicit claims will be honored.

Under these circumstances, stakeholders are frequently willing to pay a substantial premium for the claims of firms they trust. For example, IBM computers are purchased not because they offer the latest technology, longest warranties, or lowest prices, but because customers value the wide variety of implicit claims that IBM sells with its machines more highly than the implicit claims of smaller, competing manufacturers.

Because the payoffs on implicit claims are uncertain, even when the possibility of bankruptcy is remote, stakeholders who purchase implicit claims from the firm will seek to determine whether the firm has the organizational structure, management skills, and financial strength to make good on its implicit claims. Thus the value of these claims will be sensitive to information about the firm's financial condition.

Financially healthy firms typically have a strong incentive to honor their implicit claims. Myopic behavior on the part of the firm – for example, improving cash flow today by defaulting on implicit claims sold in the past – will damage the firm's reputation for quality products and reliable service, and thereby lower the price at which it can sell future implicit claims. Nevertheless, a firm having difficulty scraping up enough cash to pay its creditors may be tempted to cut corners in service and products. For such a firm, the long-run value of a strong reputation may be less important than generating enough cash to make it through the next day.

Recognizing these possibilities, stakeholders will pay less for the implicit claims of financially troubled firms. In practical terms, this means that a company in financial distress, or even one that may wind up in financial distress, will have to discount its product prices, pay more to its employees, and receive worse terms from its suppliers and distributors.[13] The net result is that companies that have difficulty convincing stakeholders of their ability or willingness to honor their implicit claims may be placed at a competitive disadvantage relative to their more financially secure rivals.

Thus, firms have clear-cut incentives to find ways of assuring the market that they will not engage in opportunistic behavior. Such mechanisms include things like the following: providing managers with incentives, such as stock options, to act in accordance with shareholder interests; bearing monitoring costs in the form of audits, specific reporting procedures and other surveillance methods; and including various restrictive convenants in bond and bank loan agreements.

The firm can also use its capital structure as a conflict management tool. Unfortunately, a financial policy designed to reduce one source of

12 Rational economic behavior implies that the firm will do whatever is in its self-interest to do after the fact. If all goes well, it will generally be in the firm's best interest to honor its commitments.

13 The costs of financial distress are elaborated on in Alan C. Shapiro and Sheridan Titman, "An Integrated Approach to Corporate Risk Management," *Midland Corporate Finance Journal*, Summer 1985, pp. 41–56.

conflict often opens the door to other conflicts. For instance, one way to lessen the opportunity of management to waste the firm's free cash flow is to reduce the scope of management discretion by issuing additional debt. Issuing more debt, however, increases potential stockholder-bondholder conflicts and also raises the probability of financial distress. On the other hand, adding equity to the capital structure will reduce conflicts between stockholders and bondholders but increase the likelihood of conflicts between management and stockholders over the disposition of free cash flow. It may also increase the government's share of the pie.

In short, any change in capital structure is likely to mitigate some problems and aggravate others. Managers must attempt to balance these effects in light of the firm's special characteristics. It is in this sense that it is meaningful to speak of financial policy for a growth company. The special characteristics of rapidly growing companies mean that some costs and conflicts are greater and others smaller than in the case of mature companies. Therefore, it makes sense first to discuss the distinctive features of a growth company and then to suggest how those features affect the choice of financial policy.

THE SPECIAL FEATURES OF GROWING COMPANIES

The most obvious sign of a rapidly growing company is its large appetite for cash. Even though income rises along with sales, cash flow is generally negative because the investment required to finance the growth in sales typically exceeds the current net operating cash flow. A company, or its division, usually begins to generate substantial free cash flow only after the business matures and sales growth slows. Therefore, the ability to locate potential sources of external funds and to arrange them in an attractive financial package are major factors affecting corporate growth. The absence of free cash flow also reduces the likelihood that this will be a source of conflict between management and shareholders.

The second prominent feature of growing companies is less obvious, but critical nonetheless in devising a financial plan. For a company to grow in value, not just in size, it must have access to investment opportunities with positive net present

values. These opportunities may be thought of as growth options.[14] Such options include the possibility of increasing the profitability of existing product lines as well as expanding into profitable new products or markets.

Growth options are typically the primary source of value in rapidly expanding firms. Such firms often have few tangible assets in place; their assets instead consist primarily of specialized knowledge and management skill. For example, Genentech, a genesplicing company, had a stock market value of over $3 billion in late 1986 even though earnings for the year were only $11 million, giving it a P/E ratio of over 270 to 1. Clearly, the market was valuing Genentech's future ability to capitalize on its research in areas such as anti-cancer therapy and blood clot dissolvers for heart attack victims.

A third key aspect of growth companies is that the market is likely to have a particularly difficult time in establishing their values. Unlike companies whose value depends primarily on familiar, straightforward projects, the value of a growth company depends on the value of growth options, for which there are no obvious comparables. Instead, such valuations must be based on expectations about future profits from yet-to-be-developed products (as in the case of Genentech) or novel market niches (as in the case of Federal Express). This difficulty in valuing growth options both exacerbates the credibility problem and increases the potential for conflicts among managers, investors, and non-investor stakeholders.

The credibility gap between management and investors is likely to be most pronounced in the case of growth companies because management in such cases will often have far better information about the future profitability of undeveloped products and untapped market niches. This greater possibility for important inside information increases the amount by which investors will discount the price of new corporate securities to compensate for their informational disadvantage.

---

14 The idea of growth options was introduced by Stewart C. Myers, "Determinants of Corporate Borrowing," *Journal of Financial Economics*, November 1977, pp. 138–147. For discussion of new techniques for valuing such options, see Volume 5 Number 1 of the *Midland Corporate Finance Journal*, which is devoted entirely to that subject.

The natural management response to this problem, which is to provide investors with additional information, is often not credible because such statements are likely to be self-serving. Nor is the provision of such information to outsiders a possible alternative in many cases, because going public with the information necessary to evaluate its investments could jeopardize the company's competitive position.

Investors must also cope with the problem of uncertainty about management's abilities and commitment. The problems of managerial shirking and misrepresentation, which are liable to exist in all firms, are especially critical in growth companies because the value of growth options is especially dependent on the performance of management. The higher the percentage of value accounted for by growth options, the worse these problems are likely to be (unless management has a sizeable equity stake in the company).

Bondholders' fears of being exploited are also magnified in the case of growth companies. Growth options often involve the possibility of future projects whose actual undertaking depends on how events unfold over time. Also, other things being equal, the riskier an investment the more valuable is an option on it. Taken together, these factors increase the risk to bondholders of opportunistic behavior on the part of shareholders of companies with substantial amounts of growth options.

Another problem for bondholders is that growth options typically have little value apart from the firm. The absence of a secondary market for such options limits their use as security for debt claims.

Stockholders and bondholders are not the only parties for whom the wider information gap besetting growth companies is an important problem. Non-investor stakeholders such as customers and suppliers must make "firm-specific investments" whose returns depend on management's ability to exploit growth options effectively. If the firm fails to expand and develop new products, those parties that chose to do business with the firm will suffer. To reassure these stakeholders, management must do more than simply promise to honor their implicit claims; it must find some means to "bond" those promises. These bonding mechanisms are particularly important for growth companies because, in most instances, management has not had the time to develop its reputation or the reputation for the firm's products.

FINANCING GROWTH COMPANIES

In the first two sections of this article, we presented a checklist of issues to guide the financial manager in his or her attempt to make financial choices that maximize the value of the firm. Some of these issues are more important for growth companies than others.

Taxes, for example, are primarily of concern to companies in the highest effective tax bracket. Companies with fairly stable or predictable incomes, and with little other means of shielding their income from taxes, know that they will be in the highest corporate tax bracket each year. Examples include consumer goods firms, utilities, some computer manufacturers, and packaged foods companies. Growth companies, by contrast, are typically unsure of their tax bracket because it is unclear whether they will have net taxable income in any given year. On average, therefore, the effective tax rate for these companies is significantly below the maximum corporate rate. Moreover, since the variability of profit is likely to be higher for a growth company, there is a lower probability that they will be able to make full use of the interest tax shield, particularly at high levels of debt. This means that the tax advantages of debt are less valuable for growth companies than for mature companies.[15]

Although growth companies are unlikely to be able to benefit from the tax advantages of debt, taxes may still play a role in their financing strategy. Specifically, low tax bracket growth companies may be able to use financing to transfer certain tax benefits to other companies that can more fully

---

15 There is another reason why the tax advantage of debt is unlikely to be significant for a growth company. Recall that Merton Miller has argued that debt will be issued in aggregate until the tax advantage at the corporate level of issuing more debt is fully offset by the higher returns demanded by investors who must pay tax on their interest receipts. Even if some tax advantage to debt remains, Miller's argument implies that only those firms that face the highest effective tax rates are likely to benefit from issuing more debt. Growth companies are unlikely to fall into this category.

utilize them in return for a lower effective cost of funds. For example, we saw earlier that low-tax-bracket companies may be able to raise funds at a lower after-tax cost with preferred stock than with debt. Similarly, leasing (rather than buying) assets allows a growth company that isn't sufficiently profitable to make current use of all its depreciation deductions to transfer these deductions to investors in higher tax brackets; in return it gets financing with a lower effective interest rate.

As discussed earlier, there are two reasons for designing innovative securities: (1) to satisfy unmet market demand for a particular security with a unique risk/return trade-off; and (2) to solve specific incentive problems and resolve potential conflicts. Only the second reason is likely to be a reliable source of value for growth companies. As also noted earlier, unmet demands for new securities are unlikely to persist for long in a competitive financial marketplace. Furthermore, a growth company may be at a disadvantage in introducing innovative securities. Because of the relatively large credibility gap that faces growth companies, investors are likely to be especially wary of new securities from such companies that promise unique risk/return trade-offs. Fearing that these securities may be designed to exploit their ignorance, investors are likely to discount them more heavily, thereby negating the benefits of innovation.

Increasing liquidity and reducing transaction costs are potentially useful ways to increase the value of a firm. However, the benefits of these actions are apt to be smaller for growth companies. Growth companies are likely to attract investors who are more interested in long-run capital appreciation. Such investors typically follow a buy-and-hold strategy, so that the benefits of increasing liquidity or reducing transaction costs are likely to be minimal. When weighed against the costs of increasing liquidity or lowering transaction costs, therefore, such measures appear to be less beneficial for growth companies than for more mature companies.

The credibility gap and the problem of financing growth companies

Growth companies, then, are not likely to have a comparative advantage in creating value by dividing up the cash flow pie. By contrast, measures designed to bridge the credibility gap are likely to be particularly valuable for growth companies. Both investor and non-investor stakeholders will be more uncertain about the future prospects of a growth company than about the prospects of a more mature firm. Measures the firm can take to resolve this uncertainty will both raise the price that investors are willing to pay for its securities and reduce potential conflicts among the various corporate stakeholders.

The problem of credibility for growth companies is so pervasive that it affects all aspects of their financing. Perhaps the best way to introduce the problem is to consider a growing firm that needs new funds to exercise a growth option. Assume the firm is making a straightforward choice of debt or equity. To make the example concrete, suppose the option is the chance to invest in the development of a new software package for word processing.

If the firm goes to the equity market today to finance development of the product, credibility will be a serious issue. How are investors to know exactly what the product will look like, and whether management will be capable of producing the product on schedule, effectively marketing it, and enhancing and supporting it? Because of this uncertainty, the firm has an incentive to delay exercising its growth option until investors become better informed.

Competitive conditions, however, provide an incentive for early exercise. Because these options are often shared with other competitors and cannot generally be traded, a company that waits to exercise a shared growth option – such as the chance to enter a new market or to invest in a new technology – may find that competitors have already seized the opportunity. For instance, a software firm that delays developing its new word processing program may find that, by the time the program ships, customers are committed to a competing product. (The problem is analogous to deciding whether to exercise an option on a dividend-paying stock before maturity; you preserve the option by waiting but forgo the dividend.)

The message here is that companies must structure their financing to remain flexible enough to exercise growth options at the opportune moment. In this regard, future flexibility may be as important as current flexibility. Many strategically important investments – such as investments in R&D, factory automation, a brand name, or a distribution network – are often but the first link in a chain of subsequent investment decisions. The company must be prepared to exercise each of these related growth options in order to fully exploit the value of the initial investment. Moreover, stakeholders will condition the price they are willing to pay for the company's implicit claims today on the company's financial capacity to exercise these growth options in the future and provide them with the services and products they expect.

For example, if our software firm decides it must have the funds today to retain its flexibility, then it must issue equity at a big discount or go to the debt market. As noted earlier, the discount on debt will be much smaller because the cash flows received by creditors are less sensitive to the performance of the firm. However, there is a cost to issuing debt which is likely to be particularly great for growing firms.

First, the cost of financial distress is apt to be particularly large for growing firms. As we have seen, much of the value of a growing company comes from growth options which, as also noted, are highly intangible assets. Such intangible assets will rapidly depreciate in value if the firm experiences – or even seems likely to experience – financial trouble. Because the probability of financial distress increases with financial leverage, the expected cost of financial distress increases with the amount of debt issued.

Recognizing the costs of financial distress, creditors of growing firms require detailed covenants to protect themselves against potential managerial opportunism and incompetence. These covenants are likely to be especially restrictive for highly-leveraged growth companies because these companies, by their nature, are engaged in high-risk activities. Although restrictive loan covenants avoid many of the potential conflicts associated with debt financing – by limiting management actions that are potentially harmful to bondholders – they also may turn out to be costly to shareholders because they constrain management's choice of operating, financial, and investment policies and reduce its capacity to respond to changes in the business environment. For example, lenders may veto certain high-risk projects with positive net present values because of the added risk they would have to bear without a corresponding increase in their own expected returns.

The opportunity cost associated with the loss of operating and investment flexibility will be especially high for firms with substantial growth options because such firms must be able to respond quickly to continually changing product and factor markets. All else being equal, therefore, the high costs of financial distress, together with the costs associated with resolving the conflicts of interest between shareholders and bondholders, reduce the optimal amount of debt in a growth firm's capital structure. For example, in explaining why his company shunned debt, the chief financial officer of Tandem Computer commented, "We were a young company competing with the likes of IBM. Not taking on debt was a marketing decision because we might not get customers if we seemed financially shaky."[16] By contrast, established firms operating in stable markets can afford more debt since their competitive stance will be less compromised by the restrictions and delays associated with high financial leverage.

Faced with this unsatisfactory trade-off between the steep discount on new equity and the restrictive covenants associated with issuing straight public debt, growth companies are well advised to look elsewhere for funds. One place to start is with a commercial bank.

The role of bank loans in financing growth companies

A banking relationship may solve many of the problems associated with public debt. The potential advantages of a bank credit are twofold: First, the firm can more readily custom-tailor a set of terms and conditions in face-to-face negotiations with its bankers than by trying to deal with a large number of smaller investors. Second, renegotiating certain covenants in response to changing circumstances is less cumbersome with a bank loan. The flexibility, discretion, and durability of these arrangements is what is termed a "banking relationship."

---

16 This statement appeared in Kate Ballen, "Has the Debt Binge Gone Too Far?" *Fortune*, April 25, 1988, pp. 87–94.

Richard K. Goeltz, Vice President-Finance of Seagram & Sons, Inc., makes this point as follows:

There is an important advantage in dealing with individual bankers rather than an amorphous capital market. One can explain a problem or need to account officers at a few institutions. Direct communications with the purchasers of [bonds] are almost impossible. These investors, as is the case for most public issues, have little feeling of commitment to the borrower or sense of continuity . . . If the borrower can modify the terms and conditions of the former more easily and inexpensively than the latter, then the bank loan will be less costly, even if the effective interest rates are identical.[17]

The advantages of a banking relationship to a growing company stem from the personal nature of the relationship between borrower and lender. Presumably, bankers, who deal directly with the borrower, have lower costs of monitoring client activities than do bondholders, who are anonymous (in the case of bearer bonds) or are not interested, as are banks, in a long-term relationship with the borrower.

Some recent research supports this assumption. The basic argument of this work is that banks play the part of delegated monitors who check on the behavior of the firm's managers.[18] Specifically, it is claimed that banks have a comparative cost advantage in information gathering and monitoring relative not only to investors in public capital markets, but relative to other financial institutions as well. This comparative advantage arises in large part from banks' ongoing deposit history with the borrower and from the short-term repeat lending activity in which banks specialize.[19]

When a firm is unable to make interest payments on time or when its financial statements indicate problems, the banker's first response is to examine the firm's condition more closely. Such examination is particularly valuable for growth companies because much of their value arises from options that will be lost if the firm cannot get financing on sufficiently flexible terms. If the banker finds that the firm's prospects are promising, he can reschedule the firm's payments, waive a covenant, or even increase the amount of the bank's loan.

The relationship with a bank can also reduce a growth company's information problem with other investors. The view that bankers, as insiders, have better information about the firm's prospects than outsiders and are better able to supervise its behavior implies that the loan approval process should convey two pieces of positive information about the borrowing firm to outside investors: (1) the bank believes the firm is sound, and (2) the bank will supervise corporate management to ensure that it behaves properly. In support of this argument, a recently published study by Christopher James (presented in a later article in this issue) documents a consistently positive stock market response to companies announcing the arrangement of loan commitments from commercial banks.[20]

Another important aspect of a banking relationship is the provision of continuous access to funds. In the typical commercial banking relationship, the bank can be viewed as writing options for its loan customer. Through such devices as credit lines or lending commitments, the borrower can choose the timing and the amount of the loan; the borrower can often prepay or refinance the loan at a nominal fee. Most important, the bank makes an implicit, and sometimes explicit, commitment to provide funds in times when the borrower finds them difficult to obtain from other sources. This flexibility is critical for growth companies because the timing of their investment program is so difficult to forecast.

Despite the advantages of bank debt, banks cannot supply all the financing required by growth companies. The difficulties are three: First, bank

17   Richard Karl Goeltz, "The Corporate Borrower and the International Capital Markets", manuscript dated March 6, 1984, p. 5.
18   The information production and monitoring services of banks are discussed, respectively, by Tim Campbell and William Kracaw, "Information Production, Market Signalling, and the Theory of Financial Intermediation," *Journal of Finance*, September 1980, pp. 863–882 and Douglas W. Diamond, "Financial Intermediation and Delegated Monitoring," *Review of Economic Studies*, August 1984, pp. 393–414.
19   For a good review of this literature, see Mitchell Berlin, "Bank Loans and Marketable Securities: How Do Financial Contracts Control Borrowing Firms?" *Business Review*, Federal Reserve Bank of Philadelphia, July/August 1987, pp. 9–18.

20   See Christopher James and Peggy Wier, "Are Bank Loans Different?," *Journal of Applied Corporate Finance* Vol. 1 No. 2, which is based in turn on Christopher James, "Some Evidence on the Uniqueness of Bank Loans," *Journal of Financial Economics*, 19 (1987).

debt is still debt, which retains many restrictive features. Second, like any form of debt, bank loans increase the probability of financial distress, with all its adverse consequences for firms trying to sell implicit claims. Third, from the standpoint of the creditor, financing high-risk investments such as growth options is not attractive. The creditor bears all the downside risk without sharing in the upside benefits. Growth options also make poor collateral; their value in liquidation is usually nil.

The role of venture capital in financing growth companies

In the case of start-ups, whose assets are comprised primarily if not exclusively of growth options, bank loans are virtually unobtainable. Venture capital has evolved as a solution to these problems. In effect, venture capitalists provide private equity. But, in return, they demand a much closer relationship, more control, and a significantly higher expected rate of return.

Venture capitalists also typically demand a financial structure that shifts a great deal of risk onto company management. In order to ensure that the founders remain committed to the business, venture capital firms try to structure the deal so that management benefits only if the firm succeeds. This usually involves modest salaries for managers, with most compensation tied to profits and the appreciation in the value of their stock.

Moreover, the venture capitalist usually buys preferred stock convertible into common shares when and if the company goes public. Besides giving the venture capitalist a prior claim on the assets of the firm in liquidation, one obvious effect of using preferred stock instead of straight equity is to transfer risk from the venture capitalist to the entrepreneur. But, this is probably not the primary reason for using convertible preferred because there are no clear net gains to the venture capitalist from simply transferring risk; if the founders have to bear more risk, they will raise the price to the venture capitalist of acquiring a given stake in the firm.

As William Sahlman argues (in the article following this one), two more likely reasons for using a financial structure that shifts a major share of the risk to the founders are as follows: (1) to force the founders to signal how strongly they believe in the forecasts contained in their business plan; and (2) to strengthen the founders' incentive to make the company succeed by ensuring that they benefit greatly only if they meet their projections. By their willingness to accept these terms, the founders increase investors' confidence in the numbers contained in the business plan. The venture capitalist, therefore, is willing to pay a higher price for his equity stake. The financial structure also motivates management to work harder and thereby increases the probability that a favorable outcome will occur.

To further limit their downside risk, venture capitalists also rarely give a start-up company all the money it needs at once. Typically, there are several stages of financing. At each stage, the venture capitalists will give the firm enough money to get it to the next product or market development milestone. By staging the commitment of capital, the venture capitalist gains the option of abandoning the project or renegotiating a lower price for future purchases of equity in line with new information.

In return for this option, the venture capitalist is willing to accept a smaller ownership share for a given investment. The founders benefit from this financing structure because it means giving up a smaller share of ownership for the needed funding. If the venture progresses according to plan, the founders will be able to bring in future capital with less dilution of their ownership share. Staged financing thus provides the founders with the option to raise capital in the future at a higher valuation.

Both of these venture capital practices, the use of convertible preferred stock and staged capital commitment, can be seen as means of overcoming the "credibility gap" that confronts all growth companies in raising capital.

The role of private placements in financing growth companies

Although bank loans and venture capital offer the benefit of flexibility that comes with a close relationship, they are both expensive. The interest rates on bank loans are generally higher than the rates on straight debt, and venture capitalists demand a high rate of return for the risks they bear and the time they invest. For this reason, growth companies have an incentive to issue securities despite the problems discussed earlier. The key is to design such securities so as to minimize the credibility gap that leads to a large discount on equity and to restrictive covenants on debt.

A growing firm that needs flexible debt financing may be able to secure such funds by way of a private placement. As in the case of bank debt, dealing directly with the ultimate investor opens the possibility for negotiation and renegotiation of the lending terms. In addition, the firm may be able to provide a few creditors with sensitive strategic information that it would not want to make publicly available.

Unfortunately, there is one major complication that arises when growing firms attempt private placements. Because privately placed securities are difficult to sell prior to maturity, investors will want to be assured at the outset that payments will be made over the life of the security. It is just such assurances that are difficult for growth companies to provide. This produces an incentive for the creditors to protect themselves with restrictive covenants and thereby leads to the same problem that exists with publicly issued debt.

The role of convertible securities in financing growth companies

Another alternative to straight debt is to issue bonds or preferred stock that are convertible into common stock at the bondholder's option. If the conversion features are set properly, convertible securities can overcome some of the problems that cause investors to demand strict covenants on straight debt. Convertibles offer investors participation in the high payoffs to equity when the firm does better than expected while simultaneously offering them the downside protection of a fixed-income security when the firm's value falls. If a firm with convertibles is expected to undertake high-risk projects, the value of the conversion option will increase (because stock price volatility increases an option's value), offsetting to some extent a decline in the value of the fixed income portion.

As Michael Brennan and Eduardo Schwartz have argued, this offset means that the value of an appropriately designed convertible should be relatively insensitive to the risk of the issuing

company.[21] This feature of convertibles is particularly valuable when investors and management disagree about the risk of a company, as is likely to be the case with rapidly growing firms. Consider the case of company which investors believe to be very risky, but which management, with privileged information, believes is only moderately risky. Assume further that management is confronted with the choice of paying a coupon rate of 12 percent on straight debt when companies that management deems of comparable risk are paying only 10 percent. In such a case, as Brennan and Schwartz illustrate, management is likely to be able to sell a convertible bond issue with the same conversion premium but only a slightly higher coupon rate (say, 8 percent relative to 7.75 percent) than the moderately risky company.

The reason, again, that the effect of the divergence in risk assessment is much less for the convertible than for straight debt is that the value of convertibles is much less sensitive to changes in risk; or, to put it a little differently, the implicit warrant in a convertible protects bondholders from large changes in risk. Thus, if the market overestimates the risk of a small growth company (and thereby undervalues the company's straight debt), it will overvalue the convertible's call option feature. In this sense, convertible securities are well suited for coping with differing assessments of a company's risk.[22]

---

21 Michael Brennan and Eduardo Schwartz, "The Case for Convertibles," *Chase Financial Quarterly*, Spring 1982, pp. 27–46: reprinted in this issue.
22 A convertible issue may also provide more advantageous financing terms if management believes the market is undervaluing the company's stock. Convertible securities can be seen as an alternative to equity which allows the firm to issue common stock at a higher price, albeit on a deferred basis, thereby avoiding current market fears that management has chosen to sell equity because it is overpriced. Even if the call option embedded in the convertible security is underpriced due to the credibility gap, when the true information is ultimately revealed, and the issue is converted into common stock, the firm will receive a higher price than it would have received had it sold equity directly.

Of course, if management truly believes that the stock market is undervaluing the company's shares, the least expensive financing option would be to issue straight debt. Thus, convertibles are the best choice in this situation only if straight debt is inappropriate under the circumstances, for example, because of the added restrictive covenants that would come along with it.

The problem with convertibles for growth firms, however, is that the very flexibility they afford investors may actually reduce management's financing flexibility. Once issued, a convertible bond is a hybrid security which effectively becomes an equity claim when times are good (and the value of the firm appreciates) but a straight debt claim when the value of the firm falls. It is, of course, precisely when times are bad that debt can cause problems for growth companies short of tangible assets. At the same time, however, the coupon reduction on convertibles relative to straight debt may significantly reduce the debt service burden and, with it, the likelihood of financial distress. Also, the less restrictive covenants associated with convertibles provide management with more flexibility in responding to unforeseen events than does straight debt.

Corporate stakeholders and the financial policy of growth companies

Capitalizing on growth options involves more than developing a new product or exploiting a new market niche. The company must develop relationships with customers, suppliers, and distributors, all of whom make "firm-specific investments" when they do business with the company. In making these commitments, as we argued before, customers and other stakeholders are in effect purchasing implicit claims for timely delivery, product support, future enhancements, and the like. The prices they pay for these claims depends on how confident they are that the company will be able to honor them.

Established firms can use reputation to "bond" their implicit claims. Customers realize that if IBM were to fail to stand behind one of its machines, the resulting damage to IBM's reputation would be very costly. They understand, therefore, that it is not in IBM's best interest to default on its implicit claims.

Unfortunately, this bonding mechanism is not available to growth companies, which by definition have not had time to develop a reputation. Therefore, growing firms must turn to alternative mechanisms for bonding implicit claims. One possibility is to use financial policy.

In a capital market with information freely available to all and without material transaction costs, financial policy would not play an important role in the firm's effort to convince stakeholders that it will honor its implicit claims. Because a company can always go to the capital markets whenever it needs to finance its growth options, all the company has to do is to convince stakeholders that it has a profitable sequence of growth options. Stakeholders will then take it for granted that the firm will go to the capital market whenever it comes time to exercise a growth option.

However, this "perfect markets" view overlooks the credibility gap problem that we have stressed throughout this paper. A growth company always faces a significant problem whenever it goes to the capital market. This problem is exacerbated if the company even *appears* likely to face financial distress. Under these circumstances, financial policy can play an important role in bonding implicit claims.

The problem from a stakeholder standpoint is as follows: If a growing firm develops a cash shortage or faces financial distress, it may be in the company's interest to default on implicit claims rather than go to the capital market. Even if the company intends to honor its implicit claims, the disruption to its operations caused by financial difficulty may not allow the company to provide stakeholders with their expected payoffs. For this reason, the firm must convince stakeholders up-front that it has the financial resources to see projects through to completion; otherwise they will not make commitments to the firm.

To reassure stakeholders, growth companies generally should maintain substantial financial resources in the form of unused debt capacity, large quantities of liquid assets, excess lines of credit, and access to a broad range of fund sources. This financial flexibility helps preserve operating flexibility. A firm that has left itself with financial reserves for contingencies can respond to an adverse turn of events by allowing long-term considerations to prevail. By contrast, a firm with a high debt-to-equity ratio, minimal liquidity, and few other financial resources might have to sacrifice its long-term competitive position to generate cash for creditors.

The critical importance of financial flexibility for growth companies

The ability to marshall substantial financial resources also signals competitors, actual and potential, that the firm will not be an easy target. Consider the alternative, a firm that is highly leveraged, with no excess lines of credit or cash reserves. In such a case, a competitor can move into the firm's market and gain market share with less fear of retaliation. In order to retaliate – by cutting price, say, or by increasing advertising expenditures – the firm will need more money. Because it has no spare cash and can't issue additional debt at a reasonable price, it will have to go to the equity market. But we have already seen that firms issuing new equity face a credibility gap. The credibility problem will be particularly acute when the firm is trying to fend off a competitive attack. Thus, a firm that lacks financial reserves faces a Hobson's choice: Acquiesce in the competitive attack or raise funds on unattractive terms.

Similarly, when opportunity knocks, a firm with substantial financial resources will be better positioned to take advantage of it than a firm with few financial resources and bound by tightly drawn debt covenants. Thus, firms with valuable growth options should place a high priority on financial flexibility.

In the attempt to preserve financing flexibility, however, management must perform what amounts to a balancing act. Recall that corporate managers historically have demonstrated a strong preference to fund new investment with the least risky sources available: first, retained earnings, next, straight debt, and, last (and only if necessary), common stock. This financial "pecking order," as Stewart Myers argues, reflects the attempt to avoid the greater information costs (in the form of larger price discounts) of riskier offerings. By adhering to the pecking order and overcoming one problem, however, management may well be creating another. The reason: a firm that issues debt today thereby increases the probability that it "must" raise equity tomorrow – perhaps on very unfavorable terms.

In short, a firm that needs to raise funds today faces a trade-off. If sources low on the pecking order (internal funds and debt) are used in the current period, then current financing costs appear to be low. But, as a result, the firm faces the hidden opportunity cost of being pushed up the pecking order in the uncertain future and thus being forced to issue more costly equity.[23] Conversely, if the firm reverses the pecking order and instead issues equity in the current period (and the funds are held as cash), then current costs may be higher, but the option to move "down" the pecking order in the future may actually provide the firm with a cheaper source of funds overall.

For growth companies, then, beginning with a substantial equity endowment and thus preserving the option to move "down" the pecking order is likely to be the favored strategy. A balance sheet heavily weighted toward equity, and perhaps including large cash balances at various times, should provide growth firms with the kind of financing flexibility necessary to exercise their "growth options."

As we saw earlier, however, too much financial flexibility may also create its own problems. For one thing, there is a tax penalty associated with investing corporate funds in marketable securities because the interest on these securities is taxed twice, once at the corporate level and again at the investor level. But potentially more important, companies with excess financial resources are more insulated from the discipline exerted by the financial marketplace.

On the other hand, the weakening of management incentives that tends to come with financial "slack" is most likely to be a problem for mature companies where managers have much smaller equity stakes than those typically held by managers of growth companies. Thus, although new equity for growth companies may be expensive to raise, providing the management of such firms with an "equity cushion" is much less likely to introduce some of the incentive problems that come with corporate age and prosperity. With growth options to finance and free cash flow generally negative, the managements of growth companies have a clear incentive to husband their funds wisely. Moreover, the knowledge that such managements typically have major equity stakes in their firms provides comfort to outside equity investors that they often do not have with large established companies.

---

23 As mentioned earlier, the financing costs referred to here are added discounts due to the credibility gap. These are costs the company must pay in addition to the normal cost of capital associated with the securities being issued.

FINANCING GROWTH COMPANIES: SUMMING UP

Despite all the complexities involved in financing a growth company, our suggestions for policy are relatively simple and straightforward. First, complicated strategies designed to divide the cash flow pie in unusual ways are unlikely to be profitable exercises for growth companies. Younger and rapidly growing firms whose credibility is not yet established are at a comparative disadvantage in this arena relative to mature firms such as General Electric or General Motors.

Second, for a rapidly expanding company, the primary role of finance should be to preserve the growth options that are its principal source of value. Growth options, which are opportunities to undertake future investments, are different from on-going projects in that their cash requirements and their future payoffs are generally more uncertain. This uncertainty compounds the credibility problem that any company faces whenever it issues new securities (Is management selling securities now, investors will ask, because it knows they are overvalued?). In addition, the potential conflicts between managers and investors, between managers and non-investor stakeholders (such as customers and suppliers), and different groups of investors (such as stockholders and bondholders) are aggravated when the company's future is hazy. These credibility problems and potential conflicts have the effect of increasing the discount at which the company can sell its securities or, alternatively, reducing the flexibility of the terms on which securities can be sold. The task confronting the financing manager is to minimize the discount while still providing the financial flexibility to allow the company to exercise its growth options at the opportune time.

One way to improve the terms of this trade-off is to develop a close working relationship with the providers of funds. This means that a banking relationship, or some other source of "private" debt, may be particularly important for those growth companies with enough tangible assets to support moderate amounts of debt. In the case of start-ups, venture capital – probably structured in

the form of convertible preferred – most likely will be the principal source. In both of these cases, the credibility problem is partly resolved by the close relationship between management and the provider of funds that allows for the exchange of information on a confidential basis. Moreover, these funding sources can negotiate financing terms which offer management considerable financial and operating flexibility while at the same applying strong pressure for performance. And by their willingness to accept such terms, management can in turn signal its confidence to the providers of capital.

If a growth firm is able to tap the public capital markets in an economical manner, the security should be carefully designed to minimize the credibility and conflict problems. For instance, convertible securities, by giving bondholders an option to convert to equity, reduce the incentive for managers to exploit bondholders by undertaking riskier-than-expected projects. They also reduce the valuation consequences of differences of opinion between management and investors about the riskiness of the company. These considerations increase the flexibility of the terms at which debt will be provided and reduce the discount demanded by investors.

Finally, a growing company cannot make financial policy without considering its non-investor stakeholders. If customers, suppliers, and distributors feel that the firm is so financially weak that its longevity is in question, they will not make the investment required to develop a relationship with the firm. Without such commitment from noninvestor stakeholders, the firm is likely to fail before it can fully develop its growth options. For this reason, a growing firm must demonstrate that it has financial strength and flexibility. Thus, the analysis in this article points to one unavoidable conclusion: A growth company needs a good deal of equity upfront (despite the steep discount at which it might be forced to issue its securities); debt is to be used with care and moderation.

CHAPTER 18

Are Banks Still Special? New Evidence on Their Role in the Corporate Capital-Raising Process

Christopher James and David C. Smith (University of Florida)

Early studies of corporate financing choices focus almost exclusively on the type of financial claims firms use to finance their investments. Typically these studies emphasize the costs and benefits of debt versus equity financing with the aim of determining a firm's optimal leverage ratio. In the past decade, financial economists have turned their attention to the costs and benefits associated with different providers of funds and, in general, to the choice between public and private sources of financing. Recent studies have attempted to provide answers to questions such as: What are the main factors that influence the choice between using privately placed debt and issuing publicly traded debt? Are corporate bonds and commercial paper close substitutes for bank borrowing for certain types of borrowers? Beyond the general choice between public and private claims, the question also arises as to whether the identity of a particular type of private lender matters. For example, are commercial loans from finance companies close substitutes for bank loans or are bank loans a unique source of debt financing?

How we answer this last question has important implications for both corporate financial policy and bank regulatory policy. For example, while it is well established that small, privately held companies benefit most from private financing, it is less clear how medium- and large-size firms should choose between private and public financing. For these firms, an understanding of the costs and benefits of private debt financing and the advantages of using certain types of lenders can lower the overall cost of capital. From a bank regulatory perspective, it is important to know whether banks are a unique or special source of financing for businesses. For if bank loans are special, then disruptions to the banking sector can reduce corporate investment and general macroeconomic activity.[1] In fact, one potential role for banks is to provide a liquidity cushion in the economy when public capital markets fail. But if public or other private debt financing sources are good substitutes for bank borrowing, then adverse changes in the banking sector will have little effect on overall investment.

Understanding the importance of lender identity can also help explain the persistent importance of private debt financing in the United States. As shown in Figure 18.1, while U.S. banks' share of total corporate financing has declined over the past two decades, the fraction of all loans (including loans from foreign banks, insurance companies, and finance companies) of total debt outstanding has held steady at around 40%. Thus despite the

---

[1] For instance, a set of theories stress the so-called bank "lending channel" as an important conduit of monetary policy stress. See Anil Kashap and Jeremy Stein "Monetary Policy and Bank Lending," in *Monetary Policy* edited by N. Gregory Mankiw, 1994 University of Chicago Press, Chicago.

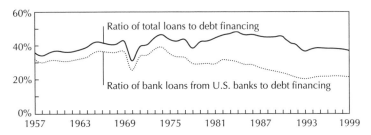

Figure 18.1 US Bank Loans and Total Loans as a Proportion of Debt Financing*
**Source*: Federal Reserve Flow of Funds, various years.

widespread perception of an increase in the importance of public debt financing, private lenders continue to be an important source of financing for U.S. businesses.

In this article, we review recent evidence on whether there is anything special or unique about bank loan financing versus public debt or commercial paper financing. We also review the evidence concerning whether bank lending is different from lending by finance companies and other private lenders. Our point of departure is an empirical study by one of the present authors entitled "Some Evidence on the Uniqueness of Bank Loans" and published in the *Journal of Financial Economics* in 1987.[2] That study (hereafter referred to as James (1987)) reported the surprising finding that the stock market responds positively on average (and in a very strong majority of cases) to announcements of new bank lending agreements. This finding offers a pointed contrast to the neutral or negative responses that have been found to accompany announcements of almost all other kinds of securities offerings, including private placements of debt, straight public debt, preferred stock, convertible debt, convertible preferred, and common stock.[3] We update the earlier article by reviewing a number of recent studies that examine whether the market reaction to loan announcements varies

with the types of borrowers, the types of loans, and the identity of the private lender.

Overall, these recent studies confirm the earlier finding of a positive market response to announcements of bank loan agreements. Nevertheless, there is also evidence that the market responds favorably to loan announcements by other types of lenders, thus suggesting that banks may not play a unique role in corporate financing.[4] It turns out that these nonbank lenders, such as finance companies, offer loans with characteristics similar to bank loans. But, as we point out later, the fact that banks continue to be the predominant providers of commitment-based loans suggests that banks have a comparative advantage in providing these types of loans.

The positive stock price reaction to new loan agreements raises another intriguing question: If bank loans are good news and public debt issues are bad news for stock market investors, why do so many companies issue publicly traded debt? The obvious answer is that for some borrowers, at least in certain circumstances, bank borrowing is more expensive than borrowing in public debt markets. To better understand the value added by banks and other private lenders, several recent studies investigate whether stock price reactions to loan announcements vary with the characteristics of the borrower or the type of loan being made. In general, these studies suggest that private lenders add the greatest value for so-called "informationally-intensive"

2 Christopher M. James, "Some Evidence on the Uniqueness of Bank Loans," *Journal of Financial Economics*, 1987, 19. A practitioner version of the study by Christopher James and Peggy Weir, entitled "Are Bank Loans Different? Some Evidence from the Stock Market," was published in this journal the following year (Summer 1988).

3 See for example, Clifford Smith's article entitled "Raising Capital: Theory and Evidence," *Midland Corporate Finance Journal* (Spring 1986).

4 See Dianna Preece and Donald Mullineaux "Monitoring by Financial Intermediaries: Banks vs. Nonbanks," *Journal of Financial Services Research*, 1994, 8 and Matthew Billett, Mark Flannery and Jon Garfinkel, "The Effect of Lender Identity on the Borrowing Firm's Equity Returns," *Journal of Finance*, 1995, 50.

Table 18.1 Comparing Bank-dependent Firms to Firms with Public Debt Based on a Sample of 250 Publicly Traded firms from 1980 to 1993*

	Bank-dependent firms		Firms with public debt	
	Mean	**Median**	**Mean**	**Median**
Assets (in 1980 $ millions)	356	55	2585	463
Leverage	.32	.29	.51	.41
Interest Coverage	17.16	4.83	5.79	3.37
Market Value Assets/Book Value Assets	1.35	1.19	1.32	1.14
Volatility in Stock Returns	2.9%	2.5%	2.7%	2.1%
Cash and Marketable Securities/Assets	.093	.052	.075	.045

*From Joel Houston and Christopher James, "Do Relationship have Limits?: Banking Relationships, Financial Constraints and Investment" December 1999, Forthcoming in *Journal of Business*.

borrowers – borrowers who face the greatest potential information problems when issuing public securities. Indeed, as we will argue below, firms seem to borrow privately when they are most likely to be undervalued by the market and turn to public financing when they are overvalued.

In the pages that follow, we start by reviewing the reasons why the identity of a firm's lenders might affect the value of corporate borrowers; and, in so doing, we review recent research on the main factors that appear to influence the choice between public and private debt financing. Next, we review important new studies of the stock market response to loan announcements and discuss the implications of these findings for the role of banks in the capital-raising process. In the final section, we focus on the characteristics of bank loan contracts and discuss why banks may have a comparative advantage in providing these types of loans.

WHY COMPANIES SHOULD CARE WHO THEIR LENDER IS

There are at least four good reasons why firms might care about who provides them with financing. First, private lenders may be better informed about the future prospects of the borrowing firm than investors in public debt or equity markets. If potential investors in new public debt issues are uncertain about the value of the securities the firm is issuing (while private lenders are confident in the company's ability to service at least a short term loan), they will require a

premium for bearing this risk, thus raising the cost of public financing relative to private financing. Second, private financing may involve greater monitoring – and, if problems arise, more active intervention – by lenders, which can serve to reduce agency conflicts that arise between the various claimants of debt-financed companies. The better control of conflicts provided by private debt contracts can lower the return that investors require for supplying funds. Third, private debt contracts may be easier to renegotiate or restructure than publicly traded debt contracts, which tends to lower financial distress costs. Finally, there may be differences in the transaction and flotation costs associated with issuing public as opposed to private debt and equity claims. For example, if there are significant economies of scale in issuing public securities, then firms with large financing needs will find it less expensive to borrow in public markets than borrowing privately.

Empirical studies of the mix of private versus public debt suggest that all four factors influence the extent of a firm's reliance on private financing. For example, in an article forthcoming in the *Journal of Business*, Joel Houston and Chris James report the results of their study of the private and public debt structure of 250 publicly traded companies over the period 1980–1993.[5] Using detailed information from the companies' financial statements, their study was able to determine the percentage of

5 Joel Houston and Christopher James, "Do Relationships Have Limits?: Banking Relationships, Financial Constraints and Investment," December 1999, Forthcoming in *Journal of Business*.

borrowing that comes from public debt, bank debt, and other types of private debt. As summarized in Table 18.1, firms that relied primarily on bank financing (so-called "bank-dependent" firms) were on average smaller, younger, less highly levered, and more likely to hold liquid assets (cash and marketable securities) than firms with public debt outstanding. Perhaps more important, the study also found that the level of investment spending by bank-dependent firms was more sensitive to the firm's internally generated cash flows – that is, for example, when operating cash flows declined, the drop in investment was proportionately greater – than in the case of firms with public debt. These results are consistent with the argument that bank-dependent firms face higher costs of external financing (arising from information or potential agency problems) than firms with public debt outstanding.

Public debt issues typically involve flotation costs that include investment banker fees, registration and filing fees, and other transactions costs. In a recent study published in the *JFE*, Sudha Krishnaswami, Paul Spindt, and Venkat Subramanian examined the importance of flotation, information, and agency costs in determining the mix of public and private debt for publicly traded firms.[6] In their paper, "private debt" refers to all forms of long-term debt that are not publicly traded, including bank loans and private placements. Krishnaswami et al. begin by noting the conventional wisdom that the fixed component of flotation costs is considerably larger for public debt issues than for private issues, thus giving public debt issues greater economies of scale. In making this point, they cite a study of the private placement market that maintains that public issues are only cost-effective when issue size exceeds $100 million.[7] Consistent with this observation, Krishnaswami et al. find that larger firms, and firms with larger average issue sizes, rely more heavily on public debt financing.

More interesting are Krishnaswami et al.'s findings that bear on how agency costs affect the choice of public versus private debt. The two agency problems that affect a firm's debt structure are known as *asset substitution* and *underinvestment*. The asset substitution problem stems from the incentives of companies with debt outstanding to substitute higher-risk for lower-risk investments. Shareholders gain by such substitutions since they receive the upside gains from the riskier projects while bondholders bear the losses if the project is unsuccessful. Faced with the potential for asset substitution, bondholders who are unable to monitor or control asset substitution will demand a higher yield to bear this risk. The underinvestment problem refers to the tendency of even shareholder-value maximizing firms with risky debt outstanding to pass up relatively low-risk, positive net present value (NPV) investments. The idea is that, for firms with risky debt outstanding, shareholders are paid out of cash flows that remain only after first paying off the claims of all debtholders. In cases where the "debt overhang" is sufficiently great, even managers acting in the interest of their shareholders will pass up positive-NPV projects whose cash flows go toward making the firm's debt less risky.

These agency problems associated with debt are generally thought to be more severe for firms with significant growth opportunities, since these firms can more easily substitute riskier projects for safe ones and are more likely to face underinvestment problems. One way to control these agency problems, while still enjoying the benefits of debt financing, is to use private debt. With the help of the tighter bond covenants that invariably come with private issues, private debtholders have a comparative advantage in monitoring and enforcing debt contracts. And, to the extent that private debt contracts are easier to renegotiate than public debt contracts, firms with greater growth opportunities will use more private debt.[8] Consistent with this argument, Krishnaswami et al. find that reliance on private borrowing is positively related to the extent of a company's growth opportunities (as measured by the ratio of a firm's market value to book value of equity).

Krishnaswami et al. do not distinguish between bank debt and other private debt claims. But since bank debt is primarily short term, and short-term

6 Sudha Krishnaswami, Paul A. Spindt, and Venkat Subramanian, "Information Asymmetry, Monitoring, and the Placement Structure of Corporate Debt," *Journal of Financial Economics*, 1999, 51.

7 See Mark Carey, Stephen Prowse, John Rhea and Gregory Udell, "The Economics of the Private Placement Markets: A New Look", *Financial Markets and Instruments*, 1993, 2.

8 Clifford Smith and Jerold Warner, "On Financial Contracting: An Analysis of Bond Covenants," *Journal of Financial Economics* 1979, 7.

debt (with monitoring) is likely to be more effective at controlling the underinvestment problem, we would expect the positive relation between reliance on private borrowing and growth opportunities to be strongest in the case of bank borrowing. Consistent with this view, a 1996 study by Joel Houston and Chris James found that a company's reliance on bank borrowing rises with increases in its market-to-book ratio.[9] At the same time, they found no relation between use of other private debt and the importance of growth opportunities, which suggests that short-term bank lending is particularly effective at mitigating agency problems of debt.

But if banks and perhaps other short-term lenders appear to add value by reducing agency costs, there appear to be limits on the flexibility bank loans provide corporate borrowers when mixed with public debt. For example, in a 1995 study of troubled debt restructurings, James found that while bankers frequently waive covenants, they rarely scale down or exchange their claims for equity if the troubled firm also has public debt outstanding.[10] During workouts involving such companies, banks scale down their claims only when public bondholders agree to do the same (and by more than the banks do). Of course, the unwillingness of banks to scale back their claims unilaterally is not at all surprising, given that most bank debt is secured while public debt claims are rarely secured.[11] Thus, one implication of this result is that for companies with some public debt

outstanding, too much bank debt may actually inhibit their attempt to restructure their debt when experiencing financial distress.

As we discuss in greater detail in the last section of this article, a distinctive feature of private debt and particularly bank loans is that they contain more comprehensive and restrictive covenants than public debt contracts. While designed to reduce agency problems and hence a firm's borrowing costs, the contractual restrictions in debt covenants can also end up reducing value by restricting a firm's flexibility when faced with a deterioration in earnings. Such considerations may be particularly important in light of banks' reluctance to restructure their claims when other, more junior debt is outstanding.

Indeed, as Stuart Gilson and Jerold Warner discuss in a recent study, junk bond issues were (and continue to be) marketed by investment bankers as an important alternative source of debt financing for growth firms that would otherwise rely heavily on bank financing.[12] Junk bonds, the argument goes, can provide flexibility because they impose fewer and looser financial restrictions and because they are typically unsecured, which gives management greater discretion in using the firm's cash flows. This flexibility may be particularly important for growth firms that anticipate bumping up against the covenants contained in their bank loan contracts.

Gilson and Warner examined whether junk bonds are issued to enhance financial flexibility by examining 164 high-yield bond issues during the period 1980 through 1992 whose proceeds were used to repay bank loans. Their study compared the covenants contained in junk bond issues to those in the bank loans the bonds were issued to replace. Virtually all bank loan contracts were found to contain covenants that restrict investment expenditures, the sale of assets, financing activities, and the issuance of senior debt claims. The bank loan contracts also typically contained covenants that specified values for financial ratios that trigger default. In contrast, the majority of junk bond contacts did not contain these types of restrictions.

9 Joel Houston and Christopher James "Bank Information Monopolies and Mix of Private and Public Debt Claims," *Journal of Finance*, 1996, 51, 1863–1890. They find that the relation between the proportion of bank debt to total debt and growth opportunities varies with the number of lenders a firm uses. Specifically, the positive relation between reliance on bank debt and growth oppurtunities is most pronouced for large firms that use multiple bank lenders or have public debt outstanding.
10 Christopher James, "When do Banks Take Equity in Debt Restructurings?," *Review of Financial Studies*, (Winter) 1995.
11 In a follow-up study published in 1996 in the *Journal of Finance*, James finds that, while banks rarely unilaterally scale down their claims, banks appear to influence the success of public debt exchange offers in financial distress. Specifically, exchange offers made in conjunction with bank concessions are characterized by significantly greater reductions in public debt outstanding and a significantly higher probability of success. See Christopher James, "Bank Debt Restructurings and the Composition of Exchange offers in Financial Distress," *Journal of Finance*, 1996, 51.

12 Stuart Gilson and Jerold Warner, "Junk Bonds, Bank Debt, and Financing Corporate Growth", Harvard University Working paper, 2000.

Table 18.2 Comparing Bank Borrowers to Finance Company Borrowers using LPC Deal Scan Data, 1987–1993

	Bank borrowers		Finance company borrowers	
	Mean	Median	Mean	Median
Panel A. Borrower Characteristics				
Assets ($ millions)	234	213	251	235
Leverage	.50	.50	.72	.75
Interest Coverage	4.37	3.60	2.39	1.87
EBITDA/Assets	.12	.13	.10	.12
Market-to-Book Ratio	1.39	1.18	1.20	1.02

Panel B. Loan Characteristics		
	Bank loans	**Finance company loans**
Loan Type (Percent)		
Line of Credit	57	51
Term Loan	29	40
Bridge Loan/Demand Loan	7	6
Standby Letter of Credit	4	1
Loan Terms		
Median Spread over LIBOR	250	402
Median Term to Maturity	24	37
Percentage of Loans Secured	70	92
Percentage of Loans with Borrowing Base Features	30	47

Data are from Mark Carey, Mitchell Post, and Steven Sharpe, "Evidence from Specialization in Private Debt Contracts," *Journal of Finance*, June, 1998, 53.

And consistent with the view that junk bonds are issued when bank loan covenants are likely to bind, Gilson and Warner reported that companies that issued junk bonds experienced significant declines in operating earnings in the year after issuance; in fact, the average change in quarterly operating income to total assets was a negative 44 percent from the quarter preceding the issue to four quarters after the issue.

Most of the recent studies of corporate debt structure do not distinguish between short-term private debt claims made by banks and by other private lenders. An important exception is a 1998 study by Mark Carey, Mitchell Post, and Steven Sharpe on the differences between bank lending and finance company lending to corporations.[13]

As the data we saw earlier in Figure 18.1 indicates, lending by finance companies and other non-bank lenders has increased in recent years. Indeed, Carey et al. report that corporate lending by finance companies increased 120% between 1985 and 1995, while commercial lending by banks increased by only 54% during this period. While much of the growth in finance company lending to businesses was in the form of equipment lending and auto-related finance (dealer financing through captive finance subsidiaries) – lending which may be qualitatively different from traditional commercial lending – finance companies have also made significant inroads into banks' traditional term and commitment-based lending areas.

The growth of finance company lending raises the question of whether this type of lending is a close substitute for bank loans or whether finance companies specialize in making certain types of loans that banks typically avoid. Using information obtained from Loan Pricing Corporation's Deal

---

13 Mark Carey, Mitchell Post and Steven Sharpe, "Evidence from Specialization in Private Debt Contracts," *Journal of Finance*, June, 1998, 53.

Scan data base, Carey et al. provide evidence that finance companies specialize in making so-called "asset-backed" loans to high risk borrowers – a segment of the lending market that banks have traditionally shied away from. As shown in Table 18.2, they found that borrowers from finance companies are more highly levered, have lower coverage ratios, and have lower operating earnings relative to assets than the average bank borrower. Consistent with the view that finance companies specialize in asset-backed loans, loans made by finance companies are also likely to be secured with borrowing amounts tied to a borrowing base.

Why do finance companies specialize in loans to high-risk borrowers, while commercial banks tend to avoid them? The most obvious explanation is that bank regulators tend to discourage this type of lending, thus leaving the field open to finance companies. But Carey et al. propose another, more subtle motivation – one that considers lenders' concern about reputation. Noting that private debt contracts provide lenders significant control through restrictive covenants, they go on to point out that borrowers are naturally worried that, if they trip a covenant, lenders may use the covenants to extract concessions as part of the renegotiation process. Moreover, for commercial bankers intent on preserving market share in such an environment, a lender's reputation for acting reasonably may be particularly important; and it is this concern about reputation that may give banks another important (non-regulatory) reason to stay out of asset-backed finance. As Carey et al. explain,

Specialization may support the conservation of reputational capital – high-risk borrowers go to lenders with a reputation for being tough and, given their clientele, such lenders will be forced to liquidate borrowers and enforce covenants with high frequency. Low-risk borrowers go to other lenders, who are better able to maintain good reputations because liquidation and enforcement actions are rarely necessary.

Overall, empirical studies of the corporate debt structure suggest that banks and other private lenders play an important role in mitigating the agency problems of debt and financial distress costs. At the same time, evidence also suggests that there are costs from using private debt relative to public debt. These costs include the costs of monitoring, higher percentage floatation costs for smaller issues, and costs of lender control (in terms of lost flexibility).

WHAT DOES THE STOCK PRICE REACTION TO BANK LOAN ANNOUNCEMENTS TELL US ABOUT WHAT BANKS DO?

While the studies reviewed in the last section provide valuable insights into the role of private lenders in the capital-raising process, they are not particularly well suited for examining the importance of banks and other private lenders in resolving information problems associated with the issuance of new claims. Information problems between managers and new investors are likely to be temporary. As a result, the debt structure of a firm at any point in time will likely reflect past information problems, but not necessarily current firm misvaluations by the market.[14] Studies of the influence of incremental borrowing decisions are more likely to detect the effect of information asymmetries on financing choice. For this reason, studies of the stock price reaction to bank loan announcements focus primarily on the role of banks in resolving adverse selection problems associated with new securities issues.

These problems are generally explained in the context of managers issuing public securities when they believe their stock is overvalued relative to its prospects.[15] Put a little differently, managers are more likely to offer securities when they expect a fall in profits after the offering (and thus think the firm is overvalued) than when they anticipate a subsequent rise in profits (and think the firm is overvalued). Of course, new investors understand management's incentives to issue new securities

---

14 In contrast, since potential agency problems are more likely to be related to the type of asset a firm holds (and the importance of growth opportunities) studies that examine cross sectional differences in the mix or structure of a firms debt structure are better at detecting the effect of agency problems and potential financial distress costs on debt structure.

15 This explanation was originally put forth by Stewart Myers and Nicholas Majluf in their paper entitled "Corporate Financing and Investment Decisions When Firms Have Information That Outsiders Do Not Have," *Journal of Financial Economics*, 1984, 13 (2).

when a firm is overvalued and they reduce the value of firms when their managers announce a public securities offering. Because of this rational market bias against new offerings, companies with profitable new projects and good future prospects face a financing problem: they penalize existing shareholders any time they try to issue securities. Although such underpricing can be avoided by using internally generated funds, such funds may be insufficient to finance new investments.

When internally generated funds are limited, the use of "inside" debt is likely to be a more cost-effective alternative. In a 1985 *Journal of Monetary Economics* article entitled "What's Different About Bank Loans?," Eugene Fama characterized inside debt as financing that comes from lenders' having access to information about the borrower that is not otherwise publicly available. Banks enjoy a unique role as inside lenders because they obtain private information through their ongoing deposit relationship with the firm. Moreover, banks can directly participate in a firm's decision-making, for example, as a member of its board of directors.[16] By contrast, "outside" debtholders in public debt markets must rely on publicly available information generated by bond rating agencies, independent audits, or analyst reports. Following this line of reasoning, firms should have a tendency to turn to inside bank debt when they are undervalued by the market and have insufficient internal funds to finance upcoming projects.

A testable implication of this view that banks loans – as a source of inside debt – mitigate adverse selection problems for undervalued firms is that announcements of bank financing should be viewed favorably by the market. As mentioned earlier, James (1987) was the first study to document a positive share price reaction to bank loan announcements. As shown in Table 18.3, the findings of three more recent studies have confirmed James's original finding. Though these three studies vary in sample size and time period, each finds that borrowers earn positive and statistically significant

Table 18.3 Two Day Abnormal Returns to Firms Announcing Loans

Study	Abnormal Return (−1,0) in %
James (1987)	1.93
Lummer and McConnell (1989)	0.61
Best and Zhang (1993)	0.32
Billett, Flannery and Garfinkel (1995)	0.68

abnormal returns upon the announcement of a bank loan.

The fact that the stock market response to bank loan announcements differs from the announcement effects of other securities issues raises a number of questions that are addressed in more recent papers. For example, if banks have an information advantage over outside investors, does this advantage arise from an established relationship with a borrower? Are banking relationships more valuable to some borrowers than others? Do loans made by nonbank lenders (such as finance companies) have the same valuation effects as bank loans? Answers to these questions are critical to understanding when bank lending is preferred to other types of borrowing.

In a 1989 study, Scott Lummer and John McConnell[17] investigated whether banks add value as part of an ongoing relationship or at the initiation of the relationship. For example, bank loans may become inside debt only over time as the banker learns about the credit quality and growth prospects of the borrower as part of an ongoing relationship.[18] If an ongoing relationship is what provides banks with an informational advantage, then announcements of new loan agreements should be associated with a smaller stock price response than renewals or extensions of existing

16 In the United States, Lender Liability may limit bank participation in corporate government. Indeed, Randall Kroszner and Philip Strahan find that bankers tend to be represented on boards of large stable firms. See, Randall Kroszner and Philip Strahan, 1999, "Bankers on Boards: Monitoring, Conflicts of Interest and Lender Liability," Working paper.

17 Scott Lummer and John McConnell, "Further Evidence on the Bank Lending Process and the Capital Market Response to Bank Loan Agreements," *Journal of Financial Economics*, 1989, 25.
18 This is what Eugene Fama had in mind when he argued that bank loans are special because of the deposit relationship borrowers maintain with their bank lender. The deposit relationship, Fama speculated, was an important way for banks to obtain nonpublic information about a customer's credit risk.

agreements. Another possibility, however, is that banks could be most valuable at the start of a credit relationship. Specifically, if banks have a comparative advantage in evaluating risky lending opportunities, then a new loan announcement may serve as a "seal of approval" concerning a prospective borrower's credit worthiness. In this case, the positive information from a bank loan should be reflected in a firm's stock price upon initiation of a new loan.

Using a sample of 728 loan announcements, Lummer and McConnell distinguished between new loan announcements and announcements about loan renewals and found that positive stock price responses to bank loan announcements occurred in the case of renewals, but not initiations. Based on this result, they inferred that bank loan announcements are informative only after firms have produced information through an ongoing relationship.

Later studies by Ronald Best and Hang Zhang and Billett et al. revisited the issue of whether the valuation effects of new loan announcements differ from the valuation effects of credit renewals.[19] In contrast to Lummer and McConnell, both papers documented positive stock price reactions for loan initiations as well as renewals, suggesting that valuable information is revealed through initial screenings by banks as well as in the renewal process. Moreover, neither study found a statistically significant difference in the reactions to initiations versus renewals once they controlled for differences in other borrower and lender characteristics, such as the precision of analysts' forecasts and the credit quality of lenders.[20]

Given the positive valuation effects of loan announcements, why do some borrowers choose to issue public securities? One explanation is that certain borrowers find bank loans advantageous while others do not. Best and Zhang addressed this question by examining whether announcement-day returns vary with the information problems borrowers face in the market. In particular, they argue that if banks produce valuable private information about borrowers, then loan announcements should convey good news to stock market investors only when public information about firm value is noisy or hard to interpret by outside investors. To test this idea, they split their sample into two groups according to the precision with which stock analysts forecast borrower earnings. Large forecast errors in earnings (measured by the difference between the most recent earnings forecast prior to the loan announcement and the firm's actual earnings) indicate a high level of noise or uncertainty about the future prospects of the borrower. As they expected, Best and Zhang found that companies experienced positive abnormal returns when analysts' forecast errors were high, but earned zero abnormal returns when forecast errors were low.

Best and Zhang took their analysis a step further and reasoned that banks will add the most value when evaluating those borrowers perceived by the public to have poor earnings prospects. There are two reasons banks might create the greatest value for such borrowers. First, borrowers perceived by the public as having poor earnings prospects are the most likely to be undervalued by the market and therefore the least likely to want to issue public securities. If banks possess inside information about the credit quality of these borrowers, their choice to borrow from the bank provides a signal to the market that they are in fact undervalued. Second, the value of bank monitoring and credit evaluation is likely to be greatest when two factors are present: (1) public information does not provide a reliable guide to a firm's prospects and (2) the firm's credit quality is suspect.[21]

---

19 Ronald Best and Hang Zhang, "Alternative Information Sources and the Information Content of Bank Loans" *Journal of Finance*, 1993, 48.

20 One reason that duplicating the results of Lummer and McConnell has been difficult is that properly classifying loan announcements as initiations or renewals is tricky because many announcements do not make this distinction. Even when new loans are classified correctly as initiations, most firms in this category will have already established a lending relationship with the bank through a previous lending arrangement or unused loan commitment. In fact, it is difficult to imagine that there are many public traded firms that do not have some sort of ongoing banking relationship.

---

21 See, Mitch Berlin and Jan Loeys "Bond Covenants and Delegated Monitoring," *Journal of Finance*, 1988, 43.

To examine this issue, Best and Zhang split their sample again, this time sorting by revisions to forecasted earnings. Consistent with the idea that bank loans are most valuable to undervalued borrowers, those companies in the high prediction error category earned the largest abnormal returns when analysts had previously revised downward their earnings forecasts for the company.

In a recent working paper, Charles Hadlock and Chris James (2000) focus on the role of banks in resolving information problems associated with new securities issues.[22] In particular, they directly examine why some firms choose to borrow from public markets while others borrow from banks, even when it appears that such firms stand to gain the most from issuing public securities because of their size and credit standing. Following James (1987), this study argues that companies seek bank financing when they perceive themselves to be undervalued by the market. Correctly valued and overvalued firms prefer to avoid the cost of bank monitoring and issue public securities instead. Hadlock and James extend this argument by considering the costs associated with bank borrowing in the form of higher flotation costs for large issues, as well as the costs of monitoring and excess control.

In this sense, Hadlock and James tie the loan announcement literature to the studies on debt structure mix. In their framework, firms choose bank loans over public financing only when there is a high degree of uncertainty about their value. Consistent with this intuition, Hadlock and James show that firms choose bank financing over public financing (1) after periods of large stock price declines and (2) when there is great uncertainty about their stock price. They also find that the size of stock price reactions to loan announcements varies directly with proxies for the degree to which a firm is undervalued by the market and inversely with the extent to which market participants anticipate that firms will choose bank loans. In other words, the stock price reaction is most positive when companies that normally find it advantageous to borrow in public markets instead announce a bank loan.

The results of Hadlock and James's study raise another interesting issue: Are the bank loans announced in the financial press typical of most firms borrowing from banks? Put differently, are the bank loans announced in the financial press those that are most likely to result in a positive share price reaction? There are at least two reasons why this question may be relevant. First, unlike public securities offerings, new bank loan agreements need be announced only when they are deemed to be "material," in accordance with guidelines established by the Securities and Exchange Commission. Thus, small agreements and those considered immaterial by the firm will not be reported to the financial press. Moreover, even when companies announce loans in a press release, newspapers like the *Wall Street Journal* may run the announcement only when the editors believe the announcement is important. Second, bank loans announced in the financial press tend to be very large (both in terms of dollar value as well as relative to the size of the firm). For example, the average value of the loans in James's original study was $72 million and constituted about 75% of the market value of the issuing firm. By comparison, the average straight debt issue in James's sample was about $100 million and represented only 26% of the market value of the issuing firm.[23] Thus, there appears to be a selection bias toward announcing the largest bank loans.

The 1995 study by Billett et al. examined the influence of lender characteristics on loan announcement abnormal returns. They considered whether shareholders perceive value in bank lending that differs from other types of non-bank private lending. For their purposes, non-bank lending consisted of loans from finance companies. James (1987) also studied the stock price reaction to announcements of non-bank private debt. He provided evidence that announcements of privately placed debt were associated with small negative abnormal returns – similar to those

---

22 Charles Hadlock and Christopher James, "Bank Lending and the Menu of Financing Options," University of Florida Working paper, 2000.

23 Later studies confirm that bank loans announced in the financial press are quite large. For example, Billett, et al. report an average loan size of $116 million (representing 77 percent of the issuing firms' common stock) and a median loan size of $45 million. By comparison, Carey et al. (1998) report that the median loan size in Loan Pricing Corporation's Deal Scan data base for Compustat-listed firms over the same period was $25 million.

associated with public debt issues. But Billett et al. found a different result. They reported positive and (marginally) significant abnormal returns to announcements of finance company loans, and were unable to statistically distinguish between the market response to bank loans from the non-bank loan announcements.[24] A 1994 study by Preece and Mullineaux reached the same conclusion. Our best guess is that the difference in findings among these three studies arises from differences in the types of non-bank loans analyzed by each study. Whereas James (1987) focused on longer-maturity private placements that resemble publicly traded debt contracts, both Billett et al. and Preece and Mullineaux examined mostly commitment-type non-bank loans made by non-bank lenders that resemble bank debt. We discuss why this distinction may be important in the next section.

In general, then, studies of the stock price reaction to new loan announcements indicate that banks play an important role in resolving adverse selection problems associated with issuing new securities. However, banks do not appear to play a unique role since borrowers from finance companies enjoy similar benefits. These findings suggest that there is something special about the type of loans that banks make, but not necessarily that the loan is from a bank. In the next section, we explore what might be different about the types of loans banks make and why this type of borrowing could enable firms to limit the adverse selection problems of issuing securities.

Why Bank Loans Are Still Special

While the benefits of issuing private debt are easy to understand, why is borrowing from a bank or finance company different from borrowing in the private placement market? One reason may be that bank-type loans have different characteristics than private placements. To investigate this possibility, we obtained some summary statistics of loans reported in Loan Pricing Corporation's (LPC) Deal Scan data. The Deal Scan data derive

Table 18.4 Characteristics of Loans based on LPC Deal Scan Data, 1987–1997

	Proportion of total (%)
Deals (15,661 observations)	
Includes a line of credit	84
Includes a term loan	37
Includes both line of credit and term loan	21

Source: Based on statistics provided by Mark Carey, Board of Governors of the Federal Reserve System.

both from SEC filings and participating lending institutions and include most loan agreements for medium-sized and large firms in the U.S. In sum, the Deal Scan data base covers over 15,000 loan "deals" involving more than 22,500 separate loans called "facilities." Each loan deal between bank and borrower can include more than one facility.[25]

The most notable feature of the LPC deals summarized in Table 18.4 is that 84% involve some form of a line of credit.[26] Like a credit card, a line of credit allows companies to borrow on demand up to a certain prespecified limit, and to choose how and when they will pay back their loans. Such commitment-based financing arrangements specify an interest rate that is a fixed mark-up over a benchmark rate such as LIBOR or the Prime Rate. Since most deals include only one loan facility, revolving lines of credit are the dominant form of bank financing to commercial borrowers. By comparison, this flexibility in the timing of borrowing and repaying is absent in privately placed loans. For example, most private placements include provisions for punitive prepayment penalties.[27]

Banks also make term loans, which appear in about a third (37%) of the LPC loan deals. Nevertheless, term loans are usually made in

24 Billett et al. also find that the identity of the bank lender is important in that loans from banks with higher bond ratings elicit a higher stock price reaction.

25 For instance, a typical deal may include the following three facilities: a three-year revolving line of credit facility, a two-year term loan that begins immediately, and a two-year term loan set to begin two years from the deal date.
26 The statistics in Table 18.4 are based on a slightly smaller sample of firms that eliminates guidance lines, which are not contractually committed loans. Here, lines of credit include standby letters of credit. Term loans include bridge loans, demand loans, trade letters of credit, bankers acceptances, and leases.
27 See Carey et al. (1993).

conjunction with a credit line. In fact, only 16% of the LPC deals contain a term loan facility without a corresponding credit line facility.

Three other characteristics distinguish bank-type loans from privately placed debt. First, bank loans are typically secured with collateral (see Table 18.2 earlier). For instance, according to a recent working paper by Philip Strahan, 78% of all lines of credit and 85% of all term loans from Deal Scan are collateralized.[28] These loans are often secured with short-term assets such as borrowers' accounts receivables and inventory. Privately placed debt can also be collateralized with asset-backed securities such as leveraged leases, collateralized trust certificates, and collateralized mortgage obligations, and with first and second mortgage bonds. However, Carey et al. (1993) report that secured debt represents less than a third of all private placements. Second, bank-type loan agreements typically carry stringent covenants that require borrowers to maintain a set of financial ratios above a certain minimum. They can also include explicit price-based covenants that tie the loan rate directly to firm performance based on financial ratios. Although covenants are also common with privately placed loans, they tend to be less restrictive and relate to levels of financial ratios only upon the occurrence of a certain event, such as a further increase in debt. Third, as mentioned earlier, bank loans tend to be short term. Strahan reports that the average maturity on lines of credit is 42 months and for term loans it is 69 months.

What, then, are the advantages of obtaining bank-type loans? For well-established companies with access to public markets, revolving lines of credit allow companies to raise private financing quickly when they view themselves to be undervalued by the market or, alternatively, when credit risk spreads look unattractive in public markets. In short, commitment-based financing provides firms with liquidity and a kind of insurance against adverse changes in the cost of borrowing. The insurance provided by commitments arises from

the fact that the rate on the commitment is a fixed mark-up over a benchmark rate.[29] This insurance is likely to be particularly valuable when there is considerable uncertainty about the value of the firm at the time it needs financing.

An excellent example of the value of the insurance provided by lines of credit was provided by the recent credit crunch in the Fall of 1998. As Marc Saidenberg and Philip Strahan noted in a recent Federal Reserve Bank of New York publication, the collapse of the Russian ruble and the problems at Long Term Capital Management precipitated an investor "flight to safety" to low risk-investments. This flight to quality in turn raised spreads between corporate bonds and similar maturity Treasury securities by 100 basis points, while short-term commercial paper spreads more than doubled.[30] As a result, through the fourth quarter of 1998, the amount of outstanding commercial paper fell by $10 billion; but during this same period, bank commercial lending increased by $20 billion. Saidenberg and Strahan show that nearly all of the increase in bank lending came from customers drawing on credit lines. Thus, in this instance, bankers provided a way for large corporations to avoid a spike in the cost of borrowing in public markets.

The fact that bank loans are collateralized, contain strict covenants, and are typically short term improves a bank's ability to monitor informationally-intensive loans. By securing a loan, banks ensure the seniority of their loans over other debt issues made by the firm. Moreover, a senior position in the payoff structure increases the return and therefore the incentives of lenders to monitor. The return to monitoring is higher for senior creditors because any benefits of monitoring (in terms of timely liquidations) go to senior creditors.[31] Similarly, a short maturity increases a bank's

28 Philip E. Strahan, "Borrower Risk and the Price and Nonprice Terms of Bank Loans", Federal Reserve Bank of New York Working Papers, October 1999.

29 The insurance is limited, however, since commitments contain so called "material adverse change" clauses that allow the bank to refuse to advance funds in the face of a marked decrease in the credit quality of the prospective borrower.
30 Marc R. Saidenberg and Philip E. Strahan, "Are Banks Still Important for Financing Large Businesses?," Current Issues in Economics and Finance, Federal Reserve Bank of New York, August 1999.
31 See, Cheol Park, "Monitoring and the Structure of Debt Contracts," Journal of Finance, forthcoming 2000.

ability to monitor the loan by requiring firms to roll over their bank debt often, which allows for frequent reevaluations by the banks.

Although the share of bank-type loans offered by banks has declined through time (as we saw in Figure 18.1), banks continue to dominate the loan market. For example, Carey et al. reported that banks accounted for approximately 90% of all bank-type loans made during the period 1987–1993. The dominance of banks in this market suggests that banks have a comparative advantage in providing loans with the characteristics described above. In a recent working paper, Anil Kashyap, Raghu Rajan, and Jeremy Stein argue that this comparative advantage arises from the dual role of banks as deposit takers and providers of highly liquid loans.[32] They point out that a revolving line of credit is the mirror image of a demand deposit in that it allows borrowers to withdraw money on demand and pay back when they want to. They argue that it is efficient for banks to offer both services together because both deposit-taking and commitment lending require banks to hold large stocks of liquid assets. So long as the liquidity needs of borrowers do not exactly match the needs of depositors, the combination of loan commitments and deposit-taking enables banks to add value by reducing the total amount of cash or liquidity necessary to perform both functions.

The Fall 1998 credit crunch provides an example of how such synergies between deposit-taking and lending work. In their flight to safety, investors transferred funds from risky securities such as corporate bonds and commercial paper into safe investments like bank deposits.[33] This flow of funds into deposits increased the liquidity stock of banks. Simply holding these liquid stocks as reserves would have been costly for banks since reserves earn small or zero returns. However, the rush to safe deposits was offset by an increase in the demand for liquidity as companies drew down their credit lines. This allowed banks to efficiently re-allocate liquid funds to their best use. Kashyap et al. hint at why banks sometimes also offer other types of loans such as term loans. The basic argument is fairly simple: once a bank has investigated a firm for a line of credit, it has a comparative advantage in offering other types of loans as well. Table 18.4 provides support for this argument by showing that, although lines of credit are frequently offered without term loans, the opposite is rarely true.

Conclusion

Bankers appear to play a special role in providing commitment-based financing to corporations. This type of lending is important not only for small firms that lack access to public debt markets but for large and medium-size firms as well. For larger companies, commitment-based financing provides flexibility that is particularly valuable when a firm faces an immediate need for financing and when interest rates in public debt markets are prohibitively high. In addition, commitment-type financing provides flexibility which may be particularly important when a firm must raise funds but believes that it is currently undervalued by the market. The fact that commitment-based financing is particularly valuable when firms are undervalued in the market is also likely to be the best explanation of why announcements of these types of loans result in a positive stock price reaction.

---

32   Anil K. Kashyap, Raghuram Rajan, and Jeremy C. Stein, "Banks as Liquidity Providers: An Explanation for the Co-Existence of Lending and Deposit-Taking," National Bureau of Economic Research working paper 6962, February 1999.
33   See Saidenberg and Strahan (1999).

CHAPTER 19

Convertible Bonds: Matching Financial and Real Options

David Mayers (University of California at Riverside)*

Why do companies issue convertible bonds instead of, say, straight bonds or common stock? The popular explanation is that convertibles provide the best of both worlds: they provide issuers with "cheap" debt in the sense that they carry lower rates than straight debt; and, if the firm performs well and the bonds convert into equity, they allow issuers to sell stock "at a premium" over the current share price. Take the case of MCI Communications Corp. In August of 1981, the company issued 20-year-convertible subordinated debentures with a 10 1/4% coupon rate (as compared to the 14 1/8% it was paying on 20-year sub bonds issued just four months earlier). The conversion price of $12.825 was set at an 18% premium over MCI's then current price of $10.875. Eighteen months later, when the stock price had risen to $40, the issue was called, the convertible bondholders chose to become stockholders, and

MCI received an infusion of equity in the midst of a major capital investment program.

But, as finance professors Michael Brennan and Eduardo Schwartz pointed out in an article published in the same year as MCI's first convertible bond issue,[1] the argument that convertibles represent cheap debt and the sale of equity at a premium involves a logical sleight of hand. It compares convertibles to straight debt in one set of circumstances (when the company's stock doesn't rise and there is no conversion) and to common stock under another (when the stock price rises and the issue converts). What the argument fails to point out is that convertible issuers may well have been better off issuing stock in the first set of circumstances and straight debt in the second. That is, if the firm performs very well, straight debt may have preserved more value for the existing shareholders by not cutting new investors into future appreciation. And, if the firm's stock performs poorly after the new issue, then common stock would have been better than convertibles – not only because there is no dilution of value, but because the firm may then have had the greatest need for equity.

---

* This research received support from the Charles A. Dice Center for Research in Financial Economics at Ohio State University. I thank Steve Buser, Peter Chung, Larry Dann, Tom George, Dan Greiner, Jeff Harris, Herb Johnson, Wayne Mikkelson, Tim Opler, John Persons, Cliff Smith, René Stulz, Ralph Walking, Jerry Warner, and especially Paul Schultz for helpful comments. I thank Arnold Cowan, Nandkumar Nayar, and Ajai Singh for graciously providing me the use of their listing of convertible bond calls.

1 Michael Brennan and Eduardo Schwartz, "The Case for Convertibles," *Chase Financial Quarterly* (Fall 1981). Reprinted in *Journal of Applied Corporate Finance* (Summer 1988).

As Brennan and Schwartz went on to say in their 1981 article, convertibles do not provide issuers with the financing equivalent of a "free lunch." Investors are willing to accept a lower coupon rate on convertibles than on straight bonds *only because* the issuer is also granting them a valuable option on the company's stock – an upside participation that can dilute the value of existing stockholders' claims. And provided the company's stock is fairly valued at the time of issue, there are no obvious reasons why convertibles should be less expensive than straight debt or equity.

But there are some less obvious reasons why convertibles may be a value-conserving financing strategy – reasons that depend on market "imperfections" such as transaction and information costs, and managerial incentives that are not fully consistent with maximizing stockholder wealth. Beginning with the pioneering paper on agency cost theory by Jensen and Meckling in 1976,[2] financial academics have proposed a number of ways that convertibles can reduce the costs arising from such imperfections. And, in a study published in 1998 in the *Journal of Financial Economics (JFE)*, I presented yet another rationale for convertibles that shows how they reduce new issue costs and agency problems facing certain kinds of companies.[3] Put as simply as possible, my explanation views convertibles as the most cost-effective way for companies with promising growth opportunities to finance a *sequence* of major corporate investments of uncertain value and timing. Financial economists, along with a steadily increasing number of corporate practitioners, refer to such future investment opportunities as "real options." Such investments are options in the sense that, although they may not be worth undertaking today (i.e., they are currently "out-of-the-money"), they may become so in the future. And if and when such options move "into the money," the company will need to have sufficient capital (or at least access to capital) to "exercise" its real options and carry out its strategic plan. Convertible bonds are likely to prove a cost-effective financing approach for companies with major growth options because of the ability they offer management to match capital inflows with expected investment outlays. In particular, as the company's real options move into the money and its stock price rises to reflect that, the call provision in convertibles effectively gives management the option to call the bonds and so force conversion into equity. And, besides eliminating the cash flow drain from servicing the debt, the new infusion of equity can in turn be used to support additional debt (or convertible) financing.

In this article, after reviewing the theory and evidence on convertibles, I show how my own explanation and findings are both consistent with and extend the previous research. Like other theories – notably, Jeremy Stein's "backdoor equity" hypothesis – my argument suggests that convertibles can be viewed as "deferred equity" offerings that add value for companies with promising future growth opportunities (that may not be fully reflected in current share prices). Unlike past theories, I show how convertibles are uniquely suited to the sequential financing problem faced by management in funding real investment options. Although there is considerable empirical support for my explanation in the past research, the most persuasive evidence comes from my recent study of the investment and financing activity of a large sample of U.S. companies around the time their convertible bonds are converted into common stock. In brief, my study of 289 conversion-forcing calls of convertible debt over the period 1971–1990 shows significant increases in corporate investment activity beginning in the year of the call and continuing for the following three years. This investment activity is matched with increased financing activity, principally new long-term debt, that is significant primarily in the year of the call. Thus, although equity is being brought in "through the back door" by the conversion process, new debt is being brought in along with it. To return to our earlier example, one month after MCI forced conversion of its first ($250 million) convertible bond issue, it floated its second convertible issue, this time raising almost $400 million.

2　See Michael C. Jensen and William H. Meckling, "Theory of the Firm: Managerial Behavior, Agency Costs, and Capital Structure," *Journal of Financial Economics* (1976), pp. 305–360.

3　See my article, "Why Firms Issue Convertible Bonds: The Matching of Financial and Real Investment Options," *Journal of Financial Economics* 47 (1998), pp. 83–102, from which article all tables and figures in this article are taken.

In short, my study suggests that convertibles are designed to facilitate the future financing of valuable real investment options.

THEORETICAL ARGUMENTS FOR CONVERTIBLES[4]

Given that financial markets are reasonably efficient and that convertibles are a fair deal for investors and issuers alike, finance theory says that the issuance of convertibles should not increase the value of the issuing company. In fact, there is even reason to believe that the market's response to the announcement of new convertible offerings should be negative, on average.

Convertibles and the market's "information asymmetry" problem

In a 1984 paper entitled "Corporate Financing and Investment Decisions When Firms Have Information That Investors Do Not Have," Stewart Myers and Nicholas Majluf offered an explanation for why the announcement of a convertibles issue is generally not good news for the company's stockholders.[5] A company's managers have at least the potential to know more about their firm's prospects than outside investors and, as representatives of the interests of existing stockholders, the managers have a stronger incentive to issue new equity when they believe the company is overvalued. Because part of a convertible issue's value consists of an option on the company's stock, the same argument holds for convertibles, although to a lesser degree. Recognizing managers' incentives to issue overpriced securities, investors respond to announcements of both equity and convertible offerings by lowering their estimates of the issuers' value to compensate for their informational disadvantage.

This argument is supported by empirical studies that show that, in the two-day period surrounding the announcement of new equity issues, a company's stock price falls by about 3%, on average. In response to announcements of convertibles, the average market response is roughly a negative 2%.[6] (By contrast, the market response to straight debt offerings is not reliably different from zero.) The negative market reactions to announcements of new equity and convertible offerings cause the new securities to be issued at a lower price than otherwise. And in those cases where management believes the firm is fairly valued (or even undervalued) prior to the announcement of the convertible offering, the negative market response effectively dilutes value of the existing stockholders' claims. In this sense, the negative market reaction represents a major cost of issuing the security (potentially much larger than the investment banker fees and other out-of-pocket costs). For example, if the stock price of a (fairly valued) firm with an equity market cap of $1 billion drops by 5% upon the announcement of a new $500 million common stock issue, the "information costs" associated with the new issue amount to 3.3% of the value of the firm (or 10% of the funds raised) – possibly a good reason not to issue common equity.

The risk insensitivity hypothesis

Up to this point, we have mentioned the information costs associated with issuing convertibles. And such costs come on top of out-of-pocket flotation costs that are estimated to run around 3.8%

---

4   This section draws heavily on Frank C.Jen, Dosoung Choi, and Seong-Hyo Lee, "Some New Evidence on Why Companies Use Convertible Bonds," *Journal of Applied Corporate Finance*, Vol. 10, No. 1 (Spring 1997).

5   S. Myers and N. Majluf, "Corporate Financing and Investment Decisions When Firms Have Information That Investors Do Not Have," *Journal of Financial Economics* 13 (1984).

6   See L. Dann and W. Mikkelson, "Convertible Debt Issuance, Capital Structure Change, and Financing-Related Information," *Journal of Financial Economics* 13 (1984); D. Asquith and P. Mullins, "Equity Issues and Offering Dilution," *Journal of Financial Economics* 15 (1986); E. Eckbo, "Information Asymmetries and Valuation Effects of Corporate Debt Offerings," *Journal of Financial Economics* 15 (1986); R. Masulis and A. Kowar, "Seasoned Equity Offerings: An Empirical Investigation," *Journal of Financial Economics* 15 (1986); W. Mikkelson and M. Partch, "Valuation Effects of Security Offerings and the Issuance Process," *Journal of Financial Economics* 15 (1986); C. Smith, "Investment Banking and the Capital Acquisition Process," *Journal of Financial Economics* 15 (1986); R. Hansen and C. Crutchley, "Corporate Earnings and Financing: An Empirical Analysis," *Journal of Business* 63 (1990); and E. Pilotte, "Growth Opportunities and Stock Price Response to New Financing," *Journal of Business* 65 (1992), among others.

(of funds raised) for the median convertible issue of $75 million.[7] What are the benefits of convertibles that would make companies willing to incur such costs? And what kinds of companies are likely to find the cost/benefit ratio for convertibles to be most favorable?

The first theoretical justification for convertibles consistent with modern finance theory was provided by Michael Jensen and William Meckling in their much-cited 1976 paper on agency costs. Among the sources of agency problems described by Jensen and Meckling are potential conflicts of interest between a company's bondholders and its stockholders (or managers acting on behalf of stockholders). In normal circumstances – that is, when operations are profitable and the firm can comfortably meet its debt service payments and investment schedule – the interests of bondholders and shareholders are united. Both groups of investors benefit from managerial decisions that increase the total value of the firm. But, in certain cases, corporate managements find themselves in the position of being able to increase shareholder value *at the expense of* bondholders. For example, management can reduce the value of outstanding bonds by increasing debt or adding debt senior to that in question. (In professional circles, this is known as "event risk"; in academic terms it is the *claims dilution problem*.) Or, in highly leveraged companies, management could also choose – as did many S&L executives – to invest in ever riskier projects after the debt is issued (the *risk-shifting or asset substitution problem*). Finally, a management squeezed between falling revenues and high interest payments might choose to pass up value-adding projects such as R&D or, if things are bad enough, basic maintenance and safety procedures (the *underinvestment problem*).[8]

Debtholders, of course, are aware that such problems can arise in leveraged firms, and they protect themselves by lowering the price they are willing to pay for the debt. For corporate management, such lower prices translate into higher interest payments, which in turn further raise the probability of financial trouble. And for high-growth firms, in particular, financial trouble can mean a large loss in value from underinvestment.

Convertibles help to control such shareholder-bondholder conflicts in two ways: First, by providing bondholders with the right to convert their claims into equity, management gives bondholders the assurance that they will participate in any increase in shareholder value that results from increasing the risk of the company's activities – whether by further leveraging, or by undertaking riskier investments. Second, by reducing current interest rates and so reducing the likelihood of financial trouble, convertibles also reduce the probability that financially strapped companies will be forced to pass up valuable investment opportunities.[9]

The role of convertibles in reducing information costs

As Brennan and Schwartz argued in their 1981 paper, convertibles also are potentially useful in resolving any disagreements between managers and bondholders about how risky the firm's activities are. As suggested above, the value of convertibles is relatively insensitive to changes in company risk. Unexpected increases in company risk reduce the value of the bond portion of a convertible, but at the same they increase the value of the embedded option on the company's stock (by increasing the "volatility" of the stock price). And, as Brennan and Schwartz went on to show, it is largely because of this risk-neutralizing effect of convertibles that convertible issuers tend to be

---

7 See I. Lee, S. Lochhead, J. Ritter, and Q. Zhao, "The Costs of Raising Capital," *The Journal of Financial Research* 19 (1996), pp. 59–74. In addition to the out-of-pocket flotation costs, there also is evidence that convertibles, like IPOs, are underpriced, by about 1% on average. See J. Kang and Y. Lee, "The Pricing of Convertible Debt Offerings," *Journal of Financial Economics* 41 (1996), pp. 231–248.
8 For an account of the underinvestment problem, see Stewart Myers, "The Determinants of Corporate Borrowing," *Journal of Financial Economics* (1977). For a more detailed examination of these sources of shareholder/debtholder conflict, see Clifford W. Smith and Jerold B. Warner, "On Financial Contracting: An Analysis of Bond Covenants," *Journal of Financial Economics*, 7 (1979), pp. 117–161.

---

9 More technically, the underinvestment problem arises from the fact that, in financially troubled firms, an outsized portion of the returns from new investments must go to helping restore the value of the bondholders claims before the shareholders receive any payoff at all. This has also been dubbed the "debt overhang" problem.

smaller, riskier, growth firms characterized by high earnings volatility.[10]

The backdoor equity financing hypothesis

The next major development in the theory came in 1992, when Jeremy Stein published a paper in the *JFE* entitled "Convertibles Bonds as Backdoor Equity Financing."[11] Beginning with the recognition that many convertible bond issuers build equity through forced conversion of convertibles, Stein developed a model that uses information asymmetry between managers and investors, and the resulting information costs, to explain why growth firms in particular find it attractive to issue convertibles. As Stein suggests, companies with limited capital and abundant growth opportunities often find themselves in a financing bind. On the one hand, they are reluctant to use significant amounts of straight debt because they face high expected costs of financial distress. Often lacking an investment-grade bond rating, the kinds of companies that issue convertibles are likely to face high coupon rates on straight debt. And, even if they are able to issue high-yield bonds or raise a significant amount through bank loans, a temporary shortfall in cash flow could force their managers to cut back on strategic investment – and tripping a covenant or failing to meet an interest payment could even mean relinquishing much of the value of the firm to creditors or other outsiders.

But if straight debt financing is very costly in these circumstances, conventional equity financing could also have significant costs. For one thing, the management of some growth firms – particularly, those in a fairly early stage of a growth trajectory – may not feel the current stock price fairly reflects the firm's growth opportunities, and so the issuance of equity would be expected to cause excessive dilution of existing stockholders' claims. And, even if the firm is fairly valued, the information asymmetry problem described earlier might cause investors to reduce the value of the company's shares upon announcement of the offering, thereby diluting value.

In such circumstances, where both straight debt and equity appear to have significant costs, managers with a great deal of confidence in their firm's growth prospects may choose to build equity by issuing convertibles and planning to use the call provision to force conversion when the stock price rises in the future. Moreover, the stock market may actually encourage the use of convertibles in the following sense: If investors are persuaded that convertible issuers have promising growth prospects but no other viable financing options (i.e., there is little additional debt capacity and a straight equity issue has been ruled out by management as too dilutive), the market is likely to respond less negatively (or, in some cases, even positively) to the announcement of a new convertible issue. That is, management's choice of a convertible bond financing may function as a "signal" to investors that management is highly confident about the firm's future, thus allowing the issuer to avoid much of the negative information costs that attend conventional equity announcements. And there is some interesting evidence to support this view. In a 1997 study published in this journal, Frank Jen, Dosoung Choi, and Seong-Hyo Lee showed that the stock market responds more favorably to announcements of convertible issues by companies with high post-issue capital expenditures and high market-to-book ratios (both plausible proxies for growth opportunities), but low credit ratings and high (post-offering) debt-equity ratios.[12] And since high capital expenditures and market-to-book ratios are also reasonable proxies for the presence of the real options I discussed earlier, such findings also provide support for my own theory of convertibles.

A NEW RATIONALE

In my 1998 article in the *JFE*, I offered a rationale for convertibles that both is consistent with and

---

10 In his 1991 Ph.D. dissertation at the University of Chicago, "Convertible Securities and Capital Structure Determinants," Stuart Essig reported that convertible bond financing tends to be used by risky firms, high-tech firms, and firms with a limited track record.
11 J. Stein, "Convertibles Bonds as Backdoor Equity Financing," *Journal of Financial Economics* 32 (1992).

12 Jen, Choi, and Lee (1997), cited above.

extends Stein's "backdoor equity" argument.[13] Stein's model addresses itself mainly to the financing problem that growth companies face at a given point in time. That is, given that the firm needs financing and cannot easily service a large amount of straight debt, how does management raise a form of equity financing that minimizes the dilution ("information costs") suffered by the current stockholders *at the time of issue*?

The problem I address is somewhat different: Given that the firm needs financing today to fund current activities and *may* also require significantly more capital in the future (depending on how things turn out in the next few years), how does management minimize dilution and other costs over the expected *sequence* of current and future financings. To cite once more the case of MCI, how does management minimize not just the costs associated with its present convertible bond issue, but also that of the issue that is expected to follow its conversion . . . and, if the latter issue is likely to be a convertible, too, perhaps even the issue that is expected to follow it. Thus, a key consideration in my theory is the extent of both managers' and investors' uncertainty about both the value and the timing of the firm's future investment opportunities. As I suggested earlier, the presence of such uncertainty means that today's future investment opportunities are really "growth options" that may (or may not) be "exercised" at some point in the future – in most cases, by raising more outside capital.

The analysis

To show how convertibles can minimize costs over a sequence of financings, my study used a "two-period model" that works essentially as follows. At time 0, the company has a (clearly) positive-NPV investment project that requires immediate funding, and it also has an investment "option" that may require funding at time 1, depending on what happens between time 0 and time 1. In addition to its positive-NPV project and investment option,

the company also has an abundant supply of negative-NPV projects (think of them as diversifying acquisitions) that management might choose to take if it has excess capital and no positive-NPV projects. All investment projects are assumed to have a life of one period.

Given these conditions, the challenge for management is to devise a financing strategy at time 0 that minimizes the costs associated with funding *both* the initial project *and* the investment option. My model assumes that there are only two major categories of costs: (1) new issue costs and (2) overinvestment costs. By new issue costs I mean not only the transactions costs associated with floating a new issue, but also the "information costs" discussed above.[14] Overinvestment costs can be described as the reduction in value that results from companies having too much capital – more than they can profitably reinvest in their core businesses. Excess capital is assumed to lead to corporate investment in negative-NPV projects because of the managerial tendency to pursue size at the expense of profitability. In my model, investors automatically assume that managers will invest excess capital in negative-NPV projects. Thus, if the firm announces its intent to raise more capital than investors think it can profitably use, investors effectively charge a higher cost for such capital by reducing the value of the firm's shares in advance of the offering.

My model also assumes that the company can choose among three debt financing alternatives available at time 0 (an equity offering is ruled out from the start as "too expensive," making some form of debt the preferred choice). It can issue two-period straight debt (that is, debt issued at time 0 and maturing at time 2); this way, the profits from the initial project can be used to help fund the second-period investment if the prospects materialize. Alternatively, the firm can finance both projects separately by sequentially issuing single-period straight debt (and forgoing the second issue if the investment option proves "out of the money"). The third possibility is that the firm can issue a convertible bond that matures at the end of the first period and must either be redeemed or converted into equity at that point.

---

13 My explanation is also similar to recent explanations for other special financing arrangements: unit initial public offerings, where warrants are issued with shares (Schultz (1993), and venture capital arrangements, where equity is provided sequentially Sahlman (1990)).

14 The issue (or "information") cost function is assumed to contain fixed and variable components, so that issue costs exhibit economies of scale, and the function is the same in each period.

First, let's consider the two-period straight-debt issue. The advantage of this financing arrangement is that the proceeds from the first-period investment are left in the firm to help finance the second-period project if it turns out to be profitable (and this would also be true of an equity offering). For example, if the proceeds from the first project are sufficient, the two-period contract provides complete financing for both projects up front and saves the entire second-period issue cost. The problem with this financing alternative, however – and this would be even more true of equity – is that the second-period project will be financed, regardless of whether the investment option turns out to be valuable or not. And because the market anticipates this behavior, the firm's securities are priced at a discount to reflect investors' uncertainty about management's use of the proceeds.

The second financing alternative – sequential issues of single-period straight debt – avoids this overinvestment problem of two-period debt (and equity) by forcing managers to return to the market to fund the second project. But this choice also has a problem: if the investment option proves profitable, the firm may be forced to bear heavy new issue costs, particularly if managers have a more optimistic view of the new investment than the market.[15] And if it turns out that the firm really needs equity to fund the investment option, such new issue costs will be even higher.

The optimal solution to this sequential financing problem – the one that both economizes on second-period issue costs and helps control the over-investment problem – is to issue a convertible bond at time 0 that matures at the end of the first period. The bond is designed such that its equity component is "out of the money" at issue and becomes "in the money" only if and when the NPV of the investment option is revealed (to investors as well as managers) to be positive. If the second-period project looks sufficiently profitable at time 1, the bondholders will convert their bonds into equity at the bond maturity date. This leaves the funds both inside the firm and transformed into equity that can

then be used to finance the second-period project. But if the project turns out not to be profitable, the bondholders do not exercise the conversion option; instead they submit their bonds for redemption, thus controlling the overinvestment problem.

The Special Role of the Call Provision. Of course, like all models, this one is clearly unrealistic in many respects. To cite one of its most artificial assumptions, the model assumes that the maturity date of the investment option occurs at the end of the first period. But what if the investment opportunity materializes before then? If the stock price has appreciated sufficiently (in part to reflect the emergence of the new opportunity) to make the bond in the money, then management can use the call provision to force the bondholders to convert into equity.[16]

Forcing conversion has a number of benefits in this situation. First of all, the bonds no longer have to be redeemed at the end of time 1, thus eliminating the need to raise new capital (and the associated issue costs) to fund the new investment project. Second, since dividend yields are typically much lower than convertible coupon rates, forcing conversion halts the cash flow drain on the firm from required interest payments and allows the savings to be channeled into the new project. Third, the resulting addition to the firm's equity base allows it to raise additional debt financing for the new project unencumbered by the outstanding debt issue. As mentioned earlier, one month after MCI forced conversion of its August 1981 10 1/4% convertible, the company issued a new 20-year convertible carrying a coupon of 7 3/4%. Thus, a major advantage of convertible debt is that immediate conversion reduces leverage, thus making it less costly to sell additional securities when more financing is required.

Extension to Debt with Warrants and Convertible Preferreds. My model of convertible bonds – and to some extent those of Stein and Brennan and Schwarz as well – can also be applied to the cases of debt with warrants

---

15   Short-term debt typically has issue costs that are quite low, and the reader may wish to solve the cost-of-issue problem by sequentially issuing short-term debt. However, the periods are assumed long term, and long-term contracts are less costly.

16   The Stein model explains the purpose of the call provision as helping to avoid possible financial distress. The call provision allows companies "to get equity into their capital structures 'through the backdoor' in situations where . . . informational asymmetries make conventional equity issues unattractive." Stein (1992, pp. 3–4).

and convertible preferreds. Like convertible bonds, issues of debt with warrants and convertible preferreds also include options that provide additional financing (by allowing the firm to retain funds it would otherwise pay out) if the options are exercised; if not, the funds are returned to investors. (And it's interesting to note that MCI issued both convertible preferreds and debt with warrants before issuing its first convertible bonds.) Indeed, the attachment of these financing options may make sense whenever a real investment option exists, regardless of whether debt, common, or preferred stock is the initial choice. Thus, for any initial security type (debt, equity, or preferred), it can be advantageous to add a financial option as a hedge against incurring additional issue costs.

THE EVIDENCE

What evidence do we have to back this theory? Consistent with the MCI story, my own recent study found striking evidence of increased investment and financing activity around the time convertible bonds are converted. But, before reporting the results of my own recent study, let me briefly review some of the relevant findings of other studies of convertibles.

The focus of past research on convertibles can be classified into the following four categories: (1) managers' professed motives for issuing convertibles; (2) the frequency and timing of convertible calls and conversions; (3) the kinds of companies that choose to issue convertibles; and (4) the stock market's reaction to announcements of new convertible issues.

The first academic research on convertibles took the form of surveys of corporate issuers. Each of the three best-known surveys, published in 1955, 1966, and 1977,[17] reported that about two-thirds of the responding managers believed that their stock prices would rise in the future and accordingly

viewed their convertible offerings as ways of obtaining deferred equity financing. Management's belief that the convertible feature will be exercised because the stock price will rise is, of course, consistent with my argument that convertible issuers have future investment "options" that will require funding if they turn out to be profitable.

And management's expectations appear to be borne out by the subsequent experience of convertible issuers. For, as shown in a 1991 study by Paul Asquith, roughly two-thirds of all convertible bonds issued (and not subsequently redeemed in a merger) are eventually converted.[18] Moreover, a 1991 study by Asquith and David Mullins showed that essentially all companies call their convertibles if the conversion value exceeds the call price and if there are cash savings from the conversion (that is, if the after-tax interest payments on the debt exceed the dividends on the new equity).[19] The fact that such a large fraction of convertible bonds is ultimately converted is consistent with my view of convertibles as part of an anticipated financing sequence.

Among studies of the kinds of companies that issue convertibles, Stuart Essig's 1991 Ph.D. dissertation showed that convertible issuers tend to have higher-than-average R&D-to-sales ratios, market-to-book ratios, and long-term debt-to-equity ratios (when the convertible issue is counted as debt).[20] They also tend to have more volatile cash flows than issuers of straight debt. At the same time, convertible issuers have lower ratios of tangible assets (property, plant and equipment, and inventories) to total assets. The association of convertibles with volatility, intangible assets, and high R&D and market-to-book ratios is consistent with convertible issuers having significant future growth opportunities, as well as considerable uncertainty about the value and timing of those opportunities. The higher leverage ratios also are consistent with my argument since higher leverage means larger potential cash flow savings from calling the bonds

17   C.J. Pilcher, "Raising Capital with Convertible Securities," *Michigan Business Studies*, 21/2 1955); Eugene Brigham, "An analysis of Convertible Debentures: Theory and Some Empirical Evidence," *Journal of Finance* 21 (1966); and J.R. Hoffmeister, "Use of Convertible Debt in the Early 1970s: A Reevaluation of Corporate Motives," *Quarterly Review of Economics and Business* 17 (1977).

18   Paul Asquith, "Convertible Debt: A Dynamic Test of Call Policy," Working paper, Sloan School of Management (1991).
19   Paul Asquith and David Mullins, Jr., "Convertible Debt: Corporate Call Policy and Voluntary Conversion, *Journal of Finance* 46 (1991), 1273–1289.
20   Stuart Essig, "Convertible Securities and Capital Structure Determinants," Ph.D. dissertation (Graduate School of Business, University of Chicago, 1991).

and replacing them with equity when additional financing is required for new investment.

As noted earlier, the stock market reaction to announcements of convertible bonds is significantly negative, on average, though less negative than in the case of equity issues. Such a finding in and of itself neither supports nor contradicts my explanation. But, as also mentioned earlier, the 1997 study by Jen, Choi, and Lee found considerable variation in the market's response to convertible offerings. The market reaction was significantly less negative to announcements of convertibles by companies with high market-to-book ratios and high (post-offering) capital expenditures. These are the kinds of companies that fit my thesis – firms with significant investment options that may pan out and require future funding, but may not.

New evidence on after-issue investment and financing activity

In my 1998 study of convertibles, I tested my sequential financing hypothesis by comparing the post-issue investment and financing activity of convertible issuers with that of their industry competitors. I began by compiling a sample of all (436) calls of convertible bonds by NYSE or AMEX companies during the period 1968–1990. After combining multiple calls by the same companies within the same year (there were 35 such cases) and deleting cases without Cusip numbers (5) or call announcement dates (2), the sample fell to 394. Finally, I was forced to drop an additional 105 cases because some firms are not listed in *Standard and Poor's Industrial Compustat* data files – my source of information about the company's investment and financing. The final sample contains 289 events that occur during the period 1971 to 1990.

Table 19.1 lists the (two-digit) industrial classification codes of the companies making the 289 calls. As the table shows, convertible issuers are not confined to just a few industries, but nor are they randomly distributed among all sectors. For example, both the oil and gas extraction and computer equipment industries have large concentrations of companies calling their convertibles. The firms in such industries would seem to fit the profile of companies with large ongoing financing requirements combined with significant investment options.

Table 19.2 contains summary statistics comparing the sample firms with their industry medians at the close of the year prior to the call. Like the findings reported in Essig's 1991 study (cited earlier), my sample of convertible-calling companies had higher leverage ratios, higher market-to-book ratios, more R&D to sales, and lower tangible to total assets than the median values in their industries. Moreover, for these sample firms, convertible bonds were an important part of the capital structure, representing on average 30% of total debt.[21]

The next issue my study addressed was the amount of time that elapses between the issuance and call of convertibles. Figure 19.1 presents a frequency distribution of the number of years between issue and call (time to call) for the 286 called convertible bonds that are identified in *Moody's Industrial Manual*. Although the original maturities of the called convertible bonds ranged from 10 to 35 years, with a median of 25 years, the time period between issue and call was relatively short. The mean and median time to call were 6.8 and 5 years, and the mode was 3 years. (MCI's 1981 convertible had a maturity of 20 years and was called in 18 months.)

I also examined the stated uses of funds reported in *Moody's* (by 279 issuers) at the time of issue. Although the most common is to repay other indebtedness (cited by 162 of the 279 issuers), most issuers mention other uses. And, in the majority of cases where debt repayment is cited, there is another use that can be interpreted as providing funding for corporate investment. For example, 95 issuers mentioned a desire to fund increases in working capital (including accounts receivable), 38 cited funding for acquisitions, and 74 mentioned various forms of investment, a category that includes "exploration," "expansion," "capital expenditure," and "new equipment." Thus, considering the relatively short time-to-call together with the stated uses of funds, it seems highly plausible that most

---

21 These companies also tended to be among the larger firms in their industries; however, I think that the more useful comparison is that between convertible issuers and issuers of straight bonds in the same industry. Other studies (e.g. Essig (1991)) have shown that across industries small firms tend to have the greatest proportion of convertible securities. This fact is also consistent with the sequential-financing hypothesis since issue costs are more important for smaller issues, and issue size should be correlated with firm size.

Table 19.1   Distribution of Two-digit Industry Affiliation of 289 Firms Calling Convertible Bonds During the Period 1971 Through 1990

Two-digit code	Industry	No.	Two-digit code	Industry	No.
01	Agriculture Production-Crops	1	48	Communications	7
10	Metal Mining	1	49	Electric, Gas, Sanitary Serv.	7
13	Oil and Gas Extraction	18	50	Durable Goods-Wholesale	7
15	Operative Builders (Bldg. Const.)	2	51	Nondurable Goods-Wholesale	7
16	Heavy Construction-Not Bldg. Const.	2	52	Bldg. Matl., Hardwr., Garden-Retl.	6
20	Food and Kindred Products	5	53	General Merchandise Stores	9
21	Tobacco Products	1	54	Food Stores	4
22	Textile Mill Products	2	56	Apparel and Accessory Stores	1
23	Apparel & Other Finished Pds.,	2	57	Cmp. and Cmp. Software Stores	1
24	Lumber and Wood Pds. - Ex. Furn.	2	58	Eating Places	4
25	Wood-Hshld. Furniture	1	59	Miscellaneous Retail	3
26	Paper and Allied Products	5	60	Depository Institutions	9
27	Printing, Publishing & Allied Products	2	61	Nondepository Credit Instn.	4
28	Chemicals & Allied Products	12	62	Security Brokers and Dealers	6
29	Petroleum Refining	10	63	Insurance Carriers	3
30	Rubber & Misc. Plastics Products	2	65	Real Estate	5
32	Abrasives, Asbestos, Misc. Minrls.	1	67	Real Estate Investment Trust	5
33	Primary Metal Industries	6	70	Hotels, Other Lodging Places	1
34	Fabr. Metal	9	73	Business Services	12
35	Indl., Comml. Machy., Computer Eq.	21	75	Auto Rent and Lease	3
36	Electr., Oth. Elec. Eq., Ex. Cmp.	12	78	Motion Pic., Videotape Prodtn.	2
37	Transportation Equipment	16	79	Misc. Amusement & Rec. Services	3
38	Meas. Instr.; Photo. Gds.; Watches	16	80	Hospitals	5
39	Misc. Manufacturing Industries	3	82	Educational Services	1
40	Railroad Transportation	2	83	Social Services	1
44	Water Transportation	1	87	Engineering Services	1
45	Transportation by Air	17		Total	289

Table 19.2   Summary Statistics Comparing Characteristics of Firms Calling Convertible Bonds During the Period 1971 through 1990 with Matching Industry Medians

	Calling firms mean/median	N	Matching industry mean/median	N	Two-sample test p-values	
					t-test	Wilcoxon
Leverage (LTD/Equity)	0.94/0.47	286	0.53/0.30	248	0.0001	0.0012
Convertible Debt/Total Debt	0.30/0.23	263	0.01/0.00	238	0.0001	0.0001
Total Convertible/Total Debt & Preferred	0.31/0.24	261	0.01/0.00	238	0.0001	0.0001
Market/Book of Equity	2.12/1.60	289	1.64/1.40	250	0.0090	0.0002
R&D/Sales	0.03/0.02	119	0.04/0.01	224	0.1842	0.0986
Tangible/Total Assets	0.97/0.99	228	0.99/1.00	250	0.0001	0.0001

convertible issuers were considering the possible need to fund future investment options when raising capital for current activities.

Post-Call Investment Activity. Having looked at corporate statements of intent and the timing of convertible calls, the next step in my study was to examine both actual investment and further financing activity around the time of the convertible bond calls. For each of the 289 companies in my sample, I collected annual data from

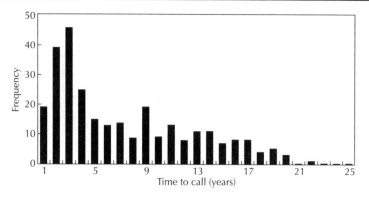

Figure 19.1 Frequency Distribution of Time to Call (Number of Years Between Issue and Call) for 286 Called Convertible Bonds, 1971–1990

Standard & Poor's Industrial Compustat files on capital expenditures (a category which represents the funds used for additions to the company's property, plant, and equipment, but excludes amounts arising from acquired companies). My data collection began five years before the convertible call (year −5) and ended four years after the year of the call (year +4). For each of the 10 years (year 0 counts as the year of the call) and for all 289 companies, I calculated (1) the level of capital expenditures as a percentage of total assets and (2) (for nine of the ten years) the change in capital expenditures as a percentage of total assets from the prior year. Then I performed the same calculations for a control sample of companies in the same four-digit industrial classification.

As shown in Table 19.3 (see columns 2 and 3), companies that call their convertibles show somewhat higher levels of capital expenditures than their industry competitors in the years leading up to the call, but sharply higher levels in the years following the call. Moreover, as can be seen most clearly in column 6, by far the largest changes in capital expenditures are reported in the year of the call (3.4%) and the year immediately following (5.0%). (MCI's increases in capital expenditures were 40.9% and 25.8% in the year of and the year following the call of its first convertible issue in 1983.) As shown in column 7, the industry-matched control firms also show their largest increases in years 0 and 1 (although the increases were only 1.5% and 1.6%). (And, to return to the MCI example, the capital spending of other telecommunications firms changed by −1.1% and 0.6% in 1983 and 1984.) Increased investment by competitors is not surprising since the profitability

of investment options for firms within industries should be correlated. That is, when one oil company decides to undertake a major expansion, the same factors are likely to drive other oil companies to do the same. But even so, both the levels of capital expenditures, and their rates of growth, are significantly higher for the companies that force conversion of their convertibles.

Financing Activity. Using the same *Compustat* source for the same sample of 289 firms, I next calculated the amount of funds received from (1) the sale of common and preferred stock, (2) the issuance of long-term debt, and (3) total sources – each as a percentage of total assets – over the same ten-year period. As shown in Table 19.4, long-term debt, common and preferred stock, and total funding sources all experience significant increases during the year of the call. For example, as shown in Panel A, the average increase in long-term debt for convertible-calling firms was 6.66% of total assets (as compared to less than 1% for the industry matched sample). And, as shown in Panel B, the increase in common and preferred stock in year 0 also is about 6%, which reflects mainly the conversion of the called convertibles into stock.[22]

---

22   I inferred this from the following procedure: Using the fractions of outstanding shares into which the bonds are convertible (about 14%), as reported in Singh, Cowan, and Nayar (1991), and the equity capitalization and total asset means from Table 19.3, I estimate that shares added through conversions on average represent 5.5% of assets. See A.K. Singh, A.R. Cowan, and N. Nayar, "Underwritten Calls of Convertible Bonds," *Journal of Financial Economics* 29 (1991), 173–196.

Table 19.3   Mean and Median Capital Expenditures and Changes in Capital Expenditures (Levels and Changes Scaled by Total Assets for Year −1) for Years Relative to the Call of Convertible Debt by 289 Firms During the Period 1971 Through 1990*

	Capital expenditures/total assets (%)				Changes in capital expenditures/total assets (%)			
	Conversion sample	Industry match			Conversion sample	Industry match	Two-sample test p-values	
Year (1)	mean/median (2)	mean/median (3)	N(sample) (4)	N(match) (5)	mean/median (6)	mean/median (7)	t-test (8)	Wilcoxon (9)
−5	5.0/3.7	4.7/4.0	227	228				
−4	5.8/4.2	5.1/4.5	241	233	1.0[a]/0.5[a]	0.4[a]/0.4[a]	0.0967	0.2106
−3	6.8/5.8	5.7/4.8	245	241	0.8[a]/0.4[a]	0.5[a]/0.4[a]	0.4285	0.6412
−2	7.6/6.4	6.6/5.7	264	253	0.8[a]/0.7[a]	0.8[a]/0.6[b]	0.9377	0.9618
−1	9.2/7.1	7.8/6.2	276	268	1.3[a]/0.6[a]	0.8[a]/0.4[a]	0.1720	0.4009
0	13.4/8.8	9.5/7.2	273	268	3.4/1.3	1.5/0.5	0.0023	0.0019
1	18.3/11.6	11.5/8.1	261	268	5.0[c]/1.8[a]	1.6/0.5	0.0001	0.0001
2	18.8/12.4	12.7/9.5	252	268	1.0[b]/0.9	0.3[a]/0.2	0.5132	0.0274
3	20.5/12.5	13.4/9.6	238	257	1.8[c]/0.9	−0.1[b]/0.2	0.0929	0.0138
4	23.2/12.2	14.6/9.7	224	249	1.3[b]/0.5[b]	0.7/0.2	0.5033	0.5719

* Tests reported in columns 6 and 7 (and indicated by the letters a, b, and c as described below) are paired mean and median tests comparing year-zero changes with the changes in other years. Thus, for example, the 3.4 mean value reported in column 6, year 0 is significantly different from the other mean values of that column in all years. The tests reported in columns 8 and 9 are the indicated two-sample tests comparing the sample and matching mean changes and distributions of changes for each year. Thus, for example, both the means and distributions differ in years 0 and 1 between the conversion sample (column 6) and the industry matches (column 7).
a indicates significance at the 0.01 level
b indicates significance at the 0.05 level
c indicates significance at the 0.10 level

But then in year 1, the percentage of equity drops sharply (by about 4%) – and the reason for this sudden drop will shortly become clear.

In the final part of my study, I also collected data from *Investment Dealer's Digest* (which reports all issues of public securities by corporations) on the financing activity of a somewhat larger sample of 365 convertible-calling companies around the time of the call. Of the 365 firms, 110 obtained new financing during the year prior to the call, while 144 raised new capital the year after the call, a significant increase of 31%. Moreover, of the 144 firms with new post-call financings, 86 issued only debt, 28 only equity, and seven only preferred – while 23 issued some combination of debt and either preferred or equity. Thus, debt is clearly the preferred instrument for financing after convertible bond calls.[23]

---

23   Further, these estimates of the relative number of firms with new debt financings are likely biased down by the omission of private financings by the *Digest*.

Another way to capture the relative importance of debt in post-call financing is to examine leverage ratios (LTD/Equity), which reflect private as well as public debt. As a result of conversion, there are significant reductions in leverage ratios by the end of year 0, the mean and median leverage ratios are 0.63 and 0.36, as compared with 0.94 and 0.47 at the end of the preceding year. But at the end of year 1, the mean and median leverage ratios have risen significantly to 0.81 and 0.39. Moreover, by the end of year 2, mean and median leverage are 1.00 and 0.43, which are indistinguishable from their values at year end −1. (And the same result is obtained using total debt rather than long-term debt in measuring the leverage ratio.) This rapid increase in leverage ratios after the call explains the sharp drop in common and preferred in year 1.

In summary, Figure 19.2 illustrates the changes in both capital expenditures and funding sources of the 289 companies over the 10-year period

Table 19.4 Mean and Median Issuances of Long-term Debt, Common and Preferred, and Total Sources of Funds (Levels and Changes Scaled by Total Assets for Year −1) for Years Relative to the Call of Convertible Debt by 289 Firms During the Period 1971 Through 1990*

	Financing activity level/total assets (%)				Changes in financing activity/total assets (%)			
	Conversion sample	Industry match			Conversion sample	Industry match	Two-sample Test p-values	
Year (1)	mean/median (2)	mean/median (3)	N(sample) (4)	N(match) (5)	mean/median (6)	mean/median (7)	t-Test (8)	Wilcoxon (9)
Panel A: issuances of long-term debt								
−5	4.4/2.6	3.6/1.3	195	224				
−4	5.0/2.8	3.9/1.6	205	229	0.8[a]/0.0[a]	0.7/0.0	0.8398	0.3640
−3	7.5/4.9	3.4/1.8	214	233	2.7[b]/0.5	−0.3[c]/0.0	0.0003	0.0012[c]
−2	7.9/5.6	3.2/1.9	220	241	0.5[a]/0.0[a]	−0.2[a]/0.0	0.4828	0.5194[b]
−1	8.9/5.0	4.3/2.3	230	253	1.3[b]/0.8[a]	0.4/0.0	0.3020	0.1939[c]
0	15.5/9.0	4.9/2.3	243	268	6.6/1.6	0.9/0.0	0.0001	0.0004
1	21.0/8.6	7.2/3.0	229	268	5.4/0.0	1.9[c]/0.0	0.1410	0.2694
2	18.1/8.5	6.7/2.6	225	268	−2.3[a]/0.0[a]	−1.5[b]/0.0	0.7622	0.6488[c]
3	20.9/7.6	9.0/2.8	219	257	2.3[b]/0.0[a]	0.6/0.0	0.4578	0.9114
4	22.4/9.1	9.6/3.2	207	250	0.2[b]/0.0	1.1/0.0	0.7038	0.7552
Panel B: issuances of common and preferred								
−5	0.9/0.1	0.3/0.0	200	224				
−4	1.4/0.1	0.6/0.0	212	229	0.4[a]/0.0[a]	0.2/0.0	0.5335	0.3864
−3	1.7/0.2	0.6/0.0	219	233	0.3[a]/0.0[a]	0.0[c]/0.0[a]	0.4362	0.0072
−2	1.8/0.2	0.6/0.0	227	241	0.0[a]/0.0[a]	0.1/0.0	0.7142	0.2078
−1	2.4/0.5	0.7/0.0	238	253	0.6[a]/0.0[a]	0.0[b]/0.0[a]	0.2119	0.0071
0	9.4/5.4	0.9/0.1	250	268	6.7/3.5	0.2/0.0	0.0001	0.0001
1	5.4/0.5	0.6/0.1	239	268	−4.0[a]/−2.4[a]	−0.3[b]/0.0[a]	0.0002	0.0001
2	3.5/0.2	0.6/0.1	232	268	−1.8[a]/0.0	−0.2/0.0[a]	0.1662	0.0037
3	4.1/0.3	0.9/0.0	220	257	0.7[a]/0.0[a]	0.1/0.0	0.5740	0.8634
4	3.8/0.2	0.7/0.0	206	250	−0.6[a]/0.0	0.0/0.0[b]	0.6038	0.3575
Panel C: Total sources of funds								
−5	13.1/11.2	14.1/11.6	210	224				
−4	15.4/12.7	16.0/12.6	219	228	2.4[a]/1.3[a]	2.2[b]/1.7[a]	0.8455	0.5159
−3	19.4/15.4	16.3/14.4	219	231	4.2[a]/3.1[a]	1.8[b]/1.7[a]	0.0180	0.0127
−2	22.8/18.5	18.3/17.2	212	236	4.0[a]/3.3[a]	1.8[b]/2.2[a]	0.0748	0.0773
−1	27.4/21.9	21.9/19.9	208	240	4.7[a]/2.8[a]	2.3/2.8[c]	0.1112	0.7692
0	43.0/34.3	29.1/22.6	212	252	16.1/12.4	7.3/3.0	0.0043	0.0001
1	47.6/33.4	31.0/24.4	185	244	3.3[a]/−1.4[a]	4.3/1.8[c]	0.7505	0.0012
2	48.1/36.7	32.9/26.1	169	221	1.8[a]/2.2[a]	0.4[a]/1.9[a]	0.6850	0.5429
3	52.9/36.9	38.7/29.4	150	200	5.0[a]/0.8[a]	3.8/2.9	0.7025	0.2585
4	60.2/38.9	40.5/32.8	129	186	7.4/2.8[a]	4.0/2.2	0.4198	0.7757

* Tests reported in columns 6 and 7 (and indicated by the letters a, b, and c as described below) are paired mean and median tests comparing year-zero changes with the changes in other years. Thus, for example, the 6.6 mean value reported in column 6, year 0 of Panel A is significantly different from the other mean values of that column and Panel in all years except year 1. The tests reported in columns 8 and 9 are the indicated two-sample tests comparing the sample and matching mean changes and distributions of changes for each year. Thus, for example, both the means and distributions differ in year 0 of Panel A between the conversion sample (column 6) and the industry matches (column 7).
a indicates significance at the 0.01 level
b indicates significance at the 0.05 level
c indicates significance at the 0.10 level

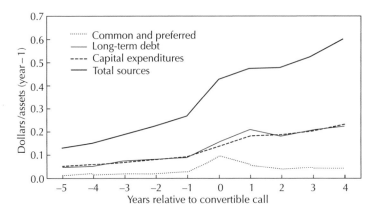

Figure 19.2   Mean Capital Expenditures and New Financing (Scaled by Assets in Year −1) for Years Relative to the Call of Convertible Debt by 289 Firms, 1971–1990

surrounding their conversions. As shown in the figure, both the level of investment and total sources of outside funding experience notable increases in the year of the call and the year after. Nevertheless, equity funding, after rising sharply in the year of conversion, declines sharply in the next two years as companies follow with new debt (or convertible) issues.

CONCLUSION

In the "new economy," a rapidly growing proportion of corporate value appears to derive not from the profits generated by companies' current activities, but from their real investment options that may prove worth pursuing, but may not. For companies whose value consists in large part of real options (and Internet and biotech stocks are likely to fall into this category), convertible bonds may offer the ideal financing match (as long as the coupon rate can be kept low enough) because of the matching financial option that they provide.

In this paper, I propose that corporations use convertible debt as a key element in a financing strategy that aims not only to fund current activities, but to enable them to "exercise" their real options by giving them access to low-cost capital should the options turn out to be valuable. In this sense, convertibles can be seen as the most cost-effective solution to a sequential financing problem – that is, how to fund not only today's

activities, but also tomorrow's opportunities. According to my analysis, the sequential financing approach is designed to control an overinvestment incentive that can arise if financing is provided before an investment option's maturity (i.e., before an investment opportunity materializes). The key considerations in my analysis are new issue costs (which include the "information costs" associated with selling underpriced securities) and the degree of uncertainty about the profitability of the firm's real investment options. The higher the new issue costs, and the greater the degree of uncertainty about the size and timing of the firm's future capital requirements, the more effective are convertibles both in controlling the overinvestment problem and minimizing costs associated with raising capital in the future.

As my analysis also shows, the critical feature of convertibles is the call provision that, provided the stock price is "in the money," effectively enables managers to force conversion of the bonds into equity. As option pricing theory suggests, the value of this call option increases directly with increases in uncertainty about both the eventual value and the maturity date of the real option. If and when the investment opportunity does materialize, exercise of the call feature gives the firm an infusion of new equity that enables it to carry out its new investment and financing plan unencumbered by the debt issue.

Because my analysis suggests the convertible feature is the key to solving a sequential-financing problem, my study examines the investment and financing activities of 289 companies around the time their convertible bonds are called and converted. Such companies made significant increases in capital expenditures (as compared to those by an industry-matched control group) starting in the year of the call and extending through three years after. These companies also showed increased financing activity following the call, mainly new long-term debt that is issued in the year of the call. These new issues of debt, which are often themselves convertible into equity, suggest that financing the exercise of real investment options is an important consideration in the design of convertible bonds.

CHAPTER 20

The Uses of Hybrid Debt in Managing Corporate Risk

Charles W. Smithson (Chase Manhattan Bank) and Donald H. Chew, Jr. (Stern Stewart & Co.)

The corporate use of hybrid debt securities – those that combine a conventional debt issue with a "derivative" such as a forward, swap, or option – increased significantly during the 1980s. And, while many of the more esoteric or tax-driven securities introduced in the last decade have disappeared, corporate hybrids now seem to be flourishing. In so doing, they are helping U.S. companies raise capital despite the restrictive financing climate of the '90s.

Hybrid debt, to be sure, is not a new concept. Convertible bonds, first issued by the Erie Railroad in the 1850s, are hybrid securities that combine straight debt and options on the value of the issuer's equity.[1] What is distinctive about the hybrid debt instruments of the 1980s is that their payoffs, instead of being tied to the issuing company's stock price, are linked to a growing variety of *general* economic variables. As illustrated in Figure 20.1, corporate hybrids have appeared that index investor returns to exchange rates, interest rates, stock market indices, and the prices of commodities such as oil, copper, and natural gas.

The recent wave of corporate hybrids began in 1973, when PEMEX, the state-owned Mexican oil producer, issued bonds that incorporated a *forward* contract on a commodity (in this case, oil). In 1980, Sunshine Mining Co. went a step further by issuing bonds incorporating a commodity *option* (on silver). In 1988, Magma Copper made yet another advance by issuing a bond giving investors a *series of commodity options* (on copper) – in effect, one for every coupon payment.

Other new hybrids, as mentioned, have had their payoffs tied to interest rates, foreign exchange rates, and the behavior of the stock market. In 1981, Oppenheimer & Co., a securities brokerage firm, issued a security whose principal repayment is indexed to the volume of trading on the New York Stock Exchange. Notes indexed to the value of equity indexes appeared in 1986, and inflation-indexed notes (tied to the CPI) were introduced in 1988.

The 1980s also saw new hybrids with payoffs that, like those of convertibles, are tied to company-specific performance. For example, the Rating Sensitive Notes issued by Manufacturer's Hanover in 1988 provide for increased payments to investors if Manny Hanny's creditworthiness declines. And the LYON™ pioneered and underwritten by Merrill Lynch in 1985 grants investors not only the option to convert the debt into equity, but also the right to "put" the security back to the firm.

---

1 The date for the introduction of convertible bonds is reported by Peter Tufano in "Financial Innovation and First-Mover Advantages," *Journal of Financial Economics*, 25, pp. 213–240.

LYON™ is a trademark of Merrill Lynch & Co.

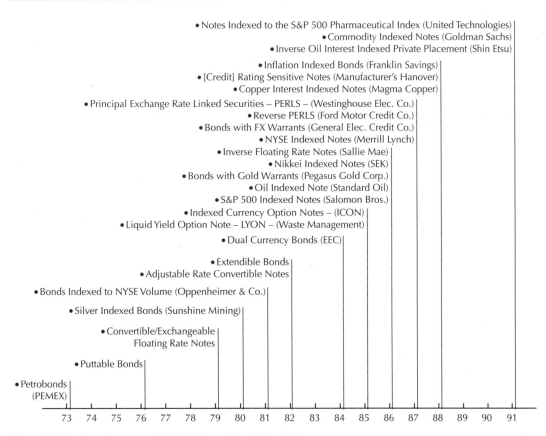

Figure 20.1   Development of Hybrid Securities: 1973–1991

The pace of hybrid innovation peaked around 1987. But hybrids are now staging a comeback. As the title of a recent *Wall Street Journal* article put it, 1991 was "A Boom Year for Newfangled Trading Vehicles."[2] The past year witnessed the introduction of notes indexed to a subset of a general equity index, Goldman Sachs' notes indexed to a commodity index, private placements incorporating options on commodities, and a boom in convertible debt.

Why do companies issue, and investors buy, such complex securities? Before the development of derivative products in the 1970s, investors may have been attracted by the prospect of purchasing a "bundle" of securities – say, debt plus warrants – that they could not duplicate themselves by purchasing both of the components separately. And this

"scarce security" or "market completion" argument also holds for some of today's debt hybrids (especially those that provide longer-dated forwards and options than those available on organized exchanges).

But, because active exchanges now provide low-cost futures and options with payoffs tied to all variety of interest rates, exchange rates, and commodity prices, markets are becoming increasingly "complete," if you will. Given the existence of well-functioning, low-cost markets for many of the components making up the hybrid debt instruments, we have to ask the following question: Is there any reason investors should be willing to pay more for these securities sold *in combination* rather than separately?

In this article, we argue that hybrid debt offers corporate treasurers an efficient means of managing a variety of financial and operating risks – risks that, in many cases, cannot be managed if the firm

---

2   December 26, 1991, p. C1. The *Journal* article dealt more with exchange-traded products than with hybrids.

issues straight debt and then purchases derivatives. By hedging such risks and thereby increasing the expected stability of corporate cash flows, hybrids may lower the issuer's overall funding costs.[3] At the same time, though, part of the present corporate preference for managing price risks with hybrids rather than derivative products stems from current restrictions on the use of hedge accounting for derivatives, as well as tax and regulatory arbitrage opportunities afforded by hybrids.

PRICE VOLATILITY: THE NECESSARY CONDITION FOR HYBRIDS

The stability of the economic and financial environment is a key determinant of the kinds of debt instruments that dominate the marketplace. When prices are stable and predictable, investors will demand – and the capital markets will produce – relatively simple instruments.

In the late 1800s, for example, the dominant financial instrument in Great Britain was the *consol*: a bond with a fixed interest rate and no maturity – it lasted forever. Investors were content to hold infinite-lived British government bonds because British sovereign credit was good and because inflation was virtually unknown. General confidence in price level stability led to stable interest rates, which in turn dictated the use of long-lived, fixed-rate bonds.

But consider what happens to financing practices when confidence is replaced by turbulence and uncertainty. As one of us pointed out in an earlier issue of this journal, in 1863 the Confederate States of America issued a 20-year bond denominated not in Confederate dollars, but in French Francs and Pounds Sterling. To allay the concern of its overseas investors that the Confederacy would not be around to service its debt with hard currency, the issue was also convertible at the option of the holder into cotton at the rate of six pence per pound. In the parlance of today's investment banker, the Confederate States issued a *dual-currency, cotton-indexed* bond.[4]

The breakdown of Bretton Woods and the new era of volatility

Throughout the 1950s and most of the 1960s, economic and price stability prevailed in the U.S., and in the developed nations generally. Investment-grade U.S. corporations responded predictably by raising capital in the form of 30-year, fixed-rate bonds (yielding around 3–4%). But, toward the end of the '60s, rates of inflation in the U.S. and U.K. began to increase. There was also considerable divergence among developed countries in monetary and fiscal policy, and thus in rates of inflation. Such pressures led inevitably to the abandonment, in 1973, of the Bretton Woods agreement to maintain relatively fixed exchanged rates. And, during the early 1970s and thereafter, the general economic environment saw higher and more volatile rates of inflation along with unprecedented volatility in exchange rates, interest rates, and commodity prices. (For evidence of such general price volatility, see Figure 20.2.)

In response to this heightened price volatility, capital markets created new financial instruments to help investors and issuers manage their exposures. Indeed, the last 20 years has seen the introduction of (1) futures on foreign exchange, interest rates, metals, and oil; (2) currency, interest rate, and commodity swaps; (3) options on exchange rates, interest rates, and oil; and (4) options on the above futures and options. Flourishing markets for these products in turn helped give rise to corporate hybrid debt securities that effectively incorporate these derivative products.

USING HYBRIDS TO MANAGE COMMODITY RISK

Unlike foreign exchange and interest rates, which were relatively stable until the 1970s, commodity prices have a long history of volatility. Thus, it is no surprise that hybrid securities designed to hedge

---

3 For preliminary evidence of the impact of issuing hybrid debt on the firm's cost of capital, see Charles Smithson and Leah Schraudenbach, "Reflection of Financial Price Risk in the Firm's Share Price," Chase Manhattan Bank, 1992.

4 Waite Rawls and Charles Smithson, "The Evolution of Risk Management Products," *Journal of Applied Corporate Finance*, Vol. 1 No. 4 (1989).

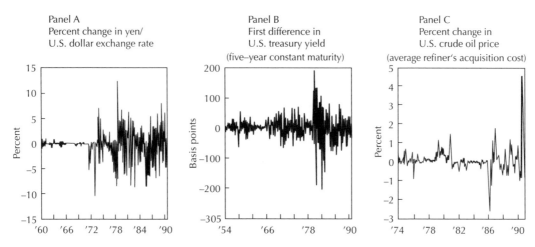

Figure 20.2   General Price Volatility

commodity price risks came well before hybrids with embedded currency and interest rate derivatives.

As mentioned earlier, the Confederacy issued a debt instrument convertible into cotton in 1863. By the 1920s, commodity-linked hybrids were available in U.S. capital markets. A case in point is the gold-indexed bond issued by Irving Fisher's Rand Kardex Corporation in 1925. Similar to the PEMEX issue described earlier, the principal repayment of this gold-indexed bond was tied directly to gold prices.[5] Fisher realized that he could significantly lower his firm's funding costs by furnishing a scarce security desired by investors – in this case, a long-dated forward on gold prices. And Fisher's successful innovation was imitated by a number of other U.S. companies during the '20s.

Like so many of the financial innovations of the 1920s, however, that wave of hybrid debt financings was ended by the regulatory reaction that set in during the 1930s.[6] Specifically, the "Gold Clause" Joint Congressional Resolution of June 5, 1933 virtually eliminated indexed debt by prohibiting "a lender to require of a borrower a different quantity or number of dollars from that loaned." And it was not until October 1977, when Congress passed the Helms Amendment, that the legal basis for commodity-indexed debt was restored.

Hybrids with option features

The hybrids issued by Rand Kardex and PEMEX represent combinations of debt securities with forward contracts; that is, the promised principal repayments were designed to rise or fall directly with changes in the prices, respectively, of gold and oil. In the case of PEMEX, moreover, this forward-like feature reduced the risk to investors that the issuer wouldn't be able to repay principal; it did so by making the *amount* of the principal vary as directly as possible with the company's oil revenues.

Unlike the PEMEX and Rand Kardex issues, Sunshine Mining's 15-year silver-linked bond issued in 1980 combined a debt issue with a *European option*[7] on silver prices. In this case, the promised principal repayment could not fall below a certain level (the face value), but would increase proportionally with increases in the price of silver price above $20 per ounce at maturity.[8] Because most of the commodity-linked hybrids that followed the Sunshine Mining issue in the '80s contain embedded options rather than forwards, let's consider briefly how the

---

5   See J. Huston McCulloch, "The Ban on Indexed Bonds," *American Economic Review* 70 (December 1980), pp. 1018–21.
6   See Merton Miller's account of financial innovation in the 1920s and 1930s in the first article of this issue.

---

7   European options can be exercised only at maturity, as distinguished from American options, which can be exercised any time before expiration.
8   From the perspective of 1991, during which the silver price has averaged $4.00 per ounce, this exercise price of $20 per ounce may seem bizarre. But keep in mind that this bond was issued in early 1980. During the period October 1979–January 1980, the price of silver averaged $23 per ounce.

embedding of options within debt issues manages risk and lowers the issuer's cost of capital.

How Hybrids with Options Manage Risk. Corporate bondholders bear "downside" risk while typically being limited to a fixed interest rate as their reward. (In the jargon of options, the bondholder is "short a put" on the value of the firm's assets.) Because of this limited upside, they charge a higher "risk premium" when asked to fund companies with more volatile earnings streams. Like the forward contract embedded in the PEMEX issue, options also provide bondholders with an equity-like, "upside" participation. In return for this upside participation, bondholders will reduce the risk premium they charge. Indeed, the greater the expected volatility of the commodity price in question, the more valuable is that embedded option to the bondholders.[9]

Unlike hybrids with forwards, hybrids with embedded options provide investors with a "floor" – that is, a minimum principal repayment or set of coupons. And, though options therefore effect a less complete transfer of risk than in the case of forwards (in the sense that the firm's financing costs don't fall below the floor in the event of an extreme decline in commodity prices), investors should be willing to pay for the floor in the form of a reduced base rate of interest. To the extent they lower the rate of interest, option-like hybrids reduce the probability of default, thus reassuring bondholders and the rating agencies.

A good example of corporate risk management with options was a 1986 issue of Eurobonds with detachable gold warrants by Pegasus Gold Corporation, a Canadian gold mining firm. In effect, this issue gave investors two separable claims: (1) a straight debt issue with a series of fixed interest payments and a fixed principal repayment; and (2) European options on the price of gold. By giving bondholders a participation in the firm's gold revenues, the inclusion of such warrants reduced the coupon rate on the bond – which in turn lowered the issuer's financial risk.

Probably the most newsworthy hybrid in 1986, however, was Standard Oil's *Oil-Indexed Note*. This hybrid combines a zero-coupon bond with a European option on oil with the same maturity. The issue not only aroused the interest of the IRS, but also succeeded in rekindling regulatory concerns about the potential for "speculative abuse" built into hybrid securities.[10]

Commodity Interest-Indexed Bonds. The commodity hybrids mentioned thus far are all combinations of debt with forwards or options with a single maturity. In effect, they link only the principal repayment to commodity prices, but not the interim interest payments. But, in recent years, hybrids have also emerged that combine debt with a *series of options* of different maturities – maturities that are typically designed to correspond to the coupon dates of the underlying bond.

In 1988, for example, Magma Copper Company issued *Copper Interest-Indexed Senior Subordinated Notes*. This 10-year debenture has embedded within it 40 option positions on the price of copper – one maturing in 3 months, one in 6 months, . . ., and one in 10 years. The effect of this series of embedded option positions is to make the company's quarterly interest payments vary with the prevailing price of copper, as shown below:

Average copper price	Indexed interest rate
$2.00 or above	21%
1.80	20
1.60	19
1.40	18
1.30	17
1.20	16
1.10	15
1.00	14
0.90	13
0.80 or below	12

In 1989, Presidio Oil Company issued an oil-indexed note with a similar structure, but with the coupons linked to the price of natural gas. And, in 1991, Shin Etsu, a Japanese chemical manufacturer, issued a hybrid with a similar structure; however, the issue was a private placement and the coupon payment floated *inversely* with the price of oil.

9   For a discussion of how the equity option embedded in convertibles could make convertible bondholders indifferent to increases in the volatility of corporate cash flow, see Michael Brennan and Eduardo Schwartz, "The Case for Convertibles," *Chase Financial Quarterly* (Fall 1981). Reprinted in *Journal of Applied Corporate Finance* (Summer 1988).

10   See James Jordan, Robert Mackay, and Eugene Moriarty, "The New Regulation of Hybrid Debt Instruments," *Journal of Applied Corporate Finance*, Vol. 2 No. 4 (Winter 1990).

THE CASE OF FOREST OIL: THE CONSEQUENCES OF NOT MANAGING RISK

It was Forest Oil, however, and not Presidio, that first considered issuing natural gas-linked debt. But Forest's management was confident that natural gas prices would go higher in the near future and thus decided that the price of the natural gas-linked debt would turn out to be too high. Unfortunately, the company's bet on natural gas prices ended up going against them. Natural gas prices since the issue was contemplated have fallen dramatically, and the company has been squeezed between high current interest costs and reduced revenues. Indeed, the squeeze has been so tight that Forest has been forced to restructure its debt.

USING HYBRIDS TO MANAGE FOREIGN EXCHANGE RISK

As Figure 20.2 suggests, exchange rates became more volatile following the abandonment of the Bretton Woods agreement in 1973. As a result, many companies have experienced foreign exchange risk arising from transaction, translation, and economic exposures.

The simplest way to manage an exposure to foreign exchange risk is by using a forward foreign exchange contract. If the firm is long foreign currency, it can cover this exposure by selling forward contracts. Or if it has a short position, it can buy forwards.

Dual Currency Bonds. Similar to PEMEX's oil-indexed issue, the simplest FX hybrid debt structure is a *Dual Currency Bond*. Such a bond combines a fixed-rate, "bullet" (that is, single) repayment bond and a long-dated forward contract on foreign exchange. For example, in 1985, Philip Morris Credit issued a dual-currency bond in which coupon payments are made in Swiss Francs while principal will be repaid US Dollars.

PERLs. A variant of the dual currency structure is the *Principal Exchange Rate Linked Security*. In 1987, Westinghouse Electric Company issued *PERLs* wherein the bondholder received at maturity the principal the USD value of 70.13 million New Zealand dollars. The issuer's motive in this case was likely to reduce its funding costs by taking advantage of an unusual investor demand for

long-dated currency forwards. Earlier in the same year, and presumably with similar motive, Ford Motor Credit Company issued *Reverse PERLs*. In this case, the principal repayment varied inversely with the value of the yen.[11]

Creating a hybrid by adding options

As in the case of commodity-linked hybrids, forward-like FX hybrids seemed to have given way to structures containing warrants or other option-like features. In 1987, for example, General Electric Credit Corporation made a public offering made up of debt and yen-USD currency exchange warrants.

Bonds with Principal Indexed (Convertible) to FX. Like bonds with warrants, convertible bonds are made up of bonds and equity options. But there is one important difference: In the case of bonds with warrants, the bondholder can exercise the option embodied in a warrant and still keep the underlying bond. With convertibles, the holder must surrender the bond to exercise the option. Sunshine Mining's Silver-Indexed Bonds and Standard Oil's Oil Indexed Notes are similar constructions. The bondholder can receive either the value of the bond or the value of the option, but not both.

When this debt structure appeared with an embedded foreign currency option, the hybrid was called an *Indexed Currency Option Note* (or *ICON*). This security, which was first underwritten by First Boston in 1985, combines a fixed rate, bullet repayment bond and a European option on foreign exchange.[12]

USING HYBRIDS TO MANAGE INTEREST RATE RISK

Some companies have significant exposures to interest rates. Take the case of firms that supply

---

11 See Michael G. Capatides, *A Guide to the Capital Markets Activities of Banks and Bank Holding Companies* (Browne & Co.), 1988, p. 132.
12 In his article in this issue, "Securities Innovation: An Overview," John Finnerty notes that ICONs "were introduced and disappeared quickly."

inputs to the housing market. When interest rates rise, the revenues of such firms tend to fall. The use of standard, floating-rate bank debt in such cases would likely increase the probability of default.

Creating a hybrid with embedded swaps

To manage interest rate risk, such companies may be best served by a debt instrument wherein the coupon payment actually declines when interest rates rise. Such an *Inverse Floating Rate Note* – or a *Yield-Curve Note*, as it was called when first issued by the Student Loan Marketing Association (Sallie Mae) in the public debt market in 1986 – can be decomposed into a floating-rate, bullet repayment note and a plain vanilla interest rate swap for twice the principal of the loan.

Creating a hybrid by adding options

Just as bondholders can be provided options to exchange their bonds for a specified amount of a commodity or foreign currency, hybrid securities have been issued that give bondholders the option to exchange a bond (typically at maturity) for another bond (typically with the same coupon and maturity).

Convertible/Exchangeable Floating Rate Notes. These hybrids, which give the holder the right to convert to (or exchange for) a fixed-rate bond at a pre-specified interest rate, first appeared in 1979. Such notes contain embedded "put" options on interest rates; that is, investors are likely to exercise their conversion or exchange rights only if interest rates fall below a certain level.

Extendible Notes. The same, moreover, is true of extendible notes, which give the holder the right to exchange the underlying bond for a bond of longer maturity. Such bonds first appeared in 1982.

USING HYBRIDS TO REDUCE CONFLICTS BETWEEN BONDHOLDERS AND SHAREHOLDERS

In "normal" circumstances – that is, when operations are profitable and the firm can comfortably

meet its debt service payments and investment schedule – the interests of bondholders and shareholders are united. Both groups of investors benefit from managerial decisions that increase the total value of the firm.

In certain cases, however, corporate managements find themselves in the position of being able to increase shareholder value *at the expense of bondholders*.[13] For example, as happened in a number of leveraged recapitalizations, management could reduce the value of outstanding bonds by increasing debt or adding debt senior to that in question. (In professional circles, this is known as *event risk*, in academic parlance it is the *claims dilution problem*.) Or, if the firm were in danger of insolvency, management could choose – as did some S&L executives – to invest in ever riskier projects in desperate attempts to save the firm (the *asset substitution problem*). Finally, a management squeezed between falling revenues and high interest payments could choose to pass up value-adding projects such as R&D or, if things are bad enough, basic maintenance and safety procedures (the *underinvestment problem*).[14]

Corporate debtholders are well aware that such problems can arise, and they accordingly protect themselves by lowering the price they are willing to pay for the debt. For corporate management, such lower prices translate into higher interest payments, which in turn further raise the probability of financial trouble.

Hybrids reduce these shareholder–bondholder conflicts by reducing current interest rates, shifting debt service payments to periods when firms are better able to pay, stabilizing cash flow, and thereby reducing the likelihood of financial distress. In so doing, they also raise the price of

13   For the seminal discussion of the effect of conflicts between shareholders and debtholders (and between management and shareholders as well) on the behavior of the firm, see Michael C. Jensen and William H. Meckling, "Theory of the Firm: Managerial Behavior, Agency Costs, and Capital Structure," *Journal of Financial Economics* (1976), pp. 305–360.

14   For an account of the underinvestment problem, see Stewart Myers, "The Determinants of Corporate Borrowing," *Journal of Financial Economics* (1977). For a more detailed examination of these sources of shareholder/debtholder conflict, see Clifford W. Smith and Jerold B. Warner, "On Financial Contracting: An Analysis of Bond Covenants," *Journal of Financial Economics*, 7 (1979), pp. 117–161.

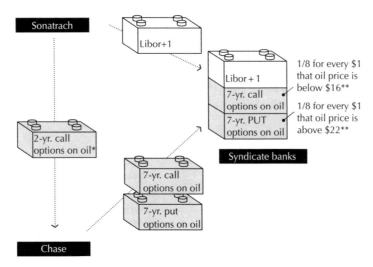

Figure 20.3   Oil-linked Credit-sensitive Syndicate
*During the first two years, if the price of oil exceeds $23, Sonatrach will pay a supplemental coupon to Chase.
**In the first year, the syndicate receives additional interest if the price of oil falls outside the range of $16–$22. In year 2, the range widens to $15–$23, then to $14–$24 in year 3, and to $13–$25 in years 4 through 7.

the corporate debt to investors and lower the overall corporate cost of capital.

Using hybrids to reduce the claims dilution problem (or protect against "event risk")

Puttable Bonds. Introduced in 1976, these bonds give their holders the option to "put" the bond back to the issuer. Such an option would be exercised only if interest rates rise or the issuer's credit standing falls. In this sense, puttable bonds give bondholders both a call option on interest rates and an option on the credit spread of the issuer.[15] Such put options thus protect bondholders not only against increases in interest rates, but also against the possibility of losses from deteriorating operating performance or leveraged recapitalizations. In the wake of the widely publicized bondholder losses accompanying the KKR buyout of RJR

Nabisco in 1989, the use of put options to protect against such "event risk" enjoyed a new vogue.

Floating Rate, Rating Sensitive Notes. These notes, issued by Manufacturer Hanover in 1988, contain explicit options on the issuer's credit standing. In this security, Manufacturer's Hanover agreed to pay investors a spread above LIBOR that increased with each incremental decline in the bank's senior debt rating.

From the standpoint of risk management, however, there is an obvious flaw in the design of this security. Although it may partially compensate investors for increases in risk, it actually increases the probability of default instead of reducing it. The security increases the corporate debt service burden precisely when the issuing firm can least afford it – when its credit rating has fallen and, presumably, its operating cash flow declined.

A hybrid structure designed to overcome this problem was a syndication of oil-indexed bonds created by Chase Manhattan for Sonatrach (the state hydrocarbons company of Algeria) in 1990. As illustrated in Figure 20.3, the transaction was structured so that Chase accepted two-year call options on oil from Sonatrach and then transformed those two-year calls into seven-year calls and puts that were passed on to the syndicate members. Investors were compensated for a

---

15   Extendible notes also provide bondholders with an option on the firm's credit standing. But, unlike puttable debt, it represents the opportunity to benefit from increases in the firm's credit standing, or decreases in the spread. In the case of extendible notes, if the credit spread of the issuer decreases, the right to extend the maturity of the note (at the old credit spread) has value.

below-market interest by a payoff structure that would provide them with higher payoffs in the event of significantly *higher or lower* oil prices.

For the issuer, however, the security requires higher payments to Chase *only in the event of higher oil prices*. If the price of oil declines, although the syndicate members receive a higher yield, the increase comes from Chase, not Sonatrach.

Using hybrids to reduce the asset substitution and underinvestment problems

Convertibles. At the outset, we noted that convertible bonds contain embedded options on the company's equity. By providing bondholders with the right to convert their claims into equity, management provides bondholders with the assurance that they will participate in any increase in shareholder value that results from increasing the risk of the company's activities – whether by leveraging up or undertaking riskier investments. By lowering current interest rates and thus reducing the likelihood of financial trouble, convertibles also reduce the probability that financially strapped companies will be forced to forgo valuable investment opportunities.[16]

Convertibles (and debt with warrants, their close substitutes) are also potentially useful in resolving disagreements between bondholders and shareholders about just how risky the firm's activities are. The value of convertibles are risk-neutral in the following sense: Unexpected increases in company risk reduce the value of the bond portion of a convertible, but at the same time increase the value of the embedded option (by increasing volatility). It is largely because of this risk-neutralizing effect – and for their role in reducing the "underinvestment problem" mentioned below – that convertible issuers tend to be smaller, newer, riskier firms characterized by high growth and earnings volatility.[17]

---

16 More technically, the underinvestment problem arises from the fact that, in financially troubled firms, an outsized portion of the returns from new investments must go to help restore the value of the bondholders' claims before the shareholders receive any payoff at all. This has also been dubbed the "debt overhang" problem.
17 For an exposition of this argument, see Michael Brennan and Eduardo Schwartz, "The Case for Convertibles," *Chase Financial Quarterly* (Fall 1981). Reprinted in *Journal of Applied Corporate Finance* (Summer 1988).

THE CASE OF LYONS

While a number of bonds are puttable or convertible, the Liquid Yield Option Note (LYON) introduced by Merrill Lynch in 1985 is both puttable and convertible. The combination of the put and conversion features are especially useful in controlling the asset substitution, or risk-shifting, problem just described.[18] For this reason, the LYONs structure should be particularly attractive to issuers with substantial capital investment opportunities and a wide range of alternative investment projects (with varying degrees of risk).

It is thus interesting to note that the LYON structure was first used to fund companies where the asset substitution problem was acute. Take the case of Waste Management, the first issuer of LYONs. Although Waste Management is today a household name among even small investors, in 1985 the company could best be viewed as a collection of "growth options." As such it posed considerable uncertainty for investors.

THE ECONOMIC RATIONALE FOR ISSUING A HYBRID SECURITY

We are still left with a fundamental question: Given the well-functioning, low-cost markets for derivative products available today, why should a corporate issuer ever prefer the "bundled" hybrid to simply issuing standard debt and buying or selling the derivatives. We now discuss the following three reasons why corporate management might choose hybrids:

(1) If the firm issuing the hybrid can provide investors with a "play" not available otherwise – that is, a derivative instrument not available in the traded derivatives markets – the issuing firm will consequently be paid a premium for "completing the market."
(2) The hybrid may enable the issuer to take advantage of tax or regulatory arbitrages that would lower the cost of borrowing.

---

18 As described at length in the next article in this issue, the put feature also enabled Merrill Lynch to tailor the security for its network of retail investors.

(3) By embedding a risk management product into a hybrid, the issuer may be able to obtain hedge accounting treatment, which may not be allowed if the derivative was bought or sold separately.

Using hybrids to provide investors with a "play"

The most straightforward reason for issuing a hybrid is to provide investors with a means of taking a position on a financial price. If the issuer provides a "play" not otherwise available, the investor will be willing to pay a premium, thereby reducing the issuer's cost of funding. (And, if the hybrid provides investors with a "scarce security" not otherwise obtainable, it may also provide corporate issuers with a hedge they can't duplicate with derivative products.)

The "play" can be in the form of a forward contract. Perhaps the best example of such is dual currency bonds, which provided investors with foreign exchange forward contracts with longer maturities than those available in the standard market. The forward contracts embedded in dual currency bonds have maturities running to 10 years, whereas liquidity in the standard foreign exchange forward market declines for maturities greater than one year, and falls very significantly beyond five years.

The "play," however, has more commonly been in the form of an option embedded in the bond – generally an option of longer maturity than those available in the standard option market. Sunshine Mining's Silver Indexed Bond fits this category, as do Standard Oil's Oil Indexed Note and the gold warrantes issued by Pegasus Gold Corporation. In 1986 long-dated options on stock market indices were introduced with the development of hybrid debt in which the principal was indexed to an equity index. While the first such debt issues were indexed to the Nikkei, Salomon Brothers' "S&P 500 Index Subordinated Notes (SPINs)" have probably received more public attention. A SPIN is convertible into the value of the S&P 500 Index, rather than into an individual equity. Since then, debt has been issued that is indexed to other equity indices (for example, the NYSE index) or subsets of indices. For example, in 1991, United Technologies issued a zero-coupon bond indexed to the S&P Pharmaceutical Index.

Using hybrids to "arbitrage" tax and/or regulatory authorities

Hybrid debt has also been used to take advantage of asymmetries in tax treatment or regulations in different countries or markets. One classic example is a case of "arbitrage" reported in *Business Week* under the provocative title, "A Way for US Firms to Make 'Free Money'." The "free money" came from two sources:

(1) A difference in tax treatment between the U.S. and Japan – the Japanese tax authorities ruled that income earned from holding a zero-coupon bond would be treated as a capital gain, thereby making interest income on the zero non-taxable for Japanese investors. In contrast, U.S. tax authorities permitted any U.S. firm issuing a zero coupon bond to deduct from current income the imputed interest payments.
(2) A regulatory arbitrage – The Ministry of Finance limited Japanese pension funds' investments in non-yen-dominated bonds issued by foreign corporations to at most 10% of their portfolios. The Ministry of Finance also ruled that dual currency bonds qualified as a yen issue, thus allowing dual currency bonds to command a premium from Japanese investors.

Consequently, U.S. firms issued zero-coupon yen bonds (to realize the interest rate savings from the tax arbitrage), and then issued a dual currency bond to hedge the residual yen exposure from the yen zero, while realizing a further interest savings from the regulatory arbitrage.

Tax-Deductible Equity. Perhaps the most thinly disguised attempt to issue tax-deductible equity was the *Adjustable Rate Convertible Debt* introduced in 1982.[19] Such convertibles paid a coupon determined by the dividend rate on the firm's common stock; moreover, the debt could be converted to common stock at the current price at any time (i.e., there was no conversion premium). Not

---

19 This point is made by John Finnerty in his article in this issue.

surprisingly, once the IRS ruled that this was equity for tax purposes, this structure disappeared.

On a less aggressive level, hybrid structures like Merril Lynch's LYON take advantage of the treatment of zero coupon instruments by U.S. tax authorities – that is, zero coupon bonds allow the issuer to deduct deferred interest payments from current income (although the holder of the bond must declare them as income). Given the impact of the IRS ruling on adjustable rate convertible debt, it is not surprising that a great deal of attention has been given to the tax status of the LYON.

Using hybrids to obtain accrual accounting treatment for risk management

If a U.S. company uses a forward, futures, swap, or option to hedge a specific transaction (for example, a loan or a purchase or a receipt), it is relatively simple to obtain accrual accounting treatment for the hedge. (Changes in the market value of the hedging instrument offset changes in the value of the asset being hedged, so there is no need to mark the hedging instrument to market.)

If, however, the firm wishes to use one of the risk management instruments to hedge expected net income or an even longer-term economic exposure, the current position of the accounting profession is that the hedge position must be marked to market. Some companies have been reluctant to use derivatives to manage such risks because this accounting treatment would increase the volatility of their reported income – *even while such a risk management strategy would stabilize their longer-run operating cash flow.*

With the use of hybrids, by contrast, which contain embedded derivatives, the firm may be able to obtain accrual accounting treatment for the entire package. Accountants are accustomed to valuing convertible debt at historical cost; and, given this precedent, they can extend the same treatment to hybrids.[20]

---

20   See J. Matthew Singleton, "Hedge Accounting: A State-of-the-Art Review," *Journal of Banking and Finance*, 5 (Fall 1991), pp. 26–32.

CONCLUDING REMARKS

Beginning in 1980 with Sunshine Mining's issue of silver-linked bonds, U.S. corporations have increasingly chosen to raise debt capital by embedding derivatives such as forwards or options into their notes and bonds. In the early '80s, such hybrids typically provided investors with payoffs (at first only principal, but later interest payments as well) indexed to commodity prices, interest rates, and exchange rates. But, in recent years, companies have begun to issue debt indexed to general stock market indices and even subsets of such indices.

Critics of such newfangled securities view them as the offspring of "supply-driven" fads. According to this view, profit-hungry investment banks set their highly-paid "rocket scientists" to designing new securities that can then be foisted on unsuspecting corporate treasurers and investors.

As economists, however, we begin with the assumption that capital market innovations succeed only to the extent they do a better job than existing products in meeting the demands of issuers and investors. The evidence presented in these pages, albeit anecdotal, suggests that hybrid debt is a capital market response to corporate treasurers' desire to manage pricing risks and otherwise tailor their securities to investor demands. In some cases, especially those in which hybrids feature long-dated forwards or options, hybrids are furnishing investors with securities they cannot obtain elsewhere.

Like the remarkable growth of futures, swaps, and options markets beginning in the late '70s, the proliferation of corporate hybrids during the '80s is fundamentally an attempt to cope with increased price volatility. The sharp increase in the volatility of exchange rates, interest rates, and oil prices – to name just the most important – during the 1970s provided the "necessary condition" for the rise of hybrids.

But another important stimulant to hybrids has come from other constraints on companies' ability to raise debt. In the early '80s, for example, when interest rates were high, hybrid debt was used by riskier firms to reduce their interest costs to manageable levels. Given the current level of interest rates today, most companies would likely choose to borrow as much straight debt as possible. But except for the highest-rated companies, many firms also now face *non-price* credit restrictions that have greatly enlarged credit spreads. In some such cases, companies are using hybrid debt to lower their risk profile and thus avoid the higher funding costs now associated with being a riskier corporate borrower. In other cases, hybrids are providing access to debt capital that would otherwise be denied on any terms.

CHAPTER 21

Using Project Finance to Fund Infrastructure Investments

Richard A. Brealey, Ian A. Cooper, and Michel A. Habib (London Business School)*

Throughout most of the history of the industrialized world, much of the funding for large-scale public works such as the building of roads and canals has come from private sources of capital. It was only toward the end of the 19th century that public financing of large "infrastructure" projects began to dominate private finance, and this trend continued throughout most of the 20th century.

Since the early 1980s, however, private-sector financing of large infrastructure investments has experienced a dramatic revival. And, in recent years, such private funding has increasingly taken the form of project finance. The principal features of such project financings have been the following:

- A project is established as a separate company, which operates under a concession obtained from the host government.
- A major proportion of the equity of the project company is provided by the project manager or sponsor, thereby tying the provision of finance to the management of the project.
- The project company enters into comprehensive contractual arrangements with suppliers and customers.

- The project company operates with a high ratio of debt to equity, with lenders having only limited recourse to the government or to the equity-holders in the event of default.

The above characteristics clearly distinguish project finance from traditional lending. In conventional financing arrangements, projects are generally not incorporated as separate companies; the contractual arrangements are not as comprehensive, nor are the debt-equity ratios as high, as those observed in the case of project finance; and the vast majority of loans offer lenders recourse to the assets of borrowers in case of default.

Our purpose in this paper is to explore some possible rationales for the distinctive characteristics of project finance, from the viewpoint of both the project sponsor and the host government. We do so in the specific context of infrastructure investments. After providing some information about the growth of project finance in funding such investments, we note that project finance is but one of several mechanisms for involving the private sector in funding and managing infrastructure projects. We show how project finance, and the complex web of contractual arrangements that such funding entails, can be used to address "agency problems" that reduce efficiency in large organizations, private as well as public. We also view the contracts among the multiple parties to project financings as risk management devices designed to shift a variety of project risks to those

* We would like to thank Joseph Blum, Carlo Bongianni, Don Lessard, Gill Raine, Mary Wan and Adam Wilson for helpful discussions. The third author would like to acknowledge the financial support of the International Programme on the Management of Engineering and Construction.

parties best able to appraise and control them. In closing, we discuss what we believe are some common misconceptions about the benefits and costs of project finance – particularly, the notion that project finance represents "expensive finance" for governments – and we contrast project finance with other private-sector options such as privatization and the use of service contracts with private-sector companies.

THE GROWTH IN PROJECT FINANCE: SOME EVIDENCE

Comprehensive data on the financing of infrastructure projects do not appear to be available. Table 21.1 does, however, provide information about the growth in the value of those projects in developing countries that have been partially financed by the International Finance Corporation (the World Bank's private sector affiliate).

Over 80% (by value) of the projects involving the IFC have been in the power and telecommunication industries, with the remainder in transportation (roads, railroads, and ports), water, and pipelines. About 50% of the projects have been in Latin America, with the bulk of the remainder in Asia.

The use of project finance has not been restricted to infrastructure investments in developing countries. Indeed, over 40% of the project finance loans reported in the 1995 survey conducted by *IFR Project Finance International* were for projects in the United States, Australia, or the United Kingdom. In the United States, the passage of the Public Utility Regulatory Power Act (PURPA) in 1978 provided a major stimulus to the use of project finance by requiring that electric utilities purchase power from independent power producers. This encouraged the formation of stand-alone power producers able to borrow large sums on the basis of the long-term power purchase agreements they had entered into with electric utilities. Since these projects do not directly involve a government or a government agency, they are somewhat beyond the scope of this article. So are projects in Australia, which have primarily been in extractive industries rather than in infrastructure.

In the U.K. by contrast, the government has been directly involved in a growing number of infrastructure projects since it announced in 1992

Table 21.1 Value of Projects Involving IFC Participation in Developing Countries

Year of approval	No. of projects	Value of projects $ million
1966–1987	7	517
1988	2	409
1989	6	704
1990	4	1279
1991	6	1103
1992	8	1384
1993	15	3699
1994 (1st 6 months)	30	5512

Source: G. Bond and L. Carter, "Financing Private Infrastructure Projects; Emerging Trends from IFC's Experience," International Finance Corporation, Discussion Paper 23, 1994.

the establishment of the Private Finance Initiative (PFI). The PFI is designed to involve the private sector in the financing and the management of infrastructure and other projects. Private finance has so far been used principally for transportation projects such as the £320 million rail link to Heathrow airport, the £2.7 billion Channel Tunnel Rail Link, a £250 million scheme to build and maintain a new air traffic control center in Scotland, and projects worth more than £500 million to design, build, finance, and operate (DBFO) trunk roads. But the potential scope of the PFI is wide. Over 1,000 potential PFI projects have been identified, and the government has signed contracts to build and maintain such diverse assets as prisons, hospitals, subway cars, and the National Insurance computer system.[1]

SOME ALTERNATIVES TO PROJECT FINANCE

A government need not involve the private sector in either the financing or the management of projects, and may choose to undertake both itself. As we will argue below, the desirability of private-sector involvement in infrastructure projects

1 See Standard & Poor's, *Global Project Finance*, July 1996, pages 24–28, and OXERA, *Infrastructure in the UK*.

depends in large part on the extent to which (1) the provision of high-powered incentives is necessary to the success of the project and (2) such incentives can be specified in a verifiable contract.

It is important to note that high-powered incentives need not always be beneficial. For example, consider the hypothetical case of privatized parking enforcement agencies. Such organizations would probably be subject to severe moral hazard problems if provided with high-powered incentives, for they may then have an incentive to claim an offence has been committed even where none has.

It should further be noted that public-sector organizations are not entirely devoid of incentives, and that these are often of the same nature as the incentives found in private-sector companies. Both voters and shareholders have an interest in efficient management, the former as taxpayers and the latter as owners. Both use their votes to discipline inefficient management, the former by voting for a new government, and the latter by voting for a new management. Nonetheless, the greater power and prevalence of incentives in private-sector organizations suggests an important role for these organizations when high-powered incentives are desired.

A government that uses project finance to fund a project obtains both private-sector funding and private-sector management. Project finance therefore reduces the need for government borrowing, shifts part of the risks presented by the project to the private sector, and aims to achieve more effective management of the project. But, as we indicate in Table 21.2, there are a number of other means of involving the private sector in infrastructure investment. The government can do so through privatization, for example, in which case the private sector provides capital and management services to an entire industry rather than to individual projects. Thus, the government can privatize a public utility that generates and distributes electric power, rather than grant a concession to a private company to generate power that is then sold to the public utility.

If the government simply wishes to benefit from private-sector management expertise, it can contract with the private sector for the provision of management services while continuing to finance the project and retaining ownership of the project's assets. Conversely, the government can simply

Table 21.2   Ways that Infrastructure Projects can be Funded and Managed

Arrangement	Finance	Management
Project finance	Private	Private
Privatization	Private	Private
Service contracts	Government	Private
Leases	Private	Government
Nationalization	Government	Government

secure finance by leasing the project's assets from the private sector, while continuing to be responsible for the management of the project.

In view of these alternatives to project finance, it is natural to ask why it has developed into such an important mechanism for funding infrastructure investments. We argue that the dominant reason for the growing importance of project finance in funding infrastructure investment is that it addresses agency problems in a way that other forms of financing do not.

PROJECT FINANCE AS A RESPONSE TO AGENCY PROBLEMS

Agency problems arise from the differing, and sometimes conflicting, interests of the various parties involved in any large enterprise. Success of the enterprise therefore requires that these parties be provided with incentives to work together for the common good. This can be achieved, to some extent at least, by the appropriate choice of a company's financial structure.

Consider, for example, the problem faced by shareholders in a public corporation who wish to motivate the CEO to work hard to increase firm value. Shareholders would like the CEO to do her utmost to increase shareholder wealth, and they may wish to write a contract that specifies what she should do in all the various circumstances that she may encounter. But such a contract would be impossible to write, if only because of the difficulty of envisaging and describing these various circumstances. Any contract between shareholders and corporate managers will therefore inevitably be incomplete. Furthermore, even if it were possible to write a complete contract that specified exactly what the CEO were to do in every circumstance, it would be very costly for shareholders to monitor the manager to ensure that she was keeping to the contract.

One solution to these problems of incomplete contracting and costly monitoring is to arrange for the manager to take an equity stake in the business. Such a stake ties the manager's wealth to her actions, thus rewarding her for hard work and penalizing her for sloth. The "residual claimancy" associated with the ownership of equity therefore serves to motivate the manager, to some extent at least, in the cases where contracts fail to do so.

The above example illustrates the role of financial structure in solving agency problems. Notice that the CEO's equity stake in the business provides her with the incentive to act in the shareholders' interest by exposing her to part of the risk of the business. The creation of incentives and the transfer of risk from the shareholders to the manager are therefore two sides of the same coin. This transfer of risk is not beneficial in itself; for the manager, unlike the shareholders, does not hold a diversified portfolio. She therefore requires a higher return than do the shareholders for bearing this risk. The transfer of risk is beneficial *only* to the extent that it improves efficiency.

In the case of project finance, a complex series of contracts and financing arrangements distributes the different risks presented by a project among the various parties involved in the project. As in the case of our simple example of the management compensation contract, these transfers of risk are rarely advantageous in themselves, but have important incentive effects. To see how this occurs, we need to look at the structure of a typical project financing.

THE MAIN PARTIES

There are numerous parties involved in the structuring of a typical project financing. As shown in Figure 21.1, besides the lenders and the project company, these parties typically include one or more project sponsors, contractors, suppliers, major customers, and a host government.

Sponsors and Investors. A separate company is established for the purpose of undertaking the project. A controlling stake in the equity of that company will typically be owned by a single project

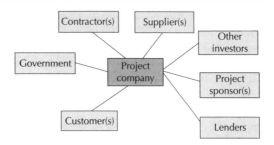

Figure 21.1 Parties to Project Financing

sponsor, or by a group of sponsors, who will generally be involved in the construction and the management of the project. Other equity-holders may be companies with commercial ties to the project, such as customers and suppliers, or they may be financial investors. For example, the shareholders of the PT. Paiton Energy Co. (PEC), which is building the Paiton 7 and 8 power stations in Indonesia, are Edison Mission Energy (40%), General Electric Capital Corp. (12.5%), Mitsui & Co. Ltd. (32.5%), and PT. Batu Hitam Perkasa (15%). As is typical of such projects, the main shareholders of the project company are the main contractor of the plant, Mitsui, and its operator, Edison Mission Energy, which will operate and maintain the plant through PT. MOMI Indonesia, the local affiliate of Mission Operation & Maintenance Inc. General Electric Co., of which General Electric Capital Corp. is the finance affiliate, will supply the steam turbine generators. The Indonesian company PT. Batu Hitam Perkasa appears to have no operational involvement in the project, but may carry political clout.

Lenders. Infrastructure projects involve substantial investments. A large fraction of the needed finance is generally raised in the form of debt from a syndicate of lenders such as banks and specialized lending institutions and, less frequently, from the bond markets. In the case of PEC, for example, equity-holders provided $680 million in equity and subordinated debt. $1.8 billion was provided in the form of senior debt, of which 90% was bank debt and 10% was senior secured bonds.

Project companies will sometimes enter into production payment arrangements instead of issuing ordinary debt. These arrangements are functionally equivalent to borrowing: a bank provides cash upfront as advance payment for a project's output, and the project company undertakes to deliver the output to the bank and arranges for the output to be repurchased at a guaranteed price.

Most infrastructure facilities have very long lives. This suggests that they should be financed with long-term debt. Yet, most infrastructure projects are financed by bank loans, which have maturities that rarely exceed 10 to 12 years, rather than by long-term bonds.

Some observers have suggested that the difficulty in arranging long-term bond financing is due to the fact that bondholders are particularly risk-averse. But, since most bondholders also hold substantial portfolios of equities, this seems improbable. Our explanation for the widespread use of bank finance, and the correspondingly limited role of bond finance, focuses instead on the ownership structures of these two forms of financing. The concentrated ownership of bank debt encourages lending banks to devote considerable resources to evaluating the project, and to monitoring its progress on a continuing basis. It also facilitates the renegotiation of the debt should the project company experience difficulties in servicing it. By contrast, the more diffuse nature of bond ownership reduces the incentives of bondholders to evaluate and monitor the progress of the project, and makes it difficult to take concerted action if covenants are breached or require modification. Thus, it does not seem surprising that many bond issues, such as the $180 million issue made by PEC, have been privately placed under rule 144a. This ensures that ownership remains in the hands of a limited number of qualified institutional buyers (or QIBs).

A bond issue to fund a green-field project is likely only in the case of a low-risk project. Even then, it is commonly enhanced by a credit guarantee from an insurance company, or a political risk guarantee from a national or supranational agency. For example, a project company established to upgrade two major roads in England was able to raise the majority of its debt by an issue of bonds that were enhanced by a Aaa/AAA guarantee from AMBAC Indemnity Corporation.

Bonds are also commonly used in project finance in one other set of circumstances. Once construction is completed and project facilities become operational, bond financing is often used to replace existing bank debt. This can be explained by the fact that the need for monitoring falls upon completion of the construction phase.

Government. The project company will in most cases need to obtain a concession from the host government to build a road or a railway, for example, or to operate a telecommunication service. The government may also need to establish a new regulatory framework, guarantee currency convertibility, and provide environmental permits.

In many cases, the project company retains ownership of the project's assets. Such arrangements are known as "build-own-operate" projects (BOOs). In other cases, ownership of the project's assets is transferred to the government at the end of the concession period. These arrangements are known as "build-operate-transfer" projects (BOTs).[2]

Contractors. As noted above, the main contractor of the plant will often hold a stake in the equity of the project company. Other contractors may also do so, although generally to a lesser extent.

Suppliers and Customers. Once the project facility has been built and has become operational, the project company will need to purchase the supplies it requires, and to sell the products it produces or the services it provides. Sometimes, as in the case of a pipeline, there will be in effect only one customer. Often in this case the customer will be a government-owned utility, or the government itself. For example, the sole customer for the electricity produced by the Paiton 7 and 8 power stations will be the Indonesian state-owned electric utility. In other cases, as in that of a toll road, there may be many possible customers.

CONTRACTUAL ARRANGEMENTS

Although a project company is unusual in that it is established to undertake a single project, there is nothing unusual about the identity of the parties involved in the project. All companies have owners, lenders, suppliers, and customers, and all have dealings with the government. The difference in the case of project finance lies in the overriding importance of the contractual and financing

---

2 It should however be noted that the terms BOO and BOT are sometimes used interchangeably.

arrangements that exist between these various parties. These are more than a series of independent bilateral arrangements. In particular, the complete package of contracts needs to be put in place before debt finance can be secured.

We discuss the contractual arrangements first. These are designed to allocate every major risk presented by a project to the party that is best able to appraise and control that risk. Because a party to a project will agree to bear a given risk at a non-prohibitive price only if it has a clear understanding of that risk, most projects involve established technologies, as is the case for power stations, roads, and airports. Project finance is less appropriate for projects that involve complex or untried technologies, as evidenced by the failure of the U.K. government to secure project financing for research and development projects.

Let us look briefly at the various ways in which contractual arrangements distribute risk among the various parties to a project:

◆ The project sponsors bear the risks of project completion, operation, and maintenance. This is achieved through a facility management contract that includes guarantees that the project facility will be completed on time, and that it will be built and operated to the desired specifications. The project sponsor may also enter into a "working capital maintenance" agreement or a "cash deficiency" agreement with the lending banks. Such agreements ensure adequate funding for the project in its early years.

◆ The lenders to the project will require the usual assurances from the project company, including security for their loans. But, especially in the early stages of the project, lenders will also have recourse to the project sponsors in the event of specific problems such as cost overruns. Lenders will particularly want to ensure that cash that can be used to service the debt is not paid out to equity-holders. The amount of debt service may therefore be linked to the project's output, and any earnings in excess of debt service requirements may be placed in a "reclaim" account and drawn on if subsequent earnings do not suffice to service the debt.

◆ The main contractor is obviously best able to ensure that construction is completed within cost and on schedule. He will therefore often enter into a turnkey contract that specifies a fixed price and penalties for delays, and he will usually be required to post a performance bond.

◆ When there is a major supplier to the project, there will be a contract with that supplier to ensure that (1) he does not abuse his possible monopoly power and (2) he produces efficiently. For example, if the project company is a major purchaser of energy from a monopolistic state-owned enterprise (SOE), the project company will enter into a long-term supply contract with the SOE. The contract purchase price will often be fixed, or indexed to inflation or some other variable that affects project revenues; and the contract may require the SOE to compensate the project company if the SOE fails to supply the contracted energy.

◆ When there are only a few potential customers for the project's output, revenue risk is likely to be transferred to those customers by means of long-term sales contracts. These will often include a take-or-pay clause or, as in the case of a pipeline, a throughput agreement that obliges the customer to make some minimum use of the pipeline. Another arrangement for transferring revenue risk to a customer is a tolling contract, whereby the customer agrees to deliver to the project company materials that it is to process and return to the customer. Some power projects, such as Navotas in the Philippines, have been structured in a similar way: the purchasing utility provides the fuel and the project company is simply paid for converting it to electricity. The purpose of transferring revenue risk to customers is to provide them with the incentive to estimate their demand for the project's output as carefully and honestly as possible.

The contract between project company and customers will as much as possible seek to ensure that the prices of the product are indexed to its costs; and, where there is considerable currency uncertainty, prices may also be indexed to exchange rates as in the case of the Paiton power project.

◆ When there are many customers, as in the case of a toll road, long-term purchase contracts with these customers may be impossible. Indeed, if alternative routes are not subject to a toll, it may be infeasible to set a price that provides the project company with a satisfactory return. For example, one of the problems in attracting private finance to the funding of rail projects within central London has been that the revenues from such projects are likely to be highly dependent on transport policy towards *other* means of transportation in the capital. In such cases, it may be possible to attract project finance only if the government guarantees some minimum payment to investors.

♦ When the government grants a concession to a project company, there will need to be a concession agreement that gives the company the right to build and operate the project facility. The concession agreement may also require the government to construct supporting facilities such as access roads. Failure to do so may lead to the failure of the project, or may decrease the return on the project. For example, the profitability of Eurostar, the company that operates rail services through the Channel Tunnel, has suffered from the delays in the construction of a promised high-speed rail link in England and a new railway station south of London. The government may also need to guarantee the performance of state-owned companies. For example, if a project sells electricity to a state-owned power utility, the government may need to guarantee the contractual obligations of that utility.

The project company will also be concerned about currency convertibility, in particular its ability to service its foreign currency debt and pay dividends to its equity-holders. The government may therefore be asked to provide guarantees or comfort letters; and, if the project has hard currency revenues, it may have to consent to having these revenues paid into an offshore escrow account.

As we have already observed, this web of contractual arrangements, which may vary over time in line with the progress of a project, is designed to allocate the various risks presented by the project to those parties that can best appraise and control those risks. An attempt to allocate a given risk to a party that is not best able to control that risk will generally fail. For example, the private financing of prisons in the U.K. ran into difficulties when the government sought to link its payments to private prisons to the number of prisoners that were sent to these prisons. The problem, of course, was that the number of prisoners was outside the control of the project companies, but at least partially within

that of the government. Conversely, failure to allocate a given risk to the party that is best able to control that risk will lead to a loss in efficiency. As one example, government guarantees of fair rates of return to utilities or project companies remove any incentive for these organizations to reduce their costs.

OWNERSHIP, CAPITAL STRUCTURE, AND INCENTIVES

We now turn to the financing arrangements observed in the case of project finance. Among the questions we address are the following:

♦ Why are projects incorporated in separate companies?
♦ Why are the operators and the main contractors of the project typically the main equity-holders in that company?
♦ Why are project companies highly leveraged?
♦ Why does this leverage take the form of non-recourse financing?

The object of the contractual arrangements that we have described above is to ensure that a project company is not exposed to an abuse of monopoly power, and to provide all parties to the project with the incentives to act efficiently by transferring the risk of poor performance to those best able to manage it. Construction risk is thus borne by the contractor, the risk of insufficient demand by the purchaser, and similarly for the other risks presented by the project.

But this does not explain the widespread practice of incorporating the project in a separate company, and tying the management of a project to its financing. Indeed, a government could easily raise money directly for infrastructure investment and contract with each party to provide the required services. But, as we pointed out earlier, there is a limit to how much can be written into a contract and how efficiently that contract can be monitored. Contractual arrangements therefore need to be complemented by financing arrangements.

Think, for example, why the operator and the main contractor of a project should be made to be equity-holders in the project. These equity holdings would not be needed if it were possible to write and monitor complete contracts with the contractor and the operator. The operation of the project could then be separated from its financing. This sometimes happens – most recently, in the case of a South African road project. But it is usually not possible to write and monitor sufficiently comprehensive contracts. In such cases, the equity holdings that the contractor and the operator have in the project company provide them with an incentive to be efficient by making them residual claimants whose profits depend on how well the project facility is built and operated.

Project companies are highly levered: the average debt ratio for IFC-financed projects, for example, is around 60%. Such leverage is used despite the fact that there is reputed to be a shortage of potential lenders for project finance, and that it is costly to structure the project to make these high debt levels possible. Furthermore, lenders lend directly to the project company rather than to the sponsors, and they have only limited recourse to the sponsors in case of default by the project company. This last observation suggests that the motive for the high leverage observed cannot be that debt is a "cheap" source of finance. If that were the case, the loans could equally well be made to the sponsors.

In their classic paper on capital structure, Miller and Modigliani showed that, in perfectly competitive capital markets, company value would be independent of the degree of leverage. Similar arguments can be used to show that, under the same restrictive set of conditions, value cannot be enhanced simply by concentrating debt in a subsidiary or an associated company. As illustrated in Exhibit 21.1 below, the total cash flow to all security holders is independent of whether debt is located in a pro-ject company or in its parent company.

Why, then, do we observe a high concentration of debt in the project company? As happens so often in discussions of capital structure, there is an abundance of possible explanations, none of which appears to be capable of explaining all the facts. Many of these explanations are related to the incompleteness of contracts. We discuss below some of the more common explanations (and summarize in Exhibit 21.2 four of the principal theoretical models of project finance).

Bankruptcy Costs. The example in Exhibit 21.1 shows that the total cash flows to investors are independent of whether the firm employs project financing when bankruptcy costs are assumed to be zero, as in an M & M world. The example also shows, however, that project finance changes the states of the world in which the debt is in default. In so doing, project finance changes the expected costs of default.

The projects undertaken by project companies typically have low bankruptcy costs. This is because their assets are largely tangible assets, which are likely to go through a bankruptcy process largely unscathed. For example, a change in ownership is unlikely to affect the efficiency with which a power station or a toll road is operated. In addition, if the bankruptcy costs of the sponsor are higher than those of the project company, it could be more efficient to isolate the debt in the project company to ensure that the sponsor's business is not damaged by a possible bankruptcy of the project.[3] A trading and construction company such as Mitsui, for example, is likely to lose much more of its operating value than the project company building the Paiton power stations, and it should therefore attempt to contain the effects of a possible project failure through the use of project finance. The low cost of bankruptcy for project companies may therefore help to explain why project companies carry heavy, non-recourse debt loads, but it does not explain why these companies enter into a variety of credit-enhancing contracts, such as insurance and hedging contracts (we return to this issue later).

Taxes. When a project is located in a high-tax country, and the project company in a lower-tax country, it may be beneficial for the sponsor to locate the debt in the high-tax country. The company maximizes its interest tax shields in so doing.

---

3   See Michel Habib and D. Bruce Johnsen, "User Specialisation and Asset Financing," working paper, London Business School, 1996. It may not simply be the sponsor's business that is damaged by bankruptcy. The management of the sponsoring company may have valuable control rights such as perquisites and an enhanced reputation, and the project may have synergies with other projects run by the same management. Management may therefore wish to isolate the project to protect its control rights. See T. Chemmanur and K. John, "Optimal Incorporation, Structure of Debt Contracts, and Limited-Recourse Project Financing," working paper, New-York University, 1992.

Exhibit 21.1   The Impact of Project Finance in an M&M World

The example below illustrates (a) that, in a Miller–Modigliani world, project finance does not affect the total value of the firm and (b) that project finance can potentially affect value when debt default is costly.

Panel 1 shows a firm with existing assets and debt undertaking a large project. Both the assets and the project give a single cash flow and have pure discount debt. Panel 2 shows the payoffs in different states of the world to debt and equity if the project is undertaken as part of the general activities of the firm. Panel 3 shows the payoffs to project debt, existing debt, and parent equity if the project is undertaken as a separate entity (project finance).

In a Miller–Modigliani world without taxes, project finance has no impact on the total value of the firm. This can be seen by comparing the final columns of Panel 2 and Panel 3, where the total cash flows accruing to all security holders are identical in all states. In a complete securities market, this guarantees that the total value of the firm is independent of the way that financial claims on the firm are structured.

The impact of project finance on default risk can be seen by comparing Panel 3 (project finance) with Panel 2. The net impact of project finance on default is to:

A. Prevent the existing assets bringing down the project in state 2.

B. Prevent the project bringing down the existing assets in state 3.

C. Make the project default in state 5 because the coinsurance of the existing assets is lost.

By thus rearranging the states of the world in which default occurs, project finance can change the associated costs of default.

		CHARACTERISTICS OF EXISTING ASSETS AND PROJECT					SECURITY PAYOFFS IN THE CASE OF TRADITIONAL FINANCE				SECURITY PAYOFFS IN THE CASE OF PROJECT FINANCE					
State	PANEL 1	Debt Face Value: Existing Assets	Debt Face Value: Project	Cash Flow: Existing Assets	Cash Flow: Project	PANEL 2	Debt	Equity	Total Cash Flow	PANEL 3	Project Debt	Project Equity	Total Cash Flow to Sponsor	Parent Debt	Parent Equity	Total Cash Flow: Project Debt + Existing Debt + Parent Equity
1		100	100	50	50		100*	0	100		50*	0	50	50*	0	100
2		100	100	50	130		180*	0	180		100	30	80	80*	0	180
3		100	100	130	50		180*	0	180		50*	0	130	100	30	180
4		100	100	130	130		200	60	260		100	30	160	100	60	260
5		100	100	300	50		200	150	350		50*	0	300	100	200	350
6		100	100	300	130		200	230	430		100	30	330	100	230	430

*Indicates default.

But the difference in tax rates does not explain why the debt has limited recourse, nor does it explain the concentration of debt in the project company when both the sponsor and the project company are located in the same jurisdiction.

Myopia. Some of the arguments for placing the debt in the project company assume that the lenders are blinkered. For example, it is sometimes suggested that the limited recourse of the debt holders to the project sponsors provides the sponsors with a free lunch, and that project finance allows the debt to be "off-balance-sheet" to the sponsors (for example, by structuring the contractual obligation as a production payment rather than as a loan). However, it is very doubtful that lenders are misled by such stratagems.

Political Risk. We have argued that the difficulty of writing complete contracts with operators and contractors provides the motive for tying project financing and management. Similarly, the difficulty of writing a comprehensive and binding concession agreement with a host government provides the need for financing arrangements that make it difficult for the government to take actions that may render the project unprofitable.

Exhibit 21.2 Theoretical Models of Project Finance

Model	Benefit of debt	Cost of debt	Benefit of project finance	Cost of project finance
Habib and Johnsen (1996)[a]: Asset specific investment by the initial user and the alternative user of an asset.	Induces both users to make the first-best investment in case the asset is to be transferred over some range of states.	May distort the asset-specific investment made by the initial user in case the asset is not to be transferred.	Avoids the distortion of asset-specific investment in the case of many assets and many alternative users.	
Chemmanur and John (1992)[b]: Private benefits of control.	Avoids selling outside equity, thus lowering the probability of losing control to outsiders.	Increases the probability of bankruptcy and the monitoring of management by debt-holders.	Avoids having a high-risk project bankrupt a low-risk project.	Loses the coinsurance property of debt.
John and John (1991)[c]: Tax benefits and agency costs of debt.	Tax savings.	Foregone growth opportunities (Myers underinvestment).	Enables trade-offs between the costs and the benefits of debt that are specific to the project and to existing assets.	
Shah and Thakor (1987)[d]: Signalling with debt.	Tax savings.	Signals high risk.	Lowers the cost of information gathering by creditors. Avoids the join credit evaluation of the projects and existing assets.	Precludes optimal leverage for the entire firm.

[a]M. Habib and D.B. Johnsen, "User Specialization and Asset Financing," Working Paper, London Business School, 1996.
[b]T. Chemmanur and K. John, "Optimal Incorporation, Structure of Debt Contracts, and Limited-Recourse Project Financing," Working Paper, New-York University, 1992.
[c]T. John and K. John, "Optimality of Project Financing: Theory and Empirical Implications in Finance and Accounting," *Review of Quantitative Finance and Accounting* 1 (1991), 51–74.
[d]S. Shah and A. Thakor, "Optimal Capital Structure and Project Financing," *Journal of Economic Theory* 42 (1987), 209–243.

One such arrangement is for the host government to take equity in the project company. Another is an extensive reliance on limited recourse financing. By arranging for the project company to issue such debt, the sponsors ensure that the cost of adverse government action falls directly on the lending banks and agencies. These generally consist of a syndicate of major banks from a wide range of countries, together with national or supranational bodies such as the export-import banks of the main industrial countries, the World Bank, the International Finance Corporation, the Asian Development Bank, and

the Inter-American Development Bank. All have considerable political clout, and can bring pressure to bear upon the host government if necessary. Moreover, the national and supranational agencies commonly hold subordinated debt that further exposes them to the consequences of adverse government actions. In contrast, the commercial banks tend to hold senior debt in the project.

In addition, the national and supranational agencies also provide loan guarantees, which are generally intended to protect lenders against political risk, but rarely provide protection against commercial risk, again illustrating the principle that risk should be allocated to those that can best manage it. For example, the World Bank may assist the project company in raising debt by offering a partial risk guarantee that covers the host government's contractual obligations and political *force majeure* risks, as in the case of the Hub power project in Pakistan. Similarly, one level of government may guarantee the performance of another. For example, the Indian central government was contractually liable for any loss to the sponsor of the Dabhol power project that was a consequence of government action. This encouraged the Indian central government to put pressure on the state government of Maharashtra to resume construction of the plant, in spite of the electoral promises of the new state government to cancel the project.

Protection against political risk may go far towards explaining the debt structure of project companies in developing countries. It does not explain why projects in politically stable countries are also heavily levered. Of course, such countries are not free from political risk. Environmental legislation or court awards in liability suits may sometimes pose serious threats to business. However, these risks generally threaten the sponsors of the project as much as the project company, and are therefore unlikely to explain the concentration of debt in the project company.

Information Costs. The granting of a loan clearly requires that the lenders evaluate the creditworthiness of the borrower, and monitor his use of the assets financed by the loan. A possible benefit of project finance, and of the associated lack of recourse, is that it allows lenders to the project to confine their evaluation and monitoring to the project only, and saves them from having to evaluate and monitor the sponsors as well.

Free Cash Flow. Michael Jensen has argued that companies with a surplus of cash and a lack of worthwhile projects have a tendency to invest this cash in negative NPV projects rather than return it to shareholders. Leverage ensures that cash is needed to service debt, and is not frittered away. That is, heavy debt financing can provide stronger incentives both to generate more cash, and to pay out what cash cannot be profitably reinvested in the company.

The above argument leaves open the question as to why the debt is located in the project company rather than in the parent companies. After all, if the parent companies assumed the debt, they would have an equally great incentive for ensuring that cash was distributed to them rather than reinvested unproductively.

There are two possible reasons why the location of the debt could matter. One is that the parent companies may find it difficult or costly to monitor the efficiency with which cash is used within the project company, and therefore cannot prevent the waste of free cash flow. The other is that, when there is more than one parent company, the owners may have different views about how to use cash. For example, if one parent is a potential supplier to the project company while another has a purely financial interest in it, the two parents may disagree about the desirability of having the company reinvest its free cash flow. By ensuring that cash flows are used to service debt, such disagreements are avoided.

INSURANCE AND HEDGING

The risk transfer contracts that we described earlier have the effect of transferring many of the project risks from the project sponsor to the other parties to the project. Further risks are transferred by a variety of insurance contracts, such as completion insurance, insurance against *force majeure*, and insurance against political risks.

Although an insurance company may have particular expertise at pricing these risks and may possibly be skillful at monitoring them, it has no control over them. An insurer cannot control whether there will be a flood, a hurricane, or other natural catastrophes. Insurance contracts therefore should have no beneficial effect, and may well have detrimental effects, on incentives, as they reduce the incentives of the project company to exert effort that would minimize the effects of such disasters. Therefore, the probable purpose of such risk transfers is simply to enable the project company to operate at higher debt ratios than it otherwise could.

In addition to the protection against firm-specific risks they purchase from insurance companies, project companies may also undertake to hedge themselves against market risks, such as any remaining currency risk, interest rate risk, and commodity price risk. These contracts too enable the project company to operate at high debt ratios.

BIDDING

Project finance is expensive to arrange. It involves establishing the project company, forming a consortium of equity-holders and lenders, gaining agreement to a complex set of contractual arrangements between the parties involved, and arranging costly documentation.

Governments commonly advertise for competing bids. Of course, in preparing their bid, companies recognize both the cost of doing so and the probability that they will not be awarded the contract. For this reason, an open auction will not necessarily result in the optimal number of bidders, or the lowest cost to the government. For example, a common complaint by contractors in the U.K. has been that they have incurred large bidding costs under the Private Finance Initiative, with a low probability of success. Bidding costs are reputed to have been up to five times higher than for private sector projects.[4]

Where each potential bidder has access to the same technology and is equally well-equipped to undertake the project, there is no gain in social welfare from inviting a large number of bids. The government needs to invite only a sufficient number of bids to avoid collusion or the exercise of monopoly power.

BUILD-OPERATE-TRANSFER

In the case of BOT (build-operate-transfer) as opposed to BOO (build-own-operate) projects, ownership of a project's assets is transferred to the government at the end of the concession period. For example, ownership of privately financed toll roads and bridges is often eventually transferred to the government.

Of course this is not a free lunch: sponsors will recognize the limited nature of the concession in their bidding. Since project sponsors need to recover their investment within the limited period of the concession, it may not be possible to arrange BOT finance even for projects that provide a satisfactory return over their complete life. An often-cited example is the early Mexican toll road program, where a 10-year concession period obliged sponsors to charge such high tolls that motorists avoided using the roads. The other danger with BOT contracts is that, as the end of the concession period approaches, there is little incentive for the sponsor to invest more in the project, and every incentive for him to take as much cash out as he can. For example, oil rights with a limited life encourage the franchisee to extract oil earlier than may be desirable.

Why, then, are some projects organized as BOT contracts? We suggest that such an arrangement makes sense where there is a need for the government to support the project by continuing infrastructure investments that cannot easily be specified by contract. Knowing that the project will eventually revert to government ownership provides an incentive for the government to invest in the supporting infrastructure.

The government sometimes has an option to terminate the concession before the end of the concession period. This may be particularly important when the original concession agreement may prevent government policy changes in (say) the regulatory framework.

CONCLUDING REMARKS

We conclude this paper by discussing what we believe are some common misconceptions about project finance, and by briefly contrasting project finance with the alternatives of privatization and service contracts.

It is sometimes argued that project finance is attractive simply because "the mobilisation of private capital is the only way in which public service is likely to be maintained,"[5] or because it saves the government money by transferring the investment expenditure from the public to the private sector. For example, the British government recently agreed to sell homes occupied by military personnel to private firms which would manage those homes and lease them back to the government. This, it was asserted would reduce government spending

---

4   *The Financial Times*, 10 November 1995.

5   As Ross Goobey argued in *The Times* (22 June 1996).

by £500 million, thus cutting the government's borrowing requirements. While this is literally correct, the sale of the homes also makes the government liable for a series of future rental payments. Unless the private sector is more efficient at managing these homes, the cash flows paid out by the government in the sale-and-leaseback arrangement can be exactly replicated by government borrowing. Of course, by using project finance rather than direct government borrowing, a government may reduce its apparent deficit and avoid contravening IMF requirements on borrowing, or rules for admission to European Monetary Union. But it is difficult to believe that such transparent dodges provide a reliable long-term basis for the use of project finance.[6]

Some *critics* of the use of project finance for infrastructure investment argue that the cheaper financing available to the government could well outweigh the gains in efficiency made possible by private-sector management. The government is said to have a lower cost of capital than do private-sector companies because it is able to borrow at blue-chip rates, whereas a project company is likely to pay a higher rate of interest on its debt and may need to offer the project sponsors a prospective return of 20 percent or 30 percent on their equity investment in the company. For example, *The Economist* quotes a report on a Scottish water project by Chemical Bank, which estimates that "if the works were privately built, owned and operated, interest rates and the need to achieve a return on equity investment would make the finance costs 50% more expensive than the £201 million costs that would be incurred under the normal public-borrowing rules. There would be no chance . . . to recoup the higher financing costs through the greater efficiency of a private operator, because the costs of running a £100m sewage work is only about £5m a year."[7] The World Bank, too, appears to subscribe to the view that governments have a

lower cost of capital than private sector companies, commenting that "[i]n infrastructure projects, the cheaper credit available to governments needs to be weighed against possible inefficiencies in channelling funds through government."[8]

The notion that the government enjoys a lower cost of capital than private sector companies is misleading. While it is certainly the case that governments can borrow more cheaply than corporations and do not have to provide a return to shareholders, this does not imply that the total cost of capital is lower to governments than it is to the private sector. The lower interest rate paid by a government simply reflects the guarantee provided by taxpayers to lenders. In the case of private sector companies, the bulk of the risk presented by a project is borne by the equity-holders, who demand a correspondingly higher rate of return. A smaller part of the risk goes to the debt-holders, who bear the risk that the firm may default on its debt payments. In contrast, government debt is risk-free in nominal terms, a characteristic that is reflected in the low rate of interest on the debt. But the risk presented by the projects does not disappear when the project is financed by the government. If cash flows from the project are unexpectedly low and do not suffice to service the debt raised by the government to finance the project, the shortfall is met by taxpayers, who play a role similar to that of equity-holders in a private sector company (but without the benefit of limited liability). Indeed, because it seems likely that the capital markets share risk better than does the tax system, the cost of capital for the government could well be *higher* than for corporations.

We believe that the argument for transferring ownership as well as management revolves around the difficulty of writing contracts that ensure that managers maximize efficiency. We have described above how contractual arrangements provide incentives for efficiency by transferring risks to those best able to control them. At the same time, we have also argued that, because the vast majority of contracts are incomplete and imperfectly monitored, an exclusive reliance on service contracts is unwise. The ultimate incentive for project managers to maximize efficiency is for them to be made residual claimants who capture the benefits

---

6 It may however be the case that project finance, by allocating the revenues from a project to the project company, serves to remove these revenues from the reach of the government, which may otherwise divert them to uses other than the repayment of the debt. This may justify the view of project finance as "off-balance-sheet" finance in the case of governments, but it does not explain why such projects should be highly leveraged.

7 "Something Nasty in the Water," The Economist, 9 September 1995, page 32.

8 World Development Report 1994, World Bank.

Exhibit 21.3   The Benefits and Costs of Project Finance*

When Project Finance Makes Sense

AGENCY EFFECTS:

- Specializes and decentralizes management.
- Makes possible the provision of separate incentives for project managers.
- Precludes the waste of project free cash flow.
- Increases the outside scrutiny of projects.
- Improves incentives for the production of information.

OWNERSHIP STRUCTURE:

- Permits joint ventures without requiring the exhaustive mutual evaluation of the creditworthiness of potential partners.
- Limits the liability of parents to projects.
- Limits the exposure of creditors to well-defined project risks.
- Allows project-specific debt ratios.

OTHER EFFECTS:

- Crystallizes project costs for regulatory purposes.
- Allows the provision of services to several companies rather than just to sponsors.
- Partially transforms a sponsor from an equity-holder in the project into a supplier to the project, thus improving the sponsor's priority ranking in case of default.
- May avoid double taxation.

When Project Finance Does *not* Make Sense

- There are complex interactions of the project with the rest of the firm.
- Default of the project is costly (lost coinsurance).
- The optimal leverage of the project is low.
- The costs of contracting for the project are high.

*This exhibit, along with some of the arguments presented in this paper, adapt and extend arguments made by John Kensinger and John Martin in "Project Finance: Raising Money the Old-Fashioned Way," *Journal of Applied Corporate Finance*, Vol. 1 No. 3 (Fall 1988).

of any improvements they make. Thus, it is desirable to tie ownership and the provision of management services whenever it is difficult to specify *ex ante* the required level of services, or the acceptable level of costs, and to monitor them. This can be achieved through the use of project finance.

Rather than hiving off individual projects in order to attract private-sector funding and management expertise to a given industry, a government can do so by privatizing the industry. Indeed, it seems likely that the growth in privatization and in the use of project finance for infrastructure investments have both been prompted by the same concerns about the efficiency of government-owned enterprises and the appropriateness of government funding for large, risky investments. However, while the recent popularity of project finance and privatization may have similar causes, there are three reasons why project finance may sometimes be preferred to privatization. First, privatization is a more complex undertaking, particularly since it involves both existing and new plant. While project finance relies on a one-off set of contractual undertakings for each plant, privatization needs a regulatory framework for the entire industry. Second, there are a number of areas, such as health or education, where it may be possible to involve private funding for particular projects but where full-scale privatization is deemed inappropriate. Third, unless the industry is to be entirely foreign-owned, privatization requires a large local capital market, in contrast to project financings, which take place piecemeal and over a period of time.

PART V

Risk Management

Wall-Street bashing is a time-honored practice, even among economists. In the first article in this section, "Financial Innovation: Achievements and Prospects," Merton Miller traces the popular skepticism about Wall Street and financial innovation to an 18th-century economic doctrine known as "Physiocracy." According to this theory, the ultimate source of national wealth lies in the production of *physical* commodities. All other forms of commercial activity are considered nonproductive, if not parasitic. "Modern-day Physiocrats," as Miller says, "automatically and enthusiastically consign to that nonproductive class all the many thousands on Wall Street and LaSalle Street now using the new instruments."

The subject of Miller's article is "the new instruments" – that is, the proliferation since the early 1970s of all variety of futures, swaps, and options. It is Miller's contention that the social benefits accruing from financial innovation far outweigh the costs.

What are these benefits? Perhaps the principal source of gain from the many securities innovations over the past 20 years has been an improvement in the allocation of risk within the financial system – which in turn has enabled the capital markets to do a better job of performing their basic task of channeling investor savings into productive corporate investment of all kinds. The foreign exchange futures market started in 1972, together with the

host of "derivative" products that have risen up since then, have dramatically reduced the cost of transferring risks to those market participants with a comparative advantage in bearing them. "Efficient risk-sharing," as Miller says, "is what much of the futures and options revolution has been all about." By functioning much like "a gigantic insurance company," the options, futures, and other derivative markets also effectively raise the price investors pay for corporate securities, thus adding to corporate investment and general economic growth.

Consider, for example, the development of a national mortgage market made possible by investment bankers' pooling and repackaging of individual mortgages into securities. Such asset securitization, which was in turn made possible by the development of financial futures necessary to hedge the investment bankers' interest rate and prepayment exposures, has accomplished a massive transfer of interest rate risk away from financial institutions to well-diversified institutional investors. Besides lowering interest rates for homeowners, such risk-shifting should also help prevent a repeat of the S&L debacle in the early 1980s.

Futures and options continue, of course, to have a big PR problem – one that stems mainly from the fact that they are used by "speculators" as well as "hedgers." But economists know that speculators serve a purpose: Besides keeping markets "efficient" by channeling information rapidly into prices, they also help supply the liquidity essential to these markets. And, as Miller argues further, the widespread charges that index futures and options are the cause of growing stock price volatility (including the crash of 1987) are contradicted by a growing weight of academic evidence. In short, popular indictments of the new instruments confound the messenger with the message: What price volatility shows up within the system is largely the reflection of fundamental events; index futures and options are simply methods allowing companies and investors to cope with it.

In "Managing Financial Risk," Charles Smithson, Cliff Smith, and D. Sykes Wilford provide a broad survey of the theory and current corporate practice of risk management. There is still a good deal of confusion in the corporate world about what constitutes – and thus about the extent of – real, economic corporate exposures to exchange rates, interest rates, and commodity prices. American corporations are accustomed to hedging accounting-based exposures that arise from contractual commitments to make future sales or purchases (known as "transaction exposures"). Many companies also attempt to smooth their earnings by hedging "contingent" exposures – that is, operating net cash flows that are relatively predictable, but not yet bound by contract and booked. Still relatively uncommon, however, are corporate efforts to quantify and manage "competitive" exposures – the longer-run effects of changes in financial variables on corporate revenues and net operating margins. Such competitive exposures are the most elusive, and potentially the most damaging, of all the corporate exposures the authors refer to collectively as "strategic risk."

The article then describes a variety of techniques for identifying and quantifying such exposures. Although gap and duration analysis are now widely used by financial institutions to measure interest rate exposures, the methods for evaluating industrial companies' exposures to interest rates and other financial variables are still in an early stage of development. Some companies such as Merck are using sophisticated quantitative methods to simulate the effect of exchange rate changes on long-run currency earnings and cash flows. Others evaluate specific exposures by means of statistical regressions that measure the strength of correlation between stock price movements and changes in financial variables.

But, as Smithson, Smith, and Sykes Wilford go on to argue, not all corporate exposures should be hedged. From the perspective of modern portfolio theory (MPT), foreign exchange risk, interest rate risk, and commodity price risk are all "diversifiable" risks. Stockholders, according to MPT, are able to manage such risks on their own simply by holding large, diversified portfolios. And thus active corporate management of these risks does not increase share values by reducing a company's cost of capital. (This would suggest, for example, that a multinational's success in reducing the volatility of its overseas earnings would not by itself cause investors to raise the P/E multiple on the stock.) But there are other important benefits from hedging that are likely to increase corporate market values: (1) a reduction in expected tax liabilities; (2) a lowering of the probability (and hence expected costs) of financial difficulty (or, alternatively, an increase in the firm's debt capacity); and (3) an improvement of management's incentives to undertake valuable long-run investments.

In the latter part of the article, Smithson, Smith, and Sykes Wilford go on to provide an introduction to the four basic instruments for managing financial risks: forwards, futures, swaps, and options. After demonstrating the close relationships among these four "financial building blocks," the article goes on to demonstrate the potential for combining these instruments to achieve virtually any desired risk position. The framework also lends itself to the analysis and pricing of complex hybrid securities by breaking them down into the basic components.

In "Rethinking Risk Management," René Stulz presents a theory of corporate risk management that uses the idea of comparative advantage in risk-bearing to go beyond the "variance-minimization" model that dominates most academic discussions. It argues that the primary goal of risk management is not to dampen swings in corporate cash flows or value, but rather to provide protection against the possibility of costly lower-tail outcomes – situations that would cause financial distress or make a company unable to carry out its investment strategy. By reducing the odds of financial trouble, risk management has the power to change not only the optimal capital structure of the firm, but its optimal ownership structure as well. For besides increasing corporate debt capacity, the reduction of downside risk also facilitates larger equity stakes for managers by shielding their investments from "uncontrollables."

The article's most significant departure from the standard theory, however, is in Stulz's suggestion that some companies may have a comparative advantage in bearing certain financial market risks – an advantage that could derive from information acquired through normal business activities. Although such specialized market information may lead some companies to take speculative positions in commodities or currencies, it is more likely to encourage "selective" hedging, a practice in which the risk manager's "view" of future price movements influences the percentage of the exposure that is hedged. But if such view-taking becomes an accepted part of a company's risk management program, managers' "bets" should be evaluated on a risk-adjusted basis and relative to the market. As Stulz notes in closing, "If [risk] managers want to behave like money managers, they should be evaluated like money managers."

In "Theory of Risk Capital in Financial Firms," Robert Merton and André Perold present a concept of risk capital that can be used to guide the capital structure, performance measurement, and strategic planning decisions of commercial and investment banks, insurance companies, and other firms engaged in principal financial activities. Ever since publication of the BIS capital guidelines, not only banks but most financial institutions have been forced to revisit the issue of capital adequacy. The concept of risk capital presented here differs significantly, however, from "both *regulatory capital*, which attempts to measure risk capital according to a particular accounting standard, and from *cash capital*, which represents the up-front cash required to execute a transaction."

After illustrating their concept of risk capital with a series of examples, Merton and Perold go on to demonstrate its application to a number of challenging problems faced by financial firms – specifically, allocating the costs of risk capital to individual businesses or projects in performance measurement and accounting for the benefits of internal diversification among business units in strategic planning.

In "Corporate Insurance Strategy," Neil Doherty and Clifford Smith describe a radical shift in British Petroleum's approach to insuring property and casualty losses, product liability suits, and other insurable events. Conventional corporate practice – and until recently the longstanding risk management policy of BP – has been to insure against large losses while "self-insuring" against smaller ones. In this article, Doherty and Smith explain why BP has chosen to flout the conventional wisdom and now insures against most smaller losses while self-insuring larger ones.

The BP decision came down to factors affecting the market *supply* of insurance as well as the corporate demand for it. On the demand side, the authors demonstrate that the primary source of demand for insurance by large public companies is not, as standard insurance textbooks assume, to transfer risk away from the corporation's owners (corporate stockholders and bondholders, it turns out, have their own means of neutralizing the effect of such risks). The demand stems rather, at least in BP's case, from insurance companies' comparative advantage in assessing and monitoring risk and in processing claims. On the supply side, the authors explain why the capacity of insurance markets to underwrite very large or highly specialized exposures is quite limited – and can be expected to remain so.

In "Value at Risk: Uses and Abuses," Merton Miller, Chris Culp, and Andrea Neves use a number of derivatives disasters to illustrate some pitfalls in using the popular risk measurement technique called "VAR" to guide a risk management program. VAR is a method of measuring the financial risk of an asset, portfolio, or exposure over some specified period of time. By facilitating the consistent measurement of risk across different assets and activities, VAR allows companies to monitor, report, and control their risks in a manner that efficiently relates risk control to desired and actual economic exposures.

Nevertheless, as the authors argue, reliance on VAR can result in serious problems when improperly used, and would-be users of VAR are advised to consider the following three pieces of advice:

◆ First, VAR is a tool for firms engaged in *total value* risk management. Companies concerned *not* with the value of a stock of assets and liabilities over a specific time horizon, but rather with the volatility of a *flow of funds*, are often better off eschewing VAR altogether in favor of a measure of cash flow volatility.

- Second, VAR should be applied very carefully to companies that practice "selective" risk management – those firms that choose to take certain risks as a part of their primary business. When VAR is reported in such situations without estimates of corresponding expected profits, the information conveyed by the VAR estimate can be extremely misleading.

- Third, as a number of derivatives disasters of the 1990s are used to illustrate, no form of risk measurement – including VAR – is a substitute for good management. Risk management as a process encompasses much more than just risk measurement. Indeed, risk measurement (whether using VAR or some of the alternatives proposed in this article) is pointless without a well-developed organizational infrastructure and IT system capable of supporting the complex and dynamic process of risk taking and risk control.

CHAPTER 22

Financial Innovation: Achievements and Prospects

Merton H. Miller (University of Chicago) *

The wonderment of Rip Van Winkle, awakening after his sleep of 20 years to a changed world, would pale in comparison to that felt by one of his descendants in the banking or financial services industry falling asleep (presumably at his desk) in 1970 and waking two decades later. So rapid has been the pace of innovation in financial instruments and institutions over the last 20 years that nothing could have prepared him to understand such now commonplace notions as swaps and swaptions, index futures, program trading, butterfly spreads, puttable bonds, Eurobonds, collateralized-mortgage bonds, zero-coupon bonds, portfolio insurance, or synthetic cash – to name just a few of the more exotic ones. No 20-year period has witnessed such a burst of innovative activity.

What could have produced this explosive growth? Has all this innovation really been worthwhile from society's point of view? Have we seen the end of the wave of innovations, or must we brace for more to come? These are the issues I now address.

WHY THE GREAT BURST OF FINANCIAL INNOVATIONS OVER THE LAST TWENTY YEARS?

Several explanations have been offered for the sudden burst of financial innovations starting some 20 years ago.[1]

The move to floating exchange rates

A popular one locates the initiating impulse in the collapse of the Bretton Woods, fixed-exchange rate regime. In the early 1970s, the U.S. government, with strong prodding from academic economists, notably Milton Friedman, finally abandoned the tie of gold to the dollar. The wide fluctuations in exchange rates following soon after added major new uncertainty to all international transactions. One response to that uncertainty was the development of exchange-traded foreign-exchange futures contracts by the Chicago Mercantile Exchange – an innovation that spawned in turn a host of

---

* This article will appear in *Japan and the World Economy*, Vol. 4 No. 2 (June, 1992).

1 See, for example, my article, "Financial Innovation: The Last Twenty Years and the Next," *Journal of Financial and Quantitative Analysis* 21 (December 1986), 459–71; and James C. Van Horne, "Of Financial Innovations and Excesses," *Journal of Finance* 40 (July 1985), 621–36.

subsequent products as the turbulence spread from exchange rates to interest rates.

But cutting the tie to gold cannot be the whole story because financial futures, influential as they proved to be, were not the only major breakthrough of the early 1970s. Another product introduced only a few months later, and almost equally important to subsequent developments, was not so directly traceable to the monetary events of that period. The reference, of course, is to the exchange-traded options on common stock of the CME's cross-town rival, the Chicago Board of Trade. That the CBOT's options did not precede the CME's financial futures was mainly luck of the bureaucratic draw. Both exchanges started the process of development at about the same time, impelled to diversify by the same stagnation in their traditional agricultural markets. Both needed the cooperation, or at least the toleration, of the appropriate regulators to break out in such novel directions.

The CME was the more fortunate in having to contend only with the U.S. Treasury and the Federal Reserve System – at a time, moreover, when both those agencies were strongly committed to the Nixon administration's push for floating exchange rates.[2] The CBOT, alas, faced the U.S. Securities and Exchange Commission, a New Deal reform agency always hypersensitive to anything smacking of speculative activity.[3] By the time the SEC had finished its detailed review of option trading, the CME had already won the race.

Computers and information technology

Another explanation for the sudden burst of financial innovation after 1970 finds the key in the information revolution and, especially, in the electronic computer. Computers in one form or another had been available since the 1950s. But only in the late 1960s, with the perfection of transistorized circuitry, did computers become cheap and reliable enough to design new products and strategies such as stock index arbitrage and collateralized mortgage obligations. And certainly the immense volume of transactions we now see regularly could not have been handled without the data-processing capacities of the computer.

But the basic and most influential innovations, financial futures and exchange-traded options, did not require computers to make them commercially feasible. Options on commodities in fact had been traded regularly on the CBOT until the U.S. Congress, in one of its periodic bouts of post-crash, anti-speculative zeal, ended the practice in 1934. That this long prior history of option trading is not better known may trace to the arcane CBOT terminology under which options were known as "privileges." But traded instruments designated with the modern terms puts and calls go back much further than that, to the Amsterdam Stock Exchange of the late 17th century.[4] Routine exchange trading of futures contracts has a history almost as long.

Innovation and world economic growth

Still another possibility, and the one I find most persuasive,[5] is that the seeming burst of innovation in the 1970s was merely a delayed return to the long-run growth path of financial improvement. The burst seems striking only in contrast to the dearth of major innovations during the long period of economic stagnation that began in the early 1930s and that for most of the world continued well into the 1950s.

The shrinkage in the world economy after 1929 was on a scale that few not actually experiencing it can readily imagine. The prolonged depression

---

2   The then Secretary of the Treasury was George P. Shultz, a former colleague and long-time friend of Milton Friedman. The Chairman of the Federal Reserve Board was Arthur Burns, another old friend. With Milton Friedman's blessing, both gave a cordial audience to Leo Melamed of the CME and at least a *nihil obstat* to his proposal for an International Monetary Exchange. (See Leo Melamed, "The International Monetary Market," in *The Merits of Flexible Exchange Rates*, ed. Leo Melamed, George Mason University Press, Fairfax, Virginia, 1988, 417–29.)

3   Under the SEC's original dispensation, only calls could be traded because puts were regarded as potentially destabilizing. Word of the put-call parity theorem had apparently not yet reached the SEC staff.

4   Joseph de la Vega, *Confusion de Confusiones*, Amsterdam, 1688, translated by Hermann Kellenbenz, 1957, reprinted by Baker Library, Harvard Business School, 1988.

5   See Miller (1986), cited in note 1.

undermined any demand pull for developing new financial instruments and markets, and the increased regulatory role of the state throttled any impulses to innovate from the supply side. Much of this new regulation, particularly in the U.S., was in fact a reaction to the supposed evils – notably the Crash of 1929 – flowing from the development of exchange-traded, and hence relatively liquid, common stock as a major investment and financing vehicle in the 1920s. Prior to the 1920s, U.S. companies had relied almost exclusively on bonds and preferred stock for raising outside capital.

Even in the depressed '30s, of course, financial innovation, though muted relative to the 1920s, did not come to a halt. But the major novelties tended to be government sponsored, rather than market induced. Examples are the special housing-related instruments such as the amortizing mortgage and the Federal Home Administration loan guarantees. Another government initiative of the '30s was the support direct and indirect of what later came to be called, rather unprophetically we now know, "thrift institutions." New U.S. Treasury instruments were developed, or at least used on a vastly expanded scale, notably Series E savings bonds for small savers and, at the other extreme, U.S. Treasury bills. Indeed, T-bills quickly became the leading short-term liquid asset for banks and corporate treasurers, displacing the commercial paper and call money instruments that had previously served that function.

Financial innovation by the private sector might perhaps have revived by the 1940s had not the War intervened. The War not only drained manpower and energy from normal market-oriented activity, but led to new regulatory restrictions on financial transactions, particularly international transactions.

Regulation and deregulation as stimuli to financial innovation

By a curious irony, the vast structure of financial regulation erected throughout the world during the 1930s and 1940s, though intended to and usually successful in throttling some kinds of financial innovation, actually served to stimulate the process along other dimensions. Substantial rewards were offered, in effect, to those successfully inventing around the government-erected obstacles. Many of these dodges, or "fiddles" as the British call them, turned out to have market potential far beyond anything dreamed of by their inventors; and the innovations thrived even after the regulation that gave rise to them was modified or abandoned.

The most striking example of such a regulation-propelled innovation may well be the swap in which one corporation exchanges its fixed-rate borrowing obligation for another's floating-rate obligation; or exchanges its yen-denominated obligations for another's mark-denominated obligations; and so on in an almost unimaginable number of permutations and combinations. Some swaps are arranged by brokers who bring the two counterparties directly together; others by banks who take the counterparty side to a customer order and then either hedge the position with forwards and futures or with an offsetting position with another customer.

The notional amount of such swaps, interest and currency, currently outstanding is in the trillions of dollars and rising rapidly. Yet, according to legend at least,[6] the arrangement arose modestly enough as vacation-home swapping by British overseas travelers, who were long severely limited in the amount of currency they could take abroad. Two weeks free occupancy of a London flat could compensate a French tourist for a corresponding stay in a Paris apartment or compensate an American for the use of a condominium at Aspen. If the ingenious British innovator happened to work for one of the merchant banks in the City, as is likely, the extension of the notion to corporate currency swaps was a natural one. The rest, as they say, is history.

The list of similar, regulation-induced or tax-induced innovations is long, and includes the Euro-dollar market, the Eurobond market, and zero-coupon bonds, to name just some of the more far-reaching loopholes opened in the restrictive

---

6 The first currency swap appears to have been arranged by Continental Illinois' London merchant bank in 1976. The precise dates and places remain problematic because the originators sought secrecy in a vain attempt to maintain their competitive advantage. See Henry T. C. Hu, "Swaps, the Modern Process of Financial Innovation and the Vulnerability of a Regulatory Paradigm," *University of Pennsylvania Law Review* 128 (December 1989), pp. 333–435 (see especially note 73, p. 363).

regulatory structure of the 1930s and 1940s.[7] Whether the private sector processes that produced the seemingly great wave of innovations after 1970 will continue to produce innovations if left unchecked is a topic to be taken up later. First let's consider some of the arguments currently being advanced for not leaving them unchecked.

HAS THE WAVE OF FINANCIAL INNOVATIONS MADE US BETTER OR WORSE OFF?

Free market economists have a simple standard for judging whether a new product has increased social welfare: are people willing to pay their hard-earned money for it? By this standard, of course, the new products of the 1970s and '80s have proved their worth many times over. But why have they been so successful? Whence comes their real "value added?" The answer, in large part, is that they have substantially lowered the cost of carrying out many kinds of financial transactions.

Consider, for example, a pension fund or an insurance company with, say, $200 million currently in a well-diversified portfolio of common stocks. Suppose that, for some good reason, the sponsors of the fund believe that the interests of their beneficiaries would be better served at the moment by shifting funds from common stocks to Treasury bills. The direct way would be first to sell the stock portfolio company by company, incurring commissions, fees, and "market impact" on each transaction. The cash proceeds, when collected, could then be put in Treasury bills, again incurring transaction costs. A second and much cheaper alternative, however, is simply to sell about 1,000 (at present price levels) S&P 500 index futures contracts. Thanks to the way the futures contracts must be priced to maintain intermarket equilibrium, that one transaction has the same consequences as the two transactions along the direct route. And at a fifth or even less of the cost in fees, commissions, and market impact!

Or, to take other kinds of financial costs, consider a bank maintaining an inventory of government bonds for resale. The availability of that inventory,

like the goods on the shelf in a supermarket, means better and faster service for the bank's customers when they come to shop. But it also means considerable risk for the bank. Bond prices can fall, sometimes very substantially, even in the course of a single day.

To protect against such losses, the bank can hedge its inventory by selling Treasury bond futures. Should the price of the bonds fall during the life of the futures contract, the gain on that contract will offset the loss on the underlying inventory. Without this opportunity to shift the risk via futures, the bank must seek other and more costly ways of controlling its inventory exposure. Some banks might find no better solution than to shrink their inventory and, hence, the quality and immediacy of the services they offer. Others might well abandon the activity altogether.

Insurance and risk management

A bank's use of futures to hedge its own inventory does not, of course, eliminate the price risk of the underlying bonds. It merely transfers that risk to someone else who *does* want to bear the risk, either because he or she has stronger nerves, or more likely, because another firm or investor somewhere wants to hedge against a *rise* in bond prices. The futures and options exchanges have greatly reduced the time (and hence cost) that each risk-shifter might otherwise have spent searching for a counterparty with the opposite risk exposure.

The combined set of futures and options contracts and the markets, formal and informal, in which they are transferred has thus been likened to a gigantic insurance company – and rightly so. Efficient risk-sharing is what much of the futures and options revolution has been all about. And that is why the term "risk management" has come increasingly to be applied to the whole panoply of instruments and institutions that have followed in the wake of the introduction of foreign exchange futures in CME's International Money Market in 1972. Honesty requires one to acknowledge, however, that this essentially benign view of the recent great innovative wave is not universally shared by the general public or even by academic economists.

7 For a fuller account of tax- and regulation-induced innovations, see Miller (1986), cited in note 1.

The case against the innovations

Some of the complaints about the harmful social consequences of the financial innovations appear to be little more than updated versions of a once-popular 18th-century economic doctrine known as Physiocracy, which located the ultimate source of national wealth in the production of physical commodities, especially agricultural commodities. Occupations other than commodity production were nonproductive. Modern-day Physiocrats, disdaining consumer sovereignty, automatically and enthusiastically consign to that nonproductive class all the many thousands on Wall Street and LaSalle Street now using the new instruments.

A related complaint is that the new instruments, by lowering transactions costs, have led to too much short-term trading – trading that not only wastes resources, but which has unduly shortened the planning horizons of both firms and investors. That the volume of trading has in fact skyrocketed in recent years there can be no doubt. But the key stimulus to the surge in trading in the underlying stocks appears to have been less the introduction of index futures and options than the ending of the regime of high fixed commissions in 1974. For Treasury bonds, the spur was the huge expansion of Federal government debt beginning in 1981.

But the critics are surely right in believing that lower trading costs will induce more trading. More trading, however, need not mean more waste from society's point of view. Trading is part of the process by which economic information, scattered as it necessarily is in isolated bits and pieces throughout the whole economy, is brought together, aggregated, and ultimately revealed to all. The prospect of trading profits is the bribe, so to speak, that society uses to motivate the collection, and ultimately the revelation, of the dispersed information about supply and demand.

Index Futures and Stock Market Volatility. Although many of the complaints against the new financial investments are merely standard visceral reactions against middlemen and speculators, some are specific enough to be tested against the available data. Notable here is the widespread view, expressed almost daily in the financial press, that stock market volatility has been rising in recent years and that stock-index futures and options are responsible. The evidence, however, fails to support this widespread public perception of surging volatility.

Volatility, measured as the standard deviation of rates of return (whether computed over monthly, weekly or even daily intervals), is only modestly higher now than during the more placid 1950s and 1960s, and is substantially below levels reached in the 1930s and 1940s.[8] Even the 1950s and 1960s had brief, transitory bursts of unusually high volatility, with a somewhat longer-lasting major burst occurring in the mid-1970s. The number of large, one-day moves (that is, moves of 3% or more in either direction) has indeed been higher in the 1980s than in any decade since the 1930s, but almost entirely due to the several days of violent movements in the market during and immediately following the crash of October 1987. Such increased volatility seems to accompany every major crash (as the Japanese stock market showed through much of 1990).

In fact, the tendency of volatility to rise after crashes and fall during booms is one of the few, well-documented facts researchers have been able to establish about the time-series properties of the volatility series. These bursts of post-crash volatility typically die out within a few months, and that has been basically the case as well for the crash of 1987. Indeed, what makes the 1930s so different from more recent experience is that the high levels of post-1929-crash volatility persisted so long into the next decade.

Index Products and the Crash of 1987. The failure to find a rising trend in volatility in the statistical record suggests that the public may be using the word volatility in a different and less technical sense. They may simply be taking the fact of the crash of 1987 itself (and the later so-called mini-crash of October 13, 1989) as their definition of market volatility. And without doubt, the 20% decline during the crash of 1987 was the largest one-day shock ever recorded. (The mini-crash of October 13, 1989, at about 6%, was high, but far from record-breaking.) If the crash of 1987 is the source of the public perception of increased volatility, the task of checking for connections

---

8   See G. William Schwert, "Why Does Stock Market Volatility Change over Time?", *Journal of Finance* 44 (December 1989), 1115–1153.

between the innovative instruments and volatility becomes the relatively straightforward one of establishing whether index futures and options really were responsible either for the occurrence or the size of the crash. On this score, signs of a consensus are emerging, at least within academia, with respect to the role of two of the most frequently criticized strategies involving futures and options, portfolio insurance and index arbitrage.

For portfolio insurance, the academic verdict is essentially "not guilty of causing the crash," but possibly guilty of the lesser charge of "contributing to the delinquency of the market." Portfolio insurance, after all, was strictly a U.S. phenomenon in 1987, and the crash seems to have gotten under way in the Far East, well before trading opened in New York or Chicago. The extent of the fall in the various markets around the world, moreover, bore no relation to whether a country had index futures and options exchanges.[9] Even in the U.S., non-portfolio insurance sales on the 19th, including sales by mutual funds induced by the cash redemptions of retail investors, were four to five times those of the portfolio insurers.

Still, portfolio insurance using futures, like some older, positive-feedback strategies such as stop-loss orders or margin pyramiding, can be shown, as a matter of theory, to be potentially destabilizing.[10] The qualification "using futures" is important here, however, because the potentially destabilizing impact of portfolio insurance is much reduced when carried out with index options (that is, essentially, by buying traded puts rather than attempting to replicate the puts synthetically with futures via craftily-timed hedges). With exchange-traded puts, the bearishness in portfolio insurance would make its presence known immediately in the market prices and implicit volatility of the puts. With futures, by contrast, or with unhedged, over-the-counter puts, the bearishness may be lurking in

the weeds, only to spring out on a less-than-perfectly forewarned public.[11]

Index Arbitrage: The New Villain. Whatever may or may not have been its role in the crash of 1987, portfolio insurance using futures rather than options has almost entirely vanished. Certainly it played no role in the mini-crash of October 13, 1989. Its place in the rogues' gallery of the financial press has been taken over by computerized "program trading" in general and by index arbitrage program trading in particular.

Why index arbitrage should have acquired such an unsavory public reputation is far from clear, however. Unlike portfolio insurance, which can be destabilizing when its presence as an information-less trade in the market is not fully understood, intermarket index arbitrage is essentially neutral in its market impact. The downward pressure of the selling leg in one market is always balanced by the equal and opposite buying pressure in the other. Only in rather special circumstances could these offsetting transactions affect either the level or the volatility of the combined market as a whole.

Index arbitrage might, possibly, increase market volatility if an initial breakout of the arbitrage bounds somehow triggered sales in the less-liquid cash market so massive that the computed index fell by more than needed to bring the two markets back into line. A new wave of arbitrage selling might then be set off in the other direction.

Despite the concerns about such "whipsawing" often expressed by the SEC, however, no documented cases of it have yet been found.[12] Careful studies find the market's behavior after program trades entirely consistent with the view that prices are being driven by "news," not mere speculative "noise" coming from the futures markets as the critics of index futures have so often charged.

Nor should these findings be considered in any way remarkable. The low cost of trading index

9 See Richard Roll, "The International Crash of October 1987," *Financial Analysts Journal* 22 (September 1988), 19–35.

10 See Michael J. Brennan and Eduardo S. Schwartz, "Portfolio Insurance and Financial Market Equilibrium," *Journal of Business* 62 (October 1989), pp. 455–72. Particularly interesting in their demonstration, however, is how small the destabilization potential really is, provided the rest of the investing public understands what is going on.

11 See Sanford J. Grossman, "An Analysis of the Implications for Stock and Futures Price Volatility of Program Trading and Dynamic Hedging Strategies," *Journal of Business* 61 (July 1988), 275–98.

12 See, for example, the very thorough searches described in Gregory Duffie, Paul Kupiec, and Patricia White, "A Primer on Program Trading and Stock Price Volatility: A Survey of the Issues and Evidence," Working Paper, Board of Governors, Federal Reserve System, Washington, D.C., 1990.

futures makes the futures market the natural entry port for new information about the macro economy. The news, if important enough to push prices through the arbitrage bounds, is then carried from the futures market to the cash market by the program trades of the arbitragers. Thanks to the electronic order routing systems of the NYSE, the delivery is fast. But arbitrage is still merely the medium, not the message.

That so much recent criticism has been directed against the messenger rather than the message may reflect only the inevitably slow reaction by the public to the vast changes that have transformed our capital markets and financial services institutions over the last 20 years. Index futures, after all, came of age less than 10 years ago. The shift from a predominantly retail stock market to one dominated by institutional investors began, in a big way, less than 15 years ago. In time, with more experience, the public's understanding of the new environment will catch up. Unless, of course, new waves of innovation are about to sweep in and leave the public's perceptions even further behind.

FINANCIAL INNOVATIONS: ANOTHER WAVE ON THE WAY?

Will the next 20 years see a continuation, or perhaps even an acceleration, in the flow of innovations that have so vastly altered the financial landscape over the last 20 years? I think not. Changes will still take place, of course. The new instruments and institutions will spread to every country in the developed world (and possibly even to the newly liberalized economies of Eastern Europe). Futures and options contracts will be written on an ever-widening set of underlying commodities and securities. But the process will be normal, slow, evolutionary change, rather than the "punctuated equilibrium" of the recent past.[13]

Long-range predictions of this kind are rightly greeted with derision. Who can forget the U.S. Patent Office Commissioner who recommended in

the early 1900s that his agency be closed down because all patentable discoveries had by then been made? We know also that regulation and taxes, those two longstanding spurs to innovation, are still very much with us despite the substantial progress, at least until recently, in deregulation and in tax rate reduction. But something important has changed. In the *avant garde* academic literature of economics and finance today, few signs can be seen of new ideas and concepts like those that bubbled up in the '60s and '70s and came to fruition later in specific innovations.

The extent to which academic thinking and criticism prefigured the great wave of financial innovations of the 1970s and 1980s is still too little appreciated. Calls for the creation of a foreign exchange futures market and analysis of the economic benefits that would flow from such an institution were common in the 1950s and 1960s, as noted earlier, in the writings of the academic supporters of floating exchange rates, especially Milton Friedman. On the common-stock front, major academic breakthroughs in the 1950s and 1960s were the Mean-Variance Portfolio selection model of Harry Markowitz and, building on it, the so-called Capital Asset Pricing Model of William Sharpe and John Lintner in which the concept of the "market portfolio" played a central role.

The notion of the market portfolio ultimately became a reality by the early 1970s when the first, passively-managed index funds were brought on line. That the world would move from there to the trading of broad market portfolios, either as baskets or as index futures and options, was widely anticipated. The fundamental Black-Scholes and Robert Merton papers on rational option pricing were published in the early 1970s, though manuscript versions of them had been circulating informally among academics well before then. These and other exciting prospects abounded in the academic literature 20 years ago. At the moment, however, that cupboard seems bare of new concepts and ideas waiting for the day of practical implementation.

Such hints of future developments as the current literature does have relate more to the structure of the exchanges themselves than to the products they trade. For academics, accustomed to spending their workdays staring at the screens of their PCs, the

---

13 Evolution also involves "extinctions." Some of the recent innovations will inevitably fail in the competitive struggle. Others may be killed by heavy-handed regulation.

near-term transition of the markets from floor trading to electronic trading is taken for granted. Frequent references can be found in the many articles on the crash of 1987 to the presumed failings of the current exchange trading systems during that hectic period. Those systems are typically characterized pejoratively as "archaic" and "obsolete," in contrast to the screen-based trading systems in such non-exchange markets as government bonds or inter-bank foreign exchange.

That screen-based trading will someday supplant floor trading seems more than likely, but whether that transition will occur even by the end of this century is far from clear. The case of the steamship is instructive. The new steam technology was clearly superior to sail-power in its ability to go up river and against winds and tides. Steam quickly took over inland river traffic but not, at first, ocean traffic. There steam was better, but vastly more expensive. Steam thus found its niche in military applications and in the high-unit-value fast passenger trade. Only as fuel costs dropped did steam take over more and more of the low-unit-value bulk trade in ocean freight. For some bulk commodities such as lumber, in fact, sail was often the lower-cost alternative up until the start of the first World War, more than 100 years after the first practical steamboat.

The same laws of comparative advantage apply to electronic trading systems. The open-outcry trading pits of the major futures exchanges may seem hopelessly chaotic and old-fashioned; but they are, for all that, a remarkably cheap way of handling transactions in large volume at great speed and frequency in a setting of high price volatility. Until recently, at least, electronic trading could not have come close to being cost-competitive in this arena. Screen trading found its niche

elsewhere. And electronic computer systems found their niche in futures in tasks such as order routing, data processing and some kinds of surveillance rather than on the trading floor.

But screen-trading technology, like that of computing technology generally, continues to advance and a possibly crucial watershed for the trading systems in futures may soon be crossed. By mid-1992 the Chicago exchanges hope finally to bring on line the long-delayed Globex electronic network for after-hours trading of futures contracts. Unlike some past experiments with screen trading of futures, the test this time will be a valid one. The contracts to be traded, Eurodollars and foreign exchange rates, have long proven viable; the underlying spot markets are themselves screen traded; and substantial potential trading demand for the contracts might well exist outside the U.S. and after U.S. trading hours.

Even a successful Globex, however, need not doom the exchanges to disappear as functioning business entities. The transactions facilities the exchanges provide through their trading floors are currently the major and certainly the most glamorous, but by no means the only, services they offer. The exchanges also provide such humdrum but critical functions as clearing and settlement, guarantees of contract performance, record-keeping and audit trails, and the collection and dissemination of price information. The market for these services in supporting financial transactions not currently carried out via exchanges is potentially huge. The futures exchanges, by virtue of their expertise and their substantial existing capital investments, are well positioned to enter and to capture a significant share of these new markets, just as they were 20 years ago when the shrinkage in their agricultural business propelled them into financial futures and options.

CHAPTER 23

Managing Financial Risk

Clifford W. Smith, Jr. (University of Rochester),
Charles W. Smithson (Continental Bank), and
D. Sykes Wilford (Chase Manhattan Bank)*

There is no doubt that the financial environment is a lot more risky today than it was in the 1950s and 1960s. With changes in some macroeconomic institutional structures – notably, the breakdown of the Bretton Woods agreement in 1972 – have come dramatic increases in the volatility of interest rates, foreign exchange rates, and commodity prices.

Such increased volatility will not come as "news" to most corporate executives. Since the 1970s, many CEOs and CFOs have watched the profitability of their firms swing widely in response to large movements in exchange rates, interest rates, and commodity prices. What may be news, however, are the techniques and tools now available for measuring and managing such financial risks.

Recognition of the increased volatility of exchange rates, interest rates, and commodity prices should lead managers of the firm to ask three questions:

1. To what extent is my firm exposed to interest rates, foreign exchange rates, or commodity prices?
2. What financial tools are available for managing these exposures?

---

* This article is an abbreviated version of Chapters 2, 3, and 19 of *Managing Financial Risk*, by C. Smithson, forthcoming Ballinger/*Institutional Investor Series*. This material is used with the permission of the publisher, The McGraw-Hill Companies.

3. If my firm is significantly exposed, how do I use the financial tools to manage the exposure?

It is with these three questions that the following discussion deals.

IDENTIFYING AND MEASURING FINANCIAL RISK

The risk profile

U.S. savings and loans (S&Ls) are a widely cited example of firms subject to interest rate risk. Because S&Ls typically fund long-lived assets (e.g., 30-year fixed-rate mortgages) with liabilities that reprice frequently (passbook deposits), their value is negatively related to interest rates. When interest rates rise, the value of S&Ls' assets declines significantly, but the value of their liabilities changes little. So, the value of shareholders' equity falls.

The resulting relation between interest rates and the value of S&Ls is portrayed graphically in a *risk profile* in Figure 23.1. The negative slope reflects the inverse relation between the financial price – i.e., interest rates – and the value of the S&L. The precise measure of the exposure is reflected by the slope of the line; and it is a measure of the slope that the techniques described below will provide.

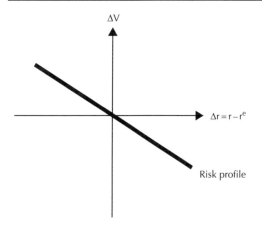

Figure 23.1 The Risk Profile for a U.S. S&L

Note: As actual interest rates, r, rise above expected rates, r^e, $\Delta r > 0$ the value of the S&L's assets declines relative to the value of its liabilities; so, the value of the firm declines, $\Delta V < 0$.

But before considering the size of the exposure, the first question is: How do we go about identifying such exposures? In the case of S&Ls, the exposure to interest rates is apparent from the firm's balance sheet; the mismatch of maturities between assets and liabilities is obvious. Many companies, however, have economic or "operating" exposures that are not reflected on their balance sheets. Take, for example, the vulnerability of building products firms to increases in interest rates. Increases in interest rates decrease the demand for building products. As sales and thus cash inflows decline – and to the extent that its costs and liabilities are fixed – the value of a building products firm declines.

We can make a similar observation about foreign exchange risk. In some instances, exposures are apparent. For example, a U.S. importer orders product from Germany and is expected to pay in Deutsche Marks (DM) for the products when they are delivered in 90 days. If, during those 90 days, the price of a DM rises – that is, the value of the dollar declines – the U.S. importer will have to pay more for the product. In this case, an increase in

the price of the foreign currency leads to a decrease in the value of the importer.

Since 1972, firms have become adept at dealing with such transaction exposures.[1] However, a firm's exposure to foreign exchange rate risk can be more subtle; even firms that have no foreign receipts or payments may still be exposed to foreign exchange risk. If the dollar is strong, the dollar price of foreign products to U.S. consumers becomes cheaper and foreign firms make inroads into the U.S. market, thereby decreasing net cash flows to the U.S. producers and thus reducing their value. The reverse is true when the value of the dollar falls. Obvious for firms like automakers, this economic or competitive (or "strategic") risk is receiving more attention by the managers of other U.S. firms as well.[2]

Not surprisingly, the same relations appear with respect to commodity price risk. The exposures can be apparent: For example, as the price of oil rises, the costs for an airline rise; so rising oil prices are linked to falling firm values. Or, the exposures can be subtle. For example, a primary input in aluminum production is electric energy. Aluminum manufacturers in Iceland use electricity generated by that country's abundant geothermal energy. As the price of oil rises, the costs of competitors rise while the costs of Icelandic producers remain unchanged, thus improving the competitive position and increasing the value of Icelandic firms. It is when oil prices fall and competitors' costs decline that Icelandic producers worry.[3]

Financial price risk, then – whether caused by changes in interest rates, foreign exchange, or commodity prices – consists of more subtle economic exposures as well as the obvious balance sheet mismatches and transactional exposures. And the *risk profile* mentioned earlier, in order to provide a useful measure of a firm's overall economic exposure, must reflect the total effect of both kinds of price risk.

The question that naturally arises, then, is: How do you determine the slope of the risk profile? That is, how do you estimate the change in firm

---

1 A transaction exposure occurs when the firm has a payment or receipt in a currency other than its home currency. A translation exposure results when the value of foreign assets and liabilities must be converted into home currency values.

2 A case in point is Kodak, which has begun to manage "overall corporate performance in the long run." See Paul Dickens, "Daring to Hedge the Unhedgeable," *Euromoney Corporate Finance*, August 1988.

3 For this useful story about Icelandic aluminum producers, we are indebted to J. Nicholas Robinson of Chase Manhattan Bank.

Table 23.1 Calculation of the Value & Duration of the Business Loan

(1) Time to receipt (Years)	(2) Cash flow	(3) Discount rate	(4) PV	(5) Weight	(6) Weight × Time
0.5	90	7.75%	86.70	0.22	0.11
1.0	90	8.00%	83.33	0.21	0.21
1.5	90	8.25%	79.91	0.20	0.31
2.0	90	8.35%	76.66	0.19	0.38
2.5	90	8.50%	73.40	0.18	0.45
			400.00 Present Value		1.45 Duration

value expected to accompany a given change in a financial price ($\Delta V / \Delta P$)?

Quantifying financial risk: a special case

Financial institutions, particularly banks, were the first to devote significant attention to quantifying financial exposures. Our S&L example is admittedly an extreme case of interest rate exposure, even for a financial institution. Nevertheless, because some mismatch between the maturities of assets and liabilities almost inevitably occurs in the normal course of their business, all financial institutions generally face some degree of interest rate risk. To measure this exposure to interest rates, financial institutions rely on two techniques: gap and duration.

GAP. The method most financial corporations use to measure their exposure to interest rate changes is called the "maturity gap" approach.[4] The approach gets its name from a procedure designed to quantify the "gap" between the market values of rate-sensitive assets (RSA) and rate-sensitive liabilities (RSL) – that is, GAP = RSA – RSL.[5]

The financial institution determines the "gapping period" – the period over which it wants to measure its interest rate sensitivity – say, 6 months, one year, five years, and so forth. Then, for each of these periods, it measures its gap as defined above. In the context of a gap model, changes in interest rates affect a financial institution's market value by changing the institution's Net Interest Income (NII). Hence, once the GAP is known, the impact on the firm of changes in the interest rate can be calculated as follows:

$$\Delta NII = (GAP) \times (\Delta r)$$

Duration. Some financial institutions use an alternative to the GAP approach called "duration analysis" to measure their interest rate exposure.[6] In essence, the duration of a financial instrument provides a measure of when on average the present value of the instrument is received.

For example, let's look at the duration of a business loan with a maturity of 2.5 years and a sinking fund. Because part of the value is received prior to maturity, the duration of the instrument is clearly less than 2.5 years. To find out how much less, we need to ask the question "When on average is the present value received?"

Table 23.1 provides an illustration. Columns 1–4 provide the present value of the bond. To determine

---

4 For a discussion of the maturity gap model, see Alden L. Toevs, "Measuring and Managing Interest Rate Risk: A Guide to Asset/Liability Models Used in Banks and Thrifts," Morgan Stanley Fixed Income Analytical Research Paper, October 1984. (An earlier version of this paper appeared in *Economic Review*, The Federal Reserve Bank of San Francisco, Spring, 1983.)

5 The assets and liabilities that are "rate sensitive" are those that will reprice during the gapping period.

6 For a discussion of duration, see George G. Kaufman, "Measuring and Managing Interest Rate Risk: A Primer," *Economic Perspectives*, Federal Reserve Bank of Chicago. See also Stephen Schaefer, "Immunisation and Duration: A Review of the Theory, Performance, and Applications," *Midland Corporate Finance Journal*, Vol. 2 No. 3, Fall 1984.

when the present value will be received, on average, we need to calculate the weighted average time of receipt. Column 5 provides the weights. Multiplying these weights (column 5) by the times the cash flows are received (column 1) and summing gives the duration of this business loan – 1.45 years.

The use of duration effectively converts a security into its zero-coupon equivalent. In addition, duration relates changes in interest rates to changes in the value of the security.[7] Specifically, duration permits us to express the percentage change in the value of the security in terms of the percentage change in the discount rate $(1 + r)$ and the duration of the security, as follows:[8]

$$\frac{\Delta V}{V} = \frac{\Delta(1+r)}{(1+r)} \times D$$

For example, if the duration of a security is 1.45 years, and the discount rate increases by 1 percent (that is, if $\Delta (1 + r)/(1 + r) = 0.01$), the market value of the 2.5 year business loan will decrease by 1.45 percent. The concept of duration, moreover, can be extended to provide a measure of the interest rate exposure of an entire bank or S&L.

Quantifying financial price risk: the general case

While gap and duration work well for financial institutions, these techniques offer little guidance in evaluating the interest rate sensitivity of a non-financial institution; and, neither gap nor duration is useful in examining a firm's sensitivity to movements in foreign exchange rates or commodity prices. What is needed is a more general method for quantifying financial price risk – a method that can handle firms other than financial institutions and financial exposures other than interest rates.

To get a measure of the responsiveness of the value of the firm to changes in the financial prices,

we must first define a measure of the value of the firm. As with interest rate risk for financial institutions, this value measure could be a "flow" measure (gap analysis uses net interest income) or a "stock" measure (duration uses the market value of the portfolio).

Flow Measures. Within a specific firm, estimation of the sensitivity of income flows is an analysis that can be performed as part of the planning and budgeting process. The trade press suggests that some firms have begun using simulation models to examine the responsiveness of their pre-tax income to changes in interest rates, exchange rates, and commodity prices.[9] Beginning with base case assumptions about the financial prices, the firm obtains a forecast for revenues, costs, and the resulting pre-tax income. Then, it considers alternative values for an interest rate or an exchange rate or a commodity price and obtains a new forecast for revenues, costs, and pre-tax income. By observing how the firm's projected sales, costs and income move in response to changes in these financial prices, management is able to trace out a risk profile similar to that in Figure 23.1.

In making such an estimation, two inherent problems confront the analyst: (1) this approach requires substantial data and (2) it relies on the ability of the researcher to make explicit, accurate forecasts of sales and costs under alternative scenarios for the financial prices. For both these reasons, such an approach is generally feasible only for analysts within a specific firm.

Stock Measures. Given the data requirements noted above, analysts outside the firm generally rely on market valuations, the most widely used of which is the current market value of the equity. Using a technique much like the one used to estimate a firm's "beta," an outside observer could measure the historical sensitivity of the company's equity value to changes in interest rates, foreign exchange rates, and commodity prices.

For example, suppose we wished to determine the sensitivity of a company's value to the following financial prices:

♦ the one-year T-bill interest rate;
♦ the Deutsche Mark/Dollar exchange rate;

---

7   Note the contrast with the gap approach, which relates changes in the interest rate to changes in net interest income.
8   The calculations in Table 1 are based on the use of MacCauley's duration. If we continue to apply MacCauley's duration (D), this equation is only an approximation. To be exact, modified duration should be used. For a development of this relation, see George G. Kaufman, G.O. Bierwag, and Alden Toevs, eds. *Innovations in Bond Portfolio Management: Duration Analysis and Immunization* (Greenwich, Conn.: JAI Press, 1983).

9   See for instance, Paul Dickens, cited in note 2.

Table 23.2   Measurements of Exposures to Interest Rate, Foreign Exchange Rates, and Oil Prices

Percentage change in	Chase Manhattan		Caterpillar		Exxon	
	Parameter estimate	T value	Parameter estimate	T value	Parameter estimate	T value
Price of 1-Year T-Bill	2.598*	1.56	−3.221**	1.76	1.354	1.24
Price of DM	−0.276	0.95	0.344	1.07	−0.066	0.35
Price of Sterling	0.281	1.16	−0.010	0.38	0.237*	1.50
Price of Yen	−0.241	0.96	0.045	0.16	−0.278**	1.69
Price of WTI Crude	0.065	1.21	−0.045	0.77	0.082***	2.33

*Significant at 90% single tailed
**Significant at 90%
***Significant at 95%

- the Pound Sterling/Dollar exchange rate;
- the Yen/Dollar exchange rate; and
- the price of oil.

We could estimate this relation by performing a simple linear regression as follows:[10]

$$R_t = a + b_1\left(\frac{\Delta P_{TB}}{P_{TB}}\right)_t + b_2\left(\frac{\Delta P_{DM}}{P_{DM}}\right)_t + b_3\left(\frac{\Delta P_{\pounds}}{P_{\pounds}}\right)_t$$
$$+ b_4\left(\frac{\Delta P_y}{P_y}\right)_t + b_5\left(\frac{\Delta P_{OIL}}{P_{OIL}}\right)_t$$

where R is the rate of return on the firm's equity; $\Delta P_{TB}/P_{TB}$ is the percentage change in the price of a one-year T-bill; $\Delta P_{DM}/P_{DM}$, $\Delta P_{\pounds}/P_{\pounds}$, and $\Delta P_y/P_y$ are the percentage changes in the dollar prices of the three foreign currencies; and $\Delta P_{OIL}/P_{OIL}$ is the percentage change in the price of crude oil. The estimate of b_1 provides a measure of the sensitivity of the value of the firm to changes in the one-year T-bill rate; b_2, b_3, and b_4 estimate its sensitivity to the exchange rates; and b_5 estimates its sensitivity to the oil price.[11]

To illustrate the kind of results this technique would yield, we present three examples: a bank, Chase Manhattan, an industrial, Caterpillar, and an oil company, Exxon. For the period January 6, 1984 to December 2, 1988 we calculated weekly (Friday close to Friday close) share returns and the corresponding weekly percentage changes in the price of a one-year T-bill rate, the dollar prices of a Deutsche Mark, a Pound Sterling, and a Yen, and the price of West Texas Intermediate crude. Using these data, we estimated our regression

---

10   In effect, this equation represents a variance decomposition. While it is a multifactor model, it is not related in any important way to the APT approach suggested by Ross and Roll. Instead, it is probably more accurate to view the approach we suggest as an extension of the market model. In its more complete form, as described in Chapter 2 of our book *Managing Financial Risk*, the regression equation would include the rate of return to the market ("beta") as well as the percentage changes in the financial prices, and would thus look as follows:

$$R_t = a + \beta R_{m,t} + b_1 PC(P_{TB}) + b_2 PC(P_{DM}) + b_3 PC(P_{\pounds})$$
$$+ b_4 PC(P_y) + b_5 PC(P_{OIL})$$

This more complete model is based on a number of earlier studies: French/Ruback/Schwert (1983) ("Effects of Nominal Contracting on Share Returns," *Journal of Political Economy*, Vol. 91 No. 1) on the impact of unexpected inflation on share returns, Flannery/James (1984) ("The Effect of Interest Rate Changes on Common Stock Returns of Financial Institutions," *Journal of Finance* Vol. 39 No. 4) and Scott/Peterson (1986) ("Interest Rate Risk and Equity Values of Hedged and Unhedged Financial Intermediaries," *Journal of Financing Research*, Vol. 9 No. 6) on the impact of interest rate changes on share prices for financial firms, and Sweeney/Warga (1986) ("The Pricing of Interest Rate Risk: Evidence from the Stock Market," *Journal of Finance*, Vol. 41 No. 2) on the impact of interest rate risk on share prices for nonfinancial firms. This model does exhibit the problems of measuring the reaction of firm value to changes in exchange rates, which

are described by Donald Lessard in "Finance and Global Competition: Exploiting Financial Scope and Coping with Volatile Exchange Rates," *Midland Corporate Finance Journal* (Fall 1986).

For expositional purposes, we use in this paper the shorter form of the equation. This abbreviated model is acceptable empirically given the small correlations which exist between the percentage changes in the financial prices and the market return.

11   These coefficients actually measure elasticities. Further, had we used the percentage change in the quantity, (1 + one-year T-bill rate), instead of the percentage change in the price of the one-year T-bill, the coefficient b_1 could be interpreted as a "duration" measure.

Table 23.2A

Bank	Estimated sensitivity	T-value
Bank of America	3.2	1.5
Bankers Trust	2.2	1.4
Chase	2.6	1.6
First Chicago	3.0	1.6
Manufacturers Hanover	3.2	1.9

Table 23.2B

	1984	1985	1986	1987	1988
Parameter Estimate for Percentage Change in Price of Yen	1.72	0.15	0.33	−1.08	−0.85
T-Value	1.59	0.31	0.65	1.08	1.53

Table 23.2C

	1984	1985	1986	1987	1988
Parameter Estimate for Percentage Change in Price of Oil	0.80	0.15	0.09	0.05	−0.01
T-Value	3.94	0.85	2.79	0.37	0.17

equation. The results of these estimations are displayed in Table 23.2.

Given the tendency of banks to accept short-dated deposits to fund longer-dated assets (loans), it is not surprising that our estimates for Chase Manhattan indicate an inverse exposure to interest rates. Although only marginally significant, the positive coefficient indicates that an increase in the one-year T-bill rate (or a decrease in the price of the T-bill) is expected to lead to a decrease in the bank's value.

Additional information can be obtained by comparing the coefficient estimates among firms in the same industry. For example, we can compare the estimated sensitivity of Chase's value to the one-year T-bill rate to the sensitivities of other banks as shown in Table 23.2.A.

In contrast to the bank's inverse exposure, Caterpillar appears to have a positive exposure to the one-year T-bill rate. That is, the negative regression coefficient indicates that increases in the one-year T-bill rate (or decreases in the price of the T-bill) lead to increases in the value of the firm.

Even more surprising, though, given much that has been written about Caterpillar's exposure to foreign currency changes, is the lack of any significant exposure to the yen. This result is more understandable if we break up this 5-year span into shorter intervals and look at Caterpillar's sensitivity to the price of the yen on a year-by-year basis. (See Table 23.2.B.) The data reflect the fact that, as Caterpillar has moved its production facilities, the firm has changed from being positively exposed to the yen (such that an increase in the value of the dollar would harm Caterpillar) to being negatively exposed to the yen (an increase in the value of the dollar now helps Caterpillar).

Unlike the other two firms, the estimate for Exxon's exposure to interest rates is not statistically significant (not, at least, to the one-year T-bill rate). Exxon does exhibit the expected positive exposure to the price of oil. But our estimates also reflect the now common view, reported in the financial press and elsewhere, that Exxon's exposure to the price of oil has been declining over time – both in size and consistency (as measured by statistical significance). (See Table 23.2.C.) Given its international production and distribution, as well as its international portfolio of assets, Exxon also exhibits marginally significant exposures to foreign exchange rates. Our estimates suggest Exxon benefits from an increase in the value of the pound but is harmed by an increase in the value of the yen.

Measuring corporate exposure: summing up

The purpose of this first section, then, has been to outline a statistical technique (similar to that used to calculate a firm's "beta") that can be used to provide management with an estimate of the sensitivity of firm value to changes in a variety of financial variables. Such measures can be further refined by using information from other sources. For example, the same regression technique can be used, only substituting changes in the firm's periodic earnings and cash flows for the changes in stock prices in our model. There are, however, two principal advantages of our procedure over the use of such accounting numbers: (1) market reactions are likely to capture the entire capitalized value of changes in firm value in response to financial price changes; and (2) regression analysis using stock prices, besides being much faster and cheaper, can be done using publicly available information.

THE TOOLS FOR MANAGING FINANCIAL RISK: A BUILDING BLOCK APPROACH[12]

If it turns out that a firm is subject to significant financial price risk, management may choose to hedge that risk.[13] One way of doing so is by using an "on-balance-sheet" transaction. For example, a company could manage a foreign exchange exposure resulting from overseas competition by borrowing in the competitor's currency or by moving production abroad. But such on-balance sheet methods can be costly and, as firms like Caterpillar have discovered, inflexible.[14]

Alternatively, financial risks can be managed with the use of off-balance-sheet instruments. The four fundamental off-balance-sheet instruments are forwards, futures, swaps, and options.

---

12   This section of the article is adapted from Charles W. Smithson, "A LEGO Approach to Financial Engineering: An Introduction to Forwards, Futures, Swaps, and Options," *Midland Corporate Finance Journal* 4 (Winter 1987).

13   In this paper we do not address the question of why public corporations hedge. For a discussion of the corporate decision whether or not to hedge financial price exposures, see Alan Shapiro and Sheridan Titman, "An Integrated Approach to Corporate Risk Management," *Midland Corporate Finance Journal* 3 (Summer 1985). For other useful theoretical discussions of the corporate hedging decision, see David Mayers and Clifford Smith, "On the Corporate Demand for Insurance," *Journal of Business* 55 (April 1982) (a less technical version of which was published as "The Corporate Insurance Decision," *Chase Financial Quarterly* (Vol. 1 No. 3) Spring 1982); Rene Stulz, "Optimal Hedging Policies," *Journal of Financial and Quantitative Analysis* 19 (June 1984); Clifford Smith and Rene Stulz, "The Determinants of Firms' Hedging Policies," *Journal of Financial and Quantitative Analysis* 20 (December 1985).

For some empirical tests of the above theoretical work, see David Mayers and Clifford Smith, "On the Corporate Demand for Insurance: Some Empirical Evidence," working paper, 1988; and Deana Nance, Clifford Smith, and Charles Smithson, "The Determinants of Off-Balance-Sheet Hedging: An Empirical Analysis," working paper 1988.

14   See "Caterpillar's Triple Whammy," *Fortune,* October 27, 1986.

When we first began to attempt to understand these financial instruments, we were confronted by what seemed an insurmountable barrier to entry. The participants in the various markets all seemed to possess a highly specialized expertise that was applicable in only one market to the exclusion of all others (and the associated trade publications served only to tighten the veil of mystery that "experts" have always used to deny entry to novices). Options were discussed as if they were completely unrelated to forwards or futures, which in turn seemed to have nothing to do with the latest innovation, swaps. Adding to the complexities of the individual markets was the welter of jargon that seems to have grown up around each, thus further obscuring any common ground that might exist. (Words such as "ticks," "collars," "strike prices," and "straddles" suddenly had acquired a remarkable currency.) In short, we seemed to find ourselves looking up into a Wall Street Tower of Babel, with each group of market specialists speaking in different languages.

But, after now having observed these instruments over the past several years, we have been struck by how little one has to dig before superficial differences give way to fundamental unity. And, in marked contrast to the specialized view of most Wall Street practitioners, we take a more "generalist" approach – one that treats forwards, futures, swaps, and options not as four unique instruments and markets, but rather as four interrelated instruments for dealing with a single problem: managing financial risk. In fact, we have come up with a little analogy that captures the spirit of our conclusion, one which goes as follows: The four basic off-balance-sheet instruments – forwards, futures, swaps, and options – are much like those plastic building blocks children snap together. You can either build the instruments from one another, or you can combine the instruments into larger creations that appear (but appearances deceive) altogether "new."

Forward contracts

Of the four instruments, the forward contract is the oldest and, perhaps for this reason, the most straightforward. A forward contract obligates its owner to buy a specified asset on a specified date at

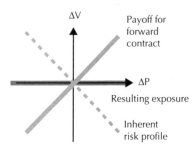

Figure 23.2 Payoff Profile for Forward Contact

a price (known as the "exercise price") specified at the origination of the contract. If, at maturity, the actual price is higher than the exercise price, the contract owner makes a profit equal to the difference; if the price is lower, he suffers a loss.

In Figure 23.2, the payoff from buying a forward contract is illustrated with a hypothetical risk profile. If the actual price at contract maturity is higher than the expected price, the inherent risk results in a decline in the value of the firm; but this decline is offset by the profit on the forward contract. Hence, for the risk profile illustrated, the forward contract provides an effective hedge. (If the risk profile were positively instead of negatively sloped, the risk would be managed by selling instead of buying a forward contract.)

Besides its payoff profile, a forward contract has two other features that should be noted. First, the default (or credit) risk of the contract is two-sided. The contract owner either receives or makes a payment, depending on the price movement of the underlying asset. Second, the value of the forward contract is conveyed only at the contract's maturity; no payment is made either at origination or during the term of the contract.

Futures contracts

The basic form of the futures contract is identical to that of the forward contract; a futures contract also obligates its owner to purchase a specified asset at a specified exercise price on the contract maturity date. Thus, the payoff profile for the purchaser of a forward contract as presented in Figure 23.2 could also serve to illustrate the payoff to the holder of a futures contract.

But, unlike the case of forwards, credit or default risk can be virtually eliminated in a futures market.

Futures markets use two devices to manage default risk. First, instead of conveying the value of a contract through a single payment at maturity, any change in the value of a futures contract is conveyed at the end of the day in which it is realized. Look again at Figure 23.2. Suppose that, on the day after origination, the financial price rises and, consequently, the financial instrument has a positive value. In the case of a forward contract, this value change would not be received until contract maturity. With a futures contract, this change in value is received at the end of the day. In the language of the futures markets, the futures contract is "marked-to-market" and "cash settled" daily.

Because the performance period of a futures contract is reduced by marking to market, the risk of default declines accordingly. Indeed, because the value of the futures contract is paid or received at the end of each day, Fischer Black likened a futures contract to "a series of forward contracts [in which] each day, yesterday's contract is settled and today's contract is written."[15] That is, a futures contract is like a sequence of forwards in which the "forward" contract written on day 0 is settled on day 1 and is replaced, in effect, with a new "forward" contract reflecting the new day 1 expectations. This new contract is then itself settled on day 2 and replaced, and so on until the day the contract ends.

The second feature of futures contracts which reduces default risk is the requirement that all market participants – sellers and buyers alike – post a performance bond called the "margin."[16] If my futures contract increases in value during the trading day, this gain is added to my margin account at the day's end. Conversely, if my contract has lost value, this loss is deducted from my margin account. And, if my margin account balance falls below some agreed-upon minimum, I am required to post additional bond; that is, my margin account must be replenished or my position will be closed out.[17]

---

15 See Fischer Black "The Pricing to Commodity Contracts," *Journal of Financial Economics* 3 (1976), 167–179.
16 Keep in mind that if you buy a futures contract, you are taking a long position in the underlying asset. Conversely, selling a futures contract is equivalent to taking a short position.
17 When the contract is originated on the U.S. exchanges, an "initial margin" is required. Subsequently, the margin account balance must remain above the "maintenance margin." If the margin account balance falls below the maintenance level, the balance must be restored to the initial level.

Panel A: an interest rate swap

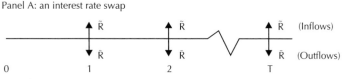

Panel B: an interest rate swap as a portfolio of forward contracts

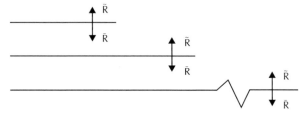

Figure 23.3

Because the position will be closed before the margin account is depleted, performance risk is eliminated.[18]

Note that the exchange itself has not been proposed as a device to reduce default risk. Daily settlement and the requirement of a bond reduce default risk, but the existence of an exchange (or clearing-house) merely serves to transform risk. More specifically, the exchange deals with the two-sided risk inherent in forwards and futures by serving as the counterparty to all transactions. If I wish to buy or sell a futures contract, I buy from or sell to the exchange. Hence, I need only evaluate the credit risk of the exchange, not of some specific counterparty.

The primary economic function of the exchange is to reduce the costs of transacting in futures contracts. The anonymous trades made possible by the exchange, together with the homogeneous nature of the futures contracts – standardized assets, exercise dates (four per year), and contract sizes – enables the futures markets to become relatively liquid. However, as was made clear by recent experience of the London Metal Exchange, the existence of the exchange does not in and of itself eliminate the possibility of default.[19]

In sum, a futures contract is much like a portfolio of forward contracts. At the close of business of each day, in effect, the existing forward-like contract is settled and a new one is written.[20] This daily settlement feature combined with the margin requirement allows futures contracts to eliminate the credit risk inherent in forwards.

---

18   Note that this discussion has ignored daily limits. If there are daily limits on the movement of futures prices, large changes in expectations about the underlying asset can effectively close the market. (The market opens, immediately moves the limit, and then is effectively closed until the next day.) Hence, there could exist an instance in which the broker desires to close out a customer's position but is not able to immediately because the market is experiencing limit moves. In such a case, the statement that performance risk is "eliminated" is too strong.

19   In November of 1985, the "tin cartel" defaulted on contracts for tin delivery on the London Metal Exchange, thereby making the exchange liable for the loss. A description of this situation is contained in "Tin Crisis in London Roils Metal Exchange," *The Wall Street Journal*, November 13, 1985.

From the point of view of the market, the exchange does not reduce default risk. The expected default rate is not affected by the existence of the exchange. However, the existence of the exchange can alter the default risk faced by an individual market participant. If I buy a futures contract for a specific individual, the default risk I face is determined by the default rate of that specific counterparty. If I instead buy the same futures contract through an exchange, my default risk depends on the default rate of not just my counterparty, but on the default rate of he entire market. Moreover, to the extent that the exchange is capitalized by equity from its members, the default risk I perceive is further reduced because I have a claim not against some specific counterparty, but rather against the exchange. Therefore, when I trade through the exchange, I am in a sense purchasing an insurance policy from the exchange.

20   A futures contract is like a portfolio of forward contracts; however, a futures contract and a portfolio of forward contracts become identical only if interest rates are "deterministic" – that is, known with certainty in advance. See Robert A. Jarrow and George S. Oldfield, "Forward Contracts and Futures Contracts," *Journal of Financial Economics* 9 (1981), 373–382; and John A. Cox, Jonathan E. Ingersoll, and Stephen A. Ross, "The Relation between Forward Prices and Futures Prices," *Journal of Financial Economics* 9 (1981), 321–346.

Swap contracts[21]

A swap contract is in essence nothing more complicated than a series of forward contracts strung together. As implied by its name, a swap contract obligates two parties to exchange, or "swap," some specified cash flows at specified intervals. The most common form is the interest rate swap, in which the cash flows are determined by two different interest rates.

Panel A of Figure 23.3 illustrates an interest rate swap from the perspective of a party who is paying out a series of cash flows determined by a fixed interest rate ($\overline{R}$) in return for a series of cash flows determined by a floating interest rate ($\tilde{R}$).[22]

Panel B of Figure 23.3 serves to illustrate that this swap contract can be decomposed into a portfolio of forward contracts. At each settlement date, the party to this swap contract has an implicit forward contract on interest rates: the party illustrated is obligated to sell a fixed-rate cash flow for an amount specified at the origination of the contract. In this sense, a swap contract is also like a portfolio of forward contracts.

In terms of our earlier discussion, this means that the solid line in Figure 23.2 could also represent the payoff from a swap contract. Specifically, the solid line in Figure 23.3 would be consistent with a swap contract in which the party illustrated receives cash flows determined by one price (say, the U.S. Treasury bond rate) and makes payments determined by another price (say, LIBOR). Thus, in terms of their ability to manage risk, forwards, futures, and swaps all function in the same way.

But identical payoff *patterns* notwithstanding, the instruments all differ with respect to default risk.

As we saw, the performance period of a forward is equal to its maturity; and because no performance bond is required, a forward contract is a pure credit instrument. Futures both reduce the performance period (to one day) and require a bond, thereby eliminating credit risk. Swap contracts use only one of these mechanisms to reduce credit risk; they reduce the performance period.[23] This point becomes evident in Figure 23.3. Although the maturity of the contract is T periods, the performance period is generally not T periods long but is instead a single period. Thus, given a swap and a forward contract of roughly the same maturity, the swap is likely to impose far less credit risk on the counterparties to the contract than the forward.

At each settlement date throughout a swap contract, the changes in value are transferred between the counterparties. To illustrate this in terms of Figure 23.3, suppose that interest rates rise on the day after origination. The value of the swap contract illustrated has risen. This value change will be conveyed to the contract owner not at maturity (as would be the case with a forward contract) nor at the end of that day (as would be the case with a futures contract). Instead, at the first settlement date, part of the value change is conveyed in the form of the "difference check" paid by one party to the other. To repeat, then, the performance period is less than that of a forward, but not as short as that of a futures contract.[24] (keep in mind that we are comparing instruments with the same maturities.)

Let us reinforce the two major points made thus far. First, a swap contract, like a futures contract, is like a portfolio of forward contracts. Therefore, the payoff profiles for each of these three instruments are identical. Second, the primary difference among forwards, futures, and swaps is the amount of default risk they impose on counterparties to the contract. Forwards and futures represent the extremes, and swaps are the intermediate case.

---

21 This section is based on Clifford W. Smith, Charles W. Smithson, and Lee M. Wakeman, "The Evolving Market for Swaps," *Midland Corporate Finance Journal* Winter (1986), 20–32.
22 Specifically, the interest rate swap cash flows are determined as follows: The two parties agree to some notional principal, P. (The principal is notional in the sense that it is only used to determine the magnitude of cash flows; is is not paid or received by either party.) At each settlement date, 1, 2, . . . , T the party illustrated makes a payment $\overline{R} = \bar{r}P$, where $\bar{r}$ is the T-period fixed rate which existed at origination. At each settlement, the party illustrated receives $\tilde{R} = \tilde{r}P$, where $\tilde{r}$ is the floating rate for that period (e.g., at settlement date 2, the interest rate used is the one-period rate in effect at period 1).

23 There are instances in a which bond has been posted in the form of collateral. As should be evident, in this case the swap becomes very like a futures contract.
24 Unlike futures, for which all of any change in contract value is paid/received at the daily settlements, swap contracts convey only part of the total value change at the periodic settlements.

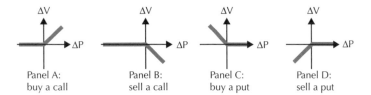

Figure 23.4 Payoff Profiles of Puts and Calls

Option contracts

As we have seen, the owner of a forward, futures, or swap contract has an *obligation* to perform. In contrast, an option gives its owner a *right*, not an obligation. An option giving its owner the right to buy an asset at a pre-determined price – a call option – is provided in Panel A of Figure 23.4. The owner of the contract has the right to purchase the asset at a specified future date at a price agreed-upon today. Thus, if the price rises, the value of the option also goes up. But because the option contract owner is not obligated to purchase the asset if the price moves against him, the value of the option remains unchanged (at zero) if the price declines.[25]

The payoff profile for the party who sold the call option (also known as the call "writer") is shown in Panel B. In contrast to the buyer of the option, the seller of the call option has the *obligation* to perform. For example, if the owner of the option elects to exercise his option to buy the asset, the seller of the option is obligated to sell the asset.

Besides the option to buy an asset, there is also the option to sell an asset at a specified price, known as a "put" option. The payoff to the buyer of a put is illustrated in Panel C of Figure 23.4, and the payoff to the seller of the put is shown in Panel D.

Pricing Options. Up to this point, we have considered only the payoffs to the option contracts.

We have side-stepped the thorniest issue – the valuation of option contracts.

The breakthrough in option pricing theory came with the work of Fischer Black and Myron Scholes in 1973.[26] Conveniently for our purposes, Black and Scholes took what might be described as a "building block" approach to the valuation of options. Look again at the call option illustrated in Figure 23.4. For increases in the financial price, the payoff profile for the option is that of a forward contract. For decreases in the price, the value of the option is constant – like that of a "riskless" security such as a Treasury bill.

The work of Black and Scholes demonstrated that a call option could be replicated by a continuously adjusting ("dynamic") portfolio of two securities: (1) forward contracts on the underlying asset and (2) riskless securities. As the financial price rises, the "call option equivalent" portfolio contains an increasing proportion of forward contracts on the asset. Conversely, the replicating portfolio contains a decreasing proportion of forwards as the price of the asset falls.

Because this replicating portfolio is effectively a synthetic call option, arbitrage activity should ensure that its value closely approximates the market price of exchange-traded call options. In this sense, the value of a call option, and thus the premium that would be charged its buyer, is determined by the value of its option equivalent portfolio.

Panel A of Figure 23.5 illustrates the payoff profile for a call option which includes the premium. This figure (and all of the option figures thus far) illustrates an "at-the-money" option – that is, an option for which the exercise price is the prevailing expected price. As Panels A and B of Figure 23.5 illustrate, an at-the-money option is paid for by sacrificing a significant amount of the firm's potential gains. However, the price of a call option falls as the exercise price increases relative to

---

25   For continuity, we continue to use the $\Delta V, \Delta P$ convention in figures. To compare these figures with those found in most texts, treat ΔV as deviations from zero ($\Delta V = V-0$) and remember that P measures deviations from expected price ($\Delta P = P-P_e$).

26   See Fischer Black and Myron Scholes, "The Pricing of Options and Corporate Liabilities," *Journal of Political Economy* 1973. For a less technical discussion of the model, see "The Black-Scholes Option Pricing Model for Alternative Underlying Instruments," *Financial Analysts Journal*, November–December, 1984, 23–30.

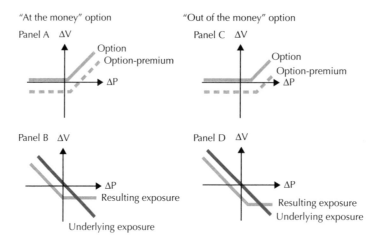

Figure 23.5

the prevailing price of the asset. This means that if an option buyer is willing to accept larger potential losses in return for paying a lower option premium, he would then consider using an "out-of-the-money" option.

An out-of-the-money call option is illustrated in Panel C of Figure 23.5. As shown in Panel D, the out-of-the-money option provides less downside protection, but the option premium is significantly less. The lesson to be learned here is that the option buyer can alter his payoff profile simply by changing the exercise price.

For our purposes, however, the most important feature of options is that they are not as different from other financial instruments as they might first seem. Options do have a payoff profile that differs significantly from that of forward contracts (or futures or swaps). But, option payoff profiles can be duplicated by a combination of forwards and risk-free securities. Thus, we find that options have more in common with the other instruments than was first apparent. Futures and swaps, as we saw earlier, are in essence nothing more than portfolios of forward contracts; and options, as we have just seen, are very much akin to portfolios of forward contracts and risk-free securities.

This point is reinforced if we consider ways that options can be combined. Consider a portfolio constructed by buying a call and selling a put with the same exercise price. As the left side of Figure 23.6 illustrates, the resulting portfolio (long a call, short a put) has a payoff profile equivalent to that of buying a forward contract on the asset. Similarly,

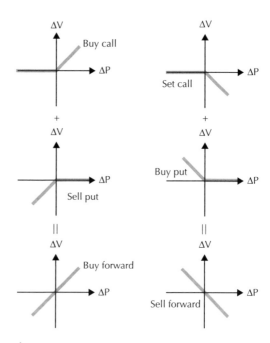

Figure 23.6

the right side of Figure 23.6 illustrates that a portfolio made up of selling a call and buying a put (short a call, long a put) is equivalent to selling a forward contract.

The relationship illustrated in Figure 23.6 is known more formally as "put-call parity." The special import of this relationship, at least in this context, is the "building block construction" it makes possible: two options can be "snapped together" to yield the payoff profile for a forward contract, which is identical to the payoff profile for futures and swaps.

At the beginning of this section, then, it seemed that options would be very different from forwards, futures, and swaps – and in some ways they are. But we discovered two building block relations between options and the other three instruments: (1) options can be replicated by "snapping together" a forward, futures, or swap contract together with a position in risk-free securities; and (2) calls and puts can be combined to become forwards.

The financial building blocks

Forwards, futures, swaps, and options – they all look so different from one another. And if you read the trade publications or talk to the specialists that transact in the four markets, the apparent differences among the instruments are likely to seem even more pronounced.

But it turns out that forwards, futures, swaps, and options are not each unique constructions, but rather more like those plastic building blocks that children combine to make complex structures. To understand the off-balance-sheet instruments, you don't need a lot of market-specific knowledge. All you need to know is how the instruments can be linked to one another. As we have seen, (1) futures can be built by "snapping together" a package of forwards; (2) swaps can also be built by putting together a package of forwards; (3) synthetic options can be constructed by combining a forward with a riskless security; and (4) options can be combined to produce forward contracts – or, conversely, forwards can be pulled apart to replicate a package of options.

Having shown you all the building blocks and how they fit together in simple constructions, we now want to demonstrate how they can be used to create more complicated, customized financial instruments that in turn can be used to manage financial risks.

ASSEMBLING THE BUILDING BLOCKS

Using the building blocks to manage an exposure

Consider a company whose market value is directly related to unexpected changes in some

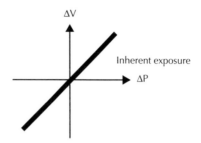

Figure 23.7
Note: The value of the firm is directly related to financial price P (i.e., interest rates or foreign exchange rates or commodity prices). If P rises, the value of the firm rises.

financial price, P. The risk profile of this company is illustrated in Figure 23.7. How could we use the financial building blocks to modify this inherent exposure?

The simplest solution is to use a forward, a futures, or a swap to neutralize this exposure. This is shown in Panel A of Figure 23.8.

But, the use of a forward, a futures, or a swap eliminates possible losses by giving up the possibility of profiting from favorable outcomes. The company might want to minimize the effect of unfavorable outcomes while still allowing the possibility of gaining from favorable ones. This can be accomplished using options. The payoff profile of an at-the-money option (including the premium paid to buy the option) is shown on the left side of Panel B. Snapping this building block onto the inherent exposure profile gives the resulting exposure illustrated on the right side of Panel B.

A common complaint about options – especially at-the-money options – is that they are "too expensive." To reduce the option premium, you can think about using an out-of-the-money option. As Panel C of Figure 23.8 illustrates, the firm has thereby given up some protection from adverse outcomes in return for paying a lower premium.

But, with an out-of-the-money option, some premium expense remains. Panel D illustrates how the out-of-pocket expense can be *eliminated*. The firm can sell a call option with an exercise price chosen so as to generate premium income equal to the premium due on the put option it wishes to purchase. In building block parlance, we snap the "buy-a-put" option onto the inherent risk profile to reduce downside outcomes; and we snap on the "sell-a-call" option to fund this insurance by giving up some of the favorable outcomes.

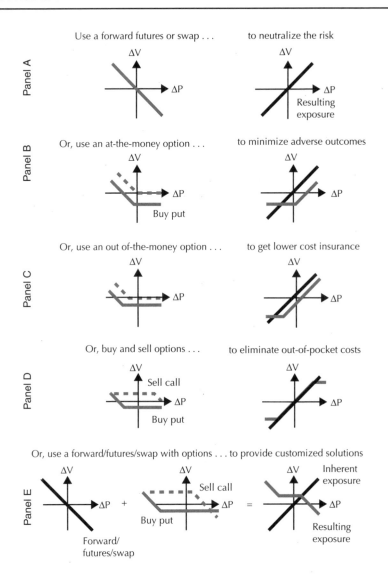

Figure 23.8

Panel E reminds us that forwards, futures, and swaps can be used in combination with options. Suppose the treasurer of the company we have been considering comes to you with the following request:

I think that this financial price, P, is going to fall dramatically. And, while I know enough about financial markets to know that P could actually rise a little, I am sure it will not rise by much. I want some kind of financial solution that will let me benefit when my predictions come to pass. But I don't want to pay any out-of-pocket premiums. Instead, I want this financial engineering product to pay me a premium.

If you look at the firm's inherent risk profile in Figure 23.7, this seems like a big request. The firm's inherent position is such that it would lose rather than gain from big decreases in P.

The resulting exposure profile shown on the right side of Panel E is the one the firm wants: it benefits from large decreases in P, is protected against small increases in P (though not against large increases) and receives a premium for the instrument.

How was this new profile achieved? As illustrated on the left side of Panel E, we first snapped a forward/futures/swap position onto the original

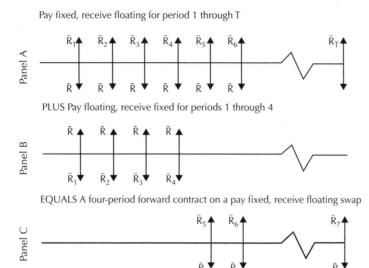

Pay fixed, receive floating for period 1 through T

PLUS Pay floating, receive fixed for periods 1 through 4

EQUALS A four-period forward contract on a pay fixed, receive floating swap

Figure 23.9

risk profile to neutralize the firm's inherent exposure. We then sold a call option and bought a put option with exercise prices set such that the income from selling the call exceeded the premium required to buy the put.

No high level math was required. Indeed, we did this bit of financial engineering simply by looking through the box of financial building blocks until we found those that snapped together to give us the profile we wanted.

Using the building blocks to redesign financial instruments

Now that you understand how forwards, futures, swaps, and options are all fundamentally related, it is a relatively short step to thinking about how the instruments can be combined with each other to give one financial instrument the characteristics of another. Rather than talk about this in the abstract, let's look at some examples of how this has been done in the marketplace.

Combining Forwards with Swaps. Suppose a firm's value is currently unaffected by interest rate movements. But, at a known date in the future, it expects to become exposed to interest rates: if rates

rise, the value of the firm will decrease.[27] To manage this exposure, the firm could use a forward, futures, or swap commencing at that future date. Such a product is known as a *forward* or *delayed start* swap. The payoff from a forward swap is illustrated in Panel C of Figure 23.9, where the party illustrated pays a fixed rate and receives floating starting in period 5.

Although this instrument is in effect a forward contract on a swap, it also, not surprisingly, can be constructed as a package of swaps. As Figure 23.9 illustrates, a forward swap is equivalent to a package of two swaps:

Swap 1 – From period 1 to period T, the party pays fixed and receives floating.

Swap 2 – From period 1 to period 4, the party pays floating and receives fixed.

Forwards with Option-like Characteristics. The addition of option-like characteristics

---

27 For example, the firm may know that, in one year, it will require funds which will be borrowed at a floating rate, thereby giving the firm the inverse exposure to interest rates, Or, the firm may be adding a new product line, the demand for which is extremely sensitive to interest rate movements – as rates rise, the demand for the product decreases and cash flows to the firm decrease.

to forward contracts first appeared in the foreign exchange markets. To see how this was done, let's trace the evolution of these contracts.

Begin with a standard forward contract on foreign exchange. Panel A of Figure 23.10 illustrates a conventional forward contract on sterling with the forward sterling exchange rate (the "contract rate") set at $1.50 per pound sterling. If, at maturity, the spot price of sterling exceeds $1.50, the owner of this contract makes a profit (equal to the spot rate minus $1.50). Conversely, if at maturity the spot price of sterling is less than $1.50, the owner of this contract suffers a loss. The owner of the forward contract, however, might instead want a contract that allows him to profit if the price of sterling rises, but limits his losses if the price of sterling falls.[28] Such a contract would be a call option on sterling. Illustrated in Panel B of Figure 23.10 is a call option on sterling with an exercise price of $1.50. In this illustration we have assumed an option premium of 5 cents (per pound sterling).

The payoff profile illustrated in Panel B of Figure 23.10 could also be achieved by altering the terms of the standard forward contract as follows:

1. Change the contract price so that the exercise price of the forward contract is no longer $1.50 but is instead $1.55. The owner of the forward contract agrees to purchase sterling at contract maturity at a price of $1.55 per unit; and

2. Permit the owner of the contract to break (i.e. "unwind") the agreement at a sterling price of $1.50.

This altered forward contract is referred to as a *break forward* contract.[29] In this break forward construction, the premium is effectively being paid by

the owner of the break forward contract in the form of the above market contract exchange rate.

From our discussion of options, we also know that a call can be paid for with the proceeds from selling a put. The payoff profile for such a situation is illustrated in Panel C of Figure 23.10. In this illustration, we have assumed that the proceeds of a put option on sterling with an exercise price of $1.56 would carry the same premium as a call option on sterling with an exercise price of $1.43.[30]

A payoff profile identical to this option payoff profile could also be generated, however, simply by changing the terms of a standard forward contract to the following:

♦ at maturity, the buyer of the forward contract agress to purchase sterling at a price of $1.50 per pound sterling;

♦ the buyer of the forward contract has the right to break the contract at a price of $1.43 per pound sterling; and

♦ the seller of the forward contract has the right to break the contract at a price of $1.56 per pound sterling.

Such a forward contract is referred to as a *range forward*.[31]

Swaps with Option-like Characteristics. Given that swaps can be viewed as packages of forward contracts, it should not be surprising that swaps can also be constructed to have option-like characteristics like those illustrated for forwards. For example, suppose that a firm with a floating-rate liability wanted to limit its outflows should interest rates rise substantially; at the same time, it was willing to give up some potential gains should there instead be a dramatic decline in short-term rates. To achieve this end, the firm could modify the interest rate swap contract as follows:

As long as the interest rate neither rises by more than 200 basis points nor falls more than 100 basis points, the firm

---

28 This discussion is adapted from Warren Edwardes and Edmond Levy, "Break Forwards: A Synthetic Option Hedging Instrument," *Midland Corporate Finance Journal* 5 (Summer 1987) 59–67.

29 According to Sam Srinivasulu in "Second-Generation Forwards: A Comparative Analysis," Business International Money Report, September 21, 1987, break forward is the name given to this construction by Midland Bank. It goes under other names: Boston Option (Bank of Boston), FOX – Forward with Optional Exit (Hambros Bank), and Cancelable Forward (Goldman Sachs).

---

30 These numbers are only for purposes of illustration. To determine the exercise prices at which the values of the puts and calls are equal, one would have to use an option pricing model.

31 As Srinivasulu, cited note 29, pointed out, this construction also appears under a number of names: range forward (Salomon Brothers), collar (Midland Montagu), flexible forward (Manufacturers Hanover), cylinder option (Citicorp), option fence (Bank of America) and mini-max (Goldman Sachs).

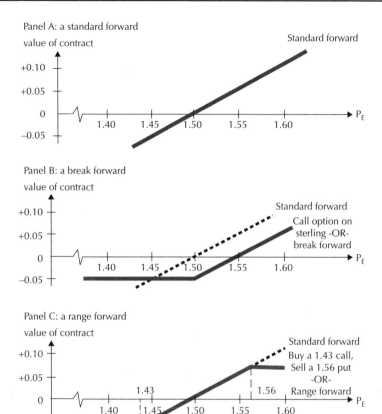

Panel A: a standard forward

value of contract

Standard forward

Panel B: a break forward

value of contract

Standard forward

Call option on sterling -OR- break forward

Panel C: a range forward

value of contract

Standard forward

Buy a 1.43 call, Sell a 1.56 put -OR- Range forward

Figure 23.10

pays a floating rate and receives a fixed rate. But, if the interest is more than 200 basis points above or 100 basis points below the current rate, the firm receives and pays a fixed rate.

The resulting payoff profile for this floating floor-ceiling swap is illustrated in Panel A of Figure 23.11.

Conversely, the interest rate swap contract could have been modified as follows:

As long as the interest rate is within 200 basis points of the current rate, the firm neither makes nor receives a payment; but if the interest rate rises or falls by more than 200 basis points, the firm pays a floating rate and receives a fixed rate.

The payoff profile for the resulting fixed floor-ceiling swap is illustrated in Panel B of Figure 23.11.

Redesigned Options. To "redesign" an option, what is normally done is to put two or more options together to change the payoff profile. Examples abound in the world of the option trader. Some of the more colorfully-named combinations are *straddles*, *strangles*, and *butterflies*.[32]

To see how and why these kinds of creations evolve, let's look at a hypothetical situation. Suppose a firm was confronted with the inherent exposure illustrated in Panel A of Figure 23.12. Suppose further that the firm wanted to establish a floor on losses caused by changes in a financial price.

As you already know, this could be done by purchasing an out-of-the-money call option on the financial price. A potential problem with this

---

32 For a discussion of traditional option strategies like straddles, strangles, and butterflies, see for instance chapter 7 of Richard M. Bookstaber, *Option Pricing and Strategies in Investing* (Addison-Wesley, 1981).

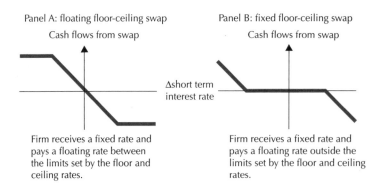

Panel A: floating floor-ceiling swap

Cash flows from swap

Panel B: fixed floor-ceiling swap

Cash flows from swap

Δshort term interest rate

Firm receives a fixed rate and pays a floating rate between the limits set by the floor and ceiling rates.

Firm receives a fixed rate and pays a floating rate outside the limits set by the floor and ceiling rates.

Figure 23.11   Pay-off Profile for Floor-ceiling Swaps

solution, as we have seen, is the premium the firm has to pay. Is there a way the premium can be eliminated?

We have already seen that buying an out-of-the-money call can be financed by selling an out-of-the-money put. However, suppose that this out-of-the-money call is financed by selling a put with precisely the same exercise price – in which case, the put would be in-the-money. As illustrated in Panel B of Figure 23.12, the proceeds from selling the in-the-money put would exceed the cost of the out-of-the-money call. Therefore, to finance one out-of-the-money call, one would need sell only a fraction of one in-the-money put.

In Panel B, we have assumed that the put value is twice the call value; so, to finance one call, you need sell only $\frac{1}{2}$ put. Panel C simply combines the payoff profiles for selling $\frac{1}{2}$ put and buying one call with an exercise price of X. Finally, Panel D of Figure 23.12 combines the option combination in Panel C with the inherent risk profile in Panel A.

Note what has happened. The firm has obtained the floor it wanted, but there is no up-front premium. At the price at which the option is exercised, the value of the firm with the floor is the same as it would have been without the floor. The floor is paid for not with a fixed premium, but with a share of the firm's gains above the floor. If the financial price rises by X, the value of the firm falls to the floor and no premium is paid. If, however, the financial price rises by less, say Y, the value of the firm is higher and the firm pays a positive premium for the floor. And, if the financial price falls, say, by Z, the price it pays for the floor rises.

What we have here is a situation where the provider of the floor is paid with a share of potential gains, thereby leading to the name of this option combination – a *participation*. This construction has been most widely used in the foreign exchange market where they are referred to as *participating forwards*.[33]

Options on other financial instruments

Options on futures contracts on bonds have been actively traded on the Chicago Board of Trade since 1982. The valuation of an option on a futures is a relatively straightforward extension of the traditional option pricing models.[34] Despite the close relation between futures and forwards and futures and swaps, the options on forwards (*options on forward rate agreements*) and options on swaps (*swaptions*) are much more recent.

More complicated analytically is the valuation of an option on an option, also known as a *compound option*.[35] Despite their complexity and

33   For more on this construction, see Srinivalsulu cited in note 29 and 31.

34   Options on futures were originally discussed by Fischer Black in "The Pricing of Commodity Options," *Journal of Financial Economics* 3 (January–March 1976). A concise discussion of the modifications required in the Black-Scholes formula is contained in James F. Meisner and John W. Labuszewski, "Modifying the Black-Scholes Option Pricing Model for Alternative Underlying Instruments," *Financial Analysts Journal* November/December 1984.

35   For a discussion of the problem of valuing compound options, see John C. Cox and Mark Rubinstein, *Options Markets* (Prentice-Hall, 1985) 412–415.

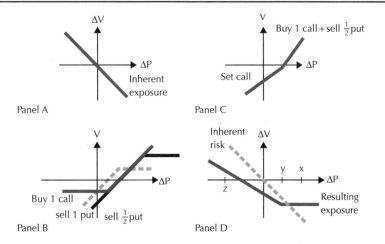

Figure 23.12

resistance to valuation formulae, some options on options have begun to be traded. These include options on foreign exchange options and, most notably, options on interest rate options (caps), referred to in the trade as *captions*.

Using the building blocks to design "new" products

It's rare that a day goes by in the financial markets without hearing of at least one "new" or "hybrid" product. But, as you should have come to expect from us by now, our position with respect to "financial engineering" is that there is little new under the sun. The "new" products typically involve nothing more than putting the building blocks together in a new way.

Reverse Floaters. One example of a hybrid security is provided in Figure 23.13. If we combine the issuance of a conventional fixed rate loan and an interest rate swap where the issuing party pays fixed and receives floating, the result is a reverse floating-rate loan. The net coupon payments on the hybrid loan are equal to twice the fixed rate ($\bar{r}$) minus the floating rate ($\tilde{r}$) times the principal (P), or

$$\text{Net Coupon} = (2\bar{r}-\tilde{r})\text{P} = 2\bar{\text{R}}-\tilde{\text{R}}$$

If the floating rate ($\tilde{r}$) rises, the net coupon payment falls.

Bonds with Embedded Options. Another form of hybrid securities has evolved from bonds with warrants. Bonds with warrants on the issuer's shares have become common. Bond issues have also recently appeared that feature warrants that can be exercised into foreign exchange and gold.

And, in 1986, Standard Oil issued a bond with an oil warrant. These notes stipulated that the principal payment at maturity would be a function of oil prices at maturity. As specified in the Prospectus, the holders of the 1990 notes will receive, in addition to a guaranteed minimum principal amount, "the excess . . . of the Crude Oil Price . . . over $25 multiplied by 170 barrels of Light Sweet Crude Oil." What this means is that the note has an embedded four-year option on 170 barrels of crude oil. If, at maturity, the value of Light Sweet Oklahoma Crude Oil exceeds $25, the holder of the note will receive (Oil Price – $25) × 170 plus the guaranteed minimum principal amount. If the value of Light Sweet Oklahoma Crude is less than $25 at maturity, the option expires worthless.[36]

The building block process has also been extended to changes in the timing of the options embedded in the bond. For a traditional bond with an attached warrant, there is only one option exerciseable at one point in time. More recent bonds have involved packages of options which can be exercised at different points in time.

36 Note that this issue did have a cap on the crude oil price at $40. Hence, the bondholder actually holds two options positions: long a call option at $25 per barrel and short a call option at $40 per barrel.

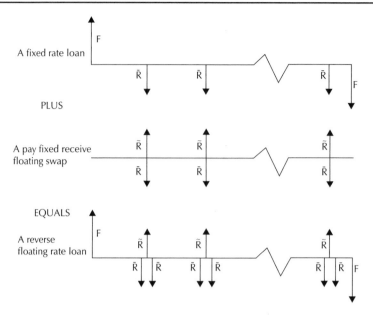

Figure 23.13   Using a Swap to Create a Reverse Floating Rate Loan

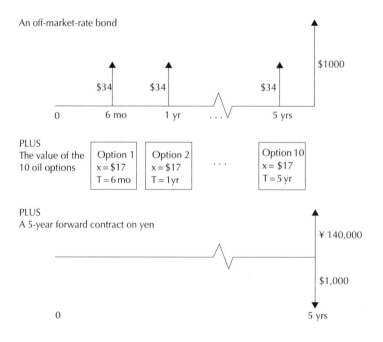

Figure 23.14

The first time we saw this extension was in Forest Oil Corporation's proposed *Natural Gas Interest Indexed Debentures*. As set forth in the issue's red herring prospectus of July 1988, Forest Oil proposed to pay a stipulated base rate plus four basis points for each $0.01 by which the average gas spot price exceeds $1.76 per MMBTU (million British Thermal Units). In effect, then, this proposed 12-year "hybrid" debenture is a package consisting of one standard bond plus 24 options on the price of natural gas with maturities ranging from 6 months to 12 years.[37]

And, if we want to get a little fancier, we can consider the possibility of an *Oil Interest-Indexed, Dual-Currency Bond*.[38] Assume that the maturity of this issue is 5 years, with the semi-annual coupon payments indexed to the price of crude oil and the final principal repayment indexed to the value of yen. More specifically, assume that, for each $1000 of principal, the bondholder receives the following: (1) the greater of $34 or the value of two barrels of Sweet Light Crude Oil at each coupon date; and (2) 140,000 yen at maturity.

How would we value such a complicated package? The answer, again, is by breaking it down into the building blocks. As shown in Figure 23.14, this oil-indexed, dual currency bond consists of three basic components: (1) a straight bond paying $34 semi-annually; (2) 10 call options on the price of oil with an exercise price of $17 per barrel ($34/2) maturing sequentially every six months over a five-year period; and (3) a five-year forward contract on yen with an exercise price of 140 yen/dollar. As it turns out, then, this complicated-looking bond is nothing more than a combination of a standard bond, a series of options, and a forward contract.

CONCLUDING REMARKS

The world is more volatile today than it was two decades ago. Today's corporate risk manager must deal with the potential impact on the firm of significant month-to-month (and sometimes day-to-day) changes in exchange rates, interest rates, and commodity prices. Volatility alone could put a well-run firm out of business, so financial price risk deserves

careful attention. As this summary has demonstrated, there now exist techniques and tools for accomplishing this task.

This article makes three major points:

First, there are simple techniques that allow management (and outsiders as well) to identify and measure a firm's exposures. Besides managing "one-off" exposures (such as interest rate exposures from floating-rate borrowings or foreign exchange transaction and translation exposures), many firms are now recognizing their economic exposures. To measure such economic exposures, we have introduced the concept of the *risk profile*. Using this concept, we have proposed simple methods for quantifying the extent of an individual firm's exposures to interest rates, foreign exchange rates, and commodity prices. In the case of a financial firm's exposure to interest rate risk, the techniques of "gap" and "duration" analysis can be applied directly. For the more general case, we demonstrate how simple regression analysis (the same technique used in calculating a firm's "beta") can be used to measure a variety of exposures.

Second, the tools for managing financial risk are more simple than they appear. These financial instruments can be viewed as building blocks. The basic component is a forward contract. Both futures and swaps are like bundles of forward contracts; forwards, in fact, can be combined to yield futures and swaps. The primary differences between these two instruments are the way they deal with default risk and the degree of customization available.

Even options, moreover, can be related to forward contracts. An option on a given asset can be created by combining a position in a forward contract on the same asset with a riskless security; in short, forwards and T-bills can be combined to produce options.[39] Finally, options can be combined to create forward positions; for example, buying a call and shorting a put produces the same positions as buying a forward contract.

Third, once you understand the four basic building blocks, it is a straightforward step to designing a customized strategy for managing your

---

37 As reported in the Wall Street Journal on September 21, 1988, Forest Oil withdrew its Natural Gas Indexed Bond in favor of a straight issue. However, in November of 1988, Magma Copper did issue senior subordinated notes on which the coupon payments were linked to the price of copper in much the same way as Forest's coupons would been linked to the price of natural gas.

38 Unlike the other structures discussed, this one has not yet been issued.

---

39 This is most often referred to as a synthetic option or as dynamic option replication.

firm's exposure. Once the exposure is identified, it can be managed in a number of ways:

- by using one of the financial instruments – for example, by using an interest rate swap to hedge a building products firm's exposure to rising interest rates;
- by using combinations of the financial instruments – for example, buying a call and selling a put to minimize the out-of-pocket costs of the hedge; or

- by combining financial instruments with a debt instrument to create a hybrid security – for example, issuing an oil-indexed bond to hedge a firm's exposure to oil prices.

Our final point in all of this is very simple. Managing financial price risk with "financial engineering" sounds like something you need a degree from Caltech or M.I.T. to do. Designing effective solutions with the financial building blocks is easy.

CHAPTER 24

Rethinking Risk Management

René M. Stulz (The Ohio State University)*

This article explores an apparent conflict between the theory and current practice of corporate risk management. Academic theory suggests that some companies facing large exposures to interest rates, exchange rates, or commodity prices can increase their market values by using derivative securities to reduce their exposures. The primary emphasis of the theory is on the role of derivatives in reducing the variability of corporate cash flows and, in so doing, reducing various costs associated with financial distress.

The actual corporate use of derivatives, however, does not seem to correspond closely to the theory. For one thing, large companies make far greater use of derivatives than small firms, even though small firms have more volatile cash flows, more restricted access to capital, and thus presumably more reason to buy protection against financial trouble. Perhaps more puzzling, however, is that many companies appear to be using risk management to pursue goals other than reducing variance.

Does this mean that the prevailing academic theory of risk management is wrong, and that "variance-minimization" is not a useful goal for

companies using derivatives? Or, is the current corporate practice of risk management misguided and in urgent need of reform? In this paper, I answer "no" to both questions while at the same time suggesting there may be room for improvement in the theory as well as the practice of risk management.

The paper begins by reviewing some evidence that has accumulated about the current practice of corporate risk management. Part of this evidence takes the form of recent "anecdotes," or cases, involving large derivatives losses. Most of the evidence, however, consists of corporate responses to surveys. What the stories suggest, and the surveys seem to confirm, is the popularity of a practice known as "selective" as opposed to "full-cover" hedging. That is, while few companies regularly use derivatives to take a "naked" speculative position on FX rates or commodity prices, most corporate derivatives users appear to allow their views of future interest rates, exchange rates, and commodity prices to influence their hedge ratios.

Such a practice seems inconsistent with modern risk management theory, or at least the theory that has been presented thus far. But there is a plausible defense of selective hedging – one that would justify the practice without violating the efficient markets tenet at the center of modern financial theory. In this paper, I attempt to explain more of the corporate behavior we observe by pushing the theory of risk

* I am grateful for extensive editorial assistance from Don Chew, and for comments by Steve Figlewski, Andrew Karolyi, Robert Whaley, and participants at a seminar at McKinsey, at the Annual Meeting of the International Association of Financial Engineers, and at the French Finance Association.

management beyond the variance-minimization model that prevails in most academic circles. Some companies, I argue below, may have a comparative advantage in bearing certain financial risks (while other companies mistakenly think and act as if they do). I accordingly propose a somewhat different goal for corporate risk management – namely, the *elimination of costly lower-tail outcomes* – that is designed to reduce the expected costs of financial trouble while preserving a company's ability to exploit any comparative advantage in risk-bearing it may have. (In the jargon of finance specialists, the fundamental aim of corporate risk management can be viewed as the purchase of "well-out-of-the-money put options" that eliminate the downside while preserving as much of the upside as can be justified by the principle of comparative advantage.)

Such a modified theory of risk management implies that some companies should hedge all financial risks, other firms should worry about only certain kinds of risks, and still others should not worry about risks at all. But, as I also argue below, when making decisions whether or not to hedge, management should keep in mind that risk management can be used to change both a company's capital structure and its ownership structure. By reducing the probability of financial trouble, risk management has the potential both to increase debt capacity and to facilitate larger equity stakes for management.

This paper also argues that common measures of risk such as variance and Value at Risk (VAR) are not useful for most risk management applications by non-financial companies, nor are they consistent with the objective of risk management presented here. In place of both VAR and the variance of cash flows, I suggest a method for measuring corporate exposures that, besides having a foundation in modern finance theory, should be relatively easy to use.

I conclude with a discussion of the internal "management" of risk management. If corporate risk management is focused not on minimizing variance, but rather on eliminating downside risk while extending the corporate quest for comparative advantage into financial markets, then much more attention must be devoted to the evaluation and control of corporate risk-management activities. The closing section of the paper offers some suggestions for evaluating the performance of risk managers whose "view-taking" is an accepted part of the firm's risk management strategy.

RISK MANAGEMENT IN PRACTICE

In one of their series of papers on Metallgesellschaft, Chris Culp and Merton Miller make an observation that may seem startling to students of modern finance: "We need hardly remind readers that most value-maximizing firms do not hedge."[1] But is this true? And, if so, how would we know?

Culp and Miller refer to survey evidence – in particular, to a Wharton-Chase study that sent questionnaires to 1,999 companies inquiring about their risk management practices.[2] Of the 530 firms that responded to the survey, only about a third answered "yes" when asked if they ever used futures, forwards, options, or swaps. One clear finding that emerges from this survey is that large companies make greater use of derivatives than smaller firms. Whereas 65% of companies with a market value greater than $250 million reported using derivatives, only 13% of the firms with market values of $50 million or less claimed to use them.

What are the derivatives used to accomplish? The only uses reported by more than half of the corporate users are to hedge contractual commitments and to hedge anticipated transactions expected to take place within 12 months. About two thirds of the companies responded that they never use derivatives to reduce funding costs (or earn "treasury profits") by arbitraging the markets or by taking a view. Roughly the same proportion of firms also said they never use derivatives to hedge their balance sheets, their foreign dividends, or their economic or competitive exposures.

1   Christopher Culp and Merton Miller, "Hedging in the Theory of Corporate Finance: A Reply to Our Critics," *Journal of Applied Corporate Finance* 8 (Spring 1995), p. 122. For the central idea of this paper, I am indebted to Culp and Miller's discussion of Holbrook Working's "carrying-charge" theory of commodity hedging. It is essentially Workings' notion – and Culp and Miller's elaboration of it – that I attempt in this paper to generalize into a broader theory of risk management based on comparative advantage in risk-bearing.
2   The Wharton School and The Chase Manhattan Bank, N.A., Survey of Derivative Usage Among U.S. Non-Financial Firms (February 1994).

The Wharton-Chase study was updated in 1995, and its results were published in 1996 as the Wharton-CIBC Wood Gundy study. The results of the 1995 survey confirm those of its predecessor, but with one striking new finding: Over a third of all derivative users said they sometimes "actively take positions" that reflect their market views of interest rate and exchange rates.

This finding was anticipated in a survey of Fortune 500 companies conducted by Walter Dolde in 1992, and published in this journal in the following year.[3] Of the 244 companies that responded to Dolde's survey, 85% reported having used swaps, forwards, futures, or options. As in the Wharton surveys, larger companies reported greater use of derivatives than smaller firms. And, as Dolde notes, such a finding confirms the experience of risk management practitioners that the corporate use of derivatives requires a considerable upfront investment in personnel, training, and computer hardware and software – an investment that could discourage small firms.

But, as we observed earlier, there are also reasons why the demand for risk management products should actually be greater for small firms than for large – notably the greater probability of default caused by unhedged exposures and the greater concentration of equity ownership in smaller companies. And Dolde's survey provides an interesting piece of evidence in support of this argument. When companies were asked to estimate what percentages of their exposures they chose to hedge, many respondents said that it depended on whether they had a view of future market movements. *Almost 90% of the derivatives users in Dolde's survey said they sometimes took a view.* And, when the companies employed such views in their hedging decisions, the smaller companies reported hedging significantly greater percentages of their FX and interest rate exposures than the larger companies.

Put another way, the larger companies were more inclined to "self-insure" their FX or interest rate risks. For example, if they expected FX rates to move in a way that would increase firm value,

they might hedge only 10% to 20% (or maybe none) of their currency exposure. But if they expected rates to move in a way that would reduce value, they might hedge 100% of the exposure.

Like the Wharton surveys, the Dolde survey also found that the focus of risk management was mostly on transaction exposures and near-term exposures. Nevertheless, Dolde also reported "a distinct evolutionary pattern" in which many firms "progress from targeting individual transactions to more systematic measures of ongoing competitive exposures."[4]

The bottom line from the surveys, then, is that corporations do not systematically hedge their exposures, the extent to which they hedge depends on their views of future price movements, the focus of hedging is primarily on near-term transactions, and the use of derivatives is greater for large firms than small firms. Many of the widely-reported derivative problems of recent years are fully consistent with this survey evidence, and closer inspection of such cases provides additional insight into common risk management practices. We briefly recount two cases in which companies lost large amounts of money as a result of risk management programs.

Metallgesellschaft

Although the case of Metallgesellschaft continues to be surrounded by controversy, there is general agreement about the facts of the case. By the end of 1993, MGRM, the U.S. oil marketing subsidiary of Metallgesellschaft, contracted to sell 154 million barrels of oil through fixed-price contracts ranging over a period of ten years. These fixed-price contracts created a huge exposure to oil price increases that MGRM decided to hedge. However, it did not do so in a straightforward way. Rather than hedging its future outflows with offsetting positions of matching maturities, MGRM chose to take "stacked" positions in short-term contracts, both futures and swaps, and then roll the entire "stack" forward as the contracts expired.

MGRM's choice of short-term contracts can be explained in part by the lack of longer-term hedging

---

3 Walter Dolde, "The Trajectory of Corporate Financial Risk Management, *Journal of Applied Corporate Finance* 6 (Fall 1993), 33–41.

4 Dolde, p. 39.

vehicles. For example, liquid markets for oil futures do not go out much beyond 12 months. But it also appears that MGRM took a far larger position in oil futures than would have been consistent with a variance-minimizing strategy. For example, one study estimated that the minimum-variance hedge position for MGRM would have required the forward purchase of only 86 million barrels of oil, or about 55% of the 154 million barrels in short-maturity contracts that MGRM actually entered into.[5]

Does this mean that MGRM really took a position that was long some 58 million barrels of oil? Not necessarily. As Culp and Miller demonstrate, had MGRM adhered to its professed strategy and been able to obtain funding for whatever futures losses it incurred over the entire 10-year period, its position would have been largely hedged.[6]

But even if MGRM's net exposure to oil prices was effectively hedged over the long haul, it is also clear that MGRM's traders had not designed their hedge with the aim of minimizing the variance of their net position in oil during the life of the contracts. The traders presumably took the position they did because they thought they could benefit from their specialized information about supply and demand – and, more specifically, from a persistent feature of oil futures known as "back-wardation," or the long-run tendency of spot prices to be higher than futures prices. So, although MGRM was effectively hedged against changes in spot oil prices, it nevertheless had what amounted to a long position in "the basis." Most of this long position in the basis represented a bet that the convenience yields on crude oil – that is, the premiums of near-term futures over long-dated futures – would remain positive as they had over most of the past decade.

When spot prices fell dramatically in 1993, MGRM lost on its futures positions and gained on its cash positions – that is, on the present value of its delivery contracts. But because the futures positions were marked to market while the delivery contracts were not, MGRM's financial statements showed large losses. Compounding this problem of large "paper losses," the backwardation of oil prices also disappeared, thus adding real losses to the paper ones. And, in response to the reports of mounting losses, MG's management chose to liquidate the hedge. This action, as Culp and Miller point out, had the unfortunate consequence of "turning paper losses into realized losses" and "leaving MGRM exposed to rising prices on its remaining fixed-price contracts."[7]

Daimler-Benz

In 1995, Daimler-Benz reported first-half losses of DM1.56 billion, the largest in the company's 109-year history. In its public statements, management attributed the losses to exchange rate losses due to the weakening dollar. One subsidiary of Daimler-Benz, Daimler-Benz Aerospace, had an order book of DM20 billion, of which 80% was fixed in dollars. Because the dollar fell by 14% during this period, Daimler-Benz had to take a provision for losses of DM1.2 billion to cover future losses.

Why did Daimler-Benz fail to hedge its expected dollar receivables? The company said that it chose not to hedge because the forecasts it received were too disperse, ranging as they did from DM1.2 to DM1.7 per dollar. Analysts, however, attributed Daimler-Benz's decision to remain unhedged to its view that the dollar would stay above DM1.55.[8]

These two brief case studies reinforce the conclusion drawn from the survey evidence. In both of these cases, management's view of future price movements was an important determinant of how (or whether) risk was managed. Risk management did not mean minimizing risk by putting on a minimum-variance hedge. Rather, it meant choosing to bear certain risks based on a number of different considerations, including the belief that a particular position would allow the firm to earn abnormal returns.

5   Mello, A., and J.E. Parsons, "Maturity Structure of a Hedge Matters: Lessons from the Metallgesellschaft Debacle," *Journal of Applied Corporate Finance*, Vol. 8 No. 1 (Spring 1995), 106–120.
6   More precisely, Culp and Miller's analysis shows that, ignoring any complications arising from basis risk and the daily mark-to-market requirement for futures, over the 10-year period each rolled-over futures contract would have eventually corresponded to an equivalent quantity of oil delivered to customers.

7   Culp and Miller, Vol. 7 No. 4 (Winter 1995), p. 63.
8   See *Risk Magazine*, October 1995, p. 11.

Is such a practice consistent with the modern theory of risk management? To answer that question, we first need to review the theory.

THE PERSPECTIVE OF MODERN FINANCE

The two pillars of modern finance theory are the concepts of efficient markets and diversification. Stated as briefly as possible, market efficiency means that markets don't leave money on the table. Information that is freely accessible is incorporated in prices with sufficient speed and accuracy that one cannot profit by trading on it.

Despite the spread of the doctrine of efficient markets, the world remains full of corporate executives who are convinced of their own ability to predict future interest rates, exchange rates, and commodity prices. As evidence of the strength and breadth of this conviction, many companies during the late '80s and early '90s set up their corporate treasuries as "profit centers" in their own right – a practice that, if the survey evidence can be trusted, has been largely abandoned in recent years by most industrial firms. And the practice has been abandoned with good reason: Behind most large derivative losses – in cases ranging from Orange County and Baring Brothers to Procter & Gamble and BancOne – there appear to have been more or less conscious decisions to bear significant exposures to market risks with the hope of earning abnormal returns.

The lesson of market efficiency for corporate risk managers is that the attempt to earn higher returns in most financial markets generally means bearing large (and unfamiliar) risks. In highly liquid markets such as those for interest rate and FX futures – and in the case of heavily traded commodities like oil and gold as well – industrial companies are unlikely to have a comparative advantage in bearing these risks. And so, for most industrial corporations, setting up the corporate treasury to trade derivatives for profit is a value-destroying proposition. (As I will also argue later, however, market efficiency does not rule out the possibility that management's information may be better than the market's in special cases.)

But if the concept of market efficiency should discourage corporations from *creating* corporate exposures to financial market risks, the companion concept of diversification should also discourage some companies from *hedging* financial exposures incurred through their normal business operations. To explain why, however, requires a brief digression on the corporate cost of capital.

Finance theory says that the stock market, in setting the values of companies, effectively assigns minimum required rates of return on capital that vary directly with the companies' levels of risk. In general, the greater a company's risk, the higher the rate of return it must earn to produce superior returns for its shareholders. But a company's required rate of return, also known as its cost of capital, is said to depend only on its non-diversifiable (or "systematic") risk, not on its total risk. In slightly different words, a company's cost of capital depends on the strength of the firm's tendency to move with the broad market (in statistical terms, its "covariance") rather than its overall volatility (or "variance").

In general, most of a company's interest rate, currency, and commodity price exposures will not increase the risk of a well-diversified portfolio. Thus, most corporate financial exposures represent "non-systematic" or "diversifiable" risks that shareholders can eliminate by holding diversified portfolios. And because shareholders have such an inexpensive risk-management tool at their disposal, companies that reduce their earnings volatility by managing their financial risks will not be rewarded by investors with lower required rates of return (or, alternatively, with higher P/E ratios for given levels of cash flow or earnings). As one example, investors with portfolios that include stocks of oil companies are not likely to place higher multiples on the earnings of petrochemical firms just because the latter smooth their earnings by hedging against oil price increases.

For this reason, having the corporation devote resources to reducing FX or commodity price risks makes sense only if the cash flow variability arising from such risks has the potential to impose "real" costs on the corporation. The academic finance literature has identified three major costs associated with higher variability: (1) higher expected bankruptcy costs (and, more generally, costs of financial distress); (2) higher expected payments to corporate "stakeholders" (including higher rates of return required by owners of closely-held firms); and (3) higher expected tax payments. The potential gains from risk management come from its

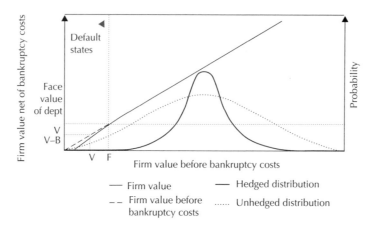

Figure 24.1 Debt, Equity, and Firm Value with Bankruptcy Costs

ability to reduce each of these three costs – and I review each in turn below.[9]

Risk management can reduce bankruptcy costs

Although well-diversified shareholders may not be concerned about the cash flow variability caused by swings in FX rates or commodity prices, they will become concerned if such variability materially raises the probability of financial distress. In the extreme case, a company with significant amounts of debt could experience a sharp downturn in operating cash flow – caused in part by an unhedged exposure – and be forced to file for bankruptcy.

What are the costs of bankruptcy? Most obvious are the payments to lawyers and court costs. But, in addition to these "direct" costs of administration and reorganization, there are some potentially larger "indirect" costs. Companies that wind up in Chapter 11 face considerable interference from the bankruptcy court with their investment and operating decisions. And such interference has the potential to cause significant reductions in the ongoing operating value of the firm.

If a company's shareholders view bankruptcy as a real possibility – and to the extent the process of reorganization itself is expected to reduce the firm's operating value – the expected present value of these costs will be reflected in a company's *current* market value. A risk management program that costlessly eliminates the risk of bankruptcy effectively reduces these costs to zero and, in so doing, increases the value of the firm.

The effects of risk management on bankruptcy costs and firm value are illustrated in Figure 24.1. In the case shown in the figure, hedging is assumed to reduce the variability of cash flow and firm value to the degree that default is no longer possible. By eliminating the possibility of bankruptcy, risk management increases the value of the firm's equity by an amount roughly equal to Bc (bankruptcy costs) multiplied by the probability of bankruptcy if the firm remains unhedged (pBU). For example, let's assume the market value of the firm's equity is $100 million, bankruptcy costs are expected to run $25 million (or 25% of current firm value), and the probability of bankruptcy in the absence of hedging is 10%. In this case, risk management can be seen as increasing the current value of the firm's equity by $2.5 million (10% × $25 million), or 2.5%. (Keep in mind that this is the contribution of risk management to firm value *when the company is healthy;* in the event that cash flow and value should decline sharply from current levels, the value added by risk management increases in absolute dollars, and even more on a percentage-of-value basis.)

---

9 For a discussion of the benefits of corporate hedging, see Clifford Smith and René Stulz, "The Determinants of Firms' Hedging Policies," *Journal of Financial and Quantitative Analysis* 20 (1985), pp. 391–405.

This argument extends to distress costs in general. For instance, as a company becomes weaker financially, it becomes more difficult for it to raise funds. At some point, the cost of outside funding – if available at all – may become so great that management chooses to pass up profitable investments. This "underinvestment problem" experienced by companies when facing the prospect of default (or, in some cases, just a downturn in earnings[10]) represents an important cost of financial distress. And, to the extent that risk management succeeds in reducing the perceived *probability* of financial distress and the costs associated with underinvestment, it will increase the current market value of the firm.

Risk management can reduce payments to "stakeholders" (and required returns to owners of closely held firms)[11]

Although the shareholders of large public companies can often manage most financial risks more efficiently than the companies themselves, the case may be different for the owners – or owner-managers – of private or closely-held companies. Because such owners tend to have a large proportion of their wealth tied up in the firm, their required rates of return are likely to reflect all important sources of risk, those that can be "diversified away" by outside investors as well as those that cannot. In such circumstances, hedging financial exposures can be thought of as adding value by reducing the owners' risks and hence their required rates of return on investment.

And it's not just the owners of closely held companies that value the protection from risk management. In public companies with dispersed ownership, non-investor groups such as managers, employees, customers, and suppliers with a large stake in the success of the firm typically cannot diversify away large financial exposures. If there is a chance that their "firm-specific" investments

could be lost because of financial distress, they are likely to require added compensation for the greater risk. Employees will demand higher wages (or reduce their loyalty or perhaps their work effort) at a company where the probability of layoff is greater. Managers with alternative opportunities will demand higher salaries (or maybe an equity stake in the company) to run firms where the risks of insolvency and financial embarrassment are significant. Suppliers will be more reluctant to enter into long-term contracts, and trade creditors will charge more and be less flexible, with companies whose prospects are more uncertain. And customers concerned about the company's ability to fulfil warranty obligations or service their products in the future may be reluctant to buy those products.

To the extent risk management can protect the investments of each of these corporate stakeholders, the company can improve the terms on which it contracts with them and so increase firm value. And, as I discuss later in more detail, hedging can also facilitate larger equity stakes for managers of public companies by limiting "uncontrollables" and thus the "scope" of their bets.

Risk management can reduce taxes

The potential tax benefits of risk management derive from the interaction of risk management's ability to reduce the volatility of reported income and the progressivity (or, more precisely, the "convexity") of most of the world's tax codes. In the U.S., as in most countries, a company's effective tax rate rises along with increases in pre-tax income. Increasing marginal tax rates, limits on the use of tax-loss carry forwards, and the alternative minimum tax all work together to impose higher effective rates of taxation on higher levels of reported income and to provide lower percentage tax rebates for ever larger losses.

Because of the convexity of the tax code, there are benefits to "managing" taxable income so that as much of it as possible falls within an optimal range – that is, neither too high nor too low. By reducing fluctuations in taxable income, risk management can lead to lower tax payments by ensuring that, over a complete business cycle, the

---

10   This argument is made by Kenneth Froot, David Scharfstein, and Jeremy Stein in "Risk Management: Coordinating Corporate Investment and Financing Policies," *Journal of Finance* 48, (1993), 1629–1658.

11   The discussion in this section and the next draws heavily on Smith and Stulz (1985), cited in footnote 9.

largest possible proportion of corporate income falls within this optimal range of tax rates.

RISK MANAGEMENT AND COMPARATIVE ADVANTAGE IN RISK-TAKING

Up to this point, we have seen that companies should not expect to make money consistently by taking financial positions based on information that is publicly available. But what about information that is not publicly available? After all, many companies in the course of their normal operating activities acquire specialized information about certain financial markets. Could not such information give them a comparative advantage over their shareholders in taking some types of risks?

Let's look at a hypothetical example. Consider company X that produces consumer durables using large amounts of copper as a major input. In the process of ensuring that it has the appropriate amount of copper on hand, it gathers useful information about the copper market. It knows its own demand for copper, of course, but it also learns a lot about the supply. In such a case, the firm will almost certainly allow that specialized information to play some role in its risk management strategy.

For example, let's assume that company X's management has determined that, when it has no view about future copper prices, it will hedge 50% of the next year's expected copper purchases to protect itself against the possibility of financial distress. But, now let's say that the firm's purchasing agents persuade top management that the price of copper is far more likely to rise than fall in the coming year. In this case, the firm's risk manager might choose to take a long position in copper futures that would hedge as much as 100% of its anticipated purchases for the year instead of the customary 50%. Conversely, if management becomes convinced that copper prices are likely to drop sharply (with almost no possibility of a major increase), it might choose to hedge as little as 20% of its exposure.[12]

Should the management of company X refrain from exploiting its specialized knowledge in this fashion, and instead adhere to its 50% hedging target? Or should it, in certain circumstances, allow its market view to influence its hedge ratio?

Although there are clearly risks to selective hedging of this kind – in particular, the risk that the firm's information may not in fact be better than the market's – it seems quite plausible that companies could have such informational advantages. Companies that repurchase their own shares based on the belief that their current value fails to reflect the firm's prospects seem to be vindicated more often than not. And though it's true that management may be able to predict the firm's future earnings with more confidence than the price of one of its major inputs, the information companies acquire about certain financial markets may still prove a reasonably reliable source of gain in risk management decisions.

The importance of understanding comparative advantage

What this example fails to suggest, however, is that the same operating activity in one company may not necessarily provide a comparative advantage in risk-bearing for another firm. As suggested above, the major risk associated with "selective" hedging is that the firm's information may not in fact be better than the market's. For this reason, it is important for management to understand the source of its comparative advantages.

To illustrate this point, take the case of a foreign currency trading operation in a large commercial bank. A foreign currency trading room can make a lot of money from taking positions provided, of course, exchange rates move in the anticipated direction. But, in an efficient market, as we have seen, banks can reliably make money from position-taking of this sort only if they have access to information before most other firms. In the case of FX, this is likely to happen only if the bank's

---

12 For a good example of this kind of selective hedging policy, see the comments by John Van Roden, Chief Financial Officer of Lukens, Inc. in the "Bank of America Roundtable on Corporate Risk Management," *Journal of Applied Corporate Finance*, Vol. 8 No. 3 (Fall 1995). As a stainless steel producer, one of the company's principal inputs is nickel; and Lukens' policy is to allow its view of nickel prices to influence how much of its nickel exposure it hedges. By contrast, although it may have views of interest rates or FX exposures, such views play no role in hedging those exposures.

trading operation is very large – large enough so that its deal flow is likely to reflect general shifts in demand for foreign currencies.

Most FX dealers, however, have no comparative advantage in gathering information about changes in the value of foreign currencies. For such firms, management of currency risk means ensuring that their exposures are short-lived. The most reliable way to minimize exposures for most currency traders is to enlarge their customer base. With a sufficient number of large, highly active customers, a trading operation has the following advantage: If one of its traders agrees to buy yen from one customer, the firm can resell them quickly to another customer and pocket the bid-ask spread.

In an article entitled "An Analysis of Trading Profits: How Trading Rooms Really Make Money," Alberic Braas and Charles Bralver present evidence suggesting that most FX trading profits come from market-making, not position-taking.[13] Moreover, as the authors of this article point out, a trading operation that does not understand its comparative advantage in trading currencies is likely not only to fail to generate consistent profit, but to endanger its existing comparative advantage. If the source of the profits of the trading room is really the customer base of the bank, and not the predictive power of its traders, then the bank must invest in maintaining and building its customer base. A trading room that mistakenly believes that the source of its profits is position-taking will take large positions that, on average, will neither make money nor lose money. More troubling, though, is that the resulting variability of its trading income is likely to unsettle its customers and weaken its customer base. Making matters worse, it may choose a compensation system for its traders that rewards profitable position-taking instead of valuable coordination of trading and sales activities. A top management that fails to understand its comparative advantage may waste its time looking for star traders while neglecting the development of marketing strategies and services.

How can management determine when it should take risks and when it should not? The best approach is to implement a *risk-taking audit*. This would involve a comprehensive review of the risks to which the company is exposed, both through its financial instruments and liability structure as well as its normal operations. Such an audit should attempt to answer questions like the following: Which of its major risks has the firm proved capable of "self-insuring" over a complete business cycle? If the firm chooses to hedge "selectively," or leaves exposures completely unhedged, what is the source of the firm's comparative advantage in taking these positions? Which risk management activities have consistently added value without introducing another source of volatility?

Once a firm has decided that it has a comparative advantage in taking certain financial risks, it must then determine the role of risk management in exploiting this advantage. As I argue below, risk management may paradoxically enable the firm to take *more* of these risks than it would in the absence of risk management. To illustrate this point, let's return to our example of company X and assume it has valuable information about the copper market that enables it to earn consistently superior profits trading copper. Even in this situation, such trading profits are by no means a sure thing; there is always the possibility that the firm will experience significant losses. Purchasing far-out-of-the-money calls on copper in such a case could actually serve to increase the firm's ability to take speculative positions in copper. But, as I argue in the next section, a company's ability to withstand large trading losses without endangering its operating activities depends not only on its risk management policy, but also on its capital structure and general financial health.

THE LINK BETWEEN RISK MANAGEMENT, RISK-TAKING, AND CAPITAL STRUCTURE

In discussing earlier the benefits of risk management, I suggested that companies should manage risk in a way that makes financial distress highly unlikely and, in so doing, preserves the financing flexibility necessary to carry out their investment strategies. Given this primary objective for risk management, one would not expect companies with little or no debt financing – and, hence, a low probability of financial trouble – to benefit from hedging.

---

13 See Alberic Braas and Charles Bralver, "How Trading Rooms Really Make Money?," *Journal of Applied Corporate Finance*, Vol. 2 No. 4 (Winter 1990).

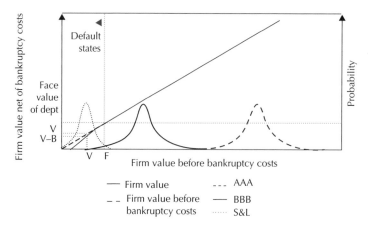

Figure 24.2 Optimal Hedging for Firms AAA, BBB, S&L

In this sense, risk management can be viewed as a direct substitute for equity capital. That is, the more the firm hedges its financial exposures, the less equity it requires to support its business. Or, to put it another way, the use of risk management to reduce exposures effectively increases a company's debt capacity.

Moreover, to the extent one views risk management as a substitute for equity capital – or, alternatively, as a technique that allows management to substitute debt for equity – then it pays companies to practice risk management only to the extent that equity capital is more expensive than debt. As this formulation of the issue suggests, a company's decisions to hedge financial risks – or to bear part of such risks through selective hedging – should be made jointly with the corporate capital structure decision.

To illustrate this interdependence between risk management and capital structure, consider the three kinds of companies pictured in Figure 24.2. At the right-hand side of the figure is company AAA, so named because it has little debt and a very high debt rating. The probability of default is essentially zero; and thus the left or lower tail of AAA's distribution of potential outcomes never reaches the range where low value begins to impose financial distress costs on the firm. Based on the theory of risk management just presented, there is no reason for this company to hedge its financial exposures; the company's shareholders can do the same job more cost-effectively. And, should investment opportunities arise, AAA will likely be able to raise funds on an economic basis, even if its cash flows should decline temporarily.

Should such a company take bets on financial markets? The answer could be yes, provided management has specialized information that would give it a comparative advantage in a certain market. In AAA's case, a bet that turns out badly will not affect the company's ability to carry out its strategic plan.

But now let's consider the company in the middle of the picture, call it BBB. Like the company shown in Figure 24.1 earlier, this firm has a lower credit rating, and there is a significant probability that the firm could face distress. What should BBB do? As shown earlier in Figure 24.1, this firm should probably eliminate the probability of encountering financial distress through risk management. In this case, even if management feels that there are occasional opportunities to profit from market inefficiencies, hedging exposures is likely to be the best policy. In company BBB's case, the cost of having a bet turn sour can be substantial, since this would almost certainly imply default. Consequently, one would not expect the management of such a firm to let its views affect the hedge ratio.

Finally, let's consider a firm that is in distress – and let's call it "S&L." What should it do? Reducing risk once the firm is in distress is not in the interest of shareholders. If the firm stays in distress and eventually defaults, shareholders will end up with near-worthless shares. In these circumstances, a management intent on maximizing shareholder value will not only accept bets that present themselves, but will *seek out* new ones. Such managers will take bets even if they believe markets are efficient because introducing new sources of volatility raises the probability of the "upper-tail" outcomes that are capable of rescuing the firm from financial distress.

Back to the Capital Structure Decision. As we saw in the case of company AAA, firms that have a lot of equity capital can make bets without worrying about whether doing so will bring about financial distress. One would therefore not expect these firms to hedge aggressively, particularly if risk management is costly and shareholders are better off without it.

The major issue that such companies must address, however, is whether they have too much capital – or, too much equity capital. In other words, although risk management may not be useful to them *given their current leverage ratios*, they might be better off using risk management and increasing leverage. Debt financing, of course, has a tax advantage over equity financing. But, in addition to its ability to reduce corporate taxes, increasing leverage also has the potential to strengthen management incentives to improve efficiency and add value. For one thing, the substitution of debt for equity leads managers to pay out excess capital – an action that could be a major source of value added in industries with overcapacity and few promising investment opportunities. Perhaps even more important, however, is that the substitution of debt for equity also allows for greater concentration of equity ownership, including a significant ownership stake for managers.

In sum, the question of what is the right corporate risk management decision for a company begs the question of not only its optimal capital structure, but optimal *ownership* structure as well. As suggested above, hedging could help some companies to increase shareholder value by enabling them to raise leverage – say, by buying back their shares – and increase management's percentage ownership. For other companies, however, leaving exposures unhedged or hedging "selectively" while maintaining more equity may turn out to be the value-maximizing strategy.

CORPORATE RISK-TAKING AND MANAGEMENT INCENTIVES

Management incentives may have a lot to do with why some firms take bets and others do not. As suggested, some companies that leave exposures unhedged or take bets on financial markets may have a comparative advantage in so doing; and, for those companies, such risk-taking may be a value-increasing strategy. Other companies, however, may choose to take financial risks without having a comparative advantage, particularly if such risk-taking somehow serves the interests of those managers who choose to expose their firms to the risks.

We have little convincing empirical evidence on the extent of risk-taking by companies, whether public or private. But there is one notable exception – a study by Peter Tufano of the hedging behavior of 48 publicly traded North American gold mining companies that was published in the September 1996 issue of the *Journal of Finance*.[14] The gold mining industry is ideal for studying hedging behavior in the sense that gold mining companies tend to be single-industry firms with one very large price exposure and a wide range of hedging vehicles, from forward sales, to exchange-traded gold futures and options, to gold swaps and bullion loans.

The purpose of Tufano's study was to examine the ability of various corporate risk management theories to explain any significant pattern of differences in the percentage of their gold price exposures that the companies choose to hedge. Somewhat surprisingly, there was considerable variation in the hedging behavior of these 48 firms. One company, Homestake Mining, chose not only to hedge none of its exposure, but to publicize its policy while condemning what it called "gold price management." At the other extreme were companies like American Barrick that hedged as much as 85% of their anticipated production over the next three years. And whereas about one in six of these firms chose to hedge none of its exposure and sold *all* of its output at spot prices, another one in six firms hedged 40% or more of its gold price exposure.

The bottom line of Tufano's study was that the only important systematic determinant of the 48 corporate hedging decisions was managerial ownership of shares and, more generally, the nature of the managerial compensation contract.

---

14 Peter Tufano, "Who Manages Risk? An Empirical Examination of the Risk Management Practices of the Gold Mining Industry, *Journal of Finance* (September, 1996).

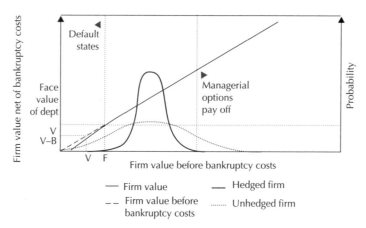

Figure 24.3 Impact of Options in Managerial Compensation Contracts

In general, the greater management's direct percentage share ownership, the larger the percentage of its gold price exposure a firm hedged. By contrast, little hedging took place in gold mining firms where management owns a small stake. Moreover, managerial compensation contracts that emphasize options or option-like features were also associated with significantly less hedging.

As Tufano acknowledged in his study, this pattern of findings could have been predicted from arguments that Clifford Smith and I presented in a theoretical paper in 1985.[15] Our argument was essentially as follows: As we saw in the case of closely held companies, managers with a significant fraction of their own wealth tied up in their own firms are likely to consider all sources of risk when setting their required rates of return. And this could help explain the tendency of firms with heavy managerial equity ownership to hedge more of their gold price exposures. In such cases, the volatility of gold prices translates fairly directly into volatility of managers' wealth, and manager-owners concerned about such volatility may rationally choose to manage their exposures. (How, or whether, such hedging serves the interests of the companies' outside shareholders is another issue, one that I return to shortly.)

The propensity of managers with lots of stock options but little equity ownership to leave their gold price exposures unhedged is also easy to

understand. As shown in Figure 24.3, the one-sided payoff from stock options effectively rewards management for taking bets and so increasing volatility. In this example, the reduction in volatility from hedging makes management's options worthless (that is, the example assumes these are well out-of-the-money options). But if the firm does not hedge, there is some probability that a large increase in gold prices will cause the options to pay off.

What if we make the more realistic assumption that the options are *at the money* instead of far out of the money? In this case, options would still have the power to influence hedging behavior because management gains more from increases in firm value than it loses from reductions in firm value. As we saw in the case of the S&L presented earlier, this "asymmetric" payoff structure of options increases management's willingness to take bets.[16]

---

15 Clifford Smith and René Stulz, "The Determinants of Firms' Hedging Policies," *Journal of Financial and Quantitative Analysis* 20 (1985), pp. 391–405.

16 Additional empirical support for the importance of the relation between the option component of managerial compensation contracts and corporate risk-taking was provided in a recent study of S&Ls that changed their organizational form from mutual ownership to stock ownership. The study finds that those "converted" S&Ls where management has options choose to increase their one-year gaps and, hence, their exposure to interest rates. The study also shows that the greater the percentage of their interest rate exposure an S&L hedges, the larger the credit risk it takes on. The authors of the study interpret this finding to argue, as I do here, that risk management allows firms to increase their exposures to some risks by reducing other risks and thus limiting total firm risk. See C.M. Schrandt and H. Unal, "Coordinated Risk Management: On and Off-balance Sheet Hedging and Thrift Conversion," 1996, unpublished working paper, The Wharton School, University of Pennsylvania, Philadelphia, PA.

But if these differences in hedging behavior reflect differences in managerial incentives, what do they tell us about the effect of risk management on shareholder value? Without directly addressing the issue, Tufano implies that neither of the two polar risk management strategies – hedging none of their gold exposure vs. hedging 40% or more – seems designed to increase shareholder value while both appear to serve managers' interests. But can we therefore conclude from this study that neither of these approaches benefits shareholders?

Let's start with the case of the companies that, like Homestake Mining, choose to hedge none of their gold price exposure. As we saw earlier, companies for which financial distress is unlikely have no good reason to hedge (assuming they see no value in changing their current capital structure.) At the same time, in a market as heavily traded as gold, management is also not likely to possess a comparative advantage in predicting gold prices. And, lacking either a motive for hedging or superior information about future gold prices, management has no reason to alter the company's natural exposure to gold prices. In further defense of such a policy, one could also argue that such a gold price exposure will have diversification benefits for investors seeking protection against inflation and political risks.

On the other hand, as Smith and I pointed out, because stock options have considerably more upside than downside risk, such incentive packages could result in a misalignment of managers' and shareholders' interests. That is, stock options could be giving managers a one-sided preference for risk-taking that is not fully shared by the companies' stockholders; and, if so, a better policy would be to balance managers' upside potential by giving them a share of the downside risk.

But what about the opposite decision to hedge a significant portion of gold price exposures? Was that likely to have increased shareholder value? As Tufano's study suggests, the managers of the hedging firms tend to hold larger equity stakes. And, as we saw earlier, if such managers have a large fraction of their wealth tied up in their firms, they will demand higher levels of compensation to work in firms with such price exposures. *Given that the firm has chosen to concentrate equity ownership*, hedging may well be a value-adding strategy. That is, if significant equity ownership for managers is expected to

add value by strengthening incentives to improve operating performance, the role of hedging is to make these incentives even stronger by removing the "noise" introduced by a major performance variable – the gold price – that is beyond management's control. For this reason, the combination of concentrated ownership, the less "noisy" performance measure produced by hedging, and the possibility of higher financial leverage[17] has the potential to add significant value. As this reasoning suggests, risk management can be used to facilitate an organizational structure that resembles that of an LBO![18]

To put the same thought another way, it is the risk management policy that allows companies with large financial exposures to have significant managerial stock ownership. For, without the hedging policy, a major price exposure would cause the scope of management's bet to be too diffuse, and "uncontrollables" would dilute the desired incentive benefits of more concentrated ownership.

Although Tufano's study is finally incapable of answering the question, "Did risk management add value for shareholders?," the study nevertheless has an important message for corporate policy. It says that, to the extent that risk-taking within the corporation is decentralized, it is important to understand the incentives of those who make the decisions to take or lay off risks.

Organizations have lots of people doing a good job, and so simply doing a good job may not be enough to get promoted. And, if one views corporate promotions as the outcome of "tournaments" (as does one strand of the academic literature), there are tremendous incentives to stand out. One way to stand out is by volunteering to take big risks. In most areas of a corporation, it is generally impossible to take risks where the payoffs are large enough to be noticeable if things go well. But the treasury area may still be an exception. When organized as a profit center, the corporate treasury was certainly a place where an enterprising executive could take such risks and succeed. To the

---

17 Although Tufano's study does not find that firms that hedge have systematically higher leverage ratios, it does find that companies that hedge less have higher cash balances.

18 For a discussion of the role of hedging in creating an LBO-like structure, see my study, "Managerial Discretion and Optimal Financing Policies," *Journal of Financial Economics* (1990), pp. 3–26.

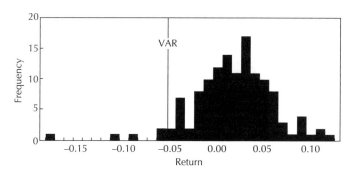

Figure 24.4 World Market Portfolio Return September 1985–December 1995

extent such possibilities for risk-taking still exist within some corporate treasuries, top management must be very careful in establishing the appropriate incentives for their risk managers. I return to this subject in the final section of the paper.

MEASURING RISK (OR, IMPROVING ON VAR)

As I mentioned at the outset, the academic literature has focused on volatility reduction as the primary objective of risk management, and on variance as the principal measure of risk. But such a focus on variance, as we have seen, is inconsistent with both most corporate practice and with the theory of risk management presented in this paper. Rather than aiming to reduce variance, most corporate risk management programs appear designed just to avoid "lower-tail outcomes" while preserving upside potential. Indeed, as I suggested earlier, some companies will hedge certain downside risks precisely in order to be able to increase their leverage ratios or to enlarge other financial exposures in ways designed to exploit their comparative advantage in risk-taking.

Many commercial banks and other financial institutions now attempt to quantify the probability of lower-tail outcomes by using a measure known as Value at Risk, or VAR. To illustrate the general principle underlying VAR, let's assume you are an investor who holds a stock portfolio that is fully diversified across all the major world markets. To calculate your Value at Risk, you will need the kind of information that is presented graphically in Figure 24.4, which is a histogram showing the distribution of monthly returns on the Morgan

Stanley Capital International world market portfolio from September 1985 through December 1995.

How risky is that portfolio? One measure is the standard deviation of the portfolio's monthly returns. Over that roughly 10-year period, the average monthly return was 1.23%, with a standard deviation of 4.3%. This tells you that, about two thirds of the time, your actual return would have fallen within a range extending from a loss of 3.1% to a gain of 5.5%.

But what if one of your major concerns is the size of your monthly losses if things turn out badly, and you thus want to know more about the bottom third of the distribution of outcomes? Let's say, for example, that you want to know the maximum extent of your losses in 95 cases out of 100 – that is, within a 95% "confidence interval." In that case, you would calculate the VAR evaluated at the 5% level, which turns out to be a loss of 5.9%. This VAR, represented by the vertical line in the middle of Figure 24.4, is obtained by taking the monthly average return of 1.23% and subtracting from it 1.65 times the standard deviation of 4.3%. And, if you wanted to know the dollar value of your maximum expected losses, you would simply multiply 5.9% times the dollar value of your holdings. That number is your monthly VAR at the 95% confidence level.

Although the VAR is now used by some industrial firms to evaluate the risks of their derivatives portfolios, the measure was originally designed by J.P. Morgan to help financial institutions monitor the exposures created by their trading activities. In fact, for financial institutions that trade in liquid markets, a *daily* VAR is likely to be even more useful for monitoring trading operations than the monthly VAR illustrated above. Use of a daily VAR would tell an institution that it could expect, in 95 cases out of 100, to lose no more than x% of its value before unwinding its positions.

The special appeal of VAR is its ability to compress the expected distribution of bad outcomes into a single number. But how does one apply such a measure to the corporate risk management we have been discussing? Despite its advantages for certain uses, VAR cannot really be used to execute the risk management goal presented in this paper – namely, the elimination of lower-tail outcomes to avoid financial distress. The fact that there is a 95% probability that a company's loss on a given day, or in a given month, will not exceed a certain amount called VAR is not useful information when management's concern is whether firm value will fall below some critical value *over an extended period of time*. The question management would like to be able to answer is this: If we define financial distress as a situation where we cannot raise funds with a rating of BBB, or where our cash flows or the value of equity fall below some target, what is the probability of distress over, say, the next three years? VAR by itself cannot answer this question – nor can traditional measures of volatility.

It is relatively simple to calculate VAR for a financial institution's portfolio over a horizon of a day or a week. It is much less clear how one would compute the VAR associated with, say, an airline's ongoing operating exposure to oil prices. In evaluating their major risks, most non-financial companies will want to know how much volatility in their cash flows or firm value an exposure can be expected to cause over periods of at least a year, and often considerably longer. Unfortunately, there are at least two major difficulties in extending the VAR over longer time horizons that may not be surmountable.

First, remember that a daily VAR at the 99th percentile is one that is expected to occur on one day out of 100. The relative precision of such a prediction makes it possible to conduct empirical checks of the validity of the model. With the large number of daily observations, one can readily observe the frequency with which the loss is equal or greater than VAR *using reasonably current data*. But, if we attempt to move from a daily to, say, a one-year VAR at the same 99th percentile, it becomes very difficult to calculate such a model, much less subject it to empirical testing. Since an annual VAR

at the 99th percentile means that the loss can be expected to take place in only one year in every 100, one presumably requires numerous 100-year periods to establish the validity of such a model.

The second problem in extending the time horizon of VAR is its reliance on the normal distribution. When one is especially concerned about "tail" probabilities – the probabilities of the worst and best outcomes – the assumption made about the statistical distribution of the gains and losses is important. Research on stock prices and on default probabilities across different classes of debt suggests that the tail probabilities are generally larger than implied by the normal distribution. A simple way to understand this is as follows. If stock returns were really normally distributed, as many pricing models assume, market declines in excess of 10% in a day would be extremely rare – say, once in a million years. The fact that such declines happen more often than this is proof that the normal distribution does not describe the probability of lower-tail events correctly.

Although this is not an important failing for most applications in corporate finance, including the valuation of most securities, it can be critical in the context of risk management. For example, if changes in the value of derivatives portfolios or default probabilities have "fatter tails" than those implied by a normal distribution, management could end up significantly understating the probability of distress.

An Alternative to VAR: Using Cash Flow Simulations to Estimate Default Probabilities. Moreover, even if we could calculate a one-year VAR for the value of the firm and be reasonably confident that the distribution was normal, the relevant risk measure for hedging purposes would not be the VAR computed at the one-year horizon. A VAR computed at the one-year horizon at the 99th percentile answers the question: What is the maximum loss in firm value that I can expect in 99 years out of 100? But when a company hedges an exposure, its primary concern is the likelihood of distress *during the year*, which depends on the value of the cumulative loss throughout the year. Thus, it must be concerned about the path of firm value during a period of time rather than the distribution of firm value at the end of the period.

Given this focus on cumulative changes in firm value during a period of time, perhaps the most practical approach to assessing a company's probability of financial distress is to conduct sensitivity analysis on the expected distribution of cash flows. Using Monte Carlo simulation techniques, for example, one could project the company's cash flows over a ten-year horizon in a way that is designed to reflect the combined effect of (and any interactions among) all the firm's major risk exposures on its default probability. The probability of distress over that period would be measured by the fraction of simulated distributions that falls below a certain threshold level of cumulative cash flow. Such a technique could also be used to estimate the expected effect of various hedging strategies on the probability of distress.[19]

One of the advantages of using simulation techniques in this context is their ability to incorporate any special properties (or "non-normalities") of the cash flows. As we saw earlier, the VAR approach assumes that the gains and losses from risky positions are "serially independent," which means that if your firm experiences a loss today, the chance of experiencing another loss tomorrow is unaffected. But this assumption is likely to be wrong when applied to the operating cash flow of a nonfinancial firm: If cash flow is poor today, it is more likely to be poor tomorrow. Simulation has the ability to build this "serial dependence" of cash flows into an analysis of the probability of financial distress.

MANAGING RISK-TAKING

As we have seen, a hedging strategy that focuses on the probability of distress can be consistent with an increase in risk-taking. With such a strategy, the primary goal of risk management is to eliminate lower-tail outcomes. Using risk management in this way, it is possible for a company to increase its volatility while also limiting the probability of a bad outcome that would create financial distress. One example of such a strategy would be to lever up the firm while at the same time buying way

out-of-the-money put options that pay off if the firm does poorly. Focusing on lower-tail outcomes is also fully consistent with managing longer-term economic or competitive exposures, as opposed to the near-term transaction exposures that most corporate risk management seems designed to hedge.

But how would the firm decide whether the expected payoff from taking certain financial bets is adequate compensation for not only the risk of losses, but also the expected costs of financial distress? And, once management decides that it is a value-increasing proposition to undertake certain bets, how would the firm evaluate the success of its risk-taking efforts?

To evaluate if the bet is worth taking, let's start by supposing that we are willing to put an explicit cost on the increase in the probability of distress resulting from betting on certain markets. In that case, the trade-off for evaluating a bet for the company becomes fairly simple: The expected profit from the bet must exceed the increase in the probability of distress multiplied by the expected cost of distress.[20] Thus, a bet that has a positive expected value and no effect on the probability of distress is one that the firm should take. But a bet with positive expected profit that significantly increases the probability of financial distress may not appear profitable if the costs of a bad outcome are too large. In such cases, it makes sense for the firm to think about using risk management to reduce the

---

19 For an illustration of the use of Monte Carlo analysis in risk management, see René Stulz and Rohan Williamson, "Identifying and Quantifying Exposures," in ed., Robert Jameson, *Treasury Risk Management* (London, Risk Publications), forthcoming.

20 One possible approach to quantifying the *expected* costs of financial distress involves the concept of American "binary options" and the associated option pricing models. An example of a binary option is one that would pay a fixed amount, say, $10, if the stock price of IBM falls below $40. Unlike standard American put options, which when exercised pay an amount equal to (the strike price of) $40 minus the actual price, the holder of a binary option receives either $10 or nothing, and exercises when the stock price crosses the $40 barrier. Such options can be priced using modified option pricing models.

The connection between binary options and risk management is this: The present value of a binary option is a function of two major variables: the probability that firm value will fall below a certain level (in this case, $40) and the payoff in the event of such a drop in value ($10). By substituting for the $10 payoff its own estimate of how much *additional* value the firm is likely to lose *once its value falls to a certain level and gets into financial trouble*, management can then estimate the expected present value of such costs using a binary option pricing model. This is the number that could be set against the expected profit from the firm's bet in order to evaluate whether to go ahead with the bet.

probability of distress. By hedging, management may be able to achieve a reduction in cash flow variability that is large enough that an adverse outcome of the bet will not create financial distress.

Given that management has decided the bet is worth taking, how does it evaluate the outcome of the strategy? Consider first the case of our firm AAA discussed earlier. Recall that this firm is not concerned about lower-tail outcomes and thus has no reason to hedge. When evaluating the outcome of the bet in this case, the appropriate benchmark is the expected gain *adjusted for risk*. It is not enough that the bet ends up earning more than the risk-free rate or even more than the firm's cost of capital. To add value for the company's shareholders, the bet must earn a return that is higher than investors' expected return on other investments of comparable risk.

For example, there is considerable evidence that holding currencies of high-interest rate countries earns returns that, on average, exceed the risk-free rate. This excess return most likely represents "normal" compensation for bearing some kind of risk – say, the higher inflation and interest rate volatility associated with high-interest-rate countries. And because such a strategy is thus *expected* to earn excess returns, it would not make sense to reward a corporate treasury for earning excess returns in this way. The treasury takes risks when it pursues that strategy, and the firm's shareholders expect to be compensated for these risks. Thus, it is only the amount by which the treasury exceeds the expected return – or the "abnormal return" – that represents *economic profit* for the corporation.

So, the abnormal or excess return should be the measure for evaluating bets by company AAA. But now let's turn to the case of company BBB, where the expected increase in volatility from the bet is also expected to raise the probability of costly lower-tail outcomes. In such a case, as we saw earlier, management should probably hedge to reduce the probability of financial trouble to acceptable levels. At the same time, however, top management should also consider subjecting its bets to an even higher standard of profitability to compensate shareholders for any associated increase in expected financial distress costs.

How much higher should it be? One method would be to assume that, instead of hedging, the firm raises additional equity capital to support the expected increase in volatility associated with

the bet. In that case, the bet would be expected to produce the same risk-adjusted return on capital as the bet taken by company AAA, but on a larger amount of imputed "risk" capital.[21]

In sum, when devising a compensation scheme for those managers entrusted with making the firm's bets, it is critical to structure their incentive payments so that they are encouraged to take only those bets that are expected to increase shareholder wealth. Managers should not be compensated for earning average returns when taking larger-than-average risks. They should be compensated only for earning more than what their shareholders could earn on their own when bearing the same amount of risk.

This approach does not completely eliminate the problem discussed earlier caused by incentives for individuals to stand out in large organizations by taking risks. But traditional compensation schemes only reinforce this problem. If a risk-taker simply receives a bonus for making gains, he has incentives to take random bets because he gets a fraction of his gains while the firm bears the losses. Evaluating managers' performance against a risk-adjusted benchmark can help discourage risk-taking that is not justified by comparative advantage by making it more difficult for the risk-taker to make money by taking random bets.

CONCLUSION

This paper presents a theory of risk management that attempts to go beyond the "variance-minimization" model that dominates most academic discussions of corporate risk management. I argue

---

21 The amount of implicit "risk capital" (as opposed to the actual cash capital) backing an activity can be calculated as a function of the expected volatility (as measured by the standard deviation) of the activity's cash flow returns. For the distinction between risk capital and cash capital, and a method for calculating risk capital, see Robert Merton and André Perold, "Theory of Risk Capital for Financial Firms," *Journal of Applied Corporate Finance*, Vol. 6 No. 3 (Fall 1993). For one company's application of a similar method for calculating risk capital, see Edward Zaik et al., "RAROC at Bank of America: From Theory to Practice," *Journal of Applied Corporate Finance*, Vol. 9 No. 2 (Summer 1996). For a theoretical model of capital budgeting that takes into account firm-specific risks, see Kenneth Froot and Jeremy Stein, "Risk Management, Capital Budgeting, and Capital Structure Policy for Financial Institutions: An Integrated Approach," Working Paper 96-030, Harvard Business School Division of Research.

that the primary goal of risk management is to eliminate the probability of costly lower-tail outcomes – those that would cause financial distress or make a company unable to carry out its investment strategy. (In this sense, risk management can be viewed as the purchase of well-out-of-the-money put options designed to limit downside risk.) Moreover, by eliminating downside risk and reducing the expected costs of financial trouble, risk management can also help move companies toward their optimal capital and ownership structure. For, besides increasing corporate debt capacity, the reduction of downside risk could also encourage larger equity stakes for managers by shielding their investments from "uncontrollables."

This paper also departs from standard finance theory in suggesting that some companies may have a comparative advantage in bearing certain financial market risks – an advantage that derives from information it acquires through its normal business activities. Although such specialized information may occasionally lead some companies to take speculative positions in commodities or currencies, it is more likely to encourage selective hedging, a practice in which the risk manager's view of future price movements influences the percentage of the exposure that is hedged. This kind of hedging, while certainly containing potential for abuse, may also represent a value-adding form of risk-taking for many companies.

But, to the extent that such view-taking becomes an accepted part of a company's risk management program, it is important to evaluate managers' bets on a risk-adjusted basis and relative to the market. If managers want to behave like money managers, they should be evaluated like money managers.

CHAPTER 25

Theory of Risk Capital in Financial Firms

*Robert C. Merton and André F. Perold (Harvard Business School)**

This paper develops a concept of risk capital that can be applied to the financing, capital budgeting, and risk management decisions of financial firms. The development focuses particularly on firms that act as a *principal* in the ordinary course of business. Principal activities can be asset-related, as in the case of lending and block-positioning; liability-related, as in deposit-taking and writing of guarantees (including insurance, letters of credit, and other contingent commitments); or both, as in the writing of swaps and other derivatives for customers.

For the purposes of this paper, principal financial firms have three important distinguishing features. The first is that their customers can be major liabilityholders; for example, policyholders, depositors, and swap counterparties are all liabilityholders as well as customers. By definition, a financial firm's customers strictly prefer to have the payoffs on their contracts as unaffected as possible by the fortunes of the issuing firm. Hence, they strongly prefer firms of high credit quality. Investors, by contrast, expect their returns to be affected by the profits and losses of the firm. Hence, they are less credit-sensitive provided, of course, they are

compensated appropriately for risk. This means that A-rated firms, for example, can generally raise the funds they need to operate, but are at a disadvantage in competing with AAA-rated firms in businesses such as underwriting insurance or issuing swaps. The presence of credit-sensitive customers thus greatly increases the importance of risk control of the overall balance sheet.[1]

A second distinguishing feature of principal firms is their *opaqueness* to customers and investors.[2] That is, the detailed asset holdings and business activities of the firm are not publicly disclosed (or, if disclosed, only with a considerable lag in time). Furthermore, principal financial firms typically have relatively liquid balance sheets that, in the

---

* An earlier version appears as "Management of Risk Capital in Financial Firms" in Samuel L. Hayes, III (1993), ed., *Financial Services: Perspectives and Challenges*, Boston: Harvard Business School Press: 215–245.

1 For an elaboration on the difference between "customers" and "investors" of the financial-service firm as a core concept, see Robert C. Merton (1992), *Continuous-Time Finance*, Revised Edition, Oxford: Basil Blackwell; R.C.Merton (1993), "Operation and Regulation in Financial Intermediation: A Functional Perspective," in Peter Englund, ed., *Operation and Regulation of Financial Markets*, Stockholm: The Economic Council: 17–67; and R. C. Merton and Zvi Bodie, "On the Management of Financial Guarantees," *Financial Management*, 21 (Winter, 1992): 87–109.

2 The notion of "opaqueness" of financial institutions is developed by Stephen Ross in "Institutional Markets, Financial Marketing, and Financial Innovation," *Journal of Finance*, 44 (July, 1989): 541–556. For further discussion, see Merton (1993), cited in note 1.

course of only weeks, can and often do undergo a substantial change in size and risk.[3] Unlike manufacturing firms, principal financial firms can enter, exit, expand, or contract individual businesses quickly at relatively low cost. These are changes that customers and investors cannot easily monitor. Moreover, financial businesses – even non-principal businesses like mutual-fund management – are susceptible to potentially enormous "event risk" in areas not easily predictable or understood by outsiders.[4]

All of this implies that principal firms will generally experience high "agency" and "information" costs in raising equity capital and in executing various types of customer transactions.[5] (We later refer to these "dissipative" or "deadweight" costs collectively as *economic costs of risk capital*, in a manner to be made more precise.) Risk management by the firm is an important element in controlling these costs.

A third distinguishing feature of principal financial firms is that they operate in competitive financial markets. Their profitability is thus highly sensitive to their cost of capital, and especially their cost of risk capital. Allocating the costs of risk capital to individual businesses or projects is a problem for organizations that operate in a more or less decentralized fashion. As we shall discuss, there is no simple way to do so. Moreover, any allocation must necessarily be *imputed*, if only because highly risky principal transactions often require little or no up-front expenditure of cash.

For example, an underwriting commitment can be executed with no immediate cash expenditure.

However, the customer counterparty would not enter into the agreement if it did not believe that the underwriting commitment would be met. The commitment made by the underwriting business is backed by the entire firm. Therefore, the strength of this guarantee is measured by the overall credit standing of the firm. The problem of capital allocation within the firm is thus effectively the problem of correctly charging for the guarantees provided by the firm to its constituent businesses.

These three distinctive features of principal financial firms – credit-sensitivity of customers, high costs of risk capital (resulting from their opaqueness), and high sensitivity of profitability to the cost of risk capital – should all be taken into account explicitly by such firms when deciding which activities to enter (or exit), how to finance those activities, and whether to hedge its various market or price exposures.

What is Risk Capital? We define *risk capital* as *the smallest amount that can be invested to insure the value of the firm's net assets against a loss in value relative to the risk-free investment of those net assets*. By *net assets*, we mean gross assets minus customer liabilities (valued as if these liabilities are default-free). Customer liabilities can be simple fixed liabilities such as guaranteed insurance contracts (GICs), or complex contingent liabilities such as property and casualty insurance policies. With fixed customer liabilities, the riskiness of net assets (as measured, for example, by the standard deviation of their change in value) is the same as the riskiness of gross assets. With contingent customer liabilities, however, the riskiness of net assets depends not only on the riskiness of gross assets, but also on the riskiness of customer liabilities and the covariance between changes in the value of gross assets and changes in the value of customer liabilities. The volatility of the change in the value of net assets is the most important determinant of the amount of risk capital.

As defined, risk capital differs from both *regulatory capital*, which attempts to measure risk capital according to a particular accounting standard, and from *cash capital*, which represents the up-front cash required to execute a transaction. Cash capital is a component of *working capital* that includes financing of operating expenses like salaries and rent. Cash capital can be large, as with the purchase of physical securities – or small, as with futures

---

3   As reported in *The Wall Street Journal*, October 24, 1991, the investment bank of Salomon Brothers reduced its total assets or "footings" by $50 billion in a period of approximately 40 days.

4   For example, consider the potentially large exposure from the "scandals" at E.F. Hutton (check writing), Merrill Lynch ("ticket in drawer"), Salomon Brothers (Treasury auction), Drexel Burnham Lambert (FIRREA/collapse of high-yield debt market), and T. Rowe Price Associates (money-market-fund credit loss).

5   For detailed development and review of the literature on asymmetric information and agency theory in a financial market context, see Amir Barnea, Robert Haugen, and Lemma Senbet (1985), *Agency Problems and Financial Contracting*, Englewood Cliffs, NJ: Prentice Hall; Michael Jensen (1986), "Agency Costs of Free Cash Flow, Corporate Finance, and Takeovers," *American Economic Review*, 76 (May): 323–329, and especially N. Strong and M. Walker (1987), *Information and Capital Markets*, Oxford: Basil Blackwell.

contracts and repurchase agreements – or even negative, as with the writing of insurance.

The organization of the paper is as follows. In the next section, a series of examples is presented to show that the amount of risk capital depends only on the riskiness of net assets, and not at all on the form of financing of the net assets. These examples further establish how risk capital funds, provided mainly by the firm's shareholders (except in the case of extremely highly leveraged firms), are then either implicitly or explicitly used to purchase asset insurance from various sources. Besides third-party guarantors, other potential issuers of asset insurance to the firm are the firm's stakeholders, including customers, debtholders, and shareholders.

We next discuss how standard methods of accounting can fail to measure risk capital and its associated costs correctly in the calculation of firm profitability, and how this can lead to an overstatement of profitability. The economic costs of risk capital to the firm are shown to be the "spreads" on the price of asset insurance arising from information costs (adverse selection and moral hazard) and agency costs. We then use this framework to establish the implications for hedging and risk-management decisions.

Finally, for multi-business firms, we discuss the problems that arise in trying to allocate the risk capital of the firm among its individual businesses. It is shown that, for a given configuration, the risk capital of a multi-business firm is less than the aggregate risk capital of the businesses on a stand-alone basis. Therefore, full allocation of risk capital across the individual businesses of the firm is generally not feasible, and attempts at such a full allocation can significantly distort the true profitability of individual businesses.

MEASURING RISK CAPITAL

We now use a series of hypothetical but concrete examples to illustrate the concept of risk capital. In the first set of examples, there are no customer liabilities, so that gross assets equal net assets. After that, we consider two cases with customer liabilities, one with fixed liabilities and the other with contingent liabilities.

Consider the hypothetical newly-formed firm of Merchant Bank, Inc., a wholly owned subsidiary of a large AAAA-rated[6] conglomerate. The firm currently has no assets. Merchant Bank's one and only deal this year will be a $100 million participation in a one-year bridge loan promising 20% interest ($120 million total payment at maturity). It does not plan to issue any customer liabilities. Merchant Bank's net assets will thus consist of this single bridge loan.

The bridge loan is a risky asset. We assume in particular that there are only three possible scenarios: A likely "anticipated" scenario, in which the loan pays off in full the promised $120 million; an unlikely "disaster" scenario, in which the borrower defaults but at maturity the lender recovers 50 cents on the dollar – that is, collects $60 million; and a rare "catastrophe" scenario, in which the lender recovers nothing.

To invest in the bridge loan requires $100 million of *cash* capital. Because this asset is risky, the firm also needs risk capital.

Merchant Bank wants to finance the cash capital by means of a one-year note issued to an outside investor. The firm wants the note to be default free. If these terms can be arranged, then at the current riskless rate of 10%, $110 million would be owed the noteholder at maturity.

In general, a firm has essentially two ways to eliminate the default risk of its debt liabilities. Both involve the purchase of insurance: The first is to do so indirectly through the purchase of insurance on its *assets*; the second and more direct method is to purchase insurance on its (debt) *liabilities*. (Combinations of these would also work.) As we shall see, the two are economically equivalent. The risk capital of the firm is equal to the smallest investment that can be made to obtain complete default-free financing of its net assets.

Risk Capital and Asset Guarantees. Suppose that Merchant Bank buys insurance on the bridge loan from a AAAA-rated bond insurer. Suppose further that, for $5 million, Merchant Bank can obtain insurance just sufficient to guarantee a return of $110 million on the bridge loan.[7]

---

6   By "AAAA-rated", we mean a firm with default-free liabilities that without question will stay that way.

7   That is, *full insurance*. The insurance would take the form of paying Merchant Bank the difference between the promised debt payments and actually received cash flows on the bridge loan.

With this asset insurance in place, the value of Merchant Bank's assets at the end of the year will equal or exceed $110 million. The noteholders of Merchant Bank are thus assured of receiving the full payment of their interest and principal, and the note will be default-free.

It follows from the definition of risk capital that the price of the loan insurance ($5 million) is precisely the amount of risk capital Merchant Bank requires if it holds the bridge loan. Merchant Bank would need to fund it with a $5 million cash equity investment from its parent. Once these transactions have been completed, Merchant Bank's accounting balance sheet will be as follows:

ACCOUNTING BALANCE SHEET A

Bridge loan	$100	Note (default free)	$100
Loan insurance (from insurance company)	5	Shareholder equity	5

If the bridge loan pays off as promised at the end of the year, Merchant Bank will be able to return a total of $10 million pre-tax to its parent ($20 million in interest income less $10 million in interest expense). If the bridge loan defaults, the asset insurance covers any shortfall up to $110 million, and Merchant Bank will just be able to meet its note obligations. There will be nothing to return to the parent. The risk capital used to purchase the insurance will have been just sufficient to protect the firm from any loss on the underlying asset (including financing expense of the cash capital). And, of course, the risk capital itself will have been lost. In this arrangement, the insurance company bears the risk of the asset; Merchant Bank's parent as shareholder bears the risk of loss of the risk capital itself.

The payoffs (cash flows) at maturity to the various stakeholders in Merchant Bank can be summarized in the following table:

Table A Payoff Structure

Bridge Loan	Loan Insurance	Bridge Loan + Insurance	Firm Stakeholders	
			Note	Shareholder
Anticipated Scenario				
120	0	120	110	10
Disaster Scenario				
60	50	110	110	0
Catastrophe Scenario				
0	110	110	110	0

Note that, in this example, Merchant Bank's accounting balance sheet corresponds to what we shall call the firm's *risk-capital balance sheet*:

RISK-CAPITAL BALANCE SHEET A

Bridge loan	$100	Note (default free)	$100
Loan insurance (from insurance company)	5	Risk capital	5

By inspection of the two balance sheets, "shareholder equity" is equal to the firm's risk capital, and the non-equity liabilities are default free. We shall see, however, that the accounting and risk-capital balance sheets are in general quite different.

Risk Capital and Liability Guarantees. A parent guarantee of the note is an alternative, and perhaps the most common, form of credit enhancement for the debt of a subsidiary such as Merchant Bank.[8] This way, the parent makes no cash equity investment in Merchant Bank. At the outset, the firm's accounting balance sheet is as follows:

ACCOUNTING BALANCE SHEET B

Bridge loan	$100	Note (default free)	$100
		Shareholder equity	0

Here Merchant Bank again obtains the necessary $100 million in cash capital through issuance of a default-free note; however, all asset risk is now borne by the parent. Thus the risk capital is merely taking the form of the parent guarantee of the note. This guarantee is an additional asset of the subsidiary – one that does not appear on its balance sheet. Suppose that the value of this guarantee is worth $G million. Then the parent's (off-balance-sheet) equity investment in Merchant Bank is worth $G million, and Merchant Bank's

---

8 This insurance could take the form of the parent either paying the noteholder the $110 million promised payment in the event of default, and then seizing Merchant Bank's assets, or paying the noteholder the difference between the promised payment and actual payments Merchant Bank is able to make. The parent guarantee avoids outside lenders becoming involved in any bankruptcy of the subsidiary, and gives the parent some "choice." For our purposes here, we can abstract from such details of structure.

balance sheet can be restated in terms of its risk-capital balance sheet as follows:[9]

RISK-CAPITAL BALANCE SHEET B

Bridge loan	$100	Note (default free)	$100
Note guarantee (from parent)	G	Risk capital	G

As in the previous example, if the bridge loan pays off as promised, Merchant Bank will be able to return a total of $10 million pre-tax to its parent ($20 million in interest income less $10 million in interest expense). If the bridge loan defaults, so too will Merchant Bank on its note, and the noteholder either collects any unpaid amounts from the parent, or the parent pays out the promised $110 million and receives back the value of the bridge-loan asset seized; either way the economic effect is the same. Merchant Bank of course will have nothing to return to its parent as equityholder. In this arrangement, the parent bears the risk of the asset as guarantor of its subsidiary's debt; the parent also bears the risk of loss of the risk capital as shareholder of Merchant Bank. Table B summarizes in terms of payoffs at maturity:

Table B Payoff Structure

Bridge loan	Note sans guarantee	Note	Note + guarantee	Shareholder
Anticipated Scenario				
120	110	0	110	10
Disaster Scenario				
60	60	50	110	0
Catastrophe Scenario				
0	0	110	110	0

A comparison of Table A and Table B demonstrates the economic equivalence of liability insurance and asset insurance.[10] In both, the noteholder bears no risk and the parent, solely in its capacity as shareholder of Merchant Bank, obtains the same cash flows: $10 million in the "anticipated" scenario and zero otherwise. Moreover, the note guarantee has the same cash flows as the bridge-loan insurance. The note guarantee therefore is also worth G = $5 million. Thus, risk capital is once again $5 million.[11]

Liabilities with Default Risk. We now turn to the more typical case where our hypothetical firm, Merchant Bank, is willing to issue liabilities with some default risk. Suppose it issues the same 10% note (promising $110 million at maturity), but without any of the credit enhancements of the previous case. This now risky note will sell at a discount $D to par (at a promised yield to maturity higher than 10%), leaving Merchant Bank $D short of its need for $100 million cash capital. The shortfall in initial funding must be supplied in the form of a cash equity investment. Merchant Bank's beginning balance sheet is as follows:

ACCOUNTING BALANCE SHEET C

Bridge loan	$100	Note (risky)	$100 − D
		Shareholder equity	D

Once again, if the bridge loan pays off as promised, Merchant Bank will be able to pay a total of $10 million pre-tax to its parent.[12] If the bridge loan defaults, so too will Merchant Bank default on its note, and the noteholder will be at risk for any shortfall on the bridge loan under $110 million. Merchant Bank will have nothing to return to its parent.

Merchant Bank's shareholder here receives the same payoffs as it did in the previous examples

---

9 For a real-world application of this "extended" balance-sheet approach to capture the "hidden" asset and corresponding equity investment arising from parent guarantees of its subsidiary's debt, see R.C. Merton, (1983), "Prepared Direct Testimony of Robert C. Merton on Behalf of ARCO Pipe Line Company," Federal Energy Regulatory Commission, Washington, D.C., Docket No. OR78-1-011 (Phase II), Exhibits II N-C-34-0-34-4 (November 28). For a similar approach to analyze corporate pension assets and liabilities and the firm's guarantee of any shortfall on the pension plan, see Zvi Bodie (1990), "The ABO, the PBO, and Pension Investment Policy," *Financial Analysts Journal*, 46 (September/October): 27–34.

10 This equivalence may not apply exactly if one takes account of the various bankruptcy costs and delays in payments which could occur, for example, if Merchant Bank sought Chapter 11 bankruptcy protection.

11 The assumption that economically-equivalent cash flows have the same value is made only for expositional convenience in this part of the paper. Later in the discussion of the management of risk capital, the assumption is relaxed to take account of differences in information and agency costs among alternative guarantors.

12 $20 million in interest income less $15 million in cash plus amortized interest expense plus $5 million return of capital.

(see Table C). This economic equivalence implies that the firm's equity must be worth D = $5 million initially. Correspondingly, the risky note will have an initial value of $95 million (with a *promised* yield to maturity of $15 on $95, or 15.8%).

To see where risk capital enters, consider the position of the debtholder. The debtholder can interpret its purchase of the risky note as equivalent to the following three-step transaction: First, the purchase of default-free debt from Merchant Bank for $100 million; second, the sale to Merchant Bank of debt insurance for $5 million; and third, the netting of payments owed the debtholder on the default-free debt against payments owed the firm if the insurance is triggered. It is perhaps easiest to see this by observing the economic identity:[13]

Risky note + note insurance = Default-free note
   so that
Risky note = Default-free note – note insurance.

As already shown (in Tables A and B), note insurance is economically equivalent to asset insurance. Thus, the debtholder can interpret its purchase of the risky note as equivalent to the purchase of default-free debt coupled with the *sale* to Merchant Bank of *asset* insurance (on the bridge loan) for $5 million. In other words:

Risky note = Default-free note – asset insurance.

This relation allows the restatement of the accounting balance sheet C in its risk-capital form:

RISK-CAPITAL BALANCE SHEET C

Bridge loan	$100	Note (default free)	$100
Asset insurance	5	Risk capital	5
(from note holder)			

The payoffs at maturity associated with this risk-capital balance sheet are shown in Table C:

Table C Payoff Structure

Bridge loan	Asset insurance	Default-free note	Risky note = Default-free note– asset insurance	Share-holder
Anticipated Scenario				
120	0	110	110	10
Disaster Scenario				
60	50	110	60	0
Catastrophe Scenario				
0	110	110	0	0

Each of the examples (A, B, C) has a different accounting balance sheet. Yet all have very similar risk-capital balance sheets. They have the same amount of risk capital – because the underlying asset requiring the risk capital is the same in all cases. They differ only in which parties bear the risk of insuring the asset: the insurance company (example A), the parent (example B), or the noteholder (example C).

A More General Case. The concept of risk capital is now further expanded by analyzing a more general balance sheet. The goals here are to illustrate the case of fixed customer liabilities and the purchase of asset insurance from multiple sources.

Consider a firm with an investment portfolio of risky assets worth $2.5 billion. The firm has customer liabilities outstanding in the form of one-year guaranteed investment contracts (GICs) promising 10% on their face value of $1 billion. Because the riskless rate is also 10%, the *default-free* value of these customer liabilities is $1 billion. The net assets – equal to assets minus the default-free value of customer liabilities – are thus worth $1.5 billion.

The riskiness of the portfolio is assumed to be such that the price of insurance to permit the portfolio to be financed risklessly for a year is $500 million. Since the customer liabilities are fixed, it follows that the price of insurance to permit the *net* assets to be financed risklessly for a year is also $500 million.[14] Therefore, $500 million is the required risk capital based on a one-year horizon.

---

13 For a full development and applications of this identify, see R.C. Merton (1990), "The Financial System and Economic Performance," *Journal of Financial Services Research*, 4 (December): 263–300; and Merton and Bodie (1992), cited in note 1.

14 By the end of the year, the *gross* assets will have experienced a loss relative to a risk-free investment if they fall below $2,750 million (110% of $2,500 million). The *net* assets will have experienced a loss relative to a risk-free investment if they fall below $1,650 million (110% of $1,500 million). Since year-end net

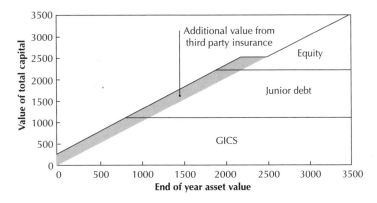

Figure 25.1 Payoffs to Firm Capital Providers

The firm's investor financings are in two forms: one-year junior debt promising 10% on its face value of $1 billion and shareholder equity. Thus, the total promised payment on fixed liabilities at the end of the year is $2.2 billion, comprised of $1.1 billion of GICs and $1.1 billion of debt that is junior to the GICs.

Suppose that the firm has formally obtained *partial* insurance on its investment portfolio, arbitrarily chosen to cover the *first* $300 million of decline of value of portfolio value below $2.5 billion. The insurance is thus structured to guarantee the portfolio value at $2.5 billion at year end, but is capped at a maximum payout of $300 million; therefore, the cap will be reached if the portfolio value falls below $2.2 billion. Assume, moreover, that the value of this "third-party" insurance is $200 million. The value of the policy appears as an additional asset on the firm's accounting balance sheet.

Figure 25.1 shows the payoffs on the various liabilities of the firm depending on the value of the investment portfolio at year end. Because the portfolio is only partially protected from loss by the firm-owned insurance policy, the junior debt and the customer liabilities are both potentially at risk to receive less than their promised payments.

As the senior liability, the GICs are most protected against a decline in the firm's asset values.

As shown in Figure 25.1, customers holding the GICs are at risk only if the value of the firm's portfolio has fallen below $800 million at year end, a decline in value of more than 68%. Accordingly, the GICs trade at only a small percentage discount to par. In our example, we assume that this discount is 1%, thus implying a price of $990 million and a promised yield to maturity of 11% ($110 on $990).

The junior debt is considerably riskier: the holders are exposed to loss if the value of the firm's portfolio falls below $1.9 billion by year end, a decline of about 24%. This debt therefore will trade at a larger discount to par. In our example, we assume that the discount is 10% for a price of $900 million, with a promised yield to maturity of 22.2% ($200 on $900). The value of the firm's equity is equal to $810 million, the difference between the value of total assets ($2.7B) and the market value of customer- and investor-held liabilities ($990 + 900 MM). The accounting balance sheet (valuing assets and liabilities at market) is thus as follows:

ACCOUNTING BALANCE SHEET D

Investment portfolio	$2,500	GICs (par $1,000)	$990
"Third-party" insurance (insurance company)	200	Debt (par $1,000)	900
		Equity	810
Total assets	2,700	Total liabilities	2,700

We now construct the risk-capital balance sheet for this firm. As in our earlier discussion of liabilities with default risk, the economic interpretation of

assets always equals year-end gross assets minus $1,100 million, any shortfall in year-end *gross* assets is exactly equal to the shortfall in year-end *net* assets, and vice versa. Therefore, the loss to the insurer of gross assets is identical to the loss to the insurer of net assets, and the prices of the two policies are the same.

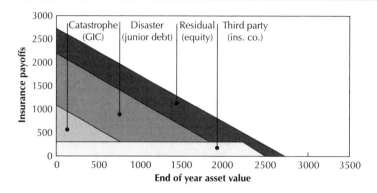

Figure 25.2 Components of Asset Insurance

the GIC holders is that, in effect, they have purchased default-free GICs and simultaneously *sold* some asset insurance to the firm, with the two transactions netted against each other. GIC holders are at risk only in the least likely of circumstances, and so they provide a kind of "catastrophe" insurance. As shown in Figures 25.1 and 25.2, the catastrophe insurance pays off only if the portfolio value falls by more than 68%. The (implicit) price of this insurance is the discount from the default-free value of the GICs, or $10 million ($1 billion – $990 million). Similarly, the debtholders' position is as if they purchased default-free debt and simultaneously sold to the firm asset insurance with a value of $100 million ($1 billion – 900 million). This insurance pays off if the firm's portfolio falls below $1.9 billion, but the maximum payoff is capped at $1.1 billion. The risk to the debtholders is greater than the risk to the GIC holders, but is still relatively small. As illustrated in Figure 25.2, it is a kind of "disaster" insurance.

We have so far accounted for total premiums of $310 million for asset insurance (third-party ($200mm) + debtholders ($100mm) + GICs ($10mm)). But we know that it takes $500 million in premiums to insure the portfolio fully. Hence, the balance of the insurance representing $190 million in premiums must effectively be provided by the equityholders. Because this insurance covers all the risks not covered by the other kinds of insurance, we call it "residual" insurance. (Figure 25.2 shows the combination of all sources of asset insurance.)

The total insurance has the same payoff structure as a *put option* on the portfolio with an exercise price equal to the current value of the portfolio

($2.5 billion) plus one year of interest at the riskless rate ($250 million), or $2.75 billion. The aggregate value of this asset insurance, or "put option," is equal to $500 million – as assumed at the outset. This is the risk capital of the firm.[15]

The equityholders can think of their $810 million investment as serving three functions: providing $500 million of default-free cash-capital financing (bringing the total cash capital to $2.5 billion), providing $500 million of risk capital to pay for asset insurance, and selling to the firm a portion of that

---

15 An alternative interpretation of the coverage provided by the four sources of insurance is as follows: The equityholders fully insure the gross assets at a level of $2.75 billion by year end, but purchase reinsurance from the insurance company that insures the assets to a level of $2.5 billion by year end. The insurance company in turn purchases reinsurance from the debtholders that insures the gross assets to a level of $1.9 billion by year end. The debtholders then purchase reinsurance from the firm's GIC customers that insures the gross assets to a level of $1.1 billion by year end. Equivalently, this can be expressed in terms of *put options*. The equityholders sell to the firm, for $500 million, a put option on the gross assets with exercise price $2.75 billion. They in turn spend $310 million of the $500 million proceeds to buy a put option from the insurance company with exercise price $2.5 billion. The insurance company then spends $110 million to buy a put option from the debtholders with exercise price $1.9 billion. Finally, the debtholders spend $10 million to purchase a put option from the GIC customers with exercise price $1.1 billion. The equityholders, insurance company, and debtholders have thus each sold a put option on the gross assets at one exercise price, and purchased reinsurance in the form of a second put option at a lower exercise price. For the formal development of the correspondence between loan guarantees and put options, see R.C. Merton (1977), "An Analytical Derivation of the Cost of Deposit Insurance and Loan Guarantees: An Application of Modern Option Pricing Theory," *Journal of Banking and Finance*, 1 (June): 3–11; see also R.C. Merton (1992, 1993), cited in note 1.

asset insurance worth $190 million. The equity-holders' net cash contribution is $500 plus $500 minus $190 million, which equals $810 million.

The risk-capital balance sheet of the firm is as follows:

RISK-CAPITAL BALANCE SHEET D

Asset portfolio	$2,500	Cash capital (default free)	
		Customers (GICs)	$1,000
Asset insurance		Debtholders	1,000
Equityholders ("residual")	190	Equityholders	500
Insurance Co ("third-party")	200	Total cash capital	2,500
Debtholders ("disaster")	100		
Customers ("catastrophe")	10	Risk capital (Equityholders)	500
Total insurance	500		
Total assets	3,000	Total Capital	3,000

This balance sheet encapsulates three basic functions of capital providers. First, *all provide cash capital*. Second, *all are sellers of asset insurance* to the firm, although in varying degrees. Customers and other senior providers of cash capital are typically sellers of catastrophe type insurance – the kind that is called upon to pay in only the rarest of instances. This level of exposure is typical because customers prefer to have their contract payoffs insensitive to the fortunes of the issuing firm. Customers will buy contracts from the firm only if they perceive the risk of default on those contracts to be very low. "Mezzanine" debtholders and equityholders are investors who provide cash capital and sell to the firm almost all the insurance not purchased from third-party providers.

The third function is the provision of risk capital, which is the cash required for the purchase of asset insurance. It is almost always performed by equityholders, as in all our illustrations. (Non-equity liabilityholders and other stakeholders in the firm will also be providers of risk capital if the market value of the underlying assets is less than the value of promised liabilities, capitalized at the riskless rate.)

A comparison of the risk-capital balance sheet with the accounting balance sheet thus illustrates that the debt and equity values of the firm need not, and generally will not, sum to the firm's cash capital; nor does the value of the equity necessarily equal the firm's risk capital. Cash capital is determined by the *assets* of the firm. Risk capital is determined by the riskiness of the *net assets* of the firm. Debt and equity, defined in the *institutional* sense, represent the netting of asset insurance against the provision of riskless cash capital and risk capital.

Contingent Customer Liabilities. As mentioned earlier, with contingent customer liabilities, the riskiness of net assets will in general differ from the riskiness of gross assets. The following example illustrates this difference.[16]

Consider again a principal financial firm with no equity, but with liabilities fully guaranteed by a AAAA parent. Suppose the firm issues a contingent liability in the form of a one-year S&P 500 index-linked note that promises to pay $100 million times the total return per dollar on the S&P index over the year. The purchaser of the note is a customer, say, a pension fund, that wants the return on its $100 million portfolio to match exactly that of the S&P 500 stock index. The customer has chosen this method of investing as an alternative to investing in an S&P 500 index fund. At the instant the transaction is consummated, the firm's accounting balance sheet is as follows:

ACCOUNTING BALANCE SHEET E

| Cash | $100 | Index-linked Note | $100 |
| | | Shareholder equity | 0 |

How the firm chooses to invest the $100 million will determine its risk capital. For instance, the firm might invest in one-year U.S. Treasury bills paying 10%. If it does so, the *gross* assets are riskless, but the *net* assets are extremely risky. In fact, the net assets are equivalent to a short position in the S&P 500.[17] By year end, the parent as guarantor will have to make up a shortfall that is equal to the total return on $100 million worth of the S&P 500 minus $10 million, the return on U.S. Treasury bills, if this amount is positive. This shortfall payment is the same payoff as that promised by a European call option on $100 million worth of the S&P 500 with a strike price of $110 million.[18,19] The risk capital of the firm – the smallest amount that can be invested to insure the

---

16 For an illustration of this point in the case of gross and net assets of a corporate pension plan, see Bodie (1990), cited in note 9.
17 Assuming the firm receives full use of the proceeds of the short sale.
18 The option must be protected from dividend payouts.
19 We saw previously that the purchase of insurance was economically equivalent to the purchase of a put option on the net assets. That is also the case here since a European call option on the S&P 500 is equivalent to a European put option on a *short* position in the S&P 500, that is, a put option on the net assets.

value of its net assets – is thus equal to the value of this call option.

As an alternative to U.S. Treasury bills, the firm might invest in the actual portfolio of stocks comprising the S&P 500. Assume it can do so costlessly. In this case, the *gross* assets are risky, but they exactly match the liabilities, so that the *net* assets are *riskless*. When the assets are invested this way, the firm's risk capital is zero.

As another alternative, the firm might invest in a customized portfolio of stocks that tracks fairly closely the S&P 500, but that omits the companies that the firm believes will underperform the S&P 500 index. In this case, the riskiness of the net assets is determined by the potential deviations in performance between the customized portfolio and the index. The risk capital of the firm will equal the value of a guarantee that pays the amount by which the customized portfolio underperforms the index, if it does so at all.[20]

These examples illustrate how the riskiness of the net assets can be significantly less than or greater than the riskiness of the gross assets. They also show that it is the riskiness of *net* assets that determines the type of insurance required to permit default-free financing for the firm, and hence it is the riskiness of net assets that determines the amount of the firm's risk capital.

ACCOUNTING FOR RISK CAPITAL IN THE CALCULATION OF PROFITS

As discussed above, risk capital is implicitly or explicitly used to purchase insurance on the net assets of the firm from a variety of potential providers. Insurance is a financial asset, and the gains or losses on this asset should be included along with the gains or losses on all other assets in the calculation of profitability. Standard methods

of accounting often fail to do this, however. For example, as discussed earlier, when a parent guarantees the performance of a subsidiary, the guarantee is not usually accounted for as an asset on the balance sheet of the subsidiary.

To illustrate, consider a securities underwriting subsidiary of a principal financial firm. The subsidiary anticipates deriving $50 million in revenues from underwriting spreads over the next year. It anticipates customary expenses of $30 million, so that its profit before tax is anticipated to be $20 million. (This profit figure assumes no mishaps such as occurred, for example, in the underwriting of British Petroleum shares in 1986.)[21] The subsidiary has an ongoing net working-capital requirement of $10 million. It has no other formal assets or liabilities and so its equity capital is $10 million.

Thus, the subsidiary's pre-tax return on equity is anticipated to be 200% for the year, and its accounting balance sheet and income statement would appear as follows:

ACCOUNTING BALANCE SHEET F

| Net working capital | $10 | Shareholder equity | $10 |

ACCOUNTING INCOME STATEMENT F

Revenues (underwriting spreads)	$50
Customary expenses	(30)
Profit before tax	20
Pre-tax ROE	200%

This accounting analysis, however, ignores risk capital, which in this case is the price of the insurance (implicitly provided by the parent) needed to ensure that the subsidiary can perform its underwriting commitments. Suppose such insurance would cost $15 million in premiums. Then the risk capital

---

20   Thus, the value of *perfect* stock-selection skills equals the value of the risk capital of the portfolio since *with such skills*, the portfolio *never* underperforms the index and its risk capital is thus reduced to zero. For a theory that equates the value of market timing to the value of a portfolio guarantee, see R.C. Merton (1981), "On Market Timing and Investment Performance Part I: An Equilibrium Theory of Value for Market Forecasts," *Journal of Business*, 54 (July): 363–406.

21   In October, 1987, prior to the stock market crash, the British government arranged to sell its $12.2 billion stake in British Petroleum to the public. The underwriting firms agreed to pay $65 per share, a full month before the offering would come to market. The shares fell to $53 post crash. According to *The New York Times*, October 30, 1987, the four U.S. underwriters collectively stood to lose in excess of $500 million. A subsequent price guarantee from the Bank of England reduced these losses to an estimated $200 million after tax.

balance sheet of the subsidiary would include the insurance as an asset, and total shareholder equity would be $25 million, consisting of $10 million of cash capital and $15 million of risk capital.

RISK-CAPITAL BALANCE SHEET F

Net working capital	$10	Cash capital	$10
Underwriting guarantee	15	Risk capital	15
(from parent)	—		—
Total Assets	25	Shareholder equity	25

After the fact, if the underwriting business performs as anticipated, the parent guarantee will not have been needed. Thus, the insurance that enabled the subsidiary to get the business in the first place will have expired worthless. As shown below in Table F, including the cost of this insurance (which expired worthless) in the income statement results in an anticipated net profit of $5 million, or a pre-tax return of 20% on *economic* equity of $25 million:

Table F Anticipated Net Profit Including Risk Capital

Revenues (underwriting spreads)	$50
Customary expenses	(30)
Underwriting insurance	(15)
Profit before tax	5
Pre-tax ROE	20%

The expensing of the $15 million cost of insurance shown in Table F is standard accounting practice if the insurance is obtained from arms-length providers. The fact that the parent provides the insurance should not change the treatment. Thus, the proper internal accounting would book the $15 million insurance premium as an expense to the underwriting subsidiary, and as revenue to the parent in its role as guarantor. Correspondingly, any "claims" paid on the guarantee should be considered revenue to the sub and an expense to the parent.

Even though this treatment of revenue and expense does not affect consolidated accounting, it can materially affect the calculated profit rates of individual businesses within the firm. In particular, the omission of risk capital "expended" on insurance overstates profits when the underlying assets perform well (because the insurance expires worthless) and understates profits when the underlying assets perform poorly (because the insurance becomes valuable).

THE ECONOMIC COST OF RISK CAPITAL

Accounting for risk capital in the calculation of actual after-the-fact profits is important for reporting and other purposes, such as profit-related compensation. For the purposes of decision-making *before the fact*, however, *expected* profits must be estimated. This requires estimation of the *expected* or *economic* cost of risk capital. Since risk capital is used to purchase insurance, and insurance is a financial asset, risk capital will not be costly in the economic sense if the insurance can be purchased at its "actuarially" fair market value. For example, the purchase of $100 worth of IBM stock is not costly in this sense if it can be purchased for $100.

Usually, however, transacting is not costless. Typically, a spread is paid over fair market value. These spread costs are "deadweight" losses to the firm. In terms of traditional use of "bid-ask" spread, the bid price from the firm's perspective is the fair value and the ask price is the amount the firm must actually pay for the insurance. The *economic cost* of risk capital to the firm is thus the spread it pays in the purchase of this insurance.

The reasons for such spreads in insurance contracts vary by type of risk coverage, but the largest component for the type discussed here generally relates to the insurer's need for protection against various forms of information risks and agency costs:

◆ *Adverse selection* is the risk insurers face in not being able to distinguish "good" risks from "bad." Unable to discriminate perfectly, they limit amounts of coverage and set prices based on an intermediate quality of risk, and try to do so to profit enough from the good risks to offset losses incurred in the underpricing of bad risks.[22]

◆ *Moral hazard* is the risk insurers face if they are not able to monitor the actions of the insured. Once covered, those insured have an incentive to increase their asset risk.

◆ *Agency costs* are the dissipation of asset values through inefficiency or mismanagement.

---

22 For a general discussion of these risks and costs in the context of insurance contracts, see Karl H. Borch (1990), *Economics of Insurance*, Amsterdam: North-Holland.

As residual claimants with few contractual controls over the actions of the firm, equity-holders bear the brunt of these costs.

Because principal financial firms are typically opaque in their structure, insurers of such firms – capital providers included – are especially exposed to these information and agency risks. Spreads for providing asset insurance to these types of firms – and hence their economic cost of risk capital – will therefore be relatively higher than for more transparent institutions.

The cost of risk capital is likely to depend on the form in which the insurance is purchased. The spreads on each form of insurance are determined differently. For example, in an all-equity firm, the required asset insurance is "sold" to the firm by its shareholders. The cost of risk capital obtained in this way will tend to reflect high agency costs (given the extensive leeway afforded to management by this structure), but little in the way of moral-hazard costs since there is no benefit to management or the firm's shareholders from increasing risk for its own sake. Debt financing, on the other hand, can impose a discipline on management that reduces agency costs. But then moral-hazard spreads can be high, especially in highly leveraged firms in which debtholders perceive a strong incentive for management to "roll the dice." The task for management is to weigh the spread costs of the different sources of asset insurance to find the most *efficient* way of "spending" the firm's risk capital.

Managing the firm most efficiently does not necessarily imply obtaining the lowest cost of risk capital. Consider the case of *signaling costs.* Firms faced with high spread charges can try to obtain lower spreads by making themselves more transparent, signaling that they are "good" firms. For example, "good" firms can report on a mark-to-market basis knowing that the cost to "bad" firms of doing so would be prohibitive (they would be seized by creditors and/or lose their customers). Transparency, however, can also impose costs of its own. For example, increasing transparency could lead to greater disclosure of proprietary strategies or self-imposed trading restraints that prevent it from taking advantage of short-lived windows of opportunity. Thus, the principal firm has to trade off between paying higher spread costs of risk capital for opaqueness and paying signaling costs and sacrificing potential competitive advantages to achieve transparency.

In calculating expected profitability for the overall firm, risk-capital costs should be expensed along with cash-capital costs. To illustrate, consider the example of Balance Sheet D in which the firm required $2.5 billion of cash capital and $500 million of risk capital. Because the cash capital is riskless, its cost is the AAAA rate (a little less than LIBOR), assumed to be 10% per annum. Suppose that the spread or economic cost of one-year risk capital for this firm is $30 million.[23] That is, the fair value "bid price" of the insurance provided by risk capital is $470 million and the "ask price" is $500 million. The $30 million spread is thus 6% of the ask price. Then total economic capital costs for the firm will be as follows:

Cash Capital costs:	$250 m	(10% of $2.5 billion)
Risk capital costs:	30 m	(6% of $500 million)

The rate paid for cash capital is the same for all firms, the riskless rate, here 10%. Risk capital costs could vary considerably among firms, and in a few special cases they could be negligible.[24]

This example differs importantly from the previous securities underwriting example (Table F). In Table F, we deducted the full "premium" expended on the purchase of insurance, while here we consider only that portion of the premium attributable to the spread or economic cost. The full insurance premium is deducted when the purpose of the analysis is to measure profits after the fact, or *expost.* But when the purpose of the analysis is to measure the cost of capital *ex ante*, only the economic cost is deducted because, *ex ante*, insurance purchased free of spread costs at its actuarial fair value is just that – costless.

We next apply our concept of risk capital to two important areas of firm management.

---

23 For an explicit model of these spread costs, see Merton (1993), cited in note 1.

24 For example, an open-end mutual fund is highly transparent. Moreover, the liabilityholders are principally customers who can redeem shares daily. Enforced by the securities laws, the selection of assets matches the promised contingent payments on customer liabilities, as expressed in the fund's prospectus. Hence *net* assets are virtually riskless.

HEDGING AND RISK MANAGEMENT

The implications of our framework for hedging and risk-management decisions are straightforward. Exposures to broad market risk – such as stock market risk, interest rate risk, or foreign exchange risk – usually can be hedged with derivatives such as futures, forwards, swaps and options. By definition, hedging away these risk exposures reduces asset risk. Thus, hedging market exposure reduces the required amount of risk capital.

Firms that speculate on the direction of the market, and therefore maintain a market exposure, will require more risk capital. By purchasing put options to insure against these market risks, the firm can maintain its desired exposures with the least amount of risk capital.

If there were no spread costs for risk capital, larger amounts of risk capital would impose no additional costs on the firm. In this case, firms may well be indifferent to hedging or not.[25] But if there are spread costs, and if these costs depend on the amount of risk capital, then a reduction in risk capital from hedging will lead to lower costs of risk capital if the hedges can be acquired at relatively small spreads.[26] That will usually be the case with hedging instruments for broad market risks where significant informational advantages among market participants are unlikely.[27]

CAPITAL ALLOCATION AND CAPITAL BUDGETING

Financial firms frequently need to consider entering new businesses or getting out of existing businesses. The cost of risk capital can be a major influence on these decisions. As always, the marginal benefit must be traded off against the marginal cost. But to evaluate the net marginal benefit

of a decision is difficult, because in principle it requires a comparison of total firm values under the alternatives being considered.

One simplifying assumption is that the incremental cost of risk capital is proportional to the incremental *amount* of risk capital. This might be reasonable, for example, if the decision does not lead to disclosures that materially change the degree of transparency or opaqueness of the firm. In this case, calculation of the economic cost of risk capital for a particular business is equivalent to the calculation of the risk capital applicable to that business.

Even if there are no economic costs of risk capital, calculation of the amount of risk capital of a particular business is still relevant. As discussed in example F, allocations of risk capital to individual businesses within the firm are necessary to calculate their after-the-fact profits. Such profit calculations can then serve, for example, as the basis for incentive compensation awards.

In general, the incremental risk capital of a particular business within the firm will differ from its risk capital determined on the basis of a stand-alone analysis. As we shall demonstrate, this results from a diversification effect that can dramatically reduce the firm's overall risk capital. The importance of this externality from risk-sharing depends on the correlations among the profits of the firm's various businesses. Its presence means that a full allocation of all the risk capital of the firm to its constituent businesses is generally inappropriate.

We illustrate with an example of a firm with three distinct businesses. Table 25.1 shows the current gross assets, customer liabilities, net assets (investor capital), and one-year risk-capital requirements of each business on a stand-alone basis.[28] The businesses all have the same amounts of gross assets, but different amounts of net assets because they have different amounts of customer liabilities.

25 Except if it changes the transparency or opaqueness of the firm, as discussed previously.
26 Merton (1993), cited in note 1, provides a model of spread costs that produces this result.
27 For example, for an explanation of the very narrow observed spreads on stock-index futures relative to the spreads on individual stocks, see James F. Gammill and and A.F. Perold (1989), "The Changing Character of Stock Market Liquidity," *The Journal of Portfolio Management*, 15 (Spring): 13–18.

28 Risk capital in this example is computed using the loan guarantee model in Merton (1977), cited in note 15, which is based on the Black-Scholes option-pricing model. Risk capital for this model will be roughly proportional to the standard deviation of profits. See the Technical Appendix for the precise calculations. See Merton (1993) and Merton and Bodie (1992), cited in note 1, for an extensive bibliography of more general models for valuing loan guarantees.

Table 25.1 ($ Millions)

Gross assets	Customer liabilities	Investor capital	Stand-alone risk capital
BUSINESS 1			
$1,000	$500	$500	$150
BUSINESS 2			
1,000	600	400	200
BUSINESS 3			
1,000	700	300	250
TOTAL			
$3,000	$1,800	$1,200	$600

Table 25.2 Correlation among Businesses

	Business 1	Business 2
Business 2	5	
Business 3	0	0

Business 1 requires substantial amounts of investor capital but relatively little stand-alone risk capital. Business 3 is the riskiest, requiring the most stand-alone risk capital; however, it has the least investor capital. Business 2 is fairly risky and requires a moderate amount of investor capital.

Table 25.2 shows how the profits of the three businesses are correlated. With a correlation coefficient of 0.5, the profit streams of Business 1 and Business 2 are fairly highly correlated. The profits of Business 3, by contrast, are completely uncorrelated with those of Businesses 1 and 2.

Because the businesses are not perfectly correlated with one another, there will be a diversification benefit: the risk of the portfolio of businesses will be less than the sum of the stand-alone risks of the businesses. Risk capital – the value of insurance on the portfolio of assets – will therefore mirror this effect, and the risk capital for the total firm will be less than the sum of the (stand-alone) risk capital necessary to support each of the three businesses. For example, based on the correlations in Table 25.2, the risk capital of the firm can be shown to be $394 million, a 34% reduction relative to the aggregate risk capital on a stand-alone basis (see Technical Appendix).

The reduction in risk capital derives from the interaction among the risks of the individual

businesses. The less-than-perfect correlation among their year-to-year profits leaves room for one business to do well while another does poorly. In effect, the businesses in the portfolio coinsure one another, thus requiring less external asset insurance.

An important implication of this risk-reduction effect is that businesses that would be unprofitable on a stand-alone basis because of high risk-capital requirements might be profitable within a firm that has other businesses with offsetting risks. Thus, the true profitability of individual businesses within the multi-business firm will be distorted if calculated on the basis of stand-alone risk capital. A decision-making process based on this approach will forgo profitable opportunities.

The alternative approach of allocating the risk capital of the combined firm across individual businesses also suffers from this problem. To show why, we examine the *marginal* risk capital required by a business. This can be done by calculating the risk capital required for the firm without this business, and subtracting it from the risk capital required for the full portfolio of businesses. Doing so for the three businesses in our example produces the results in Table 25.3.

The first line of Table 25.3 shows the required risk capital for the combination of all three businesses, taking into account the less than perfect correlations among the businesses. As already noted, this amounts to $394 million. The next three lines of Table 25.3 show the calculation of the marginal risk capital of each business. For example, in the second line, we calculate the required risk capital for a firm composed of just businesses 2 and 3, taking into account the zero correlation between these businesses. It amounts to $320 million. The difference between $320 million and the required risk

Table 25.3

Combination of businesses	Required risk capital for combination	Marginal business	Marginal risk capital
1+2+3	$294		
2+3	320	1	$74
1+3	292	2	102
1+2	304	3	90
	Summation of marginals:		$266

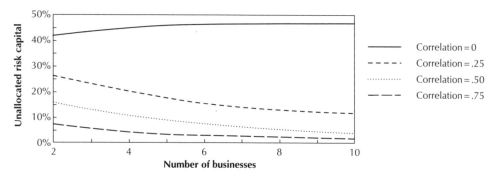

Figure 25.3 Unallocated Risk Capital*

*Percentage of total firm risk capital not accounted for by the marginal risk capital of the individual businesses. Calculations assume businesses are symmetrically correlated and have the same stand-alone risk capital.

capital for all three businesses is $74 million. This is the marginal risk capital for business 1. It is the reduction in risk capital that a firm in businesses 1, 2, and 3 would achieve by exiting business 1; or it is the additional risk capital required for a firm in businesses 2 and 3 to enter business 1.

For the purposes of making the marginal decision, the cost of marginal risk capital should be used. As shown in the last line of Table 25.3, however, the summation of marginal risk capital, $266 million, is only two thirds of the full risk capital of $394 million required for the firm. Thus, if marginal risk capital is used for allocation among businesses, $128 million (32% of total risk capital) will not be allocated to any business.[29]

The discrepancy between the total risk capital of the firm and the sum of the marginal risk capital of its businesses will of course depend on the specifics of those businesses, but it can be very large. Using the aggregate of marginal risk capital, Figure 25.3 illustrates how much of the firm's total risk capital goes unallocated as a function of the number of businesses in the firm, and the correlation among their profits. The analysis assumes that all businesses are the same size (in terms of stand-alone risk capital) and are symmetrically correlated. As

shown in Figure 25.3, the unallocated capital is larger at lower correlations. Only at the extreme of perfect correlation among the businesses is all of the capital allocated. In all other cases, at least some is not allocated. In the case of no correlation among the businesses, for example, the marginal risk capital of the individual businesses can account for as little as 50% of firm risk capital, so that as much as 50% can (and should) go unallocated.

These conclusions hold quite generally. Full allocation of the firm's risk capital overstates the marginal amount of risk capital. And the risk capital of a business evaluated on a stand-alone basis overstates the marginal risk capital by an even greater amount.[30]

Taking into account correlations among profits of individual businesses in capital-budgeting analysis may seem at odds with the traditional CAPM-based notion that the only correlations that matter are those between individual business units and the broad market. Correlations among business units matter here because, by affecting the total amount of risk capital needed to support the businesses, they ultimately affect the total

---

29 "Grossing up" the marginal allocations (by 32 percent in the example) to "fully allocate" the firm's risk capital does not solve the problem. Instead, it overstates the benefits of reductions in risk capital from dropping businesses or not starting new ones.

30 See the Technical Appendix for a formal proof of these propositions. Merton (1993) provides another extensive example. The fact that risk capital cannot be allocated stems from the "externality" arising out of the less-than-perfect correlations among the profits of individual businesses and the asymmetric risk faced by providers of insurance: limited upside and potentially large downside.

economic costs of risk capital. Per our earlier discussion, the economic cost of risk capital is the deadweight loss of spreads. The firm must expect to earn profits in excess of this cost as well as the cost of cash capital, which is the riskless rate of interest.

In traditional capital-budgeting procedures, estimates of cash flow correlations with the market portfolio are used to determine their stand-alone asset values. In our framework, these stand-alone asset values are assumed as given. Hence, correlations of business units with the broad market enter only indirectly – that is, in determining the amount of risk capital. As an insurance premium, risk capital is a function of the riskiness of the net assets as well as the value of the net assets. The *riskiness* of the net assets is affected by correlations among business units; the *value* of net assets is affected by their correlation with the broad market.

SUMMARY AND CONCLUSIONS

Financial firms that act as principal in the ordinary course of business do so in terms of asset-related as well as liability-related activities. Liability-related activities (such as deposit-taking and issuing guarantees like insurance and letters of credit) are mostly customer-driven, which makes such businesses credit-sensitive. Principal activities create a special set of financing, capital budgeting, and risk management decisions for the firm.

We have developed a framework for analyzing those decisions within the principal financial firm. The framework is built around a concept of risk capital, which we define as the smallest amount that can be invested to insure the *net* assets of the firm against loss in value relative to a risk-free investment. Using this definition of risk capital, the paper develops a number of important conclusions:

♦ The amount of risk capital is uniquely determined, and depends only on the riskiness of the net assets. It is not affected by the form of financing of net assets.
♦ Risk capital funds are provided by the firm's residual claimants, usually shareholders (except in the case of extremely highly leveraged firms). Implicitly or explicitly, this capital is used to purchase asset insurance. Potential issuers of asset insurance to the firm are third-party guarantors and the firm's

stakeholders, including customers, debtholders, and shareholders.
♦ The economic costs of risk capital to the firm are the spreads on the price of asset insurance that stem from information costs (adverse selection and moral hazard) and agency costs.
♦ For a given configuration, the risk capital of a multi-business firm is less than the aggregate risk capital of the businesses on a stand-alone basis. Full allocation of risk-capital across the individual businesses of the firm therefore is generally not feasible. Attempts at such a full allocation can significantly distort the true profitability of individual businesses.

Technical Appendix

Calculation of Risk Capital in Table 25.1 and Table 25.3

For a given business, let the value of gross assets at time t be denoted by A_t, and the default-free value of customer liabilities be denoted by L_t, for $0 \leqslant t \leqslant T$. Gross assets and customer liabilities may both have uncertain, contingent payoffs. The value of the net assets at time t is $A_t - L_t$. If the net assets were invested risklessly, they would amount to $(A_0 - L_0)\exp(rT)$ at time T, where r is the continuously-compounded riskless rate of interest. The shortfall in net assets relative to a riskless return is thus $(A_0 - L_0)\exp(rT) - (A_T - L_T)$, so that insurance to permit default-free financing of the net assets must pay $\max\{(A_0 - L_0)\exp(rT) - (A_T - L_T), 0\}$ at time T. This is the same payoff structure as a European put option on the net assets with exercise price $(A_0 - L_0)\exp(rT)$. Under the assumption that the gross assets and customer liabilities both follow geometric Brownian motions, the value of this put option, and hence the amount of risk capital, is given by:

$$\text{Risk Capital} = A_0 F(1,1,0,T,\sigma)$$

where $F(S,E,r,T,\sigma)$ is the Black-Scholes (1973) formula[31] for a European call option on a stock with initial value S, exercise price E, riskless rate r, expiration date T, and volatility σ.[32] Here, σ is the volatility of profits as measured by the volatility of

---

31   Set forth in F. Black and M. Scholes (1973), "The Pricing of Options and Corporate Liabilities," *Journal of Political Economy*, 81 (May–June): 637–654.

percentage changes in the ratio of gross assets to customer liabilities A_t/L_t (or simply the percent volatility of gross assets if customer liabilities are fixed or are non-existent.) As shown by Taylor's expansion for $\sigma\sqrt{t}$ not too large, the formula for risk capital is closely approximated by:

Risk Capital $\approx .4A_0\sigma\sqrt{T}$.

The formula used here for the variance rate of profits for a combination of N businesses is given by $\Sigma\,\Sigma w_i w_j \rho_{ij}\sigma_1\sigma_j$, where ρ_{ij} is the correlation between the profits of businesses i and j, and w_i is the fraction of gross assets in business i. The formula is an approximation that applies exactly only if investments in the businesses are continuously rebalanced so that the volatilities of the profits of the individual businesses maintain their relative proportions over the interval 0 to T. For the purposes here, this approximation has no material effect.

In Table 25.1, the volatility of business profits was assumed to be 37.5%, 50%, and 62.5% per annum, respectively. Using the above variance formula, the volatility of the profits of the combination of three businesses evaluates to 32.75% per annum. This low percentage volatility of the three businesses combined stems directly from the diversification effect. The pairwise combinations show a similar effect.

Table A shows that for the range of parameter values used here the approximation $.4A_0\sigma\sqrt{T}$ is very close to the exact Black-Scholes option value.

The Relationship of Marginal Risk Capital to Combined and Stand-Alone Risk Capital

This section establishes the general propositions that (a) the sum of the risk capital of stand-alone

Table A ($ Millions)

Gross Assets	Standard Deviation (σ)	Approximate Risk Capital ($.4A_0\,\sigma\sqrt{T}$)	"Exact" Risk Capital (Black-Scholes)
BUSINESS 1			
$1,000	37.5%	$150	$148.7
BUSINESS 2			
1,000	50.0%	200	197.4
BUSINESS 3			
1,000	62.5%	250	245.3
BUSINESS 1+2			
2,000	38.0%	304	301.4
BUSINESSES 1+3			
2,000	36.4%	292	288.8
BUSINESS 2+3			
2,000	40.0%	320	317.0
BUSINESS 1+2+3			
3,000	32.8%	394	390.8

businesses exceeds the risk capital of the businesses combined in one firm; and (b) the risk capital of a combination of businesses exceeds the sum of the marginal risk capital of each of those businesses.

As in the first part of this Appendix, let $X = (A_0 - L_0)\exp(rT) - (A_T - L_T)$ be the shortfall (or surplus if it is negative) in the net assets of a business at time T. Let there be N individual businesses, and let X_i be the shortfall for business i. From the above, insurance to permit default-free financing of the net assets of business i must pay $f(X_i) = \max\{X_1, 0\}$ at time T. Note that the function $f(.)$ is convex and satisfies $f(0) = 0$.

The sum of the insurance payoffs to the stand-alone businesses is $\Sigma f(X_i)$, and the insurance pay-off to the combined businesses is $f(\Sigma X_i)$. Since $f(.)$ is convex, we can apply Jensen's inequality to obtain:

$$\Sigma f(X_i) \geqslant f(\Sigma X_i)$$

which establishes the first proposition.[33]

To establish the second proposition, we note that $f(\Sigma_{j \neq i} X_j)$ is the insurance payoff to the firm consisting of all businesses except i. Thus the marginal

---

32 $\sigma^2 = \sigma^2_A + \sigma^2_L - \sigma_A\sigma_L\rho_{AL}$, where σ_A is the volatility of gross asset returns, σ_L is the volatility of customer liability "returns," and ρ_{AL} is the correlation between gross asset returns and customer returns. See Stanley Fischer (1978), "Call Option Pricing When the Exercise Price is Uncertain, and the Valuation of Index Bonds," *Journal of Finance*, 33 (March): 169–176; William Margrabe, 1978), "The Value of an Option to Exchange One Asset for Another," *Journal of Finance*, 33 (March): 177–186; and, especially, René Stulz (1982), "Options on the Minimum or the Maximum of Two Risky Assets: Analysis and Applications," *Journal of Financial Economics*, 10 (July): 161–185.

---

33 This is the well-known proposition that a portfolio of options always returns at least as much as the corresponding option on a portfolio of underlying securities.

insurance payoff for business i is

$$f(\Sigma X_i) - f(\Sigma_{j \neq i} X_j)$$

We now observe the identity:

$$\Sigma X_i = \Sigma_i(\Sigma_{j \neq i} X_j)/(N-1).$$

Therefore, by Jensen's inequality,

$$f(\Sigma X_i) \leq \Sigma_i f\left((\Sigma_{j \neq i} X_j)/(N-1)\right).$$

Applying Jensen's inequality a second time and using the fact that $f(0) = 0$, we obtain

$$(N-1)f(\Sigma X_i) \leq \Sigma_i f(\Sigma_{j \neq i} X_j).$$

from which it follows that

$$Nf(\Sigma X_i) - \Sigma_i f(\Sigma_{j \neq i} X_j) \leq f(\Sigma X_i)$$

or

$$\Sigma_k\{f(\Sigma X_i) - f(\Sigma_{j \neq i} X_j)\} \leq f(\Sigma X_i).$$

This proves that the sum of the marginal insurance payoffs is at most the insurance payoff to the combined firm. Therefore, the risk capital of a combination of businesses exceeds the sum of the marginal risk capital of each of those businesses.

CHAPTER 26

Corporate Insurance Strategy: The Case of British Petroleum

Neil A. Doherty (University of Pennsylvania) and Clifford W. Smith, Jr. (University of Rochester)*

Insurable events such as product liability suits, toxic torts, and physical damage to corporate assets represent major production costs for industrial corporations. For large public companies, conventional practice is to buy insurance to hedge against large potential losses while self-insuring against smaller ones. The underlying logic of this strategy, which is reflected in insurance textbooks,[1] is essentially this: For large and medium-sized corporations, small losses – the kind that stem from localized fires, employee injuries, vehicle crashes, and so forth – occur with such regularity that their total cost is predictable. To the extent such losses are predictable in the aggregate, buying insurance amounts simply to exchanging known dollars of premium for roughly equivalent and relatively known dollars of loss settlements (a practice called "trading dollars" in the profession). Larger losses, by contrast, are rare and much less predictable. Because such losses are borne by the company's owners (mainly by its stockholders but also, if the losses are large enough, by its bondholders), they should be hedged with insurance.

Recently, however, British Petroleum, one of the largest industrial companies in the world, decided upon a major change in its insurance strategy that turns the conventional wisdom on its head. In this article, we analyze why BP now insures against most smaller losses while self-insuring against the larger ones. Our analysis focuses on factors affecting the market *supply* of insurance as well as the corporate demand for it. On the demand side, we demonstrate that the primary source of demand for insurance by widely held public companies is not, as standard insurance textbooks assume, to transfer risk from the corporation's owners, but rather to take advantage of insurance companies' efficiencies in providing risk-assessment, monitoring, and loss-settlement services. On the supply side, we explain why the capacity of insurance markets to underwrite very large (or highly specialized) exposures is quite limited. Given BP's size, when losses become large enough to be of concern, they exceed the capacity of the industry. In essence, BP has a comparative advantage relative to the insurance industry in bearing large losses.

* The authors wish to thank Judith Hanratty and Rodney Insall of British Petroleum for many discussions and insightful comments.

1 See, for example, G.E. Rejda, *Principles of Insurance* (Glenview, Ill.: Scott Foresman, 1989), pp. 52–53; and C.A. Williams, *Risk Management and Insurance* (New York: McGraw Hill, 1989), Chapter 13.

A FRAMEWORK FOR EVALUATING CORPORATE INSURANCE

Before discussing the case of BP, we first provide a general framework for analyzing the corporate insurance decision – one that identifies the benefits and costs of insurance from the perspective of a corporate management intent on maximizing shareholder value.

The important difference between individual and corporate insurance[2]

Let's begin with the simplest case: the purchase of insurance by individuals. Insurance allows individuals to transfer risks to insurance companies, thus reducing uncertainty about their net worth and standard of living. In return for accepting the risk of losses, the insurance company charges a premium. The *expected cost* of the insurance, known as the "premium loading," is the difference between the premium and the present value of expected losses.

The decision to purchase insurance can be justified if the insurance company has a comparative advantage over the policyholder in bearing the risks in question. Such an advantage can derive from two sources: the reduction of risk accomplished by pooling a large portfolio of similar risks and better access to capital markets.

It is not hard to see that, relative to the risk-bearing capacity of insurance companies, the ability of most individuals to self-insure against large risks is quite limited. Private assets are not protected by the "limited liability" provision that shelters other assets of corporate stockholders. Thus, decisions by individuals to pay premiums to insure their hard assets and human capital are economically rational choices based primarily on insurance companies' advantages in pooling such risks.

Private or closely held corporations are likely to purchase insurance for the same reason – namely, their limited ability to bear certain risks relative to the risk-bearing capacity of insurance companies. The owners of such companies often have a large proportion of their wealth tied up in the firm; and, whether out of a desire to maintain control or

some other motive, they choose not to diversify their own holdings fully. For most closely-held and private companies, then, logic and experience tell us that the companies' owners will self-insure only against those risks where they have specialized expertise and, hence, their own kind of comparative advantage.

The case of large, widely held public corporations, however, presents some important differences that standard insurance textbooks fail to acknowledge. The conventional wisdom says, in effect, that because the owners of corporations (their stockholders and bondholders) are individually risk-averse,[3] financial managers should attempt to minimize their exposure to large risks. What this explanation fails to recognize, however, is that the company's stockholders and bondholders generally diversify their own portfolios of corporate securities. In so doing, they effectively diversify away the kinds of risks insurable through insurance companies.

Now, it's true that the stock market effectively assesses corporations a risk premium when setting their minimum required rates of return on capital. In general, the greater a company's risk, the higher the rate of return it must earn, on average, to produce superior returns for its shareholders. But a company's required rate of return (also known as its cost of capital) depends only on its non-diversifiable risk.[4] And because most insurable risks can be readily managed by investors through diversification,

2 This discussion draws heavily on three articles by David Mayers and Clifford Smith, "On the Corporate Demand for Insurance," *Journal of Business* (1982), 281–296; "The Corporate Insurance Decision," *Chase Financial Quarterly* (Spring 1982), 47–65; "Corporate Insurance and the Underinvestment Problem," *Journal of Risk and Insurance*, LIV (1987), 45–54.

3 In the financial economics literature, risk aversion refers to an invidual who prefers the average outcome, or the "expected value" of a gamble, to taking a chance on the distribution of possible outcomes. Thus, a risk-averse individual would pay to get out of a risky situation or, alternatively, would demand a higher rate of return for holding a riskier security.

4 One of the cardinal principles of modern finance is that, on average and over long periods of time, investors both expect and receive rewards commensurate with the risks they bear. As the bulk of the academic evidence also shows, however, average resturns on investment correlate most strongly with systematic or non-diversifiable risk. The measure of this risk, known as "beta," is a measure of the sensitivity of individual stock prices to market-wide and general economic developments; such risk cannot be eliminated by investors' diversification of their holdings. Nor is a company's systematic risk likely to be reduced by purchasing insurance – because insurable risks, to the extent they have no discernible correlation with broad economic cycles, are completely diversifiable for investors.

capital markets will not reward companies for eliminating them.

In short, insurance purchases reduce the expected variance of a company's cash flows, but not its cost of capital. Thus, corporate purchases of insurance intended solely to reduce *investors'* exposures to such risks are negative-NPV projects; the loading built into insurance premiums represents a pure transfer from the company to the insurer.

The real benefits of insurance

Why, then, do large corporations buy insurance? In this section, we describe a number of services and functions performed by insurance companies that provide the basis for a rational corporate demand for insurance – functions having nothing to do with stockholders' risk aversion. As described in sequence below, insurance purchases can increase shareholder value by:

- ♦ avoiding underinvestment and other problems faced by companies whose financial solvency (or even just liquidity) could be threatened by uninsured losses;
- ♦ transferring risk from non-owner corporate stakeholders – managers, employees, suppliers – at a disadvantage in risk-bearing;
- ♦ providing efficiencies in loss assessment, prevention, and claims processing;
- ♦ reducing taxes; and
- ♦ satisfying regulatory requirements.

Avoiding the Underinvestment (and Associated Illiquidity) Problem. Although well-diversified shareholders and bondholders may not be concerned about the prospect of uninsured losses *per se*, they will become concerned if such losses materially raise the probability of financial insolvency. Shareholders are concerned about insolvency mainly because of its potential to cause significant reductions in companies' *operating* values – that is, reductions in the present value of expected operating cash flows.

There are two important things to keep in mind about a firm's operating cash flows in this context. First, large uninsured losses do not in and of themselves reduce ongoing operating values, but should be thought of instead as one-time reductions of a company's equity, or stock of capital (a point we return to below). Second, because operating cash flows are before interest expense, a company's operating value can also be viewed as the sum of the bondholders' and the stockholders' claims on the company. This sharing of value between the two groups can create problems that end up reducing the operating value of the firm.

How does financial trouble, or just the prospect of trouble, reduce a company's operating value? To begin with the extreme case, companies that wind up in Chapter 11 face considerable interference from the bankruptcy court with their investment and operating decisions, not to mention substantial direct costs of administration and reorganization. But, even short of bankruptcy, financial difficulty can impose large indirect costs. One important source of such costs is a potential "underinvestment problem." This problem arises from conflicts of interest between stockholders and bondholders in companies with significant amounts of debt. As the example below illustrates, insurance can help manage this problem.

Consider a company with a large amount of debt outstanding that chooses not to purchase fire insurance for its plants. Suppose also that a large and highly profitable plant is destroyed at a time when a downturn in operating cash flow has depleted the company's cash reserves and driven down its stock price.

The company is then faced with a potentially difficult reinvestment decision – that is, whether and, if so, when to rebuild the plant. In these circumstances, the large casualty loss has the effect of cutting further into the firm's already deflated equity cushion, and so further raising its effective leverage ratio. This, needless to say, would be a difficult time for management to approach capital markets for funding.

In this situation, if the company's debt burden is heavy enough, a management acting on behalf of its shareholders would have an incentive to pass up

---

To the extent insurable losses do represent systematic risk, insurance will reduce the firm's cost of capital. But then insurance premiums paid must include an appropriate risk premium, which will offset any possible gain in terms of the firm's discount rate associated with competitively priced insurance. (See N.A. Doherty and S.M. Tinic. "A Note on Reinsurance under Conditions of Capital Market Equilibrium," *Journal of Finance*, 36 (1982) 949–953.)

such a positive-NPV investment. As Stewart Myers demonstrated years ago,[5] this would be a rational decision (not just the result of managerial short-sightedness) if enough of the value of the new investment went to shoring up the bondholders' position. The new equity issue would amount to a major wealth transfer from stockholders to bond-holders – and a shareholder-wealth-maximizing management would thus choose either not to rebuild the plant, or to defer it, thereby reducing overall firm value.[6]

Even if stockholders would end up sharing some of the benefits from reinvestment, such a severe liquidity problem could still tempt management to defer raising capital until the company's stock price increased. But, in this case, there would be a significant loss in operating value as a consequence of deferring the investment.

Now let's go back to the beginning of this story and assume that management instead purchases fire insurance. (In fact, debt covenants typically *require* companies to buy such insurance – in part to control this underinvestment incentive.) In that case, insurance effectively serves as a funding source. If the loss is large and the facilities must be replaced quickly, it provides a "leverage-neutral" source of financing that permits the company to avoid the costs of a hurried new issue. In so doing, insurance reduces the likelihood that management is confronted with this kind of decision.

A Note on Insurance and Capital Structure. An alternative solution to this under-investment problem, of course, would be to reduce

the amount of corporate debt. Indeed, one could argue that, as a general rule, corporate decisions to retain large exposures effectively reduce the optimal amount of debt – and, conversely, insurance purchases increase corporate debt capacity. But this conclusion, though correct as far as it goes, obscures an important feature of large casualty losses – their infrequency. Large uninsured losses, as suggested above, do not reduce ongoing operating values, but represent instead one-time reductions of a company's equity cushion. A company that chooses to self-insure such large exposures is thus making a decision that affects the adequacy of its *stock* of capital – including its ability to raise additional funds on short notice – rather than its ability to service a predictable *flow* of interest and principal payments out of regular operating cash flows.

Because large exposures are by definition infrequent events, an alternative way to manage them would be to arrange lines of credit available specifically in the event of a large uninsured loss. Such lines of credit, at least for larger, more creditworthy companies that can obtain them at reasonable cost, potentially provide a more economical, custom-tailored solution to the problem of insuring against extreme illiquidity – while allowing the firm to use its remaining debt capacity more effectively.

For smaller companies, however, insurance is likely to be more valuable. To the extent such companies have lower liquidity and face higher transactions costs for new issues, they will find insurance to be both a lower-cost funding source and an indispensable means of increasing their corporate debt capacity.

Riskshifting Within the Firm. Up to this point, we have viewed the corporation from the perspective of its investors and owners. Of course, the corporation is a vast network of contracts among various parties with conflicting as well as common interests. In addition to bondholders and stockholders, other corporate constituencies such as employees, managers, suppliers, and customers all have vested interests in the company's success.

Like the owners of private or closely-held companies, the corporation's managers, employees, suppliers, and customers may not be able to diversify insurable risks; and such risks, if not insured, can affect their future payoffs under their respective contracts. (In many cases, of course, these contracts are implied rather than explicit.) Because they are

5 More technically, insurance controls an aspect of Stewart Myers' underinvestment problem involving the joint effect of risk, limited liability, and leverage on project selection (see S.C. Myers, "Determinants of Corporate Borrowing," *Journal of Financial Economics*, 5 (1977), 147–176). With debt in the capital structure, the firm's stockholders can face incentives to turn down positive-NPV projects. An uninsured casualty loss reduces firm value, increasing the firm's leverage and thereby exacerbating this incentive. Such behavior is anticipated by rational bondholders and will be reflected *ex ante* in the bond price. Thus the loss of value from distortions in project selection falls *ex ante* on shareholders. For a discussion of [how] insurance can control such incentives, see Mayers and Smith (1987), cited in note 2.
6 Such stories can be told about corporate decisions to invest in routine maintenance and safety projects; in highly leveraged or financially distressed firms, insurance purchases effectively force managements to make necessary maintenance investments by reducing their cash premiums for so doing.

also risk-averse, these groups are likely to require extra compensation to bear any risk not assumed by the owners or transferred to an insurance company. Employees will demand higher wages (or reduce their loyalty or perhaps their work effort) at a company where the probability of layoff is greater. Managers with alternative opportunities will demand higher salaries (or maybe an equity stake in the company) to run firms where the risks of insolvency and financial embarrassment are significant. Suppliers will be more reluctant to enter into long-term contracts, and trade creditors will charge more and be less flexible, with companies whose prospects are more uncertain. And customers concerned about the company's ability to fulfil warranty obligations or service their products in the future may be reluctant to buy those products.

Because of limited liability, the amount of risk that can be allocated to the stockholders is limited by the capital stock of the company. Companies in service industries, for instance, are often thinly capitalized. And, for such companies, where the claims – and thus the risks – of managers and employees are likely to be very large relative to the claims of investors, there may be substantial benefits from transferring those risks to an insurance company.

Even if companies self-insure, the above argument can also be extended to the design of *management compensation* contracts. Effective compensation plans achieve an appropriate balance between two partly conflicting aims: strengthening managers' performance incentives and insulating them from risks beyond their control. Incentive considerations require that compensation be linked to performance measures such as share price and earnings. A potential problem with such performance proxies is that they contain significant variation (or "noise") that is unrelated to management's performance. Because uninsured losses are a potential source of such noise, companies may achieve economies in risk-bearing by excluding uninsured losses from performance measures that serve as the basis for managerial evaluations and bonuses. In so doing, though, companies should be mindful of avoidable losses and ensure that managers still have strong incentives to take sensible measures to control such risks.

Service Efficiencies. Besides transferring risk, insurance companies often provide a set of related services – and at a significantly lower cost than offered elsewhere. One obvious example, as mentioned earlier, is insurers' comparative advantage in processing and settling claims, an advantage that derives from specialization and economies of scale. Thus, we would expect part of the corporate demand for insurance to be explained by insurers' expertise and efficiency in providing low-cost claims administration.[7]

Other services for which insurance companies are likely to have a comparative advantage are the assessment of loss exposures (more precisely, estimation of the parameters of the loss distribution) and the design, administration, and auditing of safety and other loss-control programs. Although these services are occasionally priced and sold separately, they are typically bundled with insurance. When insurers accumulate large numbers of exposures, they not only reduce risks through pooling, but also achieve economies of scale and other benefits from specialization that economists typically refer to as "organizational capital."

The most tangible aspect of this organizational capital is the large data base built up by an insurance company over years of underwriting. The data base allows for extensive and precise actuarial analysis, which in turn enables the insurer to estimate and classify individual exposures more accurately and price their products appropriately.[8] Indeed, this data base constitutes one of an insurer's principal comparative advantages over its policyholders in insuring many corporate risks – namely, its greater confidence in forecasting its policyholder's loss distribution for events such as fires, vehicle collisions, and workers' injuries.

In general, then, it is the frequency of events that makes them amenable to statistical analysis. But, for

---

7 A striking confirmation of this general argument is the existence of "claims only" insurance contracts – those in which the insurance company provides only claims-management services while the insured firm pays all the claims. Claims only policies, moreover, represent only an extreme of a spectrum of insurance policies that allow the insured company to maintain a degree of self-insurance. More often employed are policies that use retrospective ratings that continually adjust the premium to reflect actual claims experience over the life of the policy. This means the insured is effectively bearing most of the risk of claims losses.
8 From the insurer's perspective, this is necessary to quote competitive insurance premiums. Failure of an insurer to categorize individuals accurately by loss expectation leads to adverse selection by policyholders.

exposures in which new or specialized technology is employed – especially if losses are infrequent – more subjective and hence less precise estimation techniques such as engineering risk assessment must take the place of statistical analysis. In these cases, the industrial companies that have developed the new technology can generally use their own organizational capital to assess the risks posed by the technology. (Also, if the company is better able to assess the risk than the insurer, adverse selection becomes a serious problem – a point we discuss below.) Hence, insurance companies are likely to operate at a competitive disadvantage in indemnifying those companies for such risks. In this sense, insurance companies' inability to apply actuarial analysis to the pricing of their products helps to define the limits of the insurance industry's products.

Similar issues of comparative advantage arise in connection with safety, loss control, and loss prevention. Insurers data bases permit them to identify common types of accidents, often enabling them to advise clients as to potential sources of risk and cost-effective means of reducing expected losses. Some specialist insurers – factory mutual insurance firms, for example – focus as much on safety audits as on the provision of insurance services. As suggested above, however, the more specialized and complex the technology, the more likely is the producer, not the insurer, to have a comparative advantage in designing and implementing a loss-prevention program. In such cases, producers are likely to perform these functions themselves.

One specific area, however, in which insurers are almost certain to have superior expertise is the defense of lawsuits. Access to the insurer's lawyers and other defense resources can reduce the expected costs of third-party liability claims. Insurers regularly defend such cases, whereas individual policyholders see them infrequently. Moreover, the adverse reputation effects that could come from vigorous defense of a lawsuit are partly shifted to the insurer that effectively conducts the case. This is particularly useful in cases where third-party claimants have a continuing relationship with the firm, as in the case of workers-compensation or product-liability claims.

Tax Benefits. The tax benefits of corporate insurance derive from the interaction of two factors: (1) the ability of corporate insurance to reduce the volatility of reported income and (2) the effective progressivity of most of the world's tax codes.

In the United States, and most other jurisdictions throughout the world, tax codes permit the deduction of both insurance premiums and of uninsured losses. Given (1) a constant marginal tax rate and (2) actuarially fair premiums, such provisions would have a neutral effect on the decision to purchase insurance. That is, the expected present value of tax deductions would be the same with insurance as without.

In practice, however, the marginal tax rate in the U.S. (and in most other jurisdictions) is not constant, but rather "convex"; that is, a company's effective tax rate rises along with increases in pre-tax income. Increasing marginal tax rates, tax shields such as depreciation allowances and interest expense, the inability to earn interest on tax-loss carry forwards, and the alternative minimum tax all work together to impose higher effective rates of taxation on higher levels of reported income and to provide lower percentage rebates for ever larger losses. Given U.S. tax treatment of insurance premiums and uninsured losses, the reductions in the volatility of taxable income resulting from insurance effectively reduce corporate taxes.

In the case of multinational corporations, tax liabilities are imposed by a number of different jurisdictions (the various countries in which they operate). Reductions in the expected tax liabilities in different jurisdictions can reduce expected taxes incurred in each, thereby reducing a multinational's overall worldwide taxes. For this reason, local purchases of insurance can add value by reducing expected local tax obligations, although they have little or no effect on the risk of aggregate corporate income.

Regulatory Requirements. Financial-responsibility laws sometimes require insurance coverage. For example, many jurisdictions require that an operator of motor vehicles have insurance or other evidence of financial capability to discharge third-party liability claims. Similar requirements are often found in workers-compensation insurance. A further example in the U.S. is the financial-responsibility requirement associated with handling hazardous materials under the Resource Control and Recovery Act of 1976.

These requirements are generally modest relative to the resources of medium to large companies. For example, in the U.S. the requirement for automobile liability insurance is typically in the range of $30,000 to $50,000. Such regulatory requirements tend to increase the demand for insurance covering relatively small losses.

The supply side of corporate insurance

As stated earlier, the gross profit to an insurer from underwriting a given policy, known as the premium loading, is defined as the difference between the expected loss and the premium. The insurance premium can be further decomposed into the expected indemnity payment, administrative costs (including the costs of providing services), a normal profit, and any rent, or "abnormal profit," that might be captured by the insurer.

Thus, some elements of the loading are not a cost to the policyholder – for example, the expected cost of various services bundled with the coverage. But other parts of the loading represent a transfer to the insurer and thus deter the purchase of insurance. This is true not only of insurer rents, but also of the component of expected indemnity payments attributable to moral hazard and adverse selection – two well-known problems confronting insurance underwriters that we discuss below. These factors affect the comparative advantage of insurance versus other risk-management strategies.

Effective Competition. Expected rents depend on the degree of competition. Some sectors of the insurance market are highly competitive; barriers to entry are low, insurers sell large numbers of homogenous policies with low correlation among payoffs, and expected losses are easily estimated. Since aggregate losses are fairly predictable, relatively little capital is required to ensure the solvency and maintain the creditworthiness of the insurer. Moreover, the routine nature of the business and the presence of established independent selling networks – that is, independent agents and brokers – serve to reduce the required investment in underwriters, actuaries, engineers, and individuals with other technical skills. Such markets include those for routine small property and liability losses incurred by large companies[9] as well as various kinds of insurance for small businesses and individuals.

In contrast, the markets for large losses and for certain specialized risks are characterized by significantly less competition. For example, writing pollution insurance requires a large investment in the ability to provide environmental audits and risk assessment; there are few U.S. insurers active in this market (A.I.G. and Reliance are the two best-known). There are also few insurers that offer coverage of very large exposures. Such business requires a large surplus – that is, equity – and substantial investment in establishing reinsurance facilities. Such an investment can be viewed as necessary reputational capital. Success in selling policies for such large exposures depends critically on the insurer's ability to assure the insured that the contract will be honored if losses occur. A large stock of equity capital may be the only credible means of backing that promise.

A significant portion of worldwide capacity for insuring very large and unusual exposures is provided by Lloyd's of London. In part, this is due to its distinctive organizational form. With unlimited liability, Lloyd's syndicates have additional implicit reserves in the form of a call on the wealth of their members. But since the value of this call depends on the net worth of the members, the ultimate capacity of Lloyd's is limited.[10] Thus, the markets for pollution and other unusual lines of insurance, for high-risk lines, and for very high levels of all lines of insurance are characterized by less competition and higher expected insurer rents.

The effective supply of insurance coverage is not limited by the financial capability of *individual* insurers. Insurance is commonly syndicated among several insurers. Alternatively, policyholders can "layer" insurance protection by purchasing separate policies from several insurers (known as "surplus-lines" insurers). In yet another alternative,

---

owning 4,000 stores. It might further improve its diversification by insuring the smaller losses on much bigger risks, small fire losses (not exceeding $500,000) on department stores, electronics manufacturers, etc.

10   There is also some question concerning the enforceability of claims against members' wealth. Following recent catastrophic loss experience in a number of syndicates, Lloyds is facing a number of lawsuits from members who are alleging negligent underwriting and challenging the call on their wealth.

---

9   For example, the fire insurer insuring 5,000 independently owned retail grocery stores will significantly improve its diversification by insuring one additional policyholder which is a chain

the capacity of individual insurers can be extended by selling secondary claims on some of its policies – or on its entire portfolio – in the reinsurance market. In most cases, some combination of these mechanisms is used to spread coverage over the market through a complex network.

Yet, in spite of these possibilities for combining insurer capacity, there are still limits to the amount of insurance protection available in the marketplace for certain kinds of exposures. For example, it is difficult to place insurance for exposures in excess of $500 million, and virtually impossible to find protection for exposures in excess of $1 billion, even on restricted terms.

Even for policies well under $500 million, the "quality" of insurance is not constant. In insurance markets, the expected value of coverage falls with the size of the claim for a number of reasons. First, a large claim can cause an insurer to become insolvent, and insurance contracts are not fully enforceable against an insolvent insurer. Even if large claims do not trigger insolvency, they often cause significant financial difficulty for insurers, especially in the surplus-lines market where the variance of claims is usually high relative to the insurer's surplus (equity). Enforcing contracts against such insurers can be very costly since they can dispute their obligations under the contract and otherwise delay settlements. The costs of enforcing contracts include legal costs of the actions as well as increases in the costs of writing future contracts because reputational capital has depreciated. These problems can be particularly acute since the expected adverse reputation consequences of disputing claims are less of a restraint on an insurer facing a higher probability of insolvency.

Moral Hazard and Adverse Selection. Moral hazard and adverse selection arise naturally in insurance markets. Moral hazard – loosely speaking, the tendency for insured parties to exercise less care and thus to experience greater losses than the uninsured – is one factor that works against insurance purchase by all potential policyholders. The expected costs of the average policyholder's actions will be built into the insurance premium. Adverse selection – the likelihood that insurers will get a riskier-than-average sample, given the tendency of less risky parties to self-insure – discourages the purchase of insurance by those policyholders that are of low risk relative to their class. The industry

practice of "experience rating" – in which the premiums for future insurance contracts are based on prior claim experience – is widely used to control moral hazard and adverse selection problems. In the case of insurable risks involving frequent losses, experience rating is an especially effective control device: it motivates the policyholder to reduce the risk of losses, thereby reducing moral hazard; and it quickly reveals loss characteristics, thus reducing the costs of adverse selection.

When losses are infrequent, however, experience rating is less useful. Simply because large losses occur much less often than small ones, the costs of adverse selection and moral hazard built into the premiums of very large insurance policies tend to be much larger than the same costs confronting purchasers of small policies.

THE CASE OF BRITISH PETROLEUM

BP comprises four operating companies. BP Exploration is the upstream company, which is responsible for exploration and development of new oil and gas resources. BP Oil is the downstream business, whose activities include refining, distribution, and retailing of petroleum products. The remaining two companies are BP Chemicals, which concentrates in petrochemicals, acetyl, and nitrates, and BP Nutrition, a relatively small company in the animal-feed business.

Perhaps the most striking feature of BP is its size. It is the largest company in the U.K., and the second largest in Europe. BP's equity capital is approximately $35 billion, and its debt is approximately $15 billion. After-tax profit has averaged $1.9 billion over the previous five years with a standard deviation of $1.1 billion.[11]

BP's major assets include exploration and extraction licenses, and scientific and technical capital specific to the oil industry in the form of rigs, pipelines, refineries, ships, road tankers and filling stations. While the company has operations worldwide (for example, it has some 13,000 service

---

11   These numbers reflect BP's balance sheet and income statement as of year-end 1991, the last full year for which data were available when the authors were assisting in the analysis of the company's insurance strategy.

Table 26.1   Actuary's Estimate of BP's Loss Distribution at 1990 (Millions of Dollars)

Loss range	Number per year	Average loss	Expected annual loss	Standard deviation
$0–$10	1845.00	$0.03	$52	$12
$10–$500	1.70	40.00	70	98
$500 plus	0.03	1000.00	35	233
Whole Distribution	1846.73	$0.66	$157	

Note: This table covers all insurable losses whether or not they were previously insured.

stations in some 50 countries), it has two major concentrations of value: its production licenses and its facilities in the North Sea and on the Alaska North Slope. This concentration of value, together with the limited range of the company's activities, imply that significant aspects of its business risk are relatively undiversified.

BP's loss exposures

BP's loss exposure ranges from routine small losses to potential losses in the multi-billion-dollar range. At the low end of this scale, there are vehicle accidents, minor shipping accidents, industrial injuries, small fires, and equipment failures. On a larger scale, potential losses include refinery fires or explosions, minor environmental damage from oil spills, and loss of (nautical) oil tankers. Very large losses could result from clean-up costs arising from major oil spills, tort claims for widespread injuries caused by release of toxic chemicals, liability for defective fuel causing a major airline disaster, and loss of an offshore rig with major loss of life (as in the Piper Alpha case). Perhaps one of the largest foreseeable losses to an oil firm would be the withdrawal of operating licenses as a consequence of political backlash in response to environmental damage.

BP employed independent actuarial consultants to estimate its loss distribution. The actuaries had access to extensive industry and BP loss data. Table 26.1 provides a summary of BP's estimated loss exposure – one that is based not only on BP's experience but also on that of other firms in the oil and chemical industries.[12]

A comparison of these figures with other BP financial statistics provides some useful insights. For example, assuming a corporate tax rate of 35%, an uninsured pretax loss of $500 million represents less than a 1% reduction of the market value of BP equity; it also amounts to only 17% of average annual after-tax earnings over the last five years, and about 30% of the standard deviation of average earnings.

Historically, BP has insured its property and liability exposures. It has also insured, to a very limited extent, business-interruption exposures where insurance coverage has been available. Liability insurance and business-interruption insurance has been placed largely with external insurers, though some insurance has been purchased from an oil-industry mutual called O.I.L. (of which BP was a joint owner). O.I.L. in turn reinsures the upper tail of its exposures. Some property has been insured directly by independent insurers, other property through a captive insurer, which also reinsures.

Thus, in the past, BP has purchased considerable external insurance protection. Virtually all of this insurance covers the first two loss ranges – those under $10 million and those between $10 and $500 million – and most has been in the $10–$500 million category. With only one or two exceptions, insurance has been unavailable above $500 million, and BP has historically self-insured in this range.

Using the cost-benefit framework presented earlier in this article, BP recently undertook

---

12   Curve fitting permits estimation of the tail of the loss distribution despite the absence (or virtual absence) of very large

losses in the loss record. Distributions such as the compound poisson are found to fit reasonably well. In addition, loss scenarios are constructed for possible large and unusual events that are not in the loss record but which nevertheless are considered to be feasible. (Note also that it would be rare for an insurer to undertake a study of this intensity to estimate the loss distribution for an individual client.)

a comprehensive re-examination of its insurance strategy. In the pages that follow, we describe BP's new approach to each of the three loss categories.

Coverage for losses below $10 million

Under the new approach, losses below $10 million are now the responsibility of the managers of the local operating unit. (Such decisions were previously made by BP's insurance subsidiary.) Where there is a demonstrable need for insurance, local managers may buy it from BP's captive insurer or seek competitive quotations in local markets.

Expected changes in firm value (and leverage ratios) resulting from uninsured losses at this level are small. The standard deviation of after-tax earnings for BP exceeds $1 billion. In comparison, self-insuring losses under $10 million increases the standard deviation of earnings by only $12 million. Thus, the expected benefits of insurance in controlling financial-distress costs are trivial at this level.

The decision to allow local managers to insure small losses reflects other considerations:

♦ Because markets for losses at this level are very competitive, market forces effectively eliminate expected insurer rents.
♦ Insurers have a comparative advantage in service-provision activities such as claims administration. Because losses within this range are frequent and routine, insurers have an informational advantage in loss assessment and control, and contract enforcement is reliable.
♦ Insurance coverage satisfies local financial-responsibility requirements.
♦ Insurance reduces noise in the performance measures employed for local managers, producing stronger incentives for good performance.
♦ Because of the localized nature of some of BP's tax liabilities, there are potential tax-related benefits of insurance.

Coverage for losses between $10 million and $500 million

Losses above $10 million are not to be insured using external insurance markets except in specific

circumstances (for example, in cases where insurance is required under existing bond indentures or joint-venture provisions). This represents a major change in policy, since most of the company's losses in the $10–$500 million range were previously insured. This strategy change reflects the following considerations:

♦ At this level, effective competition in insurance markets is limited.
♦ The costs of enforcing contracts are high.
♦ Over this range of losses, insurers do not have a comparative advantage in supplying safety and other services that are bundled with financial indemnification.
♦ The impact of such losses on total corporate value is quite limited (as shown in Table 26.1, self-insuring losses between $10 million and $500 million increases the standard deviation of annual earnings (and cash flow) by only $98 million).

Over the ten-year period ending in 1989, BP paid $1.15 billion in premiums and recovered $250 million in claims (both in present values). In effect, this amounts to a 360% loading on realized losses. This loading can be broken down into several components: (1) a reserve against catastrophe losses, (2) a payment for bundled insurance services, and (3) a payment for transaction costs, and (4) rents for the insurer. Transaction costs and bundled services typically account for 10% to 30% of premiums. We doubt that the size of this loading can be explained as a catastrophe reserve. The difference of $900 million between premiums and losses is simply too large to be accounted for by the prospect of large losses that, owing to chance, failed to materialize over the ten-year span.[13]

---

13 Suppose the total premiums paid, $1.15 billion (present values), were competitively priced in the sense that they represent the expected value of losses of $880 million plus a typical expense loading of about 20%. We can approximate this as a sequence of ten annual expected losses each having a present value of $88 million. (We cannot compare this $88 million directly with the Table 26.1 estimate of $70 million for second-tier losses since not all losses in this tier were insured.) If we use the coefficient of variation from the second tier in the table (1.4), this yields an estimate for the standard deviation of annual aggregate losses actually insured of $108.4 million. If losses are time independent, the standard deviation of the aggregate losses

Thus, we can only conclude that insurers received extraordinary rents in insuring these losses.

The explanation for this rent is found partly in the limited competition in this market. Few insurers are willing to make a market in risks the size and nature of BP's. Much of the market capacity, as mentioned earlier, is provided by Lloyd's syndicates. A large loss, however, would have a material impact on Lloyd's financial position. For example, a $500 million loss would amount to about 8% of Lloyd's total annual premia, 90% of profits, and 4% of surplus. Moreover, these statistics reflect the combined numbers of all Lloyd's syndicates, even though only a subset made a market for BP. In short, the potential for a large loss to impose financial stress on BP's insurers is great.

This problem arising from limited competition is aggravated by several contractual and institutional features of insurance markets.

Enforcement Costs. In the case of large losses, enforcement problems are higher due to the low frequency of such losses, which in turn reduces the effectiveness of reputational restraints on opportunistic behavior by insurers. To illustrate potential enforcement costs, consider that in the only large liability loss BP has filed with its insurers, settlement with the insurers was not reached until several years after settlement with the plaintiff. The insurance settlement, moreover, was only 70% of the liability claim; and, to secure this 70%, BP estimated that its expenses, legal costs, and management time in resolving this dispute amounted to approximately $1 million.

There are good reasons to view this as a representative rather than an unusual experience. Small losses occur routinely but large losses are rare. Indeed, the data in Table 26.1 contain the implication that losses greater than $500 million occur only about once every 30 years. Although insurers are

unlikely to sacrifice their reputational investments with clients for modest savings in disputing small claims, concerns about reputation are a much less effective restraint on insurers' opportunism when faced with large, infrequent losses.

Small losses also tend to come from repetitions of similar events such as damage to cars at autowashers, customer accidents, or crashes of road tankers. Given the large body of accumulated experience in negotiating past claim settlements and the experience of courts in interpreting contracts, there is little room for disagreement on coverage. Larger losses, by contrast, often present unusual facts and challenges for which there is little experience. The scope for different legal interpretations and, hence, the expected enforcement costs are correspondingly larger.

For large losses, the unlimited liability structure of the Lloyd's syndicates can make contract enforcement difficult. Lloyd's closes its accounts after three years and distributes surplus. Thus, much of a syndicate's reserves for long-gestation losses, such as liability claims, takes the form of a call on the personal wealth of the underwriting members. In recent years, attempts to recover deficits from members have met legal challenges (such as malpractice suits against the underwriter). Costly access to reserves and surplus raises expected enforcement costs.

The potential for dispute under large claims can be further increased by insurers' practice of laying off risks through the purchase of reinsurance. If a primary insurer disputes a claim and loses the ensuing litigation, the primary insurer must settle the claim to its policyholder and the reinsurer is then bound to the primary firm. However, if the primary settles a claim without a challenge, but the reinsurer considers that the loss was not covered by the primary contract language, the reinsurer might dispute its settlement to the primary. Consequently, when deciding whether to settle or fight claims, primary firms have to anticipate both the chances of being successful in litigation with their policyholder and whether they can bind their reinsurer in any settlement. (Similarly, the threat of legal challenges to syndicates at Lloyds from their members may act as an important factor in resisting settlements.) Since large losses generally involve reinsurance contracts, this further raises enforcement costs for large losses.

---

for the ten-year period is $[(10)\,(108.4)^2]^{1/2;} = \$342$ million. The realized losses for the period are $250 million, which is 1.84 standard deviations below the assumed total expected losses of $880 million. Using standard normal tables, there is only a 0.033 chance that revealed losses could be that low. This estimate is conservative since the loss distribution is skewed to the right. For such cases, use of the standard normal table will normally overestimate the probability mass in the left hand tail and underestimate the mass in the right tail.

Comparative Advantage in Risk Assessment. In operating its production, refining, and distribution activities, BP has considerable engineering and related skills. These are put to further use in safety programs that relate to design of facilities, inspection, *post mortem* on actual losses, and analysis of loss records. Given the scale and specialized nature of its operations, BP has a comparative advantage over its insurers in providing these services.

Management Incentives and Self-Insurance. The decision to self-insure against losses within this range has, however, created one problem that management has chosen to address. Uninsured losses, while posing little risk to aggregate firm value, can introduce significant "noise" into local and regional performance measures. Because such losses are infrequent and discrete events, the corporation has adopted a policy of eliminating this noise from performance measures on an *ad hoc* basis. That is, losses will not be charged against profit centers – and thereby reduce management bonuses – except insofar as the loss reflects poor management (say, a failure to enforce adequate safety standards).

Coverage for losses above $500 million

BP has chosen to continue self-insuring very large losses – primarily for supply considerations: As the size of the loss becomes material for BP, it exceeds the capacity of the insurance market.

Such expected losses, moreover, are not necessarily as large as they look because of what amount to generous co-insurance provisions in many countries' tax codes, especially the U.K.'s. Uninsured casualty losses generate tax shields, thus allowing BP to share these losses with the tax authorities. The tax code thus provides an implicit insurance policy with a coinsurance rate equal to the effective tax rate.

Losses greater than $500 million are most likely to occur in BP's two major geographical concentrations, the North Sea and the North Slope of Alaska. BP's effective tax rate for income from its North Sea production is 87%. Thus a $2 billion North Sea loss would result in only a $260 million reduction in firm value (and the expected cost of negotiation with the Inland Revenue Service over

the tax treatment for losses in this range appears modest).

Another consideration reinforcing BP's decision to self-insure very large losses is that such losses could actually lead to increases in oil prices. For example, an oilrig fire of the magnitude of the Piper Alpha disaster in the North Sea could result in new safety regulations; or a large tanker spill like the one experienced by the Exxon Valdez in Alaska could lead to the withdrawal of operating licenses. Because BP has what amounts to a very large long position in oil, the expected price increases from such supply reductions reduce BP's net exposure.

Work in progress

To manage its remaining exposure more effectively, BP is considering some additional adjustments. As one example, the three-tiered insurance strategy described above makes use of the tendency for both the costs and the benefits of insurance to increase with loss size. The tax effects just noted, however, suggest the need for some refinement of this strategy. Given the wide variation in marginal tax rates for different jurisdictions (ranging from zero to the 87% rate for North Sea production), losses of the same pre-tax value can result in widely different after-tax costs to BP. The initial allocation of exposures to the various tiers was based on pre-tax losses. This strategy is being fine-tuned to reflect after-tax costs.

A second issue to be examined more carefully is the effect of self-insurance on BP's optimal capital structure. As we observed earlier, the expected costs of financial distress can be reduced by combining a policy of self-insurance with lower financial leverage. However, the use of dedicated standby lines of credit, especially in the case of a large, creditworthy firm like BP, can be used to provide additional liquidity while limiting the required reduction in financial leverage.

In addition to lines of credit, financial instruments that include financial "shock absorbers" could also be used to lower the cost of an uninsured casualty loss. Consider, for example, the effect of substituting a convertible for a straight bond issue. A convertible bond gives bondholders, in effect, both a non-convertible bond and a call option on the stock. In return for this option, bondholders reduce the rate of interest on the bonds, thereby reducing the probability of financial difficulty.

CONCLUSION

British Petroleum, one of the largest industrial companies in the world, recently revised its corporate insurance strategy in a way that stands the conventional wisdom on its head. This change reflects recent developments in the theory of corporate finance and applications of the theory to the practice of corporate risk management.

In the past decade, financial economists have begun to re-examine the benefits and costs of corporate risk management from a shareholder-value perspective. To date, academic attention has been focused almost entirely on factors affecting the corporate *demand* for risk management products. But, in our analysis of British Petroleum's recent and marked shift in insurance strategy, we demonstrate that this new approach also depends critically on supply considerations across different sizes of potential claims.

Based on this supply-side analysis of the insurance industry as well as distinctive aspects of the *corporate* demand for insurance, this very large public company reached the conclusion that it has a substantial comparative advantage over the insurance industry in bearing the risk of its largest exposures. For this reason, BP purchases coverage only for their smallest tier of losses (under $10 million). Even in these cases, the primary motive for buying insurance is not to transfer risk, but rather to exploit the insurance industry's comparative efficiency in providing risk-assessment and claims-administration services.

Having completed and acted upon this rethinking of its insurance strategy, BP is now in the process of reviewing the way it manages its other significant exposures. In addition to property and casualty risks, oil price changes, currency fluctuations, and interest rate changes all affect the value of BP in fairly systematic ways, thus imposing risk. Over the past decade, hedging instruments such as exchange-traded futures and options and over-the-counter swaps have become available to manage these kinds of exposures. In an effort to formulate a comprehensive risk management strategy, BP is extending the analytical framework described here to weigh the benefits of managing such financial risks against the costs associated with these other forms of insurance.

CHAPTER 27

Value at Risk: Uses and Abuses

Christopher L. Culp (CP Risk Management LLC),
Merton H. Miller (University of Chicago)
and Andrea M. P. Neves (CP Risk Management LLC)*

Value at risk ("VAR") is now viewed by many as indispensable ammunition in any serious corporate risk manager's arsenal. VAR is a method of measuring the financial risk of an asset, portfolio, or exposure over some specified period of time. Its attraction stems from its ease of interpretation as a summary measure of risk and consistent treatment of risk across different financial instruments and business activities. VAR is often used as an approximation of the "maximum reasonable loss" a company can expect to realize from all its financial exposures.

VAR has received widespread accolades from industry and regulators alike.[1] Numerous organizations have found that the practical uses and benefits of VAR make it a valuable decision support tool in a comprehensive risk management process. Despite its many uses, however, VAR – like any statistical aggregate – is subject to the risk of misinterpretation and misapplication. Indeed, most problems with VAR seem to arise from what a firm *does* with a VAR measure rather than from the actual computation of the number.

Why a company manages risk affects *how* a company should manage – and, hence, should measure – its risk.[2] In that connection, we examine the four "great derivatives disasters" of 1993–1995 – Procter & Gamble, Barings, Orange County, and Metallgesellschaft – and evaluate how *ex ante* VAR measurements likely would have affected those situations. We conclude that VAR would have been of only limited value in averting those disasters and, indeed, actually might have been *misleading* in some of them.

WHAT IS VAR?

Value at risk is a summary statistic that quantifies the exposure of an asset or portfolio to market risk,

* The authors thank Kamaryn Tanner for her previous work with us on this subject.

1 *See, for example*, Global Derivatives Study Group, *Derivatives: Practices and Principles* (Washington, D.C.: July 1993), and Board of Governors of the Federal Reserve System, *SR Letter 93-69* (1993). Most recently, the Securities and Exchange Commission began to require risk disclosures by all public companies. One approved format for these mandatory financial risk disclosures is VAR. For a critical assessment of the SEC's risk disclosure rule, *see* Merton H. Miller and Christopher L. Culp, "The SEC's Costly Disclosure Rules," *Wall Street Journal* (June 22, 1996).

2 This presupposes, of course, that "risk management" is consistent with value-maximizing behavior by the firm. For the purpose of this paper, we do not consider whether firms *should be* managing their risks. For a discussion of that issue, *see* Christopher L. Culp and Merton H. Miller, "Hedging in the Theory of Corporate Finance: A Reply to Our Critics," *Journal of Applied Corporate Finance*, Vol. 8, No. 1 (Spring 1995): 121–127, and René M. Stulz, "Rethinking Risk Management," *Journal of Applied Corporate Finance*, Vol. 9, No. 3 (Fall 1996): 8–24.

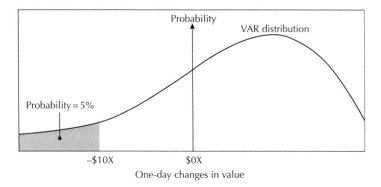

Figure 27.1

or the risk that a position declines in value with adverse market price changes.[3] Measuring risk using VAR allows managers to make statements like the following: "We do not expect losses to exceed $1 million on more than 1 out of the next 20 days."[4]

To arrive at a VAR measure for a given portfolio, a firm must generate a probability distribution of possible changes in the value of some portfolio over a specific time or "risk horizon" – *e.g.,* one day.[5] The value at risk of the portfolio is the dollar loss corresponding to some pre-defined probability level – usually 5% or less – as defined by the left-hand tail of the distribution. Alternatively, VAR is the dollar loss that is expected to occur no more than 5% of the time over the defined risk horizon. Figure 27.1, for example, depicts a one-day VAR of $10X at the 5% probability level.

The development of VAR

VAR emerged first in the trading community.[6] The original goal of VAR was to systematize the measurement of an active trading firm's risk exposures across its dealing portfolios. Before VAR, most commercial trading houses measured and controlled risk on a desk-by-desk basis with little attention to firm-wide exposures. VAR made it possible for dealers to use risk measures that could be compared and aggregated across trading areas as a means of monitoring and limiting their consolidated financial risks.

VAR received its first public endorsement in July 1993, when a group representing the swap dealer community recommended the adoption of VAR by all active dealers.[7] In that report, the Global Derivatives Study Group of The Group of Thirty urged dealers to "use a *consistent measure* to calculate daily the market risk of their derivatives positions and compare it to market risk limits. Market risk is best measured as 'value at risk' using *probability analysis* based upon a common confidence interval (*e.g.,* two standard deviations) and *time horizon* (*e.g.,* a one-day exposure). [emphasis added]"[8]

The italicized phrases in The Group of Thirty recommendation draw attention to several specific features of VAR that account for its wide-spread popularity among trading firms. One feature of VAR is its *consistent* measurement of financial risk. By expressing risk using a "possible dollar loss" metric, VAR makes possible direct comparisons of

3   More recently, VAR has been suggested as a framework for measuring credit risk, as well. To keep our discussion focused, we examine only the applications of VAR to market risk measurement.

4   For a general description of VAR, *see* Philippe Jorion, *Value at Risk* (Chicago: Irwin Professional Publishing, 1997).

5   The risk horizon is chosen exogenously by the firm engaging in the VAR calculation.

6   An early precursor of VAR was SPAN™ – Standard Portfolio Analysis of Risk – developed by the Chicago Mercantile Exchange for setting futures margins. Now widely used by virtually all futures exchanges, SPAN is a non-parametric, simulation-based "worst case" measure of risk. As will be seen, VAR, by contrast, rests on well-defined probability distributions.

7   This was followed quickly by a similar endorsement from the International Swaps and Derivatives Association. *See* Jorion, cited previously.

8   Global Derivatives Study Group, cited previously.

risk across different business lines and distinct financial products such as interest rate and currency swaps.

In addition to consistency, VAR also is *probability-based*. With whatever degree of confidence a firm wants to specify, VAR enables the firm to associate a specific loss with that level of confidence. Consequently, VAR measures can be interpreted as forward-looking approximations of potential market risk.

A third feature of VAR is its reliance on a *common time horizon* called the risk horizon. A one-day risk horizon at, say, the 5% probability level tells the firm, strictly speaking, that it can expect to lose no more than, say, $10X on the next day with 95% confidence. Firms often go on to assume that the 5% confidence level means they stand to lose more than $10X on no more than five days out of 100, an inference that is true only if strong assumptions are made about the stability of the underlying probability distribution.[9]

The choice of this risk horizon is based on various motivating factors. These may include the timing of employee performance evaluations, key decision-making events (*e.g.*, asset purchases), major reporting events (*e.g.*, board meetings and required disclosures), regulatory examinations, tax assessments, external quality assessments, and the like.

Implementing VAR

To estimate the value at risk of a portfolio, possible future values of that portfolio must be generated, yielding a distribution – called the "VAR distribution" – like that we saw in Figure 27.1. Once the VAR distribution is created for the chosen risk horizon, the VAR itself is just a number on the curve – *viz.*, the change in the value of the portfolio leaving the specified amount of probability in the left-hand tail.

Creating a VAR distribution for a particular portfolio and a given risk horizon can be viewed as a two-step process.[10] In the first step, the price or return distributions for each individual security or asset in the portfolio are generated. These distributions represent possible value changes in all the component assets over the risk horizon.[11] Next, the individual distributions somehow must be aggregated into a portfolio distribution using appropriate measures of correlation.[12] The resulting portfolio distribution then serves as the basis for the VAR summary measure.

An important assumption in almost all VAR calculations is that the portfolio whose risk is being evaluated *does not change* over the risk horizon. This assumption of no turnover was not a major issue when VAR first arrived on the scene at derivatives dealers. They were focused on one-or two-day – sometimes *intra*-day – risk horizons and thus found VAR both easy to implement and relatively realistic. But when it comes to generalizing VAR to a longer time horizon, the assumption of no portfolio changes becomes problematic. What does it mean, after all, to evaluate the *one-year* VAR of a portfolio using only the portfolio's contents *today* if the turnover in the portfolio is 20–30% per day?

Methods for generating both the individual asset risk distributions and the portfolio risk distribution range from the simplistic to the indecipherably complex. Because our goal in this paper is not to evaluate all these mechanical methods of VAR measurement, readers are referred elsewhere

---

9 This interpretation assumes that asset price changes are what the technicians call "iid," independently and identically distributed – *i.e.*, that price changes are drawn from essentially the same distribution every day.

10 In practice, VAR is not often implemented in a clean two-step manner, but discussing it in this way simplifies our discussion – without any loss of generality.

11 Especially with instruments whose payoffs are non-linear, a better approach is to generate distributions for the underlying "risk factors" that affect an asset rather than focus on the changes in the values of the assets themselves. To generate the value change distribution of an option on a stock, for example, one might first generate changes in the stock price and its volatility and *then* compute associated option price changes rather than generating option price changes "directly." For a discussion, *see* Michael S. Gamze and Ronald S. Rolighed, "VAR: What's Wrong With This Picture?" unpublished manuscript, Federal Reserve Bank of Chicago (1997).

12 If a risk manager is interested in the risk of a particular financial instrument, the appropriate risk measure to analyze is *not* the VAR of that instrument. Portfolio effects still must be considered. The relevant measure of risk is the *marginal risk* of that instrument in the portfolio being evaluated. *See* Mark Garman, "Improving on VAR," *Risk* Vol. 9, No. 5 (1996): 61–63.

for explanations of the nuts and bolts of VAR computation.[13] Several common methods of VAR calculation are summarized in the Appendix.

Uses of VAR

The purpose of any risk measurement system and summary risk statistic is to facilitate risk reporting and control decisions. Accordingly, dealers quickly began to rely on VAR measures in their broader risk management activities. The simplicity of VAR measurement greatly facilitated dealers' reporting of risks to senior managers and directors. The popularity of VAR owes much to Dennis Weatherstone, former chairman of JP Morgan & Co., Inc., who demanded to know the total market risk exposure of JP Morgan at 4:15pm every day. Weatherstone's request was met with a daily VAR report.

VAR also proved useful in dealers' risk *control* efforts.[14] Commercial banks, for example, used VAR measures to quantify current trading exposures and compare them to established counterparty risk limits. In addition, VAR provided traders with information useful in formulating hedging policies and evaluating the effects of particular transactions on net portfolio risk. For managers, VAR became popular as a means of analyzing the performance of traders for compensation purposes and for allocating reserves or capital across business lines on a risk-adjusted basis.

Uses of VAR by Non-Dealers. Since its original development as a risk management tool for active trading firms, VAR has spread outside the dealer community. VAR now is used regularly by non-financial corporations, pension plans and mutual funds, clearing organizations, brokers and futures commission merchants, and insurers.

These organizations find VAR just as useful as trading firms, albeit for different reasons.

Some benefits of VAR for non-dealers relate more to the exposure monitoring facilitated by VAR measurement than to the risk measurement task itself. For example, a pension plan with funds managed by external investment advisors may use VAR for policing its external managers. Similarly, brokers and account merchants can use VAR to assess collateral requirements for customers.

VAR AND CORPORATE RISK MANAGEMENT OBJECTIVES

Firms managing risks may be either *value risk managers* or *cash flow risk managers*.[15] A value risk manager is concerned with the firm's total value at a particular point in time. This concern may arise from a desire to avoid bankruptcy, mitigate problems associated with informational asymmetries, or reduce expected tax liabilities.[16] A cash flow risk manager, by contrast, uses risk management to reduce cash flow volatility and thereby increase debt capacity.[17] Value risk managers thus typically manage the risks of a *stock of assets*, whereas cash flow risk managers manage the risks of a *flow of funds*. A risk measure that is appropriate for one type of firm may not be appropriate for others.

Value risk managers and VAR-based risk controls

As the term *value* at risk implies, organizations for which VAR is best suited are those for which *value* risk management is the goal. VAR, after all, is intended to summarize the risk of a stock of assets

13   *See, for example,* Jorion, cited previously, Rod A. Beckström and Alyce R. Campbell, "Value-at-Risk (VAR): Theoretical Foundations," in *An Introduction to VAR*, Rod Beckström and Alyce Campbell, eds. (Palo Alto, Ca.: CAATS Software, Inc., 1995), and James V. Jordan and Robert J. Mackay, "Assessing Value at Risk for Equity Portfolios: Implementing Alternative Techniques," in *Derivatives Handbook*, Robert J. Schwartz and Clifford W. Smith, Jr., eds. (New York: John Wiley & Sons, Inc., 1997).

14   *See* Rod A. Beckström and Alyce R. Campbell, "The Future of Firm-Wide Risk Management," in *An Introduction to VAR*, Rod Beckström and Alyce Campbell, eds. (Palo Alto, Ca.: CAATS Software, Inc., 1995).

15   For a general discussion of the traditional corporate motivations for risk management, *see* David Fite and Paul Pfleider, "Should Firms Use Derivatives to Manage Risk?" in *Risk Management: Problems & Solutions*, William H. Beaver and George Parker, eds. (New York: McGraw-Hill, Inc., 1995).

16   *See, for example,* Clifford Smith and René Stulz, "The Determinants of Firms' Hedging Policies," *Journal of Financial and Quantitative Analysis*, Vol. 20 (1985): 391–405.

17   *See, for example,* Kenneth Froot, David Scharfstein, and Jeremy Stein, "Risk Management: Coordinating Corporate Investment and Financing Policies," *Journal of Finance* Vol. 48 (1993): 1629–1658.

over a particular risk horizon. Those likely to realize the most benefits from VAR thus include clearing houses, securities settlement agents,[18] and swap dealers. These organizations have in common a concern with the value of their exposures over a well-defined period of time *and* a wish to limit and control those exposures. In addition, the relatively short risk horizons of these enterprises imply that VAR measurement can be accomplished reliably and with minimal concern about changing portfolio composition over the risk horizon.

Many value risk managers have risks arising mainly from *agency* transactions. Organizations like financial clearinghouses, for example, are exposed to risk arising from intermediation services rather than the risks of proprietary position taking. VAR can assist such firms in monitoring their customer credit exposures, in setting position and exposure limits, and in determining and enforcing margin and collateral requirements.

Total vs. selective risk management

Most financial distress-driven explanations of corporate risk management, whether value or cash flow risk, center on a firm's *total risk*.[19] If so, such firms should be indifferent to the *composition* of their total risks. *Any* risk thus is a candidate for risk reduction.

Selective risk managers, by contrast, deliberately choose to manage some risks and not others. Specifically, they seek to manage their exposures to risks in which they have no comparative informational advantage – for the usual financial ruin reasons – while actively exposing themselves, at least to a point, to risks in which they *do* have perceived superior information.[20]

For firms managing total risk, the principal benefit of VAR is facilitating explicit risk control decisions, such as setting and enforcing exposure limits. For firms that selectively manage risk, by contrast, VAR is useful largely for diagnostic monitoring *or* for controlling risk in areas where the firm perceives no comparative informational advantage. An airline, for example, might find VAR helpful in assessing its exposure to jet fuel prices; but for the airline to use VAR to analyze the risk that seats on its aircraft are not all sold makes little sense.

Consider also a hedge fund manager who invests in foreign equity because the risk/return profile of that asset class is desirable. To avoid exposure to the exchange rate risk, the fund could engage an "overlay manager" to hedge the currency risk of the position. Using VAR on the *whole position* lumps together two separate and distinct sources of risk – the currency risk and the foreign equity price risk. And *reporting* that total VAR without a corresponding expected return could have disastrous consequences. Using VAR to ensure that the currency hedge is accomplishing its intended aims, by contrast, might be perfectly legitimate.

VAR AND THE GREAT DERIVATIVES DISASTERS

Despite its many benefits to certain firms, VAR is not a panacea. Even when VAR is calculated appropriately, VAR *in isolation* will do little to keep a firm's risk exposures in line with the firm's chosen risk tolerances. Without a well-developed risk management infrastructure – policies and procedures, systems, and well-defined senior management responsibilities – VAR will deliver little, if any, benefits. In addition, VAR may not always help a firm accomplish its particular risk management objectives, as we shall see.

To illustrate some of the pitfalls of using VAR, we examine the four "great derivatives disasters" of 1993–1995: Procter & Gamble, Orange County, Barings, and Metallgesellschaft.[21] Proponents of

---

18 *See* Christopher L. Culp and Andrea M.P. Neves, "Risk Management by Securities Settlement Agents," *Journal of Applied Corporate Finance* Vol. 10, No. 3 (Fall 1997): 96–103.
19 *See, for example*, Smith and Stulz, cited previously, and Froot, Scharfstein, and Stein, cited previously.
20 *See* Culp and Miller (Spring 1995), cited previously, and Stulz, cited previously.

21 In truth, Procter & Gamble was the only one of these disasters actually *caused* by derivatives. *See* Merton H. Miller, "The Great Derivatives Disasters: What Really Went Wrong and How to Keep it from Happening to You," speech presented to JP Morgan & Co. (Frankfurt, June 24, 1997) and chapter two in Merton H. Miller, *Merton Miller on Derivatives* (New York: John Wiley & Sons, Inc., 1997).

VAR often claim that many of these disasters would have been averted had VAR measurement systems been in place. We think otherwise.[22]

Procter & Gamble

During 1993, Procter & Gamble ("P&G") undertook derivatives transactions with Bankers Trust that resulted in over $150 million in losses.[23] Those losses traced essentially to P&G's writing of a put option on interest rates to Bankers Trust. Writers of put options suffer losses, of course, whenever the underlying security declines in price, which in this instance meant whenever interest rates rose. And rise they did in the summer and autumn of 1993.

The put option actually was only one component of the whole deal. The deal, with a notional principal of $200 million, was a fixed-for-floating rate swap in which Bankers Trust offered P&G 10 years of floating-rate financing at 75 basis points below the commercial paper rate in exchange for the put and fixed interest payments of 5.3% annually. That huge financing advantage of 75 basis points apparently was too much for P&G's treasurer to resist, particularly because the put was well out-of-the-money when the deal was struck in May 1993. But the low financing rate, of course, was just premium collected for writing the put. When the put went in-the-money for Bankers Trust, what once seemed like a good deal to P&G ended up costing millions of dollars.

VAR would have helped P&G, *if* P&G also had in place an adequate risk management infrastructure – which apparently it did not. Most obviously, senior managers at P&G would have been unlikely to have approved the original swap deal if its exposure had been subject to a VAR calculation. But that presupposes a lot.

Although VAR would have helped P&G's senior management measure its exposure to the speculative punt by its treasurer, much more would have been needed to stop the treasurer from taking the interest rate bet. The first requirement would have been a system for measuring the risk of the swaps *on a transactional basis*. But VAR was never intended for use on single transactions.[24] On the contrary, the whole appeal of the concept initially was its capacity to aggregate risk *across* transactions and exposures. To examine the risk of an individual transaction, the *change* in portfolio VAR that would occur with the addition of that new transaction should be analyzed. But that still requires first calculating the total VAR.[25] So, for P&G to have looked at the risk of its swaps in a VAR context, its entire treasury area would have needed a VAR measurement capability.

Implementing VAR for P&G's entire treasury function might *seem* to have been a good idea *anyway*. Why not, after all, perform a comprehensive VAR analysis on the whole treasury area and get transactional VAR assessment capabilities as an added bonus? For some firms, that *is* a good idea. But for other firms, it is not. Many non-financial corporations like P&G, after all, typically undertake risk management in their corporate treasury functions for *cash flow* management reasons.[26] VAR is a *value* risk measure, not a cash flow risk measure. For P&G to examine value at risk for its *whole* treasury operation, therefore, presumes that P&G was a *value* risk manager, and that may not have been the case. Even had VAR been in place at P&G, moreover, the assumption that P&G's senior managers would have been *monitoring* and *controlling* the VARs

---

22 The details of all these cases are complex. We thus refer readers elsewhere for discussions of the actual events that took place and limit our discussion here only to basic background. *See, for example*, Stephen Figlewski, "How to Lose Money in Derivatives," *Journal of Derivatives* Vol. 2, No. 2 (Winter 1994): 75–82.

23 *See, for example*, Figlweski, cited previously, and Michael S. Gamze and Karen McCann, "A Simplified Approach to Valuing an Option on a Leveraged Spread: The Bankers Trust, Procter & Gamble Example," *Derivatives Quarterly* Vol. 1, No. 4 (Summer 1995): 44–53.

24 Recently, some have advocated that derivatives dealers should evaluate the VAR of specific transactions *from the perspective of their counterparties* in order to determine counterparty suitability. Without knowing the rest of the counterparty's risk exposures, however, the VAR estimate would be meaningless. Even with full knowledge of the counterparty's total portfolio, the VAR number still might be of no use in determining suitability for reasons to become clear later.

25 *See* Garman, cited previously.

26 *See, for example*, Judy C. Lewent and A. John Kearney, "Identifying, Measuring, and Hedging Currency Risk at Merck," *Journal of Applied Corporate Finance* Vol. 2, No. 4 (Winter 1990): 19–28, and Deana R. Nance, Clifford W. Smith, and Charles W. Smithson, "On the Determinants of Corporate Hedging," *Journal of Finance* Vol. 48, No. 1 (1993): 267–284.

of individual swap transactions is not a foregone conclusion.

Barings

Barings PLC failed in February 1995 when rogue trader Nick Leeson's bets on the Japanese stock market went sour and turned into over $1 billion in trading losses.[27,28] To be sure, VAR would have led Barings senior management to shut down Leeson's trading operation in time to save the firm – *if they knew about it*. If P&G's sin was a lack of internal management and control over its treasurer, then Barings was guilty of an even more cardinal sin. The top officers of Barings lost control over the trading operation *not* because no VAR measurement system was in place, but because they let the same individual making the trades also serve as the recorder of those trades – violating one of the most elementary principles of good management.

The more interesting question emerging from Barings is why top management seems to have taken so long to recognize that a rogue trader was at work. For that purpose, a fully functioning VAR system would certainly have helped. Increasingly, companies in the financial risk-taking business use VAR as a monitoring tool for detecting unauthorized increases in positions.[29] Usually, this is intended for *customer* credit risk management by firms like futures commission merchants. In the case of Barings, however, such account monitoring would have enabled management to spot Leeson's run-up in positions in his so-called "arbitrage" and "error" accounts.

VAR measurements at Barings, on the other hand, would have been impossible to implement,

given the deficiencies in the *overall* information technology ("IT") systems in place at the firm. At any point in time, Barings' top managers knew only what Leeson was telling them. If Barings' systems were incapable of reconciling the position build-up in Leeson's accounts with the huge wire transfers being made by London to support Leeson's trading in Singapore, no VAR measure would have included a complete picture of Leeson's positions. And without that, no warning flag would have been raised.

Orange County

The Orange County Investment Pool ("OCIP") filed bankruptcy in December 1994 after reporting a drop in its market value of $1.5 billion. For many years, Orange County maintained the OCIP as the equivalent of a money market fund for the benefit of school boards, road building authorities, and other local government bodies in its territory. These local agencies deposited their tax and other collections when they came in and paid for their own wage and other bills when the need arose. The Pool paid them interest on their deposits – handsomely, in fact. Between 1989 and 1994, the OCIP paid its depositors 400 basis points more than they would have earned on the corporate Pool maintained by the State of California – roughly $750 million over the period.[30]

Most of the OCIP's investments involved leveraged purchases of intermediate-term securities and structured notes financed with "reverse repos" and other short-term borrowings. Contrary to conventional wisdom, the Pool was making its profits *not* from "speculation on falling interest rates" but rather from an investment play on the *slope* of the yield curve.[31] When the Federal Reserve started to

27 *See, for example,* Hans R. Stoll, "Lost Barings: A Tale in Three Parts Concluding with a Lesson," *Journal of Derivatives* Vol. 3, No. 1 (Fall 1995): 109–115, and Anatoli Kuprianov, "Derivatives Debacles: Case Studies of Large Losses in Derivatives Markets," in *Derivatives Handbook: Risk Management and Control,* Robert J. Schwartz and Clifford W. Smith, Jr., eds. (New York: John Wiley & Sons, Inc., 1997).
28 Our reference to rogue traders is not intended to suggest, of course, that rogue traders are only found in connection with derivatives. Rogue traders have caused the banks of this world far more damage from failed real estate (and copper) deals than from derivatives.
29 *See* Christopher Culp, Kamaryn Tanner, and Ron Mensink, "Risks, Returns and Retirement," *Risk* Vol. 10, No. 10 (October 1997): 63–69.

30 Miller, cited previously.
31 When the term structure is upward sloping, borrowing in short-term markets to leverage longer-term government securities generates positive cash carry. A surge in inflation or interest rates, of course, could reverse the term structure and turn the carry negative. That is the real risk the treasurer was taking. But it was not much of a risk. Since the days of Jimmy Carter in the late 1970s, the U.S. term structure has never been downward sloping and nobody in December 1994 thought it was likely to be so in the foreseeable future.

raise interest rates in 1994, the intermediate-term securities declined in value and OCIP's short-term borrowing costs rose.

Despite the widespread belief that the leverage policy led to the fund's insolvency and bankruptcy filing, Miller and Ross, after examining the OCIP's investment strategy, cash position, and net asset value at the time of the filing, have shown that the OCIP was *not* insolvent. Miller and Ross estimate that the $20 billion in total assets on deposit in the fund had a positive net worth of about $6 billion. Nor was the fund in an illiquid cash situation. OCIP had over $600 million of cash on hand and was generating further cash at a rate of more than $30 million a month.[32] Even the reported $1.5 billion "loss" would have been completely recovered within a year – a loss that was realized only because Orange County's bankruptcy lawyers forced the liquidation of the securities.[33]

Jorion has taken issue with Miller and Ross's analysis of OCIP, arguing that VAR would have called the OCIP investment program into question long before the $1.5 billion loss was incurred.[34] Using several different VAR calculation methods, Jorion concludes that OCIP's one-year VAR at the end of 1994 was about $1 billion at the 5% confidence level. Under the usual VAR interpretation, this would have told OCIP to expect a loss in excess of $1 billion in one out of the next 20 years.

Even assuming Jorion's VAR number is accurate, however, his interpretation of the VAR measure was unlikely to have been the OCIP's interpretation – at least not *ex ante* when it could have mattered. The VAR measure in isolation, after all, takes no account of the *upside* returns OCIP was receiving as compensation for that downside risk.

Remember that OCIP was pursuing a very deliberate yield curve, net cost-of-carry strategy, designed to generate high expected cash returns. That strategy had risks, to be sure, but those risks seem to have been clear to OCIP treasurer Robert Citron – and, for that matter, to the people of Orange County who re-elected Citron treasurer in preference to an opposing candidate who was criticizing the investment strategy.[35]

Had Orange County been using VAR, however, it almost certainly *would* have terminated its investment program upon seeing the $1 billion risk estimate. The reason probably would *not* have been the actual informativeness of the VAR number, but rather the fear of a public outcry at the number. Imagine the public reaction if the OCIP announced one day that it expected to lose more than $1 billion over the next year in one time out of 20. But that reaction would have far less to do with the actual risk information conveyed by the VAR number than with the lack of any corresponding expected profits reported *with* the risk number. Just consider, after all, what the public reaction would have been if the OCIP publicly announced that it would *gain* more than $1 billion over the next year in one time out of 20![36]

This example highlights a major abuse of VAR – an abuse that has nothing to do with the meaning of the value at risk number but instead traces to the presentation of the information that number conveys. Especially for institutional investors, a major pitfall of VAR is to highlight large potential losses over long time horizons *without conveying any information about the corresponding expected return*. The lesson from Orange County to would-be VAR users thus is an important one – for organizations whose mission is *to take some risks*, VAR measures of risks are meaningful *only* when interpreted alongside estimates of corresponding potential *gains*.

Metallgesellschaft

MG Refining & Marketing, Inc. ("MGRM"), a U.S. subsidiary of Metallgesellschaft AG, reported $1.3 billion in losses by year-end 1993 from its oil

32 Merton H. Miller and David J. Ross, "The Orange County Bankruptcy and its Aftermath: Some New Evidence," *Journal of Derivatives*, Vol. 4, No. 4 (Summer 1997): 51–60.
33 Readers may wonder why, then, Orange County did declare bankruptcy. That story is complicated, but a hint might be found in the payment of $50 million in special legal fees to the attorneys that sued Merrill Lynch for $1.5 billion for selling OCIP the securities that lost money. In short, *lots* of people gained from OCIP's bankruptcy, even though OCIP was not actually bankrupt. *See* Miller, cited previously, and Miller and Ross, cited previously.
34 Philippe Jorion, "Lessons From the Orange County Bankruptcy," *Journal of Derivatives* Vol. 4, No. 4 (Summer 1997): 61–66.
35 Miller and Ross, cited previously.
36 Only for the purpose of this example, we obviously have assumed symmetry in the VAR distribution.

trading activities. MGRM's oil derivatives were part of a marketing program under which it offered long-term customers firm price guarantees for up to 10 years on gasoline, heating oil, and diesel fuel purchased from MGRM.[37] The firm hedged its resulting exposure to spot price increases with short-term futures contracts to a considerable extent. After several consecutive months of *falling* prices in the autumn of 1993, however, MGRM's German parent reacted to the substantial margin calls on the losing futures positions by liquidating the hedge, thereby turning a paper loss into a very real one.[38]

Most of the arguments over MGRM – in press accounts, in the many law suits the case engendered, and in the academic literature – have focused on whether MGRM was "speculating" or "hedging." The answer, of course, is that like all other merchant firms, they were doing both. They were definitely speculating on the oil "basis" – inter-regional, intertemporal, and inter-product *differences* in prices of crude, heating oil, and gasoline. That was the *business they were in*.[39] The firm had expertise and informational advantages far beyond those of its customers or of casual observers playing the oil futures market. What MGRM did not have, of course, was any special expertise about the level and direction of oil prices generally. Here, rather than take a corporate "view" on the direction of oil prices, like the misguided one the treasurer of P&G took on interest rates, MGRM chose to hedge its exposure to oil price *levels*.

Subsequent academic controversy surrounding the case has maily been not whether MGRM was hedging, but whether they were *over*-hedging – whether the firm could have achieved the same degree of insulation from price level changes with a lower commitment from MGRM's ultimate owner-creditor Deutsche Bank.[40] The answer is that the day-to-day cash-flow volatility of the program *could* have been reduced by any number of cash flow variance-reducing hedge ratios.[41] But the cost of chopping off some cash drains when prices fell was that of losing the corresponding cash inflows when prices spiked up.[42]

Conceptually, of course, MGRM could have used VAR analysis to measure its possible financial risks. But why would they have wanted to do so? The combined marketing/hedging program, after all, was *hedged* against changes in the *level* of oil prices. The only significant risks to which MGRM's program was subject thus were basis and rollover risks – again, the risk that MGRM was *in the business of taking*.[43]

A much bigger problem at MGRM than the change in the *value* of its program was the large negative *cash flows* on the futures hedge that would have been offset by eventual gains in the future on the fixed-price customer contracts. Although MGRM's former management claims it had access to adequate funding from Deutsche Bank (the firm's leading creditor and stock holder), perhaps some benefit might have been achieved by more rigorous cash flow simulations. But even granting that, VAR would have told MGRM very little about its *cash flows* at risk. As we have already emphasized, VAR is a *value*-based risk measure.

For firms like MGRM engaged in *authorized* risk-taking – like Orange County and unlike Leeson/Barings – the primary benefit of VAR really is just as an internal "diagnostic monitoring" tool. To that end, estimating the VAR of MGRM's basis trading activities *would* have told senior managers and directors at its parent what the basis risks were that MGRM actually was taking. But remember,

---

37 A detailed analysis of the program can be found in Christopher L. Culp and Merton H. Miller, "Metallgesellschaft and the Economics of Synthetic Storage," *Journal of Applied Corporate Finance* Vol. 7, No. 4 (Winter 1995): 62–76.

38 For an analysis of the losses incurred by MRGM – as well as why they were incurred – *see* Christopher L. Culp and Merton H. Miller, "Auditing the Auditors," *Risk* Vol. 8, No. 4 (1995): 36–39.

39 Culp and Miller (Winter 1995, Spring 1995), cited previously, explain this in detail.

40 *See* Franklin R. Edwards and Michael S. Canter, "The Collapse of Metallgesellschaft: Unhedgeable Risks, Poor Hedging Strategy, or Just Bad Luck?," *Journal of Applied Corporate Finance* Vol. 8, No. 1 (Spring 1995): 86–105.

41 *See, for example,* Froot, Scharfstein, and Stein, cited previously.

42 A number of other reasons also explain MGRM's reluctance to adopt anything smaller than a "one-for-one stack-and-roll" hedge. *See* Culp and Miller (Winter 1995, Spring 1995).

43 The claim that MGRM was in the business of trading the basis has been disputed by managers of MGRM's parent and creditors. Nevertheless, the marketing materials of MGRM – on which the parent firm signed off – suggests otherwise. *See* Culp and Miller (Spring 1995), cited previously.

MGRM's parent appears to have been fully aware of the risks MGRM's traders were taking *even without a VAR number*. In that sense, even the monitoring benefits of VAR for a proprietary trading operation would not have changed MGRM's fate.[44]

ALTERNATIVES TO VAR

VAR certainly is not the *only* way a firm can systematically measure its financial risk. As noted, its appeal is mainly its conceptual simplicity and its consistency across financial products and activities. In cases where VAR may *not* be appropriate as a measure of risk, however, other alternatives *are* available.

Cash flow risk

Firms concerned *not* with the value of a stock of assets and liabilities over a specific time horizon but with the volatility of a *flow of funds* often are better off eschewing VAR altogether in favor of a measure of cash flow volatility. Possible cash requirements over a *sequence* of future dates, for example, can be simulated. The resulting distributions of cash flows then enable the firm control its exposure to cash flow risk more directly.[45] Firms worried about cash flow risk for preserving or increasing their debt capacities thus might engage in hedging, whereas firms concerned purely about liquidity shortfalls might use such cash flow stress tests to arrange appropriate standby funding.

Abnormal returns and risk-based capital allocation

Stulz suggests managing risk-taking activities using abnormal returns – *i.e.*, returns in excess of the risk free rate – as a measure of the expected profitability of certain activities. Selective risk management then can be accomplished by allocating capital on a risk-adjusted basis and limiting capital at risk accordingly. To measure the risk-adjusted capital allocation, he suggests using the cost of new equity issued to finance the particular activity.[46]

On the positive side, Stulz's suggestion does not penalize selective risk managers for exploiting perceived informational advantages, whereas VAR does. The problem with Stulz's idea, however, lies in any company's capacity actually to implement such a risk management process. More properly, the difficulty lies in the actual estimation of the firm's equity cost of capital. And in any event, under M&M proposition three, all sources of capital are equivalent on a risk-adjusted basis. The source of capital for financing a particular project thus should not affect the decision to undertake that project. Stulz's reliance on equity only is thus inappropriate.

Shortfall risk

VAR need not be calculated by assuming variance is a complete measure of "risk," but in practice this often *is* how VAR is calculated. (*See* the Appendix.) This assumption can be problematic when measuring exposures in markets characterized by non-normal (*i.e.*, non-Gaussian) distributions – *e.g.*, return distributions that are skewed or have fat tails. If so, as explained in the Appendix, a solution is to generate the VAR distribution in a manner that does *not* presuppose variance is an adequate measure of risk. Alternatively, other summary risk measures can be calculated.

For some organizations, asymmetric distributions pose a problem that VAR on its own *cannot* address, no matter how it is calculated. Consider again the OCIP example, in which the one-year VAR implied a $1 billion loss in one year out of 20. With a symmetric portfolio distribution, that would also imply a $1 billion gain in one year out of 20. But suppose OCIP's investment program had a *positively skewed* return distribution. Then, the $1 billion loss in one year out of 20 might be comparable to, say, a $5 billion gain in one year of 20.

---

44   Like P&G and Barings, what happened at MGRM was, in the end, a *management* failure rather than a *risk management* failure. For details on how management failed in the MGRM case, *see* Culp and Miller (Winter 1995, Spring 1995). For a redacted version of the story, *see* Christopher L. Culp and Merton H. Miller, "Blame Mismanagement, Not Speculation, for Metall's Woes," *Wall Street Journal Europe* (April 25, 1995).

45   *See* Stulz, cited previously.

46   *See* Stulz, cited previously.

One of the problems with interpreting VAR thus is interpreting the confidence level – *viz.*, 5% or one year in 20. Some organizations may consider it more useful *not* to examine the loss associated with a chosen probability level but rather to examine the risk associated with a *given loss* – the so-called "doomsday" return below which a portfolio must *never* fall. Pension plans, endowments, and some hedge funds, for example, are concerned primarily with the possibility of a "shortfall" of assets below liabilities that would necessitate a contribution from the plan sponsor.

Shortfall risk measures are alternatives to VAR that allow a risk manager to define a specific target value below which the organization's assets must *never* fall and they measure risk accordingly. Two popular measures of shortfall risk are below-target probability ("BTP") and below-target risk ("BTR").[47]

The advantage of BTR, in particular, over VAR is that it penalizes large shortfalls more than small ones.[48] BTR is still subject to the same misinterpretation as VAR when it is reported without a corresponding indication of possible *gains*. VAR, however, relies on a somewhat arbitrary choice of a "probability level" that can be changed to exaggerate or to de-emphasize risk measures. BTR, by contrast, is based on a real target – *e.g.*, a pension actuarial contribution threshold – and thus reveals information about risk that can be much more usefully weighed against expected returns than a VAR measure.[49]

CONCLUSION

By facilitating the consistent measurement of risk across distinct assets and activities, VAR allows firms to monitor, report, and control their risks in a manner that efficiently relates risk control to desired and actual economic exposures. At the same time, reliance on VAR can result in serious problems when improperly used. Would-be users of VAR are thus advised to consider the following three pieces of advice:

First, VAR is useful only to certain firms and only in particular circumstances. Specifically, VAR is a tool for firms engaged in *total value* risk management, where the consolidated values of exposures across a variety of activities are at issue. Dangerous misinterpretations of the risk facing a firm can result when VAR is wrongly applied in situations where total value risk management is *not* the objective, such as at firms concerned with *cash flow* risk rather than value risk.

Second, VAR should be applied very carefully to firms selectively managing their risks. When an organization deliberately takes certain risks as a part of its primary business, VAR can serve at best as a diagnostic monitoring tool for those risks. When VAR is analyzed and reported in such situations with no estimates of corresponding expected profits, the information conveyed by the VAR estimate can be extremely misleading.

Finally, as all the great derivatives disasters illustrate, no form of risk measurement – including VAR – is a substitute for good management. Risk management as a process encompasses much more than just risk measurement. Although judicious risk measurement can prove very useful to certain firms, it is quite pointless without a well-developed organizational infrastructure and IT system capable of supporting the complex and dynamic process of risk taking and risk control.

Appendix: Calculating VAR

To calculate a VAR statistic is easy *once you have generated the probability distribution for future values of the portfolio*. Creating that VAR distribution, on the other hand, can be quite hard, and the methods available range from the banal to the utterly arcane. This appendix reviews a few of those methods.

Variance-Based Approaches
By far the easiest way to create the VAR distribution used in calculating the actual VAR statistic is just to *assume* that distribution is normal (*i.e.*, Gaussian).

---

47 *See* Culp, Tanner, and Mensink, cited previously. For a complete mathematic discussion of these concepts, *see* Kamaryn T. Tanner, "An Asymmetric Distribution Model for Portfolio Optimization," manuscript, Graduate School of Business, The University of Chicago (1997).
48 BTP accomplishes a similar objective but does *not* weight large deviations below the target more heavily than small ones.
49 *See* Culp, Tanner, and Mensink, cited previously, for a more involved treatment of shortfall risk as compared to VAR.

Mean and variance are "sufficient statistics" to fully characterize a normal distribution. Consequently, knowing the variance of an asset whose return is normally distributed is all that is needed to summarize the risk of that asset.

Using return variances and covariances as inputs, VAR thus can be calculated in a fairly straightforward way.[1] First consider a single asset. If returns on that asset are normally distributed, the 5th percentile VAR is always 1.65 standard deviations below the mean return. So, the variance is a sufficient measure of risk to compute the VAR on that asset – just subtract 1.65 times the standard deviation from the mean. The risk horizon for such a VAR estimate corresponds to the frequency used to compute the input variance.

Now consider two assets. In that case, the VAR of the portfolio of two assets can be computed in a similar manner using the variances of the two assets' returns. These variance-based risk measures then are combined using the correlation of the two assets' returns. The result is a VAR estimate for the portfolio.

The simplicity of the variance-based approach to VAR calculations lies in the assumption of normality. By *assuming* that returns on all financial instruments are normally distributed, the risk manager eliminates the need to come up with a VAR distribution using complicated modeling techniques. All that *really* must be done is to come up with the appropriate variances and correlations.

At the same time, however, by assuming normality, the risk manager has greatly limited the VAR estimate. Normal distributions, after all, are symmetric. Any potential for skewness or fat tails in asset returns thus is totally ignored in the variance-only approach.

In addition to sacrificing the possibility that asset returns may *not* be normally distributed, the variance-only approach to calculating VAR also relies on the critical assumption that asset returns are totally independent across increments of time. A multi-period VAR can be calculated only by calculating a single-period VAR from the available data and then extrapolating the multi-day risk esti-

mate. For example, suppose variances and correlations are available for historical returns measured at the *daily* frequency. To get from a one-day VAR to a T-day VAR – where T is the risk horizon of interest – the variance-only approach requires that the one-day VAR is multiplied by the square root of T.

For return variances and correlations measured at the monthly frequency or lower, this assumption may not be terribly implausible. For daily variances and correlations, however, serial independence is a very strong and usually an unrealistic assumption in most markets. The problem is less severe for short risk horizons, of course. So, using a one-day VAR as the basis for a five-day VAR might be acceptable, whereas a one-day VAR extrapolated into a one-year VAR would be highly problematic in most markets.

Computing Volatility Inputs

Despite its unrealistic assumptions, simple variance-based VAR calculations are probably the dominant application of the VAR measure today. The approach is especially popular for corporate end users of derivatives, principally because the necessary software is cheap and easy to use.

All variance-based VAR measures, however, are not alike. The sources of inputs used to calculate VAR in this manner can differ widely. The next several subsections summarize several popular methods for determining these variances.[2] Note that these methods are *only* methods of computing *variances* on single assets. Correlations still must be determined to convert the VARs of individual assets into portfolio VARs.

Moving Average Volatility. One of the simplest approaches to calculating variance for use in a variance-based VAR calculation involves estimating a historical moving average of volatility. To get a moving average estimate of variance, the average is taken over a rolling window of historical volatility data. For example, given a 20-day rolling window,[3] the daily variance used for one-day VAR calculations would be the average daily variance over the most recent 20 days. To calculate this,

1   A useful example of this methodology is presented in Anthony Saunders, "Market Risk," *The Financier* Vol. 2, No. 5 (December 1995).

2   For more methods, *see* Jorion (1997), cited previously.
3   The length of the window is chosen by the risk manager doing the VAR calculation.

many assume a zero mean daily return and then just average the squared returns for the last 20 trading days. On the next day, a new return becomes available for the volatility calculation. To maintain a 20-day measurement window, the first observation is dropped off and the average is recomputed as the basis of the next day's VAR estimate.

More formally, denote the daily return from time $t-1$ to time t as r_t. Assuming a zero mean daily return, the moving average volatility over a window of the last D days is calculated as follows:

$$v_t^2 = \left[\frac{1}{D}\right] \sum_{i=0}^{D-1} r_{t-i}^2$$

where v_t is the daily volatility estimate used as the VAR input on day t.

Because moving-average volatility is calculated using equal weights for all observations in the historical time series, the calculations are very simple. The result, however, is a smoothing effect that causes sharp changes in volatility to appear as plateaus over longer periods of time, failing to capture dramatic changes in volatility.

Risk Metrics. To facilitate one-day VAR calculations and extrapolated risk measures for longer risk horizons, JP Morgan – in association with Reuters – began making available their RiskMetrics™ data sets. This data includes historical variances and covariances on a variety of simple assets – sometimes called "primitive securities."[4] Most other assets have cash flows that can be "mapped" into these simpler RiskMetrics™ assets for VAR calculation purposes.[5]

In the RiskMetrics data set, daily variances and correlations are computed using an "exponentially weighted moving average." Unlike the simple moving-average volatility estimate, an exponentially weighted moving average allows the most recent observations to be more influential in the calculation than observations further in the past. This has the advantage of capturing shocks in the market better than the simple moving average and thus is often regarded as producing a better

volatility for variance-based VAR than the equal-weighted moving average alternative.

Conditional Variance Models. Another approach for estimating the variance input to VAR calculations involves the use of "conditional variance" time series methods. The first conditional variance model was developed by Engle in 1982 and is known as the autoregressive conditional heteroskedasticity ("ARCH") model.[6] ARCH combines an autoregressive process with a moving average estimation method so that variance still is calculated in the rolling window manner used for moving averages.

Since its introduction, ARCH has evolved into a variety of other conditional variance models, such as Generalized ARCH ("GARCH"), Integrated GARCH ("IGARCH"), and exponential GARCH ("EGARCH"). Numerous applications of these models have led practitioners to believe that these estimation techniques provide better estimates of (time-series) volatility than simpler methods.

For a GARCH(1,1) model, the variance of an asset's return at time t is presumed to have the following structure:

$$v_t^2 = a_0 + a_1 r_{t-1}^2 + a_2 v_{t-1}^2$$

The conditional variance model thus incorporates a *recursive* moving average term. In the special case where $a_0 = 0$ and $a_1 + a_2 = 1$, the GARCH(1,1) model reduces *exactly* to the exponentially weighted moving average formulation for volatility.[7]

Using volatilities from a GARCH model as inputs in a variance-based VAR calculation does not circumvent the statistical inference problem of presumed normality. By incorporating additional information into the volatility measure, however, more of the actual time series properties of the underlying asset return can be incorporated into the VAR estimate than if a simple average volatility is used.

Implied Volatility. All of the above methods of computing volatilities for variance-based VAR calculations are based on historical data.

---

4   Jorion (1997), cited previously.
5   For a detailed explanation of this approach, *see* JP Morgan/ Reuters, *RiskMetrics – Technical Document*, 4th ed. (1996).

6   Robert Engle, "Autoregressive Conditional Heteroskedasticity with Estimates of the Variance of United Kingdom Inflation," *Econometrica* Vol. 50 (1982): 391–407.
7   *See* Jorion (1997), cited previously.

For more of a forward-looking measure of volatility, option-implied volatilities sometimes can be used to calculate VAR.

The implied volatility of an option is defined as the *expected future volatility* of the underlying asset over the remaining life of the option. Many studies have concluded that measures of option-implied volatility are, indeed, the *best* predictor of future volatility.[8] Unlike time series measures of volatility that are entirely backward-looking, option implied volatility is "backed-out" of actual option prices – which, in turn, are based on actual transactions and expectations of market participants – and thus is inherently forward-looking.

Any option-implied volatility estimate is dependent on the particular option pricing model used to derive the implied volatility. Given an observed market price for an option *and* a presumed pricing model, the implied volatility can be determined numerically. This variance may then be used in a VAR calculation for the asset underlying the option.

Non-Variance VAR Calculation Methods

Despite the simplicity of most variance-based VAR measurement methods, many practitioners prefer to avoid the restrictive assumptions underlying that approach – *viz.*, symmetric return distributions that are independent and stable over time. To avoid these assumptions, a risk manager must actually generate a full distribution of possible future portfolio values – a distribution that is neither necessarily normal nor symmetric.[9]

Historical simulation is perhaps the easiest alternative to variance-based VAR. This approach generates VAR distributions merely by "re-arranging" historical data – *viz.*, re-sampling time series data on the relevant asset prices or returns. This can be about as easy *computationally* as variance-based VAR, and it does *not* presuppose that everything in the world is normally distributed. Nevertheless, the approach is highly dependent on the availability of potentially massive amounts of historical data. In addition, the VAR resulting from a historical simulation is totally sample dependent.

More advanced approaches to VAR calculation usually involve some type of forward-looking simulation model, such as Monte Carlo. Implementing simulation methods typically is computationally intensive, expensive, and heavily dependent on personnel resources. For that reason, simulation has remained largely limited to active trading firms and institutional investors. Nevertheless, simulation does enable users to depart from the RiskMetrics normality assumptions about underlying asset returns without forcing them to rely on a single historical data sample. Simulation also eliminates the need to assume independence in returns over time – *viz.*, VAR calculations are no longer restricted to one-day estimates that must be extrapolated over the total risk horizon.

---

8 *See, for example,* Phillipe Jorion, "Predicting Volatility in the Foreign Exchange Market," *Journal of Finance*, Vol. 50 (1995): 507–528.

9 Variance-based approaches avoid the problem of generating a new distribution by *assuming* that distribution.

PART VI

International Finance

In "Globalization, Corporate Finance, and the Cost of Capital," René Stulz observes that "International financial markets are progressively becoming one huge, integrated, global capital market, which in turn is contributing to higher stock prices in developed as well as developing economies." Large corporations everywhere now raise funds in different financial markets throughout the world, sometimes in simultaneous offerings in domestic and overseas markets. And, as Stulz argues, for companies that are large and visible enough to attract global investors, having a global shareholder base means a lower cost of capital and a higher stock price.

How does having a global shareholder base reduce a company's cost of capital? According to Stulz, it has the potential to reduce the cost of capital and increase share values in two important ways. First might be called the *portfolio effect*. As a result of increased global capital flows, the risks of equity are now shared among more investors with different portfolio exposures and hence a different appetite for bearing certain risks. In more concrete terms, Japanese investors are likely to be willing to pay more for the shares of IBM than U.S. investors because a position in IBM helps them diversify their portfolios. Such diversification by overseas investors has the effect of reducing the equity risk premium for all U.S. companies (or, at least, all those large or promising enough to attract a global following). And, for the same reason, investments

by U.S. investors in Japanese companies effectively lower the risk premium of the Japanese market.

The second major benefit of globalization could be called the *governance effect*. When companies with less-developed capital markets list or raise capital in highly developed markets (like the NYSE or Nasdaq), they get more than lower-cost capital; they also import at least aspects of the corporate governance systems that prevail in those markets. For such firms, listing on the NYSE – or just attracting investment by large foreign institutional investors on the domestic stock exchange – can have important consequences. It is likely to mean that more sophisticated investors, with greater experience in governance issues gained from having operated within a more shareholder-friendly legal and regulatory environment, will now participate in monitoring the performance and management of such firms. And, in a virtuous cycle, more effective monitoring has the potential to build investor confidence in the companies' future performance and so improve the terms on which they raise capital.

As the article goes on to argue, conventional methods for calculating the cost of capital do not take into account these effects of globalization. Standard corporate practice is to use a "local" version of the Capital Asset Pricing Model (CAPM) that considers a stock's degree of risk in relation to its own domestic market. In place of the local CAPM, Stulz proposes a "global CAPM" that evaluates the risk of a company's stock against a world index that represents the collective wealth of all countries with well-developed, readily accessible capital markets. For example, a U.S. investor – and, for that matter, a Japanese or a Swiss investor – considering the purchase of IBM shares will evaluate the beta of IBM not in relation to the S&P 500, but rather in relation to a global index like the Morgan-Stanley World (MSCI) index. The differences between the cost of capital and share valuations produced by the two models are potentially quite large. For companies with access to global capital markets whose profitability is tied more closely to the local than to the global economy, use of the local CAPM will overstate the cost of capital because risks that are not diversifiable within a national economy can be diversified by holding a global portfolio.

But if the globalization of financial markets promises to lower the cost of capital, it has also been linked to other effects. In fact, the popular account of the Asian crisis of 1997–98 puts the blame on currency speculators like George Soros and, more generally, on financial markets. The explanation was essentially as follows: By opening their economies to large inflows of foreign capital, the Asian tigers prospered for a time. But at the first sign of trouble, speculators began to drive down currency values, which in turn caused massive capital flight and general desolation.

In the first article in this section, "Financial Markets and Economic Growth," Merton Miller attributes the problems in Asia "not to too *much* reliance on financial markets, but to too *little*." Like the U.S. economy a century ago, today's emerging Asian economies do not have well-developed capital markets and remain heavily dependent on their banking systems to finance growth. And, although banks play an important role in all economies by channeling funds from depositors to companies without access to capital markets, banking itself, as Miller argues, "is not only basically 19th-century technology, but it is disaster-prone technology." Banks' high leverage, combined with their "extreme mismatch" of maturities (funding long-term assets with short-term and, in some cases, foreign-currency-denominated liabilities) and reliance on demand deposits, makes them susceptible to massive runs – and their economies to severe, recurring credit crunches.

And, as Miller goes on to say, "in the summer of 1997 a banking-driven disaster struck in East Asia, just as it had struck so many times before in U.S. history."

In the 20th century, Miller argues, the U.S. economy has helped itself by steadily reducing its dependence on banks by developing "dispersed and decentralized" financial markets and institutions. By so doing, it has significantly reduced its vulnerability to credit crunches (for example, non-bank sources of capital were an important reason why the recession of 1990 was so mild and short-lived) while at the same time dramatically increasing the efficiency of the U.S. capital allocation process. By contrast, Japan has not reduced its economy's dependence on banks, and "its efforts to deal with its banking problems have served only to destabilize itself as well as its neighbors." Miller urges developing countries in Southeast Asia and elsewhere not to follow the Japanese example, but to take measures aimed at developing their financial markets and institutions.

Another fundamental cause of Asia's problems – one that can also be partly attributed to bank-centered systems and the absence of well-developed financial markets – is the weakness of their corporate governance systems. In "Globalization of Capital Markets and the Asian Financial Crisis," Han Kim argues that the combination of government-directed banking systems and weak corporate governance structures (including managerial incentives to increase size and market share at the expense of shareholders) in most Asian economies have resulted in systematic overinvestment and sharp declines in corporate profitability. To strengthen corporate governance, Professor Kim recommends improvements in corporate disclosure and creation of a "corporate control" market that permits hostile takeovers by foreign as well as domestic investors. To increase the productivity of capital, he suggests that Asian companies align managerial with shareholder interests by tying compensation to measures of value creation like EVA.

In "Incorporating Country Risk in the Valuation of Offshore Projects," Donald Lessard, MIT's distinguished international finance scholar, challenges the conventional practice of multinational corporations (MNCs) of using higher discount rates when evaluating overseas investments to compensate for the greater perceived risks.

Although more volatile, investments in emerging economies typically contribute significantly less to the volatility of an MNC's shareholders' portfolios than domestic projects because of the low correlation of emerging markets' performance with that of developed economies. The discount rate, according to Lessard, should reflect only "systematic" or "market covariance" risk. Political and currency risks, as well as general unfamiliarity with the local business environment, should be reflected not in the discount rate, but in downward adjustments of the levels of projected cash flows.

In "Yankee Bonds and Cross-Border Private Placements," Greg Johnson of Banc of America Securities explains why cross-border bond issuance continues at record levels and why the U.S. bond markets have become the markets of choice for many international issuers. Overseas issuers have three basic choices when tapping U.S. long-term debt markets: publicly traded "Yankee" bonds; traditional private placements; and underwritten Rule 144A private placements. In discussing the advantages and drawbacks of each, the author notes that although Yankee bonds are typically the most cost-efficient vehicle for large, investment-grade issuers, the Rule 144A market has also become a particular favorite with international issuers because of its less formal disclosure requirements and streamlined execution process.

In "Financial Risk Management for Developing Countries," Donald Lessard argues that derivatives can play an important role in managing the large and growing financial risks of emerging countries. Developing-country governments can use derivatives such as currency futures and options, and commodity and interest rate swaps and options, to stabilize their net foreign exchange earnings, their debt service, or whatever performance variable they deem most critical to maintaining their operations. By using such instruments to better align their obligations with their ability to pay, such countries can reduce their overall risk and so improve the terms on which they raise outside capital.

Take the case of oil-producing nations like Mexico and Venezuela, where the development of oil reserves has been performed largely by the state and financed by general-obligation debt, typically carrying floating rates and denominated in dollars. Such ownership and funding arrangements place huge oil price (and local currency) risks on parties who are not well-equipped to bear them – namely, local investors and taxpayers. Through the use of oil swaps or options, or the issuance of oil-linked bonds (which contains "embedded" oil options), such countries could shift much of their oil price risk to globally-diversified investors and financial institutions with a *comparative advantage* in bearing such risk. Such risk transfers, as Lessard concludes, can be expected to create "net gains in the international economy – gains that can be shared among developing and developed nations alike."

CHAPTER 28

Financial Markets and Economic Growth

Merton H. Miller (University of Chicago)*

When the title is "Financial Markets and Economic Growth" and the author is from the University of Chicago, you can be forgiven for expecting still another paean to the benefits of free markets as a way of organizing economic activity. The well-known optimality properties of markets in general will surely be stressed – how they permit goods and assets to flow to those who can utilize them most efficiently. And how in good Hayekian fashion, markets serve to aggregate, and make available to us all, the bits and pieces of private information scattered throughout the economy. Because the title emphasizes *financial* markets, additional comments are sure to follow on two critical and oft-neglected roles of financial markets – including under that heading stock markets, bond markets, future exchanges, over-the-counter markets and derivatives of all kinds. The first is the risk-transfer function of financial markets in assuring that the inevitable hazards of business life gravitate to those most willing to bear them. The second is price discovery. How much is all the non-performing real-estate collateral of the Japanese banks really worth? We don't know because the

Japanese regulatory authorities won't allow it to be sold and hence priced. The term economic growth in my title surely signals discussion of how financial markets serve to marshall the savings of the public and channel them to firms undertaking productive investments, generating still more savings and more investment in the classic virtuous circle of development. And finally, the mention of the University of Chicago certainly suggests reference will be made to free markets as an accompaniment – we would actually say an underpinning – of democracy.

These are indeed critical attributes of markets that have been stressed by economists for decades. But though it may disappoint your expectations, I don't intend to replough that familiar ground here today. Instead, I propose to take and defend a position directly counter to the anti-financial market views heard so often these days. My point will be that the recent sharp reductions in the hitherto rapid economic growth of Southeast Asia – growth being the second part of my title for this speech after all – trace not to too *much* reliance on financial markets, but to too *little*. I will argue that a well fleshed-out set of financial markets and associated institutions means a country can reduce its dependence on the banking system, which is normally far and away the dominant institution for financing economic growth in the developing countries of the world today, just as it was in the 19th century for the U.S.

* The original version of this article was presented at the Conference "Creating an Environment for Growth," in Stockholm, 11–12 June 1998. My thanks for helpful comments from my colleague Anil Kashyap.

Banking is not only basically 19th-century technology, but it is disaster-prone technology. And in the summer of 1997 a banking-driven disaster struck in East Asia, just as it had struck so many times before in U.S. history, even down to as recently as 1989–1990. That the U.S. economy did not freeze up into depression in 1989–90, as it had in 1931 and so often before that, can be credited, I believe, to the rich variety of non-bank financial markets and institutions available to American firms and households. The U.S. is now *diversified* financially, as it were, in a way that East Asia in 1997 was not. As the developing countries of Asia do diversify and reduce their over-reliance on banking, they will reap major gains not only in stability, but in economic efficiency. That's the polite way to put it, of course. I might equally well have said they would suffer less inefficiency, waste, and corruption.[1]

The positive side of banking

Before criticizing the role of banks in the East Asian disasters of the past two years, let me first restate the positive case for why such heavy reliance had been placed on that institution. Banking is often credited with the "miracle" of liquidity creation. Each bank acquires assets that are basically *illiquid* in the sense that, even under the best of conditions, converting those assets back to cash means substantial costs and delays. Yet the banks' *depositors*, who put up most of the funds for those illiquid assets, have a perfectly *liquid* investment that, again under normal circumstances, they can convert to cash immediately and at virtually no cost. Truly a miracle.[2] And that's not all. The depositors also get the services of skilled loan officers to invest their funds in illiquid assets earning far higher returns than the depositors could hope to earn on their own. What a marvelous mechanism

for channeling into productive investments the huge flow of household savings generated in those economies! Remember that those countries, including Mainland China, have savings-to-income ratios that are three, four, or even more times those we in the West have become accustomed to.

Reliance on banking: the bad news

For all its potential contributions to economic growth, however, banking remains fragile. The extreme maturity mismatch on the bank's balance sheet (long-term fixed-rate loans versus short-term, floating-rate deposits), plus the first-come-first-served nature of the deposit obligations means that the banks are inherently vulnerable to massive runs by their depositors. Banks are the classic examples of self-fulfilling prophecies. As long as every depositor believes the bank will honor its promises, the bank *will* be able to do so. The withdrawals from any one account will be offset, on average, by deposits into other accounts, buffered by small amounts of till cash. But if for any reason doubts about the safety of the deposits arise on any large scale, then *nobody* can withdraw, except for the lucky few who get to the tellers' windows before the till cash is gone.

Because this source of bank fragility – this multiple equilibrium in deposit banking as economists call it – has long been understood, most governments normally take steps to counter it. The most direct approach sees the government invoking its sovereign powers to *guarantee* the deposits. Nowhere has this approach been carried further than in the U.S., which insures all bank demand deposits up to $100,000 per account (not per individual, but per account). Because individuals can hold multiple accounts, the guarantee of household demand deposits is virtually complete.

Few other countries have gone as far as the U.S. in making the guarantees a matter of law, but the public in many other countries throughout East Asia have come to *expect* that the government *will* honor the deposit commitments of the banks. That implicit guarantee has led to much mischief. In Thailand, for example, the efforts of the Thai Central Bank to bail out the depositors of some failing banks meant increasing the Thai money

---

1   Though most of my examples in this paper will be taken from the recent Southeast Asia experience, much of the analysis applies with equal force to financing growth in Mainland China, Latin America, and Eastern Europe.

2   The classic reference is D. W. Diamond and P. H. Dybvig, "Bank Runs, Deposit Insurance and Liquidity," *Journal of Political Economy* 91 (1983), 401–419.

supply with one hand precisely at a time when the Central Bank, with the other hand, was trying to mop up local liquidity in a vain fight to discourage speculation against the baht. Talk about sending mixed signals to the market!

But whether explicit or implicit, guarantees by the government require back-up in the form of extensive regulation. Otherwise, the perverse incentives known as moral hazard take over. Banks, knowing that the government will make good their liabilities, are led to take excessive risks in selecting their assets. And why not? If the investments succeed, the stockholders get the benefits. And, if they fail, the depositors certainly won't suffer. And even the stockholders needn't suffer heavy losses of their own money, given the enormously high leverage ratios typically found in commercial banking.

Bank regulation in practice

The response of the regulators to the moral hazard problem has tended to be a two-fold one as typified, say, in the Basel agreements. On the liability side of the bank balance sheets, first-tier capital requirements of 8% have been made the accepted international norm, though that still leaves debt/equity ratios absurdly high relative to those in the rest of the economy, particularly if, as in Japan and most of the rest of Asia, you don't always write down that capital to allow for your problem loans. On the asset side, the Basel approach has sought to deal with credit risk by imposing so-called "risk-based capital requirements" under which more capital is required for holdings of real estate, say, than of government bonds.

But, as noted, these requirements plus the normal calls for caution and prudence on the part of the banks are not self-enforcing. A continual process of inspection is a feature of every country's bank regulation. In the U.S., where regulatory authority is divided among the Federal Reserve System, the Controller of the Currency and the Federal Deposit Insurance Corporation, bankers often complain that while they are saying goodbye to one group of auditors and regulators at the back door, another group is coming in the front door. This detailed process of outside review has spawned – or should I say intensified – a strong

tendency toward bureaucratization in the structure and hierarchy of most banks.

This system of elaborate national and international rules and inspections to keep banking safe failed utterly last year in most of East Asia. Paradoxically, the rule structure governing banking actually made matters *worse* by producing the credit crunch that made recovery so difficult once the collapse had occurred.[3]

THE CRIPPLING CONSEQUENCES OF BANK REGULATION: THE CASE OF JAPAN

Any indictment of banks and bank regulation for causing and prolonging the East Asia crisis must begin with Japan. Japan is far and away the biggest economy and the largest lender in the area. And Japan, of course, is the *locus classicus* of bank-driven economic growth and development. How often during the roaring 1980s did we hear hymns of praise to the Japanese *keiretsu* system linking big conglomerate firms with their lead banks? The system was widely imitated throughout East Asia, notably in Korea and was even receiving envious glances from the Mainland Chinese.[4]

In the 1990s, however, the Japanese banking system, for all its favorable aura in world publicity, had begun to have trouble meeting the international

---

3 Banking vulnerability, needless to say, is not strictly an Asian problem, and the U.S. is not and has not become a country immune to banking stresses. It's just that the U.S. already *had its* banking crises *before* 1997, first the Savings and Loan maturity mismatch crisis of the early 1980s followed by the loan quality crisis in both the S&Ls and the commercial banks in 1989–1991. (For an account of the U.S. S&L disaster of the 1980s and the "reforms" to which it led, see James R. Barth, *The Great Savings and Loan Debacle,* American Enterprise Institute, Washington, D.C.Barth (1991).) Despite such highly publicized post-1980s regulatory actions as the Financial Institutions Reform Recovery and Enforcement Act (FIRREA, 1989) and the Federal Deposit Insurance Corporation Improvement Act (FDICEA, 1991), a sudden, sharp rise in interest rates could still put U.S. banks back on the front page.

4 I discuss the role of banks in the corporate governance system of Japan in Chapter 12 (entitled "Japanese versus American Corporate Governance") of my book, *Merton Miller on Derivatives* (New York: John Wiley & Sons, Inc., 1997). The influence of the Japanese bank-driven system on China is considered in Chapter 14, "Alternative Strategies for Corporate Governance in China."

capital standards. In fact, many Japanese banks probably couldn't even have come close to those standards had they not bribed the regulators to tip them off when the supposedly random inspections were due.

Causes of the failure to meet bank capital requirements

Three main reasons can be cited for this difficulty of Japanese banks in meeting the capital standards. First, of course, was the dramatic fall of the Japanese stock market starting in early 1990 and continuing to the present day. Note in this connection that Japanese banks, unlike U.S. banks, are permitted to hold common stocks. Interlocking holdings, after all, are an integral part of the *keiretsu* system.[5]

Closely paralleling the decline in stock in Japan was the collapse in real estate prices. Some observers attribute the Japanese banks' heavy reliance on real estate lending to a deregulation-induced weakening of the *keiretsu* system under which Japanese banks had enjoyed a secure, tied source of business loans. Rather than shrink in size to meet the new realities of reduced business loan demand, as happened in the U.S., the Japanese banks, some argue, were led into new and riskier types of lending, such as real estate lending in the hope of sustaining their earnings. Perhaps so. But you really don't have to "induce" banks in East Asia to invest in real estate. That has always been their natural inclination, as is all too clear from the skylines of Bangkok, Hong Kong, and even Shanghai. The real estate investments of the Japanese banks, we know, led not to profits, but to losses. What we don't know is precisely how large these losses are on real estate loans in Japan, except that they are surely huge. So huge, in fact, that a serious attempt to force banks to recognize them, then or now, would completely blow away the capital of the banking system.

The third, and in some ways, most devastating blow to bank capital, however, came from bad commercial loans to business. One supposed beauty of banking, it will be recalled, was the expertise of specialized loan-officers in placing the depositors' money in illiquid, but high-return investments in industry. Japanese banks however had a terrible earnings record on business loans even with the supposed information advantages inherent in the *keiretsu* system. The results were even worse in places like Korea, where loans to the *chaebols* were driven not by profit considerations, but by government development objectives; or in Indonesia, the original home of "crony capitalism."

The consequences of failing to meet capital requirements

Banking regulation, alas, is not like securities regulation in which failure on some arbitrary statutory requirements might be met with reprimands or fines. A bank that fails its capital requirements because of bad loans must, in principle, either remedy its capital deficiency immediately or close its doors. Citizens of countries whose banks happen not to be in trouble at the moment are always quick to cry for the banks to write off their problem loans. That would be fine if a country were facing one or even a few insolvent banks at a time. But not if all or even most of the banks are under water simultaneously. In countries like Japan and in East Asia generally, that are so heavily dependent on bank financing, the regulators were understandably hesitant to risk strangling their economies by literal interpretation of the international capital standards for their banks – interpretations that would have forced most, or even all, banks to close. The first inclination of the regulators in such cases is always denial – that is, refusal to force recognition of the widespread losses in the hope that the losses will prove transitory. But as the losses continue to mount, that pretense wears thin and the issue of closing down bad banks or bringing in additional replacement capital has to be faced eventually by even the most stubborn regulators (which would certainly include Japan's Ministry of Finance).

One solution for the Japanese banks would have been to fill the holes in their regulatory capital by

---

5 Some of the problems caused by allowing ownership of common stocks by Japanese banks are considered in Miller (1997), especially Chapter 19 entitled "Do the Laws of Economics Apply to Japan?"

floating new equity or equity equivalents such as preferred stocks. Modern finance tells us that when the costs of new capital are measured correctly, they come essentially to *flotation* costs – a number that would be 3 or 4%, or at most 10 or 15%, of the funds raised. Cost is not always the key, however, in the cozy world of Asian banking; control is. And the existing owners (and their managers) are reluctant, to put it mildly, to share that control with outsiders, particularly with foreigners who would have to put up much of the money. They see it as merely another form of Western imperialism.

Another possibility, of course, would have been for the government to recapitalize the banks by buying big chunks of preferred stock, the strategy followed for the similarly damaged U.S. banking system in the early 1930s. But in Japan, at least, anything smacking of deliberate government bailouts out of the existing bank stockholders – not the depositors, but the stockholders – is politically out of the question.[6]

Lowering interest rates to benefit Japanese banks: the unintended consequences

Faced with the Scylla of violating the international capital standards and the Charybdis of raising new capital from foreigners, MOF in Japan had one ploy left: drive down short-term interest rates. And drive them down they did, to levels not seen since the U.S. in the 1930s. The hope was that the Japanese banks would earn such high profits on the spread between short- and long-term interest rates that they could restore their capital and begin the task of writing down their bad loans. Driving down Japanese interest rates, however, also drove down the value of the yen relative to the U.S. dollar; or, what amounts to the same thing, raised the value of the dollar in relation to the yen. Unfortunately, of course, many of the countries of Southeast Asia, notably Thailand, had tied their currencies to the U.S. dollar, so that when the

dollar surged in response to Japanese policy, those local currencies soon struck the speculators and trade hedgers as substantially overvalued and they placed their bets accordingly. The Thai baht soon gave way, losing close to 50% of its value almost overnight and dragging down with it the exchange rate of its neighbors and competitors, Malaysia, Indonesia, the Philippines, and Korea.[7] As the exchange rate went down, the real debt burden went up for those firms (and banks) that had been borrowing in dollars. Bankruptcies were threatened everywhere and few countries had the institutions, even with IMF assistance, to permit a quick restructuring of the dollar-denominated debt of hundreds of separate corporations.

In sum, efforts by the Japanese to protect the capital of their *own* banks by lowering interest rates, and by calling (or refusing to roll over) loans to Asian firms and banks, served to destabilize much of the rest of Asia – and especially the banks in the rest of Asia. Runs by depositors began occurring on a massive scale in Thailand and depositor concern was felt even in countries with "strong" banking systems like Hong Kong and Singapore. The scramble for liquidity (and the efforts by some countries to defend their currencies by raising interest rates) brought stock prices and real estate prices down sharply. Banks throughout the region and not just in Japan then faced capital compliance problems. They too responded by calling loans where they could and refusing to make new ones. Soon ordinary trade credits were being denied even to sound businesses, including companies with firm export orders in hand. Like an automobile engine that has lost its oil, the system of bank-led development was in a freeze-up.[8]

---

6 So desperate has the threat of bank runs become recently in countries like Thailand and Indonesia, however, that the governments have been forced to nationalize many failing banks.

7 The role of the depressed yen in precipitating the Southeast Asia crisis is discussed in my article, "The Current Southeast Asia Financial Crisis," *Pacific Basin Capital Market Journal* (1998). It is interesting to speculate about how different the outcome in Southeast Asia's currency markets might have been if the countries in the area had pegged their currencies to the yen rather than the dollar. Taiwan appears to be adopting just such a strategy at the moment.

8 I do not want to leave the impression, however, that the credit crunch was entirely supply-side induced. Even a bank with adequate capital won't lend to a company facing bankruptcy.

Although I am arguing that the inherent fragility of banking lies at the root of the current Asian turmoil, I intend to present here no laundry list of needed new banking regulations or reforms. Can *any* set of policies we know about guarantee the system against periodic freeze-ups? I doubt it. Remember, in this connection, that one can't simply introduce legislation and assume it will be competently and honestly administered. Japan is again the obvious object lesson there, but it is a long-held tenet of Chicago-style economics that the greater the number of government regulations the greater are the incentives to corruption.[9]

Try to lessen the vulnerability of the banking system, by all means, but recognize that for the long run, the only safe policy is to reduce the role of banks and banking in economic life. That means, among other things, the creation of market substitutes for functions now performed by banks. And, for reasons of brevity, let me mention just two such financial market instruments.[10]

FINANCIAL MARKET SUBSTITUTES FOR BANKING

Money market and other mutual funds

I begin with a simple and easily implementable substitute for bank deposits as a source of liquid accounts for the general public. That substitute, of course, is the Money Market Mutual Fund. In the U.S., at least, the deposits in such Money Market funds, most of which are transferable by check, have already surpassed the total of commercial bank deposits. Money Market Mutual Funds, unlike ordinary banks (but like Irving Fisher's

"narrow banks"), invest only in short-term, liquid money market instruments like Treasury bills, or more typically, the liquid and highly rated commercial paper of major businesses (another alternative to traditional bank loans, though the paper is often backed by bank guarantees). In the 30 years or so since the formation of Money Market Funds was generated by the idiocies of our bank regulation, in particular by the restrictions on deposit account interest payments, not a single case of failure or even massive withdrawal-runs from those institutions has occurred. And this, mind you, even though such accounts are not insured or in any way guaranteed by the sovereign credit of the U.S. government (to repeat a phrase much beloved by Alan Greenspan, the Chairman of the Federal Reserve System, when applied to the U.S. commercial banking system). Such guarantees the Funds have are provided by the reputations of the *investment* banks – not commercial banks – that sponsor the Funds. But, in some ways even more important as a discourager of runs is the abandonment of the pernicious first-come-first-served rule of ordinary commercial banks deposits.

The Money Market Mutual Funds, though they strive to maintain the value of each share at $1 at all times, are indeed *mutual* funds. If, therefore, short-term interest rates were suddenly to rise steeply; and if the market value of even the Fund's very short-term assets were to fall; and if all the depositors at once sought to be first in line at the withdrawal window, they couldn't win. A mutual fund always has the right to give withdrawers a "haircut" – that is, to give them only their aliquot share of the value of the assets. True, even though they have that right, the sponsors of some troubled Funds have found it in their interest to put in the necessary additional capital to avoid "breaking the buck," as it's called. But that is a business decision on their part, and not a matter of law. The key point is that runs can't occur as long as the depositors realize no one can benefit from running to be first to withdraw.

Mutual funds concentrating on short-term liquidity for savers are clearly one obvious and easily implemented financial institution, but mutual funds of *all* kinds – domestic stock funds, foreign stock funds, bond funds and what have you – are also urgently needed. One reason that banks are so

9 The problem of providing the correct market-driven incentives not just to bank *managers*, but to bank *regulators*, is a central theme in two articles by Edward J. Kane: "Financial Regulation and Market Forces," *Swiss Journal of Economics and Statistics* 122 (3), 325–42; and "A Market Perspective on Financial Regulation," *Cato Journal* 13 (3) (1998), 333–337.

10 In a fuller account, mention should surely be made of securitization, which permits banks or other lenders to use their expertise in *originating* loans, which are then bundled for resale in tranches of different risk to ultimate investors.

powerful in countries like Japan and China is that the average household has really no alternative to low-yield bank deposits as a way of storing wealth except, of course, putting it under the mattress (and in Japan they don't even use mattresses!). In Japan, of course, the lack of substitutes was deliberate; it was part of the Japan Inc. program of forcing the public savings into low return bank deposits for the supposed benefit of giving cheap capital to industry. The notorious technological and consumer-service backwardness of the Japanese banking industry (in Japan the ATM machines don't run on weekends!) surely traces in large part to this virtually complete absence of competition for depositors' funds.

Junk bonds

If mutual funds are a market substitute and supplement for bank deposit liabilities, junk bonds, so-called, can play an equally important role as a financial market supplement and substitute for long-term commercial loans by banks. I use the term "junk" with some trepidation because these securities, which are really nothing more than unsecured, junior debentures, have come to have bad connotations in the U.S. The term "junk" is a pejorative applied by the old-line, "white shoe" investment bankers, as we call them, working in the more dignified, high-quality end of the bond market.

Actually, of course, junk bonds in the sense of high-yield junior securities have always been with us, sometimes as the preferred stocks so beloved of J. P. Morgan in the early years of this century, but mostly of debt instruments thereafter. The modern phase of the junk bond market, however, and the one attracting the bad public image, traces to the early 1980s. At that time, a number of ambitious new communication-oriented firms, like the telephone company, M.C.I., found themselves unable to satisfy their demands for huge amounts of capital either from the investment grade bond markets – new firms like M.C.I., after all, had no previous track record – or from their regular commercial banks. Despite the supposed informational advantages of relationship banking, why should banks have been expected to put up big chunks of money for such highly speculative ventures? Bank loan

officers, after all, aren't paid to take risks. Safety is the watchword, for reasons noted earlier.

Into this breach stepped several *investment* banks. Investment bankers, unlike commercial bankers *are* paid to take risks; witness, among other things, the substantially higher salaries they command. Prominent among these investment bankers was Michael Milken at the relatively new and extremely brash firm of Drexel, Burnham, Lambert (a firm whose junk bond business was run not out of staid New York like a serious bond dealer was supposed to do, but out of Los Angeles, no less, a city with a reputation for froth and frivolity). Milken's essential innovation was not to *invent* junk bonds; they already had a long history as I have indicated, but to make them *liquid*, easily tradable, *market* instruments. He became not just a bond dealer, but a *market maker* in junk bonds.

Once the market had been made liquid, both the demand for and supply of junk bonds increased substantially. A substantial part of that new supply in the late 1980s came from what were called, again pejoratively, "corporate raiders," using junk bonds for taking over firms from complacent, entrenched managements. Although such transfers of ownership serve normally to raise shareholder value – as evidenced by the huge premiums in many hostile takeovers – entrenched corporate America, and its natural allies in Washington, struck back hard against the junk bonds they saw as the threat to their interests. Michael Milken was soon sent to jail on essentially trivial, technical charges; and major government-regulated users of junk bonds, such as savings and loan associations were forced to unload their holdings of such bonds.[11] With its main market maker thus knocked out of play and with the instrument itself under a black reputational cloud, junk bonds seemed doomed – just one more excess of the Reagan years of greed. But economics assures us that if a market does satisfy important social needs, the market will eventually surmount artificial, mainly government-induced obstacles, and resume its rightful place in the pantheon.

11 A detailed account of the government-led vendetta against Milken is given by Daniel Fischel in *Payback: The Conspiracy to Destroy Michael Milken and His Financial Revolution* (New York: Harper Business, 1995).

And that has indeed happened to the U.S. junk bond market, which has played, and which continues to play, a major role in funding the fixed capital requirements of so many firms that are growing, but whose ratings are less than triple-A (or some-times even less than single B). Innovative medium-sized firms of that kind must be relied up to resume Asia's economic growth now that the former bank/government approach to growth and the industrial dinosaurs it inevitably spawned have been so thoroughly discredited. For this necessary transition in growth modalities, a greater role for vigorous financial markets, including junk bond markets, is clearly essential.

CONCLUSION

That financial markets contribute to economic growth is a proposition almost too obvious for serious discussion at a forum this sophisticated. True, those markets are often blamed these days for causing *negative* growth, especially in Southeast Asia. But markets, because they draw so much publicity, particularly when they crash, have always been blamed for society's ills. Most Americans, even today, believe that the great depression of the 1930s was caused by the stock market crash of 1929 rather than by the inept monetary mismanagement of the Federal Reserve System. Similar folklore has sprung up about the so-called "derivatives disasters" of the 1990s – disasters which turn out, on closer examination, to be merely familiar, old-fashioned management disasters in a new disguise.[12]

I have chosen not to spend time pointing out that prices in *all* freely-functioning markets, financial and non-financial alike, are subject to crashes. Oil prices, for example, have declined far more drastically in recent months than the much ballyhooed stock market break of October 1987. Most real-world markets have time paths that are almost everywhere discontinuous, as the statisticians say (that is, that are subject to periodic abrupt shifts, *up*

as well as down). Continuously smooth price paths (which the public thinks of as normal) are actually an artifact of the specialist system of New York Stock Exchange, and even those specialists can't pull it off when sentiment shifts abruptly.

I have tried here instead to point to an often overlooked aspect of financial markets and economic growth, namely the diversification benefits that financial markets bring. Having a wide spectrum of financial markets available keeps a country from having to put all its development eggs in one basket, as it were – and, in particular, from relying too heavily on commercial banking. Commercial banking, at its best, can be an extremely efficient form of intermediation between saving and investment, particularly when a country is just starting out on its road to development. You can't expect a country to rely on a stock market, after all, until it has common stock (and the legal infrastructure that goes with it)! But, relying on banking, like relying on atomic-energy electric power, is a disaster-prone strategy requiring enormous amounts of direct government supervision to reduce the frequency of explosions (and subsequent implosions).

In fact, however, as I have attempted to argue, the regulatory apparatus designed to protect the banking system actually becomes counterproductive and leads to a credit freeze-up wherever any substantial number of banks go bad at the same time. The U.S., to its great benefit, has made itself much less vulnerable than in the past to credit crunches (and has substantially increased the efficiency of the capital allocation process) by substituting dispersed and decentralized financial markets for banking. Japan, despite having long since become a "mature" economy, still has not; and its efforts to deal with its banking problems have served only to destabilize itself as well as its neighbors. We can only hope that other developing countries, especially but not only in Southeast Asia, will not follow the Japanese example and will begin, more systematically, to substitute financial markets for banks.

---

12 The derivatives disasters are discussed in Miller (1997), especially Chapter 2 entitled "The Recent Derivatives 'Disasters': Assessing the Damage."

CHAPTER 29

Globalization, Corporate Finance, and the Cost of Capital

René M. Stulz (Ohio State University)*

When Malaysia imposed its restrictions on capital flows last year, the world financial community was stunned. Yet, for many years after World War II, such capital controls would have seemed quite normal. After the war, almost all countries had tight controls on currency conversion, which meant that outside investors could invest in foreign markets only if they could get access to often scarce foreign currencies. In addition, most countries also had explicit restrictions on foreign investment. Some countries prohibited their own citizens from buying foreign shares. In many cases, foreign investors were forbidden to buy local shares. And in countries where foreign investors were allowed to buy local shares, the shares often carried lower (or no) voting rights – and there were typically limits to the percentage of a firm's shares that could be owned by foreigners. In addition to these legal and regulatory constraints, there were also less formal deterrents to international investment. Besides political risks such as the possibility of expropriation, there were major obstacles to hedging foreign exchange rate risk as well as a near-total lack of coordination of accounting standards among countries.

Over the last 50 years, the legal and regulatory barriers to international investment have largely disappeared among developed economies. And, in the past decade, such barriers have fallen dramatically in many emerging markets. As a result of these changes, U.S. investors can now buy securities of companies in many foreign countries with almost no restrictions. Large U.S. corporations today raise funds in different financial markets throughout the world – sometimes in simultaneous offerings in onshore and offshore markets. Asian investors now worry about how the U.S. markets performed while they were asleep because they believe that the fate of their markets during the day depends on what happened in New York in the past twelve hours. And morning news shows in the U.S. routinely discuss the overnight returns of the Nikkei and Hang Seng indices in an effort to forecast the performance of U.S. markets.

Though economists and financial academics have generally welcomed this process of globalization and emphasized its benefits to investors and

* This paper presents the implications for corporate finance of my working paper entitled "Globalization of Equity Markets and the Cost of Capital," which is available at http://www.cob.ohio-state.edu/fin/faculty/stulz under the heading "working papers." I am grateful for research assistance from Ed Gladewell, Jan Jindra, and Dong Lee; and for comments from Yakov Amihud, Bernard Dumas, Peter Henry, Andrew Karolyi, John McConnell, Nils Tuchschmid, Ingrid Werner, and participants at the NYSE-Bourse de Paris Conference on Global Equity Markets in Paris and the BSI Conference in Lugano. I also thank the New York Stock Exchange and the Bourse de Paris for financial support.

corporations, many policy makers have questioned whether the process has gone too far and whether controls on capital flows should be reinstated. In this paper, I attempt to evaluate how the globalization of capital markets is affecting the corporate cost of capital and equity values.

The remainder of the paper falls into four main sections. In the first I investigate how globalization affects the discount rate that investors use in valuing a given stream of equity cash flows. In so doing, I present a number of arguments for why globalization is reducing investors' required rate of return on stocks of companies in developed as well as developing economies.

In the second section, the focus shifts to a different, generally neglected perspective on the cost of capital. John D. Rockefeller said that the greatest challenge in his career was "to obtain enough capital to do all the business I wanted to and could do" (Chernow, *Titan* (Random House, 1998)). To understand this problem of raising capital, consider a firm with a large project that management must finance. Based on the cash flows that *management* expects the project to generate, the rate of return on the project exceeds the cost of equity capital dictated by the capital markets. However, the cash flows that matter when raising equity from outside investors are the cash flows that *investors* believe they will eventually receive from the firm in the form of dividends or capital gains. If capital markets expect the project to contribute less to the value of the firm than management does, the company will be forced to sell equity at a price below what management thinks it is worth. In management's view, being forced to sell equity at a "discount" increases the effective cost of capital; and if the additional cost is large enough, management may forgo the project.

The difference between management's and investors' assessments of the project's value could exist for at least two reasons. First, management typically has more information about the profitability of a project than do investors, and it is often hard for management to communicate that information credibly. This problem is referred to by academics as the "information asymmetry" problem. Second, investors might be concerned that management will make poor use of the capital because its own objectives differ from those of investors. This shareholder-manager conflict is often called the "agency cost" problem.[1] As a result of these two problems, management might not be able to raise enough funds to launch the project. And even if the firm is able to raise the necessary funds, these two problems could make equity capital prohibitively expensive.

Because of these information and agency cost problems, a firm's cost of capital will depend critically on its corporate governance system. By corporate governance system, I mean not only the internal controls such as independent boards and effective incentive compensation plans, but also external elements such as legal protection for minority shareholders, sophisticated and activist institutional investors, and well-functioning takeover markets. My argument here, in brief, is that companies in national economies with more effective corporate governance are likely to raise capital on better terms because such firms are more likely to invest the capital wisely and to reinvest the firm's cash flows in ways that do not destroy shareholder wealth. Thus, in the second part of the paper, I maintain that globalization improves corporate governance and thereby lowers the cost of external financing by reducing information and agency costs.

The third section of the paper offers a brief review of the growing body of empirical evidence on the impact of globalization on the cost of capital. What evidence we have provides some, though by no means overwhelming, support for the above arguments – and I attempt to explain why the evidence is not more conclusive. The fourth and final section discusses the implications of the theory and evidence for corporate strategy and practice.

WHY GLOBALIZATION IS REDUCING THE COST OF CAPITAL: THE PORTFOLIO PERSPECTIVE

Consider a market that, for whatever reason, is isolated from the rest of the world. In this market, shares issued locally must be held by local

---

1 More precisely, it is called the "agency cost of managerial discretion" problem. For a detailed analysis of this problem, see my paper "Managerial Discretion and Optimal Financing Policies," *Journal of Financial Economics* (1990), 3–26.

investors, and local investors cannot diversify internationally. In such circumstances, because local investors have to bear more risk than if they were free to diversify their holdings across international markets, they will have required rates of return for holding local stocks that are higher than the rates required by well-diversified, global investors for holding the same stocks. As a consequence, the prices of local shares will be lower than if the local market were integrated with global markets.

A striking confirmation of this argument was provided by the Swiss firm Nestlé's decision, in November of 1988, to eliminate restrictions on foreign ownership on both classes of its shares. Until that time, Nestlé had two types of shares that differed only in ownership restrictions.[2] One type of shares, called *bearer shares*, was available to all investors, foreign as well as Swiss. A second type, *registered shares*, was available only to Swiss investors. Both registered and bearer shares had the same voting rights and the same dividends.

If restrictions on foreign ownership do not affect share values, one would expect the registered shares to sell for about the same amount as the unrestricted bearer shares. But the registered shares sold at a consistently large discount to the bearer shares. Indeed, the shares available only to Swiss investors were typically *only about half as valuable* as the shares available to foreign investors.

Then, on November 17, 1988, Nestlé announced that it was removing the restrictions on foreign ownership of its registered shares. During the week of the announcement, the price of the registered shares rose from SFr. 4,245 to 5,782, an increase of over 36%. And although the value of the bearer shares fell by about 25% (presumably because arbitrageurs were selling them while buying the registered shares), Nestlé's total market capitalization – the sum of the values of both classes of shares – increased by 10%.

The lesson from this example is that, where barriers to international investment segment a national capital market from global markets, the local investors bear all the risk of the economic activities in their economy. And, for bearing this

risk, such investors require a higher risk *premium* that effectively reduces the value that local investors are willing to place on the stock relative to what a globally diversified investor would pay if given the chance.

The local CAPM

To understand why investors in segmented markets are likely to require higher rates of return, consider the simple "mean-variance" model of investor behavior for which Harry Markowitz was awarded the Nobel Prize in 1990. Suppose that investors can invest only in their own countries and that, as the Markowitz model suggests, they care about only the expected return of their portfolio of assets and the variance of that return. Such investors will measure risk by the volatility of the return of their portfolio; and, as the volatility of their country's market portfolio increases, the risk premium required by investors for holding the market portfolio will increase along with it. For instance, assuming investors across countries have similar attitudes towards risk, a country where the variance of the market portfolio is twice what it is in another country will have twice the risk premium of the other country.

To estimate the cost of equity capital for a particular company operating in a segmented financial market, one could use the following "local" version of the capital asset pricing model (CAPM):

$$E(R_C) = R_f + \beta_H \times [E(R_H) - R_f],$$

where $E(R_C)$ is the required rate of return on the company's stock by local investors; R_f is the risk-free rate; β_H is the beta of the company's stock price in relation to the local or home-country market; and $E(R_H)$ is the expected return of the home country market portfolio. The cost of equity so calculated serves both as a discount rate for valuing the company's equity cash flows and, when adjusted for debt financing, as the "hurdle rate" for corporate investments. So, for example, when a firm considers whether to take on a project, the present value of the project for its shareholders is estimated by discounting the expected cash flows from the project at the CAPM-determined required rate of return.

2　There were also differences in anonymity. Investors could buy bearer shares anonymously, whereas purchasers of registered shares had to register their shares with the company to obtain full ownership rights.

Now consider what happens to the cost of capital when this country decides to open up its markets to foreign investors. To do that, let's take the real economic activities of the country as given; in other words, if a country has invested in the production of widgets, we assume that the expected value and the variance of the profits from producing widgets are not affected by globalization.[3] By keeping the degree of globalization in markets for goods and services unchanged, we can focus just on the impact of *financial* globalization.

When a country opens up its capital market to foreign investors and lets its own residents invest abroad, the residents of the country no longer have to bear all the risks associated with the economic activities of the country. They can be shared with foreign investors who, by investing in the country, bear some of these risks. In exchange, domestic investors bear foreign risks by buying foreign securities. For both groups of investors, the benefit from bearing foreign as well as domestic risks is that some of these risks offset each other through the process of diversification. By investing in many countries with economic cycles or events that are partly offsetting, investors can reduce the risk of their portfolios substantially without reducing their expected return. For example, although studies of international diversification differ as to the extent of these benefits, most conclude that exchanging a portfolio of U.S. stocks for an internationally diversified portfolio will reduce the standard deviation of the returns by at least 20%.[4]

To see the effect of diversification on investors when countries liberalize their capital markets, it is useful to consider an example. Assume there are a large number of countries integrated into world markets, that each country represents a very small fraction of the total global market, that the return on each national market portfolio has the same expected value and variance of return, and that the return on the market portfolio in each country is completely uncorrelated with the return of the market portfolio in every other country. Once the markets in all countries become open to each other, all investors (who, again, care only about the expected return and variance of their portfolios) are assumed to hold the world market portfolio to take full advantage of the benefits from diversification.

With this set of assumptions, the expected return on an investor's portfolio remains the same regardless of how his wealth is invested across countries. At the same time, the variance of the return falls with each additional country added to the portfolio. In the extreme case where the number of countries is very large, the variance of the return approaches zero, and the world market portfolio has no risk and hence no risk premium. In such a case, all stocks in all countries would be priced as if investors required only the risk free rate of return.

Of course, it is unrealistic to think that all risks could be completely diversifiable internationally. In particular, business cycles, as we saw once again during the Asian crisis,[5] have a tendency to cross country boundaries. It is also obviously a gross exaggeration to think that *all* publicly traded companies would have access to global capital markets. This would likely be true only for the largest and most visible firms – or at most those included in a major national index of stocks.

But if the above example is clearly unrealistic, it nevertheless serves to illustrate an important point: If investors truly care only about the expected return and the variance of their portfolios, they

---

3   In fact, globalization is likely to change real economic activities – and improve efficiency – by encouraging economies that have been previously segmented from global markets to focus increasingly on their areas of comparative advantage. For an article that shows how globalization allows countries to specialize more and undertake riskier projects because individuals in a country can diversify risks by investing abroad, see Maurice Obstfeld, "Risk-taking, Global Diversification, and Growth," *American Economic Review* 84 (1994), 1310–1329.

4   For a recent estimate of the benefits from diversification, see Giorgio DeSantis and Bruno Gerard, "International Asset Pricing and Portfolio Diversification with Time-varying Risk," *Journal of Finance* 52 (1997), 1881–1913.

5   Some observers have expressed concern that correlations increase during crises. For example, correlations seemed to increase during the recent Asian crisis, and then to fall afterward. More generally, there is a concern that the progressive integration of global economic activity is leading to greater synchronization of global economic cycles and rising correlations during bear markets. In a forthcoming paper, Geert Bekaert and Campbell Harvey find that when countries open their capital markets, they experience a small increase in their home market's correlation with global markets, but not sufficiently large to change our general argument about the impact of globalization on the cost of capital. (See Bekaert and Harvey, "Foreign Speculators and Emerging Markets," *Journal of Finance*, forthcoming.)

will respond to new opportunities for global diversification by creating portfolios that promise either a lower volatility for the same expected return or a higher expected return for the same volatility. And this means that risk premiums and the cost of capital can be expected to fall not only in previously segmented markets, but in long-integrated markets as well. As one would expect, the largest reductions in cost of capital resulting from globalization will be experienced by companies in liberalizing economies that are gaining access to the global markets for the first time. (Recall, again, the dramatic effect of Nestlé's decision to open its registered shares to foreign investors.) But companies in integrated economies like the U.S. are also benefiting from increasing capital flows from investors in once isolated markets because this allows the firms' risks to be shared by a much larger pool of investors with different risk exposures and hence different appetites for bearing the risks of these companies. Indeed, I would argue that globalization's effect on the cost of capital over the past decade or so is a significant contributor to the current level of U.S. stock prices.

The Global CAPM

Besides falling risk premiums in all integrated (or integrating) capital markets, the above example has a second major implication for the corporate cost of capital. As already noted, if global diversification of equity portfolios minimizes volatility and risk premiums, then investors in all countries have incentives to hold the same global portfolio that includes the equities of companies all over the world. For this reason, it is useful to think of the equity markets that are integrated with each other as forming essentially one worldwide market portfolio. And for all companies that are large or visible enough to be traded in such a global equity market, the proper risk measure, or beta, would be computed in relation not to the home-country portfolio, but to the world market portfolio. That is, in integrated markets, investors with globally diversified portfolios will measure the risk of individual stocks by how they contribute to the volatility *not* of their home-country portfolios, but to the volatility of the global portfolio. For example, a U.S. investor – and, for that matter, a Japanese or a Swiss

investor – considering the purchase of IBM shares will evaluate the beta of IBM not in relation to the S&P 500, but rather in relation to a global index like the Morgan-Stanley World (MSCI) Index.

In sum, the CAPM holds for all integrated markets together rather than on a country-by-country basis. Therefore, in calculating the cost of capital for a given firm, we should use a global CAPM like the following:

$$E(R_G) = R_f + \beta_G \times [E(R_G) - R_f],$$

where R_G denotes the required expected return on a stock when markets are global; R_f is still the local country risk-free rate, β_G is the global beta of the company in question; and R_G denotes the return of the global market portfolio (again, like the MSCI World Index).

Presented in this context, the global CAPM is especially useful in showing the two distinct effects of global diversification on the cost of capital. Besides reducing market risk premiums for both home countries and for the world equity market as a whole, gaining access to global markets also effectively reduces the betas of most companies. More precisely, globalization reduces the beta of all companies whose profits and values are more strongly correlated with their local economies than with the global economy. For example, returning to the case of Nestlé, when the company eliminated the Swiss ownership requirements on its registered shares in 1988, the company had a Swiss beta of 0.9, but a global beta of only 0.6. And even if we assume the global market risk premium was equal to (instead of lower than) the Swiss market premium, that reduction in beta alone translated into a 150 basis-point reduction of Nestlé's cost of equity capital.[6]

But, as suggested earlier, it is not only companies from once-segmented markets like Nestlé that are benefiting from globalization. Although the reduction in cost of capital is likely to be greatest for large companies based in small countries with limited capital markets, the fall in the global risk premium means that even firms in well-established

---

6   For the details of this calculation, see my 1995 article in this journal, "Globalization and the Cost of Capital: The Case of Nestlé," *Journal of Applied Corporate Finance*, Vol. 8 No. 3 (Fall 1995).

financial markets like the U.S. and U.K. are bene-fiting from the global diversification of investors' portfolios. This is a benefit that increases the value of all firms whose cost of capital is determined in global markets.

GLOBALIZATION REDUCES CAPITAL COSTS BY IMPROVING CORPORATE GOVERNANCE

The above arguments for why globalization reduces the discount rate of investors are com-pelling, but they do not capture the whole impact of globalization on the cost of capital. To under-stand why, let's focus on a company that has to raise equity to finance a new investment. In many ways, the ability of firms to raise equity from the public is a paradox. In an equity issue, the firm receives cash from outside investors without a con-tractual agreement to give anything back. For equity financing to be possible, shareholders must expect to receive sufficient cash flows to provide them with an expected return comparable to what they would expect to earn on other investments of the same risk. But, as discussed in the introduction, managers face difficulties in convincing sharehold-ers that they will receive such cash flows. This is because managers (1) have information that shareholders do not have about the firm's invest-ments and (2) have incentives both to issue equity when they feel their stock is overvalued and to take projects that do not necessarily increase shareholder value.

Because of these information and incentive problems, a firm may have good projects but be unable to finance them because its managers can-not convince shareholders that the projects are value-adding. Though we focus first on companies where shareholders are widely dispersed and man-agers are "in power," many of the issues that we discuss are the same if there is a large, controlling shareholder instead. We address the latter case toward the end of this section.

Consider a firm whose management believes it has valuable projects. In other words, if manage-ment could convince investors that the projected cash flows will materialize – and eventually accrue to them in the form of higher dividends or capital gains – the shareholders would benefit from the

firm's investment in these projects. Managers will often have difficulty convincing investors that such projects have value because managers can benefit from corporate investments even if they fail to earn the cost of capital. Managers tend to benefit – in the form of higher salaries, increased social standing, and so forth – when the firm simply gets bigger, which often leads them to invest even in unprofitable projects rather than pay out larger dividends or buy back stock.

Management will be less able to pursue its own goals at the expense of shareholders when there is effective monitoring. By "monitoring" I mean all the processes whereby boards of directors and other interested parties examine the actions and policies of management and use the outcome of their examination to influence management's actions and policies. When necessary, boards of directors, active shareholders, and potential bid-ders can all take actions to reverse managerial decisions or even replace management. And, as managers increasingly come to understand that decisions that hurt shareholders affect their own tenure and compensation, managerial decisions are more likely to be value-increasing.

But monitoring, of course, is itself a costly activ-ity and does not provide a complete solution for corporate governance. For one thing, because monitoring is costly, it is much more likely to take place after poor performance. If the firm loses money, for example, investors will often devote sig-nificant resources to figure out what is happening. But it is much harder for outsiders to figure out that managers did not take actions that would have made a successful firm even more successful. It is especially in these situations that incentives are likely to play a key role: they can lead managers to maximize shareholder wealth even when no mon-itoring takes place.

In sum, the extent to which management finds it in its own interest to maximize shareholder wealth depends critically on the firm's corporate gover-nance system. If the firm's corporate governance system makes it possible for management to be monitored efficiently – particularly when it also has strong incentives to increase value – the firm's stock price will be higher and management will find it easier to raise funds.

Let's now consider in more detail how investor monitoring of management takes place and how it is likely to be affected by globalization.[7] We consider in turn each of six important mechanisms used to monitor management:

(1) The Board of Directors. In principle, a firm's board of directors is the most direct mechanism for monitoring management. Managers report to the board and the board can fire management. Board members have a duty to be informed about what management is doing. One problem with this arrangement, however, is that when the firm has diffuse shareholders, managers generally determine the composition of the board. This clearly limits the board's ability to discipline management if it becomes necessary.

Having a board that lacks credibility may not be a problem for a company that does not need outside capital. But if the firm wants to raise funds in the capital markets, it becomes an important issue because a weak board is less likely to discipline managers – or replace them if necessary – when performance proves inadequate. For this reason, unless management has a strong track record and clear incentives to increase value, investors are likely to expect lower cash flows from companies with weak boards.

This has important implications for firms from segmented economies attempting to raise capital in *global* markets. For such firms to succeed, investors in these markets must have confidence that the use of the funds they provide will be monitored. As we are now seeing in countries like Japan and Korea – and as saw in the early 1990s in the U.S. – this demand for monitoring is leading to more active boards that are increasingly independent of management.

(2) The Capital Markets. To sell securities, managers hire investment bankers who play a key *certification* role by risking their reputations in marketing the securities to their investor clients. When raising capital in global markets, companies from less developed markets gain access to a broader range of investment banks. And provided such companies have the right qualifications and good prospects, they can choose to issue securities with banks that have stronger reputations or more

specialized knowledge about the firms' industries than their local bankers. Because such investment banks are in a better position to evaluate the firms' prospects, while also having more reputational capital at risk, securing the help of such banks conveys positive information to the markets about the companies themselves.

(3) The Legal System. The legal system plays two roles.[8] First, it limits the ability of management to expropriate resources from investors. In legal systems with few protections for (minority) shareholders, managers can almost literally steal corporate assets with something close to impunity. But, as the legal system improves, shareholders have greater recourse and the deterrents to managerial self-dealing and fraud become more effective. Second, the legal system provides a mechanism for investors to monitor management and exercise their rights. When shareholders discover management policies or actions that hurt them, they can use the legal system to force management to change those policies and, in some cases, receive compensation for lost value.

With globalization of financial markets, companies based in countries with little protection of minority shareholders that raise funds and list in countries with stronger protection expose themselves to legal actions from investors in these countries. As a result, minority shareholders in such firms end up with better legal protection than they had before.

(4) Active Shareholders. Small shareholders have little incentive to monitor management. Monitoring, as we have seen, is expensive. And since these shareholders have a small stake, even if their monitoring efforts would lead to a value-increasing improvement in management's policies, the benefits to these investors would likely be small relative to the costs incurred. Large shareholders benefit much more from their own monitoring efforts. As a result, companies with large shareholders, all else equal, are likely to be monitored more closely than firms with only small shareholders.

Globalization makes it possible for investors from other countries to take large stakes in a firm and monitor management. As suggested earlier, there is a potential problem with large shareholders: namely, their tendency to use their influence to

---

7 For a recent review of the literature on corporate governance, see Andrei Shleifer and Robert Vishny, "A Survey of Corporate Governance," *Journal of Finance* 52 (1997), 737–784.

8 See Shleifer and Vishny (1997).

obtain benefits from management that do not accrue to the other shareholders. But since the large shareholders produced by globalization are foreigners and thus presumably "outsiders," they are much more likely to perform the arm's-length monitoring that ends up increasing firm value and benefiting minority stockholders.

(5) The Market for Corporate Control. When internal governance systems fail, the market for corporate control – that is, takeovers, LBOs, and the like – makes it possible to remove management if it does not maximize shareholder wealth. Moreover, even in the absence of a takeover bid, the mere possibility of takeover has a disciplinary effect on management since it knows that if the firm performs poorly, it could become a takeover target.

Of course, takeovers are effectively, if not legally, prohibited in many national economies. But provided there is some possibility for investors to remove underperforming managers, opening up a capital market to foreign investors immediately creates a much larger pool of investors that can compete for control of firms within that market. This leads to greater competition for control among investors, which benefits existing shareholders directly. Moreover, even if takeovers are currently prohibited, the opening of capital markets to foreign investors tends to create a set of economic forces that exert pressure for opening up the market for corporate control.

(6) Disclosure. Public disclosure of information by firms is required by laws and regulations. But most larger companies would disclose information even if they were not required to do so. Failure to provide adequate information would make it very expensive, if not impossible, to raise funds from the public capital markets. In that case, the firm would have to resort to banks and other financial intermediaries – a capital-raising process in which private disclosure takes the place of public disclosure.

When a firm raises funds from public markets, it must not only provide extensive disclosure at the time of issuance, but also commit to furnish information on an ongoing basis (at least through the term of the financing). The more information a company provides initially – and the stronger its commitment to provide continuing disclosure – the less costly it is for investors to monitor

management and, hence, the more favorable the other terms and conditions of the financing.

One problem here, however, is that it is difficult for firms in countries with minimal disclosure requirements to commit themselves to ongoing disclosure. The choice of a stricter regulatory environment (say, the U.S., which means oversight by the SEC) is one way for companies to commit to continuous disclosure. Another is listing on an exchange (like the NYSE or Nasdaq) with extensive disclosure requirements. Thanks to globalization, companies can commit to higher disclosure standards simply by seeking additional listings on exchanges that have higher standards than their local market.

Of course, those firms that feel they are getting a higher stock price by maintaining their ability to conceal poor performance (say, by means of the "smoothing" allowed by the "reserve accounting" popular outside the U.S. and U.K.) are unlikely to volunteer to meet SEC requirements. But since this logic implies that firms with the best prospects are the ones most likely to choose to list on stricter exchanges, the mere announcement that a company intends to list on such an exchange tends to be interpreted by the market as good news.[9]

Why globalization increases monitoring for all companies

In this analysis, then, globalization increases the monitoring of management and thereby reduces information and agency costs. As a result, globalization reduces the costs of external finance for companies *in addition to* reducing the expected rate of return required by investors. This reduction in the costs of external finance resulting from improved corporate governance can be viewed as a decrease in the cost of capital in the following sense: it can turn value-reducing projects – projects that might otherwise have been abandoned

9 For two articles that develop theoretical models where firms reveal their good prospects by listing abroad, see Salvatore Cantale, "The Choice of a Foreign Market as a Signal," working Paper, Tulane University, 1998; and O. Fuerst, "A Theoretical Analysis of the Investor Protection Regulations: Argument for Global Listing of Stocks," Working Paper, Yale School of Management, 1998.

because of the high cost of funding them – into value-adding projects. It does so by increasing investors' estimates of the cash flows they will receive from the companies they invest in. The strengthening of corporate governance systems associated with globalization raises the probability that management will work harder and make more value-increasing decisions for its investors while having fewer opportunities to pursue goals that are not in investors' interests.

Yet, based on our analysis, one might conclude that globalization increases the monitoring of management only for those firms that decide to participate in the global capital markets. But this is not the case: Once a company has a choice between participating and not participating in global capital markets, the choice not to participate may reveal important information about the value of that firm.

To see this, let's go back to the issue of disclosure. Firms that want to participate in global markets must meet disclosure standards that allow them to compete for funds in these markets. But if a firm is large enough to access global markets and chooses not to do so mainly to avoid complying with stricter disclosure requirements, investors are likely to conclude that management prefers less disclosure because it allows them to conceal poor performance – or at least a failure to maximize value. Thus, companies that stay local and continue to meet only local disclosure requirements may be "signaling" their investors that they are worth less than previously thought. And, in this fashion, globalization can be seen as exerting pressure for better performance and greater transparency on all firms large enough to raise capital in global markets.

The special case of large shareholder-controlled firms

Our discussion has focused thus far on the case of publicly traded companies with highly fragmented ownership where management is in control. This is an apt characterization of most large, public firms in the U.S. and the U.K. But, in the case of even the largest "quoted" companies in most other countries, there tend to be large shareholders – such as banks, other corporations, and founding families – with controlling

interests.[10] As noted earlier, although such shareholders presumably have strong incentives to monitor management, they also have incentives, along with the power, to force management to take actions that benefit themselves at the expense of other shareholders and other investors. The working of such incentives can be seen clearly in recent accounts of South Korean chaebols (and also in the case study of Union Bank of Switzerland by Claudio Loderer later in this issue).

This ability of controlling shareholders to expropriate value from other investors creates a problem for firms in raising capital. For instance, outside investors who buy equity in a firm controlled by a large shareholder will discount the price they are willing to pay to reflect the fact that the firm's profits might be siphoned off to companies controlled by the large shareholder. This discount might be large enough that the firm cannot "afford" to raise new funds.

To avoid this problem, minority shareholders have to be protected. In addition to monitoring management, minority shareholders need a way to monitor the large shareholder. They can do so using all of the mechanisms discussed above except the board of directors – since the large shareholder will effectively control the board. By listing on exchanges with high standards for protecting minority shareholders, a firm expresses its commitment to respect the rights of these shareholders. In cases where the local exchange does not offer much protection for minority shareholders, globalization enables companies to seek listings on foreign exchanges that provide such protection. Such listings increase firm value both by ensuring that the firm's policies are more likely to increase shareholder wealth and by allowing the firm to raise funds on more favorable terms.

Globalization and transactions costs

Thus far, we have ignored the costs of buying and selling securities. Globalization is reducing these

---

10 See Rafael LaPorta, Florencio Lopez-de-Silanes, Andrei Shleifer, and Robert W. Vishny, "Corporate Ownership around the World," *Journal of Finance* 54 (April, 1999) 471–517.

costs for many firms, and such cost reductions increase firm value both directly and indirectly. In 1986, Yakov Amihud and Haim Mendelson published the first of several academic studies to show that the size of the bid-ask spread affects the market's required rate of return on securities.[11] The reasoning is that if investors have to pay more to transact a security, they have to be compensated with a greater expected return *before* transaction costs to offset these costs.

With globalization, one expects the bid-ask spread on securities to decrease for several reasons. For one thing, the pool of potential investors increases significantly. Second, directly related to our analysis of governance, the greater disclosure by firms associated with globalization reduces opportunities for insider trading. This means that market makers and investors without access to inside information worry less about being taken advantage of by insiders when they trade. And to the extent such assurances increase the number of investors and market makers willing to transact in a firm's securities, this leads to greater liquidity and a lower bid-ask spread.[12] In support of this proposition, a 1997 study by Katherine Smith and George Sofianos shows that firms that list abroad experience an increase in volume even in their home market, which is consistent with the argument that globalization leads to greater liquidity and hence a lower cost of capital.[13]

Third, globalization means greater competition in market-making and investment banking services. Companies that enter the global capital markets have access to investment banks that can compete for their business and hence lower prices. These firms can also choose to list on exchanges that are more efficient, thereby reducing the cost of transacting their securities.[14]

Besides reducing transactions costs, the greater liquidity resulting from globalization has an indirect impact on the monitoring of management. First, with greater liquidity, the market for a firm's equity becomes more efficient in the sense that it more quickly and accurately reflects information about the firm. This makes the firm's stock price more informative and hence more useful in monitoring management. Second, greater liquidity makes it easier for active investors to accumulate positions in a stock and to sell these positions as well.

EMPIRICAL EVIDENCE ON THE IMPACT OF GLOBALIZATION ON THE COST OF CAPITAL

Having discussed the theory of how globalization should affect the cost of capital, let's now examine the empirical evidence. We will do this in four steps: First, I review recent studies of the explanatory power of the global CAPM. Second, I discuss the problems with using traditional methods of estimating the risk premium with time-series data in order to evaluate the impact of globalization on the cost of capital. Third, I discuss indirect approaches to assessing the effect of capital market liberalization on the cost of capital. Fourth and last, I offer a number of suggestions why the measured impact of globalization – though typically statistically significant – is not greater than the studies report.

Globalization and the capital asset pricing model

Tests of the CAPM in an international setting have been conducted in two ways. First, there have been

11   Yakov Amihud and Haim Mendelson, "Asset Pricing and the Bid-ask Spread," *Journal of Financial Economics* 17 (1986), 223–249.
12   For evidence of the link between disclosure and the cost of capital – more specifically, that U.S. firms with limited analyst following that disclose more have a lower cost of capital – see Christine Botosan, "Disclosure Level and the Cost of Equity Capital," *The Accounting Review* 72 (1997), 323–349.
13   See Katherine Smith and George Sofianos, "The Impact of a NYSE Listing on the Global Trading of non-US Stocks," working paper 97-02, New York Stock Exchange, 1997.
14   Although one might think that the U.S. has not benefited from global competition in financial services, this has not been

the case. Over the last 30 years or so, the largely unregulated offshore markets have put pressure on U.S. financial service companies and played a key role in limiting their regulatory burden. To understand the importance of the offshore markets, think of the omnipresence of LIBOR in the financial industry. No U.S. institution that is active in financial markets can ignore this interest rate. While it is a dollar rate, it is not determined in the U.S. but rather in London (since it stands for the London Interbank Offer Rate). Another telling example of this offshore pressure occurred just after the LTCM crisis. The popular clamor for greater regulation of domestic hedge funds led to great concern that more regulation would drive these funds offshore.

WHEN GLOBALIZATION UNDERMINES GOVERNANCE: THE CASE OF JAPAN

Globalization does not necessarily increase the monitoring of management, at least in the short run. The reason for this is that the opening of capital markets can disrupt existing relationships within a country that once contributed to the monitoring of management or large shareholders. Take the case of Japan. In the Japanese economy, monitoring until recently took place primarily through banks, and through the networks of firms called *keiretsu* that are often organized around a bank. Japanese banks held equity stakes in their customers and played a much larger role than U.S. banks both in the financing and governance of corporate borrowers. As a result, Japan was said to have a bank-centered, "relationship-based" governance system, as contrasted with the "market-based" systems of the U.S. and U.K., with hostile takeovers as one of their central features.

Before 1980, Japanese firms were prevented by both formal and informal restrictions from raising debt in public markets – a policy that benefited Japanese banks. And, as virtually a monopoly supplier of (debt) funds to Japanese firms, the banks' ability to monitor management came in large part from their ability to threaten to withhold funds. But globalization, by enabling Japanese firms to raise funds outside of Japan

(which in turn caused restrictions on Japanese public debt markets to be eased), had a dramatic impact on Japanese corporate governance by loosening the corporate ties to banks.[15]

To the extent our theory is correct, foreign investors should begin to exert a monitoring effect on Japanese firms. In particular, a growing pool of active institutional shareholders and potential bidders should begin to emerge. But such effects, as the Japanese experience of the '90s suggests, do not happen overnight. And the continuing presence of large corporate shareholders (as distinguished from the banks) in Japanese firms, and other impediments to a well-functioning corporate control market, have made the expected monitoring benefits of globalization slow in coming.

In sum, globalization appears to have created a corporate governance vacuum in Japan – at least in the short run – by failing to substitute the monitoring power of the market for the monitoring power of banks. Nevertheless, recent developments suggest that capital markets are beginning to assume a monitoring role,[16] and that many Japanese companies are adopting important elements of Western-style corporate governance with greater attention to management incentives and stock prices.

---

tests of the global CAPM using country portfolios, and these tests have been remarkably supportive of the model. For example, a classic study by Campbell Harvey published in 1991 uses almost 20 years of historical returns of 17 different countries to assess the explanatory power of the global CAPM.[17] As noted earlier, the global CAPM

predicts that the risk premium in each country should be roughly equivalent to the risk premium on the world market portfolio multiplied by the beta of the country portfolio relative to the world market portfolio Harvey's study reports that, from February 1970 to May 1989, the average monthly return of the Morgan Stanley Capital International world index in excess of the 30-day bill was 0.553%, or 6.6% on an annualized basis. This number provides an estimate of the risk premium on the world market portfolio over that period.

Harvey's study provides support for the global CAPM in the following sense: Of the 17 countries in his sample, 14 had average excess returns that were statistically indistinguishable from the average returns predicted by the global CAPM.

---

15 See Jun-Koo Kang, Yong-Cheol Kim, K. Park, and René M. Stulz, "An Analysis of the Wealth Effects of Japanese Offshore Dollar-denominated Convertible and Warrant Bond Issues," *Journal of Financial and Quantitative Analysis* 30 (1995), 257–270.

16 Consider, for example, the recent dramatic restructuring of Nissan, brought about by pressure from its largest foreign shareholder, Renault. For an account, see Tim Burt, "Nissan Jobs to Go in $9 bn Restructuring," *Financial Times*, October 19, 1999, p. 1.

17 Campbell R. Harvey, "The World Price of Covariance Risk," *Journal of Finance* 46 (1991), 111–158.

For example, he obtains an estimate of the global beta for Germany of 0.70. And, according to the global CAPM, the risk premium for Germany is its global beta (0.70) multiplied by the risk premium on the world market portfolio of 0.55% per month, or 0.39% per month. The average monthly excess return of the market portfolio of Germany over the sample period was 0.5%, which is not statistically different from the predicted return of 0.39%.

Nevertheless, there were three countries for which the model provided a poor "fit": Japan, Norway, and Austria. For example, the global beta of Japan over the sample period was 1.42, implying a risk premium of 0.78% (1.42 × 0.55) per month. But the average excess return in Japan was a much higher 1.34% per month (clearly a statistically significant difference). The reason for the failure of the model in this case was the very large positive returns of Japanese stocks in the 1980s, which had the effect of overstating the Japanese risk premium (a problem that we take up in the next section).[18]

In a study published in 1992, K.C. Chan, Andrew Karolyi, and I tested a different prediction of the global CAPM: namely, to the extent that national capital markets are integrated, significant changes in the volatility of major components of the global portfolio should affect the risk premiums of other markets in the portfolio. In support of this proposition, we found that changes in the variance of both the Japanese stock market and the Morgan Stanley Europe, Asia and Far East Index were directly correlated with changes in the risk premium of U.S. stocks. Our findings suggest, for example, that a sharp drop in the volatility of the Japanese market can be expected to reduce the risk premium in the U.S. and, indeed, in all integrated economies.[19]

The studies on the world CAPM discussed so far focus on equity markets that are reasonably well-integrated with the global equity market. But what about countries whose markets are not part of the global markets? As suggested earlier, for securities priced in a closed market, the local CAPM should hold. But once that security begins to trade in a relatively open market, the global CAPM becomes the relevant pricing model.

One important study focuses directly on this transition. In an article published in 1995, Geert Bekaert and Campbell Harvey examine the pricing of equity in emerging markets.[20] They begin by noting that, for such markets, globalization is not a linear development. Most countries do not steadily become more integrated with world markets, but instead proceed in fits and starts – and in some cases, as the recent imposition of Malaysian capital controls suggests, they take major steps backward. As Bekaert and Harvey hypothesize in their study, when a country becomes more integrated with the world market, its cost of capital should depend more on its beta in relation to world markets; but when, like Malaysia, it takes steps that make its markets less integrated, its cost of capital should depend more on local market volatility. And their study provides considerable statistical support for this argument.

To see the implications of Bekaert and Harvey's study, let's look at the case of Chile. From 1976 to 1992, the annual average return in dollars on Chilean stocks was a very high 37%, but the standard deviation, at 40%, was also very large. In the conventional method of applying the (local) CAPM, this historical data would be used to predict future expected returns, and so a number like 37% would end up serving as an estimate of Chile's current cost of capital. Now, if Chile was still a completely closed market, one might have been justified in estimating its risk premium in this fashion. But, given the present extent of Chile's integration with world markets, 37% is clearly a gross overstatement of the country's *current* expected return. The global beta of Chile, reflecting its relatively low correlation with world markets, is generally no higher than 0.50. And, using a global CAPM, the excess expected return (in dollars) for Chile, assuming a risk-free dollar

---

18 Our discussion focuses on Table VI of Harvey (1991). He also implements his model allowing betas to change over time, and this leads to a smaller but still statistically significant mistake for Japan.

More recent support for the global CAPM was provided by DeSantis and Gerard (1997), cited earlier. Using different methods from Harvey, this study calculated monthly returns from January 1970 to December 1994 for eight large countries, and also reached conclusions that were supportive of the world CAPM.

19 K.C. Chan, G. Andrew Karolyi, and René M. Stulz, "Global Financial Markets and the Risk Premium on U.S. Equity," *Journal of Financial Economics* 32 (1992), 137–167.

20 Geert Bekaert and Campbell Harvey, "Time-varying Market Risk Premiums," *Journal of Finance* 50 (1995), 403–444.

rate of 6% and a world market risk premium of
6.6%, would be less than 10% (6% + (0.5 × 6.6%))
instead of its historical average of 37%. The key
insight here is that, if Chile's cost of capital was
once anywhere close to 37%, then the integration
of world markets must be bringing about a dramatic reduction in the cost of capital. And these
results for Chile are representative of emerging
markets in general, since these countries also tend
to have high standard deviations and low betas.[21]

But what evidence do we have that annual
expected returns in Chile, and in other emerging
markets, are now in fact closer to 10% than to 30%?
Perhaps the most suggestive piece of evidence are
the higher stock returns achieved by most of these
nations in the 1980s and 1990s, at least prior to the
Asian crisis. Such large positive returns, as I will argue
in the next section, are consistent with falling risk premiums. Also furnishing evidence of smaller risk
premiums is another study by Bekaert and Harvey
that shows that the dividend yields of emerging market equities fall as their markets become more
integrated with world markets.[22]

In sum, there is a dramatic difference in estimates of the risk premium that use historical
estimates versus those that assume the global
CAPM. And the results of Bekaert and Harvey's
study, as well as the other evidence just cited,

suggest that the global CAPM now provides a
more reliable guide to pricing emerging-market
stocks than the local CAPM. But if the global
CAPM does a good job of explaining the risk premiums of *country* portfolios, it fares less well when
applied to specific portfolios of stocks within countries. However, this should not be taken as a criticism of the global CAPM *per se*; the problems that
arise when applying the global CAPM to individual companies outside the U.S. are fundamentally
the same as those that researchers have found
when testing the local U.S. CAPM on U.S. companies. That is, the pronounced tendency of both
smaller U.S. firms and those with high book-to-
market ratios to produce higher-than-expected
returns also shows up clearly in studies of companies outside the U.S.[23]

And just as these shortcomings do not rule out
use of the CAPM for U.S. stocks, they should not
deter us from applying the global CAPM. The fact
that countries that are integrated with world markets have risk premiums that depend on their
covariances with the world market portfolio
suggests that the global CAPM offers the most
promising approach to estimating cost of capital –
at least as a first approximation. Adjustments can
then be made in cases where there are likely to be
problems – say, in the case of small firms and those
with market-to-book ratios well below 1.0.

Time-series evidence

The traditional approach to evaluating a market's
risk premium is to compute its average excess
return over a long period of time. For instance, it is
common in the U.S. to use past excess returns on
the U.S. stock market since the 1920s. The argument for proceeding this way is the presumption
that the future is likely to be similar to the past.
One has to use long periods of time because the
stock market is volatile. Over shorter periods of

21 In my working paper referenced in the first footnote of this article, I derive a condition that must be met for a country to experience a reduction in investors' required rate of return as a result of becoming integrated with world markets. The condition can be stated fairly simply: the variance of the small country market portfolio must exceeds its covariance with the world market portfolio. This condition will always be met when the small country market portfolio is much more volatile than the world market portfolio. When I tested this condition on 37 different countries using weekly returns over a 10-year period from 1988 to 1998, all 37 countries – even the U.S. and the U.K. – satisfied this condition. But, not surprisingly, some countries appear to gain much more from risk-sharing than others. Argentina is the country that over that sample period seems to gain the most from risk-sharing because of its combination of high volatility and low correlation with the world market portfolio. Interestingly, in our list of countries, the country that benefits the most from risk-sharing after Argentina is China, where the stock index is composed of the Chinese shares available to foreign investors.

22 However, Bekaert and Harvey interpret their results as consistent with a fairly modest reduction in costs of capital, less than 200 basis points. See Geert Bekaert and Campbell Harvey, "Foreign Speculators and Emerging Markets," *Journal of Finance*, forthcoming.

23 For a study that shows that a world CAPM understates the expected returns of small firms across countries, see Robert Korajczyk and Claude Viallet, "An Empirical Investigation of International Asset Pricing," *Review of Financial Studies* 2, 1989, 553–585. For a study that shows that value stocks earn a premium across countries and makes the case for a world value factor, see Eugene Fama and Kenneth French, *Journal of Finance* (1998).

time, one might conclude that the risk premium is either negative (if the market fell during the period), or extremely high (if the market increased dramatically). For instance, if you were using rolling 20-year periods to estimate the risk premium, you would conclude that the risk premium increased recently. From 1976 to 1995, the estimate of the risk premium for the U.S. using the Ibbotson data is 7.31%; but from 1978 to 1997 it is 9.36%!

A market's capitalization is the present value of the cash flow shareholders expect to receive from the securities traded in that market, where the discount rate is computed using the risk premium of the market. This implies that even if the cash flows expected by shareholders remain unchanged, when the risk premium falls, stock prices and market capitalizations will increase to reflect the reduction in investors' discount rates. And this means that there will be a negative relation between changes in the risk premium and changes in equity values.

Because of this negative relation between the risk premium and stock prices, the use of past returns to estimate the risk premium is a reliable approach only if one believes that the risk premium is relatively stable over time. In this case, the longer the period over which one estimates the risk premium, the better the estimate one obtains. Unfortunately, the variance of stock returns is high enough that, *even* when one uses fairly long periods of time, one reaches very different conclusions about the size of the risk premium depending on the estimation period chosen. For instance, the U.S. risk premium estimated over the last 70 years – about 8% (when using arithmetic averaging) – is substantially higher than the U.S. risk premium estimated over the last 200 years – about 4%.

There is little reason to believe that the risk premium is stable over long periods of time. From our discussion in the previous section, we know that there are good reasons for the risk premium to be related to the variance of returns – and this variance clearly changes over time. And, as we have seen, the market portfolio also changes over time. As markets become more integrated when barriers to international investment fall, more countries become part of the world market portfolio. And, as the world market portfolio includes more countries, its variance will continue to fall because of the benefits of international diversification.

In sum, the lack of stability in the risk premium means that the time-series averaging method for estimating cost of capital will not capture the effect of globalization on the cost of capital. Globalization has been taking place over the last 40 years; and if our theory about the impact of globalization on the cost of capital is right, the cost of capital should have been falling over that period. But, to those who ignore the impact of globalization on the cost of capital, the higher stock prices and returns associated with the past 40 years will mistakenly suggest that risk premiums have increased.

Event-study approaches

Rather than assessing the impact of globalization on the cost of capital by estimating the mean excess return on the market, one could take a more direct approach: namely, investigate the effect of particular globalization "events" on the equity capitalization of firms and countries. By "events" I mean announcements of market openings or other forms of liberalization. If equity markets incorporate information efficiently, one would expect events that lead investors to believe that an equity market will be more open to foreign investors – and that investors in a country will be better able to invest abroad – to have an immediate impact on equity values in that country.

In a recent study, Peter Henry ran a series of statistical tests designed to measure the stock market impact of capital market liberalizations in 12 countries.[24] In his first test, he considers the impact of liberalization during a period that starts four months before the announcement and ends three months after the announcement. Over that period, stock returns are higher by 4.6% per month on average, for a total cumulative abnormal return of 36.8%. He then proceeds to investigate whether this impact of globalization still holds when he controls for several variables that influence stock returns, in particular macroeconomic variables. When he does so, the impact of liberalization falls

---

24 Peter B. Henry, "Stock Market Liberalization, Economic Reform, and Emerging Market Prices, *Journal of Finance*, forthcoming.

somewhat, to about 30%, but the impact is still statistically as well as economically significant. His evidence therefore suggests that liberalization increases shareholder wealth substantially.

What does an increase in stock prices of 30% imply for the cost of capital? Because the value of equity is the present value of cash flows expected to accrue to the shareholders, we can use the following experiment to produce an estimate of the impact of globalization on the cost of capital for the countries in Henry's sample. Let's begin with a simple valuation model known as the Gordon dividend growth model. This model assumes that cash flows to shareholders consist solely of expected future dividends and that dividends are expected to grow at a constant growth rate. The model then uses the following perpetuity formula to value the future dividends as follows:

$$v = d/(r - g)$$

where V is the value of equity, d is the dividend payment at the end of the period, r is the cost of capital, and g is the growth rate of dividends.

If we assume that d and g are given (and let's set d equal to $1 and g to 5%), we can "back out" the impact of liberalization on the cost of capital from the price change by using the following formula:

Price after − Price before
$$= [d/r_{After} - g] - [d/r_{Before} - g] \qquad (1)$$

From Henry's study, we have the price change in percentage terms (again, 30%), which we define as Δ. We can then use Δ to solve the above equation to obtain:

$$r_{After} = (1/1 + \Delta) \times r_{Before} + (\Delta/1 + \Delta) \times g \quad (2)$$

Using this equation to estimate the impact on the cost of capital, we find that if the cost of capital before liberalization was, say, 20%, the 30% increase in equity capitalization reported by Henry would be consistent with a new cost of capital of 16.5%.

But this estimate of the reduction in cost of capital obtained from Henry's study should be used with some caution. First, although we keep the growth rate of dividends constant as liberalization takes place, one would expect liberalization to lead to faster growth in corporate profits, a higher

growth rate of dividends, and hence a lower estimate of the change in the cost of capital. Second, to the extent that countries liberalize after (and in part because) their stock market has done well, Henry's estimate could overstate the gains from liberalization. Third, Henry does not include all liberalization events, which might understate the total impact of liberalization. But if each of these effects is potentially important, it is not clear that they together produce any obvious bias in the estimated effect on the cost of capital.[25]

The Case of ADRs. If none of the firms in a country has access to international capital markets, the initiation of an ADR program by a single company in that country can be construed as evidence of liberalization of the capital market of that country. Nevertheless, one would expect the primary effect of initiating an ADR program to be on the cost of capital of the company that undertakes such a program. As a result, there has been a large number of studies that investigate the stock-price impact on individual firms of ADR introductions.[26]

Based on our earlier analysis, we would expect that a firm that succeeds in having its equity valued at the global market cost of capital rather than the cost of capital of a segmented market would typically experience a substantial increase in value. As an example, suppose that the risk premium of the country is 10%, the company has a beta with respect to the country market portfolio of 1.0, the dividend growth rate is 4%, and the risk free rate is 5%. Suppose further that the firm has a world beta of 0.5 and that the risk premium on the world market portfolio is only 6%. In this case, if the firm suddenly (and unexpectedly) gained access to the world markets, the global CAPM predicts that its value will increase by 57%.

Contrary to this example, empirical studies have not found evidence of large increases in firm value by focusing on a narrow window around the

25 The forthcoming study by Bekaert and Harvey, cited in note 22, also shows that liberalization leads to a significant decrease in the cost of capital – but one that is considerably smaller than that found by Henry.
26 For a review of these studies, see G. Andrew Karolyi, "Why Do Companies List Shares Abroad? A Survey of the Evidence and its Managerial Implications," *Journal of Applied Corporate Finance*, Vol. 11 No. 3 (Fall 1998).

announcement of the ADR program or the listing of the ADRs. Two recent studies – one by Stephen Foerster and Andrew Karolyi published in 1999, and another by Darius Miller in 1998[27] – investigate both the return around the announcement of an ADR program and the return around the day when the actual listing takes place. Both studies find positive returns around the announcement date *and* around the listing date. However, the returns are small. For example, in examining 153 ADR listings on the Nasdaq, AMEX, and NYSE from 1976 to 1992, Foerster and Karolyi (1999) find an abnormal return of 1.2% during the week of listing. And, for the 45 listings for which they also have an announcement date, they find an insignificant positive abnormal return of 0.2% on the day of announcement. In Miller's study, the average announcement abnormal return for 53 ADRs listed on NYSE or Nasdaq from 1985 to 1995 is 2.63%.

Miller's study also distinguishes between firms from emerging markets and firms from developed markets. To the extent that emerging markets have more barriers to international investment than developed markets, one would expect a greater abnormal return for firms from emerging markets. Confirming this expectation, Miller finds that the abnormal return of firms from emerging markets is almost twice the abnormal return of firms from developed markets.

Both Foerster and Karolyi (1999) and a study by Vihang Errunza and Darius Miller (1998) estimate returns before the initiation of an ADR program and afterwards.[28] Strikingly, Foerster and Karolyi find that firms that list experience an unexpected increase in their stock price of 19% for the year before the listing; but this increase is followed by a decrease of 14% in the year after listing. Before rushing to interpret such results, however, it is useful

to keep in mind that the significantly negative returns after listings have also been documented for U.S. firms going public on U.S. exchanges or listing on the NYSE after having traded on Nasdaq. This suggests that the negative returns after ADR listings reported by Foerster and Karolyi may have little to do with the fact that the listing is an ADR listing but much to do with the fact that firms tend to list (or go public) following exceptional performance.[29]

At the level of individual companies, it is also possible to conduct an analysis that directly compares the valuation of firms in a given country that have ADR programs with the values of those that do not. For example, a 1996 study by Denis Logue and Anat Sundaram examines changes in price-to-book, price-to-cash earnings, and price-to-earnings ratios around the month in which the firms list. The study finds that each of these three ratios increases for firms that list ADRs relative to a control group of comparable firms. Such increases in valuation ratios are all consistent with a decrease in the cost of capital.

The evidence discussed so far in this section focuses on non-U.S. firms gaining access to the global markets. But this is not the whole story. There is also evidence that U.S. companies benefit from using the global markets. Offshore markets – notably the Euro-dollar market – are playing a large and growing role in the financing of many large U.S. firms. My own study (with Yong-Cheol Kim) of the stock market reaction to offshore debt financings by U.S. companies reports significant positive returns, in contrast to the small negative reaction to announcements of U.S. domestic debt offerings.[30] And recent studies of U.S. firms that issue equity in global markets also report evidence of a more favorable stock market reaction – one that is consistent with a lower cost of capital.[31]

27 Stephen R. Foerster and G. Andrew Karolyi, "The Effects of Market Segmentation and Investor Recognition on Asset Prices: Evidence from Foreign Stocks Listing in the U.S.," *Journal of Finance* 54 (June 1999); and Darius Miller, "The Market Reaction to International Cross-listings: Evidence from Depositary Receipts," *Journal of Financial Economics* 51 (1999).
28 Vihang R. Errunza and Darius P. Miller, "Market Segmentation and the Cost of Capital in International Equity Markets," unpublished working paper, Texas A&M University, College Station, TX. (1998).

29 See Bala G. Dharan and David Ikenberry, "The Long-run Negative Drift of Post-listing Stock Returns," *Journal of Finance* 50, 1995, 1547–1574.
30 Yong-Cheol Kim and René Stulz, "The Eurobond Market and Corporate Financial Policy: A Test of the Clientele Hypothesis," *Journal of Financial Economics* 46.
31 See Susan Chaplinsky and Latha Ramchand, "The Impact of Global Equity Offerings," forthcoming in *Journal of Finance*, which shows that the average negative market reaction (of slightly more than 2%) to the announcement of equity offerings is reduced by about one third in global offerings.

Why is the decrease in the cost of capital not larger?

Although we now have considerable evidence that globalization reduces the cost of capital, the decrease in the cost of capital observed when a country liberalizes its markets or when a firm enters the global capital markets is less than one would expect. I offer a few reasons why the existing studies may not be capturing the full effect of globalization.

Because the studies just cited all investigate how stock prices react to globalization, this immediately suggests a reason why they might find smaller effects than expected. If financial markets are efficient, we expect them to incorporate information in prices very quickly, if not "instantaneously." Thus, when a country liberalizes or a firm accesses global capital markets, it is possible that the market has already anticipated this event to some degree. In the extreme case where the market knows that a firm will undertake an ADR program, the impact of that program on shareholder wealth on the date of listing will be negligible. The same holds for the liberalization of a country. For this reason, event studies of globalization have a fundamental problem. If globalization is so advantageous that it becomes largely predictable, event studies will never be able to detect its impact. To be sure, the country studies do report finding some effect. But to be able to gauge the full impact of globalization on the cost of capital from an event study, one has to have some idea of the extent to which the liberalization is anticipated – and this, of course, is very difficult to determine.

Market anticipation is not the only reason why the existing studies are likely to underestimate the benefits of globalization. The studies effectively make the assumption that a country liberalizes or a firm accesses global capital markets in such a way that they are immediately and completely integrated in world markets. But this, of course, is rarely the case. It is a well-established finding that investors are not as well-diversified internationally as the theory suggests they should be.[32] For example in 1996, U.S. investors held 90% of the value of their stock portfolio in U.S. stocks, even though

U.S. stocks represented less than half of the world market capitalization of stocks. And such a home bias exists in all foreign countries for which statistics on ownership are available.

There are several explanations that have been offered for the existence of the home bias. One focuses on the fact that, although many laws and regulations limiting foreign portfolio investment have disappeared, there are still many restrictions and additional costs faced by investors investing abroad. Information asymmetries between domestic and foreign investors, the existence of different consumption baskets, political risk, and behavioral biases can all lead to a preference for domestic assets. Political risk, for example, can make information asymmetry a major deterrent to foreign investors. The informational advantage of home country investors will depend on the disclosure and regulatory environment of a country, with weaker regimes providing a greater advantage for local investors.

As a consequence, when some countries liberalize, few foreign investors may choose to invest because the institutional "infrastructure" in such countries may be inadequate. If a country liberalizes, but markets do not expect investors to take advantage of the liberalization, then liberalization will not affect the cost of capital. If a firm starts an ADR program but foreign investors do not buy the ADRs, most of the benefits of the program will fail to materialize. In support of this view, Foerster and Karolyi (1999) show that while many ADR programs significantly expand the shareholder base, many others do not – and the extent to which an ADR program broadens the shareholder base is a crucial determinant of whether the ADR program is associated with an increase in stock price.

GLOBALIZATION, CORPORATE PRACTICE, AND CORPORATE STRATEGY

What are the lessons from the globalization of securities markets for corporations? This paper makes three important points for international financial managers:

1. International financial markets are progressively becoming one huge, integrated, global capital market, which in turn is contributing to higher stock prices in developed as well as developing economies. As a consequence of the

---

32   For these numbers, see Linda Tesar and Ingrid Werner, "The Internationalization of Securities Markets Since the 1987 Crash," Brookings-Wharton Papers on Financial Services, 1998, 281–372.

globalization of equity markets, large companies everywhere can raise capital from foreign as well as local investors. Having a global shareholder base means having a lower cost of capital and hence a greater equity value.

Shareholders benefit from globalization for two main reasons:

◆ First, the risks of equity are shared among more investors with different portfolio exposures and hence a different "appetite" for bearing certain risks. With the resulting global diversification of investor portfolios, companies with access to global markets experience a reduction in market risk premiums and hence a lower cost of capital. And a lower cost of capital means a higher stock price for a given level of cash flows or earnings.

◆ Second, when firms in countries with less-developed capital markets raise capital in the public markets of countries (like the U.S.) with highly developed markets, they get more than lower-cost capital; they also import at least aspects of the corporate governance systems that prevail in those markets. For companies accustomed to less-developed markets, raising capital overseas means that more sophisticated investors, institutions, and technologies will participate in monitoring their performance and management. And, in a virtuous cycle, more effective monitoring will increase investor confidence in companies' future profitability and so improve the terms on which such firms raise capital.

This process of globalization of equity markets continues to proceed vigorously, both at the level of national governments and capital markets and within individual companies. With the growth of the Internet, moreover, the limits to further globalization of equity markets are primarily political rather than economic or technological. Shareholders can now trade a firm's shares wherever they are, provided country governments do not prevent them from so doing.

2. Market risk premiums are not stable, and long-run past returns do not provide a reliable guide when estimating current premiums. The reduction in the cost of equity capital brought about by globalization is hard to detect when one focuses on historical data. The reason for this is that the global diversification of investor portfolios and the resulting expansion in the shareholder base (of all companies with access to global markets) has the effect of increasing equity values as it decreases the global risk premium and cost of capital. For this reason, one who uses historical returns on equity as a basis for estimating future required returns could easily conclude that the cost of equity capital has increased when in fact it has fallen. For example, using U.S. stock returns over just the last 20 years would yield estimates for the U.S. market risk premium as high as 10% – estimates that make it very hard indeed to explain the current level of U.S. stock prices. A better approach is likely to be one that computes a risk premium that is consistent with current equity valuations and reasonable growth estimates for earnings.[33]

3. In measuring the risk of individual firms and projects, use the global (not the local) CAPM. In global markets, the risk of a firm's equity depends on how the stock contributes to the volatility not of the home market portfolio, but of the world market portfolio. For companies with access to global capital markets whose profitability is tied more closely to the local than to the global economy, use of the local CAPM will overstate the cost of capital because risks that are not diversifiable within a national economy can be diversified by holding a global portfolio. Thus, to reflect the new reality of a globally determined cost of capital, all companies with access to global markets (even those in the U.S.) should consider using a global CAPM that views a company as part of the global portfolio of stocks.

Another common problem in calculating cost of capital is the tendency of managers evaluating overseas investments to add an extra risk premium – over and above the premium in the CAPM – to account for the special risks associated with foreign projects. Such an approach is hard to justify. If the extra risk premium is used to compensate for country risks, then it must be demonstrated that those risks are not diversifiable and that shareholders charge a risk premium to bear those risks. In a world where the firm has a global shareholder base, it makes little sense to think that shareholders will require a higher risk premium simply because

33 See Aswath Damodoran, "Estimating Equity Risk Premiums," Stern School of Business working paper.

the firm invests abroad. There are, to be sure, large country-specific risks in world markets; and management may well want to hedge such risks to avoid default or reduce costs associated with financial distress. But such risks should not be viewed as increasing the cost of capital for a project.

Country-specific risks may reduce the expected cash flows of a project; but as globalization progresses, a firm's shareholders care less about where the expected cash flows come from, and focus simply on how big they are – and how they affect a global portfolio.

CHAPTER 30

Globalization of Capital Markets and the Asian Financial Crisis

E. Han Kim (University of Michigan)*

With the current financial turmoil in Asia, a frequently asked question these days is, "Are open capital markets good for emerging economies?" Critics of unfettered markets point to Mexico's peso crisis in 1994 and the recent Asian currency problems to argue that emerging markets should resist the temptation of easy foreign money, or at least place regulatory restraints on capital inflows and outflows. They also cite the case of China, which has been able to avoid speculative attacks on its currency due in part to its relatively closed capital market.

One prominent critic of open markets is Joseph Stiglitz, Chief Economist of the World Bank, who recently stated that "the benefits from unimpeded capital flows are overrated, and short-term investments sometimes spark currency crises." Even Michael Camdessus, the Managing Director of the IMF, has cautioned against "a mad rush to liberalization, regardless of the risks," while urging nations to implement regulatory structures to deal with investment surges.[1]

And such arguments have been translated into actions. The most dramatic occurred on September 1, 1998, when Malaysian Prime Minister Mahathir Mohamad imposed currency controls and prevented foreign shareholders from taking their money out of the country for a year. In the same month, Taiwan also announced that, in light of Asia's financial crisis, it was reconsidering its plans for full liberalization of international capital flows by the end of the year 2000.[2] Nevertheless, not all countries are rushing for capital controls. On September 16, 1998, Chile announced the elimination of a capital constraint known as the *encaje*, which required 10% of foreign capital inflows to be kept on deposit at the central bank. Although the *encaje* has often been cited as a model for countries that need to reduce volatility and speculation in their financial markets, Carlos

* Earlier versions of this article were presented as a keynote speech at the First Joint Conference of the NFA (Nippon Finance Association) and APFA (Asia-Pacific Finance Association) on July 22, 1998, in Tokyo, and at the plenary session of the Eighth International Economics Convention of the Korea Economic Association and the Korea-America Economic Association on August 18, 1998 in Seoul. This article also draws on two previous papers I co-authored with Vijay Singal: "Stock Market Openings: Experience of Emerging Economies," University of Michigan working paper (1998); and "Are Open Markets Good for Foreign Investors and Emerging Nations?" *Journal of Applied Corporate Finance* Vol. 10, No. 3, Fall 1997. I would like to acknowledge helpful comments from Daniel Ebels and the editor Don Chew.

1 *Wall Street Journal,* July 1, 1998.
2 *Financial Times*, September 23, 1998.

Massad, head of Banco Central de Chile, stated that capital controls in Chile caused "a large increase in the cost of foreign financing for Chilean companies."[3]

In any event, the new respect for capital controls seems to be at odds with the recent move toward capital market liberalization by emerging economies. With the dissolution of the Soviet Union and the general decline in the number of centrally planned economies, politicians in developing countries have increasingly come to recognize that they can no longer ignore the global movement toward free markets. Partly to incorporate elements of market capitalism into their own economies, and partly to satisfy their need for new capital, many countries have allowed a free flow of capital across their borders, including participation by foreign investors in their stock markets.

For emerging nations, the inflow of foreign capital is essential for building infrastructure and making other investments necessary for economic progress. The industrial development of low- and middle-income countries tends to depend heavily upon capital formation. Recognizing the ability of foreign investors to provide capital and hasten the development process, many emerging economies have opened their capital markets to foreign investment. Thus, before emerging economies reverse their recent liberalization measures and implement further regulatory restraints on capital flows, it would be useful to reexamine the opportunity costs of a closed market and the risks associated with open markets.

This paper has three basic aims: (1) to analyze the impact of open capital markets on the economies of host countries; (2) to investigate the causes of the Asian financial crisis; and (3) to evaluate the likely effects of the South Korean government's recent attempts to restructure its corporate sector. These three issues are closely intertwined. In addressing the first, I summarize the findings of my recent empirical study (with Vijay Singal) that examines the experience of a sample of emerging economies around the time they first opened their stock markets for foreign investment. I then investigate the causes of the current Asian financial crisis by reviewing evidence on the role of foreign investors, host governments, and corporations in the currency crises. The results of this investigation, together with lessons from the U.S. corporate restructuring of the past 20 years, then provide a basis for evaluating the recent attempts by the Korean government to restructure its economy.

THE CASE FOR (AND AGAINST) STOCK MARKET OPENINGS

There are major benefits from having a well-functioning stock market. First of all, a market that is open to global investors reduces the cost of capital for local companies by allowing stockholders to achieve efficient diversification, thereby increasing the probability that promising new ventures will attract funding. Stock markets also lower the cost of capital by increasing the liquidity of investments. Greater liquidity not only reduces the required rate of return demanded by investors, it encourages companies with promising growth prospects to retain and reinvest earnings (instead of paying them out as dividends) *as long as* investors remain confident in their own ability to convert the retained earnings into cash by selling shares in the market.

For emerging economies, opening their stock markets to foreign investors serves as a catalyst for achieving greater efficiency in the domestic market. The catalyst is the new competition from foreign financial institutions that accompanies the opening of the market. Such competition puts pressure on host countries to import more sophisticated financial technology, to find ways to adapt the technology to the local environment, and to encourage more investment in improving information-processing and financial services.

In addition, foreign investors will demand the transparency and improved disclosure rules that enable them to monitor corporate performance and capital allocation. As part of the push for greater disclosure, investors will also demand greater accountability of management to shareholders in order to protect themselves against expropriation of wealth by the controlling investors. A coherent and convincing response to these demands will decrease investors' perception of the risk of holding stocks, which will in turn lower the cost of equity.

---

3 *The Wall Street Journal*, October 1, 1998.

Opening up the domestic stock market also offers other avenues for reducing capital costs. The cost of foreign capital tends to be lower because foreign portfolios can be more broadly diversified across national boundaries and therefore are more "efficient" in managing "country-specific" risks, resulting in a lower risk premium. The cost of foreign capital will be even lower if the newly opened market provides a unique diversification opportunity for foreign portfolios. Thus, in addition to increasing capital availability, internationalization lowers the cost of capital and generates greater efficiencies in allocating capital.

A lower cost of capital leads in turn to greater investment and employment as domestically produced goods and services become more competitive in the global marketplace. More efficient use of capital in turn leads to the value creation in the corporate sector that is necessary for sustainable economic growth.

For policymakers in emerging economies, however, such benefits must be weighed against various uncertainties associated with opening the market. One issue of major concern is the movement of so-called "hot money" – that is, international flows of funds that are highly sensitive to differences in interest rates, perceived economic growth rates, and expected returns from holding securities. Because of the sensitivity of these investments, even a small shock to the economy or revision in expectations may lead to a volatile change in fund flows, which further exacerbates the shock and destabilizes the domestic economy.

In other words, while limited inflows are good because they provide a means of funding economic development, unlimited inflows can present problems for policymakers who believe their economy cannot be left to the vagaries of unpredictable market forces that threaten sustainable growth. For instance, a large capital inflow may cause appreciation of the domestic currency, which may threaten the competitive position of export-oriented economies in the global marketplace. Policymakers are also concerned that there may not be enough investment opportunities to absorb the inflow of money and that the excess capital will fuel inflation.

Another issue of concern is that if foreign fund flows are in fact volatile, such volatility may lead to greater volatility in domestic stock prices, exchange rates, and inflation. Greater volatility in stock prices would cause investors to demand a higher risk premium, which implies a higher cost of capital and less investment. Likewise, greater volatility in exchange rates and inflation increases the risk of international trade and makes it more costly to maintain stability in the economy.

EMPIRICAL EVIDENCE

The relative merits of these opposing arguments depend on how the foreign investment flows actually affect the economies of host countries. That is, do those foreign flows of funds induce greater volatility? Or are they more likely to have a stabilizing effect on the emerging economies' stock market, inflation, and exchange rates?

In an attempt to answer such questions, Vijay Singal and I examined the economic effects of stock market liberalization on 20 emerging economies over a 10-year period surrounding their market opening dates.[4] More specifically, our study attempted to detect the effects of financial liberalization on a number of variables: (1) the level and volatility of stock returns; (2) stock market efficiency; (3) inflation; and (4) exchange rates.

In general we found that while some countries experienced undesirable side-effects from liberalization, on average the benefits to emerging economies of opening up their markets greatly outweighed the costs. Soon after market liberalization, stock prices tended to rise, reflecting both the resolution of uncertainty about the liberalization itself and the new external demand for domestic securities. Stock return volatility, rather than rising, actually decreased somewhat after the market opening.[5] And this finding of reduction in price

4   See E. Han Kim and Vijay Singal, "Stock Market Openings: Experience of Emerging Economies," University of Michigan working paper (1998).
5   The reduction in volatility becomes statistically significant when we exclude the two-year period surrounding the month of liberalization – a period of considerable uncertainty. The reason for excluding this period is that stock market openings are often accompanied by other liberalization measures and policy change, which tends to lead to greater, though short-lived, fluctuation in stock prices.

volatility makes perfect sense: It says, in effect, that when markets are opened to outsiders, the markets become more liquid and resilient due to the larger numbers of investors with diverse opinions and requirements.

We also found that stock markets become more efficient in the sense that information is more rapidly reflected in the stock price.[6] One likely reason for this increase in efficiency is foreign investors' reliance on sophisticated financial techniques to exploit market inefficiencies, which in turn puts competitive pressure on domestic investors and financial institutions to improve information-processing in pricing financial assets. Another possible reason is that stock market liberalization is often accompanied by other financial reforms, such as stricter disclosure requirements, insider trading regulations, and better investor protection.

When we examined the effects of stock market liberalization on inflation and exchange rates, the results were equally encouraging. Inflation, instead of increasing, appears to have decreased. For our entire sample, the average inflation rate fell from 1.67% per month before liberalization to 1.39% per month after liberalization.[7] And, again, our finding makes sense: If the foreign capital has been put into productive use, it would increase the supply of goods and services available to consumers, dampening inflationary pressures in the long run.

Moreover, whether measured in nominal or real terms, we found no evidence of appreciation of domestic currencies after liberalization. Emerging market currencies had been depreciating prior to market openings, and they continued to decline after the openings. But, the *rate* of exchange rate depreciation declined significantly around liberalization, from 1.44 to 0.75 per month for nominal exchange rates, and from 2.66 to 1.67% per month for real exchange rates. This decrease in the rate of exchange rate depreciation reflects an increase in investor confidence in the emerging economies that are undertaking capital market liberalization.

The volatility of inflation also fell significantly after liberalization and so did the volatility of exchange rate changes. Lower inflation volatility means that investors in the economy are less subject to inflation-related risk. Likewise, lower exchange rate volatility reduces risks associated with international trade and international borrowing and lending. Reduced volatility also means that fewer economic resources must be devoted to managing inflation and exchange rate risk.

In sum, the evidence from our study suggests that, until the recent currency crises set in, most emerging markets were successful in controlling the negative side-effects of stock market liberalization, while enjoying appreciable benefits from the participation of foreign investors. Of course, our findings should not be interpreted as the final word on this matter. Because many emerging stock markets were opened in the late 1980s and early 1990s, our post-liberalization analysis is limited to a five-year period; and to many observers a five-year period will seem to provide too little basis for making judgments about the future. And, of course, it may be years from now before we are able to offer a complete assessment of the damage inflicted on emerging economies by the latest wave of capital outflows.

But this argument should not be used as a pretext for keeping out foreign investors or restricting capital flows. There are enormous gains that can be realized by uniting foreign investors and host countries through stock market openings. But these gains provide no guarantee against the possibility of sudden outflows. Host countries can ensure that they retain foreign capital by using that capital productively and treating investors fairly.

THE ASIAN FINANCIAL CRISIS

Our finding that integrating emerging stock markets into world markets has benefited the host countries is of little comfort to countries like Thailand, Korea, Malaysia, and Indonesia that have experienced crashes in their currency values and all the ill effects of financial panic. And often the blame for the crashes goes to the hot money or hedge funds. Indeed, Prime Minister Mahathir of Malaysia singled out George Soros as *the* villain in the sharp drop in the Malaysian ringgit!

---

6   There was only one country in our sample, Pakistan, where the predictability (i.e., positive autocorrelation) of stock returns increased instead of decreasing
7   Only Pakistan, Thailand, and Turkey reported significantly higher rates of inflation.

Capital flight

But both scientific and anecdotal evidence suggest that foreign investors are neither as fickle nor as influential as they have been made out to be. During December 1994, at the height of its peso crisis, Mexico lost over $6 billion in foreign exchange reserves. But during this period, foreign investors sold only about $370 million of Mexican debt and equity. It was Mexican firms and individuals who did the rest of the selling! And net portfolio capital inflows, though down from those in 1993, still ended up at a positive $8.2 billion for the entire year of 1994.

In a similar vein, a study of the Korean stock market reported that the turnover ratio has been much higher for domestic investors than for foreign investors.[8] Based on this (and other)[9] evidence, I am tempted to suggest that foreign investors are more likely to be the *patient money*. As sophisticated investors, they are aware of the volatility, instability, and risk of the emerging stock markets – and they accordingly enter these markets with a relatively longer investment horizon.

So if the culprits are not foreign investors, who is responsible for the massive capital outflows during the Asian crisis? The Mexican experience points to domestic corporate and individual investors as the villains. As U.S. Treasury Secretary Robert Rubin observed in a recent speech about the Asian crisis,

> When these crises began, foreign investors started to withdraw capital, local companies sought to hedge hard currency exposures, exporters stopped bringing their export earnings home, and citizens moved their savings abroad. I think it has now become accepted that most of the pressure on these currencies comes from local sources and not foreign investors.[10]

As if to confirm Rubin's assertion, a recent IMF report revealed unrecorded capital flight of $20 billion from South Korea, Indonesia, Malaysia, Thailand, and the Philippines during 1997, with South Korea suffering the largest outflow of $8.7 billion.[11] Such "off-the-books" transactions, which were almost twice the recorded total net private outflow of $11 billion, tend to be conducted by local corporations and households.

The causes

It is important to note that capital flight, whether accomplished by foreign or domestic investors, is merely a symptom, not the cause, of the crisis. The list of potential causes is long, but a short list would include the following: governments' futile attempts to keep their currencies at artificially high levels; government-directed banking systems and lending

---

8 Kwang Jun, "Effects of Capital Market Liberalization in Korea: Empirical Evidence and Policy Implications," in Stijn Claessens and Sudarshan Gooptu (eds), *Portfolio Investment in Developing Countries* (The World Bank: Washington, D.C. (1993)), pp. 404–425.

9 More scientific evidence is provided in two recent working papers. In "Hedge Funds and the Asian Currency Crisis of 1987," (NBER working paper No. 6427, February 1998), Stephen Brown, William Goetzman, and James Park estimate the changing positions of the ten largest currency funds in the Malaysian ringgit and in a basket of Asian currencies. Although they find dramatic fluctuations in the net long or short positions in the ringgit or its correlates over the past four years, the fluctuations were uncorrelated with movements in the exchange rate, thus suggesting that global hedge funds did not move exchange rates. Furthermore, the estimated net positions of the major funds were neither unusually high nor low during the period of the first crash (July–September 1997); nor did the funds make abnormal profits during that period.

In the second of the two studies, "Do Foreign Investors Destabilize Stock Markets? The Korean Experience in 1997," (Ohio State University working paper 98–6, June 1998), Hyuk Choe, Bong-Chan Kho, and René Stulz use trading data to examine the impact of foreign investors on stock returns in Korea from November 30, 1996 to the end of 1997, a sample period that includes the crash of the Korean won between October and December of 1997. Although the trading data

reveal "positive feedback" trading and "herding" behavior among foreign investors, the evidence of such behavior is weaker during the crash period than during the "non-crash" period. Overall, the study finds no evidence that trades by foreign investors had a destabilizing effect on the Korean stock market.

10 Robert Rubin, Address on the Asian Financial Situation to George Washington University, Washington, D.C., January 21, 1998.

11 See "International Capital Markets: Developments, Prospects, and Key Issues," *International Monetary Fund World Economic and Financial Survey*, September 1998.

decisions; crony capitalism; massive overinvestment by corporations funded by excessive borrowing; the lack of transparency that masked the extent of problems as they developed; inadequate financial regulation and supervision; labor market "rigidities"; and a pronounced mismatch in the duration of assets and liabilities in both the corporate and banking sectors.[12]

Perhaps the two most important contributors to the current Asian crises are (1) low corporate profits and (2) policymakers' unwillingness to relinquish control. The government-directed banking systems and weak corporate governance structures (including managerial incentives to increase size and market share at the expense of shareholder value) that characterize most Asian economies have resulted in systematic overinvestment and sharp declines in corporate profitability. And the shrinking profits, besides reducing the overall value of many Asian economies, have greatly weakened the banking sectors on which many firms have historically relied for much of their funding.

Government Intervention in the Currency Market. Such effects, not surprisingly, have been accompanied by large reductions in currency values in several Asian countries, including Thailand, Indonesia, Malaysia, and South Korea. The important thing to note here is that these have not been "normal" currency devaluations. Under normal circumstances, at least in economies where the government allows the market to re-establish the exchange rate, a deterioration in an economy's prospects will be reflected in series of relatively gradual downward adjustments to the currency.

Take the case of Japan in recent times. The Japanese yen, which reached its peak of 80 per U.S. dollar in 1995, was above 140 in July 1998, thus representing a depreciation in excess of 40%. This large drop in the currency value occurred with relatively little intervention by the Japanese government; it was more or less an orderly adjustment over three years in response to market forces. With the gradual adjustment in currency value, the Japanese economy has had the time to react and so avoid the dire consequences of a financial panic that accompanies a sudden collapse in currency value (which is not, of course, to deny the major structural problems of the Japanese economy that still need to be corrected through radical reform).

Unfortunately, such was not the case for the three celebrated cases of full-fledged currency crises – those in Mexico, Thailand, and Korea. For these countries, the culprits were partial decontrol of financial markets and policymakers' unwillingness to relinquish further control.

With the move toward liberalization, many emerging economies relaxed controls on currency flows while continuing to control the exchange rate. This works fine as long as the currency value is close to its market-determined value. But when the discrepancy becomes too great, market forces can be counted on to put pressure on a government to devalue. If the government does not oblige, there will be a one-way shift in private-sector speculative currency flows that will force the currency to crash, which is precisely what has happened in the three countries.

The recent Korean experience was similar to the earlier Mexican and Thai crises. At the beginning of 1994, the Mexican peso was estimated to be about 40% overvalued; yet the government was reluctant to devalue the peso because of commitments it had made to business and labor in an agreement known as the *pacto*. Moreover, the government was preoccupied with the upcoming presidential election and was concerned that devaluation would push up inflation and generate a loss of investor confidence. But whatever the reasons for the failure to act, when President Zedillo's government assumed control in early December of 1994, it found that foreign currency reserves had been depleted by defending the peso, which forced the devaluation on December 20, 1994.

The Thai currency, the baht, was similarly overvalued. And the government similarly decided to fight market forces rather than allow an orderly depreciation, perhaps because the government

---

12 As was witnessed during the Korean crisis, a financial panic can be triggered by the refusal of foreign lenders to renew short-term loans as the mature. When domestic borrowers choose to finance long-term projects with short-term borrowings, they are building up a dangerous duration imbalance in exchange for somewhat lower financing costs. The root cause of such reckless borrowing and lending behavior is the moral hazard in the "too big to fail" legacy and the implicit role of the IMF as the lender of last resort.

thought it had sufficient foreign exchange reserves ($38.7 billion at the end of 1996) and wanted to avoid the high political costs associated with a baht devaluation. Speculators started to bet against the Thai government by borrowing baht and converting them to dollars with the expectation that, when it came time to repay the baht, it would take fewer dollars. And, of course, their expectations were realized. The Thai government spent an estimated $12 billion buying baht, but ultimately caved in on July 2, 1997. The baht was finally allowed to "float"; and, by the end of July, its value had fallen to 32 baht per dollar, down 25% since May.

Korea's case is painfully similar to those of Mexico and Thailand.[13] During the month of November 1997, the Bank of Korea spent $25 billion in a futile attempt to protect the won. It took only a few weeks to deplete most of its foreign exchange reserves (down to $6 billion) as a prelude to the collapse of the won by 50%. This collapse effectively doubled the foreign debt load of already highly leveraged Korean corporations virtually overnight and forced the Korean government into the hands of the IMF. Even though the Korean government had ample time to observe and learn from the experiences of Mexico and Thailand, it apparently didn't do any good.

Value Destruction. Although it was the ill-fated attempt by policymakers to resist market forces that transformed an otherwise normal currency depreciation into a crash, a more fundamental cause of the Asian crisis has been the widespread value destruction by Asian corporations, which has led to a lower value for the overall economy and weakened the banking sector. The countries that have been hardest hit by the Asian turmoil – Indonesia, Korea, Malaysia, and Thailand – have all seen their corporations engage in chronic over-investment with little regard to earning a rate of return adequate to compensate the suppliers of capital. In the pursuit of growth and expansion, the cost of capital was often underestimated or ignored altogether in making investment decisions.

This resulted in inefficient allocation of capital and the destruction of corporate value.

In a recent study of Korean corporations commissioned by the Korean Stock Exchange, Myeong Kyun Kim, Jaekyung Yi, and I demonstrated the widespread nature of this value destruction in the Korean economy.[14] We calculated the Economic Value Added (EVA) for 570 non-financial firms listed in the Korea Stock Exchange from 1992 through 1996. (EVA is defined as net operating profit after taxes minus cost of capital.) When we summed up the annual EVAs of each company over the five-year period (which preceded the crash), we found that only 27% of the listed companies created shareholder value; the rest, nearly three-quarters of them, destroyed value. That is, nearly three-quarters of the listed companies did not generate sufficient operating earnings to cover their capital costs during the five years preceding the crisis.

I suspect that similar value destruction has been taking place not only in the emerging economies of Thailand, Indonesia, and Malaysia, but also in Japan. And such value destruction has been clearly evident in Asian stock markets. For example, Japan's Nikkei average, which was as high as 39,000 at the end of 1989, is now in the 14,000 range, reflecting a sharp decline in the profitability of Japanese firms since the late '80s. The Korean stock market index, the KOSPI, was above 1,000 in March of 1989; now it is around 300.

Another interesting observation from our Korea Stock Exchange study is that each of three large firms (Jinro, Mando, and Halla) that went bankrupt in 1997 (and that were each part of large Korean conglomerates known as *chaebol*) had core businesses that were highly profitable. Indeed, when viewed as stand-alone companies, these three core businesses of Jinro, Mando, and Halla had cumulative EVAs that would have enabled them to rank 15th, 17th, and 28th, respectively, among the 570 firms. The failure of the three companies was thus clearly attributable to their disastrous diversification into unrelated businesses.

---

13 One difference with the Mexican case is that the crash occurred after the presidential election in Mexico, whereas it occurred a month before the election in Korea, which may have affected the outcome of the election as well as the government's effectiveness in dealing with the crash.

14 See E. Han Kim, Myeong Kyun Kim, and Jaekyung Yi, "Economic Value Added (EVA) of the Listed Companies," The Korea Stock Exchange Report 98-01, February 1998.

CORPORATE RESTRUCTURING IN KOREA

The conglomeration of Korean firms is comparable to the conglomeration of U.S. firms during the 1960s and '70s. At the time, the rationale for U.S. conglomerates was their ability to create "internal" capital markets that allowed internal funding across unrelated businesses and led to smoother growth and stable cash flows at the overall firm level. In the majority of cases, however, U.S. conglomerates ended up breeding inefficiencies that led to lower earnings and share prices. And, in the 1980s and '90s, many U.S. conglomerates were dismantled after becoming the targets of hostile takeovers and leveraged buyout (LBOs). The transfers in control that accompanied these transactions were typically followed by massive restructurings involving the selling off of unrelated businesses to pay off outstanding debt. The general aim of such restructurings was to restore operating efficiencies and improve the capital allocation process by refocusing on the remaining core businesses.[15]

The lesson to be learned from the American experience is that the creation of internal capital markets through conglomeration allowed firms to bypass the discipline of the external capital market, allowing inefficient operations to continue until the firm as a whole became a takeover candidate. And it is tempting to prescribe the same medicine for the Korean chaebol: namely, the large-scale restructuring undergone by many U.S. conglomerates during the last 15–20 years.

The "big deal"

This is presumed to be the rationale for the Korean government's current attempt to restructure the chaebol. The government is essentially demanding that the chaebol do what LBO firms did after they took over large conglomerates during the '80s: divest unprofitable (or at least non-core) businesses, use the proceeds to reduce outstanding debt, and refocus on the remaining core businesses.

But there is a crucial difference. In its efforts to implement the so-called "big deal," the Korean government is assuming the role traditionally reserved for the private market for corporate control.

The "big deal" solution is to encourage the chaebol to make large-scale swaps of entire businesses with the objective of inducing each of the chaebol to specialize in core businesses. Although the justification for the government's initiative in promoting the "big deal" is the absence of an effective market for corporate control, the important question that must be addressed is: Can the government effectively replicate the role of the market? Do government officials have incentives compatible with the private economic incentives that motivate U.S. corporate raiders to restore value?

Government officials clearly have neither the same incentives to seek out, nor the ability to identify, value-creating synergistic gains through corporate restructuring. Moreover, government-imposed "big deals" run the risk of creating monopolistic inefficiencies and negative synergies. In essence, the "big deal" policy represents yet another form of government intervention in the marketplace that is likely to lead to misallocation of resources and a net reduction in the overall efficiency of the economy.

Corporate restructuring is likely to produce the desired results only when it is pursued voluntarily by the private sector. The government's role should be limited to improving the market mechanism and enhancing competition in the markets for capital, for corporate control, and for goods and services. The Korean market for corporate control transactions could be greatly improved by increasing the efficiency of bankruptcy proceedings and by allowing hostile takeovers by foreign as well as domestic investors. And when capital markets, as well as the market for goods and services, are fully competitive with appropriate levels of transparency and accountability, corporate restructuring will become a matter of necessity for the chaebol – and market forces will then produce value-increasing restructuring decisions.

Cross-payment guarantees

Government prohibition of payment guarantees among affiliated firms also appears to be a

---

15 See E. Han Kim, "Corporate Takeovers: Winners, Losers, and Some Remaining Issues," *Recent Developments in International Banking and Finance*, Vol. IV and V, S.J. Khoury (ed.) Elsevier Science Publisher B.V. (North-Holland), 1991, pp. 101–122.

premature and therefore intrusive "reform" that interferes with contractual efficiency in the capital market. It is intrusive because loan guarantees, if executed in a transparent fashion, can reasonably be expected to increase financial flexibility and generate a joint economic benefit. For this reason, most free market economies allow payment guarantees among affiliated firms.

Korean policymakers, however, seem to believe that the chaebol cannot be trusted with payment guarantee contracts because they will be used to keep economically unprofitable businesses afloat. That is, the rationale for cutting off guarantees seems to be that it will ensure that only economically viable firms remain. Although such drastic measures may be required to prod chaebol into undertaking the necessary restructuring immediately, it is not clear that the economy can be made better off by prohibiting business practices that are considered normal in most free market economies.

For this policy to yield the desired outcome and ensure an uninterrupted supply of capital to economically viable firms, Korean capital markets would have to be capable both of distinguishing value-increasing from value-destroying firms, and of imposing the proper discipline on the latter. But due to the long history of government intervention, Korean capital markets have a long way to go in terms of increasing transparency, accountability, and ability to discriminate – not to mention liquidity and depth. Even in economies with highly advanced financial systems, such as the U.S. and Britain, there is an information "gap" between corporate insiders and the external capital market that makes it difficult to value companies with a high degree of confidence. In an economy like Korea where information problems abound, internal capital markets could have an advantage over external capital markets, at least in some circumstances.

To be sure, internal capital markets in the U.S. have often served as a pretext for allowing managers to avoid the discipline of external capital market, with lower earnings and share prices as the principal consequence. But it is equally important to note that such abuses and mistakes are likely to be corrected in the market for corporate control, where the inefficient conglomerates that run internal capital markets for "the wrong reasons" are subsequently taken over. Thus, in prohibiting

guarantees, the Korean government is attempting to correct internal abuses by decree rather than by relying on market forces.

Not only does the prohibition of payment guarantees appear to be intrusive, but it also is premature: It abolishes an internal capital market without offering an alternative. Abolishing internal capital markets in the absence of properly functioning external capital markets runs the risk of crippling the ability of Korean corporations to finance necessary investments to maintain their competitiveness in the global marketplace. Any further reduction in corporate investment activity will not only worsen the economic recession and unemployment, but will seriously weaken the foundations on which to build future growth and value.

What the government must do instead is to concentrate its efforts to strengthen the disciplinary power of the external capital market by increasing transparency, accountability, competitiveness, and fairness in the rules of the game for the participants in capital markets. When the external capital markets attain sufficient disciplinary power, the chaebol will pursue the necessary restructuring voluntarily as a matter of survival.

Other reform measures

As the Asian financial crises illustrate, an economy cannot enjoy sustainable growth while ignoring the claims of ownership. In a global capital market, the suppliers of capital will take their money elsewhere if they do not get fair rates of return. Providing equity investors with adequate rates of return, however, will require substantial increases in both operating efficiencies and the productivity of capital. So, in addition to the afore-mentioned reforms of the external capital markets, it is necessary to change the internal objectives and revise the decision-making processes inside Asian corporations.

To increase the productivity of capital, Asian corporations must realign managerial interests with the claims of shareholders by linking managerial compensation to value creation. Such a realignment will of course require abandonment of the previous goal of growth at any cost and replacement of the seniority-based egalitarian compensation system with merit-based performance pay.

Although such changes in compensation criterion are necessary, they are not in themselves sufficient. Outside investors need assurance and protection from expropriation of their wealth by the controlling investors. This requires much greater transparency in financial reporting, accountability by management, and legal protection against management and the controlling investors. For example, prior to the IMF-imposed reform measures, the chaebol were not required to file consolidated financial statements. Since the chaebol typically have 20–30 affiliated firms under their control, without consolidated financial statements they could easily disguise their true financial health by shifting funds among the affiliated firms. Furthermore, the controlling shareholders of the leading chaebol usually were not directly accountable to the public shareholders because they often did not hold an official position in any of their affiliated firms.

Much has already been accomplished by the Korean government on these accounts. To increase transparency, consolidated financial statements are required for the chaebol beginning with the 1999 fiscal year. To increase accountability, chaebol owners now must hold an official position on the Board of Directors and will be held legally responsible for their actions. To protect minority shareholders, their rights to review financial accounts, dismiss directors or auditors, and vote in the shareholder meetings have been greatly strengthened. The recent victory by the minority shareholders of Korea First Bank, in which punitive damages of 40 billion won (about $30 million) were imposed on four top former executives, should act as a bellwether in increasing accountability of management and enhancing shareholder rights.

To facilitate the exit of non-viable firms, reforms have been enacted in bankruptcy-related laws and M&A processes. Markets for corporate control and real estate have been opened up to foreign investors, allowing hostile as well as friendly takeovers. These measures, if implemented properly, will surely enhance the market mechanism for changing corporate control. In so doing, it will bring about value-increasing corporate restructuring that redeploys assets to more productive uses.

Other promising economic reform measures have been initiated or announced.[16] It is the government's stated intention to encourage competition by reducing the barriers to entry and exit, opening markets to foreigners, promoting foreign direct investment, and increasing labor market flexibility. All of these changes bode well for the future Korean economy.

CONCLUDING REMARKS

Even though the recent Asian financial crisis has led some to question the merits of open capital markets and to call for regulatory restraints on capital flows across international borders, the scientific evidence suggests that the opening of stock markets to foreign participation has been largely beneficial for the majority of emerging economies. On average, stock market liberalization has been associated with an increase in stock valuations and a reduction in stock return volatility, a reduction in inflation due to productive use of foreign capital, and a reduction in currency depreciation attributable to increased confidence among foreign investors. Furthermore, the real culprits in the currency crises are not the hedge funds or foreign speculators, as many politicians (and even some economists) would have us believe; much of the speculative pressure on currencies appears instead to have originated from local sources.

Perhaps the most fundamental cause of the crises is corporate sector value destruction caused by systematic overinvestment. Such corporate overinvestment was in turn made possible by excessive borrowing from both domestic and foreign banks. The banking sectors have historically had no qualms in funding projects regardless of their economic merit, provided the projects were sponsored by large companies that were therefore likely to be protected by the government. Domestic bankers have demonstrated the meaning of "moral hazard" in their response to the "too big to fail" legacy. And international bankers have done

---

16 For further elaboration of these points, as well as for an analysis of the current condition of various markets in Korea and reform measures announced and undertaken, see my article, "The Korean Financial Crisis and the Future of Its Economy," *Journal of Asian Business* (forthcoming).

the same with the implicit assurance that the IMF will function as the lender of last resort.

In this regard, the recent Russian default in August 1998 had the beneficial effect of reducing moral hazard by imposing painful losses on Western investors, losses which they had been able to avoid with the help of the IMF in the previous currency crises in Mexico, Thailand, and Korea. And to the extent that country defaults reduce moral hazard and restore market discipline to the international flow of capital, the Russian default is a blessing in disguise. Its importance in the international political arena makes the event highly visible, but the relatively small size of the Russian economy prevents a mortal wounding of global capital markets. Nevertheless, the disciplinary role of the capital market will not be fully effective as long as the existence of the IMF offers a potential for bailouts.

Corporate value destruction alone would not have created the crisis. For the process of currency depreciation to be accelerated into a crash, it also required governments' futile attempts to maintain the value of their currencies at artificially high levels.

The Korean government's recent initiatives to restructure the chaebol, under the name of the "big deal," have a surface resemblance to the restructuring of U.S. conglomerates during the 1980s. Unfortunately, the Korean government's plan seems to overestimate its ability to guide the market. The "big deal" runs the risk of introducing monopolistic inefficiencies and creating negative synergies. Moreover, the government's prohibition of cross-payment guarantees seems to be an attempt to undo mistakes by decree rather than by relying on market forces. Furthermore, it cuts off an existing source of funding for new value-creating ventures without offering a reasonable alternative.

These reservations notwithstanding, the various economic reform measures that the Korean government has announced or initiated to date are impressive. It will take time, however, for these reform measures to yield the desired results. In the meantime, the short-run costs of implementing reform, such as unemployment and an increase in business bankruptcies, will outweigh any short-term benefits and surely test the public's patience. But policymakers should not succumb to public pressure for quick results, as they appear to be doing in the push for "big deals" and prohibition of cross-payment guarantees.

Finally, whenever there are attempts to reform, there are powerful vested interest groups with much to lose. They will lobby hard against the changes to protect their own interests. Thus, what is required for productive change is not only the need for greater efficiency but also the consensus and the political will for reform. Korea and Thailand now appear to be moving rapidly in the direction of accepting necessary changes; and they both may benefit greatly in the long run from surrendering some domestic control of their economic policy to the IMF. This is in sharp contrast to Japan, the world's second largest economy, where lack of the will for reform may keep the nation mired in its now decade-long stagnation.

In all of the Asian economies, the economic argument for reform is apparent and compelling. But essential to the process is the political will to reform and the patience to allow the changes time to work. And it is owing to differences in these two scarce commodities that the paths of the Asian economies could diverge – and quite sharply.

CHAPTER 31

Incorporating Country Risk in The Valuation of Offshore Projects

Donald R. Lessard (Massachusetts Institute of Technology)

Offshore projects, especially those in emerging economies, are generally viewed as more risky, and thus as contributing less to shareholder value, than otherwise comparable domestic investments. Emerging economies are typically more volatile than the economies of industrialized countries. They also present a greater array of risks that are primarily of a "downside" nature, such as currency inconvertibility, expropriation, civil unrest, and general institutional instability. Further, because such risks are relatively unfamiliar to the investing companies, the companies are likely to make costly errors in early years and to require more time to bring cash flow and rates of return to acceptable steady-state levels.

To reflect these higher risks and greater unfamiliarity, many companies include an extra premium in the discount rate they apply to offshore and, particularly, to emerging-market projects. However, the basis for these discount rate adjustments is often arbitrary. Such adjustments do not properly reflect objective information available about either the nature of these risks, or about the ability of management to manage such risks. Nor do they take into account the reality that the risks stemming from unfamiliarity fall over time as the firm progresses along the learning curve.

As a result, companies often "over discount" projected cash flows in compensating for these risks, and so unduly penalize offshore projects.

More important, adjusting for country risk using arbitrary adjustments to the discount rate fails to focus management's attention on strategic and financial actions that can be taken to reduce risk – notably, actions capable of transferring some of the company's exposures to specific risks to different parties with comparative advantages in bearing those risks. Such risk-management responses range from financial hedging of currency exposures and the purchase of insurance against political risks to alternative methods of participation in emerging-economy projects such as joint ventures with local partners.

In most cases, the decision to invest cannot be separated from the participation and risk management choices, especially since the desired risk allocation in large part reflects the fact that different potential parties to the project will place different values on particular aspects of the project. Such differences in risk-bearing capacity and valuation among parties will in turn reflect differences in these parties' asset portfolios, their costs of obtaining information, their degree of control and influence over outcomes, and their vulnerability to taxes or expropriation.

As a consequence, the value of an offshore project will depend, to a much greater extent than the value of a domestic investment, on how the project is financed, who owns the various claims, and who bears the different risks associated with the project.

Thus, it is not possible to separate the overall decision neatly into a strategic problem, a capital budgeting problem, a financing problem, and a risk-management problem. Companies must attempt to address each of these aspects of the overall investment evaluation process simultaneously.

This paper proceeds as follows: I begin by developing a taxonomy of risks based on comparative advantage in risk-taking, which in turn leads to a discussion of risk allocation and participation strategies for offshore projects. The next section of the paper presents general principles of risk and valuation in the context of foreign direct investment, and I conclude with some specific suggestions for estimating discount rates for such projects.

My key findings can be summarized as follows:

- Risks should be classified in terms of whether or not the company has a comparative advantage in assuming them, which in turn depends on the firm's other assets, its information advantage (or lack thereof), and its ability to manage such risks.
- Participation strategies can increasingly be tailored through project structuring and financial engineering to allocate risks in ways that exploit these comparative advantages.
- In valuing offshore projects, how managers adjust for risk (whether by raising the discount rate or reducing expected cash flows) should depend primarily on (1) whether the risks are "one-sided" or "symmetric," and (2) whether the risks are "systematic" or instead are "diversifiable" by world capital markets. With respect to valuation, I also offer the following suggestions:
- Although more volatile, investments in emerging economies typically contribute little or no more to the volatility of a company's cash flows and its shareholders' portfolios than domestic projects because of the diversification effect.
- Political and country risks of a downside nature, such as the threat of expropriation, shifts in industrial and sectoral policy, and exchange inconvertibility, can be roughly proxied by the risk of non-payment on government bonds.
- Currency risks in general do not require additional adjustments to expected dollar cash flows or discount rates. However, they may have significant effects on these expected flows relative to most-likely levels.

- Unfamiliarity with a country should not be factored into the discount rate. The effects of unfamiliarity should decrease over time, rather than increase at a compound rate as would be implied by adjusting the discount rate.

It is important to keep in mind throughout this discussion that risk is not necessarily the enemy. The least risky countries are not necessarily the most attractive ones, nor are the most risky necessarily the least attractive. Risks clearly reduce investment attractiveness, but such risks must be weighed against the underlying sources of market attractiveness such as growth potential, as well as a firm's competitive advantage in particular countries. Risky offshore investments can add value outright by creating valuable strategic options. They can also add value in a competitive context if they create barriers to entry or provide positive-NPV investments due to comparative advantages in risk bearing. Indeed, an important part of a company's competitive advantage may be represented by the risk-management methods at its disposal. Total risk management recognizes the full range of potential responses to all sources of uncertainty.

A TAXONOMY OF RISKS

Offshore investments involve a host of risks that differ from those associated with domestic projects. These include but are not limited to the classic country risks – expropriation, civil disorder, and exchange controls and other forms of payments difficulty. Companies investing offshore also face different, though not always greater, risks of macroeconomic volatility than they do at home. They also encounter currency price risks they do not face at home, since cash flows in local currency must be translated into the home currency.

Offshore investments, especially in emerging economies, also entail various risks associated with incomplete or unstable institutions. Although expropriation and war are the most visible and dramatic forms that such political risk can take, uncertainty about local governments' economic and regulatory policies may actually lead to larger reductions in the expected values of overseas projects. Finally, offshore investments, to the extent they represent new locations for the parent company, carry the risk of

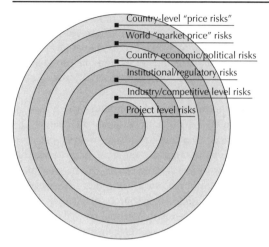

Figure 31.1 Risk Drivers Affecting International Projects

unfamiliarity with local institutional and operating conditions.

Figure 31.1 depicts, in the form of concentric circles, the various types of risk that a company faces when investing internationally. Moving from the "outer" circle toward the center, these risks are as follows: (1) world "market price" risks; (2) country macroeconomic and political risks; (3) country-level "price risks"; (4) institutional/regulatory risks; (5) industry-level risks, and (6) project/commercial risks. Most of these risks differ in degree rather than in kind from those faced at home. Indeed, the only type of risk associated exclusively with international projects are the so-called cross-border or "transfer" risks associated with commercial and financial transfers. Nevertheless, the dynamics of many of these risks are likely to be different from those faced in domestic settings. As one example, the regulatory or institutional risk of an offshore investment may differ not only because of the difference in institutions, but also because the treatment accorded a foreign company by a given set of institutions may differ from the treatment accorded a local firm (although it will not always be worse!).

Comparative advantage and allocation of risk

While most valuation approaches rest on the assumption of a common valuation platform in

which companies value projects from the perspective of "the market" (or, equivalently, completely diversified investors), there are many reasons why different clienteles of investors – or different companies acting as agents for these different clienteles of ultimate investors – may have comparative advantages in bearing various aspects of a project's risk. Although these comparative advantages are widely recognized in the risk allocation that takes place in the context of project financing,[1] such differences in risk-bearing capacity, along with their consequences for valuation, tend to be ignored when projects are not separately financed.

Comparative advantage in risk-bearing may arise for any one of three reasons (all of which are violations of assumptions that underlie the CAPM and other standard, "equilibrium-based" valuation approaches):[2] (1) information is not equally available to all investors; (2) investors may have different degrees of influence over outcomes; and (3) investors may differ in their ability to diversify risks, largely as result of reasons (1) or (2) above.

To illustrate these three considerations, take the case of an investment by a Chilean company in an Argentine independent power generating plant.[3] The investor's advantage lies largely in the successful experience it has had in Chile with 20 years of privatization and the associated institutional innovation. In this sense, the Chilean firm can be said to "know more about the future of Argentina than the Argentines." Also, given the proximity of

1 For an instructive discussion of the risk allocation that takes place in project finance, and the web of contractual arrangements it involves, see in this issue Richard Brealey, Ian Cooper, and Michel Habib, "The Use of Project Finance in Infrastructure Investments," *Journal of Applied Corporate Finance*, Vol. 9 No. 3. (Fall 1996), pp. 25–38.

2 See my earlier discussion of comparative advantage in risk bearing in my article, "Financial Risk Management for Developing Countries: A Policy Overview," *Journal of Applied Corporate Finance*, Vol. 8 No. 3. (Fall 1995). See also in this issue, René Stulz, "Rethinking Risk Management," *Journal of Applied Corporate Finance*, Vol. 9 No. 3. (Fall 1996), pp. 8–24.

3 The following example is based on public information regarding the investment of Endesa (Chile) in projects in Argentina. The example can be extended to other home/host pairs, but Chile provides an interesting setting given Chile's lead in institutional development, Argentina's greater macroeconomic and political risk, and Argentina's much larger size. Investments by, say, Thai firms in Indonesia would be quite similar.

Argentine activities to its home base, the Chilean firm may benefit from some potential for sharing costs of specialized management, technical support, and so forth.

Table 31.1 shows the comparative advantage of different players in bearing different risks associated with the project. In so doing, it provides the specifications for a value-increasing shifting of risks among different potential participants. The participation of various players in the project should be structured to give those with a comparative advantage in bearing a particular risk a larger exposure to that risk, while those with a comparative disadvantage should be shielded from such risks to the extent possible. There are many different ways to do this, and the following brief discussion presents an outline of the typical approaches for each of the six major types of risk.

Operating Risk. Based on its capabilities and experience, the Chilean firm has a clear information and influence advantage in managing operating risk as compared to both Argentine firms and "first-world" firms. Indeed, this is the primary strategic rationale for the investment.

More generally, to the extent an operating firm has a comparative advantage that derives from both better information and influence over outcomes, it will want a disproportionate exposure to operating risk. The firm, for example, could increase its operating exposure beyond that implied by its equity investment through a management contract providing for bonuses for excellent performance.

Demand Risk. Demand risks are of two types: (1) those associated with the variability of overall demand and prices; and (2) those associated with the specific demand and pricing of the project's output, which depend not only on overall conditions but also on dispatching rules, pricing conditions, and so forth. Although these risks will largely be allocated by the power purchase agreement, the stability and enforceability of that agreement will in turn depend on institutional stability. A cost-indexed "take or pay" contract, for example, will impose these demand risks completely on consumers and/or distributors, whereas contingent pricing and dispatch rules will shift some or all of these risks to the project itself.

Comparative advantage in bearing these demand risks depends largely on the stability of institutional structures. If local institutions are highly stable and thus predictable, the advantage will lie with well-diversified investors ("the market"). But in countries where there is significant regulatory or institutional uncertainty, the advantage may lie with those investors with the greatest ability to influence the process.

Chilean investors may be at a double disadvantage in bearing such demand risk. First, to the extent that Argentine and other South American projects are already a very large part of their overall portfolios, Chilean investors are likely to view such a project as contributing significantly to their total risk (that is, there are no significant diversification benefits). Second, as a visible "foreign" company in a sector with a large foreign presence, such a project may be singled out for "contract renegotiation" should the existing terms prove onerous to Argentine consumers. Therefore, they may want to shift these risks to either better-diversified international players or to investor groups with greater legitimate voice within the host country such as Argentine strategic investors or, better yet, "widows and orphans" as represented by Argentine pension funds.

Institutional Risk. This form of risk involves all of the uncertainties about how the rules of the game are likely to change. Given the recent experience of public utilities in the U.S., U.K., and other presumably "stable" countries, it is clear that these risks are not limited to emerging markets. The key questions are whether the overall structure of income and decision rights will remain in place, existing agreements will be honored, and the resulting claims will be enforced. Since most of these outcomes involve at least some element of "discretion" on the part of local policymakers, risk mitigation is a key strategic lever, and comparative advantage will again lie with those most able to influence the process. As we saw in the case of demand risk, local strategic investors and pension funds may have an advantage in taking institutional risks because of their standing within or leverage over the political processes that underpin the regulatory regime. But, because local pension funds and other passive investors are likely to be at a disadvantage in bearing operating and demand risks that require specific knowledge, they may want to limit their exposure to construction and start-up operation risks – for example, by investing

Table 31.1 Comparative Advantage in Risk Bearing – IPP Project

Risk type	Entity					
	Operator/ strategic investor	Local strategic investor	Local portfolio investor	Local public authority	Internat'l portfolio investor, market	Internat'l policy lender
Construction						
Delay	+	+?				
Cost	+	+?				
Operations						
Availability	++					
Staffing Cost	+	+				
Demand						
Overall				+	+	
Dispatch		+		+		+
Institutional						
Regulation	+	+	+			
Contract Enforcmt.	+	+	+			
Currency						
Inflation					+	
Exchange Rate					+	
Country						
Macropolitical					+	+
Macrofinancial					+	+
World Market						
Oil Prices					+	
Interest Rates					+	

in convertible bonds or preferred shares that give them an option on project equity once it is up and running.

To the extent that institutional risks are subject to mitigation by external review or pressure, it may also be in the interest of the other parties to bring international policy lenders into the project in order to mitigate these risks. The World Bank, for example, is increasingly becoming involved as a policy lender in infrastructure projects. Its participation tends to be conditional on agreements respecting institutional or regulatory behavior that, if violated, are treated as defaults on obligations to the World Bank, as well as to other lenders that have entered into cross-default clauses with the Bank.

Domestic Market Price Risks. Most prominent among such risks are those arising from changes in inflation and the exchange rate. The extent of the project's exposure to such risks will, again, depend largely on the terms and

enforceability of the power purchase agreement. Because local consumers are clearly at a disadvantage in bearing such risks, the Chilean company should explore the possibility of laying off part of such exposures on derivatives markets if the appropriate hedging instruments exist. If they do not, the company may want to seek out well-diversified global investors, for whom such risks would have minimal effect on the risk of their portfolios.

Macro Political and Economic Risks. Ultimately, an IPP project in Argentina is a bet on the viability of the Argentine economic program. Although the program has now outlasted its originator, it remains subject to many stresses. All local investors, as well as Chileans who have placed big bets on Argentina, are overexposed to this risk without any significant compensatory benefits that come with having influence over outcomes.

Thus, ironically, many of the same players that have a comparative advantage in bearing operating or regulatory risk because of their knowledge and position as insiders will be at a disadvantage relative to well-diversified world investors in bearing macro country risks. In fact, it is generally the case that those most in need of country risk insurance or other mechanisms to lay off country exposure are the local strategic investors who face unusually good investment opportunities "at home" relative to other investors because of their knowledge and influence. Local pension funds and other passive investors may also benefit from such insurance because of their similar lack of international diversification.

In this particular case, as noted earlier, Chilean strategic investors are likely to be overexposed to Argentine risk as well, since they face such good opportunities there. To reduce their exposure to overall country risk while maintaining a proportionately larger exposure to operating and institutional risks, such investors can either purchase country risk insurance or enter into hedges based on derivative instruments such as puts on traded shares of local firms. Moreover, international portfolio investors can take on pure country risk by taking the other side of these hedges as well as by investing in the project equity. To the extent that overall country risks are subject to mitigation by external pressure, it may also be in the interest of the other parties to bring international policy lenders like the World Bank into the project to mitigate these risks.

Market Price Risks. The project's exposure to world price risks such as worldwide interest rates, oil prices, and exchange rates among major currencies depends, again, largely on the power purchase agreement. In the early Argentine cases, as with many Asian countries, exchange and oil price risks were assumed by the purchaser, but world interest rate risks were not. Even though many purchase agreements provide for pass-through of oil prices, a large spike in prices would create incentives for local distributors to void the contracts and switch supply. In this sense, the project remains indirectly exposed. As we have already seen, world market price risks can be laid off to financial markets by hedging with derivatives or by encouraging investment by well-diversified global investors. In the above case, for example, buying "cheap," because well out-of-the-money, call options on oil prices might prove a valuable insurance policy.

RISK AND SHAREHOLDER VALUE: GENERAL PRINCIPLES

Within a standard, risk-adusted DCF valuation approach, risk affects shareholder value in two primary ways. Two-sided or "symmetric" risks such as fluctuations in GDP, exchange rates, or interest rates – those with similar upside and downside impacts on cash flows – reduce value only to the extent that they contribute to the volatility of the value of shareholders' total portfolios and thus increase their required rates of returns. The impact of an offshore investment on the volatility of investors' returns is measured by its "beta" relative to the benchmark home-market portfolio, just as with a domestic project.

In contrast, "asymmetric" risks – those whose potential downside impacts are significantly greater than their potential upside – reduce expected cash flows relative to their most-likely values as well, and thereby reduce value whether or not they contribute to the overall volatility of the firm or of shareholders' returns. Examples of downside risks are expropriation actions, casualty or war damage, or payments problems that may reduce cash flows but cannot increase them above the "usual" level. In practice, risks range along a continuum that runs between these two extremes, but clearly some are relatively two-sided while others have primarily downside impacts.

The impact of a particular risk on expected cash flows (relative to their most-likely level) also depends on the shape of the payoff profile of cash flows with respect to that risk. In the case of "debt-like" projects with limited upsides – as is often true of independent power projects given their fixed capacity – expected cash flows will be lower than the most-likely cash flows. This will be true even when the distributions of demand risk drivers are symmetric or even "skewed to the right." In contrast, the expected cash flows for "call option-like" projects with floors on cash flows will be higher than their most-likely value. Since the impacts of non-linear payoff profiles increase the volatility of the underlying risk drivers, proper estimation of the expected cash flows is particularly important for emerging-market projects.

The risks that will contribute most to the volatility of a U.S. shareholder's wealth, or to the value of a U.S.-based company for that matter, are those that are most closely related to the U.S. or overall world economy. By contrast, the risk of civil unrest in a small country due to purely local factors, while significantly reducing the expected cash flows from investing in that country, will have little impact on the volatility of a U.S. portfolio. Similarly, risks arising from unfamiliarity will clearly be downside risks that reduce expected cash flows. But, if the investment in question is relatively small, such risks will contribute little or nothing to the volatility of shareholder wealth or the firm's share price.

Projects whose value is determined by the variables that affect the U.S. economy as a whole will command high risk premiums. In such cases, the discount rates should be set substantially above the market interest rate. And, indeed, this is the way standard DCF analysis treats high-beta domestic projects whose cash flows and value respond sharply to changes in the levels of macroeconomic activity.

The expected cash flows from projects facing significant downside risks will be substantially lower than those projected under normal or most-likely economic and political scenarios. Although the effect of these reductions in expected cash flows is similar to the effect of increasing the discount rate, the time profile of the two sets of adjustments is quite different. This will be particularly true of cash-flow adjustments to reflect unfamiliarity. Such adjustments will be greatest in early years, instead of rising at a compound rate over time (as would be implied by an adjustment to the discount rate applicable to all periods).

In sum, country risks of a largely downside nature such as expropriation and civil disorder reduce cash flows relative to the level anticipated under normal conditions, but will have little impact on the volatility of a well-diversified portfolio (unless they are general to a large part of the world economy, such as a collapse of the world trading system as a result of a trade "war"). By contrast, risks associated with the volatility of world macroeconomic variables will typically be quite symmetrical and therefore will not have major cash-flow impacts; and, because they will contribute to the volatility of shareholders' portfolios, they will command a risk premium. Unfamiliarity, as we have seen, will have little impact of portfolio volatility, but it will reduce

expected cash flows relative to the level implied by steady-state productivity. Finally, and perhaps most counterintuitive, local variations in macroeconomic activity will have minimal effects on both cash flows and discount rates.

The weighted average cost of capital

The most common approach for valuing projects involves discounting cash flows by a weighted average discount rate that blends the cost of equity (which in turn is the interest rate plus an adjustment for market covariance risk) and the (after-tax) cost of debt:

$$NPV = \sum_{0}^{N} E(CF)_t / (1 + r)^t, \qquad \text{(eq. 1)}$$

where $E(CF)_t$ is the expected after-corporate-tax free cash flow in period t and r is the weighted average discount rate. The weighted average cost of capital, r, in turn is defined as:

$$r = r_{equity} * w_{equity} + r_{debt} * w_{debt} \\ * (1 - t_{effective}), \qquad \text{(eq. 1a)}$$

where w_{equity} and w_{debt} are the weights of debt and equity, respectively, and $t_{effective}$ is the effective tax rate on debt versus equity. The cost of equity, in turn, is defined as:

$$r_{equity} = R_f + RP, \qquad \text{(eq. 1b)}$$

where R_f is the default risk-free interest rate and RP is the risk premium for market covariance risk. This risk premium, in turn, is defined as:

$$RP = \text{project beta} * MRP, \qquad \text{(eq. 1c)}$$

where the project beta is the measure of the covariability of the project in question with the benchmark U.S. market portfolio and MRP is the risk premium on that market portfolio.

The beta of an offshore project with respect to the investing company's benchmark portfolio can be estimated in two ways: (1) directly, by regressing returns on relevant local shares against the home-market portfolio (and making adjustments for differences in financial and operating leverage);

or (2) indirectly, by estimating the beta of the project relative to the local market portfolio and multiplying the result by the *country beta*, the beta of the local market portfolio relative to the home-market portfolio. The indirect approach is an approximation that is correct only if there are no "off-diagonal" relationships between the risk exposures of the project and the benchmark home portfolio. This will, in general, be true for investments in undertakings like power generation and telecommunications that are oriented toward the local market.

Adjusting discount rates versus adjusting cash flows

Adjustments for the risks of offshore projects relative to the typical domestic project will be reflected in several components of the general valuation formula presented earlier. Differences in project betas should be reflected as adjustments to r_{equity}, which in turn will result in changes in the weighted average cost of capital. Downside risks, in theory, should be reflected as adjustments to cash flows, although under certain circumstances (as discussed below) they may also be reflected in adjustments to the weighted average cost of capital. Differences in project leverage (or the contribution of the project to the parent's potential for leverage) should be reflected in the weighting of debt in the weighted average.

It is important to note that, in principle, the cash flows in equation 1 are *unconditional* expectations of cash flows – that is, cash flows expected under each future scenario weighted by the probability of that scenario. In practice, however, the cash flow estimates used are those that are expected under the *most-likely* set of future circumstances. This lack of clarity is not a serious problem with most projects in the relatively stable home environment. But it can create serious difficulties in evaluating offshore projects that involve substantial downside risk. The reason for this is that, with downside risks, the unconditional expectation of cash flows will be smaller than the cash flows expected under the most-likely circumstances.

Consider an investment in a nuclear power plant where there is a .10 probability of a total moratorium, with zero cash flows if the moratorium

occurs. The expected cash flows from such an investment will be the expected cash flows conditional on no moratorium, multiplied by the probability of no moratorium (.9), plus the cash flows expected given that the moratorium takes place (zero), multiplied by the probability of the moratorium taking place (.1). Thus, in our simple example, expected cash flows will be .9 of the most-likely cash flows.

If the structure of downside risks is quite simple, and if their impact is expected to grow at a compound rate over time, then they can be factored into the discounted cash flow analysis either as an adjustment to cash flows (relative to the most-likely level) or as an addition to the weighted average discount rate:[4]

$$r_{adjusted} = r_{normal}$$
$$+ \text{adjustment for downside risks} \quad \text{(eq. 2)}$$

Often, though, the effects of downside risks will not be so simple, and rolling them into the discount rate will be misleading. Consider the case of the downside risk resulting from unfamiliarity with a particular market. The negative impact of this risk on expected cash flows should decrease over time as the firm gains experience. In the first year of an investment, for example, productivity may be 80% of the world norm, but by year 5 it should be 90%, and by year 10 equal to the world norm. Adjusting the discount rate upward by 20% would imply a rapidly increasing downward adjustment to cash flows. Even applying an average discount rate adjustment of 10% would overstate the cash-flow impact.

Political risks associated with regulatory uncertainty are likely to display a similarly declining or, at worst, a stable pattern over time. Even payment risks are unlikely to compound upward over time, as would be implied by adjusting discount rates by a fixed factor.

Despite these caveats, a risk-adjusted discount rate formulation may be useful as a first cut for screening offshore investments. But even so, the final evaluation of specific projects should employ expected cash flows based on various scenarios,

---

4 For a formal demonstration, see Levi, *International Finance*, Appendix 15.1

with discount-rate adjustments reflecting only market covariance risk. Even in screening applications, unfamiliarity effects should be captured in cash flows, since rolling them into discount rates is likely to involve an unacceptable degree of distortion.

Currency risks

Currency risk presents a curious problem. On the one hand, currency movements will have a large impact on the dollar value of cash flows from foreign projects. Further, to the extent that the project involves a mixture of local and international costs or revenues, currency changes will also alter the local currency cash flows. Given that the volatility of currencies is very large, often as high as two-thirds of the volatility of equity returns, these two effects will result in significant volatility in dollar cash flows.

Despite their magnitude, though, currency risks in the sense of volatility of market exchange rates do not command significant risk premiums nor do they call for major adjustments in expected cash flows (after these are properly converted into parent currency terms). There are three reasons for this. First, currency movements, when measured in real terms (that is, adjusted for relative rates of inflation), are two-sided, with as much chance of upward as downward movements. Second, since they are the relative prices of different currencies, by definition they cannot affect all assets in the same way. Third, while fluctuations in the yen, for example, affect the U.S. dollar value of Japanese securities held by U.S. investors, the opposite is true for Japanese investors; and, assuming rough balance in investment positions across countries, we should not expect forward rates to incorporate large risk premiums.

Currency risk in the sense of a depreciating trend will be reflected in forward exchange rates that are used to convert local currency cash flows into the parent currency. This is because financial markets take into account anticipated exchange movements in determining the interest rates that underlie forward rates. In theory, forward rates should be unbiased estimates of expected future spot rates – that is, they should be fair predictors, neither too high nor too low on average. In fact, however, there is now substantial evidence that this

is not exactly the case, and that forward rates themselves include small risk premiums. However, both the size and the sign of these risk premiums change over time; and, in general, such premiums are smaller than the ±2 percent accuracy typical of capital budgeting estimates.

By contrast, currency risk in the sense of exchange controls or other limitations on cross-border payments will reduce expected cash flows relative to their most-likely level. But this kind of currency risk is best thought of as political risk for this reason.

In summary, *currency volatility risks* contribute little to the market covariance risk of offshore investments and therefore do not require a separate risk premium. In fact, in some cases, currency movements actually offset variations in local currency cash flows and values. *Currency risk in the sense of expected depreciation* is already reflected in the forward exchange rates used to convert foreign currency cash flows. *Currency transfer or payment risk*, in contrast, does require an adjustment to cash flows relative to their most-likely level.

ESTIMATING DISCOUNT RATES FOR OFFSHORE PROJECTS

Offshore projects can be modeled either in the local or the parent currency. Some finance scholars have suggested, for example, that all cash flow modeling be done in nominal, local-currency terms and then transformed into the parent currency at forward rates for discounting. In a 1985 paper, I proposed a similar approach, with the difference that cash flows first be projected in real terms in the most appropriate currency (which will be local currency for the revenues and operating costs of a telecommunications firm, but may be yen or US$ for capital expenditures); second, that these flows be converted to real terms in the parent currency at projected real exchange rates; and, third, that these real parent-currency flows be converted to nominal parent-currency units using projected domestic rates of inflation in order to perform the final discounting. At the level of screening projects, the differences between these two methods will not be significant. In the discussion that follows, I assume that the cash flows have been estimated conditional on the most-likely

Table 31.2   Estimates of Country Betas of Selected Emerging Countries Relative to U.S. Market Portfolio[a]

Country	Volatility	Volatility relative to U.S.	Correlation with U.S.	Country beta relative to U.S.
Argentina	61.63	6.11	0.32	1.96
Brazil	60.86	6.04	0.40	2.42
Chile	28.54	2.83	0.23	0.65
China*	40.50	4.02	0.27	1.08
India*	28.06	2.78	0.03	0.08
Indonesia	30.55	3.03	0.26	0.79
Japan, Nikkei	26.36	2.62	0.22	0.58
Korea*	25.22	2.50	−0.03	−0.08
Malaysia	25.57	2.54	0.22	0.56
Mexico	37.90	3.76	0.22	0.83
Philippines	34.16	3.39	0.22	0.75
Taiwan, China*	38.76	3.85	0.09	0.35
Thailand	31.66	3.14	0.23	0.72
Venezuala	60.93	6.04	−0.03	−0.18
U.S., S&P 500	10.08	1.00	1.00	1.00

[a]*Source*: International Finance Corporation, *Emerging Stock Markets Factbook*, 1996. Correlations based on 50 months ending December, 1995 unless indicated by a *, where a shorter data server is used.

economic and political scenarios and converted into the parent currency at forward exchange rates – that is, the exchange rates projected by interest rate differentials.[5]

Country betas and the cost of equity for offshore investments

The first step in estimating a discount rate to be applied to an offshore investment is to determine the risk premium that should be included in the cost of equity to reflect the offshore project beta. Under the simplifying assumption that the risk of the project bears the same relation to the risks of the local economy as a comparable project in the home country, the offshore project beta can be estimated as follows:

$$\text{offshore project beta} = \text{beta of comparable home country project} * \text{country beta.} \quad \text{(eq. 3)}$$

5   If these interest differentials diverge from projected inflation differentials, as is sometimes the case, the resulting future nominal exchange rates will imply real adjustments in the exchange rate. If this real adjustment is significant, it is important to recompute the expected cash flows taking this effect into account.

This country beta is, in turn, the product of two underlying dimensions: (1) the volatility of the stock market (or of the macroeconomy of the country in question) relative to that of the U.S. and (2) the correlation of these changes in value with the U.S. benchmark portfolios.

Country betas relative to the U.S. market portfolio for 13 emerging countries (as well as Japan) are shown in Table 31.2. A coefficient of 1.0 implies that the cost of equity for a project in the country in question is equal to that for a similar project in the U.S. The coefficients obtained are considerably below 1.0 on average, showing that the market covariance risk of investments in the target countries is quite small from a U.S. perspective. In part this is due to the fact that there is little relationship between what happens in emerging economies as reflected in stock-market returns and what happens in the rest of the world.

Adjustments for downside country risks

The country betas shown in Table 31.2 capture the effect of the market risks of the target countries, but they do not reflect the potential impacts on expected cash flows of downside risks such as expropriatory action, payments difficulties, and so forth. Ideally, the impact of these risks would be estimated by combining expert assessments of possible events/scenarios with estimates of the cash flow impacts of each of these. Various services, such as Frost and Sullivan and the Economist Intelligence Unit, publish such scenarios, providing subjective assessments of the likelihood of events such as payments disruptions. The precise impact of the scenarios of cash flows would have to be assessed on the basis of relevant operating experience and large amounts of judgment and common sense. Such analysis, while absolutely essential in evaluating a specific proposal or bid, is unrealistic at the level of screening countries.

There are at least three types of data that can be used in estimating adjustments for downside risks at the screening level:

- risk premiums on government and agency bonds issued in world currencies;
- insurance premiums charged by agencies such as OPIC to insure against specific downside risks; and
- country and political risk ratings published by organizations such as Euromoney, the Economist Intelligence Unit, and Political Risk Services.

None of these estimates is completely reliable, but they are the best generally available, objective numbers. The reasons why each is at best approximate are described below.

Bond Risk Premiums. Bond risk premiums reflect the market's assessment of potential losses due to rescheduling or outright default. The events in question do not exactly match the events that would jeopardize either the local generation or the remittance of cash flows from a direct investment. Even rescheduling is not always accompanied by limits on dividend remittances. In the case of Argentina, for example, despite repeated negotiations and non-payment on sovereign debt through the 1980s (to the point that the secondary market price of this debt fell to 15% of its face value), dividends from businesses remained fully convertible. Further, even if there are limitations on remittances, a direct investor may be able to protect the value of cash flows through reinvestment or to find other channels for remitting the funds. Further, the direct investor can reap upside benefits in good times, whereas the bondholder can at best get the promised payment. Perhaps the best analogy is that of a preferred stock. External debt is like a straight preferred, whereas direct investment is cumulative participating preferred.

On the other hand, bad things can happen to the direct foreign investor without the event of default or rescheduling on government debt, especially in a regulated industry such as telecommunications. Delays or limits on rate adjustments in the face of inflation, for example, could substantially reduce cash flows without triggering an international crisis involving banks and official lenders.

Despite these caveats, bond risk premiums provide an objective measure of potentially serious payments difficulties that should be closely correlated with problems that a direct investor will encounter. Therefore, they provide first-cut measures of the impact of downside country risks. Listed below are sovereign bond risk premiums for a number of emerging countries provided by J.P. Morgan (August 30, 1996):

Country	Spread over U.S. Treasuries
South Africa	125
Poland	185
Philippines	226
Peru	434
Panama	514
Mexico	597
Brazil	610
Morocco	700
Argentina	718
Russia	765
Venezuela	811
Nigeria	1,087
Ecuador	1,113
Bulgaria	1,517

OPIC Insurance Premiums. Various government export credit agencies, such as OPIC in the U.S., insure against expropriation, war, and inconvertibility. The premiums charged by EFIC of Australia, for example, range from .2% of the investment per annum for "good risks" such as the U.K., U.S., and Japan to 1.2% per annum for the Philippines, Pakistan, India, Cambodia, and Vietnam. This insurance does not cover all

Table 31.3   ICRG Country Risk Ratings for Selected Emerging Countries*

Country	Political risk (100)	Financial risk (50)	Economic risk (50)	Composite rating (100)
Algeria	50.0	36.0	28.5	57.0
Myanmar	58.0	28.0	30.5	58.0
Russian Federation	60.0	32.0	34.0	63.0
Philippines	62.0	39.0	36.0	68.5
Brazil	64.0	34.0	32.5	65.0
Mexico	65.0	41.0	31.5	69.0
India	66.0	37.0	36.5	70.0
Indonesia	67.0	40.0	37.5	72.0
China, P.R.	68.0	38.0	39.5	73.0
Thailand	75.0	44.0	41.0	80.0
Argentina	76.0	36.0	35.5	74.0
Malaysia	78.0	44.0	42.0	82.0
Chile	80.0	43.0	40.5	82.0
Korea, Republic	81.0	46.0	41.0	84.0
Taiwan	82.0	48.0	42.5	86.0
United States	83.0	48.0	38.5	85.0
Japan	86.0	48.0	44.0	89.0
Singapore	87.0	48.0	45.0	90.0

*Source: International Country Risk Guide, Political Risk Services, August 1996.

political events; for example the denial of required rate adjustments would not be deemed an "expropriatory act," although it clearly is such from an economic perspective. Also, it covers only the book value of the investment and not expected future income stream.

Political Risk Ratings. The political risk ratings published by various services are subjective scales that bear no direct numerical correspondence to downside risks. However, they capture many dimensions of risk. Ratings for selected emerging countries, together with Japan, Singapore, and the U.S., are shown in Table 31.3.

In general, the country risk ratings correspond quite closely to the bond premiums in rank order. Country risk ratings, unfortunately, cannot be translated directly into cash flow or discount-rate adjustments since they are ranked on arbitrary dimensions. One way to transform them into percentage figures would be to regress bond yield spreads, which are correctly dimensioned, on various country risk ratings and then use the estimated values for each country in the analysis.

Combining Measures. Even if the country risk ratings were transformed into rates of return, simply adding the three risk measures would represent double counting, since all aim at capturing similar phenomena. Where risk insurance is available, in principle the adjustment for covered risks should be the minimum of the expected loss and the premiums to cover such losses. However, it is then extremely hard to estimate adjustments for the uninsurable risks since all risks are rolled together into bond risk premiums and country risk ratings.

Adjustments for unfamiliarity

As noted above, it does not make economic sense to include an adjustment for unfamiliarity in the discount rate. Instead, I suggest some standard adjustment to cash flows such as the following: Reduce operating cash flows by 10% in the first year, 8% in the second year, and so forth, declining to no reduction in fifth year. At the same time, increase capital outlays by 5% in first year declining to no increase in fifth year. An audit of actual experience in new ventures, both at home and offshore, is of course critical to assessing what these adjustments should be.

CONCLUSIONS

The free cash flows, discount rates, and the resulting present values of projects in various countries will differ because of five classes of factors:

- market and competitive factors that may be either positive or negative compared to the home-country base case;
- currency factors that may be positive (in the case of expected real appreciation) but will be generally negative relative to those of an otherwise similar home-country project;
- tax factors that may be either positive or negative compared to home-country projects;
- differences in market covariance risk that generally will be positive or neutral; and

- downside country-risk factors and unfamiliarity that will be neutral or negative.

These same sets of factors also imply competitive advantages or disadvantages for the company relative to firms based in other countries. Assuming the firm is at least equal in base skills and overhead costs to firms from these other countries, it should face significant competitive advantages in some countries, giving rise to highly profitable international diversification. There is no magic formula, of course, but it should be noted that negative aspects of countries such as monetary volatility or institutional instability are faced by all companies. Thus, the key issue is which company is best able to mitigate these risks or structure its investment to circumvent them.

CHAPTER 32

Yankee Bonds and Cross-Border Private Placements: An Update

Greg Johnson (Banc of America Securities LLC)*

As the year 2000 draws to a close, international issuers have again demonstrated the attractiveness of the U.S. long-term debt markets by setting record issuance levels. Growth in the issuance of long-term debt in the U.S. markets by international issuers is a trend that began several years ago and shows no signs of abating. Total cross-border U.S. bond issuance in 2000 is expected to exceed $350 billion, easily surpassing previous issuance levels and almost double the levels of just a few years ago.

Privatization of state-owned industries, infrastructure development, and capital investment driven by economic growth are all contributing to the worldwide demand for long-term capital. International issuers have become increasingly familiar with the benefits and depth of the U.S. bond markets, while U.S. investors have taken seemingly irreversible steps toward global diversification of their portfolios. More and more investors are learning how to evaluate country-specific

economic, foreign exchange, social, and political risks – investment skills that should stand them in good stead when confronting the higher volatility of cross-border investments.

Although issuers today face credit spreads that are at or near historic highs, U.S. Treasury yields are not far from historical lows, resulting in acceptable all-in borrowing rates. Advances in foreign exchange and interest rate swap structures allow many issuers to swap U.S. proceeds into other currencies at highly efficient all-in local currency costs. Add to the analysis relaxed regulatory reporting requirements and the prestige of accessing the deepest and longest debt markets in the world, and it is not hard to see why the U.S. bond markets are more and more frequently the markets of choice for international issuers.

Issuers and investors have three primary forms through which they can participate in these growing long-term debt markets: publicly traded, SEC registered bonds ("Yankee" bonds); traditional private placements; and underwritten Rule 144A private placements. Each of these three financing methods has distinct benefits and limitations that should be thoroughly evaluated in light of the specific objectives of the issuer. The purpose of this article is to provide a detailed analysis of each type of bond issuance and the related concerns facing a financial officer trying to determine the most appropriate source of long-term debt. We explore

*   This article is an updated version of a previously published article by Greg Johnson and Thomas Funkhouser, "Yankee Bonds and Cross-Border Private Placements," *Journal of Applied Corporate Finance*, Vol. 10 No. 3 (Fall 1997). For their contributions to this article, the author wishes to thank Arminda Aviles and Chase Cairncross, who are Associate and Analyst, respectively, in the Yankee Capital Markets Groups at Banc of America Securities.

Table 32.1 Issuance in the U.S. Long-term Debt Markets 1996-Present

Year	U.S. Public Market			U.S. Private Market			U.S. 144A Market		
	Total $B	"Yankee" Bonds	% Foreign	Total $B	For. Privates	% Foreign	Total $B	For. 144A	% Foreign
1996	545	87	16	48	17	35	103	30	30
1997	749	140	19	57	15	26	211	70	33
1998	1050	211	20	65	16	25	287	75	26
1999	1095	252	23	61	19	31	290	63	22
2000*	**990**	**270**	**27**	**50**	**16**	**32**	**200**	**70**	**35**

*Estimated; 2000 amounts are based on actual SDC levels as of 10/16/2000 for the Public and 144A markets, and on actual SDC levels as of 6/30/2000 for the Private Placement market.
Source: Securities Data Corp.

the background of these issuance methods, analyze recent trends, examine the legal characteristics, and provide a statistical comparison of the three sectors over the past several years. The mechanics of issuance in each market are discussed, including the means of addressing investment concerns of U.S. institutional investors, the importance of rating agency involvement, and the marketing, distribution, and documentation aspects of each product.

MARKET OVERVIEW

Throughout the 1990s, cross-border issuance in the U.S. long-term debt markets was on a strong growth trend. Despite significant market disruptions caused by the devaluation of the Mexican peso in late 1994, the Asian economic crisis of late 1997, and the Russian bond defaults of late 1998, the U.S. debt markets have largely remained open and an important source of debt capital for foreign issuers. The 144A market, which only began in 1990, has experienced dramatic growth and is now second in importance to only the Yankee market. By allowing foreign issuers access to a broad base of U.S. institutional investors without the time and expense of the SEC registration process, the 144A private has overcome a major drawback of the Yankee market.

Initially, yield-hungry investors pursued cross-border investments primarily as a means to improve returns, since such investments offered higher yields than those obtainable on comparably

rated domestic issues. Yield premiums for cross-border investments continue to appear under various market conditions (indeed, they were evident when this article was going to press (October 2000)). Nonetheless, investors today seem to more fully appreciate that investments in foreign companies bring a better understanding of the intricate workings of our global economy. As a result, the cross-border premium for issuers has generally declined in recent years, due in part to the high credit quality of many of the issuers accessing these markets. As issuance has increased, so has the number of investors with the expertise and authority to invest in a cross-border deal. Foreign issuance has grown to represent over 25% of the public market, roughly one-third of the traditional private market, and over one-third of the underwritten 144A market.

Long maturities at attractive rates

The U.S. bond markets are at their competitive best when an issuer is most interested in debt with a long average life. The U.S. markets tend to be deepest at the 10-year maturity, since the broadest range of investors have investment appetite at this maturity. Most other debt markets have little or no appetite for 10-year maturities, let alone longer. Maturities of 15, 20, and 30 years account for a significant portion of overall U.S. cross-border issuance, and longer offerings, including 100-year "century" bonds, have been completed on an opportunistic basis. As mentioned earlier, many of these issues are then swapped by the issuers to their local currencies resulting in attractive all-in costs.

U.S. Treasury yields are currently near historical lows as a result of low inflation and steady economic growth. Fears of an end to the economic bliss of the last decade have nonetheless led to extremely volatile market conditions. This volatility has been fueled by earnings warnings, foreign exchange losses, consolidation announcements (which constitute "event risk" for bond investors), and a perception of generally declining credit quality, resulting in a widening of credit spreads globally. In their search for higher returns, investors in the past have shown a willingness to invest despite conditions such as these and in so doing have helped drive credit spreads back to lower levels. But, as we open the new Millennium, a new consideration has moved to the forefront – one that, at least as far as the Yankee and 144A bond markets are concerned, has overtaken all others in importance. That consideration is liquidity, or lack thereof. Concerns about liquidity have led to unprecedented credit spread levels, a condition that shows little sign of improving. To understand the impact of limited liquidity on the public-style markets, one needs to better understand the investment objectives and cash flow characteristics of each of the primary groups of institutional investors.

Investor characteristics

U.S. institutional investors, which are the overwhelming majority of long-term debt buyers, vary widely in size and investment strategy. Nonetheless, they can be generally grouped into one of five main categories: life insurance companies; property and casualty insurance companies; public and private pension funds; mutual funds; and bank trust departments and money managers. Investment strategies range from a long-term "buy and hold" approach with low portfolio turnover to an actively traded, "total rate of return" approach, where assets are continually "marked to market" in order to calculate value on a real time basis. Portfolio managers must select investment categories and individual bonds based at least in part on their desired mix of liquid (actively traded, easily

Table 32.2 Investment Characteristics of U.S. Long-term Investors

Type	Maturity preference	Trading activity	Primary bond type
Life Insurance	5 to 30 yrs.	Inactive	Private/ Public
Property and Casualty Ins.	5 to 10 yrs.	Inactive	Public
Pension Funds	5 to 20 yrs.	Moderate	Private/ Public
Mututal Funds	5 to 15 yrs.	Active	Public
Bank Trust Depts./Money Mgrs.	2 to 10 yrs.	Active	Public

tradable) and illiquid (no regular listing of market prices) assets. In this manner, they balance the mix of their portfolios to reflect the anticipated need to generate cash for portfolio outflows.

Such cash outflows can be very predictable for a life insurance company using actuarial forecasts of policy payments, but very unpredictable for a mutual fund, which may need to convert its holdings to cash at any time. Not surprisingly, the most aggressive buyers of a liquid Yankee or underwritten 144A bond include those investors who need to be able to trade in and out of their holdings. During times of strong cash inflows, mutual funds dominate the public bond markets. Those investors with the most stable cash flows – insurance companies and pension funds – dominate the illiquid, traditional private placement market. In general, the five main investor groups can be said to have the investment characteristics outlined in Table 32.2.

For a portfolio manager seeking actively to manager his or her return, the inability to efficiently trade a security is unacceptable. Correctly foreseeing market developments should lead to appreciation of the value of the corporate bonds a portfolio manager is holding. Too frequently of late, however, any price appreciation has been eliminated when a portfolio manager has tried to realize the gain due to wide bid/offer levels in the secondary bond markets. This has occurred often enough in these volatile market conditions to drive some managers out of the corporate bond markets altogether. If the portfolio managers cannot achieve their desired results with corporate debt,

YANKEE BONDS

Abitibi-Consolidated Inc. is the world's largest manufacturer of newsprint and of paper used by the publishing industry. Following the acquisition of Donohue Inc. in early 2000, the company has roughly 32% of the North America newsprint market and 15% of the global newsprint market. In addition, the company has operations in value-added papers (principally uncoated ground-wood), lumber, and pulp. The company has expanded into Asia through a major joint venture and now operates a total of 29 paper mills, 24 sawmills, and 1 pulp mill.

After the acquisition of Donohue, the company was looking to refinance bank debt with longer-maturity obligations. The company was already a seasoned issuer in the Yankee markets and was widely expected to enter the markets for $1 billion or more in debt. Market conditions for low invest-ment-grade issues were less than optimal in the early spring, and the company held off issuing.

As a Baa3/BBB- issuer, the company did not want the market to conclude that the company had to issue regardless of market conditions.

Newsprint prices increased through the spring and added to the perception that the company might not issue long-term debt at all. But, when issuance slowed significantly as the July 4 holiday approached, the company took advantage of the light forward calendar. Three tranches of debt were issued, including the largest amount of 30-year bonds for a low investmentgrade issuer that year.

Abitibi-Consolidated issued $450 million of 5-year debt, $500 million of a benchmark 10-year issue, and $450 million of 30-year bonds for a total of $1.4 billion in proceeds. The trans-action pricing was tightened during the market-ing process to the point that the yield was lower that the secondary trading levels that existed on the company's outstanding debt prior to the announcement of the deal.

they will use the swap, U.S. Treasury, or other markets perceived to have more liquidity to pursue their return objectives.

YANKEE BONDS

A Yankee bond is an underwritten, dollar-denominated bond that is publicly issued in the U.S. by a foreign entity. Yankee bond offerings are those required to be registered with the SEC under the Securities Act of 1933 and are subject to dis-closure standards that are often more stringent than those required in foreign issuers' domestic markets. Due to the extensive SEC registration and rating agency requirements, a first-time Yankee offering can take anywhere from 10 to 14 weeks to complete. Yankee offerings involve more signifi-cant legal, rating, and out-of-pocket expenses than both types of private placement.

Yankee bonds can be distributed more widely than private placements and usually entail the most extensive roadshow, at least for first-time issuers or very large transactions. Yankee bonds are marketed via pre-established documentation that involves no

negotiation with investors, and typically are struc-tured with no financial covenants. The loose covenant structure reflects the diverse nature of the public investor base. Post-closing negotiations on a widely distributed issue are extremely difficult, making it impractical for an issuer to amend or adjust an issue once it is sold. The investor's lack of effective control over the issuer (due to the lack of covenants) is presumably offset by the liquidity of the public market, and by the ability of an investor to sell the position if he becomes uncomfortable with company actions or performance.

In general, individual Yankee bond offerings range in size from $200 million to $1 billion, with most issues in the $300 to $500 million range. Individual offerings are often completed in multiple tranches of $200 million or more, with most first-time issuers offering a benchmark 10-year tranche as the largest portion and with smaller amounts in the shorter and/or longer tranches. As concerns over liquidity have increased, more and more issues have been sized to assure diverse market interest and holding. Billion dollar issues, a rarity only a few years ago, have become commonplace, with 15 such "jumbo" issues already completed this year.

Mechanics of issuance

Issuance of Yankee bonds requires the hiring of one or more lead managers and typically two or more additional co-managers to market and distribute the bonds. The selection and number of underwriters in the syndicate will depend on the size of the issue and the desired breadth of distribution. The lead managers are responsible for structuring the financing and overseeing documentation of the issue as well as managing the underwriting syndicate and ensuring successful distribution of the issue. The lead managers and co-managers are expected to provide after-market trading and research support. The lead managers are often chosen based on a strong fixed-income research department (one capable of aiding investors in their investment decisions) and a strong fixed-income trading desk (capable of maintaining a liquid secondary market in the bonds). A lead manager is also usually responsible for guiding a first-time issuer through the rating agency and SEC processes.

Despite industry standards, fees charged by the underwriters will vary based on the expected level of complexity of the above responsibilities. The credit quality, industry, country of domicile, and market conditions will all affect the "gross spread" charged by underwriters (that is, the difference between the price received from investors and the proceeds to the issuer). The gross spread for an investment-grade issuer typically ranges from 50 basis points for a five-year bond to 87.5 basis points or more for a 10-year or longer bond, and is significantly higher for lower rated issuers.

Syndicate and resulting fee structures have been affected by investors' liquidity concerns and have changed dramatically in the last couple of years. To begin with, two lead managers are nearly the norm on large deals (and are the norm if one excludes self-issuance). The arguments for two or more lead managers are many, but the strongest is based in the current demand for liquidity. Use of a single lead manager limits the competitiveness of secondary market quotes, especially for infrequent issuers. With investment banks consolidating at a rapid clip, two lead managers hardly guarantee competition will exist in the secondary market over the life of a 10-year bond. In another major change, the splitting of fees in investment-grade

transactions is now being predetermined and set in direct proportion to the legal underwriting commitment of each underwriter, regardless of who actually ends up selling the bonds. This pre-agreed fee, or "100% pot," arrangement, has been a common practice in the high yield market since its inception. There is much greater market risk associated with non-investment-grade transactions, more than the underwriters are willing to assume in nearly all situations. High yield bonds are therefore completely "pre-sold" before a transaction is priced. The pre-agreed, 100% pot fee split arrangement closely aligns compensation with the legal underwriting risk of the transaction, as distinguished from the sales performance or market risk.

The traditional gross spread structure, seldom used these days even on an investment-grade transaction, had three components. A "management fee," which was paid to lead and co-managers for managing the issue, was usually 20% of the gross spread. An "underwriting fee," paid to the lead and co-managers for assuming the underwriting risk and various costs associated with the offering, was also usually 20% of the gross spread. And the "selling concession," paid *pro rata* directly to those firms that actually sold the bonds, typically represented 60% of the gross spread. In most cases, the selling concession went disproportionately to the lead underwriter by virtue of its control of the "pot" bonds. Pot bonds were usually 50% of an issue and, as a result, underwriters only retained 50% of their legal underwriting commitment for direct sale to investors. Knowing that the lead manager controlled the pot bonds as well as its own proportional retention, investors often directed orders to the lead manager to assure themselves a generous allocation. The result was that the lead underwriter typically got the lion's share of the fees, despite balanced legal underwriting commitments and incentives for each firm to sell the bonds.

Given the volatile market conditions of late, it seems unlikely that we will be returning to partial pot and traditional fee structures anytime soon. It seems more likely that, when conditions stabilize, we will see greater use of hybrid structures that try to compensate underwriters not only for their legal risk but also for their actual contribution to the sales effort.

SEC registration

The Securities Act of 1933 requires issuers of publicly offered securities to file a registration statement with the SEC and to maintain regular ongoing disclosure of prescribed business and financial information. (First-time foreign issuers generally file the registration statement on form F-1.) The filing must include a prospectus that contains strictly defined, detailed descriptions of, among other items, the issuer's operations, product lines, geographic regions, financial condition, and potential risk factors that could have a material effect on operations or on the value of the offering. Issuer's legal counsel will draft the SEC registration statement with assistance from the issuer and the underwriters. Issuers, underwriters, and their respective counsel can be held legally responsible for the accuracy of material furnished to the public in connection with a public offering.

The purpose of the strict standards set by the 1933 Act was to shift the burden of verifying the accuracy of relevant information to the sellers of the securities for the benefit of the buyers. In addition, the bond issue contains provisions that require the issuer to continue to file periodic financial information with the SEC for as long as the issue is outstanding.

Credit ratings

Buyers of public bonds rely heavily on rating agencies to conduct credit analysis, so much so that two ratings are the market standard for public bonds. Moody's and Standard & Poor's ratings are usually recommended, if not required, as a result of their longstanding market presence and established track record. Rating agencies follow an intensive and methodical process in examining all relevant aspects of an issuer's operations, management, industry position, and financial condition.

Rating methodologies are published by most rating agencies and readily available upon request. Rating agencies typically charge upfront fees of between $25,000 and $125,000 for each individual corporate credit rating, with issues over $500 million incurring additional up-front fees. Annual monitoring fees are also charged by the agencies as long as the issue is outstanding.

Timing

The preparation for a Yankee bond offering involves multiple drafting sessions in which representatives from the issuer, issuer's legal counsel, and the underwriters conduct a review of all material required for the SEC filing. At about the midpoint in the roughly 12-week process, a first draft of the registration statement is confidentially submitted to the SEC for review, and rating agency presentations are conducted by the issuer and its rating agency advisor, usually a lead manager. Rating agencies may conduct in-depth, onsite due diligence following the initial presentations.

An indication from rating agencies and comments from the SEC are typically received one to three weeks later and drafting of a revised registration statement commences. Near the end of the process, preliminary ratings are released and the registration statement is publicly filed, at which time the transaction is announced to the market and a preliminary "red herring" prospectus is distributed. An extensive roadshow will usually begin as soon as the preliminary prospectus is distributed, and the issue is typically priced within a day or two after completion of the roadshow. The financial closing of a public bond offering typically occurs within three business days of pricing, but can be longer on complex issues.

Documentation

The binding legal document for public issues is an indenture that requires a bond trustee to administer payments and take other actions on behalf of the investors. In addition to the indenture, additional important documentation requirements include a 10(b)-5 opinion by legal counsel stating that no knowledge of any material misstatement or omission exists, and an accountants' comfort letter stating that the most recent financial information is correct.

TRADITIONAL PRIVATE PLACEMENTS

A traditional private placement is a transaction that qualifies for exemption from SEC registration requirements under either Section 4(2) or

TRADITIONAL PRIVATE PLACEMENT

Cookson Group Plc is a diversified industrial materials group with three major operating divisions. The company's Electronics Division is a world leader in the supply of materials and equipment used in the manufacture of printed circuit boards and other electronic goods. The company's Ceramics Division is a world leader in the production of ceramic refractory products and systems that control, protect, and monitor liquid iron and steel. The company's Precious Metals Division is the North American leader in fabricated precious metals for the jewelry and electronics industries.

The different activities of the three divisions do not naturally lend themselves to strong synergies. Nonetheless, the company's market share and technological leadership in each of its targeted markets make for a compelling credit story. The company is best understood by analyzing each of the businesses on a stand-alone basis and by knowing management's capabilities well enough to be comfortable with their ability to profitably oversee and direct such diverse activities.

Cookson had an existing private placement of $170 million outstanding with a rating from Fitch of BBB+and a corresponding NAIC rating of 2. Recent acquisitions and pending disposals had

Cookson interested in additional long-term debt, but they wanted to avoid additional fixed rate exposure. The U.S. private placement market coupled with interest rate swaps appeared to be the most efficient means of raising long-term floating rate debt. Private placement investors were also believed to be willing to do the analysis necessary to get comfortable not only with three separate businesses but with the significant restructuring activities that were not yet finalized.

The company undertook an extensive roadshow giving private placement investors the opportunity to analyze in depth each of the company's divisions and management. Cookson entered the market for $200 million and found more than enough investor interest to complete a much larger financing. The negotiated nature of the private placement market allowed the company to accept only the most aggressive bids in each maturity. The company raised a total of $400 million in four maturities – 5, 7, 10, and 12 years. The allocations were heavily weighted toward the longer maturites, resulting in a financing with an average life exceeding 10 years. Using interest rate swaps, this 10-year fixed rate debt was then converted into floating rate financing with a very attractive rate.

Regulation D of the 1933 Act. As a consequence of the exemption, limitations are placed on the type and number of investors who can participate in an offering, and there are also restrictions on resale. A traditional private placement is the direct sale of debt or other securities by an issuer to one or more "accredited investors." As defined in Regulation D, accredited investors include banks, insurance companies, registered and small business investment companies, certain employee benefit plans, organizations with total assets in excess of $5 million, and certain wealthy individuals.

The traditional private placement market historically has offered issuers quick, discreet access to a broad base of long-term U.S. institutional investors, primarily life insurance companies and public and private pension funds. Private placement investors usually hold bonds to maturity and

are frequently repeat investors in new debt of issuers with which they have relationships.

Disclosure standards in the traditional private placement market are unregulated and significantly less well defined than those in the Yankee bond market. Transactions are typically completed on a negotiated basis, transferring to the investors much of the risk of assuring that all relevant information is available and has been considered. Investors nearly always require financial covenants in addition to numerous representations and warranties in order to protect the value of what they expect will be a very long-term holding. The need for credit ratings varies depending on the issue, but the majority of issues are completed with one or no rating. A traditional private placement for a first-time issuer can typically be completed in six to twelve weeks.

Private placements can be completed in any amount, but are usually most cost effective above $50 million and below $500 million. Most issues are in the $100 to $200 million range. Total issuance costs for a private placement can be much less than those paid for an underwritten transaction, since placement and legal fees can be as little as half those paid for an underwritten investment-grade issue.

Mechanics of issuance

Traditional private placements are executed on a best efforts basis, usually by one lead agent. The first step is typically a due diligence review by the lead agent, who then assists in the preparation of an offering memorandum that describes the offering and the issuer. The time required for preparation of a private offering memorandum is usually shorter than that required in a public transaction, mainly because the issuer has greater latitude in describing the company and its activities. While the information presented in a private placement memorandum tends to be quite similar to that required by the SEC for a public filing, there are no formal standards or requirements. Because private investors usually conduct their own due diligence review, the issuer generally has more freedom in discussing the merits, drawbacks, and prospects of its company than is possible in a public or 144A document.

Investors in a private placement recognize they have fewer protections than those afforded by regulations for public securities. Accordingly, their investigations into the merits of a particular offering can be extremely detailed. A roadshow is advisable in many instances, although it will be directed to fewer investors and will usually be oriented toward more in-depth meetings. Pricing occurs at the end of the roadshow or marketing period (if there is no roadshow), and is followed by investor due diligence and the finalizing of documentation.

Credit ratings

Ratings from a wider range of recognized rating agencies are acceptable in the traditional private placement market, and "private" ratings can be obtained that are not published or publicly disseminated. Fees charged by alternative agencies such as Fitch are similar to or slightly lower than Moody's and S&P. Since all investments purchased by insurance companies are ultimately rated by the Securities Valuation Office of the National Association of Insurance Commissioners ("NAIC"), a rating by one agency is sometimes recommended as a preemptive strategy.

Documentation

Traditional private placements were historically marketed via a term sheet, with documentation undertaken after the general provisions of the transaction had been accepted. Over the last several years, however, industry efforts to standardize documentation have been very successful, resulting in most, if not all, investment-grade transactions being completed on a "pre-documented" basis. In a pre-documented deal, legal counsel is engaged to draft the note purchase agreement (the binding legal document between the issuer and investors) prior to going to market.

If the deal is not pre-documented, drafting of the note purchase agreement is conducted after investors have "circled" the deal, during the investor due diligence stage. An "acceptance of circle" occurs when all major terms are finalized. Pre-documented deals take slightly longer to get to market but can be closed in as little as one to two weeks following circle. It may take significantly longer to close a transaction after circle if the deal is based on a summary term sheet and drafting takes place during the investor due diligence stage.

144A PRIVATE PLACEMENTS

Rule 144A was adopted in April 1990 as a means to facilitate the resale of privately placed securities and thus increase secondary trading among institutional investors of otherwise illiquid investments. Rule 144A permits resale of privately placed securities to "qualified institutional buyers," or "QIB's," which include institutions that own at least $100 million of eligible securities and dealers that own at least $10 million of such securities. When Rule 144A was first initiated, issues that were otherwise

UNDERWRITTEN RULE 144A PRIVATE PLACEMENT

Companhia Vale do Rio Doce ("CVRD") is the world's largest producer of iron ore and iron ore pellets. CVRD is also a major force in the production of aluminum and woodpulp and in the mining of copper, gold, and other minerals. Based in Brazil, the company is constrained by the sovereign debt ceiling to a non-investment-grade rating of its straight corporate debt.

The company operates two railroad networks that are linked to port facilities from which they ship their iron ore products to steel companies around the world. Iron ore is an essential element in the production of steel, and CVRD has very longstanding relationships with most of the world's steel producers. Price and volume stability coupled with the strength of CVRD's relationships with its steel customers were strong arguments for a financing based on the securitization of the company's export receivables. The structure captures payments made by certain steel companies in an offshore trust, from which interest and principal payments are made to investors before excess flows make their way back to the company. The structure allowed the company to secure investment-grade ratings for the transaction from all three of the major rating agencies.

The financing was sold in three separate tranches, including a 7-year final $25 million tranche, a 10-year final $150 million tranche, and a 7-year final MBIA-guaranteed $125 million tranche. The $300 million transaction was the largest and longest-maturity Brazilian export receivables transaction ever completed.

The underwritten 144A approach focused the marketing efforts on sophisticated institutional investors with the resources necessary to analyze the complex nature of the transaction on their own, much as one would expect with a traditional private placement. The underwritten 144A approach also allowed simultaneous marketing of the MBIA-guaranteed portion to more public style AAA investors. The company was able to consider all of its options before expanding the size of the oversubscribed $200 million transaction originally taken to market. Nearly 30 qualified institutional investors (QIB's) participated in the transaction.

---

being executed as traditional private placements had a Rule 144A provision built into the documentation to make secondary trades easier. But Rule 144A had little impact in this market because most investors who purchased such illiquid investments were looking to hold such investments to maturity anyway. Investment banks soon discovered, however, that the Rule 144A provision could be used to develop a quasi-public issue.

In an underwritten Rule 144A issue, an investment bank becomes the initial purchaser of a private placement and then resells the bonds to institutional investors under a Rule 144A exemption. A new market quickly evolved around this process, and today it closely resembles the SEC-registered market in terms of underwriting practices, including marketing, distribution, disclosure, documentation, and credit rating requirements. Foreign issuers were particularly pleased with the development of this market since it allowed them to sell large issues to U.S. institutions without complying with, among other things, the intrusive executive pay disclosure requirements of the SEC.

Transaction size range for 144A transactions is similar to that of public bonds, with transactions in the $200 to $500 million range most common Transactions such as Vodafone's $5.2 billion in bonds clearly demonstrate there is no technical limit to the size of a 144A issue. Issuance fees, including underwriting fees, are comparable to, and structured in the same manner as, fees on Yankee bonds. Because of the lack of registration requirements, 144A transactions can typically be completed in eight to twelve weeks.

Mechanics of issuance

While some complex 144A transactions are still executed as traditional private placements, the vast majority of 144A private placements are underwritten and executed by a public style syndicate similar to that required for a Yankee issue. For both under-writers and institutional investors, investment-grade Rule 144A offerings are often indistinguishable from SEC-registered transactions in terms of process and acceptance. The offering circular is prepared by issuer's counsel. Although not legally subject to the same liability standards as a public bond, it gener-ally contains the same type of information as a public prospectus. Syndication groups are formed with the same eye toward research and secondary market liquidity that one would expect for an SEC-registered issue.

The Rule 144A market underwent yet another transformation in recent years that helped propel issuance to even higher levels. Many first-time cross-border, and nearly all first-time high yield issuers, now use the Rule 144A structure with reg-istration rights, a provision that requires the issue to be registered with the SEC within a prescribed time period after issuance (usually six months). This registration requirement effectively converts the 144A into a public bond, thus conferring on the buyer the benefits of registration, including disclosure requirements and liquidity, while still allowing the issuer to come to market quickly and deal with the SEC registration process afterward. An issuer's failure to register the security in such an offering results in additional penalty interest on top of the coupon rate.

Credit ratings

Two credit ratings are generally required by 144A buyers, although one alternative agency rating coupled with an S&P or Moody's rating is some-times acceptable, depending on the nature of the transaction. Rating agency fees are consistent with those required for a Yankee issue, and the process is virtually the same.

Documentation

The binding document in a 144A private place-ment is usually a purchase agreement negotiated between the issuer and the underwriter group (ini-tial purchasers), which then resells the securities. Because Rule 144A bonds are distributed in a manner similar to public bonds, their covenants

resemble those of public bonds; that is, they are virtually non-existent. It is very difficult to negoti-ate amendments or adjustments once a transaction is sold even if the investor group cannot include individuals. Covenants are found more frequently in lower credit quality transactions, although they typically carry compliance levels that a company should be able to meet in all but the most dire of circumstances. In addition to limited or no finan-cial covenants, 144A purchase agreements typically do not require expansive representations and warranties of the issuer or provide inspection rights to the investor, as is usually the case in a traditional private placement. The same legal opinions and accountants' comfort letter required for a public offering are also generally required.

SELECTING THE MOST EFFICIENT MARKET

Yankee bonds are expected to account for roughly 76% of the $356 billion of U.S. cross-border issuance by volume in 2000, and make up an esti-mated 73% of the market when measured by the number of transactions. Given that Yankee bonds are generally utilized by the largest and most-frequent issuers, their dominance is not surprising. The importance of the 144A and traditional pri-vate placement markets is more evident if one focuses solely on corporate issuers, as opposed to all issuing entities. Sovereign, quasi-sovereign, and short-term financial institution (i.e., commercial bank) financings all inflate Yankee issuance levels compared to straight long-term corporate bond issuance.

Generalizations are dangerous in the capital markets, but for an international entity rated by Moody's and S&P, an SEC-registered bond will nearly always be the most efficient form of long-term financing available. Exceptions to this "rule" include deals that are small (under $250 million) or very unusual in structure, or which have a particu-larly cumbersome amortization schedule, or any of a number of other possible quirks. Traditional pri-vate placement and underwritten 144A investors are looking for a premium over the yield of a com-parable public issue to compensate them for the reduced liquidity of their investment, however unlikely they are to resell the securities. Accordingly, a Yankee bond should be the lowest-cost issuance method for rated issuers of any credit quality.

Why don't all issuers head to the Yankee market instead of using the underwritten 144A or traditional private placement markets? As mentioned above, the efficiency of the Yankee market is greatest for larger transactions due to the high up-front costs. Other reasons include the desire not to report to the SEC on an ongoing basis, to protect the confidentiality of results or company information, and to avoid the ongoing and continuous scrutiny of the rating agencies.

The Rule 144A structure is often used for complex structures requiring heavy rating agency involvement, such as future financial flow transactions and project financings. While the traditional private placement market has long accommodated such esoteric structures, the 144A market provides access to a wider investor base and has thus become an alternative market for issues large enough to justify the additional issuance costs. The 144A market is generally preferred over the Yankee market for this type of issue, in part because SEC registration will not notably increase the number of investors who are able or willing to analyze such credits.

Ratings plays

If a company does not yet have ratings from the two top agencies, the choice of which market is most cost efficient will require more thought. In the simplest terms, a ratings play is the ability of an issuer to position itself with investors as a higher quality credit than the issuer would be if a formal rating from Moody's and S&P were obtained. For a company with one or more debt ratings that have been made public, there is little opportunity to identify a ratings play. Nevertheless, ratings plays occur in the global debt markets on a regular basis. While one can argue that the significant funding cost differences among markets (after adjusting for differences in risk and liquidity) should be eliminated over time, in practice investors deal with imperfect market information and incomplete knowledge of rating agency opinions. For investors confident in their own investment analysis, this is often seen as much as an opportunity as a hindrance.

Institutional investors that purchase private placements are perhaps the most willing of all investor groups to help identify opportunities for ratings plays. To be sure, ratings are still important to these investors. Insurance companies, the largest sector of private placement investors, are subject to NAIC ratings on all of their investments, which in turn determine their reserve requirements. While issuers that are rated by one of the major rating agencies are nearly universally accepted by the NAIC on a comparable basis, the NAIC has on rare occasion challenged the accuracy of ratings from a rating agency. A lower rating from the NAIC will translate into higher reserve costs for the investor and much higher issuance costs for an issuer's future transactions.

Opportunities for ratings plays exist on several levels. An example is the possibility – some would say the likelihood – that one of the three primary U.S. rating agencies (or an agency in the issuer's home country or region) will provide a higher rating than both Moody's and S&P can agree upon. The reasons for a more favorable credit perspective, which are as varied as the issuers themselves, can be related to differing legal, industry, or economic outlooks, or be as basic as differences in credit philosophy.

While not anxious to encourage the phenomenon, institutions buying private placements are sophisticated investors and are aware of the incentive of an issuer to hire the rating agency that is likely to treat the issuer in the most positive light. Indeed, private investors often believe that, with sufficient covenant protection, an investment may be of higher value than a Moody's or S&P rating might suggest. Value to the investor can be measured not only in terms of the probability of timely payment of principal and interest (the overriding focus of the major rating agencies), but also in terms of covenant protection against significant events and the probability of ultimate recovery of principal and interest in the event of default.

These investors are also aware that they have to compete with alternative sources of funds that are unaware of or indifferent to U.S. rating agency viewpoints, and which may lend at very aggressive levels. Institutional investors with a more positive outlook than the major rating agencies for a given credit, industry, or country will be strong advocates for a higher NAIC rating.

Underwritten or bought

"Cost efficient," "highly liquid," and "very long" are all appropriate characterizations of the U.S. debt markets. If the inaugural bond issue of an international issuer is completed in an appropriate manner, the company will have the ability to return to the market for additional, and often longer-term, money on an expedited basis. For a first time issuer, however, the market may seem to have an unusual set of requirements and conventions.

The subtleties of the underwriting commitment an investor receives is one such issue and, indeed, a common cause of confusion among first-time issuers. Yankee or underwritten Rule 144A transactions are nearly always completed on a negotiated basis, not as competitive bids, or "bought" deals. Many international issuers approaching the U.S. markets for the first time assume "underwritten" means that the underwriters will be assuming market risk. This is not the case for a variety of reasons. One is that most U.S. deals are of relatively long maturity, as compared to debt issues in other world markets. If the bond market moves 10 basis points on a 10-year issue, the present value impact on the underwriters of a bought deal is much more significant than the impact on a 3-year Eurobond transaction of the same amount. In addition to the greater price volatility of longer-maturity issues, the time necessary to prepare for market is often longer than in other markets for reasons including the SEC review period, the rating agency review periods, and the preparation of legal opinions and documentation. The longer the lead time required to get an issue to market, the higher the market risk.

Nonetheless, bought deals do occur, albeit rarely. The downside to such transactions is not necessarily seen by an issuer immediately. Consider the progress of such a deal if market conditions move against the lead manager after it has committed to a maximum credit spread. The issue progresses as it otherwise would through the SEC, rating agencies, and roadshow process. Investor interest is determined and a book of orders is built. But because the market has moved, investor interest at the original credit spread is insufficient to sell all of the bonds and the lead manager is left holding a significant portion of the issue. After the syndicate closes and secondary trading gets underway, the lead manager will likely dump the unsold bonds to clear its balance sheet for the next issue. As a result, the bonds will trade off in price, and those investors who were most bullish on the company (the investors who liked the company enough to buy their bonds through the appropriate market-clearing level) suffer a loss on their new investment, at least on paper.

The end result is that the deal is viewed as performing badly, and the issuer is seen as having little regard for fair treatment of those investors who were most willing to support the issue. The outcome of the company's next trip to the market is likely to be a deal priced off an unfavorable secondary trading level and sold to unresponsive investors. Bought deals make sense for issuers with billions of dollars already outstanding, for which a new issue can be viewed as little more than a large secondary trade. Only a few international issuers fit the proper profile of a competitive bid issuer in the U.S. debt markets.

Documentation concerns

The private placement market was its own worst enemy over the last decade, often fighting for provisions in documents that issuers found more insulting than onerous in practice. The pre-documented aspects of the underwritten 144A and Yankee bond markets were appropriately preferred by international issuers and investment banks alike. The relatively recent development of the model note agreement – and its increased use by intermediaries to offer deals to investors on a take-it-or-leave-it basis – has helped focus issuer and investor alike on the more important aspects of documentation. Nonetheless, as issuance of lower quality credits continues to grow and now includes issues with covenants, more Yankee and Rule 144A issuers face the troubling possibility of a default on an issue – and the nearly impossible job of amendments from unknown and widely diverse investors.

IN CLOSING

The tradeoffs between issuance methods for any company considering the U.S. long-term debt markets are considerable. One product certainly does not fit all clients. Many issuers hear strong arguments only for a Yankee or underwritten 144A issue, in part because these tend to be more profitable products for many investment banks than traditional private placements. Other issuers will have preconceived notions about the difficulty of meeting ongoing SEC registration requirements, or of dealing with rating agencies, or of documenting a traditional private placement. The reality is that each product needs to be considered in the total context of the issuer's long-term financial strategy, as well as with regard to the issuer's short-term tactical needs. The product that is the right solution for one financing need of an issuer may not be the right solution for another financing need of the same issuer. We hope that this article has conveyed the message that there are significant differences in the benefits and limitations of each of these products and that careful consideration needs to be given to these issues when choosing a financing solution. After all, a financial officer is going to live with the characteristics of whichever product is chosen for a very long time.

SUMMARY OF U.S. MARKET ALTERNATIVES

Traditional private placement	Rule 144A offering	Public "Yankee" offering
Usually arranged by one agent, or occasionally two agents on larger deals	Usually three or more underwriters, depending on deal	Usually three or more underwriters, depending on deal
$50–$500 million	#250–$1000 million	$250 million–$10 billion
For investment-grade and a very few non-investment-grade issuers	For investment-grade and some non-investment-grade issuers	For investment-grade or non-investment-grade issuers
Marketed via pre-established documentation	Marketed via pre-established documentation	Marketed via pre-established documentation
Limited and/or electronic roadshow, if any	More extensive and/or electronic roadshow	Most extensive and/or electronic roadshow
Little or no negotiation of terms with investors	No negotiation of terms with investors	No negotiation of terms with investors
Credit rating may be required + wide range of options available	Two long-term credit ratings generally required	Two long-term credit ratings are required
Lowest up-front documentation costs	Considerable up-front documentation costs	Considerable up-front documentation costs
Transaction costs generally lowest	Higher transaction costs	Highest transaction costs
Usually highest credit spread	Credit spread usually slightly higher than public	Lowest credit spread
Best efforts transaction	Underwritten transaction – priced after "Book" is filled	Underwritten transaction – priced after "Book" is filled
Quick market access (interest rate can be set in a matter of days)	Longer preparation time needed before accessing the market	Longest preparation time needed before accessing the market
Convenants looser than for a bank deal; tighter than for a public or 144A deal	Covenants similar to those required for a public issue	Loosest covenant structure

CHAPTER 33

Financial Risk Management for Developing Countries: A Policy Overview

Donald R. Lessard (Massachusetts Institute of Technology)*

The demand for risk management by developing countries is now large, and it will continue to grow throughout the rest of the 1990s for several reasons.

First are the high levels of volatility of many of the key parameters of the global economy, especially interest rates, exchange rates, and commodity prices. Given the current structure of the global economy – in particular, the absence of any clear hegemonic leader, the increased globalization and hence interdependence of international business activity, the limited coordination of macroeconomic policies among major countries, and the decreasing effectiveness of the traditional tools of macroeconomic management – such volatility seems far more likely to rise than fall in coming years.

Second, as developing countries themselves become more open both in commercial and financial terms, they will also become more exposed to this volatility. Many of these national economies will become more specialized as they seek their most efficient role in the global division of labor, and such specialization will serve only to increase their financial exposures. Moreover, as the finances

of such countries are further integrated into the world economy, they will also be subject to the impact of volatility in world financial markets on their external assets and liabilities.

Third, as a result of this increasing interdependence and resulting exposure to volatility, as well as to a variety of structural issues, developing economies will remain highly risky in themselves, with pronounced variations in investor confidence and capital flows. Many will experience financial difficulties and, for most, maintaining (or restoring) country creditworthiness will continue to be a major challenge.

Fourth, there are new technologies for financial risk management – notably, derivative instruments such as currency and commodity futures, swaps, and options – that are now generally available in financial markets. Many developing-country governments are building the capabilities necessary to use such instruments to hedge large exposures to exchange rates, interest rates, and commodity prices.

Fifth, the role of developing-country governments in their own economies is rapidly changing. In most such cases, governments are reducing their direct role while increasing their role as providers of critical physical and institutional infrastructure. With respect to external commercial and financial transactions, this means a shift of the state's role from intermediating most transactions with the rest of the world to providing the financial and

* This article is a revised version of "Effective Use of Financial Markets for Risk Management by Developing Countries: A Policy Overview," which first appeared in *International Monetary and Financial Issues For The 1990s*, Research Papers for the Group of Twenty-Four, Volume V (United Nations, New York and Geneva, 1995).

contractual infrastructure that allows local companies and other autonomous entities to transact
directly – and on the most favorable terms possible –
in global capital markets. As these autonomous
players become more active internationally, the
implicit as opposed to direct risk exposures of
the state will become more important.

In recent years, international financial institutions (hereafter referred to as "IFIs") – especially
the World Bank and the International Finance
Corporation, but also the European Development
Bank and the various regional development banks –
have developed guidelines for risk management by
developing countries. Such IFIs have engaged in
training and technical assistance missions in this
regard; they are beginning to provide policy advice
along these lines; and, in limited cases, they have
actually entered into risk-shifting transactions with
developing countries or helped to structure such
transactions on their behalf. At the same time,
private providers of financial services such as commercial and investment banks have urged risk
management tools and transactions on developing
countries. And many developing countries have
themselves acquired risk management capabilities –
in their public as well as private sectors – in part as
a result of the dispersion of financial talent with
the retrenchment of New York money-center
banks in the 1980s.

The aim of this paper is to present the key
elements of risk management and to assess in
broad terms the IFIs' policy recommendations to
developing countries for managing risk. The paper
begins by defining risk management both broadly
and narrowly. In its broadest sense, risk management encompasses all the means, structural as well
as financial, that can be used to improve the risk
profile of a country, or of specific enterprises or
sectors within national economies. My primary
focus here, however, is the more narrow one
of *financial* risk management – that is, the use of
futures, options, and other derivative products to
improve these risk profiles.

The paper focuses on several questions that confront policy-makers:

◆ What is risk management?
◆ Should developing countries engage in risk
  management?
◆ Whose risk should they manage?

◆ What risks should they manage?
◆ How should they manage these risks?
◆ How should they organize their risk manage-
  ment activities?
◆ What should IFIs do to support risk manage-
  ment by developing countries?

The rest of the paper is organized in five parts.
The first provides an overview of risk management
and a detailed description of the stages of the risk
management "process." The second discusses
various sources of risk, distinguishing "exogenous"
risks – that is, those market and systematic risks
beyond the control of developing countries – from
"endogenous" risks – those created or at least ampli-
fied within the domestic economy. The third part
develops the concept of *comparative advantage in risk-
bearing*, and derives from it implications about the
optimal amounts of both *risk-pooling* within individual developing countries and *risk-shifting* between
these countries and others in the world economy.
The fourth part illustrates the various financial
mechanisms for risk management with particular
attention to the case of commodity price exposures.
The fifth and concluding section summarizes the
steps that should be taken by both developing countries and IFIs to facilitate effective risk management.

WHAT IS RISK MANAGEMENT?

Risk management is the discipline of identifying
risks in the environment, assessing their potential
impact on critical performance measures, and
employing direct and indirect means for either
reducing the exposure of underlying economic
activities to these risks or shifting some of the
exposure to others.

Risk management can take many forms, both
structural and financial. There are two basic structural forms of risk management: diversification of
real business activities and accumulation of goods
to be consumed in periods of low output or
income. Financial mechanisms involve the structuring of claims within or between countries in
ways that smooth income by shifting revenue or
costs across different circumstances. Oil producers,
for example, can use forward contracts to fix oil
prices, thereby shifting their revenues from good
economic times to bad. Conversely, oil users such

as airlines or petrochemical firms can use the same contracts to shift the burden of higher oil costs from bad times to good.

In many cases, risk management is "bundled" with financing. A farmer borrowing money to pay the costs of planting a crop may have a choice of repaying a fixed dollar amount, a fixed amount of output, or a share of his crop. By denominating the obligation in terms of a fixed physical quantity, the farmer shifts the risk of price fluctuations to the lender. By denominating it as a share of output, he also shifts output risks.

Alternatively, the farmer might undertake financing and risk management separately. That is, he might borrow from a bank on terms that are independent of the price or quantity of the crop, but at the same time lock in the price of the crop in futures markets. In so doing, he shifts the risk of price fluctuations to others; and, provided he can coordinate negotiations of these two separate transactions, the price-protected farmer is likely to get more favorable terms from his banker.

Most recent developments in risk management technologies and markets have involved the development of pure risk-shifting contracts that can be separated from financing. Forward transactions that allow "pre-contracting" of commodity prices and currency exchange rates have existed for centuries. But formal markets for futures – forward-like contracts that provide open access to such transactions with few or no preconditions regarding the creditworthiness of participants – are relatively recent, starting in the 1970s and burgeoning during the 1980s. Swaps, which are in essence nothing more than series of forward contracts, are also relatively new. Options, which provide the right but not the obligation to buy or sell a currency, commodity, or financial asset for a particular price, have existed for decades. But the range of assets covered and the depth of options markets have both increased dramatically following the development of explicit methods for pricing and hedging such instruments in the 1970s.

Thus, in principle at least, there is a broad array of instruments for managing risk. And many of these instruments are actively traded in transparent, competitive markets that should ensure fair pricing over time.

For a developing country, risk management can be applied at several levels to solve different problems.

From the perspective of a government and its agencies, risk management can be used to stabilize government receipts or external debt service, or to eliminate spikes in debt service associated with events elsewhere in the world. It could also be used to smooth net foreign exchange earnings in the face of fluctuations resulting from shifting commodity prices or swings in economic activity in other countries.

Companies or banks in developing countries can use risk management to reduce fluctuations in their operating cash flows and net worth resulting from marketable dimensions of risk, whether local or foreign. Farmers can use risk management – either directly or indirectly through local intermediaries – to protect themselves against drops in crop prices. Finally, households as investors in pension funds and other contractual savings vehicles might indirectly employ risk management techniques to shift some of the risks inherent in their own economies to others.

Stages of the risk-management process

Risk management involves a number of stages, each of which is briefly described below.

1. Specify Objects of Risk Management. The first stage of risk management is to specify the objects of risk management – those critical performance measures whose volatility the risk manager is seeking to limit. Many objects are possible, depending ultimately on whose risks are to be managed – those of the nation as a whole, those of the central government, those of a single sector, agency, or enterprise, or those of a single project.

Most important for central government will be the performance measures for which it is directly responsible – elements of the budget and net foreign settlements. But since these objects will typically be exposed to many risks, the government may choose to focus on some subset of the total object for which exposures and risk management transactions can be more readily defined. An example would be oil revenues for a country such as Venezuela or Nigeria, or debt service for highly indebted countries.

For most state-owned or private enterprises, the object will likely be *operating cash flow*, defined as the cash flows generated from current operations. Those enterprises with major capital commitments may choose instead to target their *net free cash flow,* defined as operating cash flow less financial commitments such as debt service and capital outlays necessary to meet commitments or maintain profitability. For a production sector, it might be the price of a key commodity output or input. For a pension fund, it will be the value of its assets, ideally measured in terms that reflect the consumption patterns of its intended beneficiaries. For a social or demographic group, it might be some collection of factors that have a dominant impact on income flows.

2. Identify Key Risk Dimensions and Exposures. While many risk factors influence the objects of risk management, the primary focus should be on those factors that can be managed with financial market transactions. At the present time, these are primarily exchange rates, interest rates, and prices of key commodities. Pre-conditions for the existence of deep markets for risk-shifting are that many different entities have exposures to these risks on both sides – for example, both users and producers of a commodity – and that no single party be in a position to dictate outcomes. There may also be markets that allow for more indirect management of some aggregate risk variables. As one example, the shares of Telmex provide a quite effective way to "bet on" or hedge the overall risks associated with the Mexican economy.

Assessment of exposures typically involves both structural and statistical analysis. Structural analysis means examining the forces that shape demand, supply, and prices. Statistical analysis involves testing and confirmation of these relationships from past experience. Although both these tasks are complicated by the difficulty of isolating causal effects, formal analysis is essential because seemingly commonsense solutions often turn out to be wrong on closer inspection. For example it might appear appropriate for a country exporting copper to denominate its obligations in dollars, since copper prices are quoted in dollars. However, research has shown that the dollar price of copper is sensitive to the level of the dollar vis-à-vis the yen and the DM and that, therefore, a basket of currencies would actually provide a better match.[1]

3. Estimate Risk Profiles. Once exposures of particular risk management objects to specified risk dimensions are identified, it is possible to estimate the risk profiles of these objects. These risk profiles can be expressed in many different ways, such as in terms of the volatility (standard deviation) or potential range of the performance measure, or the probability that its value will fall below some threshold level within a specified time frame.

The principle aim of this stage is to identify those exposures that appear to give rise to excessive risks for various performance measures. It is important to know whether the potential variation in an external risk variable, such as a given commodity price, is likely to result in changes in net exports or government revenues of plus or minus 5 percent or plus or minus 50 percent. A useful rule of thumb is to focus on those risks where the historical range of variations can be expected to produce fluctuations of plus or minus 10 percent or more in critical performance measures.

4. Determine Target Risk Profile. Given the risk profiles of various performance measures, it is necessary to define the desired or target profiles as guides to actual risk management transactions. Determining this desired profile, however, typically needs to be done in coordination with the next stage – the identification of risk-shifting transactions – because it is impossible to define a desired risk profile without knowing the cost of achieving it. Other things equal, less risk is of course preferable to more risk; but risk reduction for countries may come at the expense of lower revenues or higher costs on average over time and across circumstances. For this reason, a decision to undertake risk management almost always involves a trade-off between the average level of the performance measure in question and the risk associated with that measure.

There are two reasons why risk reduction may reduce average income levels or increase average debt service. First, it involves transactions costs, although these typically are small, one-eighth of a percent or less. Second, to the extent that the risks being reduced are common to the global economy, such as primary commodity prices or world interest rates, the takers of such risk will require a premium. For this reason, for example, fixed interest rates are generally higher than floating rates. Even when the risk is diversifiable at a global level, risk takers will require a premium if there are large

1 See Bernard Dumas and Phillipe Jorion, "The Optimal Composition of Debt: Application to Chile," The World Bank (1993); and, earlier, Rudiger Dornbusch, "Exchange Rates and Commodity Prices," *American Economic Review* (1987).

fixed costs of information or other factors that require them to hold undiversified portfolios.

The impact of country risk – that is, the credit risk associated with contracts with sovereigns – on the cost of risk reduction is ambiguous. It increases the cost of financial contracting in general, since enforcement depends on costly interventions by institutions capable of imposing penalties in the case of nonperformance. Nevertheless, to the extent that risk-reducing contracts better align the terms of a country's obligation with its ability or willingness to pay, overall country risk may be reduced.

5. Select Mechanisms for Risk Management. Once actual and target risks profiles are identified, alternative mechanisms for risk reduction can be evaluated. In most cases, there will be several different types of financial instruments that will shape risk profiles differently, and these instruments may each be traded with differing degrees of efficiency. An oil forward or futures contract, for example, will lock in the price for a portion of a country's oil exports (or imports). The cost of risk reduction with a forward contract, in addition to the direct transaction costs, will be the "opportunity loss" of having to sell at that price under circumstances where prices are higher. The benefit, of course, will be to receive that price when actual spot prices are lower. With a standard option, by contrast, the price of risk reduction will be in the form of a cash premium that must be paid at the outset. Range options combine some features of forwards and options, placing a floor on prices at the cost of imposing an upper limit on realized prices as well. Thus, the cost of risk reduction is the opportunity loss in particular future circumstances where prices are very high.

Risk management can also be bundled with financing and management services. If the country wishes to link risk management to financing, it may want to consider issuing oil-price-linked bonds – bonds for which the level of principal and/or interest payments are tied to the price of oil. If it wants to bring in foreign technical expertise as well, it may choose to exploit its reserves through production-sharing or other risk-sharing mechanisms. In such cases, however, outsiders will be given a voice in strategic and operating decisions along with their participation in income.

6. Execute Specific Risk Management Transactions. Actual risk management transactions, such as selling commodity forwards, purchasing put options to create floors on commodity price receipts, or swapping future commodity deliveries for fixed or price-level-indexed monetary amounts, will be performed by operational units within the various agencies. The key policy issues are to define the parameters within which these units should operate. Such parameters include the target or benchmark risk profiles, the range of discretion allowed the unit relative to these target profiles, and the way the unit's effectiveness will be measured.

7. Track Effectiveness of Risk Management. The final stage in risk management is monitoring the effectiveness of the risk management unit relative to the target profiles within the provided guidelines. Such tracking is critically important because it provides the proper incentives and accountability for risk managers.

SOURCES AND INCIDENCE OF RISK EXPOSURES

The risk exposures of developing countries are many and varied. The treasury and state agencies are directly exposed to fluctuations in commodity prices, interest rates, and exchange rates. They are also exposed to worldwide levels of economic activity through their net international settlements on commercial account and their financial settlements with the rest of the world. Moreover, they are indirectly exposed to a host of risks faced by local households, firms, and financial intermediaries through their tax receipts as well as through committed expenditures whose levels depend on some of these same factors. These exposures matter to the state not only because they aggregate into overall national exposures, but because certain exposures, if sufficiently concentrated in particular sectors or institutions, may have systemic impacts beyond the direct losses involved. Indeed, such losses could be large enough to generate pressures that will require "socialization" of the losses.

Table 33.1 identifies the typical exposures of a developing country at different levels. In addition to the *external* risks summarized in the table, the state, firms, and households will also be exposed to fluctuations in *domestic* economic activity, prices, and interest rates. While these fluctuations to some

Table 33.1 Sources of External Risk Exposures

Risk dimension/level	Commodity prices	Interest rates[a]	Exchange rates	Economic activity
Primary exports	X		?	X
Manufactured exports		?	X	X
Tourism receipts		X	X	X
Energy imports	X		?	
Debt service		X	X	
Manufactured imports			X	
Assets/liabilities of banks		X	X	
Oper. cash flows/liabils. of maj. enterprises	X	X	X	X
Earnings of key sectors, e.g. farmers, miners	X			X
Operating income of firms in general	X	X	X	X
Asset values of pension funds		X	X	
Income, wealth of households in general		X	X	

[a] Also includes share prices and other financial asset prices.

extent reflect external shocks, they differ in that many of them involve a dimension of policy or choice on the part of the developing countries themselves. Therefore, they are not purely insurable in a classic sense. Nevertheless, they should be taken into account in overall risk management.

Whose risks should the state manage?

A key question in risk management for a developing country is to define whose risk is to be managed. For a developing country, many answers are possible, and more than one is correct. From the viewpoint of an idealized, omniscient planner, the principal concern should be with the risk of the nation as a whole – that is, with the potential volatility of aggregate national income net of foreign transfers and debt service. But, given that fiscal interventions can be costly, even an omniscient planner will also be concerned about differences in risk exposures within the national economy.

In the real world, of course, there will be a multiplicity of institutions, interests, and households, each with their own exposures. The central bank will be directly concerned with the exposures of its foreign currency reserves as well as short-term projected foreign exchange inflows and outflows. It will also be concerned with the full structure of foreign

claims and other factors that could give rise to capital flows, as well as to the exposures of financial institutions whose failure would threaten the stability of the financial system for which it is responsible. The state as fiscal authority will be concerned with the exposures implicit in its projected tax revenues and in its internal and external obligations (and among such obligations are implicit commitments not only in the form of social entitlements, but also in its implied role as "backstop" to domestic firms and financial institutions should they encounter difficulties that threaten the state's economic or distributional objectives). Thus, monetary and fiscal authorities will be concerned not only with their own exposures, but with those of any entity sufficiently large to be a "squeaky wheel," and hence a candidate for bailout, in the case of failure.

The government as manager and regulator of retirement schemes will be concerned with the exposures of asset values relative to implied liabilities, not only for direct state programs but also for the full set of programs that involve implicit liabilities of the state in case of failure at any level. Individual enterprises, whether publicly or privately owned, will be concerned with the exposures of their cash flows over time. Banks and other financial institutions will focus on their net asset values; and their degree of concern, as noted, will depend in part on how much implicit backing they expect in the case of failure.

COMPARATIVE ADVANTAGE IN RISK BEARING

Just as ideal patterns of specialization and trade among countries can be defined in terms of comparative advantage, ideal patterns of financing and risk-bearing within and across countries can be defined in terms of financial comparative advantage. The comparative advantage of a specific government (or corporation) in bearing particular types of risks depends on three factors:

- the extent to which it can diversify the risk;
- the extent to which it has superior information about probable outcomes; and
- the extent to which it can mitigate the risks.

In the case of "marketable" risks, such as those arising from commodity prices, interest rates, and exchange rates of major currencies – cases where information is widely available and there are many players – the major determinant of comparative advantage is the ability to diversify risk. For example, an oil-exporting country that depends on oil revenues for a large fraction of its foreign exchange earnings and government revenues is at a comparative *dis*advantage in bearing (long) oil price risk relative to the world markets at large. Similarly, a country entirely dependent on oil imports has a comparative disadvantage in bearing (short) oil price risk.

Commercial undertakings typically involve a mixture of "exogenous," typically marketable risks and "endogenous" risks associated with national policy and company-level actions – that is, risks about which certain actors possess special information or influence. Consider oil field exploration and development. Here the major risks can be grouped into four categories: (1) risks associated with geology; (2) uncertainty about both capital and operating costs in developing commercial fields; (3) variations in oil prices; and (4), finally, uncertainty about the "take" of the host government. If we apply the same rules of comparative advantage in risk-bearing, we can identify those agents most likely to have a comparative advantage in bearing each of these risks.

With respect to geological risk, while the underlying risk structure is totally out of the control of the participants, information about that risk is the major factor creating comparative advantage. For "old" geological areas where information is fairly widely available and standard forms of analysis are applicable, both local and foreign firms will be on an equal footing. In new areas involving complex structures, however, foreign multinationals (MNCs) with experience and special skills may have a comparative advantage over local firms or state-owned enterprises. For this reason, developing-country goverments often provide public funding for exploration activities whose results are then made generally available.

Capital and operating costs, by contrast, are at least partly under the control of the operating company. Therefore, these risks are best borne by the company that incurs them. For example, if a developing country contracts for a foreign MNC's services on a cost-plus basis, it must monitor expenditures closely to see that it is not overcharged.

In the case of oil price risks, comparative advantage depends on the circumstances of the country in question. A country such as Brazil has a comparative advantage in bearing (long) oil price since it is a net importer. In contrast, countries such as Venezuela and Nigeria, which are highly dependent on oil exports, are at a strong comparative disadvantage in bearing oil price risk.

The upshot of this analysis is that there is no single appropriate contracting structure for oil exploration and development. It depends on the distribution of information and expertise among actors, the ability of the government to specify and monitor activity, and, of course, the exposure of the country in question to oil prices.[2] *A key contribution of risk management technology is to allow the bundling or unbundling of various risks to align risk exposures with the ability to bear them.*

Country-level versus project-level risks

Country-level risks are those associated with a country's overall economic performance as well as

---

2   For a discussion along these lines of alternative oil contracting arrangements, see Charles Blitzer, James Paddock, and Donald Lessard, "Risk Bearing and the Choice of Contract Forms for Oil Exploration and Development," *The Energy Journal 5* (1984).

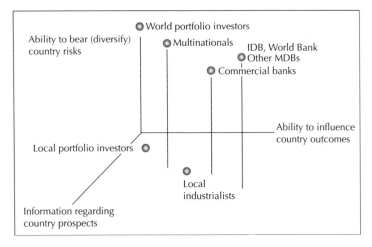

Figure 33.1 Comparative Advantage in Risk Bearing: Country-level Risks

the sovereign and political risks associated with activities undertaken within its borders. Some agents with a comparative advantage in bearing country-level risks may be at a comparative *dis*advantage in bearing commercial risks at the project or enterprise level. In exploring this possibility, let's begin by first considering just the case of country-level risks.

As illustrated in Figure 33.1, world portfolio investors are strongly advantaged in terms of their ability to diversify country risks since the typical developing country represents a trivial portion of their portfolio. At the same time, however, such investors have limited information about developing countries' prospects, no ability to influence country outcomes, and little incentive to seek to overcome these disadvantages given the small scale of developing-country opportunities.

By contrast, multinational firms have considerable information about country prospects, some ability to influence country outcomes, and also considerable ability to bear country risk. In short, they have a significant comparative advantage in bearing country-level risks.

Local industrialists, by comparison, typically have even more information about countries' prospects; and, as stakeholders in the political system, they are also able to exert a good deal more influence over country outcomes. But local industrialists also have a major disadvantage. Precisely because of their informational and influence

advantages, their financial as well as human capital is likely to be concentrated in the home country; and this means that local industrialists are likely to have very large risk exposures to country risk.

As this reasoning suggests, then, the parties most exposed to country risk in all of its forms may well be the locals, not the foreigners. And, for this reason, perhaps the whole discussion of country risk insurance should be turned on its head.

International banks have substantial information and influence, but they have portfolios that are heavily skewed toward developing-country debts. The World Bank and other regional development banks are in a somewhat similar position, typically with greater leverage because of the extensive cross-default clauses and other linkages to official actions, and also because of their broader diversification. Although their portfolios are concentrated in the obligations of less-developed countries, the sponsor governments that stand behind such IFIs are in fact well diversified.

In sum, there are three kinds of large-scale institutions – multinational firms, large commercial banks, and multilateral finance institutions – that are capable of generating information and exerting leverage while nevertheless still diversifying their holdings. And it is these three classes of institutions that should be dominant in bearing country-level risk. World portfolio investors and local industrialists have particular advantages along one dimension or another, but both of these groups are

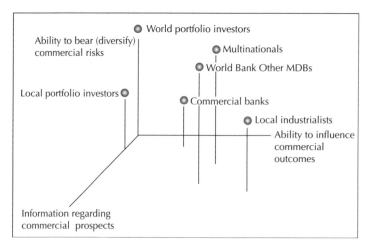

Figure 33.2 Comparative Advantage in Risk Bearing: Project-level Risks

significantly disadvantaged in others. Local portfolio investors appear to be the most disadvantaged of all the groups in bearing the risk of their own country.

But now let's consider comparative advantage in bearing *project-level* risks. As illustrated in Figure 33.2, world portfolio investors stand in the same position as they did with country-level risks. Local industrialists have even more information about specific commercial prospects along with greater influence over commercial outcomes and substantial ability to diversify across commercial risks. By comparison, international banks typically have less information about commercial prospects within less-developed countries, and typically less ability to influence commercial outcomes – though, again, they have greater ability to diversify individual project risks across industries and across countries than in the case of country risk. Multinationals come out as extremely strong in this regard, since they have both specific knowledge about commercial undertakings and the ability to influence commercial outcomes – and yet they are still able to diversify commercial risks.

The implication of this analysis, then, is that there is a mismatch in the ability of various economic agents to take on country-level and project-level risks. And this in turn means that some form of risk engineering that transfers risks among these different groups should create net gains in the international economy – gains that can be shared among developing and developed

nations alike. In an ideal world, those entities best able to take on country risks would do so. There should be a division of labor between the different actors achieved by contracting and financing mechanisms that split the risks along the lines of comparative advantage.

Moreover, our analysis of comparative advantage provides important insights into not only who should bear particular risks, but whether they can be intermediated locally or require international intermediation. As illustrated in Figure 33.3, two factors are critical in determining the ideal locus of risk intermediation. The first is whether the economy as a whole is strongly exposed to the dimension of risk in question. If so, risk-pooling to obtain diversification requires intermediation with other countries or agents that do not share this exposure. The second is whether there is a sufficient number of sophisticated autonomous actors in the domestic economy to create a market. If the number is small (fewer than, say, 30 or 40), offshore intermediation will be required for efficiency and transparency, even if in terms of aggregate exposure the risk could be pooled domestically.

MECHANISMS FOR RISK MANAGEMENT

A country with large aggregate exposures to one or more sources of risk can seek to reduce the impact of that risk in several ways. It can shift its structure

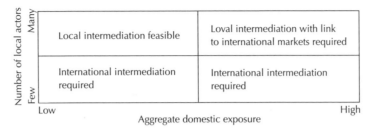

Figure 33.3   Potential for Domestic Risk Intermediation/Pooling

Table 33.2   Modes of Financial Risk Management

Instrument	Transfers risk	Provides financing	Includes management services/control
Forward contract	X		
Futures contract[a]	X		
Option	X		
Commodity bond	X	X	
Production share/prefinancing	X	X	X
General obligation finance		X	
Project finance	X	X	limited
Management contract			X
Direct investment	X	X	X

[a] A futures contract differs from a forward contract in two principal ways. It is traded on an organized exchange and requires regular (typically daily) cash settlements in line with movements in value. A forward, in contrast, is a binding agreement to lock in a price at a future date. As a result of these differences, futures are limited to relatively standard commodities and time frames, but they are much less sensitive to the credit standing of the parties.

of production and trade in ways that diversify its real business activities. It can seek through collective action with other countries to eliminate or at least stabilize the source of risk itself. Or, it can engage in financial transactions to shift some of the risk to which it is exposed to others in the world economy.

Each of these three strategies can be used either alone or in combination with the other two, and each involves different costs and benefits. Diversification will be desirable as long as it does not require significant sacrifices in terms of comparative advantage or scale economies. Price stabilization efforts will typically require real resources, and, most important, a degree of collaboration among countries that in general has not proved sustainable over time. Financial risk transfers will involve transactions costs and, in most cases (as we have seen), a reduction in the average realization of the performance variable in question over time. Ideally, a country should pursue each of

these three strategies to the point where the marginal amount of risk reduction per unit of cost provided by each is equal.

Financial risk management can be undertaken directly through "pure" risk transactions such as futures, swaps, or options. Or it can be bundled with financing, as in a commodity-linked bond or a floating-rate bond with a cap on interest rates. Further, whether bundled or alone, the contract may entitle the risk-taker to participate in the control of the operation giving rise to the risks. A futures contract or a commodity bond, for example, would not in general entitle the holder to participate in investment or operating decisions, except in the case of default on the terms of the contract. By contrast, a production share or direct equity investment combines financing, risk transfer, and management participation. (The positions of various financial instruments along these three dimensions are identified in Table 33.2.)

A fixed- or floating-rate general obligation debt is in principle a pure financing contract, although it does involve general sovereign risk of nonperformance. A forward, future, swap, or option would be a pure risk-transfer contract, providing no financing. A management contract with incentives tied to performance would be a pure right to participate. An equity investment, of course, involves all three. A production share also involves all three, but it is a more explicit contract than equity and typically limits both the risk exposures and decisions rights of the investors in ways that equity does not.

Whether developing countries should in general attempt to bundle their risk-management transactions with financing or keep them separate is largely beyond the scope of this paper.[3] Suffice it here to say that such a decision will depend, in large part, on the extent to which external parties have skills, technology, or networks that are critical to the efficient operation of the investment in question. From a risk management perspective, what is important for a developing country is to recognize its major risk exposures and consider all the various mechanisms available to it for achieving its desired risk profile.

Take the case of Indonesia, which has financed a large proportion of its oil exploration and development through production-sharing agreements with foreign MNCs. Under such arrangements, the MNCs developing the resources are effectively held responsible for the costs of operations and receive a proportion of the output in return. Besides ensuring the cost-effectiveness of the operations, such production-sharing effectively transfers a large proportion of Indonesia's oil price risk to the stockholders of the MNCs – that is, to individual and institutional investors with globally diversified portfolios.

In countries such as Mexico and Venezuela, by contrast, the exploration of oil reserves has been performed exclusively by the state and financed by general obligation money, typically borrowed at floating rates and denominated in dollars. Such ownership and funding arrangements mean that all oil price risks are borne locally. And since the

activities are financed with floating-rate debt, the oil "income" net of financing costs of these two nations is much more volatile than oil prices themselves. To reduce their oil price exposures to the level of Indonesia's, but without giving up ownership of assets, these countries could use one or more of the following risk-transfer mechanisms: (1) issue oil-price-linked bonds (which, again, effectively combines risk management with financing); (2) pre-contract for the sale of oil by selling oil futures or options, or (3) purchase options that provide floors on future oil prices.

In general, then, it will be desirable for countries to engage in bundled as well as unbundled risk transactions so that they can properly assess the relative cost of transferring risk through both methods and assure themselves of competitive pricing. In those cases where bundling limits the pool of potential investors to a very small number, some degree of unbundling will be required so that there are sufficient contenders to ensure competitive pricing. But if contracts involve risks of fulfillment by sovereign governments, they may be hard to unbundle without the intervention of IFIs, a point we discuss in the final section.

NATIONAL RISK MANAGEMENT POLICY

Risk management policy for a nation involves managing a variety of risk exposures at many different levels. Government plays several roles in addition to being directly responsible for risk management at the central bank, treasury, and public enterprise levels. As summarized in Table 33.3 and described below, these roles include regulatory oversight of risk management markets and practices, development of commercial and financial infrastructure, and provision of information. Also illustrated in Table 33.3 is the distribution of these four risk management roles across various levels within the national economy.

Oversight/regulation of risk management

Oversight or regulation of the risk management of firms and financial institutions involves both the creation of incentives for and the imposition of

---

3 For a much more detailed discussion of risk-shifting financing strategies for developing countries, see my article, "Recapitalizing Third-World Debt: Toward a New Vision of Commercial Finance for Less-developed Countries," *Midland Corporate Finance Journal*, Vol. 5, No. 3, Fall 1987.

Table 33.3   Role of Central Government[a] in Overall National Risk Management

Risk management role/level	Direct responsibility	Oversight regulation	Markets/ infrastructure	Information
Budget / revenues, mandated expenditures	X			X
Official international settlements	X			X
Total international settlements		X		X
Assets / liabilities of key banks		X	X	X
Operating cash flows / liabilities of major enterprises		X	X	X
Earnings of key sectors, e.g., farmers, miners			X	X
Asset value of pension funds		X	X	X
Income, wealth of firms, individuals in general			X	X

[a] Central government in this case refers to the treasury or to some designated overall risk management unit that may include representatives of the central bank and key state-owned enterprises as well.

requirements on non-governmental actors to induce them to manage their key risk exposures properly. The justification for such intervention goes beyond a paternalistic interest in the welfare of the parties in question. It is necessary because of potential "spillovers" of private risks to the public sphere – the possibility that private losses from unmanaged exposures could create systemic problems or force the central government to bail out the losers.

Regulation is likely to be necessary with large exposures that affect key institutions or large numbers of firms or households, especially if they are concentrated in one region. The reason is that pressures for government bailouts in case of disasters will be irresistible. As a result, private decision-making will fail to consider the costs associated with these risks, and so there will be more than the socially optimal level of losses and failures. If large banks perceive that they are "too big to fail," for example, they will gamble with the states' money in much the same way as did major U.S. money-center banks and S & Ls, thus costing taxpayers billions.

The analogy in the case of natural risks would be a prohibition on the building of homes within a flood plain. Here private decisions will be suboptimal to the extent that homeowners implicitly assume that the government will compensate them for losses in the case of a disaster affecting many homeowners at once. Of course, governments could announce that they will not compensate "foolish" homeowners, but in the modern welfare state such declarations often lack credibility. And thus governments, somewhat ironically, find themselves in the position of having to regulate private behavior to eliminate the distortions created by their own tendency to intervene.

Private actors exposed to risks may err either on the side of caution or of daring, from a social perspective. They will err on the side of caution when they take into account volatility that could be diversified at a social level – for example, in cases where there are private risks that do not fully translate into social risks (such as a large, publicly traded oil company choosing to hedge an oil price exposure that has already been "diversified away" by its shareholders). They will err on the side of daring in those cases where risks contribute more to social than to private risks, either because such risks trigger a system-wide reaction (such as a bank failure that triggers a run) or because private actors assume that society will in some way absorb their losses.

Mexico's recent crisis clearly demonstrates that limiting financial vulnerability is a key responsibility of governments in addition to their fiscal responsibility. It also underscores the importance of monitoring of such risk management by international investors and lenders.

MEASURING FINANCIAL VULNERABILITY RATHER THAN FINANCIAL POSITION: LESSONS FROM THE MEXICAN CRISIS

In a paper for the National Bureau of Economic Research, international economists Jeffrey Sachs, Andres Velasco, and Aaron Tornell analyzed the Mexican crisis as follows:

In the first quarter of 1995, Mexico found itself in the grip of an intense financial panic. Foreign investors fled Mexico despite very high interest rates on Mexican securities, an undervalued currency, and financial indicators that pointed to long-term solvency. The fundamental conditions of the Mexican economy cannot account for the entire crisis. The crisis was due to unexpected shocks that occurred in 1994, and the inadequate policy response to those shocks. In the aftermath of the March assassination, the exchange rate experienced a nominal devaluation of around 10 percent and interest rates increased by around 7 percentage points. Nevertheless, the capital outflow continued.

The policy response was to maintain the exchange rate rule, and to prevent further increases in interest rates by expanding domestic credit and by converting short-term, peso-denominated government liabilities (Cetes) falling due into dollar-denominated bonds (Tesobonos). A fall in international reserves and an increase in short-term, dollar-denominated debt resulted. The government simply ended up illiquid, and therefore financially vulnerable. Illiquidity exposed Mexico to a self-fulfilling panic.[4]

In the wake of the crisis, it is useful to ask whether investors should have anticipated events such as the worsening of the Chiapas conflict or the assassination of Colosio. Probably not. While political risk forecasters might have argued that Mexican society was more vulnerable than others to such shocks, the shocks remained surprises.

What should investors have looked at? As Sachs et al. have shown, standard aggregate economic indicators would not have done much good. Rather, investors (and those responsible for managing the Mexican economy) should have placed greater focus on financial vulnerability.

The first focus should have been on the vulnerability of individual companies and banks within the country, which in turn acted as constraints on macroeconomic choices, making the whole system more vulnerable. The Mexican banking system was highly exposed to both devaluation and an increase in interest rates, and many Mexican corporates were illiquid, highly levered with dollar borrowings.

The second focus should have been the government's vulnerability to changes in financial variables. In mopping up capital inflows by issuing short-term obligations, first in pesos but later in dollars, the government was effectively increasing its exposure to a crisis of confidence – that is, the country's liabilities were actually set up so as to increase as investor confidence (and thus the peso) declined. As such, its structure was becoming unsustainable regardless of the long-term fundamentals. Instead of issuing short-term, dollar obligations, the government should have considered longer-term financing options providing investors with, say, an upside payoff in the event of rising oil prices.

A further indication of financial vulnerability that could have been applied to Mexico would have been to classify investors in these various instruments in terms of their degree of "footlooseness." The press focused on the fact that much of Mexico's short-term funding came from foreigners, implying that this was the source of the problem. But, in fact, a recent IMF review shows that Mexican money moved as quickly, if not more quickly, than foreign money. The key issue is that footloose institutional and large-scale private investors held the bulk of this paper, as opposed to "sticky" (or buy-and-hold) local investors such as middle-class families and contractual savings plans.

The comparatively mild reaction experienced by Chile to the same shocks, though partly attributable to the country's stronger fundamentals, also reflected the fact that a very large proportion of its internal financial claims is held by sticky local investors who could not move their funds abroad without incurring large information and transaction costs. In Argentina, by contrast, a large proportion of the short-term claims on the country was held by footloose investors, Argentine as well as foreign. And, given that Argentina was forced to weather a crisis comparable to Mexico's, it seems likely that greater capital mobility played a significant role in both of these cases.

---

4 Abstract of J. Sachs, A. Velasco, and A. Tornell, "The Collapse of the Mexican Peso: What Have We Learned?," NBER Working Paper #5142, June 1995.

Market regulation / contractual infrastructure

Risk management is a complex process, with continuous introduction of new products as technology advances and as the leading providers of risk management services seek to differentiate themselves from their competitors. As a result, regulators of markets for and providers of risk management transactions, even in the most advanced countries, have a difficult time staying abreast of the practice of leading producers and users of derivative instruments.[5] Most developing countries cannot and should not expect to keep pace with this full range of developments, especially since in many cases only a handful of local institutions or enterprises will be able to make effective use of them.

A distinction should be drawn between two fundamentally different types of transactions: (1) those likely to involve many local actors, where it is important to provide broad access; and (2) those where the limited numbers of players and required levels of sophistication are such that continued reliance on international markets is required. Even where broad local access is called for, the best procedure may involve creation of a clearinghouse or other mechanism that eases the access of local actors to existing international markets rather than seeking to create local markets to take their place.

Where local markets are possible, a full regulatory context will of course be required. But, in order to limit costs and to ensure its international compatibility, the regulatory system should draw substantially on models developed elsewhere.

For those risk transfers that will be intermediated offshore, what is required is that the underlying basic contracts be recognized in local commercial codes, perhaps by interposing a clearing intermediary with the necessary legal status. To allow innovations on the part of those local actors capable of making use of them, local regulations might provide an option for firms to remain entirely within local standards or to comply fully with reporting rules of the U.S., U.K., or some other advanced country whose legal framework is closest to that of the country in question.

As we have seen, markets for risk reduce the divergence between public and private perspectives in cases where private actors face risks that can be diversified at a broader level. Such markets achieve this effect by enabling overly exposed actors to shift risks to others at prices that should reflect the overall incidence of these risks. Nevertheless, local private enterprises may lack market access because they lack creditworthiness – or because their creditworthiness is reduced by an overlay of country risk, which has the same effect. Thus, most developing countries will need to take steps to reduce costs to local actors of accessing international markets.

The most desirable situation, of course, is one with full access at the country level and a complete internal market with credit information such as that provided by Dun and Bradstreet's, reliable contract enforcement, and so forth. For those countries unable to reach this level, governments might sponsor clearinghouses to bridge the domestic institutional/contractual structure and international markets. Such a clearinghouse would require cash settlements with domestic firms, while enabling them to bypass exchange controls and other hindrances to cross-border contracting.

The role of IFIs

While risk management is a critical need and responsibility for developing country governments, it is also an area where many of them will require the assistance of international institutions such as the World Bank. Such assistance includes information about sources of risk, quantification of exposures, risk management techniques, and regulatory/institutional developments. Assistance from IFIs should also take the form of technical assistance and training; and, in some cases, IFIs will even act as intermediaries in risk-shifting financial transactions.

Information. IFIs can and should play a major role in increasing risk awareness on the part of developing countries. Increased awareness can help them keep pace with rapid changes in the risk environment, in risk management techniques, and in regulatory procedures surrounding this dynamic area of finance. One simple step for building

---

5 See, for example, the Global Derivatives Study Group, *Derivatives: Principles and Practices* (Washington, D.C., July, 1993). This study is popularly known as the "Group of Thirty" report.

risk awareness would be for statistical publications to present not only levels of key variables, but also their volatilities, and to place greater emphasis on predictions of volatility as well as future direction. A few recent World Bank documents have included such information. Studies of particular sectors or countries could also include, where possible, estimates of the sensitivity of key performance measures to particular sources of risk.

Technical Assistance. Developing countries are also likely to require technical assistance to learn to employ risk management techniques effectively. They will also require help in creating and maintaining the regulatory environment necessary to monitor the risk management activities of local financial intermediaries and other key autonomous players. Of the two, the regulatory aspects are probably the more difficult.

IFIs might provide computer-based models that provide simulations of future interest rates, exchange rates, and commodity prices, which in turn could aid countries in testing their direct risk management strategies as well as the risk positions of local intermediaries or firms that they monitor. They might also institute a common reporting system for the risk-shifting nature of countries' external obligations as well as the "off-balance-sheet" positions of governments and key national entities.

If, as suggested earlier, developing countries are to rely in large part on advanced countries for regulatory developments, they can reasonably be expected to want some voice in the formulation of these regulations. IFIs here might serve as an intermediary forum, representing the needs and interests of those countries whose size or level of financial development does not allow them to operate directly in this arena.

Intermediation. Those developing countries that have access to private world capital markets undoubtedly find themselves presented with an ample array of competitive providers of risk-shifting transactions, in which case there is no special intermediation role for IFIs. For those countries that do not have such access, however, those risk-shifting transactions like forwards and long-term swaps that imply future credit exposures are also out of reach. And although these countries still have access to organized futures markets, such instruments tend

to be relatively short term.[6] They can also employ purchased options, although the typically large up-front premiums will have to be financed.

As we noted earlier, risk management for a commodity-producing country will in general mean finding a way to transfer revenues from future circumstances when commodity prices are above average to periods when they are very low. But there is a credit problem that arises from this arrangement: namely, if the country promises to pay out very large amounts in the case of price windfalls, it probably will not be believed, since the temptation to default under those circumstances will be too great.[7]

To address this "credit-and-incentive" issue, the World Bank and other IFIs could provide such contracts on a transparent basis, without violating their "one-price-for-all" policy, by adding to their normal loan rate the cost they would incur in the market for selling a put and a capped call on the commodity in order to match the contract it wrote with the developing country. The benefit of such "bundling" would be that the World Bank would finance the premium, but would not be made worse off since it would hold an equally good or better claim against the country.

Even highly creditworthy countries might require IFI intermediation to obtain non-recourse, commodity-linked project financing – that is, financing for a project without any recourse to the state for repayment in the event that the future cash flows generated by the project are insufficient to meet the obligation. In those cases where the cash flows depend on government actions – such as, for example, imposing world prices on energy sold in local markets – the country probably would not be able to obtain project financing because of the combination of general country risk and compliance risks associated with the

---

6 Short-term transactions, however, can under many circumstances provide effective hedges against longer-term positions if the amounts covered adequately reflect the time period to be covered. For example, in order to cover a three-year exposure, say of commodity revenues, with three-month forwards, an amount equal to three years of sales would have to be rolled forward every three months.

7 For a recent analytical treatment of these issues, see Kenneth M. Kletzer, David M. Newbery, and Brian D. Wright, "Alternative Instruments for Smoothing the Consumption of Primary Commodity Exporters," The World Bank (1990).

specific arrangement. In such cases, the World Bank, by virtue of its expanded co-financing programs, is in a very strong position to take and mitigate such compliance risks, and therefore can be a very useful participant. World Bank intermediation could also deal with a series of completion and contracting risks and thus allow the country to lay off underlying price risk without providing an unconditional guarantee of repayment. Thus, by accepting and passing on a conditional state guarantee, IFIs would actually be reducing the state's credit exposure.

PART VII

International Corporate Governance

The past decade has given rise to a growing debate over the relative efficiency of different national economic systems. At the risk of oversimplifying, there are two basic corporate finance and governance systems that predominate in developed economies today. One is the Anglo-American "market-based" model, with widely dispersed shareholders and a fairly vigorous corporate control (or takeover) market. The other can be represented by the Japanese and German "relationship-based" systems, with their large bank and intercorporate holdings – and conspicuous absence of takeovers. Given the increasing globalization of business, which of these two systems can be expected to prevail over time? Or will both systems continue to coexist (which seems more plausible), while seeking to adopt the most valuable aspects of the other?

Throughout the 1980s and well into the '90s, the popular business press was telling us that U.S. companies were falling ever farther behind their global competitors – even as U.S. stock prices continued to move ever higher. We were also told that the leveraged restructuring of the '80s was adding to the American competitiveness problem by reducing investment and otherwise reinforcing the "short termism" of U.S. managers. At the same time, Japanese companies were pronounced the victors in the competitive wars, and U.S. managers and investors were urged to cultivate the patience of their Japanese counterparts.

This section begins with Merton Miller's classic defense of the "shareholder value principle" entitled "Is American Corporate Governance Fatally Flawed?" As Miller argues, the alleged shortsightedness of the U.S. stock market is not likely to be a serious problem:

. . . myopia is not the only disease of vision afflicting business managers. They may suffer from astigmatism (distorted vision) or even from hyperopia or excessive farsightedness. Looking back over the last 20 years, one may well find cases in which American firms facing strong stockholder pressures to pay out funds invested too little in some kinds of capital-intensive technology. But many Japanese firms, facing no such pressure, have clearly *over*invested during that same period in highly capital-intensive plants that will never come close to recovering their initial investment, let alone earning a positive rate of return. And I won't even mention the trillions of yen poured into land and office buildings both at home and abroad.

Japanese managers, adds Miller, are justly skeptical about using stock prices to guide their investment decisions. Because of "the heroic scale of market intervention by the Ministry of Finance (MOF), Japanese managers can be pardoned for wondering whether the stock market may be just a *Bunraku* theater, with the bureaucrats from MOF backstage manipulating the puppets."

In "The Role of Corporate Governance in South Korean Economic Reform," Stanford law and economics professor Kenneth Scott reinforces Miller's message by observing that banks and large corporations in Southeast Asia tend to be run more in the interest of the government and the controlling shareholder group than to maximize efficiency and overall shareholder wealth. In the name of full employment and other socially sanctioned goals, such organizations often pursue growth in market share and assets – and, in many cases, diversification – at the expense of profitability and value. But if ensuring growth would appear to be a more humane pursuit than profit and value maximization, the reality is quite different. The practical consequences of such "growth-at-all-cost" policies – which have become painfully clear in nations like Japan – are chronic overinvestment and bloated payrolls, which lead eventually to declining profits and stock prices, inability to service debt (in some cases), and massive downsizing and layoffs.

Much of this, of course, recalls the experience of U.S. companies – especially conglomerates – during the 1980s. But there is an important difference. By encouraging corporate raiders to initiate the necessary process of restructuring in the '80s, the U.S. market for corporate control prevented the U.S. "overinvestment" problem from escalating to its current proportions in Southeast Asia (and parts of Europe).

In Southeast Asia, as in most of continental Europe, there are few signs of a well-functioning market for corporate control. One reason for this, as Professor Scott points out, is that the typical public corporation in those regions (as well as in most emerging market economies) is closely held and, in many cases, dominated by the founder and his family or associates. External equity is a relatively small part of the capital structure, with the bulk of financing supplied by retained earnings and bank debt (often provided on a subsidized basis from government-controlled banks). Given these financing sources, along with the limited legal rights of minority stockholders, public companies face little pressure for change – or not at least until the "crisis" hits.

And so, as Scott argues, any serious attempt to reform such bank-centered economies must include significant changes in their systems of corporate governance. Perhaps most important are (1) greater legal protection for minority shareholders from transactions involving potential conflicts

of interest; and (2) a strengthening of the incentives of management and large corporate holders, such as house or main banks, to maximize shareholder value (as Scott notes in closing, "charging management or the board with a legal mandate to 'balance' the interests of various constituencies or stakeholders is merely to diminish any legally enforceable responsibility to shareholders").

In "Corporate Ownership and Control in the U.K., Germany, and France," Julian Franks and Colin Mayer characterize the U.K. and U.S. corporate ownership and governance systems as *outsider* systems with a large number of public corporations, widely dispersed ownership, and well-developed takeover markets. By contrast, the much smaller number of publicly traded German and French corporations are governed by *insider* systems – those in which the founding families, banks, or other companies have controlling interests and in which outside shareholders are not able to exert much control.

Both kinds of systems, the authors argue, have proven highly durable, and thus both are likely to have important strengths as well as weaknesses. Concentrated ownership, for example, would seem to encourage longer-term relationships between the company and its investors. But, while perhaps better suited to some corporate activities with longer-term payoffs, concentrated ownership could also lead to costly delays in undertaking necessary corrective action, particularly if the owners receive "private" benefits from owning and running a business.

In "Universal Banks Are Not the Answer to America's Corporate Governance 'Problem'," Jonathan Macey and Geoffrey Miller object to a recent tendency of legal and economic scholars to "romanticize" the corporate governance role of German universal banks and Japanese main banks. There are potential conflicts between banks' interests as lenders and as shareholders that are likely to make banks less-than-ideal monitors for outside shareholders. Macey and Miller argue that the main problems with the German and Japanese governance systems stem from their failure to produce well-developed capital markets along with active takeover markets. The main problem with U.S. corporate governance is "not that hostile takeovers are bad, but that there are not enough of them due to regulatory restrictions and misguided legal policies."

In "Which Capitalism? Lessons From the East Asian Crisis," the University of Chicago's Raghuram Rajan and Luigi Zingales offer a suggestive explanation for why bank-centered, "relationship-based" economies like Japan and Germany, while prospering in the 1980s, have faltered in recent years. Relationship-based systems tend to be more effective than market-based systems in economies with scarce capital (relative to profitable investment opportunities) and lacking a well-developed "contractual infrastructure." But problems arise in such economies when capital becomes too plentiful, particularly when they open their markets to foreign inflows and effectively become "hybrid" economies (part relationship-based, part market-based). Without the reliable price signals provided by market-based system, such economies are more than usually prone to capital misallocation (i.e., massive overinvestment), which in turn leads to capital flight (because investors have few contractual safeguards) and plummeting currencies and asset prices.

Because of this problem inherent in "hybrid" economic systems, Rajan and Zingales suggest that emerging economies may want to impose *temporary* capital controls and revert for a time to their "pure" relationship-based systems. But such steps should be clearly intended to serve only as stop-gap

measures while continuous efforts are made to develop the greater disclosure, contract enforcement, and competition essential to a market-based system. For, as the authors say in closing, the current Asian crisis may be the most opportune moment for these economies to effect the transition between systems.

In "Measuring the Effectiveness of Different Corporate Governance Systems: Toward a More Scientific Approach," Cornell's Jonathan Macey proposes three objective criteria for evaluating the effectiveness of different corporate governance systems: (1) the average premium at which the voting shares of companies with multiple classes of stock trade in relation to their non-voting shares (large premiums for voting stock suggest large "private" benefits from control that are not shared with outside, non-voting shareholders); (2) the level of IPO activity (since entrepreneurs operating in economies with weak governance systems will generally not be able to command high enough prices to want to take their firms public); and (3) the speed and reliability with which inefficient management teams are replaced, either through takeover or board action. By each of these three measures, moreover, the U.S. corporate governance system appears to be quite effective.

CHAPTER 34

Is American Corporate Governance Fatally Flawed?

Merton H. Miller (University of Chicago)*

Are the investment horizons of U.S. firms too short? Yes, was the conclusion of *Capital Choices*, a report published in August 1992 by 25 academic scholars under the leadership of Professor Michael Porter of the Harvard Business School. The Porter Report was widely acclaimed not only by the U.S. financial press, but by many Japanese observers. Mr. Katsuro Umino, for one, Vice President of the Osaka-based Kotsu Trading Company, was quoted in the Chicago *Tribune* of August 24, 1992 as saying:

It's interesting to see that somebody in America is finally waking up to the real culprit behind the decline of American corporate competitiveness. I think many of us in Japan have known for a long time that America's capital allocation system is inherently flawed.

The flaw seen by Messrs. Porter and Umino and ever so many others is the overemphasis on stock prices and shareholder returns in the American system of corporate governance. By contrast, a survey of 1,000 Japanese and 1,000 American firms by Japan's Economic Planning Agency, reported in the same Chicago *Tribune* story, finds that on a scale of 0 to 3 – 3 being most important – Japanese firms give "Higher Stock Price" a rating of only 0.02. "Increasing Market Share" gets a reported rating of 1.43 in Japan, almost twice its rating in the United States.

Surveys must never be taken too literally, of course. Japanese managers surely cannot believe that increasing market share is the overriding corporate goal. Achieving a 100 percent market share for your product is too easy: just give it away! Profitability must also and always be considered. And, indeed, the Japanese firms surveyed did give a rating of 1.24 to Return on Investment – far less than the 2.43 rating given by the American firms, but still much much more than the virtually zero weight given to Higher Stock Prices.

For all its technical limitations, however, the survey does, I believe, accurately reflect differences in managerial behavior in the two countries. American managers *are* more concerned with current movements in their own stock prices than are Japanese managers. And rightly so. The emphasis American managers place on shareholder returns is not a flaw in the U.S. corporate governance system, but one of its primary strengths.

Some of my academic colleagues believe, in fact, that American big-business management has been putting put too *little* weight on stockholder returns, leading to massive waste of both shareholder and national wealth. Their argument has not, in my view, been convincingly established. The billion-dollar losses of companies like IBM and General Motors in recent years, offered by

* My thanks for helpful comments from my colleagues Steven Kaplan and Anil Kashyap and from Donald Chew.

such critics as evidence for their case, testify less to failures in the U.S. governance system than to the vigorously competitive environment in which U.S. firms must operate.

MAXIMIZING SHAREHOLDER VALUE AS THE PRIMARY OBJECTIVE OF THE BUSINESS CORPORATION

Let me begin my defense of U.S. corporate governance by emphasizing that managerial concern with shareholder value is merely one specific application of the more general proposition that in American society the individual is king. Not the nation, not the government, not the producers, not the merchants, but the individual – and especially the individual consumer – is sovereign. Certainly that has not been the accepted view of ultimate economic sovereignty here in Japan, though the first signs of change are beginning to appear.

The connection between consumer sovereignty and corporate governance lies not just in the benefits customers derive from the firm's own output. The customers are not the only consumers the firm serves. The shareholders, the investors, the owners – however one chooses to call them – are also consumers and their consumption, actual and potential, is what drives the shareholder-value principle.

To see how and why, consider the directors of a firm debating how much of the firm's current profits, say $10 million, to pay out as dividends to the shareholders. If the $10 million is paid as dividends, the shareholders clearly have an additional $10 million in cash to spend. Suppose, however, that the $10 million is not paid out, but used instead for investment in the firm – buying machinery, expanding the factory, setting up a new branch, or what have you. The stockholders now do not get the cash, but they need not be disadvantaged thereby. That will depend on how the stock market values the proposed new investment projects.

If the market believes the firm's managers have invested wisely, the value of the shares may rise by $10 million or even more. Stockholders seeking to convert this potential consumption into actual consumption need only sell the shares and spend the proceeds. But if the market feels that the managers have spent the money foolishly, the stock value will rise by less than the forgone dividend

of $10 million – perhaps by only $5 million, or possibly not at all. Those new investments may have expanded the firm's market share; they may have vastly improved the firm's image and the prestige of its managers. But they have not increased shareholder wealth and potential consumption. They have reduced it.

Current market values and future earnings

Using the stock market's response to measure the true worth of the proposed new investments may strike many here in Japan as precisely the kind of short-termism that has led so many American firms astray. Let it be clearly understood, therefore, that, in a U.S.-style stock market, focusing on current *stock* prices is not short-termism. Focusing on current *earnings* might be myopic, but not so for stock prices, which reflect not just today's earnings, but the earnings the market expects in all future years as well.

Just how much weight expected future earnings carry in determining current stock prices always surprises those not accustomed to working with present-value formulas and, especially, with growth formulas. Growth formulas, however, whether of dividends or earnings, rarely strike my Japanese friends or my Japanese students as very compelling. Many Japanese firms, after all, pay only nominal dividends, and the formulas don't make sufficiently clear what investors are really buying when they buy a stock.

Let me therefore shift the focus from a firm's rate of sales or earnings growth to where it ought to be – namely, to the competitive conditions facing the firm over meaningful horizons. And let me, for reasons that will become clear later, measure the strength of those competitive conditions by the currently fashionable market value-to-book value ratio (also known as the "market-to-book" or "price-to-book" ratio). The book-value term in the ratio, based as it is on original cost, approximates what management actually spent for the assets the market is valuing. A market-to-book ratio of 1.0 (abstracting from any concerns about pure price inflation) is thus a natural benchmark, signifying a firm with no competitive advantage or disadvantage. The firm is expected to earn only normal profits in the economists' sense of that term, that is, profits just large enough to give the stockholders the average, risk-adjusted return for equities generally.

To sell for more than an unremarkable market-to-book ratio of 1.0 – that is, to have a positive "franchise value," as some put it – a firm must have long-term competitive advantages allowing it to earn a higher than normal rate of return on its productive assets. And that's not as easy to do as it may seem. Above-normal profits always carry with them the seeds of their own decay. They attract competitors, both from within a country and from abroad, driving profits and share prices relentlessly back toward the competitive norm. Investors buying into a firm are thus making judgments not only about whether the firm and its managers have produced a competitive advantage over their rivals, but also about how far into the future that competitive advantage can be expected to last.

Some specific numbers may help to fix ideas.[1] Consider a U.S. firm with a market-to-book ratio of 3.0 – and there still are many such. And suppose, further, that it will be plowing back its entire cash flow into investments expected to earn *twice* the normal competitive rate of return. By paying three times book value for the shares, investors are in effect anticipating that the firm will expand and stay that far ahead of its competitors *for the next 20 years*!

That's *really* forward-looking – much too forward looking, some would say, in this highly uncertain world. And perhaps that's why so many Japanese managers are instinctively skeptical about using the stock market to guide or evaluate managerial decision-making. They don't really trust the prices in the Japanese stock market where, at the height of the stock market boom of 1989, market-to-book ratios were not just 3.0 but, even after adjusting for real estate and for other corporate shares in cross-holdings, ran routinely to 5.0 or even 10.0. Such ratios implied that investors

saw opportunities for these companies to earn above-normal, competitor-proof returns for centuries to come!

Prices and market-to-book ratios have fallen substantially since then, but are still hard to take seriously because they are not completely free-market prices. The values are not only distorted by the pervasive cross-holdings of nontraded shares, but the prices of the thinly-traded minority of shares in the floating supply often reflect the heroic scale of market intervention by the Ministry of Finance (MOF). Japanese managers can be pardoned for wondering whether the stock market may be just a *Bunraku* theater, with the bureaucrats from MOF backstage manipulating the puppets.

MOF's notorious market support activities also interact in other ways with the issue of corporate governance in Japan. Many academic observers in the U.S. (myself, in particular)[2] have attributed MOF's famous P.K.O. (Price Keeping Operations, and a Japanese pun on the country's participation in the U.N.'s Peace Keeping Operations in Cambodia) to its role as cartel manager for the Japanese brokerage industry. Another motivation traces, however, to the Japanese banking industry. Japanese banks, unlike those in the U.S., can hold equity positions in the companies to which they are also lending – a dual role that, in turn, has often been cited as the real key to Japanese managerial success. The bank connection is said to reduce corporate agency costs, provide better monitoring of corporate decisions, and, above all, allow management to undertake profitable but risky long-run ventures while confident of having the continued financial support needed to carry projects through to completion.

But any gains to the Japanese economy on the governance front have come at a substantial cost on other fronts. Corporate equities can be great assets for banks when the stock market is booming as it was in Japan in the 1980s. The price appreciation

1   The calculations to follow are adapted from the finite growth model presented in Merton H. Miller and Franco Modigliani, "Dividend Policy, Growth and the Valuation of Shares," *Journal of Business*, Vol. 24, No. 4 (October 1961), pp. 411–433. I have taken the value of *rho* (the risk-adjusted cost of capital) as 10 percent (what else?) and the value of *k* (the investment-to-earnings ratio) as 1.0. A firm with a market-to-book ratio of 1.0 corresponds to a "no growth-premium firm" with average internal rate of return (*rho-star*) just equal to the cost of capital.

2   For an account of how MOF systematically uses its regulatory powers to sustain the Japanese brokerage industry cartel and to support the level of stock prices, see my articles, "The Economics and Politics of Index Arbitrage in the U.S. and Japan," *Pacific-Basin Finance Journal*, Vol. 1, No. 1 (May 1993), pp. 3–11; and "Japanese-American Trade Relations in the Financial Services Industry," Working Paper, Graduate School of Business, University of Chicago (September 1993).

then provides the banks with substantial regulatory capital to support their lending activities. But when the stock market collapses, as it did in Japan after 1989, the disappearance of those hidden equity reserves can threaten the solvency of the banks and the integrity of the country's payment system.

The prospect becomes even more frightening when we remember that shareholdings in Japan run in both directions. Not only do banks hold the firm's shares but the firms – again, presumably with a view to better governance – also hold the *banks'* shares. The result is a classic, unstable, positive-feedback asset pyramid. No wonder MOF must keep supporting stock prices and always seems to be running around, like the proverbial Dutch boy on the dikes, plugging holes and leaks in its regulations.

Stock prices and information

To say that the stock market in the U.S. is much closer to the free-market ideal than the Japanese stock market is not to suggest that valuations in the U.S. are always correct. But at least those investors with bearish opinions about particular stocks or the market as a whole can express their pessimism by selling, even selling short, without encountering the kind of anti-selling rules and taboos for which MOF has become notorious. Those pessimists may well be wrong, of course. And so in their turn may be those who are optimistically anticipating a rise in future earnings and prices.

No serious student of stock markets has ever suggested that stock prices always "correctly" measure the true "fundamentals," whatever those words might mean. The most claimed is that the prices are not systematically distorted, like those in Japan where MOF's heavy thumb often tilts the scales against selling. Nor are the prices in the U.S. just some artificial numbers driven by whims and fads, as some academics have argued (and quite unsuccessfully so, in my opinion). The evidence overwhelmingly supports the view that prices reflect in an unbiased way all the information about a company that is available to the investing public.

The word "available" is worth stressing, however. Stockholders and potential outside investors can't be expected to value management's proposed investment projects properly if they don't have the

information on which management has based those plans. And management may well hesitate to disclose that information for fear of alerting competitors. This inevitable "asymmetry" in information, to use the fashionable academic jargon, is what many see as the real flaw in the shareholder-value principle. Projects with positive net present values, possibly even with substantial net present values, may not be undertaken because outside investors cannot value the projects properly and will condemn management for wasting the stockholders' money. That, essentially, is the Porter position. As one way to deal with it, the Porter study recommends that U.S. governance rules be changed to permit firms to disclose proprietary, competitively-sensitive information *selectively* to that subset of the stockholders willing to commit to long-term investing in the company.

Can investment be discouraged by inability to disclose selectively? Possibly. Has it happened? And on what scale? That is much harder to say. The main evidence cited for its pervasiveness in the U.S. is the supposedly superior earnings and growth performance of bank-disciplined Japanese manufacturing firms relative to their impatient American stockholder-disciplined counterparts. Note that I stress Japanese *manufacturing* firms. No one has ever suggested that Japanese market-share-oriented firms were superior in the service industries, notably retailing, or in commercial banking.

And I should say that manufacturing *was* the main evidence for Japanese governance superiority cited before the current recession hit Japan. That recession, painful as has been and still is its impact on the Japanese economy, has at least served to remind us that myopia is not the only disease of vision afflicting business managers. They may suffer from astigmatism (distorted vision) or even from hyperopia or excessive far-sightedness. Looking back over the last 20 years, one may well find cases in which American firms facing strong stockholder pressures to pay out funds invested too little in some kinds of capital-intensive technology. But many Japanese firms, facing no such pressures, have clearly *over*invested during that same period in highly capital-intensive plants that will never come close to recovering their initial investment, let alone earning a positive rate of return. And I won't even mention the trillions of yen poured into land and office buildings both at home and abroad.

No form of corporate governance, needless to say, whether Japanese or American, can guarantee 20-20 vision by management. Mistakes, both of omission and of commission, will always be made. My claim is only that those American managers who *do* focus on maximizing the market value of the firm have a better set of correcting lenses for properly judging the trade-off between current investment and future benefits than those who focus on maximizing growth, market share, or some other, trendy, presumed strategic advantage.

MANAGEMENT OBJECTIVES AND STOCKHOLDER INTERESTS

Glasses help you see better, of course, only if you wear them. And the complaint of at least one wing of American academic opinion, especially in the field of finance, is precisely that U.S. managers don't always wear their stockholder-corrected lenses to work. Because ownership of American corporations is so widely dispersed among a multitude of passive individual and institutional investors, U.S. managers, so the argument runs, are left free to pursue objectives that may, but need not, conform to those of the stockholders.

Shareholders, however, are not powerless. Although neither able nor willing to perform day-by-day monitoring of management operating decisions, shareholders do have the right to elect the company's Board of Directors. And the Board, in turn, by its power to unseat management, and even more by its power to design the program for executive compensation, has command over important levers for aligning management's objectives with those of the shareholders.

Compensation packages and management incentives

The Board of Directors has a tool-box full of levers but not, alas, any simple or fool-proof set of instructions for using them. In fact, academic "agency cost" theory suggests that *no* all-purpose optimal scheme – no "first-best" as opposed to, say, second-best or even lower-best solution – really exists for aligning interests when success depends on luck as well as skill.

To see why, ask yourself how the directors could make the managers accept the stockholders' attitudes toward risk. Suppose, to be specific, that the directors try what may seem the obvious performance-based compensation strategy of giving the managers shares in the company. Will that make managers act like the shareholders would? More so, probably, than if the directors just offered a flat – and presumably high – salary supplemented with generous retirement benefits. Managers so compensated are more likely to be working for the bondholders than for the stockholders. Salaried managers clearly have little incentive to consider projects with serious downside risk.

Giving managers stock at least lets them participate in the gains from their successful moves, but still does not solve the problem of excessive managerial timidity – excessive, that is, relative to the interests of the outside stockholders. Those stockholders are, or at least in principle ought to be, well diversified. They can thus afford risking their entire investment in the company even for only 50:50 odds because their stockholding is only a small part of their total wealth. That, after all, is a key social benefit of the corporate form with fractional and easily transferable ownership interests: more efficient sharing of the business risks. But the managers are typically *not* diversified. A major fraction of their personal wealth and their human capital is tied to the corporation. Caution, not boldness, inevitably becomes their watchword.

The executive stock option was invented in the U.S. in the 1950s precisely to offset the play-it-safe tendencies of underdiversified corporate managers (though tax considerations and accounting conventions have since blurred the original incentive-driven motivation for options).[3] Stock options, suitably structured, work by magnifying the upside potential for the manager relative to the down. A bet paying $1,000 if a coin comes up heads and losing $1,000 if tails would hardly be tempting to the typical risk-averse manager. But tossing a fair coin might well seem attractive if heads brought $5,000 and tails cost only $500.

---

3 See Merton Miller and Myron Scholes, "Executive Compensation, Taxes and Incentives," in *Financial Economics: Essays in Honor of Paul Cootner*, William Sharpe and Catheryn Cootner (Eds.), Prentice-Hall, Englewood Cliffs, NJ, 1982.

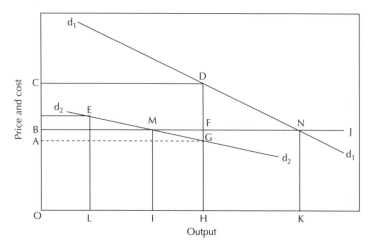

Figure 34.1   Social Versus Private Costs of Losing a Corporate Franchise Premium

Options and their many variations – including option-equivalents like highly leveraged corporate capital structures – not only can reduce management's natural risk-aversion, but may overdo it and tempt managers into excessively risky ventures. If these long-odds strategies do happen to pay off, the managers profit enormously. If not, the bulk of the losses are borne by the shareholders, and probably the bondholders and other prior claimants as well. Many observers feel that a payoff asymmetry of precisely this kind for undercapitalized owner-managers was the root cause of the U.S. Savings and Loan disaster.

The inability to align management interests and risk attitudes more closely with those of the stockholders shows up most conspicuously, some academic critics would argue, in the matter of corporate diversification. Corporate diversification does reduce risk for the managers. But because stockholders can diversify directly, they have little to gain – except perhaps for some tax benefits, large in some cases, from internal offsetting rather than carry-forward of losses – when a General Motors, say, uses funds that might otherwise have been paid as dividends to buy up Ross Perot's firm, Electronic Data Services (EDS). In fairness, however, let it be noted that the stockholders, by the same token, would have little to lose by such acquisitions unless the acquiring firm were to pay too high a price for control – which certainly has been known to happen.

Stockholders could also lose if diversification predictably and consistently means sacrificing the efficiencies from specialization. Some evidence suggests that it does – although hardly enough, in my view, to justify claims by some academic critics of corporate diversification that loss of corporate focus and related failures of governance by GM or IBM or Sears in recent years have destroyed *hundreds of billions* of dollars of their stockholders' and, by extension, of the nation's wealth.

For those firms, certainly, aggregate stock market values have declined substantially. But to treat such declines as a national disaster like some gigantic earthquake is to overlook the distinction between social costs and private costs. Consider, for example, the story told in Figure 34.1, which pictures an IBM-type firm about to be hit unexpectedly with an anti-trust suit (and let it be clearly understood that this is an illustration, and not necessarily a recommendation). The company's initial demand curve is d_1d_1, and its long-run marginal cost is BJ (assumed, for simplicity, to be constant and hence equal to its average cost). Because the firm had "market power," it set its product price at OC (i.e., above average and marginal cost), earning thereby the above-normal profits indicated by the rectangle BCDF. Those above-competitive profits will be capitalized by the stock market and the company will sell for a high market-to-book value premium.

Now let the government win its anti-trust suit against the company and immediately force the company's price and output to their competitive levels (OB for price and OK for quantity). The abnormal profits will vanish, the stock price will fall, and the market-to-book value premium will disappear. Yet no net loss in *national* wealth or welfare has occurred in this instance. Wealth and economic welfare have simply been transferred from the company's shareholders to its customers; producer surplus has been transformed into consumers' surplus. In fact, in the case pictured, society is better off on balance, not worse off. Because output increases to the competitive level, consumers gain additional consumers' surplus in the form of the ("Harberger") triangle DFN.

The social and private consequences are easily distinguished in this anti-trust scenario. But what if the decline in stock-market value is a self-inflicted wound? IBM, after all, did *not* lose its anti-trust case. Its market value was eroded by the entry of new firms with new technologies.

That kind of value erosion, however, surely cannot be the national disaster to which the governance critics are pointing. Why, after all, should society's consumers care whether the new products were introduced by IBM or by Intel or Apple; by Wal-Mart or by Sears; or, for that matter, by General Motors or by Toyota? The complaint of the critics may be rather that the managements of those firms have failed to downsize and restructure fast enough even *after* the new competition had penetrated the market. Entrenched managements, unchecked by the hand-picked sycophants on their Boards, kept pouring money into the old, money-losing lines of the firm's business rather than letting their stockholders redeploy the funds to better advantage elsewhere.

But continuing to make positive investments in a declining industry – "throwing good money after bad," as the cliché would have it – cannot automatically be taken as evidence of economic inefficiency, and certainly not of bad management. Nothing in economic logic or commonsense suggests the best exit path is always the quickest one. A firm withdraws its capital by making its *net* investment negative, that is, by holding its rate of gross investment below the rate of depreciation. The marginal rate of return on that gross investment may well be high even though the average rate of return on the past capital sunk in the division or the firm as a whole is low or even negative.

When the direct costs of exit (such as severance payments) are high, and when the firm is at least covering its variable costs (unlike many in Russia, so we are told), investing to reduce a loss can often be a highly positive net-present-value project indeed.

Suppose, however, for the sake of argument that some entrenched managers *were* too slow in downsizing. The losses reported by their firms still cannot be equated dollar for dollar with the social costs of bad governance. To see why, turn again to Figure 34.1, which can also be used to show the new condition of our original firm – that is, after the entry of the new competition attracted by its earlier high profits. The firm's demand curve is now the much more elastic demand curve d_2d_2, and its new long-run equilibrium level of output will be OL, smaller than its earlier equilibrium output level OH.

Should the firm seek to maintain its earlier market share of OH, however, net losses of ABFG will be incurred, exactly as the critics insist. But only the triangle MFG represents the social cost of the failure to downsize. The rest, given by the area ABMG is, again, merely a transfer to consumer surplus. How much of the reported loss goes one way and how much goes the other cannot be settled, of course, merely from a schematic diagram. That requires specific empirical research of a kind not yet found in the recent academic literature so critical of U.S. corporate governance.

That the losses suffered in recent years by firms like IBM or Sears or General Motors may not be social losses will be of little comfort, of course, to those stockholders who have seen so much of their retirement nest eggs in those companies vanish. One can hardly blame them for wishing that the directors had somehow prodded management to abandon their formerly successful strategies *before* the success of the newer competitive strategies had been so decisively confirmed. Fortunately, however, shareholders whose personal stake is too small to justify costly monitoring of management have another and well-tested way to protect their savings from management's mistakes of omission or commission: diversify! A properly diversified shareholder would have the satisfaction of knowing that his or her loss on IBM shares or Sears or General Motors was not even a *private* loss since it was offset in the portfolio by gains on Microsoft, Intel, Apple,

WalMart and other new-entrant firms, foreign and domestic, that did pioneer in the new technologies.

CONCLUSION

Summing up, then, we have seen two quite different views of what is wrong with American corporate management. One view, widely accepted in Japan and by the Michael Porter wing of academic opinion, is that American managers pay too much attention to current shareholder returns. The other view, widely held among U.S. academic finance specialists, is that American managers pay too little attention to shareholder returns.

Which view is right? Both. And neither. Both sides can point to specific cases or examples seeming to support their positions. But both are wrong in claiming any permanent or systematic bias for U.S. firms in the aggregate toward myopia or hyperopia, toward underinvestment or overinvestment relative either to the shareholders' or to society's best interests. There is no inherent bias because market forces are constantly at work to remove control over corporate assets from managers who lack the competence or the vision to deploy them efficiently.

We saw those forces most dramatically perhaps in the takeover battles, leveraged buyouts, and corporate restructurings of the 1980s and, more recently, in many well-publicized board-led insurgencies. But, for all their drama, those events (which often seem little more than struggles over how the corporate franchise premium is to be shared between the executives and the shareholders) represent only one part – and by no means the most important part – of the process of allocating society's productive capital among firms. The ultimate discipline for the managers of one firm in the U.S. will always be the managers of other firms, including foreign firms, competing with them head to head for customer business. As long as we continue to have plenty of *that* kind of competition in the U.S., I, for one, can't become terribly concerned about the supposedly fatal flaws in our governance system.

CHAPTER 35

The Role of Corporate Governance in South Korean Economic Reform

Kenneth Scott (Stanford University Law School)*

At the beginning of 1997, the "Asian tigers" had achieved decades of remarkable growth, and they were being held up as models for the rest of the less-developed world to follow. Their economies typically combined elements of both business free enterprise and governmental control of investment, usually exerted through the banking system. The ruling politicians directed the banks' lending policies and even individual decisions; the banks received implicit government (central bank) guarantees; the favored borrowers could expand rapidly, if not necessarily prudently; and the politicians received large contributions from the favored firms. It was a system exemplifying not Western-style party democracy and checks-and-balances, but "Asian values" of hard work, social order, and deference to authority.

The second half of 1997, however, subjected the concept of a new Asian model of economic development to a series of severe tests. Beginning in July, first Thailand and then the Philippines, Malaysia, and Indonesia were forced to abandon their attempts to control exchange rates, and to let their currencies float (and sink) in the open market.

Companies and banks with large amounts of short-term, foreign-currency-denominated debt quickly saw themselves confronting bankruptcy. The most recent, and most important, addition to this list is South Korea. In December the International Monetary Fund responded with a $57 billion loan and credit assistance package, which soon had to be supplemented with efforts to obtain another $10 billion in new credit from an international consortium of private banks.[1]

The causes and consequences of this series of Asian economic crises will be examined and debated for some time to come, and of course there are meaningful differences from one country to another. Whether the outcome will be significant and lasting reform in the way some of these economies are run remains to be seen, despite the conditions attached to IMF assistance programs. As with all bailout programs, the problem is that they also tend to perpetuate flawed institutions and relieve borrowers and lenders from some of the losses resulting from their decisions. In this respect, market discipline is undermined. But if there is such reform, one – among many – of the ingredients that will have to be considered is a change in the system of corporate governance for banks and

---

*   This article draws on a presentation at the KDI-Hoover Joint Conference, "Agenda for Economic Reform in Korea: International Perspectives," January 15–16, 1997, and on "Agency Costs and Corporate Governance," in *The New Palgrave Dictionary of Economics and the Law* (P. Newman, ed. 1998).

1   "Foreign Banks May Lend $10 Billion to Seoul," *Wall St. Journal*, Dec. 30, 1997, p. A6.

business firms. Such large enterprises are now often run more in the interest of the government and the controlling shareholder group than in the interest of efficiency and maximizing aggregate shareholder wealth.

This article will examine that general proposition in terms of the structure of corporate governance in South Korea. The IMF Staff Report on the Korean situation noted that "there is an urgent need to improve corporate governance and the corporate structure."[2] The rest of this article falls into four sections. The first discusses the threshold issues of why and when corporate governance is significant. The second looks at how corporate governance institutions function in different countries, focusing primarily on the United States, Japan, and Germany. The third undertakes to develop from the comparative analysis some criteria by which to appraise corporate governance systems. The fourth and concluding section applies the analysis specifically to South Korean institutions and attempts to evaluate the reforms now being suggested.

WHEN AND WHY CORPORATE GOVERNANCE IS IMPORTANT

To make a coherent analysis of a set of corporate governance institutions, it is necessary to specify the objective being sought. Modern corporations, to take advantage of technological progress and scale economies, are large organizations requiring heavy capital investment. The amounts of capital required often can be raised only by pooling the savings of a multitude of investors, who must rely on others to manage their investments and run the enterprise. The institutions – the particular set of legal rules, incentives, and behaviors – that support and underlie that reliance by investors constitute the system of corporate governance in a given society.

In this paper I will assume that the objective is to maximize the economic efficiency of the firm. Discussions of corporate governance sometimes appear to be addressing other concerns – such as monopolistic or oligopolistic power, the welfare of

particular constituencies, or macroeconomic stability. Those are all valid issues, but the design of corporate governance is not a very direct or effective way to deal with them. It has a real and important contribution to make to economic efficiency, but only a tangential bearing on numerous other matters.

It should be noted that other institutions and forces also come to bear on the operations of the firm, pushing it toward greater efficiency. Foremost among them are the pressures that arise from competition in the product and factor markets. Perfect competition, domestically and internationally, would work to eliminate this and many other problems, but in its absence corporate governance continues to be a matter worth attention.

In terms of economic efficiency, my focus will be on the cost of external equity capital to the firm – the price, in the sense of expected returns, that the firm must offer outside investors to get them to buy stock in the enterprise. Why are shareholders willing to turn large sums of money over to other people (managers) to invest in specialized assets on very ill-defined terms? The managers of the firm do not tell them when they will get their money returned or what compensation will be paid for its use. Others who furnish inputs to the business are not so vague about arrangements for payment.

Why are shareholders' property rights so poorly defined? The usual answer is that the stockholders' essential function necessitates that condition. They are the bearers of the residual risk of the firm, enabling others to contract with it on more definite terms; their claims come last, after all other various contingencies and claims are satisfied, and hence it is impractical to try to spell them out in detail under all states of the world. The status of stockholders provides a paradigm of the (highly) "incomplete" contract. As such, it leaves the stockholder potentially quite vulnerable to managers acting incompetently or in their own interests.

If the position of stockholders cannot be well protected by contract, then how is it made viable? There are two principal mechanisms that serve this function. One is law: fiduciary rules that require managers (agents) to act in the best interests of stockholders (principals). The other is governance: a set of provisions that enable the stockholders by exercising voting power to compel those in operating control of the firm to respect their interests.

2 International Monetary Fund Document, "Republic of Korea – Request for Stand-By Arrangement," Washington, D.C., December 3, 1997, p. 15, ¶51.

Legal fiduciary rules can best address relatively clear conflicts of interest; issues of managerial competence, except in egregious cases, fall in the domain of governance.

Obviously, corporate governance is not a problem for the 100%-owner-manager of a business. Nor is it much of a problem for the majority stockholder (or group) which controls the board of directors and can fire the managers at any time. (Protection for minority interests in such a firm will have to come primarily from fiduciary rules, since their voting power is generally ineffectual.) So corporate governance is an issue mainly for minority stockholders in companies that are controlled by the managers and where there are no significant stockholders that can easily work together. In that situation, the stockholders potentially can still exert control through the board to protect their interests, but they face formidable difficulties (in terms of transaction costs and inadequate incentives) in acting together and actually doing so.

In a practical sense, therefore, corporate governance is important as a means of reducing the "agency costs" imposed by managers acting in their own interests to the detriment of shareholders, mainly, again, in firms owned by dispersed stockholders. How large a concern is this? That depends on the prevalence of such firms in the economy, and hence will vary across countries. Reliance on external equity finance displays a wide range, from firm to firm and nation to nation. The explanations for that range constitute one of the major areas of controversy and investigation in the field of corporate finance and governance.

A starting point is to inquire why a firm would wish to rely on external equity finance at all. The usual answer is that it is cheaper to finance through the stock market because portfolio investors can diversify away the "non-systematic" or firm-specific risk, and the issuer thus pays a risk premium only for the systematic or remaining risk. Stock market equity is also believed by many to reduce the corporate cost of capital by opening up the potential supply of capital. A lower cost of capital for the firm (or a nation's economy) in turn increases, *ceteris paribus*, profitability, economic growth, and international competitiveness.

But recourse to public capital markets also means greater exposure of owners to agency costs, and thus greater need for corporate governance

institutions and rules to limit the extent to which managers can mismanage the firm, divert wealth from shareholders, and extract "control rents." If the objective seems desirable enough, then what is controversial? How best to achieve it.

A BRIEF OVERVIEW OF INTERNATIONAL CORPORATE GOVERNANCE SYSTEMS

Since all countries and economic systems face the problem of how to economize on principal-agent costs, one approach to an answer is to look around the world and see how it has been dealt with. The comparative approach, which has attracted considerable attention over the last decade, focuses on the three largest and most developed economies: the United States, Japan and Germany. Each has a distinctive set of institutions. A full description would be quite lengthy and go beyond the scope of this paper, but each is usually characterized in terms of an "ideal type" (even though it does not reflect the actual diversity and complexity to be found in each nation).

For the United States, the ideal type is the so-called Berle-Means corporation,[3] with equity ownership diffused among a multitude of small stockholders and a self-perpetuating management firmly in control under most circumstances. A degree of discipline over management is provided by the threat, and occasionally the reality, of proxy contests, hostile takeovers, and leveraged buy-outs. Legal rules also impose on directors and officers certain fiduciary duties – particularly the duty of loyalty – which "require" them in conflict-of-interest situations to act in the best interest of the stockholders rather than of themselves. That general admonition has received development in a number of recurring patterns, and is enforced through civil liability actions brought by attorneys on behalf of shareholders.

Underneath the ideal type lie many questions. How accurate is it for the U.S. economy? Institutional as opposed to individual investors now own almost half of the total U.S. equity market, but

---

3 This designation comes from Adolph Berle and Gardiner Means's 1932 classic, *The Modern Corporation and Private Property* (New York: Macmillan, 1932).

there are thousands of institutional investors (including pension funds, mutual funds, insurance companies, trust companies, foundations, charities and endowments). How much less acute is *their* collective action problem? In the 25 largest U.S. corporations, on average 27.5% of the common stock is held by the top 25 institutional investors.[4] But, as capitalization size decreases, so in general does the institutional share (though exact data on this are lacking). And various financial and securities statutes impose a set of technical legal impediments to significant holdings and coordinated action by institutional investors, although the latter were somewhat eased in 1992.

As for fiduciary duties, just how effective are they? There is a multitude of different rules for different contexts, ranging from criminal penalties for theft and embezzlement to civil liability for "unfair" self-dealing and to amorphous admonitions to treat minority shareholders with inherent fairness in a holding company formation. Enforcement also faces a collective action or free rider problem, handled with the devices of derivative suits and class actions, but the latter in turn have their own agency costs.

In Japan, the ideal type is the "keiretsu," thought of as a group of companies linked by stable cross-shareholdings and seller-buyer relationships. A parent company, or more often a main bank, is supposed to act as the administrator for the group, monitoring management performance of the member firms and intervening in cases of sufficient financial distress.[5] Non-member shareholdings constitute a substantial minority of the ownership of most of the member firms; but the public shareholders are inactive investors, and discipline exerted through market mechanisms such as hostile takeovers is almost unheard of.

Again, there are questions as to the extent to which the keiretsu pattern describes the current Japanese economy. Much of the literature is descriptive and assertive, not numerical or empirical. The role of the main bank, which cannot itself

own more than 5% in any company, was not much tested before the crash at the end of 1989. And, in part because of the propensity in Japanese accounting and bank supervision to conceal rather than disclose financial losses, the main bank system has not received definitive analysis since. It may be undergoing significant change, under current economic pressures.[6] With the main banks themselves in trouble, rescue operations for keiretsu members seem to have become hard to find.

The cross-shareholdings and transaction relationships are laden with potential conflict-of-interest dangers for the interests of outside stockholders, and it is not known how they have fared. The Japanese legal system does not rely on a general fiduciary duty of managers to act in the best interest of stockholders; instead, directors may be liable for gross negligence in performance of their duties, including the duty to supervise. The duty and liability run to the company, however, and enforcement by derivative suits is a relatively new phenomenon.

In Germany, the standard account looks at only a few hundred large firms, listed on the stock exchanges and operating under the two-tier (supervisory and management) board system required of companies with more than 2,000 employees (who elect half the supervisory board). Major (over 25%) block-holders are common. Even more significant is the role of the firm's house bank and other banks in terms of their voting power. German banks, as universal banks, can own corporate stock, unlike U.S. banks. In addition, in a system of bearer shares, German banks are the primary depositaries for public stockholders and vote their proxies; the banks also run investment funds and vote those shares. The result is that banks in 1992 cast on average 84% of the votes at the annual shareholder meetings of the 24 largest widely held stock corporations.[7]

Does this mean that in Germany banks act as effective institutional monitors on behalf of shareholders? The answer is far from clear, since the

4   Institutional Investment Report 1997, Vol. No. 2 (New York: The Conference Board, 1997) p. 36.
5   See Masahiko Aoki, "Monitoring Characteristics of the Main Bank System: An Analytical and Developmental View," in, eds., Masahiko Aoki and Hugh Patrick, *The Japanese Main Bank System* (New York: Oxford University Press, 1994).

6   See Paul Sheard, "Financial System Reform and Japanese Corporate Governance," working paper, Baring Asset Management (Japan) Limited (1997).
7   See Theodor Baums, "Universal Banks and Investment Companies in Germany," in, eds., Anthony Saunders and Ingo Walter, *Universal Banking: Financial System Design Reconsidered* (Chicago: Irwin, 1996).

same structure applies to the banks themselves. The five largest universal banks as a group cast between 54% and 64% of the votes in 1992 at their own shareholder meetings, though no one had an absolute majority at its own meeting. If the banks' managements are relatively unconstrained by other shareholders or the stock market, how is their discretion employed?

The legal system is not thought of as playing much of a role in German corporate governance. The civil law is not congenial to the broad fiduciary concepts of Anglo-American equity law. Supervisory board directors really do not have much decision-making responsibility, and co-determination has been criticized as undermining even its monitoring effectiveness.[8] Management board directors could act negligently or commit torts, but the institutions of the derivative suit or class action are unknown. For stockholders to sue management in such a situation, it would take a majority at a general meeting, or at least 10% to file a court petition; obviously it is a rare occurrence.

Suppose we leave the world of the most highly developed market economies and go to the world of the less-developed countries and emerging market economies. Now the typical pattern (to the extent the economy is not state-run) is one of companies closely held or dominated by a founder, his family, and associates. The role of external equity finance is small; the business is financed by retained earnings and heavily by debt (often on a political or subsidized basis from government-controlled banks). The effective constraints of the legal system on managers may be weak or non-existent, a condition which Russia at this point seems to exemplify.

What explains all these variations? We do not have convincing explanations, in part because we do not even have a good factual picture of corporate governance variables across the world. Of course, even in the absence of comprehensive information, one can speculate. There is a large political component in the generation of these different institutional structures. Mark Roe, among other law and economics scholars, has demonstrated how the American antipathy to private

concentrations of economic power led to statutes that geographically fragmented the banking industry and prohibited banks and insurance companies from owning stock.[9] Such restrictions, Roe argues, effectively prevented U.S. financial institutions from playing the governance role of their counterparts in Germany and Japan. Germany, in particular, had by the end of the 19th century developed large, nationwide universal banks with close relationships to industrial clients. As Roe also notes, however, the banks have both directly and indirectly stymied the growth of the public securities market, thus discouraging another potential source of corporate monitoring. In Japan, the goverment took control of the banking industry during World War II and used it to allocate capital to the industrial sector. After the war, with private capital exceedingly scarce, there was no significant stock market and government policy continued to be to finance industrial growth through bank debt, supporting the power of the main bank over its group of client firms. Such thumbnail sketches are not intended as explanations, but to suggest that understanding existing corporate governance systems goes beyond the pressures for economic efficiency to a consideration of historical "path-dependency" and other factors.

So which system is preferable? Is that even an answerable question? I have already mentioned the problem of data that are not available or have not been collected and tabulated. For no country, including the United States, can we paint a picture of the entire corporate governance structure. In comparative terms, no one has even attempted to go beyond a half dozen or so of the largest countries.[10]

But there are difficulties at a deeper level. How would one undertake to measure, in any rigorous way, the effectiveness of corporate governance across nations? How do you isolate and measure agency costs for an economy? In the 1980s, the tendency was simply to say that if economic growth rates in Japan or Germany had been higher than in the U.S., corporate governance was

---

8 See Katharina Pistor, "Co-determination in Germany," working paper, Harvard Institute for International Development, 1997.

9 Mark Roe, *Strong Managers, Weak Owners: The Political Roots of American Corporate Finance* (Princeton: University Press, 1994).
10 See Andrei Shleifer and Robert Vishny, "A Survey of Corporate Governance," *Journal of Finance* 52 (1997), pp. 737–83.

one of the factors at work and their systems might be better. If that pattern reverses over the 1990s, does the conclusion reverse? In the absence of good direct measures of corporate governance efficiency, some studies have resorted to the use of proxies, such as the rates of board turnover or management turnover, the level of discretionary spending or free cash flow, or the likelihood of takeover bids and acquisition. All proxies have their flaws, and methodology remains an issue and concern. At this time, we have more plausible stories than well-tested hypotheses.

Furthermore, critics of corporate governance systems and proposals argue that any system has costs that must be accounted for along with the expected benefits from the reduction of control rents and mismanagement. One widely alleged cost of the U.S. system is that market-based discipline creates an undesirable management orientation toward short-term stock price performance rather than long-term investment returns and growth. The argument rests on the proposition that the stock market is "myopic" – that, in pricing companies, it consistently overdiscounts longer-term expected cash flows and returns. There are various models of "asymmetric information" and accounts of short-term speculative bubbles that attempt to give more "structure" to this argument. Nevertheless, actual empirical evidence of consistent discount myopia in the stock market is weak;[11] and, even if it were persuasive, it would raise questions going far beyond matters of corporate governance.

Another criticism of corporate governance as analyzed here is that it should not be judged in terms of economic efficiency, the cost of capital, and shareholder wealth, but should take into account effects on other "constituencies" such as employees, suppliers, customers, managers, and the community at large.[12] All are characterized as "stakeholders," and the corporate governance system is to be judged by how well all interests are served. A focus on shareholders, it is argued, does not take into account costs imposed on these other stakeholders. What is invariably omitted from the

argument, however, is consideration of the extent to which these other interests can protect themselves by contract. Moreover, many of these stakeholders can not really be said to make firm-specific investments that are subject to expropriation by management. Thus, we are returned to a point with which we began: what is unique about stockholder claims is the fact that they are long-term, residual, and necessarily poorly defined.

EVALUATING DIFFERENT CORPORATE GOVERNANCE SYSTEMS

But perhaps we do not need to be able to arrive at a logical and analytical answer to the question of which set of corporate governance rules is to be preferred. We can employ the test of economic survival – does not competition in the product market force evolution toward the most efficient governance structure? We have noted one qualification of that argument; political forces can impose fundamental constraints on the available economic choices. That makes it hard to assert that the U.S. or German or Japanese system would be best for others. Still, each of those systems has worked well enough to sustain capital accumulation, investment, and economic growth in a leading economy. By looking at their common elements, rather than their differences, we may be able to draw some tentative conclusions.

First, what can we say about their legal institutions? I do not feel altogether comfortable in going beyond the United States, but can at least offer some impressions. To begin, a distinction should be made between legal rules that define and protect shareholder voting rights and their ability to assert control, and legal rules that substitute for (or supplement) shareholder control by imposing enforceable duties on managers. There is a fairly well-developed set of laws establishing voting and control rights for shareholders in each country, although it is not difficult to suggest improvements. This would seem to be a minimum requirement for any effective corporate governance system, but it is lacking in some countries.

The importance of fiduciary duties, or their equivalent, has been less studied. One can postulate a continuum of situations involving conflicts of interest between managers and owners, with the

---

11 See Jeffrey Abarbanell and Victor Bernard, "Is the U.S. Stock Market Myopic?," working paper, Michigan Business School, 1995.
12 See Oliver Williamson, *The Economic Institutions of Capitalism* (New York: The Free Press, 1985), Chapter 12.

conflict becoming less sharp (and perhaps the legal rules less essential). At one extreme would be outright theft, embezzlement, and misappropriation; without effective legal sanctions in these cases, only the gullible would part with their money. A somewhat less transparent form of achieving the same end is the self-dealing transaction between the manager and his firm. By buying too low or selling too high, the controlling party transfers wealth from the firm to himself, but the picture can be confused by intricate transactions in non-standard assets or subject to varying degrees of price unfairness. Enforcement becomes more difficult, but still seems essential if agency costs are to have any bound. The appropriation of corporate opportunities, excessive compensation, and consumption of managerial perks can be still more judgmental, and probably the legal rules are less effective, but the order of magnitude is also less. And when one reaches conflicts highly intertwined with the regular operation of the business, such as excessive diversification or self-retention by less competent managers, the fiduciary duty of loyalty (or the Japanese duty of supervision) probably offers little protection.

The United States has, it is my impression, gone considerably farther along this continuum than Japan or Germany. How effectively is hard to measure; the subject has not received much attention.[13] But it cannot simply be ignored by any corporate governance system intended to sustain external finance, particularly for companies in which there is a controlling majority shareholder or group. They may still be constrained to some extent by considerations of reputation, or the need for repeated dealings, but that is a constraint that disappears whenever the controlling party chooses to be free of it.

Second, all three systems have found methods for combining economic and control rights into large blocks, in order to overcome the ineffectualness of fragmented voting power. In Germany it takes the form of large investors, with their voting clout sometimes augmented by proxy control. In Japan, it takes the form of coordinated networks, acting through institutions like the presidents' council and the main bank. Both of those arrangements are relatively stable, whereas in the U.S. the aggregation is often ad hoc; voting power is assembled for the occasion, through a proxy contest or tender offer or leveraged buyout. The techniques differ, but they appear to be addressing a common need in an effective corporate governance system. Of course, where the arrangement is stable, it can be turned against outside minority stockholders.

In the last analysis, for many reasons we probably cannot point to an individual system as the best under all circumstances. There is some basis for identifying shortcomings or proposing improvements, but a number of quite distinctive institution arrangements seem to work at least passably and perhaps equivalently well.[14] That suggests a strategy of not adopting or entrenching any single system, but creating, if possible, the opportunity for any of them to take root and demonstrate superiority, even if only in a special niche.[15]

For the U.S., that strategy would mean removing the legal impediments to financial institutions accumulating more significant blocks, and to blockholders working together to monitor and, if necessary, to replace management. For Germany, it would mean encouraging the deepening of the securities market and the capacity of stockholders to oust management (currently usually protected in office by five-year contracts). For Japan, it would mean accepting the role of hostile tender offers and other forms of capital market discipline.

Of course, in each country there are political barriers to such reforms, led by managements and sometimes unions, and so the reforms may not be attainable. But there are also those who would benefit from enhanced corporate governance, and this might be a sensible strategy for them to follow; the tactics that would have the best prospect of success depend upon local political institutions and forces.

13   Notable very recent exceptions are Shleifer and Vishny (1997), cited in footnote 10; and Rafael LaPorta, Florencio Lopez-de-Silane, Andrei Shleifer, and Robert Vishny, "Legal Determinants of External Finance," working paper no. 5879 (Cambridge: National Bureau of Economic Research, 1997).

14   See Steven Kaplan, "Top Executives, Turnover, and Firm Performance in Germany," *Journal of Law, Economics, and Organization* 10 (1994), pp. 142–59; and Steven Kaplan, "Top Executive Rewards and Firm Performance: A Comparison of Japan and the United States," *Journal of Political Economy* 102 (1994).

15   Roe (1994), cited in footnote 9.

REFORMING THE SOUTH KOREAN GOVERNANCE SYSTEM

In conclusion, how does all of this apply to Korea? In the discussion that follows, my account of the Korean corporate governance system, as well as proposals to reform it, draws heavily on recent work by Korean governance scholars – in particular, a 1996 study by Young Ki Lee.[16]

The "ideal type" for Korea seems to be the *chaebol*, best described as a conglomerate web of firms, linked by indirect cross-shareholdings and a common founding-chairman in the core companies. The founder and his family on average own about 10%, and through cross-holdings control another 30% to 40%, of the group member firms. In those companies that are listed, financial institutions own about 30% of the equity. This is a picture of the family-dominated firm, mentioned earlier as typical for emerging economies, in which control rents are likely to be high.

Professor Lee's 1996 study does not describe the extent to which the legal system attempts to limit those control rents, beyond noting that board members do not represent outside shareholders, who are said to be "overlooked." The role of auditors is described as "atrophied." In addition, a set of managerial prerogatives known as "management right" was protected until 1997 by a prohibition of hostile tender offers, and custodians of public shares are prohibited from casting independent votes at the annual meeting (i.e., they "shadow vote").

The government has pursued a number of policies with the professed aim of "achieving wider shareholding." Listing on the first tier of the stock exchange now requires that over 40% of the company's stock be held by shareholders owning less than 1%, and that the principal owner and his family own not more than 51%. Cross-shareholdings by a firm may not exceed 25% of its net equity capital. A bank cannot without permission own over 10% of a company's shares, and no shareholder can own more than 4% of a bank. As can be seen, these rules work mainly to disperse outside shareholder voting power but do not threaten the continuance of dominance by the insider control group.

Professor Lee's study also reviews a number of proposals that have been made to improve Korean corporate governance. The suggested reforms have included strengthening the position of internal and outside auditors, allowing mergers and acquisitions approved by a panel, requiring more outside directors on boards, introducing the German supervisory board or two-tier system, and allowing banks to own greater equity shares in companies. Some of these same measures are promised in the government's request to the IMF for assistance.[17]

To aid in evaluating these and other reform proposals, there are a number of principles that we can derive, at least tentatively, from the body of experience that is available:

(1) Attention should be paid to the state of legal protection from transactions involving potential conflicts of interest. Governance in the narrow sense – the exercise of voting rights – is of little immediate help to minority shareholders confronting a controlling block. This is particularly significant if one is concerned with start-up technology firms in the Silicon Valley mode; venture capital firms are medium-term investors who need an exit for their investments in the form of an active IPO market.

(2) It is not enough to note that someone – a house bank, or main bank, or outside directors, or supervisory board – possesses the power to be an effective monitor of management. One must also examine closely their incentives to so act, and observe their performance in actual practice. Where direct incentives are mixed or weak, as in all of the above cases, it may be a mistake to have high expectations. There is no real substitute for the possession or acquisition by the outsiders of a major economic stake in the firm's success.

(3) Charging management or the board with a legal mandate to "balance" the interests of

16   See Young Ki Lee, "Corporate Governance in Korea: The Structure and Issues," working paper, Korea Development Institute, 1996; and see also Young Ki Lee and Young Jae Lim, "Corporate Governance in Korea: Issues and Prospects," working paper, Korea Development Institute, 1997.

17   International Monetary Fund Document, cited in note 2, Anx. III, p. 10, ¶30.

various constituencies or stakeholders is merely to diminish any legally enforceable responsibility to shareholders, without creating a definable obligation to any one else. In the United States, such statutes have been used by management primarily to enlarge their discretion to ignore shareholder preferences in hostile takeover situations. The result is to increase the scope of potential control rents and agency costs.

(4) Who pays for (such an increase in) agency costs? The existing owners of the firm, not new shareholders purchasing in the market – the price the new shareholders pay will reflect the reduction in their share of expected cash flows to the firm. This means that it is the owners of family firms, when they sell shares to the public at a higher price, who are the beneficiaries of effective legal rules and corporate governance. If better understood, this fact would facilitate the adoption of what are usually described as "shareholder" protections.

(5) The largest beneficiary of a more effective corporate system, however, is the nation as a whole, since the improvements in management performance and reductions in cost of capital in the economy aid it in domestic productivity and international competitiveness.

Applying these principles to the reforms being considered in South Korea suggests that the accomplishments will be modest. To begin, I am not aware of serious attention to the protection of minority shareholders from conflict-of-interest transactions, which have been commonplace in the chaebol structure. There is mention of enhanced disclosure, through consolidated balance sheets and enforcement of accounting standards in line with GAAP. But the legal rules to be applied to the disclosed transactions are a separate matter. Reliance on capital market discipline presupposes a capital market in which outside investors are willing to play a large role.

Further, capital market discipline also involves the possibility of outside investors being able to displace poorly performing management, even where it possesses a significant (though not controlling) ownership share. The only mechanism referred to in this regard is a liberalization of restrictions on mergers and acquisitions, along with the interesting promise that "bankruptcy provisions according to Korean law will be allowed to operate without government interference."[18] There is also a somewhat opaque statement that "[l]egislation concerning hostile takeovers will be submitted to the first special session of the National Assembly to harmonize Korean legislation on abuse of dominant positions in line with other industrial countries' standards."[19] It is doubtful that the chaebols' founding chairmen have much to fear.

One potentially important commitment by the government, however, is that it will discontinue directed lending and permit commercial banks to be run by their boards in the interest of their shareholders rather than the government.[20] That step, if taken, would be a rather drastic shift away from the Asian model.

---

18 International Monetary Fund Document, cited in footnote 2, Annex III, p. 45, ¶35.
19 Ibid., p. 44, ¶32.
20 Ibid., p. 45, ¶34.

CHAPTER 36

Corporate Ownership and Control in the U.K., Germany, and France

Julian Franks (London Business School), and Colin Mayer (Oxford University)*

Differences among national financial systems have been a subject of continuing debate for well over a century. The primary distinction drawn by economists has been that between "bank-based" and "market-based" systems.[1] In the stylized description of bank-based systems, companies raise most of their external finance from banks that have close, long-term relationships with their corporate customers. By contrast, the market-based systems of the U.K. and the U.S. are characterized by arm's-length relationships between corporations and investors, who are said to be concerned primarily about short-term returns.

While these distinctions cannot be dismissed, they have proved to be difficult to formulate with much precision. Empirical evidence does not provide grounds for the sharp distinction that would have been expected if there were fundamental differences in the structure and operation of national economies. Nevertheless, there is one area in which there are clear differences in the structure and conduct of economies that are deep-rooted and open to quite precise quantification. These differences concern the ownership and control of corporations.

In their 1932 classic, *The Modern Corporation and Private Property*, Adolph Berle and Gardiner Means warned that the growing dispersion of ownership of U.S. stocks was giving rise to a potentially value-reducing separation of ownership and control.[2] In 1976, the general argument of Berle and Means was given a more rigorous formulation by Michael Jensen and William Meckling in their theory of "agency costs."[3] Agency costs, loosely speaking, are reductions in value resulting from the separation of ownership from control in public corporations. Pointing to a roughly tenfold decline in the

* This paper is a revised version of a paper entitled "Ownership and Control" that was written for the International Workshop at the Kiel Institute on "Trends in Business Organization: Increasing Competitiveness by Participation and Cooperation," June 13 and 14, 1994. It is based on an inaugural lecture that was given by Colin Mayer at the University of Warwick on February 1, 1993. It is part of a project funded by the ESRC (no. W102251003) on "Capital Markets, Corporate Governance and the Market for Corporate Control." We are grateful to participants at the workshop for helpful comments and in particular to our discussant, Martin Hellwig. We are also grateful to Marc Goergen and Luis Correia da Silva for research assistance on the project.
1 For recent interesting examples of this, see F. Allen and D. Gale, "A Welfare Comparison of the German and US

Financial Systems," CEPR-Fundacion BBV Conference, April 1994; and J. Edwards and K. Fischer, *Banks, Finance and Investment in Germany* (Cambridge: Cambridge University Press, 1994).
2 A. Berle and G. Means, *The Modern Corporation and Private Property* (New York: Macmillan, 1932).
3 For the original formulation of agency theory, see M. Jensen and W. Meckling, "Theory of the Firm: Managerial Behavior, Agency Costs and Ownership Structure," *Journal of Financial Economics*, No. 3 (1976).

percentage of managerial stock ownership of large U.S. public companies between the 1930s and the 1980s, Jensen argued that dispersed ownership was leading to major inefficiencies in U.S. companies, particularly in the form of widespread conglomeration. In this view, the rise of hostile takeovers and LBOs in the 1980s was a value-increasing response by U.S. capital markets – one that reduced agency costs by removing inefficient managers and, especially in the case of LBOs, concentrating corporate ownership.[4]

More recently, however, a study by Harold Demsetz and Kenneth Lehn has argued that concentrated ownership is likely to have had significant costs as well as benefits.[5] That is, besides providing stronger incentives to maximize value, concentrated ownership can impose costs in two ways: (1) by forcing managers and other inside shareholders to bear excessive company-specific risks – risks that could be borne at lower cost by well-diversified outside stockholders; and (2) by allowing inside owners to capture private benefits at the expense of minority or outside owners. In the view of Demsetz and Lehn, ownership patterns should reflect a trade-off between the incentive benefits of concentrated ownership and the expected costs arising from excessive concentration of risk and the potential for expropriating minority holders.

In this paper, after a brief summary of existing theories of corporate ownership and control, we describe patterns of ownership in France, Germany, and the U.K. We also review the evidence (much of it our own) on the operation of the market for corporate control in the U.K. and Germany. As we conclude, none of the existing theories offers a completely satisfying explanation of the differences between the *insider* ownership systems of Germany and France, on the one hand, and the *outsider* systems of the U.S. and the U.K. on the other. Nevertheless, given the durability of the two systems, both appear to have devised effective ways of disciplining poor managers and otherwise promoting efficiency.

THEORIES OF OWNERSHIP AND CONTROL

There are two strands of literature that are relevant to this discussion. The first concerns the determinants of corporate ownership, and the second focuses on the operation of the market for corporate control.

With regard to ownership there are three classes of models. The first is the industrial economics literature on vertical relationships – for example, those between manufacturers and their suppliers. This class of models seeks to explain the tendency of upstream and downstream firms to own each other (or to remain independent companies) in terms of the "externalities" that may exist between the parties.[6] For example, upstream firms will not always take full account of the interests of downstream firms in the prices that they charge and the way in which they treat their purchasers. In such a case, joint ownership may be required to "internalize this externality" in the absence of suitable contractual alternatives.

A second, related, class of literature on ownership argues that transaction costs may make transactions through markets more costly than internal activities within the firm.[7] It may be difficult or costly to write the contracts necessary to undertake transactions between firms through the marketplace. Discouraging "opportunistic" breaches of implicit contracts may be accomplished more effectively inside the firm than through the marketplace.

A third literature on ownership is concerned with the effect of incomplete contracts on the incentives that firms have to make long-term, highly specialized investments – the kind of investments

4   See M. Jensen, "The Agency Costs of Free Cash Flow: Corporate Finance and Takeovers," *American Economic Review* 76 (May, 1986); and M. Jensen, "The Eclipse of the Public Corporation," *Harvard Business Review* (1989).

5   H. Demsetz and K. Lehn, "The Structure of Corporate Ownership: Causes and Consequences," *Journal of Political Economy*, 93 (1985), 1155–77.

6   See, for example, A. Dixit, "Vertical Integration in a Monopolistically Competitive Industry," *International Journal of Industrial Organization*, 1 (1983), 63–78; M. Salinger, "Vertical Merger and Market Foreclosure," *Quarterly Journal of Economics*, 103 (1988), 345–56; and W. Waterson, "Vertical Integration, Variable Proportions and Oligopoly," *Economic Journal*, 92 (1982), 129–44.

7   See, for example, R. Coase, "The Nature of the Firm," *Economica*, 4 (1937), 386–405; O. Williamson, *Markets and Hierarchies: Analysis and Anti-Trust Implications* (New York: Free Press, 1975); O. Williamson, *The Economic Institutions of Capitalism* (New York: Free Press, 1985); and M. Aoki, B. Gustafsson, and O. Williamson, *The Firm as a Nexus of Treaties* (London: European Sage, 1988).

that would have little value if transferred beyond the context of the particular firm.[8] Joint or vertical ownership is viewed as a means of encouraging such "firm-specific" investments by guaranteeing that important parties will honor their implicit commitments to projects involving joint effort (for example, those involving suppliers and manufacturers).

According to this theory, one would expect to see joint ownership where (1) it is difficult to use contracts to avoid expropriation of subsequent returns; (2) there is a high degree of "complementarity" between the assets of the two firms; and (3) one of the assets or one of the owners of the assets is particularly important to the other party and should therefore become the owner of both the assets. These theories suggest that we would expect patterns of ownership to reflect complementarities in production.

The second major strand of literature is concerned with corporate control. Separation of ownership and control in outsider systems like the U.S. and the U.K. has prompted the rise and refinement of a number of mechanisms designed to limit the agency problems with dispersed ownership.[9] Such mechanisms include monitoring and control by non-executive (or "outside") directors, pay-for-performance management incentive systems, and a market for corporate control.

Most financial economists' attention to date has focused on the operation of the corporate control market or, in popular parlance, the takeover market. In the standard conception of this market, corporate raiders identify companies that are not being managed so as to maximize shareholder value. Raiders launch bids for controlling

ownership that, if successful, give them the right to bring about value-increasing changes in strategy and, in many cases, top management.

PATTERNS OF OWNERSHIP IN FRANCE, GERMANY, AND THE U.K.

The stereotypical description of the structure of corporate sectors runs as follows: There are a large number of small companies that are privately owned by individuals, families, and partners; and there are a much smaller number of large companies that are quoted (or "publicly traded") on the stock market and owned by a large number of individual shareholders. Complicating this pattern somewhat, a significant fraction of the shares of quoted companies are owned by institutional investors – in particular, pension funds, life insurance firms, and mutual funds.

Corporate ownership in the U.K.

The above description fits the U.K. reasonably well. There are over 2,000 U.K. companies quoted on the stock market out of a total population of around 500,000 firms. Almost 80% of the largest 700 companies are quoted on the stock market, and the value of companies quoted on the stock market is around 81% of the GDP. Approximately two-thirds of the equity of quoted U.K. companies is held by institutions.

But this pattern of ownership is by no means universal; on the contrary, it appears to be the exception rather than the rule. Although the U.S. has more quoted companies than the U.K., in most other countries the number of quoted companies is far lower. In Germany, for example, there are fewer than 700 quoted companies and in France less than 500 (see Figure 36.1). In both countries, the value of quoted companies amounts to only 25% of GDP (Figure 36.2). In short, quoted companies in Germany and France account for a much smaller fraction of total national corporate activity than those in the U.K. and the U.S.

In the U.K. and the U.S., moreover, ownership is widely dispersed among a large number of institutions or individuals. Most of the equity of quoted U.K. companies is held by institutions, but

8   See, for example, B. Klein, R. Crawford, and A. Alchian, "Vertical Integration, Appropriable Rents and the Competitive Contracting Process," *Journal of Law and Economics*, 21 (1978), 297–326; S. Grossman and O. Hart, "The Cost and Benefits of Ownership: A Theory of Vertical and Lateral Integration," *Journal of Political Economy*, 94 (1986), 691–719; O. Hart and J. Moore, "Property Rights and the Nature of the Firm," *Journal of Political Economy*, 98 (1990), 1119–58.

9   See H. Manne, "Mergers and the Market for Corporate Control," *Journal of Political Economy* (1965), 110–20; and A. Alchian and H. Demsetz, "Production, Information Costs and Economic Organization," *American Economic Review*, 62 (1972), 777–95; and E. Fama and M. Jensen, "Separation of Ownership and Control," *Journal of Law and Economics*, No. 26 (1983).

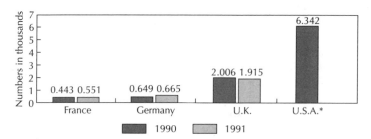

Figure 36.1 Comparison of the French, German, U.K., and U.S. Capital Markets in 1990 and 1991: Number of Domestic Listed Companies on Stock Markets
*U.S.A = NASDAQ + NYSE

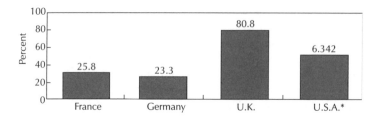

Figure 36.2 Comparison of the French, German, U.K., and U.S. Capital Markets in 1990 and 1991: Market Capitalization of Domestic Equity as a Percent of GDP
*U.S.A = NASDAQ + NYSE

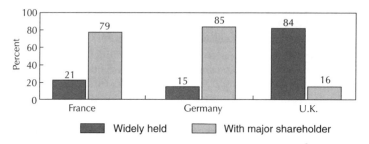

Figure 36.3 Percent of Ownership of a Sample of French, German, and U.K. Quoted Companies (Percent)

no one institution owns very much of any one company. In the U.S., the largest category of shareholders is individuals.

In most of continental Europe, however, ownership is much more concentrated. Consider the ownership pattern revealed in Figure 36.3, which shows the percentage of (approximately) the largest 170 quoted companies in France, Germany, and the U.K. with a single large (at least 25%) shareholder. In only 16% of the U.K. companies did a single shareholder own more than 25% of the shares. By contrast, in nearly 85% of the German

firms there was at least one shareholder owning more than 25%; and almost 80% of the French companies had at least one shareholder with more than 25% ownership. In short concentration of ownership is much greater in corporations based outside the U.K. and the U.S.[10]

---

10 For a comparison of ownership in Japan and the U.S. that makes a similar observation, see S. Prowse, "The Structure of Corporate Ownership in Japan," *Journal of Finance*, 47 (1992), 1121–40. In the case of Japan, the largest group of shareholders is financial institutions.

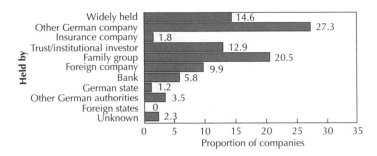

Figure 36.4   Percentage of Companies with Share Stakes in Excess of 25% in 171 German Industrial and Commercial Quoted Companies in 1990

Corporate ownership in Germany and France

In France and Germany, by far the single largest group of shareholders is the corporate sector itself. Figure 36.4 breaks down large share stakes in 171 large quoted German companies by different groups of investors – banks, investment institutions, companies, government, and so forth. It reveals that a majority of the large share stakes are held by companies. The next largest group is families, followed by trusts, institutional investors, and foreign companies.

Although there is a commonly held view that banks control corporate Germany, banks actually come far down the list of large stakeholders. Nevertheless, the control exerted by banks is significantly greater than their direct equity holdings would suggest. As holders of the bearer shares owned by their customers, they are able to exercise proxy votes on behalf of dispersed shareholders. (And, since all the companies studied here are quoted, at least a portion of the shares are widely held.)

Figure 36.5 provides more detail on the ownership of the 171 large German companies analyzed in Figure 36.4. As shown in Figure 36.5A, trusts and institutional investors are sometimes large shareholders in German companies. However, their share stakes are rarely majority holdings. The same holds for banks (Figure 36.5B): there are some large share stakes but rarely majority holdings. This contrasts with the pattern of family ownership. In almost one-third of the cases, families appear to be majority holders of German companies (Figure 36.5C).

In examining these figures, one should keep in mind that they refer to the *largest* German companies. Thus, in contrast to our earlier description of the U.K. ownership structure, large-block family ownership is a highly representative feature of the largest enterprises in Germany. This raises the interesting question (to which we return later) of how and why German (and French) families play a much more significant role in corporate ownership than, say, their U.K. counterparts.

The other group that emerges as having majority shareholdings in Germany is the German corporate sector (Figure 36.5D). Not only do German companies have many and large stakeholdings in other German firms, but also these intercorporate shareholdings are often majority ones. What makes such corporate equity stakes in other firms especially noteworthy is that these are all quoted companies, not just subsidiaries of other companies.

In sum, then, while German banks do have quite large share stakes, they are rarely majority shareholders. The pattern for insurance companies, trust, and institutional investors is very similar – some large but rarely majority shareholdings. The two dominant investor groups in German companies are families and other German firms.

A remarkably similar pattern emerges for France. First, as noted above, the proportion of large stakeholdings in total is about the same as in Germany. Figure 36.6 summarizes the ownership distribution for 155 large quoted French companies. As in the case of Germany, a majority of these stakes are held by other companies. Other large stakeholders in French firms are foreign companies, families, and banks.

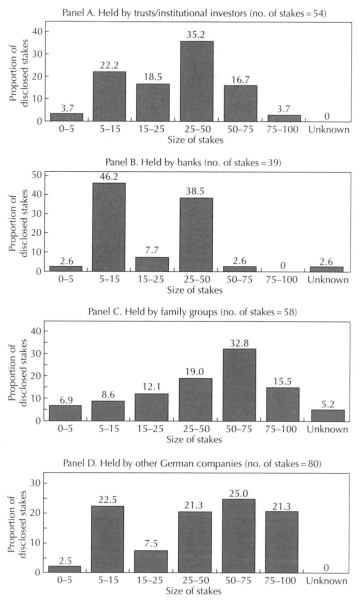

Figure 36.5 Proportion of Disclosed Stakes by Size of Stakes in 171 German Industrial and Commercial Quoted Companies in 1990

Further detail on the ownership of these 155 French companies is provided in Figure 36.7. As we saw in the case of Germany, there are some large stakes held by insurance companies but these are rarely majority holdings (Figure 36.7A). Banks have some large minority shareholdings, often in excess of 25% (Figure 36.7B). But, as in Germany,

it is French families (Figure 36.7C) and other French companies that have the largest proportion of majority shareholdings (Figures 36.7C and 36.7D).

There is, however, one notable difference between France and Germany, and that is the comparative importance of state ownership of

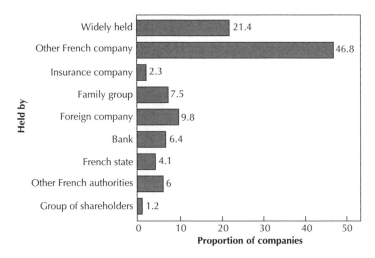

Figure 36.6   Share Stakes in Excess of 25% in 155 French Industrial and Commercial Quoted Companies in 1990

large companies. As shown in Figure 36.8, share stakes by the state are more prevalent and tend to be larger in France than in Germany.

Four cases of German and French Corporate structure

The ownership patterns of individual firms reveal a number of characteristics that are hidden in the aggregate data. Figures 36.9, 36.10, and 36.11 show the ownership structures of three prominent and representative German companies – Renk AG, Kromschröder AG, and Metallgesellschaft AG. Figure 36.12 describes the ownership of the French water company, Degrémont.

What can we learn from these exhibits?

♦   First, they show the extent of equity holdings of corporations in each other's shares. These investments are frequently in quoted companies and are often by firms in a related or the same industry. Figure 36.9, for example, shows a large holding by MAN AG, a large German engineering company that produces buses, lorries, and machines, in Renk AG, another mechanical engineering company. Ruhrgas (shown in Figure 36.10) is a gas company that owns Elster, another gas company.

♦   Second, the other corporate owners are frequently *not* trading partners. For example,

the gas company Elster holds Kromschröder, a precision mechanics and optics company.

♦   Third, banks and insurance companies often emerge higher up in the ownership tree. For example, partnerships between Allianz, which is a German insurance company, and German banks show up in a number of large corporations. Allianz and Deutsche Bank between them have a controlling interest in the holding company of Metallgesellschaft (Figure 36.11). Allianz, Allianz's life insurance company, and Commerzbank have a controlling interest in a holding company that has a large stake in MAN. And, as shown in Figure 36.12, Compagnie Financiere de Suez, Crédit Lyonnaise, and UAP all have significant holdings in Société Lyonnaise des Eaux-Dumex, which in turn owns Degrémont.

Thus, institutional owners play a prominent role in all three countries. But, whereas institutional ownership is highly dispersed in the U.K., it is highly concentrated in France and Germany. And, as the above illustrations further suggest, the corporate governance role of outside shareholders in France and Germany is even less significant than the small number of quoted companies in these countries would suggest. For, even in those cases in which companies are quoted on the stock market, controlling shareholdings often reside with other companies.

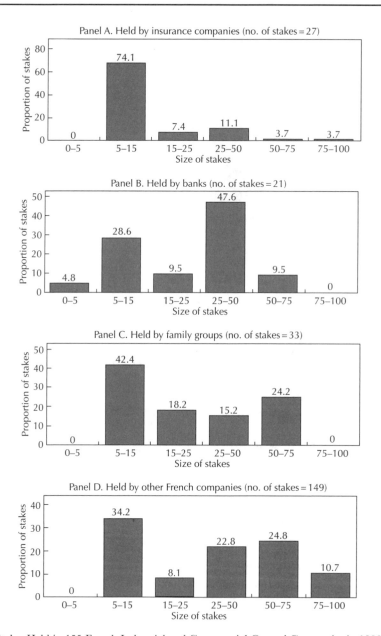

Figure 36.7 Stakes Held in 155 French Industrial and Commercial Quoted Companies in 1990

Therefore, as we noted earlier, the German and French corporate governance systems are perhaps best described as *insider* systems (see Figure 36.13). Insider systems are those in which the corporate sector has controlling interests in itself and in which outside investors, while participating in equity returns through the stock market, are not able to exert much control. By contrast, the U.K. and the U.S. are *outsider* systems of corporate control, in which there are few controlling shareholdings (what controlling blocks do exist are rarely associated with the corporate sector itself). And, as we discuss below, these differences in ownership systems give rise to very different forms of corporate control.

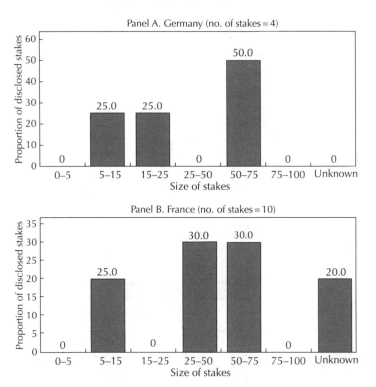

Figure 36.8 Proportion of Disclosed Stakes Held by the State in Germany[1] and France[2]
[1]In 171 German industrial and commercial quoted companies.
[2]In 155 French industrial and commercial quoted companies.

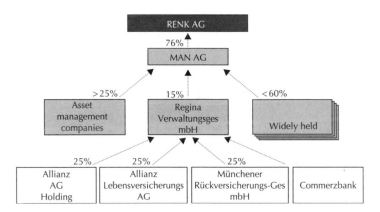

Figure 36.9

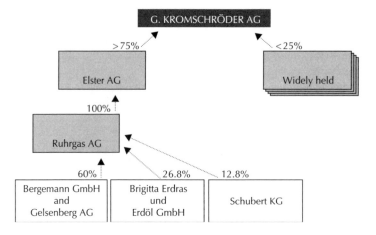

Figure 36.10

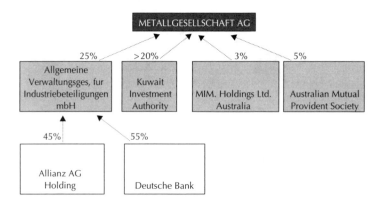

Figure 36.11

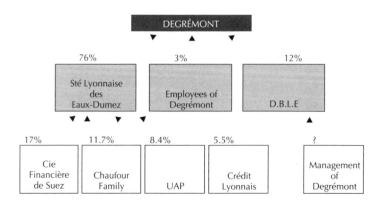

Figure 36.12

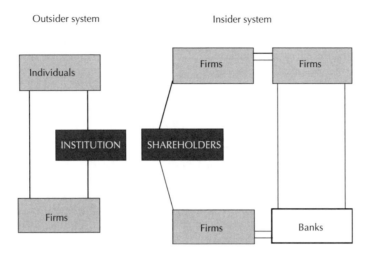

Figure 36.13   Corporate Control Systems

THE MARKET FOR CORPORATE CONTROL IN THE U.K.

The takeover market is active in the U.K. During the merger waves at the beginning of the 1970s and the end of the 1980s, as much as 4% of the total U.K. capital stock was acquired by takeover (or merger) in one year.[11] Furthermore, it has been estimated that about 25% of takeovers in the 1980s were "hostile" in the sense of being rejected initially by the incumbent management.[12] Of those bids that were hostile in nature, approximately one-half were successfully completed.

There are two empirical studies of takeovers that have attempted to distinguish takeovers designed to correct past managerial failure from those that were not. In a 1991 study of the U.S. market, Kenneth Martin and John McConnell investigated the disciplinary role of corporate takeovers in the U.S. over the period 1958 to 1984, using a sample of 253 successful tender offers. They classified a takeover as "disciplinary" if there was any change in the CEO of the target firm. Their study, somewhat surprisingly, reported no difference in bid premiums

associated with disciplinary and non-disciplinary takeovers and only moderate evidence of differences in the share price performance of targets of disciplinary and non-disciplinary bids prior to takeover.

In a study published in 1995, we reported similar results for a sample of 80 contested bids in the U.K. in 1985 and 1986.[13] We found that for a range of financial variables, including share price returns, dividends, and cash flow rates of return, the performance of targets of hostile bids in the six years prior to a bid was not statistically distinguishable from that of samples of either accepted bids or non-merging firms. In fact, the dividend performance of targets of both friendly and hostile bids was *appreciably better than* that of firms in the lowest deciles of share performance. Whereas poorly performing firms frequently reduced their dividends, targets of hostile and friendly bids rarely reduced their dividends in the two years prior to a bid.[14]

We also repeated our analysis of U.K. firms using Martin and McConnell's definition of managerial

---

11 See our article, "Corporate Ownership and Corporate Control: A Study of France, Germany and the UK," *Economic Policy* (1990).

12 T. Jenkinson and C. Mayer, *Hostile Takeovers* (London: Macmillan, 1994).

13 J. Franks and C. Mayer, "Hostile Takeovers and the Correction of Managerial Failure," *Journal of Financial Economics* 40, (1996), 162–81.

14 Although it appears inconsistent with standard explanations of the control market, such a finding is consistent with Jensen's free cash flow theory of takeovers, in which companies with excess capital tend to overinvest. See Jensen (1986), cited earlier.

failure as replacement of top management. But, again, we found found little evidence that managerial control changes in takeovers were a response to poor financial performance. The past performance of acquired firms where managers were replaced was not significantly worse than the performance of those targets in which top managers were retained.

All these results question the common association of markets for corporate control with the correction of managerial failure. Nevertheless, even in the absence of poor pre-merger performance, we did find evidence of considerable restructuring after takeovers. More precisely, we found that levels of asset disposals and restructurings were significantly higher in cases where bids were either hostile or followed by managerial control changes. Furthermore, we found that managerial dismissals were much higher in hostile than in friendly bids. Indeed, nearly 80% of executive directors either resigned or were dismissed within two years of a successful hostile bid.

In sum, then, while the market for corporate control does not appear to be associated with the correction of managerial failure as measured by past corporate performance (which we henceforth refer to as *ex post failure*), it does give rise to substantial corporate restructurings in the form of asset disposals and executive dismissals (*ex ante failure*). One possible interpretation of these results is that hostile bids can occur, even in the absence of any evidence of poor past performance, in the expectation that the acquiring firm will implement a new and more valuable policy in the future (an explanation that would fall under the classfication of *ex ante failure*). In support of this argument, we found in the previously mentioned study of takeovers that hostile bidders paid much larger premiums over market than friendly acquirers, which is consistent with higher expected benefits from the planned restructurings of targets of hostile bids.[15]

THE MARKET FOR CORPORATE CONTROL IN GERMANY

In a recently published study, we found that during the 1980s the total number of mergers in Germany

was only about one-half of those in the U.K.[16] More significantly, in contrast to the active market in corporate control in the U.K., there have been just four recorded cases of hostile takeovers in Germany since World War II, and three of those four have occurred within the last six years.

Several explanations have been suggested for the low level of hostile takeovers in Germany. The first focuses on the dominant position of banks resulting from owning corporate equity and sitting on the supervisory boards of many quoted German companies. As noted earlier, German banks' holdings of equity are a quite modest proportion of the total, but they exercise considerable control by virtue of their ability to vote in proxy contests the bearer shares they hold in custody for customers.

The second explanation is that voting right limitations prevent predators from acquiring controlling interests in firms. German companies frequently pass resolutions at shareholders' meetings limiting the voting right of any one shareholder to a maximum of 5%, 10%, or 15% of total votes, irrespective of the size of the shareholding. The justification for such voting restrictions is that, in the absence of a U.K.-style takeover code, they protect minority shareholders from predators who, after acquiring a controlling interest, attempt to dilute the value of the minority's investments.

The third explanation is that it may prove difficult to remove members of the supervisory board and thereby gain control of a company, even when a majority of the shares are tendered. The supervisory board comprises representatives of employees as well as shareholders. For an AG (public limited company), 50% of the board is composed of employee representatives, who by tradition vote with the incumbent management.

Case studies of hostile takeovers in Germany provide evidence of the effectiveness of these institutional features as barriers to takeover.[17] The unwelcome bid by Pirelli for Continental, Germany's largest tire manufacturer, was launched in September 1990. During the course of the bid, substantial share stakes were acquired by allies of the two parties: Italmobiliare, Mediobanca, and

---

15 J. Franks and C. Mayer, "Corporate Control: A Synthesis of the International Evidence," mimeo.

16 J. Franks and C. Mayer, see [13].

17 Ibid.

Sopaf in the Pirelli camp; BMW, Daimler-Benz, and Volkswagen in the Continental camp. These share stakes were in large part acquired from individual investors and investment institutions.

At the time of the Pirelli bid, there was a 5% limitation on the voting rights that could be exercised by any one shareholder. Prior to launching the bid, Pirelli attempted to have the 5% limitation removed so as not to dilute the voting rights of its own (and its partners') holdings. A motion for removal of the restriction was passed at a shareholders' meeting in March 1991, thereby paving the way for Pirelli to launch a tender bid for Continental. Nevertheless, the removal was delayed (and never implemented) due to a court action by shareholders objecting to rule violations of minority interests.

The Continental case illustrates that voting right restrictions can introduce a two-stage procedure into German takeovers. In the first stage, predators solicit the support of small shareholders to have voting right limitations removed. In the second stage, a normal tender can be launched. The Continental case suggests that the first stage can represent a significant, though not necessarily insurmountable, barrier to takeover.

Although the management board of Continental was resolutely opposed to the merger, the supervisory board showed itself more willing to explore merger possibilities with Pirelli. This difference in approach resulted in the dismissal of the chairman of the management board in May 1991. He was replaced by a chairman who was more sympathetic to merger discussions.

The Continental case suggests that neither proxy votes nor voting right restrictions are absolute defences against hostile takeovers, though the latter certainly slows down the process. Furthermore, the supervisory board may remove members of the management board, though this is less easy to achieve than in the U.K.

The main impediment, however, to an Anglo-American market for corporate control is the ownership structure of German companies. In the Continental case, there was no major shareholder who owned a stake of 25% or more, thus allowing Pirelli and its partners to build large holdings. Two other hostile takeovers in Germany – that of Feldmühle Nobel and the bid by Krupp for Hoesch – were also for firms in the small set of German companies with dispersed shareholdings. In the latter case, Krupp was able to amass a stake of 24.9% without the knowledge of Hoesch or the investment banking community. The purchase of this stake took more than five months to complete, involved purchases on the German, London, and Swiss stock exchanges, and was a crucial tactic in gaining control. Without such a stake, a merger would have proved unlikely or impossible, since all previous attempts at friendly mergers in the industry had failed.

Where ownership is concentrated, direct control is effectively exercised by boards. This is reflected in a close association between ownership and representation on supervisory boards, in particular in the all-important position of chairman. In the small proportion of companies where ownership is dispersed, bank representation on supervisory boards is more in evidence. This suggests that, in widely held companies, proxy votes and voting restrictions together permit banks to exercise effective control through board representation.

A DISCUSSION OF THE EVIDENCE

The evidence presented above on national differences between corporate ownership and control can be summarized by the following observations:

1. There are marked differences in the ownership structures of similar companies in different countries.
2. Intercorporate holdings of companies are very significant in some countries but not others.
3. Large shareholdings by families are of much greater importance in some countries than others.
4. Markets for corporate control are little in evidence in countries with concentrated ownership.
5. Even where companies are widely held, markets for corporate control are seriously restricted in some countries.
6. Bank control is associated primarily with widely held companies where the market for corporate control is restricted.
7. There is little association of the market for corporate control with poor past performance (or *ex post failure*).

8. Corporate control transactions such as takeovers lead to substantial restructuring and management changes (which can be interpreted as evidence of *ex ante failure*).

How well do the theories of ownership and the market for corporate control square with these observations? The answer is not well at all; they leave a large number of unresolved issues.

First, it would not be expected that the broadly similar production technologies that are employed in different countries would give rise to the marked variations in ownership patterns recorded in this paper. Moreover, it is difficult to imagine that there are sufficient differences in production complementarities across countries to explain much larger intercorporate holdings in some countries than in others.

Second, the large family holdings in France and Germany suggest that families in those countries either (1) possess greater managerial skills or (2) derive larger "private" benefits from control (larger at least in relation to the value they could realize by selling their controlling interest) than their English and American counterparts. It is possible that regulation may create greater private benefits in some countries, for example, by being more permissive towards insider trading or providing less protection of minority interests.[18] In this respect, regulation may have important consequences for the structure of corporate organization.

Third, if markets for corporate control improve corporate efficiency, why are they largely absent in some countries? For example, it is very difficult to understand why markets for corporate control in Germany are restricted by bank intermediation *even* in cases of widely held companies where there are weak incentives for shareholders to exert control directly themselves.

On the other hand, if the market for corporate control really does work to correct managerial failure, the puzzle posed by the U.K. is why there is so little evidence of poor pre-bid performance. And, in the absence of poor pre-bid performance, why is there so much restructuring after the takeover?

In this sense, then, current theories of ownership and control fail to provide adequate explanations for the ownership structure and operation of either U.K. or Continental European capital markets. For example, there is clearly more to the determination of ownership in the U.K., Germany, and France than complementarity in production. Moreover, the market for corporate control does not appear to perform its assumed function of correcting managerial failure – or not at least the kind of failure that manifests itself in substandard operating and shareholder returns.

One might suggest that dispersed public ownership, because of its efficiencies in risk-bearing and the liquidity of public markets, is better suited to providing capital for large-scale corporate expansions. But this ignores the reality that even companies with concentrated share ownership can raise external equity while retaining control through either the issuance of dual class shares or the "pyramiding" of intercorporate holdings (as illustrated earlier in the case of several German and French companies).[19] It also ignores the fact that active secondary markets can be (and are) organized in shares other than those that are part of the controlling block.[20]

Concentrated ownership, as suggested by Demsetz and Lehn, is likely to occur for one or both of the following reasons: (1) the greater potential for owners to exercise control over managers increases the value of the enterprise (relative to the value it would command under dispersed ownership), or (2) there are "private" benefits to owners of exercising control – that is, benefits that do not accrue to (and may even come at the expense of) minority stockholders. Both of these factors are likely to explain the extent of family ownership in Germany and France. Concentrated ownership allows investors to exert *direct* control, which is presumably much less costly than the indirect control

---

18 And differences in estate taxes may lead to differences in ownership; for example, many large family interests in U.S. companies are reportedly sold to pay estate taxes.

19 For a defense of the economic efficiency of the pyramid ownership structure, see Brian Kantor, "Shareholders as Agents and Principals: The Case for South Africa's Corporate Governance System," *Journal of Applied Corporate Finance*, Vol. 8, No. 1 (Spring 1995).

20 For a paper arguing that this may be an important source of information for structuring incentives for management, see B. Holmstrom and J. Tirole, "Market Liquidity and Performance Monitoring," *Journal of Political Economy*, 101 (1993), 678–709.

exerted by takeover markets (especially given restrictions on takeovers in Continental markets). And the private, perhaps even non-monetary, benefits of owning a large enterprise (which may include greater powers to keep minority shareholders at bay) may well be larger in France and Germany than in the U.S. or the U.K.

Nevertheless, the differences in the extent of family ownership of public corporations among these nations remain a puzzle. Unless the relative costs of direct and indirect control can be shown to vary greatly among countries, or unless families in different countries attach very different values to private benefits, the diverse forms of ownership cannot be readily explained.

The hypothesis we offer is that the different patterns of ownership across countries are associated with different forms of corporate control that allow for different kinds of correction. Large share stakes and concentrated ownership are likely to be more effective in responding to *ex post* managerial failures (poor past performance), in large part (as we will argue below) because of the "information and agency costs" that confront dispersed shareholders. And there is at least one piece of supporting evidence for this argument: In a recent study (with a colleague), we found that those companies in the bottom decile of corporate performance were far more likely to replace their managers than those with dispersed ownership.[21] By contrast, dispersed ownership seems to be more effective in correcting *ex ante failure* – that is, in bringing about valuable restructuring and management changes in cases where financial performance has been adequate, but managers have failed to maximize value.

At first sight, this argument would appear to suggest that national systems with dispersed ownership will tend to achieve more efficient resource allocations than those with concentrated ownership. Nevertheless, there is a problem presented by dispersed ownership – namely, the inability of a large number of small shareholders to make "commitments" to other key corporate stakeholders such as employees and suppliers.

A simple example illustrates the point. Consider a company with 100,000 shareholders each owning one share in a firm. An alternative prospect, for example, a proposed acquisition emerges. A sale of a majority of shares results in a change in corporate policy to the detriment of existing stakeholders (suppliers, purchasers, and employees). Individually, shareholders base their decision to sell purely on the price which they are offered since the action of any one shareholder has no effect on policy. In addition, the loss sustained by stakeholders in the event of a change in policy cannot be attributed to the actions of any one shareholder. In contrast, large shareholders know that if they sell their shares, they will affect corporate policy to the detriment of stakeholders. Their decisions will be affected by the loss of their reputation as well as the price for their shares.

According to this description, the key distinction between corporate systems concerns the degree of anonymity of shareholders. To a much greater extent than in the U.S. or the U.K., the Continental system allows a large number of small investors to buy and sell shares without having any effect on control. At the same time, large investors such as families or other companies – those who are likely to have the best information about the firm's long-run prospects – effectively guarantee the ability of the firm to make good on strategic commitments.

On the other hand, the advantage of dispersed ownership is that outside shareholders who are not bound by prior commitments are more likely to seek the highest value control group *at any point in time*. Thus, dispersed share ownership achieves value maximization, at least over the short run, although possibly at the expense of valuable long-term relationships with other stakeholders.[22]

It is in this sense, then, that the U.K. and the U.S. financial markets may be considered "short-term."

---

21 J. Franks, C. Mayer, and C. Renneboog, "The Ownership and Control of Poorly Performing Companies in the U.K.," working paper (1995).

22 This provides the basis for the Shleifer and Summers' assertion that shareholders are unable to make commitments to other stakeholders and employ managers to do this on their behalf. The observation here is that through concentrated ownership some financial systems permit investors to make commitments. (See A. Shleifer and L. Summers, "Breaches of Trust in Hostile Takeovers," in *Corporate Takeovers: Causes and Consequences*, ed. Alan Auerbach (University of Chicago Press for National Bureau of Economic Research, 1988.)

Dispersed shareholders cannot commit to the same extent as concentrated owners and cannot therefore sustain the same set of prior relations. This kind of short termism thus does not represent a mispricing of securities or excessive trading of shares, but is rather a direct result of the structure of ownership. And if the short-term orientation of dispersed shareholders limits their ability to commit to key corporate stakeholders, it also provides a potentially valuable flexibility (an ability to reduce operating leverage, if you will, by converting fixed into variable costs). For this reason, in cases where little investment is required of other stakeholders, or relationships can be sustained through explicit contracting, dispersed share ownership may well lead to more efficient allocation of resources than a concentrated ownership burdened by commitments.[23]

Moreover, while it is possible to provide a rationale for high levels of concentration of ownership, majority (or large minority) intercorporate ownership remains very hard to explain. Indeed, the main puzzle presented by the Continental ownership structure is this: Where control is retained within the corporate sector through large corporate shareholdings and corporate representatives who serve on supervisory boards, management is likely to enjoy a high degree of protection from external influences. Managerial failure will not be corrected, either directly by large outside shareholders such as families or indirectly by takeovers, as in economies with dispersed shareownership. Thus, one plausible view of the insider system holds that the complex web of intercorporate holdings in France and Germany is designed, not to promote efficiency, but to perpetuate control within the corporate sector itself.

CONCLUSIONS

There are pronounced differences in the ownership patterns of corporate sectors across countries.

The U.K. and the U.S. have large quoted sectors with share ownership dispersed across a large number of investors. (In the U.K. the dominant shareholding group is institutional investors; in the U.S. it is individual investors.)

In contrast, France and Germany have small quoted sectors. Perhaps more significant, even the largest quoted companies in France and Germany typically have at least one shareholder owning more than 25% of the equity and, in many cases, even a majority shareholding. Such large shareholdings tend to be held either by the founding family or by other corporations. In this sense, both France and Germany can be seen as having "insider systems" of corporate ownership, as contrasted with the "outsider systems" of the U.K. and the U.S.

The different ownership systems are associated with very different forms of corporate control. There is an active market for corporate control in the U.K. and the U.S., but very little in the way of a market for corporate control in France and Germany. In the case of Germany, even in the comparatively small widely held component of the quoted sector, the market for corporate control is impeded by proxy votes and voting right restrictions that effectively confer more power on banks than on the concentrated ownership segment.

Some economists have suggested that complementarities in production can make vertical relationships (including intercorporate block holdings) a cost-effective way of reducing transaction costs or "completing" incomplete contracts. Nevertheless, the patterns of intercorporate ownership we observe in France and Germany do not appear to be particularly closely associated with trading relationships. And, in further contradiction of this theory, similar companies have quite different ownership structures in the U.K., on the one hand, and France and Germany on the other.

In theory, the market for corporate control should be closely associated with the correction of managerial failure. In practice, however, there is very little evidence of a relation between the incidence of hostile takeovers and poor corporate performance. The performance of targets of hostile takeovers in the U.K. is close to that of the average quoted company. At the same time, however, hostile takeovers do result in considerable restructuring and managerial turnover. This can be

---

23 Franks and Mayer (1996), cited above, emphasize another distinguishing feature of insider and outsider systems and that is the importance of committees. Control in insider systems is exercised by committees that can reflect the interests of parties who, for credit constraint reasons, are underrepresented in ownership stakes. In Germany, stakeholder representation on boards is in part dictated by legal considerations.

construed as evidence that targets, while performing up to averages, were failing to *maximize* shareholder value.

The different patterns of ownership in the U.K. and in France and Germany create different incentives and corporate control mechanisms. Concentrated ownership would seem to encourage longer-term relationships between the company and its investors. But, while perhaps better suited to some corporate activities with longer-term payoffs, concentrated ownership could also lead to costly delays in undertaking necessary corrective action, particularly if the owners receive non-monetary benefits from owning and running a business. And although widely dispersed ownership may increase the likelihood that corrective action will be sought prematurely (that is, in cases where the firm is suffering a temporary downturn and outsiders rush to sell their shares), the presence of well-diversified public owners may also be more appropriate for riskier ventures requiring large amounts of new capital investment.

In short, different forms of ownership would appear to be suited to promoting different types of activity. Concentrated ownership may be necessary where investment by other stakeholders is important and cannot be promoted contractually, but dispersed ownership will be advantageous where little investment is required by non-investor stakeholders or where adequate contracts can be written that protect their interests. What is finally very hard to explain, however, is the high level of intercorporate holdings in the French and particularly the German systems. Such holdings, while possibly achieving some coordination benefits, are also likely to create insider systems that are largely immune to necessary corrective intervention by outside investors.

CHAPTER 37

Universal Banks Are Not the Answer to America's Corporate Governance "Problem": A Look at Germany, Japan, and the U.S.

Jonathan R. Macey (Cornell Law School), and
Geoffrey P. Miller (New York University Law School)**

Recent scholarship on the governance of the large, publicly held corporation has been critical of the American tradition. Our corporate governance is routinely depicted as having "sharply constrained the development of multidimensional governance relationships."[1] In particular, the U.S. is seen as offering mechanisms of monitoring and control of corporate managers that are grossly inferior to those operating in Germany and Japan. American firms are described disparagingly as "Berle-Means" corporations, with widespread share-ownership, separation of management and risk-bearing, and significant agency conflicts between managers and shareholders. Despite some protestations of agnosticism,[2] the tone makes it clear that the American system of corporate governance is viewed as inferior because it does not foster the sort of "relational investing" that leads to effective monitoring by sophisticated intermediaries.

This modern tendency to hold up for emulation the German and Japanese corporate governance systems turns on the role played by *commercial banks*. The dominant idea is that market forces, if allowed to function free of regulation, result in an economic system in which banks have great influence on the business affairs of borrowing corporations. However, U.S. law, "by restricting the size of banks and the scope and geographical range of their activities," has caused bank influence to wane below the optimal level.[3] Thus, for example, some commentators have been quite explicit in their view that, without major changes in American banking law and practice, "the United States is

*   This paper is a shortened version of "Corporate Governance and Commercial Banking: A Comparative Economic Perspective with Emphasis on Germany, Japan and the United States," *Stanford Law Review* Vol. 48 No. 1.

1   Ronald Gilson & Reinier Kraakman, "Investment Companies as Guardian Shareholders: The Place of the MSIC in the Corporate Governance Debate," 45 *Stan. L. Rev.* 985, 989 (1993).

2   For example, Mark Roe writes that he "examines Germany and Japan not to argue that their corporate structures are better

and should be mimicked but to show that different structures are possible." Mark Roe, "Some Differences in Corporate Structure in Germany, Japan, and the United States," 102 *Yale Law Journal* (1993), p. 1927.

3   Gilson and Kraakman, cited above, p. 990.

likely . . . to lag behind its European and Japanese competitors."[4]

Focusing on the roles played by major German banks and Japanese main banks, critics suggest that American banks should play a much larger role in the management of the firms to which they loan money. U.S. banks are said to lack the "power and incentive" to monitor their borrowers. As a consequence,

the monitoring role in the American corporate governance system is relegated to those who provide the equity capital to the corporation – the shareholders. This characteristic has forced American governance institutions to follow a unique Berle-Means pattern of successive efforts, ranging from independent directors to hostile takeovers, to bridge the separation of ownership and management in the face of dispersed shareholdings.[5]

Our objective in this article is to cast doubt on the accepted wisdom concerning the desirability of commercial bank involvement in corporate governance. We argue that current scholarship ignores important costs of the Japanese and German systems of bank-dominated corporate governance, as well as important benefits of the American system of equity-dominated corporate governance. Current theory also ignores critical differences between the monitoring incentives of equity holders and the monitoring incentives of debt holders.

Much of the confusion in the current debate stems from a failure to appreciate the economics of commercial banking. We begin by describing the conflict of interest that exists within publicly held firms between the interests of banks and other fixed claimants on the one hand, and the interests of equity claimants on the other. Understanding this conflict is critical to analyzing the supposed advantages of the German and Japanese systems over the American system. We show that the core assumption of the current thinking about the role of banks in corporate governance – namely, that what is good for a nation's banks is also good for the nation's borrowers – is flawed. Using basic principles of corporate finance, we show that to

the extent banks control the firms to which they lend money, their incentives are to reduce the levels of risk-taking below the levels that are optimal from a social perspective.

Next, we discuss the German and Japanese systems of corporate governance in light of banks' incentives as both lenders and stockholders. In both the German and Japanese systems, banks are far more influential in corporate decision-making than in the U.S. And, in both of these systems, the banks have used this influence to reduce risk-taking among borrowers and to suppress the market for corporate control. Current wisdom holds that the German and Japanese banking systems are a substitute for a robust market for corporate control in reducing agency costs and improving managerial performance. We argue that the Japanese and German bank-dominated systems of corporate governance are better viewed as the root *cause* of the lack of a robust market for corporate control in those countries.

In the final part of the article, we explore the implications of our theory for the ongoing debate about American corporate governance. We argue that simply giving banks more power over borrowers is not the answer to the perceived problems in American corporate governance. Rather we argue that strengthening the "voice" of American equity holders by eliminating restrictions on the market for corporate control would be more effective in improving firm performance. Moreover, we argue that other U.S. laws – notably, environmental law, partnership law, and lender liability rules – reduce American banks' ability to control moral hazard problems with borrowers to the same extent as European banks.

Finally, we argue that the expected "convergence" among these three national corporate governance systems does not seem likely. Despite recent weaknesses, German and Japanese banks will continue to be successful in resisting the encroachments of local capital markets onto their turf. And, in the U.S., the recent proposals to liberalize Glass Steagall and the Bank Holding Company Act may encourage some banks to play a somewhat greater role in corporate governance. But the highly developed U.S. capital and corporate control markets will continue to ensure that such a role is a relatively small one.

---

4   Anthony Saunders & Ingo Walter, *Universal Banking in the United States*, p. 236 (1994). For a widely cited expression of this view, see also Michael Porter, "Capital Disadvantages," *Harvard Business Review*, September–October 1992, pp. 76–77.

5   Gilson and Kraakman, cited above, p. 989.

BANKS AS FIXED CLAIMANTS

A fundamental contribution of modern corporate financial theory has been to analyze the conflict of interest that exists within the publicly held corporation between the interests of holders of fixed claims (such as banks) and the interests of shareholders who hold the residual claims to the firm's earnings. Among any particular set of asset allocation decisions, an investment strategy that increases risk will transfer wealth from the fixed claimants to the residual claimants. To the extent that shareholders can influence corporate decisions through their voting power, such shareholders can enrich themselves at the expense of the fixed claimants by shifting assets to risky investments. To the extent that banks and other fixed claimants can influence corporate decisions through corporate governance structures (or, as in Germany, through their ability to vote shares owned by others), these fixed claimants can enrich themselves at the expense of shareholders. A simple example illustrates this process.

Suppose that a borrower has assets of $1000 and liabilities of $500. Assume the $500 represents the principal and interest due on money borrowed from banks. This leaves the firm with $500 in shareholders' equity. The firm has the option of investment strategy A, which has an expected payoff of $2000, and investment strategy B, which has an expected payoff of $1875.

As the chart indicates, if the firm selects strategy A, there are five possible outcomes: (1) a 5% chance that the strategy will cause the firm to have a net worth of $400; (2) a 20% chance the investment will cause the firm to have a net worth of $1000; (3) a 50% chance the investment will cause the firm to have a net worth of $2000; (4) a 20% chance the investment will cause the firm to have a net worth of $3000; and (5) a 5% chance the investment will cause the firm to have a net worth of $4000. Thus, with strategy A, there is a 5% chance that there will be a small loss for the bank because, if the investment returns only $400, the firm will not be able to repay the full $500 in interest and principal due to the bank. Strategy A has a total expected (risk-adjusted) return of $495 for banks and $1525 for shareholders.

By contrast, strategy B poses absolutely no risk of loss for the bank because, even under the worst possible scenario, the strategy brings returns great enough to repay the principal and interest on the firm's bank debt in full.

However, there are two other important differences between strategies A and B. First, strategy B is significantly inferior to strategy A from the shareholders' perspective. This is because strategy B has an expected return to shareholders of only $1375, compared with the expected return of $1525 for strategy A. This result is driven by the simple fact that strategy A has both a greater upside potential than strategy B (the best possible outcome under strategy A is a firm value of $4000, as compared with only $2500 for strategy B), as well as a greater downside potential than strategy B (the worst possible outcome under strategy A is a firm value of $400, as compared with $1000 for strategy B). Since the equity claimants capture all of the gains on the upside after the bank has been repaid, but share the losses on the downside with the bank, they obviously prefer this riskier investment.

Not only is strategy B inferior from the shareholders' perspective, it also is inferior from the perspective of society as a whole. This is because the expected value of strategy A is $2020, compared with only $1875 for strategy B. Thus, if an economy were to allocate plenary authority over investment decisions to fixed claimants such as banks, productivity and gross domestic product would decline to suboptimal levels as the banks steered investments away from the highest-valued projects and toward lower-valued projects.

It is for this reason, as Frank Easterbrook and Dan Fischel have observed, that in American corporate governance structures, the shareholders, as residual claimants, retain plenary authority to guide the investment decisions of firms: *Over the broadest range of issues, it is the shareholders who have the greatest incentive to maximize the value of the firm.*[6]

Of course, just as it would be suboptimal to give plenary authority over investment decisions within

---

6 Easterbrook and Fischel, "Voting in Corporate Law," 26 *J.L.Econ.*, pp. 403–406 (1983). See also Eugene Fama, "Agency Problems and the Theory of the Firm," 88 *J. Pol. Econ.*, pp. 288–289 (1980).

STRATEGY A:

	Monetary return			Expected value		
Probability	Firm	Bank	Common	Firm	Bank	Common
.05	$400	$400	$0	$20	$20	$0
.20	$1000	$500	$500	$200	$100	$100
.50	$2000	$500	$1500	$1000	$250	$750
.20	$3000	$500	$2500	$600	$100	$500
.05	$4000	$500	$3500	$200	$25	$175
1.00				$2020	$495	$1525

STRATEGY B:

	Monetary return			Expected value		
Probability	Firm	Bank	Common	Firm	Bank	Common
.25	$1000	$500	$500	$250	$125	$125
.50	$2000	$500	$1500	$1000	$250	$750
.25	$2500	$500	$2000	$625	$125	$500
1.00				$1875	$500	$1375

STRATEGY C:

	Monetary return			Expected value		
Probability	Firm	Bank	Common	Firm	Bank	Common
.30	$0	$0	$0	$0	$0	$0
.50	$1000	$500	$500	$500	$250	$250
.20	$7500	$500	$7000	$1500	$100	$1400
1.00				$2000	$350	$1650

a firm to the firm's fixed claimants, so too would it be suboptimal to give plenary authority over *all* investment decisions within a firm to the equity claimants. This is because equity claimants have an incentive to transfer wealth to themselves by *increasing* the riskiness of the firm in which they have invested. Thus, left to their own devices, the shareholders might select strategy C with the following payoff structure:

Shifting to strategy C would increase the value of the shareholder's stake from $1525 under strategy A to $1650, but would reduce the value of the bank's investment from $495 under strategy A to $350. More important from society's point of view, it would also reduce the total value of the firm to $2000 from $2020. As before, these results are driven by adjusting the probability of particular outcomes (risk of the project). In strategy A the difference or variance between the worst and best

possible outcomes and the median outcome is small, just $3600.[7] In strategy B, which is the best investment among the three from the bank's perspective, the variance is even less, just $1,500.[8] But in strategy C, the variance is quite large, $7,500.[9] That is why strategy C is the worst investment among the three from the bank's perspective, but the best from the shareholders' perspective. The shareholders capture the lion's share of the huge upside potential associated with strategy C, but share the loss on the downside with the bank.

In a properly functioning capital market, an equilibrium emerges to resolve the incentive

---

7   The median outcome of strategy A is $2000. The best possible outcome is $4000 and the worst possible outcome is $400. $(2000-400) + (4000-2000) = 3600$.

8   $(2000-1000) + (2500-2000) = 1500$.

9   $(1000-0) + (7500-1000) = 7500$.

incompatibility problems that exist between fixed claimants, equity claimants, and, indeed, all other claimants on the firm's cash flows (such as workers, managers, suppliers, and customers). Rational banks demand to be compensated in the form of higher interest payments for the danger that they will loan money to firms with investment portfolios that resemble B, only to have the firm shift its resources towards A or C. Shareholders, on the other hand, will pay less for stock in firms whose investment patterns resemble strategy B rather than A or C.

Through their bargaining, the parties are able to improve on any equilibrium that does not maximize the overall value of the firm. Shareholders, for example, could agree to pay higher interest in exchange for giving the equity claimants the right to pursue riskier projects. Or the bondholders could agree to accept a lower interest rate in exchange for a credible promise from the shareholders not to shift their investments towards riskier projects after credit has been extended. In this fashion, the equilibrium that emerges in a properly functioning capital market not only protects both banks and equity holders, but also promotes the efficient allocation of resources within society by increasing the odds that the investment that maximizes the overall value of the firm will be pursued.

Designing mechanisms for resolving the conflicts between risk-averse banks and other fixed claimants, on the one hand, and risk-preferring residual claimants, on the other, constitutes one of the cores of the subject of corporate finance, and represents much of the added value contributed by corporate lawyers providing advice for financial transactions. Preferred stock, convertible bonds, and bond indentures can all be understood as market-driven mechanisms for controlling both excessive risk-taking by shareholders and excessive risk-aversion by fixed claimants.[10]

Two important insights come out of the preceding discussion that are relevant to the ongoing

debate about alternative corporate governance mechanisms. First, the clear conflict of interest between fixed claimants (including banks) and equity claimants suggests that banks are not the ideal institution to monitor corporate performance on behalf of shareholders. Second, legal and structural problems raise transaction costs, thereby impeding the operation of capital markets and making it more difficult for market participants to resolve the inherent conflicts between fixed claimants and residual claimants (as well as among other participants in the corporate enterprise). Managers, for example, tend to be more risk-averse than shareholders because their compensation is predominantly fixed, thus aligning their incentives more closely with fixed claimants than equity claimants. Managers' incentives for risk-taking are further reduced by their investment of "nondiversifiable" human capital in their jobs. The value of this human capital would depreciate significantly if their firms were to fail. Although stock options and other forms of executive compensation contracts can help counteract such risk-aversion, differences between managers' and shareholders' risk preferences often result in suboptimal amounts of corporate risk-taking.[11]

Legal rules and institutions can raise the costs stemming from these sources of inefficiency. For example, rules that artificially restrict the market for corporate control, or that increase the bargaining power of one group of claimants over others (for example, by guaranteeing them places on corporate boards of directors), can prevent investing parties from reaching the value-maximizing bargaining equilibrium.

ROMANTICIZING THE ROLE OF GERMAN AND JAPANESE BANKS

The critical distinction between the American model and the German and Japanese models of

---

10   For an analysis of various mechanisms that fixed claimants use to control this conflict through the interfirm contracting process, see Clifford Smith & Jerold Warner, "On Financial Contracting: An Analysis of Bond Covenants," 7 *Journal of Financial Economics*, pp. 117–119 (1979).

11   Empirical support for this argument comes from one study that shows that higher levels of debt (and hence greater risk) in corporate capital structures were associated with higher levels of managerial stock ownership. Conversely, firms where principal stockholders were not managers tended to assume lower risk levels. See Irwin Friend & Larry Lang, "An Empirical Test of the Impact of Managerial Self-Interest on Corporate Capital Structure," 43 *Journal of Finance*, p. 271 (1988).

corporate governance can be easily summarized. In Germany and Japan, there are large block share-holders that take an active role in management to reduce managerial shirking and misconduct. In contrast, the U.S. structure of corporate gover-nance focuses power in management, particularly in the chief executive officer. For this reason, outside shareholders of U.S. corporations are said to be relatively powerless to affect management decisions; they are too disaggregated even to know whether or not managements' activities are furthering their interests, much less to galvanize into effective political coalitions to oppose these activities.

The main banking system in Japan

There is a strong tendency in current scholarship to romanticize the Japanese main bank system. Japanese main banks are viewed as effective moni-tors of their debtors, and their monitoring activity is believed to be effective both in protecting clients against business failure and monitoring perform-ance on behalf of outside shareholders.[12]

The Japanese system of corporate governance is characterized by complex networks of intercor-porate equity cross-holdings known as *keiretsu*, generally organized around Japanese "main" banks. Each member of an individual *keiretsu* owns about 2% in every other firm in the group, and thus a large percentage – typically between 30% and 90% – of the stock of every firm in the *keiretsu* is owned by other members of the group.[13] At the center of the *keiretsu* are the banks, which have places on corporate boards and are thus in a posi-tion to exert pressure on corporate management, particularly when cash flows become unstable.

As a result of this pattern of intercorporate cross-holdings, hostile takeovers are virtually unknown in Japan. Nevertheless, a large number of commentators have suggested that Japanese bank

oversight acts as an effective substitute for a well-functioning market for corporate control.[14] (In the U.S., as we discuss in more detail below, the corpo-rate control market operates to reduce managerial inefficiency by means of hostile takeovers in which inefficient management teams that fail to maximize the value of their firms' equity holdings are replaced by new owners.[15])

Recent empirical work suggests that Japanese banks serve as at least a partial substitute for the mar-ket for corporate control. In their recent study of a sample of large Japanese firms in the 1980s, Randall Morck and Masao Nakamura report the following:

{P}oor stock market performance in large non-financial firms leads to an increased probability that a bank execu-tive is named to the board of directors in the subsequent year. The appointment of a new bank representative to a board is regarded as important by Japanese financial ana-lysts and the financial press. It is thought to indicate increased bank attention to the company. We also find that liquidity problems are a stronger predictor of intervention [than poor stock price performance]. Bank intervention is followed by a quick return to industry normal cash flow and liquidity levels. Sales growth and especially employ-ment growth remain low for several years but eventually return to industry levels.[16]

---

12 See Ronald Gilson and Mark Roe, "Understanding the Japanese Keiretsu: Overlaps Between Corporate Governance and Industrial Organization," 102 (1993).

13 "Watching the Boss (Survey of Corporate Governance)," *The Economist*, January 29, 1994 at 8.

14 See, for example, Paul Sheard, "The Main Bank System and Corporate Monitoring and Control in Japan," 11 *Journal of Economic Behavior and Organization* (1989); Takeo Hoshi, Anil Kashyap and David Scharfstein, "The Role of Banks in Reducing the Costs of Financial Distress in Japan," 27 *Journal of Financial Economics* (1990); Stephen Prowse, "The Structure of Corporate Ownership in Japan," 47 *Journal of Finance*, Masahiko Aoki and Paul Sheard, "The Role of the Main Bank in the Corporate Governance Structure in Japan," Stanford University Working Paper; Ronald Gilson and Mark Roe, "Comparative Corporate Governance: Focusing on the United States-Japan Inquiry," 1992 Columbia Law School Working Paper; Steven Kaplan and Bernadette Minton, "Outside Intervention in Japanese Companies: Its Determinants and its Implications for Managers," 1992 Monograph.

15 There is strong evidence that hostile takeovers discipline managers and improve corporate performance. See Michael Jensen and Richard Ruback, "The Market for Corporate Control: The Scientific Evidence," 11 *Journal of Financial Economics* (1983). Randall Morck, Andrei Shleifer and Robert Vishny, "Alternative Mechanisms for Corporate Control," 79 *American Economic Review* (1989).

16 Randall Morck and Masao Nakamura, "Banks and Corporate Control in Japan," Working Paper No. 6–92, July 26, 1993, Institute for Financial Research, Faculty of Business, University of Alberta, Edmonton, Alberta CANADA T6G 2R6, p. 3.

Three critical features of Japanese corporate governance deserve emphasis. First, large Japanese firms own blocks of shares in other Japanese firms, which such firms are unwilling to sell except in unusual circumstances. Second, Japanese banks, unlike American banks, can hold and vote substantial (up to 5%) blocks of stock in any industrial firm. (Under U.S. law, bank holding companies (but not banks) can own up to 5% of the stock in a firm that is engaged in activities unrelated to banking, but the investment must be passive.) Finally, and most important, the pattern of cross holdings prevalent in Japan was a "deliberate response by [Japanese] managers to a series of hostile raids in the early post-war years."[17]

After World War II, U.S. occupation forces broke up the large corporate groups (*zaibatsu*) that were controlled by the leading Japanese families and financed by large universal banks. The occupation forces accomplished this diffusion of ownership by compelling the families to sell their cross-holdings in each other's shares; and, by 1950, cross-holdings of shares were virtually eliminated. But when the U.S. occupation ended, cross-holdings quickly reemerged, as managers feared that the depressed prices of their shares would lead to hostile takeovers. In the mid-1960s, these new cross-holding networks, called *keiretsu*, gained in strength as depressed stock prices led to a fear of hostile takeovers, and the large banks (Fuji, Sanwa and Daichi-Kango) "began major efforts to increase cross-holdings among firms associated with them, again with the explicit aim of blocking potential hostile takeovers."[18] This pattern repeated itself in the 1970s.[19]

It is clear what *management* gains from the pattern of bank domination and cross-ownership of shares that characterizes the *keiretsu*. This corporate governance system allows incumbent management to insulate itself from the prospect of takeover, and thereby to avoid the strict discipline imposed by the takeover market. It's less clear, however, what the *banks* in Japan gain from this system. We argue that the banks in Japan gain in three ways from this pattern of share ownership. First, the banks gain

because, by avoiding hostile takeovers altogether, they are able to eliminate the threat of particularly undesirable hostile takeovers that increase the target firm's leverage and transfer wealth from the fixed claimants (the banks) to the equity claimants.[20] Consistent with this analysis, Morck and Nakamura find that highly leveraged firms are more likely to have bank representatives appointed to their boards than other firms.[21] This suggests that banks step in to control risk that might benefit shareholders at banks' expense.

In sum, over a wide range of corporate governance issues, the interests of the banks are aligned with the interests of incumbent management and opposed to the interests of shareholders. Because both managers and banks have fixed claims on the cash flows of their firms, they are both likely to care far less about maximizing the potential upside performance of their firms than about minimizing the potential downside performance. The *keiretsu* relationship benefits managers and banks by reducing the uncertainty associated with both the managers' investment of human capital and the banks' investment of fixed capital. But this implicit contract between banks and the management of publicly held borrowers comes at the expense of the outside shareholders, who would capture most of the gains from promising investments not undertaken.

More on "the deal" between the main bank and its borrowers

When corporations become part of a *keiretsu*, they limit their ability to obtain funding from outside banks. Once a borrower has associated with the main bank within a *keiretsu*, the negative "information effect" associated with switching banks makes it costly for the borrower to secure funding from

17 Ibid., p. 6.
18 Ibid., p. 7.
19 Ibid.

20 Hostile takeovers (and takeover defense) are funded primarily with debt. See Michael Jensen, "Takeovers: Their Causes and Consequences," 2 *J. of Econ. Perspectives* (1988). Debt issued before a takeover reflects a value based upon the then-existing degree of business risk and leverage. Increased leverage (more debt) results in increased risk to pre-existing debtholders, which is reflected in a decline in the value of debt and increase in the value of equity (because of the greater leverage).
21 Morch and Nakamura, cited earlier, p. 21.

another bank outside the group.[22] During the course of developing a client-bank relationship, banks acquire specialized information about their clients, including detailed – and often confidential – information about their clients' businesses, their ability to deal with business problems, and their trustworthiness. Because this information must be built up over a long period of time from repeat dealings, ending a relationship with a main bank could have a significantly negative "market-signaling" effect on a company's outside stakeholders. Customers, suppliers and investors may infer that a client is switching banks because that client is experiencing credit problems. Even if the inference is wrong, it will be costly to correct – which provides more incentive to stick with the main bank.

While not all major Japanese firms have main banks, most do. Indeed, one study reported that over 90% of the non-financial firms listed on the Japanese Stock Exchange are affiliated with a main bank.[23] Managers of these firms are willing to sacrifice a large degree of autonomy and flexibility for the dependence and safety of a relationship with a main bank. Moreover, the available data support the conclusion that Japanese firms are extraordinarily dependent on their banking relationships. For example, one study reports that Japanese firms borrow $5.33 from banks for every dollar they raise in the capital markets, whereas American firms borrow only $0.85.[24]

But Japanese firms do not necessarily borrow so much from Japanese banks because they find it economical to do so. Main banks charge their client firms higher rates of interest than the market rate.[25] Moreover, consistent with our analysis that Japanese borrowers are "captured" by the main banks within their *keiretsu*, the premium over market rates appears to be higher the greater the firm's dependence on financing from banks within the *keiretsu*.[26]

Professor Masahiko Aoki has offered an explanation that justifies such high debt costs as an "agency fee paid by individual shareholders [for the service of monitoring management]."[27] But, in light of the embedded conflicts between the interests of banks and the interests of shareholders, a more plausible explanation is that these excess fees are rents the bank obtains on its loan portfolio in exchange for (1) insulating incumbent management of borrower firms from hostile takeover and (2) accepting suboptimal returns on their equity holdings.

If banks were acting to maximize equity values in the firms in which they invested, they would intervene to deter poor stock price performance. But, as noted earlier, the study by Morck and Nakamura shows that Japanese banks intervene in the management of their clients primarily in response to cash flow and liquidity problems (which are of more concern to banks than return to equity claimants) and not poor stock performance.[28] This strongly suggests that banks are not acting primarily to protect the interests of shareholders, but rather to protect their own interests as fixed claimants.

Moreover, when the banks do intervene, the available evidence does not support the conclusion that shareholders benefit from bank involvement in

---

22   Generally, Japan has an underdeveloped monitoring system in its capital markets, especially when compared to the plethora of bond and credit-rating institutions, as well as security analysis agencies, in the United States. Sheard, cited earlier, p. 403. Main banks serve as a generalized substitute for this lack of market monitoring. Disassociation may not only indicate significant problems within the firm, but it also removes the firm from the monitoring function of the main bank.

23   Ibid., p. 401.

24   J. Mark Ramseyer, "Explicit Reasons for Implicit Contracts: The Legal Logic to the Japanese Main Bank System," Law and Economics Working Paper No. 17 (2d Series), p. 3 (August 1993). Generally, less than half of a firm's borrowed funds come directly from a main bank. See Horiuchi, "The Effect of Firm Status on banking Relationships and Loan Syndication," pp. 20–21 & Table 11 (Universita Degli Di Siena, Quaderni Del Dipartimento Di Economia Politica, 1994). The vast majority of loans to Japanese firms are arranged through loan syndicates. The long-term relationship between a main bank and firm is the foundation of the loan syndicate. Ibid. at 20.

25   R. Caves and M. Uekusa, *Industrial Organization in Japan*, Brookings Institution, Washington, D.C. 1976.

26   Morck and Nakamura, cited earlier, p. 9. Keiretsu firms also tend to have more leverage than firms not affiliated with a keiretsu (although there are few non-keiretsu firms). Ibid. This indicates that main banks 'encourage' their keiretsu affiliates to borrow somewhat more.

27   M. Aoki, "Information, Incentives, and Bargaining in the Japanese Economy," 148 (1988).

28   Morck and Nakamura, cited earlier, p. 29. Regression analysis reveals that bank intervention is 100% more likely when liquidity and cash flows are very low as compared to an industry norm than when stock performance is similarly poor.

distressed firms. Morck and Nakamura conclude that, although bank intervention improves cash flows and profitability, it has no discernible, sustained effect on share prices.[29] This supports the conclusion that the value added by banks through intervention is consumed by managers and bankers rather than by shareholders.[30]

Thus, neither the available evidence nor common sense supports the theory that Japanese main banks benefit other shareholders by conducting costly monitoring that principally benefits such shareholders. Rather, the evidence supports the view that Japanese banks use their influence to intervene to protect their own interests as fixed claimants. Because banks are highly leveraged, and because their own balance sheets are dominated by checkable deposits available on demand, banks have strong interests in ensuring that the cash flows from borrowers remain highly stable. Thus, while Japanese banks do hold equity positions in the firms to which they have loaned money, their interests as fixed claimants dominate their interests as equity claimants.

German universal banks

The role of banks in corporate governance in Germany is, if anything, even greater than the role of the main banks in Japan. Indeed, it is no exaggeration to say that the universal bank "sits at the epicenter of German corporate governance."[31] And the tendency to romanticize the effectiveness of this corporate governance structure has been equally pronounced. Commentators argue that, in sharp contrast to U.S. banks, German banks have "the position, information and power to effectively monitor the activity of management and, when necessary, to discipline management."[32] As a result, bank involvement is also supposed to improve the *profitability* of German firms.[33]

The German Aktiengesellschaft (AG) is the corporate organizational form most directly comparable to the publicly held corporation in the U.S. The distinctive feature of the AG is its two-tier board structure containing both a management and executive committee (*Vorstand*) and a supervisory board of directors (*Aufsichtsrat*). The supervisory board appoints the management committee, but has limited additional powers. But although the supervisory board cannot "even by purported delegation, take any steps in the actual management" of the firm,[34] it does screen management's investment plans, and can veto plans it disapproves. The role of the supervisory board has been described as analogous to that of the U.S. Senate to advise and consent to the President's appointments and treaty agreements.[35]

Most striking about the large German corporation is the almost complete dominance of fixed claimants on the supervisory boards of directors. German banks are strongly represented on the supervisory board of directors of German AGs; indeed, one study reported that German banks had representatives on the supervisory boards of 96 of the 100 largest German firms.[36] And, in a unique feature of the German corporate governance system known as "co-determination," companies with more than 2000 employees must provide for employee representation on the board equal to that of the shareholders.

German banks, like Japanese banks, own only a modest percentage of the shares in the firms to

---

29 Following bank intervention, the firm's liquidity sharply increases, and cash flows return relatively quickly to normal levels. Morck and Nakamura, pp. 36–37. Moreover, in the year of intervention stock return increases, on average, 6.4%; but in the year following intervention, stock return declines 6.3%. As to stock performance, bank intervention is a near-complete wash for equity holders. Ibid., pp. 34–35.

30 This conclusion is further supported by the astonishingly high entertainment expenses for firms subjected to bank intervention. In 1991, they amounted to 6.14 trillion yen ($62 billion). Morck and Nakamura, p. 34. Entertainment costs are below industry norms for firms prior to bank intervention, but are significantly more than 100% greater than in the years preceding intervention. Ibid., p. 57.

31 Ibid., p. 988.

---

32 Gilson and Kraakman, cited earlier, p. 988.

33 See John Cable, "Capital Market Information and Industrial Performance: The Role of West German Banks," 95 *Economic Journal* 118 (1985); Roe, *Yale L.J.*, cited earlier. But see Romano, A Cautionary Note on Drawing Lessons from Comparative Corporate Law, 102 *Yale L.J.* 2021 (1993).

34 Norbert Horn, *et al, German Private and Commercial Law* (1982), p. 260.

35 Roe, *Yale Law Journal*, cited earlier, p. 1942.

36 Moreover, a bank representative chaired 14 of those boards. Ibid., p. 1939.

which they lend money. But the banks exercise a degree of control significantly out of proportion to the amount of their shareholdings. Though banks account for only about 6% of large share stakes in German firms,[37] they tend to exert effective control over a majority of the shares voted in annual meetings. As one example, the direct stock holdings of three banks in Daimler-Benz were recently reported as follows: Deutsche Bank (28.2%), Dresdner Bank (1.60%), and Commerz Bank (1.6%).[38] But these banks voted considerably larger amounts of stock: Deutsche Bank (41.8%), Dresdner Bank (18.78%), and Commerz Bank (12.24%).[39] Moreover, a 1988 study reported that these same three banks controlled an average of 45% of the voting stock in 42 of the 100 largest AGs.[40]

The disparity between the small equity positions and the large voting power of German banks is attributable to a combination of three factors. First, German banks vote bearer shares that they hold as custodians on behalf of the beneficial owners who are small shareholder-clients of the banks' brokerage operations. Individual investors deposit their shares with banks, which vote by proxy at shareholders' meetings. Second, German companies frequently pass resolutions at shareholders meetings limiting the voting rights of any single shareholder to 5% to 15% of total votes, regardless of the size of its shareholding. This restriction increases the voting power of German banks because it does not apply to banks voting shares as proxy for other shareholders. Finally, German banks' voting power is enhanced beyond their actual ownership position by the banks' operation of mutual funds and right to vote the shares held by the mutual funds.

Despite their prodigious voting power, German banks' economic stake in German corporations is predominantly that of a lender. Like Japanese firms, German firms obtain far more of their external financing from bank borrowing than from the capital markets. German firms reportedly borrow $4.20 from banks for every $1.00 they obtain from capital markets, as compared to the $0.85 borrowed by U.S. firms noted earlier.[41]

This puts German banks in a significant conflict of interest. Banks have an incentive to vote the shares they control in favor of reducing the levels of risk-taking at the firms to which they have outstanding loans. It stands to reason that German banks will use their voting power over German firms to reduce aggregate levels of risk-taking below levels that are optimal from the shareholders' perspective. Moreover, the banks are not likely to be opposed in this effort by the labor representatives on the supervisory board who, like their bank counterparts, represent the interests of fixed claimants.

The above description of corporate governance in Germany makes it clear that the U.S. is not the only country to experience a separation of ownership and control. Like most individual U.S. shareholders, outside German shareholders also lack "the information, skill and incentive to monitor managers."[42] The difference appears to be that in America the managers wield the decisive power, whereas in Germany management shares this power with the banks.

In addition, German banks, like banks in Japan, use their power to protect incumbent management by effectively eliminating the market for corporate control for German firms. One study reports that the total number of takeovers in Germany during the 1980s was less than one-half of that in the U.K., and that there have only been four recorded cases of hostile takeovers in Germany since World War II.[43]

---

37   "Those German Banks and their Industrial Treasuries," *Economist*, Jan. 21, 1995, at 71 (85% of Germany's 171 largest non-financial firms have single shareholders who own more than 25% of the voting stock; only 6% of these large blocs are owned by banks). 10% of the total market capitalization is owned directly by banks. Hauck, "The Equity Market in Germany," in *Institutional Investors and Corporate Governance* 561 (Baums, ed., 1994).

38   Roe, cited earlier, p. 1998.

39   Ibid., p. 1938.

40   Arno Gottschalk, "Der Stimmrechteinfluss der Banken in den Aktionärsversammlungen der Grossunternehmen," 5 *WSI-Mitteilungen* 294, 298 (1988).

41. Ramseyer, cited earlier, p. 3.

42   Roe, cited earlier, p. 1933.

43   See (in this issue) Julian Franks and Colin Mayer, "Corporate Ownership and Control in the U.K., Germany, and France," *Journal of Applied Corporate Finance* Vol. 9 No. 4 (Winter 1997).

IMPLICATIONS FOR AMERICAN CORPORATE GOVERNANCE

We wish to stress that our point is not that the U.S. system of corporate governance is superior to the corporate governance systems in Germany and Japan. Our point is merely to show that the supposed advantages of the German and Japanese systems have been exaggerated, and the costs understated. These costs come not only in the form of excessive risk aversion, which leads to a stifling of innovation, but – perhaps more important – in the form of illiquid, undeveloped and poorly functioning capital markets.

For several reasons, the incentives for market participants to develop equity markets are far smaller in Germany and Japan than in the U.S. First, German and Japanese banks limit gains to residual claimants on the upside, thus reducing the potential gains from investing in the stock market. Second, the highly concentrated patterns of share-ownership in Germany and Japan have made hostile takeovers – a major source of potential gains for target company shareholders – practically impossible for most firms. Third, these concentrated patterns of share ownership also have reduced market liquidity, since these stable shareholdings reduce the order flow in the market, thereby depriving the market of liquidity. Finally, and perhaps most important, the core purpose of the German and Japanese corporate governance systems has been to produce stability for systems that during the immediate post-War period experienced massive uncertainty.[44] But there is growing evidence that this kind of stability is not a virtue today, when global competition and rapid technological innovation are placing a far higher premium on innovation and flexibility.

For purposes of comparing the American system of corporate governance with the Japanese and German systems, we will focus in this section on three sets of problems that exist within the American system. The first problem is the possibility of excessive risk-taking. Just as the German and Japanese bank-dominated systems may cause firms to forsake potentially profitable projects that are perceived as too risky by the banks, the American system may cause firms to undertake excessively risky projects because weak banks in America are unable to monitor and control excessive risk-taking as effectively as German and Japanese banks. Second, in recent years, American politics has increasingly interfered with the functioning of the U.S. market for corporate control, which is the central device for disciplining managers in market-oriented corporate governance systems such as those in the U.S. and the U.K. Finally, a set of seemingly minor rules in the U.S. reduces the ability of banks and other debtholders to monitor and control borrowers. Thus, while the levels of domination and control by banks in Germany and Japan are probably too high, the level of bank control in the U.S. is probably artificially low.

The problem of excessive risk-taking

Just as fixed claimants can transfer wealth to themselves from equity claimants by using their influence and control to reduce the riskiness of a firm, so too can equity claimants increase their own wealth at the expense of the fixed claimants by *increasing* the riskiness of the firm. The goal of a properly functioning corporate governance structure is to reach the appropriate bargaining equilibrium between the risk-taking proclivities of shareholders and the risk-avoidance proclivities of the fixed claimants.

Several features of the U.S. system of corporate governance, as already noted, combine to reduce the ability of shareholders to act opportunistically by increasing risk-taking. First, fixed claimants can protect themselves against this contingency through the use of loan covenants and other contractual means. Second, U.S. banks often make loans with relatively short maturities, and require borrowers to rely on revolving lines of credit. This places borrowers in a pattern of repeat dealings with particular banks because they realize that they will have to return to the banks for additional

---

44   This is especially true in Japan (see Morck & Nakamura, p. 6) despite the efforts of laws instituted by the post-war Allied Occupation Government. See Roe, cited earlier, p. 1972. Germany, which has traditionally relied heavily on central banks since Bismarck, naturally looked to central banks as sources of economic stability after the Second World War. See ibid. at 1971.

extensions of credit when their existing loans have matured. Third, by buying convertible bonds (convertible into equity claims) instead of ordinary bonds, fixed claimants can reduce borrowers' incentives to engage in excessive risk-taking because convertible bondholders share with equity claimants the gains from risky projects that turn out well. Fourth, to the extent the managers that are said to control U.S. firms have claims that resemble debt more than equity, they too have incentives to discourage excessive risk-taking.

For all of these reasons, then, the danger to American firms of excessive risk-taking does not appear nearly as great as the danger to Japanese and German firms of excessive risk-avoidance and stasis.

The market for corporate control

The market for corporate control, which takes advantage of the price-setting mechanism of the U.S. stock market, lies at the heart of the American system of corporate governance. Managers unable to produce levels of performance acceptable to shareholders may find themselves replaced by a hostile bidder with a rival management team. Between 1985 and 1990, hostile takeovers accounted for $140 billion in financial transactions in the U.S.[45] Moreover, innovations in corporate finance, such as bridge financing and junk bonds, created a competitive environment in which virtually every firm in the economy was a potential takeover target. Such a capital-market environment had the effect of increasing managerial efficiency, since a high share price is the best defense against a hostile takeover.

Contrary to critics' claims, moreover, the available evidence fails to support the hypothesis that hostile takeovers are undesirable because they induce managers to focus too much on short-term share prices to the detriment of long-term performance. In an efficient stock market – and U.S. markets are widely held to be the most efficient in the world – the share prices set by investors reflect

the present value of the corporations' expected future returns to shareholders. Thus, firms that invest heavily in promising R&D and other long-term projects do not suffer from lower share prices and increased chances of takeover because their current share prices reflect the expected future payoffs from long-term investments.

Confirming this logic, studies conclude that firms with heavy R&D investments are less likely, not more likely, to be the subject of a hostile takeover than other firms.[46] Studies also report that hostile takeovers do not lead to massive layoffs. Indeed most blue-collar workers keep their jobs after hostile takeovers. The layoffs that occur are in the ranks of middle managers, most of whom find replacement jobs surprisingly quickly.[47]

The problem with American corporate governance, then, is not that hostile takeovers are bad, but that there are not enough of them due to regulatory restrictions and misguided legal policies. The volume of hostile takeovers in the U.S. declined from a high of $46 billion in 1989 to less than $500 million in 1993. State law rules restricting takeovers have become increasingly prohibitive, a testament to the political success of incumbent management in dealing with local state legislatures at the expense of out-of-state shareholders.[48] In fact, the inability of the shareholders of U.S. public corporations to galvanize into an effective political coalition to block incumbent managements' political maneuvering against hostile takeovers is probably the most costly consequence of widely dispersed share ownership. Such political maneuvering culminated in the Pennsylvania anti-takeover law of 1990, which amounted to a massive wealth transfer from shareholders to incumbent management.

In addition to these anti-takeover laws, incumbent management has been successful in persuading state legislatures to pass so-called "other constituency" statutes. These statutes empower corporate management to take the interests of workers, local

---

45 *The Economist*, "Corporate Governance Survey," cited earlier, p. 6.

46 Jonathan R. Macey, "State Anti-Takeover Statutes: Good Politics, Bad Economics," *Wisconsin Law Review* 467 (1988).

47 See Roberta Romano, "A Guide to Takeovers: Theory, Evidence, and Regulation," 9 *Yale Law Journal* (1992); Michael C. Jensen, The Modern Industrial Revolution, Exit, and the Failure of Internal Control Systems, 48 *Journal of Finance*, 831, July 1993.

48 Ibid.

communities, suppliers and customers into account when making decisions about whether and how to resist hostile acquisition attempts.[49] In reality, such statutes are used by incumbent management to justify their efforts to protect their own interests at the expense of the shareholders'.

State court judges have provided little, if any, comfort to shareholders. In particular, they have done little to curb the use of poison pill anti-takeover devices, which can be adopted without shareholder vote by a target company board of directors. Nevertheless, in December 1993, the Delaware Supreme Court prevented Paramount from using its poison pill to prevent a hostile takeover by QVC. This decision may auger a change in attitude by courts in favor of shareholders' interests. This, in turn, could usher in a new era for hostile takeovers in the United States.

Do hostile takeovers come too late?

One legitimate complaint against hostile takeovers as a corporate governance mechanism is that "companies have to go further off course before attracting a hostile bid than they might if they were monitored continuously."[50] Hostile bids are extremely capital intensive, not only because they require a major financing commitment, but also because bidders must invest a substantial amount of resources in research to *identify* undervalued targets before ever making a bid. Unless a firm is substantially undervalued, bidders will not be able to recoup these capital and search costs.

There are at least three problems with this analysis. First, it does not really distinguish the American system of corporate governance from the German and Japanese systems. As in the U.S., German and Japanese firms must go substantially off course before attracting outside intervention. Moreover, as fixed claimants, the German and Japanese banks are less concerned than U.S. shareholders about relatively small deviations from optimal performance levels that do not threaten

payments of interest and principal (and the associated fees).

A second problem with criticizing the takeover market as too costly a system of corporate governance is that the market for corporate control affects managerial performance *even in the absence of a formally announced takeover bid*. A robust market for corporate control improves management's performance because incumbents wish to lower the probability that an outside bid will be made. This causes managers to work harder.

Finally, it is a mistake to think of takeovers as an all-or-nothing issue. Investors can take steps short of launching a full-blown tender offer that effectively put a target company in play. For example, investors can launch a proxy contest for as little as $5,000 (down from $1 million a few years ago).[51] Similarly, it is increasingly common for large institutional investors to purchase stakes in troubled firms they believe to suffer from management problems and to monitor management by using their stakes to put representatives on to corporate boards where they can "agitate for better performance."[52] Critical to the success of such strategies is the existence of a credible threat of a management change if corporate performance does not improve. The problem with the German and Japanese systems is that a lack of capital market liquidity – combined with the intense loyalty of the banks towards incumbent management – removes the ability of insurgent shareholders to make a credible threat of a hostile takeover in the event managerial performance does not improve.

This is not to suggest that the market for corporate control worked perfectly in the U.S. during the 1980s. Critics are right to say that share prices must decline too far before the market begins to function. The point, rather, is that monitors in Germany and Japan also lack the incentive to intervene before firm values have declined significantly. Moreover, if the problem with the takeover market is that firms must decline too far before the market begins to operate, the solution is to design a regulatory system that lowers the costs of intervention. This is not happening in Germany, Japan,

49 Macey and Miller, "Corporate Stakeholders: A Contractual Perspective" 43 *University of Toronto Law Journal* 401 (1993).
50 *The Economist*, "Corporate Governance Survey," p. 13.

51 Ibid., p. 16.
52 Ibid.

or the U.S., largely because of the formidable power of incumbent management to resist change.

Rules limiting monitoring and control by U.S. intermediaries

After legal impediments to the market for corporate control, our most serious criticism of the American system of corporate governance is that other legal rules prevent U.S. financial intermediaries from protecting themselves contractually against the "moral hazard problem" posed by corporate borrowers. (By moral hazard, we mean the incentive discussed earlier of managers as shareholders' representatives to increase the risk of the firm after issuing debt.) Although fixed claimants clearly have an incentive to monitor and control corporate borrowers, a variety of legal rules in the U.S. constrain the ability of lenders to do so.

In a series of important articles, Mark Roe has discussed both the historical origins and consequences of a number of these rules.[53] As Roe observes,

American legal restrictions have historically kept American banks small and weak, by banning them from operating nationally, entering commerce, affiliating with investment banks, equity mutual funds, or insurers, or from coordinating stockholdings with these other intermediaries.[54]

Our emphasis differs from Roe's. We are less interested in the ability of banks to dominate American corporate finance, but more concerned about legal restrictions that prevent U.S. banks from simply protecting their positions as fixed claimants. These restrictions raise capital costs and lower allocative efficiency by raising the costs of fixed claims to American firms.

In a nutshell, a variety of legal doctrines exist in the U.S. that expose lenders to risks of liability if they attempt to write contracts that provide protection from moral hazard by borrowers. While many of these liability rules derive from the reasonable doctrine that borrowers are protected by a generalized obligation of good faith imposed on banks, the courts often interpret them in ways that are inconsistent with basic principles of freedom of contract.[55] Expanded principles of lender liability have enabled borrowers to engage in opportunistic behavior, transferring wealth to themselves from their banks by bringing law suits against banks that threaten to enforce their contractual rights against the borrowers.[56]

When banks, for example, have merely threatened to use a management change clause (a contractual provision ostensibly allowing lenders to declare a default if top officers are appointed who do not meet their approval), borrowers have been successful in suing banks for interfering with contractual relations between the borrowers and their employees.[57] Courts have even forced banks to loan more money or give more advance notice of termination of a lending relationship than required by contract.[58] Furthermore, banks that become actively involved in the affairs of borrowers in order to protect the value of their security interests may face massive liability for environmental damage caused by the borrowers.

Bankruptcy rules further chill the incentive of U.S. banks to take an active role in the affairs of borrowers by discouraging such intervention precisely when it would be most helpful – namely, when the borrower is in distress. Specifically, U.S. bankruptcy law strips senior lenders of their claims to collateral and/or subordinates their claims to those of junior lenders if other creditors can show that the lender exercised some degree of control over the borrower. This principle, which is known as *equitable subordination*, provides a powerful disincentive for banks to play an active role in corporate governance.

In the classic *American Lumber* case, a U.S. bank assisted in restructuring a troubled debtor after it

53   Mark J. Roe, "A Political Theory of American Corporate Finance," 91 *Colum. L. Rev.* 10 (1991); Mark J. Roe. "Political and Legal Restraints on Ownership and Control of Public Companies," 27 *J. Fin. Econ.* (1990).
54   Roe, *Yale L.J.*, cited earlier, p. 1948.
55   Macey and Miller, "Banking Law and Regulation," cited earlier, p. 206.
56   Daniel R. Fischel, "The Economics of Lender Liability," 99 *Yale L.J.* 131, 141–142 (1989).
57   *State National Bank of El Paso v. Farah Manufacturing Co., Inc.*, 678 F.2d 661.
58   *K.M.C. Inc. v. Irving Trust Co.*, 757 F.2d 752, 759–763 (6th Cir. 1986).

advanced the debtor extra funds. When the debtor began to fail despite the bank's efforts, the bank tried to recover its funds. The other creditors complained of preferential treatment, and they persuaded a court to subordinate the banks' claims to theirs:

> While [the bank] argues that subordination will cause members of the financial community to feel they cannot give financial assistance to failing companies, but must instead foreclose on their security interests and collect debts swiftly, not leaving any chance for survival, the Court is singularly unimpressed.[59]

Thus, America's corporate governance problem may not stem from a lack of concentrated share blocks and powerful financial intermediaries, as Roe suggests. Rather, the problem may arise from American courts' and legislatures' unwillingness to enforce the contractual provisions that financial intermediaries and borrowers agree upon. Enforcing such contractual provisions would not only protect the banks from moral hazard, but also permit borrowers to reduce their borrowing costs.

CONVERGENCE OF THE SYSTEMS

Many commentators have argued recently that the American, German and Japanese systems of corporate governance are converging, each becoming more like the other. For such convergence to take place, however, three things would have to happen. First, German and Japanese banks would have to decrease their concentrated levels of share ownership in order to promote more liquid capital markets and the development of a market for corporate control. Second, the control over corporate funding currently enjoyed by German and Japanese banks would have to diminish in order to facilitate the development of capital markets. And finally, of course, patterns of concentrated share ownership would have to emerge in the U.S.

With regard to the decrease in concentrated levels of share ownership in Germany and Japan, it is clear that no convergence is taking place. In Germany, bank ownership of large blocks of stock

is increasing, rather than decreasing; and in Japan bank ownership of stock has remained remarkably stable over time.[60] Nevertheless, the market share of German and Japanese banks in funding corporate borrowers does appear to be falling.[61] And, taking these two facts together, it might appear that corporate governance in Germany and Japan will improve as the banks' interests as shareholders come to dominate their interests as fixed claimants. Although this is a distinct and promising possibility, we wish to emphasize that the conflicts that exist between banks and outside equity holders in Germany and Japan come not only from the banks' status as fixed claimants, but also from the banks' capital structure, which is characterized by extremely heavy leverage, and a large percentage of funding due to creditors (depositors) on demand. This capital structure requires the banks to maintain stable cash flows in order to survive. Thus, German and Japanese banks have a strong incentive to act like fixed claimants despite the fact that they hold substantial equity claims on their clients.

Finally, commentators tentatively have hypothesized that U.S. firms may be evolving "toward the German and Japanese style of ownership" because U.S. financial intermediaries are taking a more active role in the management of the firms in which they invest.[62] Warren Buffett's firm, Berkshire Hathaway, provides the model for the new form of American investor. Lazard Freres and Dillon Read, two American investment banks, offer investment funds that specialize in identifying undervalued and poorly managed companies, and contributing managerial expertise to improving performance within these firms.[63] Also worth noting are the LBO firms like KKR, Forstmann Little,

---

60 See, e.g., Mark Roe, "Some Differences in Corporate Governance in Germany, Japan, and America," in *Institutional Investors and Corporate Governance* 24 (Baums, et al. eds., 1994); and The Economist Corporate Governance Survey, at 17.

61 Ramseyer, cited earlier, "Explicit Reasons for Implicit Contracts," pp. 12–14; Roe, "Some Differences in Corporate Structure," cited earlier, p. 1960; Michael H. Best & Jane Humphries, "The City and Industrial Decline," in *The Decline of the British Economy*, pp. 223–224 (Bernard Elbaum & William Lazonick eds., 1986); Zoglin, "Stable Cross-Holding of Shares Likely to Withstand Pressures," *Japan Econ. J.*, June 21, 1986 at 7.

62 Roe, *Yale L.J.*, cited earlier, p. 1965.

63 *The Economist*, "Corporate Governance Survey," p. 16.

---

59 *In re American Lumber Co.*, 5 B.R. 470, 478 (D.C. Minn. 1980).

and Clayton & Dubilier, which have purchased controlling blocks and board positions at some large U.S. firms.

Commentators who draw an analogy between this emerging pattern of relational investing in the U.S. and the corporate governance structures of Germany and Japan fail to recognize the critical distinction between the American firms and the German and Japanese banks. The American intermediaries make largely equity investments and fund those investments with equity or long-term debt, whereas the German and Japanese banks' claims are predominantly fixed and are funded primarily with short-term debt. Thus, it stands to reason that the new American financial intermediaries will represent the interests of equity claimants more effectively than their Japanese and German counterparts, whose power and authority to monitor is compromised by conflicts of interest with the equity claimants of the firms in which they have invested.

The effectiveness of corporate governance efforts by purchasers of large blocks of shares depends on their ability to make a credible threat to displace management teams that resist their efforts at reform. Unless these large block purchasers can make a credible threat to obtain control themselves, or to transfer their block to a hostile bidder who will obtain control, incumbent management has no reason to listen to the suggestions made by these "relational investors." In other words, relational investing should be viewed as a complement to, but not as a substitute for, a robust market for corporate control.

The import of current bank reform for U.S. corporate governance

Responding to the declining market share of U.S. firms in the financial services sector of the world economy, several proposals recently have been offered to reduce the legal barriers that the Bank Holding Company Act and the Glass Steagall Act pose to affiliations between banks and securities firms. As the banking industry's share of U.S. financial assets has decreased over the last 20 years from 66% to less than 30%, and as U.S. banks have disappeared from the ranks of the world's major

financial institutions, policymakers have come to realize that allowing banks to affiliate with the providers of other financial services may enable the banking industry become viable competitors in the financial markets.

On February 2, 1995, Alfonse D'Amato, Chairman of the Senate Committee on Banking, Housing and Urban Affairs introduced the Depository Institution Affiliation Act (DIAA). And on February 27, 1995, Jim Leach, Chairman of the House Banking Committee, offered a revised version of his Financial Services Competitiveness Act of 1995. Under both of these proposals, the Bank Holding Company Act of 1956 would be renamed the "Financial Services Holding Company Act of 1995," and bank holding companies would be transformed into new financial services holding companies. The scope of permissible activities for the non-bank affiliates of these holding companies would be expanded to allow these affiliates to conduct any activities deemed by the Board of Governors of the Federal Reserve System to be "financial in nature." Under these proposals, the powers of securities affiliates of bank holding companies would be expanded to permit such affiliates to engage in the underwriting of corporate debt, equity, and mutual fund shares; and Glass-Steagall would be modified to allow commercial banks to affiliate with investment banking organizations to an unlimited extent.

We strongly favor the liberalization of the Glass-Steagall Act, and we wish to emphasize that the problems with commercial bank involvement in corporate governance that we have identified in this article are not likely to develop in the U.S. if the Glass-Steagall and Bank Holding Company Acts are liberalized to permit greater involvement by banks in the securities business, because the structure of the U.S. financial services sector will prevent bank domination of the kind that one observes in Germany, and, to a lesser extent in Japan.

First, we wish to observe that, from the perspective of U.S. banking organizations, greater involvement in the securities business will bring significant benefits in the form of lower risk through diversification, as well as lower operating costs through increased economies of scale and scope. In fact, recent studies have shown that far from increasing the riskiness of banking institutions, securities activities actually makes banks safer and less likely to fail.[64]

The economies of scope occur because the information that banks gather in the course of making credit evaluations of commercial borrowers also can be used to make decisions regarding the underwriting and selling of the securities of these commercial borrowers. Economies of scale will be achieved by combining the data processing and other back-office operations of these financial services holding companies. Similarly, the riskiness of bank lending activities can be reduced because, under the proposed legislation, banks may gain access to more extensive customer information through their affiliation with the other enterprises, which could in turn enable them to make more informed judgments in extending credit to certain borrowers.

All of these benefits can be realized without banks achieving such control over the voting shares of their corporate clients that they would be inclined to use that control in ways that would harm the interests of non-bank shareholders. There is no reason to believe that U.S. commercial banks would use their control over borrowing firms to intrude into the corporate governance of such firms. In this context, it is important to recognize that U.S. banks will not have any expanded securities powers under any of these new legislative proposals. These proposals merely allow for more extensive affiliations between U.S. banks and securities firms. And U.S. securities firms, unlike European banks, make a point of not intruding in the corporate governance of their clients. Rather, U.S. investment banks limit their activities to underwriting, trading, and general investment banking advice about mergers and acquisitions and corporate finance.

One important reason for such specialization is that the American financial services sector is uniquely characterized by both intense competition and heterogeneity. Investment banking firms that attempted to intrude into the corporate governance of their clients would quickly find themselves without clients because, unlike Japanese and German corporations, U.S. firms can switch investment banking relationships with impunity. Moreover, in the U.S., powerful, independent, non-bank institutional investors such as insurance companies, pension funds, and mutual funds would strongly object to efforts by financial services holding companies to assert themselves in the corporate governance of publicly traded companies.

Path dependence provides a final reason why the current proposals to liberalize the scope of permissible affiliations between banks and securities firms in the U.S. does not pose a serious threat of excessive bank control to the U.S. corporate governance system. Simply put, while the U.S. banking industry has languished, U.S. capital markets have filled the gap as the principal suppliers of capital to U.S. industry. Consequently, it is too late for U.S. banking organizations to use their influence over corporate governance to retard the growth of U.S. capital markets.

CONCLUSION

Perhaps the most powerful corporate governance device of all is vigorous competition in the product and labor markets. Such competition forces firms to work hard and to compete for capital. The rapid globalization of trade and investment therefore will lead to improved corporate governance throughout the world. Nevertheless, those economies with the best corporate governance structures will outperform rival economies at the margin.

The purpose of this article has been to show that the "continuous and textured" monitoring that characterizes the relational investing conducted by financial intermediaries in Japan and Germany is not a panacea. The problems posed by these systems are the result of straightforward conflicts of interests between the risk-averse fixed claimants who make loans and control the investment process,

---

64 For example, Eugene White found that the securities operations of commercial banks did not impair their stability prior to Glass-Steagall because banks that engaged in securities activities did not have any higher earning variance or lower capital ratios than banks without such operations. White also reports that, in the bank crisis during the Great Depression, more than 25% of all U.S. national banks failed, but less than 10% of banks with securities affiliates failed. Eugene White, "Before the Glass-Steagall Act: An Analysis of the Investment Banking Activities of National Banks," 23 *Explorations in Economic History* 33 (1986). See also Randall S. Kroszner and Raghuram G. Rajam, "Is the Glass-Steagall Act Justified? A Study of the U.S. Experience with Universal Banking Before 1933," 84 *American Economic Review*, pp. 810–811 at footnote 3 (1994).

and the residual claimants who put up the risk capital and have the greatest stake in the financial success of the firm. Moreover, the highly leveraged capital structure of banks, along with the fact that their liabilities are due to depositors on demand, further detract from any claim that such firms are ideal monitors. This capital structure makes these banks dependent on steady cash flows, and contributes to a high level of risk aversion, which suits the interests of incumbent management as well.

Existing theories of relational investing demonstrate an unfortunate tendency to treat all financial intermediaries alike. This tendency has resulted in a failure to distinguish between the interests of equity investors and fixed claimants. Moreover, the existing theories extolling the virtues of bank-dominated systems of corporate governance do not take sufficient account of the adverse effects such systems have had on the development of capital markets in those countries employing such systems. Put differently, the strong role played by financial intermediaries has retarded the growth of primary and secondary markets for equity, and has thereby suppressed an important source of risk-capital for firms.

The American corporate governance system is by no means perfect. In the United States, the market for corporate control is a market-generated solution to the lack of monitoring that characterizes the large American corporation with widely dispersed share ownership. Outside bidders protect the interests of shareholders by monitoring management in publicly traded firms and by launching hostile bids when firms underperform. But, in recent years, politics has interfered with the efficacy of the market for corporate control, with state antitakeover statutes dramatically reducing the number of hostile takeovers in the U.S. Especially in the absence of a healthy takeover market, the weakness of American financial intermediaries is cause for concern. Unfortunately, several U.S. legal doctrines have artificially limited the ability of banks to monitor their borrowers. As a result, while the degree of banks' influence in Germany and Japan is probably excessive, in the U.S. it is probably too low.

The problem in Germany and Japan is that the interests of equity investors are insufficiently represented in corporate governance. The problem in the U.S. is that the takeover market is too restricted and fixed claimants are unable fully to protect themselves contractually from the moral hazard posed by their borrowers. Both of these deficiencies in corporate governance structures raise the cost of capital and reduce allocational efficiency. Rather than investing resources in copying each others' systems, each system would be better off by focusing on, and repairing, its own problems.

CHAPTER 38

Which Capitalism? Lessons from the East Asian Crisis

Raghuram G. Rajan and Luigi Zingales
(University of Chicago)

Just a few years ago, it was fashionable to decry the short-sightedness of the American financial system, the widely alleged tendency of U.S. financial markets to ignore longer-term corporate prospects while focusing on quarterly earnings reports. There were repeated calls for the U.S. to adopt new laws that would permit financiers to take a longer view of their investments, and to move toward the more relationship-based investing model that prevails in Japan.[1]

It is amazing what a banking crisis or two will do to popular fashion. Now the talk is all about the virtues of "the market," the importance of competition and disclosure, and the horrors of crony capitalism.

Why did these relationship-based financial systems, which have been credited with fueling the miraculous growth of East Asia, suddenly implode? Is the current crisis a temporary setback to an otherwise successful system or does it herald its demise? Does the slow but steady ascendance of the public markets, even in Germany, suggest the eventual supremacy of the arm's-length, market-based Anglo-Saxon system?

---

1 See, for example, Michael Porter, "Capital Choices: Changing the Way America Invests in Industry," *Journal of Applied Corporate Finance*, Vol. 5 No. 2 (Summer 1992), pp. 4–16.

RELATIONSHIP VERSUS ARM'S-LENGTH SYSTEMS

To answer these questions, let's begin with a sketch of the salient features of these two kinds of systems. Like all sketches, this one has elements of caricature, but this is the price we have to pay to avoid being distracted by the details.

A financial system has two primary goals: to channel resources to their most productive uses and to ensure that an adequate portion of the return flows to the financier. The latter is, of course, crucial to the former. Without a guarantee of an adequate return, funds will not be made available for investment.

Relationship-based systems ensure a return to the financier by granting her some form of power over the firm being financed. The simplest form of power is when the financier has (implicit or explicit) ownership of the firm. The financier can also serve as the sole or main lender, supplier, or customer. In all of these forms, the financier attempts to secure her return on investment by retaining some kind of monopoly power over the firm she finances. As with every monopoly, this requires some barriers to entry. These barriers may come from regulation, or lack of transparency – or "opacity" – of the system, which substantially raises the costs of entry to potential competitors.

Contrast this with the arm's-length, Anglo-Saxon system, where the financier is protected by explicit contracts. In such systems, contracts and associated prices determine the transactions that are undertaken. As a result, institutional relationships matter less and the market becomes a more important medium in determining the terms of transactions.

An important distinction between these two systems is their different degree of reliance on legal enforcement. Relationship-based systems can survive in environments where laws are poorly drafted or contracts not enforced. The relationship is largely self-governing; parties intent on maintaining their "reputations" honor the spirit of agreements (often in the absence of any written contract) in order to ensure a steady flow of future business within the same network of firms. By contrast, the prompt and unbiased enforcement of contracts by courts is a pre-condition for the viability of a market-based system. Moreover, since contracts are typically hard to write with the wealth of detail necessary to fully govern transactions, it is important that the law offer a helping hand. Under common law, the court tries to follow the spirit rather than the letter of a contract, thus enabling contracts to offer greater protection. For this reason, it is perhaps no surprise that market-based systems are found largely in countries with a common-law tradition (hence the "Anglo-Saxon" model).[2]

Another distinction between the two systems is the relative importance of transparency. Market-based systems require transparency as a guarantee of protection. In the words of Franklin Roosevelt, "Sunlight is said to be the best of disinfectants; electric light the most efficient policemen."[3] By contrast, relationship-based systems are designed to preserve opacity, which has the effect of protecting relationships from the threat of competition.

An example: credit

Before going further, let us consider the example of a transaction – the extension of credit – in each of the two systems. In a relationship-based system, a bank will have close ties with a potential borrowing firm, perhaps because of frequent past contacts or because of ownership links. In assessing the borrowing needs of the firm and its ability to pay interest and principal, the bank will consider not only the firm's current debt-servicing capability, but also its long-term ability to repay and the various non-contractual levers the bank can push to extract repayment.[4] The interest rate charged will be repeatedly negotiated over time, and may not have a direct relationship to the intrinsic risk of the project.

In an arm's-length system, by contrast, the firm will be able to tap a wider circle of potential lenders because there will be more financial information about it. The loan will be contracted for a specific period, and the interest rate will be a competitive one that compensates the lender for time and the risk of the particular loan.

Limitations on competition in a relationship system do not just give the financier power, but also strengthen his incentive to cooperate with the borrower. Studies show that the main banks of Japanese keiretsus went out of their way to help financially distressed borrowers within their keiretsus. For example, Sumitomo Bank not only effectively guaranteed Mazda's debts when it got into trouble after the first oil shock, but also orchestrated a rescue, in part by exhorting employees within its keiretsu to buy Mazda cars.[5] Sumitomo's incentive to help would have been considerably weaker if Mazda had had the option of giving the lion's share of its business, once it emerged from distress, to some other bank. As this example suggests, the effective limitations on outside competition imposed by the keiretsu system enable lenders to "internalize" a greater share of the benefits accruing to borrowers than is possible in an arm's-length, competitive banking environment.

The absence of competition and disclosure in a relationship-based system imply that there are really no price signals to guide decisions. Unlike an

---

2   See Rafael la Porta, Florencio Lopez de Silanes, Andrei Shleifer, and Robert Vishny, "The Legal Determinants of External Finance," *Journal of Finance*, 52 (1997).
3   In Joel Seligman, *The Transformation of Wall Street*, Northeastern University Press, Boston 1995, p. 42.

4   For example, the bank may refuse to extend a blanket guarantee to the firm's other creditors, or refuse to provide new financing or even take a piece of it, if the firm is not cooperative.
5   See Takeo Hoshi, Anil Kashyap, and David Scharfstein, "The Role of Banks in Reducing the Costs of Financial Distress in Japan", *Journal of Financial Economics*, 27, 67–88 (1990).

arm's-length system, where a number of competitive lenders can give a borrowing firm independent assessments of the costs of undertaking a project, the cost a borrower faces in the relationship-based system is simply what the relationship lender and the borrower negotiate. Since there can be substantial value created in the relationship, and the negotiation and allocation of this "surplus" is a function of each party's power, the effective cost can deviate substantially from the true risk-adjusted cost over a long period.

Do Relationship-Based Systems Always Lead to Worse Investment Decisions?

But is this necessarily a bad thing? Are lending and investment decisions always inefficient if the cost of funds differs from their true cost? Are there no redeeming features of a relationship-based system? The answer to all these questions is no. In the real world with all its "imperfections," an imperfect cost of funds can sometimes produce the right investment decisions.

For instance, consider our previous example of a firm in distress. Taking into consideration all the value that the firm adds to society – to workers, customers, and local governments as well as shareholders – the company may be worth saving. But, *in the short run*, the true cost of funding may far exceed what the firm can pay without creating further investment distortions.[6] And in the competitive arm's-length system, a lender may not be able to recoup or "internalize" enough of the firm's value in the long run to be able to offer it subsidized financing in the short run. So the firm is much less likely to be bailed out in the competitive, arm's-length system. By contrast, a lender in a relationship-based system, confident in the strength of the relationship (and the protection it affords from competition), can offer a below-market rate in the short run and then recoup its losses with an above-market rate over the long run

when the firm is healthy and can afford high payouts. In sum, relationship banks can be viewed as using their monopoly power to charge above-market rates in normal circumstances in return for an implicit agreement to provide below-market financing when their borrowers get into trouble.

A recent study (involving one of the present writers) provides evidence of such relationship lending practices even in the U.S.[7] In examining bank loans to small businesses in different banking "markets" throughout the U.S.,[8] the study finds that in "concentrated" markets (those where most of the lending is done by a handful of banks) more credit is available to young firms than in more competitive banking markets. To the extent that young firms are subject to more credit "rationing," as many observers have suggested, the evidence suggests that the relationship-based system does a better job of ensuring that value-adding projects get funded.

The study also finds that the interest rates charged younger firms are lower, on average, in concentrated markets than in competitive markets, with the effect reversing for older firms. This suggests that banks in concentrated markets can offer more credit on economic terms because their relationships allow "intertemporal cross-subsidies" – that is, below-market rates for younger firms that are compensated for by above-market rates for more mature firms with greater ability to pay. Such subsidies, as suggested earlier, would not be possible in more competitive markets.

Clearly, it is this kind of ability to "internalize joint surplus" – that is, to trade off short-run losses for longer-run gains – that led so many observers, including many economists, to defend the efficiency of relationship-based systems. But it is easy to see the problems that can arise in such systems. Perhaps most important, the relationship-based system does not pay much attention to market or price signals. And this indifference to price signals becomes self-fulfilling: If investment decisions are

---

6   For example, too high an interest rate could lead the firm to take riskier, negative NPV projects. See Michael Jensen and William Meckling, "Theory of the Firm, Managerial Behavior, Agency Costs, and Capital Structure," *Journal of Financial Economics* 3 (1976).

7   See Mitchell Petersen and Raghuram Rajan, "The Effect of Credit Market Competition on Lending Relationships," *Quarterly Journal of Economics*, 110, 407–443 (1995).

8   The idea of distinct banking markets makes sense in this case because small firms rarely do business with a bank outside their local banking market; the median borrower in the above cited study is only two miles from its bank.

not driven by prices, then prices become less effective in providing economic direction because they reflect less information.

This is not to say that the arm's-length system is a perfect allocator of resources. Because outsiders have little power under normal circumstances, management can indulge in considerable "empire-building" without triggering an intervention by outsiders (a problem that has been called "the agency costs of free cash flow" by Michael Jensen). Nevertheless, the arm's-length system can use hostile takeovers and LBOs to correct this problem when it gets out of hand.[9] In relationship-based systems, by contrast, the problem of misallocation of resources due to the lack of price signals is more troublesome, because such systems lack a self-activating corrective mechanism. In fact, even if the price signals were accurate, the power structures in relationship-based system may not allow movement in the direction indicated by the prices.

Evidence of this unwillingness to respond to market signals was provided by a 1991 study by Hoshi, Kashyap, and Scharfstein.[10] The study looked at a sample of Japanese firms in the late '70s and early '80s that had close ties to banks and compared their investment behavior with a sample that had no such ties. The investments of firms that had no bank ties were very sensitive to the cash flow the firms generated from operations; when operating cash flows decreased sharply, so did investment spending – and vice versa. By contrast, the investments of firms with strong ties to the banks were significantly less sensitive to the firms' operating cash flow.

As suggested earlier, one possible interpretation of these findings is that banking relationships make it easier for firms to obtain external funding for value-adding investments, thus making them less dependent on their own cash flows. But recent events in Japan suggest a different explanation. More often than not, the companies' continuous access to bank funding on favorable terms allowed them to ignore the signal sent by their poor cash flows and to continue investing. By continuing to invest in these circumstances, such firms may well have been destroying long-term value rather than increasing or preserving it. And, even if the banks were failing to provide the managers of these firms with the right signals, it appears that the stock market was attempting to do so. For, as the study also reported, the firms with strong bank ties in their sample had lower "Tobin's q" (or market-to-replacement cost) ratios than firms without bank ties. To the extent Tobin's q is a reliable proxy for a firm's investment opportunities, the stock market was expressing skepticism about the likely payoff from such investments.

Moreover, another study of Japanese firms published in the past year suggests that such market skepticism was warranted. For although Japanese firms with close bank ties had greater access to funds when their operating cash flows declined, such access did not enable them to achieve higher profits or growth rates than their peers.[11]

Yet another recent study provides additional evidence that relationships can distort the allocation of funds.[12] In the early 1990s, Japanese banks increased their lending to the U.S. commercial real estate market. At their peak in 1992, the U.S. subsidiaries of Japanese banks accounted for one fifth of all commercial real estate loans held in the U.S. banking sector. Then, in response to a severe decline in real estate prices in Japan, the Japanese banks cut back their lending in the U.S. even as U.S. prices were rising (and lending by non-Japanese banks increasing); at the same time they expanded their lending in the domestic Japanese market, where prices were plummeting. Thus, rather than cutting their losses in Japan – or at least not abandoning their profitable opportunities in the U.S. – Japanese banks poured more money into their unprofitable Japanese relationships.

---

9 If anything, managerial empire-building may be less of a problem in relationship-based systems precisely because financiers have the power to intervene extensively and absorb free cash flows from successful firms.

10 Takeo Hoshi, Anil Kashyap, and David Scharfstein, "Corporate Structure, Liquidity, and Investment: Evidence from Japanese Bank Data," *Quarterly Journal of Economics*, 27: (1991), 33–60.

11 See David Weinstein and Yishay Yafeh, "On the Costs of a Bank Centered Financial System: Evidence from the Changing Main Bank Relations in Japan," *Journal of Finance*, 53, 635–672 (1998).

12 See Joe Peek and Eric Rosengren, "The International Transmission of Financial Shocks: The Case of Japan," *American Economic Review*, 87, 495–505 (1998).

In sum, the message from the existing research is that although relationships may increase or preserve value in some cases – particularly when contracts are hard to write or enforce – they also have the downside that they do not rely on price signals. The consequence has been a widespread and costly misallocation of resources.

By contrast, market-based economies like the U.S. and U.K. sustained high levels of corporate investment throughout most of the '90s while still producing enough profit to reward shareholders. The relative prosperity of these economies can be attributed in no small part to their reliance on market prices to allocate resources. And indeed there appears to be a virtuous cycle at work here: in the process of relying on prices for guidance, the arm's-length transactions that predominate in these economies also have the beneficial effect of making prices more informative. Thus, the more transactions that come into the market, the more likely decisions made on the basis of price are likely to be the right ones. As we will argue below, in economies with a sufficient degree of contractual "infrastructure" to support them, arm's-length transactions are likely to lead to better decisions.

THE COSTS AND BENEFITS OF CONGLOMERATES: SOME EVIDENCE OF WHEN RELATIONSHIPS ADD VALUE

But, if relationship-based systems generally allocate resources less efficiently than market-based economies, how do we account for their popularity? After all, almost all economies, including the U.S., have at some point in their history relied heavily on relationships, particularly in earlier stages of development.[13] Thus, one promising hypothesis for the durability of the relationship-based system is that it works better than an arm's-length system in relatively less developed economies – those where contracts are ineffective and price signals from the market relatively uninformative.

Some support for this argument comes from recent research on the performance of conglomerate

organizations. Conglomerates can be thought of as the ultimate relationship-based financial system in the sense that the different business units that make up the organization receive financing from an internal capital market.

Several studies of conglomerates in the U.S. have shown that they trade at substantial discounts relative to stand-alone firms.[14] Moreover, these studies – including one that we recently completed (with Henri Servaes) – show that the size of the discount is related to the extent of the conglomerate's investments in relatively unprofitable segments. In particular, our study shows that both the discount and the degree of overinvestment in unprofitable businesses increase as the diversity of businesses within a conglomerate increases.[15]

Taken together, then, the evidence on U.S. conglomerates suggests that they trade at a significant discount relative to stand-alone firms, and that such discounts appear to be a direct function of the extent of resource misallocation. But do conglomerates perform better in less-developed economies?

There is some evidence for this, most of it fairly recent. In 1995, this journal published a study showing that the South African "groups" (collections of publicly traded companies with a pyramid ownership structure) have traded at consistent premiums to their net asset values (NAVs).[16] A more recent study finds that large diversified groups in India outperformed smaller unaffiliated firms between 1989 and 1995.[17] And a 1998 study of

13 See Charles Calomiris and Carlos Ramirez, "The Role of Financial Relationships in the History of American Corporate Finance," *Journal of Applied Corporate Finance*, Vol. 9, No. 2 (Summer 1996), pp. 52–74.

14 See, for example, Larry Lang and Rene Stulz, "Tobin's q, Corporate Diversification, and Firm Performance", *Journal of Political Economy*, 102, 1248–1291 (1994); and Philip Berger and Eli Ofek, "Diversification's Effect on Firm Value," *Journal of Financial Economics*, 37, 39–65.

15 See Raghuram Rajan, Henri Servaes, and Luigi Zingales, "The Costs of Diversity: The Diversification Discount and Inefficient Investment," mimeo, University of Chicago, http://gshlgz.uchicago.edu.

16 Graham Barr, Jos Gerson, and Brian Kantor, "Shareholders As Agents And Principals: The Case for South Africa's Corporate Ownership Struture," *Journal of Applied Corporate Finance*, Vol. 8, No. 1 (Spring 1995). Part of the groups' superior performance is attributed to the opportunities for diversification they provide large South African investors – opportunities that are likely to be valuable in regimes, like South Africa's, with relatively binding capital controls.

17 See Arun Khanna and Krishna Palepu, "Corporate Scope and Institutional Context: An Empirical Analysis of Diversified Indian Groups." Harvard Business School Working Paper (1997).

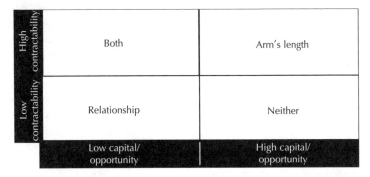

Figure 38.1 Systems Most Consistent with Different Environments

conglomerates in 35 countries reports that the relative value of diversification in a country is related to the country's income level.[18] Specifically, in low-income countries they find either a diversification *premium* or no discount, while in high-income countries they find a significant diversification discount.[19] Perhaps the most telling evidence for conglomerates, however, is the continuing dominance of this organizational form in Asia, Latin America, and much of Western Europe – indeed, almost everywhere outside the Anglo-Saxon world.[20] Of course, such dominance does not necessarily imply that they will continue to prevail, only that they have proved efficient in certain (possibly now past) circumstances.

A FRAMEWORK FOR THINKING ABOUT THE VALUE OF RELATIONSHIPS

From our discussion above, two factors seem important in determining whether relationships work well in an environment relative to arm's-length transactions. The first is the adequacy of

18   See Larry Fauver, Joel Houston and Andy Naranjo, "Capital Market Development, Legal Systems, and the Value of Corporate Diversification: A Cross Country Analysis," University of Florida Working Paper (1998).
19   This evidence should be viewed as preliminary, because Lins and Servaes find a conglomerate discount in six of the seven emerging markets they examine (see Karl Lins and Henri Servaes, "Is Corporate Diversification Beneficial in Emerging Markets?", London Business School Working Paper (1998).
20   See Khanna and Palepu, cited earlier.

the contractual "infrastructure" ("contractability" for short) in that environment. If much of the surplus value in a transaction can be contractually allocated, there is little role for a controlling financier to add value by reallocating the surplus to facilitate transactions. For this reason, the development of property rights, laws, and institutions (such as auditors and regulators) that facilitate transactions will reduce the relative value of relationships.

The second factor is the importance of price signals. In a situation of extreme capital scarcity, when it is relatively easy to determine that certain investments have positive net present values, decisions based on relationships are not likely to go very wrong. But in situations where the clearly profitable investments have been made and there is abundant capital chasing relatively few opportunities, price signals are very useful in helping to guide investment and relationships. In such cases, obscuring price signals can lead to investment that ends up destroying substantial value.

Figure 38.1 may be a useful way to summarize our framework. On the x axis is the ratio of available capital to investment opportunities, on the y axis is the degree to which institutional development facilitates contracting. As shown in the lower left corner of the figure, a relationship-based system is clearly better than an arm's-length system when there is little available capital relative to opportunities *and* when contractability is low. As shown in the upper right, an arm's-length system dominates when both are high. When the ratio of capital to opportunities is low but contractability is high, both systems work reasonably well – though, in most developed economies, the arm's-length system tends to supplant the relationship system over time.[21] This is because a well-functioning contractual system creates very good opportunities outside the relationship, and narrows the amount of give and take that is possible inside it. Finally, neither system works well when capital is relatively abundant and contractibility is low. The relationship system cannot allocate the capital effectively (it can easily lead to overinvestment) while the arm's-length system has limited ability to recover funds once they are invested.

Figure 38.1 begs the question: What brings about a change in the environment? The main force for such change appears to be major changes in investment opportunities or capital flows; institutional infrastructure changes tend to follow them, though often with a considerable lag. Moreover, there is no guarantee that institutional changes will keep pace with the changes in capital flows, or that the system itself will change to be consistent with the environment.

For example, consider a relationship system in a situation with low contractability and high capital availability relative to opportunities (in short, the condition of East Asia and most emerging economies a few years ago). An improvement in institutional infrastructure and the move towards an arm's-length system has the potential to improve matters. But there is no reason to believe that institutional change will be rapid or that the vested interests in the relationship system will permit such a move. The resulting inconsistency of the system with the environment can lead to distortions.

Let us now try and make some sense of the recent events in East Asia in the light of this framework.

MAKING SENSE OF THE ASIAN CRISIS

Until the end of the 1980s, the East Asian economies were overwhelmingly relationship-based

systems.[22] At the outset of liberalization, the volume of profitable investment opportunities greatly exceeded the available capital. This capital shortage in turn prompted a momentous change in the environment: namely, the opening up of these economies to capital flows – a development that coincided with the increased desire of Western banks and fund managers for international diversification.

But, as Figure 38.1 would suggest, there was a potential problem. A flood of foreign capital poured into these countries at a time when the institutional infrastructure was not adequately developed to permit direct contracting between these sources of capital and borrowers. Essentially, the arm's-length capital was lent to a relationship-based system that did not have adequate price signals to deploy the massive inflow of capital properly.[23] The economies moved from the lower left-hand box in Figure 38.1 to the lower right hand box, an environment where neither system can be expected to work very well.

Not only did foreign lenders not always know whether their funds were being deployed appropriately, they also did not have the institutional safeguards to protect their investment.[24] Therefore they took the next best route – they kept their loans and investments short term so that they could pull out at any indication of trouble.[25] So long as the

21 For example, even Germany is moving toward U.S. accounting standards and has recently developed a vibrant market for high-tech initial public offerings.

22 For an excellent overview of the East Asian Crisis, see the articles on Nouriel Roubini's web page at http://www.stern.nyu.edu/~nroubini/asia/AsiaHomepage.html. In particular, see Nouriel Roubini, Giancarlo Corsetti and Paolo Pesenti, "What Caused the Asian Currency and Financial Crisis?," New York University Working paper, 1998; and Steve Radelet and Jeffrey Sachs, "The Onset of the East Asian Financial Crisis," Harvard University Working Paper (1998).

23 These countries had stock markets, which could have been a source of price signals. But disclosure rules were often inadequate and the monitoring institutions that exist in more developed economies – such as auditors, analysts, and rating agencies – are still relatively undeveloped.

24 For example, even if creditors could learn enough to know the firm was defunct, bankruptcy laws existed largely on the books.

25 This is very similar to the way depositors keep bank management in check by threatening to run in case of trouble (see Charles Calomiris and Charles Kahn, "The Role of Demandable Debt in Structuring Optimal Banking Arrangements," *American Economic Review*, 81 (1991), pp. 497–513; and Douglas Diamond and Raghuram Rajan, "Liquidity Risk, Liquidity Creation and Financial Fragility: A Theory of Banking," working paper, University of Chicago).

countries could not offer adequate institutional safeguards, short-term financing was the cheapest way for the countries to obtain the large amounts of capital that were on offer. Both sides were happy provided the economies continued to hum along.

But then prospects changed. It is hard to say whether the trigger was the depreciating yen (driven down because of loose Japanese monetary policy), poor macroeconomic policies, or the realization that capital was being poorly invested by the relationship system. At any rate, once some foreign arm's-length capital started to pull out, it did not make sense for any to stay in. Since the relationship system would ensure that the pain would be spread through invisible cross-subsidies and the like, and not contained within a few specific "bad" institutions, it made sense for every outsider who could to pull out. This was not necessarily a panic, but a "rational" move to the exits by arm's-length capital providers who knew they had inadequate protection for the long run, and were not sufficiently part of the relationship system to get any of the benefits of staying. Of course, it is easy to see how the subsequent development of the crisis took place.

We do not rule out the possibility that moral hazard may have been behind some of the investment that flowed in, or that there was some panic in the search for exits. Yet it seems to us that much of what happened can be explained as the consequence of two financial systems that are essentially incompatible coming into contact with each other. Not having either the power that is the currency in relationship systems or contractual safeguards that are essential to an arm's-length system, foreign investors protected themselves by keeping the exits clear. An unexpected bad shock led them to head for the exits. The mistake, if any, may have been on the part of the East Asian countries in underestimating the risk involved in accepting such flows, without a clear plan to reform their institutions once the flows had been accepted.

One clear policy implication of this analysis is that a country faced with the prospect of substantial financial inflows has to either accept the risk of financial fragility or improve its financial infrastructure before it accepts the flows. Institutions such as exchanges and custodial services have to be set up, monitors such as rating agencies, auditors, and supervisory authorities have to be established

or strengthened, accounting standards and disclosure laws improved, and bankruptcy and contract law made more effective. Not only does such institutional development improve the way foreign inflows are invested, it also makes the system more resilient to adverse shocks by "localizing" them within a few institutions.

In short, unfettered flows should be allowed only after the financial infrastructure is in place. The notion that investors will create their own institutions after they come in is a version of Say's Law that should be laid to rest.

WHERE DO WE GO FROM HERE?

Given the flight of foreign capital and the ensuing capital shortage now confronting them, East Asian economies might appear to be justified in returning to their traditional relationship-based systems. But is a return to the old system likely to restore these economies to their former strength? And is a relationship-based system really a viable, long-run solution for these economies?

Our analysis thus far would suggest that a return to relationships is the best way to go in the short run. That is, until foreign capital shows signs of renewed interest in these economies, staying in the lower left-hand corner of Figure 38.1 would appear to be the best course of action. Yet there is a fundamental problem with relationship systems, one that we have largely glossed over until now: namely, their resistance to change. The opacity and collusive practices that sustain a relationship-based system entrench incumbents at the expense of potential new entrants. Moreover, the very lack of transparency also makes it hard for democratic forces to detect all of the abuses in the system. This strengthens the hand of incumbents in resisting reform.

One of the effects of a crisis is to create such immense problems that even the relationship system cannot hide them. The evidence of gross abuse can be a powerful weapon for democratic and liberal forces in pressing for reform. An example is the financial legislation that was rushed through Congress soon after the onset of the Great Depression, in 1933 and 1934. Of course, much of that legislation – including the Glass Steagall Act and the Securities Act of 1934 – has been attacked by economists as politically motivated[26] and a source of inefficiency in the U.S. economy.[27] What is rarely pointed out, however, is that such legislation laid the framework for the modern-U.S. financial sector. The crisis of the Great Depression provided an opportunity for democratic forces to combat the concentration of power on Wall Street; and the legislation that resulted from the crisis essentially ended relationship-based finance in the United States. In so doing, Glass Steagall and the Securities Acts can be seen as providing the initial impetus for the present variety and competitiveness of U.S. financial institutions.

In the near term, then, East Asia's crisis and capital shortage provides a rare opportunity for institutional reform. Over the longer run, however, such economies can be expected to move from their current condition of capital shortage to situations that once again test the systems' ability to allocate capital. When that day comes, the arm's-length system is likely to be more efficient. If the current crisis can be weathered, the long run need not be that long for the East Asian economies. Rather than reconstituting the old monopolies and inside deals, these economies would be well advised to follow the U.S. example in the 1930s and take advantage of the financial crisis to improve transparency and accountability in their financial system.

But how do these economies weather the short-run crisis? The problem is that while a large portion of foreign capital has fled, some is still in the system, along with domestically supplied capital. As the financial mess is untangled and the underlying problems revealed, more capital will disappear, either outside the country or under the mattress. Furthermore, there is likely to be a ratchet effect in the disclosure process. Because the markets suspect insiders of dissembling as in the past, any disclosures will be discounted as understating the true extent of the problems. But this makes it hard for reforming insiders to confess everything since the market continues to discount their disclosures.[28] For example, if the market's past experience with the system causes it to multiply the size of disclosed loan losses by two, an admission of the true size of loan losses may cause tremendous capital flight since, at least in the short run, the market might believe the true losses are twice the actual ones. Since confidence is so critical to markets, it may paradoxically be impossible to clean up the system and restore long run credibility without risking further short-run flight.

This would suggest that if there is a serious intention to clean up the system, a temporary government guarantee – with clearly defined time limits – of the financial institutions, together with a temporary restriction on capital flows, may be necessary to give the system the latitude to purge itself.[29] The danger in this course, however, is that such restrictions would make it easier to continue with the status quo because the market would no longer reflect the state of the system. Therefore, it is crucial that there be genuine political will to reform the system before such drastic measures are contemplated. Other institutional reforms should follow in the longer run, and these reforms will provide Asian economies not only with the capacity to absorb arm's-length foreign capital when fashion and sentiment turn, as surely they must, but also with the much-needed information to allocate this capital to the highest-value use. Therein lies the best hope for restoring long-term growth.

26 See George Benston, *The Separation of Commercial and Investment Banking*, Oxford: Oxford University Press (1990) and Randall Kroszner and Raghuram G. Rajan, "Is the Glass Steagall Act Justified?: Evidence from the U.S. Experience with Universal Banking 1921–1933," *American Economic Review*, Vol 84, pp 810–832 (1994).
27 See Mark Roe, *Strong Managers and Weak Owners*, Princeton University Press, Princeton, NJ (1994).
28 See Raghuram Rajan, "Why Bank Credit Policies Fluctuate: A Theory and Some Evidence," *Quarterly Journal of Economics*, 109 (1994), 399–442.
29 For another view on the necessity of capital controls, see Paul Krugman, "Saving Asia: It's Time to Get Radical," *Fortune* (September 7, 1998).

CHAPTER 39

Measuring the Effectiveness of Different Corporate Governance Systems: Toward a More Scientific Approach

Jonathan R. Macey (Cornell Law School)

Ever since publication of Berle and Means' 1932 classic, *The Modern Corporation and Private Property*,[1] many have believed that there are significant problems with the American system of corporate governance.[2] In particular, the separation of ownership and control identified with the American publicly held corporation is said to produce an organizational structure in which shareholders face collective action problems that make it impossible for them effectively to monitor and discipline the management of the firms in which they have invested.[3]

Professional managers are said to be virtually unaccountable to shareholders.

Recently scholars have suggested that institutional investors are the group most likely to resolve America's corporate governance problem.[4] Other commentators, however, have questioned the merits of having institutional investors take a more active role in corporate governance. Roberta Romano, for example, has shown that public pension funds face political constraints that are likely to prevent them from serving very effectively as monitors of corporate managers.[5] As for corporate pension funds and financial institutions, it has long been recognized that these institutions face conflicts of interest that prevent them from serving as effective representatives of the interest of outside shareholders.[6] Jack Coffee has pointed out that the kind of long-term, "relational" investing required to make institutional investors a voice in corporate governance may be too costly to such investors

---

1 Adolf A. Berle, Jr. & Gardiner C. Means, *The Modern Corporation and Private Property* (1932).

2 Mark Roe, *Strong Managers, Weak Owners: The Political Roots of American Corporate Governance* 6–17 (Princeton University Press, 1994); Bernard Black, "Agents Watching Agents: The Promise of Institutional Investor Voice," 39 *UCLA L. Rev.* 811 (1992) (Arguing that the American system of corporate governance needs to induce institutional investors to take a more active role in monitoring); Edward B. Rock, "The Logic and (Uncertain) Significance of Institutional Shareholder Activism," 79 *Geo. L. J.* 445, 454 n. 29 (1991) (discussing literature discussing collective action problems facing shareholders).

3 *See, e.g.*, Ronald J. Gilson & Reiner Kraakman, "Reinventing the Outside Director: An Agenda for Institutional Investors," 43 *Stan. L. Rev.* 863, 875 (1991) (arguing that directors lack the time, the information and the economic incentive to actively discipline management); George W. Dent, Jr., "Toward Unifying Ownership and Control in the Public Corporation," 1989 *Wis. L. Rev.* 881, 898–901 (arguing that directors' deference to management contributes further to the lack of accountability of management).

4 Bernard S. Black, "Shareholder Passivity Reexamined," 89 *Michigan L. Rev.* 520, 575–91 (1990); Gilson & Kraakman, cited in note 3.

5 Roberta Romano, "Public Pension Fund Activism in Corporate Governance Reconsidered," 93 *Colum. L. Rev.* 795 (1993).

6 John Brooks, *Conflicts of Interest: Corporate Pension Fund Asset Management: Report to the Twentieth Century Fund Steering Committee on Conflicts of Interest in the Securities Markets* 224 (Twentieth Century Fund, 1975).

because it will require them to sacrifice liquidity.[7] Jill Fisch has argued that institutional investors may not find it rational to engage in relational investing unless they are given special benefits such as special information about control transactions, sweetheart preferred stock, and preferential treatment in business transactions with the issuer – benefits which they are unlikely to receive.[8]

The previous scholarship has focused largely on the "supply side" of the debate. It has focused on the institutional investors who might become more involved in corporate governance, and it has analyzed how much, if any, good it would do to have such investors more involved in corporate governance.[9] This article starts with the premise that it is necessary to look at the "demand side" of the issue of the role of institutional investors in corporate governance. Considering the demand side of this debate requires us to address the issue of how well or poorly the existing system is working. It is clear from the existing literature that it will not be costless for the market to provide a greater supply of institutional investor monitoring.[10] To the extent that the existing corporate governance mechanisms are working well, incurring the costs of moving institutional investors into a more active role will probably not be worthwhile. On the other hand, if there are large inefficiencies associated with the corporate governance mechanisms already in place, then providing incentives for institutional investors to expand their role in corporate governance becomes a more attractive policy option.

Unfortunately, as Andrei Schleifer and Robert Vishny have pointed out,

even in advanced market economies, there is a great deal of disagreement on how good or bad the existing corporate governance mechanisms are. For example, Easterbrook and Fischel, and Romano make a very optimistic assessment of the United States' corporate governance system, while Jensen finds it deeply flawed[11]

The purpose of this article is to make two modest points that, I believe, would improve our current understanding of what our goals should be concerning the ideal role for institutional investors in corporate governance. First, I assert that the quality of the debate would be improved if we had a better empirical sense of how badly (or how well) the American system of corporate governance is functioning. More precisely, given the lack of consensus on the issue, it would be helpful to have some systematic understanding of how far away the current system of corporate governance lies from the "production possibility frontier" defined by corporate governance alternatives. If there is huge room for improvement – that is, if the American system is a long way from being the best that it could be given current technology – then perhaps radical change is warranted. But if the American system of corporate governance is already producing results close to the maximum of what is possible, then it is more doubtful that costly changes will be worth the marginal investment.

The second goal of the article is to point out that there are now marketplace alternatives for achieving all of the goals that commentators hope to accomplish by inducing institutional investors to become more involved in corporate governance. In evaluating the efficacy of greater institutional investor involvement in corporate governance, one must compare the costs and benefits of such institutional investor involvement with the costs and benefits of the available substitute governance mechanisms. Specifically, the market for corporate control and

---

7 John C. Coffee, Jr., "Liquidity versus Control: The Institutional Investor as Corporate Monitor," 91 *Colum. L. Rev.* 1277 (1977).

8 Jill E. Fisch, "Relationship Investing: Will It Happen Will It Work?," 55 *Ohio St. L. J.* 1009–1040 (1994).

9 Black, cited in note 2; Coffee, cited in note 7; Alfred F. Conard, "Beyond Managerialism: Investor Capitalism?," 22 *U. Mich. J. L. Ref.* 117 (1988); Gilson & Kraakman, cited in note 3; Martin Lipton, "Corporate Governance in the Age of Finance Corporatism," 136 *U. Pa. L. Rev.* 1 (1987); Mark J. Roe, "A Political Theory of American Corporate Finance," 91 *Colum. L. Rev.* 10 (1991).

10 Andrei Schleifer and Robert W. Vishny, "A Survey of Corporate Governance," manuscript prepared for the Nobel Symposium on Law and Finance, Stockholm, 30–37 (June, 1995) (on file with author).

11 *Ibid.* (citing Daniel R. Fischel & Frank Easterbrook, The Economic Structure of Corporate Law" (1991); Roberta Romano, "The Genius of American Corporate Law" (AEI, 1993); Michael Jensen, "Eclipse of the Public Corporation," *Harv. Bus. Rev.*, Sept–Oct., 60–70 (1989); Michael Jensen, "The Modern Industrial Revolution, Exit, and the Failure of Internal Control Systems," 48 *J. Fin.* 831–880 (1993).

leveraged financing both provide mechanisms for monitoring management that directly substitute for the monitoring offered by institutional investors. This article offers direct comparisons of the relative merits of these mechanisms.

The first section of this article sets the stage for the analysis by describing what I believe is a reasonable consensus about the goals of corporate governance. In the second part, I describe a set of objective, empirically testable criteria by which I believe we might test the operation of systems of corporate governance. In this section, I also question whether the use of institutional investors in corporate governance would do a better job than the market for corporate control in reducing the agency costs associated with investing.

THE GOALS OF CORPORATE GOVERNANCE

Corporate governance can be described as the processes by which investors attempt to minimize the transactions costs[12] and agency costs[13] associated with doing business within a firm. Andrei Schleifer and Robert Vishny framed the issue very well when they said:

Corporate governance deals with the ways in which suppliers of finance to corporations assure themselves of getting a stream of return on their investment. How do the suppliers of finance get managers to return some of the profits to them? How do they make sure that managers do not steal the capital they supply or divert it to other uses? How do suppliers of finance control managers?[14]

Early academic discussions about corporate governance in the United States focused on such things as the merits of the conglomerate merger and the hostile takeover as mechanisms for controlling agency costs.[15] More recently, there has been

renewed focus on the legal responsibilities of corporate boards of directors, the efficacy of shareholder litigation as a mechanism for controlling agency costs,[16] and, above all, the role of institutional investors as corporate monitors.[17]

Serious comparative corporate governance is an even newer phenomenon for Americans. Of great interest recently has been the efficacy of jurisdictional competition for corporate charters,[18] and, once again, the role played in corporate governance by institutional investors, particularly banks in the U.S. and abroad.[19] While there is a great deal of debate about the specifics, one can identify the general goals of the corporate governance system that has emerged.

I believe that a consensus exists on at least two important issues. There seems to be agreement among scholars and commentators about (1) the incomplete nature of the corporate contract, and the value of corporate governance principles that fill in the "gaps" in these incomplete, contingent contracts;[20] and (2) the need to control the managerial tendency to pursue interests and objectives that conflict with those of maximizing efficiency and value (i.e. to control agency costs).[21]

It is well known that corporate law provides, among other things, a set of standard, off-the-rack terms that permit participants in a corporation to economize on contracting costs. The formal contracts among entrepreneurs, managers, investors, and others are necessarily incomplete, and corporate law provides an important mechanism for supplementing the actual bargains that people make by supplying background terms and filling in the gaps in contracts.[22] Thus, while there is vigorous debate about whether the missing terms supplied by the legal system should be mandatory or enabling, there is no disagreement with the

---

12 Coase's classic explanation for the existence of the firm in a modern exchange economy focused on transaction costs, *see* Coase, "The Nature of the Firm," 4 *Economica* 386–405 (1937).
13 M.C. Jensen & William H. Meckling, "Theory of the Firm, Managerial Behavior, Agency Costs and Ownership Structure," *Journal of Financial Economics* 305–60 (1976).
14 Schleifer & Vishny, cited in note 10.
15 Henry G. Manne, "Mergers and the Market for Corporate Control," 73 *J. Pol. Econ.* 110 (1965); Frank H. Easterbrook & Daniel R. Fischel, "The Proper Role of a Target's Management in Responding to a Tender Offer," 94 *Harv. L. Rev.* 1161, 1169–1182 (1981).

16 Black, cited in note 4, at 530–553.
17 Black, cited in note 2, at 820–829.
18 Romano, cited in note 5.
19 Roe, cited in note 2; Jonathan R. Macey and Geoffrey P. Miller, "Corporate Governance and Commercial Banking: A Comparative Examination of Germany, Japan, and the United States," 48 *Stan. L. Rev.* 73–112 (1995).
20 *See generally*, American Law Institute, "Principles of Corporate Governance: Analysis and Recommendations" (1992).
21 Easterbrook & Fischel, cited in note 15, at 1170.
22 Easterbrook & Fischel, cited in note 11, at 34.

proposition that corporate governance systems should supply the missing terms.

A second goal of a properly functioning system of corporate governance is to control managerial shirking and, more generally, the failure to maximize value. While this goal can also be characterized as a subset of the first goal of enforcing contracts, it is important enough to deserve special mention. Any corporation of any size will have outside investors. The presence of these outside investors requires the separation of management and finance, commonly described as the separation of ownership and control. Takeovers, proxy fights, and public contests for control are among the ways that capital markets-oriented corporate governance systems (such as those in the U.S. and the U.K.) deal with the problem of agency costs. In corporate governance regimes with a weak or non-existent market for corporate control, but relatively strong banks, a company's relationships with its main bank, its corporate shareholders, its corporate group, and other institutional investors may substitute, to some extent, for the role played by the market for corporate control in its various incarnations.[23]

MEASURING THE PERFORMANCE OF ALTERNATIVE SYSTEMS OF CORPORATE GOVERNANCE

While there may be a measure of consensus on certain broad issues in the field of corporate governance, as discussed above, there certainly is no consensus about which corporate governance system is best. Part of this lack of consensus undoubtedly stems from the fact that there are no generally accepted criteria for the appropriate means to *measure* alternative systems of corporate governance. That is to say, there are no formalized, generally accepted criteria for determining whether a particular system of corporate governance is working. Once such criteria are developed, it

should be possible to begin serious comparative empirical work in corporate governance.

Drawing on some recent research in corporate finance, I identify three ways to measure empirically the performance of corporate governance systems. First, following the suggestion of Shleifer and Vishny (cited earlier),[24] we can categorize the performance of corporate governance systems on the basis of how effective they are in limiting managers' ability to divert firm resources to their own, private uses. The specific measure I propose, following a suggestion by Luigi Zingales,[25] is the size of the premium at which voting shares trade in relation to non-voting shares.

Second, we can compare corporate governance systems empirically on the basis of the willingness of entrepreneurs to make initial public offerings of stock. Investors who are confident that a particular system of corporate governance adequately protects them from managerial self-interest will be more inclined to make investments in the first place. Entrepreneurs in firms with ineffective governance systems will be unable to make credible commitments to the investing public that they will not act opportunistically *ex post* – that is, after the shareholders' initial investments have been made. Thus, a second empirically testable measure of corporate governance systems proposed here is the relative proclivity of firms under rival governance schemes to go public. Firms that operate under a properly functioning corporate governance system will be able to sell their shares to the public, while firms that operate under a dysfunctional system will not.

A third measure of the performance of a corporate governance system will be the functioning of internal and external markets for corporate control. Put simply, if a particular system of corporate governance is functioning properly, inefficient management will be replaced, either through a hostile takeover, or through appointments of new management by (presumably independent) directors.[26]

---

23   Misahiko Aoki, "Towards an Economic Model of the Japanese Firm," 28 *J. Econ. Lit.* 1–27 (1990); Misahiko Aoki, Hugh Patrick & Paul Sheard, "The Japanese Main Bank System: An Introductory Overview," in *The Japanese Main Bank System: Its Relevancy for Developing and Transforming Economies* (Misahiko Aoki and Hugh Patrick, eds., 1994).

24   Schleifer & Vishny, cited in note 10.
25   Zingales, infra note 27.
26   Steven N. Kaplan & Bernadette A. Minton, Appointments of outsiders to Japanese boards, Determinants and Implications for Managers, 36 *J. Fin. Econ.* 224–258 (1994).

Measuring managements' ability to obtain private benefits from control

Comparing the variations among legal systems in the size of premiums paid for voting stock relative to non-voting stock provides one empirical measure of the performance of a particular system of corporate governance. As Zingales has observed, the fact that outsiders often are willing to pay sizeable premiums for voting stock suggests that there are high private benefits to control, and that these private benefits are not shared with outside, non-voting shareholders.[27] The right to control a corporation brings with it the right to realize all of the private benefits associated with such control, particularly the right to divert wealth away from shareholders and other groups in favor of the controlling coalition. Large premiums for the shares needed to control a corporation suggest that the private benefits for control – including the ability to transfer wealth from minority shareholders – can be great. Such large premiums also indicate that the protections for outside investors in general and minority shareholders, in particular, are weak.

As Zingales observes:

The right to control a corporation is valuable per se because it guarantees the owner of this right some unique benefits. Votes allocate control. Therefore even if outside shareholders do not enjoy these private benefits, they may attribute some value to voting rights as long as there is competition among different management teams to acquire those votes. In particular, votes held by small outside shareholders become very valuable when they are pivotal, that is when they are decisive in attributing control to any of the management teams fighting for it.[28]

From an empirical perspective, therefore, a high premium paid for voting shares in companies that have voting and non-voting stock with similar economic rights is strong evidence that the expected costs of this lack of protection for non-controlling shareholders are significant. In this sense, the premium for the voting shares can be viewed as the "discount" paid by minority shareholders for the non-voting shares.

There have been several studies of differential voting rights in different countries. And while it is not entirely appropriate to make direct comparisons of their findings, some of the studies have attempted to take into account the different economic rights of the shares (in particular, the fact that the non-voting shares may have different dividend and liquidation rights).[29] In summarizing the findings of these studies, Zingales found that "voting rights are generally worth 10% to 20% of the value of the common stock."[30] Particular studies of companies in individual countries reported the following results:

Country	Premium (%)	Study[31]
U.S.	5.4	Lease, McConnell, and Mikkelson
Sweden	6.5	Rydqvist
England	13.3	Megginson
Switzerland	20.0	Horner
Canada	23.3	Robinson & White
Israel	45.5	Levy
Italy	82.0	Zingales

At least by this measure of performance, the U.S. corporate governance system appears to be functioning quite well.

---

29   See infra, note 32 and accompanying data.

30   Id. at 125.

31   Full citations for each of the studies cited above are as follows: Lease, McConnell, & Mikkelson, "The Market Value of Control in Publicly Traded Corporations," 11 *Journal of Financial Economics* 439 (1983); Rydqvist, "Takeover Bids and the Relative Prices of Shares that Differ in Their Voting Rights" (Stockholm School of Economics Working Paper, 1992); Megginson, "Restricted Voting Stock, Acquisition Premiums, and the Market Value of Corporate Control," 25 *The Fin. Rev.* 175 (1990); Horner, "The Value of the Corporate Voting Right," 12 *J. Banking & Fin.* 69 (1988); Robinson & White, "The Value of a Vote in the Market for Corporate Control" (York University Working Paper, 1990); Levy, "Economic Evaluation of Voting Power in Common Stock," 38 *J. Fin.* 79 (1982); Zingales, cited in note 27.

---

27   See generally, Luigi Zingales, The Value of the Voting Right: A Study of the Milan Stock Exchange Experience, 7 *Rev. Fin. Stud.*, no. 1, 125–148 (Spring, 1994).

28   Id. at 126.

Going public

If a corporate governance system is functioning well, then, *ceteris paribus*, public markets for capital should function well. Firms will be eager to go public, because doing so provides a low-cost method of funding projects. On the other hand, if the corporate governance system in a particular jurisdiction is not disciplining managers effectively, entrepreneurs will not be able to make credible commitments to outside investors that they will be treated fairly *ex post* – after their initial investments have been made. Thus, the fact that there are large numbers of firms that are eligible to go public but refrain from doing so suggests that the corporate governance system is not functioning well.

The analytical approach in this section builds on the "lemons problem" well-known to economists.[32] Investors won't invest in firms controlled by management without discounting the price they are willing to pay by an amount necessary to compensate themselves for any expected *ex-post* exploitation by management. This will, in turn, lead to a situation in which entrepreneurs refuse to sell their shares to the public because they can't receive an adequate price. Thus, where a corporate governance system is not performing well, there will be relatively few public offerings.

Take Italy, for example, which was the country that performed the worst in the previous measure – that is, it had the highest premium (over 80%, as compared to 5% in the U.S.) for voting shares. Of the 12,391 companies that satisfied the listing requirements of the Milan Exchange during the period 1982–1992, only 66 chose to do so.[33] The size of the median firm that goes public in Italy is four times that of its U.S. counterpart.[34] And there were approximately the same number of firms listed on the Milan Stock Exchange in October 1996 (218) as there were in 1910 (210). By contrast, there were 2907 firms listed on the New York Stock Exchange in October 1996 as compared to only

426 firms in 1910. And, of course, there are also now well over 5000 public companies whose shares trade on the NASDAQ, which was not even in existence in 1910.

In contrast to companies in Italy, most U.S. firms that are eligible to go public do, in fact, go public at some point (though there are, of course, some notable exceptions, such as Cargill, Koch Industries, and UPS). And it is precisely because so many U.S. firms have listed that the New York Stock Exchange now views its most significant opportunity for growth as being in the international arena. The NYSE's current "prospect list" today contains the names of some 2300 foreign firms, as compared to only 600 or 700 U.S. firms.[35]

It might be possible to argue that the propensity of firms to go public is not a reliable indicator of the quality of a particular corporate governance structure because it does not take into account the relative attractiveness of alternative sources of capital. The idea here is that if a certain country has a particularly strong *banking system*, then its companies might not need to have access to the public equity market because they can meet all of their capital needs through bank borrowings. But this argument runs counter to much of the learning in modern corporate finance, which posits that capital markets are more efficient sources of capital than banks. In a nutshell, modern corporate finance teaches that assets that can be securitized will be. In a recent address to a Senate committee, Alan Greenspan stated this lesson as follows:

The heart of financial intermediation is the ability to obtain and use information. The high cost of gathering and using facts in the past meant that banks and other intermediaries could profit from their cumulative store of knowledge about borrowers by making significantly more informed credit decisions than most other market participants. These other market participants were thus obliged to permit depository intermediaries to make credit decisions in financial markets and therefore allow bank credit to substitute for what would otherwise be their own direct acquisition of credit market instruments.[36]

---

32 See George A. Akerlof, The Market for 'Lemons': Quality Uncertainty and the Market Mechanism, 84 *Qrtly. J. Econ.* 488 (1970).

33 Marcano Pagano, Fabio Panetta & Luigi Zingales, "Why Do Companies Go Public? An Empirical and Legal Analysis" (NBER Working Paper 5367, November, 1995).

34 Ibid.

35 I am grateful to conversations with George Sophianis, Chief Economist of the New York Stock Exchange, for this information.

36 Alan Greenspan, Statement before the Committee on Banking, Housing, and Urban Affairs, U.S. Senate (Dec. 1, 1987) 74 Federal Reserve Bulletin 91, 99 (1988).

In an open economy with free-entry into lending markets and capital markets, it becomes difficult for banks to compete with public capital markets because "on-line databases, coupled with powerful computers and wide-ranging telecommunication facilities, can now provide potential investors with virtually the same timely credit and market information that was once available only to [banks]."[37] A variety of new securities projects, including mortgage-backed securities, consumer receivables financing, consumer loan-based securities, and commercial paper all have been introduced to replace relatively costly bank financing with relatively cheap capital market financing. In short, the argument that strong banks can replace public equity markets does not seem plausible.[38]

The market for corporate control

An important part of any system of corporate governance is some mechanism for controlling managerial inefficiency, or failure to maximize value. As Michael Jensen and William Meckling observed, because investors will discount the price they are willing to pay for a firm's shares by the expected levels of managerial "agency costs,"[39] companies must be able to make credible commitments to control such problems if the firm is to attract significant outside funds.

As noted above, there is considerable disagreement among corporate governance scholars as to whether the best mechanism for controlling managers is a robust market for corporate control (the U.S. model) or active monitoring by institutional investors (the German model). But it seems indisputable that the existence of *some* governance mechanism is critical.

As Geoffrey Miller and I have concluded in a recent study comparing the U.S., German, and Japanese governance systems, "the market for corporate control lies at the heart of the American system of corporate governance."[40] As early as

1965, Henry Manne pointed out that takeovers are the primary mechanism by which the market for corporate control disciplines managers because, unlike mergers, takeovers do not require the approval of the board of directors of the target firm.[41] Thus, outside bidders can appeal directly to target shareholders for their approval. And, as Roberta Romano has observed, takeovers provide a backstop mechanism for monitoring corporate performance when other corporate governance devices fail.[42] Hostile takeovers target poorly performing firms and replace their managers with rival management teams, thereby keeping the capital market competitive and constraining managers to maximize value for shareholders.

The basic theory, then, is simple: outside bidders have an incentive to monitor incumbent managers because they can profit by buying the shares of poorly managed firms and installing better management teams.[43] Bidders must share these gains with target-firm shareholders, but as long as bidders can earn a risk-adjusted market rate of return on their investments, they will find it in their interests to monitor target management teams on behalf of incumbent firm shareholders.

Roberta Romano has made an extensive review of the empirical evidence, and finds that it is consistent with this "inefficient management explanation of takeovers."[44] Professor Romano also finds the explanation incomplete, however, because it does not explain acquisitions in which the acquiror retains incumbent management, and particularly management-led leveraged buy-outs (so-called MBOs), in which top management is part of the acquiring group and stays on the job. But, as Romano observes, the inefficient management explanation is convincing even in these contexts. In the MBO context, superior performance after an MBO can be explained by the fact that management had weak incentives *before* the takeover because they had such a small stake in the firm they were managing. After the MBO, management's far greater equity stake, coupled with the personal guarantees that management often gives

---

37   Ibid. at 93.
38   I am grateful to Luigi Zingales for bringing this point to my attention.
39   Jensen & Meckling, cited in note 13, at 305–360.
40   Macey & Miller, cited in note 19, at 101.

41   Manne, cited in note 15.
42   Roberta Romano, "A Guide to Takeovers: Theory, Evidence and Regulation," 9 *Yale J. Reg.* 119, 129–31 (1992).
43   Manne, cited in note 15.
44   Romano, cited in note 42 at 131.

to their bankers to secure financing for the MBO transaction, provides it with very strong incentives to increase efficiency and value. Moreover, LBOs in general can also reduce agency costs insofar as the increased debt constrains managers from wasting their firms' "free cash flow."[45]

From a corporate governance perspective, one must wonder why takeovers are not a complete solution to the monitoring problems arising from the separation of ownership and control in most public U.S. corporations. One possible objection to this solution is that takeovers are costly, and that, therefore, "companies have to go further off course before attracting a hostile bid than they might if managers were monitored continuously."[46] Because it is costly to search for, identify, and then replace target managers, a firm must be substantially undervalued before a takeover bid can be attempted.

But, if takeovers are very costly, it is important to recognize that a vigorous market for corporate control has important, beneficial third-party effects. An active takeover market affects managerial performance in a positive way, *even in the absence of a formally announced takeover bid*, because target managers will want to keep their share price high to reduce the probability that they will be displaced by a hostile takeover. Thus, even if the probability of a takeover is slight, risk-averse managers can be expected to work harder when there is a positive probability that a hostile bid will be announced.[47]

Further, those who argue that takeovers are too expensive and therefore too "lumpy" to be an effective governance device ignore the fact that an investor need not launch a full-blown tender offer to put a target company effectively "in play." Investors may launch a proxy contest for as little as $5000 (down from $1 million a few years ago).

The point here is that the market for corporate control serves as a mechanism for replacing weak managers with superior managers, and for giving managers greater incentives to do a better job, which

is exactly what institutional investors are supposed to do. In fact, studies of Japanese firms show that poor performance leads to an increased probability that institutional investors – that is, in most cases, Japanese main banks – will replace incumbent officers and directors with their own nominees.[48] In their important study of the appointment of outside directors to the boards of large non-financial Japanese corporations, Steve Kaplan and Bernadette Minton conclude that their findings are

consistent with an important monitoring and disciplining role for banks, corporate shareholders, and corporate groups in Japan [and] with the view that the relationship-oriented system of corporate governance in Japan substitutes for the more market-oriented system in the U.S. Banks, corporate shareholders, and corporate groups appear to play a role that is similar to that of takeover in the U.S.[49]

My point here is not that takeovers are superior to "continued and textured monitoring by institutional investors." Rather, I want to make two different arguments. First, takeovers provide a form of continuous monitoring that substitutes for the monitoring provided by institutional investors. This monitoring may be inferior because it is costly, but it may also be superior because, unlike institutional investor monitoring in a corporate governance system that (like Japan's) lacks a market for corporate control, the market for corporate control affects *all* companies, not just the one in which an institutional investor has a stake. All companies are potential takeover candidates at all times.

The second point is that one can generalize from the above discussion in order to develop an empirical measure of corporate governance performance across different systems. In a properly functioning corporate governance system, poorly performing management teams will be replaced.[50] Consequently, comparing the sensitivity of management changes to share-price performance provides a means of testing the efficacy of alternative corporate

45 See Romano cited in note 43, at 131 (discussing Michael C. Jensen, "The Takeover Controversy: Analysis and Evidence," in *Knights, Raiders & Targets: The Impact of the Hostile Takeover*, 314 (John C. Coffee, et al. eds, 1988).
46 "Watching the Boss: A Survey of Corporate Governance," *The Economist*, January 29, 1994, at 13.
47 Macey & Miller, cited in note 19, at 104.
48 Kaplan & Minton, cited in note 26; Randall Morck & Masao Nakamura, "Banks and Corporate Control in Japan" 4–5 (Institute for Financial Research, Faculty of Business, University of Alberta, Working Paper No. 6–92, rev. July 26, 1993).
49 Kaplan & Minton, cited in note 26, at 257.
50 Manne, cited in note 15.

governance structures. A corporate governance system that does not replace poorly performing managers is not working very well.

THE MECHANISMS OF CORPORATE GOVERNANCE

One criticism that might be made of the above analysis is that, by focusing exclusively on outcomes, it ignores the mechanisms by which corporate governance can be improved. In particular, the analysis seems to ignore the ways that institutional investors can work together with other mechanisms to achieve superior corporate governance.[51] For example, in the preceding section, the case was made that a properly functioning corporate governance system will replace poorly performing management teams. In certain contexts, concentrated institutional investor ownership can make takeovers less costly by lowering the transactions costs to an outside acquirer of gaining control.

However, facilitating control transactions by selling shares, which is an exit strategy, is much different than engaging in corporate monitoring at the operational level. While there is some evidence that institutional investors have become involved in the former, there is not much evidence that they have become involved in the latter. Specifically, as Jill Fisch has observed, *"it is possible to explain the rapid growth in institutional activism as simply a second order institutional response to the takeover era.*[52] Fisch points out that institutional activism in the United States first arose in the context of corporate control transactions. The takeover wave of the 1980s was met with a combination of state anti-takeover statutes and court-sanctioned anti-takeover devices. This, in turn, was met by an increase in activism by institutional investors who opposed management efforts to erect powerful barriers to outside acquisitions.[53]

The point here is that institutional investors do not seem to be engaging in the continuous, textured monitoring that demands active involvement

in influencing corporate policy. Institutional investors, like other investors, appear to rely on market forces, particularly market forces in the form of the market for corporate control. Institutional investors do not make use of the strategy of giving corporate governance advice and guidance to firms as a means of increasing their investment returns. And there are several good reasons for this:

First, institutional investors operate in a competitive environment. It is easy to monitor *their* performance and there are a lot of them. Modern portfolio theory teaches that firm-specific risk can be diversified away by investors. The logic behind the Capital Asset Pricing Model supposes that investors will be compensated only for the non-diversifiable risks they bear. Additionally, the Efficient Capital Markets Hypothesis posits that the process of fundamental analysis of a stock's value is not going to produce superior investment results. Institutional investors should accordingly concentrate on constructing portfolios of stocks that are designed effectively to eliminate firm-specific risk, and on keeping costs down. Neither of these strategies is consistent with the continuous and textured monitoring proposed by some. Thus, it is not surprising that "American institutional investors do not have a . . . skilled pool of employees" capable of offering suggestions and advice that would improve corporate performance.[54]

Put differently, it is not clear that the human capital skills needed to be a successful fund manager are the same as the skills necessary to provide operational advice to the firms in which a fund are invested.[55] And if the skills are different – and modern financial theory suggests they are – there are no obvious synergies or economies of scale associated with having institutional investors more actively involved in corporate management.

A second reason why institutional investors – particularly mutual funds – are not actively involved with management of the firms in which they have invested is because any gains associated with this sort of activity must be shared with other

---

51   Rock, cited in note 2, at 478–501.
52   Fisch, cited in note 8, at 1030–1032.
53   Ibid., at 1030.

54   Robert G. Vanecko, "Regulations 14A and 13D and the Role of Institutional Investors in Corporate Governance," 87 *Nw. U. L. Rev.* 376, 406–408 (1992).
55   Gilson & Kraakman, cited in note 3, at 880.

investors, including rival investment funds. As Jill Fisch has pointed out, many institutional investors are evaluated by how well they do against similarly situated competitors.[56] An institution that invests a lot in efforts to increase the performance of one firm will not be able to share the costs of this investment. But the returns will have to be shared with other investors, including other institutional investors who own the same stock.

A third explanation for the observed lack of institutional involvement in corporate governance is that institutional investors do not want to sacrifice investment liquidity in order to achieve a greater voice in the activities of the firms in which they have invested.[57] In particular, board membership in a company brings responsibilities as well as information. Since it is highly doubtful that an institutional investor could use any information received in that capacity, or in any other role that could be defined as creating a fiduciary relationship, the incentives to assume an active role in corporate governance are greatly diminished.

Greater involvement in corporate governance will involve significant new costs. These costs include: (1) new investments in human capital; (2) significant free-rider problems; (3) loss of liquidity; and (4) potential legal liability for insider trading, or for breach of fiduciary duty to other shareholders where the insiders have assumed a role as a director or an active participant in management.

CONCLUSION

This article has explored the need for greater institutional investor involvement in corporate governance. In light of the fact that greater institutional involvement in corporate governance entails substantial costs and risks to institutions, the potential benefits from institutional investor involvement should be considered. One way of measuring these benefits is to measure how well the current system is performing. I suggest three ways for measuring the performance of a corporate governance system.

First, I propose measuring the private benefits of control by examining the relative share price performance of voting and non-voting shares in firms with a capital structure that includes both voting and non-voting stock.

Second, I propose looking at the willingness of firms to go public. Investors will not pay full value for firms with weak corporate governance because they will discount the price they pay for such firms by an amount sufficient to compensate them in the future for possible exploitation by management. This will, in turn, lead to a situation in which entrepreneurs refuse to sell their shares to the public because they can't receive an adequate price. Thus, where a corporate governance system is not performing well, there will be relative few public offerings.

Third and last, I argue that a good corporate governance system can be measured by the speed with which management is replaced for sustained poor performance. Systems with weak corporate governance systems won't replace management very often.

The purpose of this article has been to suggest some ways of measuring the performance of a corporate governance system. This seems superior to simply asserting that the U.S. system of corporate governance does not work. The article does not purport to fully test the performance of the U.S. system, although it does make some tentative observations. In particular, I find no evidence that the U.S. system is performing badly, and indeed, the U.S. system seems to be used as the benchmark for comparing the performance of rival systems.

It should be clear that none of the tests suggested in this article is meant to be used in isolation to measure the performance of a system of corporate governance. Rather, they should be used together, since shortcomings in one measurement can be compensated for by strengths in another. Finally, it goes without saying, I think, that the U.S.'s market-oriented system of corporate governance has been hurt in recent years by the wave of anti-takeover statutes and court decisions that are hampering the market for corporate control. One of the few salutary effects that institutional investors are having on U.S. corporate governance are their actions directed at lowering or removing some of these barriers.

---

56   Fisch, cited in note 8, at 1020.
57   Coffee, cited in note 7.

Epilogue

CHAPTER 40

Merton Miller's Contribution to Modern Finance

René M. Stulz (Ohio State University)*

> Merton Miller was a great economist. He was also a fine warrior. In the 1950s he takes up finance and engineers a stunning campaign that, after a period of years, decisively undermines the Old Guard and installs Modern Finance. That done, he brings his methods to the Real World, and becomes a strategist for Chicago's commodity crowd in their battles with New York's establishment and Washington's power brokers. He does all this with such finesse, such humor, and, above all, such devotion to economic principle that you reluctantly admire him even as he rides past you to victory.
>
> – *Fischer Black[1]*

For the last 30 years, the field of academic finance was new enough that most of its founding fathers were still active and influencing its development. And until his death last spring at the age of 77, Merton Miller stood at the center of these founding fathers. It has been impossible to work in finance without being continually reminded of his contributions and his presence.

Miller's accomplishments were many, but if we were to remember only one of his contributions to the field of finance, which would it be? Most financial economists would cite the famous "M&M" capital structure and dividend irrelevance propositions. But I will argue that although any finance scholar would be thrilled to have produced one of the M&M propositions, Miller's most important contribution to our field went well beyond the propositions themselves.

In making my case, I will start with the first Modigliani and Miller paper, "The Cost of Capital, Corporation Finance and the Theory of Investment," which was published in the *American Economic Review* in 1958. The main conclusion of that paper is the well-known M&M Proposition I, which states that "the market value of any firm is independent of its capital structure and is given by capitalizing its expected return at the rate . . . appropriate to its [risk] class."[2] In other words, changes in companies' leverage ratios should not

*   This article builds on my keynote address at the annual meeting of the Financial Management Association in Seattle this past October, and differs substantially from the version of that speech that was published as "Merton Miller and Modern Finance" in the Winter 2000 issue of *Financial Management*. I am grateful for Don Chew's considerable editorial assistance, as well as for comments from Steve Buser, Harry DeAngelo, Andrew Karolyi, Lemma Senbet, and Alex Triantis.

1   Foreword to Merton H. Miller, *Financial Innovations & Market Volatility* (Blackwell Publishers, 1991). In the first two sentences, the word "was" originally appeared as "is," since Miller was alive when Black wrote these words in 1991. Fischer Black died in 1995; had he lived three more years, he would have shared the Nobel Prize with Robert Merton and Myron Scholes in 1997.
2   Franco Modigliani and Merton Miller, "The Cost of Capital, Corporation Finance and the Theory of Investment," *American Economic Review* Vol. 48, No. 3 (1958).

affect their market values; such values are determined solely by their expected future earnings power or, more technically, by the discounted present value of their expected cash flows. And the companion to Proposition I, the dividend irrelevance proposition, maintains that changes in dividend policy should also have no effect on corporate values.

In the real world, of course, we have all seen dramatic movements in stock prices in response to announcements of dividend changes and leveraged recapitalizations. And in the last 30 years, finance scholars have provided convincing empirical evidence that changes in capital structure and dividends have fairly predictable effects on corporate values. But, as I argue below, the M&M propositions' apparent lack of predictive power in no way diminishes either the validity of their logic or their importance to our current theory of corporate finance. As Miller himself wrote in a 1988 article called "The Modigliani-Miller Propositions Thirty Years Later,"

The view that capital structure is literally irrelevant or that 'nothing matters' in corporate finance, though still sometimes attributed to us . . . is far from what we ever actually said about the real-world applications of our theoretical propositions. Looking back now, perhaps we should have put more emphasis on the other, upbeat side of the 'nothing matters' coin: showing what doesn't matter can also show, by implication, what does.

"This more constructive approach," as Miller went on to note, "has now become the standard one in teaching corporate finance."[3] That is to say, even if the M&M propositions have not been confirmed by empirical research – and it is unlikely they ever can be – they have nonetheless served as the starting point for virtually all academic research in corporate finance in the last three decades.

What has enabled the M&M propositions to transform modern finance into a serious scholarly undertaking is not their predictive power, but

rather the proofs on which the propositions rest – the way of thinking that Miller and Modigliani used in arriving at their conclusions. In the proof of Proposition I, M&M began by making a set of assumptions that, while clearly violated in practice, enable them to produce useful – and in some respects surprising – insights. They started with a set of conditions known as "perfect capital markets" (which Miller himself once referred to as "the economist's frictionless dream world"), in which there are no taxes or transactions (including bankruptcy) costs, reliable information about a company's future performance is freely available to investors, and managers' operating and investment policies are completely unaffected by financing choices. Under such conditions, as M&M demonstrated, changes in capital structure (and dividend policy) cannot affect a company's operating cash flows. And if operating cash flows – that is, the total amount of cash profits to be divided among *all* the firm's security holders – remain affected by such changes, then investors continually in quest of profit opportunities can be counted on to eliminate any differences in valuation resulting solely from differences in financial policies.

The mechanism by which investors eliminate the effects of such differences is called "arbitrage." The arbitrageur identifies two assets with identical payoffs that are trading at different prices, and then earns riskless profits by selling the higher-priced asset and buying the lower-priced one. In the words of M&M, arbitrage works as follows:

if Proposition I did not hold [and levered firms sold for, say, higher values than identical unlevered firms], an investor could buy and sell stocks and bonds in such a way as to exchange one income stream for another stream, identical in all relevant respects but selling at a lower price. The exchange would therefore be advantageous to the investor quite independently of his attitudes toward risk. As investors exploit these arbitrage opportunities, the value of the overpriced shares will fall and that of the underpriced shares will rise, thereby tending to eliminate the discrepancy between the market values of the firms.[4]

In the rest of this article, I argue that it is this concept of arbitrage that is at the center of Merton Miller's career and of his contributions to our field. Fischer Black paid tribute to Miller by

3 Merton Miller, "The Modigliani-Miller Propositions Thirty Years Later," *Journal of Economic Perspectives* (1988). A somewhat shorter version of this article was published in Volume 2 Number 1 (Spring 1989) of this journal, and all citations of this article in these pages will be from this 1989 *JACF* version of Miller's paper.

4 Modigliani and Miller (1958), p. 269.

calling him a "warrior." The cause for which Miller fought until the end of his life was the social efficacy of financial markets – the idea that financial markets, when allowed to function with minimal interference from regulators and governments, are extraordinarily effective in allocating resources in ways that create social wealth. And the arbitrage mechanism was Miller's guiding principle in thinking about what makes markets so effective. Both his research and his battles with politicians and regulators are testimony to his conviction that any substantial market mispricing of assets that presented arbitrage opportunities for investors would quickly be eliminated because market forces would soon step in to set prices right.

In what follows, I begin by considering how the idea of arbitrage has affected the development of corporate finance theory. I then go on to consider the relationship between arbitrage, market efficiency, and – a relatively new consideration in finance – liquidity, particularly in light of recent events like the failure of Long-Term Capital Management.

ARBITRAGE IN THE HISTORY OF FINANCE

Modigliani and Miller did not invent arbitrage. When their paper was published in 1958, there was already a well-developed arbitrage argument in the economics literature. Both academics and practitioners in the field of international finance knew how to price forward currency contracts based on the interest rate parity theorem (IRPT), a theorem that was proved using arbitrage arguments. The IRPT says, for example, that the value of a position in a U.S. risk-free asset (say, a one-year T-bill) and a forward contract on a foreign currency (a contract to exchange dollars for British pounds in one year) cannot deviate much from the price of the foreign currency risk-free asset with the same maturity (one-year British treasury stock). The logical appeal of the IRPT is fairly straightforward, relying as it does only on the ability of investors to hedge the exchange rate risk in a foreign bond and so transform it into its domestic currency counterpart. And the predictive power of the IRPT thus depends only on whether or not such risk-free securities really exist and can be purchased without incurring large transactions costs.

The proof of the leverage irrelevance proposition was a much more ambitious undertaking. M&M began by making the assumption that there are many companies in the same risk class. More precisely, these firms are assumed to generate operating cash flows (that is, cash flows before subtracting financing costs) that are perfectly correlated with each other, such that the stocks of these firms can be viewed by investors as perfect substitutes. M&M did not explain why it would be reasonable to assume there would always be enough companies in a given risk class to allow investors to perform this novel kind of arbitrage between risky cash flow streams. Instead, the paper went ahead and attempted to provide empirical support for the irrelevance proposition by examining the leverage ratios and stock returns of a sample of electric utilities. But, as Miller himself wrote 30 years later, "our hopes of settling the empirical issues by that route . . . have been largely disappointed."[5]

When published in 1958, the first M&M paper generated an avalanche of comments, a number of which were published in the *American Economic Review*. The response that is probably best remembered was by David Durand, then a professor of finance at MIT. Durand's position was that the propositions were logically correct, but only "in their own properly limited theoretical context."[6] His quarrel was with the realism of the assumptions that made possible the arbitrage proof of Proposition I, particularly those permitting "homemade" leverage and the absence of restrictions on margin buying.

Miller himself never denied the existence of market frictions – although the fact that M&M devised an empirical test of the proposition suggests their belief that it might have some predictive power *despite* those frictions. But perhaps a more useful way of viewing the M&M irrelevance propositions is this: They tell us what we should *expect* to see if we could somehow eliminate the effects on corporate cash flows of real-world frictions like taxes, information costs, and value-reducing managerial behavior. Despite Durand's objections, the

---

5   Miller (1989), p. 9.
6   David Durand, "The Cost of Capital, Corporation Finance, and the Theory of Investment: Comment," *American Economic Review* 49 (1959).

key assumptions of M&M have been used over and over in financial research not because they are accurate descriptions of reality, but because they have helped researchers to identify and focus on those variables that *are* likely to affect the real underlying source of value: the expected cash flows.

Besides providing a foundation for future research in corporate finance, arbitrage arguments of the kind introduced by M&M also prepared the way for other major developments in finance theory – developments that led to the derivatives revolution that has dramatically changed the practice of finance in the last 15 or 20 years. The arbitrage portfolio strategies in the M&M paper are "static" strategies in the sense that once the investor establishes an initial position, there is no need to change it. If a levered firm sells for more than an unlevered firm, investors can make a risk-free profit by selling short the levered firm and buying the unlevered firm, and then just holding that position. But with the discovery of the Black-Scholes option pricing formula and the introduction of "continuous-time" pricing models by Robert Merton in the early 1970s, finance added dynamic arbitrage strategies to its tool box. Such strategies involve continuous changes in the positions held by the arbitrageur and, in so doing, make it possible to create trading strategies that replicate the payoffs of almost any security.

This extension of the arbitrage argument was first made in the context of the option pricing model developed by Fischer Black, Robert Merton, and Myron Scholes in the early 1970s. Remarkably enough, the first sentence of the famous Black-Scholes paper makes an arbitrage argument that is exactly what one would expect from Miller: "If options are correctly priced in the market, it should not be possible to make sure profits by creating portfolios of long and short positions in options and their underlying stocks."[7]

After publication of the Black-Scholes formula, the continuous-time arbitrage approach to pricing securities quickly showed itself to have considerable predictive power and a broad range of applications. This approach made possible the pricing and hedging of all kinds of new derivatives (not just traded

options on stocks), thereby providing tremendous impetus to the growth of derivatives markets. Apart from futures contracts on agricultural commodities, derivatives were virtually unknown when the M&M paper was published in the late '50s. By the end of 1999, the notional value of over-the-counter (OTC) *financial* derivatives contracts outstanding had almost reached $90 trillion[8] – an amount that doesn't include the derivatives outstanding on the organized futures and options markets. Such derivatives are now used every day by investors and companies both to make markets more efficient and to manage major price risks.[9] In addition to their extensive use in corporate risk management, continuous-time arbitrage pricing methods are also now widely used by corporations in *real option* applications such as project valuation and strategic planning.

ARBITRAGE AND CORPORATE FINANCE

Though arbitrage arguments are now pervasive throughout finance, the more immediate impact of the arbitrage proof of Proposition I was to provide the foundation for modern *corporate* finance by demonstrating the conditions under which capital structure should not matter – and, by implication, the conditions under which it might. The M&M propositions are often identified as the beginning of modern corporate finance because they represent the first attempt to apply rigorous economic logic to corporate financial decision-making. In so doing, Miller and Modigliani started the transformation of the study of corporate finance from what then amounted to a glorified apprenticeship system into the more systematic and scientific discipline it has since become.

The basic insight of the M&M propositions is that, when viewed from a broad macro perspective,

---

7   Fischer Black and Myron Scholes, "The Pricing of Options and Corporate Liabilities," *Journal of Political Economy* Vol. 81, No. 3 (1973).

8   This is the latest estimate of the size of the over-the-counter derivatives market produced by the Bank for International Settlements.

9   In my article, "Rethinking Risk Management" (which appeared in Vol. 9 No. 3 (Fall 1996) of this journal), I argue that the primary source of value added by corporate risk management is that it enables companies to reduce major price risks they have no comparative advantage in bearing. By transferring such risks to other parties better able or more willing to bear them, risk management effectively allows management to focus more on managing those risks where they do have a comparative advantage.

differences in leverage and dividend payout ratios are simply different ways of dividing up the operating cash flows produced by the business and repackaging them for (possible) distribution to investors. And as long as "merely financial" decisions do not affect "real" decisions in any systematic way – for example, provided managers make the same investment decisions whether the debt-to-capital ratio is 10% or 90% – financial decisions do not "matter."

As mentioned earlier, the M&M propositions were developed under a restrictive set of conditions, the most important of which are these: (1) there are no taxes paid by companies or their investors; (2) there are no costs associated with bankruptcy or other forms of financial trouble; (3) reliable information about the firm's earnings prospects is freely available to investors (and, thus, what management knows about the future cannot be significantly different from what investors know); and (4) corporate investment and operating decisions are not influenced by financing or dividend choices.

What, then, do the M&M propositions have to say to corporate practitioners? There are really two distinct messages. The first is that there is no "magic" in leverage or dividends. Since the heyday of the conglomerates in the late '60s, investment bankers have been fond of showing their clients the miraculous effect of increasing leverage – whether by issuing new debt or buying back stock – on pro forma earnings per share. The message of Miller and Modigliani is that this EPS effect is an illusion. It is true that if companies issue debt and use the proceeds to retire their shares, their EPS will go up as long as the return on invested capital exceeds the after-tax corporate borrowing rate – hardly an acceptable standard of profitability. The problem with this strategy, as M&M showed, is that as companies take on more financial leverage, the risk of the equity rises commensurately. And as the risk of the equity increases, stockholders raise their *required* rate of return, and the P/E of the firm goes down. The net effect is a wash; overall value remains unchanged. In response to those who claim that investors value companies largely on the basis of dividends, M&M showed that dividends are simply a way of distributing earnings; and as long as the company's earning power remained unaffected, the shareholders' *total* return (dividends plus capital gains) should stay the same.

The second message of M&M can be seen by standing the propositions on their heads. That is, if changes in corporate financing or dividend policy are going to increase stock prices, they are likely to do so only for the following reasons: (1) they reduce taxes or transactions costs paid by the companies or their investors; (2) they reduce (the present value of) the expected costs of financial distress; (3) they reduce information asymmetries between management and investors; or (4) they provide stronger incentives for management to invest wisely and operate efficiently. It is in this sense that the M&M propositions can be seen as laying the ground work for the modern theory of corporate finance: they showed future scholars (as well as practitioners) where to look for the *real* effects of financial decisions.

The academic process of exploring these four possible sources of value added by corporate financing decisions was begun by Miller and Modigliani themselves almost 40 years ago. In the so-called "tax-adjusted" M&M proposition presented in a 1963 paper, they argued that the benefits of substituting debt with tax-deductible interest payments for equity with non-deductible (and thus potentially twice-taxed) dividend payments could push the optimal capital structure toward 100% debt.[10] But this result seemed completely at odds with the conservative corporate practices of the time. Faced with corporate debt-equity ratios in the early 1960s "that were not much higher than they were in the low-tax 1920s," Miller recalls,

we seemed to face an unhappy dilemma: either corporate managers did not know (or perhaps care) that they were paying too much in taxes; or something major was being left out of the model . . . [Our thinking] suggested that the high bond ratings in which the management took so much pride may actually have been a sign of their incompetence; that the managers were leaving too much of their stockholders' money on the table in the form of unnecessary corporate income tax payments.[11]

The initial way out of this dilemma was to focus on the costs of high leverage – and the most

---

10 Franco Modigliani and Merton Miller, "Corporate Income Taxes and the Cost of Capital: A Correction," *American Economic Review* (1963).

11 Miller (1989), p. 12.

obvious candidate was bankruptcy costs. But the findings of a much-cited study of a sample of bankrupt railroads suggested that the direct, or "out-of-pocket," costs associated with formal bankruptcy proceedings were much too low – less than 1% of total firm value, on average, for the larger firms – to explain the reluctance of companies to use more leverage.[12] This led finance scholars to explore the "indirect" costs of leverage, those costs (including predictable value-reducing changes in managers' behavior) resulting from the financial troubles of companies in situations much less extreme than bankruptcy.

The most intuitively appealing analysis of such costs was a 1977 paper by Stewart Myers called "The Determinants of Corporate Borrowing."[13] After viewing the values of all companies as the sum of two components – tangible "assets in place" and intangible "growth options" – Myers went on to demonstrate why companies whose values stem mainly from assets in place support much higher leverage ratios than firms whose values come mainly from growth options (think of today's Internet firms). The main argument against using debt to finance such growth companies was identified by Myers as the "underinvestment problem." The essence of the argument is straightforward: When faced with a downturn in operating cash flows, debt-financed companies are more likely than their equity-financed counterparts to pass up valuable investment opportunities. And since the potential loss from underinvestment is much greater for growth companies than for mature firms, growth companies have greater reason to avoid debt.[14]

To the extent that such expected "costs of financial distress" were assumed to be a major factor in financial decision-making, choice of the firm's leverage ratio could be seen as an attempt to balance such costs against the anticipated tax benefits of higher leverage. But Miller himself remained skeptical about whether distress costs were large enough to resolve the capital structure puzzle, and he proposed a different solution. In his 1976 Presidential Address to the American Finance Association entitled "Debt and Taxes,"[15] Miller pointed out that the tax savings of debt financing from the deductibility of interest (but not dividends) were exaggerated by the failure to account for the taxes paid by the *holders* of corporate debt. For individuals, interest on corporate debt is taxed as income while capital gains are taxed at a lower rate and their realization can be postponed. Miller showed that the tax savings from converting equity into debt at the corporate level are at least partly offset by the higher pre-tax promised rate of return that debtholders require as compensation for the taxes they pay on their interest income. And in the somewhat extreme situation where the debtholders' interest is fully taxed while the stockholders' gains go essentially untaxed, the entire tax benefit from debt would disappear. Based on this new development, the leverage irrelevance proposition could hold even in the presence of taxes.

In the late '70s, there was another attempt to take finance theory beyond capital structure irrelevance by exploring the possibility that corporate financing decisions provide "signals" to investors by communicating important "insider" information about the firm's earnings prospects. This theory seemed especially suited to explain the widely noted tendencies of new equity issues to meet with large price drops and of stock buybacks to cause price increases. But, as Miller himself concluded in his 1986 paper on "The Informational Content of Dividends," "none of the signaling models has provided – nor is one likely to provide – a signaling 'equilibrium' in which one dividend or financial policy is clearly superior to another."[16] That is, even though signaling theories offer

---

12 Jerold Warner, "Bankruptcy Costs: Some Evidence," *Journal of Finance*, Vol. 32 (1977).

13 Stewart Myers, "The Determinants of Corporate Borrowing." *Journal of Financial Economics*, Vol. 5 (1977).

14 At the root of this problem, as Myers demonstrated, are conflicts between shareholders and bondholders. If the firm raises funds for investment by selling new shares, the bondholders benefit because their debt becomes less risky. But this increase in the value of the firm's existing debt resulting from an equity issue represents a wealth transfer from the firm's existing shareholders, who accordingly may choose to bypass the investment rather than incur the costs of a new stock issue. In addition to Myers's discussion of the underinvestment problem, other bondholder-shareholder conflicts arise from incentives of shareholders to make the debt riskier and so less valuable (as pointed by Michael Jensen and William Meckling in their 1976 paper on "agency costs," which I discuss later in this paper).

---

15 Merton Miller, "Debt and Taxes," *Journal of Finance* (1977).

16 Merton Miller, "The Informational Content of Dividends," in *Macroeconomics and Finance: Essays in Honor of Franco Modigliani* (MIT Press, 1987).

a plausible explanation of how investors interpret *changes* in corporate leverage and payout ratios, they provide little guidance on the questions of *optimal* capital structure and dividend policy.

By the early 1980s, then, the finance profession had come up with (1) one good reason for some companies (mainly high-growth firms) to avoid debt (namely, to reduce the possibility of underinvestment), (2) one *possible* reason to increase leverage (to reduce corporate taxes), and (3) a third factor – information asymmetries – that would lead most companies to stay away from high leverage (to avoid the "information" costs associated with having to raise new equity). In sum, there was no clear message coming from the academic finance profession about how greater use of debt financing could be expected to add value.

But a new way out of the capital structure dilemma presented itself in the wave of leveraged restructurings in the 1980s. During that period, debt-equity ratios in LBOs and some "public" leveraged recaps achieved levels that Miller described as "far beyond anything we dared to use in our classroom illustrations of the tax advantage." But, as many observers suspected and research later confirmed, tax savings were not the only benefit of high leverage, nor were they probably the most important. As early as 1976, Michael Jensen and William Meckling had pointed to another possible benefit of debt financing in their pioneering paper on "agency costs."[17] Jensen and Meckling demonstrated that, in a world where managers often pursue their own interests at the expense of their shareholders, raising equity capital from outside investors can be costly. The more dispersed the firm's ownership (and the less stock owned by the firm's managers), the greater is this value-reducing conflict of interest between ownership and control. For this reason alone, replacing equity with debt (and perhaps, as in LBOs, increasing managers' stock ownership in the process) could be expected to lead to greater operating efficiency and higher firm value.

But the application of Jensen and Meckling's agency cost theory to the events of the 1980s did not come until Jensen's formulation of his "free cash flow" theory of corporate finance. Published in the *American Economic Review* in 1986, Jensen's paper argued that the massive substitution of debt for equity in leveraged takeovers, LBOs, and leveraged stock repurchases was adding value by curbing wasteful reinvestment in mature industries with few promising investment opportunities.[18] In Jensen's view, high leverage exerts a discipline on management that, while potentially costly in high-growth firms, can be a major source of value in large, mature companies with far more capital than growth opportunities.[19] As Miller himself summed up Jensen's argument: "By accepting such heavy debt-service burdens, the managers are making a binding commitment to themselves and to the other residual equity holders against yielding to the temptations to pour the firm's good money down investment ratholes."[20]

In the 1990s, the academic finance community furnished supporting evidence for Jensen's argument in the form of study after study documenting significant increases in operating efficiency and value in the LBOs and other leveraged restructurings of the '80s. But, with the collapse of the junk bond market in 1989 and the ensuing wave of defaults and bankruptcies, this was far from the popular view of leverage and financial markets. So, when Merton Miller was awarded the Nobel Prize in Economics at the end of 1990, it was not a complete surprise that he chose "Leverage" as both the title and subject of his Nobel lecture. After briefly noting the "substantial real efficiency gains" accomplished "by LBO entrepreneurs" during the 1980s "by concentrating corporate control and redeploying assets," Miller quickly turned to the main business of the speech – the use of economic logic to combat what he called the "particularly

---

17 Michael Jensen and William Meckling, "Theory of the Firm: Managerial Behavior, Agency Costs, and Ownership Structure," *Journal of Financial Economics* (1976). The view that the firm's capital structure and the ownership of its equity affect managerial behavior is central to the agency literature and started with this seminal paper by Jensen and Meckling.

18 Michael Jensen, "Agency Costs of Free Cash Flow, Corporate Finance, and Takeovers," Vol. 76 *American Economic Review* (1986).

19 One of my own papers provides a model of optimal leverage in which debt has such a disciplining role. See René Stulz, "Managerial Discretion And Optimal Financing Policies," *Journal of Financial Economics*, 1990, Vol. 26, No. 1.

20 Miller, "The M&M Propositions Thirty Years Later," *JACF*, Vol. 2, No. 1 (1989), p. 14.

virulent strain of anti-leverage hysteria" then prevailing among U.S. politicians and regulators.

The main thrust of Miller's argument, which can be traced back to the M&M propositions, is the improbability of debt financing *per se* causing significant reductions in the value of corporate America's real assets and future earnings power. This is not to deny the painful losses experienced by many investors and employees of highly leveraged companies during the early '90s. But the main culprit in many of these cases was not debt, but the downturn in the economy (a downturn made worse, as Miller said, by "regulatory overreaction to the S&L crisis" and the adverse effects of new bank capital requirements). If the highly leveraged deals of the '80s had been funded mainly with equity rather than debt, such companies would still have experienced large losses in value; but such losses would then have been borne largely by stockholders instead of being shared with the debtholders. And even those losses that could correctly be attributed to overleveraging were more likely to represent "private" than "social" costs, since the forgone investment opportunities and laid-off employees were likely to move to other (in some cases new) firms. Hence Miller's skepticism about the popular argument that a cluster of bankruptcies could lead to a general collapse of the economy:

Neither economics generally nor finance in particular offers much support for this notion of a leverage-induced "bankruptcy multiplier" or contagion effect. Bankrupt firms do not vanish from the earth. They often continue operating pretty much as before, though with different ownership and possibly on a reduced scale. Even when they do liquidate and close down, their inventory, furniture and fixtures, and employees and customers flow to other firms elsewhere in the economy. Profitable investment opportunities that one failing firm passes up will be assumed by others – if not immediately, then later when the economic climate becomes more favorable.[21]

Given the events of the past ten years, Miller's words now seem prophetic. The remarkable growth of the last decade has laid to rest the concerns about high leverage that were so prevalent in the early 1990s. Eventually, economic historians will conclude that the growth of the '90s, far from being constrained by the high leverage of the '80s, was made possible in large part by the efficiency gains accomplished by the leveraged restructurings of that period.

ARBITRAGE, FINANCIAL MARKETS, AND MARKET EFFICIENCY

Research findings based on arbitrage arguments in perfect markets are relevant only as long as one believes that market forces work. Investors must be able to take sufficient advantage of pricing mistakes that prices will not differ in a systematic way from what they would be if financial markets were perfect.

In Miller's view of the world, financial prices cannot be wrong for long because investors are always looking for riskless profits from correcting pricing errors. And when regulations or other government interference prevent investors from playing this arbitrage role, the markets tend to find innovative ways around such obstacles – in some cases, by creating new securities. In a 1986 speech to the Western Finance Association,[22] Miller argued that many if not most financial innovations are responses to regulatory impediments to the working of market forces. In making this point, he reminded his audience of Milton Friedman's role in the creation of financial futures. In the early 1970s, Friedman wanted to speculate on the British pound by taking a short position; but at that time one could take a short forward position only by going to a bank, and no bank was willing to be his counterparty. (Banks apparently did not want to be seen by their regulators as promoting currency speculation.) This experience led Friedman to advocate the creation of *financial* futures since futures markets make it just as easy for investors to take a short position as a long one. And the first currency futures began trading on the Chicago Mercantile Exchange in 1972.

---

21   Merton Miller, "Leverage," Nobel Memorial Prize Lecture delivered December 7, 1990 in Stockholm. The text of the speech was reprinted in this journal, Vol. 4, No. 2 (Summer, 1991), p. 10.

22   Merton Miller, "Financial Innovation: The Last Twenty Years and the Next," *Journal of Financial and Quantitative Analysis* 21 (1986).

Financial economists tend to regard both financial innovation and capital flows in pursuit of investment opportunities as positive forces that make markets more efficient, facilitate risk-sharing, and increase economic growth. But, outside the circle of economists, this view is highly controversial. Politicians and regulators, in particular, are generally inclined to see financial innovation and unfettered capital flows as leading to crashes and general instability. Political and regulatory attacks on financial innovation were particularly fierce in the wake of the stock market crash of 1987 and the junk bond losses in 1989. The same "anti-finance" forces mounted campaigns during the spate of derivatives disasters in the mid-1990s and the emerging-market crises in the second half of the '90s.

Whenever market forces and financial innovations were blamed for problems in financial markets, Merton Miller was there to provide careful economic analysis. For example, when portfolio insurance and index arbitrage were widely blamed for the stock market crash in October 1987, Miller chaired a blue ribbon commission set up by the Chicago exchanges to look into the causes of the crash. And the commission contributed a number of important points to the politically charged debate that took place after the crash. For example, critics of the futures markets invariably argued that prices first fell in the stock index futures markets in Chicago, with the effect then spreading to the stock markets in New York. But, as Miller pointed out, this by no means proves that the futures markets *caused* the crash. Noting that many NYSE stocks had delayed openings on October 19, Miller said that a more plausible interpretation of the day's events was that the futures market prices simply *reflected* the true state of the market that was hidden on the NYSE because of the delayed openings. In addition to emphasizing the valuable role of futures markets in "price discovery," Miller also observed that the size of portfolio insurance programs was far too small to account for the volume of selling on October 19.[23]

The debate over portfolio insurance was recently reopened with the publication of a book by Bruce Jacobs,[24] a professional portfolio manager. The main thesis of Jacobs's book is that portfolio insurance programs caused the crash of 1987 by setting off a "massive liquidation" in response to the price declines before the week of the crash. According to Jacobs, the result of this massive liquidation attempt was "a tremendous explosion – selling, understandable reluctance to buy, prices gapping down, investor panic." As the book explains, "What the participants in these strategies apparently don't realize is that, as their investments become concentrated, so does their need for liquidity. When they need to get out, they find they are stuck in illiquid positions that can be unwound only at steep discounts."

But Miller himself never argued that markets always move continuously, nor did he hold that continuous price movements were a necessary condition for market efficiency. In fact, in May of 1987 (and thus just five months before the crash), he gave a paper at the Mid-America Institute that proved to be remarkably prescient about the possibility of price gaps. In that paper, he pointed out that although greater liquidity in markets makes it possible for individuals separately to withdraw their capital whenever they wish, it is not possible for society as a whole to withdraw its investment. In normal times, individuals who sell and buy largely balance each other out. But, on occasion, there are imbalances in which many more individuals want to sell than buy. In such situations, there is a possibility that the buffer stocks of the market makers and the resources of liquidity providers will be exhausted. This creates the equivalent of a bank run in which those investors who get to sell first are the lucky winners, while those who come last cannot sell because there are no buyers.

Having acknowledged that possibility, Miller went on to explore its implications for the organization of markets. His main prescription was the importance of putting in place mechanisms that expand the capacity of exchanges to absorb the demand for transactions. But, as he warned in closing, "No economically feasible amount of added capacity will guarantee against any recurrence of

---

23 Reports showed that sales of stocks unrelated to portfolio insurance were three to five times as great as the sales driven by portfolio insurance.

24 Bruce Jacobs, *Capital Ideas and Market Realities* (Blackwell Publishers, 1999).

market brown-outs, of course; but it can at least make them even rarer events."[25]

More recently, a number of financial economists have argued that the level and volatility of stock prices experienced in the past few years are clear evidence of a "bubble." The recent debates on the level of the stock market have made extensive use of the findings of a new branch of finance known as "behavioral finance." For example, in a book published in 2000,[26] Robert Shiller uses behavioral models based on various forms of investor "irrationality" to explain how investors at times can get carried away by theories supporting high stock prices. According to Shiller, the late 1990s represent the fourth period in the 20th century in which investors have become enthralled by some version of the idea of a "new economy." The first such period was at the turn of the century, the second one led up to the crash of 1929, and the third took place in the 1960s. As Shiller points out, the previous three periods in which dramatic increases in stock prices were fueled by visions of a new economy did not end well.

But if Miller believed that prices might change with dramatic speed because of the limited capacity of financial markets to provide liquidity, he did not think that such price gaps were necessarily evidence of bubbles. In his keynote address to the Pacific-Basin Finance Association in 1989, he pointed out that stocks are securities with "theoretically infinite durations." This means that, especially in the case of low-dividend stocks, much of their value resides in cash flows that will not be produced until years into the future. And this in turn means that small changes in expectations about growth rates, interest rates, or risk premiums can lead to large changes in prices. To illustrate this point, Miller used an example in which the firm begins with a dividend yield of 3%, a discount rate of 10%, and a growth rate of dividends of 7%. Plugging these assumptions into the Gordon dividend growth model widely used by practitioners, Miller shows that the share price would be worth 33 times the current dividend. He then goes on to show that if the growth rate falls by a half

a percentage point to 6.5%, and the discount rate increases by the same amount to 10.5%, the stock price falls to 25 times dividends, a drop of 24%. As Miller's example was meant to suggest, it does not take much of a change in expectations to generate a fall in the stock prices of the magnitude of what took place on October 19, 1987.

In choosing these numbers, Miller made it clear that all he was doing was providing a set of numbers that would be *consistent* with a fundamental explanation of the crash. He did not believe it would be possible for economists to devise empirical tests capable of distinguishing between the two main hypotheses – that the crash represented (1) investor irrationality and the bursting of a bubble or (2) a rational investor response to a sudden shift in fundamentals. In summing up his position, Miller said, "We are faced with competing theories that can seemingly account for the same facts and we have no way of conducting decisive experiments that can distinguish between them."[27] And in response to this ambiguity, Miller's recommendations for policymakers concluded with the suggestion that the "wiser and ultimately more conservative policy, even for those who still believe in bubbles, is not to seek to prevent stock market crashes at all costs, but if one does occur, to localize any damage and keep it from spreading to other sectors of the economy."[28]

In Miller's world, the forces of arbitrage, broadly understood, eventually prevail. If the random or poorly understood actions of a mass of individual investors were to lead them to exit the markets in a hurry, this should create profit opportunities for other investors; and the act of exploiting such opportunities should move prices back to their proper levels. This mechanism assumes that arbitrageurs will always be there in force to prevent overshooting and systematic biases in prices relative to what they should be based on fundamentals alone.

But how can we be sure that the free fall of October 19, 1987 stopped just where it should have? How can we know that the collapses of emerging markets, or the recent drop in the value of the

25 Miller (1991), cited in note 1, p. 48.
26 Robert Shiller, *Irrational Exuberance* (Princeton University Press, 2000).

27 Miller, *Financial Innovation and Market Volatility* (1991), cited earlier, p. 103.
28 Ibid., p. 106.

Nasdaq, were not excessive? Perhaps we will never know. Such drops or gaps in markets will turn out to be consistent with market efficiency only if there are enough investors who do not succumb to panic to step in and start buying. This means that such investors must have enough capital at their disposal.

IS THERE ENOUGH CAPITAL FOR ARBITRAGE?: THE CASE OF LTCM

Investors can now make trades more quickly, and with lower transactions costs, than ever before. Although this increase in liquidity is unquestionably a great benefit for both investors and the companies in whose shares they trade, it also creates the potential for investors to herd in ways that were not possible before. We have seen dramatic reversals in investor sentiment in the last few years. For instance, capital flows to East Asian countries experienced a swing of more than $100 billion from 1996 to 1997. When such events take place, trades by a group of investors can end up destabilizing markets unless Miller's arbitrageurs stand up to the herd and profit from their behavior. But while more arbitrage capital may now be needed to allow other investors to exit from the markets at a moment's notice, developments in the last few years suggest that we may actually have less of such capital – or at least not enough.

Among recent events that seem to indicate the limitations of the arbitrage mechanism, the fall of Long-Term Capital Management (LTCM) in the fall of 1998 stands out. LTCM was mostly engaged in transactions that would qualify as M&M-type arbitrage transactions. A typical example of such a transaction was to go long in an agency bond and go short in a similar Treasury bond. Although bonds issued by government agencies typically have yields fairly close to those of Treasury bonds of the same maturity, there are times when the yield of agency bonds is considerably higher. And since the coupon payments of the agency bond exceed those of the bonds held short, a long position in an agency bond trading at par and a short position in a comparable Treasury bond will earn a positive cash flow provided (1) the federal guarantee to the agencies is strong enough that there is no default risk on the agency bonds and (2) the positions are held to maturity.

In the real world, there are three difficulties with this arbitrage transaction. First, there might be some default risk on the agency bond, although this problem could be eliminated by using a credit derivative to construct a default-free synthetic agency bond. (In this fashion, financial engineering has removed one obstacle to arbitrage.) A second difficulty is transactions costs that increase the yield differential between agency and Treasury bonds at which an arbitrage trade becomes profitable. Such costs would be increased by any restrictions on full use of the proceeds on short sales, which would force the investor to use some of his own capital to implement the trade. Third, and most important, this would be a true arbitrage trade only if it were certain that the position could be held to the bonds' maturity, at which time the values of the long position and the short position *must* converge (since both bonds are at par). To see why this condition is important, consider what happens if one month after the trade is put in place, the yield on agency bonds increases sharply relative to the yield on Treasury bonds. In that case, the value of the position becomes negative because the price of the bond held long falls by more than the increase in the value of the bond held short. And if the investor *could for some reason* be forced to liquidate the position after its value has fallen, then the arbitrage is no longer riskless – and hence it is no longer arbitrage.

The situation of LTCM in August of 1998 is well represented by this simple example of an arbitrage trade. LTCM had positions that were generating positive cash flows with a high degree of certainty, but changes in yield spreads had sharply reduced the net worth of those positions through their effect on prices. In terms of our above example, the difference between the yield spreads on agency bonds and those on more liquid Treasuries, which was large enough to attract investors like LTCM in the first place, suddenly became even larger, reflecting investors' heightened desire for liquidity. And as a result of this marketwide preference for liquidity, the values of the securities LTCM was holding long fell by more than the values of the more liquid securities they were shorting, causing a drop in the net worth of their combined positions.

Arbitrageurs with sufficient capital to allow them to hold positions for long periods of time can close the gaps created by increases in the premium for liquidity. In fact, one of the important economic functions of arbitrageurs is to provide liquidity to the markets. But, in August of 1998, many if not most such arbitrageurs stayed on the sidelines. Although still puzzling in some ways, perhaps the most important cause of the failure of arbitrage on this occasion was the major constraints faced by many of the firms and investors capable of playing such an arbitrage role. Financial institutions that could have provided liquidity and thereby earned arbitrage profits are subject to regulations that can discourage them from so doing. A good example of such regulation is the new capital requirements for the trading activities of commercial banks that were put in place at the beginning of 1998. That change in regulation created a situation in which any significant increase in volatility in global capital markets would force banks to choose between increasing the capital used to back their trading activities and cutting back the scope of those activities.

And in August of 1998, the extreme volatility of global financial markets prompted many firms that normally function as market makers to *reduce* their positions instead of providing liquidity.[29] As a result, LTCM was in fact unable to satisfy the all-important third condition of arbitrage: *the ability to hold the combined positions to maturity*. As LTCM's net worth plummeted, it found itself unable to continue financing its positions (even though many of them would still have been profitable arbitrages if carried to maturity). The fact that Warren Buffett, arguably the world's most famous arbitrageur, teamed up with Goldman and AIG to offer to buy

the fund for $250 million (as well as committing $3 billion of Berkshire Hathaway's capital to stabilize the fund after the acquisition) suggests that even when the net worth of the fund was plummeting, outsiders continued to see value in the portfolio. But Buffett's offer was not accepted and, with some prompting from the New York Fed, a consortium of commercial and investment banks provided LTCM with enough new capital to continue the operation. The banks ended up making a modest profit – about 10% – on their investments when LTCM was liquidated early in 2000.

BUILDING LIQUIDITY INTO THE MODEL

Given its role in the collapse of LTCM and the failure of portfolio insurance during the crash of '87, liquidity may well prove to be the Achilles heel of a theory of finance built on perfect market assumptions. Nevertheless, as Miller himself showed us, liquidity can be studied. In a paper published in the *Journal of Finance* in 1988,[30] Miller and Sanford Grossman offered an explanation for why liquidity can suddenly disappear even in an efficient market. They hypothesized that if many investors suddenly want to sell a security because they experience a "liquidity event" – some unanticipated need to raise cash – the price of that security will drop to attract buyers even though the underlying expected cash flows of the security are unchanged. This temporarily low price should make it attractive for other investors to step in and buy the security, causing its price to return to its previous level. Thus, in markets with a large supply of capital, a large number of investors selling for liquidity reasons would have little or no impact on price. But, as Miller and Grossman also showed in their model, if the suppliers of liquidity have limited capital, or their actions are restricted by regulations, then market makers – particularly when hit with a series of liquidity events – may exhaust their ability to provide liquidity, leading to a free fall in prices.[31]

---

29 Another problem facing publicly traded financial institutions with significant trading operations are the difficulties in communicating the reliability of trading profits to the investment community. For instance, in the middle of 1998, Salomon Smith Barney decided to sharply limit its proprietary trading operations at a time when it was contemplating the integration of its operations with the rest of the new Citigroup. The apparent reason for taking this step was that the volatility of the profits expected from such operations would be difficult to explain not only to stock analysts and the bank's regulators, but also to customers (like depositors and purchasers of insurance products) concerned about the bank's financial stability. And for this reason, as well as the regulatory problem mentioned above, a number of economists have suggested that publicly traded financial institutions are likely to be supplanted in this arbitrage role by private, unregulated investors, popularly known as "hedge funds."

---

30 Sanford Grossman and Merton Miller, "Liquidity and Market Structure," *Journal of Finance*, Vol. 43 (1988).
31 Indeed, yield spreads today on non-investment grade bonds are considerably wider today than in August of 1998, a puzzling phenomenon that has been attributed partly to the absence of market making by U.S. financial institutions.

Miller was acutely aware of the importance of liquidity in markets. But, in all his writings on the subject, his main concern was to ensure that excessive regulation not reduce liquidity, and that financial markets be allowed to perform their role of directing capital to its best uses. He always took a dim view of arguments suggesting that regulators or bureaucrats could allocate capital more effectively than the private sector under the discipline of financial markets.

What's more, he saw a fairly limited role for commercial banks in the capital allocation process. During the 1980s, when Japanese industrial companies seemed to be outperforming their U.S. and European counterparts, some financial economists began to develop theoretical models that purported to explain why bank-financed economies like Japan and Germany function more efficiently than market-based systems like the U.S. and U.K. But Miller remained squarely in the camp of those who argued that the U.S.–U.K. model of market capitalism is the most reliable way of producing consistent economic growth.

In an article published in this journal in the wake of the Asian crisis,[32] Miller argued that the problems of the Japanese economy (still very much in evidence today) stem from the same fundamental source as those afflicting the countries in Southeast Asia – namely, excessive reliance on bank financing and failure to develop well-functioning capital markets. He went on to say that banking "is not only basically 19th-century technology, but disaster-prone technology," and that "in the summer of 1997 a banking-driven disaster struck in East Asia, just as it had struck so many times before in U.S. history." In the 20th century, as Miller pointed out, the U.S. economy steadily reduced its dependence on banks by developing "dispersed and decentralized" financial markets and institutions. By so doing, it has significantly reduced its vulnerability to credit crunches (for example, non-bank sources of capital were an

important reason why the U.S. recession of 1990 was so mild and short-lived) while at the same time dramatically increasing the efficiency of the U.S. capital allocation process. In closing, Miller urged the developing countries in Southeast Asia and elsewhere not to imitate the Japanese example, but to

follow the model of the U.S. in shrinking the banking industry itself, and steadily expanding the number and variety of market alternatives to bank loans . . . If the current crises have done nothing more than to discredit the Japanese and Korean models of bank-driven economic development, then perhaps the whole episode, painful as it has been, and still is to live through, has nevertheless been worthwhile.

In sum, Miller was always ahead of the crowd in identifying important issues and using the logic of economics to come up with solutions. And, having thought the issues through, he had no equal in presenting those solutions in ways that would not only affect the thinking of his profession, but also appeal to a much broader audience. In the closing sentences of his Nobel lecture, Miller urged his colleagues to do the same:

Many in academic finance have viewed the ill-founded attacks on our financial markets, particularly the newer markets, with some dismay. But they have, for the most part, stood aside from the controversies. Unlike some of the older fields of economics, the focus in finance has not been on issues of public policy. We have emphasized positive economics rather than normative economics, striving for solid empirical research built on foundations of simple, but powerful organizing theories. Now that our field has officially come of age, as it were, perhaps my colleagues in finance can be persuaded to take their noses out of their data bases from time to time and to bring insights of our field, and especially the public policy insights, to the attention of a wider audience.[33]

In this undertaking Merton Miller had no peers, only students, and it seems safe to say that his influence on financial economists and his contribution to the field of finance will not be matched.

32 Merton Miller, "Financial Markets and Economic Growth," *Journal of Applied Corporate Finance*, Vol. 11, No. 3 (Fall 1998).

33 Miller, Nobel Prize Lecture, *JACF* (1991), p. 12.

Index